CICA Assurance and Related Services Guidelines

No.	Title (Date)
	Introduction to auditing and related services guidelines (March 1992)
AUG-1	Related party transactions and economic dependence (September 1980)
AUG-2	Audit of pension costs and obligations (November 1986)
AUG-3	(Withdrawn September 1995)
AUG-4	Services on matters relating to solvency (October 1988)
AUG-5	Compilation engagements—financial statement disclosures (December 1988)
AUG-6	Examination of a financial forecast or projection included in a prospectus or other offering document (September 1989)
AUG-7	Applying materiality and audit risk concepts in conducting an audit (March 1990)
AUG-8	Auditor's report on comparative financial statements (October 1990)
AUG-9	(Withdrawn August 1996)
AUG-10	Legislative requirements to report on the consistent application of generally accepted accounting principles (February 1991)
AUG-11	Communications with audit committees (or equivalent) (August 1991)
AUG-12	Auditor's report on pension fund financial statements filed with a regulator (March 1992)
AUG-13	Special reports on regulated financial institutions (May 1992)
AUG-14	Auditor's report on the financial statements of federally regulated financial institutions (December 1992)
AUG-15	Audit of actuarial liabilities of life insurance enterprises (February 1993)
AUG-16	Compilation of a financial forecast or projection (February 1993)
AUG-17	Transactions or conditions reportable under the "well-being reporting requirement" in federal financial institutions legislation (October 1993)
AUG-18	Criteria for non-derivative reports issued under subsection 295(5) of "an Act respecting trust companies and savings companies" in Québec (January 1994)
AUG-19	Audit of financial statements affected by environmental matters (January 1994)
AUG-20	Performance of a review of financial statements (September 1995)
AUG-21	Canada–U.S. reporting differences (August 1996)

Statements on Internal Auditing Standards
The Institute of Internal Auditors

SIAS No.		
1	1983	Control: Concepts and Responsibilities
2	1983	Communicating Results
3	1985	Deterrence, Detection, Investigation, and Reporting of Fraud
4	1986	Quality Assurance
5	1987	Internal Auditors' Relationships with Independent Outside Auditors
6	1987	Audit Working Papers
7	1989	Communicating with the Board of Directors
8	1991	Analytical Auditing Procedures
9	1991	Risk Assessment
10	1991	Evaluating the Accomplishment of Established Objectives and Goals for Operations or Programs

Auditing
& OTHER ASSURANCE ENGAGEMENTS

First Canadian Edition

Jack C. Robertson, Ph.D., C.P.A., C.F.E.
C.T. Zlatkovich, Centennial Professor
The University of Texas at Austin

Wally J. Smieliauskas, Ph.D., C.P.A., C.F.E.
University of Toronto

McGraw-Hill Ryerson

Toronto   New York   Burr Ridge   Bangkok   Bogotá   Caracas   Lisbon
London   Madrid   Mexico City   Milan   New Delhi   Seoul
Singapore   Sydney   Taipei

McGraw-Hill
Ryerson Limited

A Subsidiary of The **McGraw·Hill** *Companies*

Auditing and Other Assurance Engagements

First Canadian Edition

ISBN: 0-07-560370-5

1 2 3 4 5 6 7 8 9 10 GTC 7 6 5 4 3 2 1 0 9 8

Printed and bound in Canada

Sponsoring Editors: Roderick T. Banister and Lisa Feil
Developmental Editor: Sabira H. Charlesworth
Senior Associate Editor: Susan Calvert
Production Editor: Matthew Kudelka
Production Co-ordinator: Nicla Dattolico
Cover Photo: Gary Braasch/Tony Stone Images
Typesetter: GAC/Shepard Poorman
Printer: Transcontinental Printing Inc.

Canadian Cataloguing in Publication Data

Robertson, Jack C.
    Auditing and other assurance engagements

1st Canadian ed.
Includes bibliographical references and index.
ISBN 0-07-560370-5

1. Auditing. I. Smieliauskas, Wally. II. Title.

HF5667.R616 1998   657′.45   C98-930263-6

J. C. Robertson dedicates this book to
Charles T. Zlatkovich
Professor Emeritus
C. Aubrey Smith Professorship
Educator
Mentor
The University of Texas at Austin

W. J. Smieliauskas dedicates this book to
Fabrice and Adrian

ABOUT THE AUTHORS

Jack C. Robertson is the C.T. Zlatkovich Centennial Professor at the University of Texas at Austin, where he has been a member of the faculty since 1970. In 1988 he was the Visiting Erskine Fellow in the Department of Accountancy at the University of Canterbury in Christchurch, New Zealand. He has given invited presentations in Jerusalem, Tel Aviv, Christchurch, Dunedin, Wellington, Kyoto, and Kobe.

Professor Robertson is a Certified Public Accountant (Texas) and has worked in industry, public accounting, and government (Academic Fellow in the SEC Office of the Chief Accountant).

Professor Robertson is a member of the American Institute of CPAs, the Texas Society of CPAs, and the American Accounting Association. He has served on committees and task forces of the AICPA and TSCPA, and he has been active in the AAA—serving as secretary, vice-chairman, and chairman of the Auditing Section and as chairman of the Auditing Standards Committee and the Committee on Liaison with the SEC. In the TSCPA he has been active on the Professional Ethics Committee.

Professor Robertson's research and writing interests include auditing and financial reporting subjects. His books are *Auditing, Cost Accounting for Small Manufacturers,* and *Business Income Determination Through Use of Current Cost Accounting.* He has published numerous articles on educational and technical topics in such journals as the *Accounting Review;* the *Journal of Accountancy; Journal of Accounting, Auditing, and Finance;* the *CPA Journal; Accounting Horizons; Auditing: A Journal of Practice and Theory;* and *Research in Accounting Regulations.*

At the University of Texas, Professor Robertson has developed three new auditing courses that have served as national models for courses elsewhere. Prior to his appointment as the C.T. Zlatkovich Centennial Professor, he held the Price Waterhouse Auditing Professorship (1979–85). Professor Robertson is listed in *Who's Who in America.*

Wally J. Smieliauskas is a professor of accounting at the University of Toronto, where he has been a member of the faculty since 1979. In 1987 he served as chair of the CAAA's Expectation Gap Task Force, which made a submission to the MacDonald Commission. Also in 1987, he co-chaired the CAAA conference that had as invited speaker Nobel laureate Herbert Simon.

Professor Smieliauskas is a certified public accountant and has worked in industry and public accounting. He spent his 1986–87 sabbatical year with the firm of Deloitte & Touche.

Professor Smieliauskas is a member of the American Institute of Certified Public Accountants, the Canadian Academic Accounting Association, and the Association of Fraud Examiners.

Professor Smieliauskas's research and writing interests include auditing and the role of accounting in society. He has published numerous articles on educational and technical topics in such journals as *Accounting Review, Contemporary Accounting Research, Journal of Accounting Research, Journal of Accounting Literature,* and *Auditing: A Journal of Practice and Theory.*

At the University of Toronto, Professor Smieliauskas developed the first degree-credit introductory auditing course (in 1981) and the first advanced auditing course (in 1990). In 1988 he was the first director of the MBA Co-op Program in Professional Accounting, a position he held until 1993. The program is designed to facilitate the entry of undergraduates from various fields into the profession, and to provide a broader management education as well as specialized training in accounting, auditing, and tax topics.

CONTENTS

PART II

BASIC CONCEPTS AND TECHNIQUES OF AUDITING
103

CHAPTER 7   *Audit Sampling*   **240**

CHAPTER 8   *Auditing in a Computer Environment*   **296**

PART III

AUDIT APPLICATIONS
347

PART IV

PROFESSIONAL SERVICES AND RESPONSIBILITIES
603

CHAPTER 14   **Other Public Accounting Services and Reports**   **604**

CHAPTER 15   **Professional Ethics, Auditor Responsibilities**   **684**

CHAPTER 16   *Legal Liability*   **742**

CHAPTER 17   *Comprehensive Auditing: Public Sector and Internal Audits*   **794**

CHAPTER 18   ***Fraud Awareness Auditing***   ***854***

PART V

SPECIALIZED TOPICS

935

PREFACE

Auditing and Other Assurance Engagements bridges the gap between students' knowledge of accounting principles and the professional practice of accounting and auditing in the working world. Learning the subject of *auditing* is a new experience for students of accounting. In place of the financial accounting standards, accounting calculations, and journal entries of previous accounting courses, the focus of study becomes auditing, the process of gathering evidence and making judgments about the fair presentation of financial statement balances that have already been produced by accountants.

To familiarize students with the realities of professional practice, the text covers both the concepts and the procedures of auditing. On the conceptual level, students learn about the social role of auditing; the services offered in internal, governmental, and public accounting practice; and the professional standards for behaviour and technical competence. On the technical level, they learn about the programs and procedures for defining audit objectives, gathering evidence, making decisions, and exercising professional scepticism.

This textbook reflects the challenges inherent in accounting and auditing practice, particularly in public accounting firms. Clients who pay the fees expect *value*—consulting advice, recommendations for improvements in the business, and an audit report. On the other hand, public users of these clients' financial statements expect *effective service;* that is, they expect auditors to be objective sceptics working to monitor the business management and blow the whistle on fraudulent financial statements. These dual challenges of service to clients and service to the public merge the business and professional aspects of public accounting practice.

Throughout the 1990s, the practice of accounting and auditing expanded its horizons. This book incorporates important aspects of expansion—other assurance engagements. Everyone is becoming more interested in other assurance engagements. This text fills that void through coverage of the general concept of assurance engagements (Chapters 2 and 14) as well as specific applications (Chapters 14, 17, 18, 19 and the book appendix).

IMPORTANT FEATURES
· · · · · · · · · · · ·

This first Canadian edition has an emphasis on financial auditors' decision-making processes: (1) recognizing problems and developing audit objectives, (2) gathering evidence with audit procedures, and (3) making judgments about the fair presentation of financial statement assertions. These elements are emphasized throughout the standard sequence of audit theory chapters (Chapters 1–8) and are the focus in the chapters on audit applications (Chapters 9–13).

This book includes the following: a chapter on fraud awareness; an appendix on environmental auditing; chapter material on electronic commerce and the Internet; comprehensive coverage of the new assurance engagement concept; a theoretical framework for professional accountants' Codes of Conduct; discussion of audit of derivatives; integration of the learning objectives and the review checkpoints; and various anecdotes, asides, and "casettes."

Fraud Auditing

This book contains full-chapter coverage of fraud auditing, until now unavailable in introductory auditing books. This basic purpose of the chapter is to create awareness of, and sensitivity to, the signs and signals of potential errors, irregularities, and frauds. The chapter contains some unique insights on extended audit and investigation procedures.

Environmental Auditing

This book contains an extended appendix providing a comprehensive overview of the increasingly important topic of environmental auditing.

Learning Aids

Each chapter and section in *Auditing and Other Assurance Engagements* contains features that enhance readability, study, and learning.

Professional Standards References

Each chapter references the relevant professional standards for the chapter topics. The inside front and back covers list these standards and other library resources used by professional auditors.

Learning Objectives

Each chapter begins with the presentation of several learning objectives. These are repeated as marginal notes within the chapters.

Anecdotes and Asides

All the chapters contain illustrative anecdotes and asides. Some of these are in the flow of the chapter text; others stand alone to add realism and interest. These notes bring the real world into the textbook treatment of auditing.

Review Checkpoints

Instead of placing review questions at the end of each chapter, we have placed *review checkpoints* (questions) within each chapter so that students can test themselves as they proceed. These checkpoint islands make the text user-friendly by effectively breaking each chapter into smaller sections.

Casettes

The "casettes" are *short stories* structured to reveal error, irregularity, or fraud in an account. An *audit approach* follows. The audit approach describes an audit objective, desirable controls, test of controls procedures, and audit of balance procedures that can result in discovering the situation. The casettes are in the "applications chapters" (Chapters 9, 10, 11, 12, and 13).

The purpose of the casettes is to enliven the study of auditing. They replace the typical lengthy exposition of audit fundamentals (often tedious and boring) with illustrative situations based on real events. There are 25 casettes with audit approaches in the applications chapters. Another 20 casettes are in the end-of-chapter discussion case sections. In these, the case stories are told, and the students' assignment is to write the audit approach sections.

Key Terms

Throughout the book, key terms are highlighted in boldface print. An alphabetical key terms reference list with definitions is in the back of the book.

Kingston Company Case

The Kingston Company case is a *practice case-within-a-textbook*. The company description starts in Chapter 4 and continues through Chapter 13. Assignments related to Kingston connect many of the technical topics in a logical sequence of audit engagement activities. However, there are numerous exercises, problems, and discussion cases at the end of each chapter that are unrelated to the Kingston Company.

Behavioural Exercises

Robert Ashton (Duke University) published several thought-provoking behavioural decision cases for use in auditing courses. This textbook reproduces a selection of these cases and their variations for instructors and students who wish to probe the subtle aspects of human information processing and decision making. They are found in problems 1.42, 2.44, 3.42, 16.46, 20.36, and 20.37.

ORGANIZATION
. . . .

Part I—Introduction to Auditing and Public Practice

Part I has three chapters. They cover the basic orientation to the accounting profession; assurance standards, generally accepted auditing standards, and quality control standards; the standard unqualified audit report; and major types of qualifications (technical modifications are a chapter appendix).

Part II—Basic Concepts and Techniques of Auditing

Part II follows the normal progression of financial auditing topics. Chapter 4 sets the stage with explanations of financial assertions, general types of procedures, and working paper documentation. Chapter 5 continues the early audit planning considerations with technical material on preliminary analytical procedures, audit risk, and materiality. Chapter 6 takes up the stream of planning and performing audit work with coverage of control risk assessment. Chapter 7 maintains the flow of planning topics with generalized and nonstatistical explanations of audit sampling. Chapter 8 introduces basic concepts of computer auditing and control.

Part III—Audit Applications

Part III contains four chapters that get into the details of audit work on specific accounts and assertions, and one chapter that wraps it all up with audit completion considerations. Chapters 9–13 are the accounting-cycle chapters, and organize the control structure and account balances for comprehensive understanding. Chapter 13, aptly titled *Completing the Audit,* concentrates on client representation letters, lawyers' letters, subsequent events, subsequent discovery of facts, financial statement adjustments, and related party transactions.

Part IV—Professional Services and Responsibilities

The five chapters in Part IV can stand alone or be integrated with the preceding and following chapters. They deal separately with nonaudit services rendered by public accounting firms; the context, methodology, and reports of governmental and internal auditors; and fraud awareness auditing. The latter chapter has benefited from the author's association with the National Association of Certified Fraud Examiners. The two chapters in auditor responsibilities cover legal liability and professional codes of conduct. It was felt that these two topics are better understood after students have gained some knowledge of audit theory and practice.

Part V—Specialized Topics

Part V covers the heavy-duty technical topics. Chapter 19 covers computer audit planning and procedural applications. It fills out the introductory computer audit material in Chapter 8. Chapter 20 covers test of controls using attribute sampling, and presents a thorough treatment of variables sampling for the audit of balances, with dollar-unit sampling carrying the chapter content.

PROFESSIONAL STANDARDS
. . . .

This textbook contains numerous references to authoritative statements on auditing standards and to standards governing other areas of practice. Even so, the text tries to avoid mere repetition of passages from the standards, concentrating instead on explaining their substance and operational meaning in the context of making audit decisions. Instructors and students may wish to supplement the text with current editions of pronouncements published by the Canadian Institute of Chartered Accountants (CICA), the Certified General Accountants Association of Canada, and the Institute of Internal Auditors (IIA).

SUPPLEMENTS
. . . .

Several additional resources for introductory auditing courses are available for instructors and students.

- **Instructor's Resource Guide.** The *Instructor's Resource Guide* includes a description of the Kingston Company case and a set of syllabi for organizing topical coverage. Each chapter contains suggested answers for all the review checkpoints, multiple-choice questions, Kingston assignments, exercises and problems, and discussion cases. Blank forms for some homework assignments can be removed and copied for the students.

- **Computerized Test Bank.** The *Computerized Test Bank* contains numerous objective, short-answer, and essay questions.
- **PowerPoint® Presentation Slides.** The *PowerPoint® Presentation Slides* illustrate chapter concepts with the aid of presentation graphics software.

ACKNOWLEDGMENTS
. . . .

The Certified General Accountants Association of Canada (CGAAC), and the Canadian Institute of Chartered Accountants (CICA), have generously given permission for liberal quotations from official pronouncements and other CICA publications, all of which lend authoritative sources to the text. In addition, several publishing houses, professional associations, and accounting firms have granted permission to quote and extract from their copyrighted material. Their co-operation is much appreciated because a great amount of significant auditing thought exists in this wide variety of sources.

A special acknowledgment is due Mr. Joseph T. Wells, founder and chairman of the National Association of Certified Fraud Examiners. He created the Certified Fraud Examiner (CFE) designation. Mr. Wells is a well-known authority in the field of fraud examination education, and his entrepreneurial spirit has captured the interest of fraud examination professionals throughout North America.

This book could not have been completed without the co-operation and input of many students in my auditing courses at the University of Toronto over the years 1992 through 1997. I am particularly indebted to Peter Guo (book appendix), Dominique Barker (book appendix), Mike Saniga (Chapter 19), Neil Newaz (Chapter 17), Chris Bayley (Chapter 17), Steven Miniuk (Chapter 17), Arthur Chen (book appendix), Marian Sit (book appendix), Millie Tran (book appendix), and Rebecca Luo (Chapter 19) for material that was adapted in various forms in this book.

I am grateful for the invaluable advice provided by Sylvia Smith, Diane Hiller, Jan Munro, Greg Shields, and Karen Duggan of the CICA. My experience with these talented individuals convinced me that Canada likely has the most productive standard setters in the world on a per person basis. They are keeping Canada at the forefront of practice globally and are an important influence on international standard setting. I sincerely hope the CICA will continue to actively represent the Canadian perspective in the global arena of standard setting.

I would also like to thank my colleagues at the University of Toronto for providing a stimulating, supportive environment for this work, especially Donna Losell, Manfred Schneider, Len Brooks, Ann Kittler, and Irene Wiecek. In addition, the excellent typing provided by Maria and Michelle Raz over numerous revisions of this manuscript is greatly appreciated.

The excellent reviews and suggestions provided by several professors have been a significant help in completing this textbook. Sincere appreciation is due to Marcia McCann (Ryerson Polytechnic University), Margaret Kelly (University of Manitoba), Charlotte Heywood (Wilfrid Laurier University), Barbara Treholm (University of New Brunswick), Kate Bewley (York University), Donna Losell (University of

Toronto), John Edds (Brock University), Dani Moss (Durham College), Dan A. Simniuc (University of British Columbia), Richard D. Rennie (University of Regina), Susan McIsaac (Doane Raymond and Mount Allison University), Michael Maingot (University of Ottawa), Mohamed Ibrahim (Concordia University), and Karim Jamal (University of Alberta). Their attention to reviews greatly enhanced several portions of the text. However, we remain responsible for all errors of commission and omission.

We owe a great debt of gratitude to professional accountants in all walks of life. In particular, Jack Robertson acknowledges his indebtedness to the late Jim Tom Barton and the late Albert L. Wade; and Wally Smieliauskas acknowledges his gratitude to Don Leslie, Don Cockburn, Alistair Mason, Jim Gaston, and the late P. Howard Lyons. All are unforgettable individuals on the public accounting scene and all helped us gain a keener appreciation of the profession.

Saving the best to the end, words cannot express the extent of support given by Susan Robertson and Chantal Smieliauskas. Behind every author there is a force saying, "Get it finished so we can clean out the garage and home office!"

J.C. Robertson and W.J. Smieliauskas

PART I

Introduction to Auditing and Public Practice

CHAPTER 1

Learning Objectives

Learning objectives are statements of what you should be able to do after you have studied each chapter of this textbook, examined related professional standards, answered the review checkpoints in each chapter, and completed assigned homework problems. For example, in an auto mechanics school one learning objective would be: "Be able to take a carburetor apart and put it back together in 15 minutes."

Learning objectives for auditing, however, are not this task specific. The learning objectives are given at the beginning of each chapter and are restated within the chapter at appropriate places. As you study each part of the chapter, you can use them as general reference points.

Chapter 1 gives you an introduction to professional accounting practice. Other accounting courses helped you learn the principles and methods of accounting; now you are starting a study of the ways and means of practising accounting and auditing outside the classroom. Your objectives are to be able to:

1. Distinguish auditing from accounting.

2. Chronicle the historical development of auditing standards, including the criticisms of the profession and its responses.

3. Define and explain auditing, especially its role in information risk reduction.

4. Describe the audits and auditors in governmental, internal, and operational auditing.

5. Describe the organization of public accounting firms and identify the various services they offer.

6. Provide an overview of U.S. and international auditing (Appendix 1A).

7. Describe alternative theories of the role of auditing in society (Appendix 1B).

8. List and explain the requirements for becoming a public accountant (Appendix 1C).

9. Describe the accounting and auditing activities of the professional accounting organizations (Appendix 1C).

PROFESSIONAL PRACTICE

USER DEMAND FOR RELIABLE INFORMATION

· · · · · · · · · · · · ·

Accounting

LEARNING OBJECTIVE
1. Distinguish *auditing* from *accounting*.

The following three underlying conditions affect demand by users for accounting information:

1. **Complexity.** A company's transactions can be numerous and complicated. Users of financial information are not trained to collect and compile it themselves. They need the services of professional accountants.

2. **Remoteness.** Users of financial information are usually separated from a company's accounting records by distance and time, as well as by lack of expertise. They need to employ full-time professional accountants to do the work they cannot do for themselves.

3. **Consequences.** Financial decisions are important to the state of investors' and other users' wealth. Decisions can involve large dollar amounts and massive efforts. The consequences are so important that good information, obtained through the financial reports prepared by accountants, is an absolute necessity.

Accounting is the process of recording, classifying, and summarizing into financial statements a company's transactions that create assets, liabilities, equities, revenues, and expenses. It is the means of satisfying users' demands for financial information that arise from the forces of complexity, remoteness, and consequences. The function of **financial reporting** is to provide statements of financial position (balance sheets), statements of results of operations (income statements), statements of changes in financial position (cash flow statements), and accompanying disclosure notes (footnotes) to outside decision makers who have no internal source of information like the management of the company has. A company's accountants are the producers of such financial reports. In short, accounting tries to record and summarize economic reality for the benefit of economic decision makers (the users).

Auditing

Financial decision makers usually obtain their accounting information from companies that want to obtain loans or sell stock. This source of information creates a potential **conflict of interest**, which is a condition that creates society's demand for audit services. Users need more than just information; they need reliable information. Preparers and issuers (directors, managers, accountants, and others employed in a business) might benefit by giving false, misleading, or overly optimistic information. The potential conflict has become real often enough to create a natural skepticism on the part of users. Thus, they depend on professional auditors to serve as objective intermediaries who will lend some credibility to financial information. This "lending of credibility" is also known as **providing assurance**, and external auditing of financial statements is described as an **assurance engagement**.

Auditing does not include the function of financial report production. That function is performed by a company's accountants under the direction of its management. Auditors obtain evidence that enables them to determine whether the information in the financial statements is reliable. Auditors then report to the users that the information is reliable by expressing an opinion that the company's presentation of financial position, results of operations, and changes in financial position is in accordance with generally accepted accounting principles (GAAP), or some other disclosed basis of accounting. This opinion is the assurance provided by the assurance function, as it relates to the traditional financial statements.

Independent auditors work for clients. A **client** is the person (company, board of directors, agency, or some other person or group) who retains the auditor and pays the fee. In financial audits the client and the auditee usually are the same economic entity. **Auditee** is the actual designation of the company or other entity whose financial statements are being audited. Occasionally the client and the auditee are different. For example, if Conglomerate Corporation hires and pays the auditors to audit Newtek Company in connection with a proposed acquisition, Conglomerate is the client and Newtek is the auditee.

Reliable financial information helps make capital markets efficient and helps people understand the consequences of a wide variety of economic decisions. Independent auditors practising the assurance function are not, however, the only auditors at work in the economy. Bank examiners, Revenue Canada auditors, provincial regulatory agency auditors (e.g., auditors with a province's Commissioner of Insurance), internal auditors employed by a company, and the Auditor General of Canada: all practise auditing in one form or another.

REVIEW CHECKPOINTS

1.1 What conditions create demand for financial reports, and who produces financial reports for external users?

1.2 What is assurance? What condition creates demand for assurance to financial reports?

1.3 What is the difference between a client and an auditee?

1.4 What is the difference between auditing and accounting?

BRIEF HISTORY OF AUDITING

LEARNING OBJECTIVE
2. Chronicle the historical development of auditing standards, including the criticisms of the profession and its responses.

Auditors have been around for a long time. As long as there has been civilization, there has been a need for some types of record-keeping to implement accountability. In fact, it was the need to keep records of ownership of quantities of goods that led to the development of writing and arithmetic. The first number systems and the first written words were developed as symbols to keep track of merchandise either collected as taxes or used in trade. It was centuries later that literature and mathematics evolved separately, far removed from this initial accountability application. For example, the first proto-Greek written script, Linear B, was essentially developed for keeping records of business transactions and palace inventories in Mycenaean

Greece of 1400–1300 B.C. It was only in 800–700 B.C. that a further evolved writing system was used to record some of the earliest works of Western literature, the *Iliad* and the *Odyssey*. By then in Greece writing had evolved to the point of recording outstanding deeds and social events and not just commercial transactions. Similarly, accounting and measuring evolved into more abstract mathematics. This pattern of the gradual evolution of writing, had been seen in many even earlier civilizations, starting with the Sumerians (3000 B.C.), the Egyptians (2500 B.C.), the first Indus River civilization (2500 B.C.), and the start of the Xia dynasty in China (2300 B.C.).

Auditing accompanied the development of accounting, and the first recorded auditors were the spies of King Darius of ancient Persia (522 to 486 B.C.). These auditors acted as "the King's ears" checking on the behaviour of provincial satraps. The word *auditor* comes from the Latin word "to hear" because in ancient times auditors listened to the oral reports of responsible officials (stewards) to owners or those having authority, and confirmed the accuracy of the reports. Over the centuries this role of auditors as verifiers of official reports evolved to include that of verifying written records. By A.D. 1500 double-entry bookkeeping had evolved to the point of being documented by Luca Pacioli of Italy in the first known book on accounting. Pacioli also recommended that the accounting records be verified by auditors. By the early 19th century auditors acting as independent outside experts were frequently called upon to investigate and report on business failures or to settle business disputes. Independence is a key characteristic of the auditor that we will discuss in some detail throughout this book. For now think of it as conditions necessary to obtain an objective appraisal of the subject matter at issue. If the auditor showed any bias in his or her investigation, or even if there was merely the suspicion of bias, the effectiveness of the auditor's report would be greatly reduced.

Modern auditing began in 1844 when the British Parliament passed the Joint Stock Companies Act, which for the first time required that corporate directors report to shareholders via an audited financial statement, the balance sheet. In 1844 the auditor was required neither to be an accountant nor to be independent, but in 1900 a new Companies Act was passed that required an independent auditor.

The first public accountants' organization was the Society of Accountants in Edinburgh, organized in 1854, and Scotland and England became the leaders in establishing an accounting profession. As a result of the British lead, the first North American association of accountants, later to become the Institute of Chartered Accountants of Ontario, was organized in 1879 in Toronto. The Quebec Order became the first legally incorporated accounting association in North America in 1880. The Canadian Institute of Chartered Accountants began under federal incorporation laws in 1902. And the Certified General Accountants Association of Canada was incorporated by an Act of Parliament in 1913.

Following British precedents, the first legislation requiring audits in Canada was the Ontario Corporations Act of 1907. This was followed by the Federal Corporation Act of 1917. Until 1930 Canadian practice followed the British model, focusing on the procedures that were followed to process a transaction (transaction oriented); these procedures largely relied on internal evidence.

After the 1929 stock market crash and the Great Depression of the 1930s, Canadian practice was increasingly influenced by developments in the United States. U.S. practice had evolved since the late 19th century toward a process of collecting evidence as to assets and liabilities or what is frequently referred to as a balance sheet audit. As a result of extensive misleading financial reporting that contributed to the stock market crash of 1929 and the world depression of the 1930s, the U.S. passed legislation in 1933 and 1934 that greatly influenced auditing around the world. The U.S. Securities Acts of 1933 and 1934 created the Securities and Exchange Commission (SEC), which regulated the major stock exchanges in the U.S. Companies wishing to trade shares on the New York Stock Exchange or the American Stock Exchange were required to issue audited income statements as well as balance sheets. In addition, because of the earlier problems with misleading financial reports of the 1920s, the emphasis switched to fairness of presentation of these financial statements, and the auditor's role was to verify the fairness of presentation.

In 1941, as a result of experience in the McKesson and Robbin's fraud case (discussed in Chapter 16), the SEC recommended references to "generally accepted audit standards (GAAS)" in the auditor's report and mandated more extensive reliance on external evidence. This created a need to better define audit standards and objectives. This process was begun in 1948 by the American Institute of Certified Public Accountants (AICPA).

These developments in the United States greatly influenced Canadian auditing as well as auditing in the rest of the world. For example, in 1946 the CICA began its own standards for financial statement disclosure in Bulletin #1. A series of bulletins were issued over the next 20 years covering accounting and auditing matters. In 1968 these bulletins were reorganized into a single volume called the *CICA Handbook*. Revisions and additions have been made to the *Handbook* with such regularity since then that in the 1990s the *Handbook* was split into three volumes, one containing the accounting recommendations (*Sections* 1000 to 5000), another covering the auditing recommendations (*Sections* 5000 and higher), and a third dealing with public-sector accounting and auditing standards.

An important development of standard setting in Canada was the adoption of Bulletins of the CICA in the Ontario (1953) and Federal Corporation Acts. In 1965 the Ontario Securities Act gave the Ontario Securities Commission (OSC) responsibility to regulate the Toronto Stock Exchange, Canada's largest. In 1972 an OSC Policy Statement mandated the use of the *CICA Handbook* to determine generally accepted accounting principles (GAAP). These requirements were soon incorporated in the *Ontario Securities Act* of 1978 and the *Canadian Business Corporation Act* of 1975. As a result of these developments, the status of *Handbook Recommendations* carries the force of law in Canadian reporting.

In contrast, the accounting and auditing standards developed by the American Institute of Certified Public Accountants (AICPA) and the Financial Accounting Standards Board (FASB) do not have comparable legal status in the United States. There, the SEC has the legal authority to set accounting standards for all the U.S. stock exchanges; however, the SEC has for the most part delegated this authority to the FASB and the AICPA. See Appendix 1A for more details on U.S. developments.

The failure of two Alberta banks in the first half of the 1980s and the resultant enquiry by the Estey Commission in 1985 raised questions about the effectiveness of audit and accounting standards in Canada. In response, the CICA helped organize the Macdonald Commission, which enquired into the public accounting profession. The commission's report came out in 1988 with 50 recommendations for improving accounting and auditing practice to help reduce a perceived "expectations gap" between what the public expects of auditors and what auditors can deliver. As a result of these recommendations the CICA attempted to reduce the gap through promulgation of new standards related to the auditor's report, auditor responsibility for detecting fraud, and documentation of internal controls evaluations. These recommendations are covered in the relevant chapters throughout this text.

Similar expectations gap standards were developed in the United States as a result of business and audit failures there, especially with respect to the savings and loan industry. A fundamental difference between the U.S. and Canadian environments, however, is the extent of government involvement in monitoring the profession. In the U.S. there have been several congressional investigations in the last two decades, with pressure being exerted through the Securities and Exchange Commission, which acts as a regulator of the profession (see Appendix 1A). In Canada, on the other hand, the government and regulators by and large have relied on the CICA standard-setting process to address public concerns.

R E V I E W
C H E C K P O I N T S

1.5 What single event can be said to have prompted the development of generally accepted auditing standards?

1.6 Identify the major changes to the auditing profession since 1945.

DEFINITIONS OF AUDITING

Academic Accountants' Definition of Auditing

LEARNING OBJECTIVE
3. Define and explain auditing, especially its role in information risk reduction.

The American Accounting Association (AAA) Committee on Basic Auditing Concepts (1971) prepared a comprehensive definition of auditing:

> Auditing is a systematic process of objectively obtaining and evaluating evidence regarding assertions about economic actions and events to ascertain the degree of correspondence between the assertions and established criteria and communicating the results to interested users.

This definition contains several ideas important in a wide variety of audit practices. The first and most important concept is the perception of auditing as a systematic process which is purposeful and logical and is based on the discipline of a structured approach to decision making. Auditing is not haphazard, unplanned, or unstructured.

The audit process, according to this definition, involves obtaining and evaluating evidence which consists of all the influences that ultimately guide auditors' decisions, and relates to assertions about economic actions and events. When beginning an audit engagement, an external auditor is given financial statements and other disclosures by management and thus obtains management's assertions about economic actions and events (assets, liabilities, revenue, expense). Evidence is then acquired which either substantiates or contradicts these management assertions.

External auditors generally begin work with explicit representations from management—assertions of financial statement numbers and information disclosed in footnotes. Other auditors, however, are typically not so well provided with explicit representations. An internal auditor, for example, may be assigned to "evaluate the cost effectiveness of the company's policy to lease, rather than to purchase, heavy equipment." A governmental auditor may be assigned to determine, for example, whether goals of creating an environmental protection agency have been met by the agency's activities. Often times, these latter two types of auditors must develop the explicit standards of performance for themselves.

EXHIBIT 1–1   OVERVIEW OF FINANCIAL STATEMENT AUDITING

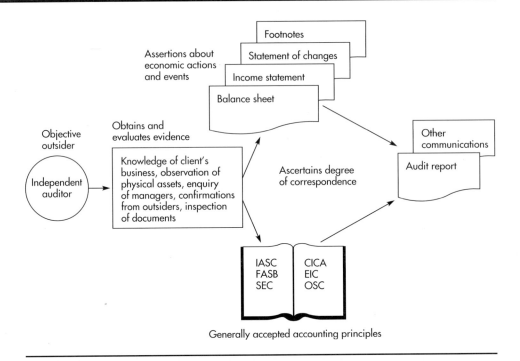

Generally accepted accounting principles

The purpose of obtaining and evaluating evidence is to ascertain the degree of correspondence between the assertions and established criteria. Auditors will ultimately communicate their findings to interested users. To communicate in an efficient and understandable manner, there must be a common basis for measuring and describing financial information. Such a basis constitutes the established criteria essential for effective communication.

Established criteria may be found in a variety of sources. For external auditors, governmental auditors, and Revenue Canada inspectors, the criteria largely consist of the generally accepted accounting principles (GAAP). Revenue Canada, Taxation, inspectors also rely heavily on criteria specified in federal tax acts. Governmental auditors may rely on criteria established in legislation or regulatory agency rules. Bank examiners and provincial insurance board auditors look to definitions and rules of law. Internal and governmental auditors rely a great deal on financial and managerial models of efficiency and economy as well as on generally accepted accounting principles (GAAP). All auditors rely to some extent on elusive criteria of general truth and fairness.

Exhibit 1–1 depicts an overview of financial statement auditing.

Audit Objective and the Auditor's Report

The American Accounting Association definition is broad and general enough to encompass external, internal, and governmental auditing. Although the Canadian Institute of Chartered Accountants (CICA) has not defined auditing, its Audit Handbook Recommendation, "Audit of Financial Statements—an introduction" (*Section* 5090), sets forth the main objective of a financial audit:

The objective of the audit of financial statements is to express an opinion whether the financial statements present fairly, in all material respects, the financial position, results of operation and changes in financial position in accordance with generally accepted accounting principles, or in special circumstances another appropriate disclosed basis of accounting. Such an opinion is not an assurance as to the future viability of an entity nor an opinion as to the efficiency or effectiveness with which its operations, including internal control, have been conducted. . . . In the performance of an audit of financial statements, the auditor complies with generally accepted auditing standards (GAAS), which (as set out in Section 5100.02) relate to the auditor's qualifications, the performance of the audit and the preparation of his or her report.[1]

The CICA statement of objective restricts auditing interest to external auditors' audit of the traditional financial statements and their footnotes. However, as the needs of users change, new audit objectives and reports are created to meet new needs. Thus, the *CICA Handbook* also offers guidance on such divergent topics as reporting on control procedures at service organizations, on matters related to solvency, and on examination of a financial forecast in a prospectus. A set of evolving ''assurance standards'' (presented in Chapter 2) may provide a framework to govern a wide range of assurance services.

The expression of the auditor's opinion on financial statements is found in the last paragraph of the audit report. A standard report is shown in Exhibit 1–2. (Chapter 3 explains this and other audit reports in more detail.)

A Definition of Auditing Relating to "Risk Reduction"

Although it is sometimes difficult to distinguish between a definition and a theory, most statements of theory begin with a definition. A theoretical viewpoint currently gaining popularity is that auditing is a ''risk-reduction activity.'' The definition that supports this view is: Auditing is a process of reducing (to a socially acceptable level) the information risk to users of financial statements.

Economic activity takes place in an atmosphere of **business risk**. This risk is the chance a company takes that inflation will rise, taxes will increase, customers will

---

E X H I B I T 1–2   **AUDITOR'S REPORT**

To the Shareholders of.....................................

I have audited the balance sheet of .... as at ...., 19....., and the statements of income, retained earnings and changes in financial position for the year then ended. These financial statements are the responsibility of the company's management. My responsibility is to express an opinion on these financial statements based on my audit.

I conducted my audit in accordance with generally accepted auditing standards. Those standards require that I plan and perform an audit to obtain reasonable assurance whether the financial statements are free of material misstatement. An audit includes examining, on a test basis, evidence supporting the amounts and disclosures in the financial statements. An audit also includes assessing the accounting principles used and significant estimates made by management, as well as evaluating the overall financial statement presentation.

In my opinion, these financial statements present fairly, in all material respects, the financial position of the company as at ...., 19....., and the results of its operations and the changes in its financial position for the year then ended in accordance with generally accepted accounting principles.

City   (signed)...................................

Date
                                                                        Chartered Accountants

---

[1] The Auditing Recommendations of the *CICA Handbook* are authoritative CICA pronouncements on auditing theory and practice.

buy from competitors, government grants will be lost, employees will go on strike, and the like. Countering these negative examples are similar risks (probabilities) that favorable events will occur. Auditors do not directly influence a company's business risk.

Information risk, on the other hand, is the risk (probability) that the financial statements distributed by a company will be materially false and misleading. Financial analysts and investors depend on financial reports for making stock purchase and sale decisions. Creditors (suppliers, banks, and so on) use them to decide whether to give trade credit and bank loans. Labour organizations use financial reports to help determine a company's ability to pay wages. Government agencies and Parliament use them in preparing analyses of the economy and in making laws concerning taxes, subsidies, and the like. These various users cannot take it on themselves to determine whether financial reports are reliable and, therefore, low on the information-risk scale. The users do not have the expertise, resources, or time to enter thousands of companies to satisfy themselves about the veracity of financial reports; thus, they hire independent auditors to perform the assurance function and reduce the information risk. Auditors assume the social role of attesting to published financial information, thereby offering users the valuable service of assurance that the information risk is low.

This risk-reduction definition may appear very general. As your study of auditing continues, you will find that auditors perform many tasks whose primary objective is to reduce the risk of giving an inappropriate opinion on financial statements. Auditors are careful to work for trustworthy clients, to gather and analyse evidence about the data in financial statements, and to take steps to ensure that audit personnel report properly on the financial statements when adverse information is known. Subsequent chapters of this book will have more to say about various information-risk-reduction activities.

. . . .

R E V I E W
C H E C K P O I N T S

1.7 Define and explain auditing. What would you answer if asked by an anthropology major: "What do auditors do?"

1.8 What is the essence of the risk-reduction theory (definition) of auditing?

1.9 Who cares about information risk reduction?

. . . .

OTHER KINDS OF AUDITS AND AUDITORS
. . . .

LEARNING OBJECTIVE
4. Describe the audits and auditors in governmental, internal, and operational auditing.

The AAA, CAAA, CICA, and the risk-reduction definitions clearly apply to the financial audit practice of independent external auditors who practise auditing in public accounting firms. The word *audit*, however, is used in other contexts to describe broader kinds of work.

The variety of audit work performed by different kinds of auditors causes some problems with terminology. Hereafter in this textbook, "independent auditor," "external auditor," "chartered accountant (CA)," "certified general accountant (CGA)," and "public accountant (PA)" will refer to people doing audit work with public accounting firms. In the governmental and internal contexts discussed below, auditors are identified as governmental auditors, operational auditors, and internal auditors. While many of these auditors are chartered accountants or certified general accountants, the initials *PA, CA,* and *CGA* in this book will refer to auditors in public practice. (Governmental and internal audit work is covered in more detail in Chapter 17.)

Operational and Internal Auditing

The Institute of Internal Auditors defined internal auditing and stated its objective as follows:

> Internal auditing is an independent appraisal function established within an organization to examine and evaluate its activities as a service to the organization. The objective of internal auditing is to assist members of the organization in the effective discharge of their obligations. To this end, internal auditing furnishes them with analyses, appraisals, recommendations, counsel, and information concerning the activities reviewed.

Internal auditing is practised by auditors employed by an organization, such as a bank, hospital, city government, or industrial company. Some internal auditing activity is known as **operational auditing**. Operational auditing (also known as **performance auditing** and **management auditing**) refers to the study of business operations for the purpose of making recommendations about the economic and efficient use of resources, effective achievement of business objectives, and compliance with company policies. The goal of operational auditing is to help managers discharge their management responsibilities and improve profitability.

Operational and internal auditors also perform audits of financial reports for internal use, much as external auditors audit financial statements distributed to outside users. Thus, some internal auditing work is similar to the auditing described elsewhere in this textbook. In addition, the expanded-scope services provided by internal auditors include: (1) reviews of control systems that ensure compliance with company policies, plans, and procedures and with laws and regulations; (2) appraisals of the economy and efficiency of operations; and (3) reviews of effectiveness in achieving program results in comparison to pre-established objectives and goals.

Operational auditing is included in the definition of internal auditing cited above. In a similar context a PA may consider operational auditing performed by independent PA firms as a distinct type of management consulting service whose goal is to help a client improve the use of its capabilities and resources to achieve its objectives. So, internal auditors consider operational auditing integral to internal auditing, and external auditors define it as a type of management consulting service offered by public accounting firms.

Internal auditors need to be independent of the line managers in an organization, much like the external auditors need to be independent of the company management. Independence helps internal auditors be objective. They can make recommendations for correction of poor business decisions and practices, and they can praise good decisions and practices. If they were responsible for making the decisions or carrying out the practices, they could hardly be credible in the eyes of upper-management officers to whom they report. Consequently, the ideal organizational arrangement is to have internal auditors with no other responsibilities than to audit and to report to a very high level in the organization, such as a financial vice president and the audit committee of the board of directors. This arrangement is a type of internal independence that enhances the appraisal function (internal audit) within a company.

Governmental Auditing

The office of the Auditor General of Canada (OAG) is an accounting, auditing, and investigating agency of Parliament, headed by the Auditor General. In one sense, OAG auditors are the highest level of internal auditors for the federal government as a whole. Many provinces have audit agencies similar to the OAG. These provincial auditors answer to provincial legislatures and perform the same types of work described under governmental auditing below. In another sense, the OAG and similar provincial auditors are really external auditors with respect to government agencies they audit because they are organizationally independent.

Many government agencies have their own internal auditors and inspectors: for example, most federal ministries (Defense Ministry, Revenue Canada) and provincial agencies (education, welfare, controller). Well-managed local governments (cities, regions, townships) also have internal audit staffs.

Governmental and internal auditors have much in common. The OAG shares with internal auditors the same elements of expanded-scope services. The OAG, however, emphasizes the accountability of public officials for the efficient, economical, and effective use of public funds and other resources. The CICA sets accounting and auditing standards for all public sector audit engagements including the federal, provincial, and local levels of government. Public sector audits can be described as comprehensive auditing as follows:

> Public Sector auditing includes financial, compliance and value-for-money (VFM) audits. . . . Financial statement audits determine (1) whether financial statements present fairly the financial position, results of operations . . . in accordance with generally accepted accounting principles, and (2) compliance audits determine whether the [audited] entity has complied with laws and regulations. . . . VFM audits include economy and efficiency and effectiveness audits.

In this definition you can see the audit function applied to financial reports and a compliance audit function applied with respect to laws and regulations. All government organizations, programs, activities, and functions were created by law and are surrounded by regulations that govern the things they can and cannot do. For example, in some provinces there are serious problems of health card abuse and fraud by ineligible persons. A hospital cannot simply provide free services to anyone since there are regulations about eligibility of tourists and visitors from other countries. A compliance audit of such a program involves a study of the hospital's procedures and performance in determining eligibility and treatment of patients. Nationwide, such programs involve millions of people and billions of taxpayers' dollars.

Also in this definition you see value-for-money or VFM audits, a category that includes economy, efficiency, and effectiveness audits. Government is always concerned about accountability for taxpayers' resources, and value-for-money audits are a means of seeking to improve accountability for the efficient and economical use of resources and the achievement of program goals. Value-for-money audits, like internal auditors' operational audits, involve studies of the management of government organizations, programs, activities, and functions.

Comprehensive governmental auditing is auditing that goes beyond an audit of financial reports and compliance with laws and regulations to include economy and efficiency and effectiveness audits. The public sector standard on the elements of comprehensive auditing is similar to the internal auditors' view. (These elaborations are presented in Chapter 17.)

SOME EXAMPLES OF VALUE-FOR-MONEY AUDITS CONDUCTED BY THE ONTARIO PROVINCIAL AUDITOR

HEALTH CARE: Stronger efforts needed to control undesirable patterns of practice by health care providers.

INSURANCE: Cost effectiveness of Ontario Insurance Commission monitoring activities was considered adequate.

EDUCATION: Need to improve procedures for availability of programs to exceptional children.

YOUNG OFFENDERS: Suggested improvements to documentation before releasing young offenders.

CRIMINAL LAW: Several recommendations made for better utilization of courtroom and judicial resources.

Source: The Office of the Provincial Auditor of Ontario.

The audit of a governmental organization, program, activity, or function may involve financial auditing, compliance auditing, or VFM auditing, or all of them (a comprehensive audit). Public Sector standards do not require all engagements to include all types of audits. The scope of the work is supposed to be determined according to the needs of those who use the audit results.

Regulatory Auditors

For the sake of clarity, other kinds of auditors deserve separate mention. You probably are aware of tax auditors employed by Revenue Canada. These auditors take the "economic assertions" of taxable income made by taxpayers in their tax returns and audit these returns to determine their correspondence with the standards found in the Tax Regulations. They also audit for fraud and tax evasion. Their reports can either clear a taxpayer's return or claim that additional taxes are due.

Federal and provincial bank examiners audit banks, trust companies, and other financial institutions for evidence of solvency and compliance with banking and other related laws and regulations. In 1985 these examiners as well as external auditors made news as a result of the failures of two Alberta banks—the first Canadian bank failures in over 60 years.

· ·

R E V I E W
CHECKPOINTS

1.10 What is operational auditing? How does the CICA view operational auditing?

1.11 What are the elements of comprehensive auditing?

1.12 What is compliance auditing?

1.13 Name some other types of auditors in addition to external, internal, and governmental auditors.

· ·

Public Accounting

· · · · · · · · · · · ·

The Accounting Profession

LEARNING OBJECTIVE

5. Describe the organization of public accounting firms and identify the various services they offer.

There are a number of professional associations representing accountants. In addition to the provincial Institutes of Chartered Accountants (the chartered accountants organization in Quebec is called Order of Chartered Accountants of Quebec), there are the Certified General Accountants Associations, the Societies of Management Accountants, and the Institute of Internal Auditors. Each of these provincial organizations also has a national coordinating and standard setting body: the Canadian Institute of Chartered Accountants (CICA), the Certified General Accountants' Association of Canada (CGAAC), Society of Management Accountants of Canada (SMAC), and the Institute of Internal Auditors (IIA) which is an international organization. Each of these organizations have developed their own professional designations as follows: the Chartered Accountants (CAs), Certified Management Accountants (CMAs), Certified General Accountants (CGAs), and Certified Internal Auditors (CIAs). The requirements for obtaining these various designations vary greatly and it is best to consult your provincial organization or local chapter for the details.

Generally the distinguishing features of these various designations are as follows: CAs have traditionally been oriented to providing auditing and related public accounting services for even the largest companies, CMAs have traditionally been oriented primarily to providing private management and internal accounting services, CIAs are oriented primarily to provide private internal audit services to larger organizations, and CAs aim to provide all types of services, although they have been prohibited from doing external audits in some provinces. There is considerable overlap among all these accounting professionals in that they provide accounting, tax, and management advisory work, with CAs and CGAs primarily oriented to providing these services to the public while CMAs and CIAs are oriented to provide these services to their full-time employer companies.

Recently, CGAs and CMAs have been obtaining public practice rights throughout Canada. The only exceptions now are the provinces of Ontario and Prince Edward Island, but even here there have been some moves toward accommodation. It is therefore more appropriate to talk about public accountants as PAs instead of CGAs in a book about external auditing. Although we will use the more generic term *PA* throughout the book, many of our illustrations will be based on standards set by the CICA. The reason for this is that the CICA's standards are given legal standing in the courts through the various Federal and Provincial Corporation Acts, and through various regulatory policy statements. In addition, when CGAs and CMAs practice public accounting, their guides refer to the use of the *CICA Handbook* standards in the performance of public accounting services. Appendix 1C provides illustrations of public accounting standard setting activities and requirements.

Public Accounting Firms

Many people think of public accounting in terms of the "big" accounting firms. (As of October 1997, there were the "Big Six": Ernst & Young, Deloitte & Touche, KPMG, Price-Waterhouse, Coopers & Lybrand, and Arthur Andersen & Co. Recent merger talks indicate that this will soon be reduced to a "Big Three.") Notwithstanding this perception, public accounting is practised in thousands of practice units ranging in size from sole proprietorships (individuals who "hang out the shingle") to international firms employing thousands of professionals. Many students look on public accounting

E X H I B I T 1–3   PA FIRM ORGANIZATION

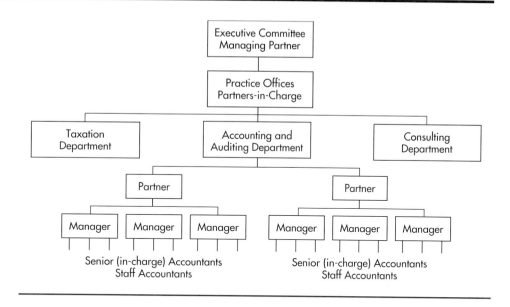

as the place to begin a career: for three to ten years they gain intimate knowledge of many different business enterprises; they then select the industry segment in which to pursue their interests. Public accounting experience provides an excellent background to almost any business career.

Public accounting firms do business in a competitive environment. They are in business to make profits, yet they are also in the profession to perform public accounting services in the public/social interest. This duality—profit motive and professional responsibility—creates tensions between the need to perform quality services and the desire to make a profit.[2] As the 1980s closed and the 1990s began, public accounting felt the lingering effects of a national recession. Business sagged in some services, and some large public accounting firms trimmed partners and staff from their payrolls. One large accounting firm in the United States actually declared bankruptcy, reportedly pushed over the brink by lawsuits looming over malpractice claims. At the same time, some public accounting firms experienced growth, particularly in their taxation and consulting services.

Public accounting as a whole is a major employer of PAs performing assurance services, tax services, and consulting services. Exhibit 1–3 shows a typical organization of a PA firm. PA firms differ in their organization. Some have other departments than those shown, such as small-business advisory and compensation consulting. Some PA firms have other names for their staff and management positions. The exhibit shows the most typical organizational structure for a larger PA firm.

Assurance Services
Audits of traditional financial statements are the most frequent type of assurance services for public companies and for most large and medium nonpublic companies. Auditing amounts to around 45 to 65 percent of the business of most large PA firms. Most of this textbook is about the audit of traditional financial statements.

---

[2] Note that this dichotomy exists in most professions: doctors often diagnose an illness and treat it; architects act on behalf of the owners of buildings and often also as general contractors.

Accounting and review services are the ''nonaudit'' or other services, performed frequently for medium and small businesses and not-for-profit organizations. A great deal of nonaudit work is done by small public accounting practice units. PAs can be associated with clients' financial statements without giving the standard audit report. They can perform compilation, which consists of writing up the financial statements from a client's books and records, without performing any evidence-gathering work. They can perform review, a semiaudit service in which some evidence-gathering work is performed, but which is lesser in scope than an audit. (Compilation and review standards are explained in more detail in Chapter 14.)

Assurance services are also performed on information in presentations other than traditional financial statements. Since assurance is the lending of credibility by an independent party (assurer, auditor) to the representations made by one person or organization to another, demand for numerous kinds of PA organizations has arisen. Public accountants have provided assurance to vote counts (Academy Awards), to the dollar amount of prizes claimed to have been given in sweepstakes advertisements, to investment performance statistics, and to characteristics claims for computer software programs. These nontraditional services are governed by special sections of the *CICA Handbook,* and proposals have been made to develop a broader set of standards for assurance engagements (explained in more detail in Chapter 2). Henceforth, any reference to *Handbook Section* or *Section* is intended to mean sections of the *CICA Handbook.*

Taxation Services

Local, provincial, national, and international tax laws are often called accountant and lawyer full-employment acts. The laws are complex, and PAs perform services of tax planning and tax return preparation in the areas of income, gift, estate, property, and other taxation. A large proportion of the practice in small accounting firms is tax practice. Tax laws change frequently, and tax practitioners must spend considerable time in continuing education and self-study to keep current with them.

Consulting Services

All accounting firms handle a great deal of consulting. The firm of Arthur Andersen & Company even separated its consulting practice under the name of Andersen Consulting. Consulting and management advisory services are the great ''open end'' of public accounting practice, placing accountants in direct competition with the non-PA consulting firms. The field is virtually unlimited, and a list of consulting activities could not possibly do justice to all of them. Indeed, accounting firms have created consulting units with professionals from other fields—doctors, actuaries, engineers, and advertising executives, to name a few. Many of the large accounting firms have tried to become ''one-stop shopping centres'' for clients' auditing, taxation, and business advice needs.

In large PA firms the consulting department is quite often independent from the auditing and accounting department, performing engagements that do not directly interact with the audits performed by other professionals. In contrast, the OAG has on staff an equally wide range of expertise; but all its combined expertise goes into the audits and studies performed for Parliament. The OAG does not distinguish audits from consulting work, instead marshalling all its abilities to study the wide range of social, agricultural, defence, engineering, and personnel activities it gets charged to investigate.

Regulation of Public Accounting

Regulation of public accounting, as with most professional groups, is a provincial matter. Most provinces have laws, public accounting acts, that specify who can be licensed to practise public accounting in the province. For example, Ontario's Public Accounting Act licenses only CAs to perform audits and reviews. This effectively allows CAs to self-regulate, within constraints brought on by the Ontario Securities Commission and other regulators, as well by as the courts. Alberta's Public Accounting Act of 1988 licenses CMAs and CGAs, as well as CAs; British Columbia and Quebec license CAs and CGAs, while Saskatchewan and Manitoba have no public accountancy laws, effectively allowing anyone to practice. In a province like Saskatchewan, the various designations act as certificates signalling to the public that certain educational and experience requirements have been met, but technically anyone is allowed to practise public accounting. In such provinces market demand determines the relative success of the various designations. There may also be other legislation such as Corporation Acts that specify, for example, that CAs must perform the annual audits of a public corporation. Such legislation effectively creates demand for public accounting services, to be provided by the affected accounting association.

The general trend in provincial public accountancy legislation in recent years has been to open up public accounting to CGAs and CMAs as well as CAs. For example, currently there is a proposal before the Attorney General of Ontario to reform the Public Accounting Act so as to allow CGAs and CMAs to practise audits under controlled conditions in order to better serve the public interest. There is a desire to increase accessibility of public accounting services at reasonable cost while maintaining standards. The concern is to protect the public interest, particularly that of vulnerable third parties.

In addition to the self-regulatory system described above, there are other factors that have great influence on the profession. These include the legal system in which the profession operates (discussed in Chapter 16) and regulators that have an impact on practising auditors. These regulators include at the federal level the Superintendent of Financial Institutions, who has the prime responsibility for monitoring and protecting the public interest vis-à-vis the financial services industry falling under the jurisdiction of the Federal Bank Act. At the provincial level there are the securities commissions, which are charged with the responsibility of investor protection and with ensuring the fairness and efficiency of the capital markets in a province. There are securities commissions in every province and territory. Due to the division of powers between the provinces and the federal government, there is no national-level securities commission in Canada comparable to the SEC in the United States.

The Ontario Securities Commission (OSC) has responsibility for the biggest and most developed capital markets in Canada. It will be used as an illustration of the impact a regulator can have on public accounting. The OSC has three principal activities in ensuring the orderly functioning of capital markets within its jurisdiction, such as the Toronto Stock Exchange:

1. Registration of persons trading in securities and commodity futures contracts.
2. Reviewing and clearing of prospectuses.
3. Enforcement of the Securities Act and Commodity Futures Act.

Activities 2 and 3 have the most impact on public accountants. The staff of the OSC include the chief accountant and a chief forensic accountant who works under the director of enforcement. The Office of the Chief Accountant is responsible for the formulation of financial reporting policy and for monitoring the application of accounting principles and auditing standards by report issuers and their auditors. Financial statements are reviewed on a selective basis, and up to one-quarter of companies reviewed receive comment letters relating to inadequacies in their financial reports. The companies' auditors are also informed of problems noted. If the financial reporting problems are severe enough, the Enforcement Branch is notified.

An example of an Enforcement Branch report affecting an auditor follows:

> An investigation of National Business Systems Inc. resulted in the withdrawal of the company's financial statements for the year ended September 30, 1987. Revised financial statements were required because of "misrepresentations, new information which either was not available or was withheld at the time of the audit of the Original 1987 Statements and matters for which the original accounting was inappropriate". The shareholders equity in the revised financial was $22 million, a reduction of $56 million from the original figure of $78 million reported to shareholders. (*OSC 1988 Annual Report*; p. 18)

The office also monitors auditing and accounting standards-setting of the CICA, and provides input on emerging issues and commentary on proposed standards. In addition, since 1989 the OSC has issued Staff Accounting Communiques (SACs), which are intended to explain the OSC staff's views on specific reporting issues. Although the SACs have no official OSC approval, OSC staff are likely to challenge any treatment that is inconsistent with an SAC. In recent years the OSC, by publishing the results of its monitoring program, and filing complaints to provincial disciplinary committees, and through its representation on CICA standard-setting boards, has made a significant, ongoing impact on the profession.

There are other regulators that touch the profession. For example, the Canadian Investor Protection Fund, which is sponsored by the Toronto, Montreal, Vancouver, and Alberta stock exchanges, and by the Toronto Future Exchange, as well as by the Investment Dealers Association of Canada, is a trust established to protect customers in the event of the financial failure of a member firm (any member of a sponsoring organization, and some American bond dealers that trade in Canada). In recent years fund staff have taken a more active supervisory role. The fund oversees regular, monthly, quarterly, and annual reporting, periodic surprise visits to the offices of a member firm, and at least one surprise financial questionnaire a year. The fund can fine and set sanctions if a member firm violates capital, reporting, or other requirements. The fund is developing policy statements that address standards for internal control within member firms. Auditors have to be aware of these standards when auditing member firms. Internal control reports are discussed in more detail in Chapter 14.

Another regulator that affects Canadian auditors whose client firms have dealings with U.S. securities markets is the SEC. In recent years many Canadian companies have gone to American and other international markets to raise cash through initial public offerings (IPOs). Many Canadian companies are finding it cheaper to raise money on public markets in other countries, because if they did so in Canada, they would need to file regulatory documents in each province. This increases the cost of financing in Canada. At this writing, Finance Minister Paul Martin is exploring the idea of creating a national securities regulation in order to make Canadian securities markets more competitive.[3] The impact of the SEC on auditors is discussed in Appendix 1A.

Finally, there are regulators such as provincial ministries of the environment and natural resources, which have an indirect impact on the profession through restrictions they place on client activities that the clients themselves may need to disclose. This is further discussed in the book appendix.

---

[3]   A. Freeman and K. Hawlett, "Keep IPO's at home: Martin." *The Globe and Mail*, Toronto (March 8, 1996), B1.

It is clear from this brief review that the profession is facing an increasingly complex regulatory environment and that auditors will have to be increasingly sensitized to regulator concerns in order to do a proper audit.

R E V I E W
C H E C K P O I N T S

1.14 Identify several types of professional accountants and their organizations.

1.15 What are some examples of assurance services rendered on representations other than traditional financial statements?

1.16 What are the three major areas of public accounting services?

SUMMARY

This chapter began by defining auditing and distinguishing it from accounting. The practice of public accounting is rooted in the history of auditing, which started in Canada shortly before 1900. Events since the mid-1970s, in the form of various company failures and related litigation and enquiries, have propelled auditors in public practice into a phase of far-reaching change.

Auditing is practised in numerous forms by various practice units including PA firms, Revenue Canada, the OAG, internal audit departments in companies, and several other types of regulatory auditors. Fraud examiners, many of whom are internal auditors and inspectors, have found a niche in auditing-related activities.

Many auditors aspire to become CAs, CGAs, CMAs, or CIAs; this involves passing rigorous examinations, obtaining practical experience, and maintaining competence through continuing professional education. Each of these groups has a large professional organization that governs the professional standards and quality of practice of its members.

When you begin a study of auditing, you may be eager to attack the nitty-gritty of doing financial statement audit work. These technical topics begin in Chapter 4. Instructors can choose to cover chapters in a different sequence than the one offered, but the next chapters introduce you to generally accepted audit standards and audit reports. Technical material starts in Chapter 4 and continues through Chapter 13. You are then introduced to other services and reports, professional ethics, legal liability, governmental and internal auditing, and fraud awareness auditing. The book concludes with more advanced coverage of computer auditing and statistics.

Although the textbook will enable you to learn about auditing, instructors are seldom able to duplicate a practice environment in a classroom setting. You may feel frustrated about knowing "how to do it." This frustration is natural because auditing is done in the field under pressure of time limits and in the surroundings of client personnel, paperwork, and accounting information systems. The textbook can provide a foundation and framework for understanding auditing, but nothing can substitute for the first few months of work when the classroom study comes alive in the field.

MULTIPLE-CHOICE QUESTIONS FOR PRACTICE AND REVIEW

1.17 When people speak of the assurance function, they are referring to the work of auditors in:

a. Lending credibility to a client's financial statements.

b. Detecting fraud and embezzlement in a company.

c. Lending credibility to an auditee's financial statements.

d. Performing a program results audit in a government agency.

1.18 Company A hired Sampson & Delila, CAs, to audit the financial statements of Company B and deliver the audit report to Megabank. Which is the client?

a. Megabank.

b. Sampson & Delila.

c. Company A.

d. Company B.

1.19 According to the CICA, the objective of an audit of financial statements is:

a. An expression of opinion on the fairness with which they present financial position, results of operations, and cash flows in conformity with generally accepted accounting principles.

b. An expression of opinion on the fairness with which they present financial position, results of operations, and cash flows in conformity with accounting standards promulgated by the Financial Accounting Standards Board.

c. An expression of opinion on the fairness with which they present financial position, result of operations, and cash flows in conformity with accounting standards promulgated by the CICA Accounting Standards Committee.

d. To obtain systematic and objective evidence about financial assertions and report the results to interested users.

1.20 Bankers who are processing loan applications from companies seeking large loans will probably ask for financial statements audited by an independent PA because:

a. Financial statements are too complex for them to analyse themselves.

b. They are too far away from company headquarters to perform accounting and auditing themselves.

c. The consequences of making a bad loan are very undesirable.

d. They generally see a potential conflict of interest between company managers who want to get loans and their needs for reliable financial statements.

1.21 Operational audits of a company's efficiency and economy of managing projects and of the results of programs are conducted by whom?

a. Management advisory services departments of PA firms in public practice.

b. The company's internal auditors.

c. Governmental auditors employed by the federal government.

d. All of the above.

1.22 Independent auditors of financial statements perform audits that reduce and control:

a. The business risks faced by investors.

b. The information risk faced by investors.

c. The complexity of financial statements.

d. Quality reviews performed by other PA firms.

1.23 The primary objective of compliance auditing is to:

a. Give an opinion on financial statements.

b. Develop a basis for a report on internal control.

c. Perform a study of effective and efficient use of resources.

d. Determine whether auditee personnel are following laws, rules, regulations, and policies.

1.24 The CICA senior committees do not have the power to:

a. Award the CICA certificate to a qualified candidate.

b. Issue enforceable statements on auditing standards.

c. Issue enforceable statements on standards for accounting and review services.

d. Make interpretations and rulings on the Rules of Professional Conduct.

1.25 Auditing standards are officially issued by the:

a. Financial Accounting Standards Board.

b. CICA Accounting and Review Services Committee.

c. CICA Accounting Standards Executive Committee.

d. CICA Auditing Standards Board.

EXERCISES AND PROBLEMS

. . . .

1.26 Controller as Auditor. The chairman of the board of Hughes Corporation proposed that the board hire as controller a PA who had been the manager on the corporation's audit performed by a firm of independent accountants. The chairman thought that hiring this person would make the annual audit unnecessary and would consequently result in saving the professional fee paid to the auditors. The chairman proposed to give this new controller a full staff to conduct such investigations of accounting and operating data as necessary. Evaluate this proposal.

1.27 Controller as Auditor. Put yourself in the position of the person hired as controller in the above situation. Suppose the chairman of the board moves to discontinue the annual audit because Hughes Corporation now has your services on a full-time basis. You are invited to express your views to the board. Explain how you would discuss the nature of your job as controller and your views on the discontinuance of the annual audit.

1.28 Logic and Method. You have 12 solid spherical objects, 11 of which have an identical weight and volume. The other sphere has a different weight. All 12 spheres look exactly alike.

You have been given a balance scale (a weighting instrument), and you have been granted three (and only three) weighing trials in which to determine (*a*) which sphere has the different weight, and (*b*) whether it is heavier or lighter than the other 11.

Required:
Develop and apply a solution approach that will produce the two determinations for all combinations of weighing trial outcomes.

1.29 Logic and Method. A census worker asked a mother the ages (years, not months) of her three children. The mother replied that the product of their ages is 36, and the sum of their ages is the same as the address (house number) to

the north. After looking at that address, the census worker returned and said to the mother: "I need more information." The mother gave one final clue, saying: "The oldest is sleeping upstairs."

Required:
What are the ages of the three children, and what is the address (house number) next door to the north? (Reprinted with permission from *Parade*, copyright 1991)

1.30 Operational Auditing. Bigdeal Corporation manufactures paper and paper products and is trying to decide whether to purchase and merge Smalltek Company. Smalltek has developed a process for manufacturing boxes that can replace other containers that use fluorocarbons for expelling a liquid product. The price may be as high as $45 million. Bigdeal prefers to buy Smalltek and integrate its products, while leaving the Smalltek management in charge of day-to-day operations. A major consideration is the efficiency and effectiveness of the Smalltek management. Bigdeal wants to obtain a report on the operational efficiency and effectiveness of the Smalltek sales, production, and research and development departments.

Required:
Who can Bigdeal engage to produce this operational audit report? Several possibilities exist. Are there any particular advantages or disadvantages in choosing among them?

1.31 Definition of Financial Position. Every independent auditor's opinion refers to the presentation of financial position in conformity with generally accepted accounting principles. Search the authoritative accounting and economics literature (or conduct interviews with practising auditors) and find the official definition of "financial position." Determine whether the definition(s) is adequate for you and defend your support or criticism of the definition.

1.32 Auditor as Guarantor. Your neighbour invited you to lunch yesterday. Sure enough, it was no "free lunch" because he wanted to discuss the annual report of the Dodge Corporation. He owns Dodge shares and just received the annual report. He says: "Price Waterhouse prepared the audited financial statements and gave an unqualified opinion, so my investment must be safe."

Required:

What misconceptions does your neighbour seem to have about the auditor's role with respect to Dodge Corporation?

1.33 Identification of Audits and Auditors. Audits may be characterized as (*a*) financial statement audits, (*b*) compliance audits—audits of compliance with control policies and procedures and with laws and regulations, (*c*) economy and efficiency audits, and (*d*) program results audits. The work can be done by independent (external) auditors, internal auditors, or governmental auditors. Below is a list of the purposes or products of various audit engagements:

1. Render a public report on the assumptions and compilation of a revenue forecast by a sports stadium/racetrack complex.
2. Determine the fair presentation in conformity with GAAP of an advertising agency's financial statements.
3. Report on how better care and disposal of vehicles confiscated by drug enforcement agents could save money and benefit law enforcement.
4. Determine costs of municipal garbage pickup services compared to comparable service subcontracted to a private business.
5. Audit tax shelter partnership financing terms.
6. Study a private aircraft manufacturer's test pilot performance in reporting on the results of test flights.
7. Conduct periodic examination of a bank for solvency.
8. Evaluate the promptness of materials inspection in a manufacturer's receiving department.

Required:

Prepare a three-column schedule showing: (1) Each of the engagements listed above; (2) the type of audit (financial statement, compliance, economy and efficiency, or program results); and (3) the kind of auditors you would expect to be involved.

1.34 Analysis and Judgment. As part of your regular year-end audit of a publicly held client, you must estimate the probability of success of its proposed new product line. The client has experienced financial difficulty during the last few years and—in your judgment—a successful introduction of the new product line is necessary for the client to remain a going concern.

There are five steps, all of which are necessary for successful introduction of the product: (1) successful labour negotiations between the construction firms contracted to build the necessary addition to the present plant and the building trades unions; (2) successful defence of patent rights; (3) product approval by the Health Branch; (4) successful negotiation of a long-term raw material contract with a foreign supplier; and (5) successful conclusion of distribution contract talks with a large national retail distributor.

In view of the circumstances, you contact experts, who have provided your audit firm with reliable estimates in the past. The labour relations expert estimates that there is an 80 percent chance of successfully concluding labour negotiations before the strike deadline. Legal counsel advises that there is a 90 percent chance of successfully defending patent rights. The expert on Health Branch product approvals estimates a 95 percent chance of approval. The experts in the remaining two areas estimate the probability of successfully resolving (*a*) the raw materials contract and (*b*) the distribution contract talks to be 90 percent in each case. Assume these estimates are reliable.

Required:

What is your assessment of the probability of successful product introduction? (Hint: You can assume the five steps are independent of each other.)

Appendix 1A

Overview of U.S. and International Auditing

. . . .

LEARNING   OBJECTIVE

6. Provide an overview of U.S. and international auditing.

In the United States the early formal development of accounting and auditing were mixed together. Working with the Federal Trade Commission, the Federal Reserve Board, and the New York Stock Exchange, the American Institute of Accountants (later renamed the American Institute of Certified Public Accountants) produced these bulletins designed to systematize accounting and auditing:

1917— Federal Reserve Board, "Uniform Accounting: A Tentative Proposal Submitted by the Federal Reserve Board."

1918— Federal Reserve Board, "Approved Methods for the Preparation of Balance Sheet Statements."

1929— Federal Reserve Board, "Verification of Financial Statements."

1934— New York Stock Exchange, "Audits of Corporate Accounts."

1936— American Institute of Accountants, "Examination of Financial Statements by Independent Public Accountants."

These first 20 years were marked by interest in both accounting and auditing and by co-operation between the American Institute and government agencies. In 1939 the American Institute went its own way by creating the Committee on Auditing Procedure to deal exclusively with auditing matters. This committee launched the Statements on Auditing Procedure series, the first of which (1939) was titled "Extensions of Auditing Procedure."

Generally accepted auditing standards, however, were not known by that name until 1947. Following an investigation of the late 1930s, McKesson and Robbins fraud and the auditors' failure to detect it, the Securities and Exchange Commission in the United States passed a rule requiring auditors to report that their audits were "in accordance with generally accepted auditing standards." The Committee on Auditing Procedure got busy (after being delayed by World War II) and published in 1947 the "Tentative Statements of Auditing Standards—Their Generally Accepted Significance and Scope."

Standard-setting for auditors has been the responsibility of the American Institute ever since, although the names have changed. In 1972 the AICPA Auditing Standards Executive Committee replaced the Committee on Auditing Procedure, and the series of auditing pronouncements was renamed Statements on Auditing Standards. Following an extensive study by the Commission on Auditors' Responsibilities (Cohen Commission), the committee's name was changed to the AICPA Auditing Standards Board (1978), which remains the AICPA's senior technical committee on auditing matters. (The name of the series, *Statements on Auditing Standards (SAS)*, was not changed.) The Cohen Commission was formed at a time when auditors were coming under criticism from the U.S. Congress. In the early 1970s several spectacular business failures and alleged audit failures drew the attention of senators and representatives, and they proposed a federal takeover of the regulation of accounting and auditing. Accountants abhor federal regulation, and the Cohen Commission report paved the way for several reforms that defused the congressional concerns, including the creation of the AICPA private companies practice section and the SEC practice section (discussed later in this appendix).

THOUGHTS FROM "THE ACCOUNTING ESTABLISHMENT"

Selected Recommendations

Congress should exercise stronger oversight of accounting practices and more leadership in establishing proper goals and practices.

Congress should amend the Federal securities laws to restore the right of individuals to sue independent auditors for negligence.

Congress should consider methods of increasing competition among accounting firms for selection as independent auditors.

The Federal Government should directly establish financial accounting standards for publicly-owned corporations.

The Federal Government should establish auditing standards used by independent auditors.

Federal standards of conduct for auditors should prohibit representation of client interests and management advisory services for audit clients.

The Federal Government should define the responsibilities of independent auditors so that they clearly meet the expectations of Congress, the public, and courts of law.

Source: Staff Study by the Subcommittee on Reports, Accounting, and Management of the Senate Committee on Government Operations, 95th Congress, Document No. 95-34, March 31, 1977.

However, trouble would not go away. In the 1980s more business and audit failures led to creation of the National Commission on Fraudulent Financial Reporting (Treadway Commission). In 1987 this commission made numerous recommendations concerning auditors' responsibilities. Many of these recommendations were enacted by the Auditing Standards Board in several Statements on Auditing Standards, known generally as the expectation gap auditing standards. The main thrust of these new statements (issued in 1988 and numbered 53–61) was to increase auditors' responsibilities for detecting and reporting errors, irregularities, illegal acts, and frauds, and to enhance accounting firms' monitoring of the quality of their audit practices.

Congressional interest in the auditing profession continues to this day. Bank and savings and loan failures have heightened this interest. The Oversight and Investigations Subcommittee of the House Energy and Commerce Committee (chaired by Representative John Dingell, Democrat, Michigan) has held many hearings focusing on the effectiveness of independent accountants who perform audits. Legislation has been introduced that would, among other things, (1) require auditors to make special reports when clients commit illegal acts, (2) require the SEC to prescribe methods to be used by auditors to detect and report illegal activities, and (3) require the SEC to prescribe methods to detect illegal acts and related party transactions, and to evaluate companies' going-concern status. Only time will tell the nature and extent of new regulation of the auditing profession.

The AICPA currently regulates itself through the Division for CPA Firms. This division consists of two sections: the Private Companies Practice Section (PCPS) and the SEC Practice Section (SECPS). Accounting firms can volunteer to join one or both of the sections. Rules for membership include requirements for an average of 40 hours of continuing professional education (CPE) each year for professional employees and a peer review every three years. A peer review or quality review is a study of a firm's quality policies and procedures followed by a report on the firm's quality of audit practice. Both sections have peer review committees that review the work and reports of the peer reviewers. In addition, the SECPS has a Public Oversight Board (POB) that is like a board of outside directors. The POB consists of prominent people who serve as representatives of the public at large, overseeing the self-regulation of firms that audit companies registered with the U.S. Securities and Exchange Commission. Auditors of SEC-registered companies are required to be members of the SEC Practice Section. (Professionals working in accounting firms that audit SEC companies and are not members of SECPS cannot remain members of the AICPA.) The goal of this requirement is to ensure the high quality of audits of public companies. The SECPS membership consists of about 1,000 accounting firms that employ about 127,000 professionals and audit the 14,000 public companies.

Quality Control Standards

From 1977 to 1982, the AICPA also had a Quality Control Standards Committee. This senior committee was dissolved after it issued its *Statement on Quality Control Standards No. 1 (QCS 1)*. The AICPA believed that, because the work of quality control and self-regulation was being handled well by the Division for Firms, a separate committee was no longer needed. Nevertheless, *QCS 1* remains as an authoritative practice standard. In 1987 the AICPA designated the Quality Review Executive Committee as a senior technical committee. This body develops policies and procedures for the peer review programs, and it currently provides the technical support for the reviews of accounting firms' quality controls.

Accredited Personal Financial Specialists

For many years the AICPA resisted proposals to accredit persons as specialists (e.g., tax specialists, consulting specialists). The ice was broken, however, in 1987. After the Colorado Society of CPAs instituted a successful specialization course and examination, the AICPA authorized the specialty designation of "Accredited Personal Financial Specialist" (APFS). Among the requirements are a one-day examination, 250 hours of personal financial planning experience in each of the past three years, and six reference letters from other professionals and clients. APFSs must also meet continuing education requirements, have valid CPA certificates in their states, and maintain membership in the AICPA. Examinations are given annually and may be given more often in the future if demand is great enough. The AICPA has a Personal Financial Planning Executive Committee that has been designated by council as a senior technical committee to make official pronouncements relating to personal financial planning practice.

International Auditing

Many of the large public accounting firms are worldwide organizations that have grown rapidly in the last few decades paralleling the increased economic integration of their global clientele. Developments such as the North American Free Trade Agreement (NAFTA), the evolution of the European Economic Union and other free trade zones, and the pervasive effects of technological change are all contributing to increased global harmonization of auditing and accounting standards. For these reasons the International Federation of Accountants (IFAC) was created in 1977. The IFAC is increasingly mirroring the activities at an international level what national institutes have been doing domestically. In particular, the IFAC publishes its own handbook on auditing standards that recommends international standards on auditing (ISAs). ISAs cover such issues as basic principles of auditing, auditor's reports, professional independence, reliance on other auditors abroad, and professional qualifications.

The issue is whether ISAs will achieve worldwide acceptance. This increasingly looks likely. For example, the *CICA Handbook* has a section (*Section* 5101) providing a comparison between the *Handbook* and ISAs. The CICA's policy is to adopt ISAs as is unless Canadian conditions require a different standard, and to keep existing practice until the CICA adopts a new ISA. *Section* 5101 either notes a significance difference between an ISA and a *Handbook Section*(*s*), or makes the statement that there is no significant difference. Generally, the remaining significant differences between the *Handbook* and the ISAs are that the ISAs tend to focus more on (1) financial information instead of financial statements, (2) procedures rather than broader standards, (3) rules of professional conduct (something not covered in the *CICA Handbook*), (4) working paper documentation, (5) engagement letters, (6) reliance on other auditors, (7) management representatives, and (8) special purpose auditor reports. The CGAs have published their own GAAP guide, which, in addition to the *CICA Handbook,* references U.S. and IASC standards and notes key differences between the Canadian requirements and those of the IASC and the United States.

As the world becomes more interdependent, many concepts and terms used in other countries will become increasingly accepted in Canadian practice. Indeed, many large firms already use manuals and training materials reflecting international practice. This textbook makes use of those terms and concepts and does not restrict itself to those currently used in the *CICA Handbook.*

Appendix 1B

Alternative Theories of the Role of Auditing in Society

. . . .

LEARNING OBJECTIVE

7. Describe alternative theories of the role of auditing in society.

In the chapter we defined *auditing* as an information risk reducing activity. This definition follows from the information hypothesis that is used to explain the demand for external audits. Under the information hypothesis, audit services are demanded to reduce the information risk to users of financial statements. Information risk is the risk that user decisions may be based on incorrect information. Thus, auditors are demanded in order to reduce losses due to faulty decisions as a result of errors or irregularities in the financial statements. Losses to investors may also arise because of failure to disclose all the facts about a firm by company management. Auditors help assess whether this information asymmetry is alleviated through proper disclosure. Less accurate information may also deter investment, so auditing may also alleviate underinvestment in the capital markets and result in better resource allocation in the economy.

Another hypothesis that has been proposed to explain the sources of demand for audits is the monitoring hypothesis. The monitoring hypothesis is based on the principal-agent framework of economic theory. Agency theory predicts that utility-maximizing agents (the managers), if unchecked, will consume more resources than optimal. However, investors with rational expectations will take such behaviour into account in pricing a firm's securities. As a result, the agents have the incentive to contract for mechanisms to monitor their opportunistic behaviour. The hiring of an external auditor is one such mechanism. This theory predicts that management will demand audits whenever the cost of monitoring their activities is less than the wage loss management suffers without the monitoring. The presumption here is that the owners of the firm will pay managers more with monitoring of their activities than without monitoring.

The insurance hypothesis predicts that auditors are demanded in order that they may be sued in case there is a business failure. Auditing thus provides investors a form of insurance. If an investor purchases securities on the basis of audited financial statements and subsequently sustains losses, the law provides some degree of recourse against the auditor. In this way the auditor can, depending on how the court's reasoning works, function as an indemnifier against investment losses.

The degree of recourse depends on the legal system in force. Under a negligence-based concept, some form of audit failure needs to be proved. Moreover, for registration statements under SEC laws (covered in Chapter 16), the burden of proof is on the auditor to demonstrate that due care was observed in the audit task. Recent court cases in the United States seem to abandon the negligence concept in favour of an implied warranty concept. Under the implied warranty concept, the issue of whether the auditor is negligent is irrelevant. The auditor is responsible once it can be proved that the audited financial statement is wrong. This concept is concerned with accident (audit failure) prevention, compensating the injured, and a better distribution of losses. Under implied warranty the audit fee may be little more than a fee for insurance against otherwise uninsurable business risk (e.g., due to management incompetence). We say "may" because it all depends on how courts interpret "wrong" financial statements: if "wrong" financial statements mean failure to anticipate *any* adverse business event, then auditors are responsible for insuring business losses. If, on the other hand, "wrong" financial statements mean failure to disclose only those adverse events for which there is information at the time of audit, then auditors are effectively liable only for information risk. So, much depends on court interpretation and the amount of damages awarded to the plaintiffs. The punitive damage award system in the United States—with its high multiples of actual damages—is close to the kind of system that would make auditors insurers of business risk. It is assumed that any auditor-insured business risk is then passed on in the form of fee increases to all clients. Clients in turn pass these costs on to society via increased prices for their products. In this way risks faced by investors are passed on to society—that is, business risk is socialized.

Each of these theories helps explain some aspect of the audit environment and some of the reasons audits are demanded. These theories also appear to apply in different degrees in different countries and different legal systems. For example, in the United States the risk of an auditor being sued has traditionally been about 10 times that of the risk in Canada. This suggests that the insurance hypothesis may be a more important explanation of the demand for audits in the American business environment than in the Canadian business environment.

Each of these theories can provide a justification for reduced information risk. Clearly under the monitoring and information hypotheses, information risk is to be reduced for the principals and other users respectively. Under the insurance hypothesis it may be less obvious why information risk should be reduced. Under a negligence-based liability system, if the auditor can prove due care in reducing information risk, then the auditor will reduce the possibility of legal liability. Even under the implied warranty concept of insurance, reduced information risk will reduce the risk of legal liability because there is a lower chance of an audit failure or "accident" to cause the liability. Thus, despite the different explanations these hypotheses provide, they all have in common the auditor's need to reduce information risk. Some estimate that information risk is a significant component of cost of capital for many firms. A reduction in information risk thus has the tangible effect of reducing a firm's cost of capital.

APPENDIX 1C

HOW TO BECOME A PA

· ·

LEARNING OBJECTIVE
8. List and explain the requirements for becoming a public accountant.

Education

First, we discuss the education requirements for the CA designation. The provincial institutes, which are regulatory agencies for each province, set the education requirements for taking the CA examination and receiving a CA designation. The majority of provinces currently require a bachelor's degree. However, some provinces are considering a policy position that all CAs admitted to membership beginning in the year 2000 or soon thereafter must have 150 semester hours (five years) of university-level education. It is interesting to note that the 150-hour requirement does not presume the completion of a master's degree, and each provincial institute can set its own policy for the number of accounting courses included in the 150 hours. In the United States the AICPA has also set the target date of the year 2000 for such a 150-hour requirement. Call or write your provincial CA institute to learn about its requirements and plans.

In addition to entry-level education requirements, the provincial institutes, in conjunction with the CICA, have available optional continuing-education courses. However, with the North American Free Trade Agreement (NAFTA) and globalization of public accounting services there will be increasing harmonization of educational requirements in public accounting. For these reasons it is instructive to look at other countries' systems, especially that of the United States, which tends to lead global practice. At present with respect to continuing professional education, the AICPA and most states require 120 contact hours (not semester or quarter-college hours) of continuing professional education (CPE) over three-year reporting periods, with no less than 20 hours in any one year. CPAs who are not in public practice generally face fewer continuing-education requirements (the AICPA requires 90 hours over three-year reporting periods with no less than 15 hours in any one year.) These continuing-education hours are obtained in a variety of ways—AICPA continuing-education courses, state CPA society-sponsored courses, in-house training in CPA firms and industry, college courses, and private-provider courses. These types of courses range in length from one hour to two days, depending on the subject. Although similar courses are also being offered by provincial institutes, at the current time CPE is done on a voluntary basis by CAs.

CGAs are more flexible in their formal education requirements. Currently, there is no university education requirement; the entire program of professional studies is available directly through the CGAs. However, there is a proposal to require a university degree or its equivalent prior to certification, to be implemented by 1998. Check with your provincial association for more detailed requirement. CMAs already have a university degree or its equivalent. Again check with your provincial society for more details.

PA Examination

The Uniform Final Examination is prepared by the Examinations Division of the CICA. It is administered in September each year in all Canadian provinces and territories. The examination covers business law, auditing, accounting practice, and accounting theory. These areas also include questions of professional ethics, legal liability of accountants, income taxation, and quantitative methods in accounting and auditing. These topics are covered in depth separately as well as being integrated in a comprehensive case format reflecting a realistic professional setting. Because qualifications for taking the CA examination vary from province to province, you should contact your provincial institute for information. CGA examinations are designed to provide an in-depth assessment of knowledge and skills in accounting, auditing, finance, and taxation. Students take the various level exams after completing a specific program of courses. In 1998 a comprehensive, integrative type of exam will be given to go along with the new educational requirements. Check your provincial association for more details. CMA students must also pass a comprehensive entrance exam on accounting and management knowledge gained through university studies, as well as a case presentation and board report upon completion of the program.

Experience

Most provinces and territories require persons who have attained the education level and passed the CA Examination to have a period of experience before they are awarded CA designations. Experience requirements vary among provinces, but the most common system requires two years for holders of bachelor's degrees and one year for holders of master's degrees. While a few provinces require that the experience be obtained in a public accounting firm, most of them accept experience in other organizations (provincial auditor, Revenue Canada) as long as the applicant performs work requiring accounting judgment and is supervised by a competent accountant, preferably a CA.

CGAs and CMAs also have experience requirements that vary among provinces.

Provincial Certificate and Licence

The CICA does not issue CA certificates or licences to practice. There is no national CA certificate. Most provinces and territories have public accountancy laws and provincial institutes to administer them. These are the agencies that make physical arrangements to give the CA examination (called the Uniform Final Examination or UFE), collect the examinations, receive the grades from the CICA grading service, and notify candidates whether they passed or failed. After satisfying provincial requirements for education and experience, successful candidates are awarded the CA designation by a province. At the same time, new CAs must pay a fee to obtain a provincial licence to practise. Thereafter, provincial institutes regulate the behaviour of CAs under their jurisdiction (enforcing provincial rules of professional conduct) and supervise practice inspection.

Provincial associations and societies regulate the practice of CGAs and CMAs respectively. This regulation includes enforcing the provincial rules of professional conduct, and administering subject area and national exams as well as the programs of professional education courses.

R E V I E W
CHECKPOINTS

1.35 Can you see any justification for requiring 150 semester-hours of university courses for PAs?

1.36 How much continuing education is required of PAs?

1.37 Why do you think experience is required by all provinces to be a PA?

1.38 What are some of the functions of a provincial institute, association, or society?

The National and Provincial Organization of PAs

. . . .

LEARNING OBJECTIVE
9. Describe the accounting and auditing activities of the professional accounting organizations.

Public recognition of PAs as professionals is enhanced by the existence of professional organizations both nationally (CICA, CGAAC, SMAC) and provincially. The provincial institutes' societies and associations have responsibility for setting and enforcing standards of qualification, standards of adherence, and standards of enforcement. The standards of qualification relate to enrolment, education, and examination of students, and each provincial institute society and association has responsibility for administering each aspect of qualification through various committees, such as in Ontario the Education Coordination Committee and Applications Committee of the ICAO. Each CICA committee is assisted by at least one full-time staff member of ICAO.

Standards of adherence relate to the system of practice inspection that a province may have to monitor the quality of audit practice. The objective is to provide feedback to members on the quality of their work, and, if needed, recommendations for additional training. There are also practice advisory services and consultation services provided to members on request, usually for sole practitioners or smaller firms. The standards of enforcement relate to the activities of professional conduct, discipline, and appeals as discussed in Chapter 15. Activities of provincial institutes also include lobbying activities with provincial governments for changes to legislation in such areas as securities regulation, corporation acts, and taxation. Since 1991 there have also been various Co-ordination Committees set up to co-ordinate issues such as rules of professional conduct and education across the various provinces. An organization chart of the Institute of Chartered Accountants of Ontario (ICAO) is shown in Exhibit 1C–1 as an illustration. This chart reflects the management and senior staff of the Institute, many of whom act in an advisory capacity to related committees.

Regulation 44 of the Canada Business Corporation Act requires that financial statements of companies subject to the Act be prepared in accordance with the recommendations of the *CICA Handbook.* Thus the CICA has primary responsibility for standards of practice, including the setting of accounting and auditing standards through the *Handbook.* However, the CICA also has other objectives, such as to maintain the highest national and international stature as a professional organization; in co-operation with the provincial Institutes, to develop and maintain a body of knowledge and to prepare the uniform final exam; and to promote international harmonization of principles, standards, and practices of the profession.

To achieve these various objectives the CICA operates through numerous committees and groups. A list of some of the more important committees follows:

1. Accounting Research and Auditing Standards Committees
2. Federal Legislation Committee
3. Management Consultants and Taxation Committees

CICA Organization

A partial organization chart is shown in Exhibit 1C–2. It highlights the CICA divisions most closely related to accounting and auditing practice.

The national organizations of CGAs and CMAs also engage in similar activities, setting national standards or guides, including programs of basic research. However, currently only the CAs have gotten to the point of developing their own audit standards.

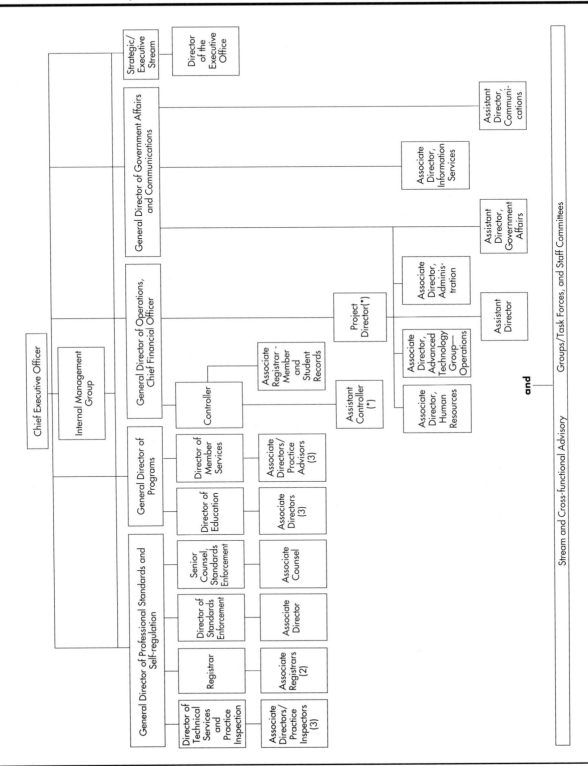

EXHIBIT 1C–2   **PARTIAL CICA ORGANIZATION CHART**
(as of December 31, 1995)

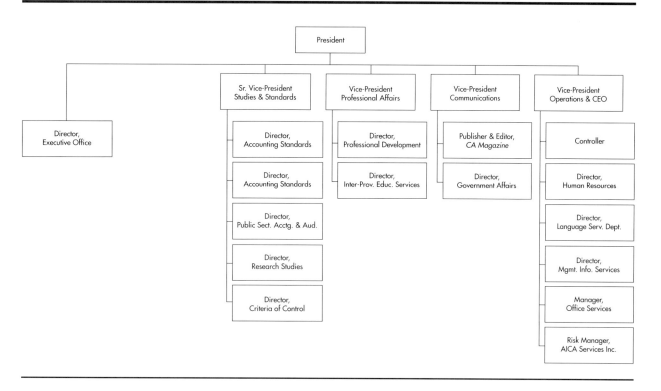

. . . .

R E V I E W
C H E C K P O I N T S

1.39 Identify the type of standards set by the CICA.

1.40 Identify the type of standards set by provincial institutes of CAs.

1.41 Identify at least two other activities of the CICA besides standard setting.

1.42 Identify two interprovincial issues that require co-ordination by provincial institutes.

. . . .

CHAPTER 2

Learning Objectives

Chapter 1 gave you a general introduction to professional accounting practice. Chapter 2 explains three sets of interrelated practice standards for audit services offered by PAs in public practice. Your objectives are to be able to:

1. Name the various practice standards for internal, governmental, and independent auditors, and identify their sources.

2. Discuss the reasons for having general assurance standards and give some examples of assurance subject matters.

3. Write and explain the eight CICA generally accepted auditing standards (GAAS), and explain how GAAS was or was not followed in specific fact situations.

4. Describe the standard unqualified audit report in terms of its communication of audit standards and other messages.

5. Interpret GAAS in the context of a computer environment.

6. Explain some characteristics of "professional scepticism."

7. List and explain the important requirements of quality control standards for a PA firm.

Assurance, Audit, and Quality Control Standards

Practice Standards

LEARNING OBJECTIVE

1. Name the various practice standards for internal, governmental, and independent auditors, and identify their sources.

Practice standards are general guides for the quality of professional work. The North American accounting and auditing profession has many sets of standards, depending upon which sets are included or excluded in a particular count. This chapter deals directly with three sets: assurance standards, as suggested by various sections of the *CICA Handbook*; generally accepted auditing standards, issued by the CICA Auditing Standards Board; and quality control standards as reflected in firm peer review, and in provincial Institutes' practice inspection manuals and the CICA's *Guide for Developing Quality Control Systems in Public Accounting*.

Other chapters in this textbook explain other sets of standards. Chapter 15 covers the Rules of Professional Conduct. The CICA Recommendations for Compilation and Review Services are explained in Chapter 14. The CICA's public sector audit standards and the internal audit standards (Institute of Internal Auditors) are in Chapter 17. *Professional Standards and Practices for Certified Fraud Examiners* (Association of Certified Fraud Examiners) are in an appendix to Chapter 18.

Another set of auditing standards is known as the International Standards of Auditing (ISA), issued by the International Auditing Practices Committee of the International Federation of Accountants. In the international community, accountants and regulators have a great interest in **harmonization**—that is, making the standards co-ordinated, if not uniform, throughout the world. The ISAs are a first step in this direction. They are not cited specifically in this textbook because they contain many standards statements that are the same as Canadian generally accepted auditing standards. Some differences exist, however. The *CICA Handbook* has summaries of the points on which the ISA's are more demanding or conflict with Canadian generally accepted auditing standards (*Section* 5101). Also CGA-Canada has prepared a guide relating CICA Standards to ISA and U.S. Standards.

You will find very few references to the accounting recommendations in this textbook. The CICA issues accounting standards; but this book concentrates on auditing and the practice of accounting, not on the accounting rules themselves. An overview of the audit standard-setting process is provided in the next section.

Overview of Auditing Standard-setting Process of CICA[1]

The Senior Vice-President Studies and Standards has overall responsibility for standard setting as indicated in Exhibit 1–1 in Chapter 1. There are five directors, each reporting to the Senior Vice-President Studies and Standards with various technical and support staff, in each of the following areas as of February 1995: (1) Accounting

---

[1] This section is based on information supplied by CICA on their standard-setting process.

Standards, (2) Auditing Standards, (3) Criteria for Control, (4) Public Sector Accounting and Auditing, and (5) Research Studies.

In order to ensure due process, a number of key steps are taken in developing standards:

1. Identification of need and setting of priorities.
2. Preliminary investigation—if necessary, by means of a Study or Report.
3. Development and approval of a Project Proposal.
4. Setting up and briefing of volunteer group (task force).
5. The development of the draft Statement of Principles.
6. The distribution of the draft Statement of Principles to "Associates."
7. Approval by the respective standard-setting board/committee of the Statement of Principles.
8. The development of the Exposure Draft.
9. Approval by the respective standard-setting board/committee of the Exposure Draft.
10. Processing of the comments on the Exposure Draft and meetings with respondents.
11. Approval by the respective standard-setting board/committee of the final Standard in English and French.
12. Production and distribution of the final Standard.[2]

The boards referred to in steps 7, 9, and 11 are made up of volunteer members, who are appointed for three-year terms as voting members, as well as staff of the CICA, who are nonvoting members. Volunteer efforts are critical to the CICA's standard-setting efforts: an estimated 5,400 volunteer days are contributed annually by some 850 volunteers. The formal objectives of the boards most relevant to this text are stated as follows:

1. The Auditing Standards Board's objective is to develop and promulgate recommended performance and reporting standards and practice guidance on auditing and related services in the best interests of the profession and the public as a whole.
2. The Public Sector Accounting and Auditing Board's objective is to recommend standards to improve and harmonize financial reporting, accounting, and auditing in the public sector in the best interests of the public, including users, preparers, and auditors of financial information.
3. The Criteria of Control Committee's objective is to develop criteria that will permit management to assess and report on control systems and publish such guidance as it considers to be in the best interests of the public, including users, preparers, and auditors of control reports.
4. The Studies Advisory Committee, which has recently been formed, provides leadership and direction to the studies activity by supporting and monitoring the progress of projects initiated by the standard-setting boards, and by identifying and stimulating research on other topics and themes that are likely to be of concern to the accounting profession.[3]

[2] Ibid, p. 5.
[3] Ibid, p. 2.

EXHIBIT 2–1   PROJECT DEVELOPMENT PROCESS

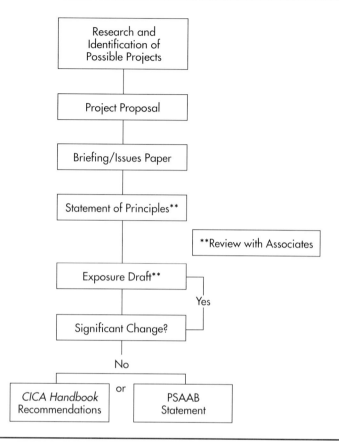

*Boards/Committees may vote not to re-expose.
**Review with associates takes place at either the draft Statement of Principles or draft Exposure Draft stage or both.

   The entire process normally takes at least two years, and projects that are preceded by studies take the longest. An overview of the process is given in Exhibit 2–1.

   More timely guidance is provided by Auditing Guidelines. Auditing Guidelines do not go through the full due process of a Standard and they do not have the same authority as *Handbook Recommendations*. The Boards issue Guidelines in order to clarify existing standards or provide guidance in their application on a timely basis.

- -

R E V I E W   2.1   What are the practice standards, and who issues them for external auditors of
CHECKPOINTS   financial statements? internal auditors? government auditors?

                  2.2   What are the practice standards, and who issues them for external nonaudit
                        assurance engagements? quality of CA firms' audit practice? fraud examination
                        work? consulting services? tax services? (Refer also to Chapter 1.)

- -

ASSURANCE STANDARDS

. . . .

LEARNING OBJECTIVE

2. Discuss the reasons for having general assurance standards and give some examples of assurance subject matters.

In March 1997 the CICA issued *Section* 5025, "Standards for Assurance Engagements." The significance of this standard, the first of its kind in the world, arises from the fact that it is intended to provide an umbrella framework for all existing and future audit-type engagements. This means the standard is intended to provide a framework for auditing and related engagements for a large variety of subject matters besides financial statement audits. Over time this framework should influence the future evolution of the rest of the *Handbook*. Its importance therefore cannot be overemphasized.

An assurance engagement is defined in *Section* 5025.03–.04 as follows:

> An engagement where, pursuant to an accountability relationship between two or more parties, a practitioner is engaged to issue a written communication expressing a conclusion concerning a subject matter for which the accountable party is responsible. An accountability relationship is a prerequisite for an assurance engagement. An accountability relationship exists when one party (the "accountable party") is answerable to and/or is responsible to another party (the "user") for a subject matter or voluntarily chooses to report to another party on a subject matter. The accountability relationship may arise either as a result of an agreement or legislation, or because a user can be expected to have an interest in how the accountable party has discharged its responsibility for a subject matter.

The assurance standard does not supersede exisiting audit and review standards, but it will probably influence future changes to more specific standards. In the meantime the assurance framework is expected to provide guidance for expanding assurance service to new "subject matters" not currently covered in the *Handbook*.

An assertion is a statement about some relevant aspect of a subject matter—for example, that a building exists as of a certain point in time. The assurance standards in *Section* 5025 are quite broad in that they can be applied to assertions that are unwritten and only implied (called direct reporting engagements) as well as to written assertions (called attestation engagements):

> In an attest engagement the practitioner's conclusion will be on a written assertion prepared by the accountable party. The assertion evaluates using suitable criteria, the subject matter for which the accountable party is responsible. In an direct reporting engagement, the practitioner's conclusion will evaluate directly using suitable criteria, the subject matter for which the accountable party is responsible. . . . In these standards, the accountable party is referred to as management. Depending on a circumstance, the user could include a variety of stakeholders such as shareholders, creditors, customers, the board of directors, the audit committee, legislators or regulators. The practitioner is the person who has overall responsibility for the assurance engagement. (*Handbook Sections* 5025.05–.06)

For example, the practitioner of *Section* 5025.06 in a financial statement assurance engagement has traditionally been referred to as an external auditor. Since most of this textbook deals with financial statement audits, we will continue using the traditional terminology for much of the text. After we have become familiarized with other assurance services in Chapter 14, we will discuss the assurance standards in more detail. For now we would like to focus on existing auditing standards and provide an overall comparison between the auditing standards (GAAS) and the new assurance standard.

The assurance standard was written long after the generally accepted auditing standards for financial statement audits (GAAS). In Exhibit 2–2 you can see the ideas borrowed from the existing GAAS.

The major differences lie in the areas of practitioner competence, internal control, and reporting. With respect to practitioner competence, the GAAS presume knowledge of accounting and require training and proficiency as an auditor (meaning an auditor of financial statements, since that was the only kind of assurance engagement being performed when the GAAS were written). On the other hand, the assurance standards are more general, requiring training and proficiency in assurance engagements and knowledge of the "subject matter of the engagement." The assurance service refers to the ability to recognize the information being asserted, to determine the evidence relevant to the assertions, and to make decisions about the correspondence of the information asserted with suitable criteria. The "knowledge of the subject matter" is not confined to accounting and financial assertions because assurance engagements may cover a wide variety of information. Note, however, that the first assurance standard does not allow auditors to provide assurance on assertions beyond their level of competence, for example, adherence to complex legal contracts.

The assurance standards, unlike GAAS, have no requirement regarding an understanding of the internal control structure for an information system. Considerations of internal control are implicit in the task of obtaining sufficient evidence. Anyway, some kinds of assured information may not have an underlying information control system in the same sense as a financial accounting and reporting system.

Reporting is different because assurance engagements on nonfinancial information do not depend upon generally accepted accounting principles. These are the only criteria for financial statement audits. The assurance standards speak of "evaluation against suitable criteria" and "accordance with generally accepted criteria" and they leave the door open for assurance engagements on a wide variety of informational assertions. An illustration of how far assurance engagements can go is provided in *The Wall Street Journal* article excerpt given in the box below.

FORE!

Wilson Sporting Goods Company is using PAs to prove that amateur golfers can hit Wilson's Ultra golf ball farther than they can hit competitors' golf balls. Wilson says the PAs certify that Wilson's Ultra outdistances its competitors by an average of 5.7 yards per drive.

Competitors aren't impressed by Wilson's accountants. "I can walk off a golf ball's distance as well as any accountant," says Harry Groome, an accountant executive with Ayer, Inc., the ad agency for the Maxfli gold balls made by Dunlop Slazenger Corporation. "Using a PA is an odd way to measure a golf drive."

Marlene Baddeloo, a manager for the Chicago office of Coopers & Lybrand, which oversees the golf-ball competitions sponsored by Wilson, agrees "that anyone could pace off a golf driving range to see how far a ball goes." But she says Coopers staffers since last May have checked that Wilson employees haven't doctored the results at more than 30 driving ranges. "We also make sure the amateurs participating aren't affiliated with Wilson or its competitors and haven't been paid to participate," she adds.

The use of accountants may upset Wilson's competitors, but it sure makes the accountants happy. "Our personnel love . . . {to} wear shorts and spend the day out in the air," says Ms. Baddeloo. "I get a lot of volunteers."

Source: Lee Burton, "After This, CPAs May Take Over Instant-Replay Duties for Football." *The Wall Street Journal,* July 19, 1991, p. B1.

E X H I B I T 2–2   COMPARISON OF ASSURANCE AND AUDIT STANDARDS
(The numbers are in the sequence of the more familiar and specific GAAS)

Assurance Standards	Auditing Standards
1. The practitioner should seek management's acknowledgment of responsibility for the subject matter as it relates to the objective of the engagement. If the practitioner does not obtain management's acknowledgment, the practitioner should: (a) obtain other evidence that an accountability relationship exists, such as a reference to legislation or a regulation; (b) consider how the lack of management's acknowledgment might affect his or her work and conclusion; and (c) disclose in his or her report that acknowledgment of responsibility has not been obtained. The assurance engagement should be performed with due care and with an objective state of mind. The practitioner and any other persons performing the assurance engagement should have adequate proficiency in such engagements. The practitioner and any other persons performing the assurance engagement should collectively possess adequate knowledge of the subject matter. In addition, when a specialist is involved, the practitioner should consider whether the practitioner's involvement in the engagement and knowledge of the subject matter elements involving the specialist is sufficient to enable the practitioner to discharge his or her responsibilities.	1. The examination should be performed and the report prepared by a person or persons having adequate technical training and proficiency in auditing, with due care and with an objective state of mind.
2. The work should be adequately planned and the practitioner should ensure that any other persons performing the assurance engagement are properly supervised.	2. The work should be adequately planned and properly executed using sufficient knowledge of the entity's business as a basis. If assistants are employed they should be properly supervised. 3. A sufficient understanding of internal control should be obtained to plan the audit. When control risk is assessed below maximum, sufficient appropriate audit evidence should be obtained through tests of controls to support the assessment.
4. the practitioner should consider the concept of significance and the relevant components of engagement risk when planning and performing the assurance engagement. Sufficient appropriate evidence should be obtained to provide the practitioner with a reasonable basis to support the conclusion expressed in his or her report.	4. Sufficient appropriate audit evidence should be obtained, by such means as inspection, observations, enquiry, confirmation, computation, and analysis, to afford a reasonable basis to support the content of the report.
5,6,7 As a minimum the practitioner's report should: (a) identify to whom the report is directed; (b) describe the objective of the engagement and the entity or portion thereof, the subject matter, and the time period covered by the engagement; (c) in an attest report, identify management's assertion; (d) describe the responsibilities of management and the practitioner; (e) identify the applicable standards in accordance with which the engagement was conducted; (f) identify the criteria against which the subject matter was evaluated; (g) state a conclusion that conveys the level of assurance being provided and/or any reservation the practitioner may have; (h) state the date of the report; (i) identify the name of the practitioner (or firm); and (j) identify the place of issue.	5. The report should identify the financial statements and distinguish between the responsibilities of management and the responsibilities of the auditor.
7. The reservation should be expressed in the form of a qualification of conclusion or a denial of conclusion when the practitioner is unable to obtain sufficient appropriate evidence to evaluate one or more aspects of the subject matter's conformity with the criteria. When the practitioner: (a) in a direct reporting engagement, concludes that the subject matter does not conform with criteria; or (b) in an attest engagement, concludes that the assertion prepared by management does not present fairly the criteria used or the conformity of the subject matter with the criteria or	7. The report should contain either an expression of opinion on the financial statements or an assertion that an opinion cannot be expressed. In the latter case, the reasons therefore should be stated.

(continued)

EXHIBIT 2–2   COMPARISON OF ASSURANCE AND AUDIT STANDARDS (continued)

Assurance Standards	Auditing Standards
essential information has not been presented or has been presented in an inappropriate manner, he or she should express a reservation in the form of a qualification of conclusion or an adverse conclusion. 8. A reservation should be expressed when the practitioner: (a) is unable to obtain sufficient appropriate evidence to evaluate one or more aspects of the subject matter's conformity with the criteria; (b) in a direct reporting engagement, concludes that the subject matter does not conform with the criteria; or (c) in an attest engagement concludes that (i) the assertion prepared by management does not present fairly the criteria used, (ii) the assertion prepared by management does not present fairly the subject matter's conformity with the criteria, or (iii) essential information has not been presented or has been presented in an inappropriate manner. A reservation should provide an explanation of the matter giving rise to the reservation and, if reasonably determinable, its effect on the subject matter.	8. Where an opinion is expressed, it should indicate whether the financial statements present fairly, in all material respects, the financial position, results of operations and changes in financial position in accordance with an appropriate disclosed basis of accounting, which except in special circumstances should be generally accepted accounting principles. The report should provide adequate explanation with respect to any reservation contained in such opinion.
A. Before undertaking an assurance engagement, the practitioner should have a reasonable basis for believing the engagement can be completed in accordance with the standards in this *Section*. B. The practitioner should identify or develop criteria that are suitable for evaluating the subject matter. When generally accepted criteria consistent with the objective of the engagement exist, the practitioner should use them in forming his or her conclusion except when and only when, the intended users of practitioner's report are an identifiable limited group of users and he or she is satisfied such users agree their needs are met by using criteria other than generally accepted criteria. In such cases, the practitioner's report should not include a reservation with respect to generally accepted criteria but should include a caution that the report is intended only for the use of the intended users. When there are no generally accepted criteria consistent with the objective of the engagement, criteria from sources in paragraph 5025.41 (d) and (e) should be used. The practitioner should assess the suitability of these criteria because they lack authoritative support. In these circumstances, the practitioner should attempt to obtain, from intended users and management, acknowledgment that the criteria are suitable for the engagement. When such acknowledgment cannot be obtained, the practitioner should consider the effect if any on his or her work and report. In no circumstances should the practitioner perform the engagement using criteria which, in his or her judgment, would result in a report that would be misleading to intended users. C. The practitioner should document matters that in his or her professional judgment are important in providing evidence to support the conclusion expressed in his or her report.	

A, B, C, designates *Section* 5025 Standards that are not directly comparable to a GAAS standard.

The assurance standards shown in Exhibit 2–2 provide guidance and a broad framework for a wide variety of assurance engagements PAs can perform in public practice.

Many people appreciate the value of auditors' assurance to historical financial statements, and they have found other representations for PAs to assure. Examples of assurance engagements accepted by PAs appear in the following box.

EXAMPLES OF ASSURANCE ENGAGEMENTS

- Insurance claims data.
- Labour data for union contract negotiation.
- Newspaper and magazine audience and circulation data.
- Integrity and security of a computer network.
- Investment performance statistics.
- GST and real estate tax bases.
- Political contributions and expenditures.
- Financial feasibility of a rapid transit system.
- Cost justification for a utility rate increase.
- Regulator's questionnaire on business ethics and conduct.

Source: Courtesy of Alan Winters.

A main objective in developing the assurance standards is to provide a general framework for, and set reasonable boundaries around, the assurance services offered by public accountants. Whether these standards actually "set boundaries" remains to be seen. After all, before the assurance standards were published, public accountants were using the GAAS audit standards as a point of departure for other assurance engagements. New assurance opportunities may well be taken anyway, only now with the assurance standards as the point of departure. As we will see in further discussion of assurance standards in Chapter 14, assurance standards are so broad that the distinction between assurance engagements and consulting engagements may become increasingly blurred.

REVIEW CHECKPOINTS

2.3 What is the purpose served by assurance standards?

2.4 What are the major differences between assurance standards and the generally accepted auditing standards?

2.5 Define an "assurance engagement."

2.6 What is the theoretical essence of an "assurance service?"

GENERALLY ACCEPTED AUDITING STANDARDS (GAAS)

LEARNING OBJECTIVE

3. Write and explain the eight CICA generally accepted auditing standards (GAAS), and explain how GAAS was or was not followed in specific fact situations.

The CICA's generally accepted auditing standards (GAAS) were first written as a short statement of eight standards. Since 1975, these eight have been augmented by additional explanations and requirements in the Auditing Recommendations of the *Handbook*. The eight basic standards are shown below, classified as the general standard, examination standards, and reporting standards.

The Auditing Recommendations of the *Handbook* are issued from time to time in a numbered series. Officially they are considered "interpretations" of the eight basic standards; but, for all practical purposes, they are also GAAS. Any auditor who does not follow *Handbook* directives can be judged to have performed a deficient audit.

The auditing standards literature also includes a series of Guidelines. Although officially considered less authoritative and less binding than the Recommendations, auditors still must justify any departures from them. For the most part, the Guidelines give technical help.

Auditing standards are quite different from auditing procedures. Auditing procedures are the particular and specialized actions auditors take to obtain evidence in a specific audit engagement. **Auditing standards** are audit quality recommendations that remain the same through time and for all audits, including audits of computerized accounting systems. Procedures may vary, depending on the complexity of an accounting system (whether manual or computerized), on the type of company, and on other situation-specific factors. This difference is the reason audit reports refer to an audit "conducted in accordance with generally accepted auditing standards," rather than in accordance with auditing procedures. Considerable judgment is required to apply audit procedures in specific situations.

GAAS General Standard

The general standard of GAAS relates to the personal integrity and professional qualifications of auditors (Section 5100.02 of the *Handbook*).

Competence

The first general standard requires competence—adequate technical training and proficiency—as an auditor. This competence starts with education in accounting, because auditors hold themselves out as experts in accounting standards and financial reporting. It continues with on-the-job training in developing and applying professional judgment in real-world audit situations. This stage is practice in performing the

---

GENERALLY ACCEPTED AUDITING STANDARDS

Generally Accepted Auditing Standards are as follows:

General standard

The examination should be performed and the report prepared by a person or persons having adequate technical training and proficiency in auditing, with due care and with an objective state of mind.

Examination standards

1. The work should be adequately planned and properly executed. If assistants are employed they should be properly supervised.
2. A sufficient understanding of internal control should be obtained to plan the audit. When control risk is assessed below maximum, sufficient appropriate audit evidence should be obtained through tests of controls to support the assessment.
3. Sufficient appropriate audit evidence should be obtained, by such means as inspection, observation, enquiry, confirmation, computation, and analysis, to afford a reasonable basis to support the content of the report.

Reporting standards

1. The report should identify the financial statements and distinguish between the responsibilities of management and the responsibilities of the auditor.
2. The report should describe the scope of the auditor's examination.
3. The report should contain either an expression of opinion on the financial statements or an assertion that an opinion cannot be expressed. In the latter case, the reason therefore should be stated.
4. Where an opinion is expressed, it should indicate whether the financial statements present fairly, in all material respects, the financial position, results of operations and changes in financial position in accordance with an appropriate disclosed basis of accounting, which except in special circumstances should be generally accepted accounting principles. The report should provide adequate explanation with respect to any reservation contained in such opinion.

assurance function, in which auditors learn to (1) recognize the underlying assertions being made by the management of a company in each element (account) in the financial statements, (2) decide which evidence is relevant for supporting or refuting the truth of the assertions, (3) select and perform procedures for obtaining the evidence, and (4) evaluate the evidence and decide whether the management assertions correspond to reality and GAAP. Auditors must be thoughtfully prepared to encounter a wide range of judgment on the part of management accountants, varying from true objective judgment to the occasional extreme of deliberate misstatement.

Objectivity

The general standard also requires an objective state of mind. In this sense objectivity is a matter of intellectual honesty and impartiality. Auditors are expected to be unbiased and impartial with respect to the financial statements and other information they audit. They are expected to be fair both to the companies and executives who issue financial information and to the outside persons who use it. This type of objectivity in assurance services is achieved through the maintenance of professional independence. There are two aspects of independence: independence in fact and independence in appearance. Independence in fact is a mental attitude that is an essential for an objective state of mind. Independence in appearance is another matter and is addressed in more detail in the Rules of Professional Conduct (Chapter 15). The appearance of independence—avoiding financial and managerial relationships with clients—is important because the appearances are all the public users of audit reports can see. They cannot see inside auditors' heads to detect the "mental attitude." Independence must be zealously guarded because the general public will grant social recognition of professional status to auditors only as long as they are perceived to be independent.

Some critics of the public accounting profession say the fact that auditors are paid by their clients is an undesirable arrangement. They argue that it is impossible to be independent from the party paying the fee. Accountants have generally not taken such criticism seriously because the alternative would be some form of public government control of accounting fees, and very few people want government involvement. In addition, as noted in Chapter 1 public accounting is not alone among professions that face such a dilemma. Medical doctors, lawyers, and architects face similar dilemmas. What is unique about auditors is that, although a company pays the auditor, the auditors' real clients are the third-party users of financial statements. The auditor therefore needs to sort out responsibilities to the company from responsibilities to third parties. Addressing such ethical conflicts in a competent manner is part of what makes public accounting a profession. See Chapter 15 for more details.

The notion of individual independence is more specific in the conduct of each audit engagement. In essence, an individual auditor must not subordinate his or her judgment to others and must stay away from influences that might bias judgment. In more specific terms, auditors must preserve their independence in the "Three Aspects" practical ways presented in the following box.

Due Professional Care

The exercise of due professional care requires observance of the general standard and the field work standards. Auditors must be competent and independent; they must plan and supervise the audit, understand the auditee's control structure, and obtain sufficient competent evidence if they are to be properly careful. Their training should

THREE ASPECTS OF PRACTICAL INDEPENDENCE

Programming Independence

Auditors must remain free from interference by client managers who try to restrict, specify, or modify the procedures auditors want to perform, including any attempt to assign personnel or otherwise control the audit work. Occasionally, client managers try to limit the number of auditors permitted in a location.

Investigative Independence

Auditors must have free access to books, records, correspondence, and other evidence. They must have the co-operation of management without any attempt to interpret or screen evidence. Sometimes, client managers refuse auditors' requests for access to necessary information.

Reporting Independence

Auditors must not let any feelings of loyalty to the client or auditee interfere with their obligation to report fully and fairly. Neither should the client management be allowed to overrule auditors' judgments on the appropriate content of an audit report. Disciplinary actions have been taken against auditors who go to a client management conference with a preliminary estimate for a financial adjustment and emerge after agreeing with management to a smaller adjustment.

---

include computer auditing techniques because of the importance and pervasiveness of computers in the business world.

Due care in an audit is best understood in the context of the prudent auditor. The idea of a prudent professional practitioner is present in other social science theories—for example, the "economic person" of economic theory and the "reasonable person" in law. Mautz and Sharaf summarized the qualities of the prudent auditor:

> A prudent practitioner [auditor] is assumed to have a knowledge of the philosophy and practice of auditing, to have the degree of training, experience, and skill common to the average independent auditor, to have the ability to recognize indications of irregularities, and to keep abreast of developments in the perpetration and detection of irregularities. Due audit care requires the auditor to acquaint himself with the company under examination, the accounting and financial problems of the company . . . to be responsive to unusual events and unfamiliar circumstances, to persist until he has eliminated from his own mind any reasonable doubts he may have about the existence of material irregularities, and to exercise caution in instructing his assistants and reviewing their work. (Mautz and Sharaf, *The Philosophy of Auditing*, American Accounting Association, 1961, p. 140.)

Due professional care is a matter of what auditors do and how well they do it. A determination of proper care must be reached on the basis of all facts and circumstances in a particular case. When an audit firm's work becomes the subject of a lawsuit, the question of due audit care is frequently at issue (as you will see in the law cases in Chapter 16).

LESSONS AUDITORS IGNORE AT THEIR OWN RISK

Litigation is an exacting and uncompromising teacher, but it provides auditors with some hard and useful lessons. The tuition is the high cost of malpractice insurance, legal fees, adverse court decisions, embarrassing publicity, and stress.

- There is no substitute for knowledge of the client's business.
- There is no substitute for effective, ongoing, substantial supervision of the work of people assigned to the engagement.
- The partner in charge of the engagement must constantly emphasize the importance of integrity, objectivity, and professional skepticism in carrying out the audit.

Source: Hall and Renner, "Lessons That Auditors Ignore at Their Own Risk," *Journal of Accountancy*, July 1988, pp. 50–58.

*All material from the *Journal of Accountancy* appearing in this textbook is reprinted with permission by the American Institute of Certified Public Accountants, Inc. Opinions of the authors are their own and do not necessarily reflect policies of the AICPA.

R E V I E W
C H E C K P O I N T S

2.7 What is the difference between auditing standards and auditing procedures?

2.8 By what standard would a judge determine the quality of due professional care? Explain.

2.9 What are the three specific aspects of independence that an auditor should carefully guard in the course of a financial statement audit?

GAAS Examination Standards

The three examination standards set forth general quality criteria for conducting an audit. Auditors cannot effectively satisfy the general standard requiring due professional care if they have not also satisfied the standards of field work.

Planning and Supervision

Section 5150 contains several lists of considerations for planning and supervising an audit. They are all concerned with (1) preparing an audit program and supervising the audit work, (2) obtaining knowledge of the client's business, and (3) dealing with differences of opinion among the audit firm's own personnel.

A written audit program is desirable. An **audit program** is a list of the audit procedures the auditors need to perform to produce the evidence needed for good audit decisions. The procedures in an audit program should be stated in enough detail to instruct the assistants about the work to be done. (You will see detailed audit programs later in this textbook.)

An understanding of the client's business is an absolute necessity. An auditor must be able to understand the events, transactions, and practices characteristic of the business and of the management that may have a significant effect on the financial statements. This knowledge helps auditors identify areas for special attention (the places where errors, irregularities, or frauds might exist), evaluate the reasonableness of accounting estimates made by management, evaluate management's representations

---

Too Late

FastTrak Corporation got mad at its auditor because the partner in charge of the engagement would not agree to let management use operating lease accounting treatment for some heavy equipment whose leases met the criteria for capitalization. FastTrak fired the auditors 10 weeks after the company's balance sheet date, then started contacting other audit firms to restart the audit. However, the audit report was due at the OSC in six weeks. Every other audit firm contacted by FastTrak refused the audit because it could not be planned and performed properly on such short notice with such a tight deadline.

---

and answers to enquiries, and make judgments about the appropriateness of accounting principles choices (*Section* 5140).

Where does an auditor get this understanding of a business? By being there; by work in other companies in the same industry; by conducting interviews with management and other client personnel; by reading extensively—CICA accounting and audit guides, the CGAAC Public Practice Manual, industry publications, other companies' financial statements, business periodicals, and textbooks; by getting a thorough familiarization presentation by the partner in charge of the audit before beginning the engagement; and by being observant and letting on-the-job experience sink into long-term memory.

There is no guarantee that all the auditors on an audit team will always agree among themselves on audit decisions, which range from inclusion or omission of procedures to conclusions about the fair presentation of an account or the financial statements as a whole. When differences of opinion arise, audit personnel should consult with one another and with experts in the firm to try to resolve the disagreement. If resolution is not achieved, the audit firm should have procedures to allow an audit team member to document the disagreement and to dissociate himself or herself from the matter. Particularly in a situation where there are disagreements, the basis for the final audit decision on the matter should be documented in the working papers for later reference.

Timing is important for audit planning. To have time to plan an audit, auditors should be engaged before the client's fiscal year-end. The more advance notice auditors can have, the better they are able to provide enough time for planning. An early appointment benefits both auditor and client. The audit team may be able to perform part of the audit at an **interim date**—a date some weeks or months before the fiscal year-end—and thereby make the rest of the audit work more efficient. At an interim date, auditors can perform preliminary analytical procedures, do a preliminary assessment of internal control risk, and audit some account balances. Advance knowledge of problems can enable auditors to alter the audit program as necessary so that year-end work (performed on and after the fiscal year-end date) can be more efficient. Advance planning for the observation of physical inventory and for the confirmation of accounts receivable is particularly important.

Internal Control Assessment

The second examination standard requires an understanding of the client's internal control. Internal control consists of a company's control environment, accounting system, and control procedures. The existence of a satisfactory internal control

---

CONTROL LAPSE CONTRIBUTES TO DUPLICATE PAYMENTS

All Points Trucking processed insurance claims on damages to shipments in transit on its trucks, paying them in a self-insurance plan. After payment, the claims documents were not marked "paid." Later, the same documents were processed again for duplicate payments to customers, who kicked back 50 percent to a dishonest All Points employee. The auditors learned that the documents were not marked "paid," concluded that the specific control risk of duplicate payments was high, extended their procedures to include a search for duplicate payments in the damage expense account, found them, and traced the problem to the dishonest employee. Embezzlements of $35,000 per year were stopped.

---

system reduces the probability of errors and irregularities in the accounts. This in turn provides the foundation for the work auditors do in an assessment of control risk. Control risk is the probability that a material misstatement (error or irregularity) could occur and not be prevented or detected on a timely basis by the company's internal control structure policies and procedures (*Section* 5210).

Internal control may be defined simply as a system's capability to prevent or detect material data processing errors or fraud and provide for their correction on a timely basis. Auditors need to know enough about the client's control system to assess the control risk.

The primary purpose of control risk assessment is to help the auditors develop the audit program, which specifies the nature, timing, and extent of the audit procedures for gathering evidence about the account balances that will go into the financial statements. The second field work standard presumes two necessary relationships: (*a*) good internal control reduces the control risk, and an auditor thus has a reasonable basis for minimizing the extent of subsequent audit procedures; (*b*) conversely, poor internal control produces greater control risk, and an auditor must increase the extent of subsequent audit procedures. If auditors were to assume no relationship between the quality of controls and the accuracy of output, then an assessment of control risk would be pointless. Audit efficiency would be lost in many cases. (Chapter 6 explains the work involved in control risk assessment.)

Sufficient, Appropriate Evidential Matter

Evidence is the heart of assurance function work for audits of financial statements and for assurance to nonfinancial information. The third examination standard requires auditors to obtain enough evidence to justify the decision about an opinion on financial statements. **Evidence** is all the influences upon the minds of auditors that ultimately guide their decisions. Evidence includes the underlying accounting data and all available corroborating information (*Section* 5300). Appropriate evidence— evidence that is reliable and relevant—may be quantitative or qualitative; it may be objective or subjective; it may be absolutely compelling to a decision or it may only be mildly persuasive. The audit team's task is to collect and evaluate sufficient appropriate evidence to afford a reasonable and logical basis for audit decisions.

The standard refers to "sufficient," rather than "absolute," evidence. Auditors do not audit all of a company's transactions and events. They audit data samples and make audit decisions by inference, in most cases.

The standard takes a broad brush to procedures for gathering evidence—inspection, observation, enquiry, and confirmation. This is not a complete enumeration of evidence-gathering procedures. (Chapter 4 contains a more thorough explanation of audit objectives and procedures.)

. . . .

R E V I E W
C H E C K P O I N T S

2.10 What three elements of planning and supervision are considered essential in audit practice?

2.11 Why does the timing of an auditor's appointment matter in the conduct of a financial statement audit?

2.12 For what reasons does an auditor obtain an understanding of the internal control system?

2.13 Define audit *evidence*.

. . . .

GAAS Reporting Standards

. . . .

LEARNING OBJECTIVE

4. Describe the standard unqualified audit report in terms of its communication of audit standards and other messages.

The ultimate objective of independent auditors—the report on the audit—is guided by the four GAAS reporting standards. These four deal with generally accepted accounting principles (GAAP), auditor and management responsibilities, adequate disclosure, and report content. Auditing standards dictate use of a "standard report." (The standard unqualified audit report is shown in Exhibit 2–3 [same as Exhibit 1–2], and you should review it in relation to the discussion that follows.)

"Unqualified," in the name of the report, means "good" in the sense that the auditors are not calling attention to anything wrong with the audit work or the financial statements. "Qualified" means "bad" in the sense that the financial statements contain a departure from GAAP. (You will study "qualified" audit reports in Chapter 3.) All standard **unqualified reports** contain these features:

E X H I B I T 2–3   **AUDITOR'S REPORT**

To the Shareholders of....................................

I have audited the balance sheet of .... as at ...., 19....., and the statement of income, retained earnings and changes in financial position for the year then ended. These financial statements are the responsibility of the company's management. My responsibility is to express an opinion on these financial statements based on my audit.

I conducted my audit in accordance with generally accepted auditing standards. Those standards require that I plan and perform an audit to obtain reasonable assurance whether the financial statements are free of material misstatement. An audit includes examining, on a test basis, evidence supporting the amounts and disclosure in the financial statements. An audit also includes assessing the accounting principles used and significant estimates made by management, as well as evaluating the overall financial statement presentation.

In my opinion, these financial statements present fairly, in all material respects, the financial position of the company as at ...., 19....., and the results of its operations and the changes in its financial position for the year then ended in accordance with generally accepted accounting principles.

City   (signed)....................................

Date   Chartered Accountant

✳ 1. **Title.** The title should refer to the auditor, thus indicating that the report is based on an audit examination and not some other types of engagement.

2. **Address.** The report shall be addressed to the client, which occasionally may be different from the auditee.

3. **Notice of audit.** A sentence should identify the financial statements and declare that they were audited. This appears in the introductory paragraph.

4. **Responsibilities.** The report should state management's responsibility for the financial statements and the auditor's responsibility for the audit report. These statements are also in the introductory paragraph.

5. **Description of the audit.** The second paragraph (scope paragraph) should declare that the audit was conducted in accordance with generally accepted auditing standards and describe the principal characteristics of an audit.

6. **Opinion.** The report shall contain an opinion (opinion paragraph) regarding conformity with generally accepted accounting principles.

7. **Signature.** The auditor shall sign the report, manually or otherwise.

8. **Date.** The report shall be dated with the date when all significant field work was completed.

Generally Accepted Accounting Principles (GAAP)

The fourth reporting standard refers to generally accepted accounting principles, or GAAP, which is used in most circumstances. In the audit report, this standard is shown to be met with the opinion sentence in the opinion paragraph: "In our opinion, the financial statements . . . present fairly in all material respects the financial position . . . and the results of operations and changes in financial position . . . in accordance with generally accepted accounting principles." In this opinion sentence, auditors make a statement of fact about their belief (opinion). Auditors are the professional experts, so users of financial statements rely upon the audit opinion.

However, determining the appropriate GAAP in a company's circumstances is not always an easy matter. Students often think of *Handbook Recommendations* on accounting standards as the complete body of GAAP. Not so. GAAP consists of all the accounting methods and procedures that have substantial authoritative support. The *Handbook* is only one source of such support, albeit the highest and most powerful. It is widely recognized that "the meaning of 'present fairly in accordance with GAAP' in the audit report" sets forth a hierarchy of authoritative support for various sources of GAAP.

Handbook Recommendations cover many accounting issues and problems. When the *Handbook* covers an issue, its standards are considered generally compelling. However, the *Handbook* has not covered all conceivable accounting matters. When a conclusion about GAAP cannot be found in *Handbook Recommendations,* auditors usually go down a hierarchy to find the next highest source of support for a client's accounting solution to a financial reporting problem. Reference can be made to positions on accounting matters by the affected provincial Securities Commission. Reference can also be made to other countries' authoritative pronouncements such as the U.S.'s Financial Accounting Standards Board (FASB) announcements, industry audit and accounting guides, consensus positions of the CICA's Emerging Issues Committee, and other accounting literature.

The unqualified opinion sentence contains these implicit messages: (*a*) the accounting principles in the financial statements have general acceptance (authoritative support); (*b*) the accounting principles used by the company are appropriate in the circumstances; (*c*) the financial statements and notes are informative of matters that may affect their use, understanding, and interpretation (full disclosure accounting principle); (*d*) the classification and summarization in the financial statements is neither too detailed nor too condensed for users; and (*e*) the financial statements are accurate within practical materiality limits (Section 5130). This last feature refers to materiality and accuracy. Auditors and users do not expect financial account balances to be absolutely accurate to the penny. Accounting is too complicated, and too many estimates are used in financial statements to expect absolute accuracy. After all, many financial reports use numbers rounded to the thousands, even millions, of dollars! Everyone agrees that financial figures are "fair" as long as they are not "materially" misstated—that is, misstated by enough to make a difference in users' decisions. (Chapter 5 discusses "materiality" in more detail.)

Consistency

The fourth reporting standard calls for explicit reporting in accordance with GAAP except in special circumstances. Prior to 1991, all audit reports contained a sentence confirming that GAAP had been "consistently applied" when no changes in the application of accounting principles had been made. This sentence referred to a company's use of the same accounting procedures and methods from year to year. However, an official pronouncement (*Handbook Section* 1506) governs the accounting and disclosure of a company's change of accounting principles.

In 1991 the fourth reporting standard was changed to allow the audit report to be silent (i.e., implicit) about consistency when no accounting changes had been made or any changes that were made were properly disclosed in the financial statements. This change has created a conflict with U.S. reporting standards for clients falling within the jurisdiction of SEC filing requirements. A CICA Guideline suggests that this conflict is best resolved by providing information on the conflict to U.S. readers in documents submitted to the SEC. See the CICA Guideline (AUG-21) on Canada–U.S. reporting differences.

Adequate Disclosure

The fourth reporting standard also has a second implicit report element. The standard requires auditors to use professional judgment to decide whether the financial statements and related disclosures contain all the important accounting information users need for their decisions. Disclosure of information not specified completely in sources of authoritative support may be necessary. Auditors may need to deal with a rare and unusual fact situation that nobody has encountered before. Using this standard, auditors have latitude for determining what is important and what is not. Likewise, users of financial statements also have the right to claim that certain information is necessary for adequate disclosure. In fact, many lawsuits are brought forward on the issue that certain necessary information was not disclosed, and auditors must show reasons for lack of disclosure.

When auditors believe that some information is necessary for adequate disclosure, yet the company refuses to disclose it, a departure from GAAP exists. A "qualified opinion" is usually written, and the reason for the departure (missing disclosure) is described in the audit report. Sometimes the missing disclosure is added to the audit report itself.

Report Content

The third reporting standard states the requirements concerning an opinion. There are two elements in the first sentence:

> 1. The report shall contain either an expression of opinion on the financial statements or an assertion that an opinion cannot be expressed.

The first sentence divides opinion statements into two classes: (*a*) opinions on statements taken as a whole (i.e., unqualified, adverse, and qualified opinions) and (*b*) the denial of opinion. An **adverse opinion** is the opposite of an unqualified opinion. It states that the financial statements are not in accordance with GAAP. A **denial of opinion** is an auditor's declaration that no opinion is given. The standard applies to financial statements as a whole, that is, the standard applies equally to a set of financial statements and footnotes and to each individual financial statement and footnote. The second sentence adds the requirement to explain why an opinion cannot be expressed:

> 2. In the latter case, the reasons therefor should be stated.

Combining reporting standards three and four, an explanation is required whenever there is a report reservation. Thus, when the adverse opinion, qualified opinion, or denial of opinion is rendered, all the substantive reasons for doing so must be explained. An additional paragraph is generally used for such an explanation.

The first two reporting standards relate to auditor responsibilities and the need to identify the financial statements covered by the opinion. Every time PAs (even when acting as accountants associated with unaudited financial statements) are associated by name or by action with financial statements, they must report on their work and responsibility. The character of the work is usually described by the standard reference to an audit in accordance with generally accepted auditing standards. But if an audit has been restricted in some way or if the statements are simply unaudited, the auditor must say so.

 The "degree of responsibility" is indicated by the form of the opinion. Auditors take full responsibility for their opinion about conformity with GAAP when they give either an unqualified or an adverse opinion. They take no responsibility whatsoever when they give a denial of opinion. They take responsibility when they give the qualified opinions for all matters except those stated as the reasons for the qualification. (Qualified and adverse opinions and denials of opinion are discussed more fully in Chapter 3.)

R E V I E W
CHECKPOINTS

2.14 What are the eight important features of a standard unqualified audit report?

2.15 Identify various authoritative support for GAAP with an indication of their ranking.

2.16 Do auditors take any responsibility for clients' choices of accounting principles?

2.17 What four kinds of audit opinion statements are identified in this chapter? What is the message of each one?

2.18 What messages are usually implicit in a standard audit report?

AUDITING STANDARDS IN A COMPUTER ENVIRONMENT

· · · · · · · · · · · ·

LEARNING   OBJECTIVE
5. Interpret GAAS in the
   context of a computer
   environment.

The auditing standards (GAAS) were written without any special reference to the use of computers in accounting. Nevertheless, the general and field work standards guide audit quality in a computer environment as well as in a manual accounting system environment. Some interpretation, however, will help you put the standards in context.

General Standard

To be considered adequately trained and proficient, auditors must have a working knowledge of the functions of computerized accounting and control systems. Levels of required knowledge include a minimum competency expected of new staff accountants; a supervisory capability expected of senior accountants, managers, and partners; and a technical expertise expected of computer audit specialists.

New staff accountants should be familiar with computer terminology, be able to comprehend the flow of transactions in clients' computerized systems, be able to read and understand system and logic flowcharts, and know the nature of common organizational arrangements in computer departments. Supervising accountants must have knowledge beyond these fundamentals so they can decide what level of technical support is needed and can review the audit plans of computer audit specialists and the results of their work in relation to the audit engagement as a whole. Computer audit specialists, usually trained in special technical courses and given extensive job experience, are the people who need to know how to work directly with the computers.

Sufficient training and proficiency in computer auditing are necessary to enable auditors to make their own evaluations and decisions about the computer operations in a client's accounting system. Without knowledge of computers, independence is threatened. An auditor must be technically proficient and exercise suitable professional scepticism to avoid being inappropriately influenced by experts' technical explanations and terminology. At the very least, supervisory auditors should know enough about computers to be able to recognize situations calling for the technical assistance of computer audit specialists. With specialists at work, the engagement can be completed as a team effort.

Examination Standards

The exercise of due audit care in an engagement depends on observance of the three examination standards. Special care is required when assigning personnel to the job and planning the audit. Among other things, the audit planner needs to know (*a*) the computer systems in use so compatible audit tools can be provided; (*b*) the extent of internal auditor involvement in reviewing and controlling computer operations so the extent of audit effort can be estimated; and (*c*) the computer department schedule so that access to the client's files and systems can be arranged. Above all, the partner in charge of the audit needs to plan ahead to arrange for the appropriate level of expertise needed for supervision of computer audit specialists and for the level of expertise needed for review of their work.

Probably the most complex task is performing an assessment of control risk. Computer audit expertise is required for all but the simplest computer systems. The ability to evaluate manual control over input data and over output distribution usually is not sufficient. Computerized accounting applications typically have control features built into both the systems and program software. Some members of the audit team must be able to evaluate the operations of such controls using the computer. Clients spend a great amount of money developing systems and controls, and they expect auditors to be able to understand them.

Computerized accounting systems lend themselves to computer-assisted methods of gathering sufficient appropriate evidence. Auditors can program a computer to scan a client's files and identify unusual items (e.g., loans receivable with credit balances, debits in revenue accounts, and credits in expense accounts), to recalculate accounting calculations (e.g., depreciation) made by the client, and to select accounts receivable for confirmation and print the confirmation information. These are examples of computer-assisted audit methods for obtaining sufficient appropriate evidential matter.

Reporting Standard

The technical problems and opportunities presented by the computer environment add complications to the general standards and field work standards. However, the reporting standards are not affected by the technology of the accounting system. It matters not whether the financial statements were produced by chiselling them on stone or by engraving them on paper with a laser beam: reporting requirements regarding conformity with generally accepted accounting principles, consistency, adequate disclosure, and report content remain the same. When a standard audit report is written, the output of the system, not its process, is the subject of the report.

· ·

R E V I E W
C H E C K P O I N T S

2.19 Do the general standards of generally accepted auditing standards apply when the client uses a computerized accounting system? examination standards? reporting standards? Explain.

2.20 What is considered the most complex task for auditing in a computer environment?

· ·

PROFESSIONAL SCEPTICISM
· · · · · · · · · · · ·

LEARNING OBJECTIVE
6. Explain some characteristics of "professional scepticism."

"Professional scepticism" is a buzz phrase that appears frequently in auditing literature and speech. **Professional scepticism** is an auditor's tendency not to believe management assertions, a tendency to ask management to "prove it" (with evidence). Professional scepticism is inherent in applying due care in accordance with the general standards. The business environment that has seen errors, irregularities, and fraud in financial reports dictates this basic aspect of professional scepticism: "A potential conflict of interest always exists between the auditor and the management of the enterprise under audit."

Holding a belief that a potential conflict of interest always exists causes auditors to perform procedures to search for errors, irregularities, and frauds that would have a material effect on financial statements. This requirement tends to make audits more extensive and more expensive. The extra work is not needed in the vast majority of audits where no errors, irregularities, or frauds exist. Nevertheless, auditors have had to react in all audits to the misdeeds perpetrated by a few people.

Even so, auditors must be careful when exercising professional scepticism and when holding a belief regarding a potential conflict of interest. Once an audit is under way and procedures that are designed to search for errors, irregularities, and frauds have been performed and none have been found, the audit team must be willing to accept the apparent fact there is no evidence that the potential conflict is a real one. Overtones of suspicion can be dispelled by evidence.

Still, due audit care requires professional scepticism on the part of auditors—a disposition to question all material assertions made by management whether oral, written, or incorporated in the accounting records. However, this attitude of scepticism must be balanced with an open mind about the integrity of management. Auditors should neither blindly assume that every management is dishonest nor thoughtlessly assume management to be perfectly honest. The key lies in auditors' objectivity and in the audit attitude toward gathering the evidence necessary to reach reasonable and supportable audit decisions.

R E V I E W
C H E C K P O I N T S

2.21 Why should auditors act as though there is always a potential conflict of interest between the auditor and the management of the enterprise under audit?

QUALITY CONTROL STANDARDS

LEARNING OBJECTIVE

7. List and explain the important requirements of quality control standards for a PA firm.

Generally accepted auditing standards must be observed in each audit engagement conducted by a PA firm. Thus, each PA firm needs to observe GAAS in conducting its entire audit practice. While GAAS relate to the conduct of each audit engagement, quality control standards govern the quality of a PA firm's audit practice as a whole. Quality control can be defined as actions taken by a public accounting firm to evaluate compliance with professional standards. And a "system of quality control" is designed to provide reasonable assurance of conforming with professional standards. Professional standards include GAAS as covered in the *CICA Handbook* as well as Provincial Rules of Conduct.

Elements of Quality Control

The Quality Control Standards Committee of the AICPA has identified nine basic elements of quality control. These are listed and explained briefly in Exhibit 2–4.

Canada currently does not have codified quality control standards. Both the 1978 Adams Report (the *Report of the Special Committee to Examine the Role of the Auditor*) and the 1988 Macdonald Commission Report (*Report of the Commission to Study the Public's Expectations of Audits*) recommended the development of quality control standards and that PA firms establish systems of quality control conforming with these standards. More recently several regulatory agencies have taken initiatives to discipline substandard performance of professional staff in PA firms and criticized the individual-level focus of the provincial disciplinary process. In response provincial Institutes are amending their bylaws to bring firms as well as individuals within

EXHIBIT 2–4   ELEMENTS OF QUALITY CONTROL

It is recommended that public accounting firms establish policies and procedures for the following elements of quality control:

1. *Independence.* Persons at all organizational levels must maintain independence to the extent required by the rules of professional conduct.

2. *Assigning Personnel to Engagements.* Assignment of personnel to engagements should provide the firm with reasonable assurance that work will be performed by persons having the degree of technical training and proficiency required in the circumstances.

3. *Consultation.* Personnel should seek assistance, to the extent required, from persons having appropriate levels of knowledge, competence, judgment, and authority.

4. *Supervision.* The conduct and supervision of work at all organizational levels should provide the firm with reasonable assurance that the work performed meets the firm's standards of quality. The responsibility of a firm for establishing policies and procedures for supervision is distinct from the responsibility of individuals to adequately plan and supervise the work on a particular engagement.

5. *Hiring.* Hiring should be conducted to provide the firm with reasonable assurance that employees possess the appropriate characteristics to enable them to perform competently. The quality of a firm's work ultimately depends on the integrity, competence, and motivation of personnel who perform and supervise the work. Thus, a firm's recruiting programs are factors in maintaining such quality.

6. *Professional Development.* Professional development should be conducted or provided to give the firm reasonable assurance that personnel will have the knowledge required to enable them to fulfill responsibilities assigned. Continuing professional education and training activities enable a firm to provide personnel with the knowledge required to fulfill responsibilities assigned to them and to progress within the firm.

7. *Advancement.* Advancement and promotion policies should provide the firm with reasonable assurance that those selected for advancement will have the qualifications necessary for fulfillment of the responsibilities they will be called on to assume. Qualifications that personnel selected for advancement should possess include, but are not limited to, character, intelligence, judgment, and motivation.

8. *Acceptance and Continuance of Clients.* Decisions of whether to accept or continue a client should be guided to minimize the likelihood of association with a client whose management lacks integrity. Prudence suggests that a firm be selective in determining its professional relationships.

9. *Inspection.* Internal inspection activities should be established to provide the firm with reasonable assurance that the procedures relating to the other elements of quality control are being effectively applied. (Internal inspection is like peer review, but it is performed by members of the firm.)

the disciplinary process. This expanded disciplinary process will require new guidelines for evaluating systems of quality control. Increasing litigation is also putting pressure on firms to develop good systems of quality control so that they can demonstrate compliance with professional standards and thus minimize the loss from litigation. Recently, the International Federation of Accountants has issued a policy statement proposing that members' bodies provide guidance on quality control systems. There is thus increasing need for developing codified quality control standards in Canada. A recent CICA study entitled "Guide for Developing Quality Control Systems in Public Accounting" proposes a quality control framework based on five key components or areas: clients, personnel, engagement procedures, practice administration, and a quality control review program.

Exhibit 2–5 illustrates the implementation of a quality control systems as proposed by the CICA study using the five key components as a framework. The study proposes that the areas of clients and engagement procedures be given top priority when implementing a system in stages. The right-hand columns in Exhibit 2–5 reflect the suggested priority in setting up a firmwide quality control system. Note in Exhibit 2–5 that the five key components or quality control areas have been subdivided into a series of refined elements that allow firms to better articulate all the different aspects of quality control. This refined list of elements may be viewed as an improvement on Exhibit 2–4 and thus as a better framework for quality control. However, the Exhibit 2–5 framework is not a standard at the current time, but indicates where a Canadian codified framework may be headed. Note that this framework can be extended to include tax and management advisory services, and one controversy is the extent to which these other services should also be considered in the quality control system.

Whatever framework is used, firms can use these or similar criteria in developing their policies and procedures for quality control, and the related documentation. When a peer review or quality review is conducted, the reviewers "audit" the

EXHIBIT 2–5*   IMPLEMENTING A QUALITY CONTROL SYSTEM

Quality Control Area/Elements	First Priority	Second Priority
A. Clients (refer to Chapter 5)		
1. Independence and Objectivity	✔	
2. Prohibited Investments	✔	
3. Conflicts of Interest	✔	
4. Confidentiality	✔	
5. Acceptance and Continuance	✔	
6. New Client Proposals		✔
B. Personnel (refer to Chapter 6)		
1. Hiring		✔
2. Assignment		✔
3. Performance Evaluation		✔
4. Advancement		✔
5. Continuing Professional Education	✔	
6. Restriction of Professional Staff Activities	✔	
C. Engagement Procedures (refer to Chapter 7)		
1. Engagement Letters	✔	
2. Planning and Execution	✔	
3. Documentation	✔	
4. Supervision and Review	✔	
5. Resolution of Differences of Opinion		✔
6. Consultation with Peers		✔
7. Independent Review	✔	
8. Management Letters	✔	
D. Practice Administration (refer to Chapter 8)		
1. Use of Firm Name		✔
2. Access to Client Files	✔	
3. Security of Confidential Information	✔	
4. Retention of Files		✔
5. Software Usage and Security		✔
6. Technical Reference Materials	✔	
7. Litigation and Professional Conduct		✔
8. Advertising and Promotion		✔
9. Solicitation of Clients	✔	
E. Quality Control Review Program (refer to Chapter 9)		
1. Internal Review		✔
2. Monitoring Client Services		✔
3. Monitoring Quality Control		✔
4. Premerger Review		✔
Total Elements	17	16

*Same as Exhibit 4–2 in CICA's *Guide for Developing Quality Control Systems in Public Accounting*, p. 35.

PA firm's statement of policies and procedures designed to ensure compliance with the elements of Exhibits 2–4 and 2–5 or similar criteria. These statements of policy and procedures may vary in length and complexity, depending on the size of the PA firm. (Students who wish to know these policies and procedures in detail when interviewing for a job should ask for a copy of the firm's "quality control document.")

Practice Inspection, Peer Review, and Quality Reviews

Practice inspection, peer review, and quality reviews are "audits of the auditors." Practice inspection is the name given to the system of reviewing and evaluating practice units' audit files and other documentation by an independent external party. The main objective of practice inspection is to evaluate conformity of members' work with the *CICA Handbook* and professional, ethical principles and rules of conduct (covered in Chapter 15). The practice unit can be an individual or an entire office, in which case the individual members of the office are evaluated relative to their level of responsibility. Provincial Institutes' practice inspection programs apply to all members and consist of several steps:

1. Selection of practice unit for inspection.
2. Completion of practice inspection questionnaires gathering general information about the practice and quality control systems of the practice unit.
3. Assignment of inspector.
4. Report of inspection.
5. Follow-up reviews.
6. A report to the professional conduct committee if necessary.[4]

There are some minor variations among provincial practice inspection programs relating to types of engagements reviewed and the way the inspection reports are prepared. The overall focus is on an individual member's performance, and the orientation is more educational than disciplinary in character, although serious deficiencies of professional practice could lead to a complaint with a professional conduct committee. This is further discussed in Chapter 15. Practice inspections are a useful complement to a firm's system of quality control. Their success is reflected in the fact that many countries have followed this Canadian model, including Ireland, Norway, Hong Kong, and Australia.

Peer reviews or quality reviews are a review and evaluation of the quality of the overall practice. They are thus aimed more at the firm level rather than at individuals. A peer review involves an extensive study of a firm's quality control document, including interviews with audit personnel and selection of audit engagements for detailed study of the quality of work and of adherence to GAAS and quality control standards. Peer reviews can cost from $500 to $50,000. A firm's peer review usually is done by another PA firm engaged by the firm reviewed. The reviewers issue a report giving conclusions about the firm's compliance with quality control standards and making recommendations about ways to improve the audit practice.

A quality review has the same objective as a peer review, but it is less extensive. Quality reviews usually are requested by the smaller PA firms. They cost from $1,000 to $5,000.

Peer reviews and quality reviews are more common in the United States, where they are mandated not only by the SEC but also by the AICPA Practice Sections (see Appendix 1A). In particular, the SEC Practice Section oversees the peer review process of firms wishing to practise for the SEC. This includes all firms issuing shares in U.S. stock exchanges and therefore affects some Canadian companies and their auditors.

SEC Practice Section members are required to report to the SEC any litigation against the firm or its personnel alleging audit deficiencies involving public companies

---

[4] CICA, *Guide for Developing Quality Control Systems in Public Accounting*, CICA, 1993, p. 17.

or regulated financial institutions. The SEC obtains lawsuit documents related to the litigation, but it does not attempt to try the case. The SEC's goal is to determine whether the litigation has any bearing on quality control deficiencies in the public accounting firm. In Canada sometimes a regulator such as the OSC will ask that a PA firm or individual be reviewed by a provincial Institute reviewer. This is usually in response to a complaint made to the regulator; but it sometimes arises from regular monitoring of annual reports and filings submitted to the regulator.

The extent of work involved in practice inspection, peer review, or quality review is greatly influenced by the quality of documentation concerning the quality control system. Generally, if the quality control documentation is good and the reviewer can rely on extensive internal monitoring of quality control, less work is required than if documentation is poor and the reviewer must rely more on his or her own detailed inspection of files.

A recent survey of one aspect of quality control, the use of accounting consultation units, among the largest five public accounting firms in Canada shows considerable variation in the characteristics of these units.[5] Accounting consultation units (ACUs) act as internal consultants at the firm's national offices. They assist practice office partners throughout the country in making difficult financial accounting judgments, including choosing among different alternatives in GAAP and disclosure issues. Some ACUs are proactive, encouraging consultation before the client enters into a transaction. These proactive ACUs tend to have more extensive staffs and databases, and emphasize creation of knowledge by compiling information on consultations already completed.

Other ACUs, however, are more passive, reacting to each consultation as a unique case and making relatively little use of databases available to them. There is no special emphasis on consultation before the client enters a transaction, and the focus is on the best technical accounting solution rather than the reasons for the transaction. There is relatively little, if any, documentation at the ACU of the consultation for future reference. These more passive ACUs tend to be driven by practice office partner needs rather than audit client needs, as is the case with the proactive ACUs. Interestingly, the proportion of proactive versus passive ACUs is evenly split among the large firms, and these differences in role are not reflected in the formal descriptions as written in the firm manuals. ACUs are an interesting example of qualitative differences among PA firms. Future research is needed to determine whether these qualitative difference in ACUs have an impact on overall audit firm performance.

· ·

R E V I E W
CHECKPOINTS

2.22 What is the meaning of quality control as it relates to a PA firm?

2.23 Consider the following quality control policy and identify the quality control element to which it relates: "Designate individuals as specialists to serve as authoritative sources; provide procedures for resolving differences of opinion between audit personnel and specialists."

2.24 What is the practice inspection, and what roles does it play in the quality control self-regulation of the profession?

· ·

[5] S. Salterio and R. Denham, "Organizational Memory in Public Accounting Firms: The Role of Accounting Consultation Units," University of Alberta Working Paper (presented at the 1995 CAAA Conference in Montreal).

SUMMARY

The assurance standards are the general framework for applying the "assurance engagements" to a wide range of subjects. They are the quality guides for general assurance work. Theoretically, they could serve as quality guides for independent audits of financial statements. However, they were created long after GAAS for audits of financial statements, and therefore GAAS remains the predominant framework for most engagements.

Financial statement auditors are most concerned with the eight GAAS standards because they are the direct guides for the quality of everyday audit practice. The general standard sets requirements for auditors' competence, objectivity, and due professional care. The three examination standards set requirements for planning and supervising each audit, obtaining an understanding of the client's internal controls, and obtaining sufficient appropriate evidence to serve as a basis for an audit report. The four reporting standards cover requirements for GAAP, auditor and management responsibilities, adequate disclosure, and report content.

These GAAS have been widely copied. When you study Chapter 17, on public sector and internal auditing, you will see that the CICA and internal audit standards incorporate all the GAAS and many elements of assurance concepts. All auditors have some common ground in generally accepted auditing standards.

GAAS are applicable in computer accounting systems as well as in manual systems. Compliance with the GAAS general and field work standards is more complex because of the technological complexity of computer systems. However, the GAAS reporting standards are not affected.

In all matters relating to financial statement audits, auditors are advised to have a sense of professional scepticism. This attitude is reflected in a "prove it with evidence" response to management representations, to answers to enquiries, and to financial statement assertions themselves.

While assurance standards and GAAS govern the quality of work on each individual engagement, the quality control elements guide a PA firm's audit practice taken as a whole. Quality control is the foundation of the self-regulatory system of peer review, practice inspection, and quality review. The nine elements of independence, assigning personnel, consultation, supervision, hiring, professional development, advancement, acceptance and continuance of clients, and inspection are usually the objects of a firm's policies and procedures for assuring that GAAS are followed faithfully in all aspects of the firm's practice.

As an auditor, you must have a thorough understanding of these practice standards, especially GAAS. All practical problems can be approached by beginning with a consideration of the practice standards in question. Auditing standards do not exist in a vacuum. They are put to work in numerous practical applications. Practical applications of the standards will be shown in subsequent chapters on audit program planning, execution of auditing procedures, gathering evidence, and making auditing decisions.

MULTIPLE-CHOICE QUESTIONS FOR PRACTICE AND REVIEW

2.25 It is always a good idea for auditors to begin an audit with the professional scepticism characterized by the assumption that:

a. A potential conflict of interest always exists between the auditor and the management of the enterprise under audit.

b. In audits of financial statements, the auditor acts exclusively in the capacity of an auditor.

c. The professional status of the independent auditor imposes commensurate professional obligations.

d. Financial statements and financial data are verifiable.

2.26 When Client Company prohibits auditors from visiting selected branch offices of the business, this is an example of interference with:

a. Reporting independence.

b. Investigative independence.

c. Auditors' training and proficiency.

d. Audit planning and supervision.

2.27 After the auditors learned of Client Company's failure to record an expense for obsolete inventory, they agreed to a small adjustment to the financial statements because the Client president told them the company would violate its debt agreements if the full amount were recorded. This is an example of a lack of:

a. Auditors' training and proficiency.

b. Planning and supervision.

c. Audit investigative independence.

d. Audit reporting independence.

2.28 The primary purpose for obtaining an understanding of the company's internal controls in a financial statement audit is:

a. To determine the nature, timing, and extent of auditing procedures to be performed.

b. To make consulting suggestions to the management.

c. To obtain direct sufficient appropriate evidential matter to afford a reasonable basis for an opinion on the financial statements.

d. To determine whether the company has changed any accounting principles.

2.29 Auditors' activities about which of these generally accepted auditing standards are not affected by the auditee's utilization of a computerized accounting system?

a. The audit report shall state whether the financial statements are presented in accordance with GAAP.

b. The work is to be adequately planned and assistants, if any, are to be properly supervised.

c. Sufficient appropriate evidential matter is to be obtained . . . to afford a reasonable basis for an opinion regarding the financial statements under audit.

d. The audit is to be performed by a person or persons having adequate technical training and proficiency as an auditor.

2.30 Which of the following is not found in the standard unqualified audit report on financial statements?

a. An identification of the financial statements that were audited.

b. A general description of an audit.

c. An opinion that the financial statements present financial position in conformity with GAAP.

d. An emphasis paragraph commenting on the effect of economic conditions on the company.

2.31 The assurance standards do not contain a requirement that auditors obtain:

a. Adequate knowledge in the subject matter of the assertions being examined.

b. An understanding of the auditee's internal control structure.

c. Sufficient evidence for the conclusions expressed in an attestation report.

d. Independence in mental attitude.

2.32 Auditor Jones is studying a company's accounting treatment of a series of complicated transactions in exotic financial instruments. She should look for the highest level of authoritative support for proper accounting in:

a. Provincial Securities Commission Staff Position Statements.

b. CICA industry audit and accounting guides.

c. CICA recommendations in the *Handbook.*

d. Emerging Issues Committee Consensus Statements.

2.33 Which one of the following services would not be considered an assurance engagement?

a. Giving an opinion on a prize promoter's claims about the amount of sweepstakes prizes awarded in the past.

b. Giving an opinion on the conformity of the financial statements of a university with generally accepted accounting principles.

c. Giving an opinion on the fair presentation of a newspaper's circulation data.

d. Giving assurance about the average drive length achieved by golfers with a client's golf balls.

2.34 An auditor's understanding of the control system in an auditee's organization contributes information for:

a. Determining whether members of the audit team have the required technical training and proficiency to perform the audit.

b. Ascertaining the independence of mental attitude of members of the audit team.

c. Planning the professional development courses the audit staff needs to keep up to date with new auditing standards.

d. Planning the nature, timing, and extent of subsequent substantive audit procedures on an audit.

2.35 Quality control standards require that auditors' independence must be maintained according to the rules in the:

a. CICA generally accepted auditing standards.

b. CICA statements on financial accounting standards.

c. Provincial rules of professional conduct.

d. Standards for assurance engagements.

Exercises and Problems

2.36 Audit Independence and Planning. You are meeting with executives of Cooper Cosmetics Corporation to arrange your firm's engagement to audit the corporation's financial statements for the year ending December 31. One executive suggests the audit work be divided among three staff members. One person would examine asset accounts, a second would examine liability accounts, and the third would examine income and expense accounts to minimize audit time, avoid duplication of staff effort, and curtail interference with company operations.

Advertising is the corporation's largest expense, and the advertising manager suggests that a staff member of your firm, whose uncle owns the advertising agency that handles the corporation's advertising, be assigned to examine the Advertising Expense account. The staff member has a thorough knowledge of the rather complex contact between Cooper Cosmetics and the advertising agency.

Required:

a. To what extent should a PA follow the client's suggestions for the conduct of an audit? Discuss.

b. List and discuss the reasons why audit work should not be assigned solely according to asset, liability, and income and expense categories.

c. Should the staff member of your PA firm whose uncle owns the advertising agency be assigned to examine advertising costs? Discuss.

2.37 Examination Standards. You have accepted the engagement of auditing the financial statements of the C. Reis Company, a small manufacturing firm that has been your client for several years. Because you were busy writing the report for another engagement, you sent a staff accountant to begin the audit, with the suggestion that she start with the accounts receivable. Using the prior year's working papers as a guide, the auditor prepared a trial balance of the accounts, aged them, prepared and mailed positive confirmation requests, examined underlying support for charges and credits, and performed other work she considered necessary to obtain evidence about the validity and collectibility of the receivables. At the conclusion of her work, you reviewed the working papers she prepared and found she had carefully followed the prior year's working papers.

Required:

The opinion rendered by a PA states that the audit was made in accordance with generally accepted auditing standards.

List the three generally accepted standards of field work. Relate them to the above illustration by indicating how they were fulfilled or, if appropriate, how they were not fulfilled.

(ICAO adapted)

2.38 Time of Appointment and Planning. Your public accounting practice is located in a town of 15,000 population. Your work, conducted by you and two assistants, consists of compiling clients' monthly statements and preparing income tax returns for individuals from cash data and partnership returns from books and records. You have a few corporate clients; however, service to them is limited to preparation of income tax returns and assistance in year-end closings where bookkeeping is deficient.

One of your corporate clients is a retail hardware store. Your work for this client has been limited to preparing the corporation income tax return from a trial balance submitted by the bookkeeper.

On December 26 you receive from the president of the corporation a letter containing the following request:

> We have made arrangements with the First National Bank to borrow $500,000 to finance the purchase of a complete line of appliances. The bank has asked us to furnish our auditor's certified statement as of December 31, which is the closing date of our accounting year. The trial balance of the general ledger should be ready by January 10, which should allow ample time to prepare your report for submission to the bank by January 20. In view

of the importance of this certified report to our financing program, we trust you will arrange to comply with the foregoing schedule.

Required:

From a theoretical viewpoint, discuss the difficulties that are caused by such a short-notice audit request.

(AICPA adapted)

2.39 Reporting Standards. PA Musgrave and his associates audited the financial statements of North Company, a computer equipment retailer. Musgrave conducted the audit in accordance with the general and field work standards of generally accepted auditing standards and therefore wrote a standard audit description in his audit report. Then he received an emergency call to fill in as a substitute tenor in his barbershop quartet.

No one else was in the office that Saturday afternoon, so he handed you the complete financial statements and footnotes and said: "Make sure it's OK to write an unqualified opinion on these statements. The working papers are on the table. I'll check with you on Monday morning."

Required:

In general terms, what must you determine in order to write an unqualified opinion paragraph for Musgrave's signature?

2.40 GAAS in a Computer Environment. The Lovett Corporation uses an IBM mainframe computer system with peripheral optical reader and high-speed laser printer equipment. Transaction information is initially recorded on paper documents (e.g., sales invoices) and then read by optical equipment that produces a magnetic disk containing the data. These data file disks are processed by a computer program, and printed listings, journals, and general ledger balances are produced on the high-speed printer equipment.

Required:

Explain how the audit standard requiring "adequate technical training and proficiency" is important for satisfying the general and field work standards in the audit of Lovett Corporation's financial statements.

2.41 Audit Report Language. The standard unqualified report contains several important sentences and phrases. Give an explanation of why each of the following phrases is used instead of the alternative language indicated.

1. Address: "To the Board of Directors and Stockholders" instead of "To Whom It May Concern."
2. "We have audited the balance sheet of Anycompany as of December 31, 1992, and the related statements of income, retained earnings, and cash flows for the year then ended" instead of "We have audited the attached financial statements."
3. "We conducted our audit in accordance with generally accepted auditing standards" instead of "Our audit was conducted with due audit care appropriate in the circumstances."
4. "In our opinion, the financial statements referred to above present fairly . . . in conformity with generally accepted accounting principles" instead of "The financial statements are true and correct."

2.42 Authoritative Support. Auditors' reports on financial statements contain an opinion on the conformity of the statements with generally accepted accounting principles (GAAP). An audit decision on GAAP includes the determination of whether an accounting treatment is "generally accepted," and this determination is made by finding the authoritative support for the accounting treatment.

Required:
List in order of priority the sources of authoritative support an auditor can consult when faced with a decision about GAAP.

2.43 Deficiencies and Omissions in an Audit Report. On completion of all field work on September 23, 1993, the following report was written by Betsy Ross to the directors of Continental Corporation.

To the Board of Directors.
Continental Corporation:

The accompanying balance sheet of Continental Corporation and the related statements of income and retained earnings as of July 31, 1993, are the responsibility of management. In accordance with your instructions, we have conducted a complete audit. We planned and performed the audit to obtain reasonable assurance about whether the financial statements are free of material misstatement. An audit includes examining, on a test basis, evidence supporting the amounts and disclosures in the financial statements. An audit also includes assessing the accounting principles used and significant estimates made by management, as well as evaluating the overall financial statement presentation. We believe that our audit provides a reasonable basis for our opinion.

In many respects this was an unusual year for the Continental Corporation. The weakening of the economy in the early part of the year and the strike of plant employees in the summer led to a decline in sales and net income. After making several tests of the sales records, nothing came to our attention that would indicate sales have not been properly recorded.

In our opinion, with the explanation given above, and with the exception of some minor errors we consider immaterial, the aforementioned financial statements present the financial position of Continental Corporation at July 31, 1993, and the results of its operations, and its cash flows for the year then ended, in conformity with generally accepted accounting principles.

Betsy Ross & Co., PA
July 31, 1998

Required:
List and explain the deficiencies and omissions in Ross's audit report.

2.44 Management Fraud Conflict of Interest. Many cases of management fraud probably go undetected even when competent annual audits are performed. The reason, of course, is that generally accepted auditing procedures are not always designed and executed specifically to detect executive-level management fraud. Please give your own estimate of the prevalence of executive-level management fraud as requested below.

1. Based on your perceptions of business, is the incidence of significant executive-level management fraud more than 10 in each 1,000 clients (i.e., 1 percent) audited by Big Six accounting firms? Answer *a* or *b*.

   a. Yes, more than 10 in each 1,000 Big Six clients have significant executive-level management fraud.
   b. No, fewer than 10 in each 1,000 Big Six clients have significant executive-level management fraud.

2. What is your estimate of the number of Big Six clients per 1,000 that have significant executive-level management fraud?

Discussion Cases

2.45 Investment Performance Assurance. Nancy Drew is the president of Mystery Capital Management, Inc. Mystery manages $1.2 billion in two mutual funds, one a stock fund and the other a bond fund. Competition for investors' money is fierce, and hundreds of money management companies compete by advertising their funds' performance statistics. Recently, the Ontario Securities Commission (OSC) has criticized the advertisements for misrepresenting the returns investors can actually earn. In addition to the investment performance statistics, money management firms also advertise the amounts of their fees, usually representing no-load or low-fee arrangements, but they often do not advertise the other expenses allowed under OSC rules.

Ms. Drew has retained your PA firm to give an opinion on the fair presentation of Mystery Capital Management's investment performance statistics and expense ratios used in its advertisements. The plan is to present your report in the company's advertisements.

Required:
For each of the assurance standards, state its applicability in relation to the engagement.

2.46 Auditing Standards Case Study. Ray, the owner of a small company, asked Holmes, PA, to conduct an audit of the company's records. Ray told Holmes that the audit was to be completed in time to submit audited financial statements to a bank as part of a loan application. Holmes immediately accepted the engagement and agreed to provide an auditor's report within three weeks. Ray agreed to pay Holmes a fixed fee plus a bonus if the loan was granted.

Holmes hired two accounting students to conduct the audit and spent several hours telling them exactly what to do. Holmes told the students not to spend time reviewing the controls but, instead, to concentrate on proving the mathematical accuracy of the ledger accounts and on summarizing the data in the accounting records that support Ray's financial statements. The students followed Holmes's instructions and after two weeks gave Holmes the financial statements, which did not include footnotes. Holmes reviewed the statements and prepared an unqualified auditor's report. The report, however, did not refer to generally accepted accounting principles or to the fact that Ray had changed to the accounting standard for capitalizing interest.

Required:
Briefly describe each of the generally accepted auditing standards and indicate how the action(s) of Holmes resulted in a failure to comply with each standard.

(AICPA adapted)

2.47 Quality Control Standards. Each of the following quality control policies and procedures is typical of ones that can be found in PA firms' quality control documents. Identify each of them with one of the elements of quality control required by the Quality Control Standards.

a. Review semiannual performance reports with individuals and assess their progress in relation to job performance, future objectives, assignment preferences, and career opportunities.

b. Publish guidelines for review of each audit report, including determination of the adequacy of evidence shown in the working papers, conformity of the report with professional standards, and review of the report by a partner not otherwise connected with the audit engagement.

c. Maintain or provide access to adequate reference libraries and designated experts by (1) maintaining technical manuals and internal technical newsletters and (2) advising staff personnel of the degree of authority accorded internal experts' opinions and the procedures to be followed for resolving disagreements with experts.

d. Consider the experience and training of the engagement personnel in relation to the complexity or other requirements of the engagement and the extent of supervision to be provided.

e. Review recruiting results annually to determine whether goals and personnel needs are being achieved.

f. Distribute new professional pronouncements (IAGs, EIC, others), and encourage personnel at all levels to take continuing professional education courses.

g. A special team will review a selection of completed audits for compliance with professional standards, including generally accepted auditing standards, generally accepted accounting principles, and the firm's quality control policies and procedures.

h. Obtain from personnel periodic, written representations listing their investments, outside business relationships, and employment of their close relatives.

i. A firm management committee shall annually review client relationships in light of changes in management, directors, ownership, legal counsel, financial condition, litigation status, nature of client's business, and scope of the engagement.

CHAPTER 3

Learning Objectives

This chapter covers the most frequent variations in audit reports.

Management has the primary responsibility for the fair presentation of financial statements in conformity with generally accepted accounting principles. Auditors have primary responsibility for their own audit reports on the financial statements. You must know the standard unqualified report as a starting place, since this chapter explains reasons for changing the standard language when auditors cannot give this "clean opinion."

Your objectives, with respect to variations in audit reports, are to be able to:

1. Determine whether an accountant is associated with financial statements.

2. Explain the general meaning of the three "levels of assurance."

3. Write a detailed description of the meaning of the scope paragraph and the opinion paragraph in a standard unqualified audit report.

4. Write a qualified, an adverse, and a disclaimer report for a given description of accounting facts and audit circumstances.

5. Write an audit report with an unqualified opinion but containing additional explanation or modified wording for specific issues allowed by auditing standards.

6. Explain why auditors have standards for reporting on the "application of accounting principles."

7. List and explain the effects of materiality on audit report choices.

8. Write an audit report in which a principal auditor refers to the work of another independent auditor (Appendix 3A).

9. Write the required modifications when a report on prior-year comparative financial statements is changed (Appendix 3A).

10. Describe the type of report issued when an audit engagement is limited (Appendix 3A).

11. Explain auditors' reporting responsibilities in connection with "other information" and supplementary information (Appendix 3A).

12. Describe the reporting requirements involved in auditors' association with condensed financial information (Appendix 3A).

REPORTS ON AUDITED FINANCIAL STATEMENTS

ASSOCIATION WITH FINANCIAL STATEMENTS

LEARNING OBJECTIVE
1. Determine whether an accountant is associated with financial statements.

Auditing standards require a report to be rendered in all cases where a PA's name is **associated with financial statements**. As a PA, you are associated with financial statements when (1) you have consented to the use of your name in connection with the statements; or (2) you have prepared or performed some other services with respect to the statements, even if your name is not used in any written report (*Handbook Section* 5020.04).

The concept of association is far-reaching. PAs are associated with financial statements and must render reports even in such cases as these: (1) financial statements are merely reproduced on an accountant's letterhead, (2) financial statements are produced by the accountant's computer as part of a bookkeeping service, and (3) a document containing financial statements merely identifies an accountant as the public accountant or auditor for the company. The reason a report is required is that most users of financial statements assume that an audit has been conducted and that "everything is OK" whenever an independent accountant is known to be involved with financial statements. Consequently, an obligation exists to inform the users about the nature of the work performed, if any, and the conclusions the accountant has made about the financial statements. This outline is summarized in more detail in Appendix 3A.

R E V I E W
CHECKPOINTS

3.1 Why should public accountants issue a report whenever they are associated with financial statements?

LEVELS OF ASSURANCE

LEARNING OBJECTIVE
2. Explain the general meaning of the three "levels of assurance."

In practice, accountants and auditors can render three basic types of conclusions about financial statements. These three are known as the **levels of assurance**. The highest level is considered to be the audit assurance exemplified by the standard unqualified report (sometimes known as the clean opinion). Its opinion sentence reads: "In our opinion, the accompanying financial statements present fairly, in all material respects." This opinion sentence is sometimes called **positive assurance** because it is a forthright and factual statement of the PA's opinion based on an audit. Although the *CICA Handbook* does not explicitly state how much assurance an auditor provides in an audit opinion, it does discuss assurance in terms of auditor objectives. (See *Handbook Section* 5130.02.)

The middle level is known as **negative assurance**. A negative assurance conclusion is typical in the review report on unaudited nonfinancial statements, thus:

E X H I B I T 3–1   LEVELS OF ASSURANCE

"Based on my review, nothing has come to my attention that causes me to believe that these financial statements are not, in all material respects, in accordance with generally accepted accounting principles" (*Section* 8200.04 of the *Handbook*). This conclusion is called negative because it uses the backdoor phrase "nothing has come to my attention" to give assurance about conformity with GAAP. Auditing standards prohibit the use of negative assurance in reports on audited financial statements because it is considered too weak a conclusion for the audit effort involved (*Section* 5400.15). However, negative assurance is permitted in reviews of unaudited financial statements, in letters to underwriters, and in reviews of interim financial information. (More details about review reports on unaudited financial statements are in Chapter 14.)

The lowest level of assurance is "no assurance." This is the **denial of opinion**, with which auditors explicitly state that they give no opinion and no assurance, thus taking no responsibility for a report on the fair presentation of financial statements in conformity with GAAP. The conclusion sentence in the denial of opinion ends as follows: "I am unable to express an opinion whether these information financial statements are presented fairly in accordance with generally accepted accounting principles." The circumstances under which denials of opinions are issued in audit engagements are explained later in this chapter.

Some nonaudit engagements also do not provide any audit assurance. The most common examples are compilation engagements, which can be considered a form of specified procedures engagements. Compilation engagements are not considered to be assurance engagements because the practitioner is not required to audit, review, or otherwise attempt to verify the accuracy or completeness of the information provided by management. The practitioner is, therefore, not expressing a conclusion on the reliability of the statements compiled. The auditors' involvement in compiling the financial statements is presumed, however, to add accounting credibility to the financial statements even though there is no audit credibility or assurance provided. (More details about compilation reports on unaudited financial statements are in Chapter 14).

The levels of assurance are depicted in Exhibit 3–1.

E X H I B I T 3–2   **AUDITOR'S REPORT** (from *Handbook Section 5400.26*)

To the Shareholders of.....................................

I have audited the balance sheet of .... as at ...., 19....., and the statements of income, retained earnings and changes in financial position for the year then ended. These financial statements are the responsibility of the company's management. My responsibility is to express an opinion on these financial statements based on my audit.

I conducted my audit in accordance with generally accepted auditing standards. Those standards require that I plan and perform an audit to obtain reasonable assurance whether the financial statements are free of material misstatement. An audit includes examining, on a test basis, evidence supporting the amounts and disclosure in the financial statements. An audit also includes assessing the accounting principles used and significant estimates made by management, as well as evaluating the overall financial statement presentation.

In my opinion, these financial statements present fairly, in all material respects, the financial position of the company as at ...., 19....., and the results of its operations and the changes in its financial position for the year then ended in accordance with generally accepted accounting principles.

City   (signed)....................................
Date   Chartered Accountant

R E V I E W
C H E C K P O I N T S

3.2 What is the most important distinction between an auditor's opinion on financial statements and an auditor's disclaimer of opinion?

3.3 What is a negative assurance? Why is it generally prohibited? When is a negative assurance permitted?

STANDARD UNQUALIFIED REPORT AND VARIATIONS

LEARNING OBJECTIVE

3. Write a detailed description of the meaning of the scope paragraph and opinion paragraph in a standard unqualified audit report.

The standard unqualified report contains three basic segments: (1) the introductory paragraph, (2) the scope paragraph, and (3) the opinion paragraph. An example is given in Exhibit 3–2. The technical details of this report were introduced in Chapter 2.

Meaning of the Introductory, Scope, and Opinion Paragraphs

Many users understand the audit report by counting the paragraphs! Crude as this may seem, it makes some sense because the three standard paragraphs are supposed to convey the same messages for all audits.

Introductory Paragraph

The introductory paragraph declares that an audit has been conducted and identifies the financial statements. These identifications are important because the opinion paragraph at the end is an opinion on these financial statements. If one or more of the basic financial statements is not identified in the introductory paragraph, the opinion paragraph likewise should not offer any opinion on it (them). The introductory paragraph also gives notice of management's responsibility for the financial statements and the auditors' responsibility for the audit report (*Handbook Section 5400.08*).

Scope Paragraph

Auditors must render a fair presentation of their own work, as well as an opinion on the financial statements. The scope paragraph is the auditor's report of the character of the work in the audit. This portion of the report is vitally important for disclosure of the quality and extent of the audit itself.

The sentence "I conducted my audit in accordance with generally accepted auditing standards" refers primarily to the general and field work standards. Its message is that (1) the auditors were trained and proficient, (2) the auditors were independent, (3) due professional care was exercised, (4) the work was planned and supervised, (5) a sufficient understanding of the internal control structure was obtained, and (6) sufficient appropriate evidential matter was obtained. To the extent that one or more of these general and field work standards is not actually satisfied during an audit, the scope paragraph must be qualified. A qualification in this paragraph means the addition of words explaining exactly which standard was not satisfied. Such qualifications may be caused by lack of independence, lack of sufficient appropriate evidence, or restrictions on procedures imposed by the client (*Section* 5510). In practice, auditors always change the standard opinion paragraph language when the scope paragraph is qualified.

The scope paragraph contains general descriptions of the audit work in addition to the reference to generally accepted auditing standards. It makes special mention of the auditors' assessment of the choice of accounting principles and the evaluation of the overall financial statement presentation.

Opinion Paragraph

Users of audited financial statements are generally most interested in the opinion paragraph. It is actually one long sentence. This sentence contains the auditors' conclusions about the financial statements. It is the public manifestation of the private audit decision process.

The third and fourth reporting standards are incorporated in the opinion sentence:

1. The standard report states that the financial statements are presented in accordance with generally accepted accounting principles.

2. The standard report, by its silence, regards the financial statement disclosures as reasonably adequate.

3. The standard report contains an expression of opinion regarding the financial statements.

4. An "overall opinion" is expressed in the standard report, so no reasons for not doing so need to be stated.

5. The scope paragraph gives the "clear-cut indication of the character of the audit examination," and the degree of responsibility is unqualified positive assurance.

With regard to the fourth reporting standard, other examples later in this chapter will show how auditors assert that an opinion cannot be expressed (denial of opinion) and how audit responsibility can be limited (qualified opinion).

When reading the reporting standards, you should understand the term "financial statements" to include not only the traditional balance sheet, income statement, and statement of changes in financial position (which is soon to be referred to as cash flows statement) but also all the footnote disclosures and additional information (e.g., earnings per share calculations) that are integral elements of the basic financial presentation required by GAAP. The first and fourth standards are explicit in the standard report. The second and third standards are effectively on an implicit reporting basis—that is, the report comments on consistency only when accounting principles have been changed *and* disclosures are considered inadequate. The adequacy of disclosures may be judged by GAAP requirements; but auditors also must be sensitive to the information needs of investors, creditors, and other users when considering the need to disclose information that is not explicitly required by GAAP. Disgruntled investors often use the "lack of informative disclosure" criterion as a basis for lawsuits.

Reservation in the Standard Unqualified Report

Subsequent sections of this chapter explain the major variations on the standard report. These are referred to as reservations in the auditor's report. There are three basic reasons for giving a report other than the standard unqualified audit report.

When the financial statements contain a departure from GAAP, including inadequate disclosure, the auditors must choose between a qualified opinion and an adverse opinion. The choice depends on the materiality (significance) of the effect of the GAAP departure.

When there is a scope limitation (extent of audit work has been limited), and the auditors have not been able to obtain sufficient appropriate evidence on a particular account balance or disclosure, the auditors must choose between a qualified opinion and a denial of opinion. The choice depends on the materiality of the matter for which evidence is not sufficient.

When the auditors lack independence, they should resign or not accept an audit engagement by the Rules of Professional Conduct (discussed in Chapter 15).

· ·

R E V I E W
C H E C K P O I N T S

3.4 Think about the standard unqualified introductory and scope paragraphs: (*a*) What do they identify as the objects of the audit? (*b*) What is meant by this sentence: "We conducted our audit in accordance with generally accepted auditing standards"?

3.5 What are the major reasons for changing the standard unqualified report?

· ·

AUDIT REPORT RESERVATIONS
· · · · · · · · · · · ·

LEARNING OBJECTIVE

4. Write a qualified, an adverse, and a disclaimer report for a given description of accounting facts and audit circumstances.

Audit reports other than the standard unqualified audit report are called audit report reservations. The most common report reservations are called **qualified reports** because they contain an opinion paragraph that does not give the positive assurance that everything in the financial statements is in conformity with GAAP. The three basic types of qualified reports are different.

GAAP Departure Reports

A company's management can decide to present financial statements containing an accounting treatment or disclosure that is not in conformity with GAAP. The reasons are varied. Management may not wish to capitalize leases and show the related debt, may calculate earnings per share incorrectly, may not accrue unbilled revenue at the end of a period, may make unreasonable accounting estimates, or may be reluctant to disclose all the known details of a contingency. Whatever the reason, the fact is a departure from GAAP. Now the auditor must decide the type of opinion to render.

If the departure is immaterial or insignificant, it can be treated as if it did not exist. The audit opinion can be unqualified. What is considered immaterial under the circumstances is a matter of auditor's professional judgment.

If in the auditor's judgment the departure is material enough to potentially affect users' decisions based on the financial statements, the opinion must be qualified. In this case, the qualification takes the "except-for" language form. The opinion sentence begins: "In my opinion, except for the [nature of the GAAP departure explained in the report], the financial statements present fairly, in all material respects . . . in accordance with generally accepted accounting principles." This except-for form of GAAP departure qualification isolates a particular departure, but says that the financial statements are otherwise in conformity with GAAP. The nature of the GAAP departure can be explained in a separate paragraph (called the reservation paragraph) in the audit report between the scope paragraph and the opinion paragraph (*Handbook Section* 5510.28).

In the except-for qualified report, the introductory and scope paragraphs are the same as the standard unqualified report. They are not changed. After all, the audit has been performed without limitation, and the auditors have sufficient appropriate evidence about the financial statements, including the GAAP departure.

GAAP-departure report examples are hard to find in published financial statements. Most published statements come under the jurisdiction of the provincial securities commissions, which require public companies to file financial statements in conformity with GAAP without any departures. Exhibit 3–3 shows a GAAP departure due to a failure to record depreciation.

E X H I B I T 3–3   **(from *Handbook Section* 5510.A, Example A)**

Departure from generally accepted accounting principles—no depreciation recorded. When the auditor has determined that a qualification is the type of reservation required, the following wording may be appropriate.

AUDITOR'S REPORT

To the Shareholders of...................................

I have audited the balance sheet of .... as at ...., 19....., and the statements of income, retained earnings and changes in financial position for the year then ended. These financial statements are the responsibility of the company's management. My responsibility is to express an opinion of these financial statements based on my audit.

I conducted my audit in accordance with generally accepted auditing standards. Those standards require that I plan and perform an audit to obtain reasonable assurance whether the financial statements are free of material misstatement. An audit includes examining, on a test basis, evidence supporting the amounts and disclosures in the financial statements. An audit also includes assessing the accounting principles used and significant estimates made by management, as well as evaluating the overall financial statement presentation.

Note..........describes the depreciation policy with respect to the company's manufacturing plants and equipment. The note also indicates that the company is not depreciating its head office building, which it acquired 5 years ago, on the grounds that it is not a producing asset and is maintaining its value as a potential rental or resale property. In this respect the financial statements are not in accordance with generally accepted accounting principles. The estimated useful life of similar buildings is usually considered to be between 30 and 40 years. If depreciation had been provided on the basis of an estimated useful life of, say, 35 years, depreciation for the current year would have been increased by $..........(19.......... $..........), net income after taxes would have been decreased by $..........(19..........$..........), accumulated depreciation would have been increased by $..........(19..........$..........) and the balance of deferred income taxes and the closing balance of retained earnings would have been reduced by $..........(19..........$..........) and $.......... (19..........$..........)respectively.

In my opinion, except for the effects of the failure to record depreciation as described in the preceding paragraph, these financial statements present fairly, in all material respects, the financial position of the company as at ...., 19.........., and the results of its operations and the changes in its financial position for the year then ended in accordance with generally accepted accounting principles.

(signed)...................................
(CHARTERED ACCOUNTANT)

However, if the GAAP departure is (1) more than material or "so significant that they overshadow the financial statements" (what we'll call here "super-material"), or (2) pervasive, affecting numerous accounts and financial statement relationships, an adverse opinion should be given. An adverse opinion is exactly the opposite of the unqualified opinion. In this type of opinion, auditors say the financial statements do not present financial position, results of operations, and changes in financial position in conformity with generally accepted accounting principles. The introductory and scope paragraphs should not be qualified because, in order to decide to use the adverse opinion, the audit team must possess all evidence necessary to reach the decision. When this opinion is given, all the substantive reasons must be disclosed in the report in the reservation paragraph(s) (*Section* 5510.28).

Because of the securities commission requirements, adverse opinions are hard to find. The example in Exhibit 3–4 is an adverse opinion due to a disagreement between the auditor and management on the carrying value of a long-term investment. The departure from GAAP is considered to be super-material, or well in excess of what would be considered material for an "except for" qualification.

As a practical matter, auditors generally require more evidence to support an adverse opinion than to support an unqualified opinion. Perhaps this phenomenon can be attributed to auditors' reluctance to be bearers of bad news. However, audit standards are quite clear on the point that, if an auditor has a basis for an adverse opinion, the uncomfortable position cannot be relieved by giving a denial of opinion.

E X H I B I T 3–4   **ADVERSE REPORT (from *Handbook Section* 5510.11)**

Departure from generally accepted accounting principles—disagreement on carrying value of a long-term investment. When the auditor has determined that an adverse opinion is the type of reservation required, the following wording may be appropriate. (For an adverse opinion, "present fairly" in the opinion paragraph, need not be modified with the phrase "in all material respects")

AUDITOR'S REPORT

To the Shareholders of...................................

I have audited the balance sheet of .... as at ...., 19....., and the statements of income, retained earnings and changes in financial position for the year then ended. These financial statements are the responsibility of the company's management. My responsibility is to express an opinion of these financial statements based on my audit.

I conducted my audit in accordance with generally accepted auditing standards. Those standards require that I plan and perform an audit to obtain reasonable assurance whether the financial statements are free of material misstatement. An audit includes examining, on a test basis, evidence supporting the amounts and disclosures in the financial statements. An audit also includes assessing the accounting principles used and significant estimates made by management, as well as evaluating the overall financial statement presentation.

The company's investment in X Company Ltd., its only asset, which is carried at a cost of $10,000,000, has declined in value to an amount of $5,850,000. The loss in the value of this investment, in my opinion, is other than a temporary decline and in such circumstances, generally accepted accounting principles require that the investment be written down to recognize the loss. If this decline in value had been recognized, the investment, net income for the year and retained earnings would have been reduced by $4,150,000.

In my opinion, because the write-down has not been made for the significant decline in value of the investment described in the preceding paragraph, these financial statements do not present fairly the financial position of the company as at ...., 19..... and the results of its operations and the changes in its financial position for the year then ended in accordance with generally accepted accounting principles.

(signed)...................................
CHARTERED ACCOUNTANT

Date
City

3.6 With reference to evidence, what extent of evidence is required as a basis for the unqualified opinion? for an adverse opinion? for an opinion qualified for GAAP departure?

3.7 What effect does the materiality of a GAAP departure have on the auditors' reporting decision?

Scope Limitation Reports

Auditors are in the most comfortable position when they have all the evidence needed to make a report decision, whether the opinion is to be unqualified, adverse, or qualified for a GAAP departure. However, two kinds of situations can create **scope limitations**, which are conditions where the auditors are unable to obtain sufficient appropriate evidence. The two arise from (1) management's deliberate refusal to let auditors perform some procedures and (2) circumstances, such as late appointment of auditor, in which some procedures cannot be performed.

If management's refusal or the circumstance affect the audit in a minor, immaterial way, the audit can be considered unaffected, and the report can be unqualified as if the limitation had never occurred.

Management's deliberate refusal to give access to documents or decision to otherwise limit the application of audit procedures is the most serious condition. It casts doubt on management's integrity. (Why does management refuse access or limit the work?) In most such cases, excluding ones in which the limitation clearly relates to financial matters already known to be immaterial, the audit report is qualified or an opinion is denied, depending upon the materiality of the financial items affected.

Exhibit 3–5 shows two reports that illustrate the auditors' alternatives. The illustrated failure to take physical counts of inventory might have been a deliberate management action, or it might have resulted from other circumstances (such as the company not anticipating the need for an audit and appointing the auditor after the latest year-end).

In Panel A the opinion is qualified, using the except-for language form. Here the lack of evidence is considered material but not "super-material" to overwhelm the meaning of a qualified audit opinion and the usefulness of the unaffected parts of the financial statements. The proper qualification phrase is: "In our opinion, except for the effects of adjustments, if any, as might have been determined to be necessary had we been able to examine evidence regarding the inventories, the financial statements present fairly, in all material respects, . . . in conformity with generally accepted accounting principles." This report "carves out" the inventory from the audit reporting responsibility, taking no audit responsibility for this part of the financial statements.

Notice that the introductory paragraph in Panel A is the same as for an unqualified report. However, the scope paragraph is qualified because the audit was not entirely completed in accordance with generally accepted auditing standards. Specifically, sufficient appropriate evidence about the inventories was not obtained. Whenever the scope paragraph is qualified for an important omission of audit work, the opinion paragraph should also be qualified.

In Panel B the situation is considered fatal to the audit opinion. The inventories are too large and too important in this case to say "except for adjustments, if any." The audit report then must be a denial of opinion.

It is very important to remember that scope limitation reservations arise only when it is not possible to obtain compensating assurance from alternative audit procedures.

EXHIBIT 3–5   **SCOPE LIMITATION REPORTS**

Panel A: Qualified Opinion

Auditor's Report

To The Shareholders of
X Company:

[Introductory paragraph same as standard unqualified report.]

In my opinion, except for the effects of such adjustments, if any, which I might have determined to be necessary had I been able to examine evidence regarding the inventories described above, the financial statements referred to above present fairly, in all material respects, the financial position of X Company at December 31, 19X2 and 19X1, and the results of operations and changes in financial position for the years then ended in accordance with generally accepted accounting principles.

/s/ Auditor signature
January 29, 19X7

Panel B: Denial of Opinion

Auditor's Report

To The Shareholders of
X Company:

[Introductory paragraph same as standard unqualified report.]

Except as discussed in the following paragraph, we conducted our audits in accordance with generally accepted auditing standards . . . (Remainder of paragraph the same as the standard unqualified scope paragraph) . . .

The Company did not make a count of its physical inventory in 19X2 or 19X1, stated in the accompanying financial statements at $10 million as of December 31, 19X2, and at $15 million as of December 31, 19X1, and we were unable to observe the physical quantities on hand. The Company's records do not permit the application of other auditing procedures to the audit of the inventories.

In view of the possible material effects on the financial statements of the matters described in the preceding paragraphs, I am unable to express our opinion on whether these financial statements are presented fairly in accordance with generally accepted accounting principles.

/s/ Auditor signature
January 29, 19X7

If, for example, in Panel A and Panel B the auditor had been able to satisfy himself or herself through alternative procedures that the inventory was materially accurate, then an unqualified opinion could have been issued for both panels. Thus, scope limitation reports are issued only if in the auditor's judgment there are insufficient alternative procedures to compensate for the restriction.

R E V I E W
C H E C K P O I N T S

3.8 What are the differences between a report qualified for a scope limitation and a standard unqualified report?

3.9 What are the differences between a report in which the opinion is denied because of scope limitation and a standard unqualified report?

3.10 What are unaudited statements? In connection with unaudited statements, which general reporting guides should the auditor follow for public companies?

OTHER RESPONSIBILITIES WITH A DENIAL

A denial of opinion because of severe scope limitation or because of association with unaudited financial statements carries some additional reporting responsibilities. In addition to the denial, these guides should be followed:

1. If the PA should learn that the statements are not in conformity with generally accepted accounting principles (including adequate disclosures), the departures should be explained in the denial.
2. If prior years' unaudited statements are presented, the denial should cover them as well as the current-year statement.

Effects of Lack of Independence

Independence is the foundation of the audit function. When independence is lacking, an audit in accordance with generally accepted auditing standards is impossible. An audit is not simply the application of tools, techniques, and procedures of auditing; it is also the independence in mental attitude of the auditors. This idea is reflected in the general standard and in provincial Codes of Professional Conduct, an example of one of which is the Ontario Institutes Rule 204, titled "Objectivity."

> Rule 204.1: A member engaged as an auditor to express an opinion on financial statements or on financial or other information shall hold himself or herself free of any influence, interest or relationship, which, in respect of the engagement, impairs the member's professional judgment or objectivity or which in view of a reasonable observer would impair the member's professional judgment or objectivity.

This rule applies to the auditors of financial statements. The criteria for determining independence are discussed in Chapter 15.

. . . .

R E V I E W
C H E C K P O I N T S

3.11 If an auditor is not independent with respect to a public company client, what should he or she do?

. . . .

UNQUALIFIED OPINION WITH EXPLANATION OR MODIFICATION

. . . .

LEARNING OBJECTIVE

5. Write an audit report with an unqualified opinion but containing additional explanation or modified wording for specific issues allowed by auditing standards.

Several circumstances may permit an unqualified opinion paragraph, but they raise the need to consider additional information and additional paragraphs to the standard report. Five such situations are covered in this section.

- Consistency. Effects of various changes in accounting and the appropriate disclosure.
- *Section* 5400.22 Report. An unqualified opinion under *Section* 5400.22, justifying a departure from an official pronouncement.

- Emphasis Paragraph(s). Additional explanatory paragraphs that "emphasize a matter" of importance.
- Uncertainty. Paragraph that draws attention to accounting and disclosure for contingencies.
- Going Concern. Paragraph that draws attention to problems of being able to continue as a going concern.

Consistency

There is no longer a need to make reference to consistency even when there are changes in accounting principles as long as the changes are properly disclosed in the financial statements (*Section* 5400.17).

Other changes that do not require consistency references in the audit report are the following: (1) changes in accounting estimates, (2) error corrections that do not involve a change in accounting principles, (3) changes in the classification or aggregation of financial statement amounts, (4) changes in the format or basis of the statement of changes in financial position (e.g., from a balancing format to a net change format), and (5) changes in the subsidiaries included in consolidated financial statements as a result of forming a new subsidiary, buying another company, spinning off or liquidating a subsidiary, or selling a subsidiary. However, failure to disclose any of these changes could amount to a GAAP departure and could present a different reason for qualifying the opinion.

When evaluating a change in accounting principle, auditors must be satisfied that management's justification for the change is reasonable. In the United States there is an additional requirement that the change be to a "preferable" principle. The U.S. standard "Accounting Changes" states:

> The presumption that an entity should not change an accounting principle may be overcome only if the enterprise justifies the use of an alternative acceptable accounting principle on the basis that it is preferable.

A change from accelerated depreciation to straight-line "to increase profits" may be preferable from management's viewpoint, but such a reason is not reasonable justification for most auditors. If the U.S. auditors cannot agree that a change in accounting principle is preferable, then an opinion qualification based on a departure from GAAP is appropriate. (The SEC in the United States requires auditors to submit a letter stating whether the change is to a preferable principle—one that provides a better measure of business operations.)

Section 5400.22 Report

The unqualified opinion depends upon GAAP for standards of financial accounting. However, *Handbook Section* 5400.22 provides for the possibility that adherence to *Handbook Recommendations* might create misleading financial statements:

> When there is a departure from a Handbook Recommendation and the auditor concludes that following the Recommendation would result in misleading financial statements, the auditor should express his or her opinion without reservation, provided the related disclosure is adequate.

E X H I B I T 3–6   EXAMPLE OF ADDITIONAL COMMENTS PARAGRAPH (from *CICA Handbook* Aug-21 Appendix)

**Comments by Auditor for U.S. Readers
on Canada-U.S. Reporting Difference**

In the United States, reporting standards for auditors require the addition of an explanatory paragraph (following the opinion paragraph) when the financial statements are affected by conditions and events that cast substantial doubt on the company's ability to continue as a going concern, such as those described in Note .... to the financial statements. My report to the shareholders dated ...., 19..... is expressed in accordance with Canadian reporting standards which do not permit a reference to such events and conditions in the auditor's report when these are adequately disclosed in the financial statements.

City   (signed)..................................
Date   CHARTERED ACCOUNTANT

Emphasis Paragraph

Sometimes auditors opt to add additional information in the auditor's report. This type of addition to the audit report is known as the **emphasis of a matter** paragraph. Beyond the standard unqualified report wording, auditors have one avenue for enriching the information content in an audit report. They can add one or more paragraphs to emphasize a matter they believe readers should consider important or useful. An emphasis paragraph can be added when the auditor intends to write an unqualified opinion paragraph. Indeed, the matter emphasized is not supposed to be mentioned in the standard unqualified opinion sentence.

Currently (May 1997) there are some limits on the content of an emphasis paragraph. For example *Handbook Sections* 5701 and 5510.19 specifically prohibit reference to contingencies on going concern issues if they are already properly disclosed in the financial statements. In addition the *Handbook* specifically mentions that the following information may be provided in a final paragraph: information required by statute (*Section* 5701.03); unaudited comparative figures (*Section* 5701.10); and comparative figures reported on by other auditors (*Section* 5701.11). However, since the time *Section* 5701 was issued, several new issues have evolved that may expand the content of an emphasis paragraph. These issues include foreign reporting requirements, use of another appropriate disclosed basis of accounting besides GAAP, and, possibly, going concern issues if the current standards are revised in conformity with international standards. An example of additional comments attached to but distinct from the auditor's report, relating to Canadian GAAP and foreign reporting requirements, is shown in Exhibit 3–6.

Reporting on Uncertainties

In an earlier part of this chapter, you studied scope limitations in which management or circumstances prevented the auditors from obtaining sufficient appropriate evidence about a part of the financial statements. A different type of evidence deficiency arises when uncertainties exist. An auditing "uncertainty" is similar to an accounting "contingency," which is defined in *Handbook Section* 3290.02:

> A contingency is . . . an existing condition, or situation, involving uncertainty as to possible gain ("gain contingency") or loss ("loss contingency") to an enterprise that will ultimately be resolved when one or more future events occur or fail to occur.

Resolution of the uncertainty may confirm the acquisition of an asset or the reduction of a liability or the loss or impairment of an asset or the incurrence of a liability.

Section 3290 sets forth accounting and disclosure standards for contingencies. One of the most common contingencies involves the uncertain outcome of litigation pending against the company. Audit uncertainties include not only lawsuits but also such things as the value of fixed assets held for sale (e.g., a whole plant or warehouse facility) and the status of assets involved in foreign expropriations.

Auditors may perform procedures in accordance with generally accepted auditing standards, yet the uncertainty and lack of evidence may persist. The problem is that it is impossible to obtain audit "evidence" about the future. The concept of audit evidence includes information knowable at the time a reporting decision is made and does not include predictions about future resolution of uncertainties. Consequently, auditors should not change (modify or qualify) the introductory, scope, or opinion paragraphs of the standard unqualified report when contingencies and uncertainties exist. When the audit has been performed in accordance with generally accepted auditing standards, and the auditor has done all the things possible in the circumstances, no alteration of these standard paragraphs is necessary as long as the uncertainty has been properly disclosed.

When significant uncertainties about future events exist about such matters as tax deficiency assessments, contract disputes, recoverability of asset costs, lawsuits, and other important contingencies, they should be explained clearly and completely in footnotes to the financial statements. These disclosures are as much a part of management's responsibility as the balance sheet, income statement, and statement of changes in financial position. *Handbook Section* 5510.46 advises that:

> when a contingency is accounted for and disclosed in accordance with GAAP it is not appropriate to draw attention to the contingency by expressing a reservation of opinion or by mentioning it in a separate paragraph following the auditor's standard report.

In the United States, however, the auditor may decide to add a paragraph to the report as a "red flag" drawing attention to the uncertainty.

Uncertainty situations may cause audit reports to be qualified for departures from GAAP, if (1) management's disclosure of the uncertainty is inadequate, (2) management uses inappropriate accounting principles to account for the uncertainty, and (3) management makes unreasonable accounting estimates in connection with the effects of the uncertainty. The audit report also may be qualified because of a scope limitation regarding available evidence about an uncertainty.

Reporting on "Going-concern" Problems

Generally accepted accounting principles are based on the going-concern concept, which means the entity is expected to continue in operation and meet its obligations as they become due, without substantial disposition of assets outside the ordinary course of business, restructuring of debt, externally forced revisions of its operations (e.g., a bank reorganization forced by the Superintendent of Financial Institutions), or similar actions. Hence, an opinion that financial statements are in conformity with GAAP means that continued existence may be presumed for a "reasonable time" not to exceed one year beyond the date of the financial statements ("The Going Concern Assumption," 1991 CICA Research Report). This one-year time horizon is reiterated in the CICA's Exposure Draft on going concern issues, released in March 1996.

"SUBJECT-TO" OPINIONS PRIOR TO 1980

From the early 1960s until 1980, auditors gave "subject-to" opinions for uncertainty situations. The opinion sentence was qualified with these words: "In our opinion, subject to the effects of such adjustments, if any, as might have been determined had the outcome of the uncertainty discussed in the preceding paragraph been known . . ." The explanatory paragraph was placed before the opinion paragraph, and the opinion was considered qualified. You may see this form of "subject to" opinion when you use reports issued in 1980 and earlier. However, the audit standards were changed in 1980, and now (1) the "subject to" wording is prohibited, (2) the explanatory paragraph is no longer used, and (3) the opinion sentence itself is unqualified.

Dealing with questions of going concern, or lack thereof, is difficult because auditors are forced to evaluate matters of financial analysis, business strategy, and financial forecasting. Most managements are unwilling to give up and close their businesses without strong attempts to survive. Sometimes, survival optimism prevails until the creditors force bankruptcy proceedings and liquidation. Auditors are generally reluctant to puncture any balloons of optimism. Managers and auditors both view news of financial troubles in an audit report (an attention-directing paragraph or a disclaimer based on going-concern doubt) as a "self-fulfilling prophecy" that causes bankruptcy. However fallacious this view might be, it still prevails and inhibits auditors' consideration of going-concern questions.

Auditors are responsible for determining whether there is a significant doubt about a company's ability to continue as a going concern. No careful auditor should ignore signs of financial difficulty and operate entirely on the assumption that the company is a going concern. Financial difficulties, labour problems, loss of key personnel, litigation, and other such things may be important signals. Likewise, elements of financial flexibility (salability of assets, lines of credit, debt extension, dividend elimination) may be available as survival strategies. (In U.S. auditing standards these elements of financial flexibility and management strategy are known as **mitigating factors** that may reduce the financial difficulties.)

Accounting and finance research efforts have produced several bankruptcy prediction models. These models use publicly available financial information to classify companies into "fail" and "nonfail" categories. At least one auditing firm uses such a model as an analytical review tool. Auditing standards, however, make no mention of research models, specifying instead many company-specific considerations and elements of internal information for analysis. (One bankruptcy prediction model is described briefly in the appendix to Chapter 5 of this textbook.)

Auditor's responsibilities for the going-concern assumption are currently the same as for contingencies (*Section* 5510.53). However, the recent CICA Research Study, "The Going Concern Assumption," gives recommendations leaning toward U.S. practice except that it quantifies key threshold probabilities whereas U.S. standards do not. The key audit recommendations of the CICA's going concern study are as follows:

1. Require auditors on every audit to perform procedures to provide reasonable assurance about the validity of the "going-concern" assumption.

2. Evaluate results of procedures performed.

3. If significant (20–50% probability) or substantial doubts (50% or greater probability) are raised, assess management's plans to address these matters, considering if they can be effectively implemented. (Note: The very existence of such plans should call "going concern" into question.)

4. Expand the auditor's reporting responsibilities when doubt about the validity of the "going-concern" assumption becomes substantial. Include an explanatory paragraph even if doubt is adequately disclosed in the notes.

5. Issue an adverse opinion where substantial doubt exists and disclosure is inadequate.

6. Issue an adverse opinion if virtually certain, and GAAP no longer applies.

According to this study five types of audit reports may be used when going-concern problems exist. The first is a standard report with no additional explanatory paragraphs as long as doubts are significant or less and properly disclosed in the notes to the financial statements. The second is a standard report with an unqualified opinion paragraph and an additional explanatory paragraph(s) to direct attention to management's disclosures about the problems. This second type of standard report would be used when there are substantial doubts and the company has properly disclosed these problems in the notes.

The third type of report is an adverse opinion that arises from failure to disclose substantial doubts, or when it is virtually certain that the company will fail to continue as a going concern, and GAAP no longer applies.

A fourth type of report is a qualification for a GAAP departure if the auditor believes the company's disclosures about financial difficulties and going-concern problems are inadequate. Such a report is shown in Exhibit 3–7. The fifth type of report is a report qualified for a scope limitation if evidence that does exist or did exist is not made available to the auditors, leading to the "except for adjustments, if any" type of qualified opinion explained earlier in this chapter. These different reports arise from the refined classification scheme reflected by the Going-concern Study recommendations. Since these recommendations have not yet gone through the due process of standard setting they are not considered GAAS. Instead, the current *Handbook* recommendations apply (*Section* 5510.53), which effectively state that if there is a "going-concern" problem, an unqualified opinion is given as long as this fact is adequately disclosed. If the facts are not adequately disclosed, then the auditor should issue a reservation of the audit opinion. An illustration of an "except for" qualification reservation is shown in Exhibit 3–7.

As of this writing (May 1997) there are Auditing (issued September 1995) and Accounting (issued March 1996) Exposure Drafts related to going concern. The Accounting Exposure Draft uses a significant doubt concept similar to that described above from the CICA Research Study. However, the Auditing Exposure Draft uses the term factors that "cast doubt" on the entity's ability to continue as a going concern. It is not clear whether "cast doubt" is comparable to "significant doubt," and perhaps this will be clarified in the final standards. One thing that is clear in the current standards is that contingencies related to going concern that are appropriately disclosed in the financial statements are specifically prohibited as a subject matter for an emphasis paragraph (*Handbook Sections* 5510.49 and 5510.52). Whether this will continue to be the case depends on the final form of the Going Concern Standards.

EXHIBIT 3–7   **QUALIFIED REPORT EXPLAINING GOING CONCERN PROBLEMS (from *Handbook Section* 5510.F)**

Departure from generally accepted accounting principles—inadequate disclosure of matters affecting the company's ability to continue as a going concern. When the auditor has determined that a qualification is the type of reservation required, the following wording may be appropriate.

AUDITOR'S REPORT

To the Shareholders of.....................................

I have audited the balance sheet of .... as at ...., 19-1 and the statements of income, retained earnings and changes in financial position for the year then ended. These financial statements are the responsibility of the company's management. My responsibility is to express an opinion on these financial statements based on my audit.

I conducted my audit in accordance with generally accepted auditing standards. Those standards require that I plan and perform an audit to obtain reasonable assurance whether the financial statements are free of material misstatement. An audit includes examining, on a test basis, evidence supporting the amounts and disclosures in the financial statements. An audit also includes assessing the accounting principles used and significant estimates made by management, as well as evaluating the overall financial statement presentation.

The accompanying financial statements, in my opinion, do not draw attention explicitly to doubts concerning the company's ability to realize its assets and discharge its liabilities in the normal course of business. These doubts arise because it is uncertain whether the company will be able to refinance long-term debt in the amount of $.......... due on ...., 19-2 in view of the existence of recurring operating losses in the past five years and the deficiency in working capital of $.......... as at ...., 19-1. If refinancing cannot be arranged, it is not known whether the company can sell its hotel property for an amount sufficient to realize its carrying value of $.......... and to generate adequate funds to repay this debt.

In my opinion, except for the omission of the disclosure described in the preceding paragraph, these financial statements present fairly, in all material respects, the financial position of the company as at ...., 19-1 and the results of its operations and the change in its financial position for the year then ended in accordance with generally accepted accounting principles.

(signed)....................................
CHARTERED ACCOUNTANT

Date
City

Reporting on the Application of Accounting Principles

· · · · · · · · · · · ·

LEARNING OBJECTIVE

6. Explain why auditors have standards for reporting on the "application of accounting principles."

The subject of "reporting on the application of accounting principles" touches a sensitive nerve in the public accounting profession. It arose from clients' shopping for an auditor who would agree to give an unqualified audit report on a questionable accounting treatment. "Shopping" often involved auditor-client disagreements, after which the client said: "If you won't agree with my accounting treatment, then I'll find an auditor who will." These disagreements often involved early revenue recognition and unwarranted expense or loss deferral. A few cases of misleading financial statements occurred after shopping resulted in clients' switching to more agreeable auditors. However, the practice is not entirely undesirable, because "second opinions" on complex accounting matters often benefit from consultation with other PAs.

Handbook Section 7600 established procedures for dealing with requests for consultation from parties other than an auditor's own clients. These parties can include other companies (nonclients who are shopping), lawyers, investment bankers, and perhaps other people. *Section* 7600 is applicable in these situations:

- When preparing a written report or giving oral advice on specific transactions, either completed or proposed.

- When preparing a written report or giving oral advice on the type of audit opinion that might be rendered on specific financial statements.
- When preparing a written report on hypothetical transactions.

The standard does not apply to conclusions about accounting principles offered in connection with litigation support engagements or expert witness work, nor does it apply to advice given to another PA in public practice. It also does not apply to an accounting firm's expressions of positions in newsletters, articles, speeches, lectures, and the like, provided that the positions do not give advice on a specific transaction or apply to a specific company.

The basic requirements are to consider the circumstances of the request for advice, its purpose, and the intended use of the report of the advice; to obtain an understanding of the form and substance of the transaction in question; to review applicable GAAP; to consult with other professionals if necessary; and to perform research to determine the existence of creditable analogies and precedents (e.g., find the authoritative support). When the request for advice comes from a business that already has another auditor, the consulting PA should consult with the other auditor to learn all the facts and circumstances.

Written reports are required and should include these elements:

- Description of the nature of the engagement and a statement that it was performed in accordance with standards for such engagements.
- Statement of relevant facts and assumptions, and the sources of information.
- Statement of the advice—the conclusion about appropriate accounting principles or the type of audit report, including reasons for the conclusions, if appropriate.
- Statement that a company's management is responsible for proper accounting treatments, in consultation with its own auditors.
- Statement that any differences in facts, circumstances, or assumptions might change the conclusions.

The purpose of the *Section* 7600 standards is to impose some discipline on the process of shopping/consultation and to make it more difficult for companies to seek out a "willing" auditor.

R E V I E W
CHECKPOINTS

3.12 Why might "opinion shopping" be suspect? beneficial?

3.13 What must a PA do when reporting on the application of accounting principles?

SUMMARY

LEARNING OBJECTIVE
7. List and explain the effects of materiality on audit report choices.

This chapter began at the beginning: setting forth the requirement that auditors must report whenever they are "associated with" financial statements. This report can take different forms in different circumstances—audit assurance, negative assurance, and no assurance. These levels of assurance are further explained in terms of (1) reports qualified for (*a*) scope limitations, and (*b*) departures from GAAP; (2) adverse

E X H I B I T 3–8   **INFLUENCE OF MATERIALITY ON AUDIT REPORTS**

Circumstances for Departure from Standard Report	Required Type of Report	
	Lesser Materiality	Greater Materiality
Departure from GAAP	Qualified "except for": Separate paragraph discloses reasons and effects.*	Adverse Opinion: Separate paragraph discloses reasons and effects.
Limitation on scope (lack of evidence)	Qualified Opinion: Refers to possible effects on financials.	Denial of Opinion: Separate paragraph explains limitations.
Uncertainty	Unqualified Opinion**	Unqualified Opinion**

*Where the departure is necessary to make the financials not misleading, an unqualified opinion is issued with an explanation of the circumstances.
**Unless there is a failure to properly disclose the uncertainty.

reports resulting from GAAP departures; and (3) denials of opinion resulting from lack of independence and lack of sufficient appropriate evidence.

Throughout this chapter's explanation of the auditors' choices of reports, the materiality dimension played an important role. When an auditor makes decisions about the audit report, immaterial or unimportant information can be ignored and treated as if it did not exist. However, when inaccuracies, departures from GAAP, accounting changes, and uncertainties have a large enough financial impact, the standard audit report must be changed. In practice, when an auditor decides a matter is material enough to make a difference, a further distinction must be made between "lesser materiality" and "greater materiality." Lesser materiality means that the item in question is important and needs to be disclosed or that the opinion needs to be qualified for it. The information cannot simply be ignored. Greater materiality means that the item in question is very important and has an extreme impact on the reporting decision.

Auditing standards refer to several basic circumstances that cause departures from the standard unqualified audit report. These circumstances are shown in Exhibit 3–8 in relation to the influence of materiality. You can see that each report qualified when the item is of lesser materiality becomes a disclaimer or an adverse report when the item involves greater materiality. The exception is the lack of independence issue, where materiality does not make a difference.

Audit reports can also be modified and expanded with additional paragraphs. Such additions to the audit report arise from the need for an "emphasis of a matter" paragraph. The final topic in the chapter is "shopping" for accounting principles and auditors. Standards exist to raise the public perception that auditors are careful about competing among one another on the basis of professional opinions.

R E V I E W
C H E C K P O I N T S

3.14 Explain the effect of greater or lesser materiality on an auditor's report when the client uses an accounting method that departs from generally accepted accounting principles.

3.15 Explain the effect of greater or lesser materiality on an auditor's report when there is a scope limitation.

3.16 Explain the effect of greater or lesser materiality on an auditor's report when there is a material uncertainty associated with the financial statements.

3.17 Identify the levels of assurance associated with auditor's reports.

3.18 Under what conditions would an auditor use an "emphasis of a matter" paragraph?

· ·

MULTIPLE-CHOICE QUESTIONS FOR PRACTICE AND REVIEW
· ·

3.19 A PA developed a system for clients to enter transaction data by remote terminal into the PA's computer. The PA's system processes the data and prints monthly financial statements. When delivered to the clients, these financial statements should include:
a. A standard unqualified audit report.
b. An adverse audit report.
c. A report containing a description of the character of the examination and the degree of responsibility the PA is taking.
d. A description of the remote terminal system and of the controls for ensuring accurate data processing.

3.20 For which of the following reports is an expression of negative assurance not permitted?
a. A review report on unaudited financial statements.
b. An audit report on financial statements that present financial position and results of operations.
c. A report in a letter to an underwriter in connection with securities transactions.
d. A review report on interim financial information.

3.21 Some of the GAAS reporting standards require certain statements in all audit reports ("explicit") and others require statements only under certain conditions ("implicit" basis). Which combination shown below correctly describes these features of the reporting standards?

Standards	(a)	(b)	(c)	(d)
1. GAAP	Explicit	Explicit	Implicit	Implicit
2. Consistency	Implicit	Explicit	Explicit	Implicit
3. Disclosure	Implicit	Implicit	Explicit	Explicit
4. Report	Explicit	Explicit	Implicit	Implicit

3.22 A PA finds that the client has not capitalized a material amount of leases in the financial statements. When considering the materiality of this departure from GAAP, the PA's reporting options are:
a. Unqualified opinion or denial of opinion.
b. Unqualified opinion or qualified opinion.
c. Emphasis paragraph with unqualified opinion or an adverse opinion.
d. Qualified opinion or adverse opinion.

3.23 An auditor has found that the client is suffering financial difficulty and that the going-concern status is seriously in doubt. Even though the client has placed good disclosures in the financial statements, the PA must choose between the following audit report alternatives:
a. Unqualified report with a going-concern explanatory paragraph or disclaimer of opinion.
b. Denial of opinion.
c. Qualified opinion or adverse opinion.
d. Standard unqualified report.

3.24 A company accomplished an early extinguishment of debt, and the auditors believe that recognition of a huge loss distorts the financial statements and causes them to be misleading. The auditors' reporting choices are:
a. Explain the situation and give an adverse opinion.
b. Explain the situation and give a denial of opinion.
c. Explain the situation and give an unqualified opinion, relying on Rules of Professional Conduct to not be associated with misleading financial statements.
d. Give the standard unqualified audit report.

3.25 Which of these situations would require an auditor to insert an explanatory paragraph about consistency in an unqualified audit report?

a. Client changed its estimated allowance for uncollectible accounts receivable.

b. Client corrected a prior mistake in accounting for interest capitalization.

c. Client sold one of its subsidiaries and consolidated six this year compared to seven last year.

d. None of the above.

3.26 Phil became the new auditor for Royal Corporation, succeeding Liz, who audited the financial statements last year. Phil needs to report on Royal's comparative financial statements and should write in his report an explanation about another auditor having audited the prior year:

a. Only if Liz's opinion last year was qualified.

b. Describing the prior audit and the opinion but not naming Liz as the predecessor auditor.

c. Describing the audit but not revealing the type of opinion Liz gave.

d. Describing the audit and the opinion and naming Liz as the predecessor auditor.

3.27 When other independent auditors are involved in the current audit on parts of the client's business, the principal auditor can write an audit report that:

a. Mentions the other auditor, describes the extent of the other auditor's work, and gives an unqualified opinion.

b. Does not mention the other auditor and gives an unqualified opinion in a standard unqualified report.

c. Places primary responsibility for the audit report on the other auditors.

d. Names the other auditors, describes their work, and presents only the principal auditor's report.

3.28 An "emphasis of a matter" paragraph inserted in an audit report causes the report to be characterized as:

a. Unqualified opinion report.

b. Divided responsibility.

c. Adverse opinion report.

d. Denial of opinion.

3.29 Under which of the following conditions can a denial of opinion never be given?

a. Going-concern problems are overwhelming the company.

b. The client does not let the auditor have access to evidence about important accounts.

c. The auditor owns shares in the client corporation.

d. The auditor has found that the client has used the NIFO (next-in, first-out) inventory costing method.

EXERCISES AND PROBLEMS

3.30 Association with Financial Statements. This series of questions is a drill on the subjects of "association with" financial statements, unaudited financial statements, and the denial of opinion. What kind of report can you give in each case?

a. Able Corporation engaged you to prepare financial statements from its books and records without performing any audit or review procedures. Able is a public company.

b. Baker Corporation, a public company, uses your computerized bookkeeping service. You deliver monthly financial statements to Baker's controller. Another PA performs the annual audit for Baker Corporation.

c. Charlie Corporation engaged you to audit its financial statements. Charlie is not a public company. You serve as the corporation's part-time financial vice president.

d. Dagmar Partnership engaged you on January 30 to audit its financial statements for the year just ended on the previous December 31. Dagmar has never been audited and has never conducted a physical inventory. Sale of manufactured goods is the major business, and inventories amount to about 75 percent of total assets.

3.31 Association with Financial Statements. For each of the situations described below, state whether the PA is or is not associated with the financial statements. What is the consequence of being associated with financial statements?

a. PA audits financial statements and his or her name is in the corporate annual report containing them.

b. PA prepares the financial statements in the partnership tax return.

c. PA uses the computer to process client-submitted data and delivers financial statement output.

d. PA uses the computer to process client-submitted data and delivers a general ledger printout.

e. PA lets client copy client-prepared financial statements on the PA's letterhead.

f. Client issues quarterly financial statements and mentions PA's review procedures but does not list PA's name in the document.

g. PA renders consulting advice about the system to prepare interim financial statements but does not review the statements prior to their release.

3.32 Reports and the Effect of Materiality. The concept of materiality is important to PAs in audits of financial statements and expressions of opinion on these statements. How will materiality influence an auditor's reporting decision in the following circumstances?

a. The client prohibits confirmation of accounts receivable, and sufficient appropriate evidence cannot be obtained using alternative procedures.

b. The client is a gas and electric utility company that follows the practice of recognizing revenue when it is billed to customers. At the end of the year, amounts earned but not yet billed are not recorded in the accounts or reported in the financial statements.

c. The client leases buildings for its chain of transmission repair shops under terms that qualify as capital leases. These leases are not capitalized as leased property assets and lease obligations.

d. The client company has lost a lawsuit. The case is on appeal in an attempt to reduce the amount of damages awarded to the plaintiffs.

3.33 Errors in an Adverse Report. Brown & Brown, PAs, was engaged by the board of directors of Cook Industries, Inc., to audit the financial statements for the year ended December 31, 1992. Joe Brown has decided an adverse report is appropriate. He has also become aware of a March 14, 1993, subsequent event, which the Cook financial vice president properly disclosed in the notes to the financial statements. Brown wants responsibility for subsequent events to be limited to this specific event after the field work was completed on March 7.

Required:

Identify the deficiencies in the draft of the report presented below. Do not rewrite the report.

Accountant's Report

To the President of
Cook Industries, Inc.:

We have audited the financial statements of Cook Industries, Inc., for the year ended December 31, 1992. We conducted our audits in accordance with generally accepted auditing standards. Those standards require that we plan and perform the audit to obtain reasonable assurance about whether the financial statements are free of material misstatement. An audit includes examining, on a test basis, evidence supporting the amounts and disclosures in the financial statements. An audit also includes assessing the accounting principles used and significant estimates made by management, as well as evaluating the overall financial statement presentation. We believe that our audit provides a reasonable basis for our opinion.

As discussed in Note K to the financial statements, the Company has properly disclosed a subsequent event dated March 14, 1993.

As discussed in Note G to the financial statements, the Company carries its property and equipment at appraisal values, and provides depreciation on the basis of such values. Further, the Company does not provide for income taxes with respect to differences between financial income and taxable income arising from the use, for income tax purposes, of the instalment method of reporting gross profit from certain types of sales.

In our opinion, the financial statements referred to above do not present fairly the financial position of Cook Industries, Inc., as of December 31, 1992, and the results of its operations and its cash flows for the year then ended in conformity with generally accepted accounting principles.

/s/ Brown & Brown
Public Accountants
March 14, 1993

(AICPA adapted)

3.34 Arguments with Auditors. Officers of the company do not want to disclose information about the product liability lawsuit filed by a customer asking $500,000 in damages. They believe the suit is frivolous and without merit. Outside counsel is more cautious. The auditors insist upon disclosure. Angered, the Kingston Company chairman of the board threatens to sue the auditors if a standard unqualified report is not issued within three days.

3.35 Errors in a Comparative Report with Change from Prior Year (Appendix 3A). The following audit report was drafted by an assistant at the completion of the audit of Cramdon, Inc., on March 1, 1993. The partner in charge of the engagement has decided the opinion on the 1992 financial statements should be modified only with reference to the change in the method of computing sales. Also, due to a litigation uncertainty, an uncertainty paragraph was included in the audit report on the 1991 financial statements, which are included for comparative purposes. The 1991 audit report (same audit firm) was dated March 5, 1992, and on October 15, 1992, the litigation was resolved in favor of Cramdon, Inc.

Auditor's Report
To the Board of Directors
of Cramdon, Inc.:

We have audited the accompanying financial statements of Cramdon, Inc., as of December 31, 1992 and 1991. These financial statements are the responsibility of the Company's Management. Our responsibility is to express an opinion on these financial statements based on our audits.

We conducted our audits in accordance with generally accepted auditing standards. Those standards require that we plan and perform the audit to obtain reasonable assurance about whether the financial statements are free of material misstatement. An audit includes examining, on a test basis, evidence supporting the amounts and disclosures in the financial statements. An audit also includes assessing the accounting principles used and significant estimates made by management, as well as evaluating the overall financial statement presentation. We believe that our audit provides a reasonable basis for our opinion.

As discussed in Note 7 to the financial statements, our previous report on the 1991 financial statements contained an explanatory paragraph regarding a particular litigation uncertainty. Due to our lawyer's meritorious defence in this litigation, our current report on these financial statements does not include such an explanatory paragraph.

In our opinion, based on the preceding, the financial statements referred to above present fairly, in all material respects, the financial position of Cramdon, Inc., as of December 31, 1992, and the results of its operations and its cash flows for the period then ended in conformity with generally accepted accounting principles consistently applied, except for the changes in the method of computing sales as described in Note 14 to the financial statements.

/s/ PA Firm
March 5, 1993

Required:
Identify the deficiencies and errors in the draft report and write an explanation of the reasons they are errors and deficiencies. Do not rewrite the report.

3.36 Using the Work and Report of Another Auditor (Appendix 3A). Landies. Michaels, PA, has been engaged to audit the financial statements of the parent company and one of the subsidiaries and to act as the principal auditor. Thomas, PA, has audited the financial statements of the other subsidiary whose operations are material in relation to the consolidated financial statements.

The work performed by Michaels is sufficient for Michaels to serve as the principal auditor and to report as such on the financial statements. Michaels has not yet decided whether to make reference to the part of the audit performed by Thomas.

Required:

a. What are the reporting requirements with which Michaels must comply if Michaels decides to name Thomas and make reference to the audit work done by Thomas?

b. What report should be issued if Michaels can neither assume responsibility for Thomas's work nor divide responsibility by referring to his work?

3.37 Reference to Another Auditor in Principal Auditor's Report (Appendix 3A). Presented below is an independent auditor's report that contains deficiencies. The Corporation being reported on is profit oriented and publishes general-purpose financial statements for distribution to owners, creditors, potential investors, and the general public:

Report of Independent Auditor

We have audited the accompanying consolidated balance sheet of Bonair Corporation and subsidiaries as of December 31, 1992, and the related statements of income, retained earnings, and cash flows for the year then ended. These financial statements are the responsibility of the Company's management. Our responsibility is to express an opinion on these financial statements based on our audit. We did not examine the financial statements of Caet Company, a major consolidated subsidiary. These statements were examined by

Corporation is a domestic company with two wholly-owned domestic subsidiar-other auditors whose report thereon has been furnished to us, and our opinion expressed herein, insofar as it relates to Caet Company, is based solely upon the report of the other auditors.

Except as stated in the paragraph above, we conducted our audit in accordance with generally accepted auditing standards. Those standards require that we plan and perform the audit to obtain reasonable assurance about whether the financial statements are free of material misstatement. An audit includes examining, on a test basis, evidence supporting the amounts and disclosures in the financial statements. An audit also includes assessing the accounting principles used and significant estimates made by management, as well as evaluating the overall financial statement presentation. We believe that our audit provides a reasonable basis for our opinion.

In our opinion, except for the matter of the report of the other auditors, the financial statements referred to above present fairly, in all material respects, the financial position of Bonair Corporation and subsidiaries December 31, 1992, and the results of their operations and their cash flows for the year then ended in conformity with generally accepted accounting principles.

Required:

Describe the reporting deficiencies, explain why they are considered deficiencies, and briefly discuss how the report should be corrected. (Exclude the addressee, signatures, and report date.) Organize your answer sheet as follows:

Deficiencies   Reason   Correction

3.38 Reporting on Supplementary and Other Information (Appendix 3A). For the separate fact situations given below, specify the appropriate form and content of the audit report on the related financial statements.

a. Mona Corporation voluntarily presented the interim financial information described in *Handbook Section* 1750.06. This year, however, time ran short, and the controller's staff was unable to present everything specified by the *Handbook*.

b. When Kinky Korp Company presented its interim financial figures in a footnote to the financial statements, the footnote was labelled "Interim Financial Results," and the closing sentence of the narrative introduction was: "Grey & Fox, CAs, reviewed the interim financial results in accordance with standards established by the Canadian Institute of Chartered Accountants."

c. Kaviar, Inc.'s president, Sharon Kaviar, wrote a management discussion and analysis section in the annual report to shareholders, in which she said: "Research and development expenses increased this year by 20 percent." Consulting the R&D expense disclosure in the financial statements, you see that the expense for last year is reported to be $3 million and for this year $3.75 million.

3.39 Uncertainty and Accounting Issues. Peaco Corporation builds pollution control equipment. In the year just ended December 31, 1992, the company had sales of $600 million and net income of $26 million. In the fourth quarter of the year, however, reported net income was $7 million or $0.84 per share, exactly the same as in the fourth quarter of 1991. Company management takes pride in the fact that earnings have increased about 10 percent each quarter of the corresponding year-earlier period for the last four years.

These fourth-quarter data were released January 20. It is now February 20, and you are about to complete your audit covering the comparative 1992 and 1991 financial statements. Only one matter remains for resolution.

During the fourth quarter of 1992, Peaco experienced difficulty with a subcontractor on a medium-sized project. The result was that the subcontractor was released, and Peaco filed lawsuits totalling $4 million for breach of contract, claiming that the company had incurred additional costs of $2.5 million as a result of the subcontrac-

tor's actions. The subcontractor has filed counterclaims for $6 million in damages. Peaco lawyers say that all this litigation will take a long time to settle in court unless it is negotiated in out-of-court agreements.

In the meantime, Peaco has accounted for its $4 million damage claims as an offset against the $2.5 million actual additional cost (an amount you have found to be materially accurate). Your problem now concerns the accounting validity of recognizing the $4 million claim. The effect of alternative accounting is that net income would be $5 million in the fourth quarter (and EPS would be 60 cents), and net income for the year would be $24 million (and EPS would be $2.88 for 1992 compared to $2.40 for 1991).

Required:

Decide what to do about the audit report and write the opinion paragraph and any explanatory or emphasis paragraphs you consider necessary. You may assume that all matters of litigation were fully described in footnote L to the financial statements.

3.40 Explain Deficiencies in an Opinion Denial. The following audit report was written by your partner yesterday. You need to describe the reporting deficiencies, explain the reasons for them, and discuss with him how the report should be corrected. This may be a hard job because he has always felt somewhat threatened because you were the first woman partner in the firm. You have decided to write up a three-column worksheet showing the deficiencies, reasons, and corrections needed. This was his report:

I made my examination in accordance with generally accepted auditing standards. However, I am not independent with respect to Mavis Corporation because my wife owns 5 percent of the outstanding common stock of the company. The accompanying balance sheet as of December 31, 1992, and the related statements of income and retained earnings and cash flows for the year then ended were not audited by me. Accordingly, I do not express an opinion on them.

Required:

Prepare the worksheet described above.

3.41 Evidence Required for Various Audit Reports. Auditors' alternatives for reporting on financial statements offer many choices among unqualified, disclaimed, modified, and expanded report language.

Required:

a. List the reports that require fully sufficient appropriate evidence.

b. List the reports that result from pervasive and massive evidence deficiencies.

c. List the reports that result from isolated evidence deficiencies.

3.42 Reporting Situations. For each of the four unrelated situations described below:

a. Specify the content of the notes, if any, you would request the client to add to the financial statements.

b. State, with reasons, whether the situation would necessitate a qualification to the standard auditor's report. Specify any changes you would make to the report.

State any assumptions inherent in your approach. Assume all circumstances are material. Do *not* write out the entire auditor's report.

a. You completed the field work for your client, Tanker Oil, on February 23, 1990. It is now March 6, 1990, and you are in a meeting with the controller of Tanker Oil, reviewing the draft of the annual report. The controller informs you that one of the company's ships was involved in a major oil spill early that morning, off the Grand Banks of Newfoundland.

    While reading the annual report, you note that in the president's message to the shareholders, she has boasted that Tanker Oil has never been involved in a major oil spill, and has a better safety record than any of its major competitors.

b. Your client, Able Manufacturing, Inc., has had steadily increasing losses since its inception in April 1987. Management feels that Able will be able to tap into the U.S. market next year due to the scheduled removal of tariffs in January 1991 relevant to its industry as negotiated under the Free Trade Agreement.

    The owners of the company have exhausted all of their personal financial resources and are hoping to obtain a large increase in their corporate demand bank loans to cover operating expenses until the tariff reduction takes place.

    Able's banker is anxiously awaiting the audited financial statements to see if the results of the year ended March 31, 1990, are any better than the previous two years' results. Able has defaulted on its last two monthly payments on its demand loan.

    Management of Able is confident the company will earn substantial profits in 1991 and is not in favour of making any disclosures that would jeopardize Able getting the increase in bank loans that it requires.

c. In addition to the audited consolidated financial statements provided to the shareholders, your client would like to attach audited nonconsolidated financial statements to its corporate income tax returns.

d. Your client, a secretarial personnel agency, has just completed its second year of operations. Due to its planned expansion in the near future, it requires audited financial statements. You performed a compilation engagement for its first year-end.

(ICAO adapted)

3.43 Departures from GAAP. On January 1, Kingston Company purchased land (the site of a new building) for $100,000. Soon thereafter, the Highway Department announced a new feeder road that would run alongside the site. The effect was a dramatic increase in local property values. Nearby, comparable land sold for $700,000 in December of the current year. Kingston shows the land at $700,000 in its accounts. After reduction for implicit taxes at 33 percent, the fixed asset total is $400,000 larger, with the same amount shown separately in a shareholder equity account titled "Current value increment." The valuation is fully disclosed in a footnote to the financial statements, along with a letter from a certified property appraiser attesting to the $700,000 value.

Required:

a. Write the appropriate audit report, assuming you believe the departure from GAAP is material but not enough to cause you to give an adverse opinion.

b. Write the appropriate report, assuming that you believe an adverse opinion is necessary.

c. For discussion: Should you (could you) issue a report conforming to Rules of Professional Conduct or equivalent rules in other provinces (association with a false or misleading information)?

3.44 Reporting on an Accounting Change. In December of the current year, Kingston Company changed its method of accounting for inventory and cost of goods sold from LIFO to FIFO. The account balances shown in the trial balance have already been recalculated and adjusted retroactively, as required by *Handbook Section* 1506.11. The accounting change and the financial effects are described in note 2 in the financial statements.

Required:

a. Assume you believe the accounting change is justified. Write the audit report appropriate in the circumstances.

b. Assume you believe the accounting change is not justified and causes the financial statements to be materially distorted. Inventories that would have been reported at $1.5 million (LIFO) are reported at $1.9 million (FIFO); operating income before tax that would have been $130,000 is reported at $530,000; current assets are revised upward 17 percent and total assets 9 percent; shareholder equity is 14 percent greater. Write

the audit report appropriate in the circumstances.

3.45 Financial Difficulty—The "Going-Concern" Problem. The Kingston Company has experienced significant financial difficulty. Current liabilities exceed current assets by $1 million, cash is down to $10,000, the interest on the long-term debt has not been paid, and a customer has sued for $500,000 on a product liability claim. Significant questions concerning the going-concern status of the company exist.

Required:

a. Write the appropriate audit report, assuming you decide that an audit opinion instead of a disclaimer is appropriate in the circumstances.

b. Write the appropriate audit report, assuming that you decide the uncertainties are significant and that the client fails to disclose properly.

Required:

Write the audit report appropriate in the circumstances.

3.46 Late Appointment of Auditor. Dalton Wardlaw, PA, has completed the field work for the audit of the financial statements of Kingston Company, for the year ended December 31, and is now preparing the audit report. Wardlaw has audited the financial statements for several years, but this year Kingston delayed the start of the audit work, and Wardlaw was busy anyway, so he was not present to observe the taking of the physical inventory on December 31. However, he performed alternative procedures, including (1) examination of shipping and receiving documents with regard to transactions since the year-end, (2) extensive review of the inventory count sheets, and (3) discussion of the physical inventory procedures with responsible company personnel. He also satisfied himself about the propriety of the inventory valuation calculations and the consistency of the valuation method. Kingston determines year-end inventory quantities solely by means of physical count.

Required:

Write Wardlaw's audit report on the balance sheet at the end of the current year under audit, and on the statements of operations, retained earnings, and cash flows for the one year then ended.

3.47 Changing the Prior Year Audit Report (Appendix 3A). In November of the prior year (1991), Kingston Company was sued by a supplier for damages and misrepresentation. The supplier sought $500,000 in judgment. In connection with the audit of the prior year, Kingston's lawyer submitted a letter stating that the company had sufficient defences to prevail in the case, and that he expected that only a minor amount would have to be paid, and then only in order to avoid prolonged and costly litigation. He estimated that no more than $20,000 would need to be paid to settle the lawsuit. The company maintained that the probability of this amount of loss was not even "reasonably possible" and accrued no liability in the financial statements for the year ended December 31, 1991. As auditors, you (Anderson, Olds & Watershed) gave an audit report containing an uncertainty explanation paragraph. On July 15 of the current year under audit (1992), after you had delivered your report dated February 10, 1992, on the prior year financial statements, the lawsuit was settled for $5,000.

Required:

Write the unqualified audit report on the comparative financial statements as of and for the years ended December 31, 1992 and 1991, making your current report (dated February 4, 1993) on the prior year (1991) financial statements not affected by the litigation uncertainty mentioned in the report delivered last year.

3.48 Using Work of Other Independent Auditors (Appendix 3A). You (Anderson, Olds & Watershed) are the principal auditor on the December 31 consolidated financial statements of Kingston Company and subsidiaries. However, other auditors do the work on certain subsidiaries for the year under audit amounting to:

	1992	1991
Total assets	29%	31%
Total revenues	36%	41%

Mr. Wardlaw investigated the other auditors, as required by auditing standards, and they furnished him with their audit reports. Wardlaw has decided to rely on their work and to refer to the other auditors in the AOW audit report. None of the audit work showed any reason to qualify any of the audit opinions.

Required:

Write the AOW audit report referring to the work and reports of the other auditors.

3.49 Other Information in a Financial Review Section of an Annual Report (Appendix 3A). Mr. Lancaster (chairman of the board) and Mr. Grace (vice president, finance) prepared the draft of the financial review section of the annual report. You are reviewing it for consistency with the audited financial statements. The draft contains the following explanation about income coverage of interest expense: "Last year, operating income before interest and income taxes covered interest expense by a ratio of 6:1. This year, on an incremental basis, the coverage of interest expense increased to a ratio of 6.588:1."

The relevant portion of the audited financial statements showed the following:

	Current Year	Prior Year
Operating income	$400,000	$360,000
Extraordinary gain from realization of tax benefits	100,000	
Interest expense	(81,250)	(60,000)
Income taxes	(127,500)	(120,000)
Net income	$291,250	$180,000

Required:

a. Determine whether the financial review section statement about coverage of interest is or is not consistent with the audited financial statements. Be able to show your conclusion with calculations.

b. Assume you find an inconsistency, and the officers disagree with your conclusions. Write the explanatory paragraph you should put in your audit report.

APPENDIX 3A

ADDITIONAL AUDIT REPORT TOPICS

Several topics in audit reporting are somewhat outside the mainstream of the basic levels of assurance and report modification topics covered in Chapter 3. However, many instructors and students have an interest in them. This appendix covers these five additional topics:

- Using the work and reports of other independent auditors.
- Reporting on comparative financial statements.
- Reporting on limited audit engagements.
- Responsibility for supplementary and other information.
- Association with condensed financial information.

Using the Work and Reports of Other Independent Auditors

LEARNING OBJECTIVE

8. Write an audit report in which a principal auditor refers to the work of another independent auditor.

Handbook Section 6930 covers those situations where one auditor (the primary auditor) relies on the work of another (the secondary auditor) when the primary auditor is reporting on the financial statements and the secondary auditor audits a subsidiary, an investee, a joint venture, or a branch or division. The primary auditor needs to obtain reasonable assurance that the secondary auditor has conducted his examination in accordance with GAAS in Canada before he can rely on the secondary auditor's report (the secondary auditor may even be from another country).

When relying on the secondary auditor, the primary auditor must obtain evidence to support such reliance. This evidence will be influenced by the nature of the arrangement with the secondary auditor—that is, by whether the arrangement is an agency one, and ongoing or temporary, and whether the component is material.

The evidence normally considered by the primary auditor is as follows:

1. The professional qualifications, competence, and integrity of the secondary auditor.

2. Communications with the secondary auditor on such matters as audit scope, and the nature of procedures indicating that his examinations are conducted in an acceptable matter to primary auditor.

3. The financial statements and auditor's report of the component audited by the secondary auditor.

4. A written representation from the secondary auditor acknowledging that the primary auditor intends to rely on his report and setting out the representation required by the primary auditor.

5. If the primary auditor has not, in his judgment, acquired the necessary audit assurance from other procedures, he should review the working papers of the secondary auditor.

When the auditor has been unable to obtain sufficient appropriate evidence to rely on the report and work of the secondary auditor, he or she should exercise a reservation of opinion. When expressing an opinion without reservation, the primary auditor should not refer to the secondary auditor in his or her report. However, the opinion paragraph must be consistent with the sufficiency and competency of evidence gathered by all the auditors. If secondary auditors have rendered opinions qualified in some way, the circumstances must be considered by the primary auditor when deciding whether to qualify, modify, or expand the report on the consolidated financial statements.

Reporting on Comparative Statements

LEARNING OBJECTIVE

9. Write the required modifications when a report on prior-year comparative financial statements is changed.

Public companies usually present comparative balance sheets for two years and comparative income statements for three years. Financial statement footnotes also usually contain disclosures in comparative form for two or three years. The auditor's opinion for the current period for the current report extends to the comparative figures only if such an extension is specifically stated in his or her report (*Handbook Section* 5701.08).

Where comparative figures from prior periods are included in the annual report and they are either unaudited or audited by a different auditor, the current auditor should assure that appropriate disclosure is made either in the footnotes or in a separate paragraph of the auditor's report following the opinion paragraph (*Section* 5701.10).

When auditors issue a report on the current-year financial statements, they update the report they previously issued on the prior-year financial statements. For example, the Chrysler Corporation auditors issued an unqualified report dated February 1990 on the 1989 and 1988 financial statements; later, after the next-year audit, they issued the report dated February 7, 1991, on the 1990 financial statements and on the 1989 statements presented in comparative form. Their updated report on the 1989 financial statements is based not only on the prior-year audit but also on information that has come to light since then (particularly in the course of the next year's audit work). An updated report may be the same as previously issued, or it may be different depending on whether current information causes a retroactive change in the auditor's reporting decision. An updated report carries the date of the end of the most recent field work, and the auditors' responsibility now runs to the more recent date (*Handbook Section* 5405.17).

An updated report differs from the reissuance of a previous report. A reissuance amounts to providing more copies of the report or giving permission to use it in another document sometime after its original delivery date. The report date of a reissued report is the original date of the end of field work on that year's audit, indicating a cutoff date for the auditors' responsibility (*Section* 5405.05).

If the company has changed auditors, the introductory paragraph will identify only the current-year statements as the ones audited by the new (successor) auditor. A sentence will be added giving facts about the former (predecessor) auditor's report: "The financial statements of the company as of December 31, 1989, were audited by other auditors whose report dated March 1, 1990, expressed an unqualified opinion on those statements." The opinion paragraph will cite only the current-year financial statements audited by the successor auditor.

Auditors can give different opinions on different financial statements in the same report. Exhibit 3–4 shows the situation in which the prior-year financial statements were considered materially misstated, but the most recent balance sheet was in conformity

EXHIBIT 3–9   **COMPARATIVE STATEMENT OPINION CHANGED FROM ADVERSE TO UNQUALIFIED**

Auditor's Report

To the Board of Directors and Shareholders,
North Country Bank

(Standard introductory paragraph here.)
(Standard scope paragraph here.)

In our report dated February 15, 1992, we expressed an opinion that the balance sheet as of December 31, 1991, and the statements of income, retained earnings, and cash flows for the year then ended did not fairly present financial position, results of operations, and cash flows in accordance with generally accepted accounting principles because the Bank did not record an additional $30,000,000 provision for possible loan losses on nonperforming loans in the Bank's portfolio as of December 31, 1991. As described in Note 2 in these financial statements, the Bank has restated its 1991 financial statements to record the additional loan loss provision in conformity with generally accepted accounting principles. Accordingly, our present opinion on the 1991 financial statements, as presented herein, is different from the opinion we expressed in our previous report.

In our opinion, the financial statements referred to above present fairly, in all material respects, the financial position of North Country Bank as of December 31, 1992 and 1991, and the results of its operations and its cash flows for the years then ended in accordance with generally accepted accounting principles.

/s/ Auditor signature
January 31, 1993

---

with GAAP. You can see that the opinion on the misstated financial statements is an adverse opinion, and the opinion on the most recent balance sheet is unqualified.

Auditors can also change the opinion given on last year's financial statements. This is known as an "opinion on prior period financial statements different from the opinion previously expressed." The auditors must have good reasons for such a change, which must be explained in the report. For example, consider the North Country Bank situation shown in Exhibit 3–9. Suppose the bank originally failed to record the additional $30 million loan loss reserve in the 1991 financial statements, and the auditors gave the adverse opinion last year. This year, assume the bank restated its 1991 financial statements, recording the additional loan loss reserve in the proper period. The report on the 1992 and 1991 comparative financial statements should contain the explanation shown in Exhibit 3–9.

Reporting on Limited Engagements

LEARNING OBJECTIVE
10. Describe the type of report issued when an audit engagement is limited.

Sometimes clients hire auditors to audit and report on only one of the financial statements and not the others. Most often, such an engagement is for the audit of the balance sheet only. Audit standards make a special exception and do not define this kind of engagement as a scope limitation. Instead, it is known as an "incomplete set of financial statements" (*Handbook Section* 5400.02). An unqualified report on only one financial statement is permitted. The auditor amends the forms of the report as appropriate. For example, in the introductory paragraph, the one statement (e.g., balance sheet or income statement) will be declared to be audited. In the opinion paragraph, the opinion will be limited to one presentation (e.g., financial position or results of operations).

Other Information and Supplementary Information

LEARNING OBJECTIVE
11. Explain auditors' re-
    porting responsibilities
    in connection with
    "other information"
    and supplementary
    information.

A great deal of financial information is distributed publicly in annual reports and in other documents containing audited financial statements. The company president's letter to shareholders, management's discussion and analysis of results of operations, interim financial statements, and supplementary schedules all contain financial information that is not mentioned explicitly in the auditors' reports. Auditors have professional responsibilities with regard to much of this information. When something is wrong, auditors may need to modify the audit report.

Other Information

All annual reports to shareholders and securities commissions filings contain such sections as a president's letter and management's discussion and analysis of operations. These sections are separate from the audited financial statements and are not covered by the audit opinion. Nevertheless, auditors have an obligation to read (study) the other information and determine whether it is inconsistent with the audited financial statements (*Handbook Section* 7500.13). However, auditors are not obligated to review press releases, analysts' interviews, or other forms of irregular financial news releases unless specifically engaged by the client to do so.

If auditors decide a material inconsistency exists in other information, such as the president's selective use of audited financial statement numbers, action is required. The appropriate actions are diagrammed in Exhibit 3–10.

Action When Other Information Is Materially Inconsistent

An example of other information is a president's letter remark: "Earnings increased from $1 million to $2 million, an increase of 50 cents per share." This statement can be corroborated by comparison to the audited financial statements. The president's comment would be considered inconsistent if the $1 million was income before an extraordinary loss and the $2 million was income after an extraordinary gain, or if the 50-cent change in EPS was the difference between last year's fully diluted EPS and this year's primary EPS. The president may have selected numbers without due regard to their meaningful comparison. Other kinds of other information, however, may not be so directly related to audited figures. For example, the marketing vice president may write: "This year's sales represent a 20 percent share of the total market for our product." If auditors detect a material misstatement of fact (not necessarily a direct inconsistency with audited financial statement numbers), the information should be discussed with the client. One example would be the marketing vice president's comment about market shares. Auditors must decide whether they have the expertise to evaluate the information in question, whether management has experts who developed the information, and whether consultation with some other expert is needed. This last step would be taken only if there were a valid basis for pursuing the matter and if it concerned information that is particularly important.

If a misstatement of material fact exists, auditing standards provide the following: (1) formally notify the client of the auditor's views, (2) consult with legal counsel

E X H I B I T 3–10   ACTION WHEN OTHER INFORMATION IS MATERIALLY INCONSISTENT

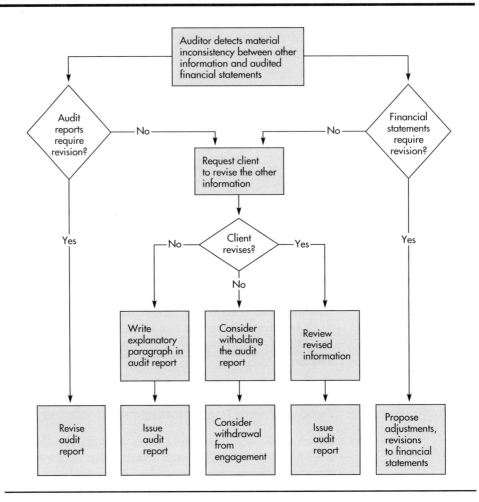

about appropriate action to take, and (3) take the action indicated by professional judgment in the particular circumstances. These three points are vague, mainly because there is no catalogue of "other information" that is not under the auditor's opinion. Auditors have latitude to decide what to do about material misstatements of other information, providing an analogy to the fourth reporting standard. (Informative disclosures in the financial statements are to be regarded as reasonably adequate unless otherwise stated in the report.)

The reporting obligation is exception reporting. The standard report is silent about other information unless an inconsistency or a material misstatement of fact exists. When something is wrong with other information, the report should be expanded with an explanatory paragraph. On the other hand, if the auditor concludes that an inconsistency between the financial statements and other information results from a material misstatement in the financial statements, then the auditor should insist on a correction to the financial statements. If the client does not correct the financial statements, the auditor should issue a report reservation for material misstatements as per *Section* 5510.

Quarterly and Supplementary Information

Accounting principles do not require interim (quarterly) financial information as a basic and necessary element of financial statements conforming to GAAP. When interim information is presented, however, it should conform to the accounting principles in *Handbook Section* 1750. The provincial securities commission, on the other hand, may require the presentation of interim information as supplementary information outside the basic financial statements. Thus, interim information is voluntary insofar as the CICA is concerned, but may be required insofar as a regulator is concerned.

Problems arise when (1) required information is omitted, (2) the information departs materially from GAAP guidelines, (3) the review procedures that auditors should perform cannot be completed, (4) management's presentation of the information indicates the auditor performed review procedures without also saying the auditor does not express an opinion on it, and (5) management places the information close to, or within, the basic financial statements (e.g., in a financial statement footnote) and does not label it unaudited. When these problems arise, auditors should expand the audit report or give a disclaimer on the information.

The expanded report for the first three cases calls attention to omission, departure from GAAP guides, or failure to review. In the latter two cases, a disclaimer of opinion on the supplementary information is added to the standard report so readers can be well informed that the auditors are not expressing an audit opinion that covers the information.

Reporting on Condensed Financial Statements

LEARNING OBJECTIVE

12. Describe the reporting requirements involved in auditors' association with condensed financial information.

Published financial statements are lengthy and complicated. Companies sometimes have occasion to present the financial statements in considerably less detail. Generally, such condensed financial statements are derived directly from full-scale audited financial statements. However, condensed financial statements are not a fair presentation of financial position, results of operations, and cash flows in conformity with GAAP. Auditors who report on such statements cannot render the standard unqualified report, even if this report was given on the full-scale financial statements.

Auditors may give a special kind of report on condensed financial statements derived from full-scale financial statements that have been audited. The report should refer to the audit report on the full financial statements, giving the date and the type of opinion, and state whether the information in the condensed financial statements is fairly stated in all material respects in relation to the complete financial statements. A hypothetical example is shown in Exhibit 3–11.

· ·

R E V I E W
C H E C K P O I N T S

3.50   Why do you think auditors are prohibited from giving a standard unqualified audit report on condensed financial statements?

3.51   What criteria define a "primary auditor"?

3.52   Is the reference in an audit report to work performed by another auditor a scope qualification? Explain.

3.53   What is an updated audit report? a reissued audit report?

E X H I B I T   3–11   **REPORT ON CONDENSED FINANCIAL STATEMENTS DERIVED FROM AUDITED FINANCIAL STATEMENTS**

Auditor's Report on Condensed Financial Statements

To the Shareholders
of X Company:

We have audited, in accordance with generally accepted auditing standards, the balance sheet of X Company as of December 31, 1992, and the related statements of income, retained earnings, and cash flows for the year then ended (not presented herein); and in our report dated February 15, 1993, we expressed an unqualified opinion on those financial statements.

In our opinion, the information set forth in the accompanying condensed financial statements is fairly stated, in all material respects, in relation to the financial statements from which it has been derived.

/s/ Auditor signature
August 21, 1993

3.54 Does an audit limited by a company to the balance sheet only cause the auditor to give an audit opinion qualified for a scope limitation?

3.55 What two kinds of disclosure problems must an auditor be alert to detect when reading "other information" in an annual report? Explain them.

3.56 When should an auditor give a denial of opinion on supplementary information in financial statements?

PART II

BASIC CONCEPTS AND TECHNIQUES OF AUDITING

CHAPTER 4

Learning Objectives

Chapter 4 and Chapter 5 cover the underlying concepts of audit field work and their role in planning an independent audit of financial statements. Chapter 4 deals with the pre-engagement arrangements for an audit, the important task of understanding the client's business and industry, the organization of financial statements and the management assertions in them, the theory of evidence, the general forms of evidence-gathering procedures, and the working papers that document the audit. After studying Chapter 4, you should be able to:

1. List and describe the activities auditors undertake before beginning an audit.

2. Identify the procedures and sources of information the auditors can use to obtain knowledge of a client's business and industry.

3. Name the principal accounts in each cycle in accounting and business processes.

4. Describe and define the five principal management assertions in financial statements, and explain their role for establishing audit objectives.

5. Explain audit evidence in terms of its appropriateness and relative strength of persuasiveness.

6. List and describe six general types of audit techniques for gathering evidence.

7. Discuss the effectiveness of various audit procedures.

8. Review an audit working paper for proper form and content.

AUDIT OBJECTIVES, PROCEDURES, AND WORKING PAPERS

AUDIT PLANNING

Many activities are involved in planning an audit of financial statements. This chapter covers some of them, and succeeding chapters cover others. For organizational purposes, the first aspects of planning are divided into activities, concepts, and tools. They are explained in Chapters 4 and 5 as follows:

Overview of Chapters 4 and 5

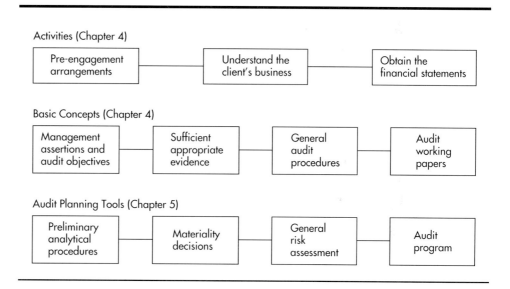

Discussion of the activities, concepts, and tools continues in Chapter 6 (Assessing Control Risk) and Chapter 7 (Audit Sampling). Technical topics of statistical sampling are in Chapter 20, and computer auditing topics are in Chapters 8 and 19. Audit applications in specific accounts and cycles are in Chapters 9 to 13.

PRE-ENGAGEMENT ARRANGEMENTS

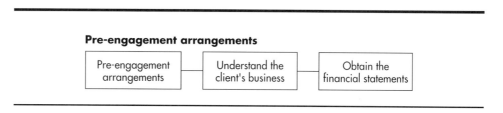

LEARNING   OBJECTIVE
1. List and describe the activities auditors undertake before beginning an audit.

Auditors undertake several activities before beginning any audit work on a client's financial statements. In general, these can be called the first risk management activities. Risk in an audit engagement generally refers to the probability of something going wrong. Auditors try to reduce risk by carefully managing the engagement. The flip side of risk management is quality management, which was discussed in Chapter 2 under the heading of "Quality Control Standards." The topics discussed next can best be understood in the context of risk management and quality management.

Client Selection and Retention

An important element of an accounting firm's quality control policies and procedures is a system for deciding to accept a new client and, on a continuing basis, deciding whether to resign from audit engagements. Accounting firms are not obligated to accept undesirable clients, nor are they obligated to continue to audit clients when relationships deteriorate or when the management comes under a cloud of suspicion. For example, an auditor may think twice about accepting an engagement with management that has a poor business reputation or where an assumption of management good faith cannot be made.

Client acceptance and retention policies and procedures include (1) obtaining and reviewing financial information about the prospective client—annual reports, interim statements, registration statements, annual information forms, and reports to regulatory agencies; (2) enquiring of the prospective client's banker, legal counsel, underwriter, or other persons who do business with the company for information about the company and its management; (3) communicating with the predecessor auditor, if any, for information on the integrity of management, on disagreements with management about accounting principles, auditing procedures, or similar matters, and on the reasons for a change of auditors; (4) considering whether the engagement would require special attention or involve unusual risks; (5) evaluating the accounting firm's independence with regard to the prospective client; and (6) considering the need for special skills (e.g., computer auditing or specialized industry knowledge).

Decisions to continue auditing a client are similar to acceptance decisions, except that the accounting firm will have more first-hand experience with the company. Retention reviews may be done periodically (say, annually) or upon occurrence of major events, such as changes in management, directors, ownership, legal counsel, financial condition, litigation status, nature of the client's business, or scope of the audit engagement. In general, conditions that would have caused an accounting firm to reject a prospective client may develop and lead to a decision to discontinue the engagement. For example, a client company may expand and diversify on an international scale to the extent that a small accounting firm may not have the competence to continue the audit. It is not unusual to see newspaper stories about accounting firms dropping clients after directors or officers admit to falsification of financial statements or to theft and misuse of corporate assets.

Communication Between Predecessor and Successor Auditors

When companies change auditors, the former auditor is the predecessor, and the new auditor is the successor. Experience has shown that clients have fired their auditors because of arguments about the scope of the audit or the acceptability of accounting principles. Sometimes these arguments involve auditors' access to necessary evidence, questions of early revenue recognition, or disputes over deferral of expenses and losses.

PEAT MARWICK RESIGNS

Coated Sales, Inc., was prospering in a tough business. The company had numbers to prove it. Revenues climbed from $10 million in 1983 to $90 million in 1987, audited without qualification. Profits grew even faster. There was one problem: Many of Coated Sales's figures were fake. Last May [1988], Peat Marwick resigned, announcing that it no longer trusted the integrity of Coated Sales management.

The company has written off half of its total reported assets and says 1987 sales were overstated. More write-downs are likely. Shareholders have seen over $160 million in market value disappear. Unsecured creditors are out $17 million. A federal grand jury is investigating, and indictments are expected soon.

Source: "Requiem for a Fraud," *Forbes,* December 26, 1988.

Peat Marwick Fired, Price Waterhouse Hired

Home Owners Federal Savings & Loan fired Peat Marwick after a rancorous dispute, replacing them with Price Waterhouse, according to filings at the Federal Home Loan Bank Board. The dispute was about Home Owner's desire to recognize a $12.7 million gain on the sale of future loan servicing profits. Peat Marwick disagreed, observing that Home Owners' proposed gain recognition would overstate the company's net income. At one point, Peat Marwick's senior partner on the engagement was ordered off the Home Owners' property and was readmitted only after the accountants said they would report the move as a bid to restrict the audit.

Source: The Wall Street Journal, February 18, 1988

More frequently, however, a change in business ownership or a concern over fees is the reason for a change.

The Rules of Professional Conduct of the provincial Institutes require a successor auditor to initiate contact with, and attempt to obtain basic information directly from, the predecessor. The reason for this is that the former auditor knows a great deal about the client and can give the new auditor information that will be useful in (1) deciding whether to accept the new client and become the successor auditor, and (2) planning the audit.

The Rules of Professional Conduct require the predecessor auditor to respond to communications from the successor. However, client consent will determine the amount of client information that is conveyed. Note that the file belongs to the auditor, not the client. However, confidentiality remains even when the auditor–client relationship ends. It is common practice for the successor auditor to explain the situation and the standards to the client and to ask that consent be given to permit the former auditor to speak. If this consent is refused, the successor auditor should be wary.

With consent, the predecessor auditor can speak freely. It is not unusual to have a cordial change of auditors and see the successor conduct interviews with the predecessor auditor's staff and obtain copies of the predecessor auditor's working papers. This exchange greatly facilitates the successor's first-time audit.

A change of auditors could cause the successor auditor's report to be modified from the standard form. It is important to note that the predecessor–successor situation is not the "using the work and reports of other independent auditors" topic explained in Appendix 3A. That situation involved the engagement of two or more audit firms auditing the financial statements for the same year. The predecessor–successor situation arises in the topic of "reporting on comparative statements" (Appendix 3A). In this case the successor auditor may be reporting on the current year, but the client may present the prior-year financial statements audited by the predecessor. The successor's report should disclose this fact in a separate paragraph of the auditor's report following the opinion paragraph or in the notes to the financial statements (*Handbook Section* 5701.11).

Engagement Letters

When a new audit client is accepted, an **engagement letter** (Exhibit 4–1) should be prepared. (The letter should be obtained each year from continuing clients.) This letter sets forth the terms of the engagement, including an agreement about the fee to be charged. Normally fees are based on the time required to perform the services. Such time estimates require some familiarity with the accounting system. The engagement letter is in effect the audit contract. It may contain special requests and assignments to be undertaken by the auditors, or it may be a rather standard letter stating that an audit of financial statements will be performed in accordance with generally accepted auditing standards. An engagement letter is highly recommended as a means of reducing the risk of misunderstandings with the client and as a means of avoiding legal liability for claims that the auditors did not perform the work promised. Also, there may be changes in fees and services provided so that it is usually advisable to prepare engagement letters even for continuing clients. A typical engagement letter is illustrated in Exhibit 4–1.[1]

Staff Assignment

When a new client is obtained, most accounting firms assign a full-service team to the new client. For larger clients, this team usually consists of the audit engagement partner (the person with final responsibility for the audit); the audit manager; one or more senior audit staff members; staff assistants or PA students; any statistics, computer, and industry specialists (if needed); a tax partner; a consulting services partner; and a second audit partner. The tax and consulting partners are consultants to the audit team if the engagement does not include other specific tax and consulting work contracted by the client. For smaller clients the team may consist of only one or two people, the partner and a staff assistant, especially if the public accounting firm itself is small.

The second audit partner reviews the work of the audit team. This partner is supposed to have a detached professional point of view because he or she is not directly responsible for keeping the client happy.[2]

[1] *International Standard on Auditing No. 2 (AU 8002),* "Audit Engagement Letters," gives detailed guidance. The international standards are issued by the International Auditing Practice Committee of the International Federation of Accountants. They are not enforceable under the provincial Rules of Conduct. Canadian generally accepted auditing standards do not require engagement letters for audits, although they are recommended for some other types of engagements.

[2] A second audit partner is required for audits of financial statements filed with the U.S. Securities and Exchange Commission. On SEC engagements, the audit engagement partner is required to rotate to other clients so that he or she does not remain in charge of a particular client for more than seven years.

EXHIBIT 4–1   **ENGAGEMENT LETTER**

Anderson, Olds, and Watershed
Public Accountants
Toronto, Ontario
July 15, 1997

Mr. Larry Lancaster,
Chairman
Kingston Company
Kingston, Ontario

Dear Mr. Lancaster:

 This will confirm our understanding of the arrangements for auditing the Kingston Company financial statements for 1997.

Our work will consist of an audit of the balance sheet at December 31, 1997, and the related statements of income, retained earnings, and changes in financial position for the year ending that date. Our audit will be made in accordance with generally accepted auditing standards and will include such tests of the accounting records and such other auditing procedures as we consider necessary.

Our audit will be conducted in accordance with generally accepted auditing standards. The audit will include examining, on a test basis, evidence supporting the amounts and disclosure in the financial statements. The audit also includes assessing the accounting principles used and significant estimates made by management, as well as evaluating the overall financial statement presentation.

We will plan the audit to detect material errors and irregularities that may affect your financial statements. However, our work is subject to the unavoidable risk that errors, irregularities, and illegal acts, including fraud and theft, if they exist, will not be detected. We expect to obtain reasonable but not absolute assurance that material misstatements do not exist in the financial statements. Our findings regarding misstatements that indicate significant weaknesses in internal control, including the design or operation of the entity's financial reporting process, will be reported to the audit committee of your board of directors in a separate letter at the close of the audit.

At your request, we will perform the following other services: (1) timely preparation of all required corporate tax returns and (2) a review and report on the company's methods for assessing your environmental performance information system in accordance with the CICA Study "Reporting on Environmental Performance."

We will provide your staff with a package of blank schedules needed by our staff during the audit. The delivery dates have been discussed and mutually agreed upon. We understand that your staff will prepare all the schedules in the package, all the financial statements and notes thereto, and the Ontario Securities Commission Annual Information Form for our review. The scope of our services does not include preparation of any of these financial statements.

Mr. Dalton Wardlaw will be the partner in charge of all work performed for you. He will inform you immediately if we encounter any circumstances that could significantly affect our fee estimate of $60,000 discussed with you on July 1, 1997. He is aware of the due date for the audit report, February 15, 1998. You should feel free to call on him at any time.

If the specifications above are in accordance with your understanding of the terms of our engagement, please sign below and return the duplicate copy to us. We look forward again to serving you as public accountants.

Sincerely yours,

Arnold Anderson, PA

Accepted by _____ Date _____

GETTING TOUGH IN THE ENGAGEMENT LETTER

Ivan F. Boesky's limited partnership is seeking a new auditing firm after Mr. Boesky's longtime auditors imposed stringent new conditions for remaining on the job. The CPA firm of Oppenheim, Appel, Dixon & Company reportedly sent an "engagement letter" to the limited partnership requesting assurances that Mr. Boesky, the general partner, and the SEC would answer all questions asked by the auditor. Such questions could involve sensitive areas the SEC is still investigating. This was one of the conditions the accounting firm presented as necessary for its continuance as auditor. [Mr. Boesky was later convicted and sentenced to prison for securities violations.]

Representatives of other accounting firms said: "If we couldn't get assurances that we would be told all the facts relevant to the audit, I doubt we would want to take the risk of taking such an engagement," and "We prefer that the Boesky limited partnership doesn't come to us; there are people we just can't afford to be associated with because we have to maintain our own reputation."

Source: The Wall Street Journal, January 23, 1987.

Time Budget

The partner and manager in charge of the audit prepare a plan for the timing of the work and set the number of hours that each segment of the audit is expected to take. This time budget is based on last year's performance for continuing clients, taking changes in the client's business into account. In a first-time audit, the budget may be based on a predecessor auditor's experience or on general experience with similar companies. A simple time budget is shown below.

	Audit Time Budget (hours)	
	Interim	Year-End
Knowledge of the business	15	
Internal audit familiarization	10	
Assessment of control risk	30	10
Audit program planning	25	
Related parties investigation	5	15
Client conferences	10	18
Cash	10	15
Accounts receivable	15	5
Inventory	35	20
Accounts payable	5	35
Representation letters		20
Financial statement review		25
Report preparation		12
Total	160	175

The time budget is illustrative, not complete. Real-time budgets are much more detailed. Some specify the expected time by level of staff people on the team (partner, manager, in-charge accountant, staff assistant, specialist). The illustration shows time at interim and at year-end.

Interim audit work refers to procedures performed several weeks or months before the balance sheet date.

Year-end audit work refers to procedures performed shortly before and after the balance sheet date. Audit firms typically spread the workload out during the year by scheduling interim audit work so that they will have enough time and people available when several audits have year-ends on the same date (December 31 is common). For many audit firms, the audit "busy season" runs from October through June of the following year. The interim work can consist of both internal control risk assessment work (*Handbook Section* 5210.20) and audit of balances as they exist at the early date (*Section* 5300.36).

Everyone who works on the audit reports the time taken to perform procedures for each segment of the audit. These time reports are recorded by budget categories for the purposes of (1) evaluating the efficiency of the audit team members, (2) compiling a record for billing the client, and (3) compiling a record for planning the next audit. Time budgets create job pressures. Staff members are under pressure to "meet the budget," and beginning auditors often experience frustration as they learn how to do audit work efficiently.

. . . .

R E V I E W
C H E C K P O I N T S

4.1 What sources of information can a PA use in connection with deciding whether to accept a new audit client?

4.2 Why does a successor auditor need to obtain the client's consent for a predecessor auditor to give information about the former audit client?

4.3 What benefits are obtained by having an engagement letter?

4.4 What persons and skills are normally assigned to a "full-service" audit team?

4.5 What is interim audit work? year-end audit work?

. . . .

Understanding the Client's Business

. . . .

Understanding the client's business

Pre-engagement arrangements	Understand the client's business	Obtain the financial statements

LEARNING   OBJECTIVE

2. Identify the procedures and sources of information that auditors can use to obtain knowledge of a client's business and industry.

Knowledge and understanding of the client's business in the context of the client's industry is very important in an audit. Therefore, auditing standards require the audit team to obtain a sufficient understanding of the business in order to plan and perform the audit work (*Handbook Section* 5140.07). The understanding and planning culminate in an audit program, which is a list of the audit procedures believed necessary to obtain sufficient, appropriate evidence that will serve as the basis for the audit report: Auditing standards state: "The auditor should document matters which in his or her opinion are important in providing evidence to support the content of his or her report" (*Handbook Section* 5140.01). A mental program "in my head" is not sufficient.

The auditor's objectives in obtaining knowledge of the business are the following:

1. Design and execute an effective audit that identifies and addresses all the significant risks of a material misstatement in the financial statements.

2. Design and execute an efficient audit that provides sufficient appropriate audit evidence in the most economical manner.

3. Enhance the accuracy of the auditor's evaluation of audit findings and the evidence supporting them.

4. Provide better ancillary services to the client[3]

In order to achieve these objectives, auditors must understand the broad economic environment in which the client operates, including such things as the effects of national economic policies (e.g., price regulations and import/export restrictions), the geographic location and its economy (Alberta's predominantly resource-based economy, Ontario's manufacturing-based economy), and developments in taxation and regulatory areas (e.g., deregulation in agriculture and air transport, approval processes in the drug and chemical industries). Industry characteristics are important. There is a great deal of difference in the production and marketing activities of banks, insurance companies, mutual funds, supermarkets, hotels, oil and gas, agriculture, manufacturing, and so forth. No auditors are experts in all these businesses. Audit firms typically have people who are expert in one or two industries and rely on them to manage audits in those industries. Indeed, some PA firms have a reputation for having many audit clients in a particular industry, while other PA firms have a larger presence in other industries.

Methods and Sources of Information

Numerous sources of information are available for obtaining the understanding of the client's business and industry. They can be categorized by the methods auditors use in practice.

Enquiry, Including Prior Working Papers

For continuing audits, specific information about the client is available in prior audit working papers. Personnel who worked on the audit in prior years are available to convey their understanding of the business. Enquiry and interviews with the company's management, directors, and audit committee can bring auditors up to date on changes in the business and the industry. Such interviews with client personnel have the multiple purposes of building personal working relationships (which includes observations about the co-operation and integrity of client managers), obtaining general understanding, and probing gently for problem areas that might harbour financial misstatements.

One very important aspect of the enquiry-based familiarization is obtaining information for planning the computer-based audit work. Almost all organizations use computers in data processing to some extent. The audit team needs to determine the

---

[3] Shields, G., "Knowledge of the Clients' Business" *CA Magazine*, August 1994, pp.56–57.

Probing Gently for Potential Trouble Spots

Aggressive management attitude in financial reporting.

Inadequate or inconsistent profitability relative to industry.

Unusual related party transactions.

Constant crisis conditions in operating areas, such as frequent/excessive back orders shortages, delays, and understaffed departments.

Bonuses or management profit based on short-term financial results.

Overemphasis on quantified targets that are linked to management compensations.

Source: CICA Handbook Section 5135A.

---

extent of computer use on significant accounting transactions, the complexity of the computer system, the organization of the computer processing activities, and the availability of data and system documentation.

Another important aspect of enquiry is to obtain an understanding of the needs of the users of the client's financial statements. Part of this is obtained when assessing whether to accept the engagement, but an important part is also obtained at this enquiry stage. The information obtained from enquiries of management, when combined with analysis of management's financial statements (covered later), helps the auditor to assess user needs in terms of what is significant for the users. The materiality concept is a way of quantifying significance for users. Materiality is discussed in more detail in Chapter 5.

Observation

At the same time that enquiries and interviews take place, the audit team can take a tour of the company's physical facilities. This is the time to keep eyes open for activities and things that should be reflected in the accounting records. For example, an auditor might notice a jumbled pile of materials and parts in the warehouse and make a mental note to check for its inventory condition and valuation. The tour is the time to see company personnel in their normal workplaces. Later, the auditors will meet these same people in more directed evidence-gathering circumstances.

Study

Numerous sources for reading material are available. A good start can be found in CICA and AICPA industry accounting and auditing guides. These guides explain the typical transactions and accounts used by various kinds of businesses and not-for-profit organizations. They were written by accountants for accountants. In addition, most industries have specialized trade magazines and journals. You may not choose to read *Canadian Grocer* for pleasure, but magazines of this special type are very valuable for learning and maintaining an industry expertise. Specific information

---

SOURCES OF BUSINESS AND INDUSTRY INFORMATION

General Information

Statistics Canada (including economic forecasts)
Dun & Bradstreet Principal International Businesses.
Standard & Poor's Register of Corporations, Directors, and Executives.
CICA Industry Guides, Audit Risk Alerts

Value Line Investment Survey.
Moody's manuals (various industries).
CFO Magazine
Standard & Poor's Corporation Records.
Analysts' reports.
Dunn & Bradstreet, *Key Business Ratios.*
Firm libraries, universities, dissertations on specialized industry topics.

Communications Media

Canadian Journal of Communication
Broadcasting-Cablecasting Yearbook (annual).
Advertising Age (twice weekly).
Broadcasting (weekly).
Publishers Weekly (weekly).
Variety (weekly).
Internet sites, trade associations, conferences.

---

about public companies can be found in registration statements and annual report filings with the provincial securities commissions.

General business magazines and newspapers often contribute insights about an industry, a company, and individual corporate officers. Many are available, including such leaders as *Canadian Business*, *Report on Business Magazine*, *Financial Times of Canada*, *The Financial Post*, *Business Week*, *Forbes*, *Harvard Business Review*, *Barron's*, *The Wall Street Journal*, and of course the business sections of newspapers such as *The Globe and Mail*. Practising auditors typically read several of these regularly. A selection of other public information sources is shown in the above box.

Other Aspects of Understanding the Business

The general understanding discussed above can lead to some specific areas for further investigation and planning.

First-time Audits

A first audit requires more work than a repeat engagement. If an existing company has been operating for a while, but has never been audited, the additional work includes an audit of the beginning balances in the balance sheet accounts. In other words, the starting place for the audited accounting must be established with reliable account balances. Such accounts as inventory, fixed assets, and intangible assets affect the current-year income and cash flow statements. This work may involve going back to audit several years' transactions that make up the permanent account balances.

Internal Auditors

Audit efficiency can be realized by working in tandem with internal auditors. Independent auditors should understand a company's internal audit activities as they relate to the system of internal control. Internal auditors can also assist with performance of parts of the audit under the supervision of the independent audit team. External auditors' co-operation with internal auditors is explained in more detail in Chapter 17.

Analysis

The auditors' own analysis of the client's financial statements can contribute a significant understanding of the business, and how it has operated for the period covered by the financial statements. Analytical procedures (e.g., ratio and comparison analyses) applied at the beginning of the audit can point out specific areas of audit risk. These applications are explained in more detail in Chapter 5.

Specialists

The understanding of the business can lead to information that indicates the need to employ specialists on the audit. **Specialists** are persons skilled in fields other than accounting and auditing—actuaries, appraisers, legal counsel, engineers, and geologists—who are not members of the audit team. Auditors are not expected to be expert in all fields of knowledge that may contribute information to the financial statements. When specialists are engaged, auditors must know about their professional qualifications and reputations. A specialist should be unrelated to the company under audit, if possible. Auditors must obtain an understanding of the specialist's methods and assumptions. Provided some additional auditing work is done on the accounting information used by the specialist, auditors may use the specialist's work in connection with audit decisions (*Handbook Section* 5360).

· ·

R E V I E W
C H E C K P O I N T S

4.6 What are some of the types of knowledge and understanding about a client's business and industry an auditor is expected to obtain?

4.7 What are some of the methods and sources of information for understanding a client's business and industry?

· ·

MANAGEMENT'S FINANCIAL STATEMENTS
· · · · · · · · · · · · ·

EXHIBIT 4–2A   KINGSTON COMPANY TRIAL BALANCE, DECEMBER 31, 1992

Revenue and collection cycle
| Acquisition and expenditure cycle
| | Production and conversion cycle
| | | Financing and investment cycle

					Debit	Credit
X	X	X	X	Cash	484,000	
X				Accounts receivable	400,000	
X				Allowance for doubtful accounts		30,000
X				Sales		8,500,000
X				Sales returns	400,000	
X				Bad debt expense	50,000	
	X	X		Inventory	1,940,000	
	X			Capital assets	4,000,000	
	X			Accum amortization		1,800,000
	X			Accounts payable		600,000
	X			Accrued expenses		10,000
	X			General expense	1,955,000	
		X		Cost of goods sold	5,265,000	
		X		Amortization expense	300,000	
			X	Bank loans		750,000
			X	Long term notes		400,000
			X	Accured interest		40,000
			X	Share capital		2,000,000
			X	Retained earnings		900,000
			X	Dividends declared	0	
			X	Interest expense	40,000	
			X	Income tax expense	196,000	
					15,030,000	15,030,000

LEARNING OBJECTIVE

3. Name the principal ac-
counts in each cycle in
accounting and business
processes.

Two points need to be made about the financial statements: (1) the management of the company is responsible for preparing them, thus they contain management's assertions about economic actions and events; and (2) the numbers in them are produced by the company's control system, which includes the accounting system, and the numbers can be found in the company's trial balance. The relation of the trial balance to the financial statements is shown in Exhibit 4–2, and the relation of the financial statements to assertions is illustrated in Exhibit 4–3. (These exhibits use the trial balance of the Kingston Company, which is the subject of the case study that begins in the problems section of this chapter.)[4]

The illustrative Kingston trial balance is short and simple. Real companies have trial balances with hundreds of accounts, and the number of them creates an organization problem for the auditors. To simplify the audit plan, auditors typically group the accounts into several cycles. A **cycle** is a set of accounts that go together in an accounting system. This book uses these four cycles: (1) revenue and collection cycle; (2) acquisition and expenditure cycle; (3) production and conversion cycle; and (4) finance and investment cycle. Briefly, cycle 1 deals with the record-keeping for the sales activities of the firm, cycle 2 deals with the record-keeping for purchasing, cycle

[4] In Exhibit 4–2 and thereafter, the term *amortization* is the general term for allocating capital asset costs over the years' benefited in accordance with *Handbook Section* 3060. Historically and internationally, specialized names for amortization have evolved in practice. *Depreciation* is amortization when applied to tangible capital assets, such as machinery and buildings, while the term *depletion* tends to be used for natural resources. In practice, amortization tends to be used in the more restricted sense of applying to intangible assets and premium or discount on long-term debt. Consistent with the *Handbook*, however, we treat all these allocations as specialized names for amortization.

EXHIBIT 4–2B   **KINGSTON COMPANY UNAUDITED FINANCIAL STATEMENTS**

BALANCE SHEET

Cash	$ 484,000	Accounts payable	$ 600,000
Accounts receivable	370,000	Accrued expenses	10,000
Inventory	1,940,000	Accrued interest	40,000
Current Assets	$2,794,000	Current Liabilities	$ 630,000
Capital assets (net)	$4,000,000	Long-term debt	$1,150,000
Accum amortization	(1,800,000)		
		Share capital	$2,000,000
Captial assets (net)	$2,000,000	Retained earnings	1,194,000
		Total Liabilities	
Total Assets	$4,994,000	and Shareholder Equity	$4,994,000

STATEMENT OF INCOME

Sales (net)	$8,100,000
Cost of goods sold	5,265,000
Gross Profit	$2,835,000
General expenses	$2,005,000
Amortization expense	300,000
Interest expense	40,000
Operating Income	
Before Taxes	$ 490,000
Income Tax Expense	196,000
Net Income	$ 294,000

NOTES TO FINANCIAL STATEMENTS
1. Accounting Policies
2. Inventories
3. Plant and Equipment
4. Long-term Debt
5. Stock Options
6. Income Taxes
7. Contingencies
Etc.

CASH FLOWS

Operations:	
Net Income	$ 294,000
Amortization	300,000
Decrease in Accounts Receivable	90,000
Increase in Inventory	(440,000)
Increase in Accounts Payable	150,000
Decrease in Accrued Expenses	(40,000)
Decrease in Accrued Interest	(20,000)
Cash Flow from Operations	$ 334,000
Investing Activities:	
Purchase Captial Assets	$ (1,000,000)
Financing Activities:	
Bank Loan	$ 750,000
Repay Notes Payable	(200,000)
Financing Activities	$550,000
Increase (Decrease) in Cash	$ (114,000)
Beginning Balance	600,000
Ending Balance	$ 484,000

3 deals with the recordkeeping for manufacturing and cost accounting, and cycle 4 deals with the recordkeeping involving all the financing activities of the firm.

Using the revenue and collection cycle as an example, the idea of the cycle organization is to group together accounts related to one another by the transactions that normally affect them all. This cycle starts with a sale to a customer and a charge to cost of goods sold, along with the recording of an account receivable, which is later collected in cash or provided in an allowance for doubtful accounts. Auditors find it easier to audit such related accounts with a co-ordinated set of procedures instead of attacking each account as if it existed alone. All the cycles are discussed in more detail in Chapters 9 through 12.

In Exhibit 4–2, the Kingston accounts are rearranged into an order not normally seen in a trial balance. This is done to illustrate the idea of the cycles. You can see that some accounts are in more than one cycle. For example, the cash account is represented in all the cycles, because: (*a*) cash receipts are involved in cash sales and collections of accounts receivable (revenue and collection cycle), (*b*) cash receipts are involved in deposit of stock issuance and loan proceeds (finance and investment cycle), (*c*) cash disbursements are involved in buying inventory and capital assets and paying for expenses (acquisition and expenditure cycle), and (*d*) cash disbursements are involved in paying wages and overhead expenses (production and conversion cycle).

When placed in the financial statements, the accounts and their descriptive titles make the assertions that are the focal points of audit procedures. Exhibit 4–2 carries the accounts forward to the financial statements.

- -

R E V I E W
C H E C K P O I N T

4.8 What are four of the major "cycles" in an accounting system? What accounts can be identified with them?

- -

MANAGEMENT ASSERTIONS AND AUDIT OBJECTIVES
- - - - - - - - - - - -

Management assertions and audit objectives

Management assertions and audit objectives	Sufficient appropriate evidence	General audit procedures	Audit working papers

LEARNING OBJECTIVE

4. Describe and define the five principal management assertions in financial statements, and explain their role for establishing audit objectives.

As you study this section, keep in mind this scheme of things:

- Management's accounting system produces a trial balance.
- Management arranges the trial balance in financial statements and thereby makes certain assertions about the financial statements.
- Auditors take the assertions as focal points for the audit work.
- The practical audit objectives are to obtain and evaluate evidence about these five assertions made by management in financial statements. We will start with five very general assertions here:
  1. Existence or occurrence.
  2. Completeness.
  3. Rights and obligations.
  4. Valuation or allocations.
  5. Presentation and disclosure.

EXHIBIT 4–3   MANAGEMENT ASSERTIONS ABOUT INVENTORY

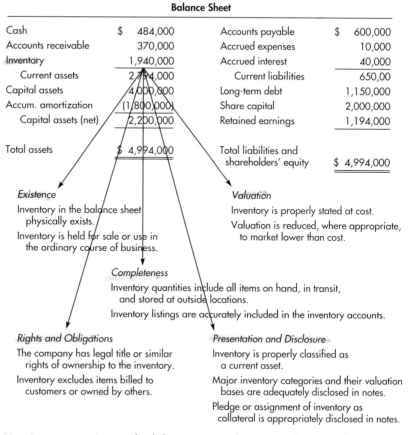

Balance Sheet

Cash	$ 484,000	Accounts payable	$ 600,000
Accounts receivable	370,000	Accrued expenses	10,000
Inventory	1,940,000	Accrued interest	40,000
Current assets	2,794,000	Current liabilities	650,00
Capital assets	4,000,000	Long-term debt	1,150,000
Accum. amortization	(1,800,000)	Share capital	2,000,000
Capital assets (net)	2,200,000	Retained earnings	1,194,000
Total assets	$ 4,994,000	Total liabilities and shareholders' equity	$ 4,994,000

Existence

Inventory in the balance sheet physically exists.

Inventory is held for sale or use in the ordinary course of business.

Valuation

Inventory is properly stated at cost.

Valuation is reduced, where appropriate, to market lower than cost.

Completeness

Inventory quantities include all items on hand, in transit, and stored at outside locations.

Inventory listings are accurately included in the inventory accounts.

Rights and Obligations

The company has legal title or similar rights of ownership to the inventory.

Inventory excludes items billed to customers or owned by others.

Presentation and Disclosure

Inventory is properly classified as a current asset.

Major inventory categories and their valuation bases are adequately disclosed in notes.

Pledge or assignment of inventory as collateral is appropriately disclosed in notes.

Note: Inventory assertions are detailed in: Existence, Valuation, Completeness, Rights and Obligations, and Presentation and Disclosure. See *Audit of Inventories*, CICA, 1986.

Exhibit 4–3 illustrates the five general assertions in some detail with relation to the inventory in the balance sheet. The sections that follow describe and define the assertions more fully.

Existence or Occurrence

The audit objective related to existence is to establish with evidence that assets, liabilities, and equities actually exist and that revenue and expense transactions actually occurred. Occurrence is the existence assertion for transactions. Thus, auditors will count cash and inventory, confirm receivables and payables, and perform other procedures to obtain evidence related to their specific objectives of determining whether cash, inventory, receivables, insurance in force, and other assets actually exist. Beginning students must be careful at this point, however, because the finding of existence alone generally proves little about the other four assertions. (Chapter 9 contains a special note on existence assertion audit procedures.)

Cutoff

A special aspect of existence or occurrence is cutoff. Cutoff refers to recognizing assets and liabilities as of a proper date and accounting for revenue, expense, and other transactions in the proper period. Simple cutoff errors can occur (1) when late December sales invoices are recorded for goods not actually shipped until January or (2) when cash receipts are recorded through the end of the week (e.g., Friday, January 4) and the last batch for the year should have been processed on December 31. In auditor's jargon, the cutoff date refers to the client's year-end balance sheet date.

Proper cutoff means accounting for all transactions that occurred during a period and neither postponing some recordings to the next period nor accelerating next period transactions into the current-year accounts.

Completeness

The objective related to completeness is to establish with evidence that all transactions and accounts that should be presented in the financial reports are included. Thus, auditors' specific objectives include obtaining evidence to determine whether, for example, all the inventory on hand is included, all the inventory consigned out is included, all the inventory consigned in is excluded, all the notes payable are reported, and so forth. Auditing this assertion means auditing what is not there, so verifying this assertion creates special difficulties for the auditor. A verbal or written management representation saying that all transactions are included in the accounts is not considered a sufficient basis for deciding whether the completeness assertion is true. Auditors need to obtain persuasive evidence about completeness. (Chapter 10 contains a special note on completeness assertion audit procedures.)

Cutoff

The completeness assertion also has a special cutoff aspect. Both completeness and cutoff mean that all the transactions of a period should be recorded in the proper period and not shifted to another. Incomplete accounting and coincident cutoff errors include such things as (1) failure to record accruals for expenses incurred but not yet paid, thus understating both expenses and liabilities; (2) failure to record purchases of materials not yet received and, therefore, not included in the ending inventory, thus understating both inventory and accounts payable; and (3) failure to accrue unbilled revenue through the fiscal year-end for customers on a cycle billing system, thus understating both revenue and accounts receivable.

Rights and Obligations

The objective related to rights and obligations is to establish with evidence that amounts reported as assets of the company represent its property rights and that the amounts reported as liabilities represent its obligations. In plainer terms the objective is to obtain evidence about ownership and owership. You should be careful about ownership, however, because the idea includes assets (rights) for which a company does not actually hold title. For example, an auditor will have a specific objective of obtaining evidence about the amounts capitalized for leased property. Likewise, the owership idea includes "accounting liabilities" a company may not yet be legally obligated to pay. For example, specific objectives would include obtaining evidence about the obligations under a capitalized lease or the estimated liability for product guarantees.

Valuation or Allocation

The objective related to valuation or allocation is to determine whether proper values have been assigned to assets, liabilities, equities, revenue, and expense. Auditors, thus, obtain evidence about specific valuations by reconciling bank accounts, comparing vendors' invoices to inventory prices, obtaining lower-of-cost-or-market data, evaluating collectibility of receivables, and so forth. Many valuation and allocation decisions amount to decisions about the proper application of GAAP.

Presentation and Disclosure

Auditors also must determine whether accounting principles are properly selected and applied and whether disclosures are adequate. This objective relates to the presentation and disclosure assertion. Specific objectives include proper current and long-term balance sheet classification, and footnote disclosure of accounting policies. The presentation and disclosure objective is the meeting place for accounting principles and audit reporting standards. Footnote disclosure is the one area where management and auditors have the most disagreements and where professional judgment is essential.

A Compliance Assertion

Although not normally listed as a separate assertion, compliance with laws and regulations is very important for a business, and disclosure of known noncompliance is sometimes necessary for presentation of financial statements in conformity with generally accepted accounting principles. Auditors gather evidence about specific objectives related to financial laws and regulations, such as provincial securities acts, tax withholding regulations, minimum wage laws, wage and price guidelines, credit allocation regulations, income tax laws, and specialized industry regulations. Compliance with legal terms of the company's private contracts (e.g., merger agreements and bond indentures) is also important for financial statement presentations. The importance of this assertion has recently been elevated through the issuance of *Section* 5136 of the *Handbook,* "Misstatements—Illegal Acts," which provides additional guidance on dealing with this assertion. When the sole purpose of an engagement is to audit compliance with various laws regulations, or rules, the engagement is called a compliance audit. This type of engagement is discussed in Chapter 14.

Compliance with laws and regulations is also a required characteristic of governmental audits, such as those by the Auditor General and provincial auditors. It is generally an objective for internal auditors with respect to managerial policies. Compliance auditing is a major topic in Chapter 17 (Governmental and Internal Auditing).

Importance of Assertions

Financial statement assertions are important and fairly complicated. They are the management assertions subject to audit and the focal points for audit procedures. When audit procedures are specified, you should be able to relate the evidence produced by each procedure to one or more specific objectives tailored to specific assertions. The way to begin planning a list of audit procedures is to ask: "Which assertion(s) does this procedure produce evidence about?" Then, "Does the list of procedures (the audit program) cover all the assertions?" The extent to which a particular procedure is used, however, will be determined by qualitative factors (discussed later in this chapter), the cost of the procedure, the risks associated with each assertion, and materiality. Risk and materiality are covered in Chapter 5.

You can simplify the five major assertions by calling them existence, completeness, ownership, valuation, and presentation. Just do not forget that each of them has additional aspects. Auditing standards explicitly identify the following assertions: existence, occurrence, completeness, ownership, valuation, measurement, and statement presentation, where measurement relates to valuation of transactions and allocation of transactions to the proper period and occurrence relates to the existence of transactions. In essence there are five assertions for assets and liabilities: existence, completeness, ownership, valuation, and statement presentation; and four assertions for revenue and expenses: occurrence, completeness, measurement, and statement presentation (*Handbook Section* 5300.17).

R E V I E W
C H E C K P O I N T S

4.9 List and briefly explain the five major assertions that can be made about assets and liabilities and auditors' objectives related to each.

4.10 Why should auditors think about a "compliance assertion" that is not listed in the auditing standards about assertions (*Handbook Section* 5300.17)?

SUFFICIENT APPROPRIATE EVIDENCE IN AUDITING

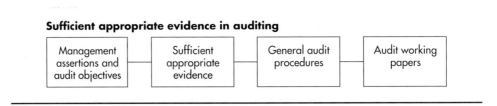

Sufficient appropriate evidence in auditing

| Management assertions and audit objectives | Sufficient appropriate evidence | General audit procedures | Audit working papers |

LEARNING OBJECTIVE

5. Explain audit evidence in terms of its appropriateness and relative strength of persuasiveness.

After obtaining the financial statements, auditors proceed to the task of specifying procedures for gathering evidence about the assertions in them. However, before studying these procedures, you need to understand some features of evidence in auditing.

The third examination standard requires auditors to obtain sufficient appropriate evidential matter as a reasonable basis for an opinion on financial statements (*Handbook Section* 5100.02). The accounting records (journals, ledgers, accounting policy manuals, computer files, and the like) are evidence of the bookkeeping/accounting process but are not sufficient appropriate supporting evidence for the financial statements. Evidence corroborating these records must be obtained through auditors' direct personal knowledge, examination of documents, and the enquiry of company personnel. The purpose of gathering and analysing evidence is to support the decision on whether the financial statements conform to GAAP.

Appropriateness of Evidence

Appropriateness of evidence relates to the qualitative aspects of evidence. To be considered **appropriate,** evidence must be relevant and reliable. To be *relevant,* audit evidence must assist the auditor in achieving the audit objectives. This means relevant evidence must relate to at least one of the assertions. If evidence does not relate to one of the management assertions, the evidence is not relevant to the auditor.

The *reliability* of audit evidence depends on its nature and source. The following hierarchy of evidential matter will help you understand the relative reliability and, when combined with relevance, the overall persuasive power or appropriateness of different kinds of evidence. The hierarchy starts with the strongest form of evidence and proceeds to the weakest.

Hierarchy of Evidential matter:

1. An auditor's direct, personal knowledge, obtained through physical observation and his or her own mathematical computations, is generally considered the most reliable evidence.

2. Documentary evidence obtained directly from independent external sources (external evidence) is considered very reliable.

3. Documentary evidence that has originated outside the client's data processing system but that has been received and processed by the client (external-internal evidence) is generally considered reliable. However, the circumstances of internal control quality are important.

4. Internal evidence consisting of documents that are produced, circulated, and finally stored within the client's information system is generally considered low in reliability. However, internal evidence is used extensively when it is produced under satisfactory conditions of internal control. Sometimes, internal evidence is the only kind available. Internal evidence is also generally easy to obtain and, therefore, tends to be less costly than other evidence.

5. Spoken and written representations given by the client's officers, directors, owners, and employees are generally considered the least reliable evidence. Such representations should be corroborated with other types of evidence.

Auditors must be careful about the appropriateness of evidence. When specifying audit procedures for gathering evidence, the best initial approach is to seek the evidence of the highest reliability. If physical observation and mathematical calculation are not relevant to the account or are impossible or too costly, then move down the hierarchy to obtain the best evidence available. Best in the sense that it is the most appropriate or persuasive evidence under the circumstances—the most reliable evidence that can be obtained in a cost-effective manner relative to a particular audit objective.

Sufficiency of Evidence

Sufficiency is a question of how much appropriate evidence is enough. The auditing profession has no official standard, leaving the matter of sufficiency to auditors' professional judgment. Realistically, however, audit decisions must be based on enough evidence to stand the scrutiny of other auditors (supervisors and reviewers)

> ## RELATED PARTIES AND THE APPROPRIATENESS OF EVIDENCE
>
> *Handbook Section* 3840 contains extensive definitions and accounting standards concerning disclosure of balances and transactions that a company has with related parties. This note, however, deals only with the audit evidence aspect of related parties.
>
> The Audit Guideline "Related Party Transactions and Economic Dependence" put the matter in perspective by stating: "The auditor should be aware that the substance of a particular transaction could be significantly different from its form and that financial statements should recognize the substance of particular transactions, rather than merely their legal form." Auditors are supposed to identify related party relationships and transactions and obtain evidence that the financial accounting and disclosure for them are proper.
>
> The audit problem with related parties is that evidence obtained from them should not be considered highly reliable in terms of persuasiveness. The source of the evidence may be biased. Hence, auditors should obtain evidence of the purpose, nature, and extent of related party transactions and their effect on financial statements; and the evidence should extend beyond enquiry of management.

and outsiders (such as critics and judges). The real test of sufficiency is whether you can persuade someone else that your evidential base is strong enough to reach the same conclusions you have reached. The fact that important evidence is difficult or costly to obtain is not an acceptable reason for failing to obtain it.

With these aspects of evidence in mind, you are now ready to study the general procedures for obtaining evidence.

- -

REVIEW
CHECKPOINTS

4.11 How are external, external-internal, and internal documentary evidence generally defined?

4.12 What's the problem with evidence obtained from related parties?

- -

GENERAL AUDIT PROCEDURES

- - - - - - - - - - -

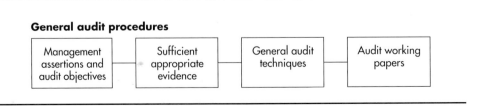

General audit procedures

Management assertions and audit objectives — Sufficient appropriate evidence — General audit techniques — Audit working papers

EXHIBIT 4–4   AUDIT TECHNIQUES AND RELATED TYPES OF EVIDENCE

Audit Techniques	Types of Evidence
1. Computation.	1. Auditor's calculations.
2. Observation.	2. Physical observation, inspection.
3. Confirmation.	3. Statements by independent parties.
4. Enquiry.	4. Statements by client personnel.
5. Inspection.	5. Documents prepared by independent parties.
6. Analysis.	6. Documents prepared by the client.
	7. Data interrelationships.

Auditors use seven basic types of evidence and auditing standards identify six general techniques to gather it. The six techniques identified in *Handbook Section 5300.22* (and also in the third examination standard) are (1) computation, (2) observation, (3) confirmation, (4) enquiry, (5) inspection, and (6) analysis. In practice many auditing firms subdivide these techniques into more specific procedures. One or more of these techniques may be used no matter what account balance, control procedure, class of transactions, or other information is under audit. Auditors arrange the techniques or more specific procedures in an audit program, which is basically a list of procedures. Exhibit 4–4 shows the seven types of evidence and the techniques most closely related to each.

Computation

Computation consists of performing independent calculations, or recalculating the calculations previously performed by a client. This produces compelling mathematical evidence. A client calculation is either right or wrong. Client calculations performed by computer programs can be recalculated using computer auditing software, with differences printed out for further audit investigation. Mathematical evidence can serve the objectives of both existence and valuation for financial statement amounts that exist principally as calculations—for example, depreciation, pension liabilities, actuarial reserves, statutory bad debt reserves, and product guarantee liabilities. Recalculation, in combination with other procedures, also is used to provide evidence of valuation for all other financial data. Computation provides the auditor with evidence that is highly reliable with respect to mathematical accuracy.

Observation

Observation consists of looking at the application of policy or procedures by others. It provides highly reliable evidence as to performance or conditions at a given point in time but does not necessarily reflect performance at other times or over long time periods. The technique of observation is utilized whenever auditors view the client's physical facilities and personnel on an inspection tour, or watch personnel carry out accounting and control activities, or participate in a surprise petty cash count or payroll distribution. Physical observation can also produce a general awareness of events in the client's offices.

Confirmation

Confirmation consists of an enquiry, usually written, to verify accounting records. Confirmation by direct correspondence with independent parties is a procedure widely used in auditing. For example, confirmation is recommended for accounts receivable by *Section* 5303 of the *CICA Handbook*. Confirmation can produce evidence of existence and ownership and sometimes of valuation and cutoff. Most transactions involve outside parties and, theoretically, written correspondence could be conducted even on such items as individual paycheques. However, auditors limit their use of confirmation to major transactions and balances about which outside parties could be expected to provide information. A selection of confirmation applications includes:

- Banks—account balances.
- Customers—receivables balances.
- Borrowers—note terms and balances.
- Agents—inventory or consignment or in warehouses.
- Lenders—note terms and balances.
- Policyholders—life insurance contracts.
- Vendors—accounts payable balances.
- Registrar—number of shares of stock outstanding.
- Legal counsel—litigation in progress.
- Trustees—securities held, terms of agreements.
- Lessors—lease terms.

The important general points about confirmations are these:

- Confirmation letters should be printed on the client's letterhead, or a facsimile, and signed by a client officer.
- Auditors should be very careful that the recipient's address is reliable and not subject to alteration by the client in such a way as to misdirect the confirmation.
- The request should seek information the recipient can supply, like the amount of a balance or the amounts of specified invoices or notes.
- Confirmations should be controlled by the audit firm, not given to client personnel for mailing. Direct communication is required by auditing standards.
- Responses should be returned directly to the audit firm, not to the client.

Confirmations of receivables and payables may take several forms. Two widely used forms are positive confirmation and negative confirmation. The positive confirmation requests a reply in all cases, whether the account balance is considered correct or incorrect. The negative confirmation requests a reply only if the account balance is considered incorrect. Auditors should try to obtain replies from all positive confirmations by sending second and third requests to nonrespondents. If there is no response to positive confirmations, or if the response to either positive or negative confirmations specifies an exception to the client's records, the auditors should investigate with other audit procedures, such as examining whether there is subsequent collection on the account or examination of internal evidence supporting the recording of the receivable. Cash and accounts receivable confirmations, as well as limitations, and issues arising from the use of faxes in confirmation procedures, are explained more

---

WHO'S LYING NOW?

This news item was released at the time of the U.S. Senate hearings on the Clarence Thomas nomination to the U.S. Supreme Court, after Anita Hill's information about sexual harassment became public (1991).

****

Psychologist Paul Ekman has spent 30 years studying the art of lying. He knows the averted eyes, fleeting facial expressions and hesitations that characterize a person at war with the truth.

After viewing the Thomas–Hill contradictory testimony, Ekman concluded: "Whichever one started out lying is now totally convinced of what they are saying. People who have an enormous stake in distorting the truth can . . . convince themselves that what they prefer to believe truly happened. Most people think they can tell when someone is lying, but they can't." A study showed that police, judges, and even FBI agents cannot reliably separate truth tellers from liars.

Source: News item from *Los Angeles Times* Service, October 13, 1991.

****

So, what can most auditors do? The best strategy is first to distinguish new assertions from "evidence." Most responses to enquiries produce more management assertions about facts, estimates, or judgments. And second, to verify the new assertions with other, independent evidence.

---

fully in Chapter 9. Accounts payable confirmations are mentioned briefly in Chapter 10, with reference to the audit of the completeness of liability recording.

Enquiry

Enquiry generally involves the collection of oral evidence from independent parties and client officials. Statements must be obtained in the written representation letter for all important enquiries. (Representation letters are covered in detail in Chapter 13.) Auditors use enquiry procedures during the early office and plant tour and when conferences are conducted. Evidence gathered by formal and informal enquiry of persons working for the client generally cannot stand alone as convincing, and auditors must corroborate responses with other findings based on other procedures. Such corroboration may include making further enquiries from other appropriate sources within the entity. Consistent responses from different sources provide an increased degree of assurance. Sometimes, however, the auditor will encounter conflicting evidence in the form of a negative statement where someone volunteers adverse information, such as an admission of theft, irregularity, or use of an accounting policy that is misleading. In these situations the auditor will have to use considerable judgment in reconciling the conflicting evidence or in deciding what additional evidence to gather. Scepticism and a critical attitude are important aspects of professional judgment, and the auditor may sometimes get into situations similar to that described in the box above. The last paragraph in the box suggests one way of dealing with conflicting evidence from enquiries.

Inspection

Inspection consists of looking at records and documents or at assets having physical substances. It encompasses procedures of varying degrees of thoroughness such as examining, perusing, reading, reviewing, scanning, scrutinizing, and vouching.

Physical inspection of tangible assets provides reliable evidence of existence and may provide tentative evidence of condition and valuation. The same is true of physical inspection of formal documents having intrinsic value, such as securities certificates. Records and documents not having an intrinsic market value, such as invoices or purchase orders, have varying degrees of reliability for different assertions depending on their source.

Much auditing work involves gathering evidence by examining authoritative documents prepared by independent parties and by the client. Such documents can provide at least some evidence regarding all the assertions.

Documents Prepared by Independent Outside Parties

A great deal of documentary evidence is external-internal. The most convincing documentation is that prepared or validated by other parties and sent to the client. The signatures, seals, engravings, and other distinctive stylistic attributes of formal authoritative documents make such sources more reliable (less susceptible to alteration) than ordinary documents prepared by outsiders. Some examples of both types of documents are listed below:

Formal Authoritative Documents	**Ordinary Documents**
1. Bank statements.	1. Vendor's invoices.
2. Cancelled cheques.	2. Customers' purchase orders.
3. Insurance policies.	3. Loan applications.
4. Notes receivable.	4. Notes receivable (on unique forms and on standard bank forms).
5. Securities certificates.	
? 6. Indenture agreements.	5. Insurance policy applications.
7. Elaborate contracts.	6. Simple contracts.
8. Title papers (e.g., autos).	7. Correspondence.

Documents Prepared and Processed Within the Entity under Audit

Documentation of this type is internal evidence. Some of these documents may be quite informal and not very authoritative or reliable. As a general proposition, the reliability of these documents depends on the quality of internal control under which they were produced and processed. Some of the most common of these documents are:

Internal Documents	
1. Sales invoice copies.	7. Shipping documents.
2. Sales summary reports.	8. Receiving reports.
3. Cost distribution reports.	9. Requisition slips.
4. Loan approval memos.	10. Purchase orders.
5. Budgets and performance reports.	11. Credit memoranda.
6. Documentation of transactions with subsidiary or affiliated companies.	12. Transaction logs.
	13. Batch control logs (computer).

A Particular Inspection Procedure: Vouching—Examination of Documents

The important point about vouching in the examination of documents is the direction of the search for audit evidence. In vouching an item of financial information is selected from an account (e.g., the posting of a sales invoice in a customer's master file record); then the auditor goes backward through the accounting and control system to find the source documentation that supports the item selected. The auditor finds the journal entry or data input list, the sales summary, the sales invoice copy, and the shipping documents, and, finally, the customer's purchase order. Vouching of documents can help auditors decide whether all recorded data are adequately supported (the existence/occurrence assertion), but vouching does not provide evidence to show whether all events were recorded. (This latter problem is covered by tracing.)

A Particular Inspection Procedure: Tracing—Examination of Documents

Tracing in the examination of documents takes the opposite direction from vouching. When an auditor performs tracing, he or she selects sample items of basic source documents and proceeds forward through the accounting and control system (whether computer or manual) to find the final recording of the accounting transactions. For example, samples of payroll payments are traced to cost and expense accounts, sales invoices to the sales accounts, cash receipts to the accounts receivable subsidiary accounts, and cash disbursements to the accounts payable subsidiary accounts.

Using tracing, an auditor can decide whether all events were recorded (the completeness assertion), and complement the evidence obtained by vouching. However, you must be alert to events that may not have been captured in the source documents and not entered into the accounting system. For example, the search for unrecorded liabilities for raw materials purchases must include examination of invoices received in the period following the fiscal year-end and examination of receiving reports dated near the year-end. (The "search for unrecorded liabilities" is explained in detail in Chapter 10.)

A Particular Inspection Procedure: Scanning

Scanning is the way auditors exercise their general alertness to unusual items and events in clients' documentation. A typical scanning directive in an audit program is "Scan the expense accounts for credit entries; vouch any to source documents."

In general, scanning is an "eyes-open" approach of looking for anything unusual. The scanning procedure usually does not produce direct evidence itself, but it can raise questions for which other evidence must be obtained. Scanning can be accomplished on computer records using computer audit software to select records to be printed out for further audit investigation. Typical items discovered by the scanning effort include debits in revenue accounts, credits in expense accounts, unusually large accounts receivable write-offs, unusually large paycheques, unusually small sales volume in the month following the year-end, and large cash deposits just prior to year-end. Scanning can contribute some evidence related to the existence of assets and the completeness of accounting records, including the proper cutoff of material transactions.

Scanning is valuable when sampling methods are applied in audit decisions. When a sample is the basis for selecting items for audit, the risk of choosing a sample that does not reflect the entire population of items always exists. Such an event may cause a decision error. Auditors subjectively reduce this detection risk by scanning items not selected in the sample.

Analysis

Analysis consists of

(a) identifying the components of a financial statement item or account so that particular characteristics of these components can be considered in designing the nature, timing and extent of other audit procedures; and

(b) performing analytical procedures, which are techniques by which the auditor:
   (i) studies and uses meaningful relationships among elements of financial and non-financial information to form expectations about what amounts recorded in the accounts should be;
   (ii) compares such expectations with the recorded amounts; and
   (iii) uses the results of this comparison to help determine what, if any, other audit procedures are needed to obtain sufficient appropriate audit evidence that the recorded amounts are not materially misstated. [*Handbook Section* 5300.01]

The difference between part (a) of the definition of analysis and scanning is that analysis relates to a higher level of aggregation—comparison of components of a financial statement—whereas scanning relates to the detail records about a particular component.

Auditors can evaluate financial statement accounts by analysis. The methods of study and comparison are known as analytical procedures. Auditors can use analysis when (a) planning the audit (i.e., at the beginning), (b) during the executing phase of the audit as a substantive procedure to verify assertions about specific account balances or classes of transactions, and (c) when performing the final review and evaluation of the financial statements before the audit report is issued (i.e., at the end of the audit). *Handbook Sections* 5301.11 and 5301.27 require that analysis be used at the planning (beginning) stage and at the end of the audit.

Analysis is the "other" category in the list of six auditing techniques. Analytical procedures are "everything else an auditor can think to do" that does not meet the definitions of computation, observation, confirmation, structured enquiry, or inspection. The procedures themselves range from simple comparisons to application of complex mathematical estimation models. They can be used to obtain evidence on any of the management assertions, but the assertions most affected are completeness, valuation, measurement or allocation, and statement presentation (D.G. Smith, *Analytical Review*, Chapter 2, CICA, 1983).

Analytical procedures can be classified into these five general forms:

1. Comparison of current-year account balances to balances of one or more comparable periods.

2. Comparison of the current-year account balances to anticipated results found in the company's budgets and forecasts.

3. Evaluation of the relationships of current-year account balances to other current-year balances for conformity with predictable patterns based on the company's experience.

4. Comparison of current-year account balances and financial relationships (e.g., ratios) with similar information for the industry in which the company operates.

5. Study of the relationships of current-year account balances with relevant nonfinancial information (e.g., physical production statistics).

SOME EXAMPLES OF ANALYTICAL PROCEDURES

Auditors noticed large quantities of rolled steel in the company's inventory. Several 30,000-kilogram rolls were entered in the inventory list. The false entries were detected because the auditor knew the company's fork-lift trucks had a 10,000-kilogram lifting capacity.

****

Auditors compared the total quantity of vegetable oils the company claimed to have inventoried in its tanks to the storage capacity reported in national export statistics. The company's "quantity on hand" amounted to 90 percent of the national supply and greatly exceeded its own tank capacity.

****

Last year's working papers showed that the company employees had failed to accrue wages payable at the year-end date. A search for the current accrual entry showed it had again been forgotten.

****

Auditors programmed a complex regression model to estimate the electric utility company's total revenue. They used empirical relations of fuel consumption, meteorological reports of weather conditions, and population census data in the area. The regression model estimated revenue within close range of the reported revenue.

Auditors need to be careful to use independent, reliable information for comparison to current-year financial accounts. Thus, the sources of information for analytical procedures are very important:

- Financial account information for comparable prior period(s). Company budgets and forecasts.
- Financial relationships among accounts in the current period.
- Industry statistics.
- Nonfinancial information, such as physical production statistics.

Because analytical procedures are loosely defined, many auditors consider the evidence they produce to be "soft." Therefore, auditors, professors, and students tend to concentrate on computation, observation, confirmation, inspection of assets, and vouching of documents that are perceived to produce "hard" evidence. However, you should resist this distinction. Analytical procedures are, in fact, quite effective.

Hylas and Ashton collected evidence on misstatements requiring financial statement adjustment in a large number of audits.[5] They were interested primarily in describing the audit procedures used to detect the misstatements. Their definition of analytical procedures was broad. It included data comparisons, predictions based on

---

[5] R.E. Hylas and R.H. Ashton, "Audit Detection of Financial Statement Errors," *Accounting Review*, October 1982, pp. 751–65.

POTHOLES IN THE AUDIT PROCEDURE ROAD

Computation:

An auditor calculated inventory valuations (quantities times price), thinking the measuring unit was gross (144 units each), when the client had actually recorded counts in dozens (12 units each), thus causing the inventory valuation to be 12 times the proper measure.

Inspection of Assets:

While inspecting the fertilizer tank assets in ranch country, the auditor was fooled when the manager was able to move them to other locations and place new numbers on them. The auditor "inspected" the same tanks many times.

Confirmation:

The insurance company executive gave the auditor a false address for a marketable securities confirmation, intercepted the confirmation, then returned it with no exceptions noted. The company falsified $20 million in assets.

Enquiry:

Seeking evidence of the collectibility of accounts receivable, the auditors "audited by conversation" and took the credit manager's word about the collection probabilities on the over-90-day past-due accounts. They sought no other evidence.

Inspection by Examination of Documents:

The auditors did not notice that the bank statement had been crudely altered. (Can you find the alteration in the bank statement in Exhibit 18–3 in Chapter 18?)

Inspection by the Scanning Procedure:

The auditors extracted a computer list of all the bank's loans over $1,000. They neglected to perform a similar scan for loans with negative balances, a condition that should not occur. The bank had data processing problems that caused many loan balances to be negative, although the trial balance balanced!

---

outside data, analyses of interrelationships among account balances, "reasonableness tests," "estimates," and cursory review of financial statements in the audit planning stage. They also had two procedure categories called expectations from prior years (which involves the carry over of analytical and detail knowledge about continuing audit clients), and discussions with client personnel.

They found that auditors gave credit for misstatement discovery to analytical procedures for 27.1 percent of all misstatements. They gave credit to "expectations" and "discussions" for another 18.5 percent. Altogether, the so-called soft procedures accounted for detection of 45.6 percent of the misstatements. All of these procedures typically are applied early in the audit, so you should not infer that other kinds of audit procedures would or would not have detected the same misstatements. The detection success of other procedures depends on the results of the early applied procedures because, as this study was designed, even a good physical observation procedure did not get credit for "discovery" of a misstatement that already had been discovered using analytical procedures.

Auditors must consider the value of analytical procedures, especially since they are usually less costly than more detailed, document-oriented procedures. Also, the "hard evidence" procedures have their own pitfalls. Auditors may not be competent

EXHIBIT 4–5   FREQUENCY OF AUDIT ADJUSTMENTS (sample of audits from one audit firm)

Number of Audit Adjustments*	Number of Audits	Percent of Audits
Zero or 1	22	12%
2–5	30	16
6–10	45	24
More than 10	89	48
Total	186	100%

*Total number of adjustments detected regardless of size or nature.

to "see" things they are supposed to observe. Clients can manipulate confirmations by giving auditors the addresses of conspirators or by asking customers just to "sign it and send it back." An audit program consists of several different types of procedures, and analytical procedures deserve a prominent place.

The box on the preceding page illustrated problems that can arise in evaluating evidence obtained with "hard evidence" procedures.

R E V I E W
C H E C K P O I N T S

4.13   What is meant by "vouching"? by "tracing"? and by "scanning"?

4.14   What can auditors do to improve the effectiveness of confirmation requests?

4.15   What are the five types of general analytical procedures?

4.16   Are analytical procedures very effective for discovering errors and irregularities?

EFFECTIVENESS OF AUDIT PROCEDURES

LEARNING   OBJECTIVE
7. Discuss the effectiveness of various audit procedures.

Audits are supposed to be designed to provide reasonable assurance of detecting misstatements that are material to the financial statements (see *Handbook Section* 5090.04). When misstatements exist, and auditors do a good job of detecting them, adjustments will be made to management's unaudited financial statements before an audit report is issued. How often does this happen? Wright and Ashton obtained information on 186 audits performed by KPMG Peat Marwick during 1984–85.[6] The reported frequency of audit adjustments is shown in Exhibit 4–5.

What kinds of misstatements did the auditors find? Wright and Ashton reported the data for 23 accounts. A selection of them is shown in Exhibit 4–6. The misstatements consisted of both understatements and overstatements. (However, you should remember that these are not "good" or "bad" descriptions. Overstatement of assets and understatement of liabilities both cause shareholders' equity to be overstated.) Since they come from respondents in one public accounting firm, these data may not be generalizable to all audits. In this case, however, the overstatements/understatements look mixed in the current assets, understatements are in the majority in the

[6] Data for Exhibit 4–5 and the other, related exhibits come from Arnold Wright and Robert H. Ashton, "Identifying Audit Adjustments with Attention-Directing Procedures," *The Accounting Review*, October 1989, pp. 710–28.

EXHIBIT 4–6   SUMMARY OF MISSTATEMENTS (selected accounts)

Account	Number of Misstatements	
	Overstatement	Understatement
Cash	6	10
Securities	21	17
Accounts receivable	48	22
Inventory	24	32
Property, plant	14	23
Other noncurrent	11	24
Accounts payable	21	25
Accrued liabilities	17	40
Other current liabilities	10	13
Long-term liabilities	12	24
Revenue	32	30
Cost of goods sold	38	45
Selling expense	11	16
Gen and admin. expense	39	52

Note: The effect of adjustments on income was that 43 percent of the adjustments reduced the reported income, while 28 percent increased the reported income. The other 29 percent of the adjustments were reclassifications that neither reduced nor increased income.

EXHIBIT 4–7   INITIAL EVENTS THAT IDENTIFIED ADJUSTMENTS

Initial Event	Number of Adjustments	Percent
Tests of details: examination of transaction amounts and descriptions, account balance details, workups to support account balances, data on various reconciliations	104	28.7%
*Expectations from the prior year	78	21.5
*Analytical procedures: comparison of current unaudited balances with balances of prior years, predictions of current balances based on exogenous data, analyses of interrelationships	56	15.5
*Client enquiry	48	13.3
Test of detail: checks for mathematical accuracy	35	9.7
General audit procedures	8	2.2

*These were the three "attention-directing procedures" that accounted for 50.3 percent of the identified adjustments.

noncurrent assets, understatements appear to be in the majority in the liabilities, and understatements appear to be in the majority in the expense accounts.

As you can see, discovery of misstatements in management's unaudited financial statements is not unusual. How do the auditors do it? What procedures do they find effective? Wright and Ashton compiled data on seven "initial events" that identified misstatements in financial statements. They were called "initial events" instead of "audit procedures" because they were the first work that identified misstatements, and all of them did not correspond exactly with specific procedures auditors would list in an audit program. Exhibit 4–7 shows the initial events that indicated misstatements that required adjustment. The so-called "soft" information from expectations based on prior-year experience, analytical procedures, and client enquiry accounted for an overall 50 percent of the discovered misstatements. (These data are consistent with the earlier Hylas-Ashton study. See footnote 5.)

Nevertheless, detail audit procedures also were effective. Wright and Ashton note that the "ordering effect" (the fact that the attention-directing procedures come first) biases the results against showing that detail procedures might have detected the misstatements if they had not already been detected. They note further that (1) few adjustments were initially signalled by confirmations or inventory observation and (2) simple methods of comparison and client enquiry detected many misstatements.

R E V I E W
C H E C K P O I N T S

4.17   Is there any pattern in auditors' experience in finding overstatements and understatements in accounts?

4.18   List several types of audit work (initial events, audit procedures) in their order of apparent effectiveness for identifying financial statement misstatements. Where would you put accounts receivable confirmation and inventory observation on the list?

AUDIT WORKING PAPERS

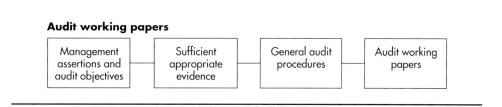

Audit working papers

| Management assertions and audit objectives | Sufficient appropriate evidence | General audit procedures | Audit working papers |

LEARNING   OBJECTIVE

8. Review an audit working paper for proper form and content.

An audit is not complete without preparation of proper working paper documentation. Working papers are the auditors' record of compliance with generally accepted auditing standards. They should contain support for the decisions regarding procedures necessary in the circumstances and all other important decisions made during the audit. Even though the auditor is the legal owner of the working papers, professional ethics require that those papers not be transferred without consent of the client because of the confidential information recorded in them. Detailed auditing standards concerning working papers are in *Handbook Section* 5145.

Working papers can be classified into three categories: (1) permanent file papers, (2) audit administrative papers, and (3) audit evidence papers. The last two categories are often called the "current file" because they relate to the audit of one year.

Permanent File Papers

The "permanent file" contains information of continuing interest over many years' audits of the same client. This file can be used year after year, whereas each year's current audit evidence papers are filed away after they have served their purpose. Documents of permanent interest and applicability include (1) copies or excerpts of the corporate charter and bylaws, or partnership agreements; (2) copies or excerpts of continuing contracts, such as leases, bond indentures, and royalty agreements; (3) a history of the company, its products, and its markets; (4) excerpts of minutes of shareholders' and directors' meetings on matters of lasting interest; and (5) continuing schedules of accounts whose balances are carried forward for several years, such as share capital, retained earnings, partnership capital, and the like. Copies of prior years' financial statements and audit reports also may be included. The permanent file is a ready source of information for new personnel on the engagement who must familiarize themselves with the client.

Audit Administrative Papers

Administrative papers contain the documentation of the early planning phases of the audit. They usually include the engagement letter, staff assignment notes, conclusions related to understanding the client's business, results of preliminary analytical procedures, initial assessments of audit risks, and initial assessments of audit materiality. Many accounting firms follow the practice of summarizing these data in an engagement planning memorandum.

Audit planning and administration also includes work on the preliminary assessment of control risk and preparation of a written audit program. In general, the following items are usually among the administrative working papers in each year's current file:

1. Engagement letter.
2. Staff assignments.
3. Client organization chart.
4. Memoranda of conferences with management.
5. Memoranda of conferences with the directors' audit committee.
6. Preliminary analytical review notes.
7. Initial risk assessment notes.
8. Initial materiality assessment notes.
9. Engagement planning memorandum.
10. Audit engagement time budget.
11. Internal control questionnaire and control analyses.
12. Management controls questionnaire.
13. Computer controls questionnaire.
14. Internal control system flowcharts.
15. Audit program.
16. A working trial balance of general ledger accounts.
17. Working paper record of preliminary adjusting and reclassifying entries.
18. Memoranda of review notes and unfinished procedures (all cleared by the end of the field work).

Audit Evidence Papers

The current-year audit evidence working papers contain the specific assertions under audit, the record of the procedures performed, the evidence obtained, and the decisions made in the course of the audit. (See Exhibit 4–8.) These papers communicate the quality of the audit, so they must be clear, concise, complete, neat, well indexed, and informative. Each separate working paper (or multiple pages that go together) must be

EXHIBIT 4–8   **CURRENT WORKING PAPER FILE**

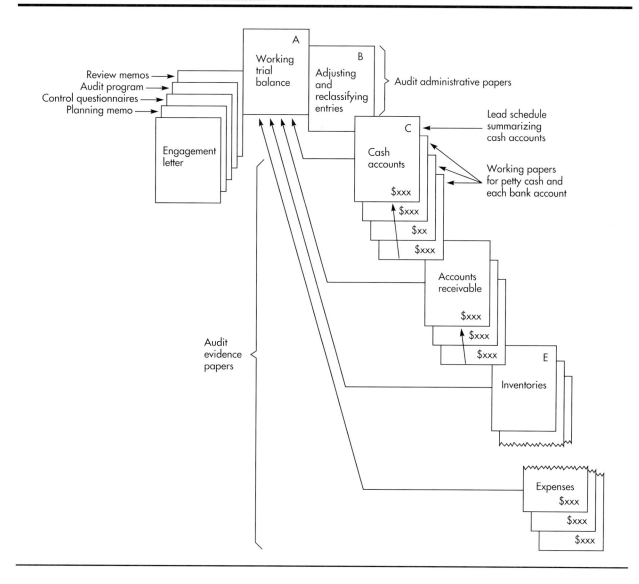

complete in the sense that it can be removed from the working paper file and considered on its own, with proper cross-reference available to show how the paper co-ordinates with other working papers. Working papers may be in the form of magnetic tape or disks, or film, or photographs; they may be handwritten or stored on computer.

The most important facet of the current audit evidence papers is the requirement that they show the auditors' decision problems and conclusions. The papers must record the management assertions that were audited (book values or qualitative disclosures), the evidence gathered about them, and the final decisions. Auditing standards (*Section* 5145) recommend that the working papers show (1) evidence that the work was adequately planned and supervised; (2) a description of audit evidence obtained include memoranda, check lists, questionnaires, flowcharts, audit programs, schedules, correspondence, and extracts of legal documents; (3) evidence of the evaluation and disposition of misstatements; and (4) copies of letters or notes concerning audit matters reported

EXHIBIT 4–9   ILLUSTRATIVE WORKING PAPER

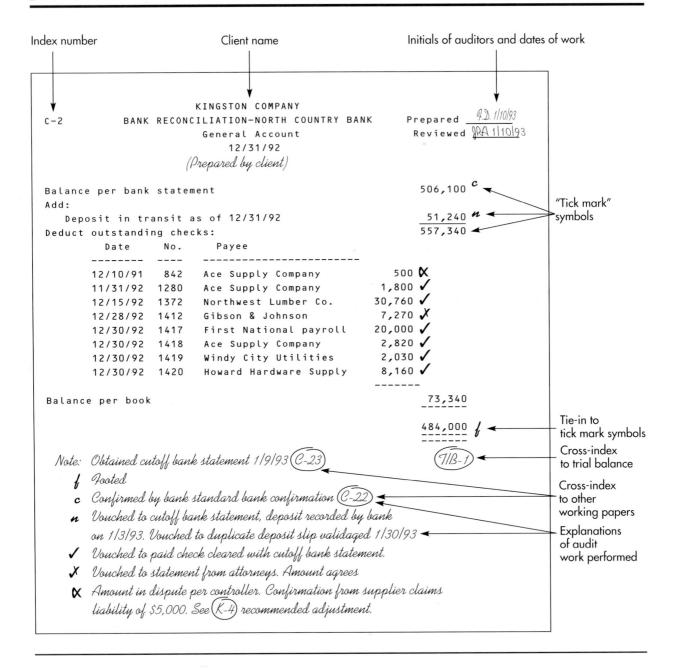

Index number   Client name   Initials of auditors and dates of work

KINGSTON COMPANY
C-2   BANK RECONCILIATION—NORTH COUNTRY BANK   Prepared _G.D. 1/10/93_
General Account   Reviewed _JRA 1/10/93_
12/31/92
(Prepared by client)

Balance per bank statement   506,100 *c*   "Tick mark" symbols
Add:
    Deposit in transit as of 12/31/92   51,240 *n*
Deduct outstanding checks: 557,340

    Date   No.   Payee
    --------   ----   --------------------
    12/10/91   842   Ace Supply Company   500 X
    11/31/92   1280   Ace Supply Company   1,800 ✓
    12/15/92   1372   Northwest Lumber Co.   30,760 ✓
    12/28/92   1412   Gibson & Johnson   7,270 ✗
    12/30/92   1417   First National payroll 20,000 ✓
    12/30/92   1418   Ace Supply Company   2,820 ✓
    12/30/92   1419   Windy City Utilities   2,030 ✓
    12/30/92   1420   Howard Hardware Supply   8,160 ✓

Balance per book   73,340

                                              484,000 *f*   Tie-in to tick mark symbols

Note: *Obtained cutoff bank statement 1/9/93 (C-23)*   (T/B-1)   Cross-index to trial balance
   f Footed   Cross-index to other working papers
   c Confirmed by bank standard bank confirmation (C-22)
   n Vouched to cutoff bank statement, deposit recorded by bank   Explanations of audit work performed
       on 1/3/93. Vouched to duplicate deposit slip validated 1/30/93
   ✓ Vouched to paid check cleared with cutoff bank statement.
   ✗ Vouched to statement from attorneys. Amount agrees
   X Amount in dispute per controller. Confirmation from supplier claims
       liability of $5,000. See (K-4) recommended adjustment.

to the client (*Handbook Section* 5145.05). Common sense also dictates that the working papers be sufficient to show that the financial statements conform to GAAP and that the disclosures are adequate. The working papers also should explain how exceptions and unusual accounting questions were resolved or treated. (Notice in Exhibit 4–9 the auditor's confirmation of the disputed account payable liability.) Taken altogether, these features should demonstrate that all the auditing standards were observed.

Working Paper Arrangement and Indexing

Every auditing organization has a different method of arranging and indexing working papers. In general, however, the papers are grouped in order behind the trial balance according to balance sheet and income statement captions. Usually, the current assets appear first, followed by fixed assets, other assets, liabilities, equities, income, and expense accounts. The typical arrangement is shown in Exhibit 4–8.

Several working paper preparation techniques are quite important for the quality of the finished product. The points explained below are illustrated in Exhibit 4–9.

- *Indexing.* Each paper is given an index number, like a book page number, so it can be found, removed, and replaced without loss.
- *Cross-indexing.* Numbers or memoranda related to other papers carry the index of other paper(s) so that the connections can be followed.
- *Heading.* Each paper is titled with the name of the company, the period under audit date, and a descriptive title of the contents of the working paper.
- *Signatures and initials.* The auditor who performs the work and the supervisor who reviews it must sign the papers so that personnel can be identified.
- *Dates of audit work.* The dates of performance and review are recorded on the working papers so that reviewers of the papers can tell when the work was performed.
- *Tick marks and explanations.* "Tick marks" are the auditor's shorthand for abbreviating comments about work performed. Tick marks always must be accompanied by a full explanation of the auditing work.

R E V I E W
CHECKPOINTS

4.19 What information would you expect to find in a permanent audit file? in the front of a current working paper file?

4.20 What is considered the most important content of the auditor's current audit working papers?

Summary

This chapter discussed two types of topics. The first was a set of activities auditors undertake when beginning an audit engagement. These pre-engagement activities start with the work of deciding whether to accept a new client and become its auditor and, on an annual basis, deciding whether to continue as auditor for existing clients. Public accounting firms are not obligated to provide audits to every organization that asks for one, and they regularly exercise discretion about the organizations with which they wish to associate. The investigation may involve the co-operative task of communicating with the former (predecessor) auditor of the organization. Once a client is accepted, the pre-engagement work continues with the preparation of an engagement letter, and the assignment of partners, managers, and staff to the job, and the preparation of a time budget for the audit.

The activities part of the chapter also covered the important process of obtaining an understanding of the client's business and industry. Methods and sources of information were explained. The last part of the activities was a brief explanation of the financial statements and of the grouping of accounts into cycles for purposes of organizing the audit.

The second set of topics in the chapter related to the basic practical concepts involved in performing audits. The financial statements were explained in terms of the primary assertions management makes in them, and these assertions were identified as the focal points of the auditors' procedural evidence-gathering work. The theory of sufficient, appropriate evidence was introduced with an explanation of the relative strengths and persuasiveness of various types of evidence. Next, the general procedures for obtaining evidence were outlined. This explanation of procedures was enriched with additional notes about the ways in which procedures can be misapplied. Analytical procedures were introduced, and their power was illustrated with some empirical research findings based on actual audit results. The chapter closed with some basic pointers about the form, content, and purpose of audit working papers.

CASE STUDY   KINGSTON COMPANY

Introduction

The following is the opening description of Kingston Company, an organization that will serve as the basis for numerous problems throughout the remaining chapters of this textbook. Problem assignments in this section follow the Kingston case in the manner auditors proceed with an audit. Additional case descriptions and problem requirements appear at the end of subsequent chapters. However, a student does not need to work all the Kingston assignments to get the sense of an audit.

Kingston Company

The Kingston Company is a regional wholesale distributor of lumber and hardware. Its products are shipped to large and small retail outlets in southern Ontario. The company stocks a wide range of products and has a large customer base of retail store and lumber company customers. Kingston operates from a large office and warehouse facility in Kingston, Ontario.

Kingston Company, incorporated in the province of Ontario, is a public corporation. Its shares are traded in the over-the-counter market. No one presently owns more than 4 percent of the outstanding common shares. The company is subject to the reporting requirements of the Ontario Securities Commission (OSC).

Organization and Personnel

Kingston Company is a medium-sized corporation. It has over 100 employees organized in five departments headed by vice presidents. The organization chart is shown in Exhibit 4–10.

KINGSTON COMPANY ORGANIZATION CHART

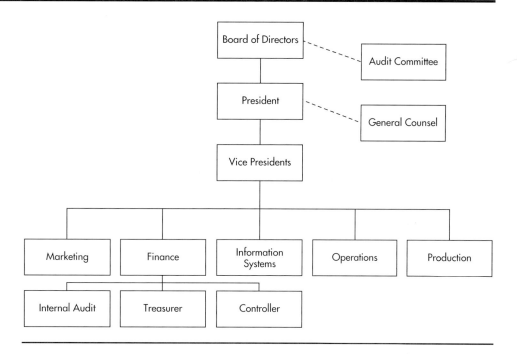

Marketing

The marketing department handles advertising and direct contact with customers. The marketing department vice president supervises the sales staff, the advertising staff, and the customer relations staff.

Finance

The finance department has three subordinate offices—the treasurer, the controller, and the internal audit function. The treasurer supervises the cashiers, the credit manager, and the cash management professionals. The director of internal audit has several staff internal auditors. The controller's office has the following departments and personnel: billing department, accounts receivable/cash receipts department, accounts payable/cash disbursements department, inventory records department, payroll department, general ledger department, and financial statement department.

Information Systems

An information systems department is being created. At present, the staff consists of a director of MIS (management information systems), a systems development project manager and two programmer/analysts, an operations manager (who also serves as the librarian and control clerk), and two machine operators. The computer has arrived and is being tested.

Production

The production department may be misnamed (because it sounds like a manufacturing operation), but the name came from the founder of the company. The department contains production planning specialists and some production control professionals, who assist the marketing department in technical matters and assist customers with product specifications. Production supervisors supervise the hourly workers, who move products from receiving, inventory, and shipping to serve customer demand. The department also supervises the timekeepers, who maintain the workers' time clocks and collect payroll time cards.

Operations

The operations department contains the critical functions of purchasing, receiving, and shipping. Inventory storekeeping responsibility is also in this department, with some inventory managers. For reasons lost to history, the department also has the mailroom and the personnel department.

Officers and Directors

The president, Larry Lancaster, is both chairman of the board of directors and chief executive officer (CEO). The vice presidents are members of the board, along with three outside (independent) directors who never worked for the Kingston organization. These three outside board members also constitute the audit committee of the board.

Kingston Case Assignments

4.21 Kingston Company Engagement Letter. Write an appropriate engagement letter addressed to Mr. Larry Lancaster, chairman of the Kingston Company board of directors. (You can see an example engagement in Exhibit 4–1.) Take under consideration the following information and the report of the meeting, which took place early in July 1992.

****

The audit firm of Anderson, Olds, and Watershed has been the independent auditor for several years. Several months before the December 31 fiscal year-end, the conversation reported below took place in a meeting attended by Ann Anderson, PA; Dalton Wardlaw, PA (partner in charge of the audit for the past two years); Julie Grace (Kingston's vice president of finance); Mila Davila (Kingston's treasurer); Sandra Carboy (Kingston's controller); and Jonathan Roberts (Kingston's director of internal audit). The three members of the audit committee of the board also were present, but they did not enter into the conversation.

Ms. Grace (VP finance): Well, here we are again, getting ready for another independent audit. Ann, will Dalton be in charge again?

Ms. Anderson (AOW managing partner): Yes, and he will be assisted by seven of our best staff, including a tax specialist and a computer systems management consultant. We need to keep up to date on your computer work.

Ms. Davila (treasurer): In the past, we have never had any unpleasant discoveries of embezzlement or theft, but we always want to be vigilant. Will you plan enough in-depth auditing to give us assurances about errors and irregularities in the accounts?

Mr. Wardlaw (partner of the audit): We will follow audit standards and base our audit work on samples of transactions. We plan the work to look for major errors and irregularities in the accounts, but cleverly hidden schemes might not be discovered. We will give you the usual separate management letter on our internal control evaluation and other related findings.

Mr. Roberts (internal auditor): Dalton, I agree, it's hard to uncover clever schemes. None of the projects I have undertaken this year shows anything amiss, other than normal human error types of mistakes.

Ms. Davilia (treasurer): This year, we want to add some work to the audit. I am short on staff time and need to have you prepare the provincial franchise tax return as well as the federal tax returns. I am also preparing, with Ms. Carboy, some current value information on our real estate subsidiary's assets. Will you review it and give us a report on how well we're doing?

Mr. Wardlaw (partner on the audit): Our tax staffperson can do the provincial and federal returns, and I will have them reviewed by Mr. Olds, our tax partner. We will review the current value information. Do you want a special audit report on it? Anything else?

Ms. Carboy (controller): Yes, and I have something else in mind. This year we also want you to do a review of our quarterly financial statistics included in the financial statement footnotes. We want to state in the footnote that the auditors have reviewed the information.

Ms. Anderson (AOW managing partner): All right, we will do a review of the interim financial information. I assume you also want us to review the OSC filing material?

Ms. Grace (VP finance): Yes. Will you need any staff help from us?

Mr. Roberts (internal auditor): Last year, Kingston saved a lot of time and audit fees when my staff prepared a stack of schedules and analyses you needed.

Mr. Wardlaw (partner on the audit): Yes, Jonathan, I will give you a package of blank schedules for various accounts. I will appreciate your having them ready when we start work in September.

Ms. Carboy (controller): Speaking of being ready, we will be able to give you a trial balance and financial statement the day after December 31.

Ms. Grace (VP finance): How much is this going to cost us?

Ms. Anderson (AOW managing partner): We cannot give a fixed fee deal like we did when we first audited Kingston, but my estimate, considering the additional work this year, is $75,000. Dalton will let you know immediately if problems arise to cause the work to be more extensive.

Ms. Grace (VP finance): Thank you. This has been a productive meeting of the minds. We look forward to your getting started next month.

4.22   Understanding Kingston Company's Business and Audit Staffing.   Additional considerations include these:

a. Based on the description of Kingston Company and the meeting reported in 4.21, do you see any need for special business knowledge in regard to the basic type of business and products Kingston manages? Specify, if any, and explain.

b. Based on the description of Kingston Company and the meeting reported in 4.21, do you see any need for special audit or accounting expertise for any of the work the auditors agreed to perform? Specify, if any, and explain.

4.23   Obtain Kingston Company's Financial Statements.   Textbook cases can only go so far in pretending to follow the time sequence of an audit engagement. According to the conversation in 4.21, the date is July 1992, but the financial statements for the whole year 1992 have already been presented in Exhibit 4–2 in the chapter! To give you a chance to "obtain" the financial statements by writing some, suppose you have the comparative trial balance shown in Exhibit 4.23–1. (The current-year column is the same 1992 trial balance that is in Exhibit 4–2.)

Required:

a. Determine whether the prior-year and current-year trial balances balance. (Add them.)

b. Write the prior-year financial statements in the format shown in Exhibit 4–2. To prepare the statement of cash flows, you need to know some balances for the year ended before the prior year. They are below; credit balances are in parentheses:

EXHIBIT 4.23-1   KINGSTON COMPANY—COMPARATIVE TRIAL BALANCE

Account	Prior-Year Debits (Credits)	Current-Year Debits (Credits)
North Country Bank	$(1,600,000)	$(2,484,000)
Trade accounts receivable	(500,000)	(400,000)
Allowance for doubtful accounts	(40,000)	(30,000)
Inventory	1,500,000	1,940,000
Other current assets	0	0
Capital assets	(3,000,000)	(4,000,000)
Accumulated amortization	(1,500,000)	(1,800,000)
Other assets	0	0
Trade accounts payable	(450,000)	(600,000)
Accrued expenses	(50,000)	(10,000)
Accrued interest	(60,000)	(40,000)
Other current liabilities	0	0
Bank loans payable	0	(750,000)
Notes payable	(600,000)	(400,000)
Deferred credits	0	0
Share capital and contributed surplus	(2,000,000)	(2,000,000)
Retained earnings—beginning	(720,000)	(900,000)
Dividends declared	0	0
Sales	(9,200,000)	(8,500,000)
Sales returns	(200,000)	(400,000)
Cost of goods sold	(6,296,000)	(5,265,000)
General expenses	(2,000,000)	(1,955,000)
Bad debt expense	(44,000)	(50,000)
Amortization expense	(300,000)	(300,000)
Interest expense	(60,000)	(40,000)
Income tax expense	(120,000)	(196,000)
Other income and expense	0	0
Total trial balance		

Cash	$ 746,500
Accounts receivable	350,000
Allowance for doubtful accounts	(31,500)
Inventory	1,550,000
Capital assets	3,000,000
Accumulated amortization	(1,200,000)
Accounts payable	(475,000)
Accrued expenses	(65,000)
Accrued interest	(80,000)
Bank loans	(275,000)
Long-term notes	(800,000)
Share capital	(2,000,000)
Retained earnings	(424,000)
Dividends declared and paid	10,000

MULTIPLE-CHOICE QUESTIONS FOR PRACTICE AND REVIEW

4.24 An audit engagement letter should normally include the following matter of agreement between the auditor and the client:

a. Schedules and analyses to be prepared by the client's employees.

b. Methods of statistical sampling the auditor will use.

c. Specification of litigation in progress against the client.

d. Client representations about availability of all minutes of meetings of the board of directors.

4.25 When a successor auditor initiates communications with a predecessor auditor, the successor should expect:

a. To take responsibility for obtaining the client's consent for the predecessor to give information about prior audits.

b. To conduct interviews with the partner and manager in charge of the predecessor audit firm's engagement.

c. To obtain copies of some or all of the predecessor auditor's working papers.

d. All of the above.

4.26 Generally accepted auditing standards require that auditors prepare and use:

a. A written engagement letter on all audits.

b. Written client consents to discuss audit matters with successor auditors.

c. A written audit program.

d. Written time budgets and schedules for performing each audit.

4.27 The revenue cycle of a company generally includes these accounts:

a. Inventory, accounts payable, and general expenses.

b. Inventory, general expenses, and payroll.

c. Cash, accounts receivable, and sales.

d. Cash, notes payable, and capital stock.

4.28 When auditing the existence assertion for an asset, auditors proceed from the:

a. Financial statement numbers back to the potentially unrecorded items.

b. Potentially unrecorded items forward to the financial statement numbers.

c. General ledger back to the supporting original transaction documents.

d. Supporting original transaction documents to the general ledger.

4.29 The objective in an auditor's review of credit ratings of a client's customers is to obtain evidence related to management's assertion about:

a. Compliance.

b. Existence or occurrence.

c. Rights and obligations

d. Valuation or allocation

4.30 Jones, PA, is planning the audit of Rhonda's Company. Rhonda verbally asserts to Jones that all the expenses for the year have been recorded in the accounts. Rhonda's representation in this regard:

a. Is sufficient evidence for Jones to conclude that the completeness assertion is supported for the expenses.

b. Can enable Jones to minimize his work on the assessment of control risk for the completeness of expenses.

c. Should be disregarded because it is not in writing.

d. Is not considered a sufficient basis for Jones to conclude that all expenses have been recorded.

4.31 The evidence considered most competent by auditors is best described as:

a. Internal documents, such as sales invoice copies produced under conditions of strong internal control.

b. Written representations made by the president of the company.

c. Documentary evidence obtained directly from independent external sources.

d. Direct personal knowledge obtained through physical observation and mathematical recalculation.

4.32 Confirmations of accounts receivable provide evidence primarily about these two assertions:

a. Completeness and valuation.

b. Valuation and rights and obligations.

c. Rights and obligations and existence.

d. Existence and completeness.

4.33 When planning an audit, which of the following is not a factor that affects auditors' decisions about the quantity, type, and content of audit working papers?

a. The auditors' need to document compliance with generally accepted auditing standards.

b. The existence of new sales contracts important for the client's business.

c. The auditors' judgment about their independence with regard to the client.

d. The auditors' judgments about materiality.

4.34 An audit working paper that shows the detailed evidence and procedures regarding the balance in the accumulated depreciation account for the year under audit will be found in the:

a. Current file evidence working papers.

b. Permanent file working papers.

c. Administrative working papers in the current file.

d. Planning memorandum in the current file.

4.35 An auditor's permanent file working papers would most likely contain:

a. Internal control analysis for the current year.

b. The latest engagement letter.

c. Memoranda of conference with management.

d. Excerpts of the corporate charter and by-laws.

Exercises and Problems

4.36 Communications between Predecessor and Successor Auditors. Assume that Kingston Company was audited last year by PA Diggs. Now, Larry Lancaster wishes to engage Anderson, Olds, and Watershed, PAs, to audit its annual financial statements. Lancaster is generally pleased with the services provided by Diggs, but he thinks the audit work was too detailed and interfered excessively with normal office routines. Anderson has asked Lancaster to inform Diggs of the decision to change auditors, but he does not wish to do so.

Required:

List and discuss the steps Anderson should follow with regard to dealing with a predecessor auditor and a new client before accepting the engagement. (Hint: Use the independence rules of conduct for a complete response to this requirement.)

4.37 Audit Planning. Walter Wolf was pleased. He had been with the firm of Riding, Hood & Co. less that a year-and-a-half since graduation from university and had received excellent performance reviews on every engagement. Now he was being given "in charge" responsibility on an audit. It was a small client, but it felt good to have the firm show such confidence in him. He planned to show that the firm had made the right decision.

Walter thought back to some of the advice his seniors had given him. Two comments in particular stood out as key steps to a successful audit:

- Careful attention to planning the audit pays dividends. Time spent on audit planning is never wasted.
- Avoid being a mechanical auditor by focusing on management's assertions embodied in the financial statements and the related audit objectives when planning audit tests.

Required:

a. Develop a list of tasks that Walter should perform in planning this audit engagement, before any audit testing begins.

Classes of Transactions	General Ledger Accounts
Cash receipts	Cash
Cash disbursements	Accounts receivable
Credit sales	Allowance for doubtful accounts
Sales returns and allowances	Inventory
Purchases on credit	Capital assets
Purchase returns	Accounts payable
Uncollectible account write-offs	Long-term debt
	Sales revenue
	Investment income
	Expenses

b. *Handbook Section* 5300 lists seven management assertions embodied in financial statements. List and briefly describe the associated audit objectives that relate to these assertions.

(ICAO adapted)

4.38 **Understand the Business—Transactions and Accounts.** In the table above, the left column names several "classes of transactions." The right column names several general ledger accounts.

Required:

Identify the general ledger accounts that are affected by each class of transactions.

Approach:

Match the classes of transactions with the general ledger accounts where their debits and credits are usually entered.

4.39 **General Audit Procedures and Financial Statement Assertions.** The seven general audit procedures produce evidence about the principal management assertions in financial statements. However, some procedures are useful for producing evidence about certain assertions, while other procedures are useful for producing evidence about other assertions. The assertion being audited may influence the auditors' choice of procedures.

Required:

Prepare a two-column table with the seven general procedures listed on the right. Opposite each one, write the management assertions most usefully audited by using each procedure.

4.40 **Financial Assertions and Audit Objectives.** You were engaged to examine the financial statements of Kingston Company for the year ended December 31.

Assume that on November 1, Kingston borrowed $500,000 from North Country Bank to finance plant expansion. The long-term note agreement provided for the annual payment of principal and interest over five years. The existing plant was pledged as security for the loan.

Due to the unexpected difficulties in acquiring the building site, the plant expansion did not begin on time. To make use of the borrowed funds, management decided to invest in stocks and bonds, and on November 16 the $500,000 was invested in securities.

Required:

What are the audit objectives for the audit of the investments in securities at December 31?

Approach:

Develop specific assertions related to securities (assets) based on the five general assertions.

4.41 **Appropriateness of Evidence and Related Parties.** Johnson & Company, PAs, audited the Guaranteed Trust Company. M. Johnson had the assignment of evaluating the collectibility of real estate loans. Johnson was working on two particular loans: (1) a $4 million loan secured by the Smith Street Apartments and (2) a $5.5 million construction loan on the Baker Street Apartments now being built. The appraisals performed by the Guaranteed Appraisal Partners, Inc., showed values in excess of the loan amounts. Upon enquiry, Mr. Bumpus, the trust company vice president for loan acquisition, stated: "I know the Smith Street loan is good because I myself own 40 percent of the partnership that owns the property and is obligated on the loan."

Johnson then wrote in the working papers: (1) the Smith Street loan appears collectible; Mr. Bumpus personally attested to knowledge of the collectibility as a major owner in the partnership obligated on the loan, (2) the Baker Street loan is assumed to be collectible because it is new and construction is still in progress, (3) the appraised values all exceed the loan amounts.

Required:

a. Do you perceive any problems with related party involvement in the evidence used by M. Johnson? Explain.

b. Do you perceive any problems with M. Johnson's reasoning or the appropriateness of evidence used in that reasoning?

4.42 Relative Appropriateness of Evidence. The third generally accepted standard of audit fieldwork requires that auditors obtain sufficient appropriate evidential matter to afford a reasonable basis for an opinion regarding the financial statements under examination. In considering what constitutes sufficient appropriate evidential matter, a distinction should be made between underlying accounting data and all corroborating information available to the auditor.

Required:

What presumptions can be made about:

a. The relative appropriateness of evidence obtained from external and internal sources.

b. The role of internal control with respect to internal evidence produced by a client's data processing system.

c. The relative persuasiveness of auditor observation and recalculation evidence compared to the external, external-internal, and internal documentary evidence.

(AICPA adapted)

4.43 Relative Appropriateness of Evidence.

1. Classify the following evidential items by type (direct knowledge, external, and so on), and rank them in order of appropriateness:

a. Amounts shown on monthly statements from creditors.

b. Amounts shown on "paid on account" in the voucher register.

c. Amount of "discounts lost expense" computed by the auditor from unaudited supporting documents.

d. Amounts shown in letters received directly from creditors.

2. Classify the following evidential items by type (direct knowledge, external, and so on), and rank them in order of appropriateness.

a. Amounts shown on a letter received directly from an independent bond trustee.

b. Amounts obtained from minutes of board of directors' meetings.

c. Auditors' computation of bond interest and amortization expense when remaining term and status of bond are audited.

d. Amounts shown on cancelled cheques.

4.44 Audit Procedures. Auditors frequently refer to the terms *standards* and *procedures*. Standards deal with measures of the quality of performance. Standards specifically refer to the generally accepted auditing standards expressed in the Statements on Auditing Standards. Procedures specifically refer to the methods or techniques used by auditors in the conduct of the examination. Procedures are also expressed in the Statements on Auditing Standards.

Required:

List seven different types of procedures auditors can use during an audit of financial statements and give an example of each.

4.45 Confirmation Procedure. A PA accumulates various kinds of evidence on which to base the opinion on financial statements. Among this evidence are confirmations from third parties.

Required:

a. What is an audit confirmation?

b. What characteristics of the confirmation process and the recipient are important if a PA is to consider the confirmation evidence competent?

4.46 Audit Procedure Terminology. Identify the types of procedures(s) employed in each situation described below (vouching, tracing, recalculation, observation, and so on):

1. An auditor uses computer software to select vendors' accounts payable with debit balances and compares amounts and computation to cash disbursements and vendor credit memos.

2. An auditor examines property insurance policies and checks insurance expense for the year. The auditor then reviews the expense in light of changes and ending balances in captial asset accounts.

3. An auditor uses computer software to test perpetual inventory records for items that have not been used in production for three months or more. The client states that the items are obsolete and have already been written down. The auditor checks journal entries to support the client's statements.

4. An auditor tests cash remittance advices to see that allowance and discounts are appropriate and that receipts are posted to the correct customer accounts in the right amounts and reviews the documents supporting unusual discounts and allowances.

5. An auditor watches the client take a physical inventory. A letter is also received from a public warehouser stating the amounts of the client's inventory stored in the warehouse. The company's cost flow assumption, FIFO, is then tested by the auditor's computer software program.

4.47 Audit Working Papers. The preparation of working papers is an integral part of a PA's audit of financial statements. On a recurring engagement, PAs review their audit programs and working papers from their prior audit while planning the current audit to determine usefulness for the current-year work.

Required:

a. (1) What are the purposes or functions of audit working papers? (2) What records may be included in audit working papers?

b. What factors affect the PA's judgment of the type and content of the working papers for a particular engagement?

c. To comply with generally accepted auditing standards, a PA includes certain evidence in his or her working papers; for example, "evidence that the audit was planned and work of assistants was supervised and reviewed." What other evidence should a PA include in audit working papers to comply with generally accepted auditing standards?

d. How can a PA make the most effective use of the preceding year's audit programs in a recurring audit?

(AICPA adapted)

Discussion Cases

4.48 Client Selection. You are a PA in a regional accounting firm that has 10 offices in three provinces. Mr. Shine has approached you with a request for an audit. He is president of Hitech Software and Games, Inc., a five-year-old company that has recently grown to $40 million in sales and $20 million in total assets. Mr. Shine is thinking about going public with a $17 million issue of common shares, of which $10 million would be a secondary issue of shares he holds. You are very happy about this opportunity because you know Mr. Shine is the new president of the Symphony Society board and has made quite a civic impression since he came to your medium-size city seven years ago. Hitech is one of the growing employers in the city.

Required:
a. Discuss the sources of information and the types of enquiries you and the firm's partners can make in connection with accepting Hitech as a new client.
b. Does the profession require any investigation of prospective clients?
c. Suppose Mr. Shine has also told you that 10 years ago his closely held hamburger franchise business went bankrupt, and upon investigation you learn from its former auditors (your own firm) that Shine played "fast and loose" with franchise-fee income recognition rules and presented such difficulties that your office in another city resigned from the audit (before the bankruptcy). Do you think the partner in charge of the audit practice should accept Hitech as a new client?

4.49 Predecessor and Successor Auditors. The president of Allpurpose Loan Company had a genuine dislike for external auditors. Almost any conflict generated a towering rage. Consequently, the company changed auditors often.

Wells & Ratley, PAs, was recently hired to audit the 1993 financial statements. The W & R firm succeeded the firm of Canby & Company, which had obtained the audit after Albrecht & Hubbard had been fired. A&H audited the 1992 financial statements and rendered a report that contained an additional paragraph explaining an uncertainty about Allpurpose Loan Company's loan loss reserve. Goodby A&H! The president then hired Canby & Company to audit the 1993 financial statements, and Art Canby started the work. But before the audit could be completed, Canby was fired, and W&R was hired to complete the audit. Canby & Company did not issue an audit report because the audit was not finished.

Required:
Does the Wells & Ratley firm need to initiate communications with Canby & Company? with Albrecht & Hubbard? with both? Explain your response in terms of the purposes of communications between predecessor and successor auditors.

4.50 Potential Audit Procedure Failures. For each of the general audit procedures of (*a*) recalculation, (*b*) physical observations, (*c*) confirmation (accounts receivable, securities, or other assets), (*d*) verbal enquiry, (*e*) examination of internal documents, and (*f*) scanning, discuss one way the procedure could be misapplied or the auditors could be misled in such a way as to render the work (audit evidence) misleading or irrelevant. Give examples different from the examples in Chapter 4.

4.51 Risk of Misstatement in Various Accounts. Based on information you have available in Chapter 4:
a. Which accounts may be most susceptible to overstatement? to understatement?
b. Why do you think a company might permit asset accounts to be understated?
c. Why do you think a company might permit liability accounts to be overstated?
d. Which direction of misstatement is most likely: income overstatement or income understatement?

4.52 Working Paper Review. The schedule in Exhibit 4.52–1 was prepared by the controller of World Manufacturing, Inc., for use by the independent auditors during their examination of World's financial statements. All procedures performed by the audit assistant were noted in the bottom "Legend" section, and it was initialled properly, dated, and indexed, and then submitted to a senior member of the audit staff for review. Internal control was reviewed and is considered to be satisfactory.

Required:

a. What information essential to the audit of marketable securities is missing from the schedule?

b. What essential audit procedures were not noted as having been performed by the audit assistant?

Approach:

Write specific assertions based on the five general assertions, then look to the working paper for documentation of evidence related to each one.

(AICPA adapted)

EXHIBIT 4.52–1 **MARKETABLE SECURITIES**
(World Manufacturing, Inc., year ended December 31, 1992)

Description of Security			Serial No.	Face Value of Bonds	General Ledger 1/1	Purchased in 1992	Sold in 1992	Cost	General Ledger 12/31	12/31 Market	Dividend and Interest		
											Pay Date(s)	Amt. Received	Accruals 12/31
Corp. Bonds	%	Yr. Due											
A	6	99	21-7	10,000	9,400a				9,400	9,100	1/15 7/15	300b,d 300b,d	275
D	4	93	73-0	30,000	27,500a				27,500	26,220	12/1	1,200b,d	100
G	9	06	16-4	5,000	4,000a				4,000	5,080	8/1	450b,d	188
Rc	5	93	08/2	70,000	66,000a		57,000b	66,000					
Sc	10	97	07-4	100,000		100,000e			100,000	101,250	7/1	5,000b,d	5,000
					106,900	100,000	57,000	66,000	140,900	141,650		7,250	5,563
					a,f	f	f	f	f,g	f		f	f
Stocks													
P 1,000 shs Common			1,044		75,00a				7,500	7,600	3/1 6/1 9/1 12/1	750b,d 750b,d 750b,d 750b,d	250
U 50 shs Common			8,530		9,700a				9,700	9,800	3/1 2/1 8/1	750b,d 800b,d 800b,d	667
					17,200				17,200	17,400		4,600	917
					a,f				f,g	f		f	f

Legends and comments relative to above:
a = Beginning balances agreed to 1991 working papers.
b = Traced to cash receipts.
c = Minutes examined (purchase and sales approved by the board of directors).
d = Agreed to 1099.
e = Confirmed by tracing to broker's advice.
f = Totals footed.
g = Agreed to general ledger.

CHAPTER 5

Learning Objectives

Chapter 5 continues the coverage of audit fieldwork planning started in Chapter 4. This chapter deals with some of the tools of planning—the application of analytical procedures at the beginning of an audit, the materiality determination and tolerable misstatement assignment decisions, and the assessment of risks with reference to the audit risk model, all leading up to the preparation of audit programs. After studying Chapter 5, you should be able to:

1. Perform analytical procedures using unaudited financial statements to identify potential problems in the accounts.

2. Analyse a materiality determination case and decide upon a maximum amount of misstatement (planning materiality) acceptable in a company's financial statements.

3. Assign an overall planning materiality amount to the tolerable misstatement amounts for particular accounts.

4. Describe the conceptual audit risk model and explain the meaning and importance of its components in terms of professional judgment and audit planning.

5. Describe the content and purpose of audit programs.

Audit Planning with Analytical Procedures,

Risks, and Materiality

Audit Planning

After the auditors finish the pre-engagement arrangements, understand the audit client's business and industry, and obtain the unaudited financial statements, certain planning tools can be used to guide and direct the audit work. In this chapter these audit tools are classified as preliminary analytical procedures, materiality decisions, general risk assessment, and audit programs. The usefulness of the first three is to help the auditors design the audit programs. For our study purposes, the topics are arranged in the following sequence.

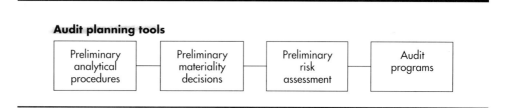

The activities, concepts, and tools introduced in Chapters 4 and 5 continue in Chapter 6 (Control Risk Assessment) and Chapter 7 (Audit Sampling). Basic sampling concepts are covered in Chapter 7 and basic computer audit concepts are covered in Chapter 8. More advanced topics in computer audit and sampling are covered in Chapters 19 and 20, respectively. Audit applications in specific accounts and cycles are in Chapters 9 to 13.

Preliminary Analytical Procedures

According to auditing standards, analytical procedures should be applied in the beginning planning stages of each audit (*Section* 5300.11) and as part of the overall evaluation at the end of the audit (*Section* 5301.27). These procedures were introduced in Chapter 4 and described in terms of five general types of procedures. For review, they are:

1. Comparison of current-year account balances to balances for one or more comparable periods.

2. Comparison of the current-year account balances to anticipated results found in the company's budgets and forecasts.

3. Evaluation of the relationships of current-year account balances to other current-year balances for conformity with predictable patterns based on the company's experience.

4. Comparison of current-year account balances and financial relationships (e.g., ratios) with similar information for the industry in which the company operates.

5. Study of the relationships of current-year account balances with relevant nonfinancial information (e.g., physical production statistics).

Analytical procedures can take many forms, ranging from simple to complex. For the more simple and easily applied procedures, auditors have begun to define a wide range of early information-gathering activity as "analytical procedures," including: (*a*) review of adjustments proposed in prior years' audits; (*b*) conversations with client personnel; (*c*) reading and study of the minutes of the meetings of directors and committees of the board of directors (e.g., executive committee, finance committee, compensation committee, audit committee); (*d*) review of the corporate charter and bylaws or partnership agreement; (*e*) review of contracts, agreements, and legal proceedings; (*f*) and many other activities that do not fit the strict definition of the five general types of analytical procedures. The purpose of this work is "attention directing"—to alert the audit team to problems (errors, irregularities) in the account balances and disclosures. The effectiveness of some of these activities was reviewed in Chapter 4 (see Exhibit 4–7).

Other analytical procedures can be complex, including mathematical time series and regression calculations, complicated comparisons of multiyear data, and trend and ratio analyses. In the sections that follow, two of the more complicated general analytical procedures are emphasized: (number 1) comparison of current year account balances to balances for one or more comparable periods, and (number 3) evaluation of the relationships of current-year account balances to other current-year balances for conformity with predictable patterns based on the company's experience.

More mathematical approaches to analytical review are covered in Chapter 20.

. . . .

R E V I E W
C H E C K P O I N T S

5.1 What are the five types of general analytical procedures?

5.2 What is the purpose of performing preliminary analytical procedures in the audit planning stage?

5.3 What official documents and authorizations should an auditor read when performing preliminary analytical procedures?

5.4 What important information can be found in directors' minutes about officers' compensation? Business operations? Corporate finance? Accounting policies and control?

. . . .

What's in the Minutes of Meetings?

Boards of directors are supposed to monitor the client's business. The minutes of their meetings and the meetings of their committees (e.g., executive committee, finance committee, compensation committee, audit committee) frequently contain information of vital interest to the independent auditors. Some examples:

- Amount of dividends declared.
- Authorization of officers' salaries.
- Authorization of stock options and other "perk" compensation.
- Acceptance of contracts, agreements, lawsuit settlements.
- Approval of major purchases of property and investments.
- Discussions of merger and divestiture progress. Authorization of financing by share issues, long-term debt, and leases.
- Approval to pledge assets as security for debts.
- Discussion of negotiations on bank loans and payment waivers.
- Approval of accounting policies and accounting for estimates and unusual transactions.
- Authorizations for individuals to sign bank cheques.

Auditors take notes or make copies of important parts of these minutes and compare them with information in the accounts and disclosures (e.g., compare the amount of dividends declared to the amount paid, compare officers' authorized salaries to amounts paid, compare agreements to pledge assets to proper disclosure in the notes to financial statements).

Because of the importance that the minutes have in determining what needs to be disclosed in order to obtain fair presentation, denial of access to the minutes of the board of directors meeting constitutes a major scope restriction by the client. Such denial is a common source of opinion reservation.

Analysis of Unaudited Financial Statements
· · · · · · · · · · · ·

Horizontal analysis refers to changes of financial statement numbers and ratios across two or more years. Vertical analysis refers to financial statement amounts expressed each year as proportions of a base, such as sales for the income statement accounts and total assets for the balance sheet accounts. Auditors look for relationships that do not make sense as indicators of problems in the accounts, and they use such indicators to plan further audit work.

Attention Directing

In the planning stage, analytical procedures are used to identify potential problem areas so that subsequent audit work can be designed to reduce the risk of missing something important. The application demonstrated below thus can be described as attention directing—pointing out accounts that may contain errors and irregularities.

The insights derived from preliminary analytical procedures do not provide direct evidence about the numbers in the financial statements. They only help the audit team plan the audit program.

An Organized Approach

With an organized approach—a standard starting place—preliminary analytical procedures can provide considerable familiarity with the client's business. Many auditors start with comparative financial statements and calculate common-size statements (vertical analysis) and year-to-year change in balance sheet and income statement accounts (horizontal analysis). This is the start of describing the financial activities for the current year under audit. Exhibit 5–1 contains financial balances for the prior year (consider them audited) and the current year (consider them unaudited at this stage). Common-size statements (vertical) are shown in parallel columns, and the dollar amount and percentage change (horizontal) are shown in the last two columns. These are some basic beginning analytical data.

Describe the Financial Activities

After generating these basic financial data, the next step is to describe the financial changes and relationships you can see in the data. According to the unaudited financial statements in Exhibit 5–1, the company increased the net income by increasing sales 10 percent, reducing cost of goods sold as a proportion of sales, and controlling other expenses. At least some of the sales growth appears to have been prompted by easier credit (larger accounts receivable) and more service (more equipment in use). The company also used much of its cash and borrowed more to purchase the equipment, to make its payment on the long-term debt, and to pay dividends.

Ask Relevant Questions

The next step is to ask: "What could be wrong?" and "What errors and irregularities, as well as legitimate explanations, could account for these financial results?" For this explanation we will limit attention to the accounts receivable and inventory accounts. At this point some other ratios can help support the analysis. Exhibit 5–2 contains several familiar ratios. (Appendix 5A at the end of this chapter contains these ratios and their formulas.)

Question: Are the accounts receivable collectible? (Alternative: Is the allowance for doubtful accounts large enough?) Easier credit can lead to more bad debts. The company has a much larger amount of receivables (Exhibit 5–1), the days' sales in receivables has increased significantly (Exhibit 5–2), the receivables turnover has decreased (Exhibit 5–2), and the allowance for doubtful accounts is smaller in proportion to the receivables (Exhibit 5–2). If the prior-year allowance for bad debts at 8 percent of receivables was appropriate, and conditions have not become worse, perhaps the allowance should be closer to $72,000 than $50,000. The auditors should work carefully on the evidence related to accounts receivable valuation.

Question: Could the inventory be overstated? (Alternative: Could the cost of the goods sold be understated?) Overstatement of the ending inventory would cause the cost of goods sold to be understated. The percentage of cost of goods sold to sales

EXHIBIT 5-1   ANYCOMPANY, INC.—PRELIMINARY ANALYTICAL PROCEDURES DATA

	Prior Year		Current Year		Change	
	Balance	Common Size	Balance	Common Size	Amount	Percent Change
Assets						
Cash	$ 600,000	14.78%	$ 200,000	4.12%	($ 400,000)	−66.67%
Accounts receivable	500,000	12.32	900,000	18.56	400,000	80.00
Allowance doubtful accounts	(40,000)	−0.99	(50,000)	−1.03	(10,000)	25.00
Inventory	1,500,000	36.95	1,600,000	32.99	100,000	6.67
Total current assets	2,560,000	63.05	2,650,000	54.63	90,000	3.52
Equipment	3,000,000	73.89	4,000,000	82.47	1,000,000	33.33
Accumulated amortization	(1,500,000)	−36.95	(1,800,000)	−37.11	(300,000)	20.00%
Total assets	$4,060,000	100.00%	$4,850,000	100.00%	$ 790,000	19.46%
Liabilities and Equity						
Accounts payable	$ 500,000	12.32%	$ 400,000	8.25%	($ 100,000)	−20.00%
Bank loans, 11%	0	0.00	750,000	15.46	750,000	
Accrued interest	60,000	1.48	40,000	0.82	(20,000)	−33.33
Total current liabilities	560,000	13.79	1,190,000	24.53	630,000	112.50
Long-term debt, 10%	600,000	14.78	400,000	8.25	(200,000)	−33.33
Total liabilities	1,160,000	28.57	1,590,000	32.78	430,000	37.07
Share capital	2,000,000	49.26	2,000,000	41.24	0	0.00
Retained earnings	900,000	22.17	1,260,000	25.98	360,000	40.00
Total liabilities and equity	$4,060,000	100.00%	$4,850,000	100.00%	$ 790,000	19.46%
Income						
Sales (net)	$9,000,000	100.00%	$9,900,000	100.00%	$ 900,000	10.00%
Cost of goods sold	6,750,000	75.00	7,200,000	72.73	450,000	6.67
Gross margin	2,250,000	25.00	2,700,000	27.27	450,000	20.00
General expense	1,590,000	17.67	1,734,000	17.52	144,000	9.06
Amortization	300,000	3.33	300,000	3.03	0	0.00
Operating income	360,000	4.00	666,000	6.46	306,000	85.00
Interest expense	60,000	0.67	40,000	0.40	(20,000)	−33.33
Income taxes (40%)	120,000	1.33	256,000	2.59	136,000	113.33
Net income	$ 180,000	2.00%	$ 370,000	3.74%	$ 190,000	105.56%

shows a decrease (Exhibits 5–1 and 5–2). If the 75 percent of the prior year represents a more accurate cost of goods sold, then the income before taxes may be overstated by $225,000 (75 percent of $9.9 million minus $7.2 million unaudited cost of goods sold). The days' sales in inventory and the inventory turnover remained the same (Exhibit 5–2), but you might expect them to change in light of the larger volume of sales. Careful work on the physical count and valuation of inventory appears to be needed.

Other questions can be asked and other relationships derived when industry statistics are available. Industry statistics can be obtained from such services as Statistics Canada, Dun & Bradstreet, and Robert Morris Associates. These statistics include industry averages for important financial yardsticks, such as gross profit margin, return on sales, current ratio, and debt/net worth. A comparison with client data may reveal out-of-line statistics, indicating a relatively strong feature of the company, a weak financial position, or possibly an error or misstatement in the client's financial statements. However, care must be taken with industry statistics. A particular company may or may not be well represented by industry averages.

E X H I B I T 5–2   ANYCOMPANY, INC.—SELECTED FINANCIAL RATIOS

	Prior Year	Current Year	Percent Change
Balance Sheet Ratios			
Current ratio	4.57	2.23	−51.29%
Days' sales in receivables	18.40	30.91	67.98
Doubtful accounts ratio	0.0800	0.0556	−30.56
Days' sales in inventory	80.00	80.00	0.00
Debt/equity ratio	0.40	0.49	21.93
Operations Ratios			
Receivables turnover	19.57	11.65	−40.47
Inventory turnover	4.50	4.50	0.00
Cost of goods sold/sales	75.00%	72.73%	−3.03
Gross margin percentage	25.00%	27.27%	9.09
Return on beginning equity	6.62%	12.76%	92.80
Financial Distress Ratios (Altman, 1968, Appendix 5A)			
Working capital/total assets	0.49	0.30	−38.89
Retained earnings/total assets	0.22	0.26	17.20
EBIT/total assets	0.09	0.14	54.87
Market value of equity/total debt	2.59	1.89	−27.04
Net sales/total assets	2.22	2.04	−7.92
Discriminant Z score	4.96	4.35	−12.32

Comparing reported financial results with internal budgets and forecasts also can be useful. If the budget or forecast represents management's estimate of probable future outcomes, planning questions can arise for items that fall short of or exceed the budget. If a company expected to sell 10,000 units of a product but sold only 5,000 units, the auditors would want to plan a careful lower-of-cost-or-market study of the inventory of unsold units. If 15,000 were sold, an auditor would want to audit for sales validity. Budget comparisons can be tricky, however. Some companies use budgets and forecasts as goals, rather than as expressions of probable outcomes. Also, meeting the budget with little or no shortfall or excess can result from managers manipulating the numbers to "meet the budget." Auditors must be careful to know something about a company's business conditions from sources other than the internal records when analysing comparisons with budgets and forecasts.

Funds Flow Analysis

If the client has not already prepared the statement of changes in financial position, the auditors can use the comparative financial statements to prepare one. The analysis of changes in financial position enables the auditors to see the crucial information of funds flow from operating, investment, and financing activities. A funds flow deficit from operations may signal financial difficulty. Companies fail when they run out of cash (no surprise) and are unable to pay their debts when they become due.

You can use the information in Exhibit 5–1 to prepare a statement of changes in financial position (or, "cash flow statement" as per the August 1996 CICA Exposure Draft). This is an exercise in a technique you learned in earlier accounting courses.

Analytical Procedures Requirements

Even though particular analytical procedures are not required by audit standards, the timing of required application is specified in two instances. Analytical procedures applicable in the circumstances are required (1) at the beginning of an audit—the planning stage application of analytical procedures discussed in this chapter—and (2) at the end of an audit when the partners in charge review the overall quality of the work and look for apparent problems.

R E V I E W
CHECKPOINTS

5.5 What are the steps auditors can use to apply comparison and ratio analysis to unaudited financial statements?

5.6 What are some of the ratios that can be used in preliminary analytical procedures?

5.7 Is anything questionable about the relationship between retained earnings and income as shown in Exhibit 5–1?

PRELIMINARY ASSESSMENT OF PLANNING MATERIALITY

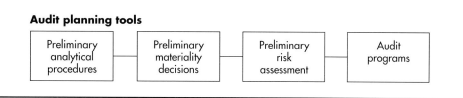

Audit planning tools

Preliminary analytical procedures → Preliminary materiality decisions → Preliminary risk assessment → Audit programs

LEARNING OBJECTIVE

2. Analyse a materiality determination case and decide upon a maximum amount of misstatement (planning materiality) acceptable in a company's financial statements.

When planning an audit, auditors should think about "planning materiality" as the largest amount of uncorrected dollar misstatement that could exist in published financial statements, yet they would still fairly present the company's financial position and results of operations in conformity with GAAP. Accounting firms, however, differ greatly on how to carry out this idea. Some believe in the "blunt instrument" approach to auditing—just beat the accounts to death for the evidence. Some of these auditors go to an engagement and start performing procedures without bothering with theoretical niceties of making preliminary materiality estimates. Some firms tell their staffs to "think about it, but don't try to put a number on it." Some firms guide their staffs with directions about how to use numbers to quantify a preliminary materiality amount.

Financial Statement Materiality

So what is materiality, and how can you deal with it? The concept of materiality pervades financial accounting and reporting in this context: Information is material and should be disclosed if it is likely to influence the economic decisions of financial statement users. The emphasis is on the users' point of view, not on accountants' and managers' points of view. Thus, material information is a synonym for important or significant information.

Financial statement measurements and information in some footnote disclosures are not perfectly accurate. However, you should not leap to the unwarranted conclusion that financial reports are inherently imprecise and inaccurate. Some numbers are not perfectly accurate because mistakes exist in them, and some are not perfectly accurate because they are based on estimates. Everyone acknowledges that people make mistakes—billing a customer the wrong amount, using the wrong prices to compile an inventory, making a mathematical mistake in an amortization calculation. Furthermore, many financial measurements are based on estimates; for example, the estimated depreciable lives of fixed assets or the estimated amount of uncollectible accounts receivable. However, this imprecise nature of accounting should not be taken as licence to be sloppy about clerical accuracy or negligent in accounting judgments (e.g., see box on next page).

Auditors are limited by the nature of accounting. Some amount of inaccuracy is permitted in financial statements because (1) unimportant inaccuracies do not affect users' decisions and hence are not material, (2) the cost of finding and correcting small errors is too great, and (3) the time taken to find them would delay issuance of financial statements. As a leading accountant once said, summing up materiality thought: "If it doesn't really matter, don't bother with it."[1] Accounting numbers are not perfectly accurate, but accountants and auditors want to maintain that financial reports are materially accurate and do not contain material misstatements.

Materiality Judgment Criteria

Many accountants wish that definitive, quantitative materiality guides could be issued, but many also fear the rigidity of such guides. The CICA offers some rules of thumb in its "Applying Materiality and Audit Risk Concepts in Conducting an Audit" Guideline (AUG–7):

1. 5–10% of income before taxes   [paragraph 6]
2. 1/2% to 1% of assets
3. 1/2% to 5% of equity   [paragraph 8]
4. 1/2% to 1% of revenue
5. 1/2% to 5% of gross profit

The CICA suggests that if income is used it should be adjusted for abnormal or extraordinary items. Also, if income is negative or close to zero a "normalized income based on some averaging could be used." But caution should be used in "normalizing" so that it is reasonable. If it is difficult to justify a normalized income if income is too small relative to other items, a different basis such as rules 2 to 5 should be used instead of rule 1. The rules of thumb can't just be applied mechanically as auditors must consider a number of factors in setting materiality. Some of the more common factors auditors use in making materiality judgments are these:

---

[1] Ernest L. Hicks, "Materiality," *Journal of Accounting Research*, Autumn 1964, p. 158.

AUDIT CONSIDERATIONS FOR ACCOUNTING ESTIMATES

An accounting estimate is an approximation of a financial statement number, and estimates are often included in financial statements. (See *Handbook Section* 5305.)

Examples include net realizable value of accounts receivable, market (lower than cost) of inventory, amortization expense, property and casualty insurance loss reserves, percentage-of-completion contract revenues, pension expense, and warranty liabilities.

Management is responsible for making accounting estimates. Auditors are responsible for determining that all appropriate estimates have been made, that they are reasonable, and that they are presented in conformity with GAAP and adequately disclosed.

Part of the audit process entails the auditors producing their own estimate and comparing it to management's estimate. Often, consideration of a range for an amount is involved. For example, management may estimate an allowance for doubtful accounts to be $50,000, and the auditors may estimate that the allowance could be $40,000 to $55,000. In this case management's estimate is within the auditors' range of reasonableness. However, the auditors should take note that the management estimate leans toward the conservative side (more than the auditors' $40,000 lower estimate, but not much less than the auditors' higher $55,000 estimate). If other estimates exhibit the same conservatism, and the effect is material, the auditors will need to evaluate the overall reasonableness of the effect of all estimates taken together.

If the auditors develop an estimate that differs (e.g., a range of $55,000 to $70,000 for the allowance that management estimated at $50,000), the preferred treatment is to consider the difference between management's estimate and the closest end of the auditors' range as an error (in this case, error = $5,000 = auditors' $55,000 minus management's $50,000). The remaining difference to the farthest end of the range ($15,000 = $70,000 − $55,000) is noted and reconsidered in combination with the findings on all management's estimates.

The best evidence of the reasonableness of estimates is the actual subsequent experience of the company with the financial amounts estimated at an earlier date. Keeping track of the accuracy of management's earlier estimates could provide the auditor with important information on the expected accuracy of future estimates.

Absolute Size

An amount of potential misstatement may be important regardless of any other considerations. Not many auditors use absolute size alone as a criterion because a given amount, say $50,000, may be appropriate in one case and too large or too small in another. Yet, some auditors have been known to say: "$1 million or some other large number is material, no matter what."

Relative Size

The relationship of potential misstatement to a relevant base number is often used. Potential misstatements in income statement accounts usually are related to net income either before or after taxes. If income fluctuates widely, a "normalized" or average income over recent years may be substituted for the current-year net income, or the relationship may be to the trend change of income. The base for nonprofit entities may be gross revenue or contributions or a figure important in the statement of changes in financial position. Potential misstatements in balance sheet accounts may be related to a subtotal number, such as current assets or net working capital. Some auditors prefer the total gross margin as a uniform base because it is less subject to year-to-year fluctuations than the net income number.

Nature of the Item or Issue

An important qualitative factor is the descriptive nature of the item or issue. An illegal payment is important primarily because of its nature as well as because of its absolute or relative amount. A misstatement in segment information may be small in relation to the total business but important for analysis of the segment. Generally, potential errors in the more liquid assets (cash, receivables, and inventory) are considered more important than potential errors in other accounts (such as capital assets and deferred charges).

Circumstances

Auditors generally place extra emphasis on lesser permitted misstatement in financial statements that will be widely used (publicly held companies) or used by important outsiders (bank loan officers). Auditors' liability is a relevant consideration. When management can exercise discretion over an accounting treatment, auditors tend to exercise more care and use a more stringent materiality criterion. Troublesome political events in foreign countries also can cause auditors to try to be more accurate with measurements and disclosures. However, these matters relate as much to risks as they do to financial statement materiality.

Cumulative Effects

Auditors must evaluate the sum of known or potential misstatements. Considering five different $15,000 mistakes that all increase net income as immaterial is inappropriate when the net income–based materiality limit is $50,000.

MATERIALITY ALLOCATION VERSUS NONALLOCATION

· · · · · · · · · · · ·

LEARNING OBJECTIVE

3. Assign an overall planning materiality amount to the tolerable misstatement amounts for particular accounts.

To plan the audit of various accounts, some auditors assign part of the planning materiality to each account. The amount assigned to an account is called the **tolerable misstatement** for that account. The tolerable misstatement is the amount by which a particular account may be misstated (error not discovered by auditors!), yet still not cause the financial statements taken as a whole to be materially misleading. Thus, tolerable misstatement for each account is based on the overall financial statement materiality.

The extent to which tolerable misstatement is "based on" the overall materiality amount may vary from auditor to auditor. One method assigns tolerable misstatement amounts that add up to twice the overall materiality. The theory is that actual financial

A POSSIBLE RELATIVE SIZE MATERIALITY DETERMINATION ILLUSTRATED

Suppose the auditors take the influence of earnings per share (EPS) on share price as an important consideration in determining materiality. For illustrative purposes, suppose the model for share price determination is a simple EPS multiple. (This is not to suggest that share prices actually are determined by such a simple method as multiplying the EPS in all cases. Analysts and investors use many other valuation models beyond the scope of this illustration.)

Assume that Anycompany, Inc., whose financial statements are in Exhibit 5–1, has 100,000 shares outstanding and its shares trade at a 14 price-earning multiple, thus indicating a share price of $51.80. (Share price = EPS ($3.70 = $370,000/ 100,000) *14 = $51.80.) The auditors must make a judgment about how much investors could overpay for the shares, yet it would not make any difference to them, say 5 percent to 10 percent.

	Low (5%)	High (10%)
Indicated share price (14 × $3.70)	$ 51.80	$ 51.80
Price materiality judgment	2.59	5.18
Adjusted share price	49.21	46.62
Adjusted earnings per share (divide by 14 multiple)	3.52	3.33
Indicated net income (multiply by 100,000 shares)	352,000	333,000
Add pretax accounts that can be audited completely:		
Interest expense	40,000	40,000
Income tax expense (40%)	234,667	222,000
Indicated pretax income*	626,667	595,000
Unaudited pretax income	666,000	666,000
Indicated planning materiality based on pretax income	39,333	71,000

*Calculate the pretax income, which, when reduced by interest expense and 40 percent income taxes, produces the indicated net income (after-tax).

misstatements in accounts can be both overstatements and understatements, and the two directions will tend to balance out. Another is to assign tolerable misstatement in amounts such that the square root of the sum of the squared tolerable misstatements is equal to the overall materiality. The theory here is that the different misstatements behave like random errors in a calculation of statistical variance. Another method is to assign tolerable misstatement amounts that exactly add up to materiality. This method assumes that the worst case is that all the errors in the account balances have the same directional effect on income (i.e., overstatement of understatement, but not some of both). All these approaches are examples of materiality allocation. The simplest approach, however, is to not allocate but to use the same overall materiality level for the entire audit. This approach also results in the least testing and is implied by the *CICA Handbook*. This simplest approach is the one used in this textbook. Thus, tolerable misstatements will be set equal to overall materiality, and there is no difference between accounting and auditing materiality.[2] These issues are covered in more detail in Chapter 20.

Consider a materiality judgment for the current-year financial information of Anycompany, Inc., shown in Exhibit 5–1. The judgment involves centring attention on the most important financial decisions that may be related to the use of the financial statements. This centre of attention can be different for different audits. In some cases the centre of attention may be the current asset-liability position of a company in financial difficulty seeking to renew its bank loans. Such a company may be experiencing operating losses, and the balance sheet, rather than the income statement, is of utmost importance. In other cases the income statement and the net income number may be the most important because the company is growing and issuing shares to the public, so that decisions based on income performance are of greatest importance. The illustration boxed earlier (Relative Size Materiality Determination Illustrated) shows a calculation of overall materiality based on an assumed effect of income misstatement on the share price. If the auditors decide the shares could be mispriced by 10 percent, and nobody would care, then the income before taxes and interest could be overstated (or understated) by as much as $71,000.

While the overall materiality assessment may frequently start with an expression of materiality for an income statement number, the materiality is audited in relation to one or more balance sheet accounts. The reason for this phenomenon is that income misstatements in the double-entry bookkeeping system leave a "dangling debit" or a "dangling credit" loose somewhere in the balance sheet accounts, and the audit challenge is to find it. If there is no dangling debit or credit, then the other side of the misstatement transaction has gone through the income statement, probably causing misstatement in two accounts (opposite directions), with no net effect on the net income bottom line. (For example, if fictitious credit sales were recorded, and the fictitious accounts receivable were written off as bad debt expense, both the revenue and expense would be overstated but the income would not be misstated.)

Even though we will not use materiality allocation in this text, readers should remember the term "tolerable misstatement." Tolerable misstatement is the part of the overall materiality number assigned to an account. Since here we do not assign overall materiality, tolerable misstatement is synonymous with overall materiality. The word "tolerable" is also frequently associated with the level of control deviations that is presumed to lead to material misstatements. Tolerable in this context is discussed in more detail in Chapter 7.

Materiality and Planning

The major reason for thinking about materiality at the planning stage is to try to fine-tune the audit for effectiveness and efficiency. Thinking about it in advance helps to avoid surprises. Suppose that near the end of an audit the partner decided that individual and aggregate misstatements over $40,000 should be considered material, but then realized that the nature, timing, and extent of audit procedures resulted in an acceptable assurance for errors only below $70,000. More work should be done, and now it is very late to do it. Conversely, an audit team might **overaudit**—perform

---

[2] Depending on factors used in setting overall materiality, there may be secondary materiality levels (less than overall materiality) necessary to satisfy the requirements of certain specific users (for example, a bank that has negotiated loan covenants as part of the loan agreement). In these situations a secondary materiality level(s) may apply to some restricted accounts (e.g., current assets) but overall materiality to all the rest. See D. Leslie's *Materiality, The Concept and Its Application to Auditing*, CICA, 1985, Chapter 2.

more audit work than is necessary, thinking in terms of detecting $70,000 in total misstatement, when accuracy to the nearest $100,000 is satisfactory.

The concept of materiality is used by auditors in three ways: (1) as a guide to planning the audit program—directing attention and audit work to the important, uncertain, or material error-prone items and accounts; (2) as a guide to evaluation of the evidence; and (3) as a guide for making decisions about the audit report. An important point is that materiality in auditing is perceived in terms of both potential misstatement (in a planning sense) and known or estimated misstatement (in an evaluation and reporting decision sense). An account, such as inventory, is not necessarily material in an audit context because of its size or its place in the financial statements. The importance derives from the potential for, and effect of, misstatements that might exist in the account. The preliminary analytical procedures should give the auditors some insights about where potential misstatements lie. Chapter 20 discusses the role of materiality in evaluating the results of audit tests on different accounts.

R E V I E W
C H E C K P O I N T S

5.8   What is "material information" in accounting and auditing? What is "planning materiality" in an audit context?

5.9   Do auditing standards require auditors to express planning materiality as a specific dollar amount?

5.10   What do you think is the best objective evidence of the reasonableness of an accounting estimate? Use the allowance for doubtful accounts receivable as an example.

5.11   What benefits are claimed for auditors' preliminary assessment of materiality as a matter of audit planning? Is $500,000 a material amount of misstatements to leave uncorrected in financial statements?

PRELIMINARY ASSESSMENT OF AUDIT RISKS

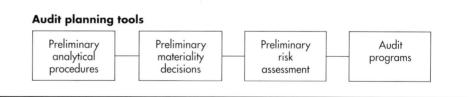

Audit planning tools

Preliminary analytical procedures	Preliminary materiality decisions	Preliminary risk assessment	Audit programs

LEARNING OBJECTIVE

4. Describe the conceptual audit risk model and explain the meaning and importance of its components in terms of professional judgment and audit planning.

Knowledge of the client's business from preliminary analytical procedures can help auditors identify problem areas and make overall risk assessments. However, some more specific risks also need to be assessed. These are known as inherent risk, control risk, detection risk, and audit risk. Since several adjectives are used to describe these risks, you should not speak of "risk" without a modifier (*inherent, control,* and so on) to specify the one you mean. Audit risk is a function of inherent risk, control risk, and detection risk. Audit risk is related to information risk (discussed in Chapter 1) associated with the financial statements. We discuss audit risk in more detail after first considering each of its components.

Inherent Risk

Inherent risk is the probability that material misstatements have occurred, regardless of the existence of internal control, in transactions entering the accounting system used to develop financial statements, or that material misstatements have occurred in an account balance (*Section* 5130.11, and Audit Guideline "Applying Materiality and Audit Risk Concepts in Conducting an Audit"). Put another way, inherent risk is the risk of material misstatements occurring in the first place. Inherent risk is a characteristic of the client's business, the major types of transactions, and the effectiveness of its accountants. Auditors do not create or control inherent risk. They can only try to assess its magnitude.

An assessment of inherent risk can be based on a variety of information. Auditors may know that material misstatements were discovered during the last year's audit, so inherent risk will be considered higher than it would be if last year's audit had shown no material misstatements. Auditors may believe the client's accounting clerks tend to misunderstand GAAP and the company's own accounting policies, thus suggesting a significant probability of mistakes in transaction processing. The nature of the client's business may produce complicated transactions and calculations generally known to be subject to data processing and accounting treatment error. (For example, real estate, franchising, and oil and gas transactions are frequently complicated and subject to accounting error. Some kinds of inventories are harder than others to count, value, and keep accurately in perpetual records.)

The concept of relative risk is closely related to inherent risk. In audit practice, relative risk refers to conditions of more or less inherent risk. Some accounts (e.g., cash and inventory) are more susceptible to embezzlement, theft, or other loss than are other accounts (e.g., land or prepaid expenses). The important relationship you should understand is that audit care and attention should be greater where relative risk and inherent risk are judged to be higher.

Auditor experience has shown that due to management optimism and bias, asset and income accounts tend to have a higher inherent risk of overstatement than understatement; and that liability accounts have a higher inherent risk of understatement than overstatement. Due to these predilections and biases, audit procedures that are more effective in detecting overstatements, such as vouching, are more widely used with asset and income accounts. At the same time, audit procedures that are more effective in detecting understatements, such as tracing subsequent payments, are more likely to be used with liability accounts. Thus, the inherent and relative risks determine the importance of various procedures for different accounts.

Control Risk

Control risk is the risk that the client's internal control will not prevent or detect a material misstatement. More specifically, control risk is the probability that the client's internal control policies and procedures will fail to detect or prevent material misstatements, provided any enter the accounting system in the first place (*Section* 5130.11, and Audit Guideline "Applying Materiality and Audit Risk Concepts in Conducting an Audit"). Auditors do not create or control the control risk. They can only evaluate a company's control system and assess the probability of failure to

INHERENT RISK ARISING FROM ECONOMIC CONDITIONS

Economic conditions have improved in 1994 and should continue to do so in 1995. Businesses are experiencing increased levels of exports, improved profitability from cost reduction activities, consumer spending increases, and a recovery in the manufacturing sector.

While this environment eliminates some of the concerns entities faced during the depths of the recession, auditors should be aware of the following factors when assessing the risk of material misstatement in an entity's financial statements.

- Increased exporting may lead to increased foreign exchange exposure with related unrecorded foreign exchange liabilities. Management may have more difficulty collecting accounts receivable arising from foreign as compared to domestic sales and fail to make adequate provision for doubtful accounts.
- Productivity improvement and cost reduction activities may have eroded the segregation of duties and increased staff workloads, bringing a drop in the attention paid to internal controls. Management's operating style, its control methods, and an entity's organization structure are three important control environment factors. Re-engineering an entity's operations may adversely affect each of these control factors.
- Lenders have become much more selective in the entities they finance, and debt covenants are more restrictive than before. This may make it more difficult for entities to finance their debt loads and expansion plans.
- Entities are introducing new technology to improve the quality of their products and reduce the costs of production. Technological obsolescence is accelerating and can affect the carrying values of productive assets, inventories, and other assets.
- Some sectors of the economy are recovering more slowly than others. Entities may continue to experience adverse operating results and find themselves in financial difficulty. In addition, many commercial and industrial buildings still have high vacancy rates and depressed selling prices. Such capital assets should be written down when the long-term expectation is that the net carrying amount will not be recovered.

Source: CICA, *Audit Risk Alert*—December 1994.

detect material misstatements. An auditor's assessment of control risk is based on the study and evaluation of the company's control system. You will study this process in detail in Chapter 6.

Inherent risk is difficult to evaluate, and sometimes its assessment can be combined with the evaluation of control risk. The problems arise from the fact that internal controls "work" only when errors, irregularities, and other misstatements occur. Exhibit 5–3 shows the combinations of original errors and control effectiveness, or lack thereof.

Control effectiveness conclusions and risk assessments may be made on a preliminary basis for planning purposes. Auditors often carry over preconceived notions

EXHIBIT 5–3   INTERNAL CONTROL CONDITIONS AND CONCLUSIONS

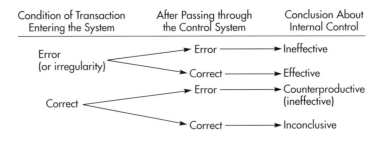

Source: Adapted from L. E. Graham, "Audit Risk-Part III," *CPA Journal*, October 1985, p. 39.

about control risk when they perform the audit on a client year after year. This carryover is known as **anchoring** the control risk assessment (starting with knowledge of last year's conclusions), and it represents (1) a useful continuity of experience with a particular client and (2) a potential pitfall if conditions change for the worse and the auditor fails to acknowledge the deterioration of control.

Control risk should not be assessed so low that auditors place complete reliance on controls and do not perform any other audit work.

Detection Risk

Detection risk is the risk that any material misstatement that has not been corrected by the client's internal control will not be detected by the auditor (*Handbook Section* 5130.10, and Audit Guideline "Applying Materiality and Audit Risk Concepts in Conducting an Audit"). In contrast to inherent risk and control risk, auditors are responsible for performing the evidence-gathering procedures that manage and control detection risk. These audit procedures represent the auditors' opportunity to detect material misstatements that can cause financial statements to be misleading.

In subsequent chapters you will study substantive procedures. These are the procedures used to detect material misstatements in dollar amounts and disclosures presented in the financial statements and footnotes. The two categories of substantive procedures are (1) audit of the details of transactions and balances and (2) analytical procedures applied to produce circumstantial evidence about dollar amounts in the accounts. Detection risk is realized when procedures in these two categories fail to detect material misstatements.

Audit Risk

In an overall sense, audit risk is the probability that an auditor will fail to express a reservation that financial statements are materially misstated. The profession assumes audit risk can at best be controlled at a low level, not eliminated, even when audits are well planned and carefully performed. The risk is much greater in poorly planned and carelessly performed audits. The relationship between audit risk and business risk was discussed in Appendix 1B. Planned audit risk may vary depending on client circumstances. Generally, the more risky the client or the more that users rely on the audited financial statements, the lower the planned audit risk. As the risk of being sued for material misstatement goes up, the planned audit risk goes down to compensate for the increased risk associated with the engagement. Many accounting firms have developed internal guidelines for setting planned levels of audit risk.

The auditing profession has no hard standard for an acceptable level of overall audit risk, except that it should be "appropriately low" and involve the exercise of professional judgment. In quantitative terms "most auditors would strive to limit such risks to no more than 5 percent" (CICA Guideline AUG-7, "Applying Materiality and Audit Risk Concepts in Conducting an Audit," paragraph 16). However, auditors would be appalled to think that even 1 percent of their audits would be bad. For a large firm with 2,000 audit clients, 1 percent would mean 20 bad audits per year! But on the other hand, not all audits have material misstatements, so using 5 percent planned audit risk on *every* engagement may lead to a much lower level of bad audits. For example, if the risk of material misstatement is 5 percent, then with 5 percent audit risk the number of bad audits would be $.05 \times .05 = .0025 = 1/4\%$.

The concept of audit risk also applies to individual account balances and disclosures. Here the risk is that material misstatement is not discovered in an account (e.g., the inventory total) or in a disclosure (e.g., a pension plan footnote explanation). Audit risk is most often utilized in practice with regard to individual balances and disclosures. You should keep this context in mind when you study the risk model summary presented next. Audit risk of 0.05 at the account level, used by many CA firms, is presented as an illustrative audit risk.

Risk Model—A Summary

The foregoing concepts of audit risks can be expressed in a model that assumes the elements of audit risk are independent. Thus, the risks are multiplied as follows:

$$\text{Audit risk (AR)} = \text{Inherent risk (IR)} \times \text{Control risk (CR)} \times \text{Detection risk (DR)}$$

Auditors want to perform an audit of a particular balance or disclosure well enough to hold the audit risk (AR) to a relatively low level (e.g., 0.05, which means that on average 5 percent of audit decisions when there is a material misstatement will be wrong). As such, AR is a quality criterion based on professional judgment. All the other risk assessments are estimates based on professional judgment and evidence.

For example, suppose an auditor thought a particular inventory balance was subject to great inherent risk of material misstatement (say, IR = 0.90) and that the client's internal control was not very effective (say, CR = 0.70). If he or she wanted to control audit risk at a low level (say, AR = 0.05), the other procedures would need to be designed so that detection risk (DR) did not exceed 0.08 (approximately). According to the model, this example would produce the following results:

$$AR = IR \times CR \times DR$$

$$0.05 = 0.90 \times 0.70 \times DR$$

$$\text{Solving for DR: DR} = 0.08$$

The practical problem here is knowing whether the audit has been planned and performed well enough to hold the detection risk as low as 0.08. Despite the simplicity of the risk model, it is only a conceptual tool. Auditors have few ways to calculate detection risk, so the model represents more of a way to think about audit risks than a way to calculate them. However, several accounting firms use this model to calculate risks and the related sample sizes.

The model produces some insights, including these:

1. Auditors cannot rely entirely on an estimate of zero inherent risk to the exclusion of other evidence-gathering procedures. Thus, you cannot have the condition:

$$AR = IR \ (=0) \times CR \times DR = 0$$

2. Auditors cannot place complete reliance on internal control to the exclusion of other audit procedures. Thus, you cannot have the condition:

$$AR = IR \times CR \ (=0) \times DR = 0$$

3. Audits would not seem to exhibit due audit care if the risk of failure to detect material misstatements were too high, for example:

$$AR = IR \ (=0.80) \times CR \ (=0.80) \times DR \ (=0.50) = 0.32$$

4. Auditors can choose to rely almost exclusively on evidence produced by substantive procedures, even if they think inherent risk and control risk are high. For example, this combination is acceptable (provided AR = 0.05 is acceptable):

$$AR = IR \ (=1.00) \times CR \ (=1.00) \times DR \ (=0.05) = 0.05$$

R E V I E W
C H E C K P O I N T S

5.12 What are the four audit risks an auditor must consider? What does each involve?

5.13 What is anchoring with regard to auditors' judgments about the quality or effectiveness of internal control?

5.14 What are some of the effects of bad economic times that produce risks that auditors should be alert to detect in clients' financial statements?

5.15 What is the difference between "audit risk in an overall sense" and "audit risk applied to individual account balances?"

PLANNING MEMORANDUM

Auditors usually prepare a **planning memorandum** summarizing the preliminary analytical review and the materiality assessment with specific directions about the effect on the audit. This planning memo also usually includes information about (1) investigation or review of the prospective or continuing client relationship, (2) needs for special technical or industry expertise, (3) staff assignment and timing schedules, (4) the assessed level of control risk, (5) significant industry or company risks, (6) computer system control environment, (7) utilization of the company's internal auditors, (8) identification of unusual accounting principles problems, and (9) schedules of work periods, meeting dates with client personnel, and completion dates. The memo summarizes all the important overall planning information.

All the planning becomes a basis for preparing the audit program. An **audit program** is a specification of procedures that auditors use to guide the work of inherent and control risk assessment and to obtain sufficient competent evidence that serves as a basis for the audit report.

AUDIT PROGRAMS

· · · · · · · · · · · ·

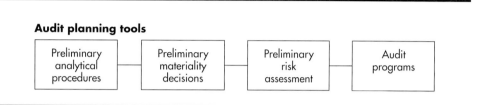

Audit planning tools

| Preliminary analytical procedures | → | Preliminary materiality decisions | → | Preliminary risk assessment | → | Audit programs |

LEARNING OBJECTIVE

5. Describe the content and purpose of audit programs.

Auditors use two kinds of audit programs, each with a different objective. One contains the specification of procedures for obtaining an understanding of the client's business and management's control system, and for assessing the inherent risk and the control risk related to the financial account balances. For identification purposes we will call this program the "internal control program." The other contains the specification of substantive procedures for gathering direct evidence on the assertions (i.e., existence, completeness, valuation, rights and obligations, presentation, and disclosure) about dollar amounts in the account balances. For identification, we will call this one the "balance-audit program."

These audit programs combine all the considerations of audit planning heretofore discussed in Chapter 4 and Chapter 5, including:

- Understanding the client's business and industry.
- Assertions and objectives embodied in the client's financial statements.
- Persuasive strengths of evidence.
- General procedures for obtaining evidence, expressed as specific procedures and directives.
- Preliminary analytical procedures for identifying specific risk areas in the unaudited financial statements.
- Preliminary materiality decisions and tolerable misstatement assignments.
- Preliminary risk assessments.

In actual field situations these audit programs are very lengthy. Special program documents may contain separate listings of procedures and questionnaires on the company's internal control environment, internal control procedures, management control, and computer control. The audit programs contain numerous detailed specifications of procedures the auditors intend to perform as the work progresses. The two boxes below abstract elements of audit programs for illustrative purposes. They put in perspective the sequence of topics you have read about in Chapter 4 and Chapter 5.

The technical parts of internal control risk assessment programs are too detailed to cover at this stage. They are explained more fully in subsequent chapters.

INTERNAL CONTROL PROGRAM

Understand the Business, Inherent Risk, Control Risk

- Communicate with predecessor auditors.
- Study prior-year audit working papers, CICA and AICPA audit and accounting guides, and industry publications concerning the company and its industry.
- Interview management with regard to business and accounting policies.
- Evaluate the competence and independence of the company's internal auditors.
- Determine the need for specialists on the engagement.
- Determine the extent of significant computer applications in the company's accounting system.
- Obtain the financial statements and make decisions about the planning materiality appropriate in the circumstances.
- Perform preliminary analytical procedures to identify risk areas in the financial statement accounts.
- Assess the inherent risk in general and with respect to particular accounts.

****

- Obtain an understanding of the company's internal control through interviews, observations, and tests of controls (more on this topic in Chapter 6).
- Perform detail test of control procedures, if necessary (more on this topic in Chapters 6 and 7, and Chapter 20 for more advanced issues).
- Assess the control risk (more on this topic in Chapters 6 and 7, and Chapter 20 for more advanced issues).
- Use the control risk assessment to design the nature, timing, and extent of substantive audit procedures (more on this topic in Chapters 6 and 7, and 20 for advanced issues).

The balance-audit program consists of several programs, each applicable to a particular account. Auditors first subdivide the financial statements into cycles (as explained in Chapter 4), then turn attention to the accounts in each cycle. The procedures in these audit programs are designed to obtain evidence about the existence or occurrence, completeness, valuation, rights and obligations, and presentation and disclosure assertions implicit in each account title and balance. The box below contains brief specifications of procedures for auditing accounts receivable. You can see in them the elements of the general techniques (e.g., confirmation, computation, enquiry, inspection, and the assertions toward which they are directed). This type of audit program is presented later in more detail in Chapter 7.

An illustration of a partial program in the revenue and collection cycle is given in the box below.

These audit procedures are intended to enable auditors to conduct the work in accordance with the three CICA examination standards concerning planning and supervision of the audit, obtaining an understanding of the control structure, and obtaining sufficient competent evidence to serve as a basis for the audit report. The

---

BALANCE SHEET AUDIT PROGRAM IN REVENUE AND COLLECTION CYCLE

Accounts Receivable

- Prepare and send confirmations on a sample of customers' accounts receivable. Analyse the returns.
- Obtain an aged trial balance of the receivables. Calculate and analyse the age status of the accounts and the allowance for uncollectible accounts.
- Interview the credit manager concerning the past-due accounts. Obtain credit reports and financial statements for independent analysis of overdue accounts.
- Vouch receivables balances to cash payments received after the confirmation date.
- Read loan agreements and make note of any pledge of receivables, sales with recourse, or other restrictions or contingencies related to the receivables.
- Read sales contracts for evidence of customers' rights of return or price allowance terms.
- Obtain written representations from the client concerning pledges for collateral, related party receivables, collectibility, and other matters related to accounts receivable.

---

exact specification of the procedures, the arrangement for their timing (i.e., when they are performed), and the determination of their extent (i.e., the sample sizes of data examined, such as the number of customer accounts receivable to confirm) all depend upon the activities, concepts, and tools of audit planning.

· ·

R E V I E W
C H E C K P O I N T S

5.16 Two kinds of audit programs have been identified. What are they? What is the objective of each?

5.17 What is meant by the terms nature, timing, and extent of audit procedures?

· ·

SUMMARY
· ·

The several topics under the heading of "audit planning" started in Chapter 4 with pre-engagement activities, understanding the client's business and industry, and obtaining the financial statements and organizing the accounts into cycles for efficient audit work. Chapter 4 also introduced the basic concepts of management assertions and audit objectives, qualities of evidence, general types of audit procedures, and audit working papers. The concepts are part of the theoretical foundation for performing audits.

Chapter 5 continued the series of audit planning topics by explaining several technical tools of planning. These tools are part of the nitty-gritty of audit work. They start with preliminary analytical procedures applied to the client's unaudited financial statements. The analytical process includes getting the financial data, calculating common-size and comparative financial statements, calculating ratios, describing the company's financial activities, and asking relevant questions. This analysis enables auditors to look for problem areas and signs of potential misstatement in the financial statements. Detecting signs of problems enables the auditors to plan procedures for the audit program to follow up and to determine whether misstatements, errors, irregularities, or frauds have affected the fair presentation of the financial balances.

The technical planning tools include auditors' determination of materiality with relation to the financial statements taken as a whole. Materiality in this sense is defined as the largest amount of uncorrected dollar misstatement that could exist in published financial statements, yet the statements would still fairly present the company's financial position and results of operations in conformity with GAAP. A method of calculating materiality based on judgments about acceptable misstatement was presented to connect income misstatement to earnings-per-share misstatements and an effect on share prices.

Risk assessment is the common language of auditing. The audit risk model was explained, and its elements of inherent risk, control risk, detection risk, and audit risk were defined. Implications of the risk model were explored in relation to limits on the risks permitted in practical applications.

The closing topic was a brief preview of audit programs. Programs were categorized as "internal control programs" and "balance-audit programs." The illustrations were not complete programs for conducting any particular audit, but they showed the general nature and content of audit programs.

Now the stage is set to take up a more detailed explanation of the theory and process of auditing internal control. The next chapter deals with the task of control risk assessment.

CASE STUDY   # KINGSTON COMPANY

The Kingston Company's business and organization was described at the end of Chapter 4. The case study continues here with assignments on the application of preliminary analytical procedures and the preliminary materiality determination. To recapitulate the information you have about the company:

- Business and organization description at the end of Chapter 4.
- Comparative trial balance of prior year (1991) audited financial balances and current year (1992) unaudited balances in Exhibit 4.23–1.
- Current year (1992) financial statements in Exhibit 4–2.
- Prior-year financial statements prepared in response to case assignment 4.23.

5.18 Kingston Company Minutes of Meetings of the Board of Directors: Attention-directing Review of Corporate Minutes. The board of directors met twice during the period under audit, January 1 through December 31 of the current year, and once in

January the next year before the audit was completed. Condensed minutes of the meetings are given below.

Meeting Held June 15, 1992

Larry Lancaster, chairman of the board, presided over the first meeting of the year, beginning at 3 P.M. All members were present:

Larry Lancaster	Archie Goodwin
Josephine Mandeville*	Fritz Brenner*
Ivan Gorr	Theodore Horstmann*
Harry Baker	Julie Grace

*Members of the audit committee.

The minutes of the December 15 meeting were reviewed and approved.

Reporting on the annual meeting of shareholders, Mr. Lancaster welcomed the newly elected board members: Josephine C. Mandeville, president of Connelly Foundation and director of Crown Cork & Seal Company; Ivan W. Gorr, CEO and director of Cooper Tire & Rubber; and Harry R. Baker, president of Marathon Electric Manufacturing Corporation and director of Wausau Paper Mills Company.

Ms. Grace presented the forecast for the year, attached herein as Exhibit 5.19–1. Sales are expected to increase 10 percent to $9,900,000, with costs of goods sold and general expenses bearing about the same relationships as experienced last year.

Mr. Brenner moved a declaration of dividends for the year ended the previous December 31. The motion died for lack of a second.

Mr. Lancaster moved and Ms. Grace seconded the approval of the officers' bonuses for the year just ended December 31. Approved by a 5–3 vote.

President, Larry Lancaster	$20,000
VP Marketing, Fred Durkin	5,000
VP Finance, Julie Grace	5,000
VP Information Systems, Lillie Rowan	5,000
VP Operations, Saul Panzer	5,000
VP Production, King Stout	5,000

Ms. Grace moved, and Mr. Lancaster seconded, officers' salary increases of 12 percent for 1992. The board approved these salaries unanimously:

President, Larry Lancaster	$127,000
VP Marketing, Fred Durkin	99,000
VP Finance, Julie Grace	97,000
VP Information Systems, Lillie Rowan	84,000
VP Operations, Saul Panzer	76,000
VP Production, King Stout	75,000
Internal Audit Director, Jonathan Roberts	70,000
Treasurer, Mila Davila	82,000
Controller, Sandra Carboy	80,000

Meeting ended 4:30 P.M.   /s/ Archie Goodwin, Secretary

Meeting Held June 15, 1992

Larry Lancaster, chairman of the board, presided over the special called meeting, beginning at 3:30 P.M. All members were present:

Larry Lancaster	Archie Goodwin
Josephine Mandeville*	Fritz Brenner*
Ivan Gorr	Theodore Horstmann*
Harry Baker	Julie Grace

*Members of the audit committee.

The minutes of the February 1 meeting were reviewed and approved.

Plans to move certain facilities from rented buildings into new office and retail space were approved. Contracts were signed to (1) acquire land for $95,000 and clear the area for $5,000; (2) authorize AllMetal Builders to build the new buildings for $285,000 on a turnkey contract; (3) purchase new equipment for $600,000, installed; and (4) overhaul old equipment moved to the new location.

Financing arrangements for a $750,000 loan to be drawn July 1, 1992, at 11 percent interest payable each June 30, were approved. The new building and equipment are to be pledged as collateral.

Ms. Grace reported that sales revenue was down because of the moving plans, and her proposal to make a personal loan to the company at zero interest was approved. Ms. Grace will loan $25,000 July 15 from funds obtained by a loan on her company-paid life insurance policy. The directors agreed to repay the loan on December 1, this year.

Meeting ended 7:30 P.M.   /s/ Archie Goodwin, Secretary

Meeting Held January 22, 1993

Larry Lancaster, chairman of the board, presided over the regular meeting, beginning at 2 P.M. All members were present:

Larry Lancaster	Archie Goodwin
Josephine Mandeville*	Fritz Brenner*
Ivan Gorr	Theodore Horstmann*
Harry Baker	Julie Grace

*Members of the audit committee.

The minutes of the June 15 meeting were reviewed and approved.

The selection by the audit committee of Anderson, Olds & Watershed as auditors was ratified.

Saul Panzer and King Stout presented a proposal for building and marketing custom privies, a novelty item for outdoor conversation gatherings. Since a similar plan to build and market custom gazebos had not been successful, the board tabled the proposal for the time being.

Sandra Carboy reported that appeals of the Revenue Canada tax assessment covering the past three years had reached the final stage. Outside counsel, Perley Stebbins, gave his opinion that Revenue Canada might ultimately win, but the recovery would be small. The company still has substantial defences yet untried.

Mr. Lancaster moved, and Ms. Grace seconded, the approval of officers' bonuses for 1992. The motion was defeated by a 6–2 vote.

Ms. Mandeville moved, and Mr. Gorr seconded, a proposal to retroactively declare a cash dividend of $50,000 payable February 15 to shareholders of record the past December 31. Approved by a vote of 6–2.

Ms. Grace was authorized to deposit $100,000 in escrow pending completion of negotiations to purchase and merge the Willie's Woods lumber business in suburbia.

Meeting ended at 8 P.M.   /s/ Archie Goodwin, Secretary

Required:

Study these minutes. Make notes in the form below for the audit working papers of matters relevant for the audit of the 1992 financial statements. Pretend you are reading the minutes of the first two meetings at the time the interim audit work just got started in October, and the minutes of the third meeting at the time of final audit work when the audit is nearing completion. Prepare a working paper with proper headings and these two columns:

Information Relevant to 1992 Audit   Audit Action Recommended

5.19   Kingston Company Preliminary Analytical Procedures.   Perform preliminary analytical procedures analysis on the financial statements using the data in Exhibits 5.19–1 and 5.19–2.

E X H I B I T 5.19–1   KINGSTON COMPANY FORECAST AND CURRENT YEAR UNAUDITED
FINANCIAL STATEMENTS

	Forecast Current Year	Current Year (unaudited)
Assets		
Cash	$ 713,200	$ 484,000
Accounts receivable	550,000	400,000
Allow doubtful accounts	(44,000)	(30,000)
Inventory	1,650,000	1,940,000
Total current assets	$2,869,200	$2,794,000
Equipment	3,000,000	4,000,000
Accumulated amortization	(1,800,000)	(1,800,000)
Total assets	$4,069,200	$4,994,000
Liabilities and Equity		
Accounts payable	$ 470,000	$ 600,000
Bank loans, 11%	0	750,000
Accrued expenses	70,000	50,000
Total current liabilities	540,000	1,400,000
Long-term debt, 10%	400,000	400,000
Total liabilities	940,000	1,800,000
Share stock	2,000,000	2,000,000
Retained earnings	1,129,200	1,194,000
Total liabilities and equity	$4,069,200	$4,994,000
Revenue and Expense		
Sales (net)	$9,900,000	$8,100,000
Cost of goods sold	6,930,000	5,265,000
Gross margin	2,970,000	2,835,000
General expense	2,248,000	2,005,000
Amortization	300,000	300,000
Operating income	422,000	530,000
Interest expense	40,000	40,000
Income taxes (40%)	152,800	196,000
Net income	$ 229,200	$ 294,000

EXHIBIT 5.19–2   KINGSTON COMPANY FINANCIAL STATEMENTS

	Prior Year (audited)	Current Year (unaudited)
Assets		
Cash	$ 600,000	$ 484,000
Accounts receivable	500,000	400,000
Allowance doubtful accounts	(40,000)	(30,000)
Inventory	1,500,000	1,940,000
Total current assets	2,560,000	2,794,000
Equipment	3,000,000	4,000,000
Accumulated amortization	(1,500,000)	(1,800,000)
Total assets	$4,060,000	$4,994,000
Liabilities and Equity		
Accounts payable	$ 450,000	$ 600,000
Bank loans, 11%	0	750,000
Accrued expenses	110,000	50,000
Total current liabilities	560,000	1,400,000
Long-term debt, 10%	600,000	400,000
Total liabilities	1,160,000	1,800,000
Share capital	2,000,000	2,000,000
Retained earnings	900,000	1,194,000
Total liabilities and equity	$4,060,000	$4,994,000
Revenue and Expense		
Sales (net)	$9,000,000	$8,100,000
Cost of goods sold	6,296,000	5,265,000
Gross margin	2,704,000	2,835,000
General expense	2,044,000	2,005,000
Amortization	300,000	300,000
Operating income	360,000	530,000
Interest expense	60,000	40,000
Income taxes (40%)	120,000	196,000
Net income	$ 180,000	$ 294,000

Required:

a. Calculate common-size financial statements and dollar amount and percent changes. (Hint: refer to Exhibit 5–1 in the chapter.)

b. Calculate selected financial ratios. Assume the market value of the common shares is $3 million in both the current and prior years. (Hint: Refer to Exhibit 5–2 in the chapter.)

c. Study the forecast prepared by Kingston for the current year (Exhibit 5.19–1). Does the comparison of the forecast to the current year unaudited statements suggest any potential problem areas? This assignment gives you some practice using the number 2 general analytical procedure discussed in the chapter: "Comparison of the current-year account balances to anticipated results found in the company's budgets and forecasts."

d. Write a brief memo addressed to the current working paper file pointing out potential problem areas.

5.20   Kingston Company Preliminary Materiality Assessment.   Auditors normally make a preliminary materiality assessment when the audit is planned—before the end of the company's year. Thus, auditors must use available interim financial information or make estimates of the full-year financial results. To make the materiality assessment problem less complex for now, you are to use the full-year financial information shown in the trial balance in Exhibit 4.23–1. For your convenience, these data are arranged in financial statement form in Exhibit 5.19–2.

Required:

a. Briefly describe independent auditors' concept of materiality.

b. What are some common relationships and other considerations used by auditors when assessing the dollar amount considered material?

c. Determine an amount you consider to be a minimum material misstatement, and allocate it to financial statement balances and audit areas. Write a memo addressed to the current working paper file justifying your decision. You should use some of the relationships and considerations you gave in answer to part (*b*) of this problem.

d. Assume Kingston company has 200,000 common shares outstanding. The market price is currently $15 per share, which represents a price-earnings multiple of about 10.2. If the auditors think the shares could be mispriced by $1.60 per share, based on a model of share price determined by a 10.2 price-earnings multiple, what dollar amount of misstatement (materiality) in the operating income before taxes and interest would be appropriate? Prepare a working paper showing your calculation.

Multiple-choice Questions for Practice and Review

5.21 Analytical procedures are generally used to produce evidence from:

a. Confirmations mailed directly to the auditors by client customers.

b. Physical observation of inventories.

c. Relationships among current financial balances and prior balances, forecasts, and nonfinancial data.

d. Detailed examination of external, external-internal, and internal documents.

5.22 Auditors perform analytical procedures in the planning stage of an audit for the purpose of:

a. Deciding the matters to cover in an engagement letter.

b. Identifying unusual conditions that deserve more auditing effort.

c. Determining which of the financial statement assertions are the most important for the client's financial statements.

d. Determining the nature, timing, and extent of audit procedures for auditing the inventory.

5.23 Which of the following match-ups of types of analytical procedures and sources of information makes the most sense?

Type of Analytical Procedure	Source of Information
a. Comparison of current account balances with prior-periods statistics	Physical production
b. Comparison of current account balances with expected balances	Company's budgets and forecasts
c. Evaluation of current account balances with relation to predictable historical patterns	Published industry ratios
d. Evaluation of current account balances in relation to nonfinancial information	Company's own comparative financial statements

5.24 Analytical procedures can be used in which of the following ways?

a. As a means of overall review at the end of an audit.

b. As "attention directing" methods when planning an audit at the beginning.

c. As substantive audit procedures to obtain evidence during an audit.

d. All of the above.

5.25 Analytical procedures used when planning an audit should concentrate on:

a. Weaknesses in the company's internal control procedures.

b. Predictability of account balances based on individual transactions.

c. Five major management assertions in financial statements.

d. Accounts and relationships that may represent specific potential problems and risks in the financial statements.

5.26 When a company that has $5 million current assets and $3 million current liabilities pays $1 million of its accounts payable, its current ratio will:
a. Increase.
b. Decrease.
c. Remain unchanged.

5.27 When a company that has $3 million current assets and $5 million current liabilities pays $1 million of its accounts payable, its current ratio will:
a. Increase.
b. Decrease.
c. Remain unchanged.

5.28 When a company that has $5 million current assets and $5 million current liabilities pays $1 million of its accounts payable, its current ratio will:
a. Increase.
b. Decrease.
c. Remain unchanged.

5.29 When a company that sells its products for a (gross) profit increases its sales by 15 percent and its cost of goods sold by 7 percent, the cost of goods sold ratio will:
a. Increase.
b. Decrease.
c. Remain unchanged.

5.30 Which of the following is not a benefit claimed for the practice of determining materiality in the initial planning stage of starting an audit?
a. Being able to fine-tune the audit work for effectiveness and efficiency.
b. Avoiding the problem of doing more work than necessary (overauditing).
c. Being able to decide early what kind of audit opinion to give.
d. Avoiding the problem of doing too little work (underauditing).

5.31 It is appropriate and acceptable under generally accepted auditing standards for an auditor to:
a. Assess both inherent and control risk at 100 percent and achieve an acceptably low audit risk by performing extensive detection work.

b. Assess control risk at zero and perform a minimum of detection work.
c. Assess inherent risk at zero and perform a minimum of detection work.
d. Decide that audit risk can be 40 percent.

5.32 Auditors are not responsible for accounting estimates with respect to:
a. Making the estimates.
b. Determining the reasonableness of estimates.
c. Determining that estimates are presented in conformity with GAAP.
d. Determining that estimates are adequately disclosed in the financial statements.

5.33 Tolerable misstatement in the context of audit planning means:
a. Amounts that should be disclosed if they are likely to influence the economic decisions of financial statement users.
b. The largest amount of uncorrected dollar misstatement that could exist in published financial statements, yet they would still fairly present the company's financial position and results of operations in conformity with GAAP.
c. Part of the overall materiality amount for the financial statements assigned to a particular account.
d. A dollar amount assigned to an account as required by auditing standards.

5.34 The risk that the auditors' own work will lead to the decision that material misstatements do not exist in the financial statements, when in fact such misstatements do exist, is:

a. Audit risk.
b. Inherent risk.
c. Control risk.
d. Detection risk.

5.35 Auditors are responsible for the quality of the work related to management and control of:
a. Inherent risk.
b. Relative risk.
c. Control risk.

d. Detection risk.

5.36 The auditors assessed a combined inherent risk and control risk at 0.75 and said they wanted to achieve a 0.15 risk of failing to detect misstatements in an account equal to the $17,000 tolerable misstatement assigned to the account. What detection risk do the auditors plan to use for planning the remainder of the audit work?

a. 0.20.
b. 0.10.
c. 0.75.
d. 0.00.

5.37 An audit program contains:

a. Specifications of audit standards relevant to the financial statements being audited.
b. Specifications of procedures the auditors believe appropriate for the financial statements under audit.
c. Documentation of the assertions under audit, the evidence obtained, and the conclusions reached.
d. Reconciliation of the account balances in the financial statements with the account balances in the client's general ledger.

Exercises and Problems

· ·

5.38 Analytical Review Ratio Relationships. The following situations represent errors and irregularities that could occur in financial statements. Your requirement is to state how the ratio in question would compare (greater, equal, or less) to what the ratio "should have been" had the error or irregularity not occurred.

a. The company recorded fictitious sales with credits to sales revenue accounts and debits to accounts receivable. Inventory was reduced and cost of goods sold was increased for the profitable "sales." Is the current ratio greater than, equal to, or less than what it should have been?

b. The company recorded cash disbursements paying trade accounts payable but held the cheques past the year-end date—meaning that the "disbursements" should not have been shown as credits to cash and debits to accounts payable. Is the current ratio greater than, equal to, or less than what it should have been? Consider cases in which the current ratio before the improper "disbursement" recording would have been (1) greater than 1:1, (2) equal to 1:1, and (3) less than 1:1.

c. The company uses a periodic inventory system for determining the balance sheet amount of inventory at year-end. Very near the year-end, merchandise was received, placed in the stockroom, and counted, but the purchase transaction was neither recorded nor paid until the next month. What was the effect on inventory, cost of goods sold, gross profit, and net income? How were these ratios affected, compared to what they would have been without the error: current ratio (remember three possible cases), gross margin ratio, cost of goods sold ratio, inventory turnover, and receivables turnover?

d. The company is loathe to write off customer accounts receivable, even though the financial vice president makes entirely adequate provision for uncollectible amounts in the allowance for bad debts. The gross receivables and the allowance both contain amounts that should have been written off long ago. How are these ratios affected compared to what they would be if the old receivables were properly written off: current ratio, days' sales in receivables, doubtful account ratio, receivables turnover, return on beginning equity, working capital/total assets?

e. Since last year, the company has reorganized its lines of business and placed more emphasis on its traditional products while selling off some marginal businesses merged by the previous go-go management. Total assets are 10 percent less than they were last year, but working capital has increased. Retained earnings remained the same because the disposals created no gains, and the net income after taxes is still near zero, the same as last year. Earnings before interest and taxes remained the same, a small positive EBIT. The total market value of the company's equity has not increased, but that is better than the declines of the past several years. Proceeds from the disposals have been used to retire long-term debt. Net sales have decreased 5 percent because the sales decrease resulting from the disposals has not been overcome by increased sales of the traditional products. Is the discriminant Z score of the current year higher or lower than that of the prior year?

5.39 Auditing an Accounting Estimate. Suppose management estimated the lower-of-cost-or-market valuation of some obsolete inventory at $99,000, and wrote it down from $120,000, recognizing a loss of $21,000. The auditors obtained the following information: The inventory in question could be sold for an amount between $78,000 and $92,000. The costs of advertising and shipping could range from $5,000 to $7,000.

Required:
a. Would you propose an audit adjustment to the management estimate? Write the appropriate accounting entry.
b. If management's estimate of inventory market (lower than cost) had been $80,000, would you propose an audit adjustment? Write the appropriate accounting entry.

5.40 Calculate a Planning Materiality Amount. The auditors were planning the work on the financial statements of the Mary Short Cosmetics Company. The unaudited financial statements showed $515,000 net income after providing an allowance of 35 percent for income taxes. The company had no debt and no interest expense. Mary Short's shares are traded over the counter, and investors have generally assigned a price-earnings multiple of 16 to the shares. Press releases by the company have enabled analysts to estimate the income for the year at about 515,000, which was forecast by the company at the beginning of the year. There are 750,000 shares outstanding, and the last quoted price for them was $11.

The auditors have decided that a 6 percent mispricing error in the shares would not cause investors to change their buying and selling decisions.

Required:
Calculate the "planning materiality" the auditors could allow, based on the income before income taxes.

5.41 Audit Risk Model. Audit risks for particular accounts and disclosures can be conceptualized in this model: Audit risk (AR) = Inherent risk (IR) × Internal control risk (CR) × Detection risk (DR). Use this model as a framework for considering the following situations and deciding whether the auditor's conclusion is appropriate.
1. Ohlsen, PA, has participated in the audit of Limberg Cheese Company for five years, first as an assistant accountant and the last two years as the senior accountant. He has never seen an accounting adjustment recommended. He believes the inherent risk must be zero.
2. Jones, PA, has just (November 30) completed an exhaustive study and evaluation of the internal control system of Lang's Derfer Foods, Inc. (fiscal year ending December 31). She believes the control risk must be zero because no material errors could possibly slip through the many error-checking procedures and review layers used by Lang's.
3. Fields, PA, is lazy and does not like audit jobs in Toronto, anyway. On the audit of Hogtown Manufacturing Company, he decided to use detail procedures to audit the year-end balances very thoroughly to the extent that his risk of failing to detect mate-

rial errors and irregularities should be 0.02 or less. He gave no thought to inherent risk and conducted only a very limited review of Philly's internal control system.

4. Shad, PA, is nearing the end of a "dirty" audit of Allnight Protection Company. Allnight's accounting personnel all resigned during the year and were replaced by inexperienced people. The controller resigned last month in disgust. The journals and ledgers were a mess because the one computer specialist was hospitalized for three months during the year. Thankfully, Shad thought, "I've been able to do this audit in less time than last year when everything was operating smoothly."

Discussion Cases

5.42 Analytical Review. Kermit Griffin, an audit manager, had begun a preliminary analytical review of selected statistics related to the Majestic Hotel. His objective was to obtain an understanding of this hotel's business in order to draft a preliminary audit program. He wanted to see whether he could detect any troublesome areas or questionable accounts that might require special audit attention. Unfortunately, Mr. Griffin caught the flu and was hospitalized. From his sickbed he sent you the schedule he had prepared (Exhibit 5.42–1). He has asked you to write a memorandum identifying areas of potential misstatements or other matters that the preliminary audit program should cover.

Required:

Write a memorandum describing Majestic's operating characteristics compared to the "industry average" insofar as you can tell from the statistics. Does this analytical review identify any areas that might present problems in the audit?

This assignment gives you some practice using the number 4 general type of analytical procedures discussed in the chapter: "Comparison of current year account balances and financial relationships (e.g., ratios) with similar information for the industry in which the company operates."

5.43 Analytical Review. The use of analytical procedure is becoming more frequent as auditors strive to improve the efficiency with which they conduct their audit examinations.

Required:

a. What are the two basic uses of analytical procedures in an audit?
b. List the basic steps in the process of performing analytical procedures.
c. What is the auditor's objective in using analytical procedures in each stage of the audit?

(CGAAC Adapted)

EXHIBIT 5.42–1   MAJESTIC HOTEL PRELIMINARY ANALYTICAL PROCEDURES FYE 3/31/8Y

The Majestic Hotel, East Apple, British Columbia, compiles operating statistics on a calendar-year basis. Hotel statistics, below, were provided by the controller, A. J. Marcello, for 199X. The parallel column contains industry average statistics obtained from the National Hotel Industry Guide.

Average annual percent of rooms occupied, Majestic (percent)

	Majestic (percent)	Industry (percent)
Sales:		
Rooms	60.4%	63.9%
Food and beverage	35.7	32.2
Other	3.9	3.9
Costs:		
Rooms department	15.2%	17.3%
Food and beverage	34.0	27.2
Administrative & general	8.0	8.9
Management fee	3.3	1.1
Advertising	2.7	3.2
Real estate taxes	3.5	3.2
Utilities, repairs, maintenance	15.9	13.7
Profit per sales dollar	17.4%	25.4%
Rooms dept. ratios to room sales dollars:		
Salaries and wages	18.9%	15.7%
Laundry	1.0	3.7
Other	5.3	7.6
Profit per rooms sales dollar	74.8%	73.0%
Food/beverage ratios to F/B sales dollars:		
Cost of food sold	42.1%	37.0%
Food gross profit	57.9	63.0
Cost of beverages sold	43.6	29.5
Beverages gross profit	56.4	70.5
Combined gross profit	57.7	64.6
Salaries and wages	39.6	32.8
Music and entertainment	—	2.7
Other	13.4	13.8
Profit per F/B sales dollar	4.7	15.3
Average annual percent of rooms occupied	62.6	68.1
Average room rate per day	$160	$120
Number of rooms available per day	$200	$148
Other	13.4	13.8
Profit per F/B sales dollar	4.7	15.3
Average annual percent of rooms occupied	62.6	68.1
Average room rate per day	$160	$120
Number of rooms available per day	$200	$148

Appendix 5A

Selected Financial Ratios

· ·

Balance Sheet Ratios	Formula*
Current ratio	$\dfrac{\text{Current assets}}{\text{Current liabilities}}$
Days' sales in receivables	$\dfrac{\text{Ending net receivables}}{\text{Credit sales}} \times 360$
Doubtful account ratio	$\dfrac{\text{Allowance for doubtful accounts}}{\text{Ending gross receivables}}$
Days' sales in inventory	$\dfrac{\text{Ending inventory}}{\text{Cost of goods sold}} \times 360$
Debt ratio	$\dfrac{\text{Current and long-term debt}}{\text{Shareholder equity}}$
Operations Ratios	
Receivables turnover	$\dfrac{\text{Credit sales}}{\text{Ending net receivables}}$
Inventory turnover	$\dfrac{\text{Cost of goods sold}}{\text{Ending inventory}}$
Cost of goods sold ratio	$\dfrac{\text{Cost of goods sold}}{\text{Net sales}}$
Gross margin ratio	$\dfrac{\text{Net sales} - \text{Cost of goods sold}}{\text{Net sales}}$
Return on beginning equity	$\dfrac{\text{Net income}}{\text{Shareholder equity (beginning)}}$

Financial Distress Ratios (Altman, 1968)	Formula*
(X_1) Working capital ÷ Total assets	$\dfrac{\text{Current assets} - \text{Current liabilities}}{\text{Total assets}}$
(X_2) Retained earnings ÷ Total assets	$\dfrac{\text{Retained earnings (ending)}}{\text{Total assets}}$
(X_3) Earnings before interest and taxes ÷ Total assets	$\dfrac{\text{Net Income} + \text{Interest expense} + \text{Income tax expense}}{\text{Total assets}}$
(X_4) Market value of equity ÷ Total debt	$\dfrac{\text{Market value of common and preferred shares}}{\text{Current liabilities and long-term debt}}$
(X_5) Net sales ÷ Total assets	$\dfrac{\text{Net sales}}{\text{Total assets}}$
Discriminant Z score (Altman, 1968)	$1.2 \times X_1 + 1.4 \times X_2 + 3.3 \times X_3 + 0.6 \times X_4 + 1.0 \times X_5$

*These ratios are shown to be calculated using year-end, rather than year-average, numbers for such balances as accounts receivable and inventory. Other accounting and finance reference books may contain formulas using year-average numbers. As long as no dramatic changes have occurred during the year, the year-end numbers can have much audit relevance because they reflect the most current balance data. For comparative purposes, the ratios should be calculated on the same basis for all the years being compared.

In the Anycompany example in Exhibits 10–1 and 10–2, the market value of the equity in the calculations is $3 million.

The discriminant Z score is an index of a company's "financial health." The higher the score, the more healthy the company. The lower the score, the closer financial failure approaches. The score that predicts financial failure is a matter of dispute. Research suggests that companies with scores above 3.0 never go bankrupt. Generally, companies with scores below 1.0 experience financial difficulty of some kind. The score can be a negative number.

CHAPTER 6

Learning Objectives

Two major themes from Chapters 4 and 5 are carried forward into this chapter. They are understanding the client's business and control risk. Chapter 6 also makes use of the concepts of management assertions and their related audit objectives, general audit procedures, and audit working papers (Chapter 4); and of risk assessment and audit programs (Chapter 5). This chapter takes these topics and molds them into the process of internal control evaluation and control risk assessment. After studying Chapter 6, you should be able to:

1. Explain primary and secondary reasons for conducting an evaluation of a client's internal controls.

2. Distinguish between management's and auditors' responsibility regarding a company's internal control structure.

3. Define and describe the three basic elements of internal control, and specify some of their component characteristics.

4. Identify and give examples of seven internal control objectives, and associate them with the five management assertions in financial account balances.

5. List and explain the control procedures companies use to achieve control objectives.

6. Explain the phases of an evaluation of control and risk assessment and the documentation and extent of audit work required.

7. Write procedures for an audit program, following the general form of a detail test of control procedure.

8. Define and explain reasonable assurance and cost-benefit in the context of control risk assessment.

9. Adapt the concepts and processes of control risk assessment to small businesses.

Internal Control Evaluation:

Assessing Control Risk

Introduction
· · · · · · · · · · ·

Internal control evaluation and control risk assessment is a very important part of the work in every audit of financial statements. Generally accepted auditing standards emphasize internal control in the second examination standard: "A sufficient understanding of internal control should be obtained to plan the audit." (*Handbook Section* 5100.02). Auditing standards describe the elements of internal controls and specify the extent of the auditors' work necessary to satisfy the second examination standard. When control risk is assessed below maximum, sufficient appropriate evidence should be obtained from tests of controls to support the assessment (*Handbook Section* 5100.02).

The elements are control environment and control systems. Control systems include accounting systems. For our purposes we will treat the accounting system as a separate element. The extent of work involves obtaining an understanding of all three elements, documenting the understanding, and performing tests of controls, if needed. Exhibit 6–1 puts these elements and this work in perspective for Chapter 6.

Chapter 6 presents a general introduction to the theory and definitions for internal control evaluation and control risk assessment. Chapter 7 (Audit Sampling) covers audit sampling for detail test of control procedures, and Chapter 20 covers the more technical topic of statistical attribute sampling for tests of controls. Computer-technical topics of the role of control in planning are covered in Chapter 8 (Auditing in a Computer Environment). Specific applications of control risk assessment are covered in the specific accounts and cycles in Chapters 9 to 13.

Reasons for Internal Control Evaluation
· · · · · · · · · · ·

LEARNING OBJECTIVE

1. Explaining primary and secondary reasons for conducting an evaluation of a client's internal controls.

Handbook Section 5200.03 defines internal control as "consisting of the policies and procedures established and maintained by management to assist in achieving its objective of ensuring, as far as practical, the orderly and efficient conduct of the entity's business." However, *Section* 5200.07 makes clear that "internal control relevant to the audit is comprised of those policies and procedures established and maintained by management that affect control risk relating to specific financial statement assertions at the account balance or class of transactions level." We will refer to these audit relevant controls as *accounting controls* and the rest of the internal control as *management controls*. The auditor is thus primarily interested in

E X H I B I T 6–1   INTERNAL CONTROL EVALUATION AND CONTROL RISK ASSESSMENT

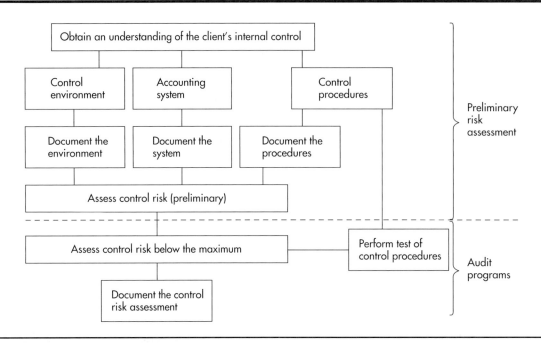

accounting controls. You can properly infer that accounting controls enable a company to safeguard its assets and prepare financial statements in conformity with generally accepted accounting principles. However, management is also interested in internal controls to assess adherence to management policy and promotion of operational efficiencies, and develops management controls to meet these objectives as well. **Control risk** arises from failures in internal control. Specifically, "control risk is the risk that the client's internal control will not prevent or detect material misstatement" (*Section* 5130.10). Control risk is a characteristic of the client's internal control. The auditors' task is to assess it; that is, to assign an evaluation to it. Many auditors conclude their internal control risk assessment decisions with descriptive assessments (e.g., high, moderate, low), and some auditors put probability numbers on them (e.g., 1.0, 0.50, 0.30).

The primary reason for conducting an evaluation of a company's internal control and assessing control risk is to give the auditors a basis for planning the audit and determining the nature, timing, and extent of audit procedures in the account balance audit program. Note that this means the auditor's primary concern with regard to internal controls is the impact controls have on safeguarding the company's assets and the accuracy of the accounting records (accounting controls). This is the basis on which the auditors have prepared a preliminary audit program and have ideas about the work they want to do. This preliminary program might be last year's audit program or an off-the-shelf "standard program" that will need to be modified for client-specific preliminary analytical review, materiality, and risk assessments. Exhibit 6–1 outlines the process. In the preliminary risk assessment phase, the auditor begins by making an assessment of the general controls associated with the overall control environment and the accounting system. If the general controls appear to be reliable, the auditor will then make a preliminary evaluation of the more specific

EXHIBIT 6-2   ACCOUNTS RECEIVABLE BALANCE-AUDIT PROGRAM (partial illustration)

Assertions/Procedures	Nature	Timing	Extent
Existence/Cutoff: Accounts receivable are authentic obligations owed to the company and represent sales made before December 31.			
1. Obtain a trial balance of customers' accounts. Select 75 for positive confirmation.	Confirmation	November 1 (interim date)	Limited sample
2. Obtain a year-end trial balance of customer accounts. Compare to the November 1 trial balance and investigate significant changes by vouching large increases to sales invoices and bills of lading.	Analytical procedures Document vouching	December 31 (year-end)	All customer accounts
3. Select all the sales invoices recorded in the last five days of the year, and vouch to bills of lading for December shipping date.	Document vouching	December 31 (year-end)	Last five days' sales
Completeness/Cutoff: Accounts receivable include all amounts owed to the company at December 31.			
4. Send positive confirmations to customers with zero balances.	Confirmation	December 31 (year-end)	All zero balance accounts
5. Select all the bills of lading dated in the last five days of the year, and trace to sales invoices recorded in December.	Document tracing	December 31 (year-end)	Last five days' shipments

procedures. Tests of controls are not performed unless the auditor feels he or she can rely on controls and most such tests relate to specific accounting cycles. The rest of this chapter discusses this process in more detail.

An **account balance audit program** is a specification (list) of procedures designed to produce evidence about the assertions in financial statements. Each procedure should have identifiable characteristics of nature, timing, and extent, as well as a direct association with one or more financial statement assertions. The **nature** of procedures refers to the six general techniques: computation, confirmation, enquiry, inspection, observation, and analysis. The **timing** of procedures is a matter of when they are performed: at "interim" before the balance sheet date or at "year-end" shortly before and after the balance sheet date. The **extent** of procedures refers to the amount of work done when the procedures are performed.

Exhibit 6–2 contains five procedures for auditing two accounts receivable assertions. These procedures are part of an account balance audit program. The existence and completeness subheadings and the columns in the exhibit were added to help you see the connections to financial statement assertions and to the nature, timing, and extent of the procedures.

Restricting Account Balance Audit Procedures

The procedures presented in Exhibit 6–2 show some restrictions of the timing and extent of work, which suggest a low control risk, specifically:

- Confirmation of a sample of customer accounts receivable before year-end, instead of confirmation of all accounts as of December 31.
- Vouching the last 5 days' recorded sales to bills of lading for cutoff evidence, instead of vouching the last 15 days' sales.
- Tracing the last 5 days' shipments to recorded sales invoices for cutoff evidence, instead of tracing the last 15 days' shipments.

You should assume the auditors think this is an efficient program. An alternative program, which would require more time and greater audit cost, would (1) confirm all the customer accounts as of December 31; (2) omit the analytical comparison of the December accounts receivable trial balance because the confirmation was done as of December 31; (3) select all the sales invoices recorded in the last 15 days for vouching to December bills of lading; (4) send positive confirmations to customers with small balances and zero balances; and (5) select all bills of lading dated in the last 15 days for tracing to December sales invoices.

The preliminary audit program presented in Exhibit 6–2, therefore, depends on a low control risk related to the company's internal control structure. The audit task is to assess the inherent and internal control risks of material misstatement (error or irregularity) that slip into the accounts receivable total through the improper or omitted recording of sales and charges to customers. If the risks are too high, some procedures may need to be changed to provide for greater extent (larger samples) and better timing (confirmation moved to December 31). Likewise, if the risk of omitted sales is not high, the confirmation of zero-balance receivables might be omitted, or negative confirmations might be used instead of positive confirmations. In general, a good system of internal control should result in less audit work than a bad system of internal control. Thus, it is possible to obtain audit efficiencies from good internal controls: less testing and audit work spread over a longer time period.

Communicating Internal Control Weaknesses

A secondary reason to evaluate internal control is to formulate constructive suggestions for improvements. Auditors become involved in system design consulting by including their suggestions in a management letter to the client. Officially, the profession considers these suggestions a part of the audit and does not define the work as a management consulting service. Clients are free to decide whether to act on the suggestions. A management letter is written at the end of the field work. (See Exhibit 13–10 in Chapter 13.) The new *Handbook Section* 5220 requires communication to management of all significant weaknesses in internal control. In addition, *Section* 5750, "Communication of Matters Identified During the Financial Statement Audit," requires the communication of (1) nontrivial misstatements, (2) fraud, and (3) consequential illegal or possibly illegal acts. However, neither of these sections requires communication in writing—oral communication is sufficient. Thus, when management letters are prepared, *Sections* 5750 and 5220 do not require that their subject matters be included in the management letter.

The management letter *can* include these identified matters; it's just that *Sections* 5750 and 5220 *do not require* management letters to do so. These sections make no explicit mention of management letters. We will call the contents of management letters reportable matters and define these as items the auditor believes should be communicated to the client in writing. (For example, see S. Smith's article, "More Than a Drop in the Bucket," in *CA Magazine,* February 1993, pp. 50–52). For some financial institution regulators, auditors have a "well-being" reporting requirement that includes reporting on significant internal control weaknesses (CICA Guideline AUG–17, "Transactions or Conditions Reportable Under the 'Well-Being Reporting Requirement' in Federal Institutions Legislation"). This Guideline uses the specific term "reportable condition." Thus, a type of reportable matter by our definition is a reportable condition. Examples of reportable conditions include:

- Absence of appropriate segregation of duties.
- Absence of appropriate reviews and approvals of transactions.
- Evidence of failure of control procedures.
- Evidence of intentional management override of control procedures by persons in authority to the detriment of control objectives.
- Evidence of wilful wrongdoing by employees or management, including manipulation, falsification, or alteration of accounting records.

Communications of reportable conditions and matters are discussed more fully in Chapter 14.

Report of Significant Weakness

Reportable matters include the serious condition called a significant weakness in internal control, which is defined as a deficiency such that a material misstatement is not likely to be prevented or detected in the current or future financial statements of the entity.

Although auditors are not obligated to provide assurance for reportable matters and significant weaknesses, they often communicate ones that come to their attention in the normal performance of the audit. Written communications are preferred, but sometimes auditors communicate reportable conditions orally, in which case a memorandum of the oral report should be placed in the working papers. However, because the potential for misinterpretation is great, *Section* 5750 recommends a carefully worded report stating that no specific matters were noted during the audit. See the following box.

"The objective of my audit was to obtain reasonable assurance that the financial statements were free of material misstatement and was not designed for the purpose of identifying matters to communicate. Accordingly my audit would not usually identify all such matters that may exist and it is inappropriate to conclude that no matters exist.

During the course of my audit of _____ for the year ended _____ I did not identify any of the following matters: misstatements, other than trivial errors; fraud; misstatements that may cause future financial statements to be materially misstated; illegal or possibly illegal acts, other than ones considered inconsequential; or significant weaknesses in internal control.

This communication is prepared solely for the information of management and is not intended for any other purpose. I accept no responsibility to a third party who relies on this communication."

Source: CICA Handbook Section 5750.22, "Communication of Matters Identified During the Financial Statement Audit" (June 1997).

· ·

R E V I E W
CHECKPOINTS

6.1 What are the primary and secondary reasons for conducting an evaluation of an audit client's internal control?

6.2 What is an account balance, substantive audit procedure? Define and explain the nature, timing, and extent features of account balance audit procedures in general.

6.3 What is a reportable condition regarding internal control?

. . . .

MANAGEMENT VERSUS AUDITOR RESPONSIBILITY

. . . .

LEARNING OBJECTIVE

2. Distinguish between management's and auditors' responsibility regarding a company's internal controls.

A company's management is responsible for its control environment, for its accounting system, and for establishing and maintaining a system of internal control procedures. Continuous managerial supervision and modification are elements of management's responsibility. Management is not only responsible for the internal control that supports the production of financial statements but also is responsible for the internal control that achieves all the other objectives of the business. This broader concept of internal control is exemplified by a definition proposed by The Institute of Internal Auditors, as shown in the box below.

External auditors' communications of *reportable* conditions and material weaknesses are intended to help management carry out its responsibilities for internal control monitoring and change. However, external auditors' observations and recommendations are usually limited to external financial reporting matters.

External auditors are not responsible for designing effective internal control for audit clients. They are responsible for evaluating existing internal controls and assessing the control risk in them. "Designing systems" refers to formulating the plan of organization, the policies and procedures, and other matters important in creating

---

INTERNAL CONTROL DEFINITION (IIA)

Internal control is the process by which an entity's board of directors, management, and/or other personnel obtain reasonable assurance that the following control objectives will be achieved:

1. Significant financial, managerial, and operating information reported internally and externally is accurate, reliable, and timely.
2. The activities of the organization are in compliance with policies, plans, standards, and procedures, and with applicable laws and regulations.
3. Resources are adequately protected.
4. Resources are acquired economically and used efficiently (or cost-effectively).
5. The organization's plans, goals, and objectives are achieved.

Commentary: Emphasis is added in number 1 (italicized words) to isolate the external auditors' primary interest in internal control. You can see by the other parts of number 1 and numbers 2 through 5 that managers' and internal auditors' interests in control are much broader.

Source: The Institute of Internal Auditors, letter to Committee of Sponsoring Organizations of the Treadway Commission (June 14, 1991).

and managing internal control. Accounting firms undertake control design as consulting engagements but consider such work to be separate and apart from the audit engagement responsibility.

External auditors' basis for knowing about reportable conditions and material weaknesses is found in their familiarity with the types of errors, irregularities, frauds, and misstatements that can occur in any account balance or class of transactions. Clearly, hundreds of innocent errors and not-so-innocent fraud schemes are possible. (Many of these are discussed in Chapter 18, on Fraud Awareness Auditing.) Instead of trying to learn hundreds of possible errors and irregularities, it is better to start with seven general categories of them. Exhibit 6–3 shows a typology of seven categories, with some examples. The external auditors' task of control risk assessment involves finding out what the company does to prevent, detect, and correct these potential errors and irregularities. You will encounter the flip side of these when you study control objectives later in the chapter.

· ·

R E V I E W
C H E C K P O I N T S

6.4   What are some of the elements of breadth that characterize managerial and internal audit interest in internal control over and above the external auditors' interest in internal control?

6.5   How do external auditors help managers meet their responsibilities for internal control?

6.6   Define control risk. What seven types of errors or irregularities is internal control intended to prevent, detect, or correct?

· ·

INTERNAL CONTROL ELEMENTS
· · · · · · · · · · · ·

Internal control structure

Obtain an understanding of the client's internal controls

| Control environment | Accounting system | Control procedures |

LEARNING   OBJECTIVE

3. Define and describe the three basic elements of internal control, and specify some of their component characteristics.

For purposes of explanation, internal control is divided into three elements: The **control environment** is a set of characteristics that defines good control working relationships in a company. The **accounting system** contains policies and procedures for recording transactions properly. The **control procedures** are specific error-checking routines performed by company personnel. In combination, these three parts provide the policies and procedures designed to prevent, detect, and correct material errors, irregularities, frauds, and misstatements.

E X H I B I T 6–3   GENERAL CATEGORIES AND EXAMPLES OF ERRORS AND IRREGULARITIES
(misstatements)

1. Invalid transactions are recorded: Fictitious sales are recorded and charged to nonexistent customers.
2. Valid transactions are omitted from the accounts: Shipments to customers never get recorded.
3. Unauthorized transactions are executed and recorded: A customer's order is not approved for credit, yet the goods are shipped, billed, and charged to the customer without requiring payment in advance.
4. Transaction amounts are inaccurate: A customer is billed and the sale is recorded in the wrong amount because the quantity shipped and the quantity billed are not the same and the unit price is for a different product.
5. Transactions are classified in the wrong accounts: Sales to a subsidiary company are recorded as sales to outsiders instead of intercompany sales, or the amount is charged to the wrong customer account receivable record.
6. Transaction accounting is incomplete: Sales are posted in total to the accounts receivable control account, but some are not posted to individual customer account records.
7. Transactions are recorded in the wrong period: Shipments made in January (next year) are backdated and recorded as sales and charges to customers in December; shipments in December are recorded as sales and charges to customers in January.

Control Environment

The control environment is characterized by management attitudes, structure (organization chart), effective communication of control objectives, and supervision of personnel and activities. The following are elements of internal control environments:

- Management's philosophy and operating style.
- Company organization structure.
- Functioning of the board of directors, particularly its audit committee.
- Methods of assigning authority and responsibility.
- Management's monitoring methods, including internal auditing. Personnel policies and practices.
- External influences (e.g., examinations by bank regulatory agencies).
- Control environment for computerized systems also includes the organizational and logical controls that control access to computers and computer files, and authorization of changes to program and data files. Generally, such environmental controls can be characterized as preventive controls in the sense that they are there to prevent misstatements from arising in the first place. Preventive controls are more cost effective than controls designed to detect or correct misstatements that have entered the system. This is one reason why auditors tend to focus the preliminary evaluation on environmental controls. Another reason is the pervasive impact environmental controls have on the accounting cycles affected.

Since management fraud in financial statements became a topic for acceptable discussion in the mid-1980s, "tone at the top" has become a buzzword for the necessary condition for good internal control. The "tone" is virtually identical to the element of control environment. A wide variety of activities characterize the control environment. Consequently, it is sometimes hard for auditors to understand it and document it.

CRITERIA OF CONTROL (COCO) BOARD OF THE CICA

All control rests ultimately on people assuming responsibility for their decisions and actions. Organizational values that people find acceptable encourage them to assume responsibility for the continuous improvement of their organization.

Shared ethical values influence all behaviour in an organization. Together with an understanding of mission and vision, they constitute the basic identity that will shape the way an individual, group, organization or board will operate, and they provide stability over time. Shared values contribute to control because they provide a guide for individual, group or team decision-making, action and policy.

The values and preferences of senior management and the board of directors greatly influence an organization's objectives and systems. These values and preferences address issues such as:

- good corporate citizenship;
- commitment to truth and fair dealing;
- commitment to quality and competence;
- leadership by example;
- compliance with laws, regulations, rules and organizational policy;
- respect for the privacy of client, organization and employee information;
- fair treatment of and respect for individuals;
- fair relationships with competitors;
- integrity of transactions and records; and
- a professional approach to financial reporting.

Ethical values are part of an organization's culture and provide an unwritten code of conduct against which behaviour is measured. A formal, written code of conduct offers a means of consistent communication of the standards of ethical behaviour. People can be asked periodically to confirm their understanding and observance of the code.

Source: COCO, *Guidance on Control* (November 1995), pp. 14, 15.

Accounting System

An accounting system processes transactions, records them in journals and ledgers (either computerized or manual), and produces financial statements without necessarily guaranteeing their accuracy. Nevertheless, the accounting policies and procedures often contain important elements of control. The accounting instruction of "Prepare sales invoices only when shipment has been made," is a control so long as the people performing the work follow the instruction. The control part of this policy could be expressed: "Prepare sales invoices and record them only when a shipping document is matched."

All accounting systems, whether computerized or manual, consist of four essential functions—data preparation, data entry, transaction processing, and report production and distribution.

Data preparation is the analysis of transactions and their "capture" for accounting purposes. The "capture" amounts to creation of source documents, such as sales invoices, credit memos, cash receipts listings, purchase orders, receiving reports, negotiable cheques, and the like. These source documents provide the information for data entry. However, in some computerized accounting systems, the paper source documents are not produced first. Transactions may be entered directly on a keyboard, or electronic equipment may capture the transaction information. Your long-distance telephone charges are initially captured by the telephone company's computers using your telephone number, the location called, and the duration of the call.

Data entry often consists of accounting personnel using a batch of source documents to enter transaction information on a keyboard into an accounting software program. This process may produce a "book of original entry," another name for a journal, such as the sales journal, purchases journal, cash receipts journal, cash disbursements journal, general journal, and others. In advanced paperless systems, electronic equipment may enter the accounting information automatically without producing an intermediate journal. Your long-distance telephone call is entered automatically into the telephone company's revenue and receivable accounts. Your monthly telephone bill is later produced from the accounting information.

Transaction processing usually refers to posting the journals to the general ledger accounts, using the debits and credits you learned in other accounting courses. The posting operation updates the account balances. When all data are entered and processed, the account balances are ready for placement in reports.

Report production and distribution is the object of the accounting system. The account balances are put into internal management reports and external financial statements. The internal reports are management's feedback for monitoring and control of operations. The external reports are the financial information for outside investors, creditors, and others.

The accounting system produces a trail of accounting operations, from transaction analyses to reports. Often, this is called the audit trail. You can visualize that it starts with the source documents and proceeds through to the financial reports. Auditors often follow this trail frontwards and backwards! They will follow it backwards from the financial reports to the source documents to determine whether everything in the financial reports is supported by appropriate source documents. They will follow it forward from source documents to reports to determine that everything that happened (transactions) got recorded in the accounts and reported in the financial statements.

Control procedures are client procedures (both computerized and manual) imposed on the accounting system for the purpose of preventing, detecting, and correcting errors and irregularities that might enter and flow through to the financial statements. For example, a control procedure related to the accounting policy cited above would be: "At the end of each day, the billing supervisor reviews all the sales invoices to see that the file copy has a bill of lading copy attached."

Minimum requirements for a good control-oriented accounting system include a chart of accounts and some written definitions and instructions about measuring and classifying transactions. In most organizations such material is incorporated in computer systems documentation, computer program documentation, systems and procedures manuals, flowcharts of transaction processing, and various paper forms. A company's internal auditors and systems staff often review and evaluate this documentation. Independent auditors may review and study their work instead of doing the same tasks over again.

Accounting manuals should contain statements of objectives, policies, and procedures. Management should approve statements of specific accounting and control objectives and ensure that appropriate procedures are used to accomplish them. In general, the overriding objective of an accounting system is to produce financial statement assertions that are correct. Therefore, the objective of accounting is to produce correct statements of existence or occurrence, completeness, valuation, rights and obligations, and presentation and disclosure. An accounting system cannot accomplish this objective without an integrated set of control procedures.

R E V I E W
C H E C K P O I N T S

6.7   What are some of the important characteristics of "tone at the top" and control environment?

6.8   Where can an auditor find a client's documentation of the accounting system?

6.9   What is the audit trail? Of what use is it in the audit process?

CONTROL OBJECTIVES AND PROCEDURES

LEARNING OBJECTIVE

4. Identify and give examples of seven internal control objectives, and associate them with the five management assertions in financial account balances.

While the objective of the accounting system is to produce correct financial statement assertions, principally in account balances, the overriding objective of control procedures is to process transactions correctly. Correctly processed transactions produce correct account balances, which in turn help produce accurate and reliable assertions in the financial statements.

These connections are shown in Exhibit 6–4. The new information in this exhibit is a list of control objectives. There are many control objective listing schemes. This is one of the shortest.

E X H I B I T 6–4   CONTROL OBJECTIVES AND FINANCIAL STATEMENT ASSERTIONS

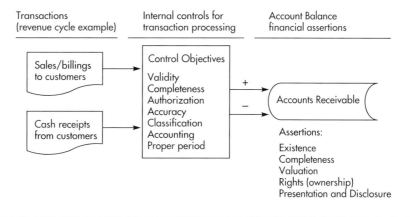

Control Objectives

Each of the control objectives is a reverse expression of the seven types of errors and irregularities shown in Exhibit 6–3. The presentation in Exhibit 6–5 summarizes each of the seven objectives, with a general statement of the objective and a specific example (accounts receivable/sales transaction processing context). The explanations that follow tell you some more about these objectives and give some examples of client procedures designed to accomplish them.

Validity refers to ensuring that recorded transactions are ones that should have been recorded. The client's procedure can be to require matching of shipping documents with sales invoices before a sale is recorded. This procedure is supposed to prevent the recording of undocumented (possibly fictitious) sales.

Completeness refers to ensuring that valid transactions are not omitted entirely from the accounting records. If sales are represented by shipments, then no shipping documents should be left unmatched with sales invoices. Transaction documents (e.g., shipping documents) are often prenumbered. Accounting for the numerical sequence of prenumbered shipping documents is a control procedure designed to achieve the completeness objective.

Authorization refers to ensuring that transactions are approved before they are recorded. Credit approval for a sale transaction is an example. Sometimes, you may need to ponder the nature of authorization for some transactions. For example, what "authorization" is needed to record a cash receipt? Usually none—companies are happy to accept payments—but a sales manager may need to approve a good customer taking a discount after the discount period has elapsed.

Management must establish criteria for recognizing transactions in the accounting system and for supervisory approval of transactions. A control system should permit accounting to proceed only for authorized transactions and should bar unauthorized transactions.

Authorization may be general and may be delegated to a fairly low level of management. For example, (1) all shipments amounting to more than $1,000 in value

EXHIBIT 6–5   INTERNAL CONTROL OBJECTIVES

Objectives	General	Specific Example (accounts receivable/sales)
Validity	Recorded transactions are valid and documented.	Recorded sales are supported by invoices, shipping documents, and customer orders.
Completeness	All valid transactions are recorded, and none are omitted.	All shipping documents are prenumbered and matched with sales invoices daily.
Authorization	Transactions are authorized according to company policy.	Credit sales over $1,000 are given prior approval by the credit manager.
Accuracy	Transaction dollar amounts are properly calculated.	Sales invoices contain correct quantities and are mathematically correct.
Classification	Transactions are properly classified in the accounts.	Sales to subsidiaries and affiliates are classified as intercompany transactions.
Accounting	Transaction accounting is complete.	All sales on credit are charged to customers' individual accounts.
Proper period	Transactions are recorded in the proper period.	Sales of the current period are charged to customers in the current period, and sales of the next period are charged in the next period.

require credit approval and (2) all sales can be recorded in the accounting department upon receipt of a copy of a shipping ticket. Some authorizations may be quite tacit. For example, listing the payments received on account when the mail is opened may be sufficient authorization to accept and record cash receipts. Some authorizations may be very important and defined specifically by the board of directors. For example, sales of major assets or responsibility for signing the company name to a loan agreement may be authorized specifically in the minutes of the board of directors.

Accuracy refers to ensuring that dollar amounts are figured correctly. A manual or computer check for billing the same quantity shipped, at the correct list price, with correct multiplication and addition of the total, is intended to control for accuracy. (This objective, rather than the completeness one, covers errors of billing at too low a price or for a smaller quantity than shipped.) **Classification** refers to ensuring that transactions are recorded in the right accounts, charged or credited to the right customers (including classification of sales to subsidiaries and affiliates, as mentioned in Exhibit 6–5), entered in the correct segment product line or inventory description, and so forth. Classification may be confused with accuracy, but remember that accuracy refers to the accounting numbers.

Accounting is a general category concerned with ensuring that the accounting process for a transaction is performed completely and in conformity with GAAP. For example, a clerk can balance the total of individual customers' receivables with the control account to determine whether all charges and credits to the control account also have been entered in individual customers' accounts. (Classification is the control over whether the entries got into the right customers' accounts, and accuracy is the control category related to use of correct numbers.) Control over accounting, in general, is a useful category if you cannot identify a control problem in one of the other categories.

Proper period refers to ensuring that the accounting for transactions is in the period in which they occur. This control objective is very closely related to the cutoff aspect of the existence and completeness assertions. Procedurally, the client's accountants must be alert to the dates of transactions in relation to month-, quarter-, and year-end. Proper period accounting (cutoff) is a pervasive problem. You will see it mentioned in relation to all kinds of transactions—sales, purchases, inventories, expense accruals, income accruals, and others.

Control Objectives and Assertions

The control objectives are closely connected to management's assertions in financial statements. An association of the control objectives with the five assertions is shown in Exhibit 6–6. The Xs in the exhibit show the primary relevance of control objectives to assertions.

To interpret Exhibit 6–6, associate the achievement of control objectives with the probability that an assertion may be materially misstated. For example, if a company has strong control over the validity of recorded sales and cash receipts transactions, if it has an effective system of credit authorization, and if it ensures that sales transactions are correctly recorded in the proper period, then the control risk related to the existence/occurrence assertions for sales and accounts receivable balances may be assessed low.

However, an auditor may find that some, but not all, of the control objectives for a particular account balance (i.e., set of assertions) are achieved. For example, the

EXHIBIT 6–6   ASSOCIATION OF CONTROL OBJECTIVES AND FINANCIAL STATEMENT ASSERTIONS

	Financial Statement Assertions				
Control Objectives	Existence, Occurrence	Completeness	Valuation	Rights, Obligations	Presentation and Disclosure
Validity	X			X	
Completeness		X		X	
Authorization	X		X	X	
Accuracy			X		
Classification					X
Accounting					X
Proper Period	X	X			

situation cited above may coexist with failure to achieve control over the completeness of recording sales transactions and accounts receivable amounts. In such a case, the preliminary audit program may be changed to require more work related to the completeness of accounts receivable (the assertion for which control risk is high) and be unchanged for the work on the existence of accounts receivable (the assertion for which control risk is low).

The final evaluation of a company's internal control is the assessment of the control risk (CR) related to each assertion. Control risk is the CR element in the audit risk model: $AR = IR \times CR \times DR$. This assessment is an auditor's expression of the effectiveness of the control system for preventing, detecting, and correcting specific errors and irregularities in management's financial statement assertions.

Control Procedures

LEARNING OBJECTIVE

5. List and explain the control procedures companies use to achieve control objectives.

Companies use numerous detailed accounting and control procedures designed to achieve the control objectives. All detail procedures are directed, one way or another, toward preventing, detecting, and correcting the seven general kinds of errors, irregularities, frauds, and misstatements that can occur.

Control procedures can be complicated. Exhibit 6–7 presents an overview of the discussion that follows. The discussion is organized under the headings of general control procedures, segregation of technical responsibilities, and error-checking procedures.

General Control Procedures

While the "tone at the top" (control environment) is pervasive, the control procedures of capable personnel, segregation of responsibilities, controlled access, and periodic comparison are always important in a company's internal controls. General controls like environmental controls are primarily preventive in nature and have a pervasive impact on the various accounting cycles. For these reasons, auditors tend to focus on environmental and general controls in the preliminary evaluation of internal controls.

Capable Personnel.   The most important feature of control is the people who make the system work. A company's personnel problems sometimes create internal control

EXHIBIT 6-7   OVERVIEW OF CONTROL PROCEDURES

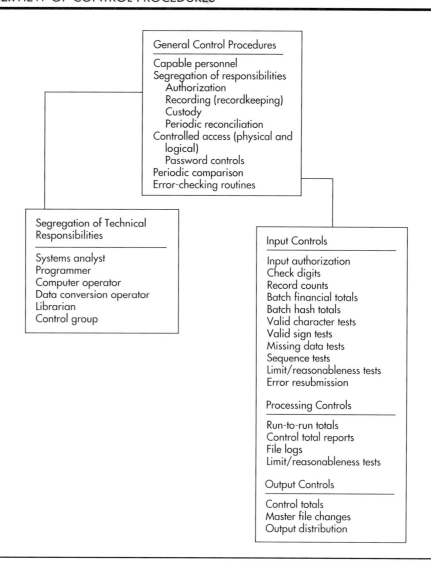

General Control Procedures

Capable personnel
Segregation of responsibilities
    Authorization
    Recording (recordkeeping)
    Custody
    Periodic reconciliation
Controlled access (physical and
    logical)
    Password controls
Periodic comparison
Error-checking routines

Segregation of Technical
Responsibilities

Systems analyst
Programmer
Computer operator
Data conversion operator
Librarian
Control group

Input Controls

Input authorization
Check digits
Record counts
Batch financial totals
Batch hash totals
Valid character tests
Valid sign tests
Missing data tests
Sequence tests
Limit/reasonableness tests
Error resubmission

Processing Controls

Run-to-run totals
Control total reports
File logs
Limit/reasonableness tests

Output Controls

Control totals
Master file changes
Output distribution

problems. High turnover in accounting jobs means that inexperienced people are doing the accounting and control tasks, and they generally make more mistakes than experienced people. New accounting officers and managers (financial vice president, controller, chief accountant, plant accountant, data processing manager) may not be familiar enough with company accounting and may make technical and judgmental errors. Sometimes accounting officers and employees are fired because they refuse to go along with improper accounting procedures desired by a higher level of management. In general, accounting personnel changes may be a warning signal.

Segregation of Responsibilities.   A very important characteristic of reliable internal control is an appropriate segregation of functional responsibilities. Sometimes this characteristic is called division of duties. Proper segregation of responsibilities is a necessary condition for making detailed clerical control procedures effective.

Four kinds of functional responsibilities should be performed by different departments, or at least by different persons on the company's accounting staff:

1. *Authorization to execute transactions.* This duty belongs to people who have authority and responsibility for initiating the recordkeeping for transactions. Authorization may be general, referring to a class of transactions (e.g., all purchases), or it may be specific (e.g., sale of a major asset).

2. *Recording of transactions.* This duty refers to the accounting and recordkeeping function (bookkeeping) which in most organizations is delegated to a computer system. (People who control the computer processing are the recordkeepers.)

3. *Custody of assets involved in the transactions.* This duty refers to the actual physical possession or effective physical control of property.

4. *Periodic reconciliation of existing assets to recorded amounts.* This duty refers to making comparisons at regular intervals and taking appropriate action with respect to any differences.

Incompatible responsibilities are combinations of responsibilities that place a person alone in a position to create and conceal errors, irregularities, and misstatements in his or her normal job. Duties should be so divided that no one person can control two or more functional responsibilities. The first and fourth responsibilities are management functions, the second is an accounting function, and the third is a custodial function. If different departments or persons are forced to deal with these different facets of transactions, then two benefits are obtained: (1) Irregularities are made more difficult because they would require collusion of two or more persons, and most people hesitate to seek the help of others to conduct wrongful acts, and (2) innocent errors are more likely to be found and flagged for correction. The old saying is that "two heads are better than one." The flip side of this is that the more people are assigned to control duties, the better are the controls and the higher the cost of the controls. Any control system will reflect compromises of benefits versus the costs.

Supervision is an important element of control procedures. You can readily imagine a company having clerks and computers to carry out the accounting and control procedures. Equally important is management's provision for supervising the work. A supervisor could, for example, oversee the credit manager's performance or could periodically compare the sum of customers' balances to the accounts receivable control account total. Supervisors or department heads can correct errors found by the clerical staff and make or approve accounting decisions. Supervision is important as management's means of monitoring and maintaining a system of internal control.

Controlled Access.   Physical access to assets and important records, documents, and blank forms should be limited to authorized personnel. Such assets as inventory and securities should not be available to persons who have no need to handle them. Likewise, access to cost records and accounts receivable records should be denied to people who do not have a recordkeeping responsibility for them.

Some blank forms are very important for accounting and control, and their availability should be restricted. Someone not involved in accounting for sales should not be able to pick up blank sales invoices and blank shipping orders. A person should not be able to obtain blank cheques (including computer-paper blank cheques) unless he or she is involved in cash disbursement activities. Sometimes, access to blank forms is the equivalent of access to, or custody of, an important asset.

For example, someone who has access to blank cheques has a measure of actual custody and access to cash. In computerized systems, controlled access is achieved through the use of physically secure hardware and software and the use of passwords to control electronic access.

Periodic Comparison.   Management has responsibility for the recorded accountability of assets and liabilities. Managers should provide for periodic comparison of the recorded amounts with independent evidence of existence and valuation. Internal auditors and other people on an accounting staff can perform periodic comparison on a regular basis. However, the people who perform these periodic comparisons should not also have responsibility for authorization of related transactions, accounting or recordkeeping, or custodial responsibility for the assets.

Periodic comparisons may include counts of cash on hand, reconciliation of bank statements, counts of securities, confirmation of accounts receivable and accounts payable, and other such comparison operations undertaken to determine whether accounting records—the recorded accountability—represent real assets and liabilities. A management that performs frequent periodic comparisons has more opportunities to detect errors in the records than a management that does not. The frequency, of course, is governed by the costs and benefits. One should not try to count, compare, or confirm assets with great frequency (say, weekly) unless those assets are especially susceptible to loss or error or unless they are unusually valuable. In other words, if the inherent risk is high the control risk should be made commensuratively lower so that the product of the two is constant, e.g., if IR = 1 then CR should be closer to .05 than if IR = .1: IR $\times$ CR = 1 $\times$ .05 = .1 $\times$ .5 = .05, assuming planned material misstatement after controls is to be maintained at a constant .05 despite variation in IR.

Subsequent action to correct differences is also important. Periodic comparison and action to correct errors lowers the risk that material misstatements will remain in the accounts. Such comparisons are frequently assigned to internal auditors and other employees.[1]

Segregation of Technical Responsibilities

Most companies use computer-based accounting and control systems. In large companies the essential separation of responsibilities involves the duties of analysts, programmers, and operators. The duties associated with these and other important roles are defined as follows:

Systems Analyst.   Analyses requirements for information. Evaluates the existing system and designs new or improved data processing. Outlines the system and prepares specifications that guide the programmers. Prepares documentation of the application system.

Programmer.   Flowcharts the logic of the computer programs required by the overall system designed by the systems analyst. Codes the logic in the computer program. Prepares documentation of the program.

Computer Operator.   Operates the computer for each accounting application system according to written operating procedures found in the computer operation instructions.

Data Conversion Operators.   Prepares data for machine processing. Previously these individuals operated keypunch machines and produced punched cards; now these

---

[1] Wayne Alderman and James Deitrick have described how companies with active internal auditors have fewer financial statement adjustments recommended by independent auditors than companies without active internal auditors. See "Internal Audit Impact of Financial Information Reliability," *The Internal Auditor*, April 1981, pp. 43–56.

PROGRAMMER AND OPERATOR COMBINED

A programmer employed by a large savings and loan association in the United States wrote a special subroutine that could be activated by a command from the computer console. The computation of interest on deposits and certificates was programmed to truncate calculations at the third decimal place. The special subroutine instructed the program to accumulate the truncated mills, and, when processing was complete, to credit the amount to the programmer-operator's savings account. Whenever this person was on duty for the interest calculation run, she could "make" several hundred dollars! She had to be on duty to manipulate the control figures "properly" so the error of overpaying interest on her account would not be detected by the control group. She was a programmer with computer operation duties.

---

operators usually convert visible source data to magnetic tape or disk, operate optical-character reading equipment, or use data transmission terminals. In advanced computer systems, the data conversion operators will likely be accounting clerks entering transactions from the accounting department into remote terminals.

Librarian.   Two types of librarian functions may be found in a computer facility—one for system and program documentation and the other for the actual programs and data files. The purpose of the system/program documentation library is to maintain control over documentation of the design and operation stages of computer information systems. The purpose of the program/data library is to maintain control over the data files and programs actually used from day to day. In many systems this second library function is done automatically with software.

Control Group.   The control group receives input from user departments, logs the input and transfers it to data conversion, reviews documentation sequence numbers, reviews and processes error messages, monitors actual processing, compares control totals to computer output, and distributes output.

Separation of the duties performed by analysts, programmers, and operators is important. The general idea is that anyone who designs a processing system should not do the technical programming work, and anyone who performs either of these tasks should not be the computer operator when "live" data is being processed. Persons performing each function should not have access to each other's work, and only the computer operators should have access to the equipment. Computer systems are susceptible to manipulative handling, and the lack of separation of duties along the lines described should be considered a serious weakness in general control. The control group or similar monitoring by the user departments can be an important compensating factor for weaknesses arising from lack of segregation of duties in computerized systems.

Error-Checking Routines

The numerous techniques used to check for errors in accounting data can be categorized as (1) input controls, (2) processing controls, and (3) output controls. The weakest point in computer systems is input—the point at which transaction data are transformed from hard-copy source documents into machine-readable cards, tape, or disk, or when direct entry is made with a communication device such as a remote terminal. When undetected errors are entered originally, they may not be detected during processing, and, if detected, they are troublesome to correct. For this reason preventive controls at *input* tend to be the most cost effective. *Processing control* refers to error-condition check routines written into the computer program. *Output control* refers primarily to control over the distribution of reports, but feedback on errors and comparison of input totals to output totals also are part of this "last chance" control point.

Input Control Procedures.   Input controls are designed to provide reasonable assurance that data received for processing by the computer department have been authorized properly and converted into machine-sensible form, and that data have not been lost, suppressed, added, duplicated, or otherwise improperly changed. These controls also apply to correction and resubmission of data initially rejected as erroneous. The following control areas are particularly important:

Input Authorized and Approved.   Only properly authorized and approved input should be accepted for processing by the computer center. Authorization usually is a clerical (noncomputer) procedure involving a person's signature or stamp on a transaction document. However, some authorizations can be general (e.g., a management policy of automatic approval for sales under $500), and some authorizations can be computer-controlled (e.g., automatic production of a purchase order when an inventory item reaches a predetermined reorder point).

Check Digits.   Numbers often are used in computer systems in lieu of customer names, vendor names, and so forth. One common type of number validation procedure is the calculation of a check digit. A check digit is an extra number, precisely calculated, that is tagged onto the end of a basic identification number, such as an employee number. The basic code with its check digit sometimes is called a self-checking number. An electronic device can be installed on a data input device or the calculation can be programmed. The device or the program calculates the correct check digit and compares it to the one on the input data. When the digits do not match, an error message is indicated on the device or printed out on an input error report. Check digits are used only on identification numbers (not quantity or value fields) to detect coding errors or keying errors such as the transposition of digits (e.g., coding 387 as 837).[2]

Data Conversion.   Conversion of data into machine-sensible form is a source of many errors. Control procedures include the following:

- **Record counts.** Counts of records are tallies of the number of transaction documents submitted for data conversion. The known number submitted can be compared to the count of records produced by the data-conversion device (e.g., the

---

[2] One check digit algorithm is the "Modulus 11 Prime Number" method:
  a. Begin with a basic number: 814973.
  b. Multiply consecutive prime number weights of 19, 17, 13, 7, 5, 3 to each digit in the basic code number:

$$
\begin{array}{cccccc}
8 & 1 & 4 & 9 & 7 & 3 \\
\times 19 & \times 17 & \times 13 & \times 7 & \times 5 & \times 3 \\
\hline
= 152 & + 17 & + 52 & + 63 & + 35 & + 9 = 328
\end{array}
$$

  Note: the sequence of weights is the same for all codes in given system.
  c. Add the result of the multiplication = 328.
  d. Determine the next higher multiple of 11, which is 330.
  e. Subtract the sum of the multiplication (330 − 328 = 2). This is the check digit.
  f. New account number: 8149732.
Now if this number is entered incorrectly, say it is keypunched as 8419732, the check digit will not equal 2 and an error will be indicated. [See J. G. Burch, Jr., F. R. Strater, Jr., and G. Grudniski, *Information Systems: Theory and Practice*, 5th ed. (New York: John Wiley & Sons, 1989), pp. 191–93.]

number of sales transactions or count of magnetic records coded). A count mismatch indicates a lost item or one converted twice. Record counts are used as batch control totals and also are used during processing and at the output stage—whenever the comparison of a known count can be made with a computer-generated count.

- **Batch financial totals.** These totals are used in the same way as record counts, except the batch total is the sum of some important quantity or amount (e.g., the total sales dollar in a batch of invoices). Batch totals are also useful during processing and at the output stage.

- **Batch hash totals.** These totals are similar to batch number totals, except the hash total is not meaningful for accounting records (e.g., the sum of all the invoice numbers on invoices submitted to the data input operator).

Edit or Validation Routines.   Various computer-programmed editing or validation routines can be used to detect data conversion errors. Some of these are listed below:

- **Valid character tests.** These tests are used to check input data fields to see if they contain numbers when they are supposed to have numbers and alphabetic letters where they are supposed to have letters.

- **Valid sign tests.** Sign tests check data fields for appropriate plus or minus signs.

- **Missing data tests.** These edit tests check data fields to see if any are blank when they must contain data for the record entry to be correct.

- **Sequence tests.** These test the input data for numerical sequence of documents when sequence is important for processing, as in batch processing. This validation routine also can check for missing documents in a prenumbered series.

- **Limit or reasonableness tests.** These tests are computerized checks to see whether data values exceed or fall below some predetermined limit. For example, a payroll application may have a limit test to flag and reject any weekly payroll time record of 50 or more hours. The limit tests are a computerized version of scanning, the general audit procedure of reviewing data for indication of anything unusual that might turn out to be an error.

Error Correction and Resubmission.   Errors should be subject to special controls. Usually the computer department itself is responsible only for correcting its own errors (data conversion errors, for example). Other kinds of errors, such as those due to improper coding, should be referred to and handled by the user departments. It is a good idea to have a control group log the contents of error reports in order to monitor the nature, disposition, and proper correction of rejected data. Unless properly supervised and monitored, the error-correction process itself can become a source of data input errors.

Processing Control Procedures.   Processing controls are designed to provide reasonable assurance that data processing has been performed as intended without any omission or double-counting of transactions. Many of the processing controls are the same as the input controls, but they are used in the actual processing phases, rather than at the time input is checked. Other important controls are the following:

- **Run-to-Run Totals.** Movement of data from one department to another or one processing program to another should be controlled. One useful control is run-to-run totals. Run-to-run refers to sequential processing operations—runs—on the same data. These totals may be batch record counts, financial totals, and/or hash totals obtained at the end of one processing run. The totals are passed to the next run and compared to corresponding totals produced at the end of the second run.

- **Control Total Reports.** Control totals—record counts, financial totals, hash totals, and run-to-run totals—should be produced during processing operations and printed out on a report. Someone (the control group, for example) should have the responsibility for comparing and/or reconciling them to input totals or totals from earlier processing runs. Loss or duplication of data thus may be detected. For example, the total of the balances in the accounts receivable master file from the last update run, plus the total of the credit sales from the current update transactions, should equal the total of the balances at the end of the current processing.

- **File and Operator Controls.** External and internal labels are means of assuring that the proper files are used in applications. The systems software should produce a log to identify instructions entered by the operator and to make a record of time and use statistics for application runs. These logs should be reviewed by supervisory personnel.

- **Limit and Reasonableness Tests.** These tests should be programmed to ensure that illogical conditions do not occur: for example, depreciating an asset below zero or calculating a negative inventory quantity. These conditions, and others considered important, should generate error reports for supervisory review. Other logic and validation checks, described earlier under the heading of input edit checks, also can be used during processing.

Output Control Procedures.   Output controls are the final check on the accuracy of the results of computer processing. These controls also should be designed to ensure that only authorized persons receive reports or have access to files produced by the system. Typical output control procedures are the following:

- **Control Totals.** Control totals produced as output should be compared and/or reconciled to input and run-to-run control totals produced during processing. An independent control group should be responsible for the review of output control totals and investigation of differences.

- **Master File Changes.** These changes should be reported in detail back to the user department from which the request for change originated because an error can be pervasive. For example, changing selling prices incorrectly can cause all sales to be priced wrong. Someone should compare computer-generated change reports to original source documents for assurance that the data are correct.

- **Output Distribution.** Systems output should be distributed only to persons authorized to receive it. A distribution list should be maintained and used to deliver report copies. The number of copies produced should be restricted to the number needed.

R E V I E W
C H E C K P O I N T S

6.10 What are some of the characteristics that distinguish among control environment, accounting system, and control procedures in an internal control system?

6.11 What four general kinds of functional responsibilities should be performed by different departments or persons in a control system with good division of duties?

6.12 Give some examples of periodic comparisons a company can perform to control the accuracy of its recorded accountability.

6.13 What is a client's control procedure?

6.14 Describe the typical duties of computer personnel.

6.15 Which duties should be segregated within the computer department?

6.16 What is a self-checking number? Can you give an example of one of your own?

6.17 Describe five types of edit or validation controls and give an example of each for fields on a sales invoice form (e.g., customer name and number, dollar amount of the sale, shipping document number field, invoice number).

. . . .

PHASES OF A CONTROL EVALUATION
. . . .

LEARNING   OBJECTIVE

6. Explain the phases of an evaluation of control and risk assessment and the documentation and extent of audit work required.

The following sections describe the process of control evaluation in three phases. A major goal in audits is to be efficient. This means performing the work in minimum time and cost while still doing high-quality work to obtain sufficient, competent evidence. The allocation of work times between control evaluation and "year-end audit work" (e.g., the procedures in Exhibit 6–2) is a cost-benefit trade-off. Generally, the more auditors know about good controls, the less substantive year-end work they need to do. However, auditors do not necessarily need to determine the actual quality of a company's internal control structure. They only need to know enough to plan the other audit work. They can obtain only a minimum understanding of the control structure, assess a high control risk, and perform extensive substantive balance-audit work. Alternatively, they can perform a complete evaluation of control, assess control risk to be low, and minimize the balance-audit work. This trade-off is illustrated in Exhibit 6–8.

The three phases of work are described as if they are separate and distinct work packages performed before any account balance (substantive) audit work is started. In practice, work on the phases is often overlapping, and account balance-audit work is often done at a date before the company's fiscal year-end, at the same time some of the control evaluation work is being done. However, the analytical thinking process follows the sequence described hereafter.

PHASE 1: UNDERSTANDING THE INTERNAL CONTROL
. . . .

Exhibit 6–9 puts the internal control evaluation phases in perspective. In Phase 1 documentation of the auditors' understanding of internal control is required, but the audit team can halt the control evaluation process for the efficiency or effectiveness reasons explained below. However, if the auditors want to justify a low risk assessment to restrict the substantive audit procedures, the evaluation must be continued in Phase 3, the testing phase.

Nature and Timing of Phase 1 Work

The Phase 1 obtaining-an-understanding work should be done early. It gives auditors an overall acquaintance with the control environment, the flow of transactions

EXHIBIT 6–8   AUDIT COST TRADE-OFF

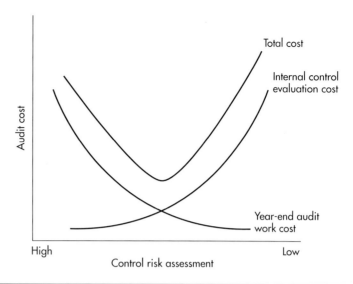

EXHIBIT 6–9   PHASES OF RISK ASSESSMENT DIAGRAM

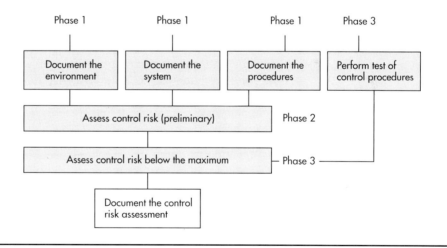

through the accounting system, and the effectiveness of some control procedures. It should produce general knowledge of the control environment along these lines:

- Managers' and directors' attitudes and actions regarding control.
- The client's organizational chart and personnel assignments.
- The segregation of functional responsibilities. Methods used to communicate responsibility and authority.
- Methods used to monitor and supervise the accounting system and the control procedures and to control access to assets and documents.
- The work assignments of internal auditors, if any.

It should also produce general knowledge of the flow of transactions through the accounting system along the following lines:

- The various classes of significant accounting transactions.
- The types of material errors and irregularities that could occur.
- Methods by which each significant class of transaction is:
  Authorized and initiated.
  Documented and recorded.
  Processed in the accounting system.
  Placed in financial reports and disclosures.

Auditors obtain an understanding of the internal controls through several sources of information. These sources include (1) previous experience with the company as found in last year's audit, (2) responses to enquiries directed to client personnel, (3) inspection of documents and records, and (4) observation of activities and operations made in a "walk-through" of one or a few transactions. Such "walk-through" tests of one transaction have traditionally been used to verify the accuracy of the auditor's flowchart or other description of the system.

The following box illustrates an actual system so bad it was considered unauditable.

UNDERSTANDING THE AUDITABILITY OF THE ACCOUNTS

Bad Books Block Audit for County: Travis County commissioners kept such poor financial records for four nonprofit corporations they controlled that an audit cannot be done, commissioners were told Tuesday. The four corporations are conduits for more than $630 million in low-interest financing for businesses. Public Accountant D. Holliday of Holliday & Associates struggled to find words to describe the corporations' records. "To say they are horrid is stretching it, because there weren't any records," Holliday told Commissioners Court members.

Among the findings were: (1) No records were kept of purchase and redemption of certificates of deposit for hundreds of thousands of dollars, (2) there may be certificates of deposit the county officials do not know exist, (3) bank statements were not kept, (4) checking accounts were not reconciled.

The former treasurer of the corporations said: "We had a very simple bookkeeping system. Money went in and went out. The system wasn't sophisticated because it wasn't needed."

Source: Austin American Statesman, August 19, 1987.

Stopping the Risk Assessment Work

Auditors can decide to stop the evaluation work in Phase 1 for either of two reasons, both of them co-ordinated with the final audit program. First, the audit team might conclude that no more evidence is needed to show that control is too poor to justify restrictions of subsequent audit procedures. This conclusion is equivalent to assessing

E X H I B I T 6-10   PHASES OF INTERNAL CONTROL EVALUATION

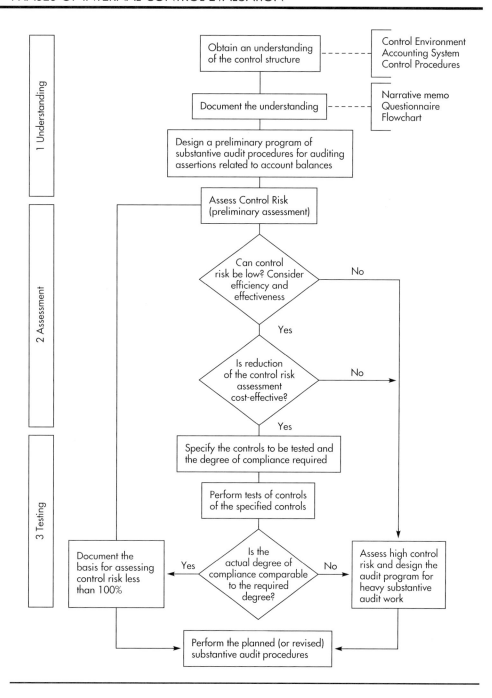

control risk at 1.0 (100 percent) and specifying extensive account balance-audit procedures, such as confirmation of all customer accounts as of December 31. Essentially, this decision is a matter of audit **effectiveness**.

Second, the audit team might decide that more time and effort would be spent evaluating controls to lower the control risk assessment than could be saved through being able to justify less account balance work (providing the controls turn out to be working well). In other words, the cost of obtaining a low control risk assessment may be high. In this case the conclusion is also equivalent to assessing control risk at or near 1.0, but this time because the auditors lack knowledge about the controls and not because they have decided controls are poor. However, the result is the same: extensive year-end account balance-audit procedures are specified. For example, suppose the extensive evaluation of controls over the validity of charges to customers would take 40 hours. If controls were excellent, suppose then the sample confirmation as of November 1 (with subsequent review of the December 31 trial balance) would take 30 hours less to perform than confirmation of all accounts as of December 31. The additional work on controls is not economical. The decision to stop work on control risk assessment in this case is a matter of audit **efficiency**—deciding not to work 40 hours in order to save 30 hours.

Documentation of the Control Elements

Working paper documentation of a decision to assess control risk as 1.0 (no reliance on the control structure to restrict procedures) can consist only of a memorandum of that fact. However, for future reference in next year's audit, many firms prepare a memorandum explaining the effectiveness-related or efficiency-related reasons.

Working paper documentation also should include records showing the audit team's understanding of the internal controls. The understanding can be summarized in the form of questionnaires, narratives, and flowcharts.

Internal Control Questionnaire and Narrative

The most efficient means of gathering evidence about the control structure is to conduct a formal interview with knowledgeable managers, using the checklist type of **internal control questionnaire** illustrated in Exhibit 6–11. This questionnaire is organized under headings that identify the control environment questions and the questions related to each of the seven control objectives. All questionnaires are not organized like this, so auditors need to know the general categories in order to know whether the questionnaire is complete. Likewise, if you are assigned to write a questionnaire, you will need to be careful to include questions about each control objective.

Internal control questionnaires are designed to help the audit team obtain evidence about the control environment and about the accounting and control procedures that are considered good error-checking routines. Answers to the questions, however, should not be taken as final and definitive evidence about how well control actually functions. Evidence obtained through the interview-questionnaire process is hearsay evidence because its source is generally a single person who, while knowledgeable, is still not the person who actually performs the control work. This person may give answers that reflect what he or she believes the system should be, rather than what it really is. The person may be unaware of informal ways in which duties have been changed or may be innocently ignorant of the system details. Nevertheless, interviews and questionnaires are useful when a manager tells of a weak feature. An admission of weak control is fairly convincing.

EXHIBIT 6-11   INTERNAL CONTROL QUESTIONNAIRE—SALES TRANSACTION PROCESSING

Client _____ Audit Date _____

Client Personnel Interviewed _____

Auditor _____ Date Completed _____

Reviewed by _____ Date Reviewed _____

Question	Answer			
	NA	Yes	No	Remarks
Environment:				
1. Is the credit department independent of the marketing department?				
2. Are sales of the following types controlled by the same procedures described below? Sales to employees, COD sales, disposals of property, cash sales, and scrap sales.				
Validity Objective				
3. Is access to sales invoice blanks restricted?				
4. Are prenumbered bills of lading or other shipping documents prepared or completed in the shipping department?				
Completeness Objective				
5. Are sales invoice blanks prenumbered?				
6. Is the sequence checked for missing invoices?				
7. Is the shipping document numerical sequence checked for missing bills of lading numbers?				
Authorization Objective				
8. Are all credit sales approved by the credit department prior to shipment?				
9. Are sales prices and terms based on approved standards?				
10. Are returned sales credits and other credits supported by documentation as to receipt, condition, and quantity, and approved a responsible officer?				
Accuracy Objective				
11. Are shipped quantities compared to invoice quantities?				
12. Are sales invoices checked for error in quantities, prices, extensions and footing, freight allowances, and checked with customer's orders?				
13. Is there an overall check on arithmetic accuracy of period sales data by a statistical or product-line analysis?				
14. Are periodic sales data reported directly to general ledger accounting independent of accounts receivable accounting?				
Classification Objective				
15. Does the accounting manual contain instructions for classifying sales?				
Accounting Objective				
16. Are summary journal entries approved before posting?				
Proper Period Objective				
17. Does the accounting manual contain instructions to date sales invoices on the shipment date?				

A strong point about questionnaires is that an auditor is less likely to forget to cover some important point. Questions generally are worded so that a "no" answer points out some weakness or control deficiency, thus making analysis easier.

One way to tailor these enquiry procedures to a particular company is to write a narrative description of each important control subsystem. Such a narrative would simply describe all the environmental elements, the accounting system, and the control procedures. The narrative description may be efficient in audits of very small businesses.

Accounting and Control System Flowcharts

Another method for documenting auditors' understanding of accounting and control systems is to construct a flowchart. Many control-conscious companies will have their own flowcharts, and the auditors can use them instead of constructing their own. Flowcharting is used widely by auditors. The advantages of flowcharts can be summarized by an old cliché: "A picture is worth a thousand words." Flowcharts can enhance auditors' evaluations, and annual updating of a chart is relatively easy—simply add or delete symbols and lines.

Construction of a flowchart takes time because an auditor must learn about the operating personnel involved in the system and gather samples of relevant documents. Thus, the information for the flowchart, like the narrative description, involves a lot of legwork and observation. When the flowchart is complete, however, the result is an easily evaluated, informative description of the system.

Exhibit 6–12 contains a few simple flowchart symbols. For any flowcharting application, the chart must be understandable to an audit supervisor. He or she should not need to consult a lengthy index of symbols to decipher a flowchart. A flowchart should be drawn with a template and ruler or with computer software. A messy chart is hard to read. The starting point in the system should, if possible, be placed at the upper left-hand corner. The flow of procedures and documents should be from left to right and from top to bottom, as much as is possible. Narrative explanations should be written on the face of the chart as annotations or be written in a readily available reference key.

The flowchart should communicate all relevant information and evidence about segregation of responsibilities, authorization, and accounting and control procedures in an understandable, visual form. Exhibit 6–13 contains a flowchart representation of the beginning stages of a sales and delivery processing system. This is a partial flowchart. The outconnectors shown by the circled *A* and *B* indicate continuation on other flowcharts. Ultimately, the flowchart ends showing entries in accounting journals and ledgers.

In Exhibit 6–13 you can see some characteristics of flowchart construction and some characteristics of this accounting system.[3]

By reading down the columns headed for each department, you can see that transaction initiation authority (both credit approval and sales invoice preparation) and custody of assets are separated. Notice that all documents have an intermediate or final resting place in a file. (Some of these files are in the flowcharts connected to *A* and *B*.) This flowchart feature gives auditors information about where to find audit evidence later.

A technological development that has helped make flowcharting more cost effective is specialized software that automates the flowcharting process. The box on page 216 illustrates some software used in practice.

---

[3] Accounting firms have various methods for constructing flowcharts. The illustrations in this book take the approach of describing an accounting subsystem completely. Some accounting firms use more efficient methods to flowchart only the documents, information flows, and controls considered important for the audit.

EXHIBIT 6–12   STANDARD FLOWCHART SYMBOLS

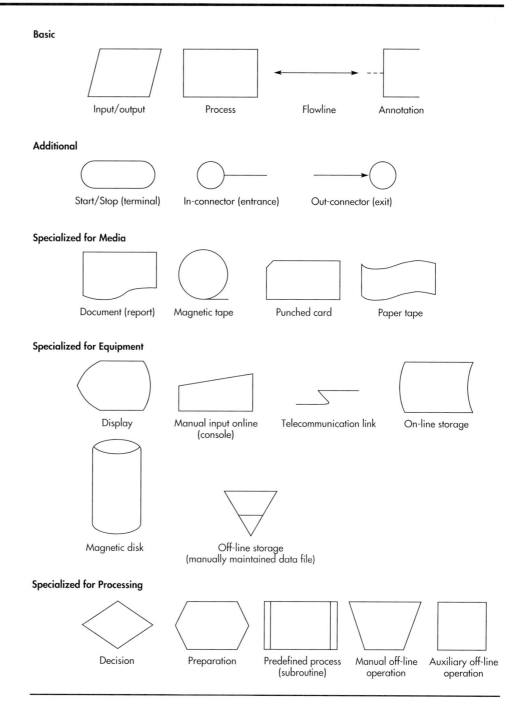

Basic

Input/output   Process   Flowline   Annotation

Additional

Start/Stop (terminal)   In-connector (entrance)   Out-connector (exit)

Specialized for Media

Document (report)   Magnetic tape   Punched card   Paper tape

Specialized for Equipment

Display   Manual input online (console)   Telecommunication link   On-line storage

Magnetic disk   Off-line storage (manually maintained data file)

Specialized for Processing

Decision   Preparation   Predefined process (subroutine)   Manual off-line operation   Auxiliary off-line operation

EXHIBIT 6–13   CREDIT APPROVAL AND SALES PROCESSING, SHIPMENT, AND DELIVERY

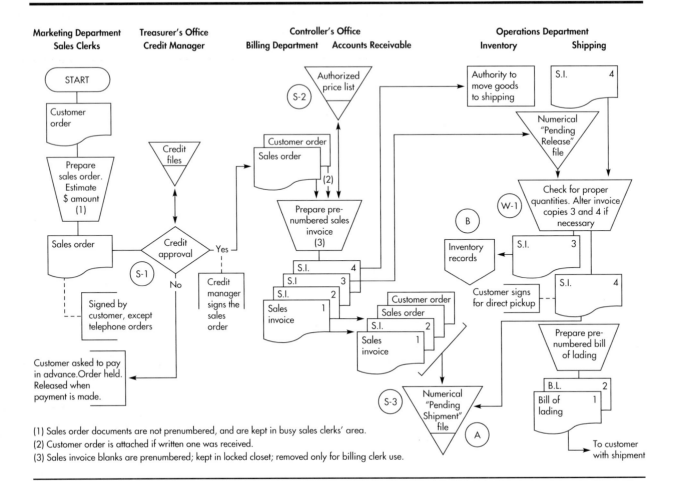

Marketing Department — Sales Clerks
Treasurer's Office — Credit Manager
Controller's Office — Billing Department, Accounts Receivable
Operations Department — Inventory, Shipping

(1) Sales order documents are not prenumbered, and are kept in busy sales clerks' area.
(2) Customer order is attached if written one was received.
(3) Sales invoice blanks are prenumbered; kept in locked closet; removed only for billing clerk use.

ANALYSING AND DOCUMENTING INTERNAL CONTROL

We can bring to bear a variety of techniques and tools to assist clients in strengthening internal control. The most exciting of these methodologies is INFOCUS, our microcomputer package for analysing portions of an entity's internal controls and graphically portraying potential weaknesses. INFOCUS harnesses the microcomputer to combine flowcharting and narratives, blending attributes of both to achieve a unique approach to documenting and evaluating internal controls that is applicable regardless of size, complexity, type of business, or nature of the entity.

Source: Grant Thornton open letter to clients, May 20, 1991.

PHASE 2: ASSESSING THE CONTROL RISK

. . . .

After completing Phase 1—obtaining an understanding of the internal control and designing a preliminary audit program—the audit team should be able to make a preliminary assessment of the control risk. One way to make the assessment is to analyse the control strengths and weaknesses. **Strengths** are specific features of good detail controls that would prevent, detect, or correct material misstatements. **Weaknesses** are the lack of controls in particular areas that would allow material errors to get by undetected. The auditors' findings and preliminary conclusions should be written up for the working paper files.

Strengths and weaknesses should be documented in a working paper sometimes called a bridge working paper, so called because it connects (bridges) the control evaluation to subsequent audit procedures. The major strengths and weaknesses apparent in the flow chart (Exhibit 6–13) can be summarized as shown in Exhibit 6–14. On the flowchart the strengths are indicated by *S-*, and the weaknesses by *W-*. In the bridge working paper, the "audit program" column contains test of controls procedures for auditing the control strengths and suggestions about substantive account balance audit procedures related to the weaknesses (the last column in Exhibit 6–14). Auditors do not need to perform test of controls audit procedures on weaknesses just to prove they are weak places. Doing so would be inefficient.

In terms of control risk assessment, at this stage the control risk related to the inventory balance might be set very high (e.g., 0.8 or 0.9). The three control strengths, however, relate to good control over sales validity and accounts receivable accuracy. The auditors probably will want to rely on these controls to reduce the accounts receivable balance audit work. Test of controls procedures ought to be performed to obtain evidence about whether the apparent strengths actually are performed well. The "audit program" segment of Exhibit 6–14 for each of the strengths is a statement of a test of controls audit procedure. Test of controls auditing (Phase 3) consists of procedures designed to produce evidence of how well the controls worked in practice. If they pass the auditor's criteria (the required degree of compliance), control risk can be assessed low. If they fail the test, the final conclusion is to assess a high control risk, revise the account balance audit plan to take the control weakness into account, and then proceed with the audit work. In summary, Phases 1 and 2 can be described as dealing with the evaluation of the *design* of the system assuming it operates properly, whereas Phase 3 is a test of the actual operation of the systems.

PHASE 3: PERFORMING TEST OF CONTROLS AUDIT PROCEDURES

. . . .

LEARNING OBJECTIVE

7. Write procedures for an audit program, following the general form of a detail test of control procedure.

By the time auditors reach the third phase of an evaluation of internal control, they will have identified specific controls on which risk could be assessed very low (e.g., the strengths shown in Exhibit 6–14). To reduce the final risk assessment to a low level, auditors must determine (1) the required degree of company compliance with the control policies and procedures and (2) the actual degree of company compliance. The **required degree of compliance** is the auditors' decision criterion for good control performance. Knowing that compliance cannot realistically be expected to be perfect, auditors might decide, for example, that evidence of using bills of lading (shipping documents) to validate sales invoice recordings 96 percent of the time is

E X H I B I T 6–14   **BRIDGE WORKING PAPER**

Index _____   By _____ Date _____
                                               Reviewed _____ Date _____

KINGSTON COMPANY
Credit Approval, Sales Processing, Shipment, and Delivery Control
December 31, 1992

	Strength/Weakness	Audit Implication	Audit Program
S-1	Credit approval on sales order.	Credit authorization reduces risk of bad debt loss and helps check on validity of customer identification.	Select a sample of recorded sales invoices, and look for credit manager signature on attached sales order.
S-2	Unit prices are taken from an authorized list.	Prices are in accordance with company policy, minimizing customer disputes.	Using the S-1 sample of sales invoices, vouch prices used thereon to the price lists.
S-3	Sales are not recorded until goods are shipped.	Cutoff will be proper and sales will not be recorded too early.	Using the S-1 sample of sales invoices, compare the recording date to the shipment date on attached bill of lading or copy 4. (Also, scan the "pending shipment" file for old invoices that might represent unrecorded shipments.)
W-1	Shipping personnel have transaction alteration (initiation) authority to change the quantities on invoices, as well as custody of the goods.	Dishonest shipping personnel can alone let accomplices receive large quantities and alter the invoice to charge them for small quantities. In this system, sales and accounts receivable would be understated, and inventory could be overstated.	The physical count of inventory will need to be observed carefully (extensive work) to detect material overstatement.

sufficient to assess a low control risk for the audit of accounts receivable (looking for overstatement in receivables and sales).

Now the auditors can perform **test of controls procedures** to determine how well the company's controls actually functioned during the period under audit. A test of controls audit procedure is a two-part statement. Part 1 is an identification of the data population from which a sample of items will be selected for audit. Part 2 is an expression of an action taken to produce relevant evidence. In general, the action is (1) determine whether the selected items correspond to a standard (e.g., mathematical accuracy), and/or (2) determine whether the selected items agree with information in another data population. The test of controls procedures in Exhibit 6–14 show this two-part design.

One other important aspect of these audit procedures is known as the direction of the test. The procedures described in Exhibit 6–14 provide evidence about control over the validity of sales transactions. However, they do not provide evidence about control over completeness of recording all shipments. Another data population—the shipping documents—can be sampled to provide evidence about completeness. The direction of the test idea is illustrated in Exhibit 6–15. If completeness control is found to be strong, the auditors can omit the year-end procedure of confirming customers' zero-balance accounts to search for unrecorded assets.

Some test of controls procedures involve **reperformance**—the auditors perform again the arithmetic calculations and the comparisons the company people were

E X H I B I T 6–15   DIRECTION OF THE TEST OF CONTROLS AUDIT PROCEDURES

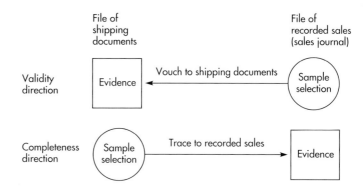

TEST OF CONTROLS NECESSARY FOR ASSESSING LOW CONTROL RISK

Enquiry alone generally will not provide sufficient evidential matter to support a conclusion about the effectiveness of design or operation of a specific [client] control procedure. When the auditor determines that a specific [client] control procedure may have a significant effect in reducing control risk to a low level for a specific assertion, he or she ordinarily needs to perform additional tests [of controls] to obtain sufficient evidential matter to support the conclusion about the effectiveness of the design or operation of that [client] control procedure.

Source: Handbook Section 5205.23.

---

supposed to have performed. Some accountants, however, believe mere **inspection** is enough—the auditors just look to see whether the documents were marked with an initial, signature, or stamp to indicate they had been checked. They maintain that reperformance is not necessary.[4]

Some test of controls procedures depend on documentary evidence, like a sales entry supported by a bill of lading. Documentary evidence in the form of signatures, initials, checklists, reconciliation working papers, and the like provides better evidence than procedures that leave no documentary tracks. Some control elements, such as segregation of employees' duties, may leave no documents behind. In this case, the best kind of procedures—reperformance of control operations—cannot be done, and the second procedure—observation—must be used. This procedure amounts to an auditor's unobtrusive eyewitness observation of employees at their jobs performing control operations.

---

[4] When you go to work for an audit organization, one preference will prevail, but many auditors believe good evidence requires reperformance, where feasible, at least for part of the controls testing.

Tests of controls procedures, when performed, should be applied to samples of transactions and control procedures executed throughout the period under audit. The reason for this requirement is that the conclusions about controls will be generalized to the whole period under audit.

· ·

R E V I E W
C H E C K P O I N T S

6.18 Must the Phase 1 obtaining-an-understanding work of an evaluation of internal control always be followed by assessment and testing phases? Explain.

6.19 What are the advantages and disadvantages of documenting internal control by using (1) an internal control questionnaire, (2) a narrative memorandum, and (3) a flowchart?

6.20 What is a bridge working paper? Describe its content and its connection to the test of controls and account balance audit programs.

6.21 What is a test of controls audit procedure? What two parts are important in a written procedure?

6.22 What is the difference between inspection and reperformance in test of controls audit procedures?

· ·

CONTROL EVALUATION AND COST/BENEFIT
· · · · · · · · · · · · ·

LEARNING OBJECTIVE

8. Define and explain reasonable assurance and cost-benefit in the context of control risk assessment.

An assessment of control risk should be co-ordinated with the final audit plan. The final account balance audit plan includes the specification (list) of **substantive audit procedures**, which were defined in Chapter 5 as the transaction detail audit and analytical procedures designed to detect material misstatements in account balances and footnote disclosures.

Internal controls are subject to cost-benefit considerations. Controls possibly could be made perfect, or nearly so, at great expense. A fence could be erected; locks could be installed; lighting could be used at night; television monitors could be put in place; guards could be hired. Each of these successive safeguards costs money, as does extensive supervision of clerical personnel in an office. At some point the cost of protecting the inventory from theft (or of supervisors' catching every clerical error) exceeds the benefit of control. Hence, control systems generally do not provide absolute assurance that the objectives of internal control are satisfied. **Reasonable assurance** is thought to be enough, and has been defined as follows: "The concept of reasonable assurance recognizes that the cost of an entity's internal [controls] should not exceed the benefits that are expected to be derived." The *CICA Handbook* notes this concept when it recognizes that internal control is designed to assist management to optimize the use of resources (*Sections* 5200–5220C).

Notwithstanding the common sense of the concept of reasonable assurance, auditors must be careful to determine whether a system contains any internal control weakness. Business managers can make estimates of benefits to be derived from controls and weigh them against the cost. Managers are perfectly free to make their own judgments about the necessary extent of controls. Managers can decide the degree of business risk they are willing to accept (refer to Appendix B of *Handbook Sections* 5200–5220). However, auditors should be aware that the "cost-benefit" and "reasonable assurance" concepts can sometimes be used loosely by a management to tolerate control deficiencies.

Since preparation of the final account balance audit plan is the primary aim and purpose, the evaluation of internal control must be documented in audit working papers. Documentation of the understanding of the internal control and the control risk assessment is required. These audit working papers can include internal control questionnaires, narrative descriptions, flowcharts, specifications of controls and compliance criteria, and the evidence produced by test of controls audit procedures.

You have studied tests of controls and substantive balance audit procedures as if they were easily distinguishable. Be advised, however, that the six general audit techniques described in Chapter 4 can be used both as test of controls procedures and as substantive procedures. Actually, you would be better advised to think in terms of test of controls and substantive **purposes** of a procedure instead of test of controls and substantive procedures. A single procedure may produce both control and substantive evidence and, thus, serve both purposes (hence the name **dual-purpose tests**, *Handbook Section* 5210.21). For example, a selection of recorded sales entries could be used (1) to vouch sales to supporting bills of lading and (2) to calculate the correct dollar amount of sales. The first datum is relevant information about control compliance. The second is dollar-value information that may help measure an amount of misstatement in the book balance of sales. Another example is the confirmation of accounts receivable procedure. This procedure has a primary substantive purpose, but, when confirmation replies tell about significant or systematic errors, the evidence is relevant to control evaluation as well as to dollar-value measurement. Most audit procedures serve dual purposes and yield evidence both about controls and about financial statement assertions.

. . . .

R E V I E W
C H E C K P O I N T S

6.23 What is the concept of reasonable assurance? Who is responsible for assessing it?

6.24 What audit problems can arise over management's beliefs about reasonable assurance?

6.25 What purposes are served by a "dual-purpose test?"

. . . .

INTERNAL CONTROL IN SMALL BUSINESS

. . . .

LEARNING   OBJECTIVE

9. Adapt the concepts and processes of control risk assessment to small businesses.

The foregoing explanations of internal control characteristics contain an underlying thread of bureaucratic organization theory and a large-business orientation. A company must be large and employ several people (about 10 or more) to have a theoretically appropriate segregation of functional responsibilities and its accompanying high degree of specialization of work. Supervision requires people. The paperwork and computer control necessary in most large systems is extensive. Control theory also suggests that people perform in accounting and control roles and do not engage in frequent personal interaction across functional responsibility boundaries. None of these theoretical dimensions fit small business very well.

Auditors should be careful to recognize the bureaucratic, large-business orientation of internal control theory. When the business under audit is small, some allowances must be made for size, the number of people employed, and the control attitude expressed by important managers and owners. Although one should keep in mind that the extensive downsizing taking place in the nineties has had a generally adverse impact on the general control environment with the consequence that critical elements of the control environment are taking on more relevance for larger businesses.

The key person in internal control in a small business is the owner-manager. Because the business is small, it does not exhibit the complexity that creates demand for elaborate internal control. A diligent owner-manager may be able to oversee and supervise all the important authorization, recordkeeping, and custodial functions. He or she also may be able to ensure satisfactory data processing accuracy. Thus, an auditor evaluating control risk will study the extent of the owner-manager's involvement in the operation of the accounting and control system and evaluate the owner-manager's competence and integrity. This latter task emphasizes the importance of the "competent personnel" quality characteristic of internal control. Internal control questionnaires designed specifically for small businesses contain more items related to the owner-manager and other key personnel than do large-business questionnaires. The reason for this is that although small businesses may lack key elements of formal control such as segregation of duties, management involvement can compensate for lack of more formal controls.

As a small business begins to grow from, say, 4 people to 10 or 15, the transition to more formalized internal control tends to lag behind. The owner-manager may become overburdened with control duties and may tacitly delegate these to others. The intermediate-size stage represents a turning point where both owner-manager and auditor need to be very careful. At this point such measures as limited specialization and surety bonding of employees may help make the transition, and an auditor may offer many suggestions to the owner-manager as an added service.

R E V I E W
CHECKPOINTS

6.26   Is the general theory of internal control embodied in the basic characteristics of reliable internal control equally applicable to large and small enterprises? Discuss.

6.27   What are the two main features of internal control in a small business?

Auditor's Responsibility to Detect and Communicate Misstatements

After the auditor's evaluation of internal controls, the auditor is in a strong position to assess the likelihood of material misstatements. Perhaps this then is a good point to review auditor responsibilities for detecting and communicating misstatements as per the new guidance in *Handbook Section* 5135.

Financial misstatements can arise from error, fraud, or other irregularities. A financial error is defined as an unintentional misstatement, whereas fraud and other irregularities are defined as intentional misstatements.

Intent is difficult to prove and for that reason "a misstatement arising from management's bias in selecting and applying accounting principles or in making accounting estimates would be considered an error." However, the audit also needs to be performed with professional scepticism, meaning the auditor:

1. should be aware of factors that increase the risk of misstatement (see appendix); and

2. should be sensitized to evidence that contradicts the assumption of management's good faith.

Note that many of the risk factors relate to poor internal controls.

If there are enough "red flags" present, the auditor will assess a higher inherent risk, and if control risk is also high, these higher assessments will cause auditor to:

1. Obtain more reliable evidence.

2. Expand the extent of audit procedures performed.

3. Apply audit procedures closer to or as of the balance sheet date.

4. Require more extensive supervision of assistants and/or assistants with more experience and training.

In essence, if the auditor suspects that the financial statements are misstated, she or he should perform procedures to confirm or dispel that suspicion. These procedures are discussed in more detail in subsequent chapters.

Generally, the auditor is less likely to detect material misstatements arising from fraud because of the deliberate concealment involved. (Procedures for fraud detection are discussed in more detail in Chapter 18 and in various examples, which we call "casettes" in this book.) The auditor should inform the appropriate level of management whenever he or she obtains evidence of a nontrivial misstatement, and of weaknesses in internal control. The audit committee or board of directors should be informed of all significant misstatements.

The auditor should consider obtaining legal advice if he or she has doubts about communicating misstatements to third parties, particularly if the auditor resigned, or was removed, or was unable to report on the financial statements.

Summary
. . . .

This chapter explained the theory and practice of auditors' involvement with a client's "internal control." The purposes of auditor involvement are to assess the control risk in order to plan the substantive audit program and to report control deficiencies to management and the board of directors.

In theory a control system consists of three elements—the control environment, the accounting system, and the client's control procedures. Each of these is evaluated and documented in the audit working papers. The control environment was explained in terms of understanding the client's business. Elements of the accounting system were explained in conjunction with control procedures designed to prevent, detect, and correct misstatements that occur in transactions. These misstatements were systematized in a set of seven categories of errors and irregularities that can occur. A reverse expression of them yielded the seven control objectives a company wishes to achieve. The control objectives were related to management's assertions found in financial statements.

Control procedures were covered extensively. They were organized under the headings of general control procedures (i.e., capable personnel, segregation of responsibilities, controlled access, periodic comparison, and error-checking routines), segregation of technical responsibilities (computer-related jobs), and error-checking routine detail (11 input controls, 4 processing controls, and 3 output controls). The explanations of these controls integrated computerized accounting systems with control practice.

Documentation of a control system was explained with reference to control questionnaires, flowcharts, and narratives. Questionnaires and flowcharts were demonstrated. The understanding and the documentation were taken one step further to the test of controls phase and the cost reduction reasons for doing work to obtain a low control risk assessment. The assessed control risk was connected to the CR in the control risk model (Chapter 5).

Control evidence was linked to audit programs with a bridge working paper presentation. The nature of test of controls procedures was explained in terms of a two-part statement that dictated identification of the data population, from which control evidence is drawn, and the action taken to produce the relevant evidence.

The chapter closed with sections on cost-benefit and reasonable assurance considerations and on adaptation of control theory to small businesses. The Chapter 6 treatment of control risk assessment provided some basis for the theory and practice of audit sampling, which is covered next in Chapter 7.

CASE STUDY   KINGSTON COMPANY

Introduction

The descriptions below continue the Kingston Company case started in Chapters 4 and 5. Your job now is to evaluate internal control to the extent it is described below. These descriptions are part of the Revenue and Collection Cycle, which is explained in more detail in Chapter 9.

Kingston Accounting and Control Systems: Revenue and Collection Cycle

As evident in the company organization chart (Exhibit 4–10), Kingston has several departments and offices concerned with management, accounting, and control. The company also has an abbreviated accounting and control manual and a chart of accounts. Officers and employees have described accounting and control procedures informally under the heading of several transaction cycles. Their descriptions—transcripts of conversations—start below.

Credit Approval and Sales Processing

Customer orders are received in the mail, over the telephone, and over the counter by salesclerks in the marketing department. The clerks prepare written sales orders for telephone and counter customers, signing each one and asking the counter customers to sign in person. The sales orders contain the customer name, a customer number (assigned immediately for new customers), customer address, identification of products, and the quantity ordered. The sales order forms are kept in the salesclerks' working area through which many people pass during the day. The sales order documents used in the offices are not prenumbered.

The salesclerks prepare an estimate of the dollar amount of the order and write it on the form. The sales orders are then hand-carried to the credit manager in the treasurer's office. The credit manager checks the customers' accounts receivable balances and other credit file information using a computer-based enquiry system. If credit is approved, the credit manager signs the sales order.

If credit is not approved, the customer is asked to pay in advance, and the sales order is held until notification of payment is received from the cashier. The sales order is stamped "paid" and sent to the billing department. Likewise, when customers pay cash over the counter, the money is taken by the cashier, and the sales order is stamped "paid" and sent to the billing department. For bookkeeping convenience, these "cash" sales are treated the same as credit sales, with the invoice amount being charged to an account receivable set up for the customer, and the customer's payment being applied immediately to the same account.

After credit has been approved, or a payment received, the sales orders are sent to the billing department in the controller's office. The billing clerks produce a four-copy sales invoice on a prenumbered invoice form. Using a screen facsimile on a microcomputer, they insert the customer and product information from the customer order, the date, and the product unit prices from an approved price list. Sales taxes, delivery charges, and the invoice total are computed and put on the invoice. The sales invoice forms are kept in a locked closet in the billing department, and sheets in the numerical sequence are removed only for billing clerks' immediate loading onto the computer printer.

Copy 1 and copy 2 of the sales invoice, the customer order, and the sales order are sent to the accounts receivable accounting department, which is also in the controller's office. These documents are held in invoice numerical order in a "pending shipment" file, awaiting matching with copy 4 of the invoice, which was first sent to the inventory stores department as authority for the storeskeeper to put the order together and move it to the shipping department. Copy 3 of the invoice is sent to the shipping department, where it is initially held in a "pending release" file.

Shipment and Delivery

The inventory storeskeeper supervises removal of products from shelves and bins upon receipt of an invoice copy 4, which serves as the authorization to move goods to the shipping area. Copy 4 is sent to the shipping area with the products. In the shipping area, shipping employees remove copy 3 from the "pending release" file. They check both copy 3 and copy 4 for the correct quantity of each product, then pack the order in suitable boxes. Copy 3 is sent to the inventory records department in the controller's office, where it serves as the source of entries to reduce the perpetual inventory records. If any items shown on the invoice are not shipped, the handlers are supposed to alter the invoice copies to show the correct quantity.

When customers are on the premises, they can pick up their own orders at the shipping area, where they are asked to sign copy 4 as acknowledgement of receipt. Otherwise, a prenumbered bill of lading is filled out in two copies for shipments by contract truckers. Copy 1 of the bill of lading is attached to the shipment. Copy 2 of the bill of lading is sent with invoice copy 4 to the accounts receivable accounting department.

ACCOUNTING AND CONTROL PROCEDURE MANUAL

Sales and Accounts Receivable

Daily batches of sales invoices shall be analysed by sales totals in the lumber and hardware product lines. Sales credits are coded to these two product line sales revenue accounts.

Charges to customer accounts should be dated the date of shipment. When sales invoices are recorded, the numerical sequence shall be checked by an accounts receivable clerk, and the items shipped shall be compared to the items billed for proper quantity, price, and other sales order terms.

The general ledger supervisor shall compare the copy 2 daily batch total with the copy 4 individual accounts posting total sent from the accounts receivable department. Discrepancies shall be investigated to help ensure that the customer subsidiary accounts are posted for the same total amount posted to the control account.

At the end of each month, the total of the trial balance of customer account balances (prepared by the accounts receivable department) shall be reconciled to the general ledger control account by the general ledger supervisor.

Sales invoice batches shall be dated with the date of shipment, and totals of batches (including product line sales for lumber and hardware) shall be accumulated each month and recorded in the accounts receivable control and sales revenue accounts. The general ledger supervisor shall approve all monthly summary entries before they are posted to the general ledger.

The treasurer shall approve all cash refunds and allowance credits for sales returns, after initiation by customer relations personnel.

The marketing vice president shall periodically analyse sales activity by product lines in comparison to budgets and forecasts and prior years activity.

Cash Management

The monthly bank statements shall be mailed to the cash management department in the treasurer's office. Personnel use the duplicate deposit slips retained when bank deposits were made, the cash receipts journal listing, and the cash disbursements listing to reconcile the general bank accounts. The payroll bank account is also reconciled, utilizing the payroll register retained by the treasurer's office.

Cash management personnel shall compare cash receipts journal daily deposit records with the bank deposits and duplicate deposit slips when the general bank account reconciliation is performed.

At the discretion of the director of internal audit, internal auditors will occasionally make unannounced reviews of the bank account reconciliations. They may also prepare reconciliations without prior notice given to cash management personnel.

Cash Receipts and Accounts Receivable Processing

All cash receipts from customers related to sales shall be credited to accounts receivable individual and control accounts.

The accounts receivable department shall post credits to individual customer accounts, dating the entries with the date of the remittance list.

Statements of accounts receivable balances shall be mailed to customers each month by the accounts receivable accounting department. Customers' reports of disputes or differences shall be handled by customer relations personnel in the marketing department.

Cash Disbursements

All disbursements shall be made by cheque, signed by the treasurer, including reimbursements of the petty cash funds.

Cheques shall be made payable to a named payee and not to "cash." Blank cheque stock shall be kept under lock and key in the accounts payable accounting department. Under no circumstances may blank cheques be signed by the treasurer.

Voided and spoiled cheques shall be transmitted to the treasurer for inspection and later filed in numerical order with paid cheques.

Cash disbursements journal entries shall be dated with the date of the cheque. The related monthly general ledger summary entries shall carry the date of the month summarized.

Inventory Perpetual Records

Inventory additions shall be dated with the date of the receiving report.

Inventory issues shall be dated with the date of shipment.

Capital Asset Records and Transactions

When acquisition costs exceed the capital budget authorization by 10 percent or more, the additional expenditure shall be approved by the treasurer and board of directors, in advance if possible.

Zero salvage values shall be used in all depreciation calculations.

Useful life and amortization method assignments for financial statement calculations shall follow these general guidelines:

Furniture and fixtures	Straight line	5–10 years
Computer equipment	Straight line	3–5 years
Automobiles, trucks	SYD	5 years
Production machinery	SYD	10–12 years
Buildings	Straight line	35 years

All repair, maintenance, capital additions, and the like of $1,000 or less shall be expensed. Amounts between $1,000 and $5,000 may be capitalized at the judgment of the accounts payable accounting department personnel. Amounts over $5,000 should always be capitalized unless unusual conditions point to proper expensing.

Capital asset acquisition dates in the detail and control accounts should be the date assets are placed in use, which may be different from the liability incurrence date.

Kingston Company Chart of Accounts

100	Asset Accounts

Current Assets
101	North Country General Account
103	North Country Payroll Account
105	Trade Accounts Receivable
109	Allowance for Doubtful Accounts
111	Inventory Control—Lumber
113	Inventory Control—Hardware
115	Other Current Assets

Property, Plant, and Equipment, and Other Assets
121	Buildings
123	Accumulated Amortization—Buildings
125	Equipment
127	Accumulated Amortization—Equipment
129	Land
140	Other Assets

200	Liability Accounts

Current Liabilities
201	Trade Accounts Payable
203	Accrued Expenses Payable (except interest)
205	Accrued Interest Payable
207	Dividends Payable
209	Income Taxes Payable
211	Other Current Liabilities
213	Bank Loans Payable

Long-Term Liabilities and Deferred Credits
220	Notes Payable
230	Deferred Credits

300	Shareholder Equity Accounts

301	Share Capital
303	Contributed Surplus
305	Retained Earnings
307	Dividends Declared

400	Revenue Accounts

401	Sales—Lumber
403	Sales—Hardware

Kingston Company Chart of Accounts
(concluded)

500   Expense Accounts

501   Cost of Goods Sold—Lumber
503   Cost of Goods Sold—Hardware
505   Wages and Salaries
507   Payroll Tax Expense
509   Amortization Expense
511   Rent Expense
513   Utilities Expense
515   Advertising Expense
517   Professional Fees
519   Insurance Expense
521   Property Taxes
523   Repairs and Maintenance
525   Other Expenses
527   Interest Expense
529   Bad Debts Expense
531   Income Tax Expense
533   Sales Returns and Allowances
535   Other Income and Expense

6.28   Kingston Company: Understanding the Control Environment.   This requirement involves only one element of the understanding phase—the company organization chart.

Required:
Using the Kingston Company description of organization and personnel, expand the organization chart in Exhibit 6–10 by showing the offices, personnel, and departments under each vice president.

6.29   Kingston Company: Identification of Errors and Irregularities.   The major classes of transactions started in the parts of the business described above are (*a*) inventory issues (goods delivered to customers) and (*b*) sales (sales invoices prepared). When you work the requirement below, be careful to confine your responses to these transactions to the extent they are described.

Required:
Prepare a working paper for the audit of Kingston Company as of December 31, 1992, showing (1) headings for each general type of error or irregularity that can occur and (2) specific descriptions of each such error and irregularity for each of the two major classes of transactions. (For example: 1. Invalid transactions may be recorded. (*a*) Inventory issues: Goods may be shown as shipped/delivered to customers, when in fact they have not been shipped. (*b*) Sales: Sales invoices may be prepared for goods no customer ordered.)

6.30   Kingston Company: Specification of Controls.   The essence of this problem is to think: "What keeps the errors and irregularities identified in problem 6.29 from happening and, if they nevertheless happen, what catches them?" With a little experience, you will be able to answer these questions in your head, but, this first time, you should do it in writing.

Required:

Prepare a homework report cross-indexed to your problem 6.29 working paper by 1(*a*), 1(*b*), 2(*a*), 2(*b*), and so on. For each error or irregularity you identified, explain the environmental element, accounting procedure, or control procedure that will serve to prevent, detect, or correct it. These elements of a control structure need not necessarily be specified or provided in the Kingston case description. You can use your imagination as well.

6.31   Kingston Company: Internal Control Questionnaire.   This problem gives you some practice with a questionnaire. You should be able to answer most of the questions using the transaction system descriptions and the accounting and control procedure manual.

Required:

Obtain a Sales Transaction Processing internal control questionnaire from your instructor. Answer the questions, leaving blank the items for which information is missing.

6.32   Kingston Company: System Flowchart Documentation.   Use the transaction system descriptions and your internal control questionnaire from problem 6.31 as information sources to document the accounting and control system.

Required:

Draw a flowchart of the credit approval/sales processing and shipment/delivery systems. You should be able to put the flowchart on one or two pages. Use a template and ruler. [Hint: The department designations across the top of the flowchart should be (from left to right): Sales Clerks, Credit Manager, Billing Department, Accounts Receivable Department, Inventory Stores, and Shipping.]

6.33   Kingston Company: Control Evaluation.   After doing the control evaluation work, you should be ready to reach some conclusions about control strengths and weaknesses. At this stage you are not expected to be proficient at writing account balance audit program procedures, but you can start a bridge working paper.

Required:

Prepare a working paper for the audit of Kingston Company as of December 31, 1992, with columns for (1) an index number (*S*-? or *W*-?) cross-referenced to your flowchart prepared in problem 6.32; (2) descriptions of each strength or weakness; (3) audit implications related to transactions or accounts reported in the financial statements; and (4) procedures for the test of controls or account balance audit program. Ask your instructor about the extent/detail you are expected to write in the audit procedures program column.

MULTIPLE-CHOICE QUESTIONS FOR PRACTICE AND REVIEW

6.34 The primary purpose for obtaining an understanding of an audit client's internal control structure is to:
   a. Provide a basis for making constructive suggestions in a management letter.
   b. Determine the nature, timing, and extent of tests to be performed in the audit.
   c. Obtain sufficient appropriate evidential matter to afford a reasonable basis for an opinion on the financial statements under examination.
   d. Provide information for a communication of internal control structure-related matters to management.

6.35 Restrictions of audit procedures can be characterized by:
   a. Selecting larger sample sizes for audit.
   b. Moving audit procedures to the fiscal year-end date.

c. Deciding to obtain external evidence instead of internal evidence.

d. Selecting smaller sample sizes for audit.

6.36 Which of the following can an auditor observe as a general control procedure used by companies?

a. Segregation of functional responsibilities.

b. Management philosophy and operating style.

c. Open lines of communication to the audit committee of the board of directors.

d. External influences such as federal bank examiner audits.

6.37 A client's control procedure is:

a. An action taken by auditors to obtain evidence.

b. An action taken by client personnel for the purpose of preventing, detecting, and correcting errors and irregularities in transactions.

c. A method for recording, summarizing, and reporting financial information.

d. The functioning of the board of directors in support of its audit committee.

6.38 The control objective intended to reduce the probability that fictitious transactions get recorded in the accounts is:

a. Completeness.

b. Authorization.

c. Proper period.

d. Validity.

6.39 The control objective intended to reduce the probability that a credit sale transaction will get debited to cash instead of accounts receivable is:

a. Validity.

b. Classification.

c. Accuracy.

d. Completeness.

6.40 Which of the following employees normally would be assigned the operating responsibility for designing a computerized accounting system, including documentation of application systems?

a. Computer programmer.

b. Data processing manager.

c. Systems analyst.

d. Internal auditor.

6.41 When erroneous data are detected by computer program controls, such data may be excluded from processing and printed on an error report. The error report should most probably be reviewed and followed up by the:

a. Control group.

b. Systems analyst.

c. Supervisor of computer operations.

d. Computer programmer.

6.42 Totals of amounts in computer-record data fields that are not usually added but are used only for data processing control purposes are called:

a. Record totals.

b. Hash totals.

c. Processing data totals.

d. Field totals.

6.43 In updating a computerized accounts receivable file, which one of the following would be used as a batch control to verify the accuracy of the posting of cash receipts remittances?

a. The sum of the cash deposits plus the discounts less the sales returns.

b. The sum of the cash deposits.

c. The sum of the cash deposits less the discounts taken by customers.

d. The sum of the cash deposits plus the discounts taken by customers.

6.44 In most audits of large companies, internal control risk assessment contributes to audit efficiency, which means:

a. The cost of year-end audit work will exceed the cost of control evaluation work.

b. Auditors will be able to reduce the cost of year-end audit work by an amount more than the control evaluation costs.

c. The cost of control evaluation work will exceed the cost of year-end audit work.

d. Auditors will be able to reduce the cost of year-end audit work by an amount less than the control evaluation costs.

6.45 Which of the following is a device designed to help the audit team obtain evidence about the control environment and about the accounting and control procedures of an audit client:

a. A narrative memorandum describing the control system.
b. An internal control questionnaire.
c. A flowchart of the documents and procedures used by the company.
d. A well-indexed file of working papers.

6.46 A bridge working paper shows the connection between:

a. Control evaluation findings and subsequent audit procedures.
b. Control objectives and accounting system procedures.
c. Control objectives and company control procedures.
d. Financial statement assertions and test of control procedures.

6.47 Test of control audit procedures are required for:

a. Obtaining evidence about the financial statement assertions.
b. Accomplishing control over the validity of recorded transactions.
c. Analytical review of financial statement balances.
d. Obtaining evidence about the operating effectiveness of client control procedures.

EXERCISES AND PROBLEMS

6.48 Costs and benefits of control. The following questions and cases deal with the subject of cost-benefit analysis of internal control. Some important concepts in cost-benefit analysis are:

1. Measurable benefit. Benefits or cost savings may be measured directly or may be based on estimates of expected value. An expected loss is an estimate of the amount of a probable loss multiplied by the frequency or probability of the loss-causing event. A measurable benefit can arise from the reduction of an expected loss.
2. Qualitative benefit. Some gains or cost savings may not be measurable, such as company public image, reputation for regulatory compliance, and customer satisfaction.
3. Measurable costs. Controls may have direct costs such as wages and equipment expenses.
4. Qualitative cost factors. Some costs may be indirect, such as lower employee morale created by overcontrolled work restrictions.
5. Marginal analysis. Each successive control feature may have marginal cost and benefit effects on the control problem.

Case A:

Porterhouse Company has numerous bank accounts. Why might management hesitate to spend $10,000 (half of a clerical salary) to assign someone the responsibility of reconciling each account every month for the purpose of catching the banks' accounting errors? Do other good reasons exist to justify spending $10,000 each year to reconcile bank accounts monthly?

Case B:

Harper Hoe Company keeps a large inventory of hardware products in a warehouse. Last year, $500,000 was lost to thieves who broke in through windows and doors. Josh Harper figures that installing steel doors with special locks and burglar bars on the windows at a cost of $25,000 would eliminate 90 percent of the loss. Hiring armed guards to patrol the building 16 hours a day at a current annual cost of $75,000 would eliminate all the loss, according to officials of the Holmes Security Agency. Should Josh arrange for one, both, or neither of the control measures?

Case C:

The Merry Mound Cafeteria formerly collected from each customer as he or she reached the end of the food line. A cashier, seated at a cash register, rang up the amount (displayed on a digital screen) and collected money. Management changed the system, and now a clerk at the end of the line operates an adding machine and gives each customer a paper tape. The adding machine accumulates a running total internally. The customer presents the tape at the cash register on the way out and pays.

The cafeteria manager justified the direct cost of $10,000 annually for the additional salary and $500 for the new adding machine by pointing out that he could serve 4 more people each weekday (Monday through Friday) and 10 more people on Saturday and Sunday. The food line now moves faster and customers are more satisfied. (The average meal tab is $6, and total costs of food and service are considered fixed.) "Besides," he said, "my internal control is better." Evaluate the manager's assertions.

Case D:

Assume, in the Merry Mound situation cited above, that the better control of separating cash custody from the end-of-food-line recording function was not cost beneficial, even after taking all measurable benefits into consideration. As an auditor, you believe the cash collection system deficiency is a material weakness in internal control, and you have written it as such in your letter concerning reportable conditions, which Merry Mound's central administration engaged you to deliver. The local manager insists on inserting his own opinion on the cost-benefit analysis in the preface to the document that contains your report. Should you, in your report, express any opinion or evaluation on the manager's statement?

6.49 Cash Receipts Control. Sally's Craft Corner was opened in 1983 by Sally Moore, a fashion designer employed by Bundy's Department Store. Sally is employed full-time at Bundy's and travels frequently to shows and marts in Vancouver, Montreal, and Toronto. She enjoys crafts, wanted a business of her own, and saw an opportunity in Vancouver. The Corner now sells regularly to about 300 customers, but business only began to pick up in 1990. The staff presently includes two salespeople and four office personnel, and Sally herself helps out on weekends.

Sales have grown, as has the Corner's reputation for quality crafts. The history is as follows:

	Sales	Discounts and Allowances	Net Sales
1986	$16,495	$500	$15,995
1987	18,575	550	18,025
1988	17,610	520	17,090
1989	18,380	570	17,810
1990	23,950	950	23,000
1991	29,470	1,480	27,990
1992	37,230	$2,230	35,000

With an expanding business and a need for inventory, the Corner is now cash poor. Prices are getting higher every month, and Sally is a little worried. The net cash flow is only about $400 per month after allowance of a 3 percent discount for timely payments on account. So she has engaged you as auditor and asks for any recommendations you might have about the cash flow situation. The Corner has never been audited.

During your review of internal control, you have learned the following about the four office personnel:

Janet Bundy is the receptionist and also helps customers. She is the daughter of the Bundy Department Store owner and a longtime friend of Sally. Janet helped Sally start the Corner. They run around together when Sally is in town. She opens all the mail, answers most of it herself, but turns over payments on account to Sue Kenmore.

Sue Kenmore graduated from high school and started working as a bookkeeper-secretary at the Corner in 1990. She wants to go to university but cannot afford it right now. She is very quiet in the office, but you have noticed she has some fun with her friends in her new BMW. In the office she gets the mailed-in payments on account from Janet, takes payments over the counter in the store, checks the calculations of discounts allowed, enters the cash collections in the cash receipts journal, prepares a weekly bank deposit (and mails it), and prepares a list (remittance list) of the payments on account. The list shows amounts received from each customer, discount allowed, and amount to be credited to customers' account. She is also responsible for approving the discounts and credits for merchandise returned.

Ken Murphy has been the bookkeeper-clerk since 1986. He also handles other duties. Among them, he receives the remittance list from Sue, posts the customers' accounts in the subsidiary ledger, and gives the remittance list to David Roberts. Ken also prepares and mails customers' monthly statements. Ken is rather dull, interested mostly in hunting on weekends, but is a steady worker. He always comes to work in a beat-up pickup truck—an eyesore in the parking lot.

David Roberts is the bookkeeping supervisor. He started work in 1987 after giving up his small practice as a PA. He posts the general ledger (using the remittance list as a basis for cash received entries) and prepares monthly financial statements. He also approves and makes all other ledger entries and reconciles the monthly bank statement. He reconciles the customer subsidiary records to the accounts receivable control each month. David is very happy not to have to contend with the pressures he experienced in his practice as a PA.

Required:
a. Draw a simple flow chart of the cash collection and bookkeeping procedures.
b. Identify any reportable conditions or material weakness in internal control Explain any reasons why you might suspect that errors or irregularities may have occurred.
c. Recommend corrective measures you believe necessary and efficient in this business.

6.50 Tests of Control Procedure Specifications. In order to conduct tests of con-

trols of a client's internal control procedures, auditors design a test of controls audit program. This audit program is a list of procedures to be performed, and each is directly related to an important client control procedure. Auditors perform the procedures to obtain evidence about the operating effectiveness of the client's control procedures.

The controls listed below relate to a system for processing sales transactions. Each numbered item indicates an error or irregularity that could occur and specifies a control procedure that could prevent or detect it.

Required:
a. Identify the control objective satisfied by the client's control procedure.
b. Write the audit program of test of controls procedures by specifying an effective procedure to produce evidence about the client's performance of the control procedure. [Hint: A test of controls procedure is a two-part statement consisting of (1) identification of a data population from which a sample can be drawn and (2) expression of an action to take.]
1. The company wants to avoid selling goods on credit to bad credit risks. Poor credit control could create problems with estimating the allowance for bad debts and a potential error by overstating the realizable value of accounts receivable. Therefore, the control procedure is: Each customer order is to be reviewed and approved for 30-day credit by the credit department supervisor. The supervisor then notes the decision on the customer order, which eventually is attached to copy 2 of the sales invoice and filed by date in the accounts receivable department. The company used sales invoices numbered 20,001 through 30,000 during the period under review.
2. The company considers sales transactions complete when shipment is made. The control proce-

dures are: Shipping department personnel prepare prenumbered shipping documents in duplicate (sending one copy to the customer and filing the other copy in numerical order in the shipping department file). The shipping clerk marks up copy 3 of the invoice indicating the quantity shipped, the date, and the shipping document number and sends it to the billing department where it is taken as authorization to complete the sales recording. Copy 3 is then filed in a daily batch in the billing department file. These procedures are designed to prevent the recording of sales (1) for which no shipment is made, or (2) before the date of shipment.

3. The company wants to control unit pricing and mathematical errors that could result in overcharging or undercharging customers, thus producing the errors of overstatement or understatement of sales revenue and accounts receivable. The accounting procedures are: Billing clerks use a catalogue list price to price the shipment on invoice copies 1, 2, and 3. They compute the dollar amount of the invoice. Copy 1 is sent to the customer. Copy 2 is used to record the sale and later is filed in the accounts receivable department by date. Copy 3 is filed in the billing department by date.

4. The company needs to classify sales to subsidiaries apart from other sales so the consolidated financial statement eliminations will be accurate. That is, the company wants to avoid the error of understating the elimination of intercompany profit and, therefore, overstating net income and inventory. The control procedure is: A billing supervisor reviews each invoice copy 2 to see whether the billing clerk im-

printed sales to the company's four subsidiaries with a big red "9" (the code for intercompany sales). The supervisor does not initial or sign the invoices.

6.51 **Test of Controls Procedures and Errors/Irregularities.** The four questions below are taken from an internal control questionnaire. For each question, state (*a*) one test of controls procedure you could use to find out whether the control technique was really used, and (*b*) what error or irregularity could occur if the question were answered "no," or if you found the control was not effective.
1. Are blank (sales) invoices available only to authorized personnel?
2. Are (sales) invoices checked for the accuracy of quantities billed? Prices used? Mathematical calculations?
3. Are the duties of the accounts receivable bookkeeper separate from any cash functions?
4. Are customer accounts regularly balanced with the control account?

6.52 **Control Objectives and Procedures Associations.** Exhibit 6.52–1 contains an arrangement of examples of transaction errors (lettered *a–g*) and a set of client control procedures and devices (numbered 1–15). You should photocopy the Exhibit 6.52–1 page or obtain a full-size copy from your instructor for the following requirements.

Required:
a. Opposite the examples of transaction errors lettered *a–g*, write the name of the control objective clients wish to achieve to prevent, detect, or correct the error.
b. Opposite each numbered control procedure, place an *X* in the column that identifies the error(s) the procedure is likely to control by prevention, detection, or correction.

6.53 **Control Objectives and Assertion Associations.** Exhibit 6.52–1 contains an arrangement of examples of transaction errors (lettered *a–g*) and a set of client control procedures and devices (numbered 1–15).

E X H I B I T 6.52–1

a.	Sales recorded, goods not shipped
b.	Goods shipped, sales not recorded
c.	Goods shipped to a bad credit risk customer
d.	Sales billed at the wrong price or wrong quantity
e.	Product line A sales recorded as Product line B
f.	Failure to post charges to customers for sales
g.	January sales recorded in December

Control Procedures

1. Sales order approved for credit

2. Prenumbered shipping doc prepared, sequence checked

3. Shipping document quantity compared to sales invoice

4. Prenumbered sales invoices, sequence checked

5. Sales invoice checked to sales order

6. Invoiced prices compared to approved price list

7. General ledger code checked for sales product lines

8. Sales dollar batch totals compared to sales journal

9. Periodic sales total compared to same period accounts receivable postings

10. Accountants have instructions to date sales on the date of shipment

11. Sales entry date compared to shipping document date

12. Accounts receivable subsidiary totalled and reconciled to accounts receivable control account

13. Intercompany accounts reconciled with subsidiary company records

14. Credit files updated for customer payment history

15. Overdue customer accounts investigated for collection

Required:

For each error/control objective, identify the financial statement assertion most benefited by the control.

6.54 Client Control Procedures and Audit Test of Control Procedures. Exhibit 6.52–1 contains an arrangement of examples of transaction errors (lettered *a–g*) and a set of client control procedures and devices (numbered 1–15).

Required:

For each client control procedure numbered 1–15, write an auditor's test of control procedure that could produce evidence on the question of whether the client's control procedure has been installed and is in operation.

DISCUSSION CASES

6.55 Obtaining a "Sufficient" Understanding of Internal Control. The 12 partners of a regional-sized PA firm met in special session to discuss audit en- gagement efficiency. Jones spoke up, saying:

"We all certainly appreciate the firmwide policies set up by Martin and

Smith, especially in connection with the audits of the large clients that have come our way recently. Their experience with a large national firm has helped build up our practice. But I think the standard policy of conducting reviews and tests of internal control on all audits is raising our costs too much. We can't charge our smaller clients fees for all the time the staff spends on this work. I would like to propose that we give engagement partners discretion to decide whether to do a lot of work on assessing control risk. I may be an old mossback, but I think I can finish a competent audit without it."

Discussion on the subject continued but ended when Martin said, with some emotion: "But we can't disregard generally accepted auditing standards like Jones proposes!"

What do you think of Jones's proposal and Martin's view of the issue? Discuss.

6.56 Starting the "Logical Approach." One of the things you can do in a "logical approach" to the evaluation of internal control is to imagine what types of errors or irregularities could occur with regard to each significant class of transactions. Assume a company has the significant classes of transactions listed below. For each one, identify one or more errors or irregularities that could occur and specify the accounts that would be affected if proper controls were not specified or were not followed satisfactorily.

1. Credit sales transactions.
2. Raw materials purchase transactions.
3. Payroll transactions.
4. Equipment acquisition transactions.
5. Cash receipts transactions.
6. Leasing transactions.
7. Dividend transactions.
8. Investment transactions (short term).

6.57 Irregularity Opportunities. The Simon Blfpstk Construction Company has two divisions. The president, Simon, manages the roofing division. Simon has delegated authority and responsibility for management of the modular manufacturing division to John Gault. The company has a competent accounting staff and a full-time internal auditor. Unlike Simon, however, Gault and his secretary handle all the bids for manufacturing jobs, purchase all the materials without competitive bids, control the physical inventory of materials, contract for shipping by truck, supervise the construction activity, bill the customer when the job is finished, approve all bid changes, and collect the payment from the customer. With Simon's tacit approval, Gault has asked the internal auditor not to interfere with his busy schedule.

Required:

Discuss this fact situation in terms of internal control and identify irregularities that could occur.

Appendix 6A

Examples of Factors That Might Increase the Risk of Material Misstatements

The importance of the factors considered in assessing inherent and control risks, including the examples shown below, varies depending upon the size, complexity, and ownership characteristics of the entity. The auditor assesses the risk of material misstatement in the financial statements by considering factors collectively. The presence of an individual factor would not necessarily indicate increased risk.

Corporate Environment

Ineffective board of directors or audit committee.

Management's poor business reputation.

Management operating and financial decisions dominated by a single person.

Aggressive management attitude in financial reporting.

Lack of formal code of conduct or its enforcement.

Financial Pressures

Business or industry decline (revenue or market share).

Inadequate or inconsistent profitability relative to industry.

Financial difficulties.

High debt-to-equity ratio, especially if the result of a recent acquisition.

Forthcoming debt or share offering.

Bonuses or management profit-sharing arrangements based on short-term financial results.

Existence of financial debt covenants.

Management places undue emphasis on meeting financial targets.

Overemphasis of quantified targets that are linked to management compensation.

Unrealistic budget pressures.

Rapidly changing conditions in entity's industry.

Sensitivity of operating results to economic factors, such as inflation, interest rates, and unemployment.

Management Style

Constant crisis conditions in operating areas such as frequent/excessive back orders, shortages, delays, understaffed departments.

Turnover in key financial positions.

Organization decentralized without adequate monitoring.

Changed control, especially if a high price was paid.

Engagement Characteristics

Poor internal control.

Ineffective internal audit function.

Company does not correct material weaknesses that are possible to correct.

Inadequate control over accounting estimates (personnel lack of knowledge due to carelessness, inexperience, or inadequate review).

Inadequate policies and procedures for security of assets, such as not limiting access to authorized employees, not investigating employees before hiring, or not bonding employees.

Difficult-to-substantiate amounts or transactions.

New client, with no previous audit history or none available from predecessor.

Unusual related party transactions.

Nature of misstatements in prior period's financial statements.

Susceptibility of assets to misappropriation.

Source: From Appendix to *Handbook Section* 5135.

CHAPTER 7

Learning Objectives

Chapters 4 and 5 introduced several activities, concepts, and tools for audit planning, and Chapter 6 introduced the theory and practice of control risk assessment. We now take up the general topic of audit sampling, which relies heavily on the concepts of materiality and risk—audit risk, inherent risk, control risk, and detection risk. Audit sampling is not an audit procedure in the same class of the techniques explained in Chapter 4. It is a method of organizing the application of audit procedures and a method of organizing auditors' thoughts for decision making.

Chapter 7 introduces audit sampling as a general topic. Later, Chapter 20 will take you into the mathematical details of statistical sampling in auditing. After you study Chapter 7, you should be able to:

1. Define and explain the terms unique to audit sampling, including the fundamental technical differences between statistical sampling and nonstatistical sampling.

2. Identify audit work considered to be audit sampling and distinguish it from work not considered to be audit sampling.

3. Develop a simple audit program for a test of controls audit of a client's internal control procedures.

   a. Specify objectives, deviation conditions, populations, and sampling units.

   b. Determine sample size and select sampling units.

   c. Evaluate evidence from a test of controls audit.

4. Develop a simple audit program for an account balance audit considering the influence of risk and tolerable misstatement.

   a. Specify objectives and define a population for data.

   b. Determine sample size and select sampling units.

   c. Evaluate monetary error evidence from a balance audit sample.

AUDIT SAMPLING

INTRODUCTION TO AUDIT SAMPLING

LEARNING OBJECTIVE

1. Define and explain the terms unique to audit sampling, including the fundamental technical differences between statistical sampling and nonstatistical sampling.

Audit sampling is the application of an audit procedure to less than 100 percent of the items within an account balance population or class of transactions for the purpose of evaluating some characteristic of the balance or class. Testing is synonymous with sampling.[1] You have already seen the sampling idea incorporated in the explanation of a test of controls audit procedure, which was defined as a two-part statement consisting of (1) an identification of the data population from which a sample of items will be selected for audit and (2) an expression of an action taken to produce relevant evidence. To understand the definition of audit sampling, you must keep the following definitions in mind: **Audit procedure** refers to actions described as past audit techniques in Chapter 4 (computation, observation, confirmation, enquiry, inspection, and analysis). An **account balance** refers to a control account made up of many constituent items; for example, an accounts receivable control account representing the sum of customers' accounts, an inventory control account representing the sum of various goods in inventory, a sales account representing the sum of many sales invoices, or a long-term debt account representing the sum of several issues of outstanding bonds. A **class of transactions** refers to a group of transactions having common characteristics, such as cash receipts or cash disbursements, but which are not simply added together and presented as an account balance in financial statements.

Other definitions: A **population** is the set of all the elements that constitute an account balance or class of transactions. Each of the elements is a **population unit**; and when an auditor selects a sample, each element selected is called a sampling unit. A **sampling unit** can be a customer's account, an inventory item, a debt issue, a cash receipt, a cancelled cheque, and so forth. A **sample** is a set of sampling units.

Sampling and the Extent of Auditing

Three aspects of auditing procedures are important—their nature, timing, and extent. **Nature** refers to the six general techniques (computation, observation, confirmation, enquiry, inspection, and analysis). **Timing** is a matter of when procedures are performed. More will be said about timing later in this chapter. Audit sampling is concerned primarily with matters of **extent**—the amount of work done when the procedures are performed. In the context of auditing standards, nature and timing relate most closely to the appropriateness of evidential matter, while extent relates most closely to the sufficiency (sample size) of evidential matter. The concept of testing is important to auditors because it is uneconomical to test client files exhaustively in many situations. It is common for client files on inventory and accounts

---

[1] *Terminology for Accountants*, 4th Ed., CICA, Toronto, 1992.

receivable to contain thousands of accounting records. Testing is a means of gaining assurance that the amount of errors in large files is not material. The formal theory supporting the concept of testing is statistical sampling. However, courts approved the concept of testing long before statistical theories were introduced to auditing. The majority of testing in auditing was once done on a judgmental basis. But as accounting populations increased in size auditors became aware that statistical sample sizes could be much smaller than intuition would suggest. For this reason statistical sampling became increasingly popular in the 1970s and 1980s. Both judgmental and statistical testing methods are equally acceptable by auditing standards. The reason for the focus on statistics here is that there is a formal theory underlying statistics that is similar to the reasoning used in pure judgmental testing. Note that both audit programs below can be performed on a statistical or nonstatistical basis.

TWO KINDS OF AUDIT PROGRAMS: TWO PURPOSES FOR AUDIT SAMPLING

Test of Controls Audit Program	Balance-Audit Program
Purpose Obtain evidence about client's control objective compliance	Purpose Obtain evidence about client's financial statement assertions
Validity Completeness Authorization Accuracy Classification Accounting Proper period	Existence/Occurrence Completeness Valuation Rights and obligations (ownership and owership) Presentation and disclosure
Sample Usually from a class of transactions (population), such as:	Sample Usually from items in an asset or liability balance (population), such as:
Cash receipts Cash disbursements Purchases (inventory additions) Inventory issues Sales on credit Expense details Welfare payments (eligibility)	Accounts receivable Loans receivable Inventory Small tool fixed assets Depositors' savings accounts Accounts payable Unexpired magazine subscriptions

Inclusions and Exclusions Related to Audit Sampling

Look again at the audit sampling definition and to that part about audit sampling being "for the purpose of evaluating some characteristics of the balance or class." The meaning of these words is: An application of audit procedures is considered audit sampling if and only if the auditors' objective is to reach a conclusion about the entire account balance or transaction class (the population) on the basis of the evidence obtained from the audit of a sample drawn from the balance or class. If the entire population is audited, or if the purpose is only to gain general familiarity, the work is not considered to be audit sampling.

Perhaps the distinction between audit sampling and other methods can be perceived more clearly in terms of the following work that is not considered audit sampling.

- Complete (100 percent) audit of all the elements in a balance or class, by definition, does not involve sampling.

- Analytical procedures, in the nature of overall comparisons, ratio calculations, and the like, are normally not applied on a sample basis.

- A **walk-through**—following one or a few transactions through the accounting and control systems in order to obtain a general understanding of the client's systems—is not audit sampling because the objective is not to reach a conclusion about a balance or class.

- Several procedures do not lend themselves to sampling methods; for example, enquiry of employees, obtaining written representations, obtaining enquiry responses in the form of answers on an internal control questionnaire, scanning accounting records for unusual items, and observation of personnel and procedures.[2]

Several procedures are typically used in audit sampling applications. They are recalculation, physical observation of tangible assets, confirmation, and document examination. These procedures most often are applied to the audit of details of transactions and balances.

Why Auditors Sample

Auditors utilize audit sampling when (1) the nature and materiality of the balance or class does not demand a 100 percent audit, (2) a decision must be made about the balance or class, and (3) the time and cost to audit 100 percent of the population would be too great. So, auditors use sampling because they need to perform efficient audits on a timely basis and cannot do so by auditing 100 percent. The two sampling designs used by auditors are statistical sampling and nonstatistical sampling.

Statistical Sampling

Auditors define **statistical sampling** as audit sampling that uses the laws of probability for selecting and evaluating a sample from a population for the purpose of reaching a conclusion about the population. The essential points of this definition are that (1) a statistical sample is selected at random, and (2) statistical calculations are used to measure and express the results. Both conditions are necessary for a method to be considered statistical sampling rather than nonstatistical sampling.

A **random sample** is a set of sampling units so chosen that each population item has an equal likelihood of being selected in the sample. You can use a random sample in a "nonstatistical sampling" design. However, you cannot use statistical calculations with a nonrandom sample. The mathematical laws of probability are not applicable for nonrandom samples, and basing such calculations on a nonrandom sample would be wrong.

A statistical calculation of sample size is not necessary for a method to be considered statistical sampling. You can use any sample size you feel appropriate in the circumstances. However, a preliminary estimate of sample size can be calculated using statistical models. (More on this subject is in Chapter 20.) A sampling method is statistical by virtue of random selection of the sample coupled with statistical calculation of the results.

[2] "Audit Sampling," *Audit and Accounting Guide* (AICPA, 1983), pp. 1–3.

WHEN TO USE STATISTICAL SAMPLING

Random numbers can be associated with population items.
Objective results that can be defended mathematically are desired.
Auditor has insufficient knowledge about the population to justify a basis for a nonstatistical sample.
A representative (random) sample is required.
Staff are adequately trained in statistical auditing.

Advantages of Statistical Sampling

Requires a precise and definite approach to the audit problem.
Incorporates evaluation that calculates a direct relation between the sample results and the entire population under audit.
Requires auditors to specify, and even quantify, particular judgments on risk and materiality.
Does not eliminate or reduce auditors' professional judgment.
Allows more objective control of audit risks. Results in better planning and documentation when properly implemented (but can be more time-consuming and costly because of the greater formalism required).

Nonstatistical Sampling

A good definition of **nonstatistical (judgmental) sampling** is audit sampling in which auditors do not utilize statistical calculations to express the results. The sample selection technique can be random sampling or some other selection technique not based on mathematical randomness. Auditors are fond of saying that nonstatistical sampling involves "consideration of sampling risk in evaluating an audit sample without using statistical theory to measure that risk." "Consideration" in this context means "giving sampling risk some thoughtful attention" without direct knowledge or measurement of its magnitude.

Sampling and Nonsampling Risk

Be careful not to confuse sampling and nonsampling risk with statistical and nonstatistical sampling. They are not related. When auditors perform procedures on a sample basis and obtain sufficient evidence, a conclusion about the population characteristic can still be wrong. For example, suppose an auditor selected 100 sales invoices for audit and found no errors or irregularities in any of them. The conclusion that a significant incidence of errors and irregularities does not exist in the entire population of sales invoices from which the sample was drawn might be wrong. How, you ask? Simple: The sample might not reflect the actual condition of the population. No matter how randomly or carefully the sample was selected, it might not be a good representation of the extent of errors and irregularities actually in the population.

Sampling risk is defined as the probability that an auditor's conclusion based on a sample might be different from the conclusion based on an audit of the entire

WHEN TO USE NONSTATISTICAL SAMPLING

Association of population items with random numbers is difficult and expensive.

Strictly defensible results based on mathematics are not necessary.

Auditor has sufficient knowledge about the population to justify a basis for a nonstatistical sample with expectation of a reasonable conclusion about the population.

A representative (random) sample is not required; for example, because an efficient nonstatistical sample of large items leaves an immaterial amount unaudited.

The population is known to be diverse, with some segments especially error-prone.

Advantages of Nonstatistical Sampling

Permits a less rigidly defined approach to unique problems that might not fit into a statistical method.

Permits the auditors to reapply evaluation judgments based on factors in addition to the sample evidence.

Permits auditors to be vague and less than definite about, and omit quantification of, particular judgments on risk and materiality.

Permits auditors to assert standards of subjective judgment. (Thus, the alternative name is ''judgment sampling.'')

---

population. You could audit a sample of sales invoices and decide, based on the sample, that the population of sales invoices contained few errors and irregularities. However, suppose some auditors with more time could audit all the sales invoices and find a large number of errors and irregularities. In such a case, your sample-based decision would have been proved wrong. Your sample apparently did not represent the population very well. Sampling risk expresses the probability of making a wrong decision based on sample evidence, and it exists in both statistical and nonstatistical sampling methods. You cannot escape it in audit sampling. With statistical sampling, you can measure it, and you can control it by auditing sufficiently large samples. With nonstatistical sampling, you can ''consider'' it without measuring it. However, considering sampling risk without measuring it requires experience and expertise. Special aspects of sampling risk are discussed later in the sections on auditing control compliance and account balances.

Nonsampling risk is all risk other than sampling risk. You need to refer to the audit risk model (Chapter 5) to grasp the breadth of this definition:

Risk Model: $AR = IR \times CR \times DR$

Nonsampling risk can arise from:

- Misjudging the inherent risk (IR). An auditor who mistakenly believes that few material errors or irregularities occur in the first place will tend to do less work and, therefore, may fail to detect problems.

Mᴀɴɪꜰᴇꜱᴛᴀᴛɪᴏɴꜱ ᴏꜰ Nᴏɴꜱᴀᴍᴘʟɪɴɢ Rɪꜱᴋ

Performing inappropriate procedures: Auditors based the evaluation of inventory obsolescence on forecasted sales without adequately evaluating the forecast assumptions.

Failure to consider test results adequately: Auditor did not adequately investigate discrepancies in inventory counts and pricing, failing to draw the appropriate conclusions.

Neglecting the importance of analytical review: Auditor might have discovered client's failure to eliminate intercompany profits if year-to-year product mix, gross profit, and recorded eliminations had been studied.

Failure to maintain control over audit procedures: Auditors' loose attitude permitted client employees to tamper with records selected for confirmation.

Lack of professional scepticism: Auditors accepted client's unsupported verbal representations instead of gathering independent evidence.

Source: Audit Risk, Coopers & Lybrand.

- Misjudging the control risk (CR). An auditor who is too optimistic about the ability of controls to prevent, detect, and correct errors and irregularities will tend to do less work, with the same results as misjudging the inherent risk.
- Poor choice of procedures and mistakes in execution—related to detection risk (DR). Auditors can select procedures inappropriate for the objective (e.g., confirming recorded accounts receivable when the objective is to find unrecorded accounts receivable), can fail to recognize errors or irregularities when vouching supporting documents, or can sign off as having performed procedures when the work actually was not done.

Nonsampling risk also represents the possibility of making a wrong decision. It exists both in statistical and in nonstatistical sampling. The problem is that nonsampling risk cannot be measured. Auditors control it—and believe it is reduced to a negligible level—through adequate planning and supervision of audit engagements and personnel, by having policies and procedures for quality control of their auditing practices, and by having internal monitoring and external peer review of their own quality control systems.

One other distinction is important: External critics (judges, juries, peer reviewers) have few grounds for criticizing auditors who fall victim to sampling risk, provided that an audit sampling application is planned and executed reasonably well. Auditors are more open to criticism and fault-finding when erroneous audit decisions result from nonsampling risk.

Sampling Methods and Applications

Audit sampling is concerned with the amount of work performed and the sufficiency of audit evidence obtained. Audit sampling terminology contains many new concepts and definitions. The ones presented above, however, are general and apply to all phases of audit sampling. You need to know them so you can "speak the language."

Auditors design audit samples to deal with (1) auditing control for the purpose of assessing control risk and (2) auditing account balances for the purpose of getting direct evidence about financial statement assertions. The next major sections of this chapter explain these two designs. Each of the sections is organized in terms of (1) planning, (2) performing, and (3) evaluating audit sampling.

This chapter is presented in general terms, avoiding the mathematics of sampling, along the same lines as the *CICA Handbook Section* 5130 and Auditing Guideline "Applying Materiality and Audit Risk Concepts in Conducting an Audit," and the AICPA audit and accounting guide entitled "Auditing Sampling." If you want to crunch numbers, Chapter 20 (attribute sampling and variables sampling) should appeal to your technical needs. Chapter 20 can be viewed as a series of lengthy appendices to this chapter. Its coverage is limited mostly to technical details.

R E V I E W
C H E C K P O I N T S

7.1 Why do auditors sample?

7.2 What are the primary distinctions between statistical and nonstatistical sampling?

7.3 What is nonsampling risk? Give some examples.

7.4 What are test of controls audit procedures in general? What purpose do they serve?

7.5 Why must an audit sample be representative of the population from which it is drawn?

7.6 What control objectives should be achieved by a company's control structure?

7.7 What two types of audit programs are ordinarily used as written plans for audit procedures?

Test of Controls for Assessing Control Risk

Auditors must assess the control risk to determine the nature, timing, and extent of other audit procedures. Final evaluations of internal control are based on evidence obtained in the review and testing phases of an evaluation. Auditors' assessments of control risk are hard to describe because they always depend entirely on the circumstances in each specific situation. The judgments are usually very specific. For example, an auditor might learn that a company's validity control procedure to prevent recording of fictitious sales is to require the bookkeeper to match a shipping order with each sales invoice before recording a sale—good control, as specified. Now suppose the test of control audit procedure of selecting recorded sales invoices and vouching them to shipping orders shows a number of mistakes (invoices without supporting shipping orders)—poor control, as performed. Sales might be overstated. One way to take this control deficiency into account is to perform more extensive work on accounts receivable using confirmation and enquiries and analytical review related to collectibility. (If sales are overstated, one result could be overstatement of receivables—the debit side of the accounting entry.)

E X H I B I T 7–1   **AUDITOR'S ASSESSMENT OF CONTROL RISK**

	Judgment Expression of Control Risk	
Evaluation of Internal Control	Nonquantitative	Quantitative
Excellent control, both as specified and in compliance.	Low (1)	10%–30%
Good control, but lacks something in specification or compliance.	Moderate (2)	20%–70%
Deficient control, either in specification or compliance or both.	High (3)	60%–95%
Little or no control.	Maximum	100%

If combining inherent and control risk evaluation is easier, then "low," "moderate," and "high" mean:
1. Low combined inherent and control risk.
2. Moderate combined inherent and control risk.
3. High combined inherent and control risk.

The example above related a specific control (the validity-related control procedure of matching sales invoices with shipping orders) to a specific set of other audit procedures directed toward a possible problem (overstatement of sales and receivables). In a more general sense, auditors reach judgments about control risk along the lines shown in Exhibit 7–1. Some situations may call for a nonquantitative expression, and auditors sometimes need a quantitative expression. The quantitative ranges overlap so you will not get the idea that auditors really can put exact numbers on these kinds of evaluations.

Audit sampling can be used as a method and plan for conducting the test of controls audit procedures. The application of sampling in test of controls auditing is a structured, formal approach embodied in seven steps. The seven-step framework helps auditors plan, perform, and evaluate test of controls audit work. It also helps auditors accomplish an eighth step—careful documentation of the work—by showing each of the seven areas to be described in the working papers. The first seven steps are:

1. Specify the audit objectives.
2. Define the deviation conditions.
3. Define the population.
4. Determine the sample size.
5. Select the sample.
6. Perform the test of controls procedures.
7. Evaluate the evidence.

Plan the Procedures

LEARNING OBJECTIVE
3A. Specify objectives, deviation conditions, populations, and sampling units.

The first three steps are planning steps that represent the **problem-recognition** phase of the sampling method. When a client describes the control system, the implicit assertion is: "These controls work; people comply with the control procedures and achieve the control objectives." The auditors' question (problem) is: "Is it so? Are the validity (and other) control objectives achieved satisfactorily?"

Test of controls audit work is always directed toward producing evidence of the client's performance of its own control procedures. Thus, auditors' procedures should produce evidence about the client's achievement of the seven control objectives.

1. Specify the Audit Objectives

Take a control procedure under the validity objective as an example—namely, the client's procedure of requiring a shipping order to be matched with a sales invoice before a valid sale is recorded. The specific objective of an auditor's test of controls audit procedure would be: Determine whether recorded sales invoices are supported by matched shipping orders. The audit procedure itself would be: Select a sample of recorded sales invoices and vouch them to supporting shipping orders.

The client's matching of sales invoices to shipping orders in the example is a **key control**—it is important. Auditors should identify and audit only the key controls. Incidental controls that are not important will not be relied on to reduce control risk and need not be audited for compliance. Auditing them for compliance just wastes time if they really do not have much impact on the control risk assessment.

2. Define the Deviation Conditions

The terms **deviation**, **error**, **occurrence**, and **exception** are synonyms in test of controls sampling. They all refer to a departure from a prescribed internal control procedure in a particular case: for example, an invoice is recorded with no supporting shipping order (bill of lading). Defining the deviation conditions at the outset is important, so the auditors doing the work will know a deviation when they see one. As an assistant accountant, you would prefer to be instructed: "Select a sample of recorded sales invoices, vouch them to supporting shipping orders, and document cases where the shipping order is missing" instead of "Check recorded sales invoices for any mistakes." The latter instruction does not define the deviation conditions well enough.

The example we are using is oversimplified. However, this vouching procedure for compliance evidence can be used to obtain evidence about several control objectives at the same time. The invoice can be compared to the shipping order for evidence of actual shipment (validity), reviewed for credit approval (authorization), prices compared to the price list (authorization and accuracy), quantity billed compared to quantity shipped (accuracy), recalculated (arithmetic accuracy), compared for correspondence of shipment date and record date (proper period), and traced to postings in the general ledger and subsidiary accounts (accounting). Exhibit 7–2 shows these deviation conditions laid out in a working paper designed to record the results of a test of controls audit of a sample of sales invoices.

Time for some more terminology: Test of controls audit sampling also is called **attribute sampling**. Attribute sampling is audit sampling in which auditors look for the presence or absence of a control condition. In response to the audit question: "For each sales invoice in the sample, can a matched shipping order be found?" the answer can be only yes or no. With this definition, auditors can count the number of deviations and use the count when evaluating the evidence.

3. Define the Population

The specification of test of controls (compliance) audit objectives and the definition of deviation conditions usually define the **population**, which is the set of all elements in the balance or class of transactions. In the example the population consists of all the recorded sales invoices, and each invoice is a **population unit**. In **classical attribute sampling**, a sampling unit is the same thing as a population unit.[3]

---

[3] Dollar-unit sampling, however, defines a different sampling unit. Dollar-unit sampling (DUS) is discussed in Chapter 20.

EXHIBIT 7–2   TEST OF CONTROLS AUDIT DOCUMENTATION

Index **M 10.3**   By **J C**   Date **11-11-92**
                                                                                    Review **J.D.**   Date **11-15-92**

KINGSTON COMPANY
Test of Controls Over Recorded Sales
December 31, 1992

Invoice number	Date	Amount	Bill of lading	Credit approved	Approved prices	Quantities match	Arithmetic accurate	Dates match	Posted to customer
35000	Mar. 30	$ 3,000							
35050	Mar. 31	$ 800			X				
35100	Apr. 2	$ 1,200					Y		
35150	Apr. 3	$ 1,500			Y				
35200	Apr. 5	$ 400							
35250	Apr. 6	$ 300	X			X	Y	X	
32100	Jan. 3	$ 1,000							
32150	Jan. 4	$ 200							
34850	Mar. 25	Missing	X	X	X	X	X	X	
34900	Mar. 26	$ 100			Y				
34950	Mar. 27	$ 200							
Sample = 200		$98,000							
Uncorrected deviations			4	9	5	6	3	7	0

X = Uncorrected deviation.
Y = Deviation occurred but was detected and corrected later.

Population definition is important because audit conclusions can be made only about the population from which the sample was selected. For example, evidence from a sample of recorded sales invoices (the population for our illustrative procedure) cannot be used for a conclusion about completeness. Controls related to the completeness objective (in this case, control over failure to record an invoice for goods shipped) can only be audited by sampling from a population representing goods shipped (the shipping order file) and not by sampling from the population of recorded invoices.

A complicating factor in population definition is the timing of the audit work. Test of controls audit procedures ideally should be applied to transactions executed throughout the period under audit because auditors want to reach a conclusion about control risk during the entire period. However, auditors often perform test of controls procedures at an **interim date**—a date some weeks or months before the client's year-end date—and at that time the entire population (say, recorded sales invoices for the year) will not be available for audit. Nothing is wrong with doing the work at an interim date, but auditors still cannot ignore the remaining period between the

---

A BALANCE-AUDIT APPLICATION OF ATTRIBUTE SAMPLING

Previous presentations have said that attribute test of controls samples usually are drawn from a class of transactions in order to obtain evidence about compliance with control objectives. Attribute sample also can be used sometimes for balance-audit purposes. This example suggests an attribute sample to obtain evidence about an ownership (rights) financial statement assertion.

Question: A lessor is in the business of leasing autos, large trucks, tractors, and trailers. Is it necessary for the auditors to examine the titles to all the equipment?

Answer: It is not necessary, unless some extraordinary situation or circumstance is brought to light, for the auditors to examine titles to all the equipment. Random test verification of title certificates or proper registration of vehicles should be made.

Source: AICPA Technical Practice Aids, 8330.02.

---

interim date and the year-end. Strategies for considering control in the period after the interim date are explained later.

Another complicating factor in population definition is the need to determine the correspondence of the **physical representation of the population** to the population itself. The physical representation of the population is the auditor's frame of reference for selecting a sample. It can be a journal listing of recorded sales invoices, a file drawer full of invoice copies, a magnetic disk file of invoices, or another physical representation. The sample actually will be selected from the physical representation, so it must be complete and correspond with the actual population. The physical representation of the recorded sales invoice as a list in a journal is fairly easy to visualize. However, an auditor should make sure that periodic listings (e.g., monthly sales journals) are added correctly and posted to the general ledger sales accounts. Now, a selection of individual sales invoices from the sales journal is known to be from the complete population of recorded sales invoices. You should be careful, however. Some physical frames may not be so easy to assess for complete correspondence to a population of interest.

Perform the Procedures

LEARNING   OBJECTIVE

3B. Determine sample size and select sampling units.

The next three performance steps represent the **evidence-collection** phase of the sampling method. These steps are performed to get the evidence.

The sample size determination and sample selection steps explained in this section might be considered planning steps; but since they require a little more action, they also can be considered performance. The distinction is not crucial. They are merely the next things to do.

4. Determine the Sample Size

Sample size—the number of population units to audit—should be determined thoughtfully. Some auditors operate on the "magic number theory" (e.g., select 30, because that's what we have always used on this audit). Be careful, however, because a magic number may or may not satisfy the need for enough evidence. A magic number may also be too large. Auditors must consider four influences on sample size: sampling risk, tolerable deviation rate, expected population deviation rate, and population size.

Sampling Risk.   Earlier, sampling risk was defined as the probability that an auditor's conclusion based on a sample might be different from the conclusion based on an audit of the entire population. In other words, when using evidence from a sample, an auditor might reach a wrong conclusion. He or she might decide that (1) control risk is very low when, in fact, it is not, or (2) control risk is very high when, in fact, it is not so bad. The more you know about a population (from a larger sample), the less likely you are to reach a wrong conclusion. Thus, the larger the sample, the lower the sampling risk of making either of the two decision errors. More will be said about these risks in the section on evaluation.

In terms of our example, the important sampling risk is the probability that the sample will reveal few or no recorded sales invoices without supporting shipping orders when, in fact, the population contains many such deviations. This result leads to the erroneous conclusion that the control worked well. The probability of finding few or no deviations when many exist is reduced by auditing a larger sample. Thus, sample size varies inversely with the amount of sampling risk an auditor is willing to take.

Tolerable Deviation Rate.   Auditors should have an idea about the correspondence of rates of deviation in the population with control risk assessments. Perfect control compliance is not necessary, so the question is: What rate of deviation in the population signals control risk of 10 percent? 20 percent? 30 percent? and so forth, up to 100 percent? Suppose an auditor believes that $90,000 of sales invoices could be exposed to control deviations without causing a minimum material misstatement in the sales and accounts receivable balances. If the total gross sales is $8.5 million, this judgment implies a **tolerable deviation rate** of about 1 percent ($90,000/$8.5 million). Since this 1 percent rate marks the minimum material misstatement, it indicates a low control risk (say, 0.05), and it justifies a great deal of reliance on internal control in the audit of the sales and accounts receivable balances.

However, there can be more than one tolerable deviation rate. Each successively higher rate is associated with a higher control risk. Continuing with our example, higher tolerable deviation rates could be associated with higher control risks as follows:[4]

Deviation Rate	Control Risk
1%	0.05
2	0.10
4	0.20
6	0.30
8	0.40
10	0.50
12	0.60
14	0.70
16	0.80
18	0.90
20	1.00

[4] Accounting firms have different policies for associating tolerable deviation rates with control risk categories. Some start with a minimum rate of 1 percent, and others start with higher rates.

Since sample size varies inversely with the tolerable deviation rate, the auditor who wants to assess control risk at 0.05 (tolerable rate = 1 percent) will need to audit a larger sample of sales transactions than another auditor who is willing to assess control risk at 0.40 (tolerable rate = 8 percent). The desired control risk level and its tolerable rate is a matter of auditor choice.

The tolerable rate is not a fixed rate until the auditor decides what control risk assessment suits the audit plan. Then it becomes a decision criterion involved in the sampling application. Some auditors express the tolerable rate as a number (necessary for statistical calculation of sample size), while others do not put a number on it. Chapter 20 contains more explanation about the determination of various tolerable rates.

Expected Population Deviation Rate.   Auditors usually know or suspect some control performance conditions. Sometimes they have last year's audit experience with the client; sometimes they have information from a predecessor auditor. They have information about the client's personnel, the working conditions, and the general control-environment. This knowledge contributes to an **expectation about the population deviation rate**, which is an estimate of the ratio of the number of expected deviations to population size. Suppose the auditors discovered 1 percent deviation in last year's audit. The expected population deviation rate could then be 1 percent. Auditors can also stipulate a zero expected deviation rate, which will produce a minimum sample size for audit.

The expected rate is important in a commonsense perspective. If auditors had reason to expect more deviations than they could tolerate, there would be no reason to perform any test of controls audit procedures. Thus, the expected rate must be less than the tolerable rate. Also, the closer the expected rate is to the tolerable rate, the larger the sample will need to be to reach a conclusion that deviations do not exceed the tolerable rate. Consequently, the sample size varies directly with the expected deviation rate (especially in terms of larger samples when the expected rate nears the tolerable rate). Some auditors will express the expected rate as a number (necessary for statistical calculations of sample size), while others will not put a number on it.

Population Size.   Common sense probably tells you that samples should be larger for bigger populations (a direct relationship). Strictly speaking, your common sense is accurate. As a practical matter, however, an appropriate sample size for a population of 100,000 units may be only 2 or 3 sampling units larger than an appropriate sample size for a 10,000-unit population. Not much difference! The power of the mathematics of probability is at work. The explanations in Chapter 20 are based on populations of 1,000 or more. However, you will need to be careful and make extra calculations when dealing with populations of fewer than 1,000 units.

The preceding discussion of sample size determinants is intended to give you a general understanding of the four influences on sample size. These influences are applicable to both statistical and nonstatistical sampling. A summary is presented in Exhibit 7–3. For further information about how to calculate a sample size, refer to Chapter 20.

5. Select the Sample

Auditing standards express two requirements for samples: (1) Sampling units must be selected from the population to which an audit conclusion will apply, ideally from transactions executed throughout the period under audit, and (2) a sample must be representative of the population from which it is drawn. In this context a **representative sample** is one that mirrors the characteristics of the population. Auditors,

E X H I B I T 7–3   SAMPLE SIZE RELATIONSHIPS: TEST OF CONTROLS AUDITING

| | Predetermined Sample Size Will Be | | |
Sample Size Influence	High Rate or Large Population	Low Rate or Small Population	Sample Size Relationship
1. Acceptable sampling risk	Smaller	Larger	Inverse
2. Tolerable deviation rate	Smaller	Larger	Inverse
3. Expected population deviation rate	Larger	Smaller	Direct
4. Population	Larger*	Smaller*	Direct

*Effect on sample size is quite small for population of 1,000 or more.

however, cannot guarantee representativeness. After all, that is what sampling risk is all about—the probability that the sample might not mirror the population well enough.

Auditors can try to attain representativeness by selecting random samples. A sample is considered **random** if each unit in the population has an equal probability of being included in the sample.

Intentional or accidental exclusion of a segment of a population can render a sample nonrepresentative. A popular way to select random samples is to associate each population unit with a unique number (easily done if the population units are prenumbered documents), then obtain a selection of random numbers to identify the sample units. You can use a printed random number table (see Appendix 20A) or a computerized random number generator to obtain a list of random numbers. This method is known as **unrestricted random selection**.

Another popular method is called **systematic random selection**. You need to know the population size and have a predetermined sample size to use it. The process is (1) obtain a random starting place in the physical representation (list of sales invoices recorded in a sales journal, for example) and select that unit, then (2) count through the file and select every kth unit, where k = Population size divided by Sample size. For example, if 10,000 invoices, numbered from 32071 to 42070, were issued, and you want a sample of 200, first use a random number table to get a starting place, say at invoice #35000, then select every kth = 10,000 divided by 200 = 50th invoice. So the next would be #35050, then #35100 . . . , then #42050, then #32100, #32150, and so on. (At the end of the list, you cycle back through the invoices #32071 through #34950.) Most systematic samples are selected using five or more random starts, as described in Chapter 20. (See the example in Exhibit 7–2).

Sample selection is the first step where a distinction between statistical and nonstatistical audit sampling is crucial. For statistical sampling evaluation, the sample must be random.

In nonstatistical plans, auditors sometimes use sample selection methods whose randomness and representativeness cannot be evaluated easily. **Haphazard selection** refers to any unsystematic way of selecting sample units; for example, closing your eyes and dipping into a file drawer of sales invoices to pick items. The problem is that you may pick only the dog-eared ones that stick out, and they may be different from most of the other invoices in the drawer. Also, you cannot describe your method so someone else can **replicate** it—reperform your selection procedure and get the same sample units. Some auditors describe haphazard sampling as a method of choosing items without any special reason for including or excluding items, thus obtaining a representative sample. However, haphazard selection should be considered only as a last resort because it is hard to document and impossible to replicate.

Another method is **block sampling**, which is the practice of choosing segments of contiguous transactions; for example, choosing the sales invoices processed on randomly chosen days, say February 3, July 17, and September 29. Implicitly, the block sampling auditor has defined the population unit as a business day (260 to 365 of them in a year) and has selected three—not much of a sample. Block sampling is undesirable because it is hard to get a representative sample of blocks efficiently. When you have enough blocks, you have a huge number of invoices to audit for compliance.

6. Perform the Test of Controls Procedures

Now you are ready to obtain the evidence. A **test of controls audit program** consists of procedures designed to produce evidence about the effectiveness of a client's internal control performance. The test of controls procedures listed in the box on the next page can be performed to determine how well the control procedures were followed on the transactions affecting accounts receivable. After each action part of a procedure, the parenthetical note tells you the control objective the auditor is testing.

· ·

R E V I E W
C H E C K P O I N T S

7.8 In test of controls auditing, why is it necessary to define a compliance deviation in advance? Give seven examples of compliance deviations.

7.9 Which judgments must an auditor make when deciding on a sample size for test of controls audit sampling? Describe the influence of each judgment on sample size.

7.10 What criterion must be met if a sample is to be considered random?

7.11 Name and describe four sample selection methods.

· ·

7. Evaluate the Evidence

LEARNING OBJECTIVE
3C. Evaluate evidence from a test of controls audit.

The final step represents the **evidence evaluation** phase of the sampling method. First, you recognized the problem as the task of determining whether each specified key control procedure worked satisfactorily. Then you gathered relevant compliance evidence. Now you need to evaluate the evidence and make justifiable decisions about the control risk.

Test of controls audit sampling is undertaken to provide evidence of whether a client's internal control procedures are being followed satisfactorily. Compliance evidence, therefore, is very important for the conclusion about control risk. When auditors evaluate sample-based compliance evidence, they run the sampling risks of making one of two decision errors: assessing the control risk too low or assessing the control risk too high. These two decision errors are related to the idea of sampling risk presented earlier.

The **risk of assessing the control risk too low** is the probability that the compliance evidence in the sample indicates low control risk when the actual (but unknown) degree of compliance does not justify such a low control-risk assessment. Assessing the control risk too low can lead to auditors' failure to do additional work

TEST OF CONTROLS AUDITING

1. Select a sample of recorded sales invoices and:
   a. Determine whether a bill of lading is attached (evidence of validity).
   b. Determine whether credit was approved (evidence of authorization).
   c. Determine whether product prices on the invoice agree with the approved price list (evidence of authorization and accuracy).
   d. Compare the quantity billed to the quantity shipped (evidence of accuracy).
   e. Recalculate the invoice arithmetic (evidence of accuracy).
   f. Compare the shipment date with the invoice record date (evidence of proper period).
   g. Trace the invoice to posting in the general ledger control account and in the correct customer's account (evidence of accounting).
   h. Note the type of product shipped and determine proper classification in the right product-line revenue account (evidence of classification).
2. Select a sample of shipping orders and:
   a. Trace them to recorded sales invoices (evidence of completeness).
   b. The procedures in 1b, 1c, 1d, 1e, 1f, and 1h also could be performed on the sales invoices produced by this sample. However, the work need not be duplicated.
3. Select a sample of recorded cash receipts and:
   a. Trace them to deposits in the bank statement (evidence of validity).
   b. Vouch discounts taken by customers to proper approval or policy (evidence of authorization).
   c. Recalculate the cash summarized for a daily report or posting (evidence of accuracy).
   d. Trace the deposit to the right cash account (evidence of classification).
   e. Compare the date of receipt to the recording date (evidence of proper period).
   f. Trace the receipts to postings in the correct customers' accounts (evidence of accounting).
4. Select a sample of daily cash reports or another source of original cash records and:
   a. Trace to the cash receipts journal (evidence of completeness).
   b. The procedures in 3b, 3c, 3d, 3e, and 3f also could be performed on this cash receipts sample. However, the work need not be duplicated.
5. Scan the accounts receivable for postings from sources other than the sales and cash receipts journals (e.g., general journal adjusting entries, credit memos). Vouch a sample of such entries to supporting documents (evidence of validity, authorization, accuracy, and classification).

This program describes the **nature** of the procedures. Each is a specific application of one of the general techniques.

that should be done. Assessing the control risk too low creates a threat to the effectiveness of the audit.

The **risk of assessing the control risk too high** is the probability that the compliance evidence in the sample indicates high control risk when the actual (but

> ## Superseded Terminology: Overreliance and Underreliance
>
> Several years ago, professional terminology was changed from reference to "reliance on control" to "assessment of control risk." However, old habits die hard, and you will probably encounter these uses of control terminology:
>
> **Overreliance** is the result of realizing the risk of assessing control risk too low. When auditors think control risk is low, when in fact it is higher, they will *overrely* on internal control and restrict other audit procedures when they actually should perform more work.
>
> **Underreliance** is the result of realizing the risk of assessing control risk too high. When auditors think control risk is high, when in fact it is lower, they will *underrely* on internal control and perform more audit work when less work would suffice.

unknown) degree of compliance would justify a lower control-risk assessment. Assessing the control risk too high tends to trigger more audit work than was planned originally. Assessing the control risk too high threatens the efficiency of the audit.

Audit efficiency is certainly important, but audit effectiveness is considered more important. For this reason, auditing standards require auditors to allow for a low level of risk of assessing the control risk too low, especially when this decision error could cause an auditor to do significantly less work on the related account balances. These risks and decisions are illustrated in Exhibit 7–4. Keeping these risks in mind, the evaluation of evidence consists of calculating the sample deviation rate, comparing it to the tolerable rate, and following up all the deviations discovered.

Calculate the Sample Deviation Rate

The first piece of hard evidence is the sample deviation rate. Suppose an auditor selected 200 recorded sales invoices and vouched them to shipping orders (bills of lading), finding four without shipping orders. The sample deviation rate is 4/200 = 2 percent. This is the best single-point estimate of the actual, but unknown, deviation rate in the population. However, you cannot say that the deviation rate in the population is exactly 2 percent. Chances are the sample is not exactly representative; the actual but unknown population deviation rate could be lower or higher.

Judge the Deviation Rate in Relation to the Tolerable Rate and the Risk of Assessing the Control Risk Too Low

Suppose the auditor in the example believed the tolerable rate was 8 percent to justify a control risk assessment of CR = 0.40. In a nonstatistical sampling application, this auditor is supposed to think about the sample deviation rate (2 percent) in relation to the tolerable rate (8 percent), and he or she is supposed to think about the risk (of assessing control risk too low) that the actual, but unknown, deviation rate in the population exceeds 8 percent. The decision in a nonstatistical evaluation depends on the auditor's experience and expertise. In our example a nonstatistical auditor might conclude that the population deviation rate probably does not exceed 8 percent because the sample deviation rate of 2 percent is so much lower.

EXHIBIT 7-4   THE TEST OF CONTROLS AUDIT SAMPLING DECISION MATRIX

Decision Alternatives (based on sample evidence)	Less Than Tolerable Rate	Greater Than Tolerable Rate
The deviation rate is less than the tolerable rate, so the control is performed satisfactorily.	Correct decision.	Control risk too low decision error.
The deviation rate is greater than the tolerable rate, so the control is not performed satisfactorily.	Control risk too high decision error.	Correct decision.

In a statistical sample evaluation, an auditor does things that are more explainable in a textbook. He or she establishes decision criteria by (1) assigning a number to the risk of assessing the control risk too low, say 10 percent, and (2) assigning a number to the tolerable rate, say 8 percent. Then a statistical table is used to calculate a sampling error-adjusted upper limit, which is the sample deviation rate adjusted upward to allow for the idea that the actual population rate could be higher. In this example the adjusted limit (call it UEL for "upper error limit") can be calculated to be 4 percent. This finding can be interpreted to mean: "The probability is 10 percent that the actual but unknown population deviation rate is greater than 4 percent." The decision criterion was: "The actual but unknown population deviation rate needs to be 8 percent or lower, with 10 percent risk of assessing the control risk too low." So the decision criterion is satisfied, and the control risk assessment (0.40) associated with the 8 percent tolerable rate can be justified.[5]

Follow Up All the Deviations

All the evaluation described so far has been mostly quantitative in nature, involving counts of deviations, deviation rates, and tolerable rate and risk judgment criteria. Qualitative evaluation is also necessary in the form of following up all the deviations to determine their nature and cause. A single deviation can be the tip of the iceberg—the telltale sign of a more pervasive deficiency. Auditors are obligated by the standard of due audit care to investigate known deviations so that nothing important will be overlooked.

The qualitative evaluation is sometimes called **error analysis** because each deviation from a prescribed control procedure is investigated to determine its nature, cause, and probable effect on financial statements. The analysis is essentially judgmental and involves auditors' determination of whether the deviation is (1) a pervasive error in principle made systematically on all like transactions or just a mistake on the particular transaction; (2) a deliberate or intentional control breakdown, rather than unintentional; (3) a result of misunderstanding of instructions or careless inattention to control duties; or (4) directly or remotely related to a money amount measurement in the financial statements. You can see that different qualitative perceptions of the seriousness of a deviation would result from error analysis findings.

---

[5] Changing the example to suppose 11 deviations were found creates a problem for the nonstatistical sampler. He or she must think harder about the evidence (a 5.5 percent sample rate) in relation to the tolerable rate (8 percent) and acceptable risk. The statistical sampler can measure the UEL at 8.3 percent, which is greater than the 8 percent tolerable rate at 10 percent risk of overreliance. The control fails the decision criterion test. Chapter 20 contains more information about making these calculations using statistical tables and formulas.

When the decision criteria are not satisfied and the preliminary conclusion is that the control risk is high, the auditors need to decide what to do next. The deviation follow-up can give auditors the obligation to do more account balance audit work by changing the nature, timing, and extent of other audit procedures—that is, by not limiting the work in reliance on the client's particular internal control procedures. If the audit manager hesitates to make this commitment to do more audit work, he or she can enlarge the sample and perform the test of controls audit procedures on more sample units in hopes of deciding that the control risk is actually lower. However, when faced with the preliminary "nonreliance" decision, you should never manipulate the quantitative evaluation by raising the tolerable rate or the risk of assessing the control risk too low. Supposedly, these two decision criteria were carefully determined in the planning stage, so now only new information would be a good basis for easing them.

Timing of Test of Controls Audit Procedures

Earlier in the chapter, you learned that auditors can perform the test of controls audit procedures at an interim date—a date some weeks or months before the client's year-end date. When test of controls auditing is timed early, an audit manager must decide what to do about the remaining period (e.g., the period October through December after doing test of controls auditing in September for a December 31 year-end audit).

The decision turns on several factors: (1) The results of the work at interim might, for example, indicate poor control performance and high control risk; (2) enquiries made after interim may show that a particular control procedure has been abandoned or improved; (3) the length of the remaining period may be short enough to forego additional work or long enough to suggest a need for continuing the test of controls audit; (4) the dollar amounts affected by the control procedure may have been much larger or much smaller than before; (5) evidence obtained about control as a byproduct of performing substantive procedures covering the remaining period may show enough about control performance that separate work on the control procedure performance may not be necessary; or (6) work performed by the company's internal auditors may be relied on with respect to the remaining period.

Depending on the circumstances indicated by these, an audit manager can decide to (1) continue the test of controls audit work because knowledge of the state of control performance is necessary to justify restriction of other audit work or (2) stop further test of controls audit work because (*a*) compliance evidence derived from other procedures provides sufficient evidence or (*b*) information shows the control has failed, control risk is high, and other work will not be restricted. Whatever the final judgment, considerations of audit effectiveness and efficiency should always be uppermost in the audit manager's mind.

R E V I E W
CHECKPOINTS

7.12 Why should auditors be more concerned in test of controls auditing with the risk of assessing the control risk too low (overreliance) than with the risk of assessing the control risk too high (underreliance)?

7.13 What important decision must be made when test of controls auditing is performed and control risk is evaluated at an interim date several weeks or months before the client's fiscal year-to-date?

SUBSTANTIVE PROCEDURES FOR AUDITING ACCOUNT BALANCES

. . . .

When audit sampling is used for auditing the assertions in account balances, the main feature of interest is the monetary amount of the population units, not the presence or absence of control deviations, as is the case with attribute sampling. Test of controls auditing is a part of the evaluation of internal control. **Substantive tests of details auditing** is the performance of procedures to obtain direct evidence about the dollar amounts and disclosures in the financial statements.

Substantive-purpose procedures include (1) analytical procedures and (2) test (audit) of details of transactions and balances. Analytical procedures involve overall comparisons of account balances with prior balances, financial relationships, nonfinancial information, budgeted or forecasted balances, and balances derived from estimates calculated by auditors (refer to the discussion of analytical procedures in Chapters 4 and 5). Analytical procedures are usually not applied on a sample basis. So, substantive procedures for auditing details are the normal procedures used in account balance audit sampling.

Risk Model Expansion

Up to now you have worked with a conceptual risk model that had a single term for "detection risk"—DR. The detection risk is actually a combination of two risks: Analytical procedures risk (APR) is the probability that analytical procedures will fail to detect material errors, and the risk of incorrect acceptance (RIA) is the probability that test-of-detail procedures will fail to detect material errors. The two types of procedures are considered independent, so detection risk is $DR = APR \times RIA$, and the expanded risk model is:

$$AR = IR \times CR \times APR \times RIA$$

This model is still a conceptual tool. The expansion of it did not make auditing any less professional. It can now be used to help you understand some elements of sampling for auditing the details of account balances. First, recognize that auditors exercise professional judgment in assessing the inherent risk (IR), control risk (CR), analytical procedures risk (APR), and audit risk (AR). If these four risks are given, you can then manipulate the model to express the risk of incorrect acceptance (RIA):

$$RIA = \frac{AR}{IR \times CR \times APR}$$

With AR, IR, and APR held constant, RIA varies inversely with CR; that is, the higher the control risk (CR), the lower the risk of incorrect acceptance (RIA), and vice versa.

More About Sampling Risk

Substantive-purpose procedures are performed to produce the evidence necessary to enable an auditor to decide whether an account balance is or is not fairly presented in conformity with GAAP. Thus, auditors run the sampling risks of making one of two decision errors. The **risk of incorrect acceptance (RIA)** represents the decision to accept a balance as being materially accurate when, in fact (unknown to the auditor), the balance is materially misstated. The other decision error risk is the **risk of**

E X H I B I T 7–5   THE ACCOUNT BALANCE AUDIT SAMPLING DECISION MATRIX

	Unknown Actual Account Balance is	
Decision Alternatives (based on sample evidence)	Materially* accurate.	Materially* misstated.
The book value of the account is materially accurate.	Correct decision.	Incorrect acceptance.
The book value of the account is materially misstated.	Incorrect rejection.	Correct decision.

*Materially in this context refers to the "material misstatement" assigned to the account balance.

incorrect rejection, and represents the decision that a balance is materially misstated when, in fact, it is not. These sampling risk relationships are shown in Exhibit 7–5.

Incorrect Acceptance

The risk of incorrect acceptance is considered the more important of the two decision error risks. When an auditor decides an account book balance is materially accurate (hence, needs no adjustment or change), the audit work on that account is considered finished, the decision is documented in the working papers, and the audit team proceeds to work on other accounts. When the account is, in fact, materially misstated, an unqualified opinion on the financial statements may well be unwarranted. Incorrect acceptance damages the effectiveness of the audit.

Incorrect Rejection

When an auditor decides an account book balance is materially misstated, some more audit work on that account is performed to determine the amount of an adjustment to recommend. The risk is that the book balance really is a materially accurate representation of the (unknown) actual value. At this point the event of incorrect rejection is about to be realized, and the audit manager may be inclined to recommend an adjustment that is not needed.

Incorrect rejection is not considered to be as serious an error as incorrect acceptance. When auditors first begin to think a balance may contain a material misstatement, efforts will be made to determine why the misstatement occurred and to estimate the amount. Thus, more evidence will be sought by the audit team or provided by the client. The data will be reviewed for a source of systematic error. The amounts of discovered errors will be analysed carefully. Client personnel may be assigned to do a complete analysis to determine a more accurate account balance.

If the initial decision was, in fact, a decision error of incorrect rejection, this other work should allow the auditors to determine whether the recorded amount is really misstated or the sample was not representative. Hence, incorrect rejection is not considered as serious as incorrect acceptance because steps will be taken to determine the amount of error and the erroneous decision has a chance to be reversed. Incorrect rejection thus affects the efficiency of an audit by causing unnecessary work.

Materiality and Tolerable Misstatement

Determining a threshold for the materiality of misstatements in financial statements is a tough problem under any circumstances. Audit sampling for substantive audit of particular account balances adds another wrinkle. Auditors also must decide on an amount of material misstatement, which is a judgment of the amount of monetary misstatement that may exist in an account balance or class of transactions and cause the financial statements to be materially misstated. Audit risk (AR in the risk model), therefore, is the risk that all the audit work on an account balance will not result in discovery of actual misstatement equal to the material misstatement. This concept is further discussed in Chapter 20.

SAMPLING STEPS FOR ACCOUNT BALANCE AUDIT

Audit sampling for the audit of account balances is structured much like the steps you studied in connection with test of controls audit sampling. As the steps are explained, an example related to auditing receivables is used. Remember, the example used with regard to test of controls sampling was the audit of a control procedure designed to prevent the recording of sales invoices without shipping orders. Now we move on to the next stage of work that can produce independent evidence of sales overstatement resulting from a breakdown of the control or from other causes. The seven-step framework explained in the next sections helps auditors plan, perform, and evaluate account balance detail audit work. It also helps auditors accomplish an eighth step—careful documentation of the work—by showing each of the seven areas to be described in the working papers. The first seven steps are the following:

1. Specify the audit objectives.
2. Define the population.
3. Choose an audit sampling method.
4. Determine the sample size.
5. Select the sample.
6. Perform the substantive-purpose procedures.
7. Evaluate the evidence.

Plan the Procedures

LEARNING OBJECTIVE
4A. Specify objectives and define a population for data.

The three planning steps represent the **problem-recognition** phase of the sampling method. When a client presents the financial statements, the assertions include (for example): "The trade accounts receivable exist and are bona fide obligations owed to the company" (ownership); "All the accounts receivable are recorded" (completeness); "They are stated at net realizable value" (valuation); and "They are properly classified as current assets, presented, and disclosed in conformity with GAAP." Each assertion represents a hypothesis (problem) to be tested; for example, "The trade accounts receivable exist as bona fide obligations owed to the company." A test of this hypothesis is the objective. The set of recorded accounts receivable is the population of data.

1. Specify the Audit Objectives
When performing accounts receivable confirmations on a sample basis, the specific objective is to decide whether the client's assertions about existence, rights (ownership), and valuation are materially accurate. In this context the auditing is viewed as **hypothesis testing**—the auditors hypothesize that the book value is materially accurate about existence, ownership, and valuation. The evidence will enable them to

accept or reject the hypothesis. The audit objective is to determine the monetary misstatement found by comparing the recorded balances to the balances determined from the evidence.

Accountants can use similar sampling methods for **dollar-value estimation objective**, which is the job of helping a client obtain an estimate of an amount. Examples include estimation of inventory FIFO values and data for current cost accounting information.[6] In dollar-value estimation, the objective is to develop a basic measurement, not to audit the balance or amount. Audit sampling, in the following discussion, adopts the objective of hypothesis testing.

2. Define the Population

Auditors need to be sure the definition of the population matches the objectives. Defining the population as the recorded accounts receivable balances suits the objective of obtaining evidence about existence, ownership, and valuation. This definition also suits the related objective of obtaining evidence about sales overstatement. In the case of accounts receivable, each customer's account balance is a population unit. However, if the objectives were to obtain evidence about completeness and sales understatement, the recorded accounts receivable would be the wrong population.

Ordinarily, the sampling unit is the same as the population unit. Sometimes, however, it is easier to define the sampling unit as a smaller part of a population unit. For example, if the client's accounting system keeps track of individual invoices charged to customers, an auditor may want to audit a sample of invoices by confirming them with customers instead of working with each customer's balance.

Since a sample will be drawn from a physical representation of the population (e.g., a printed trial balance or magnetic disk file of customers' accounts), the auditors must determine whether it is complete. Footing the trial balance and reconciling it to the control account total will accomplish the job.

Auditing standards require auditors to use their judgment to determine whether any population units should be removed from the population and audited separately (not sampled) because taking sampling risk (risk of incorrect acceptance or incorrect rejection) with respect to them is not justified. Suppose the accounts receivable in our example amounted to $400,000, but six of the customers had balances of $10,000 or more, for a sum of $100,000. The next-largest account balance is less than $10,000. The six accounts are considered **individually significant items** because each of them exceeds the material misstatement amount, and they should be removed from the population and audited completely.

In the jargon of audit sampling related to account balances, subdividing the population is known as **stratification**. The total population is subdivided into subpopulations by account balance size. For example, a small number of accounts totalling $75,000 may be identified as the first (large balance) stratum when four strata are defined. Three more strata may be defined, each containing a total of approximately $75,000 of the recorded balances, but each made up of a successively larger number of customer accounts whose average balance is successively smaller. Stratification can be used to increase audit efficiency (smaller total sample size). A stratification example appears in the following box.

[6] Don Leslie, Albert Teitlebaum, and Rodney Anderson, *Dollar Unit Sampling* (Toronto: Copp, Clark, Pitman, 1979), pp. 244–249.

STRATIFICATION EXAMPLE

The stratification below subdivides the population into a first stratum of six individually significant accounts and four other strata, which each have approximately one-fourth ($75,000) of the remaining dollar balance. You can see the typical situation in which the accounts of smaller value are more numerous.

The example also shows one kind of allocation of a sample size of 90 to the last four strata. When each stratum gets one-fourth of the sample size, the sample is skewed toward the higher-value accounts: The second stratum has 23 in the sample out of 80 in the stratum, and the fifth stratum has 23 out of 910 in the stratum.

Stratum	Book Value	Number	Amount	Sample
1	Over $10,000	6	$100,000	6
2	$625–$9,999	80	75,068	23
3	$344–$624	168	75,008	22
4	$165–$343	342	75,412	22
5	$1–$164	910	74,512	23
		1,506	$100,000	96

This kind of stratification takes care of the normal situation in which the variability of the account balances and errors in them tend to be larger in the high-value accounts than in the low-value accounts. As a consequence, the sample includes a larger proportion of the high-value accounts (23/80) and a smaller proportion of the low-value accounts (23/910). In addition to size or variability, stratification can be based on other qualitative characteristics the auditor considers important, such as transactions stratified by individual, location, date, product, and so forth.

3. Choose an Audit Sampling Method

You already have been introduced to statistical and nonstatistical sampling methods. At this point, an auditor must decide which to use. If he or she chooses statistical sampling, another choice needs to be made. In statistical sampling, classical variables sampling methods that utilize normal distribution theory are available. Dollar-unit sampling, which utilizes attribute sampling theory, also can be used. Some of the technical characteristics of the statistical methods are explained more fully in Chapter 20.

The calculation examples shown later in this chapter use the dollar-unit sampling method. This calculation is relatively simple and illustrates the points adequately. Moreover, dollar-unit sampling is used more often in practice.

Perform the Procedures

LEARNING OBJECTIVE
4B. Determine sample size and select sampling units.

The next three steps represent the **evidence-collection** phase of the sampling method. These steps are performed to get the evidence.

Figuring sample size for account balance auditing requires consideration of several influences. The main reason for figuring a sample size in advance is to help guard against underauditing (not obtaining enough evidence) and overauditing (obtaining more evidence than needed). Another important reason is to control the cost of the audit. An arbitrary sample size could be used to perform the accounts receivable confirmation procedures; but if it turned out to be too small, sending and processing more confirmations might be impossible before the audit report deadline. Alternative procedures then could become costly and time-consuming. A predetermined sample size is not as important in other situations where the auditors can increase the sample simply by choosing more items available for audit in the client's office.

4. Determine the Sample Size

Whether using statistical or nonstatistical sampling methods, auditors first need to establish decision criteria for the risk of incorrect acceptance, the risk of incorrect rejection, and the material misstatement. Also, auditors may want to estimate the expected dollar amount of misstatement. These decision criteria should be determined before any evidence is obtained from a sample.

a. Risk of Incorrect Acceptance (RIA).   This risk is assessed in terms of the audit risk model, which can be your guide. An acceptable risk of incorrect acceptance depends on the assessments of inherent risk, control risk, and analytical procedures risk. The risk of incorrect acceptance varies inversely with the combined product of the other risks. The larger the combined product of the other risks, the smaller is the allowable risk of incorrect acceptance.

Suppose, for example, two different auditors independently assess the client's control risk and their own analytical procedures and arrive at the following conclusions. Assume both auditors believe an appropriate audit risk—AR—is 0.05:

Auditor A believes the inherent risk is high (IR = 1.0), the control risk is moderate (CR = 0.50), and analytical procedures will not be performed (APR = 1.0). Audit procedures need to be so planned that the risk of incorrect acceptance will be about 10 percent.

$$RIA = AR/(IR*CR*APR) = 0.05/(1.0*0.50*1.0) = 0.10$$

Auditor B believes the inherent risk is high (IR = 1.0), the control risk is very low (CR = 0.20), and analytical procedures will not be performed (APR = 1.0). Audit procedures need to be so planned that the risk of incorrect acceptance will be about 25 percent.

$$RIA = AR/(IR*CR*APR) = 0.05/(1.0*0.20*1.0) = 0.25$$

Use the model with caution. The lesson you should learn from these examples is that auditor A's account balance sampling work must provide less risk than that of auditor B. Since sample size varies inversely with the risk of incorrect acceptance, auditor A's sample will be larger. In fact, when the control risk is lower, as in auditor B's evaluation, the acceptable risk of incorrect acceptance (RIA) is higher. Thus, auditor B's sample of customers' accounts receivable can be smaller than auditor A's sample.

b. Risk of Incorrect Rejection.   Like the risk of incorrect acceptance, the risk of incorrect rejection exists both in statistical and nonstatistical sampling applications. It can be controlled, usually by auditing a larger sample. So, sample size varies inversely with the risk of incorrect rejection. The determination of the risk of incorrect rejection is discussed in Chapter 20.

EXHIBIT 7–6   SAMPLE SIZE RELATIONSHIPS: AUDIT OF ACCOUNT BALANCES

| | Predetermined Sample Size Will Be | | |
Sample Size Influence	High Rate or Large Amount	Low Rate or Small Amount	Sample Size Relation
1. Risk of incorrect acceptance	Smaller	Larger	Inverse
2. Risk of incorrect rejection	Smaller	Larger	Inverse
3. Tolerable misstatement	Smaller	Larger	Inverse
4. Expected misstatement	Larger	Smaller	Direct
5. Population variability	Larger	Smaller	Direct
6. Population size	Larger	Smaller	Direct

c. Material Misstatement.   The material misstatement—usually the same as the overall materiality of misstatements—also must be considered in nonstatistical as well as statistical sampling applications. In statistical sampling, material misstatement must be expressed as a dollar amount or as a proportion of the total recorded amount. The sample size varies inversely with the amount of misstatement considered material. The greater the material misstatement, the smaller the sample size needed.

d. Expected Dollar Misstatement.   Auditors may want to estimate an "expected dollar misstatement" amount. The estimate may be based on last year's audit findings or on other knowledge of the accounting system. Expectations of dollar misstatement have the effect of increasing the sample size. The more dollar misstatement expected, the larger the sample size should be. Sample sizes should be larger when more dollar misstatement is expected. So, sample size varies directly with the amount of expected dollar misstatement.

e. Variability Within the Population.   Auditors using nonstatistical sampling must take into account the degree of dispersion among unit values in a population. The typical skewness of some accounting populations needs to be taken into account. **Skewness** is the concentration of a large proportion of the dollar amount in an account in a small number of the population items. In our illustration, $100,000 (25 percent) of the total accounts receivable is in six customers' accounts while the remaining $300,000 is in 1,500 customers' accounts.

As a general rule, auditors should be careful about populations whose unit values range widely, say from $1 to $10,000. Obtaining a representative sample in such a case, as you might imagine, would take a larger sample than if the range of the unit values were only from $1 to $500. Sample size should vary directly with the magnitude of the variability of population unit values. Populations with high variability should be stratified, as previously shown in the stratification example.

Auditors using classical statistical sampling methods must obtain an estimate of the population **standard deviation**, which is a measure of the population variability. When using dollar-unit sampling, the variability is taken into account with the expected dollar misstatement, and no separate estimate of a standard deviation needs to be made.

These five influences, plus the influence of population size on sample size, are summarized in Exhibit 7–6.

5. Select the Sample

As was the case with test of controls audit samples, account balance samples must be representative. Nothing is new about the selection methods. You can use unrestricted random selection and systematic selection to obtain the random samples necessary for statistical applications. Haphazard and block selection methods have the same drawbacks as they have in test of controls audit samples.

6. Perform the Substantive-purpose Procedures

The basic assertions in a presentation of accounts receivable are that they exist, they are complete (no receivables are unrecorded), the company has the right to collect the money, they are valued properly at net realizable value, and they are presented and disclosed properly in conformity with GAAP. A **substantive-purpose audit program** consists of account balance–related procedures designed to produce evidence about these assertions. The substantive-purpose procedures listed in the following box can be performed to obtain the evidence. The parenthetical notes identify the assertion addressed by the procedure.

The confirmation procedures should be performed for all the sampling units. The other procedures should be performed as necessary to complete the evidence relating to existence, ownership, and valuation. The important thing is to audit all the sample units. You cannot simply discard one that is hard to audit in favour of adding to the sample a customer whose balance is easy to audit. This action might bias the sample. Sometimes, however, you will be unable to audit a sample unit. Suppose a customer did not respond to the confirmation requests, sales invoices supporting the balance could not be found, and no payment was received after the confirmation date. Auditing standards contain the following guidance:

- If considering the entire balance to be misstated will not alter your evaluation conclusion, then you do not need to work on it anymore. Your evaluation conclusion may be to accept the book value, as long as the account is not big enough to change the conclusion. Your evaluation conclusion already may be to reject the book value, so that considering another account misstated just reinforces the decision.

- If considering the entire balance to be misstated would change an acceptance decision to a rejection decision, you need to do something about it. Since the example seems to describe a dead end, you may need to select more accounts (expand the sample), perform the procedures on them (other than confirmation), and re-evaluate the results.

. . . .

R E V I E W
C H E C K P O I N T S

7.14 Write the expanded risk model. What risk is implied for "test of detail risk" when inherent risk = 1.0, control risk = 0.40, analytical procedures risk = 0.60, audit risk = 0.048, tolerable misstatement = $10,000, and the estimated standard deviation in the population = $25?

7.15 When auditing account balances, why is an incorrect acceptance decision considered more serious than an incorrect rejection decision?

7.16 What should be the relationship between tolerable misstatement in the audit of an account balance and the amount of monetary misstatement considered material to the overall financial statements?

Account Balance Auditing

1. Confirm a sample of the receivables, investigate exceptions, and follow up nonrespondents by vouching sales charges and cash receipts to supporting documents (evidence of existence, rights, and valuation).
2. Obtain an aged trial balance of the receivables. Audit the aging accuracy on a sample basis. Calculate and analyse the age status of the accounts and the allowance for uncollectible accounts in light of current economic conditions and the company's collection experience (evidence of valuation).
3. Discuss past-due accounts with the credit manager. Obtain credit reports and financial statements for independent analysis of large overdue accounts (evidence of valuation).
4. Vouch receivables balances to cash received after the cutoff date (evidence of existence, rights, and valuation).
5. Distinguish names of trade customers from others (officers, directors, employees, affiliates) and determine that the two classifications are reported separately (evidence of presentation and disclosure).
6. Read loan agreements and note any pledge of receivables, sales with recourse, or other restrictions or contingencies related to the receivables (evidence of presentation and disclosure).
7. Read sales contracts for evidence of customers' rights of return or price allowance terms (evidence of presentation and disclosure).
8. Obtain written representations from the client concerning pledges for collateral, related party receivables, collectibility, and other matters relating to accounts receivable (detail assertions in writing).

This program describes the **nature** of the procedures. Each is a specific application of one of the seven general procedures. However, this list does not include a procedure dealing explicitly with the completeness assertion. You can obtain completeness evidence with the dual-purpose nature of the completeness procedures done in the test of controls audit work (see test of controls procedures 2 and 4). The list also excludes analytical procedures based on interrelationships with budget, forecast, industry, or historical data. More specific situational facts would need to be known in order to be specific about analytical procedures work.

7.17 What general set of audit objectives can you use as a frame of reference to be specific about the particular objectives for the audit of an account balance?

7.18 What audit purpose is served by stratifying an account balance population and by removing some units from the population for 100 percent audit attention?

7.19 What is the influence on dollar-value variables sample sizes of the risk of incorrect acceptance? of the risk of incorrect rejection? of the tolerable misstatement? of the population variability and the population size?

7. Evaluate the Evidence

LEARNING OBJECTIVE
4C. Evaluate monetary
     error evidence from a
     balance audit sample.

The final step represents the **evidence evaluation** and decision-making phase of the sampling method. Your decisions about existence, ownership, and valuation need to be justifiable by sufficient, competent quantitative and qualitative evidence. You should be concerned first with quantitative evaluation of the evidence. Qualitative follow-up is also important and is discussed later. The basic steps in quantitative evaluation are these:

- Figure the total amount of actual monetary error found in the sample. This amount is the **known misstatement**.
- Project the known misstatement to the population. The projected amount is the **likely misstatement**.
- Compare the likely misstatement (also called the "projected misstatement") to the material misstatement for the account and consider: the risk of incorrect acceptance that likely misstatement is calculated to be less than material misstatement even though the actual misstatement in the population is greater; or the risk of incorrect rejection that likely misstatement is calculated to be greater than material misstatement, even though the actual misstatement in the population is smaller.

Amount of Known Misstatement

Now you need some illustrative numbers. Hypothetical audit evidence from a sample is shown in Exhibit 7–7. The example cited earlier said that total accounts receivable is $400,000, and $100,000 of the total is in six large balances, which are to be audited separately. The remainder is in 1,500 customer accounts whose balances range from $1 to $9,999. Suppose the audit team selected 90 of these accounts and applied the confirmation or vouching procedures to each of them. The evidence showed $136 of actual misstatement representing net overstatement of the recorded amounts (Exhibit 7–7). This amount is the known misstatement for this sample of 90 customer accounts.

Project the Known Misstatement to the Population

To make a decision about the population, the known misstatement in the sample must be projected to the population. The key requirement for projecting the known misstatement to the population is that the sample must be representative. If the sample is not representative, a projection produces a nonsense number. Take an extreme example: Remember that all of the six largest accounts ($100,000 in total) were audited. Suppose one of them contained a $600 disputed amount. Investigation showed the customer was right, management agreed, so the $600 is the amount of known misstatement. If an auditor takes this group of six accounts as being representative of the population, projecting the $100 average misstatement to 1,506 accounts ($100 × 1,506) would project a total misstatement of $150,600, compared to the recorded accounts receivable total of $400,000. This projection is neither reasonable nor appropriate. The six large accounts are not representative of the entire population of 1,506 accounts. Nothing is wrong with the calculation method. The nonrepresentative "sample" is the culprit in this absurd result.

A projection based on a sample applies only to the population from which the sample was drawn. Consider the sample of 90 accounts from the population of 1,500. The average difference is $1.51 (overstatement of the recorded amount), so the

EXHIBIT 7-7　　　HYPOTHETICAL SAMPLE DATA

Sample Item	Audited Amount	Recorded Amount	Difference* (Recorded − Audited)
1	$ 691	$ 691	$ 0
*	*	*	*
*	*	*	*
*	*	*	*
6	372	508	136
*	*	*	*
*	*	*	*
*	*	*	*
23	136	141	5
*	*	*	*
*	*	*	*
*	*	*	*
50	62	62	0
*	*	*	*
*	*	*	*
*	*	*	*
90	135	130	(5)
Totals	$18,884	$19,020	$136
Averages:			
Audited amount	$209.82		
Recorded amount		$211.33	
Difference			$1.51

*A positive difference is an account overstatement, and a negative difference is an account understatement.

projected likely misstatement is $2,267 (overstatement), provided the sample is representative. This projection method is called the average difference method, expressed in equation form as:

Projected likely misstatement (under the average difference method) =
((Dollar amount of misstatement in the sample)/(Number of sampling units)) *
(Number of population units)

In the example:

Projected likely misstatement (under the average difference method) =
($136/90)*1,500 = $2,267 (overstatement)

How can you tell whether a sample is representative? You cannot guarantee representativeness, but you can try to attain it by selecting a random sample and by carefully subdividing (stratifying) the population according to an important characteristic, such as the size of individual customers' balances. When the population is stratified, each stratum is more homogeneous according to account size than the population as a whole, and the known misstatement in each can be projected. Combining them into a single projection is shown in the stratification calculation example shown below.

You can also inspect the sample to see whether it shows the characteristics of the population. In the example, for instance, the average recorded amount of the population is $200 ($300,000 divided by 1,500); the average in the illustrative unstratified

STRATIFICATION CALCULATION EXAMPLE

Projected Likely Misstatement: Average Difference Method

Stratification of a population is said to be more efficient because you can usually calculate a smaller projected likely misstatement with the same sample size than would have been used in an unstratified sample (as illustrated in this chapter), or you can usually calculate the same projected likely misstatement with a smaller stratified sample. The example below illustrates a typical situation of finding larger misstatements in the larger accounts, resulting in a projected likely misstatement smaller than the $7,350 illustrated in the chapter for an unstratified sample ($600 in the six largest customers plus $6,750 projected from the sample of 90 from the other 1,500 customers).

The calculation of projected likely misstatements (PLM), using the difference method, is applied separately to each stratum. Then, the amounts are added to get the whole sample result.

Stratum	Number	Amount	Sample	Misstatement*	PLM
1	6	$100,000	6	$ −600	$ −600
2	80	75,068	23	−274	−953
3	168	75,008	22	−66	−504
4	342	75,412	22	−88	−1,368
5	910	75,512	23	23	910
	1,506	$400,000	96	$−1,005	$−2,515

*A positive misstatement indicates overstatement of the book value, and a negative misstatement indicates understatement.

sample is $211.33 (a little high). You also can look to see whether the sample contains a range of recorded amounts similar to the population that ranged from $1 to $9,999. With statistics you can calculate the standard deviation of the sample recorded amounts and compare it to the standard deviation of the population.

The dollar-unit sampling projection method automatically takes into account the stratification of the population. You can project using the dollar-unit sampling method, expressed in equation form as follows:

Projected likely misstatement (dollar-unit method) = (Sum of the proportionate amount of misstatements or taintings of all dollar units in error in the sample) * (Recorded amount in the population)

Taintings are discussed in more detail in Chapter 20. In the example here:

Projected likely misstatement (dollar-unit method) =
$300,000 * (1/90) * ((136/508) + (5/141) − (5/130)) = $883 (overstatement)

The difference in the two projected likely misstatements illustrates the importance of having representative sampling. Auditors also need to be very careful about the adequacy of the sample size. You can see that small samples which produce large or small dollar differences can distort both the average difference and the average dollar-unit ratio, thus distorting the projected likely misstatement. One way to exercise care is to take the sampling risks into account.

Consider Sampling Risks

The risks of making wrong decisions (incorrect acceptance or incorrect rejection) exist in both nonstatistical and statistical sampling. The smaller the sample, the greater both risks. Common sense tells you that the less you know about a population because of a small sample, the more risk you run of making a wrong decision.

The problem is to consider the risk that the projected likely misstatement ($883 overstatement for the sample of 90 accounts in the example using the dollar-unit sampling method) could have been obtained even though the actual total misstatement in the population is greater than the material misstatement ($10,000 in the example). Auditing guidance suggests you can use your experience and professional judgment to consider the risk. If the projected likely misstatement is considerably less than tolerable misstatement, chances are good that the total actual misstatement in the population is not greater than tolerable misstatement. However, when projected likely misstatement is close to tolerable misstatement (say, $9,000, compared to $10,000), the chance is not so good, and the risk of incorrect acceptance may exceed the acceptable risk (RIA) that an auditor initially established as a decision criterion.

A similar situation exists with respect to the risk of incorrect rejection. Suppose the sample results had produced a projected likely misstatement of $15,000 overstatement. Now the question is: "What is the risk that this result was obtained even though the actual misstatement in the population is $10,000 or less?" Again, the judgment depends on the size of the sample and the kinds and distribution of misstatements discovered.

Auditors take the rejection decision as a serious matter and conduct enough additional investigation to determine the amount and adjustment required. Hence, the risk of incorrect rejection is mitigated by additional work necessary to determine the amount and nature of an adjustment. In the example, if the sample of 90 customers' accounts had shown total misstatement of $900 (yielding the $15,000 projected misstatement using the average difference method), most auditors would consider the evidence insufficient to propose a significant adjustment. (Incidentally, however, correction of the $900 should not by itself be a sufficient action to satisfy the auditors.)

When using nonstatistical sampling, auditors utilize their experience and expertise to take risks into account. Statistical samplers can add statistical calculations to these considerations of sampling risk. Further explanation of statistical calculations is in Chapter 20.

Qualitative Evaluation

The numbers are not enough. Auditors are required to follow up each monetary difference to determine whether it arose from (*a*) misunderstanding of accounting principles, (*b*) simple mistakes or carelessness, (*c*) an intentional irregularity, or (*d*) management override of an internal control procedure. Auditors also need to relate the differences to their effect on other amounts in the financial statements. For example, overstatements in accounts receivable may indicate overstatement of sales revenue.

Likewise, you should not overlook the information that can be obtained in account balance auditing about the performance of internal control procedures—the dual-purpose characteristic of auditing procedures. Deviations (or absence of deviations) discovered when performing substantive procedures can help confirm or contradict an auditor's previous conclusion about control risk. If many more monetary differences arise than expected, the control risk conclusion may need to be revised, and more account balance auditing work may need to be done.

Knowledge of the source, nature, and amount of monetary differences is very important. Such knowledge is required to explain the situation to management and to direct additional work to areas where adjustments are needed. The audit work is not complete until the qualitative evaluation and follow-up is done.

Evaluate the Amount of Misstatement

Handbook Section 5130 and the CICA Auditing Guideline on Materiality and Audit Risk requires the aggregation of known misstatement ("identified misstatement" in the Guideline) and projected likely misstatement ("likely aggregate misstatement" in the Guideline). The aggregation is the sum of (*a*) known misstatement in the population units identified for 100 percent audit (in the example, the six accounts totalling $100,000, with $600 overstatement discovered), and (*b*) the projected likely misstatement for the population sampled (in the example, the $883 overstatement projected using the dollar-unit sampling method). The theory underlying (*b*) is that the projected likely misstatement is the best single estimate of the amount that would be determined if all the accounts in the sampled population had been audited. You can see the importance of sample representativeness in this regard. This aggregation ($883 overstatement in the example) should be judged in combination with other misstatements found in the audit of other account balances to determine whether the financial statements taken as a whole need to be adjusted and, if so, in what amount.

The evaluation of amounts is not over yet, however. One thing that cannot be said about the projected likely misstatement is that it is the exact amount that would be found if all the units in the population were audited. The actual amount might be more or less, and the problem arises from **sampling error**—the amount by which a projected likely misstatement amount could differ from an actual (unknown) total as a result of the sample not being exactly representative. Of course, auditors are most concerned with the possibility that the actual total misstatement might be considerably more than the projected likely misstatement.

This sampling phenomenon gives rise to the concept of **possible misstatement** (the third kind, in addition to known and likely misstatement), which is interpreted in auditing standards as the further misstatement remaining undetected in the units not selected in the sample. Nonstatistical auditors resort to experience and professional judgment in considering additional possible misstatement. Statistical auditors, however, can utilize some statistical calculations to measure possible misstatement, as explained in Chapter 20.

In Chapter 20 the basic example shows how to calculate a possible misstatement. For the illustration here the possible misstatement is in the amount of $6,331. Thus, the aggregation of known, projected, and possible misstatement is $600 + $884 + $6,331 = $7,814. This total suggests that the misstatement in the account does not exceed the amount considered material ($10,000). If the possible misstatement were higher, say $9,000, the total would be $10,483, and the evidence would suggest that the misstatement in the account exceeds $10,000.

Timing of Substantive Audit Procedures

Account balances can be audited, at least in part, at an interim date. When this work is done before the company's year-end date, auditors must extend the interim-date audit conclusion to the balance sheet date. The process of **extending the audit conclusion** amounts to nothing more (and nothing less) than performing substantive-purpose audit procedures on the transactions in the remaining period and on the year-end balance to produce sufficient competent evidence for a decision about the year-end balance.

Substantive procedures must be performed to obtain evidence about the balance after the interim date. You cannot audit a balance (say, accounts receivable) as of

Balance-audit Sampling Failure

The company owned surgical instruments that were loaned and leased to customers. The auditors decided to audit the existence of the assets by confirming them with the customers who were supposed to be holding and using them. From the population of 880 instruments, the auditors selected 8 for confirmation, using a sampling method that purported to produce a representative selection.

Two confirmations were never returned, and the auditors did not follow up on them. One returned confirmation said the customer did not have the instrument in question, and the auditors were never able to find it. Nevertheless, the auditors concluded that the $3.5 million recorded amount of the surgical instrument assets was materially accurate.

Judges who heard complaints on the quality of the audit work concluded that it was not performed in accordance with generally accepted auditing standards (GAAS) because the auditors did not gather sufficient evidence concerning the existence and valuation of the surgical instruments. GAAS requires auditors to project the sample findings to the population. The auditors did not do so. They never calculated (nonstatistical) the fact that $1,368,750 of the asset amount could not be confirmed or found to exist. The sample of eight was woefully inadequate both in sample size and in the proportionately large number of exceptions reported. There was a wholly insufficient statistical basis for concluding that the account was fairly stated under generally accepted accounting principles.

Source: U.S. Securities and Exchange Commission, *Administrative Proceeding File No. 3-6579* (Initial Decision, June 1990).

September 30, then without further work accept the December 31 balance. Internal control must be well designed and performed adequately. If the company's internal control over transactions that produce the balance under audit is not particularly strong, you should time the substantive detail work at year-end instead of at interim.

If rapidly changing business conditions might predispose managers to misstate the accounts (try to slip one by the auditors), the work should be timed at year-end. In most cases careful scanning of transactions and analytical review comparisons should be performed on transactions that occur after the interim date.

As an example, accounts receivable confirmation can be done at an interim date. Subsequently, efforts must be made to ascertain whether controls continued to be reliable. You must scan the transactions of the remaining period, audit any new large balances, and update work on collectibility, especially with analysis of cash received after the year-end.

Audit work is performed at interim for two reasons: (1) to spread the accounting firms' workload so that not all the work on clients is crammed into December and January and (2) to make the work efficient and enable companies to report audited financial results soon after the year-end. Some well-organized companies with well-planned audits report their audited figures as early as five or six days after their fiscal year-ends.

R E V I E W
CHECKPOINTS

7.20 What kind of evidence evaluation consideration should an auditor give to the dollar amount of a population unit that cannot be audited?

7.21 What are the three basic steps in quantitative evaluation of monetary amount evidence when auditing an account balance?

7.22 What are two methods of projecting the known misstatement to the population?

7.23 What are some of the signs that an unstratified random sample is actually representative of the population from which it was drawn?

7.24 The projected likely misstatement may be calculated, yet further misstatement may remain undetected in the population. How can auditors take the further misstatement under consideration when completing the quantitative evaluation of monetary evidence?

7.25 What additional considerations are in order when auditors plan to audit account balances at an interim date several weeks or months before the client's fiscal year-end date?

SUMMARY

Audit sampling was explained in this chapter as an organized method to make decisions. Two kinds of decisions were shown—assessment of control risk and the decision about whether financial statement assertions in an account balance are fairly presented. The method is organized by two kinds of audit programs to guide the work on these two decisions—the test of controls audit program and the balance-audit program. The audit sampling itself can be attribute sampling for test of controls, and balance-audit (variables) sampling for auditing the assertions in an account balance.

Audit sampling is a method of organizing the application of audit procedures and a disciplined approach to decision problems. Both types of sampling were explained in basic terms of planning the audit procedures, performing the audit procedures, and evaluating the evidence produced by the audit procedures. The latter process was reinforced with some difference and dollar-unit sampling projections of misstatement amounts. Mathematical consideration of sampling error ("possible misstatement," "further misstatement remaining undetected") was postponed to Chapter 20.

Risk in audit decisions was explained in the context of nonsampling and sampling risk, with sampling risk further subdivided into two types of decision errors: (1) assessing control risk too low and incorrect acceptance of a balance and (2) assessing control risk too high and incorrect rejection of an account balance. The first pair damages the effectiveness of audits, and the second pair damages the efficiency of audits.

Dollar-valued materiality was incorporated in the balance-audit sampling in terms of the material misstatement assigned to the audit of a particular account. The connection of material misstatement to the tolerable deviation rate in test of controls sampling was postponed to Chapter 20.

Audit programs for test of controls procedures and balance-audit procedures were illustrated. Separate sections explained the application of procedures at an interim date. Thus, the chapter covered the nature, timing, and extent of audit procedures.

One of the goals of this chapter was to enable students to be able to understand these procedural programs in the context of audit sampling.

CASE STUDY   # KINGSTON COMPANY

Introduction

This portion of the Kingston Company case expands the data and builds on the casework done in Chapters 4, 5, and 6. The case requirements below are phrased and presented in terms of nonstatistical sampling. These same requirements are extended in Chapter 20 to deal with statistical calculations.

The company description, organization, and personnel, and information about the current audit engagement, are in the case sections of Chapters 4 and 5. This information was used to write an engagement letter, make a preliminary materiality assessment, and perform preliminary analytical procedures.

Accounting and Control Systems

The description of part of the revenue and collection cycle (credit approval and sales processing, and shipment and delivery), the accounting and control procedure manual, and the chart of accounts are in the Kingston case section at the end of Chapter 6. This information was used to prepare a company organization chart, identify possible errors and irregularities, specify controls, complete an internal control questionnaire, document the system with a flowchart, and evaluate part of the control system with a bridge workpaper.

Test of Controls Audit

Without prejudice to your conclusions on case assignments in previous chapters, assume you have made the conclusions described next.

Your preliminary materiality assessment produced the conclusion that a $71,000 understatement or overstatement of operating income will be material, and a tolerable misstatement of $10,000 for sales under- or overstatement will suit your purposes for planning the audit of sales. Your preliminary analytical procedures show that net sales are down 10 percent ($900,000) from last year, and gross accounts receivable are down 20 percent ($100,000) to $400,000. Operating income increased 47 percent, mainly because cost of goods sold declined proportionately more than sales declined. It looks like the greatest risk is in the inventory and cost of goods sold accounts, but you still need to audit the accounts receivable, in case some sales overstatement is stuck in receivables to mask an actual greater decline in the sales total.

Assume you obtained the following responses to these selected questions from the internal control questionnaire:

4.	Are prenumbered bills of lading or other shipping documents prepared or completed in the shipping department?	Yes.
8.	Are all credit sales approved by the credit department prior to shipment?	Yes. Sales orders approved.

9.	Are sales prices and terms based on approved standards?	Yes. Approved price list.
11.	Are shipped quantities compared to invoice quantities?	Yes. In shipping and A/R.
12.	Are sales invoices checked for error in quantities, prices, extensions and footing, and freight allowances, and checked with customers' orders?	Yes. By A/R department.
17.	Does the accounting manual contain instructions to date sales invoices on the shipment date?	Yes.
18.	(From accounts receivable control questionnaire): Does someone reconcile the accounts receivable subsidiary to the control account regularly to determine whether all entries are made to customers' accounts?	Yes.

In your bridge workpaper, you concluded that all the specifications in these internal control questionnaire items represent potential control strengths, provided company personnel comply with them properly. Now you need to audit a sample of sales transactions for control compliance. The objectives of your work will be to (1) obtain control evidence about the validity, authorization, accuracy, and proper period recording of recorded sales and (2) obtain control evidence about the accuracy and classification of sales postings to customer accounts receivable, so you can justify auditing customer accounts receivable on a sample basis.

Kingston Case Assignments

7.26   Kingston Company: Test of Controls Audit Program.   Assume that 10,000 sales invoices were processed during the year ended December 31, and you are performing the test of controls audit on the entire population. The first invoice number this year was 32071 and the last was 42070.

Required:

a. Write an audit program (specify the population from which a sample will be taken, and specify the audit actions) for the test of controls audit of sales transactions for the attributes shown in the columns in Exhibit 7–2. (Hint: The sample documents should be recorded sales invoices, and all the actions can be taken with reference to the sales invoices and other documents that support the sales invoices.)

b. Make a decision about the size of the sample. To facilitate your instructor's presentation of solutions, select one of these sample sizes: 30, 60, 80, 90, 120, 160, 220, 240, 260, 300.

7.27   Kingston Company: Test of Controls Sampling Documentation.   Assume you plan to select a random sample by associating each invoice number in the sequence 32071–42070 with a random number from the table in Appendix 13A.

Required:

Using a copy of the Test of Controls Sampling Data Sheet (Exhibit 7.27–1, or obtain a copy from your instructor), fill in the client name and the period covered, specify (define) the objectives of your work, describe the population to be sampled, and describe the sample selection process. Under the column headed "Definition of Deviations," write a brief statement of the deviations of interest. Under the heading labelled "Sample Size," insert the sample size you decided in assignment 7.26 above. For the time being, ignore the Sampling Data Sheet column headings related to statistical sampling. (Hint: When defining the deviations, refer to the column headings in Exhibit 7–2.)

E X H I B I T 7.27–1   **TEST OF CONTROLS SAMPLING DATA SHEET**

Client _____ By _____
Period covered _____ Date_____
Define the objective(s) _____
_____
_____
_____

Population description _____
Random selection procedures _____
_____

| Definition of Deviations | Risk Assess Control Risk Too Low | Tolerable Rate | Expected Deviation Rate | Sample Results | | | |
				Sample Size	Deviations	Sample Rate	CUL
1.							
2.							
3.							
4.							
5.							
6.							
7.							
8.							
9.							
10.							

Audit Conclusions
A. Effect on audit plan: _____
_____
_____

B. Recommendation to management: _____
_____

C. Other action: _____

When you complete this requirement, you will have completed the first four steps of the test of controls audit process. Keep this Sampling Data Sheet for requirements in other case problems.

7.28   Kingston Company: Perform Test of Controls Procedures.   Assume that your random sample was selected using Appendix 20A by starting at the upper left corner, reading four-digit numbers down the column, then proceeding to the top of the next column. This selection method "subtracts a constant (32,071)" and causes the random numbers 0000 through 9999 to be "associated with" the invoice numbers. You get the invoice numbers by adding the constant back to the four-digit random number. For example, the first three numbers and associations are:

Table	Constant	Invoice
3294	+32071	35365
0741	+32071	32812
5998	+32071	38069

Exhibit 7.28–1 contains a list of simulated deviations related to the invoices. This list is designed to accommodate a sample size up to 300 invoices, so please do not try to "audit" a

EXHIBIT 7.28–1   **KINGSTON COMPANY: RANDOM ORDER, INVOICE, DATE, AMOUNT, CUSTOMER, DEVIATION DESCRIPTION**

Order	Invoice	Month	Day	Amount	Customer	Deviation
21	39918	Sep.	23	$5,000	Gonzo	Wrong quantity. Overcharge $250. CM Nov. 5.
37	39357	Aug.	28	$600	Zlat	No credit approval. Unpaid as of Dec. 31.
50	35669	Apr.	18	$700	Grundey	No credit approval. Paid in full on time.
51	41612	Dec.	10	$800	Quilt	No credit approval. Unpaid as of Dec. 31.
52	42056	Dec.	28	$626	#5	Wrong quantity. Overcharge $200. No CM. Unpaid.
61	40812	Nov.	3	$150	Mucho	No credit approval. Unpaid as of Dec. 31.
66	39684	Sep.	13	$500	Fred	No credit approval. Paid in full on time.
67	33762	Feb.	21	$200	Dogg	No credit approval. Paid in full on time.
72	40004	Sep.	27	$3,600	Hiccup	Wrong quantity. Overcharge $180. CM Nov. 4.
79	41985	Dec.	28	$700	#264	Wrong quantity. Overcharge $200. CM Jan. 15.
86	40256	Oct.	8	$150	Ink	No credit approval. Unpaid as of Dec. 31.
89	34233	Mar.	5	$500	Elbert	No credit approval. Paid in full on time.
91	39640	Sep.	11	$9,900	Eric	Arithmetic error. Overcharge $8,100. CM Nov. 1.
104	39036	Aug.	14	$550	Tinker	Wrong price. Overcharge $50. CM Sept. 12.
109	41326	Nov.	27	$250	Only	No credit approval. Unpaid as of Dec. 31.
112	39113	Aug.	17	$500	Vickery	Wrong price. Overcharge $50. CM Sept. 1.
116	41754	Dec.	16	$900	Risky	No credit approval. Unpaid as of Dec. 31.
121	33430	Feb.	11	$300	Charley	Missing BL. Paid in full on time.
123	41774	Dec.	17	$1,100	Stealth	No credit approval. Paid in full on time.
125	37526	June	14	$350	Kirk	No credit approval. Paid in full on time.
132	42065	Dec.	29	$4,500	#863	Arithmetic error. Overcharge $450. CM Jan. 15.
133	33217	Feb.	4	$3,000	Baker	No credit approval. Paid in full on time.
134	41887	Dec.	22	$600	#1106	Held for shipment. BL dated Jan. 4.
137	40725	Oct.	30	$350	Luck	No credit approval. Paid in full on time.
140	41800	Dec.	18	$400	#1352	Held for shipment. BL dated Jan. 4.
143	39160	Aug.	19	$1,100	Xenia	Wrong price. Overcharge $220. CM Sept. 30.
148	39130	Aug.	18	$550	Welsch	Wrong price. Overcharge $50. CM Sept. 20.
154	42042	Dec.	28	$6,000	#109	Wrong quantity. Overcharge $600. No CM. Unpaid.
161	38488	July	19	$1,400	Monkey	No credit approval. Paid in full 60 days.
161	38488					Wrong price. Overcharge $700. CM Aug. 5.
166	38816	Aug.	4	$3,000	Smith	Wrong price. Overcharge $2,000. CM Sept. 10.
180	41898	Dec.	22	$300	Viceroy	No credit approval. Paid in full Jan. 15.
186	39163	Aug.	19	$1,800	Yant	Wrong price. Overcharge $1,650. CM Oct. 4.
190	41341	Nov.	27	$100	Peace	No credit approval. Paid in full on time.
191	38669	July	27	$600	Onan	Wrong price. Overcharge $100. CM Aug. 15.
193	35969	Apr.	24	$200	Hall	Missing BL. Paid in full on time.
225	39439	Aug.	31	$650	Blatz	No credit approval. Paid in full on time.
228	38191	July	6	$800	Lane	No credit approval. Paid in full on time.
228	38191					Wrong price. Overcharge $100. CM Aug. 6.
232	36111	May	1	$9,000	Inmann	No credit approval. Paid in full on time.
234	39485	Sep.	4	$350	Chris	No credit approval. Paid in full on time.
238	40425	Oct.	16	$600	Jack	No credit approval. Paid in full on time.
240	32270	Jan.	6	$1,500	Able	No credit approval. Paid in full on time.
242	37498	June	13	$250	Johnson	No credit approval. Paid in full on time.
245	41306	Nov.	26	$300	Never	No credit approval. Unpaid as of Dec. 31.
252	38582	July	23	$500	Nalle	No credit approval. Paid in full on time.
259	39057	Aug.	14	$4,000	Uecker	Missing BL. Paid in full on time.
265	39578	Sep.	8	$200	Danilof	No credit approval. Unpaid as of Dec. 31.
268	35100	Apr.	1	$950	Figge	No credit approval. Paid in full on time.
269	38773	Aug.	1	$300	Roberts	Wrong price. Overcharge $35. CM Aug. 22.
280	38744	Aug.	1	$750	Quick	Wrong price. Overcharge $25. CM Aug. 10.
289	39436	Aug.	31	$1,150	Action	No credit approval. Paid in full on time.
291	38740	Aug.	1	$1,500	Pell	Wrong price. Overcharge $500. CM Aug. 22.
292	41976	Dec.	28	$450	#719	No credit approval. Unpaid as of Dec. 31.
292	41976					Arithmetic error. Overcharge $350. CM Jan. 15.
296	40686	Oct.	28	$75	Kinko	No credit approval. Unpaid as of Dec. 31.

larger sample. The deviations described opposite each invoice number represent the evidence you would obtain if you actually audited the documents. The order of the invoice numbers is the random sample order you obtain by using the selection method described above.

Since this is a "pretend audit," and the Exhibit 7.28–1 deviation list will accommodate different sample size decisions, you will need to be careful not to "cheat": You are entitled to audit only the sample size you select in the first place. Remember that sampling costs time and money. Thus, you must not pay attention to deviations described on invoices that are not in your sample. You will find your proper stopping place in Exhibit 7.28–1 when you get to the last numbered sample item ("Order" column at left) in your sample size. All subsequent invoices are not in your sample.

Required:

a. Show how invoice number 39918 (number 21 in the "Order" column of Exhibit 7.28–1) was selected in the random number table (Appendix 20A).

b. Use Exhibit 7.28–1 to find your sample-based test of controls audit results. Enter the results in the Sampling Data Sheet you started in assignment 7.27. Evaluate the results quantitatively and qualitatively. Assign an evaluation to control risk related to the probability of sales overstatement being in the accounts receivable balances.

Other information about the simulated samples in Exhibit 7.28–1:

1. You found all the invoices in the sample. None were missing.
2. All the invoices were properly posted to the general ledger sales and accounts receivable control accounts, and each was posted to the right customer's individual account.
3. The invoices not listed in Exhibit 7.28–1 had no deviations related to other documents, recalculations, or comparisons.
4. "No credit approval" means that the expected credit approval notation could not be found in the documents.
5. When "Wrong quantity billed" appears, a description of the effect follows.
6. "CM (date)" means the customer notified Kingston of an error and a credit memo was issued on the subsequent date (after December 31 on some occasions). All credit memos generate debits to a sales returns account and credits to accounts receivable.
7. "Unpaid as of Dec. 31" and "Unpaid" means the customer has not yet paid the invoice. "Paid in full on time" means the customer paid the invoice when it was due.
8. "Missing BL" means the bill of lading (shipping document) could not be found.
9. "Wrong price" means the clerks put the wrong unit price on the invoice and billed the customer incorrectly.
10. "Arithmetic error" means you found the invoice multiplied and added to show an incorrect total.
11. "Held for shipment," followed by a bill of lading (BL) date, means the goods were in the shipping area on December 31, and shipped on the BL date.

7.29 Auditing the Trade Accounts Receivable Balance.   Jack and Fred are the auditors. They are getting ready to audit Kingston's trade accounts receivable.

Jack: Where's the trial balance?

Fred: Here it is. Kingston lists 1,506 customer balances, totaling $400,000. The balances range from $1 to $25,000.

Jack: Yesterday we decided the tolerable misstatement in receivables could be $10,000. That is, we want to audit for sales and receivables overstatement so we won't miss more than $10,000, if that much misstatement is in the account.

Fred: Monetary misstatements are a possibility. Last year, we audited 500 customer accounts selected at random and found $2,000 in overstatements. That computed to a projected likely misstatement of $4,000. Maybe $4,000 overstatement misstatement is in this year's balance, too.

Jack: Mmmmm (thoughtfully). Any individually big balances this year?

Fred: Kingston shows six balances over $10,000 for a total of $100,000. We ought to pull them out of the population for complete audit.

Jack: Agreed. No use taking chances.

Fred: Our analytical procedures related to receivables didn't show much. The total is down, consistent with the sales decline, so the turnover is up a little. If any misstatement is in the receivables total, it may be too small to be obvious in the ratios.

Jack: That's good news if the problems are immaterial. Too bad we can't say analytical procedures reduce our audit risk. What about internal control?

Fred: I say it's about a 50–50 proportion. Sometimes control seemed to work well, sometimes it didn't. I noticed a few new people doing the invoice processing last week when we were here for a conference. Incidentally, I lump the inherent risk problems and internal control risk problems together when I think about control risk. Anyway, firm policy is to plan a sample for a low overall audit risk for the receivables.

Jack: According to the audit program, we will confirm a sample of customer accounts, send second requests after a week, then chase down all the nonrespondents by vouching all the charges and credits in the account to supporting documents or vouching to the customers' payments in January. I'm sorry about the time it takes, and our audit cost, of doing these procedures.

Fred: I am, too. If our first sample is not large enough, we won't have time to send more confirmations. Adding accounts to the sample means we will need to audit them the same way we audit nonrespondents, and that costs more than confirmations.

Jack: Let's take a chance on needing to add to the sample. If it all works out all right, we'll save a lot of time and meet our time budget for the work.

Fred: Well, the team took a large sample last year. Let's think about it.

The auditors decided to audit all six of the customer balances over $10,000, and they discovered the following:

Account No.	Balance	Confirmation and Document Examination
109	$12,337	Wrong quantity billed on invoice ?42042, December 28, overcharged $600.
458	12,129	No error.
859	25,000	No error.
863	16,129	Arithmetic error in invoice ?42065, December 29, overcharged $450.
1092	15,005	No error.
1456	19,400	No error.

Required:
Using the information in the auditors' dialogue, but without using statistical calculations, decide on and justify a sample size from the other 1,500 accounts receivable. (To facilitate your instructor's presentation of solutions, choose one of the following sample sizes: 100, 150, 200, 220, 230, 240, 260, 280, 300, 320, 340, 360, 380, or 400.) Assume that the audit of each customer's account in the initial sample costs an average of $8, and each one added later costs $19.

7.30   Kingston Company: Calculation of Quantitative Evidence.   Study the dialogue in Kingston assignment 7.29.

a. If you choose to audit a nonstatistical sample consisting of the largest accounts, your sample will not be considered random, although you will cover a large dollar amount of the total. Exhibit 7.30–1 contains a list and totals of the differences you could discover with each sample size. The customer accounts with no differences are not listed, but their total is included in each sample subtotal in the "Balance" column.

E X H I B I T 7.30–1   **KINGSTON COMPANY: 400 LARGEST ACCOUNTS RECEIVABLE WITH MONETARY ERRORS**

Account No.	Size Order	Balance	Wrong Quantity	Wrong Math	Wrong Date	All Error	Confirmation and Document Examination
741	5	$3,698		$100		$100	Arithmetic error invoice #41476.
264	7	$1,906	$200			$200	Wrong quantity invoice #41985, Dec. 28.
1106	8	$1,555			$600	$600	Shipped to us on Jan. 4, invoice #41887.
1352	28	$700			$400	$400	Shipped to us on Jan. 4, invoice #41800.
5	78	$626	$200			$200	Wrong quantity invoice #42056, Dec. 28.
1147	81	$623	$123			$123	Wrong quantity billed invoice #41474.
720	82	$622			$125	$125	Shipped to us on Jan. 4, invoice #41891.
444	83	$621	$106			$106	Wrong quantity billed invoice #41482.
1421	85	$539			$138	$138	Shipped to us on Jan. 4, invoice #41895.
775	86	$538	$139			$139	Wrong quantity billed invoice #41490.
1428	89	$536			$126	$126	Shipped to us on Jan. 4, invoice #41900.
1199	90	$536	$133			$133	Wrong quantity billed invoice #41498.
378	91	$536			$148	$148	Shipped to us on Jan. 4, invoice #41903.
1265	93	$534	$108			$108	Wrong quantity billed invoice #41506.
1485	95	$532			$132	$132	Shipped to us on Jan. 4, invoice #41907.
50	96	$531	$119			$119	Wrong quantity billed invoice #41514.
1096	97	$528			$128	$128	Shipped to us on Jan. 4, invoice #41911.
403	99	$525	$115			$115	Wrong quantity billed invoice #41522.
Sample =	100	$86,082	$1,243	$100	$1,797	$3,140	
1206	101	$524			$119	$119	Shipped to us on Jan. 4, invoice #41916.
955	102	$521	$102			$102	Wrong quantity billed invoice #41530.
486	103	$519			$129	$129	Shipped to us on Jan. 4, invoice #41919.
483	104	$519	$119			$119	Wrong quantity billed invoice #41538.
148	107	$518			$115	$115	Shipped to us on Jan. 4, invoice #41920.
774	109	$517			$140	$140	Shipped to us on Jan. 4, invoice #41929.
1434	110	$517	$127			$127	Wrong quantity billed invoice #41547.
476	112	$514			$114	$114	Shipped to us on Jan. 4, invoice #41931.
1118	113	$511	$145			$145	Wrong quantity billed invoice #41554.
292	115	$508			$136	$136	Shipped to us on Jan. 4, invoice #41935.
465	117	$507	$136			$136	Wrong quantity billed invoice #41562.
890	118	$506			$122	$122	Shipped to us on Jan. 4, invoice #41939.
1127	119	$504	$140			$140	Wrong quantity billed invoice #41570.
1497	121	$503	$133			$133	Wrong quantity billed invoice #41578.
25	122	$503			$115	$115	Shipped to us on Jan. 4, invoice #41943.
535	124	$500			$107	$107	Shipped to us on Jan. 4, invoice #41947.
21	127	$499	$116			$116	Wrong quantity billed invoice #41586.
845	128	$499			$111	$111	Shipped to us on Jan. 4, invoice #41951.
482	129	$498	$120			$120	Wrong quantity billed invoice #41594.
165	130	$498			$108	$108	Shipped to us on Jan. 4, invoice #41958.
943	132	$494	$112			$112	Wrong quantity billed invoice #41602.
725	133	$494			$119	$119	Shipped to us on Jan. 4, invoice #41959.
366	134	$492			$112	$112	Shipped to us on Jan. 4, invoice #41963.
1223	136	$492	$108			$108	Wrong quantity billed invoice #41610.
1047	138	$490			$100	$100	Shipped to us on Jan. 4, invoice #41967.
412	140	$489			$133	$133	Shipped to us on Jan. 4, invoice #41972.
468	141	$489	$109			$109	Wrong quantity billed invoice #41619.
330	142	$489	$99			$99	Wrong quantity billed invoice #41626.
654	144	$482			$137	$137	Shipped to us on Jan. 4, invoice #41974.
1387	145	$482	$139			$139	Wrong quantity billed invoice #41637.

EXHIBIT 7.30–1   (*continued*)

Account No.	Size Order	Balance	Wrong Quantity	Wrong Math	Wrong Date	All Error	Confirmation and Document Examination
632	147	$476	$130			$130	Wrong quantity billed invoice #41644.
374	148	$476			$117	$117	Shipped to us on Jan. 4, invoice #41979.
843	150	$475			$128	$128	Shipped to us on Jan. 4, invoice #41983.
Sample =	150	$111,087	$3,078	$100	$3,959	$7,137	
436	151	$471	$128			$128	Wrong quantity billed invoice #41653.
1490	153	$470			$117	$117	Shipped to us on Jan. 4, invoice #41987.
820	154	$470	$132			$132	Wrong quantity billed invoice #41660.
530	156	$469			$144	$144	Shipped to us on Jan. 4, invoice #41991.
380	158	$467	$117			$117	Wrong quantity billed invoice #41668.
1504	159	$467			$104	$104	Shipped to us on Jan. 4, invoice #41995.
452	161	$461	$111			$111	Wrong quantity billed invoice #41679.
662	163	$460			$116	$116	Shipped to us on Jan. 4, invoice #41999.
173	165	$458	$115			$115	Wrong quantity billed invoice #41688.
580	167	$457			$107	$107	Shipped to us on Jan. 4, invoice #42003.
1200	168	$456	$139			$139	Wrong quantity billed invoice #41695.
44	170	$450			$105	$105	Shipped to us on Jan. 4, invoice #42007.
719	171	$450		$350		$350	Arithmetic error invoice #41976, Dec. 28.
160	172	$449			$118	$118	Shipped to us on Jan. 4, invoice #42013.
1458	173	$449	$126			$126	Wrong quantity billed invoice #41709.
1308	176	$448	$120			$120	Wrong quantity billed invoice #41716.
386	179	$445	$114			$114	Wrong quantity billed invoice #41723.
924	181	$398	$112			$112	Wrong quantity billed invoice #41731.
959	184	$394	$109			$109	Wrong quantity billed invoice #41740.
308	187	$394			$125	$125	Shipped to us on Jan. 4, invoice #42014.
236	188	$393			$113	$113	Shipped to us on Jan. 4, invoice #42019.
1464	189	$391	$101			$101	Wrong quantity billed invoice #41746.
1005	193	$388			$89	$89	Shipped to us on Jan. 4, invoice #42023.
822	194	$387	$187			$187	Wrong quantity billed invoice #41755.
145	197	$383			$78	$78	Shipped to us on Jan. 4, invoice #42027.
Sample =	200	$132,611	$4,689	$450	$5,175	$10,314	
902	201	$382	$102			$102	Wrong quantity billed invoice #41768.
1242	205	$380			$67	$67	Shipped to us on Jan. 4, invoice #42031.
616	207	$379	$100			$100	Wrong quantity billed invoice #41770.
1246	212	$378			$72	$72	Shipped to us on Jan. 4, invoice #42034.
379	220	$367			$67	$67	Shipped to us on Jan. 5, invoice #42039.
Sample =	220	$140,122	$4,891	$450	$5,381	$10,722	
1463	226	$364			$64	$64	Shipped to us on Jan. 5, invoice #42044.
Sample =	230	$143,760	$4,891	$450	$5,445	$10,786	
239	233	$357			$58	$58	Shipped to us on Jan. 5, invoice #42047.
422	235	$353	$114			$114	Wrong quantity billed invoice #41775.
1466	239	$351			$59	$59	Shipped to us on Jan. 5, invoice #42051.
Sample =	240	$147,297	$5,005	$450	$5,562	$11,017	
1079	246	$346			$50	$50	Shipped to us on Jan. 5, invoice #42053.
1013	249	$342	$50			$50	Wrong quantity billed invoice #41782.
368	252	$337		$17		$17	Arithmetic error invoice #41475.
4	257	$330	$98			$98	Wrong quantity billed invoice #41791.

EXHIBIT 7.30–1 (concluded)

Account No.	Size Order	Balance	Wrong Quantity	Wrong Math	Wrong Date	All Error	Confirmation and Document Examination
Sample =	260	$154,085	$5,153	$467	$5,612	$11,232	
1046	261	$326			$66	$66	Shipped to us on Jan. 5, invoice #42059.
1266	262	$326		$12		$12	Arithmetic error invoice #41484.
507	266	$319	$80			$80	Wrong quantity billed invoice #41801.
986	269	$313		$14		$14	Arithmetic eror invoice #41492.
787	273	$311	$77			$77	Wrong quantity billed invoice #41810.
867	277	$306		$11		$11	Arithmetic error invoice #41501.
Sample =	280	$160,362	$5,310	$504	$5,678	$11,492	
1363	281	$303			$43	$43	Shipped to us on Jan. 5, invoice #42064.
1274	282	$302	$82			$82	Wrong quantity billed invoice #41815.
59	284	$301		$14		$14	Arithmetic error invoice #41510.
417	291	$293			$53	$53	Shipped to us on Jan. 5, invoice #42067.
1494	292	$291	$65			$65	Wrong quantity billed invoice #41822.
293	294	$288		$13		$13	Arithmetic error invoice #41519.
349	299	$284		$14		$14	Arithmetic error invoice #41528.
Sample =	300	$166,218	$5,457	$545	$5,774	$11,776	
1088	301	$283	$78			$78	Wrong quantity billed invoice #41830.
900	307	$280		$12		$12	Arithmetic error invoice #41537.
131	309	$280	$69			$69	Wrong quantity billed invoice #41838.
1402	316	$276	$76			$76	Wrong quantity billed invoice #41847.
243	317	$276		$15		$15	Arithmetic error invoice #41546.
1114	320	$272			$32	$32	Shipped to us on Jan. 5, invoice #42069.
Sample =	320	$164,280	$5,478	$572	$5,600	$11,650	
1124	326	$267		$15		$15	Arithmetic error invoice #41555.
157	328	$264	$63			$63	Wrong quantity billed invoice #41855.
942	334	$260	$59			$59	Wrong quantity billed invoice #41860.
487	336	$259		$10		$10	Arithmetic error invoice #41564.
Sample =	340	$177,055	$5,802	$597	$5,806	$12,205	
67	343	$254	$66			$66	Wrong quantity billed invoice #41868.
15	345	$253		$15		$15	Arithmetic error invoice #41573.
1409	352	$246	$52			$52	Wrong quantity billed invoice #41876.
933	353	$245		$12		$12	Arithmetic error invoice #41582.
1101	359	$241	$62			$62	Wrong quantity billed invoice #41885.
Sample =	360	$182,003	$5,982	$624	$5,806	$12,412	
121	363	$237		$11		$11	Arithmetic error invoice #41591.
387	367	$232	$55			$55	Wrong quantity billed invoice #41894.
539	373	$229		$10		$10	Arithmetic error invoice #41600.
401	377	$227	$57			$57	Wrong quantity billed invoice #41905.
Sample =	380	$186,627	$6,094	$645	$5,806	$12,545	
204	382	$224		$11		$11	Arithmetic error invoice #41609.
333	385	$222	$32			$32	Wrong quantity billed invoice #41915.
605	390	$212		$14		$14	Arithmetic error invoice #41618.
338	394	$210	$50			$50	Wrong quantity billed invoice #41924.
1322	397	$206	$56			$56	Wrong quantity billed invoice #41923.
168	399	$205		$12		$12	Arithmetic error invoice #41627.
Sample =	400	$190,899	$6,232	$682	$5,806	$12,720	

Required:
Use the sample data for the sample size you selected. Analyse the amount and nature of the dollar differences and decide whether the $300,000 recorded amount in the 1,500 accounts is or is not materially misstated. (Question requirements part *b* is continued on page 286.)

b. If you choose to audit an unrestricted, unstratified random sample of the customer accounts, you will be able to project the likely misstatement using (1) the difference method, and (2) the ratio method. Exhibit 7.30–2 contains a list of the misstatements you could find in one random selection. The list is subdivided to show totals at the various sample sizes. The customer accounts with no differences are not listed, but their total is included in each sample subtotal in the "Balance" column.

Required:
Use the sample data for the sample size you selected. (1) Determine the dollar amount of known misstatement. (2) Calculate the projected likely misstatement using (*a*) the difference method, and (*b*) the ratio method. (3) Analyse the nature of the dollar differences. (4) Decide whether the $300,000 recorded amount in the 1,500 customer accounts is or is not materially misstated.

EXHIBIT 7.30–2   **KINGSTON COMPANY: MISSTATEMENTS IN RANDOM SAMPLE OF 400 ACCOUNTS RECEIVABLE**

Account No.	Random Order	Account Balance	Wrong Quantity	Wrong Math	Wrong Date	All Error	Confirmation and Document Examination
292	6	$508			$136	$136	Shipped to us on Jan. 4, invoice #41935.
591	11	$153		$6		$6	Arithmetic error invoice #41825.
4	15	$330	$98			$98	Wrong quantity billed invoice #41791.
362	23	$141		$5		$5	Arithmetic error invoice #41899.
1079	28	$346			$50	$50	Shipped to us on Jan. 5, invoice #42053.
465	30	$507	$136			$136	Wrong quantity billed invoice #41562.
725	31	$494			$119	$119	Shipped to us on Jan. 4, invoice #41959.
820	39	$470	$132			$132	Wrong quantity billed invoice #41660.
225	55	$117		$11		$11	Arithmetic error invoice #41744.
1160	57	$147		$6		$6	Arithmetic error invoice #41862.
1096	93	$528			$128	$128	Shipped to us on Jan. 4, invoice #41911.
165	97	$498			$108	$108	Shipped to us on Jan. 4, invoice #41958.
Sample =	100	$21,336	$366	$28	$541	$935	
308	102	$394			$125	$125	Shipped to us on Jan. 4, invoice #42014.
50	106	$531	$119			$119	Wrong quantity billed invoice #41514.
1274	113	$302	$82			$82	Wrong quantity billed invoice #41815.
1494	115	$291	$65			$65	Wrong quantity billed invoice #41822.
386	119	$445	$114			$114	Wrong quantity billed invoice #41723.
506	122	$162		$7		$7	Arithmetic error invoice #41771.
1387	133	$482	$139			$139	Wrong quantity billed invoice #41637.
473	149	$175	$25			$25	Wrong quantity billed invoice #42063.
1402	150	$276	$76			$76	Wrong quantity billed invoice #41847.
Sample =	150	$30,800	$986	$35	$666	$1,687	
1141	153	$148		$8		$8	Arithmetic error invoice #41853.
1047	154	$490			$100	$100	Shipped to us on Jan. 4, invoice #41967.
954	156	$185	$45			$45	Wrong quantity billed invoice #42011.
1352	157	$700			$400	$400	Shipped to us on Jan. 4, invoice #41800.
242	162	$132		$7		$7	Arithmetic error invoice #41955.
841	163	$178	$38			$38	Wrong quantity billed invoice #42043.
1320	170	$134		$6		$6	Arithmetic error invoice #41945.

E X H I B I T 7.30–2   *(concluded)*

Account No.	Random Order	Account Balance	Wrong Quantity	Wrong Math	Wrong Date	All Error	Confirmation and Document Examination
654	172	$482			$137	$137	Shipped to us on Jan. 4, invoice #41974.
486	192	$519			$129	$129	Shipped to us on Jan. 4, invoice #41919.
417	197	$293			$53	$53	Shipped to us on Jan. 5, invoice #42067.
Sample =	200	$38,709	$1,069	$56	$1,485	$2,610	
663	214	$176	$36			$36	Wrong quantity billed invoice #42058.
959	217	$394	$109			$109	Wrong quantity billed invoice #41740.
Sample =	220	$42,852	$1,214	$56	$1,485	$2,755	
Sample =	230	$48,556	$1,214	$56	$1,485	$2,755	
160	234	$449			$118	$118	Shipped to us on Jan. 4, invoice #42013.
440	237	$120		$12		$12	Arithmetic error invoice #42015.
Sample =	240	$50,957	$1,214	$68	$1,603	$2,885	
378	241	$536			$148	$148	Shipped to us on Jan. 4, invoice #41903.
780	254	$177	$47			$47	Wrong quantity billed invoice #42050.
349	256	$284		$14		$14	Arithmetic error invoice #41528.
Sample =	260	$54,765	$1,261	$82	$1,751	$3,094	
145	262	$383			$78	$78	Shipped to us on Jan. 4, invoice #42027.
157	269	$264	$63			$63	Wrong quantity billed invoice #41855.
632	275	$476	$130			$130	Wrong quantity billed invoice #41644.
Sample =	280	$59,224	$1,454	$82	$1,829	$3,365	
798	284	$136		$10		$10	Arithmetic error invoice #41927.
59	290	$301		$14		$14	Arithmetic error invoice #41510.
539	298	$229		$10		$10	Arithmetic error invoice #41600.
651	300	$179	$60			$60	Wrong quantity billed invoice #42035.
Sample =	300	$61,995	$1,514	$116	$1,829	$3,459	
774	305	$517			$140	$140	Shipped to us on Jan. 4, invoice #41929.
1114	315	$272			$32	$32	Shipped to us on Jan. 4, invoice #42069.
1370	317	$160		$8		$8	Arithmetic error invoice #41789.
280	319	$162		$9		$9	Arithmetic error invoice #41780.
Sample =	320	$65,672	$1,514	$133	$2,001	$3,648	
330	335	$489	$99			$99	Wrong quantity billed invoice #41626.
Sample =	340	$68,732	$1,613	$133	$2,001	$3,747	
1026	343	$115		$5		$5	Arithmetic error invoice #42045.
943	355	$494	$112			$112	Wrong quantity billed invoice #41602.
Sample =	360	$71,126	$1,725	$138	$2,001	$3,864	
535	379	$500			$107	$107	Shipped to us on Jan. 4, invoice #41947.
Sample =	380	$73,719	$1,725	$138	$2,108	$3,971	
1377	384	$179		$12		$12	Arithmetic error invoice #41735.
Sample =	400	$76,069	$1,725	$150	$2,108	$3,983	
Total		$76,069	$1,725	$150	$2,108	$3,983	
Number of differences			20	17	17	54	
Average			$86.25	$8.82	$124.00	$73.76	

MULTIPLE-CHOICE QUESTIONS FOR PRACTICE AND REVIEW

7.31 In an audit sampling application, an auditor:
  a. Performs procedures on all the items in a balance and makes a conclusion about the whole balance.
  b. Performs procedures on less than 100 percent of the items in a balance and formulates a conclusion about the whole balance.
  c. Performs procedures on less than 100 percent of the items in a class of transactions for the purpose of becoming familiar with the client's accounting system.
  d. Performs analytical procedures on the client's unaudited financial statements when planning the audit.

7.32 Auditors consider statistical sampling to be characterized by the following:
  a. Representative sample selection and nonmathematical consideration of the results.
  b. Carefully biased sample selection and statistical calculation of the results.
  c. Representative sample selection and statistical calculation of the results.
  d. Carefully biased sample selection and nonmathematical consideration of the results.

7.33 In audit sampling applications, sampling risk is:
  a. Characteristic of statistical sampling applications but not of nonstatistical applications.
  b. The probability that the auditor will fail to recognize erroneous accounting in the client's documentation.
  c. Probability that accounting errors will arise in transactions and enter the accounting system.
  d. The probability that an auditor's conclusion based on a sample might be different from the conclusion based on an audit of the entire population.

7.34 When auditing the client's performance of control to accomplish the completeness objective related to ensuring that all sales are recorded, auditors should draw sample items from:

  a. The sales journal list of recorded sales invoices.
  b. The file of shipping documents.
  c. The file of customer order copies.
  d. The file of receiving reports for inventory additions.

7.35 Nelson Williams was considering the sample size needed for a selection of sales invoices for the test of controls audit of the LoHo Company's internal controls. He presented the following information for two alternative cases:

	Case A	Case B
Acceptable risk of underreliance	High	Low
Acceptable risk of overreliance	High	Low
Tolerable deviation rate	High	Low
Expected population deviation rate	Low	High

Nelson should expect the sample size for Case A to be:
  a. Smaller than the sample size for Case B.
  b. Larger than the sample size for Case B.
  c. The same as the sample size for Case B.
  d. Not determinable relative to the Case B sample size.

7.36 Nelson next considered the sample size needed for a selection of customers' accounts receivable for the substantive audit of the total accounts receivable. He presented the following information for two alternative cases:

	Case X	Case Y
Acceptable risk of incorrect acceptance	Low	High
Acceptable risk of incorrect rejection	Low	High
Tolerable dollar misstatement in the account	Small	Large
Expected dollar misstatement in the account	Large	Small
Estimate of population variability	Large	Small

Nelson should expect the sample size for Case X to be:

a. Smaller than the sample size for Case Y.

b. Larger than the sample size for Case Y.

c. The same as the sample size for Case Y.

d. Not determinable relative to the Case Y sample size.

7.37 Which of the following should be considered an audit procedure for obtaining evidence?

a. An audit sampling application in accounts receivable selection.

b. The accounts receivable exist and are valued properly.

c. Sending a written confirmation on a customer's account balance.

d. Nonstatistical consideration of the amount of difference reported by a customer on a confirmation response.

7.38 When calculating the total amount of misstatement relevant to the analysis of an account balance, an auditor should add to the misstatement discovered in individually significant items the following:

a. The projected likely misstatement and the additional possible misstatement estimate.

b. The known misstatement in the sampled items.

c. The known misstatement in the sampled items, the projected likely misstatement, and the additional possible misstatement estimate.

d. The additional possible misstatement estimate.

7.39 Eddie audited the LoHo Company's inventory on a sample basis. She audited 120 items from an inventory compilation list and discovered net overstatement of $480. The audited items had a book (recorded) value of $48,000. There were 1,200 inventory items listed, and the total inventory book amount was $490,000. Which of these calculations is (are) correct:

a. Known misstatement of $4,800 using the difference method.

b. Projected likely misstatement of $480 using the ratio method.

c. Projected likely misstatement of $4,900 using the ratio method.

d. Projected likely misstatement of $4,800 using the difference method.

7.40 Steve Katchy audited the client's accounts receivable, but he could not get any good information about customer 102's balance. The customer responded to the confirmation saying, "Our system does not provide detail for such a response." The sales invoice and shipping document papers have been lost, and the customer has not yet paid. Steve should:

a. Get another customer's account to consider in the sample.

b. Treat customer 102's account as being entirely wrong (overstated), if doing so will not affect his audit conclusion about the receivables taken altogether.

c. Require adjustment of the receivables to write off customer 102's balance.

d. Treat customer 102's account as accurate because there is no evidence saying it is fictitious.

7.41 The risk of incorrect acceptance in balance-audit sampling and the risk of assessing control risk too low in test of controls sampling both relate to:

a. Effectiveness of an audit.

b. Efficiency of an audit.

c. Control risk assessment decisions.

d. Evidence about assertions in financial statements.

7.42 An advantage of statistical sampling is that it helps an auditor:

a. Eliminate nonsampling risk.

b. Reapply evaluation judgments based on factors in addition to the sample evidence.

c. Be precise and definite in the approach to an audit problem.

d. Omit quantification of risk and materiality judgments.

7.43 To determine the sample size for a balance-audit sampling application, an auditor should consider the tolerable misstatement, the risk of incorrect acceptance, the risk of incorrect rejection, the population size, and the:

a. Expected monetary misstatement in the account.

b. Overall materiality for the financial statements taken as a whole.

c. Risk of assessing control risk too low.

d. Risk of assessing control risk too high.

EXERCISES AND PROBLEMS

7.44 Sampling and Nonsampling Audit Work. The accounting firm of Mason & Jarr performed the work described in each separate case below. The two partners are worried about properly applying standards regarding audit sampling. They have asked your advice.

Required:

Write a report addressed to them, stating whether they did or did not observe the essential elements of audit sampling standards in each case:

a. Mason selected three purchase orders for raw materials from the LIZ Corporation files. He started at this beginning point in the accounting process and traced each one through the accounting system. He saw the receiving reports, purchasing agent's approvals, receiving clerks' approvals, the vendors' invoices (now stamped paid), the entry in the cash disbursement records, and the canceled checks. This work gave him a firsthand familiarity with the cash disbursement system, and he felt confident about understanding related questions in the internal control questionnaire completed later.

b. Jarr observed the inventory taking at SER Corporation. She had an inventory list of the different inventory descriptions with the quantities taken from the perpetual inventory records. She selected the 200 items with the largest quantities and counted them after the client's shop foreman had completed his count. She decided not to check out the count accuracy on the other 800 items. The shop foreman miscounted in 16 cases. Jarr concluded the rate of miscount was 8 percent, so as many as 80 of the 1,000 items might be counted wrong. She asked the foreman to recount everything.

c. CSR Corporation issued seven series of short-term commercial paper notes near the fiscal year-end to finance seasonal operations. Jarr confirmed the obligations under each series with the independent trustee for the holders, studied all seven indenture agreements, and traced the proceeds of each issue to the cash receipts records.

d. At the completion of the EH&R Corporation audit, Mason obtained written representations, as required by auditing standards, from the president, the chief financial officer, and the controller. He did not ask the chief accountant at headquarters or the plant controllers in the three divisions for written representations.

7.45 Test of Controls Audit Procedure Objectives and Control Deviations. This exercise asks you to specify test of controls audit procedure objectives and define deviations in connection with planning the test of controls audit of Kingston Company's internal controls. (In assignment 7.50, the requirement is to specify the client's control objectives and write test of controls audit procedures.)

Required:

a. For each control cited below, state the objective of an auditor's test of controls audit procedure.

b. For each control cited below, state the definition of a deviation from the control.

1. The credit department supervisor reviews each customer's order and approves credit by making a notation on the order.
2. The billing department must receive written notice from the shipping department of actual shipment to a customer before a sale is recorded. The sales record date is supposed to be the shipment date.
3. Billing clerks carefully look up the correct catalogue list prices for goods shipped and calculate and recheck the amounts billed on invoices for the quantities of goods shipped.
4. Billing clerks review invoices for intercompany sales and mark each one with the code "9," so that they will be posted to intercompany sales accounts.

7.46 Timing of Test of Controls Audit Procedures. Auditor Magann was auditing the authorization control over cash disbursements. She selected cash disbursement entries made throughout the year and vouched them to paid invoices and cancelled cheques bearing the initials and signatures of people authorized to approve the disbursements. She performed the work on September 30, when the company had issued cheques numbered from 43921 to 52920. Since 9,000 cheques had been issued in nine months, she reasoned that 3,000 more could be issued in the three months before the December 31 year-end. About 12,000 checks had been issued last year. She wanted to take one sample of 100 disbursements for the entire year, so she selected 100 random numbers in the sequence 43921 to 55920. She audited the 80 cheques in the sample that were issued before September 30, and she held the other 20 randomly selected cheque numbers for later use. She found no deviations in the sample of 80—a finding that would, in the circumstances, cause her to assign a low (20 percent) control risk to the probability that the system would permit improper charges

to be hidden away in expense and purchase/inventory accounts.

Required:
Take the role of Magann and write a memo to the audit manager (dated October 1) describing the audit team's options with respect to evaluating control performance for the remaining period, October through December.

7.47 Evaluation of Quantitative Test of Controls Evidence. Assume you audited control compliance in the Kingston Company for the deviations related to a random selection of sales transactions, as shown below. For different sample sizes, the number of deviations was as follows:

	Sample Sizes				
	30	60	80	90	120
Missing sales invoice	0	0	0	0	0
Missing bill of lading	0	0	0	0	0
No credit approval	0	3	6	8	10
Wrong prices used	0	0	0	0	2
Wrong quantity billed	1	2	4	4	4
Wrong invoice arithmetic	0	0	0	0	1
Wrong invoice date	0	0	0	0	0
Posted to wrong account	0	0	0	0	0
Posted to wrong account	160	220	240	260	300
Missing sales invoice	0	0	0	0	0
Missing bill of lading	1	2	2	3	3
No credit approval	14	17	23	26	31
Wrong prices used	4	8	9	9	12
Wrong quantity billed	5	5	5	5	5
Wrong invoice arithmetic	2	2	2	2	3
Wrong invoice date	2	2	2	2	2
Posted to wrong account	0	0	0	0	0

Required:
For each deviation and each sample, calculate the rate of deviation in the sample (sample deviation rate).

7.48 Stratification Calculation of Projected Likely Misstatement Using the Ratio Method. The stratification calculation example in the chapter shows the results of calculating the projected likely misstatement using the difference method. Assume the results shown in Exhibit 7.48–1 were obtained from a stratified sample.

Required:
Apply the ratio calculation method to each stratum to calculate the projected likely misstatement (PLM). What is PLM for the entire sample?

EXHIBIT 7.48–1

				Sample Results	
Stratum	Population Size	Recorded Amount	Sample	Recorded Amount	Misstatement Amount*
1	6	$100,000	6	$100,000	$ –600
2	80	75,068	23	21,700	–274
3	168	75,008	22	9,476	–66
4	342	75,412	22	4,692	–88
5	910	74,512	23	1,973	23
	1,506	$400,000	96	$137,841	$–1,005

* A negative misstatement indicates overstatement of the book value, and a positive misstatement indicates understatement.

7.49 Determining Risk of Incorrect Acceptance. In the dialogue between the Kingston auditors, Fred said: "Our analytical procedures related to receivables didn't show much. The total is down, consistent with the sales decline, so the turnover is up a little. If any misstatement is in the receivables total, it may be too small to be obvious in the ratios." Then Jack said: "That's good news if the problems are immaterial. Too bad we can't say analytical procedures reduce our audit risk. What about internal control?" Fred responded: "I say it's about a 50–50 proposition. Sometimes control seemed to work well, sometimes it didn't. I noticed a few new people doing the invoice processing last week when we were here for a conference. Incidentally, I lump the inherent risk problems and internal control risk problems together when I think about internal control risk. Anyway, firm policy is to plan a sample for a low overall audit risk for the receivables."

Required:
Based on this dialogue information, use the expanded risk model to determine a test of detail risk. Relate this risk to sample size determination.

DISCUSSION CASES

7.50 Application to Accounts Receivable. Toni Tickmark has been assigned to plan the audit of the Cajuzzi Corporation, and is currently planning the circularization (confirmation) of accounts receivable. Cajuzzi sells a number of products in the personal health care field but its mainstay is a portable whirlpool unit for use in bathtubs called the "Ecstasizer." Offering the same therapeutic muscle-relaxing benefits as built-in units costing up to four times more, the Ecstasizer has been an outstanding success and is largely responsible for the 14% jump in sales this year.

Cajuzzi has five major categories of customers: wholesalers, department store chains, drug stores, hardware stores, and sporting goods stores. Because the health care industry is highly competitive and a number of "clones" are appearing on the market, Cajuzzi has an aggressive sales strategy coupled with fairly liberal credit policies. Viewing on-site store displays as its primary advertising media, Cajuzzi actually gives each customer a display unit for demonstration purposes. These costs are charged to promotion expense. It is the stated objective of the company to have every store in the country displaying its products.

New customers are extended credit using a very liberal credit policy and terms are net 30. Cajuzzi will not stop shipments unless balances are more than 120 days old. Customers' credit status is returned to normal as soon as the overdue balances are paid. Cajuzzi is loathe to write off any account unless the customer is actually insolvent or has given intent not to pay.

Schedule A contains a five-year summary of key financial data, and Schedule B has a summary of accounts receivable at the year-end circularization date (06/30/97).

This is the second year that Toni's firm has been the auditor of Cajuzzi, and her first year on the engagement. Last year's working papers showed that the 50 largest accounts were circularized, which was coverage of 20% ($2,600,000). Overstatement of accounts receivable of $190,000 was discovered, but no adjustment was proposed as the error was deemed immaterial.

Required:

a. Critique last year's approach to the circularization of receivables and the subsequent disposition of errors discovered.

b. What is meant by random (representative) selection, and why is it the most fundamental principle of sampling theory? Under what conditions is nonrandom selection appropriate?

c. What is meant by the terms *sampling error* and *non-sampling error?* What steps can the auditor take to control these?

d. Design a sampling plan for the circularization of receivables for Cajuzzi at 06/30/87.

Cajuzzi's product line includes the following:

- Bathtub whirlpool units.
- Exercise equipment (rowers, bikes, and mini-gyms).
- Heating pads, massage units, and footbaths.
- Air purifiers and ionizers.
- "Healthware" cooking utensils.
- Skin care products and vitamin supplements.
- Track suits, footwear and sportswear.

SCHEDULE A
Cajuzzi—Five-year Financial Summary
(in $000s)

	1993	1994	1995	1996	1997
Sales	84,000	85,000	83,000	86,000	98,000
A/R (6/30)	11,000	12,500	12,000	13,000	18,000
Allowance for doubtful accounts	1,260	1,275	1,245	1,290	1,470
Pre-tax income	3,300	2,400	3,200	3,900	5,000
Total assets	25,000	25,000	26,000	26,000	29,000

SCHEDULE B
Cajuzzi—Accounts Receivable Summary
June 30, 1987

Range	Number of Customers	Total $
$100,000–$500,000	6	$ 1,800,000
75,000–99,999	20	1,700,000
50,000–74,999	35	2,000,000
25,000–49,999	30	1,100,000
15,000–24,999	100	1,900,000
10,000–14,999	120	1,400,000
Less than 10,000	16,220	8,100,000
	16,531	$18,000,000

| Cajuzzi—Aged Trial Balance at 06/30/87 | | | | |
0–30 days	31–60 days	61–90 days	91–120 days	More than 120 days
$8,350,000	$5,740,000	$2,105,000	$1,350,000	$455,000

(ICAO adapted)

7.51 Statistical Confirmation of Receivables. You are about to commence the audit of Delta Ltd. This is the first time you have worked in the field without direct supervision by a senior, and you are of course anxious to do a good job. The senior has preceded you in visiting the client and has left you an audit file containing the following:

- An internal control questionnaire indicating no serious deficiencies in internal control over accounts receivable.
- An aged accounts receivable listing prepared by the client.
- A confirmation control schedule.
- Returned confirmations.

The confirmation control shows the following information:

- Number of accounts in the receivables subledger at December 31 = 65.
- Number of positive confirms mailed = 15.
- Number of negative confirms mailed = 30.

The client year-end, December 31, was selected as the circulation date. Trade terms are 2/10, net/30. Confirmation results are as follows:

1. 8 positive confirms returned indicating full agreement.
2. 1 positive confirm returned indicating the balance was correct but this is the outstanding balance as at November 30, 1985, not December 31, 1985.
3. 1 positive confirm returned stating the balance was correct but should also reflect a credit memo issued January 5, 1986.
4. 1 positive confirm returned stating the company uses an open invoice system and is unable to respond.
5. 1 positive confirm responding that the amount shown is incorrect because it does not reflect the 2% cash discount taken January 3, 1986.
6. 1 positive and 3 negative confirms returned by the post office marked "No Such Address."
7. 1 positive confirm stating that the balance was correct but that the company refuses to pay because of defective product quality.
8. 1 positive confirm not returned, even after two follow-up requests.
9. 2 negative confirms returned with no notations made by customers.
10. 1 negative confirm returned stating the customer owed more than the balance shown.
11. 1 negative confirm returned stating that the balance was correct but asking for an extension of credit terms.
12. 1 negative confirm returned stating "sue us."

The *first* page of the aged trial balance supplied by the client for Delta as at December 31 is shown in the table on the next page.

Notes made by the senior indicate the following additional information:

- Abbey is an employee of Delta.
- The $700 Babbitt account represents a consignment shipment.
- The $500 October balance of Cabal has been formalized by a note receivable.
- The Cadenza balance represents a deposit. No shipments have been made to them yet.

Another note in the working paper file indicates that the client asked you not to send confirmation requests to Dacron Ltd. because they are worried about jeopardizing the ongoing collection efforts for the $3,000 past-due balance. Also, you were requested not to circularize Cadaver because Delta is extremely happy to have such a large account and wants to avoid bothering them in any way.

Required:

Analyse the evidence already obtained and describe any further procedures re-

quired to complete the audit of accounts receivable.

(ICAO adapted)

Account	Balance	Dec	Nov	Oct	Prior
	(CR)				
Aardwark Enterprises	$ 4,200	$ 2,100	$2,100		
Abacus Inc.	900				$ 900
Abalone Co.	5,500	1,000	3,200	$1,200	
Abbey, Fred	<600>	<600>			
Abstract Enterprises	1,100	500	400		200
Babbitt Inc.	700	700			
Bacchus Co.	6,000	2,000	4,000		
Cabal Ltd.	1,000			500	500
Cacao Enterprises	<900>				<900>
Cadaver Inc.	30,000	30,000			
Cadenza Co.	<1,200>	<1,200>			
Dacron Ltd.	3,100	100		3,000	
Subtotal (first page)	$49,800	$34,600	$9,700	$4,700	$ 800

7.52 Projected Likely Misstatement. When Marge Simpson, PA, audited the Candle Company inventory, a random sample of inventory types was chosen for physical observation and price testing. The sample size was 80 different types of candle and candle-making inventory. The entire inventory contained 1,740 types, and the amount in the inventory control account was $166,000. Simpson already had decided that a misstatement of as much as $6,000 in the account would not be material. The audit work revealed the following eight errors in the sample of 80.

Book Value	Audit Value	Error Amount
$600.00	$622.00	$(22.00)
15.50	14.50	(1.00)
65.25	31.50	(33.75)
83.44	53.45	(29.99)
16.78	15.63	(1.15)
78.33	12.50	(65.83)
13.33	14.22	$(.89)
93.87	39.87	(54.00)
$966.50	$803.67	$(162.83)

The negative difference indicates overstatement of the recorded amount.

Required:

Calculate the projected likely misstatement using the difference method. Discuss the decision choice of accepting or rejecting the $166,000 book value (recorded amount) without adjustment.

CHAPTER 8

Learning Objectives

Computers are used by almost all audit clients. Thus, computer auditing is practiced, to a greater or lesser extent, in almost all audits. Computers introduce electronic technology in four phases of the audit process: (1) planning the audit, (2) obtaining an understanding of the control structure and control risk, (3) testing controls, and (4) using the computer to obtain substantive evidence about account balances.

Chapter 8 covers the basic concepts in all four phases with focus on simple systems. Chapter 19 covers topics related to more complex computer systems. After you study Chapter 8, you should be able to:

1. Explain how a computer accounting system differs from a manual accounting system.

2. List and discuss additional matters of planning auditors should consider for clients who use computers.

3. Describe how the phases of control risk assessment are affected by computer processing.

4. Describe and explain general control procedures and place the application control procedures covered in Chapter 6 in the context of computerized "error checking routines."

5. Describe the characteristics and control problems of micro-minicomputer installations.

6. Explain the differences between auditing around the computer, auditing through the computer, and auditing with the computer.

7. Explain how the auditor can perform the test of control's audit of computerized controls in a simple computer system.

8. Describe the use of generalized audit software.

9. Describe how microcomputers can be used as an audit tool.

Auditing in a Computer Environment

Computer Environment
. . . .

LEARNING OBJECTIVE

1. Explain how a computer accounting system differs from a manual accounting system.

This chapter does not mark the first place you have seen the computer environment mentioned. A computer orientation and computer terminology has been integrated in several prior chapters. The first was in the Chapter 2 section "Auditing Standards in a Computer Environment." It would be a good idea to review those few pages now to set the stage for Chapter 8. Later, you will see references to Chapter 6 and several computer control procedures.

The *CICA Handbook* prefers the use of the term "electronic data processing," or EDP for short, when referring to computer systems. Here we use the term "computer auditing/processing" interchangeably with "EDP auditing/processing."

An auditing text cannot describe fully all the complexities of computer or EDP processing of business transactions. This chapter assumes you have had a course in computer concepts and general computer data processing. The purpose of this section is to review the basic elements of a computer system, to define some terms that will be used subsequently, and to describe some of the control considerations unique to automated systems.

Although the term "computer auditing" has a certain mystique, there is no fundamental difference between computer auditing and the auditing described elsewhere in this book. To be more specific, when a computer is used to process the transactions:

- The definition of auditing is not changed.
- The purposes of auditing are not changed.
- The generally accepted auditing standards are not changed.
- The assertions of management embodied in financial statements are not changed.
- The control objectives are not changed.
- The requirement to gather sufficient appropriate evidence is not changed.
- The independent auditor's report on financial statements is not changed.

Therefore, everything you have learned from previous chapters is valid; only the method of processing and storing accounting data has changed. When the automation of transactions becomes more complex, auditing firms need to employ audit specialists who understand computer technology and who are aware of basic audit purposes. These "computer auditors" are members of the audit team and are called upon when the need for their skills arises, just as statistical sampling specialists or industry specialists are available when their expertise is needed. All auditors should have enough familiarity with computer processing and controls to enable them to complete the audit of simple systems and to work with computer audit specialists. (From EDP Audit Guideline "Auditing in an EDP Audit Environment." Henceforth such Guidelines will be referred to as they are in the *CICA Handbook* as "EDP–" with an appropriate number, in this case EDP–1.)

Elements of a Computer-based System

In a manual accounting system, transaction processing can be readily followed and typically is supported by paper documents—approvals, vouchers, invoices, and records of accountability, such as perpetual inventory records. Similar documents often exist in a computer system, but in many cases they are available only in machine-sensible form. Further, the basic records (ledgers and journals) of a computer-based accounting system frequently are machine-sensible data files that cannot be read or changed without a computer.

A computer-based hardware system includes the following elements:

1. *Hardware.* The physical equipment or devices that constitute a computer. These may include the central processing unit, optical reader, tape drives, disk devices, printers, terminals, and other devices.

2. *Software.*
   a. *System programs.* Programs that perform generalized functions for more than one application. These programs, sometimes referred to as supervisory programs, typically include "operating systems," which control, schedule, and maximize efficient use of the hardware; "data management systems," which perform standardized data-handling functions for one or more application programs; and "utility" programs that can perform basic computer operations, such as sorting records. System programs generally are developed by the hardware supplier or by software development companies. Examples of system programs include the many versions of DOS, Windows, and WARP.
   b. *Application (user) programs.* Sets of computer instructions that perform data processing tasks. These programs usually are written within the organization or purchased from an outside supplier.

3. *Documentation.* A description of the system and its control structure in relation to input, data processing, output, report processing, logic, and operator instructions.

4. *Personnel.* Persons who manage, design, program, operate, or control data processing systems.

5. *Data.* Transactions and related information entered, stored, and processed by the system.

6. *Control Procedures.* Procedures designed to ensure the proper recording of transactions and to prevent or detect errors and irregularities.

According to auditing standards, the establishment and maintenance of internal controls is an important responsibility of management (see *Handbook Section 5200.03*). The policies and procedures included as elements of a computer-based system are part of that responsibility. The audit team's responsibility is to make an assessment of the control risk in the system. Management can meet its responsibility and assist auditors in the following ways: (1) by ensuring that documentation of the system is complete and up to date, (2) by maintaining a system of transaction processing that includes an audit trail, and (3) by making computer resources and knowledgeable personnel available to the auditors to help them understand and audit the system.

Effect of Computer Processing

The method used to process accounting transactions will affect a company's organizational structure and will influence the procedures and techniques used to accomplish the objectives of internal control. When computers are used, special control considerations are relevant for evaluating the control environment and control procedures. The following are characteristics that distinguish computer processing from manual processing:

- *Transaction trails.* Some computer systems are so designed that a complete transaction trail useful for audit purposes may exist only for a short time or only in computer-readable form. (A transaction trail is a chain of evidence provided through coding, cross-references, and documentation connecting account balances and other summary results with the original transaction documents and calculations.)

- *Uniform processing of transactions.* Computer processing uniformly subjects like transactions to the same processing instructions. Consequently, computer processing virtually eliminates the occurrence of random errors normally associated with manual processing. Conversely, programming errors (or other similar systematic errors in either the computer hardware or software) will result in all like transactions being processed incorrectly when those transactions are processed under the same conditions. This uniformity of processing characteristics causes a subtle change in the nature of audit testing of controls. The stress in auditing computerized files will be to test a small number of unusual or exceptional transactions rather than a large number of similar transactions, as is the case in manual systems. Of course, the test transactions should also include examples of the most typical, common transactions.

- *Segregation of functions.* Many internal control procedures once performed by different individuals in manual systems may be concentrated in computer systems. Therefore, individuals who have access to the computer may be in a position to perform incompatible functions. As a result, other control procedures may be required in computer systems to achieve the degree of control ordinarily accomplished by segregating functions in manual systems. These may include such techniques as use of password control procedures to prevent incompatible functions from being performed by individuals who have access to assets and access to records through an on-line terminal. The concentration of record-keeping activities normally associated with computer centres requires a change in the approach to auditing that puts more emphasis on the evaluation of internal controls of the computer centre.

- *Potential for errors and irregularities.* The potential for individuals, including those performing control procedures, to gain unauthorized access or alter data without visible evidence, as well as to gain access (direct or indirect) to assets, may be greater in computerized accounting systems than in manual systems (partly due to the lack of segregation of duties noted above). Less human involvement in handling transactions processed by computers can reduce the potential for observing errors and irregularities. Errors or irregularities made in designing or changing application programs can remain undetected for long periods.

- *Potential for increased management supervision.* Computer systems offer management a wide variety of analytical tools that may be used to review and supervise the operations of the company. The availability of these additional controls may enhance the entire system of internal control and, therefore, reduce the control risk. For example, traditional comparisons of actual operating ratios with those budgeted, as well as reconciliation of accounts, frequently are available for management review on a more timely basis when such information is computerized. Additionally, some programmed applications provide computer operating statistics that may be used to monitor the actual processing of transactions.

- *Initiation or subsequent execution of transactions by computer.* Certain transactions may be initiated or executed automatically by a computer system. The authorization of these transactions or procedures may not be documented in the same way as those in a manual accounting system, and management's authorization of those transactions may be implicit in its acceptance of the design of the system.

R E V I E W
CHECKPOINTS

8.1 How can management meet its responsibility for establishing and maintaining an internal control system and assist the auditors at the same time?

8.2 What are the important differences between manual and computer accounting systems?

PLANNING

LEARNING OBJECTIVE

2. List and discuss additional matters of planning auditors should consider for clients who use computers.

In addition to the audit planning considerations presented in Chapters 4 and 5, auditors should consider the methods employed by a client to process significant accounting information, including the use of such outside organizations as data processing service centres. The client's methods influence the design of the accounting system and the nature of the internal control procedures.

The extent to which computer processing is used in significant accounting applications as well as the complexity of the processing also may influence the nature, timing, and extent of audit procedures (EDP–1). Accordingly, when evaluating the effect of a client's computer processing on an audit of financial statements, auditors should consider such matters as:

- The extent to which the computer is used in each significant accounting application (e.g., sales and billing, payroll).
- The complexity of the computer operations used by the entity (e.g., batch processing, on-line processing, outside service centres).
- The organizational structure of the computer processing activities.
- The availability of data required by the auditor.
- The computer-assisted audit techniques available to increase the efficiency of audit procedures.
- The need for specialized skills.

Extent to Which Computers Are Used

The extent to which computers are used in each significant accounting application should be considered in audit planning. Significant accounting applications are those relating to accounting information that can materially affect the financial statements. When computers are used to process significant accounting applications, the audit team may need computer-related skills to understand the flow of these transactions. The nature, timing, and extent of audit procedures also may be affected by the level of computer use. Computer applications are so common and pervasive that virtually every transaction is typically computerized. Traditionally, payroll, accounts receivable, accounts payable, and inventory were the first applications to be computerized.

Complexity of Computer Operations

The complexity of the computer operations used by a client, including the use of an outside service centre, should be considered in audit planning. When assessing the complexity of computer processing, the audit manager should consider his or her training and experience relative to the methods of data processing used by the client. If significant accounting applications are processed at outside service centres, it may be necessary to co-ordinate audit procedures with service auditors. (Refer to Chapter 14 for a discussion of service auditors.)

Other matters may be considered when assessing the complexity of computer processing. The computer hardware utilized by the entity may show the degree of complexity involved. The degree to which various computerized systems appear to share common files or are otherwise integrated affects the complexity of computer operations because these characteristics may cause all such integrated systems to be considered significant accounting applications. In some computerized systems a transaction trail may be available only in computer-readable form for short periods and possibly in a complex form.

Organizational Structure of Computer Processing

The organizational structure of a client's computer processing activities can have significant effects on how the auditor plans to conduct the work. Clients differ greatly in their approaches to organizing these activities. The degree of centralization inherent in the organizational structure especially may vary.

A highly centralized organizational structure generally will have all significant computer processing activities controlled and supervised at a central location. The control environment, the computer hardware, and the computer systems may be uniform throughout the company. Auditors may be able to obtain most of the necessary computer processing information by visiting the central location. At the other extreme, a highly decentralized organizational structure generally allows various departments, divisions, subsidiaries, or geographical locations to develop, control, and supervise computer processing activities in an autonomous fashion. In this situation the computer hardware and the computer systems usually will not be uniform throughout the company. Thus, auditors may need to visit many locations to obtain the necessary audit information. To assess the potential for appropriate segregation of functions, auditors may wish to consider the number of people involved with computer processing activities within the company, as well as the apparent level of computer-related knowledge possessed by these personnel.

Availability of Data

Computer systems provide an ability to store, retrieve, and analyse much more data than is practical in manual systems. Input data, certain computer files, and other data required by the audit team may exist only for short periods or only in computer readable form. In some computer systems hard-copy input documents may not exist at all because information is entered directly. The data retention policies adopted by a client may require auditors to arrange for some information to be retained for review. Alternatively, auditors may need to plan to perform audit procedures at a time when the information is still available.

In addition, certain information generated by the computer system for management's internal purposes may be useful in performing analytical procedures. For example, due to the ease of storage, the client may save sales information by month, by product, and by salesman. Such information can be used with analytical procedures to determine whether the revenue amounts are reasonable.

Use of Computer-assisted Audit Techniques

Computer-assisted audit techniques (CAATs per EDP–1 and EDP–2) may be used to increase the efficiency of certain audit procedures and also may provide auditors with opportunities to apply certain procedures to an entire population of accounts or transactions. There are two main categories of CAATs: (1) audit software and (2) test data (EDP–2). The use of these techniques requires advance planning and may require individuals with specialized skills as members of the audit team. These techniques are further discussed later in this chapter.

Need for Specialized Skills

To determine the need for specialized computer skills, all aspects of a client's computer processing should be considered. In planning the engagement, the audit manager may conclude that certain specialized skills are needed to consider the effect of computer processing on the audit, to understand the flow of transactions, or to design and perform audit procedures. For example, specialized skills relating to various methods of data processing, programming languages, software packages, or computer-assisted audit techniques may be needed. Audit managers and partners should possess sufficient computer knowledge to know when to call on specialists and to understand and supervise their work.

R E V I E W
CHECKPOINTS

8.3 In addition to the planning matters considered in a manual accounting system, what additional ones should be considered when computer processing is involved?

8.4 What are the general characteristics of transactions that are typically computerized? typically not computerized?

Phase 1: Computer System Understanding
. . . .

LEARNING OBJECTIVE

3. Describe how the phases of control risk assessment are affected by computer process-ing.

The purpose of the Phase 1 understanding is to obtain sufficient knowledge of the control environment, the accounting system, and the control procedures to determine whether internal control provides a basis for planning the nature, timing, and extent of substantive audit procedures. The Phase 1 obtaining-an-understanding work should be designed to provide an understanding of the control environment and the flow of transactions through the accounting system, including a general knowledge of (*a*) the organizational structure, (*b*) the methods used by the client to communicate responsibility and authority, and (*c*) the methods used by management to supervise the system, including the existence of an internal audit function, if any. Each of these elements of the control environment may be affected by computer processing.

The Organizational Structure

The auditors' understanding of the organizational structure of a company should include an understanding of the organization of its computer function. This under-standing should contribute to the overall assessment of control risk. In reviewing the organization structure of a company's computer function, auditors should obtain and evaluate:

- A description of the company's computer resources, including details of com-puter equipment used, the use of an outside services centre, if any, and locations from which the computer resources can be accessed.

- A description of the organizational structure of computer operations as it relates to personnel within the computer department, and the interaction with person-nel in other departments.

The description of computer resources should give auditors (1) an overview of computer operating activities, (2) knowledge of access to computer resources used to process accounting information, and (3) knowledge of company policies regarding access only by authorized personnel. Auditors should enquire about the division of responsibilities between systems and programming staff and operations personnel to assess the segregation of duties. They should understand the existence and organiza-tion of the control function and its assigned responsibilities. Auditors should identify the position the computer function has in the overall organization structure, as well as understand the interaction between user departments and the computer department.

Methods Used to Communicate Responsibility and Authority

In connection with understanding the methods used by the client to communicate responsibility and authority, the auditor should obtain information about the exis-tence of (*a*) accounting and other policy manuals, including computer operations and user manuals, and (*b*) formal job descriptions for computer department personnel. Related user personnel job descriptions may be helpful. Auditors should gain an understanding of how the client's computer resources are managed and how priori-ties for their use are determined. Auditors also should gain an understanding of the extent to which other departments within the company have a clear understanding of how they must comply with computer processing-related standards and procedures.

Methods Used by Management to Supervise the System

As part of the Phase 1 review, auditors should learn the procedures management uses to supervise the computer operation, including:

- The existence of systems design and documentation standards and the extent to which they are used.
- The existence and quality of procedures for system and program modification, systems acceptance approval, and output modification (such as changes in reports or files).
- The procedures limiting access to authorized information, particularly with respect to sensitive information.
- The availability of financial and other reports, such as budget/performance reviews for use by management.
- The existence of an internal audit function and the degree of its involvement in reviewing computer-produced accounting records and related controls and its involvement in systems development control evaluation and testing.

After the audit team gains an understanding of the control environment, the obtaining-an-understanding phase should be continued by obtaining an understanding of the accounting system—the flow of transactions.

Understanding the Accounting System

An understanding of the flow of transactions through the accounting system is required to support the design of substantive audit procedures. Gaining the understanding of the flow of transactions for each significant accounting application begins with referring to the client's description of the accounting applications. When a computer system is used in significant accounting applications, descriptions should include the user's manuals and instructions, file descriptions, system flowcharts, and narrative descriptions.

The audit team may find that internal audit personnel or other client personnel already have prepared documentation relating to the flow of transactions. This documentation may be adequate for purposes of understanding the accounting system. Early in the audit planning, the internal auditors and other client personnel should be consulted to determine whether they have documentation that can be useful.

PHASE 2: ASSESSING THE CONTROL RISK

The distinction between the understanding phase and the control risk assessment phase is useful for your understanding of the audit work. However, most auditors in practice do the two together, not as separate and distinct work packages.

Control risk assessment, when a computer is used, involves:

- Identifying specific control objectives based on the types of misstatements that may be present in significant accounting applications.
- Identifying the points in the flow of transactions where specific types of misstatements could occur.

COMPUTER IMPACT ON INTERNAL CONTROL

Traditional segregation of duties may be impaired because an individual employee may be able to perform incompatible functions, such as making and concealing an error.

The number of people who handle a transaction is typically reduced, often to just the individual employee who enters the data into the computer. Control can be maintained only if additional controls are in the computer system.

In a simple environment, an individual manager can be responsible for managing and ensuring the quality of the gathering, processing, and use of data. In computer systems, an individual manager may be responsible for only a portion of the processing and control. Unless carefully defined and monitored, this sharing of control responsibilities can result in loss of overall control.

Source: Adapted from Deloitte & Touche handbook.

- Identifying specific control procedures designed to prevent or detect these misstatements.
- Identifying the control procedures that must function to prevent or detect the misstatements.
- Evaluating the design of control procedures to determine whether it suggests a low control risk and whether test of controls audit procedures on them may be cost effective.

Identifying specific control objectives is no different than in a manual data processing system. However, the process of identifying the points in the flow of transactions where misstatements could occur is different in a computer system in comparison to a manual system. For example, when a computer is used, these points (see Exhibit 8–1) are places where misstatements could occur:

1. Activities related to source data preparation are performed, causing the flow of transactions to include authorization and initial execution.
2. Noncomputerized procedures are applied to source data, such as a manual summarization of accounting data (preparation of batch totals).
3. Source data are converted into computer-readable form.
4. Input files are identified for use in processing.
5. Information is transferred from one computer program to another.
6. Computer-readable files are used to supply additional information relating to individual transactions (e.g., customer credit reports).
7. Transactions are initiated by the computer.
8. Output files are created or master files are updated.
9. Master files are changed (records added, deleted, or modified) outside the normal flow of transactions within each cycle through file maintenance procedures.
10. Output reports or files are produced.
11. Errors identified by control procedures are corrected.

EXHIBIT 8–1   COMPUTER ACCOUNTING: POINTS OF VULNERABILITY TO
MISSTATEMENT ERRORS

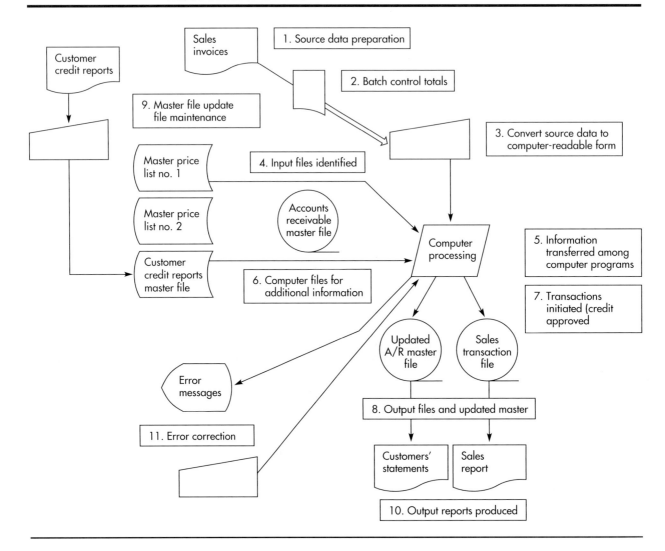

Once the audit team has identified the points where a misstatement might occur, specific control objectives can be related to such points. For example, one possible misstatement might involve billing customers with incorrect prices because a wrong file has been used. One way to state a control objective relating to this type of misstatement is: "Appropriate price information should be used during the billing process." As will be discussed later in this chapter, the controls associated with prevention, detection, or correction of these misstatements can be grouped into three broad categories: input, processing, and output controls. Input controls are the ones associated with preventing misstatements of the type numbered 1 through 4 above. Processing controls are primarily designed to detect misstatements of the type numbered 5 through 8 above. Output controls are primarily designed to correct misstatements of the type numbered 9 through 11 above.

Once points where misstatements could occur in the flow of transactions are identified, auditors should focus on specific control procedures that may prevent or detect such misstatements. Control procedures should be considered in terms of specific control objectives. For example, for the objective of using appropriate price information, one control procedure might be "The billing application program should identify the correct price file through matching the file name in the program to the name on the header label." (Header labels are described later.)

In a computerized accounting system, control procedures may have characteristics that differ from manual control procedures designed to accomplish the same control objectives. For example, in a manual system, credit approval usually is indicated by affixing an authorized signature to a source document, such as a customer's order or invoice. In a computerized system, however, approval can be accomplished by utilizing an approved password that releases a credit sale transaction by assigning a special code to it. The password provides access to programs that permit initiating a specific type of transaction or changing master files. In such a case, although the control objective is identical in the manual and computerized systems, the methods used to achieve the objective and the visible evidence of conformity with authorized procedures differ considerably and the audit approach may be significantly different.

The information gathered about the client's control environment, the accounting system, and the control procedures should enable the auditor to reach one of the following conclusions about control risk:

- Control risk may be assessed low, and it seems efficient to perform tests of controls audit procedures. Control procedures designed to prevent or detect misstatements apparently can be audited for compliance in a cost-effective manner. In this situation the auditors continue with test of controls auditing discussed later in this chapter.

- Control risk may be assessed low, but audit inefficiencies would occur if controls were tested. Control policies and procedures appear to be good, but test of controls auditing is not cost effective. In this case the auditors would concentrate attention on the substantive audit procedures.

- Control risk may be assessed high. Control structure policies and procedures do not appear to be sufficient to prevent or detect material misstatements. In this case the auditors will concentrate on substantive audit procedures.

If controls do not appear to be good, the auditors should proceed with the design of substantive audit procedures. In making this evaluation, it may be possible to identify specific control procedures that provide a low risk assessment with regard to some but not all assertions. In such situations the auditors may achieve some audit objectives through a combination of tests of controls and substantive auditing, while other audit objectives may be achieved through substantive procedures alone.

R E V I E W
CHECKPOINTS

8.5 How is the understanding of the control environment affected when a computer is used in data processing?

8.6 What sources of information can auditors use to obtain an understanding of the flow of transactions through a client's computerized accounting system?

8.7 What five general tasks are involved in computer system control risk assessment?

8.8 Categorize the 11 points of vulnerability to misstatement errors in terms of manual input, computer processing, and error correction activities in a computer system.

. . . .

Simple Computer Systems: Characteristics and Control Considerations

. . . .

LEARNING OBJECTIVE
4. Describe and explain general control procedures and place the application control procedures covered in Chapter 6 in the context of computerized "error checking routines."

The controls described in this section relate to a simple computer system, although many of the controls are applicable to more advanced systems described in Chapter 19. A simple system is one where all processing occurs at a central processing facility in a batch mode.

Characteristics of a Simple Computer System

Batch processing (also called **serial** or **sequential processing**) means that all records to be processed are collected in groups (batches) of like transactions. The computer operator (or the operating system) obtains the programs and master files from the computer library. Following the instructions in the run manual, all like transactions then are processed utilizing the same programs and the same master files. For example, all payroll records are run at one time, and the input is in the form of a magnetic tape containing employees' identification numbers and hours worked. The programs edit and validate the input and match good transactions against the employee master file for pay rate and deduction information. Programs will execute the processing to compute the payroll, print cheques, update year-to-date records, and summarize payroll information for management. After completion of the run, the programs and data files will be returned to storage (magnetic), and the output of cheques and reports will be distributed.

Batches may be collected at a central computer site or other locations. Input transactions may be entered via terminals and stored on magnetic tape or disks. Regardless of the method, batch processing is characterized by grouping like transactions to be processed in batches, all using the same programs. The master files take the place of subsidiary and general ledgers in manual systems. The batches of transactions are similar to journals in a manual system. All transactions in a batch may be listed in printed output. However, the detail of transactions usually is not printed and the familiar journal is nonexistent. Instead, summary entries are prepared for updating general ledger master files. Many smaller systems now provide the on-line processing capability that traditionally has been associated with advanced systems (see Chapter 19). *On-line* has a variety of meanings as discussed in Chapter 19, but a meaning that is relevant for all systems is the following: Data processing is termed on-line (or direct access or random) where transactions can be input into computer processing from the point of origin without first being sorted.

Master files contain records with two general types of fields—**static** fields, such as employee number and pay rate, and **dynamic** fields, such as year-to-date gross pay and account balances. Most of the computer processing of accounting data involves changing these fields in the master file records. The dynamic fields are changed in **update** processing, as was described for batch processing of payroll, Update processing does not change the static fields. The static fields are changed by **file maintenance** processing, which will add or delete entire records (e.g., add new employee) or change fields (e.g., new pay rate). Auditors are concerned with authorization and controls over both types of changes.

General Control Procedures

Control procedures in a computerized accounting system may be classified into two types—general controls and application controls (EDP–3). **General control procedures** relate to all or many computerized accounting activities—for example, controls over access to computer programs and data files. **Application control procedures** relate to individual computerized accounting applications—for example, programmed validation controls for verifying customers' account numbers and credit limits. The general controls are presented first because they usually are considered early in the audit.

Organization and Physical Access

The proper segregation of functional responsibilities—authority to authorize transactions, custody of assets, recordkeeping, and periodic reconciliation—is as important in computer systems as in manual systems. However, computer systems involve such functions as systems analysis, programming, data conversion, library functions, and machine operations that are unique. Therefore, further separation of duties is recommended. These separate functions were explained in Chapter 6, but they are also an integral part of computer system control. It is a good idea to review the Chapter 6 section "Segregation of Technical Responsibilities" at this time.

The physical security of computer equipment, and limited access to computer program files and data files, are as important as segregation of technical responsibilities. Access controls help prevent improper use or manipulation of data files, unauthorized or incorrect use of computer programs, and improper use of the computer equipment.

The librarian function or librarian software should control access to systems documentation and access to program and data files by using a checkout log (a record of entry and use) or password to record the use by authorized persons. Someone who possesses both documentation and data files will have enough information to alter data and programs for his or her own purposes.

Locked doors, security passes, passwords, and check-in logs (including logs produced by the computer) can be used to limit access to the computer system hardware. Having definite schedules for running computer applications is another way to detect unauthorized access, because the computer system software can produce reports that can be compared to the planned schedule. Variations then can be investigated for unauthorized use of computer resources.

Weakness or absence of organizational and access controls decreases the overall integrity of the computer system. The audit team should be uncomfortable when such deficiencies exist and should weigh their impact when evaluating control risk. Some typical questions asked by auditors are shown in the box below. A full set of questions, of which these are a part, is one method that auditors use to review and document the organization and access control of a computer facility.

Documentation and Systems Development

Documentation is the means of communicating the essential elements of the data processing system. The following purposes may be served by computer system documentation:

- Provide for management review of proposed application systems.
- Provide explanatory material for users.
- Instruct new personnel by providing background on previous application systems and serve as a guideline for developing new applications.

ORGANIZATION AND PHYSICAL ACCESS: SELECTED
QUESTIONNAIRE ITEMS

Preliminary

Prepare or have the client prepare a "Computer Profile," which should include an organization chart, hardware and peripheral equipment, communication network, major application processes (batch or on-line), significant input and output files, software used, and a layout of the data centre.

Organization

Are the following functions performed by different individuals so that proper segregation of duties exists?

> *a.* Application programming, computer operation, and control of data files?
> *b.* Application programming and control and reconciliation of input and output?
> Are computer operators rotated periodically from shift to shift?
> Are programmers and systems analysts rotated periodically from application to application?

Data and Procedural Control

Is there a separate group within the computer department to perform control and balancing of input and output?
> Are there written procedures for setting up input for processing?
> Is there a formal procedure for distribution of output to user departments?

Access Control

Is access to the computer room restricted to authorized personnel?
> Are operators restricted from access to program and application documentation?
> Does access to on-line files require that specific passwords be entered to identify and validate the terminal user?

- Provide the data necessary for answering enquiries about the operation of a computer application.
- Serve as one source of information for an evaluation of controls.
- Provide operating instructions.
- Simplify program revision by providing details of processing logic.
- Supply basic information for planning and implementing audit software or other auditing techniques.[1]

Auditors review the documentation to gain an understanding of the system and to determine whether the documentation is adequate. Of utmost importance in this area of the review is whether systems development and documentation standards have

---

[1] Gordon B. Davis, Donald L. Adams, and Carol A. Schaller, *Auditing and EDP*, 2nd ed. (New York: AICPA, 1983), p. 59.

DOCUMENTATION AND SYSTEMS DEVELOPMENT: SELECTED
QUESTIONNAIRE ITEMS

Development

Does a written priority plan exist for development of new systems and changes to old systems?

Do the design and development of a new system involve the users as well as computer personnel?

Is there a formal review and approval process at the end of each significant phase in developing a new system?

Documentation

Do written standards exist for documentation of new systems and for changing documentation when existing systems are revised?

Does the following documentation exist for each application?

- System flowchart.
- Record layouts.
- Program edit routines.
- Program source listing.
- Operator instructions.
- Approval and change record.

---

been established by the client. Unless written standards exist, it is very difficult to determine whether the systems development controls and the documentation are adequate. The **systems development and documentation standards manual** prepared by management should contain standards that ensure (1) proper user involvement in the systems design and modification process, (2) review of the specifications of the system, (3) approval by user management and data processing management, and (4) controls and auditability.

Armed with the manual describing systems development standards, auditors first evaluate the standards to determine whether they are adequate and then review the documentation to determine whether the standards are followed. This review actually accomplishes a test of controls audit of systems development standards (and controls), as well as providing an understanding of how a particular system works. This kind of work may require the knowledge and skills of a computer audit specialist.

Auditors are interested in the following elements of the documentation of accounting applications: application description, problem definition, programs description, acceptance testing records, computer operator instructions, user department manual, change and modification log, and listing of controls. For example, the **application description** usually contains system flowcharts, description of all inputs and outputs, record formats, lists of computer codes, and control features. The application system flowcharts frequently can be adapted to audit working paper flowcharts where the flow of transactions can be followed and control points noted.

Copies of record formats of significant master files frequently are obtained for use in computer-assisted audit techniques described later.

The **program description** should contain a program flowchart, a listing of the program source code (such as COBOL, RPG, and BASIC), and a record of all program changes. Auditors should review this documentation to determine whether programmed controls such as input validations exist.

The **acceptance testing records** may contain test data that can be used by auditors when performing their own tests of controls audit procedures. The users' manual should indicate manual procedures and controls in the user departments that submit transactions and receive the output. The log of changes and modifications is important to auditors because it should provide assurance that the application systems have been operating as described for the period under review and that all changes and modifications have been authorized.

The **controls section** of the documentation also is very important. Here all the computer controls described in other sections are repeated along with manual controls that affect the application program. Careful review by auditors of this section should provide a complete overview of the entire control over the processing of transactions in a particular application and of how the general controls are carried out in the application.

Hardware

Modern computer equipment is very reliable. Machine malfunctions that can go undetected are relatively rare. You are not expected to be a computer systems engineer, but you should be familiar with some of the hardware controls so that you can converse knowledgeably with computer personnel.

The most important hardware control now incorporated in all computers is a **parity check**. The parity check ensures that the coding of data internal to the computer does not change when it is moved from one internal storage location to another. An additional hardware control commonly found is an **echo check**. It involves a magnetic read after each magnetic write "echoing" back to the sending location and comparing results. Many computers also contain dual circuitry to perform arithmetic operations twice. Auditors (and management) cannot do much about the absence of such controls but should be concerned primarily with operator procedures when such errors occur (for example, the Pentium processor chip flaw that was widely publicized in late 1994 and early 1995). Modern computers are largely self-diagnostic. Therefore, written procedures should exist for all computer malfunctions, and all malfunctions should be recorded along with their causes and resolutions.

Another significant area of auditor interest is **preventive maintenance**. Auditors should determine whether maintenance is scheduled and whether the schedule is followed and documented. Maintenance frequently is under contract with the computer vendor. In such cases, auditors should review the contract as well as the record of regular maintenance work. Other general evidence on hardware reliability may be obtained from a review of operating reports and downtime logs.

Data File and Program Control and Security

Controls over physical access to the computer hardware were described earlier in this chapter in conjunction with organization controls. Equally important and sensitive is control over access, use, and security of the data files and programs. Since magnetic storage media can be erased or written over, controls are necessary to ensure that the proper file is being used and that the files and programs are appropriately backed up.

Backup involves a retention system for files, programs, and documentation so that master files can be reconstructed in case of accidental loss and so that processing can continue at another site if the computer centre is lost to fire or flood. Thus, backup files must be stored offsite, away from the main computer.

Some of the more important security and retention control techniques and procedures are listed and explained next.

External Labels.   These labels are paper labels on the outside of a file (diskettes, cartridges, portable disk packs, or magnetic tapes). The label identifies the contents, such as "Accounts Receivable Master File," so the probability of using the file inappropriately (e.g., in the payroll run) is minimized.

Header and Trailer Labels.   These labels are special internal records on magnetic tapes and disks. They are magnetic records on the tape or disk; but, instead of containing data, they hold label information similar to the external file label. Therefore, the header and trailer labels are sometimes called **internal labels**. Their function is to prevent use of the wrong file during processing. The header label will contain the name of the file and relevant identification codes. The trailer label gives a signal that the end of the file has been reached. Sometimes these trailer labels are designed to contain accumulated control totals to serve as a check on loss of data during operation; for example, the number of accounts and the total balance of an accounts receivable file.

File Security.   Security is enhanced by many physical devices, such as storage in fireproof vaults, backup in remote locations, and files sorted in computer-readable, printed, or microfilm form. In the majority of cases, the exposure to risk of loss warrants insurance on program and data files.

File Retention.   Retention practices are related closely to file security; but, in general, retention may provide the first line of defence against relatively minor loss, while security generally consists of all measures taken to safeguard files against total loss. In essence, the problem is how to reconstruct records and files once they have been damaged. One of the most popular methods is the **grandfather-father-son** concept. This involves the retention of backup files, such as the current transaction file and the prior master file, from which the current master file can be reconstructed. Exhibit 8–2 illustrates the file retention plan. Particularly important files may be retained to the great-grandfather generation if this is considered necessary.

Disk files are more difficult to reconstruct than tape files because the process of updating old records with new information is "destructive." The old or superseded data on a record are removed (destroyed) when new data are entered in the same place on a disk. One means of reconstruction is to have a disk file "dumped" onto tape periodically (each day or each week). This file copy, along with the related transaction file also retained, can serve as the father to the current disk file (son).

Application Control Procedures

In this book the computerized application control procedures have been integrated with the introduction to control risk assessment topics in Chapter 6. Exhibit 6–6 in Chapter 6 gives a summary list of the "error checking routines," and the chapter text explains them. These are the application control procedures. It would be a good idea to review them at this time and put them in the context of technical computer auditing.

EXHIBIT 8–2 GRANDFATHER, FATHER, AND SON IN MAGNETIC TAPE FILES

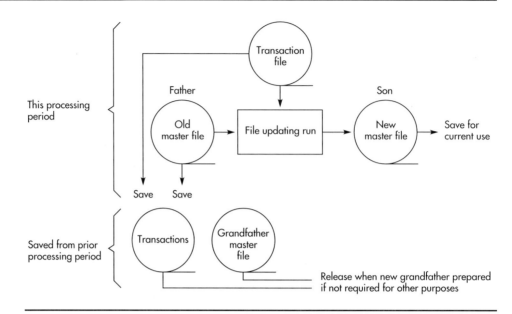

The designation "application controls" comes from the fact that they are used in each "application"—sales and billing, purchasing, payroll, and other specific accounting applications. The application controls are organized under three categories—input controls, processing controls, and output controls. The brief sections below put some computer system questionnaire items in the context of these control procedures.

Input Controls

In Chapter 6 the input controls procedures are:

- Input authorization.
- Check digits.
- Record counts.
- Batch financial totals.
- Batch hash totals.
- Valid character tests.
- Valid sign tests.
- Missing data tests.
- Sequence tests.
- Limit/reasonableness tests.
- Error resubmission.

Some typical questionnaire items that may be asked during a review of input controls are shown in the next box. These questions should be asked about each significant accounting application. Input controls are primarily preventive in nature, and with the

---

Input Control Procedures: Selected Questionnaire Items

Authorization of Transactions

Have procedures been established to ensure that only authorized transactions are accepted, such as (*a*) written approval on source documents? (*b*) general authorizations to process all of the user's transactions? and (*c*) use of identification numbers, security codes, and passwords for remote terminal users?

Completeness of Input

Are control totals established by the user prior to submitting data for processing?

Does someone verify that input data are received on a timely basis from the user and physically controlled in the computer centre?

Data Conversion

Have procedures been established to exercise proper control over processing rejected transactions, including (*a*) positive identification of rejected records? (*b*) review of the cause of rejection? (*c*) the correction of rejected records? (*d*) review and approval of the correction? and (*e*) prompt reentry of the correction at a point where it will be subjected to the same input controls as the original data?

---

increasing complexity of computer systems, auditors are placing increasing importance on the input controls. This follows from the "garbage in, garbage out" or GIGO philosophy. It is generally more cost effective for a system to prevent misstatements rather than detect and correct misstatements once they have entered the system.

Processing Controls

In Chapter 6, the processing control procedures are:

- Run-to-run totals.
- Control total reports.
- File logs.
- Limit/reasonableness tests.

Processing controls are primarily oriented to detecting misstatements. Some typical questionnaire items are in the first two boxes on the next page.

Output Controls

In Chapter 6 the output control procedures are:

- Control totals.
- Master file changes.
- Output distribution.

Output controls are primarily oriented to correcting misstatements already in the system. Some typical questionnaire items are in the third box on the next page.

Processing Control Procedures: Selected Questionnaire Items

Completeness

Are programmed control procedures (run-to-run totals) included in each job step during the processing cycle?

Do application programs test the terminal identification or password, or both, for access authorization to that specific program?

Are control totals maintained on all files, and are these verified by the update or file maintenance application program each time a file is used in processing?

File Control

Do application programs check for internal header and trailer labels?

Are tape or disk files subjected to adequate on-site and off-site backup support?

Are test data files documented, up to date, and kept separate from live data files?

Output Control Procedures: Selected Questionnaire Items

Are input control totals reconciled to output totals?

Are input changes to master files compared item by item to output reports of these changes?

Do written distribution lists exist for all output reports from each application?

Are all output files appropriately identified with internal and external labels?

Control Risk Assessment in Simple Computer Systems

Apparent weakness in any of the input, processing, and output control procedures is a matter of concern. However, absence of a control at the input stage may be offset by other controls at later stages (EDP–3). For example, if check digits are not calculated when the input is prepared, but transaction numbers are compared to master file numbers and nonmatches are rejected and printed in an error report, the control is likely to be satisfactory and effective. Of course, it usually is more efficient to catch errors early, rather than late; but control still can be considered effective for the accounting records and financial statements. Internal auditors, however, may be very interested in when controls are applied, since they are concerned about the efficiency of computer operations.

Material weaknesses in manual and computer controls become a part of the independent auditor's assessment of control risk. Lack of input controls may permit data to be lost or double-counted, and poor processing control can permit accounting calculation, allocation, and classification errors to occur. Poor output controls over distribution of reports and other output (negotiable cheques, for example) can be the source of misstatements that could make financial statements materially misleading.

The purpose of the review of internal control is to gain an understanding of the flow of transaction processing and to determine strengths (controls) and weaknesses (lack of controls) that need to be considered in planning substantive audit procedures. In a computer environment the general control procedures must be reviewed if any application system contains important computer controls. Based on the audit documentation (working papers) of the computer controls and manual controls, the audit manager must determine whether processing is accurate and complete. The audit documentation may consist of questionnaires, such as those illustrated in this chapter, and flowcharts. The general control procedures and the controls in each application system may be subject to tests of controls auditing to determine whether the controls operate effectively. Generally, most auditors find it cost effective to follow a strategy of evaluating general and environmental controls before evaluating the more specific application controls. The reasoning for this is that the controls having a more pervasive impact and preventive in nature are the more important controls.

· ·

R E V I E W
C H E C K P O I N T S

8.9 What are the four categories of general control procedures?

8.10 What general familiarity do auditors obtain with the preliminary information sought in the ''organization and physical access'' questionnaire?

8.11 What is the typical content of application description documentation for a computerized accounting system? of the program description documentation? of the acceptance testing records documentation? of the controls section documentation?

8.12 What is the difference between an external label and an internal label in magnetic file media? What is the purpose of each?

8.13 What aspects of documentation, file security, and retention control procedures are unique to computer systems?

8.14 Describe the purposes of computer system documentation. Why should the auditor review the computer system documentation?

8.15 What does an auditor need to know about computer hardware controls?

8.16 What is a self-checking number? Can you give an example of one of your own? (Refer to Chapter 6.)

· ·

MICRO/MINICOMPUTER ENVIRONMENT (SMALL BUSINESS)

· · · · · · · · · · · ·

LEARNING OBJECTIVE
5. Describe the charac-
   teristics and control
   problems of micro-
   minicomputer installa-
   tions.

The term "micro-minicomputer" is used herein to describe a family of computers that includes small business computers, microcomputers, and intelligent terminals (EDP–4). These small computers can have any or all of the characteristics of advanced systems.

Computer activity involving micro-minicomputers should be included in the assessment of control risk. Since the control objectives do not change, the internal control questionnaires illustrated in this chapter and the audit techniques discussed in Chapter 19 are relevant but may have to be tailored to the micro-minicomputer installation. The following explanations are designed to assist you in appreciating how the questionnaires, flowcharts, and audit techniques may have to be modified by directing attention to potential problems and controls normally affecting mini-computers.

Major Characteristics

Micro-minicomputers may be elements of a distributed system or a stand-alone system doing all the data processing for a business. The latter is considered here. The control environment, and not the computer technology, is the important aspect for auditors (EDP–4). Many small businesses get along well with computers for ac-counting purposes by using these resources:

- *Utility programs.* Purchased utility programs are used extensively to enter and change data.
- *Diskettes.* Floppy diskettes are used extensively for accounting file storage.
- *Terminals.* Terminals and minicomputers are used for transaction data entry, enquiry, and other interactive functions.
- *Software packages.* Purchased software packages are used extensively, rather than internally developed application software.
- *Documentation.* Available system, program, operation, and user documentation may be limited or nonexistent.
- *Tape backup.* Is used extensively as long-term backup file storage.

In a micro-minicomputer installation with these limited computer resources, the most significant control weakness is a lack of segregation of duties. This potential weakness may be compounded by the lack of control procedures in the operating system and application programs. Simply turning on the system may provide access to all the files and programs, with no record of use. The next box highlights these control problems.

Micro/minicomputer Control Considerations

Most of the control problems can be traced to the lack of segregation of duties and the lack of computerized control procedures. It follows that most of the auditors' control considerations and techniques are designed to overcome these deficiencies. Auditors should consider the entire control structure, including manual controls, and look for compensating control strengths that might offset apparent weaknesses. The various control considerations and techniques are discussed below under headings similar to the general control procedures discussed previously—organizational, operations and processing, and systems development and modification.

Control Problems in Micro/ Minicomputer Environments

Lack of Segregation of Accounting Functions

People in user departments may initiate and authorize source documents, enter data, operate the computer, and distribute output reports.

Lack of Segregation of Computer Functions

Small organizations may not separate the functions of programming and operating the computer. Programs and data are often resident on disk at all times and accessible by any operator.

Lack of Physical Computer Security

The computer often is located in the user department instead of in a separate secure area. Ease of access and use is desired, and access to hardware, programs, and data files may not be restricted.

Lack of Computer Knowledge

Individuals responsible for data processing sometimes have limited knowledge of computers, relying instead on packaged software and utility programs with convenient user manuals. Computer professionals may be assigned to monitor mainframe systems but not the micro-minicomputers.

Organizational Control Procedures

The environment in a micro-minicomputer installation is similar to the one-person bookkeeping department because the systems analysis, design, and programming operations can be performed by one or two people. The main controls involve limiting the concentration of functions, to the extent possible, and establishing proper supervision. The situation is a computerized version of internal control in a small business as described in Chapter 6. You should review that section at this time if you do not recall it. The implementation of the other control procedures discussed below will help offset control weaknesses caused by lack of segregation of duties.

Operation Control Procedures

In micro-minicomputer installations, the most important controls are those over on-line data (accounting transactions) entry.

Restricting Access to Input Devices.   Terminals may be physically locked and keys controlled. The utilization of various levels of passwords to access files, initiate changes, and invoke programs should be strictly followed.

Standard Screens and Computer Prompting.   The computer can be programmed to produce a standard screen format when a particular function is called. The operator must complete all blanks as prompted by the computer, thus ensuring that complete transactions are entered before they are processed.

On-line Editing and Sight Verification.   The input edit and validation controls discussed previously can be programmed to occur at time of input. In some installations the data on the screen are not released until the data have been sight-verified and the operator signals the computer to accept the entire screen.

Processing Control Procedures

The processing can be controlled by artificially creating the files equivalent to the grandfather-father-son retention concept found in batch systems. The procedures that could ensure that the data processed are in balance, that an adequate audit trail is maintained, and that recovery is possible include the following.

Transaction Logs.   Transaction entry through the terminal should be captured automatically in a computerized log. The transaction logs (for each terminal or each class of terminals) should be summarized into the equivalent of batch totals (counts of transactions, financial totals, or hash totals).

Control Totals.   Master files should contain records that accumulate the number of records and financial totals. The update processing automatically should change these control records.

Balancing Input to Output.   The summary of daily transactions and the master file control totals from the micro-minicomputer should be balanced to manual control totals maintained by the accounting department. If this external balancing is not feasible, techniques similar to the auditor's analytical procedures can be employed to test for reasonableness.

Audit Trail.   The transaction logs and periodic dumps of master files should provide an audit trail and means for recovery. In addition, some micro-minicomputer installations have systems software that can provide a log of all files accessed and all jobs processed.

Systems Development and Modification

The control objectives and techniques in a micro-minicomputer installation are no different than on a larger system, even though the environment is different. Many application programs will be purchased from computer manufacturers or software vendors not completely familiar with control techniques. Purchased programs should be reviewed carefully and tested before acquisition and implementation.

There are a variety of programming languages and application generators used in micro/minicomputer systems (C, DBase) and programming ability may develop within the user group. Most microcomputers have "menu-type" micro-instructions, which are simple to use without technical training. Further, the programming is in an interpretative language, which means it remains in the computer program library in source code form that is easy to change. Development standards and modification authorization become even more important than in larger systems. Since most programming will be done through terminals, special passwords should be required to access programs and only authorized personnel should be issued these passwords. The next box identifies key issues of general controls in small business systems.

There is some controversy about the effect of computerization in small businesses and whether such computerization increases or decreases control risk. The International Federation of Accountants suggests that computerization in small businesses leads to increased control risk because of the increased risk of incompatible duties being performed. However, S. J. Gaston argues that adequate general controls can be achieved with "appropriate segregation of duties of only three or four employees"

Three types of systems are encountered in small businesses: microcomputers, local area networks (LANs), and curtain multi-user systems. Where microcomputers are used to process accounting records, the computers often "stand alone" and run a single software package purchased from a software vendor. Where computers are linked together, they form a LAN, again usually running packaged software. In fewer cases, the computers are linked together using a multi-user operating system, such as UNIX, and run custom software especially developed for the business, usually by an outside developer or consultant.

Access controls are important for all of these scenarios, as are backup procedures. The greater the number of users, the greater the opportunity for using access controls for enforcing division of duties. Program development controls are significant only for custom software.

As a minimum, a small business audit file should include a brief memo addressing each of these areas, identifying, for example, whether passwords are being used and how they are administered; whether and by whom programs are changed; and whether backups are made and stored off site. The more complex the system, the more fully the areas need to be addressed.

Source: Trites, G. *Audit of a Small Business,* CICA, 1994, pp. 46–47.

when combined with proper use of user identification and password capabilities.[2] Such general controls, when combined with "reasonably effective application controls," can result in a reduced level of control risk.[3]

R E V I E W
CHECKPOINTS

8.17 Which important duties are generally not segregated in small business computer systems?

8.18 What control techniques can a company use to achieve control over the operation of a micro-minicomputer accounting system?

8.19 What control techniques can a company use to achieve control over the computer processing of accounting data in a micro-minicomputer system?

8.20 What are the major characteristics and control problems in micro-minicomputer installations?

Evaluation Approaches for Computer Systems

LEARNING OBJECTIVE

6. Explain the differences between auditing around the computer, auditing through the computer, and auditing with the computer.

When businesses started using computers, two terms were coined to describe the nature of auditing work on computer systems. The first term, "auditing around the computer," came to mean that auditors were attempting to isolate the computer—to treat it like a "black box"—and to find audit assurance by vouching data from output to source documents and by tracing from source documents to output. As long as

---

[2] S. J. Gaston, *Managing and Controlling Small Computer Systems Including LANS* (Toronto, CICA, 1992) p. XIX

[3] G. Trites, *Audit of a Small Business* (Toronto, CICA, 1994), pp. 47–48.

the computer was used as a speedy calculator, this method generally was considered adequate. In fact, it may be satisfactory today in a case where the computer system is used simply as a calculator and printer. Nothing is inherently wrong with auditing around the computer if auditors are satisfied with the control structures and are able to gather sufficient evidence. However, auditing around the computer becomes unacceptable if this approach is used because of lack of auditor expertise regarding computer processing.

The second term that has evolved is "auditing through the computer." It refers to the auditor's actual evaluation of the hardware and software to determine the reliability of operations that cannot be viewed by the human eye. Auditing through has become more common in practice because more and more computer systems do not operate as speedy calculators but have significant control procedures built into their systems. Thus, ignoring a computer system and the controls built into it would amount to ignoring important features of internal control.

More recently, two new terms have been used to describe the auditor's approach to computer systems: (1) "auditing without the computer" and (2) "auditing with the computer." The first approach consists of using visible evidence, such as the input source data, the machine-produced error listings, the visible control points (e.g., use of batch totals), and the detailed printed output. The second approach is also referred to as computer-assisted audit techniques (CAATs) as per EDP–1 and EDP–2. When auditing a simple computer system, CAATs refers to such audit techniques as the use of the following (EDP–2):

- Tests of details of transactions and balances—for example, the use of audit software to test all (or a sample) of the transactions in a computer file.

- Analytical review procedures—for example, the use of audit software to identify unusual fluctuations or items.

- Compliance tests of general EDP controls—for example, the use of test data to test access procedures to the program libraries.

- Compliance tests of EDP application controls—for example, the use of test data to test the functioning of a programmed procedure.

Exhibit 8–3 shows the scheme of auditing around the computer. The auditors select a sample of source documents for a tracing procedure to test the controls over recording sales transactions. The client's computer system processes the transactions, but the auditor treats it like a "black box," interested only in the correspondence of the input (customer's order, quantity shipped, and amount billed) to the output (debit to accounts receivable, credit to sales revenue).

TESTS OF COMPUTER CONTROLS IN SIMPLE BATCH SYSTEMS

LEARNING OBJECTIVE

7. Explain how the auditor can perform the test of controls audit of computerized controls in a simple computer system.

In the simple batch systems described earlier, adequate evidence of control performance frequently exists in the printed output and logs (thus, auditing around the computer is possible). For example, input error reports usually will contain examples of each type of error the edit routines are designed to detect. A sample of each type of error can be traced to the error log maintained by the computer control group and to evidence of correction and resubmission. Likewise, printed documentation may exist of compliance with authorized procedures required for execution of transactions or for changes to master files.

EXHIBIT 8–3   EXAMPLE OF AUDITING AROUND THE COMPUTER

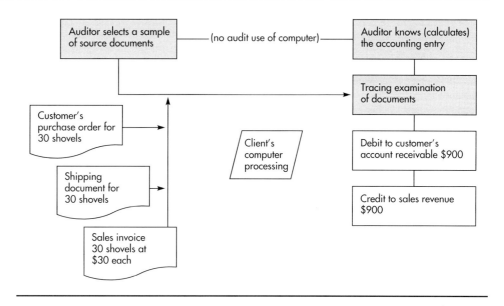

However, external auditors occasionally must use the computer as an audit tool to test the controls within the application programs of even simple systems. (Internal auditors more frequently utilize these techniques.) Thus, a consideration of the use of the computer as an "auditor's assistant" in test of controls audit procedures is the next topic for you to study.

Two Approaches for Using the Computer in Test of Controls Audit Procedures

Auditors can use two approaches to audit through the computer and with the computer to test controls: (1) audit the programmed processing controls with simulated data and (2) audit the programmed controls with live data reprocessed with an audit program. The auditing of programmed control procedures with simulated data generally is referred to as test data, while the reprocessing of live data to test program controls is called parallel simulation.

Test Data
The basic concept of test data is that once a computer is programmed to handle transactions in a certain logical way, it will faithfully handle every transaction exactly the same way. This is the uniformity principle we introduced at the beginning of the chapter. Therefore, the audit team need only prepare a limited number of simulated transactions (some with "errors" and some without) to determine whether each control operates as described in the program documentation.

A **test deck** is a sample of one of each possible combination of data fields that may be processed through the real system. Test deck is a term that refers to the earliest days of computer system operation when all input was prepared on punched card media. Today, simulated test data will more likely be on tape or disk. Test data also may be entered into an on-line system through computer terminals. The purpose of using test data is to determine whether controls operate as described in questionnaire responses and program flowcharts. Test transactions may consist of abstractions from real transactions and of simulated transactions generated by the auditors' imagination.[4] The auditors must prepare a worksheet listing each transaction and the predicted output based on the program documentation. Then these test transactions must be converted to the normal machine-sensed input form, and arrangements must be made to process the transactions with the actual program used for real transactions.

Auditors must be very familiar with the nature of the business and the logic of the programs to anticipate all data combinations that might exist as transaction input or that might be generated by processing. They must be able to assign degrees of audit importance to each kind of error-checking control method. Further, they must ensure that the test data do not get commingled with real transactions and change the actual master files.

Consider an example of processing sales transactions. Assume that the objective of the test is to check the controls over accuracy of input data. The problem is to assemble a set of transactions that includes important error conditions in order to determine whether the input and processing controls can detect them.

For example, the audit team can create hypothetical transactions with the following conditions:

1. No customer code number.
2. Invalid customer code number (wrong check digit).
3. Bill of lading document number not entered.
4. Sales amount greater than $25,000.
5. Sales amount equal to zero.
6. Sales amount less than zero.

These six conditions generate many possible combinations of transactions. An example of 15 of them is shown in a decision table presented with problem 19.24 (Exhibit 19.24–1) at the end of Chapter 19. The auditors know that transactions having no customer number or no bill of lading document number (missing data test), an invalid customer code number (self-checking number test), a sales amount greater than $25,000 (limit test), a sales amount equal to zero (missing data test), or a sales amount less than zero (sign test) should produce error messages. Transactions with valid conditions should not. The auditors arrange to run these simulated transactions on the client's system and to find out whether the controls operate.

Test data are processed at a single point in time with the client program that is supposed to have been used during the period under audit. After the analysis of test output, the audit manager still must make an inference about processing throughout the entire period. In order to do so, he or she must be satisfied by a review of documentation that any program changes have been authorized and correctly made. Some auditors occasionally perform test data procedures on an irregular, surprise basis during the year.

Exhibit 8–4 shows the scheme of testing controls with test data. (You should compare it to Exhibit 8–3, the example of auditing around the computer.) The auditors create source document input that can contain accurate as well as erroneous

---

[4] This may be an oversimplification because computer systems may have multiple controls that create thousands of error combinations and possible test transactions. Computerized test data generators are available to help auditors overcome the magnitude of the test data creation task.

EXHIBIT 8–4   EXAMPLE OF AUDITING CONTROLS WITH TEST DATA (through the computer)

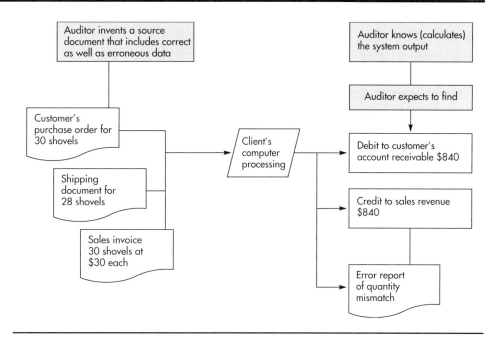

conditions, in this case a shipment of fewer units than the customer ordered. The auditors know the desired outcome—an error message that the quantity shipped and the quantity billed do not match, perhaps with an accounting entry to charge the customer for the shipped quantity. If this result does not appear from the processing of the test data, the auditors can conclude that the processing control over accurate sales recording contains a deficiency (weakness). The auditors are testing the control procedures embedded in the computer program, and they are using the actual processing program for the test. When using test data, the auditor can focus on unusual transactions or error conditions rather than a large number of similar transactions. The reasoning is that if the program handles one transaction correctly, then it will handle other similar transactions the same way. However, the test deck provides a control test only at a specific point in time. In order to rely on the program controls for a period of time, the auditor will also need to obtain assurance that general controls such as controls over program changes are in place and operating over the same time period.

Parallel Simulation

In parallel simulation the audit team prepares a computer program (utilizing generalized audit software described later in this chapter) designed to process client data properly. The result of the auditors' processing of real client data is compared with the result of the real data processed by the actual client program. The concept of this method is illustrated in Exhibit 8–5.

To test the controls contained in computer programs, auditors have the options of (1) using the client's real programs, (2) having client personnel write special programs, or (3) writing their own special programs to collect evidence that the controls

E X H I B I T   8–5   SYSTEM CONCEPT OF PARALLEL SIMULATION

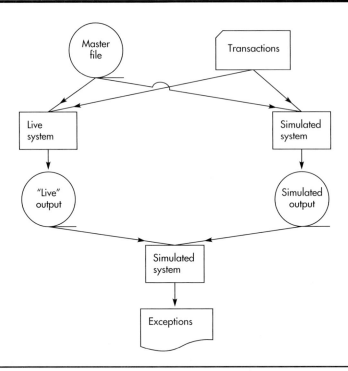

work. The first option would be used in the test data technique described in the previous section. The second option requires close supervision and testing to ensure that the client's personnel have prepared the audit program correctly. The third option is parallel simulation, and it requires significant programming expertise of the audit staff or close liaison with expert independent programmers.

However, with **generalized audit software** the parallel simulation option has become much more attractive. The generalized audit software programs consist of numerous prepackaged subroutines that can perform most tasks needed in auditing and business applications. The auditor's programming task consists of writing simple instructions that call up one or more of the subroutines. Thus, there is no need to write complete, complex programs, and the expertise to use the generalized software can be acquired in one week of training. (You will get a closer look at these generalized audit software programs and their capabilities later in this chapter.)

Using the generalized audit program capabilities, an auditor can construct a system of data processing that will accept the same input as the real program, use the same files, and attempt to produce the same results. This simulated system will contain all the controls the auditor believes appropriate, and, in this respect, the thought process is quite similar to the logic that goes into preparing test data. The simulated-system output then is compared to the real-system output for correspondence or difference, and at this point the audit evidence is similar to the evidence obtained by using test data with the real program: conclusions can be reached about the error-detection capabilities of the real system.

Another way to create a parallel system is to conduct a thorough technical audit of the controls in the client's actual program, then keep a copy of it secure in the auditors' files. Actual client data later can be processed using this audited copy of the client's program (e.g., at times later in the year under audit or in the following year audit). The goal is to determine whether output from the program the client actually used in processing data produces satisfactory accounting output when compared to the output from the auditors' controlled copy of the program. This approach is often called **controlled reprocessing**, and it is a version of parallel simulation.

The first audit application of parallel simulation may be very costly, although it probably will be more efficient than auditing without the computer or utilizing test data. Real economies are realized, however, in subsequent audits of the same client.

The audit team must take care to determine that the real transactions selected for processing are "representative." Thus, some exercise in random selection and identification of important transactions may be required in conjunction with parallel processing. The illustration in the box below is based on the illustrative sales–accounts receivable system described in the Kingston Company case study at the end of this chapter.

Parallel Simulation

A parallel simulation of Kingston Company's sales invoice and accounts receivable processing system revealed that invoices that showed no bill of lading or shipment reference were processed and charged to customers with a corresponding credit to sales. Further audit of the exceptions showed that the real-data processing program did not contain a missing-data test and did not provide error messages for lack of shipping references. This finding led to (1) a more extensive test of the sales invoice population with comparison to shipping documents and (2) a more extensive audit of accounts receivable for customers who were charged with such sales.

The ultimate goal of the computer methods of test of controls auditing is to reach a conclusion about the actual operation of controls in a computer system. This conclusion allows the audit manager to assess the control risk and determine the nature, timing, and extent of substantive audit procedures for auditing the related account balances. This control risk assessment decision is crucial, particularly in computer systems, because subsequent audit work may be performed using machine readable files that are produced by the computerized information system. The data processing control over such files is important since their content is utilized later in computer-assisted work using generalized audit software.

· ·

R E V I E W
C H E C K P O I N T S

8.21 What is the difference between auditing "through the computer" and auditing "with the computer"?

8.22 What is the difference between the computerized test of controls audit procedures of "test data" and "parallel simulation"?

8.23 "The use of the test data technique to test the client's application control procedures is unprofessional. We don't enter fake transactions into a client's manual system. Why should we do it in their computer system?" Evaluate this position and question posed by an audit partner.

8.24   What is "controlled reprocessing?"

8.25   Why is the auditors' test of computer controls and assessment of related control risk considered "crucial?"

. . . .

Generalized Audit Software

LEARNING   OBJECTIVE
8. Describe the use of generalized audit software.

Generalized audit software (GAS) programs are a set of functions that may be utilized to read, compute, and operate on machine-readable records. Audit software provides access to audit evidence that otherwise would be unavailable. This part of the chapter builds on the computer-related concepts and terminology, and the tests of controls auditing covered in the previous sections of this chapter. However, the emphasis is shifted from the assessment of control risk to the techniques of using the computer to assist with gathering substantive evidential matter about transaction details and account balances.

You need to know about generalized audit software (GAS) because it is used on most audits where the client's accounting records are stored in computer files or a database. The following material does not attempt to prepare you to use any particular generalized audit software because each audit organization has its own GAS and will provide the training to use its particular package. Instead, this section provides you with an understanding of what GAS packages can accomplish and, most important, where the general auditor needs to be involved in a GAS application.

Auditing with the Computer

The audit problems following assessment of control risk in a computer environment are to gain access to machine-readable detail records, to select samples of items for manual or computer audit procedures, to perform calculations and analyses of entire data files, and to produce audit working papers of the work performed. GAS packages were first developed by CA firms in the mid-1960s for specific application to audit engagements and have been improved and adapted with the changes in technology. The essential advantages of a generalized audit software package are:

Original programming is not required. The generalized package consists of a set of preprogrammed editing, operating, and output subroutines.

The required programming is easy. A simple, limited set of programming instructions using preprinted specification forms is used to call up the subroutines in the package. Training time is short. About one week of intensive training is sufficient to learn how to program a GAS package.

For special-purpose analysis of data files, GAS is more efficient than special programs written from scratch because of the little time required for writing the instructions to call up the appropriate functions of the generalized audit software package. Also, the same software can be used on various clients' computer systems. Control and specific tailoring are achieved through the auditors' own ability to program and operate the system. A large number of GAS packages are currently available through CA firms and consulting firms.

Audit Procedures Performed by Generalized Audit Software

Computer accounting applications capture and generate voluminous amounts of data that usually are available only on machine-readable records. GAS can be used to access the data and organize it into a format useful to the audit team. Audit software can be used with four of the six basic audit techniques of *Section* 5100.02 of the *Handbook.*[5]

1. Computation.   Verification of calculations can be done by the computer with more speed and accuracy than by hand. The audit software can be used to test the accuracy of client computations and to perform analytical procedures to evaluate the reasonableness of account balances. Examples of this use are to (*a*) recalculate depreciation expense, (*b*) recalculate extensions on inventory items, (*c*) compute file totals, and (*d*) compare budgeted, standard, and prior-year data with current-year data.

2. Confirmation.   Auditors can program statistical or judgmental criteria for selecting customers' accounts receivable, loans, and other receivables for confirmation. The GAS can be used to print the confirmations and get them ready for mailing. It can do everything except carry them to the post office!

3a. Inspection.   GAS can compare audit evidence from other sources to company records efficiently. The audit evidence must be converted to machine-readable form and then can be compared to the company records on computer files. Examples are (*a*) comparing inventory test counts with perpetual records, (*b*) comparing adjusted audit balances on confirmed accounts receivable to the audit file of book balances, and (*c*) comparing vendor statement amounts to the company's record of accounts payable.

3b. Inspection.   Auditors can use GAS to examine records to determine quality, completeness, consistency, and correctness. This is the computer version of scanning the records for exceptions to the auditors' criteria. For example, GAS can scan (*a*) accounts receivable balances for amounts over the credit limit, (*b*) inventory quantities for negative or unreasonably large balances, (*c*) payroll files for terminated employees, and (*d*) loan files for loans with negative balances.

4a. Analysis.   Comparing data on separate files can be accomplished by GAS to determine whether compatible information is in agreement. Differences can be printed out for investigation and reconciliation. Examples are comparing (*a*) payroll details with personnel records, (*b*) current and prior inventory to details of purchases and sales, (*c*) paid vouchers to check disbursements, and (*d*) current and prior-year fixed asset records to identify dispositions.

4b. Analysis.   GAS can summarize and sort data in a variety of ways. Examples are (*a*) preparing general ledger trial balances, (*b*) sorting inventory items by location to facilitate observations, and (*c*) summarizing inventory turnover statistics for obsolescence analysis.

Using Generalized Audit Software

For the most part, the widely used GAS packages are very similar. Regardless of the particular GAS used, five distinct phases are involved in developing a GAS application: (1) define audit objectives, (2) plan the application, (3) design the application, (4) code and test the application, and (5) process the application and evaluate the results.

[5] CICA, *Application of Computer-Assisted Audit Techniques Using Microcomputers,* CICA (Toronto, 1994), p. 16.

1. Define the Audit Objective

The first step in applying GAS is to determine specific audit objectives. GAS should be viewed as a special tool providing auditors with a means to accomplish their objectives, not as an objective in itself.

For example, the general audit objectives might be to audit management's assertions that the accounts receivable balance represents detail accounts which exist, are complete, and are valued correctly. Based on these general objectives, specific procedures may include footing the accounts subsidiary ledger master file, selecting a sample of accounts for confirmation, preparing an aged trial balance, and investigating accounts with overdue balances.

2. Feasibility and Planning

Feasibility should be considered in three ways: (1) Is the use of audit software technically feasible? (2) Are alternative ways to accomplish the audit task available? (3) Which of the alternatives is the most practical and economical? If the use of GAS is technically feasible, other considerations as listed in the next box must be weighed.

FEASIBILITY CONSIDERATIONS

Cost-effectiveness of hardware and software.
Technical complexity including access to client data.
Availability of qualified audit software staff.
Other issues including client concern about data security.

Source: Application of Computer-Assisted Audit Techniques Using Microcomputers, CICA (Toronto, 1994), p. 20.

Audit software may be the most practical way to achieve the audit objective, but it is seldom the only way. Audit resources (qualified people and their time) must be allocated carefully to achieve efficient and effective results. Using GAS requires considerable investment in time and effort and may be efficient only when repeated use is anticipated on return engagements. Obviously the data must be available. The desired files, especially detailed transaction files, often are retained only for a short time. The availability of data files and the degree of client co-operation normally would be determined during the general and application controls review. Client co-operation in turn could be affected by such issues as client concerns over the security of confidential or sensitive data, including the risk of auditors introducing computer viruses into client computers.

After determining the feasibility of using GAS, the audit manager should determine specifically how it will be used, establish control procedures for all subsequent steps, and arrange the logistics with the data center. Specific planning steps are listed in the next box.

The planning phase is also the time to define the workpapers that will document the GAS application. The audit manager, not the computer auditor specialist, should determine what computer output representing coding and testing should be retained in the workpapers. The computer output may be in the form of computer-readable workpapers, such as audit files on diskette.

Planning Steps

Set application objectives.
Determine content and accessibility of the client's files.
Define transactions to test procedures and output requirements.
Identify client personnel to provide technical assistance.
Determine computer and software needs.
Prepare GAS application budgets and timetables.
Execute GAS application.
Evaluate the results.

Source: EDP Audit Guideline on Computer-Assisted Audit Techniques (EDP–2, p. 7).

3. Application Design

Developing a GAS application is much like the client's procedures for developing a new application system. However, a complete description of the application phase is beyond the scope of this book. It should be undertaken only by specially trained audit staff. The application design expands the ideas developed during the feasibility and planning stage into detailed descriptions necessary for preparing coded computer instructions. The documentation of the application design phase includes the GAS application system flowchart, logic descriptions, detailed report layouts, list of control points and procedures, record formats, and a test plan. Frequently, the auditor must obtain a computer dump of a few records of each client file to ensure that subsequent coding is based on accurate information. The application must be thoroughly tested with sample client data or simulated data until the audit manager is confident that the GAS application works as desired. The client's file should not be used for testing; the auditor should obtain a copy for testing purposes.

4. Coding and Testing

Most GAS packages have an extensive repertoire of powerful instructions to facilitate processing data files and preparing audit output. The coding is done on specially designed forms (or computer screens for on-line coding).

Coding converts the application design into specific operational requirements (computer language) of the package in use. As coding progresses, the sequence and the logic should be challenged and reviewed. The coding must be converted to a machine-readable form, and all syntax errors must be removed (errors due to failure to follow the rules of the package). Then the coded instructions must be compiled (converted into the hardware machine language like any computer program).

Once the coding errors are removed, the logic must be tested. Testing is very similar to the test data approach used in test of controls auditing of client programs described earlier in this chapter. The test plan defined in the design phase should be extensive enough to test each logic path and anticipate all variations of client data.

5. Processing and Evaluation

The foregoing phases are usually accomplished during interim work—before the year-end. Thus, everything is tested and ready for processing of the year-end balances. The processing phase involves (1) verifying that the status of the client file has not changed, (2) obtaining a copy of the client file, (3) processing the GAS application against the copy of the client's file(s), and (4) reviewing results, updating working papers, and retaining audit files. The audit team should carefully monitor and control the actual processing and the output. Control procedures established during the design phase should be followed. Planned totals should be compared to results and the totals logged on control working papers. The audit manager should review the output for reasonableness and clarity. Finally, the documentation workpapers of the application must be completed and filed.

Special care must be taken to leave adequate documentation for subsequent use on a repeat engagement. (In a sense this documentation is the "audit trail of the audit.") The working papers frequently will contain a list of suggested modifications for next year's audit.

In summary, following the feasibility and planning phase, a GAS application should be designed to achieve specific audit objectives. The reliability of general application computer controls, the availability of client files, access to the computer and technical assistance, and estimated costs and the availability of GAS-trained audit staff must be evaluated. The noncomputer-trained auditor should be actively involved in the definition of audit objectives and the application plan. The computer auditor will utilize the application design to link the coding and testing to the planning phase. Results of testing should be reviewed by the audit manager. In the processing phase audit software is run under control of the computer auditor to process copies of client files and produce audit results.

Planning and testing are the most critical tasks in the development of a GAS application. If planning is not adequate, the audit objectives may not be achieved. Problems are likely to occur in subsequent phases and require excessive time and effort to correct. Testing must be adequate or the probability of success is low. Once processing is commenced after year-end, it is extremely difficult to correct errors and deficiencies.

Many larger companies have internal auditors skilled in using GAS. Independent (external) auditors may utilize the internal auditors to develop and run the GAS application under supervision and review of the external audit manager.

Generalized Audit Software Limitations

Notwithstanding the powers of the computer, several good auditing procedures are outside its reach. The computer cannot observe and count physical things (inventory, for example), but it can compare auditor-made counts to the computer records.

The computer cannot examine external and internal documentation; thus, it cannot vouch accounting output to sources of basic evidence. An exception would exist in an advanced computer system that stored the basic source documents on magnetic media. The auditor would have to test the controls over creation of the files but then would have no choice but to treat the file as a basic "document" source. This is further discussed in Chapter 19. When manual vouching is involved, computer-assisted selection of sample items is a great efficiency. Probably the biggest problem auditors encounter in using CAATs is obtaining the data in a format that can be used on their computers. Issues that must be addressed in advance include compatibility of the client's with the auditor's system, data structures in the client's system, and availability of client staff to download the data for use by the auditor.[6] Finally, the computer cannot conduct an enquiry in the limited sense that the enquiry procedure refers to questionnaires and conversations.

---

[6] Trites, G. *Audit of a Small Business*, CICA (Toronto, 1994), pp. 50–51.

8.26 What is generalized audit software?

8.27 What advantages are derived from using generalized audit software to perform recalculations? to select samples and print confirmations?

8.28 What are five audit procedures that can be performed using generalized audit software?

8.29 What are the phases of developing an application using generalized audit software? What are the noncomputer auditor's responsibilities in each phase.

8.30 Why are the testing and planning tasks the most critical when using generalized audit software?

8.31 When a generalized audit software application is planned, which member of the audit team should have the responsibility of deciding about the computer output that should be retained in the working papers?

8.32 Evaluate the following statement by a senior computer auditor: "The time to be thinking about generalized audit software procedures is at the beginning when we obtain an understanding of the control structure."

USING THE MICROCOMPUTER AS AN AUDIT TOOL

LEARNING OBJECTIVE
9. Describe how the microcomputer can be used as an audit tool.

The microcomputer has revolutionized auditing. You have probably already learned to use the microcomputer to prepare accounting schedules with spreadsheet software and to use word processing software to prepare your class papers. The audit microcomputer software makes use of these same microcomputer software tools to prepare auditing working papers, audit programs, and audit memos.

Several GAS have been designed for use on microcomputers, two of the most common in Canada being Interactive Data Extraction and Analysis (IDEA), which is sold and supported by the CICA, and ACL, which is sold by a West Coast vendor. These programs are relatively easy to use since little or no programming is required to use these packages.[7]

The microcomputer is being used regularly in small and large public accounting firms to perform such clerical steps as preparing the working trial balance, posting adjusting entries, grouping accounts that represent one line item on the financial statement into lead schedules, computing comparative financial statements and common ratios for analytical review, preparing supporting workpaper schedules, and producing draft financial statements. Many of the large firms also are using the microcomputer to assess control risk, perform sophisticated analytical functions on individual accounts, access public and firm databases for analysis of unusual accounting and auditing problems, and utilize decision support software in making complex evaluations. Exhibit 8–6 illustrates the different phases a typical public accounting firm or internal audit department may go through in the use of the microcomputer as an audit tool.

In addition to the various uses of the microcomputer listed in Exhibit 8–6, you can expect a highly integrated microcomputer-based audit process, one that will allow

___

[7] Ibid, p. 50.

E X H I B I T 8–6   PHASES FOR THE USE OF THE MICROCOMPUTER AS AN AUDIT TOOL

Applications	Goals and Objectives	Software Available
Phase 1: Automating the Audit Process		
Trial balance and working papers	Overall audit efficiency.	Automated workpapers vendor supplied, developed by PA firms and others.
Adjusting and updating financial data	Automation of time-consuming activities.	
Time and budget data	Improved control.	Vendor supplied.
Audit program, memo, and report generation	Efficient and more readable.	Word processing.
Phase 2: Basic Auditing Functions		
Spreadsheet analysis working papers	Efficiency in common working papers.	Vendor supplied, firm-developed uses.
Analytical review	Improved overall analysis	Part of automated workpaper packages.
Sampling planning, selection, and evaluation	Evidence collection and evaluation efficiency.	Statistical, firm developed.
Phase 3: Advanced Auditing Functions		
Analytical procedures for specific accounts	Improved auditor analysis.	Firm developed.
Access to client files on larger computers	Ability to download directly into automated workpaper software.	Vendor supplied or firm developed.
Access to firm and public databases	Provide auditor with reference information.	Micro as a terminal, telecommunication.
GAS functions	Mainframe GAS workpapers downloaded to micro.	Firm developed.
Modelling and decision support systems	Improved auditor decisions.	Firm-developed decision support systems.
Audit-file collection Continuous monitoring	Use the techniques in Chapter 19.	Embedded Audit Modules

Source: Adapted from Clinton E. White, "The Microcomputer as an Audit Tool," *Journal of Accountancy*, December 1983, p. 117 (as modified).

future auditors to control and document the audit from the engagement letter to the audit report and accompanying financial statements. The preliminary audit program will be generated automatically following answers to internal control questionnaires and other programmed audit risk evaluators. The accounting data for the trial balance will be entered into the microcomputer workpapers automatically, and all lead schedules and supporting workpapers will be generated. Related analytical procedure workpapers will be produced using not only client data but also related industry data (most likely downloaded from the Internet), with suggestions made to update the preliminary audit program. Virtually every element of this integrated microcomputer audit is currently in use or being developed. The integration and the degree of sophistication will develop further uses of the microcomputer as an audit tool. In particular, the availability of audit software enables the auditor to:

- simulate all or part of the process by which the data supporting management's assertions were compiled.
- extract information for substantive tests and tests of controls, based on the client's data supporting the subject matter of the engagement.

- prepare information directly relevant to high inherent and control risk items (e.g., approvals of limits for high risk customers).[8]

As a result of acquisition of microcomputers or computer services by even the smallest businesses, information in electronic format has become very common. As a result it has become more feasible for auditors to make effective use of microcomputers in small business audits. Some of the opportunities for using a microcomputer in a small business audit relate to trial balance and financial statement software, preparation of audit programs, planning and administration, and computer-assisted audit techniques (CAATs). Common applications of CAATs in small businesses include accounts receivable, confirmation and aging, footing and extending inventory files, and selecting inventory items for price testing. The ability of CAATs to check an entire file with little additional effort is a major advantage because it allows the auditor to obtain a higher degree of audit assurance, at little additional cost.

R E V I E W
C H E C K P O I N T S

8.33 What audit tasks can be accomplished with microcomputer word processing?

8.34 Describe automated workpaper software that can be used with microcomputers.

8.35 How could microcomputer spreadsheet packages be used to generate supporting workpapers, such as bank reconciliations, that could be used on more than one audit?

SUMMARY

Computer auditing is not something for future consideration. It is encountered in almost all audits today. Even though computer technology changes the accounting system and the control environment, it does not change the basic auditing standards. Qualities of competence, independence, due care, planning, control risk assessment, and sufficient competent evidence are not changed. However, the nuances and aspects of achieving them must be tailored to a world of computers.

It is very tempting to compare computer accounting systems and computer-oriented auditing to manual accounting and manual auditing. Chapter 8 tried to avoid overworking these comparisons because computers are a way of life, not a departure from a basic manual world. Nevertheless, audit planning begins with learning about a client's extent of computer use—the type of personnel organization, computer equipment, and the significant accounting applications.

Numerous general and specific control procedures were explained, starting with the "general control procedures" and proceeding to the "application control procedures." However, the application control procedures were not in Chapter 8. They were introduced in Chapter 6, where internal control was also introduced; thus, computer control concepts were intergrated with control considerations in all audits.

---

[8] CICA, *Application of Computer-Assisted Audit Techniques Using Microcomputers*, CICA, 1994, p. 17.

These application procedures were then cross-referenced in Chapter 8 for review/ study from Chapter 6. Some control questionnaire items were added to them in Chapter 8.

A useful distinction was made in this chapter between simple computer systems and advanced computer systems. The simple systems are characterized as batch systems, and the advanced systems are ones that have sophisticated data communication, database integration, automatic transaction initiation, or an unconventional audit trail. The brief introduction to advanced systems serves as a warning about the complexities of large-scale computer systems.

This chapter also had a section with a small business orientation to micro-minicomputer systems. Their characteristics and typical control problems were described. This section was similar to the small business section in Chapter 6, where students were warned not to expect to find all the bureaucratic features of big business control in small clients.

CASE STUDY	KINGSTON COMPANY

Computer Introduction

The description of the Kingston Company in Chapters 4 and 5 mentioned a new information systems department. To make the case more realistic to actual data processing methods used by a business of this size, the case now introduces you to Kingston's computerized accounting system.

The information systems department became active in July. At that time the director, Lynn Thomas, was promoted to vice president. Kingston obtained its Hewlett-Packard (HP) minicomputer soon after and began testing the hardware and software. Lynn decided to use the HP accounting software. The testing of the HP computer system progressed throughout the early fall with the accounting processing run on both the old manual system and the new computer system for the month of September. On October 1 Kingston converted to the HP system.

As the new computer system was designed and customized to Kingston's needs, every effort was made to keep as many as possible of the procedures and business documents used in the manual system. This made the transition to the computer system easy for the employees, thus reducing training and employee objections to the computer. Further, most of the controls and duties previously described were retained.

Hardware Description

You will not be too concerned with the computer hardware in this case; however, to make the case realistic, a Hewlett-Packard Business Computer System is assumed. The main memory of the computer has 320 MB (megabytes, or 320 million bytes) of storage capacity. This system can support 400 terminals, although fewer are used by Kingston. The system utilizes several disk drives on which the computer software and the active accounting databases are stored. Two tape drives are on-line to provide the logging of transactions and to provide means to back up the data on the disk drives. The computer room contains two printers—a laser printer and a 1,000-lines-per-minute contact printer. A 200-characters-per-second printer is located in the accounting department.

Accounting Software

The financial accounting software is an integrated application combining a comprehensive set of general ledger, accounts receivable, and accounts payable functions. The package is used through a series of menu screens that appear on the user's terminals. The accounting personnel are guided through each application by these means. By pressing a key labelled with a particular function (function key), users are guided up and down the menu hierarchy.

```
                            HP FINANCIAL ACCOUNTING

General Accounting Menu                                              GA MENU
--------------------------------------------------------------------------

    Company C100            Company Name: Kingston Company

    GL MAIN MENU            General Ledger Module

    AR MAIN MENU            Accounts Receivable Module

    AP MAIN MENU            Accounts Payable Module

    PAR MENU               Global and module specific parameter

    MODIFY DEFAULTS       Modify company default

    BYE                    Return to security screen


    --------------------------------------------------------------------------



    GL MAIN     AR MAIN     AP MAIN    PAR              modify        BYE
     MENU        MENU        MENU      MENU            defaults
```

Two levels of security are provided in the system. The terminals require a special password to allow their use. Access to any function (data entry, data review, report invocation) for each unique set of transactions is controlled by another set of passwords. Thus, allowed operations are isolated to the department that must enter and use the data. For example, the order entry accounting clerks cannot access the cash disbursement records or enter cash disbursement transactions without knowledge of the appropriate passwords.

The financial accounting system allows on-line entry with on-line data validation and on-line posting. However, to provide better control, Kingston has elected to utilize batch entry, deferred validation, and deferred posting. In this mode the data are not validated at the time of entry. A special input validation routine, which reports all validation errors, is employed after the batches are balanced. The erroneous entries can be corrected through maintenance functions. The transfers of transactions from the accounts receivable and accounts payable modules to the general ledger module also are done in batch mode. Batches are validated and posted every night; thus, the detailed accounting records are never more than one day from being accurate. Jonathan Roberts, the internal audit manager, insisted that Kingston start the accounting processing in this mode to establish control. As employees become more familiar with the terminal entry and control over transaction entry proves adequate, he will consider moving to on-line data entry and on-line input validation.

Organization and Duties of Information Systems Personnel

The information systems department consists of the director of MIS (management information systems), Lynn Thomas, a systems development project manager, and two programmer/analysts, an operations manager (who also serves as the librarian and control clerk), and two machine operators. Following is a brief summary of the responsibilities and duties of each.

Director of MIS

The director of MIS is responsible for the overall computer processing. Included in her responsibilities are long-range planning, setting policy and procedures for information systems (IS) employees, approving all equipment purchases, and preparing the department budget. The director also provides the primary contact with other department vice presidents and has overall responsibility for training other department personnel in the use of the new system. She works with the systems development manager and the various users to set priorities for the programmer/analysts.

Systems Development Project Manager

The project manager is primarily responsible for all modifications to the financial accounting system and other systems development projects. He creates the specifications for projects after consultation with the users and assigns projects to the programmer/analysts. Other responsibilities include interface with the users on a one-to-one basis to resolve their problems and consider their requests for modifications, education of the programmer/analysts, and working with the HP service representatives on software problems.

Operations Manager

The operations manager's primary responsibilities are to ensure that the computer is operating properly and to direct the work of the two operators. Additional duties include system security, librarian, database administrator, and control clerk. The operations manager also is the person who works with HP hardware service and maintenance personnel.

Kingston Case Assignments

8.36   Effect of the Kingston Computer on Planning.   Anderson, Olds & Watershed (AOW) were aware of the pending computer installation. In fact, the planned conversion was discussed and AOW was advised of the conversion process by the director of internal audit.

Mr. Wardlaw, the AOW engagement partner, has called you into his office to discuss the planning and staffing of the Kingston engagement. He is particularly concerned with how the processing of the last quarter's transactions by the computer will affect AOW's audit this year.

Required:

Assume you are the senior for the Kingston audit. Draft a memo to Mr. Wardlaw indicating how planning might be affected by the computer processing of accounting transactions. Organize your memo by the planning considerations mentioned in this chapter (extent computer used, complexity of computer operations, organization structure of computer activities, availability of data, computer-assisted audit techniques, and need for specialized skills). You will find it helpful to review the chapter material on the micro-minicomputer environment.

8.37   Kingston Company Information Systems Department Duties.

One of Mr. Wardlaw's specific concerns is whether there is adequate separation of duties within the information systems department. He is not very knowledgeable about computers and computer accounting processing and, therefore, is relying on you to educate him on the proper separation of computer duties and whether AOW should have concerns about the organization of Kingston's new information systems department.

Required:

Draft a memo to Mr. Wardlaw indicating (*a*) proper separation of duties in any computer data processing department and (*b*) a description of the deficiencies in separation of duties that exist in the Kingston Company's information systems department.

8.38   Documentation of Kingston Company's Computer Processing.

Documentation of the computer accounting system was described in this chapter as a primary source of information for the auditor in understanding the system as part of the preliminary review. Although the case description in this chapter did not mention documentation, there is documentation describing the system, especially since the hardware and accounting software was purchased from Hewlett-Packard.

Required:

Prepare a list of hardware and software documentation that you would expect to find at the Kingston Company that describes its new computer accounting system and that would be useful to you as an auditor in understanding the flow of transactions and the computer controls.

MULTIPLE-CHOICE QUESTIONS FOR PRACTICE AND REVIEW

8.39 In an electronic data processing system, automated equipment controls or hardware controls are designed to:
   a. Arrange data in a logical sequential manner for processing purposes.
   b. Correct errors in the computer programs.
   c. Monitor and detect errors in source documents.
   d. Detect and control errors arising from use of equipment.

8.40 A good example of application (user) computer software is:
   a. Payroll processing program.
   b. Operating system program.
   c. Data management system software.
   d. Utility programs.

8.41 Which of the following statements most likely represents a disadvantage for a company that performs its accounting using microcomputers?
   a. It is usually difficult to detect arithmetic errors.
   b. Unauthorized persons find it easy to access the computer and alter the data files.
   c. Transactions are coded for account classifications before they are processed on the computer.
   d. Random errors in report printing are rare in packaged software systems.

8.42 A procedural control used in the management of a computer centre to minimize the possibility of data or program

file destruction through operator error includes:
a. Control figures.
b. Crossfooting tests.
c. Limit checks.
d. External labels.

8.43 Which of the following is not a characteristic of a batch-processed computer system?
a. The collection of like transactions that are sorted and processed sequentially against a master file.
b. Keyboard input of transactions, followed by machine processing.
c. The production of numerous printouts.
d. The posting of a transaction, as it occurs, to several files, without intermediate printouts.

8.44 What is the computer process called when data processing is performed concurrently with a particular activity and the results are available soon enough to influence the particular course of action being taken or the decision being made?
a. Batch processing.
b. Real-time processing.
c. Integrated data processing.
d. Random access processing.

8.45 The client's computerized exception-reporting system helps an auditor to conduct a more efficient audit because it:
a. Condenses data significantly.
b. Highlights abnormal conditions.

c. Decreases the tests of computer controls requirements.
d. Is efficient computer input control.

8.46 Auditors often make use of computer programs that perform routine processing functions, such as sorting and merging. These programs are made available by software companies and are specifically referred to as:
a. Compiler programs.
b. Supervisory programs.
c. Utility programs.
d. User programs.

8.47 In the weekly computer run to prepare payroll cheques, a cheque was printed for an employee who had been terminated the previous week. Which of the following controls, if properly utilized, would have been most effective in preventing the error or ensuring its prompt detection?
a. A control total for hours worked, prepared from time cards collected by the timekeeping department.
b. Requiring the treasurer's office to account for the numbers of the prenumbered cheques issued to the computer department for the processing of the payroll.
c. Use of the check digit for employee numbers.
d. Use of a header label for the payroll input sheet.

Exercises and Problems

8.48 Computer Internal Control Questionnaire Evaluation. Assume that, when conducting procedures to obtain an understanding of the control structure in the Denton Seed Company, you checked "No" to the following internal control questionnaire items (selected from those illustrated in the chapter):
- Does access to on-line files require specific passwords to be entered to identify and validate the terminal user?

- Are control totals established by the user prior to submitting data for processing? (Order entry application subsystem.)
- Are input control totals reconciled to output control totals? (Order entry application subsystem.)

Required:
Describe the errors, irregularities, or misstatements that could occur due to the weaknesses indicated by the lack of controls.

8.49 Check Digit. Suppose that a credit sale was made to John Q. Smyth, customer account number 8149732. The last digit is a check calculated by the "Modulus 11 Prime Number" method. The data entry operator made an error and keyed in the customer as 8419732.

Required (refer to Chapter 11):
a. Calculate the check digit for the number that was keyed in.
b. How would the self-checking number control detect this data input error?

8.50 Explain Computer Control Procedures. At a meeting of the corporate audit committee attended by the general manager of the products division and you, representing the internal audit department, the following dialogue took place:

Jones (committee chair): Mr. Marks had suggested that the internal audit department conduct an audit of the computer activities of the products division.

Smith (general manager): I don't know much about the technicalities of computers, but the division has some of the best computer people in the company.

Jones: Do you know whether the internal controls protecting the system are satisfactory?

Smith: I suppose they are. No one has complained. What's so important about controls anyway, as long as the system works?

Jones turns to you and asks you to explain computer control policies and procedures.

Required:
Address your response to the following points:
a. State the principal objective of achieving control over (1) input, (2) processing, and (3) output.
b. Give at least three methods of achieving control over (1) source data, (2) processing, and (3) output.

8.51 File Retention and Backup. You have audited the financial statements of the Solt Manufacturing Company for several years and are making preliminary plans for the audit for the year ended June 30. This year, however, the company has installed and used a computer system for processing a portion of its accounting data.

The following output computer files are produced in the daily processing runs:
1. Cash disbursements sequenced by check number.
2. Outstanding payables balances (alphabetized).
3. Purchase journals arranged by (*a*) account charged and (*b*) vendor.

Company records, as described above, are maintained on magnetic tapes. All tapes are stored in a restricted area within the computer room. A grandfather-father-son policy is followed in retaining and safeguarding tape files.

Vouchers (with supporting invoices, receiving reports, and purchase order copies) are filed by vendor code. Another purchase order copy and the checks are filed numerically.

Required:
a. Explain the grandfather-father-son policy. Describe how files could be reconstructed when this policy is used.
b. Discuss whether company policies for retaining and safeguarding the tape files provide adequate protection against losses of data.

8.52 Separation of Duties and General Control Procedures. You are engaged to examine the financial statements of Horizon Incorporated, which has its own computer installation. During the preliminary understanding work, you found that Horizon lacked proper segregation of the programming and operating functions. As a result, you intensified the evaluation of the internal control structures surrounding the computer and concluded that the existing compensating general control procedures provided reasonable assurance that the objectives of internal control were being met.

Required:
a. In a properly functioning computer environment, how is the separation

of the programming and operating functions achieved?

b. What are the compensating general control procedures that you most likely found?

(AICPA adapted)

8.53 Advanced Computer Systems Control Procedures. The revenue ministry of one province is developing a new computer system for processing provincial income tax returns of individuals and corporations. The new system features direct data input and enquiry capabilities. Identification of taxpayers is provided by using the Social Insurance number for individuals and the federal identification number for corporations. The new system should be fully implemented in time for the next tax season. The new system will serve three primary purposes as described below:

1. Data will be input into the system directly from tax returns through terminals located at the central headquarters of the Department of Taxation.

2. The returns will be processed using the main computer facilities at central headquarters. The processing includes:

   a. Verification of mathematical accuracy.

   b. Auditing the reasonableness of deductions, tax due, and so forth through the use of edit routines; these routines also include a comparison of the current year's data with the prior year's data.

   c. Identification of returns that should be considered for audit by revenue agents of the department.

   d. Issuing refund cheques to taxpayers.

3. Enquiry service will be provided to taxpayers on request through the assistance of Tax Department personnel at five regional offices. A total of 50 terminals will be placed at the regional offices. A taxpayer will be allowed to determine the status of his or her return or get information from the last three years' returns by calling or visiting one of the department's regional offices.

The provincial revenue minister is concerned about data security over and above protection against natural hazards such as fire and flood. He is concerned with protection against the loss or damage of data during data input or processing. Also, both he and the provincial attorney general have discussed the general problem of data confidentiality. Both officials want to have all potential problems identified before the system is fully developed and implemented so that the proper controls can be incorporated into the new system.

Required:

a. Describe the potential confidentiality problems that could arise in each of the following three areas of processing and recommend the corrective action(s) to solve the problem: (1) Data input. (2) Processing of returns. (3) Data enquiry.

b. The provincial revenue minister wants to incorporate control procedures to provide data security against the loss, damage, or improper input or use of data during data input and processing. Identify the potential problems (other than of natural hazards such as fire and flood) for which the Department of Taxation should develop controls, and recommend the possible controls for each problem identified.

(CMA adapted)

8.54 Computer Frauds and Missing Control Procedures. The following are brief stories of actual employee thefts and embezzlements perpetrated using computers.

Required:

What kind of control procedures were missing or inoperative that might have prevented or detected the fraud?

a. An accounts payable terminal operator at a subsidiary company fabricated false invoices from a fictitious vendor, and entered them in the parent company's central accounts payable/cash disbursement system. Five cheques totalling $155,000 were issued to the "vendor."

b. A bank provided custodial and recordkeeping services for several mutual funds. A proof-and-control department employee substituted his own name and account number for those of the actual purchasers of some shares. He used the computerized recordkeeping and correction system to conceal and shift balances from his name and account to names and accounts of the real investors when he needed to avoid detection because of missing amounts in the investors' accounts.

c. The university computer system was entered. Vandals changed many students' first name to "Susan," student telephone numbers were changed to the number of the university president, grade point averages were modified, and some academic files were deleted completely.

d. A computer operator at a state-run horse race betting agency set the computer clock back three minutes. After the race was won, he quickly telephoned bets to his girlfriend, an input clerk at the agency, gave her the winning horse and the bet amount, and won every time!

Discussion Cases

· ·

8.55 Control Weaknesses and Recommendations—Frontenac Sales Corporation. George Beemster, CPA, is examining the financial statements of the Frontenac Sales Corporation, which recently installed a computer. The following comments have been extracted from Mr. Beemster's notes on computer operations and the processing and control of shipping notices and customer invoices:

To minimize inconvenience, Frontenac converted without changing its existing data processing system, which utilized tabulating equipment. The computer company supervised the conversion and provided training to all computer department employees in systems design, operations, and programming.

Each computer run is assigned to a specific employee who is responsible for making program changes, running the program, and answering questions. This procedure has the advantage of eliminating the need for records of computer operations because each employee is responsible for her or his own computer runs.

At least one computer department employee remains in the computer room during office hours, and only computer department employees have keys to the computer room.

Systems documentation consists of those materials furnished by the computer company—a set of record formats and program listings. These and the tape library are kept in a corner of the computer department.

The company considered the desirability of programmed controls but decided to retain the manual controls from its existing system.

Company products are shipped directly from public warehouses, which forward shipping notices to general accounting. There, a billing clerk enters the prices of the items and accounts for the numerical sequence of shipping notices from each warehouse. The billing clerk also prepares daily adding machine tapes ("control tapes") of the units shipped and the unit prices.

Shipping notices and control tapes are forwarded to the computer department for input and processing. Extensions are made on the computer. Output consists of invoices (in six copies) and a daily sales register. The daily sales register shows the aggregate totals of units shipped and unit prices, which the computer operator compares to the control tapes.

All copies of the invoice are returned to the billing clerk. The clerk mails three copies to the customer, forwards one copy to the warehouse, maintains one copy in a numerical file, and retains one copy in an open invoice file that serves as a detail accounts receivable record.

Required:

Describe the weaknesses in the internal control structure over information and data flows and the procedures for processing shipping notices and customer invoices. Recommend some improvements in these control policies and procedures. Organize your answer sheet with two columns, one headed "Weaknesses" and the other headed "Recommended Improvements."

(AICPA adapted)

8.56 Flowchart Control Points. Each number of the flowchart in Exhibit 8.56–1 locates a control point in the labour processing system. Make a list of the control points, and for each point, describe the type or kind of internal control procedure that ought to be specified.

8.57 Internal Control Considerations in a Microcomputer Environment.

INTRODUCTION

The second standard of field work requires that an audit include "a sufficient understanding of the internal control to plan the audit and to determine the nature, timing, and extent of tests to be performed."

Given the increasing use of microcomputers by many businesses today, auditors must know about the potential internal control weaknesses inherent in a microcomputer environment. Such knowledge is crucial if the auditor is to make a proper assessment of the related control risk and to plan an effective and efficient audit approach.

Required:

In the following case study, assume that you are participating in the audit of Calgary Appliance Company and that the background information below has been obtained during the planning

phase. You have been asked to (1) consider the potential effects on internal control that have been introduced by the microcomputer application and (2) assess how those internal control effects may alter the audit plan for the current year.

BACKGROUND INFORMATION

Calgary Appliance is a wholesale distributor of electric appliances. The company's sales in each of the last two years have been approximately $40 million. All accounting applications are handled at the company's corporate office.

The data processing operations have historically centred around an on-site minicomputer. The computer applications include accounts payable and cash disbursements, payroll, inventory, and general ledger. Accounts receivable and fixed asset records have been prepared manually in the past. Internal controls in all areas have been considered strong in the last few years.

During the past year, financial management decided to automate the processing of sales, accounts receivable, and fixed asset transactions and accounting. Management also concluded that purchasing a microcomputer and related available software was more cost effective than increasing the minicomputer capacity and hiring a second computer operator. The controller and accounting clerks have been encouraged to find additional uses for the microcomputer and to "experiment" with it when they are not too busy.

The accounts receivable clerk is enthusiastic about the microcomputer, but the fixed asset clerk seems somewhat apprehensive about it because he has no prior experience with computers. The accounts receivable clerk explained that the controller had purchased a "very easy to use" accounts receivable software application program for the microcomputer, which enables her to input the daily information regarding billings and payments received quickly and easily. The controller has added some programming of his own to the software to give it better report-writing features.

EXHIBIT 8.56–1

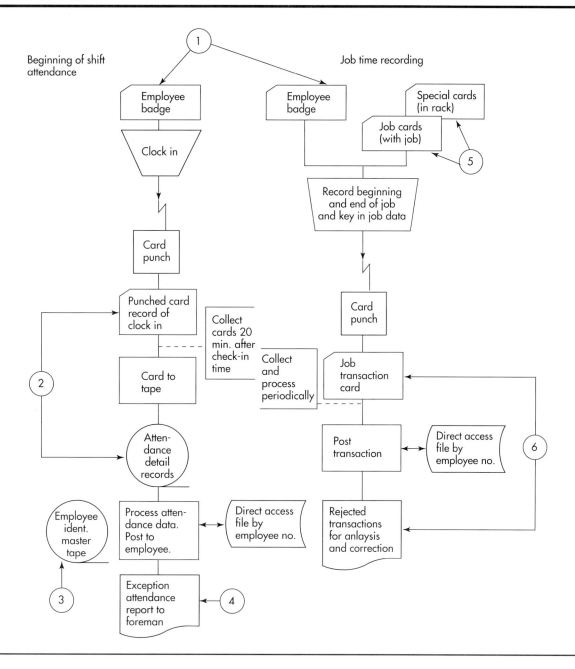

During a recent demonstration, the accounts receivable clerk explained that the program required her only to input the customer's name and invoice amount in the case of billings, or the customer's name and cheque amount in the case of payments. The microcom-puter then automatically updates the respective customer's account balance. At the end of every month, the accounts receivable trial balance is printed and reconciled by the clerk to the general ledger balance. The reconciliation is reviewed by the controller.

The fixed asset program also was purchased from an outside vendor. The controller indicated that the software package had just recently been put on the market and that it was programmed to compute tax depreciation based on recent changes in the federal tax laws. He also stated that, because of the fixed asset clerk's reluctance to use the microcomputer, he had input all the information from the fixed asset manual records. He indicated, however, that the fixed asset clerk would be responsible for the future processing related to the fixed assets files and for generating the month-end and year-end reports used to prepare the related accounting entries.

The various accounts receivable and fixed asset diskettes are all adequately labelled as to the type of program or data file. They are arranged in an organized manner in a diskette holder located near the microcomputer.

(Adapted from a case contributed by Price Waterhouse to The Auditor's Report.*)*

8.58 Use of CAATs. Jane Ford has just joined the public practice firm in which you are employed as a junior staff member. The two of you are meeting with Jay Birch, who will be the senior on your next (starting tomorrow) audit. Jane is very enthusiastic about her first audit assignment, which will provide an opportunity to use CAATs. She says to Jay, "We should use CAATs for every audit of a client who has an EDP system. That's the only way to go."

Jay relies, "It's not quite that simple—there are a number of considerations we have to bear in mind when we're deciding whether to use CAATs."

Required:
Elaborate on Jay's comment to Jane.

(CGAAC adapted)

8.59 General Controls. Les Tough has been assigned to assist you with the audit of Nercando Inc. Les will be making an initial visit to the client's office in a few days to familiarize himself with the company's operations. Nercando is an owner-managed business that has its accounting applications performed in a microcomputer environment. One of Les's tasks will be to make a preliminary assessment of Nercando's EDP internal control system and inform you so that you may incorporate that information into your audit planning. Les is somewhat unsure of what he should be looking for with respect to the EDP internal control system, and asks you for some direction.

Required:
Draft a memo to Les giving him guidance as to how to evaluate the general EDP internal control environment and the concerns that may exist in the case of a small, owner-managed company such as Nercando.

(CGAAC adapted)

PART III

AUDIT APPLICATIONS

CHAPTER 9

Learning Objectives

This chapter contains a concise overview of a cycle for processing customer orders and making sales, delivering goods and services to customers, accounting for customer accounts receivable, and collecting and depositing cash received from customers, and reconciling bank statements. A series of short cases is used to show the application of audit procedures in situations where errors, irregularities, and frauds might be discovered. The chapter ends with special technical notes on the existence assertion, using confirmations, and auditing bank reconciliations. After completing this chapter, you should be able to:

1. Describe the revenue and collection cycle, including typical source documents and controls.

2. Give examples of detail test of controls procedures for auditing control over customer credit approval, delivery, accounts receivable accounting, cash receipts accounting, and bank statement reconciliation.

3. Describe some common errors, irregularities, and frauds in the revenue and collection cycle, and design some audit and investigation procedures for detecting them.

4. Explain the importance of the existence assertion for the audit of cash and accounts receivable, and describe some procedures for obtaining evidence about the existence of assets.

5. Identify and describe considerations for using confirmations in the audit of cash and accounts receivable.

6. Design and perform substantive audit procedures for the audit of a bank statement reconcilation, and tell how auditors can search for lapping and kiting.

REVENUE AND COLLECTION CYCLE

REVENUE AND COLLECTION CYCLE: TYPICAL ACTIVITIES

LEARNING OBJECTIVE

1. Describe the revenue and collection cycle, including typical source documents and controls.

Exhibit 9–1 shows the activities and transactions involved in a revenue and collection cycle. The basic activities are (1) receiving and processing customer orders, including credit granting; (2) delivering goods and services to customers; (3) billing customers and accounting for accounts receivable; (4) collecting and depositing cash received from customers; and (5) reconciling bank statements. As you follow the exhibit, you can track some of the highlighted elements of a control structure.

Sales and Accounts Receivable Authorization

Exhibit 9–2 represents a computerized system for processing customer orders. Company personnel receive the customer's purchase order and create a sales order, entering it in a computer terminal. The computer system then performs automatic authorization procedures—determining whether the customer is a "regular" or a new customer, approving credit, and checking the availability of inventory to fill the order. (If inventory is short, a back order is entered.) When these authorizations are imbedded in a computer system, access to the master files for additions, deletions, and other changes must be limited to responsible persons. If these controls fail, orders might be processed for fictitious customers, credit might be approved for bad credit risks, and packing slips might be created for goods that do not exist in the inventory.

When a customer order passes these authorizations, the system (1) creates a record in the pending order master file, (2) produces a packing slip that is transmitted to the stockroom and shipping department, and (3) updates the inventory master file to show the commitment (removal) of the inventory. At this stage the pending order and the packing slip should be numbered in a numerical sequence so that the system can determine later whether any transactions have not been completed (completeness objective of control). The packing slip is the storeskeeper's authorization to release goods to the shipping department and the shipping department's authorization to release goods to a trucker or to the customer.

Another authorization in the system is the price list master file. It contains the product unit prices for billing customers. Persons who have power to alter this file have the power to authorize price changes and customer billings.

Custody

Physical custody of goods starts with the storeroom or warehouse where inventory is kept. Custody is transferred to the shipping department upon the authorization of the packing slip that orders storeskeepers to release goods to the shipping area. As long as the system works, custody is under accountability control. However, if the storeskeepers or the shipping department personnel have the power to change the quantity shown on the packing slip, they can cause errors in the system by billing the customer for too small or too large a quantity. (This power combines custody with a

E X H I B I T 9–1   REVENUE AND COLLECTION CYCLE

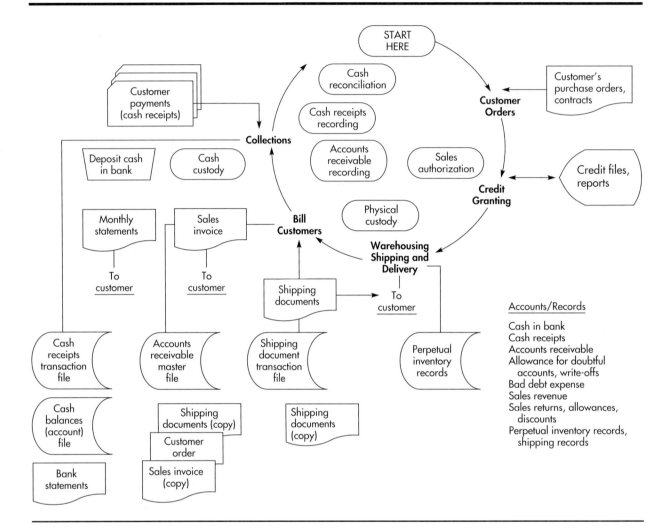

recording function. A computer record or "log" of such changes will create an electronic paper trail.)

"Custody" of accounts receivable records themselves implies the power to alter those records directly or to enter transactions to alter them (e.g., transfers, returns and allowance credits, write-offs). Personnel with this power have a combination of authorization and recording responsibility. (A computer "log" of such entries will create an electronic paper trail).

Recording
When delivery or shipment is complete, the shipping personnel enter the completion of the transaction in a terminal, and the system (1) produces a bill of lading shipping document, which is evidence of an actual delivery/shipment; (2) removes the order from the pending order master file; and (3) produces a sales invoice (prenumbered the same as the order and packing slip) that bills the customer for the quantity shipped, according to the bill of lading. Any personnel who have the power to enter or alter these transactions or to intercept the invoice that is supposed to be mailed to

EXHIBIT 9-2   SALES AND ACCOUNTS RECEIVABLE: COMPUTER PROCESSING

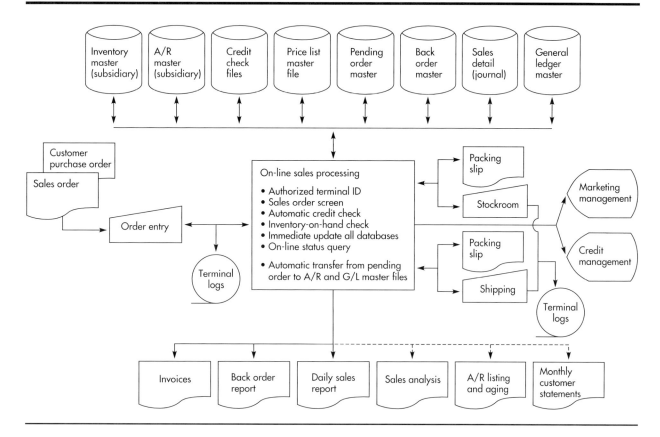

the customer have undesirable combinations of authorization, custody, and recording responsibilities; they can "authorize" transaction changes and record them by making entries in systems under their control.

Periodic Reconciliation

The most frequent reconciliation is the comparison of the sum of customers' unpaid balances with the accounts receivable control account total. Usually, this reconciliation is done with an aged trial balance. An aged trial balance is a list of the customers and their balances, with the balances classified in columns headed for different age categories (e.g., current, 10–30 days past due, 31–60 days past due, 61–90 days past due, over 90 days past due). Internal auditors can perform periodic comparison of the customers' obligations (according to the customers) with the recorded amount by sending confirmations to the customers. (Refer to the special note on confirmations at the end of this chapter.)

Cash Receipts and Cash Balances Authorization

There are numerous ways to receive cash—over the counter, through the mail, by electronic funds transfer, and by receipt in a "lockbox." In a lockbox arrangement, a fiduciary (e.g., a bank) opens the box, lists the receipts, deposits the money, and sends the remittance advices (stubs showing the amount received from each

PRICE FIXING

The company's computer programmer was paid off by a customer to cause the company to bill the customer at prices lower than list prices. The programmer wrote a subroutine that was invoked when the billing system detected the customer's regular code number. This subroutine instructed the customer billing system to reduce all unit prices 9.5 percent. The company relied on the computer billing system, and nobody ever rechecked the actual prices billed.

SHIPPING EMPLOYEE CAUGHT BY COMPUTER!

A customer paid off a shipping department employee to enter smaller quantities than actually shipped on the packing slip and bill of lading. This caused the customer's invoices to be understated. Unknown to the employee, a computer log recorded all the entries that altered the original packing slip record. An alert internal auditor noticed the pattern of "corrections" made by the shipping employee. A trap was laid by initiating fictitious orders for this customer, and the employee was observed making the alterations.

customer) to the company. Most companies need little "authorization" to accept a payment from a customer! However, authorization is important for approving customers' discounts and allowances taken, claiming to pay the bill in full. Exhibit 9–3 shows some cash receipts processing procedures in a manual accounting setting. (It is easier to describe these procedures as manual ones instead of as a variety of computerized procedures.) You can see the "approval of discounts" noted in Exhibit 9–3.

Custody

Someone always gets the cash and cheques in hand and thus has custody of the physical cash for a time. Control over this custody can vary. Companies can rotate people through the custody responsibility so that one person does not have this custody all the time; they can have rotating teams of two or more people so that they would need to collude with one another to steal money; they can make arrangements outside the company for actual cash custody (e.g., the lockbox arrangement). Since this initial custody cannot be avoided, it is always good control to prepare a list of the cash receipts as early in the process as possible, then separate the actual cash from the bookkeeping documents. The cash goes to the cashier or treasurer's office, where a bank deposit is prepared and the money is sent to the bank. The list goes to the accountants, who record the cash receipts. (This list simply may be a stack of the remittance advices received with the customers' payments. You yourself prepare a "remittance advice" each time you write the "amount enclosed" on the top part of your credit card billing, tear it off, and enclose it with your cheque.)

EXHIBIT 9–3   CASH RECEIPTS PROCESSING

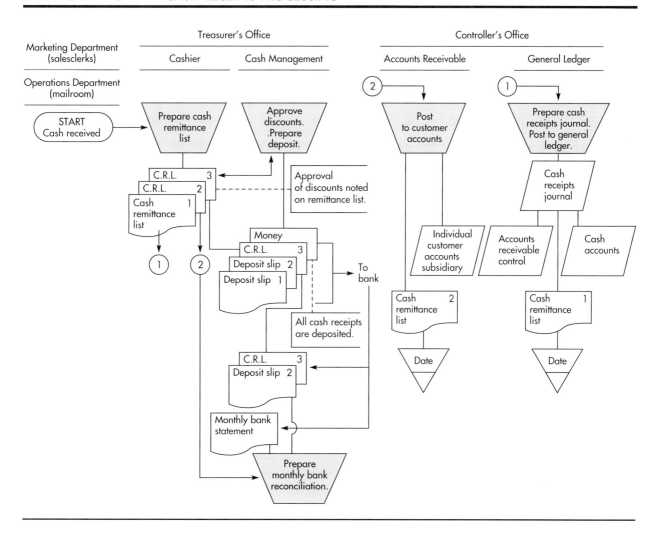

Recording
The accountants who record cash receipts and credits to customer accounts should not handle the cash. They should use the remittance list to make entries to the cash and accounts receivable control accounts and to the customers' accounts receivable subsidiary account records. In fact, it is a good error-checking procedure to have control account and subsidiary account entries made by different people; then later the accounts receivable entries and balances can be compared (reconciled) to determine whether the proper source documents (remittance lists) were used to make error-free accounting entries. Some computerized accounting programs post the customers' accounts automatically by keying in the customer identification number.

Periodic Reconciliation
It is important that bank account reconciliations be prepared carefully. Deposit slips should be compared to the details on cash remittance lists, and the totals should be traced to the general ledger entries. Likewise, paid cheques should be traced to the cash disbursements listing (journal). This care is required to establish

CAREFUL RECONCILIATION
(Refer to Exhibit 9–3)

Suppose the cashier who prepares the remittance list had stolen and converted Customer A's cheques to personal use. It might work for a short time until Customer A complained that the company had not given credit for payments. The cashier knows this. So, the cashier later puts Customer B's cheques in the bank deposit, but shows Customer A on the remittance list; thus, the accountants give Customer A credit. So far, so good for preventing Customer A's Complaint. But now Customer B needs to be covered. This "lapping" of customer payments to hide an embezzlement can be detected by a bank reconciliation comparison of the cheques deposited (Customer B) with the remittance credit recorded (Customer A).

that all receipts recorded in the books were deposited and that credit was given to the right customer. (Refer to the special note on auditing bank reconciliations at the end of this chapter.)

R E V I E W
CHECKPOINTS

9.1 What is the basic sequence of activities and accounting in a revenue and collection cycle?

9.2 What purpose is served by prenumbering sales orders, shipping documents (packing slips and bills of lading), and sales invoices?

9.3 Why is controlled access to computer terminals and master files (such as credit files and price lists) important in a control structure?

9.4 Why should a list of cash remittance be made and sent to the accounting department? Wouldn't it be easier to send the cash and cheques to the accountants so that they can enter the credits to customers' accounts accurately?

AUDIT EVIDENCE IN MANAGEMENT REPORTS AND DATA FILES

Computer processing of revenue and cash receipts transactions makes it possible for management to generate several reports that can provide important audit evidence.

Pending Order Master File
This file contains sales transactions that were started in the system but are not yet completed, thus not recorded as sales and accounts receivable. Old orders may represent shipments that actually were made, but for some reason the shipping department did not enter the shipping information (or entered an incorrect code that did not match the pending order file). The pending orders can be reviewed for evidence of the completeness of recorded sales and accounts receivable.

PEAKS AND VALLEYS

During the year-end audit, the independent auditors reviewed the weekly sales volume reports classified by region. They noticed that sales volume was very high in Region 2 the last two weeks of March, June, September, and December. The volume was unusually low in the first two weeks of April, July, October, and January. In fact, the peaks far exceeded the volume in all the other six regions. Further investigation revealed that the manager in Region 2 was holding open the sales recording at the end of each quarterly reporting period in an attempt to make the quarterly reports look good.

Credit Check Files

The computer system may make automatic credit checks, but up-to-date maintenance of the credit information is very important. Credit checks on old or incomplete information are not good credit checks. A sample of the files can be tested for current status. Alternatively, the company's records on updating the files can be reviewed for evidence of updating operations.

Price List Master File

The computer system may produce customer invoices automatically; but if the master price list is wrong, the billings will be wrong. The computer file can be compared to an official price source for accuracy. (The company should perform this comparison every time the prices are changed.)

Sales Detail (sales journal) File

This file should contain the detail sales entries, including the shipping references and dates. The file can be scanned for entries without shipping references (ficti-tious sales?) and for match of recording dates with shipment dates (sales recorded before shipment?). This file contains the population of debit entries to the accounts receivable.

Sales Analysis Reports

A variety of sales analyses can be produced. Sales classified by product lines is information for the business segment disclosures. Sales classified by sales employee or region can show unusually high or low volume that may bear further investigation if error is suspected.

Accounts Receivable Aged Trial Balance

The list of accounts receivable balances is the accounts receivable. If the control account total is larger than the sum in the trial balance, too bad. A receivable amount that cannot be identified with a customer cannot be collected! The trial balance is used as the population for selection of accounts for confirmation. (See the special note on the existence assertion and the special note on using confirma-tions at the end of this chapter.) The aging information is used in connection with assessing the allowance for doubtful accounts. (An aged trial balance is in Exhibit 9–8, presented later.)

Cash Receipts Journal

The cash receipts journal contains all the detail entries for cash deposits and credits to various accounts. It contains the population of credit entries that should be reflected in the credits to accounts receivable for customer payments. It also contains the adjusting and correcting entries that can result from the bank account reconciliation. These entries are important because they may signal the types of accounting errors or manipulations that happen in the cash receipts accounting.

R E V I E W
C H E C K P O I N T S

9.5 What computer-based files could an auditor examine to find evidence of unrecorded sales? of inadequate credit checks? of incorrect product unit prices?

9.6 Suppose you selected a sample of customers' accounts receivable and wanted to find supporting evidence for the entries in the accounts. Where would you go to vouch the debit entries? What would you expect to find? Where would you go to vouch the credit entries? What would you expect to find?

Control Risk Assessment

LEARNING OBJECTIVE

2. Give examples of detail test of controls procedures for auditing control over customer credit approval, delivery, accounts receivable accounting, cash receipts accounting, and bank statement reconciliation.

Control risk assessment is important because it governs the nature, timing, and extent of substantive audit procedures that will be applied in the audit of account balances in the revenue and collection cycle. These account balances (listed in the corner of Exhibit 9–1) include:

Cash in bank.

Accounts receivable.

Allowance for doubtful accounts.

Bad debt expense.

Sales revenue.

Sales returns, allowances, discounts.

General Control Considerations

Control procedures for proper segregation of responsibilities should be in place and operating. By referring to Exhibit 9–1, you can see that proper segregation involves authorization of sales and credit by persons who do not have custody, recording, or reconciliation duties. Custody of inventory and cash is in persons who do not directly authorize credit, record the accounting entries, or reconcile the bank account. Recording (accounting) is performed by persons who do not authorize sales or credit, handle the inventory or cash, or perform reconciliations. Periodic reconciliations should be performed by people who do not have authorization, custody, or recording duties related to the same assets. Combinations of two or more of these responsibilities in one person, one office, or one computerized system may open the door for errors, irregularities, and frauds.

FICTITIOUS REVENUE

A Mississauga computer peripheral equipment company was experiencing slow sales, so the sales manager entered some sales orders for customers who had not ordered anything. The invoices were marked "hold," while the delivery was to a warehouse owned by the company. The rationale was that these customers would buy the equipment eventually, so why not anticipate the orders! (However, it's a good idea not to send them the invoices until they actually make the orders, hence the "hold.") The "sales" and "receivables" were recorded in the accounts, and the financial statements contained overstated revenue and assets.

A common feature of cash management is to require that persons who handle cash be insured under a fidelity bond. A fidelity bond is an insurance policy that covers most kinds of cash embezzlement losses. Fidelity bonds do not prevent or detect embezzlement, but the failure to carry the insurance exposes the company to complete loss when embezzlement occurs. Auditors may recommend fidelity bonding to companies that do not know about its coverage.

In addition, the control structure should provide for detail control checking procedures. For example: (1) policy should provide that no sales order should be entered without a customer order; (2) a credit-check code or manual signature should be recorded by an authorized means; (3) access to inventory and the shipping area should be restricted to authorized persons; (4) access to billing terminals and blank invoice forms should be restricted to authorized personnel; (5) accountants should be under orders to record sales and accounts receivable when all the supporting documentation of shipment is in order, and care should be taken to record sales and receivables as of the date the goods and services were shipped and the cash receipts on the date the payments are received; (6) customer invoices should be compared with bills of lading and customer orders to determine that the customer is sent the goods ordered at the proper location for the proper prices, and that the quantity being billed is the same as the quantity shipped; (7) pending order files should be reviewed in a timely fashion to avoid failure to bill and record shipments; and (8) bank statements should be reconciled in detail monthly.

Information about the control structure often is gathered by completing an internal control questionnaire. Control risk assessment was introduced in Chapter 6. You should now refer to Exhibit 6–9 to review an internal control questionnaire for sales transaction control. A selection of other questionnaires for both general (manual) controls and computer controls over cash receipts and accounts receivable is in Appendix 9A. You can study these questionnaires for details of desirable control policies and procedures. They are organized under headings that identify the important control objectives—environment, validity, completeness, authorization, accuracy, classification, accounting, and proper period recording.

Another way to obtain general information about internal controls is called a "walk-through," or a "sample of one." In this work the auditors take a single example of a transaction and "walk it through" from its initiation to its recording in the accounting records. The revenue and collection cycle walk-through involves following a sale from the initial customer order through credit approval, billing, and delivery of goods, to the entry in the sales journal and subsidiary accounts receivable records, and finally to its subsequent collection and cash deposit. Sample documents are collected, and employees in each department are questioned about their specific duties. The purposes of a walk-through are to (1) verify or update the auditors' understanding of the client's sales/accounts receivable accounting system and control procedures and (2) learn whether the controls the client reported in the internal control questionnaire are actually in place. The walk-through, combined with enquiries, can contribute evidence about appropriate separation of duties, which might be a sufficient basis for assessing control risk slightly below the maximum. However, a walk-through is too limited in scope to provide evidence of whether the client's control procedures were operating effectively during the period under audit. Usually, a larger sample of transactions for detail testing of control performance is necessary to justify a low control risk assessment based on actual control performance evidence.

Detail Test of Controls Audit Procedures

An organization should have input, processing, and output control procedures in place and operating to prevent, detect, and correct accounting errors. You studied the general control objectives in Chapter 6 (validity, completeness, authorization, accuracy, classification, accounting, and proper period recording). Exhibit 9–4 puts these in the perspective of revenue cycle activity with examples of specific objectives. You should study this exhibit carefully. It takes control objectives out of the abstract and expresses them in specific examples related to controlling sales accounting.

EXHIBIT 9–4   **INTERNAL CONTROL OBJECTIVES: REVENUE CYCLE (sales)**

General Objectives	Examples of Specific Objectives
1. Recorded sales are *valid* and documented.	Customer purchase orders support invoices. Bills of lading or other shipping documentation exist for all invoices. Recorded sales in sales journal supported by invoices.
2. Valid sales transactions are *recorded* and none omitted.	Invoices, shipping documents, and sales orders are prenumbered and the numerical sequence is checked. Overall comparisons of sales are made periodically by a statistical or product-line analysis.
3. Sales are *authorized* according to company policy.	Credit sales approved by credit department. Prices used in preparing invoices are from authorized price schedule.
4. Sales invoices are *accurately* prepared.	Invoice quantities compared to shipment and customer order quantities. Prices checked and mathematical accuracy independently checked after invoice prepared.
5. Sales transactions are properly *classified*.	Sales to subsidiaries and affiliates classified as intercompany sales and receivables. Sales returns and allowances properly classified.
6. Sales transaction *accounting* is proper.	Credit sales posted to customer's individual accounts. Sales journal posted to general ledger account. Sales recognized in accordance with generally accepted accounting principles.
7. Sales transactions are recorded in the *proper period*.	Sales invoices recorded on shipment date.

Auditors can perform detail test of controls audit procedures to determine whether controls that are said to be in place and operating actually are being performed properly by company personnel. A detail test of control procedure consists of (1) identification of the data population from which a sample of items will be selected for audit and (2) an expression of the action that will be taken to produce relevant evidence. In general, the actions in detail test of control audit procedures involve vouching, tracing, observing, scanning, and recalculating. A specification of such procedures is part of an audit program for obtaining evidence useful in a final control risk assessment. If personnel in the organization are not performing their control procedures very well, auditors will need to design substantive audit procedures to try to detect whether control failures have produced materially misleading account balances.

Test of controls audit procedures can be used to audit the accounting for transactions in two directions. This dual-direction testing involves samples selected to obtain evidence about control over completeness in one direction and control over validity in the other direction. The completeness direction determines whether all transactions that occurred were recorded (none omitted), and the validity direction determines whether recorded transactions actually occurred (were valid). An example of the first direction is the examination of a sample of shipping documents (from the file of all shipping documents) to determine whether invoices were prepared and recorded. An example of the second direction is the examination of a sample of sales invoices (from the file representing all recorded sales) to determine whether supporting shipping documents exist to verify the fact of an actual shipment. The content of each file is compared with the another. The example is illustrated in Exhibit 9–5. (The A-1-b and A-3-b codes correspond to the test of controls procedures in Exhibit 9–6).

Exhibit 9–6 contains a selection of test controls audit procedures. Many of these procedures can be characterized as steps taken to verify the content and character of sample documents from one file with the content and character of documents in another file. These steps are designed to enable the audit team to obtain objective evidence about the effectiveness of controls and about the reliability of accounting records. These samples are usually attribute samples designed along the lines you studied in Chapter 7.

EXHIBIT 9–5   DUAL DIRECTION OF TEST AUDIT SAMPLES

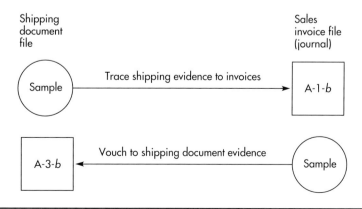

EXHIBIT 9–6   TEST OF CONTROLS AUDIT PROCEDURES FOR SALES, CASH RECEIPTS, AND RECEIVABLES

	Control Objective
A. Sales	
1. Select a sample of shipping documents:	
a. Scan for missing numbers.	Completeness
b. Trace to related sales invoices.	Completeness
2. Scan sales invoices for missing numbers in the sequence.	Completeness
3. Select a sample of recorded sales invoices (sales journal):	
a. Perform recalculations to verify arithmetic accuracy.	Accuracy
b. Vouch to supporting shipping documents. Note dates and quantities.	Validity Accuracy Proper period
c. Vouch prices to approved price lists.	Authorization
d. Vouch credit approval.	Authorization
e. Trace posting to general ledger and proper customer account.	Accounting
4. Observe customer order handling and invoice preparation work.	Environment
B. Cash Receipts	
1. Select a sample of recorded cash receipts (cash receipts journal):	
a. Vouch to deposit slip and remittance list.	Validity
b. Trace to bank statement.	Validity
c. Trace posting to general ledger accounts.	Accounting
d. Trace posting to subsidiary accounts.	Accounting
2. Select a sample of remittance lists (or daily cash reports):	
a. Trace to cash receipts journal.	Completeness
b. Trace journal posting to general ledger.	Accounting
c. Trace to bank statement.	Accuracy
3. Observe the work habits of cashiers and their interactions with persons who keep cash records.	Environment
C. Accounts Receivable	
1. Trace sales invoices to accounts receivable posting (procedure A-3e above).	Accounting
2. Trace cash receipts to accounts receivable posting (procedure B-1d above).	Accounting
3. Select a sample of credit memos.	
a. Review for proper approval.	Authorization
b. Trace to posting in customers' accounts.	Accounting
4. Select a sample of customers' accounts:	
a. Vouch debits to supporting sales invoices.	Validity
b. Vouch credits to supporting cash receipts documents and approved credit memos.	Validity
5. Observe mailing of monthly customer statements.	Validity

On the right, Exhibit 9–6 shows the control objectives tested by the audit procedures. Thus, the test of controls procedures produce evidence that helps auditors determine whether the specific control objectives listed in Exhibit 9–4 were achieved.

Summary: Control Risk Assessment

The audit manager must evaluate the evidence obtained from an understanding of the internal control structure and from test of controls audit procedures. The initial process of obtaining an understanding of the control structure and the later process of obtaining evidence from actual test of controls are two of the phases of control risk assessment work (see Exhibit 6–8 in Chapter 6).

If the control risk is assessed very low, the substantive audit procedures on the account balances can be limited in cost-saving ways. For example, the accounts receivable confirmations can be sent on a date prior to the year-end, and the sample size can be fairly small.

On the other hand, if tests of controls reveal weaknesses (such as posting sales without shipping documents, charging customers the wrong prices, and recording credits to customers without supporting credit memos), the substantive procedures will need to be designed to lower the risk of failing to detect material error in the account balances. For example, the confirmation procedure may need to be scheduled on the year-end date with a large sample of customer accounts. Descriptions of major deficiencies, control weaknesses, and inefficiencies may be incorporated in a management letter to the client.

R E V I E W
C H E C K P O I N T S

9.7   What account balances are included in a review and collection cycle?

9.8   What specific control policies and procedures (in addition to separation of duties and responsibilities) should be in place and operating in a control structure governing revenue recognition and cash accounting?

9.9   What is a "walk-through" of a sales transaction? And how can the walk-through work complement the use of an internal control questionnaire?

9.10   What are the two important characteristics of a detail test of control procedure? What "actions" are typically contemplated by such a procedure?

9.11   What is "dual direction test of controls sampling?"

Audit Cases: Substantive Audit Procedures

LEARNING   OBJECTIVE

3. Describe some common errors, irregularities, and frauds in the revenue and collection cycle, and design some audit and investigation procedures for detecting them.

The audit procedures to gather evidence on account balances are called "substantive procedures." Some amount of substantive audit procedures ought to follow the assessment of control risk. Auditors should not place total reliance on controls to the exclusion of other procedures. Substantive audit procedures differ from test of controls audit procedures in their basic purpose. Substantive procedures are designed to obtain direct evidence about the dollar amounts in account balances, while test of controls procedures are designed to obtain evidence about the company's performance of its own control procedures. Sometimes an audit procedure can be used for both purposes simultaneously, and then it is called a **dual-purpose procedure.**

The goal in performing substantive procedures is to detect evidence of errors, irregularities, and frauds if any exist in the accounts as material overstatements or understatements of account balances. In the remainder of this part of the chapter, the approach is to use a set of casettes (little cases) that contain specific examples of test of controls and substantive audit procedures (recalculation, observation, confirmation, enquiry, vouching, tracing, scanning, and analytical review). The case stories are used instead of listing schemes and detection procedures in the abstract. If you like lists of details, a selection of detail substantive procedures for cash and accounts receivable is in Appendix 9B.

DUAL-PURPOSE NATURE OF ACCOUNTS RECEIVABLE CONFIRMATIONS

Accounts receivable confirmation is a substantive procedure designed to obtain evidence of the existence and gross amount (valuation) of customers' balances directly from the customer. If such confirmations show numerous exceptions, auditors will be concerned with the controls over the details of sales and cash receipts transactions even if previous control evaluations have seemed to show little control risk.

The "casettes" follow a standard format, which first tells about an error, irregularity, or fraud situation. This part is followed by an audit approach section that tells about the audit objective (assertion), controls, test of controls, and audit of balances (substantive procedures) that could be considered in an approach to the situation. The audit approach section presumes that the auditors do not know everything about the situation. (As a student of the case, you have "inside information.") These are the parts of the case situation description for each casette:

Method: A cause of the misstatement (accidental error, intentional irregularity, or fraud attempt), which usually is easier to make because of some kind of failure of controls.

Paper trail: A set of telltale signs of erroneous accounting, missing or altered documents, or a "dangling debit" (the false or erroneous debit that results from an overstatement of assets).

Amount: The dollar amount of overstated assets and revenue, or understated liabilities and expenses.

The audit approach section contains these parts:

Audit objective: A recognition of a financial statement assertion for which evidence needs to be obtained. The assertions are about existence of assets, liabilities, revenues, and expenses; their valuation; their complete inclusion in the account balances; the rights and obligations inherent in them; and their proper presentation and disclosure in the financial statements. (These assertions were introduced in Chapter 4.)

Control: A recognition of the control procedures that should be used by an organization to prevent and detect errors and irregularities.

Test of controls: Ordinary and extended procedures designed to produce evidence about the effectiveness of the controls that should be in operation.

Audit of balances: Ordinary and extended substantive procedures designed to find signs of errors, irregularities, and frauds in account balances and classes of transactions.

At the end of the chapter, some similar discussion cases are presented, and you can write the audit approach to test your ability to design audit procedures for the detection of errors, irregularities, and frauds.

CASETTE 9.1
THE CANNY CASHIER

Problem

Cash embezzlement caused overstated accounts receivable, overstated customer discounts expense, and understated cash sales. Company failed to earn interest income on funds "borrowed."

Method

D. Bakel was the assistant controller of Sports Equipment, Inc. (SEI), an equipment retailer. SEI maintained accounts receivable for school districts in the region; otherwise, customers received credit by using their own credit cards.

Bakel's duties included being the company cashier, who received all the incoming mail payments on school accounts and the credit card account and all the cash and cheques taken over the counter. Bakel prepared the bank deposit (and delivered the deposit to the bank), listing all the cheques and currency, and also prepared a remittance worksheet (daily cash report) that showed amounts received, discounts allowed on school accounts, and amounts to credit to the accounts receivable. Bakel also reconciled the bank statement. No one else reviewed the deposits or the bank statements except the independent auditors.

Bakel opened a bank account in the name of Sport Equipment Company (SEC), after properly incorporating the company in the Department of Corporate Affairs' office. Over-the-counter cash and cheques and school district payments were taken from the SEI receipts and deposited in the SEC account. (None of the customers noticed the difference between the rubber stamp endorsements for the two similarly named corporations, and neither did the bank.) SEC kept the money awhile, earning interest; then Bakel wrote SEC cheques to SEI to replace the "borrowed" funds, in the meantime taking new SEI receipts for deposit to SEC.

Bakel also stole payments made by the school districts, depositing them to SEC. Later, Bakel deposited SEC cheques in SEI, giving the schools credit, but approved an additional 2 percent discount in the process. Thus, the schools received proper credit later, and SEC paid in less by the amount of the extra discounts.

Paper Trail

SEI's bank deposits systematically showed fairly small currency deposits. Bakel was nervous about taking too many cheques, so cash was preferred. The deposit slips also listed the SEC cheques because bank tellers always compare the deposit slip listing to the cheques submitted. The remittance worksheet showed different details: Instead of showing SEC cheques, it showed receipts from school district and currency, but not many over-the-counter cheques from customers. The transactions became complicated enough that Bakel had to use the microcomputer in the office to keep track of the school districts that needed to get credit. There were no vacations for this hard-working cashier because the discrepancies might be noticed by a substitute, and Bakel needed to give the districts credit later.

Amount

Over a six-year period, Bakel built up a $150,000 average balance in the Sport Equipment Company (SEC) account, which earned a total of $67,500 interest that should have been earned by Sports Equipment, Inc. (SEI). By approving the "extra" discounts, Bakel skimmed 2 percent of $1 million in annual sales, for a total of $120,000. Since SEI would have had net income before taxes of about $1.6 million over this six years (about 9 percent on the sales dollar), Bakel's embezzlement took about 12.5 percent of the income.

AUDIT APPROACH

Objective

Obtain evidence to determine whether the accounts receivable recorded on the books represent claims against real customers in the gross amounts recorded.

Control

Authorization related to cash receipts, custody of cash, recording cash transactions, and bank statement reconciliation should be separate duties designed to prevent errors, irregularities, and frauds. Some supervision and detail review of one or more of these duties should be performed as a next-level control designed to detect errors, irregularities, and frauds if they have occurred. For ex-

ample, the remittance worksheet should be prepared by someone else, or at least the discounts should be approved by the controller; the bank reconciliation should be prepared by someone else.

Bakel had all the duties. (While recording was not actually performed, Bakel provided the source document—the remittance worksheet—the other accountant used to make the cash and accounts receivable entries.) According to the company president, the "control" was the diligence of "our" long-time, trusted, hard-working assistant controller. Note: An auditor who "thinks like a crook" to imagine ways Bakel could commit errors, irregularities, or fraud could think of this scheme for cash theft and accounts receivable lapping.

Test of Controls

Since the "control" purports to be Bakel's honest and diligent performance of the accounting and control procedures that might have been performed by two or more people, the test of controls is an audit of cash receipts transactions as they relate to accounts receivable credit. The dual-direction samples and procedures are these:

Validity direction: Select a sample of customer accounts receivable, and vouch payment credits to remittance worksheets and bank deposits, including recalculation of discounts allowed in comparison to sales terms (2 percent), classification (customer name) identification, and correspondence of receipt date to recording date.

Completeness direction: Select a sample of remittance worksheets (or bank deposits), vouch details to bank deposit slips (trace details to remittance worksheets if the sample is bank deposits), and trace forward to complete accounting posting in customer accounts receivable.

Audit of Balance

Since there is a control risk of incorrect accounting, perform the accounts receivable confirmation as of the year-end date. Confirm a sample of school district accounts, using positive confirmations.

Blank confirmations may be used. Since there is a control risk, the "sample" may be all the accounts, if the number is not too large.

As prompted by notice of an oddity (noted in the discovery summary below), use the telephone book, chamber of commerce directory, and a visit to a local Ministry of Industry and Trade office to determine the location and identity of Sport Equipment Company.

Discovery Summary

The test of controls samples showed four cases of discrepancy, one of which looked like this:

Bank Deposit Slip

Jones	25
Smith	35
Hill Dist.	980
Sport Equip	1,563
Currency	540
Deposit	3,143

Cash Remittance Report

Name	Amount	Discount	AR	Sales
Jones	25	0	0	25
Smith	35	0	0	35
Hill Dist.	980	20	1,000	0
Marlin Dist.	480	20	500	0
Waco Dist.	768	32	800	0
Currency	855	0	0	855
Totals	3,143	72	2,300	915

The auditors sent positive confirmations on all 72 school district accounts. Three of the responses stated that the districts had paid the balances before the confirmation date. Follow-up procedures on their accounts receivable credit in the next period showed they had received credit in remittance reports, and the bank deposits had shown no cheques from the districts but had contained a cheque from Sports Equipment Company.

Investigation of SEC revealed the connection of Bakel, who was confronted and then confessed.

CASETTE 9.2
THE TAXMAN ALWAYS RINGS TWICE

Problem

Overstated receivables for property taxes in a school district because the tax assessor stole some taxpayers' payments.

Method

J. Shelstad was the tax assessor–collector in the Ridge School District, serving a large metropolitan area. The staff processed tax notices on a computer system and generated 450,000 tax notices each October. An office copy was printed and used to check off "paid" when payments were received. Payments were processed by computer, and a master file of "accounts receivable" records (tax assessments, payments) was kept on the computer hard disk.

Shelstad was a good personnel manager, who often took over the front desk at lunchtime so the teller staff could enjoy lunch together. During these times, Shelstad took payments over the counter, gave the taxpayers a counter receipt, and pocketed some of the money, which was never entered in the computer system.

Shelstad resigned when he was elected to the Ridge school board. The district's assessor–collector office was eliminated upon the creation of a new regionwide tax agency.

Paper Trail

The computer records showed balances due from many taxpayers who had actually paid their taxes. The book of printed notices was not marked "paid" for many taxpayers who had received counter receipts. These records and the daily cash receipts reports (cash receipts journal) were available at the time the independent auditors performed the most recent annual audit in April. When Shelstad resigned in August, a power surge permanently destroyed the hard disk receivables file, and the cash receipts journals could not be found.

The new regional agency managers noticed that the total of delinquent taxes disclosed in the audited financial statements was much larger than the total turned over to the region's legal counsel for collection and foreclosure.

Amount

Shelstad had been the assessor–collector for 15 years. The "good personnel manager" pocketed 100–150 counter payments each year, in amounts of $500–$2,500, stealing about $200,000 a year for a total of approximately $2.5 million. The district had assessed about $800–$900 million per year, so the annual theft was less than 1 percent. Nevertheless, the taxpayers got mad.

AUDIT APPROACH

Objective

Obtain evidence to determine whether the receivables for taxes (delinquent taxes) represent genuine claims collectible from the taxpayers.

Control

The school district had a respectable system for establishing the initial amounts of taxes receivable. The professional staff of appraisers and the independent appraisal review board established the tax base for each property. The school board set the price (tax rate). The computer system authorization for billing was validated on these two inputs.

The cash receipts system was well designed, calling for preparation of a daily cash receipts report (cash receipts journal that served as a source input for computer entry). This report was always reviewed by the "boss," Shelstad.

Unfortunately, Shelstad had the opportunity and power to override the controls and become both cash handler and supervisor. Shelstad made the decisions about sending delinquent taxes to the county attorney for collection, and the ones known to have been paid but stolen were withheld.

Test of Controls

The auditors performed dual-direction sampling to test the processing of cash receipts.

Validity direction: Select a sample of receivables from the computer hard disk, and vouch (1) charges to the appraisal record, recalculating the amount using the authorized tax rate and (2) payments, if any, to the cash receipts journal and bank deposits. (The auditors found no exceptions.)

Completeness direction: Select a sample of properties from the appraisal rolls, and determine that tax notices had been sent and tax receivables (charges) recorded in the computer file. Select a sample of cash receipts reports, vouch them to bank deposits of the same amount and date, and trace the payments forward to credits to taxpayers' accounts. Select a sample of bank deposits, and trace them to cash receipts reports of the same amount and date. In one of these latter two samples, compare the details on bank deposits to the details on the cash receipts reports to determine whether the same taxpayers appear on both documents. (The auditors found no exceptions.)

Audit of Balance

Confirm a sample of unpaid tax balances with taxpayers. Response rates may not be high, and follow-up procedures determining the ownership (county title files) may need to be performed, and new confirmations may need to be sent.

Determine that proper disclosure is made of the total of delinquent taxes and the total of delinquencies turned over to the region's legal counsel for collection proceedings.

Discovery Summary

Shelstad persuaded the auditors that the true "receivables" were the delinquencies turned over to the region's legal counsel. The confirmation sample and other work was based on this population. Thus, confirmations were not sent to fictitious balances that Shelstad knew had been paid, and the auditors never had the opportunity to receive "I paid" complaints from taxpayers.

The new managers of the regional tax district were not influenced by Shelstad. They questioned the discrepancy between the delinquent taxes in the audit report and the lower amount turned over for collection. Since the computer file was not usable, the managers had to use the printed book of tax notices, where paid accounts had been marked "paid." (Shelstad had not marked the stolen ones "paid" so the printed book would agree with the computer file.) Tax due notices were sent to the taxpayers with unpaid balances, and they began to show up bringing their counter receipts and loud complaints.

In a fit of audit overkill, the independent auditors had earlier photocopied the entire set of cash receipt reports (cash journal). They were thus able to determine that the counter receipts (all signed by Shelstad) had not been deposited or entered. Shelstad was prosecuted and sentenced to a jail term.

CASETTE 9.3
BILL OFTEN, BILL EARLY

Problem

Overstated sales and receivables, understated discounts expense, and overstated net income resulted from recording sales too early and failure to account for customer discounts taken.

Method

McGossage Company experienced profit pressures for two years in a row. Actual profits were squeezed in a recessionary economy, but the company reported net income decreases that were not as severe as other companies in the industry.

Sales were recorded in the grocery products division for orders that had been prepared for shipment but not actually shipped until later. Employees backdated the shipping documents. Gross profit on these "sales" was about 30 percent. Customers took discounts on payments, but the company did not record them, leaving the debit balances in the customers' accounts receivable instead of charging them to discounts and allowances expense. Company accountants were instructed to wait 60 days before recording discounts taken.

The division vice president and general manager knew about these accounting practices, as did a significant number of the 2,500 employees in the division. The division managers were under orders from headquarters to achieve profit objectives they considered unrealistic.

Paper Trail

The customers' accounts receivable balances contained amounts due for discounts the customers already had taken. The cash receipts records showed payments received without credit for discounts. Discounts were entered monthly by a special journal entry.

The unshipped goods were on the shipping dock at year-end with papers showing earlier shipping dates.

Amount

As misstatements go, some of these were on the materiality borderline. Sales were overstated 0.3 percent and 0.5 percent in the prior and current year, respectively. Accounts receivable were overstated 4 percent and 8 percent. But the combined effect was to overstate the division's net income by 6 percent and 17 percent. Selected data were:

	One Year Ago		Current Year	
	Reported	Actual	Reported	Actual
Sales	$330.0	$329.0	$350.0	$348.0
Discounts expense	1.7	1.8	1.8	2.0
Net income	6.7	6.3	5.4	4.6

AUDIT APPROACH

Objective

Obtain evidence to determine whether sales were recorded in the proper period and whether gross accounts receivable represented the amounts due from customers at year-end. Obtain evidence to determine whether discounts expense was recognized in the proper amount in the proper period.

Control

The accounting manual should provide instructions to record sales on the date of shipment (or when title passes, if later). Management subverted this control procedure by having shipping employees date the shipping papers incorrectly.

Cash receipts procedures should provide for authorizing and recording discounts when they are taken by customers. Management overrode this control instruction by giving instructions to delay the recording.

Test of Controls

Questionnaires and enquiries should be used to determine the company's accounting policies. It is possible that employees and managers would lie to the auditors to conceal the policies. It is also possible that pointed questions about revenue recognition and discount recording policies would elicit answers to reveal the practices.

For detail procedures: Select a sample of cash receipts, examine them for authorization, recalculate the customer discounts, trace them to accounts receivable input for recording of the proper amount on the proper date. Select a sample of shipping documents and vouch them to customer orders, then trace them to invoices and to recording in the amounts receivable input with proper amounts on the proper date. These tests follow the tracing direction—starting with data that represent the beginning of transactions (cash receipts, shipping) and tracing them through the company's accounting process.

Audit of Balance

Confirm a sample of customer accounts. Use analytical relationships of past years' discount expense to a relevant base (sales, sales volume) to calculate an overall test of the discounts expense.

Discovery Summary

The managers lied to the auditors about their revenue and expense timing policies. The sample of shipping documents showed no dating discrepancies because the employees had inserted incorrect dates. The analytical procedures on discounts did not show the misstatement because the historical relationships were too erratic to show a deficient number (outlier). However, the sample of cash receipts transactions showed that discounts were not calculated and recorded at time of receipt. Additional enquiry led to discovery of the special journal entries and knowledge of the recording delay. Two customers in the sample of 65 confirmations responded with exceptions that turned out to be unrecorded discounts.

Two other customers in the confirmation sample complained that they did not owe for late invoices on December 31. Follow-up showed the shipments were goods noticed on the shipping dock. Auditors taking the physical inventory noticed the goods on the shipping dock during the December 31 inventory-taking. Inspection revealed the shipping documents dated December 26. When the auditors traced these shipments to the sales recording, they found them recorded "bill and hold" on December 29. (These procedures were performed and the results obtained by a successor audit firm in the third year!)

Casette 9.4
Thank Goodness It's Friday

Problem

Overstated sales caused overstated net income, retained earnings, current assets, working capital, and total assets. Overstated cash collections did not change the total current assets or total assets but they increased the amount of cash and decreased the amount of accounts receivable.

Method

Alpha Brewery Corporation generally has good control policies and procedures related to authorization of transactions for accounting entry, and the accounting manual has instructions for recording sales transactions in the proper accounting period. The company regularly closes the accounting process each Friday at 5 p.m. to prepare weekly management reports. The year-end date (cutoff date) is December 31, and, in 1990, December 31 was a Monday. However, the accounting was performed through Friday as usual, and the accounts were closed for the year on January 4.

Paper Trail

All the entries were properly dated after December 31, including the sales invoices, cash receipts, and shipping documents. However, the trial balance from which the financial statements were prepared was dated December 31, 1990, even though the accounts were actually closed on January 4. Nobody noticed the slip of a few days because the Friday closing was normal.

Amount

Alpha recorded sales of $672,000 and gross profit of $268,800 over the January 1–4 period. Cash collections on customers' accounts came in the amount of $800,000.

AUDIT APPROACH

Objective

Obtain evidence to determine the existence, completeness, and valuation of sales for the year ended December 31, 1990, and the cash and accounts receivable as of December 31, 1990.

Control

The company had in place the proper instructions to people to date transactions on the actual date on which they occurred and to enter sales and cost of goods sold on the day of shipment and to enter cash receipts on the day received in the company offices. An accounting supervisor should have checked the entries through Friday to make sure the dates corresponded with the actual events, and that the accounts for the year were closed with Monday's transactions.

Test of Controls

In this case the auditors need to be aware of the company's weekly routine closing and the possibility that the intervention of the December 31 date might cause a problem. Asking the question "Did you cut off the accounting on Monday night this week?" might elicit the "Oh, we forgot!" response. Otherwise, it is normal to sample transactions around the year-end date to determine whether they were recorded in the proper accounting period.

The procedure: Select transactions 7–10 days before and after the year-end date, and inspect the dates on supporting documentation for evidence of accounting in the proper period.

Audit of Balance

The audit for sales overstatement is partly accomplished by auditing the cash and accounts receivable at December 31 for overstatement (the dangling debit location). Confirm a sample of accounts receivable. If the accounts are too large, the auditors expect the debtors to say so, thus leading to detection of sales overstatements.

Cash overstatement is audited by auditing the bank reconciliation to see whether deposits in transit (the deposits sent late in December) actually cleared the bank early in January. Obviously, the January 4 cash collections could not reach the bank until at least Monday, January 7. That's too long for

a December 31 deposit to be in transit to a local bank.

The completeness of sales recordings is audited by selecting a sample of sales transactions (and supporting shipping documents) in the early part of the next accounting period (January 1991). One way that sales of 1990 could be incomplete would be to postpone recording December shipments until January, and this procedure will detect them if the shipping documents are dated properly.

The completeness of cash collections (and accounts receivable credits) are audited by auditing the cash deposits early in January to see whether there is any sign of holding cash without entry until January.

In this case the existence objective is more significant for discovery of the problem than the completeness objective. After all, the January 1–4 sales, shipments, and cash collections did not "exist" in December 1990.

Discovery Summary

The test of controls sample from the days before and after December 31 quickly revealed the problem. Company accounting personnel were embarrassed, but there was no effort to misstate the financial statements. This was a simple error. The company readily made the following adjustment:

	Debit	Credit
Sales	$672,000	
Inventory	403,200	
Accounts receivable	800,000	
Accounts receivable		$672,000
Cost of goods sold		403,200
Cash		800,000

R E V I E W
C H E C K P O I N T S

9.12 What are the goals of dual-direction sampling in regard to an audit of the accounts receivable and cash collection system?

9.13 In the case of The Canny Cashier, name one bank reconciliation control procedure that could have revealed signs of embezzlement.

9.14 What feature(s) of a cash receipts internal control system would be expected to prevent the cash receipts journal and recorded cash sales from reflecting more than the amount shown on the daily deposit slip?

9.15 In the case of The Taxman Always Rings Twice, what information could have been obtained from confirmations directed to the real population of delinquent accounts?

9.16 In the case of Bill Often, Bill Early, what information might have been obtained from enquiries? from detail test of controls procedures? from observations? and from confirmations?

9.17 With reference to the case of Thank Goodness It's Friday, what contribution could an understanding of the business and the management reporting system have made to discovery of the open cash receipts journal cutoff error?

Special Note: The Existence Assertion

LEARNING OBJECTIVE

4. Explain the importance
of the existence asser-
tion for the audit of cash
and accounts receivable,
and describe some pro-
cedures for obtaining
evidence about the exis-
tence of assets.

When considering assertions and obtaining evidence about accounts receivable and other assets, auditors must put emphasis on the existence and rights (ownership) assertions. (For liability accounts, the emphasis is on the completeness and obligations assertions, as will be explained in Chapter 10.) This emphasis on existence is rightly placed because companies and auditors sometimes have gotten into malpractice trouble by giving unqualified reports on financial statements that overstated assets and revenues and understated expenses. For example, credit sales recorded too early (fictitious sales?) result in overstated accounts receivable and overstated sales revenue; failure to amortize prepaid expense results in understated expenses and overstated prepaid expenses (current assets).

Discerning the population of assets to audit for existence and ownership is easy because the company has asserted their existence by putting them on the balance sheet. The audit procedures described in the following sections can be used to obtain evidence about the existence and ownership of accounts receivable and other assets.

Recalculation

Think about the assets that depend largely on calculations. They are amenable to auditors' recalculation procedures. Expired prepaid expenses are recalculated, using auditors' vouching of basic documents, such as loan agreements (prepaid interest), rent contracts (prepaid rent), and insurance policies (prepaid insurance). Goodwill and deferred expenses are recalculated by using original acquisition and payment document information and term (useful life) estimates. A bank reconciliation is a special kind of calculation, and the company's reconciliation can be audited. (See the special note on auditing a bank reconciliation later in this chapter.)

Physical Observation

Inventories and fixed assets can be inspected and counted (more on inventory observation is in Chapter 10). Titles to autos, land, and buildings can be vouched, sometimes using public records in a regional government office. Petty cash and undeposited receipts can be observed and counted, but the cash in the bank cannot. Securities held as investments can be inspected if held by the company.

Confirmation

Letters of confirmation can be sent to banks and customers, asking for a report of the balances owed the company. Likewise, if securities held as investments are in the custody of banks or brokerage houses, the custodians can be asked to report the names, numbers, and quantity of the securities held for the company. In some cases inventories held in public warehouses or out on consignment can be confirmed with the other party. (Refer to the special note on confirmations later in this chapter.)

Verbal Enquiry

Enquiries to management usually do not provide very convincing evidence about existence and ownership. However, enquiries always should be made about the company's agreements to maintain compensating cash balances (may not be classifiable as "cash" among the current assets), about pledge or sale of accounts receivable

---

SIMPLE ANALYTICAL COMPARISON

The auditors prepared a schedule of the monthly credit sales totals for the current and prior years. They noticed several variations, but one, in November of the current year, stood out in particular. The current-year credit sales were almost twice as large as in any prior November. Further investigation showed that a computer error had caused the November credit sales to be recorded twice in the control accounts. The accounts receivable and sales revenue were materially overstated as a result.

---

with recourse in connection with financings, and about pledge of other assets as collateral for loans.

Examination of Documents (vouching)
Evidence of ownership can be obtained by studying the title documents for assets. Examination of loan documents may yield evidence of the need to disclose assets pledged as loan collateral.

Scanning
Assets are supposed to have debit balances. A computer can be used to scan large files of accounts receivable, inventory, and fixed assets for uncharacteristic credit balances. Usually, such credit balances reflect errors in the recordkeeping—customer overpayments, failure to post purchases of inventory, depreciation of assets more than cost. The names of debtors can be scanned for officers, directors, and related parties, amounts for which need to be reported separately or disclosed in the financial statements.

Analytical Procedures
A variety of analytical comparisons may be employed, depending on the circumstances and the nature of the business. Comparisons of asset and revenue balances with recent history may help detect overstatements. Such relationships as receivables turnover, gross margin ratio, and sales/asset ratios can be compared to historical data and industry statistics for evidence of overall reasonableness. Account interrelationships also can be used in analytical review. For example, sales returns and allowances and sales commissions generally vary directly with dollar sales volume, bad debt expense usually varies directly with credit sales volume, and freight expense varies with the physical sales volume. Accounts receivable write-offs should be compared with earlier estimates of doubtful accounts.

R E V I E W
C H E C K P O I N T S

9.18 Why is it important to place emphasis on the existence and rights (ownership) assertions when auditing cash and accounts receivable?

9.19 Which audit procedures are usually the most useful for auditing and existence and rights assertions? Give some examples.

A Decision Not to Use Accounts Receivable Confirmations

Sureparts Manufacturing Company sold all its production to three auto manufacturers and six aftermarket distributors. All nine of these customers typically paid their accounts in full by the 10th day of each following month. The auditors were able to vouch the cash receipts for the full amount of the accounts receivable in the bank statements and cash receipts records in the month following the Surepart year-end. Confirmation evidence was not considered necessary in these circumstances.

Special Note: Using Confirmations

· · · · · · · · · · · ·

LEARNING OBJECTIVE
5. Identify and describe considerations for using confirmations in the audit of cash and accounts receivable.

The confirmation audit procedure was introduced in Chapter 4. This special note gives some details about using confirmations in the audit of cash and accounts receivable. In general, the use of confirmations for cash balances and trade accounts receivable is considered a required generally accepted audit procedure (*Section* 5303.28). However, auditors may decide not to use them if suitable alternative procedures are available and applicable in particular circumstances. Auditors should document justifications for the decision not to use confirmations for trade accounts receivable in a particular audit. Justifications include (1) receivables are not material; (2) confirmations would be ineffective, based on prior years' experience or knowledge that responses could be unreliable; and (3) other substantive test of details procedures provide sufficient appropriate evidence and the auditor has assessed the combined level of inherent risk and control risk associated with the financial statement assertions being audited as low.

Confirmations of Cash and Loan Balances

The standard bank confirmation form is shown in Exhibit 9–7. This form is used to obtain bank confirmation of deposit and loan balances. (Other confirmation letters are used to obtain confirmation of contingent liabilities, endorsements, compensating balance agreements, lines of credit, and other financial instruments and transactions. The standard form and illustrative letters are reproduced in the PA's Professional Engagement Manuals.) A word of caution is in order: While financial institutions may note exceptions to the information typed in a confirmation and may confirm items omitted from it, the auditor should not put sole reliance on the form to satisfy the completeness assertion, insofar as cash and loan balances are concerned. Officers and employees of financial institutions cannot be expected to search their information systems for balances and loans that may not be immediately evident as assets and liabilities of the client company. However, it is a good idea to send confirmations on accounts the company represents as closed during the year to get the bank to confirm zero balances. (If a nonzero balance is confirmed by a bank, the auditors have evidence that some asset accounting has been omitted in the company records.)

Bank Confirmation

Areas to be completed by client are marked §, while those to be completed by the financial institution are marked †

FINANCIAL INSTITUTION § (Name, branch and full mailing address)	CLIENT (LEGAL NAME) § The financial institution is authorized to provide the details requested herein to the below-noted firm of accountants § _____ Client's authorized signature Please supply copy of the most recent credit facility agreement (initial if required) § _____
CONFIRMATION DATE § (All information to be provided as of this date) (See Bank Confirmation Completion Instructions)	

1. LOANS AND OTHER DIRECT AND CONTINGENT LIABILITIES (If balances are nil, please state)

NATURE OF LIABILITY/ CONTINGENT LIABILITY †	INTEREST (Note rate per contract)		DUE DATE †	DATE OF CREDIT FACILITY AGREEMENT †	AMOUNT AND CURRENCY OUTSTANDING †
	RATE †	DATE PAID TO †			

ADDITIONAL CREDIT FACILITY AGREEMENT(S) _____
Note the date(s) of any credit facility agreement(s) not drawn upon and not referenced above † _____

2. DEPOSITS/OVERDRAFTS

TYPE OF ACCOUNT §	ACCOUNT NUMBER §	INTEREST RATE §	ISSUE DATE (If applicable) §	MATURITY DATE (If applicable) §	AMOUNT AND CURRENCY (Brackets if Overdraft) †

EXCEPTIONS AND COMMENTS (See Bank Confirmation Completion Instructions)†

STATEMENT OF PROCEDURES PERFORMED BY FINANCIAL INSTITUTION †
The above information was completed in accordance with the Bank Confirmation Completion Instructions.

_____   BRANCH CONTACT   _____
Authorized signature of financial institution   Name and telephone number

Please mail this form directly to our chartered accountant in the enclosed addressed envelope.

Name:
Address:

Telephone:
Fax:

Developed by the Canadian Bankers Association and The Canadian Institute of Chartered Accountants

EXHIBIT 9-8   ACCOUNTS RECEIVABLE AGED TRIAL BALANCE

```
D-2                        KINGSTON COMPANY              Prepared  JD
PG. 1 OF 15              ACCOUNTS RECEIVABLE             Date     1-12-93
                         December 31, 1992              Reviewed  Terri Tough
                                                        Date      1-17-93


                 ---------  ------- Aged -------   Jan. 1993 Collection
                           30-60   61-90  Over 90                    Past
                 Current   Days    Days   Days    Total   Current    Due
-------------------------------------------------------------------------------
Able Hardware    12,337 X                         12,337 Xpc"12,337
Baker Supply        712                              712        712
Charley Company   1,486 X   420 X                  1,906 Xpc 1,486    420
Dogg General Store                         755       755

-------------------------------------------------------------------------------
Welsch Windows                      531 X          531 X NC           531
Zlat Stuff Place                           214      214              214

Balance per books 335,000 30,000 20,000 15,000 400,000 320,000 25,000
                                                        ⑨
Billing errors    (11,000)        (1,000)      (12,000) ①
                 -------------------------------------------
Adjusted balance  324,000 30,000 19,000 15,000 388,000
```

   X Traced to accounts receivable subsidiary ledger.

   pc Positive confirmation mailed Jan. 4. Replies D-2.3

   NC Negative confirmation mailed Jan. 4. Replies D-2.4

   " No reply to positive confirmation, vouched charges to invoices.

   ∂ Traced to general ledger control account.

   ① Billing error adjustment explained on working paper D-2.2

Note: See D-2.2 for analysis of doubtful accounts and our test
      of reasonableness

Confirmation of Accounts and Notes Receivable

Confirmations provide evidence of existence and, to a limited extent, of valuation of accounts and notes receivable. The accounts and notes to be confirmed should be documented in the working papers with an aged trial balance. (An aged trial balance is shown in Exhibit 9–8, annotated to show the auditor's work.) Accounts for confirmation can be selected at random or in accordance with another plan consistent with the audit objectives. Statistical methods may be useful for determining the sample size. Generalized audit software to access computerized receivables files may be utilized to select and even to print the confirmations.

Two widely used confirmation forms are positive confirmations and negative confirmations. An example of a positive confirmation is shown in Exhibit 9–9. A variation of the positive confirmation is the blank form. A blank confirmation does not contain the balance; customers are asked to fill it in themselves. The blank

EXHIBIT 9–9   POSITIVE CONFIRMATION LETTER

D-2.3

KINGSTON COMPANY
Kingston, Ontario

January 5, 1993

Charley Company
Lake and Adams
Chicago, Illinois

Gentlemen:

Our auditors, Anderson, Olds, and Watershed, are making their regular audit of our financial statements. Part of this audit includes direct verification of customer balances.

PLEASE EXAMINE THE DATA BELOW CAREFULLY AND EITHER CONFIRM ITS ACCURACY OR REPORT ANY DIFFERENCES DIRECTLY TO OUR AUDITORS USING THE ENCLOSED REPLY ENVELOPE.

This is not a request for payment. Please do not send your remittance to our auditors.

Your prompt attention to this confirmation request will be appreciated.

Sandra Carboy

Sandra Carboy, Controller

The balance due Kingston Company as of December 31, 1992, is $1,906. This balance is correct except as noted below:

It's correct. Will send payment as soon

as possible

Date: *Jan. 7, 1993*   By: *P. "Charley" O'Quirk*

Title: *President*

positive confirmation may produce better evidence because the recipients need to get the information directly from their own records instead of just signing the form and returning it with no exceptions noted. (However, the effort involved may cause a lower response rate.)

The negative confirmation form for the same request shown in Exhibit 9–9 is in Exhibit 9–10. The positive form asks for a response. The negative form asks for a response only if something is wrong with the balance; thus, lack of response to negative confirmations is considered evidence of propriety.

The positive form is used when individual balances are relatively large or when accounts are in dispute. Positive confirmations may ask for information about either the account balance or specific invoices, depending on knowledge about how customers maintain their accounting records. The negative form is used mostly when inherent risk and control risk are considered low, when a large number of small balances is involved, and when the client's customers can be expected to consider the

EXHIBIT 9–10   **NEGATIVE CONFIRMATION LETTER**

▲▲▲
KINGSTON COMPANY
Kingston, Ontario

January 5, 1993

Charley Company
Lake and Adams
Chicago, Illinois

Gentlemen:

Our auditors, Anderson, Olds, and Watershed, are making their regular audit of our financial statements. Part of this audit includes direct verification of customer balances.

PLEASE EXAMINE THE DATA BELOW CAREFULLY AND COMPARE THEM TO YOUR RECORDS OF YOUR ACCOUNT WITH US. IF OUR INFORMATION IS NOT IN AGREEMENT WITH YOUR RECORDS, PLEASE STATE ANY DIFFERENCES ON THE REVERSE SIDE OF THIS PAGE, AND RETURN DIRECTLY TO OUR AUDITORS IN THE RETURN ENVELOPE PROVIDED. IF THE INFORMATION IS CORRECT, NO REPLY IS NECESSARY.

This is not a request for payment. Please do not send your remittance to our auditors.

Your prompt attention to this confirmation request will be appreciated.

Sandra Carboy
Sandra Carboy, Controller

As of December 31, 1992, balance due to Kingston Company: $1,906
Date of Origination: November and December, 1992
Type: Open trade account

---

confirmations properly. Frequently, both forms are used: positive confirmations are sent on some customers' accounts and negative confirmations on others. According to *Handbook Section* 6020.09: "For many audit engagements, a combination of positive requests for at least a sample of large accounts and negative requests for at least a sample of smaller accounts will provide a suitable coverage."

Getting confirmations delivered to the intended recipient is a problem that requires auditors' careful attention. Auditors need to control the confirmations, including the addresses to which they are sent. Experience is full of cases where confirmations were mailed to company accomplices, who provided false responses. The auditors should consider carefully features of the reply, such as postmarks, fax and telegraph responses, letterhead, electronic mail, telephone, or other characteristics, that may suggest false responses. Auditors should follow up electronic and telephone responses to determine their origin (e.g., returning the telephone call to a known number, looking up telephone numbers to determine addresses, or using a criss-cross directory to determine the location of a respondent). Furthermore, the lack of response to a negative confirmation is no guarantee that the intended recipient received it unless the auditor carefully controlled the mailing.

The **response rate** for positive confirmations is the proportion of the number of confirmations returned to the number sent, generally after the audit team prompts recipients with second and third requests. Research studies have shown response rates ranging from 66 to 96 percent. Recipients seem to be able to detect account misstatements to varying degrees. Studies have shown **detection rates** (the ratio of the number of exceptions reported to auditors to the number of account errors intentionally reported to customers) ranging from 20 to 100 percent. Negative confirmations seem to have lower detection rates than positive confirmations. Also, studies show somewhat lower detection rates for misstatements favourable to recipients (i.e., an accounts receivable understatement). Overall, positive confirmations appear to be more effective than negative confirmations; but results depend on the type of recipients, the size of the account, and the type of account being confirmed. Effective confirmation practices depend on attention to these factors and on prior years' experience with confirmation results on a particular client's accounts.

Effective confirmation also depends on using a "bag of tricks" to boost the response rate. Often, auditors merely send out a cold, official-looking request in a metered mail envelope and expect customers to be happy to respond. However, the response rate can be increased by using (1) a postcard sent in advance, notifying that a confirmation is coming; (2) special delivery mail; (3) first-class stamp postage (not metered); and (4) an envelope imprinted "Confirmation Enclosed: Please Examine Carefully." These devices increase the cost of the confirmation procedure, but the benefit is a better response rate.[1]

The audit team should try to obtain replies to all positive confirmations by sending second and third requests to nonrespondents. If there is no response or if the response specifies an exception to the client's records, the auditors should carry out document-vouching procedures to audit the account.

These alternative procedures include the vouching direction of finding sales invoice copies, shipping documents, and customer orders that signal the existence of sales charges. They also include the tracing direction of finding evidence of customers' payments in subsequent cash receipts.

When sampling is used, all accounts in the sample should be audited. It is improper to substitute an easy-to-audit customer account not in the sample for one that does not respond to a confirmation request.

Confirmation of receivables may be performed at a date other than the year-end. When confirmation is done at an interim date, the audit firm is able to spread work throughout the year and avoid the pressures of overtime that typically occur around December 31. Also, the audit can be completed sooner after the year-end date if confirmation has been done earlier. The primary consideration when considering confirmation of accounts before the balance sheet date is the client's internal control over transactions affecting receivables. When confirmation is performed at an interim date, the following additional procedures should be considered:

1. Obtain a summary of receivables transactions from the interim date to the year-end date.

---

[1] CICA, *Confirmation of Accounts Receivable, An Audit Technique Study* (Toronto, 1980), Chapter 5. See also Paul Caster, "The Role of Confirmations as Audit Evidence," *Journal of Accountancy*, February 1992, pp. 73–76.

2. Obtain a year-end trial balance of receivables, compare it to the interim trial balance, and obtain evidence and explanations for large variations.

3. Consider the necessity for additional confirmations as of the balance sheet date if balances have increased materially.

One final note about confirmations: Confirmations of accounts, loans, and notes receivable may not produce sufficient evidence of ownership by the client (rights assertion). Debtors may not be aware that the auditor's client has sold their accounts, notes, or loans receivable to financial institutions or to the public (collateralized securities). Auditors need to perform additional enquiry and detail procedures to get evidence of the ownership of the receivables and of the appropriateness of disclosures related to financing transactions secured by receivables.

Summary: Confirmations

Confirmations of cash balances, loans, accounts receivable, and notes receivable are required, unless auditors can justify substituting other procedures in the circumstances of a particular audit. The bank confirmation is a standard positive form. Confirmations for accounts and notes receivable can be in positive or negative form, and the positive form may be a blank confirmation.

Auditors must take care to control confirmations to ensure that responses are received from the real debtors and not from persons who can intercept the confirmations to give false responses. Responses by fax, telegraph, electronic mail, telephone, or other means not written and signed by a recipient should be followed up to determine their genuine origins. Second and third requests should be sent to prompt responses to positive confirmations, and auditors should audit nonresponding customers by alternative procedures. Accounts in a sample should not be left unaudited (e.g., "They didn't respond"), and easy-to-audit accounts should not be substituted for hard-to-audit ones in a sample. Various "tricks" can be used to raise the response rate.

Confirmations yield evidence about existence and gross valuation. However, the fact that a debtor admits to owing the debt does not mean the debtor can pay. Other procedures must be undertaken to audit the collectibility of the accounts. Nevertheless, confirmations can give some clues about collectibility when customers tell about balances in dispute. Confirmations of accounts, notes, and loans receivable should not be used as the only evidence of the ownership (rights assertions) of these financial assets.

R E V I E W
C H E C K P O I N T S

9.20 List the information a PA should solicit in a standard bank confirmation enquiry sent to an audit client's bank.

9.21 Distinguish between "positive" and "negative" confirmations. Under what conditions would you expect each type of confirmation to be appropriate?

9.22 Distinguish between confirmation "response rate" and confirmation "detection rate."

9.23 What methods can be used to increase the response rate for receivables confirmations?

9.24 What are some of the justifications for not using confirmations of accounts receivable on a particular audit?

9.25 What special care should be taken with regard to examining the sources of accounts receivable confirmation responses?

. . . .

SPECIAL NOTE: AUDIT OF BANK RECONCILIATIONS WITH ATTENTION TO LAPPING AND KITING

. . . .

LEARNING OBJECTIVE

6. Design and perform substantive audit procedures for the audit of a bank statement reconciliation, and tell how auditors can search for lapping and kiting.

The company's bank reconciliation is the primary means of valuing cash in the financial statements. The amount of cash in the bank is almost always different from the amount in the books (financial statements), and the reconciliation purports to explain the difference. The normal procedure is to obtain the company-prepared bank reconciliation and audit it. Auditors should not perform the company's control function of preparing the reconciliation.

A client-prepared bank reconciliation is shown in Exhibit 9–11. The bank balance is confirmed and cross-referenced to the bank confirmation working paper (Exhibit 9–7). The reconciliation is recalculated, the outstanding cheques and deposits in transit are footed, and the book balance is traced to the trial balance (which has been traced to the general ledger). The reconciling items should be vouched to determine whether outstanding cheques really were not paid and that deposits in transit actually were mailed before the reconciliation date. The auditor's information source for vouching the bank reconciliation items is a **cutoff bank statement,** which is a complete bank statement including all paid cheques and deposit slips. The client requests the bank to send this bank statement directly to the auditor. It is usually for a 10– to 20–day period following the reconciliation date. (It also can be the next regular monthly statement, received directly by the auditors.)

The vouching of outstanding cheques and deposits in transit is a matter of comparing cheques that cleared in the cutoff bank statement with the list of outstanding cheques for evidence that all cheques that were written prior to the reconciliation date were on the list of outstanding cheques. The deposits shown in transit should be recorded by the bank in the first business days of the cutoff period. If recorded later, the inference is that the deposit may have been made up from receipts of the period after the reconciliation date. For large outstanding cheques not clearing in the cutoff period, vouching may be extended to other documentation supporting the disbursement. These procedures are keyed and described by tick marks in Exhibit 9–11.

Accounts Receivable Lapping

When the business receives many payments from customers, a detailed audit would include comparison of the cheques listed on a sample of deposit slips (from the reconciliation month and other months) to the detail of customer credits listed on the day's posting to customer accounts receivable (daily remittance list or other record of detail postings). This procedure is a test for accounts receivable lapping. It is an attempt to find credits given to customers for whom no payments were received on the day in question. An example of this type of comparison is in the discovery summary section of Casette 9.1 (The Canny Cashier).

E X H I B I T 9–11   BANK RECONCILIATION

```
                          KINGSTON COMPANY
   C-2            BANK RECONCILIATION—NORTH COUNTRY BANK        Prepared  J.D. 1/10/93
                          General Account                      Reviewed  JRA 1/10/93
                             12/31/92
                       (Prepared by client)

 Balance per bank statement                           506,100  c
 Add:
    Deposit in transit as of 12/31/92                  51,240  n
 Deduct outstanding checks:                           -------
                                                      557,340
       Date      No.    Payee
      --------   ----   ---------------------
      12/10/91    842   Ace Supply Company          500  ✗
      11/31/92   1280   Ace Supply Company        1,800  ✓
      12/15/92   1372   Northwest Lumber Co.      30,760  ✓
      12/28/92   1412   Gibson & Johnson           7,270  ✗
      12/30/92   1417   North Country payroll     20,000  ✓
      12/30/92   1418   Ace Supply Company         2,820  ✓
      12/30/92   1419   Windy City Utilities       2,030  ✓
      12/30/92   1420   Howard Hardware Supply     8,160  ✓
                                                  -------
 Balance per book                                  73,340
                                                  -------
                                                  484,000  f
                                                  -------
```

Note: Obtained cutoff bank statement 1/9/93 (C-23) (T/B-1)
   f   Footed
   c   Confirmed by bank, standard bank confirmation (C-22)
   n   Vouched to cutoff bank statement, deposit recorded by bank
       on 1/3/93. Vouched to duplicate deposit slip validaged 1/3/93
   ✓   Vouched to paid check cleared with cutoff bank statement.
   ✗   Vouched to statement from attorneys.
   ✗   Amount in dispute per controller.

Cheque Kiting

Auditors also should be alert to the possibility of "kiting." **Cheque kiting** is the practice of building up apparent balances in one or more bank accounts based on uncollected (float) cheques drawn against similar accounts in other banks. Kiting involves depositing money from one bank account to another, using a hot cheque. The depository bank does not know the cheque is on insufficient funds, but the deficiency is covered by another hot cheque from another bank account before the first cheque clears. Kiting is the deliberate floating of funds between two or more bank accounts. By this method a bank customer uses the time required for cheques to clear to obtain an unauthorized loan without any interest charge.

Professional money managers working for cash-conscious businesses try to have minimal unused balances in their accounts, and their efforts sometimes can look like cheque kites. Tight cash flows initiate kites, and intent to kite is the key for criminal charges. Kites evolve to involve numerous banks and numerous cheques. The more banks and broader geographical distance, the harder a perpetrator finds it to control a kite scheme.

Here is a simple illustration of how a kite scheme works:

Start with no money in Bank A and Bank B, and draw $5,000 cheques on each to "deposit" in the other:

	Bank A	BankB	Total
Apparent balances	$5,000	$5,000	$10,000
Actual balances	0	0	0

Do it again with $8,000 cheques:

	Bank A	Bank B	Total
Apparent balances	$13,000	$13,000	$26,000
Actual balances	0	0	0

Make a $6,000 down payment on a Mercedes from Bank A:

	Bank A	Bank B	Total
Apparent balances	$ 7,000	$13,000	$20,000
Actual balances	(6,000)	0	(6,000)

At the same time that the first cheques for $5,000 clear, write some more, this time for $9,000 each:

	Bank A	Bank B	Total
Apparent balances	$11,000	$17,000	$28,000
Actual balances	(6,000)	0	(6,000)

Pay the balances ($28,000) to a travel agent and take a long trip (preferably to a country with no extradition treaty!):

	Bank A	Bank B	Total
Apparent balances	0	0	0
Actual balances	$(17,000)	$(17,000)	$(34,000)

These are some characteristic signs of cheque kiting schemes:

- Frequent deposits and cheques in same accounts.
- Frequent deposits and cheques in round amounts.
- Frequent deposits with cheques written on the same (other) banks.
- Short time lag between deposits and withdrawals.
- Frequent ATM account balance enquiries.
- Many large deposits made on Thursday or Friday to take advantage of the weekend.
- Large periodic balances in individual accounts with no apparent business explanation.
- Low average balance compared to high level of deposits.
- Many cheques made payable to other banks.
- Bank willingness to pay against uncollected funds.
- "Cash" withdrawals with deposit cheques drawn on another bank.
- Cheques drawn on foreign banks with lax banking laws and regulations.

Auditors can detect the above signs of cheque kiting by reviewing bank account activity. The only trouble is that criminal cheque kiters often destroy the banking documents. If a company cannot or will not produce its bank statements, with all deposit slips and cancelled cheques, the auditors should be wary.

If these cash transfers are recorded in the books, a company will show the negative balances that result from cheques drawn on insufficient funds. However, perpetrators may try to hide the kiting by not recording the deposits and cheques. Such manoeuvres may be detectable in a bank reconciliation audit. If auditors notice some sign of kiting, yet no uncleared items are on the reconciliation, a schedule of interbank transfers can be constructed from the cancelled cheques and the cleared deposits in the bank statements. This schedule shows each cheque amount, the name of the paying bank (with the book recording date and the cheque clearing date), and the name of the receiving bank (with the book deposit date and the bank clearing date). The purpose of this schedule is to see that both sides of the transfer transaction are recorded in the same period (and in the proper period). (An example is in Exhibit 9.62–1 with Discussion Case 9.62 at the end of the chapter.)

Summary: Bank Reconciliations, Lapping, and Kiting

The combination of all the procedures performed on the bank reconciliation provides evidence of existence, valuation, and proper cutoff of the bank cash balances. Auditors use a cutoff bank statement to obtain independent evidence of the proper listing of outstanding cheques and deposits in transit on a bank reconciliation.

Additional procedures can be performed to try to detect attempts at lapping accounts receivable collections and kiting cheques. For lapping these procedures include auditing the details of customer payments listed in bank deposits in comparison to details of customer payment postings (remittance lists). For kiting these procedures include being alert to the signs of kites and preparing a schedule of interbank transfers.

R E V I E W
C H E C K P O I N T S

9.26 What is a cutoff bank statement? How is it used by auditors?

9.27 What is "lapping?" What procedures can auditors employ for its detection?

9.28 What is "cheque kiting?" How might auditors detect kiting?

Summary

The revenue and collection cycle consists of customer order processing, credit checking, shipping goods, billing customers and accounting for accounts receivable, and collecting and accounting for cash receipts. Companies reduce control risk by having a suitable separation of authorization, custody, recording, and periodic reconciliation duties. Error-checking procedures of comparing customer orders and shipping documents are important for billing customers the right prices for the delivered quantities. Otherwise, many things could go wrong—ranging from making sales to fictitious customers or customers with bad credit to erroneous billings for the wrong quantities at the wrong prices at the wrong time.

Cash collection is a critical point for asset control. Many cases of embezzlement occur in this process. Illustrative cases in this chapter told the stories of some of these cash embezzlement schemes, including the practice of "lapping" accounts receivable.

Three topics were given special technical notes in the chapter. The existence assertion is very important in the audit of cash and receivables assets because misleading financial statements often have contained overstated assets and revenue. The use of confirmations got a special section in this chapter because confirmation is frequently used to obtain evidence of asset existence from outside parties, such as customers who owe on accounts receivable. The audit of bank reconciliations was covered in the context of an audit opportunity to recalculate the amount of cash for the financial statements and to look for signs of accounts receivable lapping and cheque kiting.

CASE STUDY   KINGSTON COMPANY

Kingston Case Assignments

9.29   ICQ Items: Objectives and Errors from Control Weaknesses.   Anderson, Olds & Watershed auditors began the assessment of control risk by considering the possible errors and irregularities that could occur in the Kingston revenue and collection cycle.

Required:

Refer to the internal control questionnaire on cash receipts (Appendix 9A–1) and assume the answer to each question is no. Prepare a table matching the questions to the possible "errors" or "irregularities" that could occur because of the absence of the control. The column headings of your table should be:

Question Number	Possible Error or Irregularity Due to Control Weakness

9.30   ICQ Sales Transaction Processing.

The internal control questionnaire (on the next page) for the sales processing of the Kingston Company is from Appendix 9A-2. The Anderson, Olds & Watershed audit senior prefers questionnaires that are organized by control objectives and has prepared this one for you to determine the proper answers.

Required:

Prepare the answers to the questionnaire on sales transactions. You do not need to write the questions; simply identify the question number and your response on the description of the sales transaction processing described in the Kingston case at the end of Chapters 4 and 5. For yes answers, add a comment stating which department and clerk does the function.

9.31   Bridge Working Paper for Cash Receipts.

A bridge working paper was described in Chapter 6 as a means of connecting the control evaluation to subsequent test of controls and substantive procedures. The major strengths are related to the test of controls procedures, and the major weaknesses require suggestions for the substantive procedures. (See Exhibit 6–12 for an example.)

Required:

The audit senior has directed you to evaluate the controls over cash receipts for Kingston Company using the company description at the end of Chapter 4 and 5, Exhibit 9–3 (cash receipts processing flowchart), and Appendix 9A-1 (cash receipts processing internal control questionnaire). Prepare the bridge working paper for cash receipts. You will find it helpful to refer to Exhibit 9–6 (test of controls audit procedures) and Appendix 9B-1 (substantive procedures for cash).

9.32   Matching ICQ Questions to Test of Controls Audit Program.

The internal control questionnaires have been organized by control objectives. These control objectives become audit objectives when the controls are tested. The senior on the Kingston audit has another assignment for you. She wants the ICQ questions cross-referenced to the audit program.

Required:

Prepare a table listing the question numbers for the ICQ in Appendix 9A-3 (accounts and notes receivable), and opposite each question number list the related test of controls audit procedure number(s) from the audit program in Exhibit 9–6.

9.33   Accounts Receivable Confirmations.

The Kingston Company maintains the accounts receivable subsidiary ledger on a computer database. Assume that 93 negative confirmations have been mailed. Also, six positive confirmations were sent to the customers with the largest balances.

Required:

Prepare a memo addressing the following issues:

a. Identify and describe the two forms of accounts receivable confirmation requests and indicate what factors should be considered in determining when to use each.

b. Two of the customers who received positive confirmations never replied, even to a second request. What ''alternative procedures'' could you use to verify the existence of these accounts and the gross value of the receivables?

Multiple-choice Questions for Practice and Review

9.34 Which of the following would be the best protection for a company that wishes to prevent the lapping of trade accounts receivable?
a. Segregate duties so that the bookkeeper in charge of the general ledger has no access to incoming mail.
b. Segregate duties so that no employee has access to both cheques from customers and currency from daily cash receipts.
c. Have customers send payments directly to the company's depository bank.
d. Request that customer's payment cheques be made payable to the company and addressed to the treasurer.

9.35 Which of the following internal control procedures will most likely prevent the concealment of a cash shortage from the improper write-off of a trade account receivable?
a. Write-off must be approved by a responsible officer after review of credit department recommendations and supporting evidence.
b. Write-offs must be supported by an aging schedule showing that only receivables overdue several months have been written off.
c. Write-offs must be approved by the cashier who is in a position to know if the receivables have, in fact, been collected.
d. Write-offs must be authorized by company field sales employees who are in a position to determine the financial standing of the customers.

9.36 Auditors sometimes use comparisons of ratios as audit evidence. For example, an unexplained decrease in the ratio of gross profit to sales may suggest which of the following possibilities?
a. Unrecorded purchases.
b. Unrecorded sales.
c. Merchandise purchases being charged to selling and general expense.
d. Fictitious sales.

9.37 An auditor is auditing sales transactions. One step is to vouch a sample of debit entries from the accounts receivable subsidiary ledger back to the supporting sales invoices. What would the auditor intend to establish by this step?
a. Sales invoices represent bona fide sales.
b. All sales have been recorded.
c. All sales invoices have been properly posted to customer accounts.
d. Debit entries in the accounts receivable subsidiary ledger are properly supported by sales invoices.

9.38 To conceal defalcations involving receivables, the auditor would expect an experienced bookkeeper to charge which of the following accounts?
a. Miscellaneous income.
b. Petty cash.
c. Miscellaneous expense.
d. Sales returns.

9.39 Which of the following would the auditor consider to be an incompatible operation if the cashier receives remittances?
a. The cashier prepares the daily deposit.
b. The cashier makes the daily deposit at a local bank.
c. The cashier posts the receipts to the accounts receivable subsidiary ledger cards.
d. The cashier endorses the cheques.

9.40 The audit working papers often include a client-prepared, aged trial balance of accounts receivable as of the balance sheet date. The aging is best used by the auditor to:
a. Evaluate internal control over credit sales.
b. Test the accuracy of recorded charge sales.
c. Estimate credit losses.
d. Verify the existence of the recorded receivables.

9.41 Which of the following might be detected by an auditor's cutoff review and examination of sales journal entries for several days prior to the balance sheet date?

a. Lapping year-end accounts receivable.

b. Inflating sales for the year.

c. Kiting bank balances.

d. Misappropriating merchandise.

9.42 Confirmation of individual accounts receivable balances directly with debtors will, of itself, normally provide evidence concerning the:

a. Collectibility of the balances confirmed.

b. Ownership of the balances confirmed.

c. Existence of the balances confirmed.

d. Internal control over balances confirmed.

9.43 Which of the following is one of the better auditing techniques an auditor might use to detect kiting between intercompany banks?

a. Review composition of authenticated deposit slips.

b. Review subsequent bank statements.

c. Prepare a schedule of the bank transfers.

d. Prepare a year-end bank reconciliation.

9.44 The best reason for prenumbering in numerical sequence such documents as sales orders, shipping documents, and sales invoices is:

a. Enables company personnel to determine the accuracy of each document.

b. Enables personnel to determine the proper period recording of sales revenue and receivables.

c. Enables personnel to check the numerical sequence for missing documents and unrecorded transactions.

d. Enables personnel to determine the validity of recorded transactions.

9.45 When a sample of customer accounts receivable are selected for the purpose of vouching debits therein for validity evidence, the auditors will vouch them to:

a. Sales invoices with shipping documents and customer sales invoices.

b. Records of accounts receivable write-offs.

c. Cash remittance lists and bank deposit slips.

d. Credit files and reports.

9.46 In the audit of cash and accounts receivable, the most important emphasis should be on the:

a. Completeness assertions.

b. Existence assertion.

c. Obligations assertion.

d. Presentation and disclosure assertion.

9.47 When accounts receivable are confirmed at an interim date, the auditors need not be concerned with:

a. Obtaining a summary of receivables transactions from the interim date to the year-end date.

b. Obtaining a year-end trial balance of receivables, comparing it to the interim trial balance, and obtaining evidence and explanations for large variations.

c. Sending negative confirmations to all the customers as of the year-end date.

d. Considering the necessity for some additional confirmations as of the balance sheet date if balances have increased materially.

9.48 The negative request form of accounts receivable confirmation is useful particularly when the:

	Assessed level of control risk relating to receivables is:	Number of small balances is:	Proper consideration by the recipient is:
a.	Low	Many	Likely
b.	Low	Few	Unlikely
c.	High	Few	Likely
d.	High	Many	Likely

(AICPA adapted)

9.49 When an auditor selects a sample of shipping documents and takes the tracing direction of a test to find the related sales invoice copies, the evidence is relevant for deciding:

a. Shipments to customers were invoiced.

b. Shipments to customers were recorded as sales.

c. Recorded sales were shipped.

d. Invoiced sales were shipped.

(AICPA adapted)

EXERCISES AND PROBLEMS

9.50 Cash Receipts: Control Objectives and Control Examples. Prepare a table similar to Exhibit 9–4 (internal control objectives) for cash receipts.

9.51 Internal Control Questionnaire for Book Buy-back Cash Fund. Taylor, a PA, has been engaged to audit the financial statements of University Books, Incorporated. University Books maintains a large, revolving cash fund exclusively for the purpose of buying used books from students for cash. The cash fund is active all year because the nearby university offers a large variety of courses with varying starting and completion dates throughout the year.

Receipts are prepared for each purpose. Reimbursement vouchers periodically are submitted to replenish the fund.

Required:

Construct an internal control questionnaire to be used in evaluating the system of internal control over University Books's buying back books using the revolving cash fund. The internal control questionnaire should elicit a yes or no response to each question. Do not discuss the internal controls over books that are purchased.

(AICPA adapted)

9.52 Test of Controls Audit Procedures for Cash Receipts. You are the in-charge auditor examining the financial statements of the Gutzler Company for the year ended December 31. During late October you, with the help of Gutzler's controller, completed an internal control questionnaire and prepared the appropriate memoranda describing Gutzler's accounting procedures. Your comments relative to cash receipts are as follows:

All cash receipts are sent directly to the accounts receivable clerk with no processing by the mail department. The accounts receivable clerk keeps the cash receipts journal, prepares the bank deposit slip in duplicate, posts from the deposit slip to the subsidiary accounts receivable ledger, and mails the deposit to the bank.

The controller receives the validated deposit slips directly (unopened) from the bank. She also receives the monthly bank statement directly (unopened) from the bank and promptly reconciles it.

At the end of each month, the accounts receivable clerk notifies the general ledger clerk by journal voucher of the monthly totals of the cash receipts journal for posting to the general ledger.

Each month, with regard to the general ledger cash account, the general ledger clerk makes an entry to record the total debits to cash from the cash receipts journal. In addition, the general ledger clerk, on occasion, makes debit entries in the general ledger cash account from sources other than the cash receipts journal—for example, funds borrowed from the bank. Certain standard auditing procedures listed below already have been performed by you in the audit of cash receipts:

All columns in the cash receipts have been totalled and cross-totalled.

Postings from the cash receipts journal have been traced to the general ledger.

Remittance advices and related correspondence have been traced to entries in the cash receipts journal.

Required:

Considering Gutzler's internal control over cash receipts and the standard auditing procedures already performed, list all other auditing procedures that should be performed to obtain sufficient audit evidence regarding cash receipts control and give the reasons for each procedure. Do not discuss the procedures for cash disbursements and cash balances. Also, do not discuss the extent to which any of the procedures are to be performed. Assume adequate controls exist to ensure that all sales transactions are recorded. Organize your answer sheet as follows:

Other Audit Procedures	Reason for Other Audit Procedures

(AICPA adapted)

9.53 Cash Receipts: Weaknesses and Recommendations. The Pottstown Art League operates a museum for the benefit and enjoyment of the community. During hours when the museum is open to the public, two volunteer clerks positioned at the entrance collect a $5 admission fee from each nonmember patron. Members of the Art League are permitted to enter free of charge on presentation of their membership cards.

At the end of each day, one of the clerks delivers the proceeds to the treasurer. The treasurer counts the cash in the presence of the clerk and places it in a safe. Each Friday afternoon, the treasurer and one of the clerks deliver all cash held in the safe to the bank, and they receive an authenticated deposit slip that provides the basis for the weekly entry in the cash receipts journal.

The board of directors of the Pottstown Art League has identified a need to improve the system of internal control over cash admission fees. The board has determined that the cost of installing turnstiles or sales booths or otherwise altering the physical layout of the museum will greatly exceed any benefits that may be derived. However, the board has agreed that the sale of admission tickets must be an integral part of its improvement efforts.

Required:

The board of directors has requested your assistance. Prepare a report for presentation and discussion at their next board meeting that identifies the weaknesses in the existing system of cash admission fees and suggests recommendations.

(AICPA adapted)

9.54 Control Weaknesses: Computer. Ajax, Inc., an audit client, recently installed a new computer system to process the shipping, billing, and accounts receivable records more efficiently. During interim work, an assistant completed the review of the accounting system and the internal controls. The assistant determined the following information concerning the new computer systems and the processing and control of shipping notices and customer invoices.

Each major computerized function (i.e., shipping, billing, accounts receivable) is permanently assigned to a specific computer operator who is responsible for making program changes, running the program, and reconciling the computer log. Responsibility for the custody and control over the various databases and system documentation is randomly rotated among the computer operators on a monthly basis to prevent any one person from having access to the database and documentation at all times. Each computer programmer and computer operator has access to the computer room via a magnetic card and a digital code that is different for each card. The systems analyst and the supervisor of computer operators do not have access to the computer room.

The computer system documentation consists of the following items: program listings, error listings, logs, and database dictionaries. To increase efficiency, batch totals and processing controls are not used in the system.

Ajax ships its products directly from two warehouses, which forward shipping notices to general accounting. There, the billing clerk enters the price of the item and accounts for the numerical sequence of the shipping notices. The billing clerk also prepares daily adding machine tapes of the units shipped and the sales amounts. Shipping notices and adding machine tapes forwarded to the computer department for processing the computer output consist of:

a. A three-copy invoice that is forwarded to the billing clerk.

b. A daily sales register showing the aggregate totals of units shipped and sales amounts that the computer operator compares to the adding machine tapes.

The billing clerk mails two copies of each invoice to the customer and retains the third copy in an open invoice file that serves as a detail accounts receivable record.

Required:

a. Prepare a list of weaknesses in internal control (manual and computer), and for each weakness make one or more recommendations.

b. Suggest how Ajax's computer processing over shipping and billing could be improved through the use of remote terminals to enter shipping notices. Describe appropriate controls for such an on-line data entry system.

CASH: SUBSTANTIVE AUDIT PROCEDURES

9.55 Bank Reconciliation. The following client-prepared bank reconciliation is being examined by you during an audit of the financial statements of Cynthia Company:

CYNTHIA COMPANY
Bank Reconciliation
Village Bank Account 2
December 31, 1992

Balance per bank (a):		$18,375.91
Deposits in transit (b):		
12/30	$1,471.10	
12/31	2,840.69	4,311.79
Subtotal		22,687.70
Outstanding cheques (c):		
837	6,000.00	
1941	671.80	
1966	320.00	
1984	1,855.42	
1985	3,621.22	
1987	2,576.89	
1991	4,420.88	(19,466.21)
Subtotal		3,221.49
NSF cheque Returned 12/29 (d):		200.00
Bank charges		5.50
Error cheque no. 1932		148.10
Customer note collected by the bank ($2,750 plus $275 interest (e):		(3,025.00)
Balance per books (f):		$ 550.09

Required:

Indicate one or more audit procedures that should be performed in gathering evidence in support of each of the items (a) through (f) above.

(AICPA adapted)

9.56 Sales Cutoff and Cutoff Bank Statement.

a. You wish to test Houston Corporaton's sales cutoff at June 30. Describe the steps you should include in this test.

b. You obtain a July 10 bank statement directly from the bank. Explain how this cutoff bank statement should be used:

(1) In your review of the June 30 bank reconciliation.

(2) To obtain other audit information.

(AICPA adapted)

9.57 Bank Reconciliation—Cash Shortage. The Patrick Company had poor internal control over its cash transactions. Facts about its cash position at November 30 were the following:

The cash books showed a balance of $18,901.62, which included undeposited receipts. A credit of $100 on the bank statement did not appear on the books of the company. The balance according to the statement was $15,550.

When you received the cutoff bank statement on December 10, the following cancelled cheques were enclosed: no. 6500 for $116.25, no. 7126 for $150.00, no. 7815 for $253.25, no. 8621 for $190.71, no. 8623 for $206.80, and no. 8632 for $145.28. The only deposit was in the amount of $3,794.41 on December 7.

The cashier handles all incoming cash and makes the bank deposits personally. He also reconciles the monthly bank statement. His November 30 reconciliation is shown below.

Balance, per books, November 30		$18,901.62
Add: Outstanding cheques:		
8621	$190.71	
8623	206.80	
8632	145.28	442.79
		19,344.41
Less: Undeposited receipts		3,794.41
Balance per bank, November 30		15,550.00
Deduct: Unrecorded credit		100.00
True cash, November 30		$15,450.00

Required:

a. You suspect that the cashier has stolen some money. Prepare a schedule showing your estimate of the loss.
b. How did the cashier attempt to conceal the theft?
c. Based only on the information above, name two specific features of internal control that apparently were missing.
d. If the cashier's October 31 reconciliation is known to be in order and you start your audit on December 5, what specific auditing procedures could you perform to discover the theft?

(AICPA adapted)

RECEIVABLES AND REVENUES: SUBSTANTIVE AUDIT PROCEDURES

9.58 Alternative Accounts Receivable Procedures. Several accounts receivable confirmations have been returned with the notation "verification of vendors statements is no longer possible because our data processing system does not accumulate each vendor's invoices." What alternative auditing procedures could be used to audit these accounts receivable?

(AICPA adapted)

9.59 Receivables Audit Procedures. The ABC Appliance Company, a manufacturer of small electrical appliances, deals exclusively with 20 distributors situated throughout the country. At December 31 (the balance sheet date) receivables from these distributors aggregated $875,000. Total current assets were $1.3 million.

With respect to receivables, the auditors followed the procedures outline below in the course of the annual audit of financial statements:

1. Reviewed the system of internal control and found it to be exceptionally good.
2. Reconciled the subsidiary and control accounts at year-end.
3. Aged accounts. None were overdue.
4. Examined details sales and collection transactions for the months of February, July, and November.
5. Received positive confirmations of year-end balances.

Required:

Criticize the completeness or incompleteness of the above program, giving reasons for your recommendations concerning the addition or omission of any procedures.

(AICPA adapted)

9.60 Rent Revenue. You were engaged to conduct an audit of the financial statements of Clayton Realty Corporation for the year ending January 31. The examination of the annual rent reconciliation is a vital portion of the audit.

The following rent reconciliation was prepared by the controller of Clayton Realty Corporation and was presented to you. You subjected it to various audit procedures:

CLAYTON REALTY CORPORATION
Rent Reconciliation
For the Year Ended January 31

Gross apartment rents (Schedule A)	$1,600,800*
Less vacancies (Schedule B)	20,000*
Net apartment rentals	1,580,300
Less unpaid rents (Schedule C)	7,800*
Total	1,572,500
Add prepaid rent collected (Schedule D)	500*
Total cash collected	$1,573,000*

Schedules A, B, C, and D are available to you but have not been illustrated. You have conducted an assessment of the control risk and found it to be low. Cash receipts from rental operations are deposited in a special bank account.

Required:
What substantive audit procedures should you employ during the audit in order to substantiate the validity of each of the dollar amounts marked by an asterisk(*)?

(AICPA adapted)

DISCUSSION CASES

9.61 Trinity Company—Defalcations. Assume that you are participating in the audit of the Trinity Company's financial statements. The situations described below came to your attention when you performed certain substantive audit procedures of account balance details.

1. The July sales journal indicated that customers were billed $140,000 during that month. This amount was posted as a debit to accounts receivable and a credit to sales. However, you tested the footing of the July sales journal and determined that the correct sum of the customer billings was $144,500.

2. You noted that an $8,500 debit posting had been entered in the miscellaneous expense account, but you could not vouch this posting to any "preceding" record (such as a purchases journal, payroll journal, or general journal).

3. When you examined a voucher for the purchase of office supplies, you

noted that the cheque signer had initialed the vendor's invoice to indicate her approval, but the purchase order and receiving report had not been initialed or otherwise cancelled.

4. When you audited the reconciliation of the company's chequing account at year-end, you noted that a $6,000 cheque had been omitted from the list of outstanding cheques. The cheque had been issued and recorded as a disbursement during the previous month, but it had not yet cleared the bank.

Required:
1. Describe how each situation may indicate an attempted concealment of a defalcation.
2. Answer the following general questions:
   a. Are certain types of concealment "temporary" in the sense that further actions will be required to prevent detection?

EXHIBIT 9.62–1   SCHEDULE OF INTERBANK TRANSFERS

C-5

EVERREADY CORPORATION
Schedule of Interbank Transfers
December 31, 1992

Prepared _____
Date _____
Reviewed _____
Date _____

	Disbursing Account				Receiving Account		
Check #	Bank	Amount	Date per Books	Date per Bank	Bank	Date per Books	Date per Bank
1417	North Country	10,463✓	24-Dec	24-Dec˜	North Country payroll	24-Dec r	24-Decx
1601	North Country	11,593✓	31-Dec✗	31-Dec˜	North Country payroll	31-Dec r	31-Decx
1982	North Country	9.971✓	08-Jan	08-Jan˜	North Country payroll	08-Jan r	08-Janx

✓Traced from cash disbursements journal.
✗Cheque properly listed as outstanding on bank reconciliation.
˜Vouched to cheque cleared in bank statement.
rTraced from cash receipts journal.
xVouched deposit cleared in bank statement.
Note: We scanned the cash disbursements and cash receipts journals for cheques to and deposits from other bank accounts.

b. How might the direction of audit testing (testing for over- or understatement) be influenced by the auditor's responsibility to search for material defalcations?

c. Can auditors rely exclusively on a good internal control structure to fulfil the responsibility to search for and detect material misstatements?

d. Can auditors rely exclusively on analytical procedures to fulfil the responsibility to search for and detect material misstatements?

(Adapted from the case contributed by Deloitte Haskins & Sells to the Auditor's Report)

9.62 Interbank Transfers. EverReady Corporation is in the home building and repair business. Construction business has been in a slump, and the company has expierenced financial difficulty over the past two years. Part of the problem lies in the company's desire to avoid laying off its skilled crews of bricklayers and cabinetmakers. Meeting the payroll has been a problem.

The auditors are engaged to audit the 1992 financial statements. Knowing of EverReady's financial difficulty and its business policy, the auditors decided to prepare a schedule of interbank transfers covering the 10 days before and after December 31, which is the company's balance sheet date.

First, the auditors used the cash receipts and disbursements journals to prepare part of the schedule shown in Exhibit 9.62–1. They obtained the information for everything except the dates of deposit and payment in the bank statements (disbursing date per bank and receiving date per bank). They learned that EverReady always transferred money to the payroll account at North Country Bank from the general account at North Country Bank. This transfer enabled the bank to clear the payroll cheques without delay. The only bank accounts in the EverReady financial statements are the two at North Country Bank.

Next, the auditors obtained the December 1992 and January 1993 bank statements for the general and payroll accounts at North Country Bank. They recorded the bank disbursement and receipt dates in the schedule of interbank transfers. For each transfer these dates are identical because the accounts are in the same bank. An alert auditor noticed that the North Country Bank general account bank statement also contains deposits received from Commerce

Bank and cancelled cheque number 1799 dated January 5 payable to Commerce Bank. This cheque cleared the Commerce Bank account on January 8 and was marked "transfer of funds." This led to new information.

NEW INFORMATION

Asked about the Commerce Bank transactions, EverReady's chief financial of-ficer readily admitted the existence of an off-books bank account. He explained that it was used for financing transactions in keeping with normal practice in the construction industry. He gave the auditors the December and January bank statements for the account at Commerce Bank. In it, the auditors found the following:

Commerce Bank Cheque #	Payable to	Amount	Dated	Cleared Bank
4050	North Country	10,000	23-Dec	29-Dec
4051	Chase Bank	12,000	28-Dec	31-Dec
4052	North Country	12,000	30-Dec	05-Jan
4053	Chase Bank	14,000	04-Jan	07-Jan
4054	North Country	20,000	08-Jan	13-Jan

Deposits		
Received from	Amount	Dated
Chase Bank	11,000	22-Dec
Chase Bank	15,000	30-Dec
North Country	10,000	05-Jan
Chase Bank	12,000	07-Jan

When asked about the Chase Bank transactions, EverReady's chief financial officer admitted the existence of another off-books bank account, which he said was the personal account of the principal shareholder. He explained that the shareholder often used it to finance EverReady's operations. He gave the auditors the December and January bank statements for this account at Chase Bank; in it, the auditors found the following:

Chase Bank Cheque #	Payable to	Amount	Dated	Cleared Bank
2220	Commerce Bank	11,000	22-Dec	28-Dec
2221	Commerce Bank	15,000	30-Dec	05-Jan
2222	Commerce Bank	12,000	07-Jan	12-Jan

Deposits		
Received from	Amount	Dated
Commerce Bank	12,000	28-Dec
Commerce Bank	14,000	04-Jan

An abbreviated calendar for the period is in Exhibit 9.62–2.

Required:

a. Complete the schedule of interbank transfers (working paper C-5, Exhibit 9.62–1) by entering the new information.

b. What is the actual cash balance for the four bank accounts combined, considering only the amounts given in this case information, as of December 31, 1992 (before any of the December 31 payroll cheques are cashed by employees)? As of January 8, 1993 (before any of the January 8 payroll cheques are cashed by employees)? (Hint: Prepare a schedule of "apparent balances" and "actual balances" illustrated in Chapter 17 to explain cheque kiting.)

E X H I B I T   9.62–2   **CALENDAR**

	S	M	T	W	T	F	S
December	20	21	22	23	24	25	26
1992	27	28	29	30	31	1	2
January	3	4	5	6	7	8	9
1993	10	11	12	13	14	15	16

9.63 Manipulated Bank Reconciliation. Caulco, Inc., is the audit client. You have obtained the client-prepared bank reconciliation as of February 29, 1988. (The bank statement and, thus, the dates are actual documents, although the situation is contrived for the purposes of this problem.)

Required:

Cheque #2231 was the first cheque written in February. All earlier cheques cleared the bank, some in the January bank statement and some in the February bank statement.

Assume that the only February-dated cancelled cheques returned in the March bank statement are #2231; #2239 and #2231; #2240, showing the amounts listed in the February bank reconciliation. They cleared the bank on March 3 and March 2, respectively. The first deposit on the March bank statement was $1,097.69, credited on March 3. Assume further that all cheques entered in Caulco's cash disbursements journal through February 29 have either cleared the bank or are listed as outstanding cheques in the February bank reconciliation.

Examine the February bank statement in Exhibit 18–3 (Chapter 18). Determine whether anything is wrong with the bank statement and the bank recon-ciliation. If anything is wrong, prepare a corrected reconciliation and explain the problem.

9.64 Employee Embezzlement via Cash Receipts and Payment of Personal Expenses (duplicated in Chapter 18, Case 18.52). Instructions for Discussion Cases 9.64 and 9.65.

These cases are designed like the ones in the chapter. They give the problem, the method, the paper trail, and the amount. Your assignment is to write the audit approach portion of the case, organized around these sections:

Objective: Express the objective in terms of the facts supposedly asserted in financial records, accounts, and statements. (Refer to discussion of assertions in Chapter 4).

Control: Write a brief explanation of desirable controls, missing controls, and especially the kinds of "deviations" that might arise from the situation described in the case.

Test of controls: Write some procedures for getting evidence about existing controls, especially procedures that could discover deviations from controls. If there are no controls to test, then there are no procedures to perform; go then to the next section. A "procedure" should instruct someone about

CAULCO, INC.
Bank Reconciliation
February 29, 1988

Balance per bank				$7,374.93
Deposit in transit				1,097.69
Outstanding cheques				
#	Date	Payee	Amount	
2239	Feb. 26	Alpha Supply	500.00	
2240	Feb. 29	L.C. Stateman	254.37	
Total outstanding				(754.37)
General ledger balance Feb. 29, 1988				$7,718.25

the source(s) of evidence to tap and the work to do.

Audit of balance: Write some procedures for getting evidence about the existence, completeness, valuation, ownership, or disclosure assertions identified in your objective section above.

Discovery summary: Write a short statement about the discovery you expect to accomplish with your procedures.

THE EXTRA BANK ACCOUNT

Problem: Cash receipts pocketed and personal expenses paid from business account.

Method: The Ourtown Independent School District, like all others, had red tape about school board approval of cash disbursements. To get around the rules, and to make timely payment of some bills possible, the superintendent of schools had a school bank account that was used in the manner of a petty cash fund. The board knew about it and had given blanket approval in advance for its use to make timely payment of minor school expenses. The board, however, never reviewed the activity in this account. The business manager had sole responsibility for the account, subject to the annual audit. The account got money from transfers from other school accounts and from deposit of cafeteria cash receipts. The superintendent did not like to be bothered with details, and he often signed blank cheques so that the business manager would not need to run in for a signature all the time. The business manager sometimes paid her personal American Express credit card bills, charged personal items to the school's VISA account, and pocketed some cafeteria cash receipts before deposit.

Paper trail: An informant called the state education audit agency and told the story that this business manager had used school funds to buy hosiery. When told of this story, the superintendent told the auditor to place no credibility in the informant, who is "out to get us." (The informant had been fired after an

accusation of improper behaviour and later faced a similar charge at the next place of employment.) The business manager had in fact used the account to write cheques to "cash" (herself), put her own American Express bills in the school files (the school district had a VISA card, not American Express), and signed on the school card for gasoline and auto repairs during periods when school was not in session. (As for the hosiery, she purchased $700 worth with school funds one year.) The superintendent was genuinely unaware of the misuse of funds.

Amount: The business manager had been employed for six years, was trusted, and stole an estimated $15,000.

Required:

Write the audit approach section according to the instructions at the beginning of 9.64. You can assume that you received the informant's message.

9.65 Overstated Sales and Accounts Receivable. Follow the instructions given with Case 17.64. Write the audit approach section.

RING AROUND THE REVENUE

Problem: Sales were recorded early, sometimes at fictitiously high prices, overstating sales revenue, accounts receivable, and income.

Method: Mattox Toy Manufacturing Company had experienced several years of good business. Income had increased steadily, and the common shares were a favourite among investors. Management had confidently predicted continued growth and prosperity. But business turned worse instead of better. Competition became fierce.

In earlier years Mattox had accommodated a few large retail customers with the practice of field warehousing coupled with a "bill and hold" accounting procedure. These large retail customers executed noncancellable written agreements, asserting their purchase of toys and their obligation to pay. The toys were not actually shipped because the customers did not have available warehouse space. They were set aside in segregated areas on the Mattox premises and identified as the customers' property. Mattox would later drop-ship the toys to various retail locations upon instructions from the customers. The "field warehousing" was explained as Mattox serving as a temporary warehouse and storage location for the customers' toys. In the related bill-and-hold accounting procedure, Mattox prepared invoices billing the customers, delivered them to the customers, and recorded the sales and accounts receivable.

When business took the recent downturn, Mattox expanded its field warehousing and its bill-and-hold accounting practices. Invoices were recorded for customers who did not execute the written agreements used in previous arrangements. Some customers signed the noncancellable written agreements with clauses permitting subsequent inspection, acceptance, and determination of discounted prices. The toys were not always set aside in separate areas, either, and this failure later gave shipping employees problems when it came to identifying shipments of toys that had been "sold" earlier and those that had not.

Mattox also engaged in overbilling. Customers who ordered close-out toys at discounted prices were billed at regular prices, even though the customers' orders showed the discounted prices agreed by Mattox sales representatives.

In a few cases, the bill-and-hold invoices and the close-out sales were billed and recorded in duplicate. In most cases the customers' invoices were addressed and mailed to specific individuals in the customers' management instead of the routine mailing to the customers' accounts payable departments.

Paper trail: The field warehousing arrangements were well known and acknowledged in the Mattox accounting manual. Related invoices were stamped "bill and hold." Customer orders and agreements were attached in a document file. Sales of close-out toys were stamped "close-out," indicating the regular prices (bases for salespersons' commissions) and the invoice prices.

Otherwise, the accounting for sales and accounts receivable was unexceptionable. Efforts to record these sales in January (last month of the fiscal year) caused the month's sales revenue to be 35 percent higher than the January of the previous year.

In the early years of the practice, inventory sold under the field warehousing arrangements (both regular and closeout toys) was segregated and identified. The shipping orders for these toys left the "carrier name" and "shipping date" blank, even though they were signed and dated by a company employee in the spaces for the company representative and the carrier representative signature.

The lack of inventory segregation caused problems for the company. After the fiscal year-end, Mattox solved the problem by reversing $6.9 million of the $14 million bill and hold sales. This caused another problem because the reversal was larger than the month's sales, causing the sales revenue for that month to be a negative number!

Amount: Company officials' reasons for the validity of recognizing sales revenue and receivables on the bill-and-hold procedure and field warehousing were persuasive. After due consideration of the facts and circumstances, the company's own accountants agreed that the accounting practices appropriately accounted for revenue and receivables.

It was Mattox's abuse of the practices that caused financial statements to be materially misstated. In January of the year in question, the company overstated sales by about $14 million, or 5 percent of the sales that should have been recorded. The gross profit of $7 million on these sales caused the income to be overstated by about 40 percent.

9.66 Cut-off Tests for Sales. In connection with an audit of the financial statements of a wholesale food distributor, a PA will perform cutoff tests in several areas, including merchandise receipts, sales transactions, and cash.

Required:

a. Explain the general purpose of a cut-off test. To which management assertion(s) are such tests related?

b. Assume the financial statements of the wholesale distributor have never been audited. Must cutoff tests be performed for both the beginning and end, or only at the end of the fiscal year? Explain.

c. List four procedures the PA could perform in testing the cutoff of sales revenue at the end of the fiscal year. All of the company's sales are made on account.

d. Explain how the PA should test the cutoff of cash receipts at the end of the fiscal year.

(CGAAC adapted)

9.67 Audit of Receivables. You are the auditor of North Shore Linen Supply Company, which performs laundry services for restaurants and similar businesses. The company's drivers deliver clean linens (tablecloths, towels, uniforms, etc.) to each customer on a weekly basis, while picking up soiled goods for laundering and delivery the following week. All linens are the property of the customer, and the drivers carry a stock of standard items that are sold to customers who need to replace damaged goods, etc. You are planning your examination of the company's accounts receivable balances and determine the following:

1. There are 50 separate routes; each route consists of 25 to 40 customers, the number that can be serviced by a driver in one day.

2. Each driver maintains a route book. This consists of a loosely bound volume that, among other things, shows the detailed charges and credits to each customer's account.

3. Charges for laundry services are recorded on a preprinted, prenumbered invoice form at the plant and also recorded in the route book. The driver delivers the invoice to the customer with the clean goods. Charges for any linens sold are entered in the route books directly by the drivers.

4. Drivers are authorized to collect cash. Amounts collected are recorded in the route book, and the cash is remitted to a cashier at the plant at the end of each route. When collecting the cash, the cashier verifies that the amount remitted agrees with the total credits recorded to the customers' accounts by the driver that day.

5. Some customers pay their accounts by cheque sent directly to the plant. The route books are updated when these cheques are received.

6. Last year's audit program for the selection of accounts receivable for confirmation states: "Select two accounts from each route by opening the route book twice, at random."

Required:

a. List six weaknesses in internal controls in the system as described in the case. Do not include suggestions for improvements.

b. Would the procedure used last year to select a sample of accounts for confirmation produce a statistically valid random sample? Explain.

c. What form of customer confirmation request would be most appropriate in this situation? Discuss.

d. Would dollar-unit sampling be an appropriate method of determining sample size and selecting a sample of customer accounts for confirmation in this situation? Discuss.

(CGAAC adapted)

Appendix 9A

Internal Control Questionnaires

· ·

E X H I B I T   9A–1   INTERNAL CONTROL QUESTIONNAIRE—CASH RECEIPTS PROCESSING

Environment:
  1. Are receipts deposited daily, intact, and without delay?
  2. Does someone other than the cashier or accounts receivable bookkeeper take the deposits to the bank?
  3. Are the duties of the cashier entirely separate from recordkeeping for notes and accounts receivable? From general ledger recordkeeping?
  4. Is the cashier denied access to receivables records or monthly statements?

Validity objective:
  5. Is a bank reconciliation performed monthly by someone who does not have cash custody or recordkeeping responsibility?
  6. Are the cash receipts journal entries compared to the remittance lists and deposit slips regularly?

Completeness objective:
  7. Does the person who opens the mail make a list of cash received (a remittance list)?
  8. Are currency receipts controlled by mechanical devices? Are machine totals checked by the internal auditor?
  9. Are prenumbers sales invoice or receipts books used? Is the numerical sequence checked for missing documents?

Authorization objective:
 10. Does a responsible person approve discounts taken by customers with payments on account?

Accuracy objective:
 11. Is a duplicate deposit slip retained by the internal auditor or someone other than the employee making up the deposit?
 12. Is the remittance list compared to the deposit by someone other than the cashier?

Classification objective:
 13. Does the accounting manual contain instructions for classifying cash receipts credits?

Accounting objective:
 14. Does someone reconcile the accounts receivable subsidiary to the control account regularly (to determine whether all entries were made to
     customers' accounts)?

Proper period objective:
 15. Does the accounting manual contain instructions for dating cash receipts entries the same day as the date of receipt?

E X H I B I T   9A–2   INTERNAL CONTROL QUESTIONNAIRE—SALES

Environment:
  1. Is the credit department independent of the marketing department?
  2. Are sales of the following types controlled by the same procedures described below? Sales to employees, COD sales, disposals of propety,
     cash sales, and scrap sales.

Validity objective:
  3. Is access to sales invoice blanks restricted?
  4. Are prenumbered bills of lading or other shipping documents prepared or completed in the shipping department?

Completeness objective:
  5. Are sales invoice blanks prenumbered?
  6. Is the sequence checked for missing invoices?
  7. Is the shipping document numerical sequence checked for missing bills of lading numbers?

Authorization objective:
  8. Are all credit sales approved by the credit department prior to shipment?
  9. Are sales prices and terms based on approved standards?
 10. Are returned sales credits and other credits supported by documentation as to receipt, condition, and quantity, and approved by a responsible
     officer?

Accuracy objective:
 11. Are shipped quantities compared to invoice quantities?
 12. Are sales invoices checked for error in quantities, prices, extensions and footing, freight allowances, and checked with customers' orders?
 13. Is there an overall check on arithmetic accuracy of period sales data by a statistical or product-line analysis?
 14. Are periodic sales data reported directly to general ledger accounting independent of accounts receivable accounting?

Classification objective:
 15. Does the accounting manual contain instructions for classifying sales?

Accounting objective:
 16. Are summary journal entries approved before posting?

Proper period objective:
 17. Does the accounting manual contain instructions to date sales invoices on the shipment date?

E X H I B I T 9A–3 INTERNAL CONTROL QUESTIONNAIRE—ACCOUNTS AND NOTES RECEIVABLE

Environment:
1. Are customers' subsidiary records maintained by someone who has no access to cash?
2. Is the cashier denied access to the customers' records and monthly statements?
3. Are delinquent accounts listed periodically for review by someone other than the credit manager?
4. Are written-off accounts kept in a memo ledger or credit report file for periodic access?
5. Is the credit department separated from the sales department?
6. Are notes receivable in the custody of someone other than the cashier or accounts receivable recordkeeper?
7. Is custody of negotiable collateral in the hands of someone not responsible for handling cash or keeping records?

Validity objective:
8. Are customers' statements mailed monthly by the accounts receivable department?
9. Are direct confirmations of accounts and notes obtained periodically by the internal auditor?
10. Are differences reported by customers routed to someone outside the accounts receivable department for investigation?
11. Are returned goods checked against receiving reports?

Completeness objective:
(Refer to completeness questions in the sales and cash receipts questionnaires.)
12. Are credit memo documents prenumbered and the sequence checked for missing documents?

Authorization objective:
13. Is customer credit approved before orders are shipped?
14. Are write-offs returns, and discounts allowed after discount date subject to approval by a responsible officer?
15. Are large loans or advances to related parties approved by the directors?

Accuracy objective:
16. Do the internal auditors confirm customer accounts periodically to determine accuracy?

Classification objective:
17. Are receivables from officers, directors, and affiliates identified separately in the accounts receivable records?

Accounting objective:
18. Does someone reconcile the accounts receivable subsidiary to the control account regularly?

Proper period objective:
(Refer to proper period objective questions in the sales and cash receipts questionnaires.)

E X H I B I T 9A–4 SALES AND ACCOUNTS RECEIVABLE COMPUTER CONTROLS

- Each terminal performs only designated functions. For example, the terminal at the shipping dock cannot be used to enter initial sales information or to access the payroll database.
- An identification number and password (issued on an individual person basis) is required to enter the sales and each command that a subsequent action has been completed. Unauthorized entry attempts are logged and immediately investigated. Further, certain passwords have "ready only" (cannot change any data) authorization. For example, the credit manager can determine the outstanding balance of any account or view on-line "reports" summarizing overdue accounts receivable, but cannot enter credit memos to change the balances.
- All input information is immediately logged to provide restart processing should any terminal become inoperative during the processing.
- A transaction code calls up on the terminals a full screen "form" that appears to the operator in the same format as the original paper documents. Each clerk must enter the information correctly or the computer will not accept the transaction. This is called **on-line input validation** and utilizes validation checks, such as missing data, check digit, and limit tests.
- All documents prepared by the computer are numbered, and the number is stored as part of the sales record in the accounts receivable database.
- A daily search of the pending order database is made by the computer, and sales orders outstanding more than seven days are listed on the terminal in marketing management.

APPENDIX 9B

SUBSTANTIVE AUDIT PROGRAMS

· ·

E X H I B I T 9B–1   **AUDIT PROGRAM—SELECTED SUBSTANTIVE PROCEDURES—CASH**

1. Obtain confirmations from banks (standard bank confirmation).
2. Obtain reconciliations of all bank accounts.
   a. Trace the bank balance on the reconciliation to the bank confirmation.
   b. Trace the reconciled book balance to the general ledger.
   c. Recalculate the arithmetic on client-prepared bank reconciliations.
3. Review the bank confirmation for loans and collateral.
4. Ask the client to request cutoff bank statements to be mailed directly to the audit firm.
   a. Trace deposits in transit on the reconciliation to bank deposits early in the next period.
   b. Trace outstanding cheques on the reconciliation to cheques cleared in the next period.
5. Prepare a schedule of interbank transfers for a period of 10 business days before and after the year-end date. Document dates of book entry transfer and correspondence with bank entries and reconciliation items, if any.
6. Count cash funds in the presence of a client representative. Obtain a receipt for return of the funds.
7. Obtain written client representations concerning compensating balance agreements.

E X H I B I T 9B–2   **AUDIT PROGRAM FOR ACCOUNTS AND NOTES RECEIVABLE AND REVENUE: SELECTED SUBSTANTIVE PROCEDURES**

A. Accounts and Notes Receivable.
   1. Obtain an aged trial balance of individual customer accounts. Recalculate the total and trace to the general ledger control account.
   2. Send confirmations to all accounts over $X. Select a random sample of all remaining accounts for confirmation.
      a. Investigate differences reported by customers.
      b. Perform alternative procedures on accounts that do not respond to positive confirmation requests.
         (1) Vouch cash receipts after the confirmation date for subsequent payment.
         (2) Vouch sales invoices and shipping documents.
   3. Evaluate the adequacy of the allowance for doubtful accounts.
      a. Vouch a sample of *current* amounts in the aged trial balance to sales invoices to determine whether amounts aged current should be aged past due.
      b. Compare the current-year write-off experience to the prior-year allowance.
      c. Vouch cash receipts after the balance sheet date for collections on past-due accounts.
      d. Obtain financial statements or credit reports and discuss with the credit manager collections on large past-due accounts.
      e. Calculate an allowance estimate using prior relations of write-offs and sales, taking under consideration current economic events.
   4. Review the bank confirmations, loan agreements, and minutes of the board for indications of pledged, discounted, or assigned receivables.
   5. Inspect or obtain confirmation of notes receivable.
   6. Recalculate interest income and trace to the income account.
   7. Obtain written client representations regarding pledge, discount, or assignment of receivables, and about receivables from officers, directors, affiliates, or other related parties.
   8. Review the adequacy of control over recording of all charges to customers (completeness), audited in the sales transaction test of controls audit program.
B. Revenue
   1. Select a sample of recorded sales invoices and vouch to underlying shipping documents.
   2. Select a sample of shipping documents and trace to sales invoices.
   3. Obtain production records of physical quantities sold and calculate an estimate of sales dollars based on average sale prices.
   4. Compare revenue dollars and physical quantities with prior-year data and industry economic statistics.
   5. Select a sample of sales invoices prepared a few days before and after the balance sheet date and vouch to supporting documents for evidence of proper cutoff.

CHAPTER 10

Learning Objectives

This chapter contains a concise overview of a cycle for the acquisition of goods (inventory) and services (expenses), the acquisition of property, plant, and equipment (fixed assets), and the expenditure of cash (cash disbursements) in connection with paying for the purchases and acquisitions. A series of short cases is used to show the application of audit procedures in situations where errors, irregularities, and frauds might be discovered. The chapter ends with special notes on inventory observation and accounts payable completeness. After completing this chapter, you should be able to:

1. Describe the acquisition and expenditure cycle, including typical source documents and controls.

2. Give examples of detail test of controls procedures for auditing the controls over purchase of inventory and services, acquisition of fixed assets, and disbursement of cash.

3. Describe some common errors, irregularities, and frauds in the acquisition and expenditure cycle, and design some audit and investigation procedures for detecting them.

4. Explain the importance of the completeness assertion for the audit of accounts payable liabilities, and list some procedures for a "search for unrecorded liabilities."

5. Identify and describe considerations involved in the audit observation of physical inventory-taking.

ACQUISITION AND EXPENDITURE CYCLE INCLUDING AUDIT

OF ACCOUNTS PAYABLE AND INVENTORY EXISTENCE

ACQUISITION AND EXPENDITURE CYCLE: TYPICAL ACTIVITIES

LEARNING OBJECTIVE
1. Describe the acquisition and expenditure cycle, including typical source documents and controls.

Exhibit 10–1 shows the activities and transactions involved in an acquisitions and expenditure cycle. The exhibit also lists the accounts and records typically found in this cycle.

The basic acquisition and expenditure activities are (1) purchasing goods and services and (2) paying the bills. As you follow the exhibit, you can track the elements of a control structure described in the sections below.

Authorization

Purchases are requested (requisitioned) by people who know the needs of the organization. A purchasing department seeks the best prices and quality and issues a purchase order to a selected vendor. Obtaining competitive bids is a good practice because it tends to produce the best prices and involves several legitimate suppliers in the process.

Cash disbursements are authorized by an accounts payable department's assembly (voucher) of purchase orders, vendor invoices, and internal receiving reports to show a valid obligation to pay. Accounts payable obligations usually are recorded when the purchaser receives the goods or services ordered.

Cheques are signed by a person authorized by the management or the board of directors. A company may have a policy to require two signatures on cheques over a certain amount (e.g., $1,000). Vouchers should be marked "paid" or otherwise stamped to show that they have been processed completely so that they cannot be paid a second time.

Custody

A receiving department inspects the goods received for quantity and quality (producing a receiving report), then puts them in the hands of other responsible persons (e.g., inventory warehousing, fixed asset installation). Services are not "received" in this manner, but they are accepted by responsible persons. Cash "custody" rests largely in the hands of the person or persons authorized to sign cheques.

Another aspect of "custody" involves access to blank documents, such as purchase orders, receiving reports, and blank cheques. If unauthorized persons can obtain blank copies of these internal business documents, they can forge a false purchase order to a fictitious vendor, forge a false receiving report, send a false invoice from a fictitious supplier, and prepare a company cheque to the fictitious supplier, thereby accomplishing an embezzlement.

E X H I B I T 10–1   ACQUISITION AND EXPENDITURE CYCLE

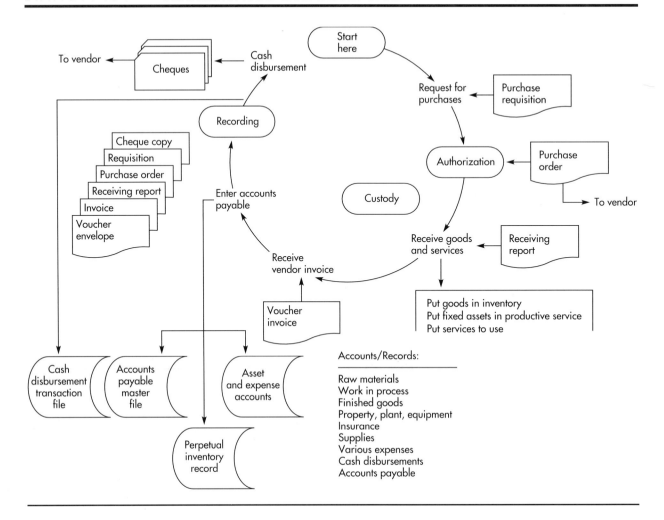

Recording
When the purchase order, vendor's invoice, and receiving report are in hand, accountants enter the accounts payable, with debits to proper inventory, fixed asset, and expense accounts and with a credit to accounts payable. When cheques are prepared, entries are made to debit the accounts payable and credit cash.

Periodic Reconciliation
A periodic comparison or reconciliation of existing assets to recorded amounts is not shown in Exhibit 10–1, but it occurs in several ways, including physical inventory-taking to compare inventory on hand to perpetual inventory records, bank account reconciliation to compare book cash balances to bank cash balances, inspection of fixed assets to compare to detail fixed asset records, preparation of an accounts payable trial balance to compare the detail of accounts payable to the control account, and internal audit confirmation of accounts payable to compare vendors' reports and monthly statements to recorded liabilities.

Too Much Trouble

A trucking company self-insured claims of damage to goods in transit, processed claims vouchers, and paid customers from its own bank accounts. Several persons were authorized to sign cheques. One person thought it "too much trouble" to stamp the vouchers PAID and said: "That's textbook stuff anyway." Numerous claims were recycled to other cheque signers, and $80,000 in claims were paid in duplicate before the problem was discovered.

Classify the Debits Correctly

Invoices for expensive repairs were not clearly identified, so the accounts payable accountants entered the debits that should have been repairs and maintenance expense as capitalized fixed assets. This initially understated expenses and overstated income by $125,000 one year, although the incorrectly capitalized expenses were written off as depreciation in later years.

Audit Evidence in Management Reports
· · · · · · · · · · · ·

Computer processing of acquisition and payment transactions makes it possible for management to generate several reports that can provide important audit evidence.

Open Purchase Orders
Purchase orders are "open" from the time they are issued until the goods and services are received. They are held in an "open purchase order" file. Generally, no liability exists to be recorded until the transactions are complete. However, auditors may find evidence of losses on purchase commitments in this file if market prices have fallen below the purchase price shown in purchase orders.

Unmatched Receiving Reports
Normally, liabilities should be recorded on the date the goods and services are received and accepted by the receiving department or by another responsible person. Sometimes, however, vendor invoices arrive later. In the meantime, the accounts payable department holds the receiving reports "unmatched" with invoices, awaiting enough information to record an accounting entry. Auditors can inspect the "unmatched receiving report" file report to determine whether the company has material unrecorded liabilities on the financial statement date.

Unmatched Vendor Invoices
Sometimes, vendor invoices arrive in the accounts payable department before the receiving processing is complete. Such invoices are held "unmatched" with receiving reports, awaiting information that the goods and services were actually received and accepted. Auditors can inspect the "unmatched invoice file" and compare it to

---

THINKING AHEAD

Lone Moon Brewing purchased bulk aluminum sheets and manufactured its own cans. To ensure a source of raw materials supply, the company entered into a long-term purchase agreement for 3 million kilos of aluminum sheeting at 80 cents per kilo. At the end of this year, 1.5 million kilos have been purchased and used, but the market price had fallen to 64 cents per kilo. Lone Moon was on the hook for a $240,000 (1.5 million kilos × 16 cents) purchase commitment in excess of current market prices.

---

the "unmatched receiving report" file to determine whether liabilities are unrecorded. Systems failures and human coding errors can cause "unmatched" invoices and related "unmatched" receiving reports to sit around unnoticed when all the information for recording a liability is actually at hand.

Accounts Payable Trial Balance

This trial balance is a list of payable amounts by vendor, and the sum should agree with the accounts payable control account. (Some organizations keep records by individual invoices instead of vendor names, so the trial balance is a list of unpaid invoices. The sum still should agree with the control account balance.) The best kind of trial balance for audit purposes is one that contains the names of all the vendors with whom the organization has done business, even if their balances are zero. The audit "search for unrecorded liabilities" should emphasize the small and zero balances, especially for regular vendors, because these may be the places where liabilities are unrecorded.

All paid and unpaid accounts payable should be supported by a "voucher" or similar document. A "voucher" is a cover sheet, folder, or envelope that contains all the supporting documents—purchase requisition (if any), purchase order (if any), vendor invoice, receiving report (if any), and cheque copy (or notation of cheque number, date, and amount), as shown in Exhibit 10–1.

Purchases Journal

A listing of all purchases may or may not be printed out. It may exist only in a computer transaction file. In either event it provides raw material for (1) computer-audit analysis or purchasing patterns, which may exhibit characteristics of errors and irregularities, and (2) sample selection of transactions for detail test of controls audit of supporting documents for validity, authorization, accuracy, classification, accounting, and proper period recording. (A company may have already performed analyses of purchases, and auditors can use these for analytical evidence, provided the analyses are produced under reliable control conditions.)

Inventory Reports (trial balance)

Companies can produce a wide variety of inventory reports useful for analytical evidence. One is an item-by-item trial balance that should agree with a control account (if balances are kept in dollars). Auditors can use such a trial balance (1) to scan for unusual conditions (e.g., negative item balances, overstocking, and valuation

---

THE SIGN OF THE CREDIT BALANCE

Auto Parts & Repair, Inc., kept perpetual inventory records and fixed assets records on a computer system. Because of the size of the files (8,000 parts in various locations and 1,500 asset records), the company never printed reports for visual inspection. Auditors ran a computer-audit "sign test" on inventory balances and fixed asset net book balances. The test called for a printed report for all balances less than zero. The auditors discovered 320 negative inventory balances caused by failure to record purchases and 125 negative net asset balances caused by depreciating assets more than their cost.

---

problems) and (2) as a population for sample selection for a physical inventory observation (audit procedures to obtain evidence about the existence of inventory shown in the account). The scanning and sample selection may be computer-audit applications on a computer-based inventory report file.

Fixed Asset Reports

These reports are similar to inventory reports because they show the details of fixed assets in control accounts. They can be used for scanning and sample selection, much like the inventory reports. The information for depreciation calculation (cost, useful life, method, salvage) can be used for the audit of depreciation on a sample basis or by computer applications to recalculate all the depreciation.

Cash Disbursements Report

The cash disbursements process will produce a cash disbursements journal, sometimes printed out, sometimes maintained only on a computer file. This journal should contain the date, cheque number, payee, amount, account debited for each cash disbursement, and a cross-reference to the voucher number (usually the same as the cheque number). This journal is a population of cash disbursement transactions available for sample selection for detail test of controls audit of supporting documents in the voucher for validity, authorization, accuracy, classification, accounting, and proper period recording.

· ·

R E V I E W
C H E C K P O I N T S

10.1 What is a voucher?

10.2 How can the situation where the same supporting documents are used for a duplicate payment be prevented?

10.3 Where could an auditor look to find evidence of losses on purchase commitments? Unrecorded liabilities to vendors?

10.4 List the main supporting source documents used in an acquisition and expenditure cycle.

10.5 List the management reports that can be used for audit evidence. What information in them can be useful to auditors?

· ·

Control Risk Assessment

. . . .

2. Give examples of detail test of controls procedures for auditing the controls over purchase of inventory and services, acquisition of fixed assets, and disbursement of cash.

Control risk assessment is important because it governs the nature, timing, and extent of substantive audit procedures that will be applied in the audit of account balances in the acquisition and expenditure cycle. These account balances include:

Inventory.

Capital assets.

Depreciation expense.

Accumulated depreciation.

Accounts and notes payable.

Cash disbursements part of cash balance auditing.

Various expenses:

Administrative: supplies, legal fees, audit fees, taxes.

Selling: commissions, travel, delivery, repairs, advertising.

Manufacturing: maintenance, freight in, utilities.

General Control Considerations

Control procedures for proper segregation of responsibilities should be in place and operating. By referring to Exhibit 10–1, you can see that proper segregation involves authorization (requisitioning, purchase ordering) by persons who do not have custody, recording, or reconciliation duties. Custody of inventory fixed assets and of cash is in persons who do not directly authorize purchases or cash payments, record the accounting entries, or reconcile physical assets and cash to recorded amounts. Recording (accounting) is performed by persons who do not authorize transactions or have custody of assets or perform reconciliations. Periodic reconciliations should be performed by people who do not have authorization, custody, or recording duties related to the same assets. Combinations of two or more of these responsibilities in one person, one office, or one computerized system may open the door for errors, irregularities, and frauds.

In addition, internal controls should provide for detail control checking procedures. For example: (1) Purchase requisitions and purchase orders should be signed or initialed by authorized personnel. (Computer-produced purchase orders should come from a system whose master file specifications for reordering and vendor identification are restricted to changes only by authorized persons.) (2) Inventory warehouses and fixed asset locations should be under adequate physical security (storerooms, fences, locks, and the like). (3) Accountants should be under orders to record accounts payable only when all the supporting documentation is in order; and care should be taken to record purchases and payables as of the date goods and services were received, and to record cash disbursements on the date the cheque leaves the control of the organization. (4) Vendor invoices should be compared to purchase orders and receiving reports to determine that the vendor is charging the approved price and that the quantity being billed is the same as the quantity received.

Information about the control structure often is gathered initially by completing an internal control questionnaire. A selection of questionnaires for both general (manual) controls and computer controls is in Appendix 10A. These questionnaires can be

---

Purchase Order Splitting

The school district authorized its purchasing agent to buy supplies in amounts of $1,000 or less without getting competitive bids for the best price. The purchasing agent wanted to favour local businesses instead of large chain stores, so she broke up the year's $350,000 supplies order into numerous $900–$950 orders, paying about 12 percent more to local stores than would have been paid to the large chains.

---

studied for details of desirable control policies and procedures. They are organized under headings that identify the important control objectives—environment, validity, completeness, authorization, accuracy, classification, accounting, and proper period recording.

Detail Test of Controls Audit Procedures

An organization should have detail control procedures in place and operating to prevent, detect, and correct accounting errors. You studied the general control objectives in Chapter 6 (validity, completeness, authorization, accuracy, classification, accounting, and proper period recording). Exhibit 10–2 puts these in the perspective of purchasing activity with examples of specific objectives. You should study this exhibit carefully. It expresses the general control objectives in specific examples related to purchasing.

Auditors can perform detail test of controls audit procedures to determine whether controls that are said to be in place and operating actually are being performed properly by company personnel. A **detail test of control procedure** consists of (1) identification of the data population from which a sample of items will be selected for audit and (2) an expression of the action that will be taken to produce relevant evidence. In general, the actions in detail test of control audit procedures involve vouching, tracing, observing, scanning, and recalculating. A specification of such procedures is part of an audit program for obtaining evidence useful in a final control risk assessment. If personnel in the organization are not performing their control procedures very well, auditors will need to design substantive audit procedures to try to detect whether control failures have produced materially misleading account balances.

Exhibit 10–3 contains a selection of detail test of controls audit procedures for controls over purchase, cash disbursement, and accounts payable transactions. The samples are usually attribute samples designed along the lines to be studied in Chapters 12 and 13. On the right the exhibit shows the control objectives tested by the audit procedures.

Detail Test of Controls for Inventory Records

Many organizations have material investments in inventories. In many engagements auditors need to determine whether they can rely on the accuracy of perpetual inventory records. Tests of controls over accuracy involve tests of the additions (purchases) to the inventory detail balances and tests of the reductions (issues) of the

E X H I B I T   10–2   INTERNAL CONTROL OBJECTIVES (PURCHASES)

General Objectives	Examples of Specific Objectives
1. Recorded purchases are *valid* and documented.	Recorded vouchers in the voucher register supported by completed vouchers. Voucher for purchases of inventory (or fixed assets) supported by vendor invoices, receiving reports, purchase orders, and requisitions (or approved capital budget).
2. Valid purchase transactions are *recorded* and none omitted.	Requisitions, purchase orders, receiving reports, and vouchers are prenumbered and numerical sequence is checked. Overall comparisons of purchases are made periodically by statistical or product-line analysis.
3. Purchases are *authorized* according to company policy.	All purchase orders are supported by requisitions from proper persons (or approved capital budgets). Purchase made from approved vendors or only after bids are received and evaluated.
4. Purchase orders are *accurately* prepared.	Completed purchase order quantities and descriptions independently compared to requisitions and vendors' catalogues.
5. Purchase transactions are properly *classified*.	Purchases from subsidiaries and affiliates classified as intercompany purchases and payables. Purchase returns and allowances properly classified. Purchases for repairs and maintenance segregated from purchases of fixed assets.
6. Purchase transaction *accounting* is complete and proper.	Account distribution on vouchers proper and reviewed independent of preparation. Freight-in included as part of purchase and added to inventory (or fixed-assets) costs.
7. Purchase transactions are recorded in the *proper period*.	Perpetual inventory and fixed asset records updated as of date goods are received.

item balances. Exhibit 10–4 pictures the "direction of the test" for detail test of controls audit procedures. The samples from the source documents (receiving reports, issues documents) meet the completeness direction requirement to determine whether everything received was recorded as an addition, and whether everything issued was recorded as a reduction of the balance. The sample from the perpetual inventory records meets the validity direction requirement for determining whether everything recorded as an addition or reduction is supported by receiving reports and issue documents. (The symbols A-1, A-2, A-3-a, and A-3-b are cross-references to the procedures in Exhibit 10–5.)

Exhibit 10–5 is similar to Exhibit 10–3 in that it contains a selection of detail test of controls audit procedures for controls over perpetual inventory records. As before, the samples are usually attribute samples designed along the lines to be studied in Chapters 12 and 13. On the right the exhibit shows the control objectives tested by the audit procedures.

Summary: Control Risk Assessment

The audit manager or senior accountant in charge of the audit should evaluate the evidence obtained from an understanding of the internal controls and from the test of controls audit procedures. If the control risk is assessed very low, the substantive audit procedures on the account balances can be limited in cost-saving ways. For example, the inventory observation test-counts can be performed on a date prior to the year-end, and the sample size can be fairly small. On the other hand, if tests of

EXHIBIT 10–3   TEST OF CONTROLS AUDIT PROCEDURES FOR PURCHASES,
CASH DISBURSEMENTS, AND ACCOUNTS PAYABLE

	Control Objective
A. Purchases	
1. Select a sample of receiving reports:	
a. Vouch to related purchase orders, and note missing receiving reports (missing numbers).	Authorization Completeness
b. Trace to inventory record posting of additions.	Completeness
2. Observe the work habits of purchasing department personnel.	Environment
B. Cash Disbursements and Other Expenses:	
1. Select a sample of cash disbursement vouchers (or cash disbursement cheque numbers):	
a. Scan for missing documents (missing numbers).	Completeness
b. Vouch supporting documentation for evidence of accurate mathematics, correct classification, proper approval, and proper date of entry.	Accuracy Classification Authorization Proper period
c. Trace disbursement debits to general and subsidiary ledger accounts.	Accounting
2. Select a sample of recorded expenses from various accounts and vouch them to (a) cancelled cheques, and (b) supporting documentation.	Validity Classification
C. Accounts Payable	
1. Select a sample of open accounts payable and vouch to supporting documents of purchase (purchase orders, vendors' invoices).	Validity
2. Trace debits arising from accounts payable transactions for proper classification.	Classification
3. Select a sample of accounts payable entries recorded after the balance sheet date and vouch to supporting documents for evidence of proper cutoff—evidence that a liability should have been recorded as of the balance sheet date.	Proper period

EXHIBIT 10–4   DUAL DIRECTION OF TEST AUDIT SAMPLES

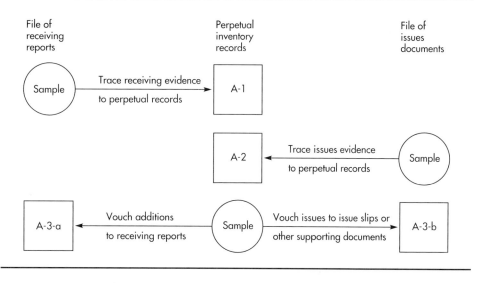

E X H I B I T 10–5   TEST OF CONTROLS AUDIT PROCEDURES FOR INVENTORY RECORDS

	Control Objective
A. Inventory Receipts and Issues	
1. Select a sample of receiving reports:	
a. Trace to perpetual inventory record entry of receipt.	Authorization Completeness
2. Select a sample of sales invoices, bills of lading or other shipping documents, or produce requisitions:	
a. Trace to perpetual inventory record entry of issue.	Authorization Completeness
3. Select a sample of inventory item perpetual records:	
a. Vouch additions to receiving reports.	Validity
b. Vouch issues to invoices, bills of lading, or other shipping documents, or production requisitions.	Validity
4. Observe work habits of inventory recordkeeping department personnel.	Environment
B. Cost of Sales	
1. With the sample of issues in A-2 above:	
a. Review the accounting summary of quantities and prices for mathematical accuracy.	Accuracy
b. Trace posting of amounts of general ledger.	Completeness
2. Obtain a sample of cost of goods sold entries in the general ledger and vouch to supporting summaries of finished goods issues.	Validity
3. Review (recalculate) the appropriateness of standard costs, if used, to price inventory issues and cost of goods sold. Review the disposition of variances from standard costs.	Accuracy

controls reveal weaknesses, the substantive procedures will need to be designed to lower the risk of failing to detect material error in the account balances. For example, the inventory observation may need to be scheduled on the year-end date with the audit team making a large number of test counts. Descriptions of major deficiencies, control weaknesses, and inefficiencies may be incorporated in a management letter to the client.

. . . .

R E V I E W
C H E C K P O I N T S

10.6   What are the primary functions that should be segregated in the acquisition and expenditure cycle?

10.7   What feature of the acquisition and expenditure control would be expected to prevent an employee's embezzling cash through creation of fictitious vouchers?

10.8   How could an auditor determine whether the purchasing agent had practised "purchase order splitting"?

10.9   Describe the two general characteristics of a test of controls audit procedure.

10.10 How is the information from the shipping department, receiving department, and warehouse used to update perpetual inventory records?

10.11 In fixed asset management and accounting, which functional responsibilities should be delegated to separate departments or management levels?

. . . .

AUDIT CASES: SUBSTANTIVE AUDIT PROCEDURES

. . . .

The audit of account balances consists of procedural efforts to detect errors, irregularities, and frauds that may exist in the balances, thus making them misleading in financial statements. If such misstatements exist, they are characterized by the following features:

Method: A cause of the misstatement (accidental error, intentional irregularity, or fraud attempt), which usually is easier to make because of some kind of failure of controls.

Paper trail: A set of telltale signs of erroneous accounting, missing or altered documents, or a "dangling debit" (the false or erroneous debit that results from an overstatement of assets).

Amount: The dollar amount of overstated assets and revenue, or understated liabilities and expenses.

The "casettes" tell about an error, irregularity, or fraud situation in terms of the method, the paper trail, and the amount. The first part of each casette gives you the "inside story" that auditors seldom know before they perform the audit work. The next part is an audit approach section, which tells about the audit objective (assertion), controls, test of controls, and test of balances (substantive procedures) that could be considered in an approach to the situation. The audit approach section presumes that the auditors do not know everything about the situation. The audit approach part of the casette contains these parts:

Audit objective: A recognition of a financial statement assertion for which evidence needs to be obtained. The assertions are about existence of assets, liabilities, revenues, and expenses; their valuation; their complete inclusion in the account balances; the rights and obligations inherent in them; and their proper presentation and disclosure in the financial statements. (These assertions were introduced in Chapter 4.)

Control: A recognition of the control procedures that should be used by an organization to prevent and detect errors and irregularities.

Test of controls: Ordinary and extended procedures designed to produce evidence about the effectiveness of the controls that should be in operation.

Audit of balance: Ordinary and extended substantive procedures designed to find signs of errors, irregularities, and frauds in account balances and classes of transactions.

At the end of the chapter, some similar discussion cases are presented, and you can write the audit approach to test your ability to design audit procedures for the detection of errors, irregularities, and frauds.

CASETTE 10.1
PRINTING (COPYING) MONEY

Problem

Improper expenditures for copy services charged to motion picture production costs.

Method

Argus Productions, Inc., a motion picture and commercial production company, assigned M. Welby the authority and responsibility for obtaining copies of scripts used in production. Established procedures

permitted Welby to arrange for outside script copying services, receive the copies, and approve the bills for payment. In effect, Welby was the "purchasing department" and the "receiving department" for this particular service. To a certain extent, Welby was also the "accounting department" by virtue of approving bills for payment and coding them for assignment to projects. Welby did not make the actual accounting entries or sign the cheques.

M. Welby set up a fictitious company under the registered name of Quickprint Company with himself as the incorporator and shareholder, complete with a post office box number, letterhead stationery, and nicely printed invoices, but no printing equipment. Legitimate copy services were "subcontracted" by Quickprint with real printing businesses, which billed Quickprint. Welby then wrote Quickprint invoices billing Argus, usually at the legitimate shop's rate, but for a few extra copies each time. Welby also submitted Quickprint bills to Argus for fictitious copying jobs on scripts for movies and commercials that never went into production. As the owner of Quickprint, Welby endorsed Argus's cheques with a rubber stamp and deposited the money in the business bank account, paid the legitimate printing bills, and took the rest for personal use.

Paper Trail

Argus's production cost files contained all the Quickprint bills, sorted under the names of the movie and commercial production projects. Welby even created files for proposed films that never went into full production, and thus should not have had script copying costs. There were no copying service bills from any shop other than Quickprint Company.

Amount

M. Welby conducted this fraud for five years, stealing $475,000 in false and inflated billings. (Argus's net income was overstated a modest amount because copying costs were capitalized as part of production cost, then amortized over a 2–3 year period.)

AUDIT APPROACH

Objective

Obtain evidence of the valid existence (occurrence) and valuation of copying charges capitalized as film production cost.

Control

Management should assign the authority to request copies and the purchasing authority to different responsible employees. The accounting, including coding cost assignments to projects, also should be performed by other persons. Managerial review of production results could result in notice of excess costs.

The request for the quantity (number) of copies of a script should come from a person involved in production who knows the number needed. This person should sign off for the receipt (or approve the bill) for this requested number of copies, thus acting as the "receiving department." This procedure could prevent waste (excess cost), especially if the requesting person were also held responsible for the profitability of the project.

Actual purchasing always is performed by a company agent, and in this case, the agent was M. Welby. Purchasing agents generally have latitude to seek the best service at the best price, with or without bids from competitors. Requirements to obtain bids is usually a good idea, but much legitimate purchasing is done with sole-source suppliers without bid.

Someone in the accounting department should be responsible for coding invoices for charges to authorized projects, thus making it possible to detect costs charged to projects not actually in production.

Someone with managerial responsibility should review project costs and the purchasing practices. However, this is an expensive use of executive time. It was not spent in the Argus case. Too bad.

Test of Controls

In gaining an understanding of the control structure, auditors could learn of the trust and responsibility vested in M. Welby. Since the embezzlement was about $95,000 per year, the total copying cost under Welby's control must have been around $1 million or more. (It might attract unwanted attention to inflate a cost more than 10 percent.)

Controls were very weak, especially in the combination of duties performed by Welby and in the lack of managerial review. For all practical purposes, there were no controls to test, other than to see whether Welby had approved the copying cost bills and coded them to active projects. This provides an opportunity, since proper classification is a control objective.

Procedures: Select a sample of project files, and vouch costs charged to them to support in source documents (validity direction of the test). Select a sample of expenditures, and trace them to the project cost records shown coded on the expenditures (completeness direction of the test).

Audit of Balance

Substantive procedures are directed to obtaining evidence about the existence of film projects, completeness of the costs charged to them, valuation of the capitalized project costs, rights in copyright and ownership, and proper disclosure of amortization methods. The most important procedures are the same as the test of controls procedures; thus, when performed at the year-end date on the capitalized cost balances, they are dual-purpose audit procedures.

Either of the procedures described above as test of controls procedures should show evidence of projects that had never gone into production. (Auditors should be careful to obtain a list of actual projects before they begin the procedures.) Chances are good that the discovery of bad project codes with copying cost will reveal a pattern of Quickprint bills.

Knowing that controls over copying cost are weak, auditors could be tipped off to the possibility of a Welby-Quickprint connection. Efforts to locate Quickprint should be taken (telephone book, chamber of commerce, other directories). Enquiry with the provincial ministry of Consumer and Commercial Relations for names of the Quickprint incorporators should reveal Welby's connection. The audit findings can then be turned over to a trained investigator to arrange an interview and confrontation with M. Welby.

Discovery Summary

In this case internal auditors performed a review of project costs at the request of the manager of production, who was worried about profitability. They performed the procedures described above, noticed the dummy projects and the Quickprint bills, investigated the ownership of Quickprint, and discovered Welby's association. They had first tried to locate Quickprint's shop but could not find it in telephone, chamber of commerce, or other city directories. They were careful not to direct any mail to the post office box for fear of alerting the then-unknown parties involved. A sly internal auditor already had used a ruse at the post office and learned that Welby rented the box, but they did not know whether anyone else was involved. Alerted, the internal auditors gathered all the Quickprint bills and determined the total charged for nonexistent projects. Carefully, under the covert observation of a representative of the local union prosecutor's office, Welby was interviewed and readily confessed.

CASETTE 10.2
REAL CASH PAID TO PHONY DOCTORS

Problem

Cash disbursement fraud. Fictitious medical and dental benefit claims were paid by the company, which self-insured up to $50,000 per employee for health and dental costs not covered by the provincial plan. The expense account that included legitimate and false charges was "employee medical benefits."

Method

As manager of the claims payment department, Martha Lee was considered one of Beta Magnetic's best employees. She never missed a day of work in 10 years, and her department had one of the company's best efficiency ratings. Controls were considered good, including the verification by a claims processor that (1) the patient was a Beta employee, (2) medical treatments were covered in the plan, (3) the charges were within approved guidelines and not covered by the provincial plan, (4) the cumulative claims for the employee did not exceed $50,000 (if over $50,000, a claim was submitted to an insurance company), and (5) the calculation for payment was correct. After verification processing, claims were sent to the claims payment department to pay the doctor directly. No payments ever went directly to employees. Martha Lee prepared false claims on real employees, forging the signature of various claims processors, adding her own review approval, naming bogus doctors who would be paid by the payment department. The payments were mailed to various post office box addresses and to her husband's business address.

Nobody ever verified claims information with the employee. The employees received no reports of medical benefits paid on their behalf. While the department had performance reports by claims processors, these reports did not show claim-by-claim details. No one verified the credentials of the doctors.

Paper Trail

The falsified claims forms were in Beta's files, containing all the fictitious data on employee names, processor signatures, doctors' bills, and phony doctors and addresses. The cancelled cheques were returned by the bank and were kept in Beta's files, containing "endorsements" by the doctors. Martha Lee and her husband were somewhat clever: They deposited the cheques in various banks in accounts opened in the names and identification of the "doctors."

Martha Lee did not stumble on the paper trail. She drew the attention of an auditor who saw her take her 24 claims-processing employees out to an annual staff appreciation luncheon in a fleet of stretch limousines.

Amount

Over the last seven years, Martha Lee and her husband stole $3.5 million, and until the last, no one noticed anything unusual about the total amount of claims paid.

AUDIT APPROACH

Objective

Obtain evidence to determine whether employee medical benefits "existed" in the sense of being valid claims paid to valid doctors.

Control

The controls are good as far as they go. The claims processors used internal data in their work—employee files for identification, treatment descriptions submitted by doctors and dentists with comparisons to plan provisions, and mathematical calculations. This work amounted to all the approval necessary for the claims payment department to prepare a cheque.

There were no controls that connected the claims data with outside sources, such as employee acknowledgment or doctor investigation.

Test of Controls

The processing and control work in the claims processing department can be audited for deviations from controls.

Procedure: Select a sample of paid claims and reperform the claims processing procedures to verify the employee status, coverage of treatment, proper guideline charges, cumulative amount less than $50,000, and accurate calculation. However, this procedure would not help answer the question: "Does Martha Lee steal the money to pay for the limousines?"

"Thinking like a crook" points out the holes in the controls. Nobody seeks to verify data with external sources. However, an auditor must be careful in an investigation not to cast aspersions on a manager by letting rumours start by interviewing employees to find out whether they actually had the medical claim paid on their behalf. If money is being taken, the company cheque must be intercepted in some manner.

Audit of Balance

The balance under audit is the sum of the charges in the employee medical benefits expense account, and the objective relates to the valid existence of the payments.

Procedure: The first procedure can be: Obtain a list of doctors and dentists paid by the company and look them up in the provincial medical and dental association directories. Look up their addresses and determine whether they are valid business addresses. You might try comparing claims processors' signatures on various forms but this is hard to do and requires training. An extended procedure would be: Compare the doctors' addresses to addresses known to be associated with Martha Lee and other claims-processing employees.

Discovery Summary

The comparison of doctors to the association directories showed eight "doctors" who were not licensed in the current period. Five of these eight had post office box addresses, and discrete enquiries and surveillance showed them rented to Martha Lee. The other three had the same mailing address as her husband's business. Further investigation, involving the Crown attorney and police, was necessary to obtain personal financial records and reconstruct the thefts from prior years.

CASETTE 10.3
RECEIVING THE MISSING OIL

Problem

Fuel oil supplies inventory and fuel expense inflated because of short shipments.

Method

Johnson Chemical started a new contract with Madden Oil Distributors to supply fuel oil for the plant generators on a cost-plus contract. Madden delivered the oil weekly in a 20,000-litre-tank truck and pumped it into Johnson's storage tanks. Johnson's receiving employees were supposed to observe the pumping and record the quantity on a receiving report, which was then forwarded to the accounts payable department, where it was held pending arrival of Madden's invoice. The quantities received then were compared to the quantities billed by Madden before a voucher was approved for payment and a cheque prepared for signature by the controller. Since it was a cost-plus contract, Madden's billing price was not checked against any standard price.

The receiving employees were rather easily fooled by Madden's driver. He mixed sludge with the oil; the receiving employees did not take samples to check for quality. He called out the storage tank content falsely (e.g., 4,000 litres on hand when 8,000 were actually in the tank); the receiving employees did not check the gauge themselves; and the tank truck was not weighed at entry and exit to determine the amount delivered. During the winter months, when fuel oil use was high, Madden ran in extra trucks more than once a week, but pumped nothing when the receiving employees were not looking. Quantities "received" and paid during the first year of the contract were (in litres):

Jan.	124,000	May	72,000	Sept.	84,000
Feb.	112,000	June	56,000	Oct.	92,000
Mar.	92,000	July	60,000	Nov.	132,000
Apr.	76,000	Aug.	56,000	Dec.	144,000

Paper Trail

The Johnson receiving reports all agreed with the quantities billed by Madden. Each invoice had a receiving report attached in the Johnson voucher files. Even though Madden had many trucks, the same driver always came to the Johnson plant, as evidenced by his signature on the receiving report (along with the Johnson company receiving employees' initials). Madden charged $.45 per litre, making the charges for the 1,100,000 litre a total of $495,000 for the year. Last year, Johnson paid a total of $360,000 for 900,000 litres, but nobody made a complete comparison with last year's quantity and cost.

Amount

During the first year, Madden shorted Johnson on quantity by 160,000 litres (loss = 160,000 × $.45 = $72,000) and charged 5 cents per gallon more than competitors (loss = 940,000 litres × $0.05 = $47,000) for a total overcharge of $119,000, not to mention the inferior sludge mix occasionally delivered.

AUDIT APPROACH

Objective

Obtain evidence to determine whether all fuel oil billed and paid was actually received in the quality expected at a fair price.

Control

Receiving employees should be provided the tools and techniques they need to do a good job. Scales at the plant entrance could be used to weigh the trucks in and out and determine the amount of fuel oil delivered. (The weight per gallon is a well-known measure.) They could observe the quality of the oil by taking samples for simple chemical analysis.

Instructions should be given to teach the receiving employees the importance of their job so they can be conscientious. They should have been instructed and supervised to read the storage tank gauges themselves instead of relying on Madden's driver.

Lacking these tools and instructions, they were easy marks for the wily driver.

Test of Controls

The control procedure supposedly in place was the receiving report on the oil delivered. A procedure to (1) take a sample of Madden's bills, and (2a) compare quantities billed to quantities received, and (2b) compare the price billed to the contract would probably not have shown anything unusual (unless the auditor became suspicious of the same driver always delivering to Johnson).

The information from the "understanding the control structure" phase would need to be much more detailed to alert the auditors to the poor receiving practices.

Procedure: Make enquiries with the receiving employees to learn about their practices and work habits.

Audit of Balance

The balances in question are the fuel oil supply inventory and the fuel expense.

The inventory is easily audited by reading the tank storage gauge for the quantity. The price is found in Madden's invoices. However, a lower-of-cost-or-market test requires knowledge of market prices of the oil. Since Johnson Chemical apparently has no documentation of competing prices, the auditor will need to make a few telephone calls to other oil distributors to get the prices. Presumably, the auditors would learn that the price is approximately $.40 per litre.

The expense balance can be audited like a cost of goods sold number. With knowledge of the beginning fuel inventory, the quantity "purchased," and the quantity in the ending inventory, the fuel oil expense quantity can be calculated. This expense quantity can be priced at Madden's price per gallon.

Analytical procedures applied to the expense should reveal the larger quantities used and the unusual pattern of deliveries, leading to suspicions of Madden and the driver.

Discovery Summary

Knowing the higher expense of the current year and the evidence of a lower market price, the auditors obtained the fuel oil delivery records from the prior year. They are shown below, and the numbers in parentheses are the additional gallons delivered in the current year:

Having found a consistent pattern of greater "use" in the current year, with no operational explanation, the auditors took to the field. With the co-operation of the receiving employees, the auditors read the storage tank measure before the Madden driver arrived. They hid in an adjoining building and watched (and filmed) the driver call out an incorrect reading, pump the oil, sign the receiving report, and depart. Then they took samples. These observations were repeated for three weeks. They saw short deliveries, tested inferior products, and built a case against Madden and the driver.

Jan. 112,000 (12,000)	May 52,000 (20,000)	Sept. 60,000 (24,000)
Feb. 96,000 (16,000)	June 44,000 (12,000)	Oct. 80,000 (12,000)
Mar. 80,000 (12,000)	July 40,000 (20,000)	Nov. 112,000 (20,000)
Apr. 68,000 (8,000)	Aug. 36,000 (20,000)	Dec. 120,000 (24,000)

CASETTE 10.4
GO FOR THE GOLD

Problem

Fixed assets in the form of mining properties were overstated through a series of "flip" transactions involving related parties.

Method

In 1989 Alta Gold Company was a public "shell" corporation that was purchased for $1,000 by the Blues brothers.

Operating under the corporate names of Diamond King and Pacific Gold, the brothers purchased numerous mining claims in auctions conducted by the Ministry of Natural Resources. They invested a total of $40,000 in 300 claims. Diamond Kind sold limited partnership interests in its 175 Northwest Territories diamond claims to local investors, raising $20 million to begin mining production. Pacific Gold then traded its 125 British Columbia gold mining claims for all the Diamond King assets and partnership interests, valuing the diamond claims at $20 million. (Diamond King valued the gold claims received at $20 million as the fair value in the exchange.) The brothers then put $3 million obtained from dividends into Alta Gold and, with the aid of a bank loan, purchased half of the Diamond King gold claims for $18 million. The Blues brothers then obtained another bank loan of $38 million to merge the remainder of Diamond King's assets and all of Pacific Gold's mining claims by purchase. They paid off the limited partners. At the end of 1989, Alta Gold had cash of $16 million and mining assets valued at $58 million, with liabilities on bank loans of $53 million.

Paper Trail

Alta Gold had in its files the partnership offering documents, receipts, and other papers showing partners' investment of $20 million in the Diamond King limited partnerships. The company also had Pacific Gold and Diamond King contracts for the exchange of mining claims. The $20 million value of the exchange was justified in light of the limited partners' investments.

Appraisals in the files showed one appraiser's report that there was no basis for valuing the exchange of Diamond King claims, other than the price limited partner investors had been willing to pay. The second appraiser reported a probable value of $20 million for the exchange based on proved production elsewhere, but no geological data on the actual claims had been obtained. The $18 million paid by Alta to Diamond King also had similar appraisal reports.

Amount

The transactions occurred over a period of 10 months. The Blues brothers had $37 million cash in Diamond King and Pacific Gold, as well as the $16 million in Alta (all of which was the gullible bank's money, but the bank had loaned to Alta with the mining claims and production as security). The mining claims that had cost $40,000 were now in Alta's balance sheet at $58 million, the $37 million was about to flee, and the bank was about to be left holding the bag containing 300 mining claim papers.

AUDIT APPROACH

Objective

Obtain evidence of the existence, valuation, and rights (ownership) in the mining claim assets.

Control

Alta Gold, Pacific Gold, and Diamond King had no control structure. All transactions were engineered by the Blues brothers, including the hiring of friendly appraisers. The only control that might have been effective was at the bank in the loan-granting process, but the bank failed.

Test of Controls

The only vestige of control could have been the engagement of competent, independent appraisers. Since the auditors will need to use (or try to use) the appraisers' reports, the procedures involve investigating the reputation, engagement terms, and independence of the appraisers. The auditors can use local business references, local financial institutions that keep lists of approved appraisers, mem-bership directories of the professional appraisal associations, and interviews with the appraisers themselves.

Audit of Balances

The procedures for auditing the asset values include analyses of each of the transactions through all their complications, including obtaining knowledge of the owners and managers of the several companies and the identities of the limited partner investors. If the Blues brothers have not disclosed their connection with the other companies (and perhaps with the limited partners), the auditors will need to enquire at the Ministry of Consumer and Commercial Relations offices where Pacific Gold and Diamond King are incorporated and try to discover the identities of the players in this flip game. Numerous complicated premerger transactions in small corporations and shells often signal manipulated valuations.

Loan applications and supporting papers should be examined to determine the representations made by Alta in connection with obtaining the bank loans. These papers may reveal some contradictory or exaggerated information.

Ownership of the mining claims might be confirmed with the Resources Ministry auctioneers or be found in the local deed records (spread all over the Northwest Territories and British Columbia).

Discovery Summary

The inexperienced audit staff was unable to unravel the Byzantine exchanges, and they never questioned the relation of Alta to Diamond King and Pacific Gold. They never discovered the Blues brothers' involvement in the other side of the exchange, purchase, and merger transactions. They accepted the appraisers' reports because they had never worked with appraisers before and thought all appraisers were competent and independent. The bank lost $37 million. The Blues brothers changed their names.

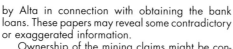

CASETTE 10.5
RETREAD TIRES

Problem

Inventory and income overstated by substitution of retread tires valued for inventory at new tire prices.

Method

Ritter Tire Wholesale Company had a high-volume truck and passenger car tire business in Hamilton, Ontario (area population 500,000). J. Lock, the chief accountant, was a longtime trusted employee who had supervisory responsibility over the purchasing agents as well as general accounting duties. Lock had worked several years as a purchasing agent before moving into the accounting job. In the course of normal operations, Lock often prepared purchase orders; but the manufacturers were directed to deliver the tires to a warehouse in Milton (a town of 30,000 population 30 kilometres north of Hamilton). Ritter Tire received the manufacturers' invoices, which Lock approved for payment. Lock and an accomplice (brother-in-law) sold the tires from the Milton warehouse and pocketed the money. At night, Lock moved cheaper retreaded tires into the Ritter warehouse so the space would not seem to be empty. As chief accountant, Lock could override controls (e.g., approving invoices for payment without a receiving report), and T. Ritter (president) never knew the difference because the cheques presented for signature were not accompanied by the supporting documents.

Paper Trail

Ritter Tire's files were well organized. Each cheque copy had supporting documents attached (voucher, invoice, receiving report, purchase order), except the misdirected tire purchases had no receiving reports. These purchase orders were all signed by Lock, and the shipping destination on them directed delivery to the Milton address. There were no purchase requisition documents because "requisitions" were in the form of verbal requests from salespersons.

There was no paper evidence of the retreaded tires because Lock simply bought them elsewhere and moved them in at night when nobody else was around.

Amount

Lock carried out the scheme for three years, diverting tires that cost Ritter $2.5 million, which Lock sold for $2.9 million. (Lock's cost of retread tires was approximately $500,000.)

AUDIT APPROACH

Objective

Obtain evidence of the existence and valuation of the inventory. (President Ritter engaged external auditors for the first time in the third year of Lock's scheme after experiencing a severe cash squeeze.)

Control

Competent personnel should perform the purchasing function. Lock and the other purchasing agents were competent and experienced. They prepared purchase orders authorizing the purchase of tires. (The manufacturers required them for shipments.)

A receiving department prepared a receiving report after counting and inspecting each shipment by filling in the "quantity column" on a copy of the purchase order. (A common form of receiving report is a "blind" purchase order that has all the purchase information except the quantity, which is left blank for the receiving department to fill in after an independent inspection and count.) Receiving personnel made notes if the tires showed blemishes or damage.

As chief accountant, Lock received the invoices from the manufacturers and approved them for payment after comparing the quantities with the receiving report and the prices with the purchase order. The cheques for payment were produced automatically on the microcomputer accounting system when Lock entered the invoice payable in the system. The computer software did not void transactions for lack of a receiving report reference because many other expenses legitimately had no receiving reports.

The key weakness in the control structure was the fact that no one else on the accounting staff had the opportunity to notice missing receiving reports in vouchers that should have had them, and Ritter never had the vouchers when cheques were signed. Lock was a trusted employee.

Test of Controls

Because the control procedures for cross-checking the supporting documents were said to have been placed in operation, the external auditors can test the controls.

Procedure: Select a sample of purchases (manufacturers' invoices payable entered in the microcomputer), and (1) study the related purchase order for (*i*) valid manufacturer name and address; (*ii*) date: (*iii*) delivery address; (*iv*) unit price, with reference to catalogues or price lists; (*v*) correct arithmetic; and (*vi*) approval signature. Then (2) compare purchase order information to the manufacturers' invoice; and (3) compare the purchase order and invoice to the receiving report for (*i*) date, (*ii*) quantity and condition, (*iii*) approval signature, and (*iv*) location.

Audit of Balance

Ritter Tire did not maintain perpetual inventory records, so the inventory was a "periodic system" whereby the financial statement inventory figure was derived from the annual physical inventory count and costing compilation. The basic audit procedure was to observe the count by taking a sample of locations on the warehouse floor, recounting the employees' count, controlling the count sheets, and inspecting the tires for quality and condition (related to proper valuation). The auditors kept their own copy of all the count sheets with their test count notes and notes identifying tires as "new" or "retread." (They took many test counts in the physical inventory sample as a result of the test of controls work, described below.)

Discovery Summary

Forty manufacturers' invoices were selected at random for the test of controls procedure. The auditors were good. They had reviewed the business operations, and Ritter had said nothing about having operations or a warehouse in Milton, although a manufacturer might have been instructed to "drop ship" tires to a customer there. The auditors noticed three missing receiving reports, all of them with purchase orders signed by Lock and requesting delivery to the same Milton address. They asked Lock about the missing receiving reports, and got this response: "It happens sometimes. I'll find them for you tomorrow." When Lock produced the receiving reports, the auditors noticed these were in a current numerical sequence (dated much earlier), filled out with the same pen, and signed with an illegible scrawl not matching any of the other receiving reports they had seen.

The auditors knew the difference between new and retread tires when they saw them, and confirmed their observations with employees taking the physical inventory count. When Lock priced the inventory, new tire prices were used, and the auditors knew the difference.

Ritter took the circumstantial evidence to a trained investigator who interviewed the manufacturers and obtained information about the Milton location. The case against Lock led to criminal theft charges and conviction.

CASETTE 10.6
AMORTIZE "THE DRUM" SLOWLY

Problem

Net asset values (unamortized cost of films) was overstated by taking too little amortization expense.

Method

Candid Production Company was a major producer of theatrical movies. The company usually had 15–20 films in release at theatres across the nation and in foreign countries. Movies also produced revenue from video licences and product sales (T-shirts, toys, and the like).

Movie production costs are capitalized as assets, then amortized to expense as revenue is received from theatre and video sales and from other sources of revenue. The amortization depends on the total revenue forecast and the current-year revenue amount. As the success or failure of a movie unfolds at the box office, revenue estimates are revised. (The accounting amortization is very similar to depletion of a mineral resource, which depends upon estimates of recoverable minerals and current production.)

Candid Production was not too candid. For example, its recent film of *Bang the Drum Slowly* was forecast to produce $50 million total revenue over six years, although the early box office returns showed only $10 million in the first eight months in the theatres. (Revenue will decline rapidly after initial openings, and video and other revenues depend on the box office success of a film.)

Accounting "control" with respect to film cost amortization resides in the preparation and revision of revenue forecasts. In this case they were overly optimistic, showing the expense recognition and overstating assets and income.

Paper Trail

Revenue forecasts are based on many factors, including facts and assumptions about number of theatres, ticket prices, receipt-sharing agreements, domestic and foreign reviews, and moviegoer tastes. Several publications track the box office records of movies. You can see them in newspaper entertainment sections and in industry trade publications. Of course, the production companies themselves are the major source of the information. However, company records also show the revenue realized from each movie.

Revenue forecasts can be checked against actual experience, and the company's history of forecasting accuracy can be determined by comparing actual to forecast over many films and many years.

Amount

Over a four-year period, Candid Productions postponed recognition of a $20 million amortization expense, thus inflating assets and income.

AUDIT APPROACH

Objective

Obtain evidence to determine whether revenue forecasts provide a sufficient basis for calculating film cost amortization and net asset value of films.

Control

Revenue forecasts need to be prepared in a controlled process that documents the facts and underlying assumptions built into the forecast. Forecasts should break down the revenue estimate by years, and the accounting system should produce comparable actual revenue data so that forecast accuracy can be assessed after the fact. Forecast revisions should be prepared in as much detail and documentation as original forecasts.

Test of Controls

The general procedures and methods used by personnel responsible for revenue forecasts should be studied (enquiries and review of documentation), including their sources of information both internal and external. Procedures for review of mechanical aspects (arithmetic) should be tested: Select a sample of finished forecasts and recalculate the final estimate.

Specific procedures for forecast revision also should be studied in the same manner. A review of the accuracy of forecasts of other movies with hindsight on actual revenues helps in a circumstantial way, but past accuracy on different film experiences may not directly influence the forecasts on a new, unique product.

Audit of Balance

The audit of amortization expense concentrates on the content of the forecast itself. The preparation of forecasts used in the amortization calculation should be studied to distinguish underlying reasonable expectations from "hypothetical assumptions." A hypothetical assumption is a statement of a condition that is not necessarily expected to occur, but nonetheless is used to prepare an estimate. For example, a hypothetical assumption is like an "if-then" statement: "If *Bang the Drum Slowly* sells 15 million tickets in the first 12 months of release, then domestic revenue and product sales will be $40 million, and foreign revenue can eventually reach $10 million." Auditors need to assess the reasonableness of the basic 15-million ticket assumption. It helps to have some early actual data from the film's release in hand before the financial statements need to be finished and distributed. For actual data, industry publications ought to be reviewed, with special attention paid to competing films and critics' reviews (yes, movie reviews!)

Discovery Summary

The auditors were not skeptical enough about optimistic revenue forecasts, and they did not weigh unfavourable actual/forecast history comparisons heavily enough. Apparently, they let themselves be convinced by exuberant company executives that the movies were comparable with *Gone with the Wind*! The audit of forecasts and estimates used in accounting determinations is very difficult, especially when company personnel have incentives to hype the numbers, seemingly with conviction about the artistic and commercial merit of their productions. The postponed amortization expense finally came home to roost in big write-offs when the company management changed.

- -

R E V I E W
CHECKPOINTS

10.12 Give some examples of "receiving departments."

10.13 When is a "blind purchase order" used as a receiving report document?

10.14 The cases on Printing (Copying) Money, on Real Cash Paid to Phony Doctors, and on Retread Tires all included fictitious people, businesses, and locations. Where can an auditor obtain information about them?

10.15 How can analytical procedures be used for discovery of excess costs (Receiving the Missing Oil) and understated expenses (Amortize "The Drum" Slowly)?

10.16 What impact can related party transactions have in some cases of asset valuation?

10.17   How can it help an auditor to know the physical characteristics of inventoried assets?

10.18   Why is "professional skepticism" important for auditors? Give two case examples.

10.19   What evidence could the "verbal enquiry" audit procedure produce in Printing (Copying) Money? Receiving the Missing Oil? Go for the Gold? Retread Tires?

. . . .

SPECIAL NOTE: THE COMPLETENESS ASSERTION
. . . .

LEARNING   OBJECTIVE

4. Explain the importance of the completeness assertion for the audit of accounts payable liabilities, and list some procedures for a "search for unrecorded liabilities."

When considering assertions and obtaining evidence about accounts payable and other liabilities, auditors must put emphasis on the completeness and obligations assertions. (For asset accounts the emphasis is on the existence and rights assertions.) This emphasis on completeness is rightly placed because companies typically are less concerned about timely recording of expenses and liabilities than they are about timely recording of revenues and assets. Of course, generally accepted accounting principles require timely accrual of liabilities and their associated expenses.

Evidence is much more difficult to obtain to verify the completeness assertion than the existence assertion. Auditors cannot rely entirely on a management assertion of completeness, even in combination with a favourable assessment of control risk. Substantive procedures, tests of details, or analytical procedures ought to be performed. The **search for unrecorded liabilities** is a set of procedures designed to yield audit evidence of liabilities that were not recorded in the reporting period. Such a search ought normally to be performed up to the report date in the period following the audit client's balance sheet date.

The following is a list of procedures useful in the search for unrecorded liabilities. The audit objective is to search all the places where evidence of them might exist. If these procedures reveal none, the auditors can conclude that all material liabilities are recorded.

1. Scan the open purchase order file at year-end for indications of material purchase commitments at fixed prices. Obtain current prices and determine whether any adjustments for loss and liability for purchase commitments are needed.

2. List the unmatched vendor invoices and determine when the goods were received, looking to the unmatched receiving report file and receiving reports prepared after the year-end. Determine which invoices, if any, should be recorded.

3. Trace the unmatched receiving reports to accounts payable entries, and determine whether ones recorded in the next accounting period need to be adjusted to report them in the current accounting period under audit.

4. Select a sample of cash disbursements from the accounting period following the balance sheet date. Vouch them to supporting documents (invoice, receiving report) to determine whether the related liabilities were recorded in the proper accounting period.

5. Trace the liabilities reported by financial institutions to the accounts. (See the bank confirmation in Exhibit 9–7, Chapter 9. However, a bank really is not

expected to search all its files to report all client liabilities to auditors, so the bank confirmation is not the best source of evidence of unrecorded debts.)

6. Study Revenue Canada notices of assessment for evidence of income or other taxes in dispute, and decide whether actual or estimated liabilities need to be recorded.

7. Confirm accounts payable with vendors, especially regular suppliers showing small or zero balances in the year-end accounts payable. These are the ones most likely to be understated. (Vendors' monthly statements controlled by the auditors also may be used for this procedure.) Be sure to verify the vendors' addresses so that confirmations will not be misdirected—perhaps to conspirators in a scheme to understate liabilities.

8. Study the accounts payable trial balance for indications of dates showing fewer payables than usual recorded near the year-end. (A financial officer may be stashing vendor invoices in a desk drawer instead of recording them.)

9. Review the lawyers' responses to requests for information about pending or threatened litigation, and about unasserted claims and assessments (see Chapter 13). The lawyers' information may signal the need for contingent liability accruals or disclosures. *Handbook Section* 6560.07 recommends that such an enquiry letter be prepared by the client and sent by the auditor.

10. Use a checklist of accrued expenses to determine whether the company has been conscientious about expense and liability accruals, including accruals for wages, interest, utilities, sales and excise taxes, payroll taxes, income taxes, real property taxes, rent, sales commissions, royalties, and warranty and guarantee expense.

11. When auditing the details of sales revenue, pay attention to the terms of sales to determine whether any amounts should be deferred as unearned revenue. (Enquiries directed to management about terms of sales, such as enquiries about customers' rights of cancellation or return, can be used to obtain initial information.)

12. Prepare or obtain a schedule of casualty insurance on fixed assets, and determine the adequacy of insurance in relation to asset market values. Inadequate insurance and self-insurance should be disclosed in the notes to the financial statements.

13. Confirm life insurance policies with insurance companies to ask whether the company has any loans against the cash value of the insurance. In this confirmation, request the names of the beneficiaries of the policies. If the insurance is for the benefit of a party other than the company, the beneficiaries may be creditors on unrecorded loans. Make enquiries about the business purpose of making insurance proceeds payable to other parties.

14. Review the terms of debt due within one year but classified long-term because the company plans to refinance it on a long-term basis. Holders of the debt or financial institutions must have shown (preferably in writing) a willingness to refinance the debt before it can be classified long-term. Classification cannot be based solely on management's expressed intent to seek long-term financing.

15. Apply analytical procedures appropriate in the circumstances. In general, accounts payable volume and period-end balances should increase when the company experiences increases in physical production volume or engages in

inventory stockpiling. Some liabilities may be functionally related to other activities, for example, sales taxes are functionally related to sales dollar totals, payroll taxes to payroll totals, excise taxes to sales dollars or volume, and income taxes to income.

R E V I E W
CHECKPOINTS

10.20   Describe the purpose and give examples of audit procedures in the "search for unrecorded liabilities."

10.21   Explain the difference in approach in confirmation of accounts receivable and accounts payable.

10.22   In substantive auditing, why is the emphasis on the completeness assertion for liabilities instead of on the existence assertion as in the audit of assets?

SPECIAL NOTE: PHYSICAL INVENTORY OBSERVATION

LEARNING OBJECTIVE

5. Identify and describe considerations involved in the audit observation of physical inventory-taking.

In an audit engagement, the audit procedures for inventory and related cost of sales accounts frequently are extensive. A 96-page joint CICA–AICPA auditing technique study entitled *Audit of Inventories* (CICA, 1986) describes many facets of inherent risk and control risk, and of the process of obtaining evidence about inventory financial statement assertions. The significance of inventories is acknowledged in the following quotation:

> Generally, inventories reflect the characteristics of a business more than any other asset. Significant to manufacturing, wholesale, and retail organizations, inventories frequently are also material to the financial statements of service organizations. It has been estimated that, for some types of businesses, inventories constitute 20 to 25 percent of total assets and represent the largest current asset.[1]

A material error or irregularity in inventory has a pervasive effect on financial statements. Errors in inventory cause misstatements in current assets, working capital, total assets, cost of sales, gross margin, and net income. While analytical procedures can help indicate inventory presentation problems, the auditors' best opportunity to detect inventory errors and irregularities is during the physical observation of the client's inventory count taken by company personnel. (Auditors observe the inventory-taking and make test counts, but they seldom actually take (count) the entire inventory.) Auditing standards express the requirement for inventory observation in *Section* 6030.04: "Usually, the checking of the quantities is accomplished most conveniently by observing and noting the counts made by the client's staff, but actual test counts are often undertaken by the auditors, before, during, or after the client's physical stocktaking."

The remainder of this special note gives details about auditors' observation of physical inventory-taking. The first task is to review the client's inventory-taking instructions. The instructions should include the following:

1. Names of client personnel responsible for the count.
2. Dates and times of inventory-taking.

---

[1] James Carty, "Ask the Right Questions about Inventory," *World Accounting Report*, January 1984, p. 20.

3. Names of client personnel who will participate in the inventory-taking.

4. Instructions for recording accurate descriptions of inventory items, for count and double-count, and for measuring or translating physical quantities (such as counting by measures of litres, barrels, meters, dozens).

5. Instructions for making notes of obsolete or worn items.

6. Instructions for the use of tags, punched cards, count sheets, or other media devices and for their collection and control.

7. Plans for shutting down plant operations or for taking inventory after store closing hours, and plans for having goods in proper places (such as on store shelves instead of on the floor, or in a warehouse rather than in transit to a job).

8. Plans for counting or controlling movement of goods in receiving and shipping areas if those operations are not shut down during the count.

9. Instructions for computer compilation of the count media (such as tags, punch cards) into final inventory listings or summaries.

10. Instructions for pricing the inventory items.

11. Instructions for review and approval of the inventory count; notations of obsolescence or other matters by supervisory personnel.

These instructions characterize a well-planned counting operation. As the plan is carried out, the independent auditors should be present to hear the count instructions being given to the client's count teams and to observe the instructions being followed.

Many physical inventories are counted at the year-end when the auditor is present to observe. The auditors can perform dual-direction testing by (1) selecting inventory items from a perpetual inventory master file, going to the location, and obtaining a test count, which produces evidence for the existence assertion; and (2) selecting inventory from locations on the warehouse floor, obtaining a test count, and tracing the count to the final inventory compilation, which produces evidence for the completeness assertion. If the company does not have perpetual records and a file to test for existence, the auditors must be careful to obtain a record of all the counts and use it for the existence-direction tests.

However, the following other situations frequently occur.

Physical Inventory Not on Year-End Date

Clients sometimes count the inventory on a date other than the balance sheet date, either before or after. When the auditors are present to make their physical observation, they follow the procedures outlined above for observation of the physical count. However, with a time period intervening between the count date and the year-end, additional roll-forward or rollback auditing procedures must be performed on purchase, inventory addition, and issue transactions during that period. The inventory on the count date is reconciled to the year-end inventory by appropriate addition or subtraction of the intervening receiving and issue transactions.

Cycle Inventory Counting

Some companies count inventory on a cycle basis or use a statistical counting plan but never take a complete count on a single date. In these circumstances the auditors must understand the cycle or sampling plan and evaluate its appropriateness. In this type of situation the auditors are present for some counting operations. Only under unusual circumstances and as an "extended procedure" are auditors present every month (or more frequently) to observe all counts. Businesses that count inventory in this manner purport to have accurate perpetual records and carry out the counting as a means of testing the records and maintaining their accuracy.

The auditors must be present during some counting operations to evaluate the counting plans and their execution. The procedures for an annual count enumerated above are utilized, test counts are made, and the audit team is responsible for a conclusion concerning the accuracy (control) of perpetual records.

Auditors Not Present at Client's Inventory Count

This situation can arise on a first audit when the audit firm is appointed after the beginning inventory already has been counted. The auditors must review the client's plan for the already completed count as before. Some test counts of current inventory should be made and traced to current records to make a conclusion about the reliability of perpetual records. If the actual count was recent, intervening transaction activity may be reconciled back to the beginning inventory.

However, the reconciliation of more than a few months' transactions to unobserved beginning inventories may be very difficult. The auditors may employ procedures utilizing such interrelationships as sales activity, physical volume, price variation, standard costs, and gross profit margins for the decision about beginning inventory reasonableness. Nevertheless, much care must be exercised in "backing into" the audit of a previous inventory. If the auditors cannot satisfy themselves as to the beginning inventory balance, then a reservation in the auditor's report is normally called for (*Section* 6030.17).

Inventories Located Off the Client's Premises

The auditors must determine where and in what dollar amounts inventories are located off the client's premises, in the custody of consignees, or in public warehouses. If amounts are material and if control is not exceptionally strong, the audit team may wish to visit these locations and conduct on-site test counts. However, if amounts are not material and/or if related evidence is adequate (such as periodic reports, cash receipts, receivables records, shipping records) and if control risk is low, then direct confirmation with the custodian may be considered sufficient appropriate evidence of the existence of quantities (*Section* 6030.07). Note that confirmation is normally expected by the CICA for two items—accounts receivable and off-premise inventories.

INVENTORY COUNT AND MEASUREMENT CHALLENGES

Examples	Challenges
Lumber.	Problem identifying quality or grade.
Piles of sugar, coal, scrap steel.	Geometric computations, aerial photos.
Items weighed on scales.	Check scales for accuracy.
Bulk materials (oil, grain, liquids in storage tanks).	Climb the tanks. Dip measuring rods. Sample for assay or chemical analysis.
Diamonds, jewellery.	Identification and quality determination problems. Ask a specialist.
Pulp wood.	Quantity measurement estimation. Aerial photos.
Livestock.	Movement not controllable. Count critter's legs and divide by four (two for chickens).

Source: (adapted): CICA, Audit of Inventories, *Auditing Procedure Study* (1986), p. 28.

Inventory Existence and Completeness

The physical observation procedures are designed to audit for existence and completeness (physical quantities) and valuation (recalculation of appropriate FIFO, specific item or other pricing at cost, and lower-of-cost-or-market write-down of obsolete or worn inventory). After the observation is complete, auditors should have sufficient appropriate evidence of the following physical quantities and valuations:

- Goods in the perpetual records but not owned were excluded from the inventory compilation.

- Goods on hand were counted and included in the inventory compilation.

- Goods consigned-out or stored in outside warehouses (goods owned but not on hand) were included in the inventory compilation.

- Goods in transit (goods actually purchased and recorded but not yet received) were added to the inventory count and included in the inventory compilation.

- Goods on hand already sold (but not yet delivered) were not counted and were excluded from the inventory compilation.

- Goods consigned-in (goods on hand but not owned) were excluded from the inventory compilation.

R E V I E W
C H E C K P O I N T S

10.23 In the review of a client's inventory-taking instructions, for what characteristics are the auditors looking?

10.24 Explain dual-direction sampling in the context of inventory test counts.

10.25 What procedures are employed to audit inventory when the physical inventory is taken on a cycle basis or on a statistical plan, but never a complete count on a single date?

SUMMARY

The acquisition and expenditure cycle consists of purchase requisitioning, purchase ordering, receiving goods and services, recording vendors' invoices and accounting for accounts payable, and making disbursements of cash. Companies reduce control risk by having a suitable separation of authorization, custody, recording, and periodic reconciliation duties. Error-checking procedures of comparing purchase orders and receiving reports to vendor invoices are important for recording proper amounts of accounts payable liabilities. Supervisory control is provided by having a separation of duties between preparing cash disbursement cheques and actually signing them. Otherwise, many things could go wrong, ranging from processing false or fictitious purchase orders to failing to record liabilities for goods and services received.

Cash disbursement is a critical point for asset control. Many cases of embezzlement occur in this process. Illustrative cases in the chapter told of some embezzlement schemes, mostly involving payment of fictitious charges to dummy companies set up by employees.

Two topics had special technical notes in the chapter. The completeness assertion is very important in the audit of liabilities because misleading financial statements often have contained unrecorded liabilities and expenses. The "search for unrecorded liabilities" is an important set of audit procedures. The physical inventory observation audit work received a special section because actual contact with inventories (and fixed assets, for that matter) provides auditors with direct eyewitness evidence of important tangible assets.

CASE STUDY   KINGSTON COMPANY

Note from the Authors

The following problems are concerned with errors, procedures, searches, and adjustments—just some of the risky matters to be examined by the auditor at work.

10.26   Purchase Control Objectives Related to Possible Errors and Test of Controls Audit Procedures.
Each of the seven control objectives could be stated in the negative; for example, authorization: "Unauthorized transactions should not be recorded." Viewed in this way, you can see that a "deviation" from a client control procedure could exist if Kingston personnel recorded an unauthorized transaction. Thus, each category of control objectives also has a related "deviation" that can result from (1) failure of the client to install adequate control procedures or (2) failure of client's personnel to perform specified procedures.

The audit manager does not think the audit has given enough attention to the possible errors or irregularities that could occur in the purchases processing and, therefore, the control risk over purchase transactions has been assessed too low. He directs you to prepare a workpaper listing the major errors that could occur in the purchasing system and to describe the test of controls procedures for auditing related purchasing controls to determine whether reliable controls exist.

Required:
For each of the objectives listed in the evaluation table of control objectives and control examples for purchases (Exhibit 10–2):

a. Reword the objectives in the negative to identify "deviations."

b. For each objective indicate the monetary error that could occur in the accounts if the client did not have control procedures to accomplish the objective.

c. For each objective, indicate at least one test of controls audit procedure that could reveal deviations from the client's controls (listed as examples in Exhibit 10–2). See Exhibit 10–3 for examples of test of controls audit procedures for obtaining evidence about purchase controls.

10.27   Kingston Company: Search for Unrecorded Liabilities.
Dalton Wardlaw, the engagement partner, has reviewed the audit working papers completed thus far. He is very upset over the search for unrecorded liabilities and is quite sure there are more. You are directed to re-examine all vouchers and cash disbursements that were recorded with a date after December 31. Further, you are to examine documents in the open purchase order file, the unmatched receiving report file, and the unmatched invoice file (a procedure omitted in the initial search audit procedures). You found the following information:

1. In the open invoice file, you found an invoice from Bass Hardware Company, dated December 30, for $5,000. However, no receiving report could be located in the unmatched

receiving reports file. You located the related purchase order in the open receiving reports file. Later, on January 6, the goods were received with bill of lading showing a January 3 shipping date.

2. An examination of the cheque register and the vouchers payable journal uncovered the following:

    a. The cheque register indicated that the utilities were paid on January 10, for $2,100. Locating the appropriate voucher revealed that the voucher also was dated January 10, and this was for December electricity consumed.

    b. A voucher was entered in the vouchers payable journal January 2, for $57,000 for an inventory purchase. The open voucher and the supporting documents indicate the goods had been shipped in December and were received January 2, FOB destination (when title passed to Kingston).

    c. Another voucher entry on January 2 was for an inventory purchase of $75,000. There was a receiving report dated December 31. Upon enquiring of the accounts payable clerk about this, he indicated that the office party was held the afternoon of the 31st and that the receiving report was probably not forwarded until the next working day.

    d. A third voucher entry on January 2 was for rent of $5,000. The cheque date column indicated that it was paid on January 2. Locating the paid voucher indicated that the rent was the monthly rent, paid in advance.

    e. A review of the bank confirmation and the interest expense accounts showed that interest on the bank loan had not been accrued.

Required:

Prepare a working paper list of the unrecorded liabilities. Prepare a recommended adjusting entry if one is necessary.

10.28   Kingston Company: Inventory Cutoff and Adjustment.   In your audit of the Kingston Company's inventory, you find the following information:

1. Lumber costing $57,000 was received on January 3, and the related purchase invoice was recorded January 5. The invoice shows that the shipment was made from Northwest Lumber Company on December 29, "FOB Kingston Company, Kingston." Shipping costs of $200 were paid by Kingston.

2. Hardware costing $6,000 was received on December 28, and the invoice was not recorded. You locate the invoice in the hands of the purchasing agent; it is marked "on consignment."

3. A packing case containing hardware costing $10,000 was standing in the shipping room when the physical inventory was taken. It was not included in the inventory because it was marked "Hold for shipping instructions." Your investigation reveals that the customer's order was dated December 18, but the case was shipped and the customer was billed on January 10. The hardware was a stock item of Kingston.

4. Lumber received from Southern Lumber Company on January 6 costing $3,000 was entered in the vouchers payable journal on January 7. The invoice shows that the lumber was shipped December 31, "FOB Eastern Lumber Company, Aylmer." Kingston paid rail shipping charges of $500. Since it was not on hand December 31, it was not included in the inventory.

5. A lot of walnut lumber special ordered for a customer (walnut lumber is not normally carried in inventory by Kingston) was on the shipping dock on December 31. The purchase had been recorded. The customer was billed for $4,500 on that date, and the lumber was excluded from inventory, although it was shipped on January 4.

6. A stack of lumber was found to be warped and looked very old. Further investigation reveals that this lumber could not be sold at the original price but might be sold as scrap for an estimated 20 to 40 percent of cost. Perpetual inventory records indicate this stack of lumber is carried at a cost of $20,000.

EXHIBIT 10.29–1   TEST COUNT WORKING PAPER

F-2.5
pg 1 of 12

KINGSTON COMPANY
Inventory Test Counts
December 31, 1992

Prepared _____
Date _____
Reviewed _____
Date _____

Tag number	Code	Description	Unit Measure	Client Quantity	Audit Quantity	Comments
87001	11530	1 × 4 6' #3 pine	unit	12500	12500	
87004	11636	1 × 4 12' #3 pine	unit	6500	6500	
87008	11782	1 × 6 8' #3 pine	unit	10335	10435	Client recounted and changed tag.
87015	12128	1 × 8 #3 pine	unit	5750	5750	200 aged and warped.
87501	51583	8d Gal. Nails	50lb. box	1250	1250	
87515	51230	36" Fence Fabric	50' roll	250	250	
87532	51331	6' T-Post	units	552	555	Client to change tag to correct count.

Required:

Assume that each of the amounts is material:

a. State whether the merchandise should be included in the client's inventory and at what value.

b. Give your reasons for your decision on each item in (a) above.

c. Prepare a recommended adjusting journal entry.

10.29   Kingston Company: Inventory Test Count.   Assume you were present to observe the physical count of Kingston Company's lumber (other members of the staff observed the count of the hardware). You put the results on your test counts on a spreadsheet working paper similar to that illustrated in Exhibit 10.29–1. However, you have not added the tick marks, nor have you written a memo describing your observation procedures. (Your instructor can give you a form.) The audit program procedures for the observation of the inventory-taking are in the box on the next page.

Required:

a. Complete the worksheet presented in Exhibit 10.29–1. Assume you have completed the procedures. Indicate that you have completed these procedures with appropriate tick marks and tick mark explanations at the bottom of the worksheet.

b. Some of the procedures are not appropriate for entering on the working paper, such as the last shipments and purchases and those that relate to observations. Assume the information for sheets (g) and (h) were recorded on other working papers (references F-4-3 and F-4-4). Prepare a memo describing the procedures you followed in the observation of Kingston's count of lumber, referring to your workpapers by reference number where appropriate.

10.30   Kingston Company: Property, Plant, and Equipment—Adjustments.   Kingston Company moved into new quarters and acquired substantial new equipment on July 1, 1992. Previously, the company had rented a building. The cost of the new building is recorded in the Buildings account (#123), $300,000, and the equipment in the Equipment account (#125), $600,000. The company also acquired the land for $100,000 (account #129). In your audit of these accounts, you find the following material items:

INVENTORY OBSERVATION PROCEDURES

a. Observe the Kingston manager giving instructions to the count teams and compare the oral instructions to the planned instructions in the memo in the planning working paper file.

b. Observe each team counting and recording the count on prenumbered tags.

c. Recount numerous counts made by each team and compare your count to theirs, noting especially the proper description and measurement on the tags.

d. Record a sample of your test counts (working paper provided).

e. Record the inclusive numbers of the tags filled in. All other numbered tags should be blank when the count is completed (assume 87001-87532).

f. Trace the test counts into Kingston's final inventory compilation.

g. Record the last several shipments made (bill of lading information) and the last several purchases received (receiving report information). Note any lumber in the shipping or receiving area that is not counted by Kingston.

h. Record any lots of lumber that appear to be unsalable due to poor condition.

---

1. Commissions of $7,310 were paid to real estate agents to acquire the land. These commissions were expensed (Miscellaneous expense, account o525) and are excluded from Land.

2. Clearing costs of $5,000 were incurred to make the land ready for construction. These costs were included in the $100,000 Land cost.

3. A group of machines was purchased for $25,000 to cut lumber to sizes desired by customers and to do other limited processing work. The cost of the machines, freight cost, unloading charges, and setup and adjustment costs were capitalized and are included in the Equipment account.

4. Kingston borrowed $750,000 with an 11 percent note to finance the acquisition of the assets. The interest on this loan was not included in the Building account.

5. Using materials from Kingston's inventory, Kingston employees took three months to build a major part of the yard sheds where lumber is stored. The direct labour and material costs of $15,000 are included in the Building account.

6. Some of the old equipment used in the former leased space had to be relocated to the new building. During the moving process, many pieces of equipment were overhauled to extend their useful life. The $23,000 cost of this overhaul and reconditioning was charged to the Repairs and Maintenance account (#523).

Required:

a. Describe (summarize) the generally accepted accounting principles that determine what should be capitalized when new facilities are acquired or constructed.

b. Indicate whether each of the above items numbered 1 to 6 requires one or more audit adjustments or reclassifications, and explain why such adjustments or reclassifications are required or not required. Organize your answer to part (*b*) as follows:

Item Number	Is Audit Adjustment or Reclassification Required?	Reasons Why Audit Adjustment or Reclassification Is Required or Is Not Required
	Yes or No	

MULTIPLE-CHOICE QUESTIONS FOR PRACTICE AND REVIEW

10.31 When verifying debits to the perpetual inventory records of a nonmanufacturing company, an auditor would be most interested in examining a sample of purchase:
a. Approvals.
b. Requisitions.
c. Invoices.
d. Orders.

10.32 Which of the following is an internal control weakness for a company whose inventory of supplies consists of a large number of individual items?
a. Supplies of relatively little value are expensed when purchased.
b. The cycle basis is used for physical counts.
c. The warehouse manager is responsible for maintenance of perpetual inventory records.
d. Perpetual inventory records are maintained only for items of significant value.

10.33 An effective internal control procedure that protects against the preparation of improper or inaccurate cash disbursements would be to require that all cheques be:
a. Signed by an officer after necessary supporting evidence has been examined.
b. Reviewed by the treasurer before mailing.
c. Sequentially numbered and accounted for by internal auditors.
d. Perforated or otherwise effectively cancelled when they are returned with the bank statement.

10.34 A client's purchasing system ends with the recording of a liability and its eventual payment. Which of the following best describes the auditor's primary concern with respect to liabilities resulting from the purchasing system?
a. Accounts payable are not materially understated.
b. Authority to incur liabilities is restricted to one designated person.

c. Acquisition of materials is not made from one vendor or one group of vendors.
d. Commitments for all purchases are made only after established competitive bidding procedures are followed.

10.35 Which of the following is an internal control procedure that would prevent a paid disbursement voucher from being presented for payment a second time?
a. Vouchers should be prepared by individuals who are responsible for signing disbursement cheques.
b. Disbursement vouchers should be approved by a least two responsible management officials.
c. The date on a disbursement voucher should be within a few days of the date the voucher is presented for payment.
d. The official signing the cheque should compare the cheque with the voucher and should stamp "paid" on the voucher documents.

10.36 Which of the following procedures would best detect the theft of valuable items from an inventory that consists of hundreds of different items selling for $1 to $10 and a few items selling for hundreds of dollars?
a. Maintain a perpetual inventory of only the more valuable items with frequent periodic verification of the validity of the perpetual inventory record.
b. Have an independent CPA firm prepare an internal control report on the effectiveness of the administrative and accounting controls over inventory.
c. Have separate warehouse space for the more valuable items with frequent periodic physical counts and comparison to perpetual inventory records.

10.37 Budd, the purchasing agent of Lake Hardware Wholesalers, has a relative who owns a retail hardware store.

Budd arranged for hardware to be delivered by manufacturers to the retail store on a COD basis, thereby enabling his relative to buy at Lake's wholesale prices. Budd was probably able to accomplish this because of Lake's poor internal control over:

a. Purchase requisitions.
b. Cash receipts.
c. Perpetual inventory records.
d. Purchase orders.

10.38 Which of the following is the best audit procedure for determining the existence of unrecorded liabilities?

a. Examine confirmation requests by creditors whose accounts appear on a subsidiary trial balance of accounts payable.
b. Examine a sample of cash disbursements in the period subsequent to the year-end.
c. Examine a sample of invoices a few days prior to and subsequent to the year-end to ascertain whether they have been properly recorded.
d. Examine unusual relationships between monthly accounts payable and recorded purchases.

10.39 When evaluating inventory controls with respect to segregation of duties, a PA would be least likely to:

a. Inspect documents.
b. Make enquiries.
c. Observe procedures.
d. Consider policy and procedure manuals.

10.40 An auditor will usually trace the details of the test counts made during the observation of the physical inventory taking to a final inventory compilation. This audit procedure is undertaken to provide evidence that items physically present and observed by the auditor at the time of the physical inventory count are:

a. Owned by the client.
b. Not obsolete.
c. Physically present at the time of the preparation of the final inventory schedule.
d. Included in the final inventory schedule.

10.41 Which of the following procedures is least likely to be performed before the balance sheet date?

a. Observation of inventory.
b. Review of internal control over cash disbursements.
c. Search for unrecorded liabilities.
d. Confirmation of receivables.

10.42 The physical count of inventory of a retailer was higher than shown by the perpetual records. Which of the following could explain the difference?

a. Inventory items had been counted but the tags placed on the items had not been taken off the items and added to the inventory accumulation sheets.
b. Credit memos for several items returned by customers had not been recorded.
c. No journal entry had been made on the retailer's books for several items returned to its suppliers.
d. An item purchased "FOB shipping point" had not arrived at the date of the inventory count and was not reflected in the perpetual records.

10.43 From the auditor's point of view, inventory counts are more acceptable prior to the year-end when:

a. Internal control is weak.
b. Accurate perpetual inventory records are maintained.
c. Inventory is slow moving.
d. Significant amounts of inventory are held on a consignment basis.

10.44 To determine whether accounts payable are complete, an auditor performs a test to verify that all merchandise received is recorded. The population for this test consists of all:

a. Vendors' invoices.
b. Purchase orders.
c. Receiving reports.
d. Cancelled cheques.

10.45 Which of the following internal control procedures most likely addresses the completeness assertion for inventory?

a. The work in process account is periodically reconciled with subsidiary inventory records.

b. Employees responsible for the custody of finished goods do not perform the receiving function.

c. Receiving reports are prenumbered and the numbering sequence is checked periodically.

d. There is a separation of duties between the payroll department and inventory accounting personnel.

(AICPA adapted)

EXERCISES AND PROBLEMS

10.46 The essential characteristic of the liabilities control system is to separate the authorization and approval to initiate a transaction from the responsibility for recordkeeping. What would constitute the authorization for vouchers (accounts) payable recording? What documentary evidence could auditors examine as evidence of this authorization?

10.47 The use of prenumbered documents is an important feature for control to ensure that all valid transactions are recorded and none are omitted. How could auditors gather evidence that the control for completeness of cash disbursements was being used properly by a company?

10.48 Two "automatic transactions" can be produced in a computerized accounting system: (1) cheque printing and signature and (2) purchase order at a preprogrammed stock reorder point. Assume management is uncomfortable with the computer creating transactions. How could management delay these transactions until they were "viewed" and authorized?

10.49 Why should auditors be concerned with the adequacy of casualty insurance coverage of a client's physical property?

10.50 What evidence regarding inventories and cost of sales can the auditor typically obtain from verbal enquiry?

10.51 Auditors plan their audit procedures to gather evidence about management's assertions in the financial statements. In addition to the broad assertions, such as existence and completeness, specific assertions are made for each major account area. List 9 or 10 examples of such specific assertions for the fixed assets and related accounts.

10.52 Why should the Repairs and Maintenance expense account be audited at the same time as the fixed asset accounts?

10.53 Audit procedures may be classified as:
Physical observation.
Recalculation.
Confirmation.
Examination of documents (vouching and tracing).
Verbal enquiry.
Scanning.
Analytical procedures.

Required:
Describe how each procedure may be used to gather evidence on fixed assets and which broad financial statement assertion(s) (existence, completeness, rights, valuation or allocation, and presentation and disclosure) is being addressed by the use of the procedure.

TEST OF CONTROLS AUDIT PROCEDURES

10.54 Payable ICQ Items: Control Objectives, Test of Controls Procedures, and Possible Errors or Irregularities. Listed below is a selection of items from the internal control questionnaire on payables shown in Appendix 10A.
1. Are invoices, receiving reports, and purchase orders reviewed by the cheque signer?
2. Are cheques dated in the cheque register with the date of the cheque?

EXHIBIT 10.55–1   MAYLOU CORPORATION—DOCUMENT FLOWCHART FOR PURCHASES

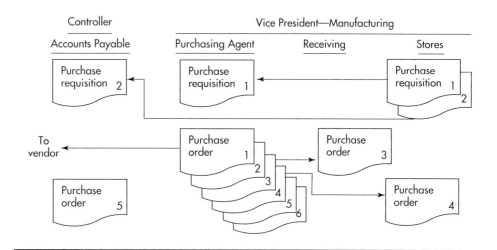

3. Are quantity and quality of goods received determined at time of receipt by receiving personnel independent of the purchasing department?

4. Are vendors' invoices matched against purchase orders and receiving reports before a liability is recorded?

Required:

For each one:

a. Identify the control objective to which it applies.

b. Specify one test of controls audit procedure an auditor could use to determine whether the control was operating effectively.

c. Using your business experience, your logic, or your imagination, or all three, give an example of an error or irregularity that could occur if the control was absent or ineffective.

10.55 Purchasing Control Procedures. Long, PA, has been engaged to examine and report on the financial statements of Maylou Corporation. During the review phase of the study of Maylou's system of internal control over purchases, Long was given the following document flowchart for purchases (see Exhibit 10.55–1).

Required:

Identify the procedures relating to purchase requisitions and purchase orders that Long would expect to find if Maylou's system of internal control over purchases is effective. For example, purchase orders are prepared only after giving proper consideration to the time to order and quantity to order. Do not comment on the effectiveness of the flow of documents as presented in the flowchart or on separation of duties.

(AICPA adapted)

10.56 Test of Controls Procedures for Cash Disbursements. The Runge Controls Corporation manufactures and markets electrical control systems: temperature controls, machine controls, burglar alarms, and the like. Electrical and semiconductor parts are acquired from outside vendors, and systems are assembled in Runge's plant. The company incurs other administrative and operating expenditures. Liabilities for goods and services purchased are entered in a vouchers payable journal, at which time the debits are classified to the asset and expense accounts to which they apply. The company has specified control procedures for approving vendor invoices for payment, for signing cheques, for keeping records, and for reconciling the chequing accounts. The procedures appear to be well specified and placed in operation. You are the senior auditor on the engagement, and you need to specify a program (list) of test of controls procedures to audit the effectiveness of the controls over cash disbursements.

Required:

Using the seven general internal control objectives, specify two or more

test of controls procedures to audit the effectiveness of typical control procedures. (Hint: From one sample of recorded cash disbursements, you can specify procedures related to several objectives. See Exhibit 10–3 for examples of test of controls procedures over cash disbursements.) Organize your list according to the example shown below for the "completeness" objective.

(AICPA adapted)

Completeness Objective	Test of Controls Program
All valid cash disbursements are recorded and none are omitted.	Determine the numerical sequence of cheques issued during the period and scan the sequence for missing numbers. Scan the accounts payable records for amounts that appear to be too long outstanding indicating liabilities for which payment may have been made but not recorded properly).

LIABILITIES: SUBSTANTIVE PROCEDURES

10.57 Unrecorded Liabilities Procedures. You were in the final stages of your audit of the financial statements of Ozine Corporation for the year ended December 31, 1992, when you were consulted by the corporation's president. The president believes there is no point to your examining the 1993 voucher register and testing data in support of 1993 entries. He stated: (1) bills pertaining to 1992 that were received too late to be included in the December voucher register were recorded as of the year-end by the corporation by journal entry; (2) the internal auditor made tests after the year-end; and (3) he would furnish you with a letter certifying that there were no unrecorded liabilities.

Required:

a. Should your procedures for unrecorded liabilities be affected by the fact that the client made a journal entry to record 1992 bills that were received later? Explain.

b. Should your test for unrecorded liabilities be affected by the fact that a letter is obtained in which a responsible management official certifies that to the best of his knowledge all liabilities have been recorded? Explain.

c. Should your test for unrecorded liabilities be eliminated or reduced because of the internal audit work? Explain.

d. What sources, in addition to the 1993 voucher register, should you consider to locate possible unrecorded liabilities?

(AICPA adapted)

10.58 Accounts Payable Confirmations. Clark and his partner, Kent, both PAs, are planning their audit program for the audit of accounts payable on the LeClair Corporation's annual audit. Saturday afternoon they reviewed the thick file of last year's working papers, and both of them remembered all too well the six days they spent last year on accounts payable.

Last year, Clark had suggested that they mail confirmations to 100 of LeClair's suppliers. The company regularly purchases from about 1,000 suppliers and these account payable balances fluctuate widely, depending on the volume of purchase and the terms LeClair's purchasing agent is able to negotiate. Clark's sample of 100 was designed to include accounts with large balances. In fact, the 100 accounts confirmed last year covered 80 percent of the total accounts payable.

Both Clark and Kent spent many hours tracking down minor differences reported in confirmation responses. Nonresponding accounts were investigated by comparing LeClair's balance with monthly statements received from suppliers.

Required:

a. Identify the accounts payable audit objectives that the auditors must consider in determining the audit procedures to be performed.

b. Identify situations when the auditors should use accounts payable confirmations, and discuss whether they are required to use them.

c. Discuss why the use of large dollar balances as the basis for selecting accounts payable for confirmation may not be the most efficient approach, and indicate a more efficient sample selection procedure that could be followed when choosing accounts payable for confirmation.

INVENTORY AND FIXED ASSETS: SUBSTANTIVE PROCEDURES

10.59 Inventory Count Observation: Planning and Substantive Audit Procedures. Sammy Smith is the partner in charge of the audit of Blue Distributing Corporation, a wholesaler that owns one warehouse containing 80 percent of its inventory. Sammy is reviewing the working papers that were prepared to support the firm's opinion on Blue's financial statements. Sammy wants to be certain essential audit procedures are well documented in the working papers.

Required:

a. What evidence should Sammy expect to find that the audit observation of the client's physical count of inventory was well planned and that assistants were properly supervised?

b. What substantive audit procedures should Sammy find in the working papers that document management's assertions about existence and completeness of inventory quantities at the end of the year? (Refer to Appendix 18B for procedures.)

(AICPA adapted)

10.60 Sales/Inventory Cutoff. Your client took a complete physical inventory count under your observation as of December 15 and adjusted the inventory control account (perpetual inventory method) to agree with the physical inventory. Based on the count adjustments as of December 15 and after review of the transactions recorded from December 16 to December 31, you are almost ready to accept the inventory balance as fairly stated.

However, your review of the sales cutoff as of December 15 and December 31 disclosed the following items not previously considered:

Cost	Sales Price	Shipped	Date Billed	Credited to Inventory Control
$28,400	$36,900	12/14	12/16	12/16
39,100	50,200	12/10	12/19	12/10
18,900	21,300	1/2	12/31	12/31

Required:

What adjusting journal entries, if any, would you make for each of these items? Explain why each adjustment is necessary.

(AICPA adapted)

10.61 Statistical Sampling Used of Estimate Inventory. ACE Corporation does not conduct a complete annual physical count of purchased parts and supplies in its principal warehouse but, instead, uses statistical sampling to estimate the year-end inventory. Ace maintains a perpetual inventory record of parts and supplies. Management believes that statistical sampling is highly effective in determining inventory values and is sufficiently reliable that a physical count of each item of inventory is unnecessary.

Required:

a. List at least 10 normal audit procedures that should be performed to verify physical quantities whenever a client conducts a periodic physical count of all or part of its inventory (see Appendix 18B for procedures).

b. Identify the audit procedures you should use that change or are in addition to normal required audit procedures (in addition to those listed in your solution to part [a]) when a client utilizes statistical sampling to determine inventory value and does not conduct a 100 percent annual physical count of inventory items.

(AICPA adapted)

10.62 Inventory Procedures Using Generalized Audit Software. Your are conducting an audit of the financial statements of a wholesale cosmetics distributor with an inventory consisting of thousands of individual items. The distributor keeps its inventory in its own distribution centre and in two public warehouses. A perpetual inventory computer database is maintained on a computer disk. The database is updated at the end of each business day. Each individual record of the perpetual inventory database contains the following data:

Item number.

Location of item.

Description of item.

Quantity on hand.

Cost per item.

Date of last purchase.

Date of last sale.

Quantity sold during year.

You are planning to observe the distributor's physical count of inventories as of a given date. You will have available a computer tape, provided by the client, of the above items taken from their database as of the date of the physical count. Your firm has a generalized audit software package that will run on the client's computer.

Required:

List the basic inventory auditing procedures and, for each, describe how the use of the general-purpose audit software package and the tape of the perpetual inventory database might be helpful to the auditor in performing such auditing procedures. (See Appen-

dix 10B for substantive audit procedures for inventory.)

Organize your answer as follows:

Basic inventory auditing procedures	How general purpose audit software package and tape of the inventory tape file date might be helpful

(AICPA adapted)

10.63 Manufacturing Equipment and Accumulated Depreciation. In connection with a recurring examination of the financial statements of the Louis Manufacturing Company for the year ended December 31, you have been assigned the audit of the fixed assets accounts (Manufacturing Equipment, Manufacturing Equipment—Accumulated Depreciation, and Repairs to Manufacturing Equipment). Your review of Louis's policies and procedures has disclosed the following pertinent information:

1. The Manufacturing Equipment account includes the net invoice price plus related freight and installation costs for all of the equipment in Louis's manufacturing plant.

2. The Manufacturing Equipment and Accumulated Depreciation accounts are supported by a subsidiary ledger, which shows the cost and accumulated depreciation for each piece of equipment.

3. An annual budget for capital expenditures of $1,000 or more is prepared by the executive committee and approved by the board of directors. Capital expenditures over $1,000 that are not included in this budget must be approved by the board of directors, and variations of 20 percent or more must be explained to the board. Approval by the supervisor of production is required for capital expenditures under $1,000.

4. Company employees handle installation, removal, repair, and rebuilding of the machinery. Work orders are prepared for these activities and are subject to the same budgetary control as other expenditures. Work orders are not required for external expenditures.

Required:

a. Prepare a list of the major specific objectives (assertions) for your audit of the Manufacturing Equipment, Manufacturing Equipment—Accumulated Depreciation, and Repairs of Manufacturing Equipment accounts. Do not include in this listing the auditing procedures designed to accomplish these objectives.

b. Prepare the portion of your audit program applicable to the review of current-year additions to the Manufacturing Equipment account. (You will find Appendix 18B helpful, although it does not specifically mention manufacturing equipment.)

(AICPA adapted)

DISCUSSION CASES

· ·

10.64 Peacock Company: Incomplete Flowchart of Inventory and Purchasing Control Procedures. Peacock Company is a wholesaler of soft goods. The inventory is composed of approximately 3,500 different items. The company employs a computerized batch processing system to maintain its perpetual inventory records. The system is run each weekend so that inventory reports are available on Monday morning for management use. The system has been functioning satisfactorily for the past 15 months, providing the company with accurate records and timely reports.

The preparation of purchase orders has been automatic as a part of the inventory system to ensure that the company will maintain enough inventory to meet customer demand. When an item of inventory falls below a predetermined level, a record of the inventory items is written. This record is used in conjunction with the vendor file to prepare the purchase orders.

Exception reports ar prepared during the update of the inventory and the preparation of the purchase orders. These reports list any errors or exceptions identified during the processing. In addition, the system provides for management approval of all purchase orders exceeding a specified amount. Any exceptions or items requiring management approval are handled by supplemental runs on Monday morn-

ing and are combined with the weekend results.

A system flowchart of Peacock Company's inventory and purchase order procedure is in Exhibit 10.64–1.

Required:

a. The illustrated system flowchart (Exhibit 10.64–1) of Peacock Company's inventory and purchase order system was prepared before the system was fully operational. Several steps that are important to the successful operations of the system were inadvertently omitted from the chart. Now that the system is operating effectively, management wants the system documentation complete and would like the flowchart corrected. Describe the steps that have been omitted and indicate where the omissions have occurred. The flowchart does not need to be redrawn.

b. In order for Peacock's inventory/purchase order system to function properly, control procedures should be included in the system. Describe the type of control procedures Peacock Company should use in its system to ensure proper functioning, and indicate where these procedures would be placed in the system.

(CMA adapted)

10.65 Inventory Evidence and Long-Term Purchase Contracts. During the audit of Mason Company, Inc., for the calendar year 1992, you noticed that the

EXHIBIT 10.64–1   PEACOCK COMPANY—INVENTORY AND PURCHASE ORDER PROCEDURE

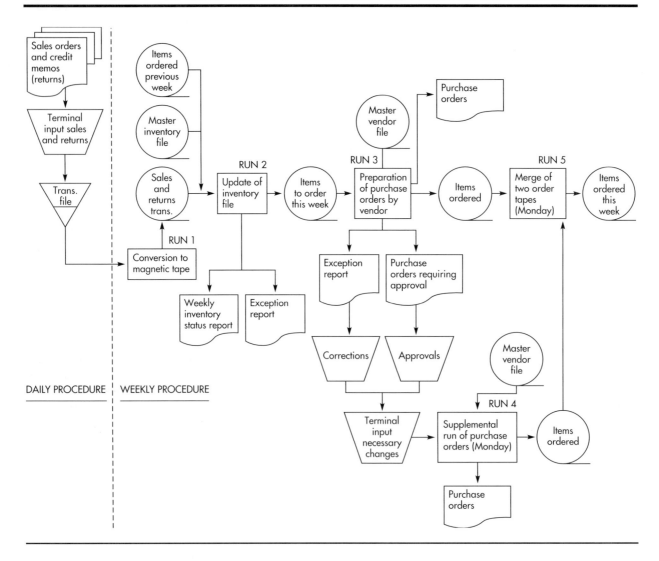

DAILY PROCEDURE | WEEKLY PROCEDURE

company produces aluminum cans at the rate of about 40 million units annually. On the plant tour, you noticed a large stockpile of raw aluminum in storage. Your inventory observation and pricing procedures showed this stockpile to be the raw materials inventory of 400 tons valued at $240,000 (LIFO cost). Enquiry with the production chief yielded the information that 400 tons was about a four-month supply of raw materials.

Suppose you learn that Mason had executed a firm long-term purchase contract with All Purpose Aluminum Company to purchase raw materials on the following schedule:

| | *Quantity* | |
Delivery Date	Quantity (tons)	Total Price
January 30, 1993	500	$300,000
June 30, 1993	700	420,000
December 30, 1993	1,000	500,000

Because of recent economic conditions, principally a decline in the demand for raw aluminum and a consequent oversupply, the price stood at 40 cents per pound as of January 15, 1993. Commodities experts predict that this low price will prevail for 12 to 15 months or until there is a general economic recovery.

Required:

a. Describe the procedures you would employ to gather evidence about this contract (including its initial discovery).

b. What facts recited in the problems are ones that you would have to discover for yourself in an audit?

c. Discuss the effect this contract has on the financial statements.

10.66 Deake Corporation: Property Accounting System. Deake Corporation is a medium-sized, diversified manufacturing company. Recently, Jack Richards was promoted to manager of the property accounting section. Richards is having difficulty responding to some of the requests from individuals in other departments for information about the company's fixed assets. Some of the requests are:

1. The controller has requested schedules of individual fixed assets to support the balances in the general ledger. Richards has furnished the necessary information, but it was late. The manner in which the records are organized makes it difficult to obtain information easily.

2. The maintenance manager wishes to verify the existence of a punch press he thinks was repaired twice. He has asked Richards to confirm the asset number and location of the press.

3. The insurance department wants data on the cost and book values of assets to include in its review of current insurance coverage.

4. The tax department has requested data that can be used to determine when Deake should switch depreciation methods for tax purposes.

5. The company's internal auditors have spent a significant amount of time in the property accounting section recently, attempting to audit the annual depreciation expense.

The property account records consist of a set of manual books. These records show the date the asset was acquired, the account number for the asset, the dollar amount capitalized, and the estimated useful life of the asset for depreciation purposes.

After many frustrations, Richards has realized that his records are inadequate and that he cannot supply data when requested. He has decided to discuss his problem with the controller, Jim Castle.

Richards: Jim, something has got to give. My people are working overtime and can't keep up. You worked in property accounting before you became controller. You know I can't tell the tax, insurance, and maintenance people everything they need to know from my records. Also, that internal auditing team is living in my area and that slows down the work pace. The requests of these people are reasonable, and we should be able to answer these questions and provide the needed data. I think we need a computerized property accounting system. I would like to talk to the information systems people to see if they can help me.

Castle: Jack, I think you have a good idea, but be sure you are personally involved in the design of any system so you get all the information you need.

Required:

a. Identify and justify four major objectives Deake Corporation's computerized property accounting system should possess to provide the data necessary to respond to requests for information by company personnel.

b. Identify the data that should be included in the computer record for each asset included in the property account.

(CMA adapted)

10.67 Grover Manufacturing—Purchasing Defalcation. On January 11 at the beginning of your annual audit of the Grover Manufacturing Company's financial statements for the year just ended December 31, the company president confides to you that an employee is living on a scale in excess of that which his salary would support.

The employee has been a buyer in the purchasing department for six years and has charge of purchasing all general materials and supplies. He is authorized to sign purchase orders for amounts up to $2,000. Purchase orders in excess of $2,000 require the countersignature of the general purchasing agent.

The president understands that the usual audit of financial statements is not designed to disclose immaterial fraud or conflicts of interest, although such events may be discovered. The president authorizes you, however, to expand your regular audit procedures and to apply additional audit procedures to determine whether there is any evidence that the buyer has been misappropriating company funds or has been engaged in activities that are a conflict of interest.

Required:

List the audit procedures that you would apply to the company records and documents in an attempt to:

1. Discover evidence within the purchasing department of defalcations being committed by the buyer. Give the purpose of each audit procedure.

2. Provide leads about possible collusion between the buyer and suppliers. Give the purpose of each audit procedure.

INSTRUCTIONS FOR DISCUSSION CASES 10.68–10.71.

These cases are designed like the ones in the chapter. They give the problem, the method, the paper trail, and the amount. Your assignment is to write the audit approach portion of the case, organized around these sections:

Objective: Express the objective in terms of the facts supposedly asserted in financial records, accounts, and statements. (Refer to discussion of assertions in Chapter 9.)

Control: Write a brief explanation of desirable controls, missing controls, and especially the kinds of "deviations" that might arise from the situation described in the case.

Test of controls: Write some procedures for getting evidence about existing controls, especially procedures that could discover devia-

tions from controls. If there are no controls to test, then there are no procedures to perform; go then to the next section. A "procedure" should instruct someone about the source(s) of evidence to tap and the work to do.

Audit of balance: Write some procedures for getting evidence about the existence, completeness, valuation, ownership, or disclosure assertions identified in your objective section above. (Refer to Appendix 10B for suggestions.)

Discovery summary: Write a short statement about the discovery you expect to accomplish with your procedures.

10.68 Financial Reporting: Overstated Inventory and Profits (duplicated in Chapter 18: Case 18.56). Follow the instructions above. For this case, recalculate the income (loss) before taxes using the correct inventory figures. (Assume the correct beginning amount two years ago was $5.5 million.)

THE PHANTOM OF THE INVENTORY

Problem: Overstated physical inventory caused understated cost of goods sold and overstated net income, current assets, total assets, and retained earnings.

Method: All Bright Company manufactured lamps. Paul M., manager of the Katherine Street plant, was under pressure to produce profits so that the company could maintain its loans at the bank. The loans were secured by the inventory of 1,500 types of finished goods, work in process, and parts used for making lamps (bases, shades, wire, nuts, bolts, and so on). Paul arranged the physical inventory counting procedures and accompanied the external audit team while the external auditors observed the count and made test counts after the company personnel had recorded their counts on tags attached to the inventory locations. At the auditors' request, Paul directed them to the "most valuable" inventory for their test count, although he did not show them all of the most valuable types. When the auditors were looking the other way, Paul raised the physical count on inventory tags the auditors would not include in their test counts. When everyone had finished each floor of the multistory warehouse, all the tags were gathered and sent to data processing for computer compilation and pricing at FIFO cost.

Paper trail: All Bright had no perpetual inventory records. All the record of the inventory quantity and pricing was in the count tags and the priced compilation, which was produced by the data processing department six weeks later. The auditors traced their test counts to the compilation and did not notice the raised physical quantities on the inventory types they did not test count. They also did not notice some extra (fictitious) tags Paul had handed over to data processing.

Amount: Paul falsified the inventory for three years before the company declared bankruptcy. Over that period, the inventory was overstated by $1 million (20 percent, two years ago), $2.5 million (45 percent, one year ago), and $3 million (42 percent, current year). The financial statements showed the following (dollars in 000s):

	Two Years Ago	One Year Ago	Current Year
Sales	$ 25,000	$ 29,000	$ 40,000
Cost of good sold	(20,000)	(22,000)	(29,000) Expenses
	(5,000)	(8,000)	(9,000)
Income (loss) before taxes	0	$ (1,000)	$ 2,500
Ending inventory	$ 6,00	$ 8,000	$ 10,200
Other current assets	9,000	8,500	17,500
Total assets	21,000	21,600	34,300
Current liabilities	5,000	5,500	13,000
Long-term debt*	5,500	6,600	9,300
Shareholder equity	10,500	9,500	12,000

*Secured by inventory pledged to the bank.

10.69 Purchase Kickbacks. Follow the instructions preceding Case 10.68. This time, let your initial objective be to select one vendor for investigation. Instead of a "test of controls" section, name the one vendor you would select from those in Exhibit 10.69–1 and tell your reasons. In the "test of balances" section, tell how you would investigate the situation. In the "discovery summary" section, speculate about how your investigation might reveal the culprit.

PURCHASING STARS

Problem: Kickbacks taken on books or supplies inventory purchases caused inflated inventory, cost of goods sold, and expenses.

Method: Bailey Books, Inc., is a retail distributor of upscale books, periodicals, and magazines. Bailey has 431 retail stores throughout the southeastern states. Three full-time purchasing agents work at corporate headquarters. They are responsible for purchasing all the inventory at the best prices available from wholesale jobbers. They can purchase with or without obtaining competitive bids. The three purchasing agents are R. McGuire in charge of purchasing books, M. Garza in charge of purchasing magazines and periodicals, and L. Collins (manager of purchasing) in charge of ordering miscellaneous items, such as paper products and store supplies.

One of the purchasing agents is suspected of taking kickbacks from vendors. In return, Bailey is thought to be paying inflated prices, which first go to inventory and then to cost of goods sold and other expense accounts as the assets are sold or used.

L. Collins is the manager in charge. Her duties do not include audit or inspection of the performance of the other two purchasing agents. No one audits or reviews Collins's performance.

EXHIBIT 10.69–1 SUMMARY OF PURCHASING ACTIVITY

Bailey Books, Incorporated
Selected Purchases 1990-1992

Vendor	Items Purchased	1990	1991	1992	Date of Last Bid	Percent of Purchases Bid (3-yr. Period)
Armour	Books	683,409	702,929	810,100	12/01/92	87%
Burdick	Sundries	62,443	70,949	76,722	—	—
Canon	Magazines	1,404,360	1,947,601	2,361,149	11/03/92	94
DeBois, Inc.	Paper	321,644	218,404	121,986	06/08/92	57
Elton books	Books	874,893	781,602	649,188	07/21/92	91
Fergeson	Books	921,666	1,021,440	1,567,811	09/08/92	81
Guyford	Magazines	2,377,821	2,868,988	3,262,49	10/08/92	81
Hyman, Inc.	Supplies	31,640	40,022	46,911	10/22/92	—
Intertec	Books	821,904	898,683	949,604	11/18/92	86
Jerrico	Paper	186,401	111,923	93,499	10/04/92	72
Julian-Borg	Magazine	431,470	589,182	371,920	02/07/92	44
King Features	Magazines	436,820	492,687	504,360	11/18/92	89
Lycorp	Sundries	16,280	17,404	21,410	—	—
Medallian	Books	—	61,227	410,163	12/15/92	99
Northwood	Books	861,382	992,121	—	12/07/91	—
Orion Corp.	Paper	86,904	416,777	803,493	11/02/91	15
Peterson	Supplies	114,623	—	—	N/A	N/A
Quick	Supplies	—	96,732	110,441	11/03/92	86
Robertson	Books	2,361,912	3,040,319	3,516,811	12/01/92	96
Steele	Magazines	621,490	823,707	482,082	11/03/92	90
Telecom	Sundries	81,406	101,193	146,316	—	—
Union Bay	Books	4,322,639	4,971,682	5,368,114	12/03/92	97
Victory	Magazines	123,844	141,909	143,286	06/09/92	89
Williams	Sundries	31,629	35,111	42,686	—	—

Paper trail: The purchasing system is computerized, and detail records are retained. An extract from these records is in Exhibit 10.69–1.

Amount: This kickback scheme has been going on for two or three years. Several hundred thousand dollars may have been overpaid by Bailey Books.

(NACFE adapted)

10.70 Fictitious vendors, Theft, and Embezzlement. Follow the instructions preceding Case 10.68. Write the Audit Approach section.

LIKE A SON

Problem: Fictitious purchases, overstated inventory, and inflated costs and expenses, causing misstated financial statements and operating losses.

Method: Simon Construction Company had two divisions. Simon, the president, managed the roofing division. Simon delegated authority and responsibility for management of the modular manufacturing division to John G. A widower, Simon had virtually adopted John when he ran away from an orphanage 20 years earlier, treating him like the son he never had, even building him a fine house on the outskirts of the city.

John and his secretary handled all the bids for manufacturing jobs, purchased all the material, controlled the physical inventory of materials, contracted for shipping by truck, supervised the construction activity, billed the customers when jobs were in progress and finished, approved all bid changes, and collected payments from the customers. With Simon's approval, John asked the company internal auditor not to interfere with his busy schedule. The secretary entered all the division's transactions into the computerized accounting system from a dedicated terminal in the manufacturing division office.

John did everything crooked, and the secretary was an accomplice. He rigged low bids and gave kickbacks to customers' purchasing agents, paid high prices to suppliers and took kickbacks, set up dummy companies to sell materials to Simon Construction at inflated prices, removed excess materials inventory and sold it and took the money, manipulated the inventory accounts to overstate the inventory and hide the thefts, and caused Simon Construction to pay trucking bills for a side business he owned. Simon exercised no control over John's operations.

Paper trail: Paper evidence was plentiful, if somebody looked for it. Bid records showed original low bids, later raised for basic construction (e.g., adding second floor, when the original request for bid included a second floor). Cheques payable to "cash" were endorsed by people known to be customers' purchasing agents. Prices paid for materials and supplies were higher than the list prices shown in the competing suppliers' price books kept in the manufacturing division library. John's kickbacks were deposited in his own bank account. Dummy companies were incorporated in the same province, with John and the secretary listed as original incorporators. The physical inventory shown in the accounts simply did not exist. Trucking bills showed deliveries to locations where the manufacturing division had no jobs in progress.

Amount: John drained $1.2 million from Simon Construction over a nine-year period before he was caught. Auditors were engaged to analyse the situation when Simon finally noticed the reported losses in the manufacturing division and had a violent argument with John.

10.71 Liability Understatement. Follow the instructions preceding Case 10.68. This time, along with your procedural solution, specify the discrepancies you notice by studying the excerpt from the accounts payable trial balance in Exhibit 10.71–1. Also, recalculate the income before taxes and write the adjusting journal entry you would propose.

THE BULGING DESK DRAWERS

Problem: Failure to record purchases of raw materials and expense items caused understated accounts payable, understated cost of goods sold, understated expenses, and overstated income.

Method: All Bright Company manufactured lamps. L. Mendoza, the company financial vice president, knew the company was under pressure to produce profits in order to maintain its loans at the bank. One of the surest ways accountants know to produce profits with a pencil is to fail to record purchases. This keeps expenses off the books and understates cost of goods sold figured on a periodic inventory basis. (Cost of good sold = Beginning inventory + Purchases − Ending inventory.)

Mendoza opened the mail each day and removed the invoices from suppliers, putting them in the office desk drawer. Later, when the company could "afford it," some invoices were sent to the accounts payable department for recording. Mendoza did not always get them in sequence of arrival, but that didn't matter much to her. Anyway, the desk drawers were getting full.

The clerks in the accounts payable department knew about this manipulation. They would go through periods with very little to record, then a large stack of invoices would be delivered for recording. (Must have made a big sale, they gossiped.)

The clerks followed control procedures about matching invoices with receiving reports, and they always had

E X H I B I T 10.71–1   **EXCERPT FROM ACCOUNTS PAYABLE TRIAL BALANCE: DECEMBER 31, 1992**

Voucher #	Vendor Name	Invoice #	Date Invoice	Date Due	Amount
26695	Industrial Uniforms	66681	01-Oct-92	01-Nov-92	112.11
26694	Industrial Uniforms	67127	08-Oct-92	08-Nov-92	112.11
27209	Industrial Uniforms	67582	15-Oct-92	15-Nov-92	112.11
27208	Industrial Uniforms	67981	22-Oct-92	22-Nov-92	112.11
27210	Industrial Uniforms	68462	29-Oct-92	29-Nov-92	112.11
27552	Industrial Uniforms	68972	05-Nov-92	05-Dec-92	112.11
27553	Industrial Uniforms	69463	12-Nov-92	12-Dec-92	112.11
27854	Industrial Uniforms	69851	19-Nov-92	19-Dec-92	112.11
29123	industrial Uniforms	70851	03-Dec-92	03-Jan-93	112.11
28095	Industrial Uniforms	71353	10-Dec-92	10-Jan-93	112.11
29437	Industrial Uniforms	71831	17-Dec-92	17-Jan-93	112.11
Vendor total					1,233.21
27484	B&B Experimental Co	17490	04-Nov-92	04-Dec-92	2,354.50
27550	B&B Experimental Co	17492	04-Nov-92	04-Dec-92	371.25
27559	B&B Experimental Co	17495	08-Nov-92	08-Dec-92	148.50
27560	B&B Experimental Co	17493	08-Nov-92	08-Dec-92	396.00
27741	B&B Experimental Co	17502	09-Nov-92	09-Dec-92	560.25
27475	B&B Experimental Co	17508	12-Nov-92	12-Dec-92	145.11
29494	B&B Experimental Co	17512	16-Nov-92	16-Dec-92	1,284.25
27556	B&B Experimental Co	17474	18-Nov-91	18-Nov-92	265.50
27662	B&B Experimental Co	17514	22-Nov-92	22-Dec-92	519.75
28084	B&B Experimental Co	17523	26-Nov-92	26-Dec-92	938.34
28085	B&B Experimental Co	17546	30-Nov-92	20-Dec-92	893.62
28086	B&B Experimental Co	17549	06-Dec-92	06-Jan-93	1,607.72
Vendor total					9,484.79
29377	Cameo Corp	44298	06-Dec-92	28-Feb-93	1,429.02
29379	Cameo Corp	44300	06-Dec-92	28-Feb-93	1,747.93
29378	Cameo Corp	44413	07-Dec-92	28-Feb-93	259.33
29374	Cameo Corp	44412	07-Dec-92	28-Feb-93	808.33
29380	Cameo Corp	44415	07-Dec-92	28-Feb-93	844.71
29382	Cameo Corp	44414	07-Dec-92	07-Feb-93	1,553.19
29372	Cameo Corp	44596	09-Dec-92	28-Feb-93	3,781.01
29371	Cameo Corp	44682	10-Dec-92	28-Feb-93	1,262.59
29383	Cameo Corp	44684	10-Dec-92	10-Feb-93	4,094.82
29381	Cameo Corp	44681	10-Dec-92	28-Feb-93	926.51
29385	Cameo Corp	44685	10-Dec-92	28-Feb-93	3,750.44
29373	Cameo Corp	44680	10-Dec-92	28-Feb-93	1,124.78
29370	Cameo Corp	44983	10-Dec-92	28-Feb-93	3,973.39
Vendor total					25,556.05
27120	Central Pension		15-Apr-92	15-Apr-92	10,558.23
27121	Central Pension		15-May-92	15-May-92	10,558.23
27122	Central Pension		15-Jun-92	15-Jun-92	10,558.23
27123	Central Pension		15-Jul-92	15-Jul-92	10,558.23
27124	Central Pension		15-Aug-92	15-Aug-92	10,558.23
27125	Central Pension		15-Sep-92	15-Sep-92	10,558.23
27126	Central Pension		15-Oct-92	15-Oct-92	10,588.23
	Vendor total				73,907.61

a full file of "unmatched receiving reports" awaiting the arrival of invoices. Mendoza had the power to override controls that called for the timely recording of purchases, and the clerks could not record invoices they had not yet received.

Paper trail: The accounts payable clerks gave each invoice-receiving report-purchase order set a voucher number in numerical sequence. They dated the accounts payable and related debit recordings on the day they processed the vouchers. Their vouchers were always complete because they were under strict orders not to record any payables that were not supported by source documents.

The problem with the paper trail is that the recording did not get started until Mendoza delivered the invoices. However, there was a file of the unmatched receiving reports in the accounts payable department, forwarded from the receiving employees, and there was a trial balance of accounts payable produced for the auditors.

An excerpt from this trial balance is in Exhibit 10.71–1. The total accounts payable on the trial balance, not shown in Exhibit 10.71–1, was $1.8 million for the year ended December 31, 1992. (The signs of delayed recording of accounts payable are in the exhibit. Can you find them?)

Amount: Mendoza held back the recording of accounts payable for two years (the current year 1992, and one year ago 1991). One year ago, the accounts payable were understated by $500,000, of which $200,000 was unrecorded purchases for inventory and $300,000 was unrecorded operating expenses. In the current year (1992), the accounts payable were understated at December 31 by $750,000, of which $450,000 was for inventory purchases, and $300,000 was unrecorded operating expenses. The financial statements showed the following (dollars in 000s):

	Two Years Ago	One Year Ago	Current Year
Sales	$ (25,000)	$ 29,000)	$ (40,500)
Cost of goods sold	(20,000)	(22,000)	(29,000)
Expenses	(5,000)	(8,000)	(9,000)
Income (loss) before taxes	0	$ (1,000)	$ (2,500)
Ending inventory	$ (6,000)	$ (8,000)	$ (10,200)
Current assets	(9,000)	(8,500)	(17,500)
Total assets	(21,000)	21,600)	(34,300)
Current liabilities	(5,000)	(5,500)	(13,000)
Long-term debt*	(5,500)	(6,600)	(9,300)
Shareholder equity	(10,500)	(9,500)	(12,000)

*Secured by inventory pledged to the bank.

10.72 Audit of Capital Assets. At the beginning of her examination of the financial statements of Nuclear Data Ltd., a small manufacturer of nuclear particle analysers used in university research laboratories and the like, a PA and her audit team studied the company's business and industry. The company's shares were recently listed on the Vancouver Stock Exchange.

While performing analytical procedures, the PA noted that Nuclear Data's debt-to-equity ratio had increased substantially from 1:2 to 2:1 during the year. However, the rate of return on common equity also increased.

Profitability was improved relative to the previous year primarily because of excellent results in the fourth quarter. Not only were quarterly sales about 25% greater than in the previous fiscal year, but the gross margin also increased. The controller pointed out that one reason for the profitability improvement was the use of percentage-of-completion method to account for certain large pieces of equipment being built on special order for a major university. The equipment was about 75% complete at year-end, and 75% of the expected gross profit was therefore recorded in the current fiscal year.

A preliminary review of internal control showed that the documents and records were adequate, and that there was a system of authorization and approval for major purchases, sales, cash receipts, and cash disbursements. However, because of the small size of the company, the number of personnel involved in processing transactions was very limited. Moreover, top management was by and large neither involved nor interested in the internal control system, concentrating instead on marketing, production, and other operation matters.

Required:

a. Identify the various elements of the audit risk model and explain how (if at all) each element is affected in this case (that is, would increase or decrease relative to a normal or typical audit).

b. List six substantive audit procedures the PA should perform with respect to the items being accounted for on a percentage-of-completion basis in the financial statements.

c. The PA is thinking of using physical units attribute sampling in performing certain audit tests. Do you think the use of attribute sampling is appropriate in this case? Explain.

(CGAAC adapted)

Appendix 10A

Internal Control Questionnaires

EXHIBIT 10A-1   PURCHASING AND ACCOUNTS PAYABLE

Environment:

1. Is the purchasing department independent of the accounting department, receiving department, and shipping department?
2. Are receiving report copies transmitted to inventory custodians? To purchasing? To the accounting department?

Validity objective:

3. Are vendors' invoices matched against purchase orders and receiving reports before a liability is recorded?

Completeness objective:

4. Are the purchase order forms prenumbered and is the numerical sequence checked for missing documents?
5. Are receiving report forms prenumbered and is the numerical sequence checked for missing documents?
6. Is the accounts payable department notified of goods returned to vendors?
7. Are vendors' invoices listed immediately upon receipt?
8. Are unmatched receiving reports reviewed frequently and investigated for proper recording?

Authorization objective:

9. Are competitive bids received and reviewed for certain items?
10. Are all purchases made only on the basis of approved purchase requisitions?
11. Are purchases made for employees authorized through the regular purchases procedures?
12. Are purchase prices approved by a responsible purchasing officer?
13. Are all purchases, whether for inventory or expense, routed through the purchasing department for approval?
14. Are shipping documents authorized and prepared for goods returned to vendors?
15. Are invoices approved for payment by a responsible officer?

Accuracy objective:

16. Are quantity and quality of goods received determined at the time of receipt by receiving personnel independent of the purchasing department?
17. Are vendors' monthly statements reconciled with individual accounts payable accounts?
18. In the accounts payable department, are invoices checked against purchase orders and receiving reports for quantities, prices, and terms?

Classification objective:

19. Does the chart of accounts and accounting manual give instructions for classifying debit entries when purchases are recorded?

Accounting objective:

20. Is the accounts payable detail ledger balanced periodically with the general ledger control account?

Proper period objective:

21. Does the accounting manual give instructions to date purchase/payable entries on the date of receipt of goods?

EXHIBIT 10A–2   **CASH DISBURSEMENTS PROCESSING**

Environment:

1. Are persons with cash custody or cheque-signing authority denied access to accounting journals, ledgers, and bank reconciliations?
2. Is access to blank cheques denied to unauthorized persons?
3. Are all disbursements except petty cash made by cheque?
4. Are cheque signers prohibited from drawing cheques to cash?
5. Is signing blank cheques prohibited?
6. Are voided cheques mutilated and retained for inspection?

Validity objectives:

7. Are invoices, receiving reports, and purchase orders reviewed by the cheque signer?
8. Are the supporting documents stamped "paid" (to prevent duplicate payment) before being returned to accounts payable for filing?
9. Are cheques mailed directly by the signer and not returned to accounts payable department for mailing?

Completeness objective:

10. Are blank cheques prenumbered and is the numerical sequence checked for missing documents?

Authorization objective:

11. Do cheques require two signatures? Is there dual control over machine signature plates?

Accuracy objective:

12. Are bank accounts reconciled by personnel independent of cash custody or recordkeeping?

Classification objective:

13. Do the chart of accounts and accounting manual give instructions for determining debit classifications of disbursements not charged to accounts payable?
14. Is the distribution of charges double-checked periodically by an official? Is the budget used to check on gross misclassification errors?
15. Are special disbursements (e.g., payroll and dividends) made from separate bank accounts?

Accounting objective:

16. Is the bank reconciliation reviewed by an accounting official with no conflicting cash receipts, cash disbursements, or recordkeeping responsibilities?
17. Do internal auditors periodically conduct a surprise audit of bank reconciliations?

Proper period objective:

18. Are cheques dated in the cash disbursements journal with the date of the cheque?

EXHIBIT 10A–3   **ACQUISITION AND EXPENDITURE COMPUTER CONTROLS**

- Each terminal performs only designated functions. For example, the receiving clerk's terminal cannot accept a purchase order entry.
- An identification number and password (used on an individual basis) is required to enter the nonautomatic purchase orders, vendors' invoices, and the receiving report information. Further, certain passwords have "read only" authorization. These are issued to personnel authorized to determine the status of various records, such as an open voucher, but not authorized to enter data.
- All input immediately is logged to provide restart processing should any terminal become inoperative during the processing.
- The transaction codes call up a full-screen "form" on the terminals that appears to the operators in the same format as the original paper documents. Each clerk must enter the information correctly (on-line input validation) or the computer will not accept the data.
- All printed documents are computer numbered and the number is stored as part of the record. Further, all records in the open databases have the vendor's number as the primary search and matching field key. Of course, status searches could be made by another field. For example, the inventory number can be the search key to determine the status of a purchase of an item in short supply.
- A daily search of the open databases is made. Purchases outstanding for more than 10 days and the missing "document" records are printed out on a report for investigation of the delay.
- The cheque signature is printed, using a signature plate that is installed on the computer printer only when cheques are printed. A designated person in the treasurer's office maintains custody of this signature plate and must take it to the computer room to be installed when cheques are printed. This person also has the combination to the separate document storage room where the blank cheque stock is kept and is present at all cheque printing runs. The printed cheques are taken immediately from the computer room for mailing.

EXHIBIT 10A–4   INVENTORY TRANSACTION PROCESSING

Environment:
  1. Are perpetual inventory records kept for raw materials? Supplies? Work in process? Finished goods?
  2. Are perpetual records subsidiary to general ledger control accounts?
  3. Do the perpetual records show quantities only? Quantities and prices?
  4. Are inventory records maintained by someone other than the inventory stores custodian?
  5. Is merchandise or materials on consignment-in (not the property of the company) physically segregated from goods owned by the company?
Validity objective:
  6. Are additions to inventory quantity records made only on receipt of a receiving report copy?
  7. Do inventory custodians notify the records department of additions to inventory?
Completeness objective:
  8. Are reductions of inventory record quantities made only on receipt of inventory issuance documents?
  9. Do inventory custodians notify inventory records of reductions of inventory?
Authorization objective:
    Refer to question 6 above (additions).
    Refer to question 8 above (reductions).
Accuracy objective:
10. If standard costs have been used for inventory pricing, have they been reviewed for current applicability?
Classification objective?
11. Are periodic counts of physical inventory made to correct errors in the individual perpetual records?
Accounting objective:
12. Is there a periodic review for overstocked, slow-moving, or obsolete inventory? Have any adjustments been made during the year?
13. Are perpetual inventory records kept in dollars periodically reconciled to general ledger control accounts?
Proper period objective:
14. Does the accounting manual give instructions to record inventory additions on the date of the receiving report?
15. Does the accounting manual give instructions to record inventory issues on the issuance date?

EXHIBIT 10A–5   FIXED ASSET AND RELATED TRANSACTIONS PROCESSING

Environment:
  1. Are detailed property records maintained for the various fixed assets?
Validity objective:
  2. Is the accounting department notified of actions of disposal, dismantling, or idling of a productive asset? For terminating a lease or rental?
  3. Are fixed assets inspected periodically and physically counted?
Completeness objective:
  4. Is casualty insurance carried? Is the coverage analysed periodically? When was the last analysis?
  5. Are property tax assessments periodically analysed? When was the last analysis?
Authorization objective:
  6. Are capital expenditure and leasing proposals prepared for review and approval by the board of directors or by responsible officers?
  7. When actual expenditures exceed authorized amounts, is the excess approved?
Accuracy objective:
  8. Is there a uniform policy for assigning depreciation rates, useful lives, and salvage values?
  9. Are depreciation calculations checked by internal auditors or other officials?
Classification objective:
10. Does the accounting manual contain policies for capitalization of assets and for expensing repair and maintenance?
11. Are subsidiary fixed assets records periodically reconciled to the general ledger accounts?
12. Are memorandum records of leased assets maintained?
Proper period objective:
13. Does the accounting manual give instructions for recording fixed asset additions on a proper date of acquisition?

EXHIBIT 10A–6   **SELECTED COMPUTER QUESTIONNAIRE ITEMS: GENERAL AND APPLICATION CONTROLS (capital assets)**

General controls:

1. Are computer operators and programmers excluded from participating in the input and output control functions?
2. Are programmers excluded from operating the computer?
3. Is there a database administrator who is independent of computer operations, systems, programming, and users?
4. Are computer personnel restricted from initiating, authorizing, or entering transactions or adjustments to the general ledger master database or the subsidiary ledger master database?
5. Is access to the computer room restricted to authorized personnel?
6. Is on-line access to data and programs controlled through the use of department account codes, personal ID numbers, and passwords?
7. Are systems, programs, and documentation stored in a fireproof area?
8. Can current files, particularly master files, be reconstructed from files stored in an off-site location?

Fixed asset application controls:

1. Is terminal entry of fixed asset data done on the basis of up-to-date written instructions?
2. Are important fixed asset data fields subject to input validation tests—missing data tests, limit and range tests, check digits, valid codes, and so forth?
3. Does the computer print an input error report? Is this returned to the accounting department for correction of errors?
4. Is an accounting department person assigned the responsibility for promptly correcting errors in fixed asset input data and re-entering the data for inclusion with the next batch?
5. Are batch control totals used to reconcile computer-processed fixed asset output to input control data?
6. Is fixed asset computer output reviewed for reasonableness, accuracy, and legibility by the computer department personnel and the fixed asset accounting personnel?

APPENDIX 10B

SUBSTANTIVE AUDIT PROGRAMS

E X H I B I T 10B–1   **AUDIT PROGRAM FOR INVENTORY AND COST OF GOODS SOLD**

A. Inventory

1. Conduct an observation of the company's physical inventory count. Count a sample of inventory items and trace these counts to the final inventory compilation.
2. Select a sample of inventory items. Vouch unit prices to vendors' invoices or other cost records. Recalculate the multiplication of unit times price.
3. Scan the inventory compilation for items added from sources other than the physical count and items that appear to be large round numbers or systematic fictitious additions.
4. Recalculate the extensions and footings of the final inventory compilation for clerical accuracy.
5. For selected inventory items and categories, determine the replacement cost and the applicability of lower-of-cost-or-market valuation.
6. Determine whether obsolete or damaged good should be written down:
   a. Enquire about obsolete, damaged, unsalable, slow-moving items.
   b. Scan the perpetual records for slow-moving items.
   c. During the physical observation, be alert to notice damaged or scrap inventory.
   d. Compare the listing of obsolete, slow-moving, damaged, or unsalable inventory from last year's audit to the current inventory compilation.
7. At year-end, obtain the numbers of the last shipping and receiving documents for the year. Use these to scan the sales, inventory/cost of sales, and accounts payable entries for proper cutoff.
8. Read bank confirmations, debt agreements, and minutes of the board, and make enquiries about pledge or assignment of inventory to secure debt.
9. Enquire about inventory out on consignment and about inventory on hand that is consigned in from vendors.
10. Confirm or inspect inventories held in public warehouses.
11. Recalculate the amount of intercompany profit to be eliminated in consolidation.
12. Obtain written client representations concerning pledge of inventory as collateral, intercompany sales, and other related party transactions.

B. Cost of Sales

1. Select a sample of recorded cost of sales entries and vouch to supporting documentation.
2. Select a sample of basic transaction documents (such as sales invoices, production reports) and determine whether the related cost of goods sold was figured and recorded properly.
3. Determine whether the accounting costing method used by the client (such as FIFO, LIFO, standard cost) was applied properly.
4. Compute the gross margin rate and compare to prior years.
5. Compute the ratio of cost elements (such as labour, material) to total cost of goods sold and compare to prior years.

EXHIBIT 10B–2   **AUDIT PROGRAM FOR CAPITAL ASSETS AND RELATED ACCOUNTS**

A. Capital Assets
1. Summarize and foot detail capital asset subsidiary records and reconcile to general ledge control accounts(s).
2. Select a sample of detail fixed asset subsidiary records:
   a. Perform a physical observation (inspection) of the assets recorded.
   b. Inspect title documents, if any.
3. Prepare, or have client prepare, a schedule of capital asset additions and disposals for the period:
   a. Vouch to documents, indicating proper approval.
   b. Vouch costs to invoices, contracts, or other supporting documents.
   c. Determine whether all costs of shipment, installation, testing, and the like have been properly capitalized.
   d. Vouch proceeds (on dispositions) to cash receipts or other asset records.
   e. Recalculate gain or loss on dispositions.
   f. Trace amounts to detail fixed asset records and general ledger control account(s).
4. Prepare an analysis of capital assets subject to investment tax credit for correlation with tax liability audit work.
5. Observe a physical inventory-taking of the capital assets and compare with detail capital assets records.
6. Obtain written representations from management regarding pledge of assets as security for loans and leased assets.

B. Depreciation
1. Analyse amortization expense for overall reasonableness with reference to costs of assets and average depreciation rates.
2. Prepare, or have client prepare, a schedule of accumulated amortization showing beginning balance, current amortization, disposals, and ending balance. Trace to amortization expense and asset disposition analyses. Trace amounts to general ledger account(s).
3. Recalculate amortization expense and trace to general ledger account(s).

C. Other Accounts
1. Analyse insurance for adequacy of coverage.
2. Analyse property taxes to determine whether taxes due on assets have been paid or accrued.
3. Recalculate prepaid and/or accrued insurance and tax expenses.
4. Select a sample of rental expense entries. Vouch to rent/lease contracts to determine whether any leases qualify for capitalization.
5. Select a sample of repair and maintenance expense entries and vouch them to supporting invoices for evidence of property that should be capitalized.

EXHIBIT 10B–3   **AUDIT PROGRAM FOR ACCOUNTS PAYABLE**

1. Obtain a trial balance of recorded accounts payable as of year-end. Foot it and trace the total to the general ledger account. Vouch a sample of balances to vendors' statements. Review the trial balance for related-party payables.
2. When concerned about the possibility of unrecorded payables, send confirmations to creditors, especially those with small or zero balances and those with whom the company has done significant business.
3. Conduct a search for unrecorded liabilities by examining open vouchers, vendors' invoices an statements received, and cash payments made for a period after year-end.
4. Enquire about terms that justify classifying payables as long term instead of current.
5. For estimated liabilities, such as warranties, determine and evaluate the basis of estimation, and recalculate the estimate.
6. Obtain written client representations about related party payables and pledges of assets as collateral for liabilities.

EXHIBIT 10B–4   **AUDIT PROGRAM FOR PREPAID, DEFERRED, AND ACCRUED EXPENSES**

---

1. Obtain a schedule of all prepaid expenses, deferred coasts, and accrued expenses.
2. Determine whether each item is properly allocated to the current or future accounting periods.
3. Select significant additions to deferred and accrued amounts, and vouch them to supporting invoices, contracts or calculations.
4. Determine the basis for deferral and accrual, and recalculate the recorded amounts.
5. Study the nature of each item, enquire of management, and determine whether the remaining balance will be recovered from future operations.
6. In other audit work on income and expenses, be alert to notice items that should be considered prepaid, deferred, or accrued, and allocated to current or future accounting periods.
7. Scan the expense accounts in the trial balance and compare to prior year. Investigate unusual differences that may indicate failure to account for a prepaid or accrual item.
8. Study each item to determine the proper current or noncurrent balance sheet classification.

Appendix 10C

EDI Systems and Accounts Payable Audits

Rapid changes in information technology have had a great impact on how audits are conducted in various accounts. The CICA has recently documented some of these changes in an audit testing study, *Confirmation of Accounts Payable* (CICA, 1996). Advanced computerized systems are discussed in general terms in Chapter 19; this appendix provides merely a brief overview of the effects EDI systems have on accounts payable audits. EDI stands for electronic data interchange and is defined in the study as "an exchange of electronic business documents between economic trading partners, computer to computer, in a standard format."

The significance of EDI for the audit approach to accounts payable is summarized in pages 35–40 of the study as follows (the numbers in the margins indicate paragraph numbers from the study):

Partnership with Suppliers

10 EDI has introduced a new way of doing business, that is, business in partnership. EDI implementation requires the support of customers and/or suppliers, and they must agree with the entity on how transactions will be carried out. With respect to purchases, the entity must enter into agreements with each of its suppliers willing to trade by EDI. Depending on the integration level of applications, discussions deal with the various documents to be exchanged, as well as supply, delivery, billing or payment methods. It becomes preferable for entities to buy a given product from a limited number of suppliers, and they will thus forge closer business relationships. In some cases, the partnership goes even further: the customer communicates the sales or production forecasts for a product to the supplier to help the latter plan for the supply of the product and improve customer service ...

Elimination of statements of account

11 Given these new ties between partners, certain documents, such as statements of account currently issued by suppliers, are no longer useful. As accounts payable balances become less significant and purchase terms are set in agreements, the partners will probably no longer feel the need for documents that summarize transactions and balances. The elimination of statements of account, however, also eliminates reliable external audit evidence regarding accounts payable at the end of the accounting period cycle. Several of the substantive procedures the auditor normally uses to audit accounts payable are based on this evidence. To obtain the required audit evidence, the auditor must now perform procedures based on other forms of evidence ...

Billing of accounts payable

13 Systems integration and partnerships with suppliers can also change the way goods are billed. For example, price information can be extracted from a price catalogue managed jointly by the trading partners and incorporated into their respective applications. In such a case, the supplier does not send an electronic invoice. The pricing of purchases is based on information contained in the electronic notice of receipt issued by the customer (or in the electronic notice of shipment issued by the supplier) and the price catalogue. The auditor can no longer use supplier invoices, which previously constituted external evidence, and will probably have to rely on the proper functioning of the pricing process. The auditor will most likely verify application controls (as well as manual and physical controls), for example, controls to access and/or modify the price catalogue ...

Audit Approach

Importance of controls in an integrated EDI environment

17 With EDI, entities depend more on computer systems, and while effective systems can lessen the risk of human error, the impact of any weakness in control may be magnified. Moreover, the accuracy, authorization and completeness of data produced by integrated EDI systems are ensured mainly by programmed controls intended to prevent, rather than only detect, errors. It will be difficult to rely on evidence available essentially only in electronic form without auditing the functioning of controls—mainly programmed controls—which ensure the reliability and authenticity of such evidence.

18 The factors mentioned in the previous paragraph, the complexity of integrated EDI systems and the difficulty of implementing detection controls that involve external evidence can increase detection risk, and it is possible that an essentially substantive approach will no longer be efficient. By obtaining the assurance that control systems have operated effectively during the entire period, the auditor will be able to reduce control risk below maximum and accept a higher level of detection risk for a comparable audit risk. Under this approach, it will be necessary to design tests of controls to verify the effectiveness of controls. Since, in an integrated EDI environment, existing controls are, for the most part, electronic, the auditor will have to use computer-assisted audit techniques more frequently, for example, integrated test facilities, concurrent audit tools and embedded audit modules. In addition, tests of controls will probably have to be performed in real time and at different times during the period, so that the auditor can assess the effectiveness of internal control throughout the period and not only at one particular moment, such as the interim audit. In short, for entities whose EDI applications are integrated with other applications, it will likely be more effective to audit financial information using a control-based approach and computer-assisted audit techniques ...

Confirmation

24 One might question the usefulness of accounts payable confirmation in an integrated EDI environment. If statements of account from suppliers are not available, if the value of accounts payable is no longer material and if other procedures can be used to verify balances more effectively, the auditor might decide that accounts payable confirmation is unnecessary.

25   Where the combined inherent and control risk associated with accounts payable is high, the auditor may need to perform substantive procedures that will provide more reliable audit evidence than that gathered from the review of subsequent payments. Accounts payable confirmation could be used to attain that objective. The fact that a supplier may be unable to determine the account balance at a specific date could be a major problem. To overcome this difficulty, the auditor could ask the client whether an agreement could be reached with the suppliers whereby they would retain (for a certain period of time) balance-related data at the client's year-end date ...

27 Eventually, auditors, too, will probably use EDI in the performance of their duties. Confirmation requests could then take the form of electronic documents, and be transmitted by EDI to suppliers. In turn, the suppliers will forward their responses to the auditor's electronic mailbox, possibly through a value-added network. If auditors are to use EDI to confirm accounts payable, however, a set of standardized electronic documents will have to be developed.

CHAPTER 11

Learning Objectives

In the production and payroll cycle, materials, labour and overhead are converted into finished goods and services. This chapter breaks the production and payroll cycle into two sections. Part I covers the production cycle, dealing with inventory valuation, amortization, and cost of goods sold accounting. The audit of payrolls and labour cost accounting is in Part II. A few short cases are used to show the application of audit procedures in situations where errors, irregularities, and frauds may be discovered. After completing this chapter, you should be able to:

1. Describe the production cycle, including typical source documents and controls.

2. Give examples of detail test of controls procedures for auditing the controls over conversion of materials and labour in a production process.

3. Describe some common errors, irregularities, and frauds in the accounting for production costs and related cost of goods sold, and design some audit and investigation procedures for detecting them.

4. Describe the payroll cycle, including typical source documents and controls.

5. Give examples of detail test of controls procedures for auditing the controls over payroll.

6. Describe some common errors, irregularities, and frauds in payroll, and design some audit and investigation procedures for detecting them.

456

PRODUCTION AND PAYROLL CYCLE INCLUDING AUDIT OF

INVENTORY VALUATION AND CAPITAL ASSETS

PART I: PRODUCTION CYCLE TYPICAL ACTIVITIES

Exhibit 11–1 shows the activities and accounting involved in a production cycle. The basic activities start with production planning, including inventory planning and management. Production planning can range from use of a sophisticated computerized long-range plan with just-in-time (JIT) inventory management to a simple ad hoc method ("Hey, Joe, we got an order today. Go make 10 units!"). Most businesses try to estimate or forecast sales levels and seasonal timing, and they try to plan facilities and production schedules to meet customer demand. As shown in Exhibit 11–1, the production cycle interacts with the acquisition cycle (Chapter 10) and the payroll cycle (later in this chapter) for the acquisition of fixed assets, materials, supplies, overhead, and labour.

The physical output of a production cycle is inventory (starting with raw materials, proceeding to work-in-process, thence to finished goods). Most matters of auditing inventory and physical inventory-taking were explained in Chapter 9 and Chapter 10. Exhibit 11–1 shows the connection of inventory to the revenue and collection cycle (Chapter 9) in terms of orders and deliveries.

Most of the "transactions" in a production cycle are cost accounting allocations, unit cost determinations, and standard cost calculations. These are internal transactions produced entirely within the company's accounting system. Exhibit 11–1 shows the elements of depreciation cost calculation, cost of goods sold determination, and job cost analysis as examples of these transactions.

As you follow Exhibit 11–1, you can track the following elements of a control structure.

Authorization

The overall production authorization starts with production planning, which usually is based on a sales forecast. Production planning interacts with inventory planning to produce production orders. These production orders specify the materials and labour required and the timing for the start and end of production. Managers in the sales/marketing department and production department usually sign off their approval on plans and production orders. Since sales volume and inventory requirements change with economic conditions and company success or failure, these plans and approvals are dynamic. They are amended according to changing needs.

Authorization also can include plans and approvals for subcontracting work to other companies. The process of taking bids and executing contracts can be a part of the planning-authorization system.

EXHIBIT 11-1   PRODUCTION CYCLE

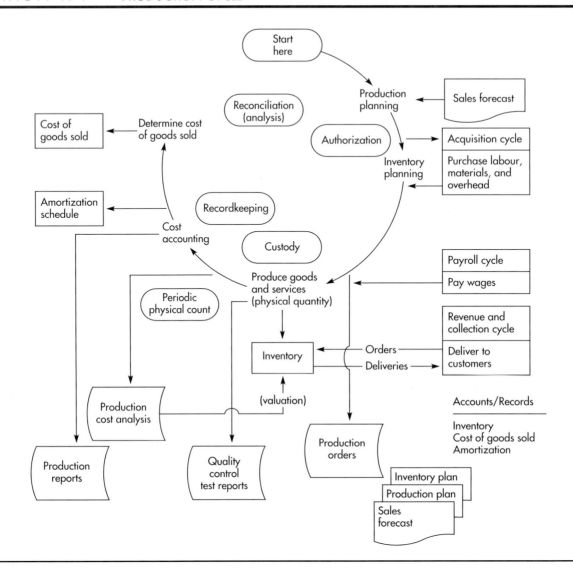

The production order usually includes a bill of materials (a specification of the materials authorized for the production). This bill of materials is the source of authorization for the preparation of materials requisitions, and these requisitions are the authorization for the inventory custodian to release raw materials and supplies to the production personnel. These documents are the inventory recordkeepers' authorizations to update the raw materials inventory files to record the reductions of the raw materials inventory.

Later, when production is complete, the production reports, along with the physical units and the quality control test reports, are the authorizations for the finished goods inventory custodian to place the units in the finished goods inventory. These same documents are the inventory recordkeepers' authorization to update the inventory record files to record the additions to the finished goods inventory.

Custody

Supervisors and workers, skilled and unskilled, have physical custody of materials, equipment, and labour while the production work is performed. They can requisition materials from the raw materials inventory, assign people to jobs, and control the pace of work. In a sense they have custody of a "moving inventory." The work in process (an inventory category) is literally "moving" and changing form in the process of being transformed from raw materials into finished goods.

Control over this custody is more difficult than control over a closed warehouse full of raw materials or finished goods. Control can be exercised by holding supervisors and workers accountable for the use of materials specified in the production orders, for the timely completion of production, and for the quality of the finished goods. This accountability can be achieved with good cost accounting, cost analysis, and quality control testing.

Recordkeeping (cost accounting)

When production is completed, production orders and the related records of material and labour used are sent forward to the cost accounting department. Since these accounting documents may come from the production personnel, the effective separation of the recordkeeping function depends upon its receiving independent notices from other places, especially notifications of materials issued from the inventory custodian and the labour costs assigned by the payroll department.

The cost accounting department produces analyses of cost-per-unit, standard cost, and variances. Cost accounting also may determine the allocation of overhead to production in general, to production orders, and to finished units. Depending on the design of the company's accounting system, these costs are used in inventory valuation and ultimately in determination of the cost of goods sold. Often the cost accounting department also is responsible for calculating the depreciation of fixed assets and the amortization of intangibles.

Periodic Reconciliation

The function of periodic reconciliation generally refers to comparison of actual assets and liabilities to the amounts recorded in the company accounts (e.g., comparing the physical count of inventory to the perpetual inventory records, comparing vendors' monthly statements to the recorded accounts payable). Exhibit 11–1 shows the periodic reconciliation of physical inventory to recorded amounts. The features and audit considerations of this reconciliation were covered in Chapter 10. The work in process inventory also can be observed, although the "count" of partially completed units is very judgmental. It can be costed at the labour, materials, and overhead assigned to its stage of completion.

Most other periodic reconciliations in the production cycle take the form of analyses of internal information. After all, with the exception of the physical inventory, no external transactions or physical units are unique to production and cost accounting. These analyses include costing the production orders, comparing the cost to prior experience or to standard costs, and determining lower-of-cost-or-market (LCM) valuations. In a sense the LCM calculations are a "reconciliation" of product cost to the external market price of product units.

OVERHEAD ALLOCATION

The cost accounting department at Pointed Publications, Inc., routinely allocated overhead to book printing runs at the rate of 40 percent of materials and labour cost. The debit was initially to the finished books inventory, while the credit went to an "overhead allocated" account that was offset against other entries in the cost of goods sold calculation, which included all the actual overhead incurred. During the year 10 million books were produced and $40 million of overhead was allocated to them. The auditors noticed that actual overhead expenditures were $32 million, and 3 million books remained in the ending inventory.

The finding resulted in the conclusion that the inventory was overstated by $2.4 million, the cost of goods sold was understated by $2.4 million, and the income before taxes was overstated by 8.2 percent.

	Company Accounting	Proper Accounting
Books produced	10 million	10 million
Labour and material cost	$100 million	$ 100 million
Overhead allocated	$ 40 million	$ 32 million
Cost per book	$ 14.00	$ 13.20
Cost of goods sold		
Labour and materials cost	$100 million	$ 100 million
Overhead allocated to books	40 million	
Overhead incurred	32 million	32 million
Overhead credited to cost	(40 million)	
Ending inventory	(42 million)	(39.6 million)
Total cost of goods sold	$ 90 million	$92.4 million

11.1 What are the functions normally associated with the production and conversion cycle?

11.2 Why is an understanding of the production process, including the related data processing and cost accounting, important to auditors evaluating the control structure as part of their assessment of control risk?

11.3 Describe a "walk-through" of a production transaction from production orders to entry in the finished goods perpetual inventory records. What document copies would be collected? What controls noted? What duties separated?

11.4 Describe how the separation of (1) authorization of production transactions, (2) recording of these transactions, and (3) physical custody of inventories can be specified among the production, inventory, and cost accounting departments.

11.5 What features of the cost accounting system would be expected to prevent the omission of recording materials used in production?

AUDIT EVIDENCE IN MANAGEMENT REPORTS AND FILES
· · · · · · · · · · · ·

Most production accounting systems produce timely reports that managers need to supervise and control production. These reports can be used by auditors as supporting evidence for assertions about work in process and finished goods inventories and about cost of goods sold.

Sales Forecast
Management's sales forecast provides the basis for several aspects of business planning, notably the planning of production and inventory levels. If the auditors want to use the forecast for substantive audit decisions, some work to obtain assurance about its reasonableness needs to be performed. This work is not an examination or compilation of a forecast as contemplated by the assurance services standards. All the auditors need to accomplish is to learn about the assumptions built into the forecast for the purpose of ascertaining their reasonableness. In addition, some work on the mechanical accuracy of the forecast should be performed to avoid an embarrassing reliance on faulty calculations.

Forecasts can be used in connection with knowing the shape of management's plans for the year under audit, most of which will have already passed when the audit work begins. It will help the auditors understand the nature and volume of production orders and the level of materials inventory. Forecasts of the following year can be used in connection with valuing the inventory at lower-of-cost-or-market (e.g., slow-moving and potentially obsolete inventory), which influences the amount of cost of goods sold that is shown in the financial statements. Special care must be taken with using the forecast for the next year in connection with inventory valuation because an overly optimistic forecast can lead to a failure to write down inventory, accelerate the depreciation of capital assets, and account for more cost of goods sold.

Production Plans and Reports
Based on the sales forecast, management should develop a plan for the amount and timing of production. The production plan provides general information to the auditors, but the production orders and inventory plan associated with the production plan are even more important. The production orders carry the information about requirements for raw materials, labour, and overhead, including the requisitions for purchase and use of materials and labour. These documents are the initial authorizations for control of the inventory and production.

Production reports record the completion of production quantities. When coupled with the related cost-accounting reports, they are the company's record of the cost of goods placed in the finished goods inventory. In most cases auditors will audit the cost reports in connection with determining the cost valuation of inventory and cost of goods sold.

Amortization Schedule
The cost accounting department may be charged with preparing a schedule of the amortization (depreciation) of capital assets. In many companies such a schedule is long and complicated, involving large dollar amounts of asset cost and calculated amortization expense. It is not unusual to find the amount of amortization expense exceeding a company's net income. (In the statement of changes in financial position, the amortization added back to calculate the cash flow from operations

---

The SALY Forecast

The auditors were reviewing the inventory items that had not been issued for 30 days or more, considering the need to write some items down to market lower than cost. The production manager showed them the SALY forecast that indicated continuing need for the materials in products that were expected to have reasonable demand. The auditors agreed that the forecasts supported the prediction of future sales of products at prices that would cover the cost of the slow-moving material items.

Unfortunately, they neglected to ask the meaning of SALY in the designation of the forecast. They did not learn that it means "Same As Last Year." It is not a forecast at all. The products did not sell at the prices expected, and the company experienced losses the following year that should have been charged to cost of goods sold earlier.

---

can be larger than the net income carried forward from the income statement.) An abbreviated illustration of a fixed asset and amortization schedule is in the following table.

Fixed Assets and Amortization

	Asset Cost (000s)				Accumulated Amortization (000s)			
Description	Beginning Balance	Added	Sold	Ending Balance	Beginning Balance	Added	Sold	Ending Balance
Land	10,000			10,000				
Bldg 1	30,000			30,000	6,857	857		7,714
Bldg 2		42,000		42,000		800		800
Computer A	5,000		5,000	0	3,750	208	3,958	0
Computer B		3,500		3,500		583		583
Press	1,500			1,500	300	150		450
Auto 1	15		15	0	15		15	0
Auto 2		22		22		2		2
Total	46,515	45,522	5,015	87,022	10,922	2,600	3,973	9,549

The amortization schedule is audited by recalculating the amortization expense, using the company's methods, estimates of useful life, and estimates of residual value. (Problem 11.54 at the end of the chapter requires some work on the schedule presented above.) The asset acquisition and disposition information in the schedule gives the auditors points of departure for auditing the asset additions and disposals. When the schedule covers hundreds of assets and numerous additions and disposals, auditors can (*a*) use computer auditing methods to recalculate the amortization expense and (*b*) use sampling to choose additions and disposals for test of controls and substantive audit. The beginning balances of assets and accumulated amortization should be traced to the prior year's audit working papers. This schedule can be made into an audit working paper and placed in the auditor's files for future reference.

· ·

<table>
<tr><td>R E V I E W
C H E C K P O I N T S</td><td>

11.6 When auditors want to use a client's sales forecast for general familiarity with the production cycle or for evaluation of slow-moving inventory, what kind of work should be done on the forecast?

11.7 If the actual sales for the year are substantially lower than the sales forecasted at the beginning of the year, what potential valuation problems may arise in the production cycle accounts?

11.8 What production cycle documentation supports the valuation of manufactured finished goods inventory?

11.9 What items in a client's fixed asset and amortization schedule give auditors points of departure (assertions) for audit procedures?

</td></tr>
</table>

· ·

CONTROL RISK ASSESSMENT
· · · · · · · · · · · ·

LEARNING   OBJECTIVE

2. Give examples of detail test of controls procedures for auditing the controls over conversion of materials and labour in a production process.

Control risk assessment is important because it governs the nature, timing, and extent of substantive audit procedures that will be applied in the audit of account balances in the production cycle. These account balances include:

Inventory:
  Raw materials.
  Work in process.
  Finished goods.

Cost of goods sold.

Amortization:
  Amortization expense.
  Accumulated amortization.

Several aspects of the audit of purchased inventories and physical quantities are covered in Chapter 10 (acquisition and expenditure cycle). With respect to inventory valuation, this chapter points out the cost accounting function and its role in determining the cost valuation of manufactured finished goods.

General Control Considerations

Control procedures for proper segregation of responsibilities should be in place and operating. By referring to Exhibit 11–1, you can see that proper segregation involves authorization (production planning and inventory planning) by persons who do not have custody, recording, or cost accounting and reconciliation duties. Custody of inventories (raw materials, work in process, and finished goods) is in the hands of persons who do not authorize the amount or timing of production or the purchase of materials and labour, or perform the cost accounting recordkeeping, or prepare cost analyses (reconciliations). Cost accounting (a recording function) is performed by persons who do not authorize production or have custody of assets in the process of production. However, you usually will find that the cost accountants prepare various analyses and reconciliations directly related to production activities. Combinations of two or more of the duties of authorization, custody, or cost accounting in one person, one office, or one computerized system may open the door for errors, irregularities, and frauds.

In addition, the control structure should provide for detail control checking procedures. For example: (1) production orders should contain a list of materials and their quantities, and they should be approved by a production planner/ scheduler; (2) materials requisitions should be compared in the cost accounting department with the list of materials on the production order, and the materials requisitions should be signed by the production operator and the materials inventory storekeeper; (3) labour time records on jobs should be signed by production supervisors, and the cost accounting department should reconcile these cost amounts with the labour report from the payroll department; (4) production reports of finished units should be signed by the production supervisor and finished goods inventory custodian and forwarded to cost accounting. These control operations track the raw materials and labour from start to finish in the production process. With each internal transaction, the responsibility and accountability for assets are passed from one person or location to another.

Complex computer systems to manage production and materials flow are found in many companies. Even though the technology is complex, the basic management and control functions of ensuring the flow of labour and materials to production and controlling waste should be in place. Manual signatures and paper production orders and requisitions may not exist. They may all be imbedded in computer-controlled manufacturing systems. Matters of auditing in a complex computer environment will need to be considered (refer to Chapter 19).

Internal Control Questionnaire

Information about the production cycle control structure often is gathered initially by completing an internal control questionnaire (ICQ). An ICQ for general (manual) controls is in Appendix 11A–1. This questionnaire can be studied for details of desirable control policies and procedures. It is organized with headings that identify the important control objectives—environment, validity, completeness, authorization, accuracy, classification, accounting, and proper period recording. Problem 11.51 at the end of the chapter asks you to describe the errors and irregularities that can occur if certain ICQ items are not specified by a company. Problem 11.62 at the end of the chapter presents a computerized payroll system and asks for identification of control weaknesses (reference to control features in Chapters 6 and 8 will help).

Production Management—JIT

Considerable interest has arisen in just-in-time (JIT) manufacturing. JIT has been implemented in many companies, and auditors need to be familiar with its precepts and implications for auditing. Appendix 11B contains a brief explanation of JIT manufacturing.

> ## Overcharging the Government
>
> Government contracting periodically gets in the news, through exposés of companies charging unrelated costs to government contracts of various kinds. Although the production plans and orders do not specify allowable costs for building the company baseball field or paying the company president's kennel fees while on business trips, costs like these have found their way into government contract reimbursement claims. Government contract auditors have found them, and companies have incurred penalties and requirements to reimburse the costs wrongly charged. Some companies summarily fire cost accountants who engage in cost manipulation on government contracts (McDonnell Douglas Company in the United States). Other organizations suffer in the glare of adverse publicity (Northrop Corporation, Massachusetts Institute of Technology, Stanford University).

Detail Test of Controls Audit Procedures

An organization should have detail control procedures in place and operating to prevent, detect, and correct accounting errors. You studied the general control objectives in Chapter 6 (validity, completeness, authorization, accuracy, classification, accounting, and proper period recording). Exhibit 11–2 puts these in the perspective of production activity with examples of specific objectives. You should study this exhibit carefully. It expresses the general control objectives in specific examples related to production.

Auditors can perform detail test of controls audit procedures to determine whether controls that are said to be in place and operating actually are being performed properly by company personnel. A detail test of control procedure consists of (1) identification of the data population from which a sample of items will be selected for audit and (2) an expression of the action that will be taken to produce relevant evidence. In general, the actions in detail test of control audit procedures involve vouching, tracing, observing, scanning, and recalculating. A specification of such procedures is part of an audit program for obtaining evidence useful in a final control risk assessment. If personnel in the organization are not performing their control procedures very well, auditors will need to design substantive audit procedures to try to detect whether control failures have produced materially misleading account balances.

Exhibit 11–3 contains a selection of detail test of controls audit procedures for auditing controls over the accumulation of costs for work in process inventory. This is the stage of "inventory" while it is in the production process. Upon completion, the accumulated costs become the cost valuation of the finished goods inventory. The illustrative procedures presume the existence of production cost reports that are updated as production takes place, labour reports that assign labour cost to the job, materials-used and materials requisitions charging raw materials to the production order, and overhead allocation calculations. Some or all of these documents may be in the form of computer records. The samples are usually attribute samples designed

E X H I B I T 11–2   **CONTROL OBJECTIVES (PRODUCTION CYCLE)**

General Objectives	Examples of Specific Objectives
1. Recorded production transactions are *valid* and documented.	Cost accounting separated from production, payroll, and inventory control. Material use reports compared to raw material stores issue slips. Labour use reports compared to job time tickets.
2. Valid production transactions are *recorded* and none omitted.	All documents prenumbered and numerical sequence reviewed.
3. Production transactions are *authorized*.	Material use and labour use prepared by foreman and approved by production supervisor.
4. Production job cost transactions computations contain *accurate* figures.	Job cost sheet entries reviewed by person independent of preparation. Costs of inventory used and labour used reviewed periodically.
5. Labour and materials are *classified* correctly as direct or indirect.	Production foreman required to account for all material and labour used as direct or indirect.
6. Production *accounting* is complete.	Open job cost sheets periodically reconciled to the work-in-process inventory accounts.
7. Production transactions are recorded in the *proper period*.	Production reports of material and labour used prepared weekly and transmitted to cost accounting. Job cost sheets posted weekly and summary journal entries of work in process and work completed prepared monthly.

E X H I B I T 11–3   **TEST OF CONTROLS AUDIT PROCEDURES FOR WORK-IN-PROCESS INVENTORY**

	Control Objective
1. Reconcile the open production cost reports to the work-in-process inventory control account.	Completeness
2. Select a sample of open and closed production cost reports:	
a. Recalculate all costs entered.	Accuracy
b. Vouch labour costs to labour reports.	Validity
c. Compare labour reports to summary of payroll.	Accounting
d. Vouch material costs to issue slips and materials-used reports.	Validity
e. Vouch overhead charges to overhead analysis schedules.	Accuracy
f. Trace selected overhead amounts from analysis schedules to cost allocations and to invoices or accounts payable vouchers.	Validity
3. Select a sample of issue slips from the raw materials stores file:	
a. Determine if a matching requisition is available for every issue slip.	Completeness
b. Trace materials-used reports into production cost reports.	Completeness
4. Select a sample of clock timecards from the payroll file. Trace to job time tickets, labour reports, and production cost reports.	Completeness
5. Select a sample of production orders:	
a. Determine whether production order was authorized.	Authorization
b. Match to bill of materials and manpower needs.	Completeness
c. Trace bill of materials to material requisitions, material issue slips, materials-used reports, and production cost reports.	Completeness
d. Trace manpower needs to labour reports, and production cost reports.	Completeness

along the lines you studied in Chapter 7. On the right, Exhibit 11–3 shows the control objectives tested by the audit procedures.

Direction of the Test of Controls Procedures

The test of controls procedures in Exhibit 11–3 are designed to test the production accounting in two directions. One is the completeness direction, in which the control performance of audit interest is the recording of all the production that was ordered to be started. Exhibit 11–4 shows that the sample for this direction is taken from the population of production orders found in the production planning department. The procedures trace the cost accumulation forward into the production cost reports in the cost accounting department. The procedures keyed in the boxes (5-*a*, *b*, *c*, *d*) are cross-references to the procedures in Exhibit 11–3. A potential finding with these procedures is the cancellation of some production because of technical or quality problems, which should result in write-off or scrap of some partially completed production units.

The other direction is the validity direction of the test. The control performance of interest is the proper recording of work in process and finished goods in the general ledger. Exhibit 11–5 shows that the sample for this test is from the production reports (quantity and cost) recorded in the inventory accounts. This sample yields references to production cost reports filed in the cost accounting department. From these basic records the recorded costs can be recalculated, vouched to labour reports, compared to the payroll, and vouched to records of material used and overhead incurred. The procedures keyed in the boxes (2-*a*, *b*, *c*, *d*, *e*, *f*) are cross-references to the procedures in Exhibit 11–3. A potential finding with these procedures is improper valuation of the recorded inventory cost.

EXHIBIT 11–4   **TEST OF PRODUCTION COST CONTROLS: COMPLETENESS DIRECTION**

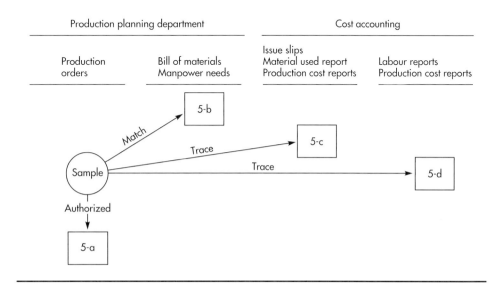

EXHIBIT 11–5   TEST OF PRODUCTION COST CONTROLS: VALIDITY DIRECTION

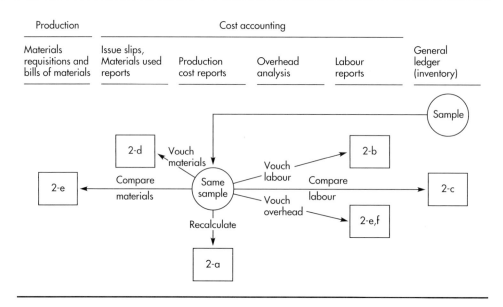

IMPROPER PRODUCTION LOSS DEFERRALS

According to the SEC, Litton Corporation incurred cost overruns on its ship-building contracts and postponed writing off a $128 million cost overrun by classifying it as an asset for financial reporting purposes. If it had been written off timely, the net income of $1 million for the year would have become a substantial loss. Litton wrote off the $128 million later.

****

According to the SEC, International Systems & Controls Corporation (ISC) recorded and reported cost overruns on fixed price contracts, claims for price escalation, and kickback arrangements with suppliers as unbilled receivables. Additional uncollectible contract costs, which indicated losses on fixed price contracts, were buried in other unrelated contracts. ISC used the unbilled receivables account as a dumping ground for improper and questionable payments on the contracts. It tried to show them as legitimate reimbursable contract costs in order to avoid (*a*) writing them off as expense and (*b*) showing the true nature of the items. ISC used the unbilled receivables account to record cost overruns on fixed price contracts, misrepresenting them as an escalation payment due from the owner, but the contract did not provide for any such payment.

Source: I. Kellog, *How to Find Negligence and Misrepresentation in Financial Statements* (New York: Shepard's/McGraw-Hill, 1983), pp. 208–9, 302–3.

Summary: Control Risk Assessment

The audit manager or senior accountant in charge of the audit should evaluate the evidence obtained from an understanding of the internal control structure and from the test of controls audit procedures. If the control risk is assessed very low, the substantive audit procedures on the account balances can be limited in cost-saving ways. For example, the inventory valuation substantive tests can be limited in scope (i.e., smaller sample size), and overall analytical procedures can be used with more confidence in being able to detect material misstatements not otherwise evident in the accounting details.

On the other hand, if tests of controls reveal weaknesses, amortization calculation errors, and cost accumulation errors, the substantive procedures will need to be designed to lower the risk of failing to detect material error in the inventory and cost of goods sold account balances. For example, the amortization cost may need to be completely recalculated and reviewed again by the auditors. A large number of inventoried production reports may need to be selected for valuation calculations. Cost overruns will need to be investigated with reference to contract terms to determine whether they should be carried as assets (e.g., inventory or unbilled receivables) or written off. Descriptions of major deficiencies, control weaknesses, and inefficiencies may be incorporated in a management letter to the client.

Computerized production cycle records are encountered frequently. Their complexity may range from simple batch systems, which automate the data processing, to transaction-driven integrated systems, which capture the production progress directly from automated devices on the production line. Computer audit techniques, such as test data, frequently are employed to audit controls in such systems, and generalized audit software may be employed to match data on different files. (Refer to Chapter 8 for these subjects.)

· ·

R E V I E W
C H E C K P O I N T S

11.10 What are the primary functions that should be segregated in the production cycle?

11.11 Describe the two general characteristics of a test of controls audit procedure.

11.12 How does the production order document (or computer record) provide a control over the quantity of materials used in production?

11.13 Where might an auditor find accounting records of cost overruns on contracts? of improper charges? of improperly capitalized inventory?

11.14 Evaluate the following statement made by an auditing student: "I do not understand cost accounting; therefore, I want to get a job with an auditing firm where I will only have to know financial accounting."

11.15 From what population of documents would an auditor sample to determine whether all authorized production was completed and placed in inventory or written off as scrap? to determine whether finished goods inventory was actually produced and properly costed?

· ·

Audit Cases: Substantive Audit Procedures

. . . .

LEARNING OBJECTIVE

3. Describe some common errors, irregularities, and frauds in the accounting for production costs and related cost of goods sold, and design some audit and investigation procedures for detecting them.

The audit of account balances consists of procedural efforts to detect errors, irregularities, and frauds that may exist in the balances, thus making them misleading in financial statements. If such misstatements exist, they are characterized by the following features:

Method: A cause of the misstatement (accidental error, intentional irregularity, or fraud attempt), which is usually made easier by some kind of failure of controls.

Paper trail: A set of telltale signs of erroneous accounting, missing or altered documents, or a "dangling debit" (the false or erroneous debit that results from an overstatement of assets).

Amount: The dollar amount of overstated assets and revenue, or understated liabilities and expenses.

Each audit program for the audit of an account balance contains an audit approach that may enable auditors to detect misstatements in account balances. Each application of procedures contains these elements:

Audit objective: A recognition of a financial statement assertion for which evidence needs to be obtained. The assertions are about existence of assets, liabilities, revenue, and expenses; their valuation; their complete inclusion in the account balances; the rights and obligations inherent in them; and their proper presentation and disclosure in the financial statements. (These assertions were introduced in Chapter 4.)

Control: A recognition of the control procedures that should be used by an organization to prevent and detect errors and irregularities.

Test of controls: Ordinary and extended procedures designed to produce evidence about the effectiveness of the controls that should be in operation.

Audit of balance: Ordinary and extended substantive procedures designed to find signs of errors, irregularities, and frauds in account balances and classes of transactions.

The next portion of this chapter consists of two "casettes" (little cases) that first set the stage with a story about an error, irregularity, or fraud—its method, paper trail (if any), and amount. This part of the casette gives you the "inside story," which auditors seldom know before they perform the audit work. The second part of the casette, under the heading of the audit approach, tells a structured story about the audit objective, desirable controls, test of control procedures, audit of balance procedures, and discovery summary. The audit approach segment illustrates how audit procedures can be applied and the discoveries they may enable auditors to make. At the end of the chapter, some similar discussion cases are presented, and you can write the audit approach to test your ability to design audit procedures for the detection of errors, irregularities, and frauds.

Casette 11.1
Unbundled Before Its Time

Problem

Production "sold" as finished goods before actual unit completion caused understated inventory, overstated cost of goods sold, overstated revenue, and overstated income.

Method

Western Corporation assembled and sold computer systems. A systems production order consisted of hardware and peripheral equipment specifications and software specifications with associated performance criteria. Customer contracts always required assembly to specifications, installation, hardware testing, software installation, and software testing, after which the customer could accept the finished installation and pay the agreed price for the entire package. Completion of an order usually took three to eight months.

For internal accounting purposes, Western "unbundled" the hardware and software components of the customer orders. Production orders were split between the two components. Standard production processing and cost accounting were performed as if the two components were independent orders. When the hardware was installed and tested (with or without customer acceptance), Western recorded part of the contract price as sales revenue and the related cost of goods sold. The amount "due from customers" was carried in an asset account entitled "unbilled contract revenue." No billing statement was sent to the customer at this time.

When the software component was completed, installed, tested, and accepted, the remainder of the contract price was recorded as revenue, and the cost of the software was recorded as cost of goods sold. A billing statement was sent to the customer. The "unbilled contract revenue," which now matched the customer's obligation, was moved to "accounts receivable."

During the time either or both of the order components were in process (prior to installation at the customer's location), accumulated costs were carried in a work-in-process inventory account.

Paper Trail

Customer orders and contracts contained all the terms relating to technical specifications, acceptance testing, and the timing of the customer's obligation to pay. Copies of the technical specification sections of the contracts were attached to the separate hardware and software production orders prepared and authorized in the production planning department. During production, installation, and testing, each of these production orders served as the basis for the production cost accumulation and the subsidiary record of the work-in-process inventory. At the end the production report along with the accumulated costs became the production cost report and the supporting documentation for the cost of goods sold entry.

Amount

Western Corporation routinely recorded the hardware component of contracts too early, recognizing revenue and cost of goods sold that should have been postponed until later when the customer accepted the entire system. In the last three years, the resulting income overstatement amounted to 12 percent, 15 percent, and 19 percent of the reported operating income before taxes.

AUDIT APPROACH

Objective

Obtain evidence of the actual occurrence of cost of goods sold transactions, thereby yielding evidence of the completeness of recorded inventory.

Control

The major control lies in the production planning department approval of orders that identify a total unit of production (in this case, the hardware and software components combined). Nothing is wrong with approving separate orders for efficiency of production, but they should be cross-referenced so that both production personnel and the cost accounting department can see them as separate components of the same order unit.

Test of Controls

While the company conducted a large business, it had relatively few production orders (200–250 charged to cost of goods sold during each year). A sample of completed production orders should be taken and vouched to the underlying customer orders and contracts. The purpose of this procedure includes determining the validity of the production orders in relation to customer orders and determining whether the cost of goods sold was recorded in the proper period. (Procedures to audit the accuracy and completeness of the cost accumulation also are carried out on this sample.)

Even though the auditors can read the customer contracts, enquiries should be made about the company's standard procedures for the timing of revenue and cost of goods sold recognition.

Audit of Balances

The sample of completed production orders taken for the test of controls also can be used in a "dual purpose test" to audit the details of the cost of goods sold balance. In connection with the balance audit, the primary points of interest are the validity and completeness of the dollar amounts accumulated as cost of the contracts and the proper cutoff for recording the cost.

The existence of the "unbilled contract revenue" asset account in the general ledger should raise a red flag. Such an account always means that management has made an estimate of a revenue amount that has not been determined according to contract and has not yet been billed to the customer in accordance with contract terms. Even though the revenue is "unbilled," the related cost of goods sold still should be in the cost of goods sold account. While accounting theory and practice permit recognizing unbilled revenue in certain cases (e.g., percentage of completion for construction con-

tracts), the accounting has been known to harbour abuses in some cases.

Discovery Summary

When the company decided to issue shares to the public, a new audit firm was engaged. These auditors performed the dual-purpose procedures outlined above, made the suggested enquiries, and investigated the "unbilled contract revenue" account. They learned about management's unbundling policy and insisted that the policy be changed to recognize revenue only when all the terms of the contract were met. (The investigation yielded the information about prior years' overstatements of revenue, cost of goods sold, and income.) Part of the reason for insisting on the change of policy was the finding that Western did not have a very good record of quality control and customer acceptance of software installation. Customer acceptance was frequently delayed several months while systems engineers debugged software. On several occasions Western solved the problems by purchasing complete software packages from other developers.

Casette 11.2
When in Doubt, Defer!

Problem

SaCom Corporation deferred costs under the heading of work in process, military contract claims, and R&D test equipment, thus overstating assets, understating cost of goods sold, and overstating income. Disclosure of the auditor's fees was manipulated and understated.

Method

SaCom manufactured electronic and other equipment for private customers and government military defence contracts. Near the end of the year, the company used a journal entry to remove $170,000 from cost of goods sold and to defer it as tooling, leasehold improvements, and contract award and acquisition costs.

The company capitalized certain expenditures as R&D test equipment ($140,000) and as claims for reimbursement on defence contracts ($378,000).

In connection with a public offering of securities, the auditors billed SaCom $125,000 for professional fees. The underwriters objected. The auditors agreed to forgive $70,000 of the fees, and SaCom agreed to pay higher fees for work the following year (150 percent of standard billing rates). SaCom disclosed audit fees in the registration statement in the amount of $55,000. This amount was paid from the proceeds of the offering.

Paper Trail

The $170,000 deferred costs consisted primarily of labour costs. The company altered the labour time records in an effort to provide substantiating documentation. The auditors knew about the alterations. The cost was removed from jobs that were left with too little labour cost in light of the work performed on them.

The R&D test equipment cost already had been charged to cost of goods sold with no notice of deferral when originally recorded. Deferral was accomplished with an adjusting journal entry. The company did not have documentation for the adjusting entry, except for an estimate of labour cost (44 percent of all labour cost in a subsidiary was capitalized during the period).

The claim for reimbursement on defence contracts did not have documentation specifically identifying the costs as being related to the contract. (Auditors know that defence department auditors insist on documentation and justification before approving such a claim.)

The audit fee arrangement was known to the audit firm, and it was recorded in an internal memorandum.

Amount

SaCom reported net income of about $542,000 for the year, an overstatement of approximately 50 percent.

AUDIT APPROACH

Objective

Obtain evidence of the validity of production costs deferred as tooling, leasehold improvements, contract award and acquisition costs, R&D test equipment, and claims for reimbursement on defence contracts.

Control

The major control lies in the procedures for documenting the validity of cost deferral journal entries.

Test of Controls

The test of controls procedure is to select a sample of journal entries, suspect ones in this case, and vouch them to supporting documentation. Experience has shown that nonstandard adjusting journal entries are the source of accounting errors and irregularities more often than standard repetitive accounting for systematic transactions. This phenomenon makes the population of adjusting journal entries a ripe field for control and substantive testing.

Audit of Balances

The account balances created by the deferral journal entries can be audited in a "dual-purpose procedure" by auditing the supporting documentation. These balances were created entirely by the journal entries, and their "existence" as legitimate assets, deferrals, and reimbursement claims depends on the believability of the supporting explanations. In connection with the defence contract claim, auditors can review it with knowledge of the contract and the extent of documentation required by government contract auditors. (As a separate matter, the auditors could "search for unrecorded liabilities," but they already know about the deferred accounting fees, anyway.)

Discovery Summary

By performing the procedures outlined above, the manager and senior and staff accountants on the engagement discovered all the questionable and improper accounting. However, the partners in the firm insisted on rendering unqualified opinions on the SaCom financial statements without adjustment. One partner owned 300 shares of the company's stock in the name of a relative (without the consent or knowledge of the relative). Another audit partner later arranged a bank loan to the company to get $125,000 to pay past-due audit fees. This partner and another, and both their wives, guaranteed the loan. (When the bank later disclosed the guarantee in a bank confirmation obtained in the course of a subsequent SaCom audit, the confirmation was removed from the audit working paper file and destroyed.)

The SEC investigated, and, among other things, barred the audit firm for a period (about six months) from accepting new audit clients who would file financial statements with the SEC. The SEC also barred the partners involved in supervising various portions of the audit work from involvement with new audit clients for various periods of time. (Adapted: ASR 196.) In addition the partners had violated several rules of professional conduct and are therefore subject to disciplinary action by their provincial institute (see Chapter 15 for discussion of Rules of Professional Conduct).

R E V I E W
C H E C K P O I N T S

11.16 In a production situation similar to the Western Corporation in the "Unbundled Before Its Time" case, what substantive audit work should be done on a sample of completed production orders (cost reports) recorded as cost of goods sold?

11.17 What red flag is raised when a company has an "unbilled contract revenue" account in its general ledger?

11.18 Why should auditors always select the client's adjusting journal entries for detail audit?

11.19 Is there anything wrong about auditors helping clients obtain bank loans to pay their accounting firm's fees?

PART II: PAYROLL CYCLE TYPICAL ACTIVITIES
· · · · · · · · · · · ·

LEARNING OBJECTIVE

4. Describe the payroll cycle, including typical
   source documents and
   controls.

Every company has a payroll. It may include manufacturing labour, research scientists, administrative personnel, or all of these. Subsidiary operations, partnerships, and joint ventures may call it "management fees" charged by a parent company or general partner. Payroll can take different forms. Personnel management and the payroll accounting cycle not only include transactions that affect the wage and salary accounts but also the transactions that affect pension benefits, deferred compensation contracts, compensatory stock option plans, employee benefits (such as health insurance), payroll taxes, and related liabilities for these costs.

Exhibit 11–6 shows a payroll cycle. It starts with hiring (and firing) people and determining their wage rates and deductions, then proceeds to attendance and work (timekeeping), and ends with payment followed by preparation of governmental (tax) and internal reports. One of these internal reports is a report of labour cost to the cost accounting department, which is how the payroll cycle is linked with cost

EXHIBIT 11–6   PAYROLL CYCLE

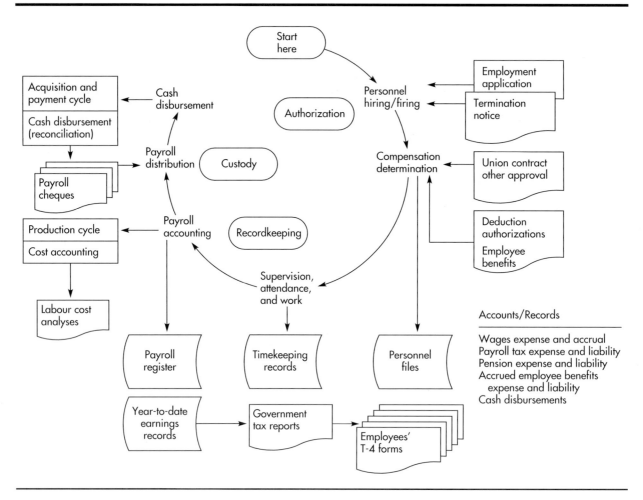

Approval of Fictitious Overtime

A supervisor at Austin Stoneworks discovered that she could approve overtime hours even though an employee had not worked 40 regular-time hours. She made a deal with several employees to alter their work timecards and split the extra payments. Over a 12-year period, the supervisor and her accomplices embezzled $107,000 in excess payments.

The employees' time cards were not reviewed after being approved by the supervisor. The company's payroll computer program did not have a valid data combination test that paid overtime only after 40 regular-time hours were paid.

---

accounting in the production cycle. Five functional responsibilities should be performed by separate people or departments. They are:

- Personnel and Labour Relations—hiring and firing.
- Supervision—approval of work time.
- Timekeeping and Cost Accounting—payroll preparation and cost accounting.
- Payroll Accounting—cheque preparation and related payroll reports.
- Payroll Distribution—actual custody of cheques and distribution to employees.

The elements that follow are part of the payroll control structure.

Authorization

A personnel or labour relations department that is independent of the other functions should have transaction initiation authority to add new employees to the payroll, to delete terminated employees, to obtain authorizations for deductions (such as insurance, saving bonds, withholding tax exemptions on federal form TD1), and to transmit authority for pay rate changes to the payroll department.

Authorization also takes place in the supervision function. All pay base data (hours, job number, absences, time off allowed for emergencies, and the like) should be approved by an employee's immediate supervisor.

Authorization is also a feature of the timekeeping and cost accounting function. Data on which pay is based (such as hours, piece-rate volume, incentives) should be accumulated independent of other functions.

Custody

The main feature of custody in the payroll cycle is the possession of the paycheques, cash, or electronic transfer codes used to pay people. (Electronic transfer codes refer to the practice by some organizations of transferring pay directly into employees' bank accounts.) A payroll distribution function should control the delivery of pay to employees so that unclaimed cheques, cash, or incomplete electronic transfers are not returned to persons involved in any of the other functions.

There are elements of custody of important documents in the supervision function and in the timekeeping function. Supervisors usually have access to time cards or time sheets that provide the basis for payment to hourly workers. Likewise, the timekeeping devices (e.g., time clocks, supervisory approval of time cards or time sheets, electronic punch-in systems) have a type of custody of employees' time-base for payroll calculations.

Recordkeeping

The **payroll accounting** function should prepare individual paycheques, pay envelopes, or electronic transfers using rate and deduction information supplied by the personnel function and base data supplied by the timekeeping-supervision functions. Persons in charge of the authorization and custody functions should not also prepare the payroll. They might be tempted to pay fictitious employees.

Payroll accounting maintains individual year-to-date earnings records and prepares the provincial and federal tax reports (income tax and Canada or Quebec Pension Plan withholding, unemployment insurance reports, and annual T-4 forms). The payroll tax returns (e.g., federal T-4 summary that reports taxes withheld, unemployment insurance returns) and the annual T-4 summary to employees are useful records for audit recalculation and overall testing (analytical) procedures. They should correspond to company records. Most company employees responsible for these reports are reluctant to manipulate them.

Periodic Reconciliation

The payroll bank account can be reconciled like any other bank account. Otherwise, there is not much to count or observe in payroll to accomplish a traditional reconciliation—comparing "real payroll" to recorded wage cost and expense. However, one kind of reconciliation in the form of feedback to the supervision function can be placed in operation. Some companies send to each supervisor a copy of the payroll register, showing the employees paid under the supervisor's authority and responsibility. The supervisor gets a chance to reapprove the payroll after it is completed. This provides an opportunity to notice whether any persons not approved have been paid and charged to the supervisor's accountability.

The payroll report sent to cost accounting can be reconciled to the labour records used to charge labour cost to production. The cost accounting function should determine whether the labour paid is the same as the labour cost used in the cost accounting calculations.

Employees on Fixed Salary

The functional duties and responsibilities described above relate primarily to non-salaried (hourly) employees. For salaried employees, the system is simplified by not having to collect timekeeping data. In nonmanufacturing businesses, the cost accounting operations may be very simple or even nonexistent.

The relative importance of each of the above five areas should be determined for each engagement in light of the nature and organization of the company's operations.

· ·

R E V I E W
C H E C K P O I N T S

11.20 What functional responsibilities are associated with the payroll cycle?

11.21 Describe a "walk-through" of the payroll transaction flow from hiring authorization to payroll cheque disbursement. What document copies would be collected? What controls noted?

11.22 In a payroll system, which duties should be separated?

NOT ENOUGH CONTROL, NO FEEDBACK, BYE-BYE MONEY

Homer had been in payroll accounting for a long time. He knew it was not uncommon to pay a terminated employee severance benefits and partial pay after termination. Homer received the termination notices and the data for the final paycheques. But Homer also knew how to keep the terminated employee on the payroll for another week, pay a full week's compensation, change the electronic transfer code, and take the money for himself. The only things he could not change were the personnel department's copy of the termination notices, the payroll register, and the individual employee pay records used for withholding tax and TD1 forms.

Fortunately, nobody reconciled the cost accounting labour charges to the payroll. The supervisors did not get a copy of the payroll register for postpayment approval, so they did not have any opportunity to notice the extra week. Nobody ever reviewed the payroll with reference to the termination notices. Former employees never complained about more pay and withholding reported on their T-4s than they actually received.

Homer and his wife Marge retired comfortably to a villa in Spain on a nest egg that had grown to $450,000. After his retirement, the company experienced an unexpected decrease in labour costs and higher profits.

11.23 What features of a payroll system can be expected to prevent or detect payment of a fictitious employee? omission of payment to an employee?

· ·

AUDIT EVIDENCE IN MANAGEMENT REPORTS AND FILES
· · · · · · · · · · · · ·

Payroll systems produce numerous reports. Some are internal reports and bookkeeping records. Others are government tax reports.

Personnel Files
The personnel and labour relations department keeps individual employee files. The contents usually include an employment application, a background investigation report, a notice of hiring, a job classification with pay rate authorization, and authorizations for deductions (e.g., health insurance, life insurance, retirement contribution, union dues, T-4 form for income tax exemptions). When employees retire, quit, or are otherwise terminated, appropriate notices of termination are filed. These files contain the raw data for important pension and post-retirement benefit accounting involving an employee's age, tenure with the company, wage record, and other information used in actuarial calculations.

A personnel file should establish the reality of a person's existence and employment. The background investigation report (prior employment, references, Social Insurance number validity check, credentials investigation, perhaps a private investi-

---

WHERE DID HE COME FROM?

The controller defrauded the company for several million dollars. As it turned out, he was no controller at all. He didn't know a debit from a credit. The fraudster had been fired from five previous jobs where money had turned up missing. He was discovered one evening when the president showed up unexpectedly at the company and found a stranger in the office with the controller. The stranger was doing all of the accounting for the bogus controller.

Source: National Association of Certified Fraud Examiners, "Auditing for Fraud."

---

gator's report) is important for employees in such sensitive positions as accounting, finance, and asset custody. One of the primary system controls is capable personnel. Experience is rich with errors, irregularities, and frauds perpetrated by people who falsify their credentials (identification, education, prior experience, criminal record, and the like). An additional protection from this risk is to obtain a suretyship bond for employees through an insurance company.

Timekeeping Records

Employees paid by the hour or on various incentive systems require records of time, production, piecework, or other measures of the basis for their pay. (Salaried employees do not require such detail records.) Timekeeping or similar records are collected in a variety of ways. The old-fashioned time clock is still used. It accepts an employee's time card and imprints the time when work started and ended. More sophisticated systems perform the same function without the paper time card. Production employees may clock in for various jobs or production processes in the system for assigning labour cost to various stages of production. These records are part of the cost accounting for production labour.

Timekeeping records should be approved by supervisors. This approval is a sign that employees actually worked the hours (or produced the output) reported to the payroll department. The payroll department should find a supervisor's signature or initials on the documents used as the basis for periodic pay. In computer systems this approval may be automatic by virtue of the supervisory passwords used to input data into a computerized payroll system.

Payroll Register

The payroll "register" is a special journal. It typically contains a row for each employee with columns for the gross regular pay, gross overtime pay, income tax withheld, Employment Insurance (EI) and Canada Pension Plan (CPP) or Quebec Pension Plan (QPP) withheld, other deductions, and net pay. The net pay amount usually is transferred from the general bank account to a special imprest payroll bank account. The journal entry for the transfer of net payroll, for example, is:

```
Payroll Bank Account . . . . . . . . . . . . . . . . . . . . . 25,774
        General Bank Account . . . . . . . . . . . . . . . . . . . . . . . . . 25,774
```

The payroll cheque amounts are accumulated to create the payroll posting to the general ledger, like this example:

Look at the Endorsements

An assistant accountant was instructed to "look at" the endorsements on the backs of a sample of cancelled payroll cheques.

She noticed three occurrences of the payee's signature followed by a second signature. Although scrawled almost illegibly, the second signatures were identical and were later identified as the payroll accountant's handwriting. The payroll accountant had taken unclaimed cheques and converted (stolen) them. When cashing these "third-party cheques," banks and stores had required the payroll accountant to produce identification and endorse the cheques that already had been "endorsed" by the employee payee.

The lesson: Second endorsements are a red flag.

Wages clearing account 40,265
     Employee income taxes payable 7,982
     Employee Canada Pension plan 3,080
     Employment Insurance premium
        payable 2,100
     Life insurance premium payable 1,329
     Payroll bank account 25,774

The payroll register is the primary original record for payroll accounting. It contains the implicit assertions that the employees are real company personnel (existence assertion), that they worked the time or production for which they were paid (rights/ownership assertion), that the amount of the pay is calculated properly (valuation assertion), and that all the employees were paid (completeness assertion). The presentation and disclosure assertion depends on the labour cost analysis explained below.

Payroll department records also contain the cancelled cheques (or a similar electronic-deposit record). The cheques will contain the employees' endorsements on the back.

Labour Cost Analysis

The cost accounting department can receive its information in more than one way. Some companies have systems that independently report time and production work data from the production floor directly to the cost accounting department. Other companies let their cost accounting department receive labour cost data from the payroll department. When the data is received independently, it can be reconciled in quantity (time) or amount (dollars) with a report from the payroll department. This is a type of reconciliation to make sure the cost accounting department is using actual payroll data and that the payroll department is paying only for work performed.

The cost accounting department (or a similar accounting function) is responsible for the "cost distribution." This is the most important part of the presentation and disclosure assertion with respect to payroll. The cost distribution is an assignment of payroll to the accounts where it belongs for internal and external reporting. Using its input data, the cost accounting department may make a distribution entry like this:

Beware the "Clearing Account"

"Clearing accounts" are temporary storage places for transactions awaiting final accounting. Like the wages clearing account illustrated in the entries above, all clearing accounts should have zero balances after the accounting is completed.

A balance in a clearing account means that some amounts have not been classified properly in the accounting records. If the wages clearing account has a debit balance, some labour cost has not been properly classified in the expense accounts or cost accounting classifications. If the wages clearing account has a credit balance, the cost accountant has assigned more labour cost to expense accounts and cost accounting classifications than the amount actually paid.

Production job A	14,364
Production job B	3,999
Production process A	10,338
Selling expense	8,961
General and administrative expense	2,603
Wages clearing account	40,265

Payroll data flows from the hiring process, through the timekeeping function, into the payroll department, thence to the cost accounting department, and finally to the accounting entries that record the payroll for inventory cost determination and financial statement presentation. The same data is used for various governmental and tax reports.

Governmental and Tax Reports
Payroll systems have complications introduced by the provincial and federal income and pension plan laws. Several reports are produced. These can be used by auditors in tests of controls and substantive tests of the balances produced by accumulating numerous payroll transactions.

Year-to-date Earnings Records
The year-to-date (YTD) earnings records are the cumulative subsidiary records of each employee's gross pay, deductions, and net pay. Each time a periodic payroll is produced, the YTD earnings records are updated for the new information. The YTD earnings records are a subsidiary ledger of the wages and salaries cost and expense in the financial statements. Theoretically, like any subsidiary and control account relationship, their sum (e.g., the gross pay amounts) should be equal to the costs and expenses in the financial statements. The trouble with this reconciliation idea is that there are usually many payroll cost/expense accounts in a company's chart of accounts. The production wages may be scattered about in several different accounts, such as inventory (work in process and finished goods), selling, general, and administrative expenses.

However, these YTD records provide the data for periodic governmental and tax forms. They usually can be reconciled to the tax reports.

Companies in financial difficulty have been known to try to postpone payment of employee taxes, UIC, and CPP or QPP withheld. However, the consequences can be serious. Revenue Canada can and will padlock the business and seize the assets for nonpayment. After all, the withheld taxes belong to the employee's accounts with the government, and the employers are obligated to pay over the amounts withheld from employees along with a matching share for the Canada Pension Plan.

Employee T-4 Reports

The T-4 slip is the annual report of gross salaries and wages and the income, pension plan, and Employment Insurance withheld. Copies are filed with the Canada (or Quebec) Pension Plan and Revenue Canada, and copies are sent to employees for use in preparing their income tax returns. The T-4s contain the annual YTD accumulations for each employee. They also contain each employee's address and Social Insurance number. In certain procedures (described later), auditors can use the name, address, Social Insurance number, and dollar amounts to obtain evidence about the existence of employees. The T-4s can be reconciled to the payroll tax reports.

· ·

R E V I E W
C H E C K P O I N T S

11.24   What important information can be found in employees' personnel files?

11.25   What is important about background checks using the employment applications submitted by prospective employees?

11.26   What payroll cycle documentation supports the validity and accuracy of payroll transactions?

11.27   Which government tax returns can be reconciled in total with employees' year-to-date earnings records? reconciled in total, but not in detail?

11.28   What is the purpose of examining endorsements on the back of payroll cheques?

· ·

CONTROL RISK ASSESSMENT

· · · · · · · · · · · · ·

LEARNING   OBJECTIVE

5. Give examples of detail test of controls procedures for auditing the controls over payroll.

The major risks in the payroll cycle are:

- Paying fictitious "employees" (invalid transactions, employees do not exist).
- Overpaying for time or production (inaccurate transactions, improper valuation).
- Incorrect accounting for costs and expenses (incorrect classification, improper or inconsistent presentation and disclosure).

The assessment of payroll system control risk normally takes on added importance because most companies have fairly elaborate and well-controlled personnel and payroll functions. The transactions in this cycle are numerous during the year yet result in small amounts in balance sheet accounts at year-end. Therefore, in most audit engagements the review of controls and test of controls audit of transaction details constitute the major portion of the evidence gathered for these accounts. On most audits the substantive audit procedures devoted to auditing the payroll-related account balances are very limited.

General Control Considerations

Control procedures for proper segregation of responsibilities should be in place and operating. By referring to Exhibit 11–6, you can see that proper segregation involves authorization (personnel department hiring and firing, pay rate and deduction authorizations) by persons who do not have payroll preparation, paycheque distribution, or reconciliation duties. Payroll distribution (custody) is in the hands of persons who neither authorize employees' pay rates or time, nor prepare the payroll cheques. Recordkeeping is performed by payroll and cost accounting personnel who do not make authorizations or distribute pay. Combinations of two or more of the duties of authorization, payroll preparation and recordkeeping, and payroll distribution in one person, one office, or one computerized system may open the door for errors, irregularities, and frauds.

In addition, the control structure should provide for detail control checking procedures. For example: (1) periodic comparison of the payroll register to the personnel department files to check hiring authorizations and terminated employees not deleted, (2) periodic rechecking of wage rate and deduction authorizations, (3) reconciliation of time and production paid to cost accounting calculations, (4) reconciliation of YTD earnings records with tax returns, and (5) payroll bank account reconciliation.

Computer-based Payroll

Complex computer systems to gather payroll data, calculate payroll amounts, print cheques, and transfer electronic deposits may be found in many companies. Even though the technology is complex, the basic management and control functions of ensuring a flow of data to the payroll department should be in place. Various paper records and approval signatures may not exist. They may all be imbedded in computerized payroll systems. Matters of auditing in a complex computer environment will need to be considered (refer to Chapter 19).

Internal Control Questionnaire

Information about the payroll cycle control structure often is gathered initially by completing an internal control questionnaire (ICQ). An ICQ for general (manual) controls is in Appendix 11A–2. This questionnaire can be studied for details of desirable control policies and procedures. It is organized with headings that identify the important control objectives—environment, validity, completeness, authorization, accuracy, classification, accounting, and proper period recording. Problem 11.62 at the end of the chapter presents a computerized payroll system and asks for identification of control weaknesses (reference to control features in Chapters 6 and 8 will help).

Detail Test of Controls Audit Procedures

An organization should have detail control procedures in place and operating to prevent, detect, and correct accounting errors. You studied the general control objectives in Chapter 6 (validity, completeness, authorization, accuracy, classification, accounting, and proper period recording). Exhibit 11–7 puts these in the perspective of the payroll functions with examples of specific objectives. You should study this exhibit carefully. It expresses the general control objectives with specific examples related to payroll.

EXHIBIT 11–7   CONTROL OBJECTIVES (personnel and payroll cycle)

General Objectives	Examples of Specific Objectives
1. Recorded payroll transactions are *valid* and documented.	Payroll accounting separated from personnel and timekeeping. Time cards indicate approval by supervisor's signature. Payroll files compared to personnel files periodically.
2. Valid payroll transactions are *recorded* and none are omitted.	Employees' complaints about paycheques investigated and resolved (written records maintained and reviewed by internal auditors).
3. Payroll names, rates, hours, and deductions are *authorized*.	Names of new hires or terminations reported immediately in writing to payroll by the personnel department. Authorization for deductions kept on file. Rate authorized by union contract, agreement, or written policy and approved by personnel officer.
4. Payroll computations contain *accurate* gross pay, deductions, and net pay.	Payroll computations checked by person independent of preparation. Totals of payroll register reconciled to totals of payroll distribution by cost accounting.
5. Payroll transactions are *classified* correctly as direct or indirect labour or other expenses.	Employee classification reviewed periodically. Overall charges to indirect labour compared to direct labour and total product costs periodically.
6. Payroll transaction *accounting* is complete.	Details of employee withholding reconciled periodically to liability control accounts and tax returns. Employee tax expense and liabilities prepared in conjunction with payroll.
7. Payroll costs and expenses are recorded in the *proper period*.	Month-end accruals reviewed by internal auditors. Payroll computed, paid, and booked in timely manner.

Auditors can perform detail test of controls audit procedures to determine whether controls that are said to be in place and operating actually are being performed properly by company personnel. A detail test of control procedure consists of (1) identification of the data population from which a sample of items will be selected for audit and (2) an expression of the action that will be taken to produce relevant evidence. In general, the actions in detail test of control audit procedures involve vouching, tracing, observing, scanning, and recalculating. A specification of such procedures is part of an audit program for obtaining evidence useful in a final control risk assessment. If personnel in the organization are not performing their control

---

COVERT SURVEILLANCE

This sounds like spy work, and it indeed has certain elements of it.

Auditors can test controls over employees' clocking into work shifts by making personal observations of the process—observing whether anybody clocks in with two time cards or with two or more electronic entries, or leaves the premises after clocking in.

The auditors need to be careful not to make themselves obvious. Standing around in a manufacturing plant at 6 A.M. in the standard blue pinstripe suit uniform is as good as printing "Beware of Auditor" on your forehead. People then will be on their best behaviour, and you will observe nothing unusual.

Find an unobtrusive observation post. Stay out of sight. Use a video camera. Get a knowledgeable office employee to accompany you to interpret various activities. Perform an observation that has a chance of producing evidence of improper behaviour.

procedures very well, auditors will need to design additional procedures to try to detect whether control failures have produced payments to fictitious employees, overpayments for time or production, or incorrect accounting for costs and expenses.

Exhibit 11–8 contains a selection of detail test of controls audit procedures for auditing controls over payroll. Most of the illustrative procedures involve manual records, and B-5 refers to computerized systems. The samples are usually attribute samples designed along the lines you studied in Chapter 7, although payroll testing also can be designed in terms of variables sampling for substantive evidence of dollar errors and irregularities (also in Chapter 7). On the right, Exhibit 11–8 shows the control objectives tested by the audit procedures.

E X H I B I T   11–8   TEST OF CONTROLS AUDIT PROCEDURES FOR PAYROLL

	Control Objective
A. Personnel Files and Compensation Documents	
1. Select a sample of personnel files:	
a. Review personnel files for complete information on employment date, authority to add to payroll, job classification, wage rate, and authorized deductions.	Authorization Classification Authorization
b. Trace pay rate to union contracts or other rate authorization. Trace salaries to directors' minutes for authorization.	Authorization Authorization
c. Trace pay rate and deduction information to payroll department files used in payroll preparation.	Completeness
2. Obtain copies of pension plans, stock options, profit sharing, and bonus plans. Review and extract relevant portions that relate to payroll deductions, fringe benefit expenses, accrued liabilities, and financial statement disclosure.	Validity Completeness Authorization Accuracy Accounting
B. Payroll	
1. Select a sample of payroll register entries:	
a. Vouch employee identification, pay rate, and deductions to personnel files or other authorizations.	Authorization
b. Vouch hours worked to clock time cards and supervisor's approval.	Validity Authorization
c. Recalculate gross pay, deductions, net pay.	Accuracy
d. Recalculate a selection of periodic payrolls.	Accuracy
e. Vouch to cancelled payroll cheque. Examine employees' endorsement.	Accuracy Validity
2. Select a sample of clock time cards. Note supervisor's approval and trace to periodic payroll registers.	Authorization Completeness
3. Vouch a sample of periodic payroll totals to payroll bank account transfer vouchers and vouch payroll bank account deposit slip for cash transfer.	Accounting
4. Trace a sample of employees' payroll entries to individual payroll records maintained for tax reporting purposes. Reconcile total of employees' payroll records with payrolls paid for the year.	Completeness Accuracy
5. Review computer-printed error messages for evidence of the use of check digits, valid codes, limit tests, and other input, processing, and output application controls. Investigate correction and resolution of errors.	
6. Trace payroll information to management reports and to general ledger account postings.	Accounting
7. Obtain control of a periodic payroll and conduct a surprise distribution of paycheques.	Validity
C. Cost Distribution Reports	
1. Select a sample of cost accounting analyses of payroll:	
a. Reconcile periodic totals with payroll payments for the same periods.	Completeness
b. Vouch to time records.	Validity
2. Trace cost accounting labour cost distributions to management reports and postings in general ledger and subsidiary account(s).	Accounting Classification
3. Select a sample of labour cost items in (a) ledger accounts and/or (b) management reports. Vouch to supporting cost accounting analyses.	Validity

Direction of the Test of Controls Procedures

The test of controls procedures in Exhibit 11–8 are designed to test the payroll accounting in two directions. One is the completeness direction, in which the control performance of audit interest is the matching of personnel file content to payroll department files and the payroll register. Exhibit 11–9 shows that the sample for this direction is taken from the population of personnel files. The procedures trace the personnel department authorizations to the payroll department files (procedure A-1–c).

The other direction is the validity direction of the test. The control performance of interest is the preparation of the payroll register. Exhibit 11–9 shows that the sample for this test is from the completed payroll registers. The individual payroll calculations are vouched to the personnel files (procedure B-1–a).

Computerized Payroll Processing

Payroll processing and payroll register preparation are usually the first computer applications a business implements. Payroll preparation is basically the same for all businesses, and many off-the-shelf computer programs are available. The files in a personnel and payroll database and the related record files (data elements) auditors should expect to find include:

- Reference files:
    Personnel master—employee name and number, date hired, education, skills, employment history, tax withholding factors.
    Payroll master—employee number, name, department, address, compensation class, deduction codes.
    Compensation table—compensation classes matched to hourly rates.
    Deduction tables—deduction codes matched to amounts or formulas.

E X H I B I T   11–9   **DUAL DIRECTION TEST OF PAYROLL CONTROLS**

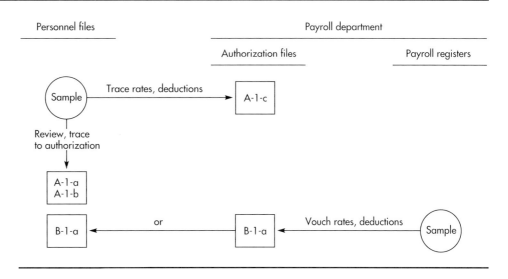

Overt Surveillance

Surprise Payroll Distribution

Auditors may perform a surprise observation of a payroll distribution in connection with tests for overstatement. Such an observation involves taking control of paycheques and accompanying a company representative as the distribution takes place. The auditor is careful to see that each employee is identified and that only one cheque is given to each individual. Unclaimed cheques are controlled, and in this manner the auditor hopes to detect any fictitious persons on the payroll. Auditors need to be extremely careful to notice any duplication of employee identification or instance of one person attempting to pick up two or more cheques.

- Dynamic files:

    Employee earnings records—employee number, compensation class, gross pay (YTD), deductions (YTD), net pay (YTD).

    Deduction, withholding, and tax—employee number, Social Insurance number, tax (QTD and YTD).

    Time card transactions—employee number, compensation class, hours (regular and overtime), time period, shop, or department.

    Cost distribution—job or department, employee number, job or process number, labour costs, benefit costs.

Generalized audit software can be used extensively in the test of controls procedures in the payroll cycle. Files can be matched (e.g., personnel master file and payroll master file), and unmatched records and differences in common fields can be printed out. Statistical samples of files can be selected and printed for vouching to union contracts or to other authorizations. Statistical samples can be selected for recalculation, using the generalized software or printed out as working papers for tracing and vouching, using the procedures in Exhibit 11–8.

In both manual and computer systems, the test of controls audit of transaction details is highly important because the evidence bears heavily on the reliability of internal management reports and analyses. In turn, reliance on these reports and analyses, along with other analytical relationships, constitutes a major portion of the substantive audit of payroll, compensation costs, and labour costs assigned to inventory and costs of goods sold.

The test of controls procedures are designed to produce evidence of the following:

- Adequacy of personnel files, especially the authorizations of pay rate and deductions used in calculating pay.

- Accuracy of the periodic payrolls recorded in accounts and in employees' cumulative wage records. The procedures tend to centre on the periodic payroll registers.

- Accuracy of cost accounting distributions and management reports. The cost accounting for labour costs must be reasonably accurate because good management reports contribute to cost control. The auditor who wishes to rely on the cost accounting system must determine whether it contains and transmits accurate information.

Computerized payroll and cost accounting systems are encountered frequently. Their complexity, however, ranges from an application of simply writing payroll cheques to an integrated system that prepares management reports and cost analyses based on payroll and cost distribution inputs. Computerized audit techniques, such as the use of test data, frequently are employed to test controls in such systems. Parallel simulation may be applied efficiently to test an integrated system. Refer to Chapter 8 for an explanation of these computerized procedures.

Summary: Control Risk Assessment

The audit manager or senior accountant in charge of the audit should evaluate the evidence obtained from an understanding of the internal control structure and from the test of controls audit procedures. If the control risk is assessed very low, the substantive audit procedures on the account balances can be limited in cost-saving ways. As examples: a surprise payroll distribution may be considered unnecessary; the auditors may decide it is appropriate to place considerable reliance on management reports generated by the payroll system.

On the other hand, if tests of controls reveal weaknesses, improper segregation of duties, inaccurate cost reports, inaccurate tax returns, or lax personnel policies, then substantive procedures will need to be designed to lower the risk of failing to detect material error in the financial statements. The problem in payroll is that the irregularities of paying fictitious employees and overpaying for fraudulent time records do not normally misstate the financial statements as long as the improper payments are expensed. (The losses are expensed, as they should be!) The only misstatement is failing to distinguish and disclose "payroll fraud losses" from legitimate wages expense and cost of goods sold, but such losses are usually immaterial in a single year's financial statements, anyway. Nevertheless, auditors habitually perform procedures designed to find payroll fraud. It is more of a service to clients than a crucial part of the effort to detect material misstatements in financial statements.

. . . .

R E V I E W
C H E C K P O I N T S

11.29 What are the most common errors and irregularities in the personnel and payroll cycle? Which control characteristics are auditors looking for to prevent or detect these errors?

11.30 What's wrong with an auditor standing by the plant gate and time clock at starting time to observe employees checking in for work shifts?

11.31 How can an auditor determine whether the amount of labour cost charged to production was actually paid to employees?

11.32 Why might an auditor conduct a surprise observation of a payroll distribution? What should be observed?

11.33 Assume the processing of payroll is accomplished with a computer utilizing the files described in this chapter. Which files could be matched for audit purposes utilizing generalized audit software?

· ·

AUDIT CASES: SUBSTANTIVE AUDIT PROCEDURES
· · · · · · · · · · · ·

LEARNING OBJECTIVE

6. Describe some common errors, irregularities, and frauds in payroll, and design some audit and investigation procedures for detecting them.

The audit of account balances consists of procedural efforts to detect errors, irregularities, and frauds that may exist in the balances, thus making them misleading in financial statements. If such misstatements exist, they are characterized by the following features:

Method: A cause of the misstatement (accidental error, intentional irregularities, or fraud attempt), which usually is made easier by some kind of failure of controls.

Paper trail: A set of telltale signs of erroneous accounting, missing or altered documents, or a "dangling debit" (the false or erroneous debit that results from an overstatement of assets).

Amount: The dollar amount of overstated assets and revenue, or understated liabilities and expenses.

Each audit program for the audit of an account balance or class of transactions like payroll contains an audit approach that may enable auditors to detect errors, irregularities, and frauds. Each application of procedures contains these elements:

Audit objective: A recognition of a financial statement assertion for which evidence needs to be obtained. The assertions are about existence of assets, liabilities, revenue, and expenses; their valuation, their complete inclusion in the account balances; the rights and obligations inherent in them; and their proper presentation and disclosure in the financial statements. (These assertions were introduced in Chapter 9.)

Control: A recognition of the control procedures that should be used by an organization to prevent and detect errors and irregularities.

Test of controls: Ordinary and extended procedures designed to produce evidence about the effectiveness of the controls that should be in operation.

Audit of balance: Ordinary and extended substantive procedures designed to find signs of errors, irregularities, and frauds in account balances and classes of transactions.

The next portion of this chapter consists of two "casettes" (little cases) that first set the stage with a story about an error, irregularity, or fraud—its method, paper trail (if any), and amount. This part of the casette gives you the "inside story," which auditors seldom know before they perform the audit work. The second part of the casette, under the heading of the audit approach, tells a structured story about the audit objective, desirable controls, test of control procedures, audit of balance procedures, and discovery summary. The audit approach segment illustrates the manner in which audit procedures can be applied and the discoveries they may enable auditors to make. At the end of the chapter, some similar discussion cases are presented, and you can write the audit approach to test your ability to design audit procedures for the detection of errors, irregularities, and frauds.

CASETTE 11.3
TIME CARD FORGERIES

Problem

False claims for work time caused the overpayment of wages.

Method

A personnel leasing agency assigned Nurse Jane to work at Municipal Hospital. She claimed payroll hours on agency time cards, which showed approval signatures of a county nursing shift supervisor. The shift supervisor had been terminated by the county several months prior to the periods covered by the time cards in question. Nurse Jane worked one or two days per week but submitted time cards for a full 40-hour work week.

    The leasing agency paid Nurse Jane, then billed Municipal Hospital for the wages and benefits. Supporting documents were submitted with the leasing agency's bills.

Paper Trail

Each hospital work station keeps ward shift logs, which are sign-in sheets showing nurses on duty at all times. Nurses sign in and sign out when going on and going off duty.

    Municipal Hospital maintains personnel records showing, among other things, the period of employment of its own nurses, supervisors, and other employees.

Amount

Nurse Jane's wages and benefits were billed to the hospital at $22 per hour. False time cards overcharging about 24 extra hours per week cost the hospital $528 per week. Nurse Jane was assigned to Municipal Hospital for 15 weeks during the year, so she caused overcharges of about $7,900. However, she told three of her crooked friends about the procedure, and they overcharged the hospital another $24,000.

AUDIT APPROACH

Audit Objective

Obtain evidence to determine whether wages were paid to valid employees for actual time worked at the authorized pay rate.

Control

Control procedures should include a hiring authorization putting employees on the payroll. When leased employees are used, this authorization includes contracts for nursing time, conditions of employment, and terms including the contract reimbursement rate. Control records of attendance and work should be kept (ward shift log). Supervisors should approve time cards or other records used by the payroll department to prepare paycheques.

    In this case the contract with the leasing agency provided that approved time cards had to be submitted as supporting documentation for the agency billings.

Test of Controls

Although the procedures and documents for control were in place, the controls did not operate because nobody at the hospital ever compared the ward shift logs to time cards, and nobody examined the supervisory approval signatures for their validity. The scam was easy in the leasing agency situation because the nurses submitted their own time cards to the agency for payment. The same scam might be operated by the hospital's own employees if they, too, could write their time cards and submit them to the payroll department.

    Auditors should make enquiries (e.g., internal control questionnaire) about the error-checking procedures performed by hospital accounting personnel. Test of control audit procedures are designed to determine whether control procedures are followed properly by the organization. Since the comparison and checking procedures were not performed, there is nothing to test.

    However, the substantive tests described below are identical to the procedures that could be called "tests of controls," but in this case they are performed to determine whether nurses were paid improperly (a substantive purpose).

Audit of Balances

Select a sample of leasing agency billings and their supporting documentation (time cards). Vouch rates billed by the agency to the contract for agreement to proper rate. Vouch time claimed to hospital work attendance records (ward shift logs). Obtain handwriting examples of supervisors' signatures and compare them to the approval signatures on time cards. Use personnel records to determine whether supervisors were actually employed by the hospital at the time they approved the time cards. Use available work attendance records to determine whether supervisors were actually on duty at the time they approved the time cards.

Discovery Summary

The auditors quickly found that Nurse Jane (and others) had not signed in on ward shift logs for days they claimed to have worked. Further investigation showed that the supervisors who supposedly signed the time cards were not even employed by the hospital at the time their signatures were used for approvals. Handwriting comparison showed that the signatures were not written by the supervisors.

The leasing agency was informed and refunded the $31,900 overpayment proved by the auditors. The auditors continued to comb the records for more! (Adapted from vignette published in *Internal Auditor*, April 1990.)

Casette 11.4
The Well-padded Payroll

Problem

Embezzlement with fictitious people on the payroll.

Method

Maybelle had responsibility for preparing personnel files for new hires, approval of wages, verification of time cards, and distribution of payroll cheques. She "hired" fictitious employees, faked their records, and ordered cheques through the payroll system. She deposited some cheques in several personal bank accounts and cashed others, endorsing all of them with the names of the fictitious employees and her own.

Paper Trail

Payroll creates a large paper trail with individual earnings records, T-4 tax forms, payroll deductions for taxes, insurance, and pension plans, and payroll tax reports. She mailed all the T-4 forms to the same post office box.

Amount

Maybelle stole $160,000 by creating some "ghosts," usually 3 to 5 out of 112 people on the payroll, and paying them an average of $256 per week for three years. Sometimes the ghosts quit and were later replaced by others. But she stole "only" about 2 percent of the payroll funds during the period.

AUDIT APPROACH

Objective

Obtain evidence of the existence and validity of payroll transactions.

Control

Different people should be responsible for hiring (preparing personnel files), approving wages, and distributing payroll cheques. "Thinking like a crook" leads an auditor to see that Maybelle could put people on the payroll and obtain their cheques.

Test of Controls

Audit for transaction authorization and validity. Random sampling may not work because of the small number of ghosts. Look for the obvious. Select several weeks' cheque blocks, account for numerical sequence (to see whether any cheques have been removed), and examine cancelled cheques for two endorsements.

Audit of Balances

There may be no "balance" to audit other than the accumulated total of payroll transactions, and the total may not appear out of line with history because the fraud is small in relation to total payroll and has been going on for years.

Conduct a surprise payroll distribution; follow up by examining prior cancelled cheques for the missing employees. Scan personnel files for common addresses.

Discovery Summary

Both the surprise distribution and the scan for common addresses provided the names of 2–3 exceptions. Both led to prior cancelled cheques (which Maybelle had not removed and the bank reconciler had not noticed) that carried Maybelle's own name as endorser. Confronted, she confessed.

R E V I E W
C H E C K P O I N T S

11.34 What good are control documents and control procedures if company personnel do not use them to prevent, detect, and correct payroll errors, irregularities, and frauds?

11.35 How can an auditor find out whether payroll control documents and control procedures were followed by client personnel?

11.36 Give some examples of payroll control omissions that would make it easy to "think like a crook" and see opportunities for errors, irregularities, and frauds.

11.37 What difference is there, if any, between tests of controls and tests (audit) of balances in the payroll area?

SUMMARY

The production and payroll cycle consists of two parts that are closely related. Production involves production planning, inventory planning, acquisition of labour, materials, and overhead (acquisition and payment cycle), custody of assets while work is in process and when finished products are stored in inventory, and cost accounting. Payroll is a part of every business and an important part of every production cycle. Management and control of labour costs are important. The payroll cycle consists of hiring, rate authorization, attendance and work supervision, payroll processing, and paycheque distribution.

Production and payroll information systems produce many internal documents, reports, and files. A dozen or more of these sources of audit information were described in the chapter. This cycle is characterized by having mostly internal documentation as evidence and by having relatively little external documentary evidence. Aside from the physical inventory in the production process, the accounts in the production and payroll cycle are intangible. They cannot be observed, inspected, touched, or counted in any meaningful way. Most audit procedures for this cycle are analytical procedures and dual-purpose procedures that test both the company's control procedures and the existence, valuation, and completeness assertions made by accumulating the results of numerous labour and overhead transactions.

Companies reduce control risk by having a suitable separation of authorization, custody, recording, and periodic reconciliation duties. Error-checking procedures of analysing production orders and finished production cost reports are important for proper determination of inventory values and proper valuation of cost of goods sold. Without these procedures, many things could go wrong, ranging from overvaluing the inventory to understating costs of production by deferring costs that should be expensed.

Cost accounting is a central feature of the production cycle. Illustrative cassettes in this chapter told the stories of financial reporting manipulations and of the audit procedures that detected them.

Payroll accounting is a critical operation for expenditure control. Many cases of embezzlement occur during this process. Illustrative cassettes in the chapter told the stories of some fictitious employee and false-time embezzlements and thefts.

KINGSTON COMPANY

Kingston Case Assignments

11.38 Kingston Company: Payroll Flowchart. The audit manager wants you to prepare a flowchart of the manual payroll system in use for the first part of the year under audit. As you prepare the flowchart, she wants you to enter the circled S- and W-symbols for strengths and weaknesses, as was done in the flowchart in Exhibit 6–11 in Chapter 6.

You have been able to determine the following Kingston personnel and payroll procedures from interviews and from reading Kingston's accounting procedures manual:

1. All hourly employees (clerical and warehouse personnel) are paid biweekly based on hours recorded on time cards maintained by a time clock machine. The time cards are approved by the supervisors. The supervisors take the approved time cards to the payroll department. Salaried employees also are paid biweekly based on a salary schedule approved by the finance committee of the board of directors.

2. The personnel department must approve all new hires, terminations, and hourly rate changes. Forms for each of these actions also are approved by appropriate supervisors and are kept in the personnel office. The personnel clerks notify payroll of the changes by a "payroll change" document.

3. The payroll department maintains the individual employees' payroll records and the forms signed by employees for all pay deductions.

4. Every two weeks, Martha, a clerk in the payroll department, prepares the payroll register (multicopy) from the time cards and the information in the individual payroll records. Martha uses a "write-it-once" system that also prepares a form indicating gross pay, each deduction, net pay, and year-to-date totals. Martha calls this form the "take-home sheet." Willie, a second clerk, checks Martha's work and recalculates the gross pay and all deductions.

5. Two copies of payroll register and the take-home sheets are sent to the accounts payable department, where they are used to prepare a separate voucher for each payroll take-home sheet. The cheques then are prepared. (There is no separate payroll bank account.) Both copies of the payroll register, the voucher, the cheques, and the accompanying take-home sheets are sent to the treasurer's office.

6. Fred Davila, the treasurer, reviews the payroll register and the take-home sheets and compares them to the cheques and signs the cheques. His secretary takes the hourly employees' cheques (and accompanying take-home sheets) to their supervisor for distribution. The salaried employees pick up their cheques from the treasurer's office. One copy of the payroll register representing paid cheques is filed in the treasurer's office. The second copy and the vouchers are marked paid and returned to accounts payable.

7. The supervisors distribute the cheques, holding those not claimed until the employee returns to work.

Required:

a. Prepare the flowchart of the flow of transactions and documents for the Kingston Company. Indicate on the flowchart the strengths (with a circle and the strength number, e.g., S-1) and the weaknesses (with a circle and the weakness number, e.g., W-1).

b. Make a list of any other information you wish you had collected relating to Kingston's payroll procedures.

11.39 Kingston Company: Payroll Bridge Working Paper. The flowchart prepared in 11.38 above is incomplete without a bridge working paper similar to the one illustrated in Chapter 6 (Exhibit 6–12).

Required:

Prepare a bridge working paper describing the strengths and weaknesses identified by number on the payroll flowchart. For each strength, describe at least one test of controls audit procedure that may be used to gather evidence on the control. For each weakness indicate the effect on year-end substantive audit procedures. (You will find some of the test of controls audit procedures in Exhibit 11–8 helpful.)

MULTIPLE-CHOICE QUESTIONS FOR PRACTICE AND REVIEW

11.40 When an auditor tests a company's cost accounting system, the auditor's procedures are designed primarily to determine that:
   a. Quantities on hand have been computed based on acceptable cost accounting techniques that reasonably approximate actual quantities on hand.
   b. Physical inventories are in substantial agreement with book inventories.
   c. The system is in accordance with generally accepted accounting principles and is functioning as planned.
   d. Costs have been properly assigned to finished goods, work in process, and cost of goods sold.

11.41 The auditor tests the quantity of materials charged to work-in-process by vouching these quantities to:
   a. Cost ledgers.
   b. Perpetual inventory records.
   c. Receiving reports.
   d. Material requisition.

11.42 Effective internal control over the payroll function should include procedures that segregate the duties of making salary payments to employees and:
   a. Controlling unemployment insurance claims.
   b. Maintaining employee personnel records.
   c. Approving employee fringe benefits.
   d. Hiring new employees.

11.43 Which of the following is the best way for an auditor to determine that every name on a company's payroll is that of a bona fide employee presently on the job?
   a. Examine personnel records for accuracy and completeness.
   b. Examine employees' names listed on payroll tax returns for agreement with payroll accounting records.
   c. Make a surprise observation of the company's regular distribution of paycheques.
   d. Control the mailing of annual T-4 tax forms to employee addresses in their personnel files.

11.44 It would be appropriate for the payroll accounting department to be responsible for which of the following functions?
   a. Approval of employee time records.
   b. Maintenance of records of employment, discharges, and pay increases.
   c. Preparation of periodic governmental reports as to employees' earnings and withholding taxes.
   d. Temporary retention of unclaimed employee paycheques.

11.45 One of the auditor's objectives in observing the actual distribution of payroll cheques is to determine that every name on the payroll is that of a bona fide employee. The payroll observation is an auditing procedure that is generally performed for which of the following reasons?
   a. The professional standards that are generally accepted require the auditor to perform the payroll observation.

b. The various phases of payroll work are not sufficiently segregated to afford effective internal control.

c. The independent auditor uses personal judgment and decides to observe the payroll distribution on a particular audit.

d. The standards that are generally accepted by the profession are interpreted to mean that payroll observation is expected on an audit unless circumstances dictate otherwise.

11.46 During the year, a bookkeeper perpetrated a theft by preparing erroneous T-4 forms. The bookkeeper's UIC withheld was overstated by $500 and the UIC withheld from all other employees was understated. Which of the following is an audit procedure that would detect such a fraud?

a. Multiplication of the applicable rate by the individual gross taxable earnings.

b. Utilizing Form T-4 and withholding charts to determine whether deductions authorized per pay period agree with amounts deducted per pay period.

c. Footing and crossfooting of the payroll register followed by tracing postings to the general ledger.

d. Vouching cancelled cheques to federal tax report.

11.47 A common audit procedure in the audit of payroll transactions involves vouching selected items from the payroll journal to employee time cards that have been approved by supervisory personnel. This procedure is designed to provide evidence in support of the audit proposition that:

a. Only bona fide employees worked and their pay was properly computed.

b. Jobs on which employees worked and their pay was properly computed.

c. Internal controls relating to payroll disbursements are operating effectively.

d. All employees worked the number of hours for which their pay was computed.

11.48 To minimize the opportunities for fraud, unclaimed cash payroll should be:

a. Deposited in a safe deposit box.

b. Held by the payroll custodian.

c. Deposited in a special bank account.

d. Held by the controller.

11.49 An effective client internal control procedure to prevent lack of agreement between the cost accounting for labour cost is and the payroll paid is:

a. Reconciliation of totals on production job time tickets with job reports by the employees responsible for the specific jobs.

b. Verification of agreement of production job time tickets with employee clock cards by a payroll department employee.

c. Preparation of payroll transaction journal entries by an employee who reports to the personnel department director.

d. Custody of pay rate authorization forms by the supervisor of the payroll department.

(AICPA adapted)

11.50 In a computerized payroll system, an auditor would be least likely to use test data to test controls related to:

a. Missing employee numbers.

b. Proper signature approval of overtime by supervisors.

c. Time tickets with invalid job numbers.

d. Agreement of hours per clock card with hours on time tickets.

(AICPA adapted)

EXHIBIT 11.54–1

Fixed Assets and Amortization

		Asset Cost (000s)				Accumulated Amortization (000s)		
Description	Beginning Balance	Added	Sold	Ending Balance	Beginning Balance	Added	Sold	Ending Balance
Land	10,000			10,000				
Bldg. 1	30,000			30,000	6,857	857		7,714
Bldg. 2		42,000		42,000		800		800
Computer A	5,000		5,000	0	3,750	208	3,958	0
Computer B		3,500		3,500		583		583
Press	1,500			1,500	300	150		450
Auto 1	15		15	0	15		15	0
Auto 2		22		22		2		2
Total	46,515	45,522	5,015	87,022	10,922	2,600	3,973	9,549

EXERCISES AND PROBLEMS

· ·

PRODUCTION AND CONVERSION CYCLE

11.51 ICQ Items: Possible Error or Irregularity Due to Weakness. Refer to the internal control questionnaire (Appendix 11A–1) and assume the answer to each question is no. Prepare a table matching questions to errors or irregularities that could occur because of the absence of the control. Your column headings should be:

Question	Possible Error or Irregularity Due to Weakness

11.52 Test of Controls Audit Procedures Related to Controls and Objectives. Each of the following test of control audit procedures may be performed during the audit of the controls in the production and conversion cycle. For each procedure: (*a*) identify the internal control procedure (strength) being tested, and (*b*) identify the internal control objective(s) being addressed.

1. Balance and reconcile detail production cost sheets to the work-in-process inventory control account.
2. Scan closed production cost sheets for missing numbers in the sequence.
3. Vouch a sample of open and closed production cost sheet entries to (*a*) labour reports and (*b*) issue slips and materials-used reports.
4. Locate the material issue forms. Are they prenumbered? kept in a secure location? available to unauthorized persons?
5. Select several summary journal entries in the work-in-process inventory: (*a*) vouch to weekly labour and material reports and to production cost sheets, and (*b*) trace to control account.
6. Select a sample of the material issue slips in the production department file. Examine for:
   a. Issue date/materials-used report date.
   b. Production order number.
   c. Foreman's signature or initials.
   d. Name and number of material.
   e. Raw material stores clerk's signature or initials.
   f. Matching material requisition in raw material stores file. Note date of requisition.
7. Determine by enquiry and inspection if cost clerks review dates on report of units completed for accounting in the proper period.

11.53 Control over Departmental Labour Cost in a Job-cost System. The Brown Printing Company accounts for the services it performs on a job-cost basis. Most jobs take a week or less to complete and involve two or more of Brown's five operating departments. Actual costs are accumulated by job. To ensure timely billing, however, the company prepares sales invoices based on cost estimates.

Recently, several printing jobs have incurred losses. To avoid future losses, management has decided to focus on cost control at the department level. Since labour is a major element of cost, management has proposed the development of a department labour cost report. This report will originate in the payroll department as part of the biweekly payroll and then go to an accounting clerk for comparison to total labour cost estimates by department. If the actual total department labour costs in a payroll are not much more than the estimated total departmental labour cost during that period, the accounting clerk will send the report to the department foreman. If the accounting clerk concludes that a significant variance exists, the report will be sent to the assistant controller. The assistant controller will investigate the cause when time is available, and recommend corrective action to the production manager.

Required:

Evaluate the proposal:

a. Give at least three common aspects of control with which the department labour cost report proposal complies. Give an example from the case to support each aspect cited.

b. Give at least three common aspects of control with which the departmental labour cost report proposal does not comply. Give an example from the case to support each aspect cited.

(CIA adapted)

11.54 Audit the Fixed Asset and Depreciation Schedule. Bart's Company has prepared the fixed asset and depreciation schedule shown in Exhibit 11.54–1. The following information is available:

- The land was purchased eight years ago when Building 1 was erected. The location was then remote but now is bordered by a major freeway. The appraised value is $35 million.
- Building 1 has an estimated useful life of 35 years and no residual value.
- Building 2 was built by a local contractor this year. It also has an estimated useful life of 35 years and no residual value. The company occupied it on May 1 this year.
- The Computer A system was purchased January 1 six years ago, when the estimated useful life was eight years with no residual value. It was sold on May 1 for $500,000.
- The Computer B system was placed in operation as soon as the Computer A system was sold. It is estimated to be in use for six years with no residual value at the end.
- The company estimated the useful life of the press at 20 years with no residual value.
- Auto 1 was sold during the year for $1,000.
- Auto 2 was purchased on July 1. The company expects to use it five years and then sell it for $2,000.
- All amortization is calculated on the straight-line method using months of service.

Required:

a. Audit the amortization calculations. Are there any errors? Put the errors in the form of an adjusting journal entry, assuming 90 percent of the amortization on the buildings and the press has been charged to cost of goods sold and 10 percent is still capitalized in the inventory, and the other amortization expense is classified as general and administrative expense.

b. List two audit procedures for auditing the fixed asset additions.

c. What will an auditor expect to find in the "gain and loss on sale of assets" account? What amount of cash flow from investing activities will be in the statement of cash flows?

PAYROLL CIRCLE

11.55 ICQ Items: Errors That Could Occur from Control Weaknesses. Refer to the internal control questionnaire on a payroll system (Appendix 11A–2) and assume the answer to each question is no. Prepare a table matching the questions to errors or irregularities that could occur because of the absence of the control. Your column headings should be:

Question Number	Possible Error or Irregularity Due to Weakness

11.56 ICQ Items: Control Objectives, Test of Controls Procedures, and Possible Errors or Irregularities. Listed below is a selection of items from the payroll processing internal control questionnaire in Appendix 11A–2.

1. Are names of terminated employees reporting in writing to the payroll department?
2. Are authorizations for deductions, signed by the employees, on file?
3. Is there a timekeeping department (function) independent of the payroll department?
4. Are timekeeping and cost accounting records (such as hours, dollars) reconciled with payroll department calculations of wage and salaries?

Required:
For each question above:

a. Identify the control objective to which the question applies.

b. Specify one test of controls audit procedure an auditor could use to determine whether the control was operating effectively (see Exhibit 11–8 for procedures).

c. Using your business experience, your logic, and/or your imagination, give an example of an error or irregularity that could occur if the control were absent or ineffective.

11.57 Test of Controls Audit Procedures, Evaluation of Possible Diversion of Payroll Funds. The Generous Loan Company has 100 branch loan offices. Each office has a manager and four or five subordinates who are employed by the manager. Branch managers prepare the weekly payroll, including their own salaries, and pay employees from cash on hand. Employees sign the payroll sheet signifying receipt of their salary. Hours worked by hourly personnel are inserted in the payroll register sheet from time cards prepared by the employees and approved by the manager.

The weekly payroll register sheets are sent to the home office along with other accounting statements and reports. The home office compiles employee earnings records and prepares all federal and provincial salary reports from the weekly payroll sheets.

Salaries are established by home office job-evaluation schedules. Salary adjustments, promotions, and transfers of full-time employees are approved by a home office salary committee based on the recommendations of branch managers and area supervisors. Branch managers advise the salary committee of new full-time employees and terminated employees. Part-time and temporary employees are hired without advising the salary committee.

Required:

a. Prepare a payroll audit program to be used in the home office to audit the branch office payrolls of the Generous Loan Company. See Exhibit 11–8 for sample audit procedures.

b. Based on your review of the payroll system, how might funds for payroll be diverted?

(AICPA adapted)

11.58 Major Risks in Payroll Cycle. Prepare a schedule of the major risks in the payroll cycle. Identify the control objectives and the financial statement assertions related to each. Lay out a three-column schedule like this:

Payroll
Cycle
Risk   Control
                  Objective   Assertion

11.59 Payroll Authorization in a Computer System. Two accountants were discussing control procedures and test of control auditing for payroll systems. The senior accountant in charge of the engagement said: "It is impossible to determine who authorizes transactions when the payroll account is computerized."

Required:
Evaluate the senior accountant's statement about control in a computerized payroll system. List the points in the flow of payroll information where authorization takes place.

11.60 Payroll Processed by a Service Bureau. Assume that you are the audit senior conducting a review of the payroll system of a new client. In the process of interviewing the payroll department manager, she makes the following statement: "We don't need many controls since our payroll is done outside the company by Automated Data Processing, a service bureau."

Required:
Evaluate the payroll department manager's statement and describe how a service bureau affects an auditors' review of controls. You may want to refer to Chapter 6.

Discussion Cases

. . . .

11.61 Croyden Factory, Inc.: Evaluation of Flowchart for Payroll Control Weaknesses. A PA's audit working papers contain a narrative description of a segment of the Croyden Factory, Inc., payroll system and an accompanying flowchart (Exhibit 11.61–1) as follows:

NARRATIVE:
The internal control system, with respect to the personnel department, is well functioning and is not included in the accompanying flowchart.

At the beginning of each workweek, payroll clerk no. 1 reviews the payroll department files to determine the employment status of factory employees. Clerk no. 1 then prepares clock time cards and distributes them as each individual arrives at work. This payroll clerk, who also is responsible for custody of the cheque signature stamp machine, verifies the identity of each payee before delivering signed cheques to the foreman.

At the end of each workweek, the foreman distributes payroll cheques for the preceding workweek. Concurrent with this activity, the foreman reviews the current week's employee timecards, notes the regular and overtime hours worked on a summary form, and initials the clock time cards. The foreman then delivers all time cards and unclaimed payroll cheques to payroll clerk no. 2.

Required:
a. Based on the narrative and accompanying flowchart (Exhibit 11.61–1), what are the weaknesses in the system of internal control?
b. Based on the narrative and accompanying flowchart, what enquiries should be made with respect to clarifying the existence of possible additional weaknesses in the system of internal control?

Note: Do not discuss the internal control system of the personnel department.

(AICPA adapted)

EXHIBIT 11.61–1   CROYDEN, INC., FACTORY PAYROLL SYSTEM

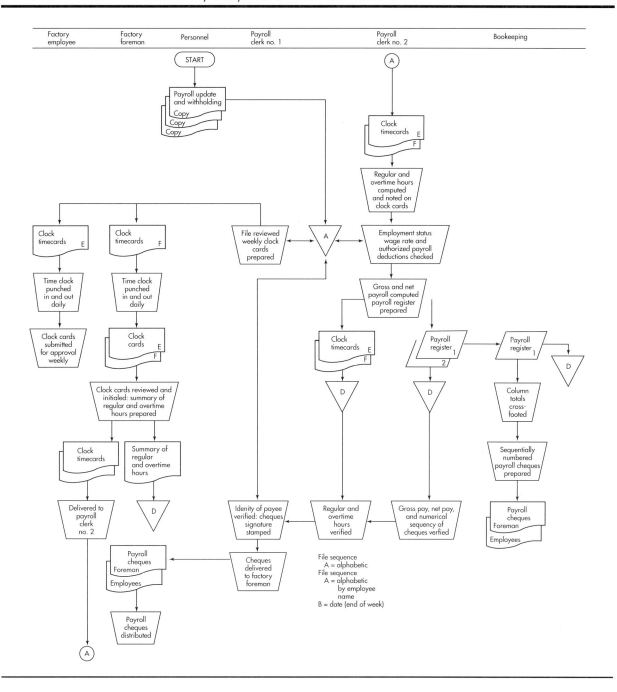

Factory employee	Factory foreman	Personnel	Payroll clerk no. 1	Payroll clerk no. 2	Bookeeping

File sequence
A = alphabetic
File sequence
A = alphabetic by employee name
B = date (end of week)

11.62 Vane Corporation: Control Weaknesses in Computerized Payroll System. The Vane Corporation is a manufacturing concern that has been

in business for the past 18 years. During this period, the company has grown from a very small family-owned operation to a medium-sized manufacturing concern with several departments. Despite this growth, a substantial number of the procedures employed by Vane have been in effect since the business was started. Just recently, Vane has computerized its payroll function.

The payroll function operates in the following manner. Each worker picks up a weekly time card on Monday morning and writes in his or her name and identification number. These blank cards are kept near the factory entrance. The workers write on the time card the times of their daily arrival and departure. On the following Monday, the factory foremen collect the completed time cards for the previous week and send them to data processing.

In data processing the time cards are used to prepare the weekly payroll transaction file. This file is used to update the master payroll file, which is maintained on magnetic tape sequenced by worker identification number. After the payroll file is updated and the cheques are prepared, the cheques are written by the computer on the regular chequing account and imprinted by a signature plate with the treasurer's signature. The cheques are sent to the factory foremen who distribute them to the workers or hold them for absent workers to pick up later.

The foremen notify data processing of new employees and terminations. Any changes in hourly pay rate or any other changes affecting payroll usually are communicated to data processing by the foremen.

The workers also complete a job time ticket for each individual job they work on each day. The job time tickets are collected daily and sent to cost accounting, where they are used to prepare a cost distribution analysis.

Further analysis of the payroll function reveals the following:

1. A worker's gross wages never exceed $300 per week.
2. Raises never exceed 55 cents per hour for the factory workers.
3. No more than 20 hours of overtime are allowed each week.
4. The factory employs 150 workers in 10 departments.

The payroll function had not been operating smoothly for some time but even more problems have surfaced since the payroll was computerized. The foremen have indicated that they would like a weekly report indicating worker tardiness, absenteeism, and idle time, so that they can determine the amount of productive time lost and the reason for the lost time. The following errors and inconsistencies have been encountered the past few pay periods:

1. A worker's paycheque was not processed properly because he had transposed two numbers in his identification number when he filled out his time card.
2. A worker was issued a cheque for $1,531.80 when it should have been $153.18.
3. One worker's paycheque was not written, and this error was not detected until the paycheques for that department were distributed by the foreman.
4. Part of the master payroll file was destroyed when the tape reel was inadvertently mounted on the wrong tape drive and used as a scratch tape. Data processing attempted to reestablish the destroyed portion from original source documents and other records.
5. One worker received a paycheque for an amount considerably larger than he should have. Further investigation revealed that 84 had been keyed instead of 48 for hours worked.
6. Several records on the master payroll file were skipped and not included in the updated master payroll file. This was not detected for several pay periods.
7. In processing nonroutine changes, a computer operator included a pay rate increase for one of his friends in the factory. By chance, this was discovered by another employee.

Required:

Identify the control weaknesses in Vane's payroll procedures and in the computer processing as it is now conducted. Recommend the necessary changes to correct the system. Arrange your answer in the following columnar format:

Control Weaknesses	Recommendations
1.	1.

11.63 Payroll Test of Controls. The diagram in Exhibit 11.63–1 describes several payroll test of control procedures. It shows the direction of the tests, leading from samples of clock cards, payrolls, and cumulative year-to-date earnings records to blank squares.

Required:

For each blank square in Exhibit 11.63–1, write a payroll test of controls procedure and describe the evidence it can produce. (Hint: Refer to Exhibit 11–8 in Chapter 11.)

EXHIBIT 11.63–1   DIAGRAM OF PAYROLL TEST OF CONTROLS

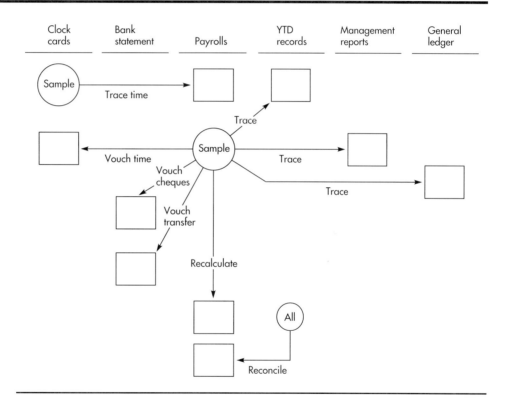

11.64 Cost Accounting Test of Controls. The diagram in Exhibit 11.64–1 describes several cost accounting test of control procedures. It shows the direction of the tests, leading from samples of cost accounting analyses, management reports, and the general ledger to blank squares.

Required:

For each blank square in Exhibit 11.64–1, write a cost accounting test of controls procedure and describe the evidence it can produce. (Hint: Refer to Exhibit 11–8 in Chapter 11.)

EXHIBIT 11.64–1   DIAGRAM OF COST ACCOUNTING TEST OF CONTROLS

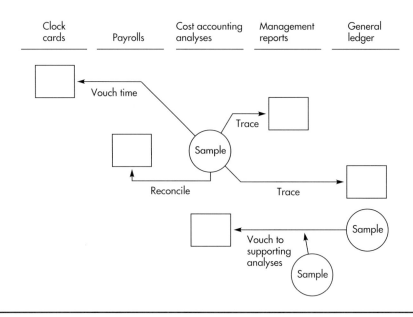

11.65 Inventory and Deferred Cost Over-statement.

INSTRUCTIONS FOR DISCUSSION CASES 11.65–11.67:

These cases are designed like the ones in the chapter. They give the problem, the method, the paper trail, and the amount. Your assignment is to write the audit approach portion of the case organized around these sections:

Objective: Express the objective in terms of the facts supposedly asserted in financial records, accounts, and statements. (Refer to discussion of assertions in Chapter 4.)

Control: Write a brief explanation of desirable controls, missing controls, and especially the kinds of "deviations" that may arise from the situation described in the case.

Test of controls: Write some procedures for getting evidence about existing controls, especially procedures that could discover deviations from controls. If there are no controls to test, then there are no procedures to perform; go then to the next section. A "procedure" should instruct someone about the source(s) of evidence to tap and the work to do.

Audit of balance: Write some procedures for getting evidence about the existence, completeness, valuation, ownership, or disclosure assertions identified in your objective section above.

Discovery summary: Write a short statement about the discovery you expect to accomplish with your procedures.

TOYING AROUND WITH THE NUMBERS

Problem: Mattel, Inc., a manufacturer of toys, failed to write off obsolete inventory, thereby overstating inventory, and improperly deferred tooling costs, both of which understated cost of goods sold and overstated income.

Method: "Excess" inventory was identified by comparing types of toys (wheels, general toys, dolls, games), parts, and raw materials with the forecasted sales or use. Lower-of-cost-or-market (LCM) determinations then were made to calculate the obsolescence write-off. Obsolescence was expected, and the target for the year was

$700,000. The first comparison computer run showed $21 million "excess" inventory! The company "adjusted" the forecast by increasing the quantities of expected sales for many toy lines. (Forty percent of items had forecasted sales greater than the recent actual sales experience.) Another "adjustment" was to forecast toy closeout sales not at reduced prices but at regular prices. Also, certain parts were labelled "interchangeable" without the normal reference to a new toy product. These "adjustments" to the forecast reduced the "excess" inventory exposed to LCM valuation and write-off.

The cost of setting up machines, preparing dies, and other preparations for manufacture are "tooling costs." They benefit the lifetime run of the toy manufactured. The company capitalized them as prepaid expenses and amortized them in the ratio of current-year sales to expected product lifetime sales (much like a natural resource depletion calculation). To get the amortization cost lower, the company transferred unamortized tooling costs from toys with low forecasted sales to ones with high forecasted sales. This caused the year's amortization ratio to be smaller, the calculated cost write-off lower, and the cost of goods sold lower than it should have been.

Paper trail: The computer-forecast runs of expected use of interchangeable parts provided a space for a reference to the code number of the new toy where the part would be used. Some of these references contained the code number of the part itself, not a new toy. In other cases the forecast of toy sales and parts use contained the quantity on hand, not a forecast number.

In the tooling cost detail records, unamortized cost was classified by lines of toys (similar to classifying asset cost by asset name or description). Unamortized balances were carried forward to the next year. The company changed the classifications shown at the prior year-end to other toy lines that had no balances or different balances. In other words, the balances of unamortized cost at the end of the prior year did not match the beginning balances of the current year, except that the total prepaid expense amount was the same.

Amount: For lack of obsolescence write-offs, inventory was overstated $4 million. The company recorded a $700,000 obsolescence write-off. It should have been about $4.7 million, as later determined.

The tooling cost manipulations overstated the prepaid expense by $3.6 million.

The company reported net income (after taxes) of $12.1 million in the year before the manipulations took place. If pretax income was in the $20–$28 million range in the year of the misstatements, the obsolescence and tooling misstatements alone amounted to about 32 percent income overstatement.

11.66 Inadequate Payroll Time Records.
Follow the instructions accompanying Discussion Case 11.65.

PAYROLL IN THE BLUE SKY

Problem: SueCan Corporation deferred costs under the heading of defence contract claims for reimbursement and deferred tooling labour costs, thus overstating assets, understating cost of goods sold, and overstating income.

Method: SueCan manufactured electronic and other equipment for private customers and government defence contracts. Near the end of the year, the company used a journal entry to remove $110,000 from cost of goods sold and defer it as deferred tooling cost. This $110,000 purported to be the labour cost associated with preparing tools and dies for long production runs.

The company opened a receivables account for "cost overrun reimbursement receivable" as a claim for reimbursement on defence contracts ($378,000).

Paper trail: The company altered the labour time records for the tooling costs in an effort to provide substantiating documentation. Company employees prepared new work orders numbered in the series used late in the fiscal year and attached labour time records dated much earlier in the year. The production orders originally charged with the labour cost were left completed but with no labour charges!

The claim for reimbursement on defence contracts did not have documentation specifically identifying the labour costs as being related to the contract. There were no work orders. (Auditors know that Defence Ministry auditors insist on documentation and justification before approving such a claim.)

Amount: SueCan reported net income of about $442,000 for the year, an overstatement of approximately 60 percent.

11.67 Employee Embezzlement via Padded Payroll. Follow the instructions accompanying Discussion Case 11.65. In this case (11.67, aka 18.53) your assignment is to analyse the payroll register and see if you can identify any of the ghosts. (This register is short, and you can try to do the analysis visually.

This case is a duplication of Discussion Case 18.53 in Chapter 18 (Ghost Riders on the Payroll). It involves an examination of some payroll information for fictitious employees using fraud auditing knowledge from Chapter 18. Case 18.53 is at the end of Chapter 18.

Required:
Analyse the payroll register in Exhibit 18.53–1 and identify the questionable employees who might be ghosts on the payroll.

11.68 Payroll Flowchart Control Points. This is a cross-reference to Discussion Case 8.47 in Chapter 8 (Audit Planning in a Computer Environment). Case 8.47 presents a flowchart of a computerized payroll process and asks for a list of the control points and control procedures.

11.69 Audit of Inventory. During his examination of the inventories and related accounts of Consumer Electronics, manufacturer and distributor of small appliances, a PA encountered the following:

a. During the inventory observation, the PA noticed several trucks loaded with finished goods parked at the shipping dock. He noted that the contents of the trucks were excluded from the physical inventory.

b. The finished goods inventory at the company's plant included several products for which there was a high volume of goods on hand, with many of the cartons being old and covered with dust. In response to the PA's questions, the plant manager stated that there was no problem as "all of these goods will eventually be sold although some price incentives may be necessary."

c. While reviewing the complex calculations used to develop the unit production costs of items in finished goods, the PA noted that the costs of the company's electrical engineering department, which had been treated as period expenses in previous years, were included as part of manufacturing overhead in the current year.

d. The company installed a computerized perpetual inventory system during the year. The PA noted that numerous year-end quantities as per the perpetual records differed from the actual physical inventory counts. In part because of these problems, the company took a complete physical inventory at year-end.

Required:
Describe the additional audit procedures (if any) that the PA should perform to obtain sufficient appropriate evidence in each of the above situations.

(CGAAC adapted)

APPENDIX 11A

INTERNAL CONTROL QUESTIONNAIRES

· ·

E X H I B I T   11A–1   **PRODUCTION AND COST ACCOUNTING TRANSACTION PROCESSING**

Environment:

1. Is access to blank production order forms denied to unauthorized persons?
2. Is access to blank bills of materials and manpower needs forms denied to unauthorized persons?
3. Is access to blank material requisitions forms denied to unauthorized persons?

Validity objective:

4. Are material requisitions and job time tickets reviewed by the production supervisor after the foreman prepares them?
5. Are the weekly direct labour and materials-used reports reviewed by the production supervisor after preparation by the foreman?

Completeness objective:

6. Are production orders prenumbered and the numerical sequence checked for missing documents?
7. Are bills of materials and manpower needs forms prenumbered and the numerical sequence checked for missing documents?
8. Are material requisitions and job time tickets prenumbered and the numerical sequence checked for missing documents?
9. Are inventory issue slips prenumbered and the numerical sequence checked for missing documents?

Authorization objective:

10. Are production orders prepared by authorized persons?
11. Are bills of materials and manpower needs prepared by authorized persons?

Accuracy objective:

12. Are differences between inventory issue slips and materials-used reports recorded and reported to the cost accounting supervisor?
13. Are differences between job time tickets and the labour report recorded and reported to the cost accounting supervisor?
14. Are standard costs used? If so, are they reviewed and revised periodically?
15. Are differences between reports of units completed and products-received reports recorded and reported to the cost accounting supervisor?

Classification objective:

16. Does the accounting manual give instructions for proper classification of cost accounting transactions?

Accounting objective:

17. Are summary entries reviewed and approved by the cost accounting supervisor?

Proper period objective:

18. Does the accounting manual give instructions to date cost entries on the date of use? Does an accounting supervisor review monthly, quarterly, and year-end cost accruals?

E X H I B I T 11A–2   **PAYROLL PROCESSING**

Environment:

1. Are all employees paid by cheque?
2. Is a special payroll bank account used?
3. Are payroll cheques signed by persons who neither prepare cheques nor keep cash funds or accounting records?
4. Is the payroll bank account reconciled by someone who does not prepare, sign, or deliver paycheques?
5. Are payroll department personnel rotated in their duties? required to take vacations? bonded?
6. Is there a timekeeping department (function) independent of the payroll department?

Validity objective:

7. Are names of terminated employees reported in writing to the payroll department?
8. Is the payroll compared to personnel files periodically?
9. Are cheques distributed by someone other than the employee's immediate supervisor?
10. Are unclaimed wages deposited in a special bank account or otherwise controlled by a responsible officer?
11. Do internal auditors conduct occasional surprise distributions of paycheques?

Completeness objective:

12. Are names of newly hired employees reported in writing to the payroll department?
13. Are blank payroll cheques prenumbered and the numerical sequence checked for missing documents?

Authorization objective:

14. Are all wage rates determined by contract or approved by a personnel officer?
15. Are authorizations for deductions, signed by the employees, on file?
16. Are time cards or piecework reports prepared by the employee approved by his or her supervisor?
17. Is a time clock or other electromechanical or computer system used?
18. Is the payroll register sheet signed by the employee preparing it and approved prior to payment?

Accuracy objective:

19. Are timekeeping and cost accounting records (such as hours, dollars) reconciled with payroll department calculations of hours and wages?
20. Are payrolls audited periodically by internal auditors?

Classification objective:

21. Do payroll accounting personnel have instructions for classifying payroll debit entries?

Accounting objective:

22. Are individual payroll records reconciled with quarterly tax reports?

Proper period objective:

23. Are monthly, quarterly, and annual wage accruals reviewed by an accounting officer?

Appendix 11B

Just-in-Time Manufacturing

. . . .

Just-in-time (JIT) manufacturing has been implemented by many companies and is being promoted by management consultants. The presentation in this appendix is a management consulting explanation intended to promote an accounting firm's expertise. As you study this explanation, notice that the 10 principles deal with matters of efficiency and effectiveness of production operations. They are not phrased in terms of audit interest; even so, the design of manufacturing operations is always of interest for auditors.

Following the 10 principles, you can notice mention of some standard production accounting documents (e.g., bills of materials, routing orders, inventory records, production forecasts). JIT alters the management of production, but it retains many familiar features of production accounting.

Just-in-Time: Eliminating Waste and Reducing Cost*

In manufacturing, waste is defined as anything other than the minimum amount of equipment, materials, space, and workers' time needed to make a product. It is anything that does not add value to the final product.

The more waste a manufacturer cuts from his operations, the more time he can devote to assuring product quality, reducing lead time, cutting costs, and increasing profitability.

That's why increasing numbers of companies are adopting just-in-time (JIT) manufacturing as a strategy to achieve a competitive advantage and increased profit.

JIT can be applied to manufacturing operations of any size or configuration. Any process or activity that adds value is a candidate for JIT, whether it is performed by a small job shop or a large mass-production facility.

JIT enables managers to solve deep-rooted operating problems. It enables management to stop "putting out fires," running from one crisis to another and papering over problems by accumulating inventory.

Instead, it can uncover root cause problems, solve them, and allow the company to move on to new challenges.

The 10 Principles

JIT is based on 10 principles.

1. **Reduce manufacturing lead time.** Ideally, a manufacturer's cycle time or lead time should equal its process time. Any additional time is "waste." If it takes eight days to produce a product, but only one hour to actually make it on a machine, the remaining seven days and 23 hours are waste.

2. **Cut inventories to a minimum.** Companies use inventory to hide problems. They increase inventory to hide problems. They increase inventory to make certain product is available when problems occur. Eliminate the inventory and management will be forced to solve problems.

---

*Source: *Manufacturing Issues*, vol. 3, no. 1 (Winter 1992), (Chicago: Grant Thornton). Reprinted with permission of Grant Thornton.

3. Synchronize all production processes to the rate of customer demand. If a customer orders 10 pieces, but a manufacturer can make 100 more economically, it makes 100; 90 of them go to inventory.

   This is wasteful. Make the manufacturing of 10 pieces the most economical lot size.

4. Use demand flows to control the shop. Today, most factories operate on a "push" system: If operator 2 produces his product faster than operator 3 needs it, the product is "pushed" to operator 3 and waits in a queue.

   JIT is a "pull" system: When operator 3 is done with his work, he sends signals to operator 2 and requests more work.

5. Reduce lot sizes and setup times. Most manufacturers produce a variety of products. If they slash inventories and work-in-process, they must be prepared to produce these various products more often and in small lot sizes. That means they must reduce setup time.

6. Strive for linear production. Instead of labouring all week to ship everything in a mad rush on Friday, maintain the same pace of production, day in and day out. Match the production pace with consumer demand.

   JIT optimizes the total operation. Each department performs at the same level to meet customer requirements. No longer do departments have individual performance requirements. The entire organization is measured against common performance criteria.

7. Make it right the first time. Rejects and scrap are pure waste.

8. Eliminate waste, in the form of rework.

9. Dedicate work cells to product families. Have the same workers work on a family of related products. It's a more efficient use of their time and your facilities.

10. Form partnerships with vendors. Have vendors guarantee more-frequent deliveries, in smaller quantities, with higher quality. In exchange, you will be in the position to give the vendor more business.

    Some ways to go about this include reducing the number of vendors for a given part, issuing a blanket order to a vendor for a year's worth of product, or involving key vendors in production planning.

    The end result will be a successful partnership with both companies in a win-win situation.

Implementing JIT

The biggest obstacle to implementing JIT is people's natural resistance to change.

The best way to overcome this resistance is to conduct a JIT pilot program on a specific family of products. Pick a pilot of modest difficulty. Its success has the best chance of convincing nonbelievers, which could be most of the factory.

To oversee the pilot program, create a steering committee, task groups, and continuous improvement teams. They do not replace line management; their job is to implement JIT.

The steering committee consists of people who can allocate resources, make decisions, and review or approve recommendations made to them. The committee may or may not include the CEO, but will likely include the plant manager and should definitely include a union representative (if applicable). The steering committee appoints a co-ordinator, who will direct the JIT implementation.

The task groups are made up of line management and workers. Their job is to solve specific problems and achieve improvements within a given time frame. Once they've identified their problems and defined and implemented the solutions, they disband.

The continuous improvement teams are an ongoing group. They focus on continually trying to improve the process and to eliminate waste in a given area of activity.

The steering committee should meet once or twice a month, but the task groups and continuous improvement teams should meet more frequently. Once a week or more frequently is typical for both.

Education and human relations programs about JIT are essential for effective implementation. Explain to your employees what you are trying to do and how it will affect them.

Understand their concerns about the change and do everything possible to eliminate their anxieties. Be sure that the union representatives, where applicable, are involved in important decisions.

Be open and upfront with all employees about the progress of the implementation and any problems encountered. Invite their help and ideas. You are trying to instill in them a sense of teamwork. Their ideas and insights are crucial to the success of the implementation. Recognize and reward ideas and initiatives generated by team members.

Taking the Steps

Once the task groups are in place, their job is to look at the operations included in the pilot program and to tear them down into components. Everything should be open to review and possible change. There should be no "sacred cows."

The task group should identify all the steps in the manufacturing process and the equipment involved. It ought to examine bills of materials, routing, inventories, setup time, and staffing levels. It should compare production forecasts for the pilot project with capabilities.

Performance measures then are benchmarked prior to implementation, and all improvement is measured against that performance.

Goals are established to enable the employees to view their improvement on a day-to-day basis. Team leaders and management should be positive and respond promptly to issues raised in the task groups and teams.

Once a pilot has been implemented, the continuous improvement team takes over. It monitors the area's performance and works to improve it even more. The team should have the authority to make changes. The quickest way for them to fail at their job is to deny them that authority.

Continuous improvement teams are crucial to the success of JIT. They insure that the hard-won gains made by the other committees are held to and continually improved on. They insure that the company continues to expand the waste-cutting benefits of the JIT philosophy.

Generally, it takes about 14 weeks to 21 weeks to implement a JIT pilot program. The biggest and most time-consuming step is diagnosing the things that need to be changed.

But the process gets easier. Once the first pilot project is completed, the next one will take less time and effort. All involved will have learned a great deal from the pilot.

CHAPTER 12

Learning Objectives

The finance and investment cycle comprehends a company's ways and means of planning for capital requirements and raising the money by borrowing, selling shares, and entering into acquisitions and joint ventures. Dividend, interest, and income tax payments are in this cycle. It also includes the accounts for investments in marketable securities, joint ventures and partnerships, and subsidiaries. The finance part of the cycle deals with getting money into the company. The investment part of the cycle deals with the disposition of money in investment accounts. After completing this chapter, you should be able to:

1. Describe the finance and investment cycle, including typical source documents and controls.

2. Give examples of test of controls procedures for obtaining information about the controls over debt and owner equity transactions and investment transactions.

3. Describe some common errors, irregularities, and frauds in the accounting for capital transactions and investments, and design some audit and investigation procedures for detecting them.

FINANCE AND INVESTMENT CYCLE

FINANCE AND INVESTMENT CYCLE: TYPICAL ACTIVITIES

· · · · · · · · · · ·

The finance and investment cycle contains a large number of accounts and records, ranging across tangible and intangible assets, liabilities, deferred credits, shareholders' equity, gains and losses, expenses, and related taxes such as income tax, goods and service tax (GST), and provincial sales tax (PST). The major accounts and records are listed in Exhibit 12–1. These include some of the more complicated topics in accounting—equity method accounting for investments, consolidation accounting, goodwill, income taxes, and financial instruments, to name a few. It is not the purpose of this chapter to explain the accounting for these balances and transactions. The chapter concentrates on a few important aspects of auditing them. Exhibit 12–1 shows a skeleton outline of the finance and investment cycle. Its major functions are financial planning and raising capital; interacting with the acquisition and expenditure, production and payroll, and revenue and collection cycles; and entering into mergers, acquisitions, and other investments.

Debt and Shareholder Equity Capital

Transactions in debt and shareholder equity capital are normally few in number but large in monetary amount. They are handled by the highest levels of management. The control-related duties and responsibilities reflect this high-level attention.

Authorization

Financial planning starts with the chief financial officer's (CFO's) cash flow forecast. This forecast informs the board of directors and management of the business plans, the prospects for cash inflows, and the needs for cash outflows. The cash flow forecast usually is integrated with the capital budget, which contains the plans for asset purchases and business acquisitions. A capital budget approved by the board of directors constitutes the authorization for major capital asset acquisitions (acquisition cycle) and investments.

Sales of share capital and debt financing transactions usually are authorized by the board of directors. All the directors must sign registration documents for public securities offerings. However, authority normally is delegated to the CFO to complete such transactions as periodic renewals of notes payable and other ordinary types of financing transactions without specific board approval of each transaction. Auditors should expect to find the authorizing signatures of the chief executive officer (CEO), CFO, chair of the board of directors, and perhaps other high-ranking officers on financing documents.

Many financing transactions are "off the balance sheet." Companies can enter into obligations and commitments that are not required to be recorded in the accounts. Examples of such authorizations include leases, endorsements on discounted

E X H I B I T 12–1   FINANCE AND INVESTMENT CYCLE

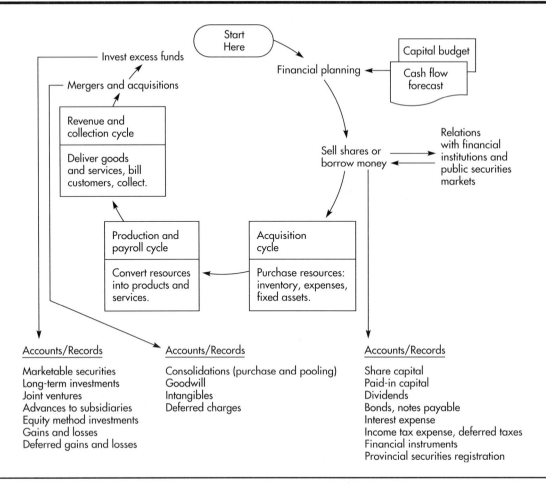

notes or on other companies' obligations, letters of credit, guarantees, repurchase or remarketing agreements, commitments to purchase at fixed prices, commitments to sell at fixed prices, and certain kinds of stock options. These are among the business and financing options available to companies. They cause problems in financial reporting and disclosure.

Custody

In large companies custody of share certificate books is not a significant management problem. Large companies employ banks and trust companies to serve as registrars and transfer agents. A registrar keeps the shareholder list and, from time to time, determines the shareholders eligible to receive dividends (shareholders of record on a dividend record date) and those entitled to vote at the annual meeting. A transfer agent handles the exchange of shares, cancelling the shares surrendered by sellers and issuing new certificates to buyers. It is not unusual to find the same bank or trust company providing both services.

Small companies often keep their own shareholder records. A share certificate book looks like a chequebook. It has perforated stubs for recording the number of

---

THE BRE-X SCANDAL
Shares close at 8.5¢ – 'it's just a shell now'

Bre-X Minerals Ltd. stock plunged 98% in minutes yesterday as angry investors wiped almost $700 million off the company's market capitalization and sent the the one-time market darling back to the ranks of the penny stocks.

It was the first time Bre-X shares have traded since the report by **Strathcona Mineral Services Ltd.** blew the whistle on a massive "falsification of assay values" at the supposedly huge Busang gold find in Indonesia.

The volume was so heavy it choked the Toronto Stock Exchange's communications system, leading officials to halt Bre-X trades and leave shareholders cooling their heels for more than an hour before trading in the stock resumed.

When the dust settled, the Calgary exploration company—valued at $6.8 billion a year ago—saw its market capitalization reduced to $18.6 million from $707.4 million on Friday.

Bre-X president David Walsh has insisted he was not part of any scam, and has hired former assistant RCMP commissioner Rod Stamler and forensic accountant Robert Lindquist to search out an explanation.

Bre-X's New York public relations firm, Hill & Knowlton Inc., left the account after viewing the Strathcona report that said the fraud was on a scale "without precedent in the history of mining."

A New York law firm, Wechsler Harwood Halebian & Feffer LLP, yesterday become at least the 10th to file a class-action suit against Bre-X.

Shaken investors on both sides of the border were lining up to get into lawsuits as they struggled to come to terms with their losses. [The sheer size of the damage claims against Bre-X ranks Busang among the biggest financial frauds in history, larger than the collapse of Barings Securities, the Bank of Credit and Commerce International and the Sumitomo copper trading scam.]

"What do I hope to recover? I guess all of it," said Dan Depaola, a Toronto sales representative who bought 3,000 shares about a month ago, after the stock collapsed. "But that's impossible, I know that. So anything, really. It's such a blow."

He didn't take the chance to dump his shares yesterday. "What's the point? The commissions are going to cost more."

Source: Sandra Rubin, *The Financial Post,* May 7, 1997, p. 6.

---

shares, the owner's name and other identification, and the date of issue. Actual unissued share certificates are attached to the stubs, like unused cheques in a chequebook. The missing certificates are the ones outstanding in the possession of owners. Custody of the share certificate book is important because the unissued certificates are like money or collateral. If improperly removed, they can be sold to buyers who think they are genuinely issued or can be used as collateral with unsuspecting lenders.

Lenders have custody of debt instruments (e.g., leases, bonds, and notes payable). A CFO may have copies, but they are merely convenience records. However, when a company repurchases its debt instruments, these come into the custody of trustees or

---

A New Meaning for "Recycling"

Something strange must have happened on the way to the dump. Hundreds of issues of long-term bonds were redeemed early and presented to Citicorp's Citibank in New York, acting as agent for the issues, according to the FBI. Many of the bonds still had not reached the maturity date marked on them. Citibank sent about $1 billion of cancelled U.S. corporate bonds to a landfill dump in New Jersey. But in the past year, some of those bonds have been turning up at banks in Europe and the United States. The banks have had a disturbing surprise: The bonds are worthless, though they still might look genuine to a layman or even to some bankers.

An FBI spokesman says a defunct company in New Jersey is being investigated. The company had a contract to destroy the bonds.

Note: Companies obtain a "destruction certificate" when bonds and stock certificates are cancelled. The certificate obtained by Citibank apparently was fraudulent.

Source: The Wall Street Journal. March 3, 1992.

---

company officials, usually the CFO. Until they are cancelled and destroyed, it is possible to misuse them by improperly reselling them to unsuspecting investors.

Recordkeeping

Records of notes and bonds payable are maintained by the accounting department and the CFO or controller. The recordkeeping procedures should be similar to those used to account for vendor accounts payable: payment notices from lenders are compared to the accounting records, due dates are monitored, interest payments are set up in vouchers for payment, and accruals for unpaid interest are made on financial reporting dates. If the company has only a few bonds and notes outstanding, no subsidiary records of notes are kept. All the information is in the general ledger accounts. (Companies with a large number of bonds and notes may keep control and subsidiary accounts, as is done for accounts receivable.) When all or part of the notes become due within the next year, the CFO and controller have the necessary information for properly classifying current and long-term amounts.

Another class of credit balances is treated here under the heading of "recordkeeping," for which the functions of authorization, custody, and reconciliation are not easy to describe. They are the "calculated liabilities and credits"—lease obligations, deferred income taxes, pension and post-retirement benefit liabilities, and foreign currency translation gains and losses, to name a few. These are accounting creations, calculated according to accounting rules and using basic data from company plans and operations. Management usually enjoys considerable discretion in structuring leases, tax strategies, pension plan and employee benefit terms, foreign holdings, and the like. These accounting calculations often involve significant accounting estimates made by management. Company accountants try to capture the economic reality of these calculated liabilities by following generally accepted accounting principles.

The Little Lease That Could

The Park 'n Fly commuter airline was struggling. According to its existing debt covenants, it could not incur any more long-term liabilities. The company needed a new airplane to expand its services, so it "rented" one. The CFO pointed out that the deal for the $12 million airplane was a noncancellable operating lease because (1) Park 'n Fly does not automatically own the plane at the end of the lease; (2) the purchase option of $1,500,000 is no bargain; (3) the lease term of 133 months is 74 percent, not 75 percent, of the estimated 15-year economic life; and (4) the present value of the lease payments of $154,330 per month, discounted at the company's latest borrowing rate of 14 percent, is $10.4 million, which is less than the 90 percent of fair value ($0.90 \times $12 million $= $10.8 million) criterion in the CICA pronouncements (*Section* 3065.06).

The CFO did not record a long-term lease obligation (liability). Do you agree with this accounting conclusion?

Periodic Reconciliation

A responsible person should periodically inspect the share certificate book to determine whether the only missing certificates are the ones known to be outstanding in the possession of bona fide owners. If necessary, company officials can confirm the ownership of shares with the holders of record. Reports with similar information content can be obtained from registrars and transfer agents to verify that the company's record of the number of shares outstanding agrees with the registrars' number. (Without this reconciliation, counterfeit shares handled by the transfer agent and recorded by the registrar might go unnoticed.)

Ownership of bonds can be handled by a trustee having duties and responsibilities similar to those of registrars and transfer agents. Confirmations and reports from bond trustees can be used to reconcile the trustee's records to the company's records.

Investments and Intangibles

A company can have many investments or only a few, and can have a large variety or a limited set of types of investments. Intangible assets may be in the form of purchased assets (e.g., patents, trademarks) or in the form of accounting allocations (e.g., goodwill, deferred charges). The sections below are phrased in the context of a manufacturing or service company for which investments and intangibles are fairly incidental in the business. Financial institutions (banks, trust companies), investment companies, mutual funds, insurance companies, and the like have more elaborate systems for managing their investments and intangibles.

Authorization

All investment policies should be approved by the board of directors or its investment committee. It is not unusual to find board or executive committee approval required for major individual investment transactions. However, auditors should expect to find a great deal of variation across companies as to the nature and amount of transactions that must have specific high-level approval. The board of

---

AUTHORIZATION: HERE TODAY, GONE TOMORROW

The treasurer of Travum County had many responsibilities as a chief financial officer. She invested several million dollars of county funds with a California-based investment money manager. Soon thereafter, news stories of the money manager's expensive personal lifestyle and questionable handling of client's funds began to circulate, indicating that clients could lose much of their investments. At the same time, news stories about the treasurer's own credit-card spending habits were published locally, indicating that she had obtained a personal credit card by using the county's name.

Although no county funds were lost and no improper credit-card bills were paid, the county commissioners temporarily suspended the treasurer's authority to choose investment vehicles for county funds.

---

directors always is closely involved in major acquisitions, mergers, and share buy-back plans.

Custody

Custody of investments and intangibles depends on the nature of the assets. Some investments, such as shares and bonds, are represented by negotiable certificates. The actual certificates may be kept in a brokerage account in a "house name" (the brokerage company), and, in this case, "custody" rests with the company official who is authorized to order the buy, sell, and delivery transactions. They also may be in the actual possession of the owner (client company). If they are kept by the company, they should be in a safe or a bank safe-deposit box. Only high-ranking officers (e.g., CFO, CEO, president, chair of board) should have combinations and keys.

Other kinds of investments do not have formal negotiable certificates, and "custody" may take the form of "management responsibility" instead of actual physical handling. Examples are joint ventures and partnerships in which the client company is a partner. Venture and partnership agreements are evidence of these investments, but they usually are merely filed with other important documents. Misuse of them is seldom a problem because they are not readily negotiable. Real custody rests with management's supervision and monitoring of the venture or partnership operations.

Having "custody" of most intangibles is like trying to keep Jell-O in your pocket—good in theory but messy in practice. However, patents, trademarks, copyrights, and similar legal intangible rights may be evidenced in legal documents and contracts. These seldom are negotiable, and they usually are kept in ordinary company files. Accounting intangibles like goodwill and deferred charges (deferred tax credits and pension obligations on the liability side) are in the custody of the accountants who calculate them. Company mangers may be assigned responsibility to protect exclusive rights granted by various intangibles.

Recordkeeping

The procedures for purchase of share and bond investments involve the voucher system described in the acquisition and expenditure cycle (Chapter 10). Authorization by the board of directors or other responsible officials is the approval for the accounting department to prepare the voucher and the cheque. The treasurer or CFO signs the cheque for the investment. If the company has few investments, no subsidiary records are maintained and all information is kept in the general ledger accounts. If the company has many investments, a control account and subsidiary ledger may be maintained.

The recordkeeping for many kinds of investments and intangibles can be complicated. The complications arise not so much from the original recording of transactions as from the maintenance of the accounts over time. This is the place where complex accounting standards for equity method accounting, consolidations, goodwill, intangibles amortization and valuation, deferred charges, deferred taxes, pension and postretirement benefit liabilities, and various financial instruments enter the picture. High-level accountants who prepare financial statements get involved with the accounting rules and the management estimates required to account for such investments and intangibles. Management plans and estimates of future events and minute interpretations of the accounting standards often become elements of the accounting maintenance of these balances. These decisions are ripe areas for overstatement of assets, understatement of liabilities, and understatement of expenses.

Periodic Reconciliation

The most significant reconciliation opportunity in the investments and intangibles accounts is the inspection and count of negotiable securities certificates. This reconciliation is similar to a physical inventory in that it consists of an inspection of certificates on hand, along with comparison to the information recorded in the accounts. (When securities are held by a brokerage firm, the "inspection" is accomplished with a written confirmation.)

A securities count is not a mere handling of bits of paper. A securities count "inventory" should include a record of the name of the company represented by the certificate, the interest rate for bonds, the dividend rate for preferred shares, the due date for bonds, the serial numbers on the certificates, the face value of bonds, the number or face amount of bonds and shares, and notes on the name of the owner shown on the face of the certificate or on the endorsements on the back (should be the client company). Companies should perform this reconciliation reasonably often and not wait for an annual visit by the independent auditors. A securities count in a financial institution that holds thousands of shares in multimillion-dollar asset accounts is a major undertaking.

When auditors perform the securities inspection and count, the same kind of information should be recorded in the audit working papers. An example of these elements in an audit working paper is in Problem 4.52 at the end of Chapter 4. You can see several elements of evidence in the information: existence is established by handling the securities, ownership is established by viewing the client name as owner, valuation evidence is added by finding the cost and market value (see the example in Problem 4.52). If a security certificate is not available for inspection, it may be pledged as collateral for a loan and in the hands of a creditor. It can be confirmed or inspected, if the extended procedure of visiting the creditor is necessary. The pledge as collateral may be important for a disclosure note. A securities count and reconciliation is important for management and auditors because companies have been known to try to substitute others' securities for missing ones. If securities have been sold, then replaced without any accounting entries, the serial numbers will show that the certificate recorded in the accounts is not the same as the ones on hand.

R E V I E W
CHECKPOINTS

12.1 Do you believe that losses hidden by fraudulent overstatement of assets should be corrected with prior period adjustment accounting after discovery?

12.2 When a management carefully crafts a lease agreement to barely fail the tests for lease capitalization and liability recognition, do you believe that auditors should insist on capitalization anyway?

12.3 What would constitute the authorization for notes payable? What documentary evidence could auditors examine as evidence of this authorization?

12.4 Define and give five examples of "off-balance-sheet information." Why should auditors be concerned with such items?

12.5 What features of a client's share capital are of importance in the audit?

12.6 What information about share capital could be confirmed with outside parties? How could this information be corroborated by the auditors?

12.7 What procedures can auditors employ in the audit of investment securities to obtain the names of the issuers, the number of shares held, certificate numbers, maturity value, and interest and dividend rates?

12.8 Describe the procedures and documentation of a controlled count of client's investment securities. What information should be included in an audit working paper?

12.9 What is a "destruction certificate?"

CONTROL RISK ASSESSMENT

LEARNING OBJECTIVE

2. Give examples of test of controls procedures for obtaining information about the controls over debt and owner equity transactions and investment transactions.

In the finance and investment cycle, auditors look for control procedures, such as authorization, custody, recordkeeping, and periodic reconciliation. They especially look for information about the level of management involved in these functions. Tests of controls generally amount to enquiries and observations related to these features. Samples of transactions for detail tests of control performance are not normally a part of the control risk assessment work as they can be in the revenue and collection cycle, in the acquisition and expenditure cycle, and in the production and payroll cycle. Because finance and investment transactions are usually individually material, each transaction usually is audited in detail. Reliance on control does not normally reduce the extent of substantive audit work on finance and investment cycle accounts. However, lack of control can lead to performance of significant extended procedures.

General Control Considerations

Control procedures for suitable handling of responsibilities (note the avoidance of the idea of "proper segregation") should be in place and operating. By referring to the discussion accompanying Exhibit 12–1, you can tell that these responsibilities are basically in the hands of senior management officials. You also can tell that different companies may have widely different policies and procedures.

It is hard to have a strict segregation of functional responsibilities when the principal officers of a company authorize, execute, and control finance and investment activities. It is not very realistic to maintain that a CEO can authorize investments but cannot have access to shareholder records, securities certificates, and the like. Real segregation of duties can be found in middle management and lower ranks, but it is hard to create and enforce in upper-level management.

In light of this problem of control, a company should have compensating control procedures. A compensating control is a control feature used when a standard control procedure (such as strict segregation of function responsibilities) is not specified by the company. In the area of finance and investment, the compensating control feature is the involvement of two or more persons in each kind of important functional responsibility.

If involvement by multiple persons is not specified, then oversight or review can be substituted. For example, the board of directors can authorize purchase of securities or creation of a partnership. The CFO or CEO can carry out the transactions, have custody of certificates and agreements, manage the partnership or the portfolio of securities, oversee the recordkeeping, and make the decisions about valuations and accounting (authorizing the journal entries). These are rather normal management activities, and they combine several responsibilities. The compensating control can exist in the form of periodic reports to the board of directors, oversight by the investment committee of the board, and internal audit involvement in making a periodic reconciliation of securities certificates in a portfolio with the amounts and descriptions recorded in the accounts.

Control over Accounting Estimates

An accounting estimate is the amount included in financial statements to approximate the effect of past business transactions or events on the present status of an asset or liability. The use of accounting estimates in financial reporting is common. Examples include such items as allowance for doubtful receivables, loss provisions, and amortization of capital assets. Accounting estimates can have a significant or pervasive effect on reported results, either individually or when considered in the aggregate (*Handbook Section* 5305.02).

Accounting estimates often are included in basic financial statements because (1) the measurement of some amount of valuation is uncertain, perhaps depending upon the outcome of future events, or (2) relevant data cannot be accumulated on a timely, cost-effective basis. Some examples of accounting estimates in the finance and investment cycle are shown in the box on the next page.

A client's management is responsible for making estimates and should have a process and control structure designed to reduce the likelihood of material misstatements in them. Specific relevant aspects of such a control structure include:

- Management communication of the need for proper accounting estimates.
- Accumulation of relevant, sufficient, and reliable data for estimates.
- Preparation of estimates by qualified personnel.
- Adequate review and approval by appropriate levels of authority.
- Comparison of prior estimates with subsequent results to assess the reliability of the estimation outcomes.
- Consideration by management of whether particular accounting estimates are consistent with the company's operational plans.

FINANCE AND INVESTMENT CYCLE ESTIMATES

Financial instruments: Valuation of securities, classification into trading versus investment portfolios, probability of a correlated hedge, sales of securities with puts and calls.

Accruals: Compensation in stock option plans, actuarial assumptions in pension costs.

Leases: Initial direct costs, executory costs, residual values, capitalization interest rate.

Rates: Imputed interest rates on receivables and payables.

Other: Losses and net realizable value on segment disposal and business restructuring, fair values in nonmonetary exchanges.

Auditors' test of controls over the production of estimates amounts to enquiries and observations related to the features listed immediately above. Such enquiries are: Who prepares estimates? When are they prepared? What data are used? Who reviews and approves the estimates? Have you compared prior estimates with subsequent actual events? Observations include study of data documentation, study of comparisons of prior estimates with subsequent actual experience, and study of intercompany correspondence concerning estimates and operational plans.

The audit of an estimate starts with the test of controls, much of which has a bearing on the substantive quality of the estimation process and of the estimate itself. Further substantive audit procedures include recalculating the mathematical estimate, developing an auditor's own independent estimate based on alternative assumptions, and comparing the estimate to subsequent events to the extent they are known before the end of the field work.

Control Risk Assessment for Notes Payable

From the preceding discussion, you can tell that test of controls audit procedures take a variety of forms—enquiries, observations, study of documentation, comparison with related data, such as tax returns, and detail audit of some transactions. The detail audit of transactions, however, is a small part of the test of controls because of the nature of the finance and investment transactions, their number (few), and their amount (large). However, some companies have numerous debt financing transactions, and in such cases a more detailed approach to control risk assessment can be used, including the selection of a sample of transactions for control risk assessment evidence.

An internal control questionnaire for notes payable is in Exhibit 12–2. It illustrates typical questions about the control objectives. These enquiries give auditors insights into the client's specifications for review and approval of major financing transactions, the system of accounting for them, and the provision for error-checking review procedures.

Auditors can select a sample of notes payable transactions for detail test of controls, provided that the population of notes is large enough to justify sample-based auditing. Exhibit 12–3 lists a selection of such procedures, with notation of the relevant control objectives shown on the right.

E X H I B I T   12–2   INTERNAL CONTROL QUESTIONNAIRE: NOTES PAYABLE

Environment:

1. Are notes payable records kept by someone who cannot sign notes or cheques?

Validity objective:

2. Are paid notes cancelled, stamped "paid," and filed?

Completeness objective:

3. Is all borrowing authorization by the directors checked to determine whether all notes payable are recorded?

Authorization objective:

4. Are direct borrowings on notes payable authorized by the directors? by the treasurer or by the chief financial officer?

5. Are two or more authorized signatures required on notes?

Accuracy objective:

6. Are bank due notices compared with records of unpaid liabilities?

Classification objective:

7. Is sufficient information available in the accounts to enable financial statement preparers to classify current and long-term debt properly?

Accounting objective:

8. Is the subsidiary ledger of notes payable periodically reconciled with the general ledger control account(s)?

Proper period objective:

9. Are interest payments and accruals monitored for due dates and financial statement dates?

E X H I B I T   12–3   TEST OF CONTROLS AUDIT PROCEDURES FOR NOTES PAYABLE

	Control Objective
1. Read directors' and finance committee's minutes for authorization of financing transactions (such as short-term notes payable, bond offerings).	Authorization
2. Select a sample of paid notes:	
a. Recalculate interest expense for the period under audit.	Accuracy
b. Trace interest expense to the general ledger account.	Completeness
c. Vouch payment to cancelled cheques.	Validity
3. Select a sample of notes payable:	
a. Vouch to authorization by directors or finance committee.	Authorization
b. Vouch cash receipt to bank statement.	Validity

Summary: Control Risk Assessment

The audit manager or senior accountant in charge of the audit should evaluate the evidence obtained from an understanding of the internal control structure and from test of controls audit procedures. These procedures can take many forms because management systems for finance and investment accounts can be quite varied among clients. The involvement of senior officials in a relatively small number of high-dollar transactions makes control risk assessment a process tailored specifically to the company's situation. Some companies enter into complicated financing and investment transactions, while others keep to the simple transactions.

However, some control considerations can be generalized. Control over management's production of accounting estimates is characterized by some common features. In some cases, such as a company with numerous notes payable transactions, samples of transactions for detail testing can be used to produce evidence about compliance with control policies and procedures.

An Estimated Valuation Based on Future Development

Gulf & Western Industries (G&W) sold 450,000 shares of Pan American stock from its investment portfolio to Resorts International (Resorts). Resorts paid $8 million plus 250,000 shares of its unregistered common stock. G&W recorded the sale proceeds as $14,167,500, valuing the unregistered Resorts shares at $6,167,500, which was approximately 67 percent of the market price of Resorts shares at the time ($36.82 per share). G&W reported a gain of $3,365,000 on the sale.

Four years later, Resorts shares fell to $2.63. G&W sold its 250,000 shares back to Resorts in exchange for 1,100 acres of undeveloped land on Grand Bahamas Island. For its records, Resorts got a broker-dealer's opinion that its 250,000 shares were worth $460,000. For property tax assessment purposes, the Bahamian government valued the undeveloped land at $525,000.

G&W valued the land on its books at $6,167,500, which was the previous valuation of the Resorts shares. The justification was an appraisal of $6,300,000 based on the estimated value of the 1,100 acres when ultimately developed (i.e., built into an operating resort and residential community). However, G&W also reported a loss of $5,527,000 in its tax return (effectively valuing the land at $640,500).

The SEC accused G&W of failing to report a loss of $5.7 million in its financial statements. Do you think the loss should have appeared in the G&W income statement?

Source: I. Kellog, *How to Find Negligence and Misrepresentation in Financial Statements* (New York: Shepard's/McGraw Hill, 1983), p. 279.

In general, substantive audit procedures on finance and investment accounts are not limited in extent. It is very common for auditors to perform substantive audit procedures on 100 percent of these transactions and balances. The number of transactions is usually not large, and the audit cost is not high for complete coverage. Nevertheless, control deficiencies and unusual or complicated transactions can cause auditors to adjust the nature and timing of audit procedures. Complicated financial instruments, pension plans, exotic equity securities, related party transactions, and nonmonetary exchanges of investment assets call for procedures designed to find evidence of errors, irregularities, and frauds in the finance and investment accounts. The next section deals with some of the finance and investment cycle assertions, and it has some cases for your review.

. . . .

R E V I E W
C H E C K P O I N T S

12.10 What is a compensating control? Give some examples for finance and investment cycle accounts.

12.11 What are some of the specific relevant aspects of management's control over the production of accounting estimates? What are some enquiries auditors can make?

12.12 When a company has produced an estimate of an investment valuation based on a nonmonetary exchange, what source of comparative information can an auditor use?

12.13 If a company does not monitor notes payable for due dates and interest payment dates in relation to financial statement dates, what misstatements can appear in the financial statements?

12.14 Generally, how much emphasis is placed on adequate internal control in the audit of long-term debt? of share capital? of contributed surplus? and of retained earnings?

• •

ASSERTIONS, SUBSTANTIVE PROCEDURES, AND AUDIT CASES
• • • • • • • • • • • •

LEARNING OBJECTIVE

3. Describe some common errors, irregularities, and frauds in the accounting for capital transactions and investments, and design some audit and investigation procedures for detecting them.

This part of the chapter covers the audit of various account balances and gains and losses. It is presented in three sections—owners' equity, long-term liabilities and related accounts, and investments and intangibles. As in previous chapters, some casettes illustrating errors, irregularities, and frauds are used to describe useful audit approaches. In addition, this chapter gives some assertions and procedures related to accounts in the cycle.

The cases begin with a description containing these elements:

Method: A cause of the misstatement (mistaken estimate or judgment, accidental error, intentional irregularity or fraud attempt), which usually is made easier by some kind of failure of controls.

Paper trail: A set of telltale signs of erroneous accounting, missing or altered documents, or a "dangling debit" (the false or erroneous debit that results from an overstatement of assets).

Amount: The dollar amount of overstated assets and revenue, or understated liabilities and expenses.

Each audit program for the audit of an account balance contains an Audit Approach that may enable auditors to detect misstatements in account balances. Each application of procedures contains these elements:

Audit objective: A recognition of a financial statement assertion for which evidence needs to be obtained. The assertions are about the existence of assets, liabilities, revenue, and expenses; their valuation; their complete inclusion in the account balances; the rights and obligations inherent in them; and their proper presentation and disclosure in the financial statements. (These assertions were introduced in Chapter 4.)

Control: A recognition of the control procedures that should be used by an organization to prevent and detect errors and irregularities.

Test of controls: Ordinary and extended procedures designed to produce evidence about the effectiveness of the controls that should be in operation.

Audit of balance: Ordinary and extended substantive procedures designed to find signs of mistaken accounting estimates, errors, irregularities, and frauds in account balances and classes of transactions.

The cases first set the stage with a story about an accounting estimate, error, irregularity, or fraud—its method, paper trail (if any), and amount. This part of the casette gives you the "inside story," which auditors seldom know before they perform the audit work. The second part of the casette, under the heading of Audit Approach, tells a structured story about the audit objective, desirable controls, test of control procedures, audit of balance procedures, and discovery summary. The Audit Approach segment illustrates how audit procedures can be applied and the discoveries they may enable auditors to make. At the end of the chapter, some similar discussion cases are presented, and you can write the Audit Approach to test your ability to design audit procedures for the detection of mistaken accounting estimates, errors, irregularities, and frauds.

Owners' Equity

Management makes assertions about the existence, completeness, rights and obligations, valuation, and presentation and disclosure of owners' equity. Typical specific assertions include:

1. The number of shares shown as issued is in fact issued.
2. No other shares (including options, warrants, and the like) have been issued and not recorded or reflected in the accounts and disclosures.
3. The accounting is proper for options, warrants, and other share issue plans, and related disclosures are adequate.
4. The valuation of shares issued for noncash consideration is proper, in conformity with accounting principles.
5. All owners' equity transactions have been authorized by the board of directors.

An illustrative program of substantive audit procedures for owners' equity is in Appendix 12A–1.

Documentation

Owners' equity transactions usually are well documented in minutes of the meetings of the board of directors, in proxy statements, and in securities offering registration statements. Transactions can be vouched to these documents, and the cash proceeds can be traced to the bank accounts.

Confirmation

Share capital may be subject to confirmation when independent registrars and transfer agents are employed. Such agents are responsible for knowing the number of shares authorized and issued and for keeping lists of shareholders' names. The basic information about share capital—such as number of shares, classes of shares, preferred dividend rates, conversion terms, dividend payments, shares held in the company name, expiration dates, and terms of warrants and share dividends and splits—can be confirmed with the independent agents. Many of these items can be corroborated by the auditors' own inspection and reading of share certificates, charter authorizations, directors' minutes, and registration statements. However, when there are no independent agents, most audit evidence is gathered by vouching share record documents (such as certificate book stubs). When circumstances call for extended procedures, information on outstanding shares may be confirmed directly with the holders.

CASETTE 12.1
UNREGISTERED SALE OF SECURITIES

Problem

A. T. Bliss & Company (Bliss) sold investment contracts in the form of limited partnership interests to the public. These "securities" sales should have been under a public registration filing with the OSC, but they were not.

Method

Bliss salespeople contacted potential investors and sold many of them limited partnership interests. The setup deal called for these limited partnerships to purchase solar hot water heating systems for residential and commercial use from Bliss. All the partnerships entered into arrangements to lease the equipment to Nationwide Corporation, which then rented the equipment to end users. The limited partnerships were, in effect, financing conduits for obtaining investors' money to pay for Bliss's equipment. The investors depended on Nationwide's business success and ability to pay under the lease terms for their return of capital and profit.

Paper Trail

Bliss published false and misleading financial statements, which used a non-GAAP revenue recognition method and failed to disclose cost of goods sold. Bliss overstated Nationwide's record of equipment installation and failed to disclose that Nationwide had little cash flow from end users (resulting from rent-free periods and other inducements). Bliss knew—and failed to disclose to prospective investors—the fact that numerous previous investors had filed petitions with the federal tax court to contest the disallowance by Revenue Canada of all their tax credits and benefits claimed in connection with their investments in Bliss's tax-sheltered equipment lease partnerships.

Amount

Not known, but all the money put up by the limited partnership investors was at risk largely not disclosed to the investors.

AUDIT APPROACH

Audit Objective

Obtain evidence to determine whether capital fund-raising methods comply with provincial securities laws and whether financial statements and other disclosures are not misleading.

Control

Management should employ experts—lawyers, underwriters, and accountants—who can determine whether securities and investment contract sales do or do not require registration.

Test of Controls

Auditors should learn the business backgrounds and securities-industry expertise of the senior managers. Study the minutes of the board of directors for authorization of the fund-raising method. Obtain and study opinions rendered by lawyers and underwriters about the legality of the fund-raising methods. Enquire about management's interaction with the OSC in any presale clearance. (The OSC will give advice about the necessity for registration.)

Audit of Balances

Auditors should study the offering documents and literature used in the sale of securities to determine whether financial information is being used properly. In this case the close relationship with Nationwide and the experience of earlier partnerships give reasons for extended procedures to obtain evidence about the representations concerning Nationwide's business success (in this case, lack of success).

Discovery Summary

The auditors gave unqualified reports on Bliss's materially misstated financial statements. They apparently did not question the legality of the sales of the limited partnership interests as a means of raising capital. They apparently did not perform procedures to verify representations made in offering literature respecting Bliss or Nationwide finances. Two partners in the audit firm were enjoined from violations of the securities laws. They resigned from practice before the OSC and were ordered not to perform any assurance services for companies making filings with the OSC. They later were expelled from the ICAO for failure to co-operate with the Disciplinary Committee in its investigation of alleged professional ethics violations.

CASETTE 12.2
TAX LOSS CARRYFORWARDS

Problem

Aetna Life & Casualty Insurance Company had losses in its taxable income operations in 1981 and 1982. Confident that future taxable income would absorb the loss, the company booked and reported a tax benefit for the tax loss carryforward. The OSC maintained that the company understated its tax expense and understated its liabilities (Aetna reported the tax benefit as a negative liability). Utilization of the loss carryforward was not "virtually certain," as required by *Handbook Section* 3470.46.

Method

Aetna forecasted several more years of taxable losses (aside from its nontaxable income from tax-exempt investments), then forecasted years of taxable income, eventually offsetting the losses and obtaining the benefit of the tax law allowing losses to be carried forward to offset against future taxable income. The company maintained there was no reasonable doubt that the forecasts would be achieved.

Paper Trail

The amounts of tax loss were clearly evident in the accounts. Aetna made no attempt to hide the facts. The size of the portfolio of taxable investments and all sources of taxable income and deductions were well known to the company accountants, management, and independent auditors.

Amount

At first, the carryforward tax benefit was $25 million, soon growing to over $200 million, then forecast to become an estimated $1 billion before it was forecast to reverse by being absorbed by future taxable income. In 1983, the first full year affected, Aetna's net income was 35 percent lower than 1981, instead of 6 percent lower with the carryforward benefit recognized.

AUDIT APPROACH

Audit Objective

Obtain evidence to determine whether realization of the benefits of the tax loss carryforward are "virtually certain."

Control

The relevant control in this case concerns the assumptions and mathematics involved in preparing the forecasts used to justify the argument for recording the tax loss carryforward benefit. These forecasts are the basis for an accounting estimate of "virtually certain realization."

Test of Controls

Auditors should make enquiries and determine: Who prepared the forecasts? When were they prepared? What data were used? Who reviewed and approved the forecast? Is there any way to test the accuracy of the forecast with actual experience?

Audit of Balances

Aside from audit of the assumptions underlying the forecast and recalculations of the compilation, the test of balances amounted to careful consideration of whether the forecast, or any forecast, could meet the test required by accounting standards. The decision was a judgment of whether the test of "virtually certain realization" was met.

The auditors should obtain information about other situations in which recognition of tax loss carryforward benefits were allowed in financial statements. Other companies have booked and reported such benefits when gains from sales of property were realized before the financial statement was issued and when the loss was from discontinuing a business line, leaving other businesses with long profit histories and prospects in operation.

Discovery Summary

The OSC was tipped off to Aetna's accounting recognition of the tax loss carryforward benefit by a story in *Financial Post* magazine, which described the accounting treatment. Aetna and its auditors argued on the basis of the forecasts. The OSC countered with the theory that forecasts were not sufficient to establish "virtually certain realization." The OSC won the argument. Aetna revised its previously issued quarterly financial statements, and the company abandoned the attempt to report the tax benefit.

Long-term Liabilities and Related Accounts

The primary audit concern with the verification of long-term liabilities is that all liabilities are recorded and that the interest expense is properly paid or accrued. Therefore, the assertion of completeness is paramount. Alertness to the possibility of unrecorded liabilities during the performance of procedures in other areas frequently will uncover liabilities that have not been recorded. For example, when fixed assets are acquired during the year under audit, auditors should enquire about the source of funds for financing the new asset.

E X H I B I T 12–4   OFF-BALANCE SHEET COMMITMENTS

Type of Commitment	Typical Procedures and Sources of Evidence
1. Repurchase or remarketing agreements.	1. Vouching of contracts, confirmation by customer, enquiry of client management.
2. Commitments to purchase at fixed prices.	2. Vouching of open purchase orders, enquiry of purchasing personnel, confirmation by supplier.
3. Commitments to sell at fixed prices.	3. Vouching of sales contracts, enquiry of sales personnel, confirmation by customer.
4. Loan commitments.	4. Vouching of open commitment file, enquiry of loan officers.
5. Lease commitments.	5. Vouching of lease agreement, confirmation with lessor or lessee.

Management makes assertions about existence, completeness, rights and obligations, valuation, and presentation and disclosure. Typical specific assertions relating to long-term liabilities include:

1. All material long-term liabilities are recorded.
2. Liabilities are properly classified according to their current or long-term status. The current portion of long-term debt is properly valued and classified.
3. New long-term liabilities and debt extinguishments are properly authorized.
4. Terms, conditions, and restrictions relating to noncurrent debt are adequately disclosed.
5. Disclosures of maturities for the next five years and the capital and operating lease disclosures are accurate and adequate.
6. All important contingencies are either accrued in the accounts or disclosed in footnotes.

An illustrative program of substantive audit procedures for notes payable and long-term debt is in Appendix 12A–2.

Confirmation

When auditing long-term liabilities, auditors usually obtain independent written confirmations for notes and bonds payable. In the case of notes payable to banks, the standard bank confirmation may be used. The amount and terms of bonds payable, mortgages payable, and other formal debt instruments can be confirmed by requests to holders or a trustee. The confirmation request should include questions not only of amount, interest rate, and due date but also about collateral, restrictive covenants, and other items of agreement between lender and borrower. Confirmation requests should be sent to lenders with whom the company has done business in the recent past, even if no liability balance is shown at the confirmation date. Such extra coverage is a part of the search for unrecorded liabilities. (Refer to Chapter 10 for more on the "search for unrecorded liabilities.")

Off-Balance Sheet Financing

Confirmation and enquiry procedures may be used to obtain responses on a class of items loosely termed "off-balance sheet information." Within this category are terms of loan agreements, leases, endorsements, guarantees, and insurance policies (whether issued by a client insurance company or owned by the client). Among these items is the difficult-to-define set of "commitments and contingencies" that often pose evidence-gathering problems. Some common types of commitments are shown in Exhibit 12–4.

Footnote disclosure should be considered for the types of commitments shown in Exhibit 12–4. Some of them can be estimated and valued and, thus, can be recorded in the accounts and shown in the financial statements themselves (such as losses on fixed-price purchase commitments and losses on fixed-price sales commitments).

Analytical relationships interest expense generally is related item by item to interest-bearing liabilities. Based on the evidence of long-term liability transactions (including those that have been retired during the year), the related interest expense amounts can be recalculated. The amount of debt, the interest rate, and the time period are used to determine whether the interest expense and accrued interest are properly recorded. By comparing the audit results to the recorded interest expense and accrued interest accounts, auditors may be able to detect (1) greater expense than their calculations show, indicating some interest paid on debt unknown to them, possibly an unrecorded liability; (2) lesser expense than their calculations show, indicating misclassification, failure to accrue interest, or an interest payment default; or (3) interest expense equal to their calculations. The first two possibilities raise questions for further study, and the third shows a correct correlation between debt and debt-related expense. Examples of working papers showing this interrelationship and recalculation of interest expense and other notes payable procedures are presented in Problems 12.27 and 12.56 at the end of the chapter.

Deferred Credits—Calculated Balances

Several types of deferred credits depend on calculations for their existence and valuation. Examples include (1) deferred profit on installment sales involving the gross margin and the sale amount; (2) deferred income taxes and investment credits involving tax-book timing differences, tax rates, and amortization methods; and (3) deferred contract revenue involving contract provisions for prepayment, percentage-of-completion revenue recognition methods, or other terms unique to a contract. All of these features are incorporated in calculations that auditors can check for accuracy.

CASETTE 12.3
OFF-BALANCE SHEET INVENTORY FINANCING

Problem

Verity Distillery Company used the "product repurchase" ploy to convert its inventory to cash, failing to disclose the obligation to repurchase it later. Related party transactions were not disclosed.

Method

Verity's president incorporated the Veritas Corporation, making himself and two other Verity officers the sole shareholders. The president arranged to sell $40 million of Verity's inventory of whiskey in the aging process to Veritas, showing no gain or loss on the transaction. The officers negotiated a 36-month loan with a major bank to get the money Veritas used for the purchase, pledging the inventory as collateral. Verity pledged to repurchase the inventory for $54.4 million, which amounted to the original $40 million plus 12 percent interest for three years.

Paper Trail

The contract of sale was in the files, specifying the name of the purchasing company, the $40 million amount, and the cash consideration. Nothing mentioned the relation of Veritas to the officers. Nothing mentioned the repurchase obligation. However, the sale amount was unusually large.

Amount

The $40 million amount was 40 percent of the normal inventory. Verity's cash balance was increased 50 percent. While the current asset total was not changed, the inventory ratios (e.g., inventory turnover, day's sales in inventory) were materially altered. Long-term liabilities were understated by not recording the liability. The ploy was actually a secured loan with inventory pledged as collateral, but this reality was neither recorded nor disclosed. The total effect would be to keep debt off the books, to avoid recording interest expense, and later to record inventory at a higher cost. Subsequent sale of the whiskey at market prices would not affect the ultimate income results, but the unrecorded interest expense would be buried in the cost of goods sold. The net income in the first year when the "sale" was made was not changed, but the normal relationship of gross margin to sales was distorted by the zero-profit transaction.

	Before Transaction	Recorded Transaction	Should Have Recorded
Assets	$530	$530	$570
Liabilities	390	390	430
Shareholder Equity	140	140	140
Debt/equity ratio	2.79	2.79	3.07

AUDIT APPROACH

Audit Objective

Obtain evidence to determine whether all liabilities are recorded. Be alert to undisclosed related party transactions.

Control

The relevant control in this case would rest with the integrity and accounting knowledge of the senior officials who arranged the transaction. Authorization in the board minutes might detail the arrangements; but, if they wanted to hide it from the auditors, they also would suppress the telltale information in the board minutes.

Test of Controls

Enquiries should be made about large and unusual financing transactions. This may not elicit a response because the event is a sales transaction, according to Verity. Other audit work on controls in the revenue and collection cycle may turn up the large sale. Fortunately, this one sticks out as a large one.

Audit of Balances

Analytical procedures to compare monthly or seasonal sales probably will identify the sale as large and unusual. This identification should lead to an examination of the sales contract. Auditors should discuss the business purpose of the transaction with knowledgeable officials. If being this close to discovery does not bring out an admission of the loan and repurchase arrangement, the auditors nevertheless should investigate further. Even if the "customer" name is not a giveaway, a quick enquiry at the corporate search branch of the provincial ministry of consumer and commercial relations for corporation records (on-line in some databases) will show the names of the officers, and the auditors will know the related party nature of the deal. A request for the financial statements of Veritas should be made.

Discovery Summary

The auditors found the related party relationship between the officers and Veritas. Confronted, the president admitted the attempt to make the cash position and the debt/equity ratio look better than they were. The financial statements were adjusted to reflect the "should have recorded" set of figures shown above.

Investments and Intangibles

Companies can have a wide variety of investments and relationships with affiliates. Investments accounting may be on the cost method, equity method without consolidation or full consolidation, depending on the size and influence represented by the investment. Purchase-method consolidations usually create problems of accounting for the fair value of acquired assets and the related goodwill. Specific assertions typical of a variety of investment account balances are these:

1. Investment securities are on hand or are held in safekeeping by a trustee (existence).
2. Investment cost does not exceed market value (valuation).
3. Significant influence investments are accounted for by the equity method (valuation).
4. Purchased goodwill is properly valued (valuation).
5. Capitalized intangible costs relate to intangibles acquired in exchange transactions (valuation).

6. Research and development costs are properly classified (presentation).
7. Amortization is properly calculated (valuation).
8. Investment income has been received and recorded (completeness).
9. Investments are adequately classified and described in the balance sheet (presentation).

An illustrative program of substantive audit procedures for investments, intangibles, and related accounts is in Appendix 12A–3.

Unlike the current assets accounts, which are characterized by numerous small transactions, the noncurrent investment accounts usually consist of a few large entries. This difference has internal control and substantive audit procedure implications. The impact on the auditors' consideration of the control environment is concentration on the authorization of transactions, since each individual transaction is likely to be material in itself and the authorization will give significant information about the proper classification and accounting method. The controls usually are not reviewed, tested, and evaluated at an interim date but are considered along with the year-end procedures when the transactions and their authorizations are audited.

A few of the trouble spots in audits of investments and intangibles are in the box below.

Confirmation

The practice of obtaining independent written confirmation from outside parties is fairly limited in the area of investments, intangibles, and related income and expense accounts. Securities held by trustees or brokers should be confirmed, and the confirmation request should seek the same descriptive information as that obtained in a physical count by the auditor (described earlier in this chapter).

Enquiries about Intangibles

Company counsel can be queried about knowledge of any lawsuits or defects relating to patents, copyrights, trademarks, or trade names. This confirmation can be sought by a specific request in the enquiry letter to the law firm. (Chapter 13 contains more information regarding the enquiry letter to the law firm.)

Income from Intangibles

Royalty income from patent licences received from a single licencee may be confirmed. However, such income amounts usually are audited by vouching the licencee's reports and related cash payment.

Inspection

Investment property may be inspected in a manner similar to the physical inspection of fixed assets. The principal goal is to determine actual existence and condition of the property. Official documents of patents, copyrights, and trademark rights can be inspected to see that they are, in fact, in the name of the client.

TROUBLE SPOTS IN AUDITS OF INVESTMENTS AND INTANGIBLES

- Valuation of investments at lower of cost, market, or value impairment that is other than temporary.
- Determination of significant influence relationship for equity method investments.
- Proper determination of goodwill in purchase-method consolidations. Reasonable amortization life for goodwill.
- Realistic distinction between purchase and pooling consolidations.
- Capitalization and continuing valuation of intangibles and deferred charges.
- Realistic distinctions of research, feasibility, and production milestones for capitalization of software development costs.
- Adequate disclosure of restrictions, pledges, or liens related to investment assets.

Documentation Vouching

Investment costs should be vouched to brokers' reports, monthly statements, or other documentary evidence of cost. At the same time, the amounts of sales are traced to gain or loss accounts, and the amounts of sales prices and proceeds are vouched to the brokers' statements. Auditors should determine what method of cost-out assignment was used (i.e., FIFO, specific certificate, or average cost) and whether it is consistent with prior-years' transactions. The cost of real and personal property likewise can be vouched to invoices or other documents of purchase, and title documents (such as on land, buildings) may be inspected.

Market valuation of securities may be required in some cases. While a management may assert that an investment valuation is not impaired, subsequent sale at a loss before the end of audit field work will indicate otherwise. Auditors should review investment transactions subsequent to the balance sheet date for this kind of evidence about lower-of-cost-or-market valuation.

Vouching may be extensive in the areas of research and development (R&D) and deferred software development costs. The principal evidence problem is to determine whether costs are properly classified as assets or as R&D expense. Recorded amounts generally are selected on a sample basis, and the purchase orders, receiving reports, payroll records, authorization notices, and management reports are compared to them. Some R&D costs may resemble non-R&D cost (such as supplies, payroll costs), so auditors must be very careful in the vouching to be alert for costs that appear to relate to other operations.

External Documentation

By consulting quoted market values of securities, auditors can calculate market values and determine whether investments should be written down. If quoted market values are not available, financial statements related to investments must be obtained and analysed for evidence of basic value. If such financial statements are unaudited, evidence indicated by them is considered to be extremely weak.

Income amounts can be verified by consulting published dividend records for quotations of dividends actually declared and paid during a period (e.g., Moody's and Standard & Poor's dividend records). Since auditors know the holding period of securities, dividend income can be calculated and compared to the amount in the account. Any difference could indicate a cutoff error, misclassification, defalcation, or failure to record a dividend receivable. In a similar manner, application of interest rates to bond or note investments produces a calculated interest income figure (making allowance for amortization of premium or discount if applicable).

Equity Method Investments

When equity method accounting is used for investments, auditors will need to obtain financial statements of the investee company. These should be audited statements. Inability to obtain financial statements from a closely held investee may indicate that the client investor does not have the significant controlling influence required by *Handbook* Section 3050.06–.08. When available, these statements are used as the basis for recalculating the amount of the client's share of income to recognize in the accounts. In addition, these statements may be used to audit the disclosure of investees' assets, liabilities, and income presented in footnotes (a disclosure recommended when investments accounted for by the equity method are material).

Amortization Recalculation

Amortization of goodwill and other intangibles should be recalculated. Like depreciation, amortization expense owes its existence to a calculation, and recalculation based on audited costs and rates is sufficient audit evidence.[1]

Merger and acquisition transactions should be reviewed in terms of the appraisals, judgments, and allocations used to assign portions of the purchase price to tangible assets, intangible assets, liabilities, and goodwill. In the final analysis, nothing really substitutes for the inspection of transaction documentation, but verbal enquiries may help auditors to understand the circumstances of a merger.

Questions about lawsuits challenging patents, copyrights, or trade names may produce early knowledge of problem areas for further investigation. Likewise, discussions and questions about research and development successes and failures may alert the audit team to problems of valuation of intangible assets and related amortization expense. Responses to questions about licensing of patents can be used in the audit of related royalty revenue accounts.

Enquiries About Management Intentions

Enquiries should deal with the nature of investments and the reasons for holding them. Management's expressed intention that a marketable security investment be considered a long-term investment may be the only available evidence for classifying it as long term and not as a current asset. The classification will affect the accounting treatment of market values and the unrealized gains and losses on investments.

---

[1] Under section 3060.31 of the *Handbook* the official terminology is now "capital assets" and "amortization" although "depreciation" still receives common use when reference is to amortization of tangible capital assets.

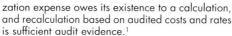

CASETTE 12.4
A CONSOLIDATION BY ANY OTHER NAME

Problem

Digilog, Inc., formed another company named DBS International (DBSI), controlled it, and did not consolidate its financial position and results of operations in the Digilog financial statements. Digilog income was overstated, and assets and liabilities were understated.

Method

Digilog, Inc., formed DBSI as a separate corporation to market Digilog's microcomputer equipment. DBSI was formed separately to avoid the adverse impact of reporting expected startup losses in Digilog's financial statements. Instead of owning shares in DBSI, Digilog financed the company with loans convertible at will into 90 percent of DBSI's stock. (Otherwise, the share ownership was not in Digilog's name.) Since Digilog did not control DBSI (control defined as 50 percent or more ownership), DBSI was not consolidated, and the initial losses were not reported in Digilog's financial statements. See *Handbook Section* 1590.08 for the usual presumptions concerning the level of ownership leading to control.

Paper Trail

Formation of DBSI was not a secret. It was authorized. Incorporation papers were available. Loan documents showing the terms of Digilog's loans to DBSI were in the files.

Amount

Several hundred thousand dollars of losses in the first two years of DBSI operations were not consolidated. Ultimately, the venture became profitable and was absorbed into Digilog.

AUDIT APPROACH

Audit Objective

Obtain evidence to determine whether proper accounting methods (cost, equity, consolidation) are used for investments.

Control

The relevant control in this case would rest with the integrity and accounting knowledge of the senior officials who arranged the transaction. Proper documentation of authorization and financing and operating transactions between the two corporations should be in the companies' files.

Test of Controls

Enquiries should be made about large and unusual financing transactions. Minutes of the board of directors' meetings should be studied to find related authorizations. These authorizations and supporting papers signal the accounting issues and the interpretations of generally accepted accounting principles required in the circumstances.

Audit of Balances

The central issue in this case was the interpretation of accounting standards regarding required consolidation. Existence, completeness, valuation, and ownership were not problematic audit issues. Unless these are extenuating factors (*Handbook Section* 1590.08), accounting standards require consolidation of over-50 percent owned subsidiaries, and prohibits consolidation of subsidiaries owned less than 50 percent. Digilog's purpose in financing DBSI with loans instead of direct share ownership was to skirt the 50 percent "ownership" criterion, thus keeping the DBSI losses out of the Digilog consolidated financial statements. The "test of the balance" (decision of whether to require consolidation) amounted to an interpretation of the substance versus form of "ownership" through convertible notes instead of direct shareholding.

Discovery Summary

Digilog, with concurrence of its independent audit firm, adopted the narrow interpretation of "ownership." Since Digilog did not "own" DBSI stock, DBSI was not "controlled," and its assets, liabilities, and results of operations were not consolidated. The regulator disagreed and took action on the position that the convertible feature of the loans and the business purpose of the DBSI formation were enough to attribute control to Digilog. The company was enjoined from violating certain reporting and antifraud provisions of the provincial securities act and was required to amend its financial statements for the years in question (consolidating DBSI). The regulator also took action against the audit firm partner in charge of the Digilog audit.

R E V I E W
CHECKPOINTS

12.15 What are some of the typical assertions found in owners' equity descriptions and account balances?

12.16 How can confirmations be used in auditing shareholder capital accounts? in auditing notes and bonds payable?

12.17 What are some of the typical assertions found in the long-term liability accounts?

12.18 What procedures do auditors employ to obtain evidence of the cost of investments? of investment gains and losses? of investment income?

12.19 Why are auditors interested in substantial investment losses occurring early in the period following year-end?

12.20 What is the concept of "substance versus form" in relation to financing and investment transactions and balances? (Refer to the off-balance sheet and consolidation cases in the chapter.)

12.21 What are some of the "trouble spots" for auditors in the audits of investments and intangibles?

OTHER ASPECTS OF CLEVER ACCOUNTING AND FRAUD

The types of clever accounting and fraud that must be considered are those affecting the fair presentation of material equity accounts, investments, and intangibles. Improper accounting presentations are engineered more frequently by senior officials than by middle management or lower ranks. Top management personnel who deal with the transactions involved in investments, long-term debt, and shareholders' equity are not subject to the same kind of control as lower-level employees, and they generally are able to override detail procedural controls.

Long-term Liabilities and Owners' Equity

The kinds of clever accounting and fraud connected with liability and owners' equity accounts differ significantly from those associated with asset and revenue accounts.

Few employees are tempted to steal a liability, although fictitious liabilities may be created as a means of misdirecting cash payments into the hands of an officer. Auditors should be alert for such fictions in the same sense that they are alert to the possibility of having fictitious accounts receivable.

Although there are opportunities for employee fraud against the company, the area of liabilities and owners' equity also opens up possibilities for company fraud against outsiders. This class of fraud is most often accomplished through material misrepresentations or omissions in financial statements and related disclosures.

Officers and employees can use share or bond instruments improperly. Unissued shares or bonds and treasury stock may be used as collateral for personal loans. Even though the company may not be damaged or suffer loss by this action (unless the employee defaults and the securities are seized), the practice is unauthorized and is contrary to company interests. Similarly, employees may gain access to shareholder lists and unissued coupons and cause improper payments of dividends and interest on securities that are not outstanding.

Proper custodial control of securities (either by physical means, such as limited-access vaults, or by control of an independent disbursing agent) prevents most such occurrences. An auditing procedure of reconciling authorized dividend and interest payments (calculated using declared dividend rates, coupon interest rates, and known quantities of outstanding securities) to actual payments detects unauthorized payments. If the company did not perform this checking procedure, auditors should include it among their own analytical recalculation procedures. Many liability, equity, and off-balance-sheet transactions are outside the reach of normal internal control procedures, which can operate effectively over ordinary transactions (such as purchases and sales) processed by clerks and machines. Auditors generally are justified in performing extensive substantive auditing of long-term liability, equity, and other high-level managed transactions and agreements since control depends in large part on the integrity and accounting knowledge of management.

Income tax evasion and fraud result from actions taken by managers. Evasion and fraud may be accomplished (1) by simple omission of income, (2) by unlawful deductions (such as contributions to political campaigns, capital cost allowance on nonexistent assets, or capital cost allowance in excess of cost), or (3) by contriving sham transactions for the sole purpose of avoiding taxation. Auditors should be able to detect errors of the first two categories if the actual income and expense data have been sufficiently audited in the financial statements. The last category—contrived sham transactions—is harder to detect because a dishonest management can skilfully disguise them. Some of the procedures outlined in Chapter 18 may be useful and effective.

Financial statements may be materially misstated by reason of omission or understatement of liabilities and by failure to disclose technical defaults on loan agreement restrictions. These restrictions or test covenants can be very important to the viability of the client because if they are violated, creditors can force the client into bankruptcy. Hence auditor knowledge of these restrictions and comparison with the client's current financial condition is very important for pinpointing audit risk areas and for properly assessing the going concern assumption. The procedures you have learned to discover unrecorded liabilities through a "search for unrecorded liabilities" may be used to discover such omissions and understatements (Chapter 10). If auditors discover that loan agreement terms have been violated, they should bring the information to the client's attention and insist on proper disclosure in notes to the financial statements. In both situations (liability understatement and loan default disclosure), management's actions, reactions, and willingness to adjust the financial figures and to make adverse disclosures are important insights for auditors' subjective evaluation of managerial integrity. An accumulation of inputs relevant to managerial integrity can have an important bearing on the auditors' perceptions of relative risk for the audit engagement taken as a whole.

Intent is difficult to prove and for that reason "a misstatement arising from management's bias in selecting and applying accounting principles or in making accounting estimates would be considered an error" (*Section* 5135). However, the audit also needs to be performed with professional skepticism, meaning the auditor:

(*a*) should be aware of factors that increase the risk of misstatement; and

(*b*) should be sensitized to evidence that contradicts the assumption of management's good faith.

If there are enough "red flags" present, the auditor will assess a higher inherent risk and for a given control risk these higher assessments will cause the auditor to:

(*a*) obtain more reliable evidence.

(*b*) expand the extent of audit procedures performed.

(*c*) apply audit procedures closer to or as of the BS date.

(*d*) require more extensive supervision of assistants and/or assistants with more experience and training.

In essence, if the auditor suspects that the financial statements are misstated, he or she should perform procedures to confirm or dispel that suspicion.

Generally, the auditor is less likely to detect material misstatements arising from fraud because of the deliberate concealment involved.

The auditor should inform the appropriate level of management whenever he or she obtains evidence of a nontrivial misstatement; and the audit committee or board of directors should be informed of all significant misstatements (*Section* 5135).

A company, its individual managers, and the auditors can violate securities regulations if they are not careful. Chapter 16 covers the general framework of regulation by provincial securities commissions. Auditors must know the provisions of the securities laws to the extent that they can identify situations that constitute obvious fraud, and so that they can identify transactions that may be subject to the law. Having once recognized or raised questions about a securities transaction, auditors should not act as their own lawyer. The facts should be submitted to competent legal counsel for an opinion. Even though auditors are not expected to be legal experts, they have the duty to recognize obvious instances of impropriety and to pursue investigations with the aid of legal experts.

Similarly, auditors should assist clients in observing securities commission rules and regulations on matters of timely disclosure. In general, the timely disclosure rules are phrased in terms of management's duties, and they do not require auditors to carry out any specific procedures or to make any specific disclosures. The regulations' purpose is to require management to disseminate to the public any material information, whether favourable or unfavourable, so that investors can incorporate it in their decision making. Various rule provisions require announcements and disclosures very soon after information becomes known. Often, relevant situations arise during the year when the independent auditors are not present, so, of course, they cannot be held responsible or liable. However, in other situations, auditors may learn of the information inadvertently or the auditors' advice may be sought by the client.

In such cases auditors should advise their clients, consistent with the requirements of law and regulations.

Presently, pressures are on the auditors to discover more information about off-balance sheet contingencies and commitments and to discover the facts of management involvement with other parties to transactions. Auditors' knowledge of contingencies and commitments that are not evidenced in accounting records depends in large part on information the management and its legal counsel will reveal. Nevertheless, certain investigative procedures are available (Chapter 18). The current pressures on auditors to discover more information is a part of the public pressure on auditors to take more responsibility for fraud detection.

Investments and Intangibles

Theft, diversion, and unauthorized use of investment securities can occur in several ways. If safekeeping controls are weak, securities simply may be stolen, in which case the theft becomes a police problem rather than an auditing problem. Somewhat more frequent are diversions, such as using securities as collateral during the year, returning them for a count, then giving them back to the creditor without disclosure to the auditor. If safekeeping methods require entry signatures (as at a safe-deposit vault), auditors may be able to detect the in-and-out movement. The best chance of discovery is that the creditor will confirm the collateral arrangement. In a similar manner, securities may be removed by an officer and sold, then repurchased before the auditors' count. The auditors' record of the certificate numbers should reveal this change, since the returned certificates (and their serial numbers) will not be the same as the ones removed. The rapid growth in use of derivative securities as investments and hedges has created new and rather unique problems for auditors, not the least of which is lack of familiarity with these financial instruments. Appendix 12A–4 provides an overview of the recent global problems in this area.

Cash receipts from interest, royalties on patent licences, dividends, and sales proceeds may be stolen. The accounting records may or may not be manipulated to cover the theft. In general, this kind of defalcation should be prevented by cash receipts control; but, since these receipts usually are irregular and infrequent, the cash control system may not be as effective as it is for regular receipts on trade accounts. If the income accounts are not manipulated to hide stolen receipts, auditors will find less income in the account than the amount indicated by their audit calculations based on other records, such as licence agreements or published dividend records. If sales of securities are not recorded, auditors will notice that securities are missing when they try to inspect or confirm them. If the income accounts have been manipulated to hide stolen receipts, vouching of cash receipts will detect the theft, or vouching may reveal some offsetting debit buried in some other account.

Accounting values may be manipulated in a number of ways, involving purchase of assets at inflated prices, leases with affiliates, acquisitions of patents for shares given to an inventor or promoter, sales to affiliates, and fallacious decisions about amortization. Business history has recorded several cases of non-arm's-length transactions with promoters, officers, directors, and controlled companies (even "dummy" companies) designed to drain the company's resources and fool the auditors.

In one case a company sold assets to a dummy purchaser set up by a director to bolster sagging income with a gain. The auditors did not know that the purchaser was a shell. All the documents of sale looked in order, and cash sales proceeds had been deposited. The auditors were not informed of a secret agreement by the seller to repurchase the assets at a later time. This situation illustrates a very devious manipulation. All transactions with persons closely associated with the company (related parties) should be audited carefully with reference to market values, particularly when a nonmonetary transaction is involved (such as shares exchanged for patent rights). Sales and lease-back and straight lease transactions with insiders likewise should be audited carefully.

R E V I E W
CHECKPOINTS

12.22 What is the single most significant control consideration in connection with clever accounting and fraud in finance and investment cycle accounts?

12.23 Which is more likely to exist in the finance and investment cycle accounts: (1) fraud against the company? or (2) fraud by the company in financial or tax reporting? Explain.

12.24 What should an auditor do when violation of securities laws is suspected?

12.25 What is the danger for auditors when company officials engage in undisclosed related party transactions?

Summary

The finance and investment cycle contains a wide variety of accounts—share capital, dividends, long-term debt, interest expense, tax expenses and deferred taxes, financial instruments, marketable securities, equity method investments, related gains and losses, consolidated subsidiaries, goodwill, and other intangibles. These accounts involve some of the most technically complex accounting standards. They create most of the difficult judgments for financial reporting.

Transactions in these accounts generally are controlled by senior officials. Therefore, internal control is centred on the integrity and accounting knowledge of these officials. The procedural controls over details of transactions are not very effective because the senior managers can override them and order their own desired accounting presentations. As a consequence, auditors' work on the assessment of control risk is directed toward the senior managers, the board of directors, and their authorizations and design of finance and investment deals.

Fraud and clever accounting in the finance and investment cycle get directed most often to producing misleading financial statements. While theft and embezzlement can occur, the accounts in this cycle frequently have been the ones subject to manipulation and spurious valuation for the purpose of reporting financial position and results of operations better than the reality of companies' situations. Off-balance-sheet financing and investment transactions with related parties are explained as ripe areas for fraudulent financial reporting.

This chapter ends the book's coverage of audit applications for various cycles and their accounts. Chapter 13 contains several topics involved in putting the finishing touches on an audit.

KINGSTON COMPANY

12.26   Kingston Company: Long-Term Liabilities and Owners' Equity Adjustments.

In your audit of the long-term liabilities and owners' equity, you discovered the following items:

1. The 11 percent bank loan of $750,000 was obtained July 1 of the year under audit (1992). Interest is payable annually on each June 30. No interest was accrued as of December 31.

2. The $400,000 in notes payable represents the balance of the $600,000 borrowed in January 1991, to finance the new building, which was mortgaged to the noteholders. The original agreement that accompanied the notes provides for interest at 10 percent paid annually each January and a $200,000 annual payment to a bank trustee each year to retire the notes.

   The $200,000 was paid on time (January 1992), as was the interest payment. On examination of the interest expense account, you find a balance of $40,000, representing the accrual for 1992.

3. Your review of the minutes of the board of directors for the January 1993 meetings reveals that dividends of $50,000 had been declared to be distributed to shareholders of record on December 31, 1992, to be paid February 15.

4. The January board minutes also include a discussion of the opportunity to purchase another lumber company in Sudbury, Ontario. The board authorized Julian Greene to deposit $100,000 in an escrow bank account to hold the offer until the board has more information.

Required:

a. Prepare adjusting and reclassification entries to propose to Kingston management based on the information above. Be sure to include a sufficient explanation of each entry you propose.

b. Describe the disclosure you would suggest for the items listed above.

12.27   Kingston Company: Notes Payable and Interest Working Paper.   Exhibit

12.27–1 is a working paper prepared by the client for the company's notes payable and interest expense. It has been given to you for your information. This is part of the help the client's personnel provide in connection with the audit.

Required:

Make a copy of Exhibit 12.27–1. Using the tick marks shown at the bottom of the working paper, indicate alongside the data in the working paper the work you will perform as an auditor. Complete the working paper for the audit files. Assume that you performed the work on January 26, 1993, and that it was reviewed by T. Townsend on January 30, 1993.

MULTIPLE-CHOICE QUESTIONS FOR PRACTICE AND REVIEW

12.28 Jones was engaged to examine the financial statements of Gamma Corporation for the year ended June 30, 1993. Having completed an examination of the investment securities, which of the following is the best method of verifying the accuracy of recorded dividend income?

a. Tracing recorded dividend income to cash receipts records and validated deposit slips.

b. Utilizing analytical review techniques and statistical sampling.

c. Comparing recorded dividends with amounts appearing on federal tax returns.

E X H I B I T   12.27–1   **NOTES PAYABLE AND INTEREST EXPENSE**

```
M-2                        KINGSTON COMPANY              Prepared _____
                   NOTES PAYABLE AND INTEREST EXPENSE    Date _____
                          December 31, 1992              Reviewed _____
                                                         Date _____
---------------------------------------------------------------------------
                             First      Mutual                    a/c/527
                             National   Insurance   Liability     Interest
                             Bank       Co.         Total         Expense
---------------------------------------------------------------------------

Balance 12-31-91:
   10% Long-term note                   600,000     600,000
      due 1994

Additions:
   11% note dated 7-1-92     750,000                750,000
      unsecured, due 6-30-93

Repayments:
   1-1-92                               (200,000)   (200,000)
                                        -----------------------------------

Balance 12-31-92            750,000     400,000     1,150,000
                                        -----------------------------------
```

α Per prior year's working papers.

c Obtained Bank Confirmation. See C-2.1

R Recalculated interest expense.

u Vouched to cancelled cheque.

✗ Traced to BOD authorization. PF-10.

✓ Vouched to bank transfer notice and bank statement.

✗ Kingston neither paid nor accrued this interest expense.

𝒯/ℬ Traced to general ledger.

---

d. Comparing recorded dividends with a standard financial reporting service's record of dividends.

12.29 When a large amount of negotiable securities is held by the client, planning by the auditor is necessary to guard against:

a. Unauthorized negotiation of the securities before they are counted.

b. Unrecorded sales of securities after they are counted.

c. Substitution of securities already counted for other securities which should be on hand but are not.

d. Substitution of authentic securities with counterfeit securities.

12.30 In connection with the audit of an issue of long-term bonds payable, the auditor should:

a. Determine whether bondholders are persons other than owners, directors, or officers of the company issuing the bond.

b. Calculate the effective interest rate to see if it is substantially the same as the rates for similar issues.

c. Decide whether the bond issue was made without violating state or local law.

d. Ascertain that the client has obtained the opinion of counsel on the legality of the issue.

12.31 Which of the following is the most important consideration of an auditor when examining the shareholders' equity section of a client's balance sheet?

a. Changes in the share capital account are verified by an independent share transfer agent.

b. Stock dividends and stock splits during the year under audit were approved by the shareholders.

c. Stock dividends are capitalized at par or stated value on the dividend declaration date.

d. Entries in the share capital account can be traced to resolutions in the minutes of the board of directors' meetings.

12.32 If the auditor discovers that the carrying amount of a client's investments is overstated because of a loss in value that is other than a temporary decline in market value, the auditor should insist that:

a. The approximate market value of the investments be shown in parentheses on the face of the balance sheet.

b. The investments be classified as long term for balance sheet purposes with full disclosure in the footnotes.

c. The loss in value be recognized in the financial statements.

d. The equity section of the balance sheet separately shows a charge equal to the amount of the loss.

12.33 The primary reason for preparing a reconciliation between interest-bearing obligations outstanding during the year and interest expense in the financial statements, is to:

a. Evaluate internal control over securities.

b. Determine the validity of prepaid interest expense.

c. Ascertain the reasonableness of imputed interest.

d. Detect unrecorded liabilities.

12.34 The auditor should insist that a representative of the client be present during the inspection and count of securities in order to:

a. Lend authority to the auditor's directives.

b. Detect forged securities.

c. Co-ordinate the return of all securities to proper locations.

d. Acknowledge the receipt of securities returned.

12.35 When independent share transfer agents are not employed and the corporation issues its own shares and maintains share records, cancelled share certificates should:

a. Be defaced to prevent reissuance and attached to their corresponding stubs.

b. Not be defaced, but segregated from other share certificates and retained in a cancelled certificates file.

c. Be destroyed to prevent fraudulent reissuance.

d. Be defaced and sent to the federal finance minister.

12.36 When a client company does not maintain its own share capital records, the auditor should obtain written confirmation from the transfer agent and registrar concerning:

a. Restrictions on the payment of dividends.

b. The number of shares issued and outstanding.

c. Guarantees of preferred share liquidation value.

d. The number of shares subject to agreements to repurchase.

(AICPA adapted)

12.37 All corporate share capital transactions should ultimately be traced to the:

a. Minutes of the board of directors.

b. Cash receipts journal.

c. Cash disbursements journal.

d. Numbered share certificates.

12.38 A corporate balance sheet indicates that one of the corporate assets is a patent. An auditor will most likely obtain evidence of this patent by obtaining a written representation from:

a. A patent lawyer.

b. A regional patent office.

c. The patent inventor.

d. The patent owner.

12.39 An audit program for the examination of the retained earnings account should include a step that requires verification of the:

a. Market value used to charge retained earnings to account for a two-for-one share split.

b. Approval of the adjustment to the beginning balance as a result of a write-down of an account receivables.

c. Authorization for both cash and share dividends.

d. Gain or loss resulting from disposition of treasury shares.

EXERCISES AND PROBLEMS

· ·

INVESTMENTS AND INTANGIBLES

12.40 ICQ for Equity Investments. Cassandra Corporation, a manufacturing company, periodically invests large sums in marketable equity securities. The investment policy is established by the investment committee of the board of directors. The treasurer is responsible for carrying out the investment committee's directives. All securities are stored in a bank safe-deposit vault.

Your internal control questionnaire with respect to Cassandra's investments in equity securities contains the following three questions:

1. Is investment policy established by the investment committee of the board of directors?

2. Is the treasurer solely responsible for carrying out the investment committee's directive?

3. Are all securities stored in a bank safe-deposit vault?

Required:

In addition to the above three questions, what questions should your internal control questionnaires include with respect to the company's investment in marketable equity securities? (Hint: Prepare questions to cover the control objectives—validity, completeness, authorization, accuracy, classification, accounting, and proper period.)

(AICPA adapted)

12.41 Noncurrent Investment Securities. You are engaged in the audit of the financial statements of Bass Corporation for the year ended December 31, and you are about to begin an audit of the noncurrent investment securities. Bass's records indicate that the company owns various bearer bonds, as well as 25 percent of the outstanding common shares of Commercial Industrial, Inc. You are satisfied with evidence that supports the presumption of significant influence over Commercial Industrial, Inc. The various securities are at two locations as follows:

1. Recently acquired securities are in the company's safe in the custody of the treasurer.

2. All other securities are in the company's bank safe deposit box. All securities in Bass's portfolio are actively traded in a broad market.

Required:

a. Assuming that the system of internal control over securities is satisfactory, what are the objectives (specific assertions) for the audit of the noncurrent securities?

b. What audit procedures should you undertake with respect to the audit of Bass's investment securities?

(AICPA adapted)

12.42 Securities Examination and Count. You are in charge of the audit of the financial statements of the Demot Corporation for the year ended December 31. The corporation has had the policy of investing its surplus funds in marketable securities. Its share and bond certificates are kept in a safe-deposit box in a local bank. Only the president and the treasurer of the corporation have access to the box.

You were unable to obtain access to the safe-deposit box on December 31 because neither the president nor the treasurer was available. Arrangements were made for your assistant to accompany the treasurer to the bank on January 11 to examine the securities. Your assistant has never examined securities that were being kept in a safe-deposit box and requires instructions. Your assistant should be able to inspect all securities on hand in an hour.

Required:

a. List the instructions that you would give to your assistant regarding the examination of the share and bond certificates kept in the safe-deposit box. Include in your instructions the details of the securities to be examined and the reasons for examining these details.

b. After returning from the bank, your assistant reports that the treasurer had entered the box on January 4 to remove an old photograph of the corporation's original building. The photograph was loaned to the local chamber of commerce for display purposes. List the additional audit procedures that are required because of the treasurer's action.

(AICPA adapted)

12.43 Securities Procedures. You were engaged to examine the financial statements of Ronlyn Corporation for the year ended June 30. On May 1 the corporation borrowed $500,000 from the Second National Bank to finance plant expansion. However, due to unexpected difficulties in acquiring the building site, the plant expansion had not begun as planned. To make use of the borrowed funds, management decided to invest in shares and bonds; on May 16 the $500,000 was invested in securities.

Required:

In your audit of investments, how would you:

a. Audit the recorded dividend or interest income?

b. Determine market value?

c. Establish the authority for security purchases?

(AICPA adapted)

12.44 Research and Development. The Hertle Engineering Company depends on innovation of new product development to maintain its position in the market for drilling tool equipment. The company conducts an extensive research and development program for this purpose, and it consistently charges research and development costs to current operations in accordance with Statement on Financial Accounting Standards No. 2.

The company began a project called Project Able in January 1991 with the goal of patenting a revolutionary drilling bit design. Work continued until October 1992 when the company applied for a patent. Costs were charged to the research and development expense account in both years, except for the cost of a computer program that engineers plan to use in Project Baker, scheduled to start in December 1992. The computer program was purchased from Computeering, Inc., in January 1991 for $45,000.

Required:

a. Give an audit program for the audit of research and development costs on Project Able. Assume that you are auditing the company for the first time at December 31, 1992.

b. What evidence would you require for the audit of the computer program that has been capitalized as an intangible asset? As of December 31, 1992, this account has a balance of $40,000 (cost less $5,000 amortized as a part of Project Able).

(AICPA adapted)

12.45 Intangibles. Sorenson Manufacturing Corporation was incorporated on January 3, 1991. The corporation's financial statements for its first year's operations were not examined by a PA. You have been engaged to audit the financial statements for the year ended December 31, 1992, and your examination is substantially completed.

A partial trial balance of the company's accounts is given below:

SORENSON MANUFACTURING CORPORATION Trial Balance at December 31, 1992		
	Trial Balance	
	Debit	Credit
Cash	$11,000	
Accounts receivable	42,500	
Allowance for doubtful accounts		$ 500
Inventories	38,500	
Machinery	75,000	
Equipment	29,000	
Accumulated depreciation		10,000
Patents	85,000	
Leasehold improvements	26,000	
Prepaid expenses	10,500	
Organization expenses	29,000	
Goodwill	24,000	
Licensing Agreement No. 1	50,000	
Licensing Agreement No. 2	49,000	

The following information relates to accounts which may yet require adjustment:

1. Patents for Sorenson's manufacturing process were purchased January 2, 1992, at a cost of $68,000. An additional $17,000 was spent in December 1992 to improve machinery covered by the patents and charged to the patents account. The patents had a remaining legal term of 17 years.
2. On January 3, 1991, Sorenson purchased two licensing agreements, which at that time were believed to have unlimited useful lives. The balance in the licensing agreement no. 1 account included its purchase price of $48,000 and $2,000 in acquisition expenses. licensing agreement no. 2 also was purchased on January 3, 1991, for $50,000, but it has been reduced by a credit of $1,000 for the advance collection of 1988 revenue from the agreement.

   In December 1991 an explosion caused a permanent 60 percent reduction in the expected revenue-producing value of licensing agreement no. 1, and in January 1992 a flood caused additional damage, which rendered the agreement worthless.

   A study of licensing agreement no. 2 made by Sorenson in January 1992 revealed that its estimated remaining life expectancy was only 10 years as of January 1, 1992.
3. The balance in the goodwill account includes $24,000 paid December 30, 1991, for an advertising program, which it is estimated will assist in increasing Sorenson's sales over a period of four years following the disbursement.
4. The leasehold improvement account includes (*a*) the $15,000 cost of improvements, with a total estimated useful life of 12 years, which Sorenson, as tenant, made to leased premises in January 1991; (*b*) movable assembly line equipment costing $8,500, which was installed in the leased premises in December 1992; and (*c*) real estate taxes of $2,500 paid by Sorenson which, under the terms of the lease, should have been paid by the landlord. Sorenson paid its rent in full during 1992. A 10-year nonrenewable lease was signed January 3, 1991, for the leased building that Sorenson used in manufacturing operations.
5. The balance in the organization expenses account includes preoperating costs incurred during the organizational period.

Required:
Prepare adjusting entries as necessary.

(AICPA adapted)

LONG-TERM LIABILITIES AND COMMITMENTS

12.46 Long-term Note. You were engaged to examine the financial statements of Ronlyn Corporation for the year ended June 30. On May 1 the corporation borrowed $500,000 from the Second National Bank to finance plant expansion. The long-term note agreement provided for the annual payment of principal and interest over five years. The existing plant was pledged as security for the loan.

Due to unexpected difficulties in acquiring the building site, the plant expansion had not begun as planned. To make use of the borrowed funds, management decided to invest in shares and bonds, and on May 16 the $500,000 was invested in securities.

Required:

a. What are the audit objectives in the examining of long-term debt?

b. Prepare an audit program for the examination of the long-term note agreement between Ronlyn and Second National Bank.

(AICPA adapted)

12.47 Long-Term Financing Agreement. You have been engaged to audit the financial statements of Broadwall Corporation for the year ended December 31, 1992. During the year, Broadwall obtained a long-term loan from a local bank pursuant to a financing agreement, which provided that:

1. Loan was to be secured by the company's inventory and accounts receivable.
2. Company was to maintain a debt-to-equity ratio not to exceed 2:1.
3. Company was not to pay dividends without permission from the bank.
4. Monthly instalment payments were to commence July 1, 1992.

In addition, during the year the company also borrowed, on a short-term basis, from the president of the company, substantial amounts just prior to the year-end.

Required:

a. For the purposes of your audit of the financial statements of erty which is security for this debt within the time provided by law for payment without penalty and shall deposit receipted tax bills or equally acceptable evidence of payment of same with the trustee."

4. "A sinking fund shall be deposited with the trustee by semiannual payments of $300,000, from which the trustee shall, in his discretion, purchase bonds of this issue."

(AICPA adapted)

Broadwall Corporation, what procedures should you employ in examining the described loans? Do not discuss internal control.

b. What financial statement disclosures should you expect to find with respect to the loan from the president?

12.48 Bond Indenture Covenants. The following covenants are extracted from the indenture of a bond issue. The indenture provides that failure to comply with its terms in any respect automatically advances the due date of the loan to the date of noncompliance (the regular date is 20 years hence). Give any audit steps or reporting requirements you believe should be taken or recognized in connection with each of the following:

1. "The debtor company shall endeavour to maintain a working capital ratio of 2:1 at all times, and, in any fiscal year following a failure to maintain said ratio, the company shall restrict compensation of officers to a total of $500,000. Officers for this purpose shall include chairman of the board of directors, president, all vice presidents, secretary, and treasurer."

2. "The debtor company shall keep all property which is security for this debt insured against loss by fire to the extent of 100 percent of its actual value. Policies of insurance comprising this protection shall be filed with the trustee."

3. "The debtor company shall pay all taxes legally assessed against prop-

OWNERS' EQUITY

12.49 Common Share and Treasury Share Audit Procedures. You are the continuing auditor of Sussex, Inc., and are beginning the audit of the common share and treasury share accounts. You have decided to design substantive audit procedures with reliance on internal controls.

Sussex has no-par, no-stated-value common shares, and acts as its own registrar and transfer agent. During the past year, Sussex both issued and reacquired shares of its own common stock, some of which the company still owned at year-end. Additional common share transactions occurred among the shareholders during the year.

Common share transactions can be traced to individual shareholders' accounts in a subsidiary ledger and to a share certificate book. The company has not paid any cash or share dividends. There are no other classes of shares, share rights, warrants, or option plans.

Required:

What substantive audit procedures should you apply in examining the common share and treasury share accounts? Organize your answer as a list of audit procedures organized by the financial statement assertions. (See Appendix 20A–1 for examples of substantive procedures for owners' equity.)

(AICPA adapted)

12.50 **Shareholders' Equity.** You are a PA engaged in an examination of the financial statements of Pate Corporation for the year ended December 31. The financial statements and records of Pate Corporation have not been audited by a PA in prior years.

The shareholders' equity section of Pate Corporation's balance sheet at December 31 follows:

Shareholders' equity:	
Share capital—10,000 shares of $10 par value authorized; 5,000 shares issued and outstanding	$50,000
Capital contributed in excess of par value of share capital	32,580
Retained earnings	47,320
Total shareholders' equity	$129,900

Pate Corporation was founded in 1982. The corporation has 10 shareholders and serves as its own registrar and transfer agent. There are no capital share subscription contracts in effect.

Required:

a. Prepare the detailed audit program for the examination of the three accounts composing the shareholders' equity section of Pate Corporation's balance sheet. Organize the audit program under broad financial statement assertions. (Do not include in the audit program the audit of the results of the current year's operations.)

b. After every other figure on the balance sheet has been audited, it may appear that the retained earnings figure is a balancing figure and requires no further audit work. Why don't auditors audit retained earnings as they do the other figures on the balance sheet? Discuss.

(AICPA adapted)

Discussion Cases

12.51 **Oil Leases Exchanged for Capital Shares.** Al and Billy Bob formed the Wildcat Corporation and transferred to it oil leases owned equally by them for which they had paid $30 in capitalized fees. They also had paid $1,280 for delay lease rentals, which they had charged to expense in the year paid by them as individuals. Al and Billy Bob had no other costs or expenses applicable to these leases.

At the time of the transfer, there were favourable geological and geophysical reports on the property, but there had been no production in the area. The board of directors of the Wildcat Corporation issued $300,000 par value common shares for the leases, one half the shares going to Al and one half to Billy Bob. Al and Billy Bob then donated one half of their respective shares to the corporate treasury to be sold at par for working capital.

Required:

a. Discuss the proper balance sheet presentation of the leases and of the capital and donated shares.

b. What audit procedures would you apply to the leases? (Consider the audit objectives in planning the proper audit procedures.)

c. Must this share issue be reported or registered with the SEC? Explain.

(AICPA adapted)

12.52 Intercompany and Interpersonal Investment Relations. You have been engaged to audit the financial statements of Hardy Hardware Distributors, Inc., as of December 31. In your review of the corporate nonfinancial records, you have found that Hardy Hardware owns 15 percent of the outstanding voting common shares of Hardy Products Corporation. Upon further investigation, you learn that Hardy Products Corporation manufactures a line of hardware goods, 90 percent of which is sold to Hardy Hardware.

Mr. James L. Hardy, president of Hardy Hardware, has supplied you with objective evidence that he personally owns 30 percent of the Hardy Products voting shares and that the remaining 70 percent is owned by Mr. John L. Hardy, his brother and president of Hardy Products. James L. Hardy also owns 20 percent of the voting common shares of Hardy Hardware Distributors. Another 20 percent is held by an estate of which James and John are beneficiaries, and the remaining 60 percent is publicly held. The shares are listed on the American Stock Exchange.

Hardy Hardware consistently has reported operating profits greater than the industry average. Hardy Products Corporation, however, has a net return on sales of only 1 percent. The Hardy Products investment always has been reported at cost, and no dividends have been paid by the company. During the course of your conversations with the Hardy brothers, you learn that you were appointed as auditor because the brothers had a heated disagreement with the former auditor over the issues of accounting for the Hardy Products investment and the prices at which goods have been sold to Hardy Hardware.

For Discussion:

a. Identify the issues in this situation as they relate to (1) conflicts of interest and (2) controlling influences among individuals and corporations.

b. Should the investment in Hardy Products Corporation be accounted for on the equity method?

c. What evidence should the auditor seek with regard to the prices paid by Hardy Hardware for products purchased from Hardy Products Corporation?

d. What information would you consider necessary for adequate disclosure in the financial statements of Hardy Hardware Distributors?

INSTRUCTIONS FOR DISCUSSION CASES 12.53–12.54—.

These cases are designed like the ones in the chapter. They give the problem, the method, the paper trail, and the amount. Your assignment is to write the Audit Approach portion of the case, organized around these sections:

Objectives: Express the objective in terms of the facts supposedly asserted in financial records, accounts, and statements. (Refer to discussion of assertions in Chapter 4.)

Control: Write a brief explanation of control considerations, especially the kinds of manipulations that may arise from the situation described in the case.

Test of controls: Write some procedures for getting evidence about existing controls, especially procedures that could discover management manipulations. If there are no controls to test, then there are no procedures to perform; go then to the next section. A "procedure" should instruct someone about the source(s) of evidence to tap and the work to do.

Audit of balance: Write some procedures for getting evidence about the existence, completeness, valuation, ownership, or disclosure assertions identified in your objective section above.

Discovery summary: Write a short statement about the discovery you expect to accomplish with your procedures.

12.53 Related Party Transaction "Goodwill."

HIDE THE LOSS UNDER THE GOODWILL

Problem: A contrived amount of goodwill was used to overstate assets and disguise a loss on discontinued operations.

Method: Gulwest Industries, a public company, decided to discontinue its unprofitable line of business of manufacturing sporting ammunition. Gulwest had capitalized the start-up cost of the business, and, with its discontinuance, the $7 million deferred cost should have been written off.

Instead, Gulwest formed a new corporation named Amron and transferred the sporting ammunition assets (including the $7 million deferred cost) to it in exchange for all the Amron shares. In the Gulwest accounts the Amron investment was carried at $12.4 million, which was the book value of the assets transferred (including the $7 million deferred cost).

In an agreement with a different public company (Big Industrial), Gulwest and Big created another company (BigShot Ammunition). Gulwest transferred all the Amron assets to BigShot in exchange for (1) common and preferred shares of Big, valued at $2 million, and (2) a note from Big-Shot in the amount of $3.4 million. Big Industrial thus acquired 100 percent of the shares of BigShot. Gulwest management reasoned that it had "given" Amron shares valued at $12.4 million to receive shares and notes valued at $5.4 million, so the difference must be goodwill. Thus, the Gulwest accounts carried amounts for Big Industrial shares ($2 million), Big-Shot note receivable ($3.4 million), and goodwill ($7 million).

Paper trail: Gulwest directors included in the minutes an analysis of the sporting ammunition business's

lack of profitability. The minutes showed approval of a plan to dispose of the business, but they did not use the words "discontinue the business." The minutes also showed approval of the creation of Amron, the deal with Big Industrial along with the formation of BigShot, and the acceptance of Big's shares and Bigshot's note in connection with the final exchange and merger.

Amount: As explained above, Gulwest avoided reporting a write-off of $7 million by overstating the value of the assets given in exchange for the Big Industrial shares and the BigShot Ammunition note.

12.54 Related Party Transaction Valuation. Follow the instructions accompanying Case 12.53. Write the audit approach section of the case.

IN PLANE VIEW

Problem: Whiz corporation overstated the value of shares given in exchange for an airplane and, thereby, understated its loss on disposition of the shares. Income was overstated.

Method: Whiz owned 160,000 Wing Company shares, carried on the books as an investment in the amount of $6,250,000. Whiz bought a used airplane from Wing, giving in exchange (1) $480,000 cash and (2) the 160,000 Wing shares. Even though the quoted market value of the Wing shares was $2,520,000, Whiz valued the airplane received at $3,750,000, indicating a share valuation of $3,270,000. Thus, Whiz recognized a loss on disposition of the Wing shares in the amount of $2,980,000.

Whiz justified the airplane valuation with another transaction. On the same day it was purchased, Whiz sold the airplane to the Mexican subsidiary of one of its subsidiary companies (two layers down; but Whiz owned 100 percent of the first subsidiary, which in turn owned 100 percent of the Mexican subsidiary). The Mexican subsidiary paid Whiz with US$25,000 cash and a promissory note for US$3,725,000 (market rate of interest).

Paper trail: The transaction was within the authority of the chief executive officer, and company policy did not require a separate approval by the board of directors. A contract of sale and correspondence with Wing detailing the terms of the transaction were in the files. Likewise, a contract of sale to the Mexican subsidiary, along with a copy of the deposit slip, and a memorandum of the promissory note was on file. The note itself was kept in the company vault. None of the Wing papers cited a specific price for the airplane.

Amount: Whiz overvalued the Wing shares and justified it with a related party transaction with its own subsidiary company. The loss on the disposition of the Wing shares was understated by $750,000.

12.55 Loss Deferral on Hedged Investments. This case contains complexities that preclude writing the entire Audit Approach according to the instructions accompanying Case 12.53. Instead, respond to these requirements:

a. What is the objective of the audit work on the investment account described in the Sharp Hedge Clippers case?

b. What is your conclusion about the propriety of deferring the losses on the hedged investments sales and the futures contracts? about the proper carrying amount of the investment in the balance sheet?

c. Do you believe the successor auditors were independent? competent? Discuss the practice of "shopping around" for an unqualified audit report.

SHARP HEDGE CLIPPERS

Problem: Southeastern Savings & Loan Company (Southeastern) overstated its assets and income by improperly deferring losses on hedged investment transactions.

Method: In the course of its normal operations, Southeastern held investments in 15 percent and 16 percent GNMA certificates. Fearing an increase in interest rates and a consequent loss in the market value of these investments, Southeastern sought to hedge by selling futures contracts for U.S. Treasury bonds. If market interest rates increased, the losses in the GNMA investments would be offset by gains in the futures contracts.

However, interest rates declined, and Southeastern was caught in an odd market quirk. The value of the GNMAs increased with the lower interest rates, but not very much. (GNMAs are certificates in pools of government-backed mortgages, which pass through the interest and principle collections to the certificate holders.) As interest rates declined, the market perceived that the underlying mortgages would be paid off more quickly, that investors would receive all their proceeds earlier than previously expected, and that they would need to reinvest their money at the now-lower interest rates. Consequently, the 15 percent and 16 percent GNMAs held by Southeastern began trading as if the expected maturity were 4–5 years instead of the previously expected 8–12 years, which means that their prices did not rise as much as other interest-sensitive securities. On the other hand, the U.S. Treasury bonds with fixed maturity dates fell in price, and the futures hedge generated large losses.

Southeastern sold its 15 percent and 16 percent GNMAs and realized a $750,000 gain. Before and after these sales, the company purchased 8.0–12.5 percent GNMAs. The goal was to be invested in substantially different securities, ones that had a market return and the normal 8–12-year expected life payout. Later, Southeastern closed out its Treasury bond futures and realized a loss of $3.7 million. Still later, Southeastern sold GNMA futures contracts to hedge the investment in the 8.0–12.5 percent GNMA investments. The net loss of about $3 million was deferred in the balance sheet, instead of being recognized as a loss in the income statement.

Paper trail/accounting principles: The accounting for these transactions is complex and requires some significant judgments. In general, no gain or loss is recognized when the security sold is simultaneously replaced by the same or substantially the same security (a "wash" transaction), provided that any loss deferral does not result in carrying the investment at an amount greater than its market value. When a futures hedge is related to the securities sold, gains and losses on the futures contracts must be recognized when the hedged securities are sold, unless the sale of the hedged securities is part of a wash sale.

The significant accounting judgment is the identification of the disposition and new investment as a wash transaction. In turn, this requires a determination of whether the sale and reinvestment is "simultaneous" and involves "substantially the same security."

The "paper trail" is littered with information relevant to these judgments:

Criterion	Southeastern Transaction
Timing: Simultaneous sale/purchase or purchase/sale.	Some of the 15 percent and 16 percent GNMAs were sold six weeks after the 8.0–12.5 percent GNMAs were purchased.
Substantial similarity: Same issuer.	Both the securities sold and the securities purchased were GNMAs.
Similar market yield.	The yields on the two different GNMA series differed by about 3 percentage points.
Similar contractual maturity date.	The contractual maturity dates were the same.
Similar prospects for redemption.	The market priced and sold the 15 percent and 16 percent GNMAs as though payback would occur in 4–5 years and the 8.0–12.5 percent GNMAs as though payback would occur in 8–12 years.
Carrying value: Asset carrying amount, including any deferred loss, shall not exceed securities' market value.	Asset value in financial statements exceeded the market value.

Paper trail/auditor involvement:
Southeastern's independent auditors

concluded that the losses should not be deferred. Southeastern fired the auditors and reported the disagreement in the 8-K report filed with the SEC. After consulting other auditors, who agreed with the former auditors, Southeastern found a PA firm whose local partners would give an unqualified audit report on financial statements containing the deferral.

In February the auditors who disagreed with the deferral were fired. The new auditors were hired on February 18 to audit the financial statements for the year ended the previous December 31. The unqualified audit report was dated March 28, 39 days after the new auditors were engaged by Southeastern's audit committee.

The new auditors were well aware of the accounting judgments required. They knew the former auditors and another PA firm had concluded that the losses should not be deferred. They saw memoranda of the disagreement and the conclusion in the predecessor's working papers. They spoke with the predecessor partner on the engagement.

12.56 Long-Term Debt Working Paper Review. The long-term debt working paper in Exhibit 12.56–1 was prepared by client personnel and audited by AA, an audit staff assistant, during the calendar year 1992 audit of Canadian Widgets, Inc., a continuing audit client. You are the engagement supervisor, and your assignment is to review this working paper thoroughly.

Required:
Identify and prepare a list explaining the deficiencies that should be discovered in the supervisory review of the long-term debt working paper.

(AICPA adapted)

12.57 Audit of Pension Expense. Clark, PA, has been engaged to perform the audit of Kent Ltd.'s financial statements for the current year. Clark is about to commence auditing Kent's employee pension expense. Her preliminary enquiries concerning Kent's pension plan lead her to believe that some of the actuarial computations and assumptions are so complex that they are beyond the competence ordinarily required of an auditor. Clark is considering engaging Lane, an actuary, to assist with this portion of the audit.

Required:

a. According to CGA–Canada Guideline No. 1. Audit Evidence or Other Standards, what is the confidence required for reliance to be placed on other professionals? What is the additional condition for reliance on other auditors?

b. What are Clark's responsibilities with respect to the findings of Lane, if she wishes to rely on those findings?

c. Distinguish between the circumstances where it is and is not appropriate for Clark to refer to Lane in the auditor's report.

(CGAAC adapted)

E X H I B I T 12.56–1

CANADIAN WIDGETS, INC.
Working Papers December 31, 1992

Index		K-1
	Initials	Date
Prepared by	AA	3.22.92
Approved by		

	Lender	Interest Rate	Payment Terms	Collateral	Balance 12/31/91	1992 Borrowings	1992 Reductions	Balance 12/31/92	Interest paid to	Accrued Interest Payable 12/31/92		Comments
①	First Commerical Bank	12%	Interest only on 25th of month, principal due in full 1/1/96, no prepayment pentaly	Inventories	$ 50,000	$300,000 A 1/31/92	$100,000 ⊕ 6/30/92	$ 250,000 CX	12/25/92	$2,500	NR	Dividend of $80,000 paid 9/2/92 (W/P N-3) violates a provision of the debt agreement, which thereby permits lender to demand immediate payment; lender has refused to waive this violation.
①	Lender's Capital Corp.	Prime plus 1%	Interest only on last day of month, principal due in full 3/5/94	2nd Mortgage on Park St. Building	100,000 √	50,000 A	—	200,000 C	12/31/92	—		
①	Gigantic Building & Loan Assoc.	12%	$5,000 principal plus interest due on 5th of month, due in full 12/31/03	1st Mortgage on Park St. Building	720,000 √	—	60,000 ⊖	660,000 C	12/5/92	5,642	R	
①	J. Lott, majority shareholder	0%	Due in full 12/31/95	Unsecured	300,000 √	—	100,000 N	200,000 C	—	—		
					$170,000 √ F	$350,000 F	$260,000 F	$1,310,000 T/B F		$8,142 T/B F		

Prime rate was 8% to 9% during the year.

Reclassification entry for current portion proposed (See RJE-3).

Borrowed additional $100,000 from J. Lott on 1/7/93.

Tick-mark legend

F   Readded, foots correctly.
C   Confirmed without exception, W/P K-2.
CX   Confirmed with exception, W/P K-3.
NR   Does not recompute correctly.
A   Agreed to loan agreement, validated bank deposit ticket, and board of directors authorization, W/P W-7.
⊖   Agreed to cancelled cheques and lender's monthly statements.
N   Agreed to cash disbursements journal and cancelled cheques dated 12/31/92, clearing 1/8/93.
T/B Traced to working trial balance.
√   Agreed to 12/31/91 working papers.
①   Agreed interest rate, term, and collateral to copy of note and loan agreement.
⊕   Agreed to cancelled cheques and board of director's authorization, W/P W-7.

Interest costs for long-term debt

Interest expense for year	$ 281,333 T/B
Average loan balance outstanding	$1,406,667 R

Five year maturities (for disclosure purposes)

Year end	12/21/93	$ 60,000
	12/31/94	260,000
	12/31/95	260,000
	12/31/96	310,000
	12/31/97	60,000
	Thereafter	360,000
		$1,310,000
		F

Overall Conclusions

Long-term debt, accrued interest payable, and interest expense are correct and complete at 12/31/92.

APPENDIX 12A

SUBSTANTIVE AUDIT PROGRAMS

. . . .

EXHIBIT 12A–1   **AUDIT PROGRAM FOR OWNERS' EQUITY**

---

1. Obtain an analysis of owners' equity transactions. Trace additions and reductions to the general ledger.
   a. Vouch additions to directors' minutes and cash receipts.
   b. Vouch reductions to directors' minutes and other supporting documents.
2. Read the directors' minutes for owners' equity authorization. Trace to entries in the accounts. Determine whether related disclosures are adequate.
3. Confirm outstanding common and preferred shares with share registrar agent.
4. Vouch stock option and profit-sharing plan disclosures to contracts and plan documents.
5. Vouch treasury stock transactions to cash receipts and cash disbursement records and to directors' authorization. Inspect treasury stock certificates.
6. When the company keeps its own share records:
   a. Inspect the share record stubs for certificate numbers and number of shares.
   b. Inspect the unissued certificates.
   c. Obtain written client representations about the number of shares issued and outstanding.

EXHIBIT 12A–2   **AUDIT PROGRAM FOR NOTES PAYABLE AND LONG-TERM DEBT**

---

1. Obtain a schedule of notes payable and other long-term debt (including capitalized lease obligations) showing beginning balances, new notes, repayment, and ending balances. Trace to general ledger accounts.
2. Confirm liabilities with creditor: amount, interest rate, due date, collateral, and other terms. Some of these confirmations may be standard bank confirmations.
3. Review the standard bank confirmation for evidence of assets pledged as collateral and for unrecorded obligations.
4. Read loan agreements for terms and conditions that need to be disclosed and for pledge of assets as collateral.
5. Recalculate the current portion of long-term debt and trace to the trial balance, classified as a current liability.
6. Study lease agreements for indications of need to capitalize leases. Recalculate the capital and operating lease amounts for required disclosures.
7. Recalculate interest expense on debts and trace to the interest expense and accrued interest accounts.
8. Obtain written representations from management concerning notes payable, collateral agreements, and restrictive covenants.

EXHIBIT 12A–3   **AUDIT PROGRAM FOR INVESTMENTS AND RELATED ACCOUNTS**

A. Investments and related accounts.
   1. Obtain a schedule of all investments, including purchase and disposition information for the period. Reconcile with investment accounts in the general ledger.
   2. Inspect or confirm with a trustee or broker the name, number, identification, interest rate, and face amount (if applicable) of securities held as investments.
   3. Vouch the cost of recorded investments to brokers' reports, contracts, cancelled cheques, and other supporting documentation.
   4. Vouch recorded sales to brokers' reports and bank deposit slips, and recalculate gain or loss on disposition.
   5. Recalculate interest income and look up dividend income in a dividend reporting service (such as Moody's or Standard & Poor's annual dividend record).
   6. Obtain market values of investments and determine whether any write-down or write-off is necessary. Scan transactions soon after the client's year-end to see if any investments were sold at a loss. Recalculate the unrealized gains and losses required for marketable equity securities disclosures.
   7. Read loan agreements and minutes of the board, and enquire of management about pledge of investments as security for loans.
   8. Obtain audited financial statements of joint ventures, investee companies (equity method of accounting), subsidiary companies, and other entities in which an investment interest is held. Evaluate indications of significant controlling influence. Determine proper balance sheet classification. Determine appropriate consolidation policy in conformity with accounting principles.
   9. Obtain written representations from the client concerning pledge of investment assets as collateral.

E X H I B I T   12A–3   *(concluded)*

B. Intangibles and related expenses.
   1. Review merger documents for proper calculation of purchased goodwill.
   2. Enquire of management about legal status of patents, leases, copyrights, and other intangibles.
   3. Review documentation of new patents, copyrights, leaseholds, and franchise agreements.
   4. Vouch recorded costs of intangibles to supporting documentation and cancelled cheque(s).
   5. Select a sample of recorded R&D expenses. Vouch to supporting documents for evidence of proper classification.
   6. Recalculate amortization of goodwill, patents, and other intangibles.

E X H I B I T   12A–4   **DERIVATIVE SECURITIES—AN EXAMPLE OF NEW RISKS THAT MANAGEMENT AND AUDITORS FACE**

Unless otherwise indicated this Appendix exhibit is a composite of the following articles:

John Saunders, "Derivatives: The biggest betting game," *The Globe and Mail.* March 4, 1994, A1, A10.

Douglas Gould, "Questions Mount in Barings Saga," *The Globe and Mail.* February 28, 1995, B10.

Bonnie McKennon, "Derivatives Rules Adequate: Palmer," *The Globe and Mail.* March 3, 1995, B4.

John Putridge, "Trader Incentives Under Attack," *The Globe and Mail.* March 3, 1995, B4.

Madelaine Drohan, "Barings Trader Lands in German Court," *The Globe and Mail.* March 3, 1995, B1, B4.

An increasingly important aspect of many larger company operations is derivative trading. The reason for this growth is that derivatives allow companies to manage risks better; however, as recent events at Orange County, California, and Barings Bank in the United Kingdom have shown, derivatives can also create risks where none existed previously. Derivatives are "securities" whose values depend on the values of other more basic variables. An IBM stock option is a derivative security because its value depends on the price of IBM shares; a wheat futures contract is a derivative security because its value depends on the price of wheat and so on.[2]

When derivatives are used to offset natural business risks, such as fluctuations in the price of commodities, interest rates, or currency exchange rates, they are called hedges. Hedges play an important role in optimizing business risks, and derivatives trading room operations of many corporations are becoming an increasingly critical function for the success (or failure) of the corporations. Thus, the control of derivatives trading within a company is becoming increasingly critical to the success and well-being of the entire company. For example, when things go wrong it's usually because employees "go rogue" (engage in a covert gamble) or simply do not know what they are doing—the Barings Bank case appears to be a classic example. There you had England's oldest (233 years old) bank, Barings PLC, which played a key role in financing the completion of the CP transcontinental railway in 1885—suddenly collapsed because it lost $1.26 billion in three weeks before anyone noticed. How could this happen? A Barings employee, Mr. Leeson, with or without the approval of others—facts that are to be determined in court—was able to commit the bank to ruinous speculations on the direction of Tokyo's Nikko 225 stock index, among other things.

"It appears that over a period of a few weeks Barings Singapore office acquired thousands of futures contracts representing billions of dollars on the Singapore International Monetary Exchange and on the Osaka futures market.

"Most of Barings exposure apparently was in 'long' contracts which means Barings was obliged to buy Nikkon index stocks at current prices, before the contracts expired at March 10, 1995. Obviously, Barings hoped the market would rise so it could sell the contracts at a profit. The Japanese stock market had been weak for quite a while and Barings gambled that the market would rebound when it kept weakening, Barings gambled further by selling more long contracts. Unfortunately for Barings throughout the period the Nikkei index kept dropping."[3]

The Barings episode is only one in a series of huge losses in derivatives experienced by various organizations around the world: Orange County California, Proctor & Gamble Co., the German Conglomerate Metallgesellschaft AG, Kashima Oil in Japan, Wall Street Investment firm Kidder Peabody & Co. Inc. Derivative trading has mushroomed in popularity around the world despite these risks. For example, the daily volume of derivatives trading on the London International Financial Futures Exchange has grown from 100,000 derivatives in 1987 to 600,000 in 1994.

A unique aspect of the Barings case is that the transactions went through exchanges that involved intermediaries who acted as guarantors. These should have required Barings to provide deposits on both the Osaka and Singapore exchanges. The Barings fiasco will provide an interesting "stress test" on the clearing corporations in Singapore and Osaka to see whether they and their members will be able to meet the obligations they have guaranteed.

Part of the problem in assessing derivatives risk is that so many new transactions have evolved that the actual risks and obligations and rights have not had time to be tested in the courts.

There are two major types of derivatives transactions, over the counter and open markets. Over the counter or off-exchange derivatives are individually tailored and privately negotiated contracts. They are frequently crafted by investment banks or brokerage firms for their client's special needs.

EXHIBIT 12A-4   *(continued)*

Canadian banks have been identified as having particularly strong internal controls to prevent the types of collapses as Barings. John Palmer, the federal Superintendent of Financial Institutions, commented that Canadian banks have been more conservative in engaging in derivatives transactions, as well as financially stronger than their foreign rivals. However, because of the increased derivatives activities, the office is working with the industry in drafting guidelines for internal controls to control risks by ensuring that bets are adequately hedged and not concentrated in any one country or stock exchange. It is important that these controls be closely monitored too so that they maintain their strength.

Since derivatives transactions take place with lightning speed involving thousands of daily transactions with huge amounts of money, it creates new challenges for management and regulators. A major part of the problem is that "derivatives basically enable you to execute transactions more efficiently and save the economy money. For example, through swap transactions banks can protect themselves against interest rate changes that could turn financing mismatches into disasters. The benefit to Canadians is five-year, fixed rate mortgage loans based on short-term, low-cost savings deposits.

"Derivatives get their beauty and deadliness from the same sources: speed and power. They came into their own with the advent of desktop computers, which make split-second calculations feasible. For better or worse, they generally let players commit themselves to large positions faster and with greater leverage (and thus risks)—a bigger bang for the buck—than is possible in other markets.

"But that is also why both dealers and customers need to maintain tight controls."

Selling uncovered options is a particularly risky game because the buyer pays only a specific sum, while the seller's losses are almost unlimited if the bet goes the wrong way.

Normally treasurers get involved in these transactions—or ought to get involved in them—as a function of a hedging strategy, and one of the things that amazes me is the lack of understanding at a basic level of management in otherwise sophisticated corporations.

One risk is what I would call the hero syndrome, where you've got the guy who's making so much money (for the firm) that everyone's afraid to question him.

Another temptation is to bend the rules in quest of a big win and then double up on losing bets. It's like gambling with other people's money. You think I'll win it back tomorrow and put it back in the kitty, but you never do. Desperate people do desperate things. . . . You just don't know what will make somebody snap."

To minimize risk, traders must be kept on a short lease, according to the director of trading room operations at the Mutual Group. No trader should be allowed to handle payment or recordkeeping functions as Mr. Leeson is suspected to have done in Singapore, possibly with the help of his wife, Lisa, who worked in the back office.

All traders should take at least four weeks' vacation a year, partly to get them away from the office long enough that secret schemes are likely to come to light and partly to relieve the stress of the job.

One result of the recent derivatives fiasco is the rethinking of the practice of paying instant rewards to market high flyers. You're beginning to get incentive structures to senior people in investment houses that go toward medium-term performance, in other words, deferred compensation and bonuses. Conceivably one effect of the Barings collapse would be to cut down on frequent moves and on immediate incentives and immediate gratification. The collapse of Barings was not only a function of "control problems" but also "the trading and investment bank culture." It's a world where players can earn hundreds of thousands, even millions of dollars a year in bonuses, and where, increasingly, they are moving from firm to firm lured by even bigger rewards.

There is a breed of young, aggressive traders and the real problem is not that they are trying to make money but that the system puts a tremendous amount of pressure on the short-run realization of profits. And the bonus structure itself forces a lot of this on individual performance inside firms.

Regulators in the United Kingdom concerned about explosive growth and a handful of big losses in the derivatives business may limit the amount of speculative trading commercial banks can do for their own account.

A *Financial Times* editorial said regulators should try to prevent bank deposits covered by taxpayer financial deposit insurance from being used for speculation. "There is no reason why taxpayers' money should be used to support banks' taste for gambling," it said.

The attitude of Canadian regulators, on the other hand, is that little can be done on a day-to-day basis other than monitoring bank controls. Regulators can oversee how the banks' own controls are working, but they can't monitor the hundreds of traders and thousands of daily transactions that financial institutions make. The regulators' focus is to ensure that controls are in place and that procedures are in place to monitor adherence to these controls.

The Canadian regulators' view is that the Barings collapse was caused by a series of blunders, not inadequate controls.

According to Susan LaBorge, "Derivatives are an essential part of risk management and so if you didn't do certain kinds of things with derivatives, you'd actually increase the risk to a bank. You'd have far more volatility in results because of interest rate mismatches and various risks on foreign exchange that we really don't want our institutions to take, so derivatives are a very useful risk-management tool."

She does worry that small institutions, such as trust companies, may lack the skills and internal safeguards required for some types of derivatives trading. In fact, the fact that Barings traditionally was not a big player in the market and hadn't developed the internal controls for dealing with it explains part of the apparent weaknesses in internal controls

E X H I B I T 12A–4   **(concluded)**

at the Barings bank. An interesting aspect of the Barings case is that until the full extent of Baring's management involvement in Mr. Leeson's deals becomes clearer, it's impossible to determine whether his trading broke any law.

Part of the problem is that organizations often ask traders to monitor their own derivatives exposure. This lax monitoring system gives traders leeway to play with valuations.

Banks have more stringent systems in place to prevent tellers from executing fraudulent transactions, than they have for traders. This reflects the rapidity with which trader activities have grown in terms of importance and risks. Such rapidity that management and regulators only now are aware of the potentially new risks being created by trader activities.

Optimal control of these new risks is not achieved by banning derivatives—derivatives bring too many benefits. Instead the optimal approach is to more carefully monitor and control exposure to the new risks. The right expertise is needed to put the right restraint in place, and this requires new types of professionals that are only now becoming identified.

Problems with derivatives trading are also evident in Canada. According to a March 4, 1995, article in the *Toronto Star*, the following are some signs of trading fiascos in Canada.

- In April 1994 CIBC Wood Gundy fired its interim head of capital markets trading. His strategy on a portfolio of financial derivatives based on Canadian interest rates cost the brokerage an estimated $12 million.

- Also in April 1994 a derivatives trader at Credit Swiss Canada "hit the bricks" after reportedly losing between $15 million and $21 million.

- In July 1994 the Bank of Montreal U.S. subsidiary, Harris Bancorp Inc., wrote off $46 million in trading-related losses.

And according to an article in *Report on Business*, A10, March 4, 1995, an investigative accountant in Canada helped to reconstruct dealings in which a Canadian company treasurer blew "several million dollars" about three years ago selling uncovered foreign exchange options.

The loss did not destroy the company, but it could have done. Apparently it was only luck of the market forces that losses were over only several million rather than several hundred millions, yet the risks were there nonetheless.[4]

In fact, these derivatives' losses are part of a longer tradition of trading losses that have plagued Canadian financial institutions over the decades. A March 4, 1995, article in the Business Section of the *Toronto Star* entitled, "So It Can't Happen Here, Eh?" details an Ontario financial institutional failure similar to Barings. For example, the Ontario Bank failure of 1906 ($1 million in damages—$7 million at current dollars) and the Osler brokerage failure of 1987 ($57 million in damages), as well as the more recent derivatives' trading losses all have in common good regulation but poor enforcement. A trusted employee is loosely supervised and breaches the trust. Something goes wrong and there's an overwhelming urge to win it back. That means placing bigger bets, which lead to bigger losses.[5]

Greed will always be around. But one way of reducing speculative trading risk is to change the way top traders are rewarded. Instead of instant payoffs, some of the bonus money could be deferred over several years. That reduces short-run pressures and the temptation to make the big play. However, with respect to derivatives trades, special technical controls also need to be developed: a framework for evaluating the effects of derivatives dealings on firm capital, regular audited reports on credit risks assumed by the firm in their derivative tradings, and last but not least, making sure hedge positions do not get over-exposed. Overexposure results in creation of new risk rather than risk minimization through proper hedging. Hence, there should be "very" close monitoring of hedging activities. For example, the very fact that a hedged position produces a gain means there is an exposed position. Just as easily as you produce gains, therefore, you can also produce losses. Hence, constant monitoring of trading activities to test if they meet firm objectives and operate within firm guidelines is a key to controlling trading losses. Since many of these trades take place very quickly and electronically, this suggests that many of the controls should be built into the electronic network so that, for example, if a capital requirement is violated, a trade should be automatically terminated. Such sophisticated computer controls can only be implemented at the design stage of system development and only through extensive consultation with management and finance specialists so that both operating control and auditability objectives of electronic trading can be met with reasonable effectiveness. This is just another example of the increased complexity of the environment the auditor must learn to operate in.

In a recent audit alert (see box below) the CICA provided suggestions to PAs on auditing derivatives, given the high-profile risks in this area.

---

[2]John Hull, *Introductions to Future and Option Markets*, Prentice Hall, Englewood Cliffs, New Jersey, 1991, p. 12.
[3]Douglas Gould, "Questions Mount in Barings Saga," *Globe and Mail*, February 28, 1995, p. B10.
[4]Ibid, p. A10.
[5]Adam Mayers, "So It Can't Happen Here, Eh?" *Toronto Star*, March 4, 1995, pp. C1 and C3.

The following are examples of unique, inherent risk factors associated with derivatives:

- Many derivatives are not recognized in the financial statements. As a result, there is an increased risk that derivatives, and related fees, premiums, commissions, receivables, and payables will not be collected and recorded by control systems.
- Because derivatives are financial instruments whose values are derived from underlying market rates or indexes, their values change as those rates or indexes change. Increase in the volatility of interest rates, commodity prices and foreign currency rates may cause wide fluctuations in the values of derivatives.
- Entities use derivatives to (*a*) manage risk—that is to hedge, and (*b*) to speculate. Derivatives used for hedging purposes may be accounted for differently from those used to speculate.

The following are steps that the auditor might consider taking when auditing an entity involved with derivative financial instruments.

- Obtain an understanding of the nature and extent of the use of derivatives to determine whether they may have a significant effect on the audit or on the financial statements.
- Make preliminary decisions on the materiality of derivatives and the level of inherent risk during the planning stage of the audit.
- Ensure that audit staff who will be performing audit procedures on derivatives have an appropriate level of knowledge and experience.
- Consider whether it is necessary to use the work of a specialist (see "Using the work of a specialist," *Section* 5360 of the *CICA Handbook* for guidance).
- Consider the extent to which it is appropriate to use the work of internal audit (see *Section* 5230, "Using the work of internal audit").
- Obtain an understanding of the control-environment factors affecting derivative activities (see *Section* 5200.11 of the *Handbook* for examples).

The extent of an entity's use of derivatives and the relative complexity of the instruments used are important in determining the level of sophistication that is necessary for an entity's control and monitoring systems for derivative activities. To assist the auditor in understanding the control environment, the following questions, adapted from material developed by the American Institute of Certified Public Accountants, could be used in discussion with top management, the board of directors, and the audit committee:

- Has the board established a clear and internally consistent risk management policy, including appropriate risk limits? In particular, if the entity is a financial institution, has the entity incorporated into its risk management programs the guidance issued by Office of the Superintendent of Financial Institutions' Derivatives Best Practices and the Canada Deposit Insurance Corporation's Standards of Sound Business Practice?

— Are management's strategies and implementation policies consistent with the board's authorization?

— Do controls exist to ensure that only authorized transactions take place and that unauthorized transactions are quickly detected and appropriate action is taken?

— Are the magnitude, complexity, and risks of the entity's derivatives commensurate with the entity's objectives?

— Are personnel with authority to engage in and monitor derivative transactions well qualified and appropriately trained?

— Do the right people have the right information to make decisions?

Source: "Auditing derivatives financial instruments," Studies and Standards Alert, *CA Magazine,* January/February 1995, p. 66.

As part of the new bank confirmation format introduced in May 1997, the CICA recommends that the sample letter in the following box be used for confirming information related to derivative instruments.

Sample Letter 2

REQUEST FOR STATEMENT DETAILING
OUTSTANDING DERIVATIVE INSTRUMENTS

[Client letterhead]

[Date]

[Financial institution official responsible for account]
[Financial institution name]
[Financial institution address]

Dear [financial institution official responsible for account]:

In connection with their audit of our financial statements for the year ended March 31, 1997, our auditors, CA & Co. have requested a statement summarizing all derivative financial instruments entered into by the company and outstanding at March 11, 1997. Derivative financial instruments include futures, foreign exchange contracts, forward rate agreements, interest rate swaps, and options contracts, or other financial instruments with similar characteristics.

In your response, please include the following information for each instrument:
1. The principal, stated, face or other similar amount (sometimes also referred to as the notional amount) on which future payments are based.
2. The date of maturity, expiration, or execution.
3. Any early settlement options, including the period in which, or date at which, the options may be exercised and the exercise price or range of prices.
4. Any options to convert the instrument into, or exchange it for, another financial instrument or some other asset or liability, including the period in

which, or date at which, the options may be exercised and the conversion or exchange ratio(s).

5. The amount and timing of scheduled future cash receipts or payments of the principal amount of the instrument, including installment repayments and any sinking fund or similar requirements.
6. The stated rate or amount of interest, dividend or other periodic return on principal and the timing of payments.
7. Any collateral held or pledged.
8. The currency of the cash flows if these are other than Canadian funds.
9. Where the instrument provides for an exchange, information noted in 1 to 8 above for the instrument to be acquired in the exchange.
10. Any condition of the instrument or an associated convenant that, if contravened, would significantly alter any of the other terms.

Please mail the above noted information directly to our auditors in the enclosed addressed envelope. Should you wish to discuss any details of this confirmation request with our auditors, please contact (name of audit staff member) at (111) 222-3333, or by fax at (111) 222-3334.

Yours truly,

[Authorized signatory of the client]

Source: CICA and Canadian Bankers Association

CHAPTER 13

Learning Objectives

This chapter covers the process of completing the field work and gathering up the loose ends of the audit. The following principal items are covered:

- Completing the audit of revenue and expense.
- Consideration of contingencies and obtaining letters from the client's lawyers.
- Obtaining written client representations.
- Events subsequent to the balance sheet date and events subsequent to the audit report date.
- Final wrap-up of the audit (audit review).

Your learning objectives relative to these topics are to be able to:

1. Describe the related balance sheet account group where the audit of the major revenue and expense accounts normally is associated.

2. Describe the use of analytical procedures to audit revenue and expense accounts.

3. Explain the use of the client representation letter and the lawyer's letter as an audit is completed.

4. Describe the reasons why written client representations are obtained, and list the four items that are included without regard to a materiality criterion.

5. Given a set of facts and circumstances, classify a subsequent event by type and describe the proper treatment in the financial statements.

6. Specify the sequence of decisions and actions auditors must consider upon discovery (after the issuance of the report) of information about facts that may have existed at the date of the auditors' report.

7. Specify the considerations and procedures applied by auditors upon concluding (after the audit report date) that one or more auditing procedures were omitted.

8. Explain the final audit steps involving adjusting entries, second-partner review, and the management letter.

COMPLETING THE AUDIT

INTRODUCTION
. . . .

This chapter covers the completion of the audit cycle. The chapter reviews the issues, techniques, procedures, and documents that are normally considered in effectively and efficiently completing an audit. At the completion of the audit, the audit opinion should be properly supported by the audit evidence as reflected in the audit files. The audit of the nominal or flow accounts reflected in the income statement, statement of changes in financial position, and statement of changes in retained earning cannot be completed until year-end when all the transactions for the period have also been completed. As a result some year-end audit procedures relate to revenue and expense accounts for the period. This part of the year-end audit is covered in the first half of the chapter.

As well, some audit procedures relate to the year-end amounts on the balance sheet. The audit of these amounts has already been covered in the earlier part of this text relating to the different accounting cycles. However, there are procedures unique to the year-end such as audit for subsequent events, contingencies, commitments or contractual obligations, overall evaluation of audit results, proper presentation, and disclosure issues that need to be considered before signing off on the audit file. These and related issues are covered in the second half of the chapter.

AUDIT OF REVENUE AND EXPENSE
. . . .

LEARNING OBJECTIVE
1. Describe the related balance sheet account group where the audit of the major revenue and expense accounts normally is associated.

As the field work nears its end, the major revenue and expense accounts will have been audited in connection with related balance sheet accounts. Now auditors need to consider other revenue and expense accounts. The broad financial statement assertions are the bases for specific assertions and audit objectives for these accounts. Typical specific assertions for the revenue and expense accounts are:

1. Revenue accounts represent all the valid transactions recorded correctly in the proper account, amount, and period.
2. The accounting for consignments and goods sold with rights of return is in conformity with accounting principles.
3. Expense accounts represent all the valid expense transactions recorded correctly in the proper account, amount, and period.
4. Revenues, expenses, cost of goods sold, and extraordinary, unusual, or infrequent transactions are adequately classified and disclosed.

Revenue
The following types of revenue and related topics already will have been audited, either in whole or in part, at the completion stage of the engagement.

Revenue and Related Topics	**Related Account Groups**
Sales and sales returns.	Receivables.
Lease revenue.	Capital assets and receivables.
Franchise revenue.	Receivables, intangibles.
Dividends and interest.	Receivables, investments.
Gain, loss on asset disposals.	Fixed assets, receivables, and investments.
Rental revenue.	Receivables and investments.
Royalty and licence revenue.	Receivables and investments.
Long-term sales commitments.	Revenue and receivables.
Product line reporting.	Revenue and receivables.
Accounting policy disclosure.	Revenue and receivables.

To the extent these revenue items already have been audited, the working papers should show cross-reference indexing to the revenue account in the trial balance. The accounts that have not been audited completely will be evident. Auditors should ascertain by reference to the trial balance that they have a list of all the revenue and gain or loss accounts and their amounts.

Audit Procedures

LEARNING   OBJECTIVE

2. Describe the use of analytical procedures to audit revenue and expense accounts.

According to the CICA study "Analytical Review" (authored by D.G. Smith, 1983), analytical procedures can be used at these points during the audit: 1. at the planning stage, 2. during the overall evaluation of the financial statements at the end of the audit, and 3. as a substantive test procedure. The use of analytical procedures as part of the overall evaluation at the end of the audit is the most common use of analytical review in practice. This overall verification "can be an effective means of obtaining assurance as to the reasonableness of reported results. There is a broad spectrum of overall verification procedures, many particular to a specific industry, which provides a range of assurance from virtually 100% assurance to reasonable approximation" (D.J. Smith [1983; p. 3]). *Section* 5301.27 requires use of analytical procedures to assist in evaluating the overall financial statement presentation upon substantial completion of the audit.

Analytical procedures can be used to compare the revenue accounts and amounts to prior-year data and to multiple-year trends to ascertain whether any unusual fluctuations are present. Comparisons also should be made to budgets, monthly internal reports, and forecasts to ascertain whether events have occurred that require explanation or analysis by management. These explanations would then be subjected to audit. For example, a sales dollar increase may be explained as a consequence of a price increase that can be corroborated by reference to price lists used in the test of controls audit of sales transactions.

Auditors also should ascertain whether account classifications, aggregations, and summarizations are consistent with those of the prior year. This information will have a bearing on the consistency issue in financial reporting.

All "miscellaneous" or "other" revenue accounts and all "clearing" accounts with credit balances should be analysed. Account analysis in this context refers to the identification of each important item and amount in the account, followed by document vouching and enquiry to determine whether amounts should be classified

E X H I B I T 13–1   **AUDIT PROGRAM FOR REVENUES AND EXPENSES**

REVENUES
1. Obtain analyses of sales, cost of goods sold, and gross profit by product line, department, division, or location.
   a. Trace amounts to the general ledger.
   b. Compare the analyses to prior years and seek explanations for significant variations.
   c. Determine one or more standard markup percentages and calculate expected gross profits. Enquire for explanations of significant variations compared to actual results.
2. Co-ordinate procedures for audit of revenue with evidence obtained in other audit programs:

Sales and sales returns.	Sales control.	Gain, loss on asset disposals.	Fixed assets.
	Cash receipts control.		Investments.
	Accounts receivable.	Rental revenue.	Accounts receivable.
Lease revenue.	Capital assets.		Investments.
	Accounts receivable.	Royalty and licence revenue.	Accounts receivable.
Franchise revenue.	Accounts receivable.		Investments.
	Intangibles.	Long-term sales commitments.	Accounts receivable.
Dividends and interest.	Accounts receivable.		Inventory.
	Investments.		

3. Scan the revenue accounts for large and unusual items and for debit entries. Vouch items to supporting documentation.
4. Obtain written client representation about terms of sales, rights of return, consignments, and extraordinary, unusual, or infrequent transactions.

EXPENSES
5. Obtain schedules of expense accounts comparing the current year with one or more prior years.
   a. Trace amounts to the general ledger.
   b. Compare the current expenses to prior years and seek explanations for significant variations.
   c. Be alert to notice significant variations that could indicate failure to defer or accrue expenses.
6. Compare the current expenses to the company budget, if any. Enquire and investigate explanations for significant variances.
7. Co-ordinate procedures for audit of expenses with evidence obtained in other audit programs:

Purchases, cost of goods sold.	Acquisition control.	Bad debt expense.	Accounts receivable.
	Cash disbursement control.	Depreciation expense.	Fixed assets.
	Inventory.	Property taxes, insurance.	Prepaids and accruals.
Inventory valuation losses.	Inventory.		Fixed assets.
Warranty and guarantee expense.	Inventory.	Lease and rental expense.	Fixed assets.
	Prepaids and accruals.	Repairs and maintenance.	Fixed assets.
	Accounts payable.	Interest expense.	Long-term liabilities.
Royalty and licence expense.	Inventory.	Pension and retirement benefits.	Liabilities.
Marketing and product R&D.	Investments.		Payroll control.
	Intangibles.	Payroll and compensation.	Payroll control.
Investment value losses.	Investments.	Sales commissions.	Payroll control.
Rental property expenses.	Investments.		
Amortization of intangibles.	Intangibles.		

8. Prepare analyses of sensitive expense accounts, such as legal and professional fees, travel and entertainment, repairs and maintenance, taxes, and others unique to the company. Vouch significant items therein to supporting invoices, contracts, reimbursement forms, tax notices, and the like for proper support and documentation.
9. Scan the expense accounts for large and unusual items and for credit entries. Vouch items to supporting documentation.
10. Obtain written client representations about long-term purchase commitments, contingencies, and extraordinary, unusual, or infrequent transactions.

---

elsewhere. All clearing accounts should be eliminated and the amounts classified as revenue, deferred revenue, liabilities, deposits, or contra-assets.

Miscellaneous revenue and other suspense accounts can harbour many accounting errors. Proceeds from sale of assets, insurance premium refunds, insurance proceeds, and other receipts simply may be credited to such an account. Often, such items reveal unrecorded asset disposals, expiration of insurance recorded as prepaid, or other asset losses covered by insurance. Exhibit 13–1 lists common audit procedures for revenue accounts.

Unusual Transactions

Significant audit evidence and reporting problems can arise with transactions designed by management to manufacture earnings. Frequently, such transactions are run through a complicated structure of subsidiaries, affiliates, and related parties. Generally, the amounts of revenue are large. The transactions themselves may not be concealed, but certain guarantees may have been made by management and not revealed to the auditors. The timing of the transactions may be arranged carefully to provide the most favourable income result.

These unusual transactions contain a wide variety of characteristics and are difficult to classify for useful generalization. Controversies have arisen in the past over revenue recognized on the construction percentage-of-completion method, over sales of assets at inflated prices to management-controlled dummy corporations, over sales of real estate to independent parties with whom the seller later associates for development of the property (making guarantees on indemnification for losses), and over disclosure of revenues by source. These revenue issues pose a combination of evidence-gathering problems and reporting-disclosure problems. Three illustrations of such problems are given below.

Expenses

Although many major expense items will have been audited in connection with other account groupings, numerous minor expenses may still remain unaudited. As a brief review, the following major expenses may have been audited in whole or in part as the audit nears its end.

Expenses	Related Account Groups
Purchases, cost of goods sold.	Inventories.
Inventory valuation losses.	Inventories.
Warranty and guarantee expense.	Inventories and liabilities.
Royalty and licence expense.	Inventories.
Marketing and product R&D.	Investments and intangibles.
Investment value losses.	Investments and intangibles.
Rental property expenses.	Investments and intangibles.
Amortization of intangibles.	Investments and intangibles.
Bad debt expense.	Receivables.
Amortization expense.	Capital assets.
Property taxes, insurance.	Capital assets and liabilities.
Lease and rental expense.	Capital assets.
Repairs and maintenance.	Capital assets and liabilities.
Legal and professional fees.	Liabilities and equity.
Interest expense.	Liabilities.
Pension and retirement benefits.	Liabilities, equity, and payroll.
Payroll and compensation costs.	Payroll.
Sales commissions.	Payroll.

As with the revenue accounts mentioned in the previous section, if audit work is complete for expense accounts, the working papers should show cross-reference

Unusual Revenue Transactions

Merger

National Fried Chicken, Inc., a large fast-food franchiser, began negotiations in August to purchase Provincial Hot Dog Company, a smaller convenience food chain. At August 1, 19X1, Provincial's net worth was $7 million, and National proposed to pay $8 million cash for all the outstanding shares. In June 19X2, the merger was consummated and National paid $8 million, even though Provincial's net worth had dropped to $6 million. Consistent with prior years, Provincial lost $1 million in the 10 months ended June 1; as in the past, the company showed a net profit of $1.5 million for June and July. At June 1, 19X2, the fair value of Provincial's net assets was $6 million, and National accounted for the acquisition as a purchase, recording $2 million goodwill. National proposed to show in consolidated financial statements the $1.5 million of post-acquisition income and $50,000 amortization of goodwill.

Audit Resolution. The auditors discovered that the purchase price was basically set at 16 times expected earnings and that management had carefully chosen the consummation date in order to maximize goodwill (and reportable net income after amortization in fiscal 19X2). The auditors required that $1 million of "goodwill" be treated as prepaid expenses which expired in the year ended July 31, 19X2, so that bottom-line income would be $500,000.

Real Estate Deal

In August, a company sold three real estate properties to BMC for $5,399,000 and recognized profit of $550,000. The agreement that covered the sale committed the company to use its best efforts to obtain permanent financing and to pay underwriting costs for BMC. The agreement provided BMC with an absolute guarantee against loss from ownership and a commitment by the company to complete construction of the properties.

According to the provincial securities commission accountant, the terms of this agreement made the recognition of profit improper because the company had not shifted the risk of loss to BMC.

Real Estate Development, Strings Attached

In December 19X1, Black Company sold one half of a tract of undeveloped land to Red Company in an arm's-length transaction. The portion sold had a book value of $1.5 million, and Red Company paid $2.5 million in cash. Red Company planned to build and sell apartment houses on the acquired land. In January 19X2, Black and Red announced a new joint venture to develop the entire tract. The two companies formed a partnership, each contributing its one half of the total tract of land. They agreed to share equally in future capital requirements and profits or losses.

Audit Resolution. The $1 million profit from the sale was not recognized as income in Black's 19X1 financial statements but, instead, was classified as a deferred credit. Black's investment in the joint venture was valued at $1.5 million. Black's continued involvement in development of the property and the uncertainty of future costs and losses were cited as reasons.

indexing from the working papers to the trial balance. Some of the expenses may not have been audited completely (such as property tax expense), and some finishing-touch vouching of supporting documents may be required.

Audit Procedures

Several minor expenses, such as office supplies, telephone, utilities, and similar accounts, are not audited until late in the engagement. Generally, the dollar amounts in these accounts are not material (taken singly), and the relative risk is small that they may be misstated in such a way as to create misleading financial statements. Auditors usually audit these kinds of accounts with substantive **analytical procedures.** These procedures include making a list of the expenses with comparative balances from one or more prior periods. The dollar amounts are then reviewed for unusual changes (or lack of unusual changes if reasons for change are known). This analysis of comparative balances may be enough to decide whether the amounts are fairly presented.

On the other hand, questions may be raised and additional evidence sought. In this case auditors may **vouch** some expenses to supporting documents (invoices and cancelled cheques). Some documentary vouching evidence already may be available about these minor expenses. If the auditors performed detail test of controls procedures on a sample of expenditure transactions in the acquisition and expenditure cycle audit program, a few expense transactions were selected for testing the client's compliance with control objectives (validity, completeness, authorization, accuracy, classification, accounting, and proper period). This evidence should be used.

Analytical comparisons to budgets, internal reports, and forecasts also may be made. Variations from budget already may have been subject to management explanation, or the auditors may need to investigate variations.

All "miscellaneous" or "other" expense accounts and "clearing" accounts with debit balances should be analysed by listing each important item on a working paper and vouching it to supporting documents. Miscellaneous and other expenses may include abandonments of property, items not deductible for tax purposes, and payments that should be classified in other expense accounts. Clearing accounts should be analysed and items therein classified according to their nature or source so that all clearing account balances are removed and accounted for properly.

Advertising expense, travel, entertainment expense, and contributions are accounts that typically are analysed in detail. These accounts are particularly sensitive to management policy violations and income tax consequences. Travel, entertainment, and contributions must be documented carefully if they are to stand the Revenue Canada auditor's examination. Questionable items may have an impact on the income tax expense and liability. Travel and entertainment sometimes harbour abuses of company policy respecting expense allowances. Minor embezzlements or cheating can be detected by careful auditors. However, a detailed audit of expense-account payments may be of greater interest to the efficiency-minded internal auditor than to the independent auditor. As far as independent auditors are concerned, even if employees did overstate their reimbursable expenses, the actual paid-out amount still is fairly presented as a financial fact. If there is evidence of expense-account cheating, independent auditors may present the data to management. Exhibit 13–1 illustrates some of the common audit procedures for expenses.

. . . .

R E V I E W
C H E C K P O I N T S

13.1 Certain revenue and expense accounts usually are audited in conjunction with related balance sheet accounts. For the following revenue and expense accounts, list the most likely related balance sheet accounts: lease revenue, franchise revenue, royalty and licence revenue, amortization expense, repairs and maintenance expense, interest expense.

13.2 Why are many of the revenue and expense accounts only audited by analytical procedures and not by other procedures?

13.3 Why can "usual revenue transactions" cause significant audit evidence and reporting problems?

13.4 What procedures can be used to obtain information about the material accuracy of balances in minor expense accounts?

. . . .

A Sequence of Audit Events

. . . .

LEARNING OBJECTIVE

3. Explain the use of the client representation letter and the lawyer's letter as an audit is completed.

Based on the material presented on the organization of the audit, you could easily visualize some audit work being done at an interim period sometime before a balance sheet date followed by completion of the work on the magic balance sheet date. True, much audit work is done months before the balance sheet date, with auditors working for a time, leaving the client's offices, and then returning for the year-end work. Actually, auditors may not even do any work on the balance sheet date itself, but they always perform evidence-gathering after that date—sometimes as much as several months afterwards.

Interim and Final Audit Work in Independent Auditing

In the "interim" audit work period, the auditor evaluates internal control with questionnaires, flowcharts, and/or written narratives; identifies strengths and deficiencies; and completes the test of controls part of the audit. Some test of controls procedures usually are performed at interim, and tentative judgments about control risk for certain transaction cycles are made early. Also, auditors can apply audit procedures for substantive audit of balances as of an interim date; in this way a significant amount of recalculating, vouching, tracing, observing, and confirming can be performed early. (Refer to Chapters 5, 6, and 7 for a more complete discussion.)

When the audit team returns after year-end and receives the final unaudited financial statements (or trial balance) prepared by the client personnel, they can start where they left off at interim and complete the work on control risk assessment and audit of balances.

However, the procedures of obtaining the lawyer's letter and the written client representations are deferred until the end of field work. These written representations are dated at the end of the field work (audit report date) because the auditors are responsible for determining whether important events that occurred after the balance sheet date are properly entered in the accounts or disclosed in the financial statement notes.

Contingencies and Lawyer's Letters

One of the most important confirmations is the response known as the lawyer's representation letter. Some difficulties had arisen over lawyers' willingness to respond to auditors' requests for information about contingencies, litigation, claims, and assessments. Lawyers themselves have faced legal liability for failure to respond properly.

Handbook Section 6560, "Communications With Law Firms," requires auditors to make certain enquiries designed to elicit information on claims and possible claims as part of the auditor's examination of financial statements. Exhibit 13–2 is an example of a letter (the enquiry letter) the auditor would request the client to send to all lawyers who had performed work for the client during the period under audit. The client must make this request because it informs the lawyer that his or her client is waiving the privilege of communications between the lawyer and his or her client and giving the lawyer permission to give information to the auditors.

As implied by the client's letter to the lawyers in Exhibit 13–2, questions about contingencies, litigation, claims, and assessments should be directed not only to legal counsel but also to management, because an auditor has the right to expect to be

---

EXHIBIT 13–2   **FROM *HANDBOOK SECTION* 6560.A, SCHEDULE A**

Schedule A
(Enquiry Letter)[1]

Version 1—when there are claims or possible claims to be listed
(On client letterhead)

(To law firm)   (Date)

Dear Sir(s):

In connection with the preparation and audit of our financial statements for the fiscal period ended (date), (which include the accounts of the following entities)[2], we have made the following evaluations of claims and possible claims with respect to which your firm's advice or representation has been sought:

Description	Evaluation
(name of entity, name of other party, nature, amount claimed and current status)	(indicate likelihood of loss (or gain) and estimated amount of ultimate loss (or gain), if any; or indicate that likelihood is not determinable or amount is not reasonably estimable)

Would you please advise us, as of (effective date of response), on the following points:
   (a) Are the claims and possible claims properly described?
   (b) Do you consider that our evaluations are reasonable?
   (c) Are you aware of any claims not listed above which are outstanding? If so, please include in your response letter the names of the parties and the amount claimed.

This enquiry is made in accordance with the Joint Policy Statement of January 1978 approved by The Canadian Bar Association and the Auditing Standards Committee of the Canadian Institute of Chartered Accountants.

Please address your reply, marked "Privileged and Confidential", to this company and send a signed copy of the reply directly to our auditor, (name and address of auditor).

                                                                                     Yours truly,

c.c. (name of auditor)

---

[1]The letter should be appropriately modified if the client advises that certain matters have been excluded in accordance with paragraph 12 of the Joint Policy Statement.
[2]Delete if inapplicable. If applicable, refer to paragraph 11 re signing of the enquiry letter.

informed by management about all material contingent liabilities. Audit procedures useful in this regard include the following:

- Enquire and discuss with management the policies and procedures for identifying, evaluating, and accounting for litigation, claims, and assessments.
- Obtain from management a description and evaluation of litigation, claims, and assessments.
- Examine documents in the client's possession concerning litigation, claims, and assessments, including correspondence and invoices from lawyers.
- Obtain assurance from management that it has disclosed all material unasserted claims that the lawyer has advised them are probable of litigation.
- Read minutes of meetings of shareholders, directors, and appropriate committees. Read contracts, loan agreements, leases, and correspondence from taxing or other governmental agencies.
- Obtain information concerning guarantees from bank confirmations.

The enquiry letter serves as a major means to learn of material contingencies. Even so, a devious or forgetful management or a careless lawyer may fail to tell the auditor of some important factor or development. Auditors have to be alert and sensitive to all possible contingencies so that they can ask the right questions at the right time.

If management or its lawyers fail to provide adequate information about lawsuit contingencies, the auditor should consider whether this represents a scope limitation on the audit. A serious audit scope limitation requires a qualification in the audit report or a disclaimer of opinion.

Auditors have a natural conservative tendency to look out for adverse contingencies. However, potentially favourable events also should be investigated and disclosed (such as the contingency of litigation for damages wherein the client is the plaintiff). In an effort to assist management in observing the law and to provide adequate disclosure of information in financial statements, the auditor should be alert to all types of contingencies.

Client Representations

LEARNING OBJECTIVE
4. Describe the reasons written client representations are obtained, and list the four items that are included without regard to a materiality criterion.

Management makes numerous responses to auditors' enquiries during the course of an audit. Many of these responses are very important. To the extent that additional evidence is obtainable through other procedures, auditors should corroborate client representations.

In addition, auditors should obtain written client representations on matters of audit importance. The written representations take the form of a letter on the client's letterhead, addressed to the auditor, signed by responsible officers (normally the chief executive officer, chief financial officer, and other appropriate managers), and dated as of the date of the auditor's report. Thus, the letter, referred to as the "client's rep letter" in practice, covers events and representations running beyond the balance sheet date up to the end of all important field work. These written representations, however, are not substitutes for corroborating evidence obtainable by applying other auditing procedures.

In most cases the written client representations are merely more assertions, like the ones already in the financial statements (perhaps more detailed, in some cases). In

INTERPRETING THE LAWYERS' LETTERS

Lawyers take great care making responses to clients' requests for information to be transmitted to auditors. This care causes problems of interpretation for auditors. The difficulty arises over lawyers' desire to preserve lawyer-client confidentiality yet co-operate with auditors and the financial reporting process that seeks full disclosure.

The Canadian Bar Association policy statement (HB 6560A.14) observes: It is in the public interest that the confidentiality of lawyer-client communications be maintained. Accordingly, the law firm will not indicate in the response letter any possible claims which are omitted from the enquiry letter.

Consequently, lawyers' responses to auditors may contain vague and ambiguous wording. Auditors need to determine whether a contingency is "likely, unlikely, or not determinable" (*Section* 3290.15). Although there are no comparable Canadian guidelines, in the United States the following lawyer responses can be properly interpreted to mean "remote," even though the word is not used:

- We are of the opinion that this action will not result in any liability to the company.
- It is our opinion that the possible liability to the company in this proceeding is nominal in amount.
- We believe the company will be able to defend this action successfully. We believe that the plaintiff's case against this company is without merit.
- Based on the facts known to us, after a full investigation, it is our opinion that no liability will be established against the company in these suits.

However, auditors should view the following response phrases as unclear—providing no information—about the probable, reasonably possible, or remote likelihood of an unfavourable outcome for a litigation contingency (adapted from AU 9337):

- We believe the plaintiff will have serious problems establishing the company's liability; nevertheless, if the plaintiff is successful, the damage award may be substantial.
- It is our opinion the company will be able to assert meritorious defences. ["Meritorious," in lawyer language, apparently means "the judge will not summarily throw out the defences."]
- We believe the lawsuit can be settled for less than the damages claimed.
- We are unable to express an opinion on the merits of the litigation, but the company believes there is absolutely no merit.
- In our opinion the company has a substantial chance of prevailing. ["Substantial chance," "reasonable opportunity," and similar phrases indicate uncertainty of success in a defence.]

this context they are not "evidence" for auditors. They are not good defences against criticisms for failing to perform audit procedures independently. ("Management told us in writing that the inventory costing method was FIFO and adequate allowance for obsolescence was provided" is not a good excuse for failing to get the evidence from the records and other sources!) However, in some cases the written management

ROOM FOR IMPROVEMENT IN LITIGATION
CONTINGENCY DISCLOSURES

American research on 126 lawsuits lost by public companies examined the disclosures about the suits in prior years' financial statements. The contingencies involved material, uninsured losses. Subsequent failure in the defence indicates the contingencies to have been "reasonably possible," calling for FASB 5 (comparable to *Section* 3290) disclosure. For the 126 cases, wide disclosure diversity existed. As indicated in the table below, the majority of cases carried satisfactory disclosure while the lawsuits were in progress, but a significant minority did not.

	Number	Percent
Satisfactory disclosure:		
Disclosure conceded the possibility of liability	60	47.6%
Disclosure included an estimate of the related liability	5	4.0
Disclosure along with booked liability	7	5.6
Total	72	57.2%
Unsatisfactory disclosure:		
No mention of the litigation	45	35.7%
Litigation mentioned but with a strong disclaimer of liability	9	7.1
Total	54	42.8%

Among the types of lawsuits covered in the 126 cases, the ones dealing with securities law violations had the highest frequency of satisfactory disclosure (8 out of 11, 73 percent). The ones dealing with fraud or misrepresentation had the lowest frequency of satisfactory disclosure (2 out of 8, or 25 percent).

Speculations about the reasons company officials and lawyers have difficulty providing auditors with appropriate information include:

- High level of emotion surrounding the lawsuits.
- Fear that financial statement disclosure will be construed as an admission of guilt.
- The legal framework for evaluating litigation outcomes varies significantly from the framework used by auditors.
- More appropriate channels exist for disclosure of litigation information [e.g., business press].
- FASB 5 disclosure requirements are viewed as only a guide and, therefore, need not be taken literally.

Source: "Disclosure of Litigation Contingencies Faulted," *Journal of Accountancy*, July 1990, pp. 15–16.

representations are the only available evidence about important matters of management intent. For example: (1) "We will discontinue the parachute manufacturing business, wind down the operations, and sell the remaining assets" (i.e., accounting for discontinued operations); and (2) "We will exercise our option to refinance the maturing debt on a long-term basis" (i.e., classifying maturing debt as long-term).

One of the major purposes of the management representation letter is to impress upon the management its primary responsibility for the financial statements. These representations also may establish an auditor's defences if a question of management integrity arises later. If the management lies to the auditors, the management representation letter captures the lies in writing. Auditors draft the management representation letter to be prepared on the client's letterhead paper for signature by company representatives. This draft is reviewed with senior client personnel, then finalized.

The management representation letter generally deals only with material matters. Notwithstanding, auditing standards provide that the following four representations must appear in the letter without limitation based on materiality:

1. Management's acknowledgment of primary responsibility for fair presentation of financial statements in conformity with generally accepted accounting principles.

2. Availability of all financial records and related data.

3. Completeness of the minutes of meetings of shareholders, directors, and important committees.

4. Irregularities involving management or employees.

A U.S. Standard, SAS 19 (AU 333), contains a list of 16 other items and discussions of several other points that may be included. While the *CICA Handbook* does not specifically require a letter of representation (except with regard to law firms), such letters are recommended with prospectuses (*Section* 7100) and review engagements (AUG–20). Exhibit 13–3 shows a typical Canadian representation letter used by the Canadian CA firm of Doane Raymond.

Audit of Related Party Transactions

One of the questions typically asked in an engagement letter is whether the client has engaged in any related party transactions (see Question F3 in Exhibit 13–3). Auditors have a responsibility to obtain reasonable assurance that related parties have been identified and that there is appropriate disclosure with such parties in the financial statements (AUG–1). Related party transactions are particularly important in Canada because of the high degree of concentration of corporate ownership. The problem with related party transactions is that since they are not arm's length they may not reflect the normal terms of trade that occur with most transactions with external parties. *Handbook Section* 3840 provides the measurement and disclosure standards for related party transactions of profit-oriented enterprises. The major problem for the auditor is identifying related party transactions. The most important procedure is to enquire of management (as in Exhibit 13–3). Other important procedures include reading the minutes of meetings of shareholders', directors', executive, and audit committees, as well as acquiring a general knowledge of the client's business (AUG–1, para. 6).

Auditors should watch for unusual transactions in the course of the audit. According to AUG–1, para. 7:

Example of circumstances that might indicate the existence of undisclosed related parties include

(*a*) abnormal terms of trade, such as unusual prices, interest rates, guarantees, and repayment terms;

(*b*) transactions which are unusual as to nature or size, particularly those that:

     (i)   have been recognized at or near the balance sheet date;

     (ii) have been made with unfamiliar enterprises; and

     (iii) appear to lack a logical reason for their occurrence; and

  (*c*) transactions whose substance appear to differ from their form.

Also, "related parties exist when one party has the ability to exercise directly or indirectly, control, joint control or significant influence over the other. Two or more parties are related when they are subject to common control, joint control, or common significant influence. Related parties include management and immediate family members" (*Section* 3840.03).

As noted earlier, auditor's knowledge of the business can help identify transactions between related parties. One important type of related party arises when there is "economic dependence." *Section* 3841.03 defines economic dependence as follows:

> A situation where an enterprise may have a significant volume of its business with another party, such as a sole or major customer, supplier, franchiser, franchisee, distributor, general agent, or leader. Sometimes, the enterprises are related because one enterprise has significant influence, joint control or control over the other.

The auditor needs to disclose not only any significant related party transactions but also any economic dependence that may exist. AUG–1, para. 13, describes how this disclosure responsibility can be met:

> During his examination, the auditor needs to obtain sufficient appropriate audit evidence to enable him to assess the reasonableness of management's determinations as to whether economic dependence exists (ECONOMIC DEPENDENCE, *Section* 3841). In considering whether the viability of a reporting entity depends on the continuance of business with another party, the auditor would assess the likely impact of a withdrawal of business on the reporting entity, considering such matters as:
>
>   (*a*) the ability to place this business with another party; and
>
>   (*b*) the ability of the reporting entity to continue its present activities without replacing the business.
>
> If the auditor concludes that economic dependence exists, and management does not disclose that fact, he would consider the effect on the content of his report. The auditor need not consider the provision of essential public services such as electricity, telephone and mail, as constituting economic dependence.

Summary of Audit Correspondence

Many types of formal correspondence have been mentioned in this book. Since you are learning the final procedures to complete the audit, this is a good place to summarize these various correspondence items. Exhibit 13–4 is a summary of audit correspondence. The management letter will be covered later in this chapter.

· ·

R E V I E W
C H E C K P O I N T S

13.5 What is the purpose of a client representation letter? What representations would you request management to make in a client rep letter with respect to receivables? to inventories? to minutes of meetings? to subsequent events?

13.6 Why are written client representations and lawyers' letters obtained near the end of the audit field work and dated on or near the audit report date?

EXHIBIT 13–3

Doane Raymond

Gentlemen:

In connection with your audit of the (consolidated) financial statements of _____,
for the year ending _____, 19___, we represent, to the best of our knowledge and belief, and to the extent
that they have or may have a material effect on the financial statements, the following:

A. Financial Statements and Financial Records

1. As members of management of the company, we understand that the purpose of your examination of the (consolidated) financial statements is to express an opinion thereon and that your audit procedures, including your tests of accounting records, were limited to those that you considered necessary in the circumstances. We also understand that such tests would not necessarily detect fraud, irregularities and error even if material in amount.

2. As members of management of the company, we are responsible for the preparation of the (consolidated) financial statements in accordance with generally accepted accounting principles.

3. The significant accounting policies adopted in the preparation of the (consolidated) financial statements are fully and fairly described in the financial statements.

4. We have not knowingly withheld any financial records and related data requested by you.

5. As members of management we believe that the company has an internal control structure adequate to permit the preparation of accurate financial statements in accordance with generally accepted accounting principles.

B. Ownership

1. The company has good title to (or lease interest in), all assets recorded in the accounts and these assets are free from hypothecation, liens, and encumbrances (except: [specify]).

C. Valuation

1. Our present plans and intentions are appropriately reflected by the carrying value and classification of the company's assets and liabilities.

2. Adequate provisions have been recorded in the accounts for all anticipated losses (including those related to accounts receivable, inventory and capital assets).

3. The company has considered the effect of environmental matters and the carrying value of the relevant assets is recognized, measured and disclosed as appropriate in the (consolidated) financial statements.

D. Existence and Completeness

1. All assets which are owned by the company are recorded in the accounts.

2. All goods shipped or services rendered prior to the year end have been recorded as sales of that year except that no amount has been included in sales and accounts receivable for goods shipped on consignment, on approval, or subject to repurchase agreements.

3. No abnormal returns have been received since the year end or are expected in respect to goods shipped prior to the year end.

4. Inventory does not include:
   a) items not paid for and for which no liability has been recorded in the accounts at year end
   b) goods on consignment from others or
   c) goods invoiced to customers.

5. All charges to capital assets (and additions under capital leases) during the year represent actual additions and no expenditures of a capital nature have been charged to expense during the year.

6. All capital assets sold or dismantled (and all capital lease terminations) during the year have been properly accounted for in the accounts.

7. Capital and other assets with a limited life are being depreciated, amortized, or otherwise written off as a charge to income in a rational and systematic manner appropriate to the nature of the assets and their use by the company.

8. All liabilities of the company at the year end have been recorded in the accounts (including provisions for such items as salaries, wages and commissions, royalties, employee benefits (including pension costs), warranties, professional service, taxes, etc. and long-term debt and obligations under capital leases).

9. At the year end there were no contingent liabilities (except [specify]) and all claims which are outstanding and possible claims have been disclosed to you, whether or not such claims have been discussed with our lawyers.

10. At the year end, the company had no unusual commitments or contractual obligations of any sort which were not in the ordinary course of business and which might have an adverse effect on the company (except [specify]).

11. There were no material transactions during the year that have not been properly reflected in the accounts.

12. The company has complied with all aspects of contractual agreements that would have a material effect on the financial statements in the event of noncompliance including all covenants, conditions, or other requirements of all outstanding debt.

E X H I B I T   13–3   **(continued)**

13. With respect to environmental matters
    a) at year end, there were no liabilities or contingencies that have not already been disclosed to you;
    b) liabilities or contingencies have been recognized, measured and disclosed, as appropriate, in the (consolidated) financial statements; and
    c) commitments have been measured and disclosed, as appropriate, in the (consolidated) financial statements.

E. Consolidated accounts and equity-accounted investments

1. All significant intercompany transactions have been identified and properly eliminated in the consolidated financial statements.
2. The cost of acquisition of investments has been assigned in the financial statements to the purchased assets (including goodwill, after adjustment for minority interest) and liabilities in accordance with their several values at the dates of acquisition.
3. Goodwill is being amortized over its estimated life.
4. Appropriate loss provisions have been provided in the accounts where there has been a permanent impairment in the value of unamortized goodwill.

F. General

1. The minute books presented to you contain complete and authentic minutes of all meetings of shareholders and directors (including committees thereof) held throughout the year to the most recent meetings on the following dates: (specify).
2. None of the directors, officers, or shareholders were indebted to the company, other than in the ordinary course of business, at the year end or at any time during the year.
3. With respect to related parties, we have disclosed to you in the financial statements:
    a) all transactions with such parties including sales, purchases, loans, transfers of assets, liabilities and services, leasing arrangements, guarantees, etc. and
    b) all balances due to or from such parties at year end. These are as follows: (specify).
4. No fraud and other irregularities have occurred and nothing has come to light which might reflect upon the honesty or integrity of any employee, agent, or officer of the company.
5. There have been no communications from regulatory agencies concerning non-compliance with laws or regulations which could have a material effect on the financial statements except: (specify).
6. We are not aware of any illegal or possibly illegal acts which have not been disclosed to you, the consequences of which should be considered for inclusion in the financial statements as a liability, contingency or commitment.

G. Events subsequent to the year-end

1. No events have occurred or are pending or in prospect and no facts have been discovered as at the present date which are of such significance in relation to the company's affairs as to make the financial statements not present fairly the financial position or results of operations of the company (except: [specify]).

Company/Organization   Date

Per: Officer

13.7 In addition to the lawyer's letter, what other procedures can be used to gather evidence regarding contingencies?

13.8 The following was included in a letter auditors received from the client's lawyers, in response to a letter sent to them similar to Exhibit 13–2: "Several agreements and contracts to which the company is a party are not covered by this response since we have not advised or been consulted in their regard." How might the auditor's report be affected by such a statement in a letter from the client's lawyer regarding a pending lawsuit against a client? Explain.

13.9 Why might companies and auditors experience difficulty making appropriate disclosures about litigation contingencies?

EXHIBIT 13–4   **AUDIT CORRESPONDENCE**

Type	From	To	Time
Engagement letter (acceptance)	Auditor (client)	Client (auditor)	Before engagement
Internal control weaknesses	Auditor	Client	Interim or after audit
Confirmations (replies)	Client (third parties)	Third parties (auditor)	Throughout the audit
Lawyer's letter (reply)	Client Lawyer	Lawyer (auditor)	Near end of audit
Client rep letter	Client	Auditor	End of field work
Management letter	Auditor	Client	After audit
Communication with client audit committee	Auditor	Directors	Before or after audit report

EVENTS SUBSEQUENT TO THE BALANCE SHEET DATE

· · · · · · · · · · · ·

LEARNING   OBJECTIVE
5. Given a set of facts and
    circumstances, classify
    a subsequent event by
    type and describe the
    proper treatment in the
    financial statements.

Certain material events that occur subsequent to the balance sheet date but before the end of field work (thus, before issuance of the audit report) require disclosure in the financial statements and related notes. Auditors (and management) are responsible for gathering evidence on these subsequent events and evaluating the proposed disclosure. Material subsequent events have been classified into two types, which are disclosed differently. The first type (Type I) requires adjustment of the dollar amounts in the financial statements and appropriate disclosure (financial statement notes), while the second (Type II) requires note disclosure and sometimes pro forma financial statements.

Type I: Adjustment of Dollar Amounts Required

This type of subsequent event provides new information regarding a financial condition that existed at the date of the balance sheet. The subsequent event information affects the numbers and requires adjustment of amounts in the financial statements for the period under audit.

The following are examples of Type I subsequent events:

- A loss on uncollectible trade accounts receivable as a result of bankruptcy of a major customer. (The customer's deteriorating financial condition existed prior to the balance sheet date.)

- The settlement of litigation for an amount different than estimated (assuming the litigation had taken place prior to the balance sheet date).

Type II: No Adjustment of Financial Statements, but Disclosure Required

The second type of subsequent event involves occurrences that had both their cause and their manifestation arising after the balance sheet date. Recall that the auditor's responsibility for adequate disclosure runs to the date marking the end of the field

---

SUBSEQUENT EVENT STOCK SPLIT

The company approved on February 15 a two-for-one stock split to be effective on that date. The fiscal year-end was the previous December 31, and the financial statements as of December 31 showed 50 million shares authorized, 10 million shares issued and outstanding, and earnings per share of $3.

Audit Resolution. Note disclosure was made of the split and of the relevant dates. The equity section of the balance sheet showed 100 million shares authorized, 20 million shares issued and outstanding. The income statement reported earnings per share of $1.50. Earnings per share of prior years were adjusted accordingly. The note disclosed comparative earnings per share on the predividend shares. The audit report was dated February 1, with a double-date of February 15 for the note disclosure.

---

work. Consequently, even for events that occurred after the balance sheet date and that are not of the first type requiring financial statement adjustment, auditors must consider their importance and may insist that disclosure be made. Type II events that occur after the balance sheet date may be of such magnitude that disclosure is necessary to keep the financial statements from being misleading as of the report date. Disclosure normally is in a narrative note. Occasionally, however, an event may be so significant that the best disclosure is pro forma financial data. **Pro forma** financial data is the presentation of the financial statements "as if" the event had occurred on the date of the balance sheet. Such pro forma data are given in a note disclosure. For example, in addition to historical financial statements, pro forma financial data may be the best way to show the effect of a business purchase or other merger or the sale of a major portion of assets.

Examples of Type II subsequent events are:

- Loss on an uncollectible trade receivable resulting from a customer's fire or flood loss subsequent to the balance sheet date (as contrasted with a customer's slow decline into bankruptcy cited as a Type I event above).

- Sale of a bond or share capital issue.

- Settlement of litigation when the event giving rise to the claim took place subsequent to the balance sheet date.

- Loss of plant or inventories as a result of fire or flood.

The aspect of retroactive recognition of the effect of stock dividends and splits is an exception that may be explained briefly with an example. The problem is one of timing and one of informative communication to financial statement users. When the financial statements reach the users, the stock dividend or split will have been completed, and to report financial data as if it had not occurred might be considered misleading.

Double-dating in the Audit Report

Double-dating refers to dating the audit report as of the end of field work along with an additional later date attached to disclosure of a significant Type II subsequent event. Sometimes it happens that, after completion of field work but before issuance of the report, a significant event comes to the audit team's attention. For example, imagine that in the illustration given in the preceding box, field work had been completed on February 1 and the audit report was to be so dated. However, before the report was typed and delivered, the auditors learned of the two-for-one stock split. In this case the report would be dated "February 1 except as to footnote X which is dated February 15" (where footnote X is the disclosure of the stock split). The accounting treatment would be the same as described in the illustration above.

The purpose of double-dating is twofold: (1) to provide a means of inserting important information in the financial statement footnote disclosures learned after field work is complete and (2) to inform users that the auditor takes full responsibility for all subsequent events only up to the end of field work (February 1 in the example) and for the specifically identified later event (the stock split disclosed in the note in the example, which occurred on February 15). However, responsibility is not taken for other events that may have occurred after the end of field work.

Actually, double-dating in the audit report is not required. In the example the auditors could have used one date (February 15) for the audit report, avoiding the complication of the double-dating. However, the consequence is that the auditors then take responsibility for performing the subsequent event audit procedures through February 15. That is, the auditors extend the field work responsibility two weeks. Double-dating is used to cut off the subsequent event procedural responsibility at the earlier date.

Audit Program for the Subsequent Period

Some audit procedures performed in the period subsequent to the balance sheet date may be part of the audit program for determining cutoff and proper valuation of balances as of the balance sheet date (Part A in Exhibit 13–5). However, the procedures specifically designed for gathering evidence about the two types of subsequent events are different and are apart from the rest of the audit program (Part B in Exhibit 13–5).

REVIEW CHECKPOINTS

13.10   What are the two types of "subsequent events"? In which way(s) are they treated differently in the financial statements?

13.11   What treatment is given stock dividends and splits that occur after the balance sheet date but before the audit report is issued? Explain.

13.12   What is the purpose of "double-dating" an audit report?

13.13   Generally, what additional actions should auditors take in the period between the audit report date and the effective date of a registration statement?

RESPONSIBILITIES AFTER THE AUDIT REPORT HAS BEEN ISSUED

The next two topics do not deal with responsibilities or concerns during the audit, but with responsibilities after the audit is completed and the report has been issued. They are covered here because they are related to subsequent event responsibilities. The topics are (1) subsequent discovery of facts existing at the date of the audit report and (2) consideration of the omission of audit procedures discovered after the report date.

E X H I B I T   13–5   **AUDITING PROCEDURES FOR THE PERIOD SUBSEQUENT TO THE BALANCE SHEET DATE**

A. Procedures performed in connection with other audit programs.
   1. Use a cutoff bank statement to:
      a. Examine cheques paid after year-end that are, or should have been, listed on the bank reconciliation.
      b. Examine bank posting of deposits in transit listed on the bank reconciliation.
   2. Vouch collections on accounts receivable in the month following year-end for evidence of existence and collectibility of the year-end balances.
   3. Trace cash disbursements of the month after year-end to accounts payable for evidence of any liabilities unrecorded at year-end.
   4. Vouch write-downs of fixed assets after year-end evidence that such valuation problems existed at the year-end date.
   5. Vouch sales of investment securities, write-downs, or write-offs in the months after the audit date for evidence of valuation at the year-end date.
   6. Vouch and trace sales transactions in the month after year-end for evidence of proper sales and cost of sales cutoff.
B. Auditing procedures for subsequent events.
   1. Read the latest available interim financial statements, compare them with the financial statements being reported on, and make any other comparisons considered appropriate in the circumstances.
   2. Enquire of officers and other executives having responsibility for financial and accounting matters about whether the interim statements have been prepared on the same basis as that used for the statements under examination.
   3. Enquire of and discuss with officers and other executives having responsibility for financial and accounting matters (limited where appropriate to major locations):
      a. Whether any substantial contingent liabilities or commitments existed at the date of the balance sheet being reported on or at the date of enquiry.
      b. Whether there was any significant change in the share capital, long-term debt, or working capital to the date of enquiry.
      c. The current status of items in the financial statements being reported on that were accounted for on the basis of tentative, preliminary, or inconclusive data.
      d. Whether any unusual adjustments have been made during the period from the balance sheet date to the date of enquiry.
   4. Read the available minutes of meetings of shareholders, directors, and appropriate committees; enquire about matters dealt with at meetings for which minutes are not available.
   5. Request that the client send a letter to legal counsel enquiring about outstanding claims, possible claims, and management's evaluation, with the reply to be sent directly to the auditor.
   6. Obtain a letter of representation, dated as of the date of the auditor's report, from appropriate officials, generally the chief executive officer and chief financial officer, about whether any events occurred subsequent to the date of the financial statements that, in the officer's opinion, would require adjustment or disclosure in these statements.
   7. Make such additional enquiries or perform such procedures as considered necessary and appropriate to dispose of questions that arise in carrying out the foregoing procedures, enquiries, and discussions.

LEARNING   OBJECTIVE
6. Specify the sequence of decisions and actions auditors must consider upon discovery (after the issuance of the report) of information about facts that may have existed at the date of the auditor's report.

The most important thing to remember is that auditors have an active, procedural responsibility for discovering Type I and Type II subsequent events and for their proper disclosure, but they are not required to perform procedures after the audit report date. However, auditors have responsibilities once they become aware of the facts or omitted procedures.

Subsequent Discovery of Facts Existing at the Date of the Auditor's Report

Auditing standards actually deal with two subsequent things: (*a*) events that occur after the balance sheet date and (*b*) knowledge gained after the audit report date of events that occurred or conditions that existed on or before the audit report date. The subsequent event or subsequently acquired knowledge may arise (1) before

E X H I B I T 13–6   SUBSEQUENT EVENTS AND SUBSEQUENT DISCOVERY

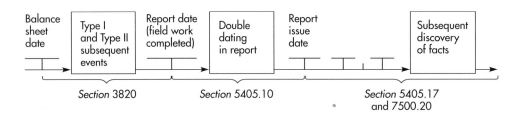

the end of audit field work, (2) after the end of field work but before issuance of the report, or (3) after the audit report is issued. Exhibit 13–6 shows a time continuum of these combinations with a key to the auditing standards sections that deal with them.

Auditors are under no obligation to continue performing any auditing procedures past the report date (except when engaged on an SEC registration statement). However, when they happen to learn of facts that are important, they have the obligation to (1) determine whether the information is reliable and (2) determine whether the facts existed at the date of the report. When both of these conditions are affirmed and the auditors believe persons are relying on the report, steps should be taken to withdraw the first report, issue a new report, and inform persons currently relying on the financial statements. These measures are facilitated by co-operation on the part of the client. However, the auditors' duty to notify the public that an earlier report should not be relied on is not relieved by client objections.[1]

A sequence of decisions is explained in Exhibit 13–7. Basically, the decisions relate to the importance and impact of the information, the co-operation of the client in taking necessary action, and the actions to be taken.

Consideration of Omitted Procedures After the Report Date

LEARNING OBJECTIVE
7. Specify the considerations and procedures applied by auditors upon concluding (after the audit report date) that one or more auditing procedures were omitted.

Although auditors have no responsibility to continue to review their work after the audit report has been issued, the report and working papers may be subjected to postissuance review by an outside peer review or practice inspection or by the firm's internal inspection program. A peer review is a quality assurance review by another auditing firm of an audit firm's quality control policies and procedures and the compliance thereof. Practice inspection is to ensure that all members in public practice maintain appropriate levels of professional standards. Practice inspection is primarily educational in focus, to help practitioners improve their professional standards where necessary. For example, in Ontario approximately 25 percent of all offices are inspected each year by the Provincial Institutes Office of the Director of Practice Inspection.[2]

---

[1] The discussion here is cast in terms of subsequent discovery of facts while the auditor remains engaged by the client. However, the responsibilities to determine whether the subsequent information is reliable and whether the facts existed at the date of the already-issued report remain in force even when the auditor has resigned from the engagement or has been fired by the client.

[2] *Practice Inspection Program,* ICAO, November 1992.

Notification of Audit Report Withdrawal

Endotronics, Inc., reported net income of $1.3 million for its fiscal year ended September 30, 1986. In March 1987 FBI agents who searched the company's warehouses testified that many of the company's cell-replicating machines reported as sold actually remained under Endotronics' control. Soon thereafter (March 1987), Peat, Marwick, Mitchell & Company (KPMG Peat Marwick) withdrew its audit report, saying: "In light of . . . serious questions about the company's revenue figure, we cannot satisfy ourselves about the facts of the situation."

Source: The Wall Street Journal, March 23, 1987.

Handbook Section 5405, "Date of Auditor's Report," provides guidance for such subsequent discovery of material misstatement situations. A possible sequence of decisions is presented in Exhibit 13–8. Because of legal implications of some of the actions proposed, consultation with the firm's legal counsel is advised. The relevance of the omitted procedure (and the evidence the auditors failed to obtain) should be measured against the auditors' present ability to support the previously expressed opinion. It may be that, after a review of the working papers and discussions with audit staff personnel, other procedures may be shown to have produced the evidence needed. In such circumstances the omitted procedure is not considered to impair the report.

However, if the other procedures did not produce sufficient appropriate evidence, and, therefore the previously expressed opinion cannot be supported, further action is necessary. As with subsequent discovery of facts, the next step is to determine whether the auditors' report is still being relied on. If reliance is still possible, the omitted procedure (or alternative procedures) should be undertaken promptly to provide a basis for the audit opinion. If such work reveals facts that existed at the date of the original report, then the actions related to subsequent discovery of facts (Exhibit 13–7) must be taken.

REVIEW CHECKPOINTS

13.14   What is the difference between a "subsequent event" and a "subsequent discovery of fact existing at the report date"? Describe the auditors' responsibility for each.

13.15   If, subsequent to issuance of a report, the audit partner discovers information that existed at the report date and materially affects the financial statements, what actions should the partner take if the client consents to disclose the information? What action should be taken if the client (including the board of directors) refuses to make disclosure?

13.16   What are the steps an auditor should take if, after the report has been issued, someone discovers that an important audit procedure was omitted?

E X H I B I T 13–7   SUBSEQUENT DISCOVERY OF FACTS EXISTING AT THE DATE OF THE
AUDITOR'S REPORT

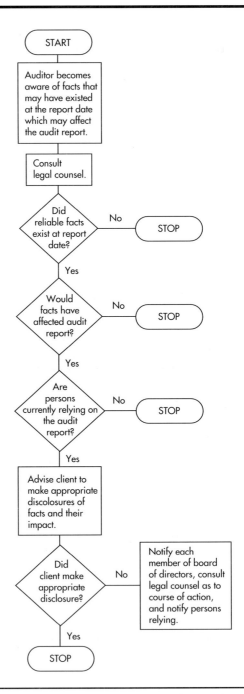

EXHIBIT 13–8 CONSIDERATION OF OMITTED PROCEDURES AFTER THE REPORT DATE

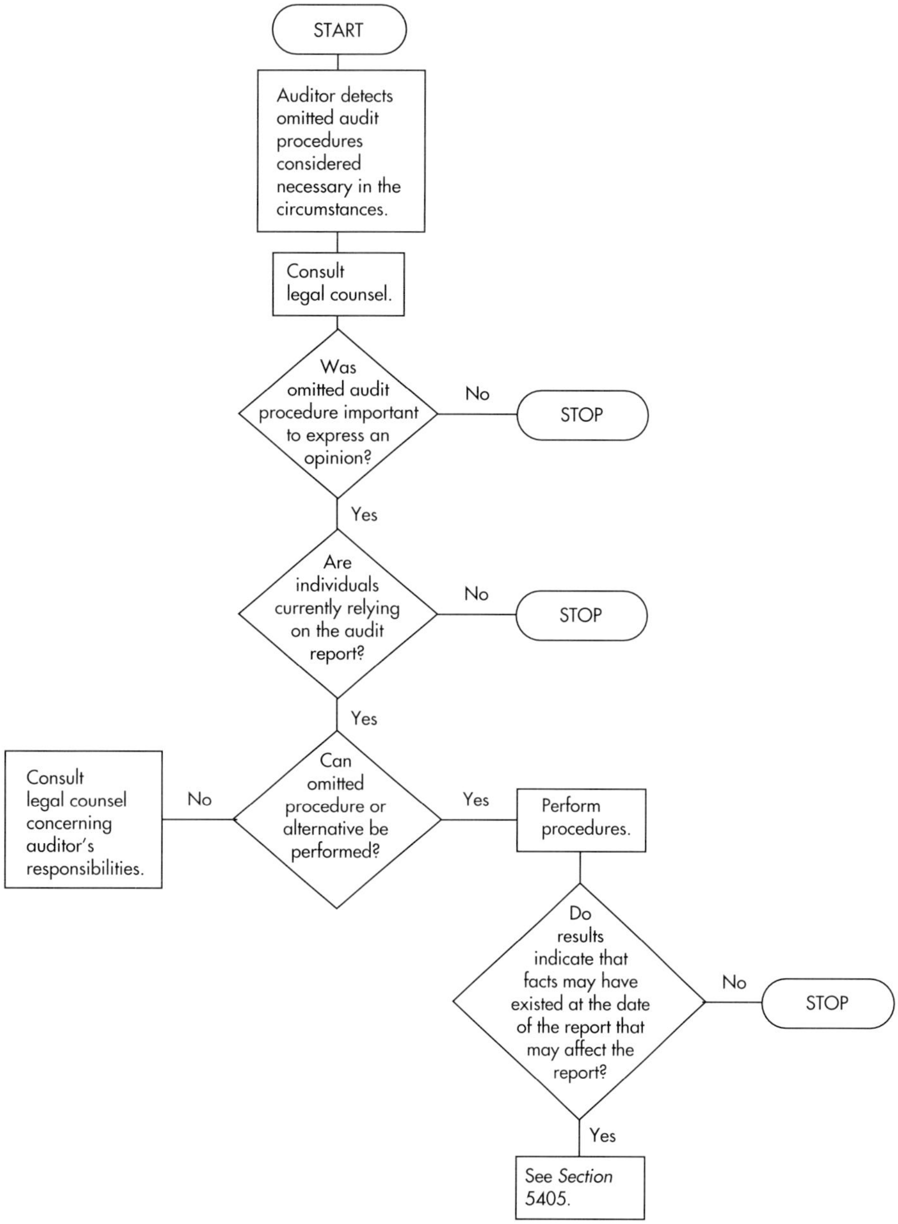
START
Auditor detects omitted audit procedures considered necessary in the circumstances.
Consult legal counsel.
Was omitted audit procedure important to express an opinion?
No
STOP
Yes
Are individuals currently relying on the audit report?
No
STOP
Yes
Consult legal counsel concerning auditor's responsibilities.
No
Can omitted procedure or alternative be performed?
Yes
Perform procedures.
Do results indicate that facts may have existed at the date of the report that may affect the report?
No
STOP
Yes
See Section 5405.

Source: *CPA Journal*, March 1984, p. 37. Copyright © 1984 by the New York Society of Certified Public Accountants.

FINAL WRAP-UP

. . . .

Several items must be completed before an audit can be considered finished. The client must approve of the proposed adjusting entries and the financial statement notes, and the audit work must be reviewed.

Communications with Audit Committees (or equivalent)

The auditor should review with management in advance the information to be covered with the audit committee. On certain matters (e.g., company operations), management should report to the audit committee and the auditor then comments; on other matters, such as audit findings, the auditor should report to the audit committee and management then comments. Both should be present in meetings with the audit committee to discuss the reports, which may be written or oral. When the auditor communicates in writing, the report should indicate that it is intended solely for use by the audit committee.

In some instances the auditor may identify matters to discuss with the audit committee without the presence of management.

The auditor should keep notes of audit committee discussions at which the auditor is present. These notes should be compared to the minutes of the audit committee. Any inconsistencies should be resolved with the audit committee or board of directors.

The auditor should communicate all matters affecting approval of the annual financial statements to the board of directors prior to such approval. Normally, the auditor should work within the audit committee's regular cycle of meetings.

The audit committee's expectations need to be clarified and put in writing. The most important matters arising from the audit of financial statements that the auditor should communicate to the audit committee include:

1. Auditor's responsibility under GAAP.
2. The planning of the current audit.
3. Deficiencies in internal controls.
4. Illegal acts.
5. Fraud.
6. Significant accounting principles and policies.
7. Management judgments and accounting estimates.
8. Misstatements.
9. Other information in annual reports (e.g., narrative information).
10. Disagreements with management.
11. Consultation with other accountants by management.
12. Major issues that influence the audit appointment.
13. Difficulties encountered in performing the audit (e.g., unreasonable delays in obtaining information from management).

The auditor's responsibility is to communicate (or determine that management has communicated) matters of concern to the audit committee. If the auditor considers the audit committee's action seriously inappropriate, the auditor may need to communicate directly with the board of directors, and in some cases has an obligation to report to outside regulatory authorities. For example, the "well-being reporting requirement" under federal financial institutions legislation described in AUG–17 may require the auditor to report to the Superintendent of Financial Institutions "any significant weaknesses in internal control which have the potential to jeopardize the financial institution's ability to continue as a going concern." Since there is the issue of client confidentiality, the auditor should seek legal advice concerning the best manner of reporting to outside authorities.

Client Approval of Adjusting Entries and Financial Statement Disclosure

The financial statements, including the notes to the financial statements, are the responsibility of management, although auditors frequently draft them. The adjusting entries shown in Exhibit 13–9 are labelled "proposed" to indicate this responsibility of management.

EXHIBIT 13–9   **PROPOSED ADJUSTING JOURNAL ENTRIES (illustrative scoresheet working paper)**

	Income Statement		Balance Sheet	
	Debit	Credit	Debit	Credit
(1) Unrecorded cash disbursements:				
Accounts payable			$42,000	
Cash				$42,000
(2) Improper sales cutoff:				
Sales	$13,000			
Inventory			7,800	
Cost of goods sold (60%)		$7,800		
Accounts receivable				13,000
(3) Inventory write-off:				
Cost of goods sold	21,000			
Inventory				21,000
(4) Unrecorded liabilities:				
Utilities expense	700			
Commissions expense	3,000			
Wages	2,500			
Accounts payable				700
Accrued expenses payable				5,500
(5) Amortization calculation error:				
Accumulated amortization			17,000	
Amortization expense		17,000		
(6) Reclassify current portion of long-term debt:				
Notes payable			50,000	
Current portion of debt				50,000
(7) Income tax @ 40%:				
Income tax refund receivable			6,160	
Income tax expense		6,160		
	$40,200	$30,960	$122,960	$132,200
Net income change		($9,240)		
Current assets change				($62,040)
Current liabilities change				$14,200
Working capital change				($76,240)

Many of the adjusting entries will be approved by management as they are prepared during the work on an area; others will await the final wrap-up to be approved. A formal list of all approved adjusting entries should be given to the client so that formal entries can be made in the accounting records to bring them into balance with the financial statements.

In a like manner, approval of all disclosure in notes must be obtained from the client. The notes considered necessary usually are drafted as proposed notes by auditors performing the audit procedures. They must be considered carefully by the audit manager and partner before being presented to the client management for acceptance as the company's disclosures.

Exhibit 13–9 is a summary worksheet ("scoresheet") showing the end-of-audit consideration of proposed adjusting journal entries. Auditors can prepare this summary to see how the proposed adjustments affect the financial statements. This review helps auditors decide which adjustments must be made to support an unqualified audit report and which adjustments may be passed. A passed adjustment is a proposed adjustment on which the auditors decide not to insist because it does not have a material effect on the financial position and results of operations.

In the exhibit the illustrative proposed adjustments are (1) recording cheques written and mailed but not recorded in the books; (2) reversing recorded sales for goods shipped after the balance sheet date, and reversing the 60 percent cost of goods sold; (3) writing off obsolete and damaged inventory; (4) recording the amounts found in the search for unrecorded liabilities; (5) correcting an amortization calculation error; (6) reclassifying the current portion of long-term debt from the long-term classification; and (6) recording a tax refund asset for overpaid income taxes (could be a debit to tax liability if all the taxes for the year had not already been paid). Some summary effects on income, current assets, current liabilities, and working capital are appended to the bottom of the exhibit.

OVERALL EVALUATION OF AUDIT TESTS

The important thing about the audit tests is that they are the basis for deciding if the amount of unadjusted error is material at the end of the audit. The adjusted errors by definition have been corrected, so the real issue at the end of the audit is whether the uncorrected errors are material in amount. A minimal way to estimate this is on the basis of known uncorrected errors as in Exhibit 13–9. We refer to this as minimal because it is based on known errors, not most likely or possible errors (with which the client may disagree). We cover adjustments based on most likely and possible errors in Chapter 20 because they are less common in practice.

The principle of audit decision making based on known unadjusted errors is to aggregate these in various ways to see if they total to a material amount. If the audit is based on cycles, then special work sheets must be prepared to aggregate errors in specific ways on which the materiality assessment is based. For example, say materiality is based on net income and is assessed to be 10 percent of recorded net income. Then the auditor will need to aggregate all errors affecting net income. This can be done on the basis of either (1) changes in net assets (assets-liabilities), or equivalently, or (2) revenues minus expenses. Both approaches should yield the same number. Note that, due to the nature of the double-entry system, in both cases understatements in liabilities/expenses must be *added* to over- or understatements of assets/revenues, while overstatements in liabilities/expenses must be subtracted from over- or understatements of assets/revenues.

Perhaps this is better explained by example than in words. Refer to Exhibit 13–9. The way to compute net effect of unadjusted (uncorrected) known errors on net income in this illustration is as follows:

Errors in net income = Errors in changes in net assets = Errors in changes in assets minus errors in changes in liabilities + $42,000_{(A)}$ + $13,000_{(A)}$ + $21,000_{(A)}$ − $7800_{(A)}$ − $17,000_{(A)}$ − $6160_{(A)}$ − (+ $42,000_{(L)}$ − $700_{(L)}$ − $5500_{(L)}$ + $50,000_{(L)}$ − $50,000_{(L)}$) = 9240 = Errors in revenues minus errors in expenses = $13,000_{(R)}$ − ($6160_{(E)}$ + $7800_{(E)}$ − $21,000_{(E)}$ − $700_{(E)}$ − $3,000_{(E)}$ − $2,500_{(E)}$ + $17,000_{(E)}$) = 9240 = Total net errors in net income (overstatement, i.e., to eliminate all error the adjusting entry must reduce client's proposed net income by 9240). This 9240 is then compared to predetermined overall materiality. If 9240 is less than material, then the auditor concludes that he or she does not need to make any more adjustments.

To reiterate, the above analysis is based on known uncorrected errors only and is therefore perfectly appropriate whenever the auditor tests 100 percent of the transactions. This 100 percent testing is likely for cash, capital assets, noncurrent liabilities, and the owner's equity section. It is less likely for inventory, receivables, and payables, which can represent large populations of individual items, thus the auditor may wish to use sampling theory concepts for adjusting these accounts by most likely and possible error. We cover adjustments and decision making based on these sampling situations in Chapter 20.

One final point on overall evaluation: how does materiality relate to assertions? Materiality is defined as the amount of errors *from all sources* that would affect a user decision. Thus materiality can be viewed as the minimum error that financial statement users find unacceptable from all assertions that have been violated. In other words, it is presumed users don't care which assertion is violated, only that aggregate violations from all sources are less than material. Again, review Exhibit 13–9 and note the assertions affected by the errors—they include completeness, valuation, existence, and presentation assertions.

Working Paper and Report Review

The audit supervisor makes a final review to ensure that all accounts on the trial balance have a working paper reference index (an indication that the audit work has been finished for that account) and that all procedures in the audit program are "signed off" with a date and initials.

The working papers of the audit staff are reviewed soon after being completed by the audit supervisor and sometimes by the audit manager. This review is to ensure that all tick-mark notations are clear, that all procedures performed are adequately documented, and that all necessary procedures were performed with due professional care.

The review by the audit manager and engagement partner will focus more on the overall scope of the audit. The audit manager and engagement partner are very involved with the planning of the audit, and they perform some of the field work on difficult areas. However, they are usually not involved in preparing the detail working papers. Even though the working papers are reviewed by the on-site audit supervisor, the review by the partner who is going to sign the audit report is essential. Review "to-do lists" are prepared during these reviews citing omissions or deficiencies that must be cleared before the final work is completed.

Audit firms vary in their treatment of the "to-do lists." Some firms prefer to destroy the lists after the work is performed and documented in the working papers. After all, they want to "clean up" the working papers, and the to-do lists were merely notes directing the staff to tie a neat ribbon around any loose ends or difficult issues. Other firms prefer to keep the lists as signed off and cross-referenced for the work performed. They believe that the lists are "working papers" that show evidence of careful review and completion of the audit. Sometimes, retained to-do lists backfire on auditors by showing questions raised but not resolved.

The working papers and financial statements, including footnotes, are given a final review on large engagements by a partner not responsible for client relations. This **second-partner review** ensures that the quality of audit work and reporting is in keeping with the quality standards of the audit firm.

The final audit time reports must be prepared and the working papers prepared for storage. At the completion of the field work, performance evaluation reports of the staff auditors usually are prepared by the audit supervisor.

Management Letter

During the audit work (especially the evaluation of the control structure and assessment of the control risk), matters are noted that can be made as recommendations to the client. When field work is completed, and in some cases after the audit report is delivered, these items are evaluated and written in a letter (commonly referred to as the **management letter**) to be sent to the client. One firm calls this communication a letter of client advisory comments and characterizes it as a voluntary and constructive dimension of an audit designed to provide clients with an important value-added service. The firm encourages consulting and tax professionals to participate with the auditors in preparing the letter.

The management letter is not required by professional standards and should not be confused with the communication of matters identified during the financial statement audit, which is now required by auditing standards (*Handbook Section* 5750, discussed in Chapter 6) or with significant weaknesses in internal control, which must be reported to the audit committee under *Handbook Section* 5220. Management letters are a service provided as a by-product of the audit. The management letter is an excellent opportunity to develop rapport with the client and to make the client aware of other business services offered by the accounting firm. Wallace read over 100 management letters and concluded that public accounting firms frequently miss opportunities to impress clients with their wide range of services.[3] Many of the letters failed to "sell." A brief management letter formulated along the lines of her suggestions is shown in Exhibit 13–10.

· ·

R E V I E W
C H E C K P O I N T S

13.17 Why are auditors' drafts of adjusting entries and note disclosures always labelled "proposed" near the end of the audit? Why shouldn't auditors just write them in final form and give them to the client?

---

[3] W.A. Wallace, "More Effective Management Letters," *CPA Journal*, December 1983, pp. 18–28.

EXHIBIT 13–10 **MANAGEMENT LETTER**

Anderson, Olds & Watershed
Chartered Accountants
Toronto, Ontario
April 1, 1992

Mr. Larry Lancaster, Chairman
Kingston Company
Kingston, Ontario

Dear Mr. Lancaster:

During our audit of the Kingston Company financial statements for the year ended December 31, 1992, we observed certain matters we believe should be brought to your attention. Our audit work was not designed to be a study of the overall efficiency and economy of the management and operation of Kingston Company, but ordinary audit procedures nevertheless enabled us to notice some actions that could enhance the profitability of the Company.

Summary

When we audited the physical inventory and compared the quantities actually on hand to the quantities shown in the perpetual inventory records, we noted several shortages. Follow-up with your warehouse personnel revealed that the "shortages" were usually in the assembly department, where numerous items of custom lawn maintenance equipment were being assembled for customers prior to delivery. The removal of the inventory from the records was routinely entered when the assembled equipment was delivered. These procedures eventually maintained the records accurately, but the delay in posting the inventory records has resulted in lost sales and some customer dissatisfaction with the custom-assembly service.

The Problem

The warehouse personnel remove parts according to the specification of custom-assembly work orders, moving the parts to the assembly area. If another customer orders these parts soon thereafter, the inventory records show them on hand, and the new customer is told that the order can be filled. Shortly thereafter, warehouse personnel find that the parts are actually not on hand, and the customer is disappointed when informed of a delay. Sales department personnel confirmed that several (20-25 during the last six months) withdrew their orders and bought the parts from a competitor. They estimated that approximately $25,000 was lost in sales during the last six months, amounting to about $9,000 in lost profits.

Custom-Assembly Losses

The inventory "shortages," noticed by warehouse personnel when they try to fill new orders, causes another difficulty. People spend extra time looking around for the parts, and usually their enquiries reach the assembly area, where workers leave their jobs unfinished while trying to help locate the "missing" parts. This helpfulness causes assembly jobs to be delayed, customers get dissatisfied, and, in one case, a customer refused to pay because of late delivery. This one case resulted in lost profits of $10,000 because the equipment had to be disassembled and returned to the inventory.

Recommendation

We discussed the following recommendation with Mr. James Worthy in the warehouse, and he agrees that it can be a practical solution. We recommend that you design a form for "Work in Progress," which will be used to make accounting and inventory entries to remove parts from the main inventory as soon as they are transferred to the assembly area. At that stage, the cost would be classified as "work in progress," which will be entered in cost of goods sold as soon as the assembly is completed and the goods are delivered. Judging from our limited knowledge of the extent of the problem during the year under audit, we estimate that you might produce $20,000-$30,000 additional profit per year, while development and use of the form should cost about $3,000.

Conclusion

AO&W has expertise in system development and operation in our management services department, and we will be happy to assist you in reviewing a new form and a systems plan for your implementation. If you wish to discuss this matter further, please inform Mr. Dalton Wardlaw.

Very truly yours,

Anderson, Olds & Watershed

13.18 What are review "to-do" lists? Cite several items that such lists might contain. Why must such lists be cleared before the field work is considered completed?

13.19 What is a good reason for keeping the "to-do list" in the audit working paper files?

13.20 Describe a "second-partner review." What is its purpose?

13.21 What is a management letter? Is a management letter required by generally accepted auditing standards?

13.22 Which PA firm personnel should participate in preparing a management letter at the end of an audit?

13.23 How can well-prepared management letters lead to additional client services besides audit engagements?

SUMMARY

This chapter covered several aspects of completing an audit. As the work draws to a close, several income and expense accounts may remain to be audited. Analytical comparisons of their balances with prior years and current expectations accomplish this auditing in most cases. Large and significant revenues and expenses usually have already been audited in connection with the audit of other accounts in the cycles. At this late stage in the audit, it is always a good idea to "step back" and review large and unusual revenue and gain transactions recorded near the end of the year. These often have been the vehicles for income statement manipulation. Some examples were given in the chapter.

Two of the most important topics for the audit completion work involve the client's written representation letter and the lawyer's letter. These submissions to the auditors are virtually required for an unqualified audit report. Without them, the audit scope is considered limited. Several requirements for the client representation letter were specified in the chapter. A special insert described particular problems interpreting lawyers' letters. Information from lawyers is especially important for getting evidence about litigation contingencies and their disclosure according to *Handbook Section* 3290. Some descriptive research on *Handbook Section* 3290 U.S. disclosure experience was provided to emphasize the difficulties faced by managers and auditors.

"Subsequent events" topics were explained in considerable detail, including (1) procedural responsibility for events following the balance sheet date; (2) the dual-dating alternative for reporting on events that occurred between the end of field work and the delivery of the report; (3) auditors' discovery, after a report was delivered, of facts that existed at the balance sheet date; and (4) auditors' finding, after a report was delivered, that one or more audit procedures they thought were performed were not actually performed.

This chapter closed this text's adventures in auditing with explanation of proposed adjusting journal entries and disclosure notes, working paper review, and the management letter. All that remains is the audit report itself, which was explained in Chapter 3. The next chapter will discuss other types of engagements that are common in public practice.

CASE STUDY	KINGSTON COMPANY

Kingston Case Assignments

Here are three assignments on client representation letters, subsequent events, and financial statement adjustment with report preparation.

13.24   Kingston Company: Client's Rep Letter.   Based on the audit program, there are still two major areas to complete: the client's rep letter and the search for subsequent events. You decide to draft a proposed client rep letter to be prepared on Kingston's letterhead stationery for the partner in charge, Dalton Wardlaw, to review when he returns.

Required:

Prepare a proposed client representation letter to be sent to Anderson, Olds & Watershed from Kingston's CEO and CFO. Include all the required items and any additional points you think are necessary based on the following:

1. There were no irregularities or violations of laws by either management or employees.
2. There are several legal cases pending, which are covered in the lawyer's letter that has been received.
3. There are several subsequent events that the client had disclosed to you (see Assignment 13.25).
4. There are no share capital repurchase options, compensating balances, or agreements to repurchase assets previously sold.

13.25   Kingston Company: Subsequent Events.   In connection with your audit of the financial statements of Kingston Company, management revealed the following items:

1. You learned in January of a $25,000 loan to Kingston from Mr. Grace, the vice president of finance. The loan was made on July 15, and the funds were obtained by him with a loan on his personal life insurance policy. The loan was recorded in the account notes payable. Kingston pays the premiums on the life insurance policy, and Mrs. Grace is the owner and beneficiary of the policy. Kingston repaid Mr. Grace on December 29, 1992, and Mr. Grace loaned the $25,000 back to Kingston on January 12, 1993.
2. As a result of reduced sales, the lumberyard activity was curtailed in mid-January and some workers were laid off. On February 5 all the remaining workers went on strike. To date the strike is unsettled.
3. An opportunity to purchase another lumber company, Willie's Woods, came to Kingston's attention. The board of directors authorized Mr. Grace to put $100,000 in an escrow account as earnest money to hold the deal until it is investigated further.
4. The content of a shipment of pine lumber en route on December 31 was determined to be number 1 pine. The shipment was recorded at year-end as number 2 pine in the amount of $23,600. The final liability to the vendor is based on the actual grade of pine, and in this case the vendor billed Kingston for $29,000.

Required:

a. Prepare an explanation for your staff, of the reasons subsequent events must be disclosed in the financial statements even though they occurred after the balance sheet date. Include in your explanation the difference between the disclosure of Type I and Type II subsequent events.

b. Give the audit procedures, in addition to verbal enquiry and the client's rep letter, that should be performed as part of the subsequent event audit work.

c. Discuss the accounting and/or disclosure, if any, you would recommend for the items listed above, stating all details that should be disclosed.

13.26 Kingston Company: Adjusting Journal Entries and Standard Unqualified Report.

You need to propose the adjustments to the financial statements you believe necessary for you (Dalton Wardlaw, partner in the CA firm of Anderson, Olds & Watershed) to give the standard unqualified report on the Kingston Company financial statements. This report is to cover only the balance sheet for the year ended December 31, 1992, and the statements of results of operations, retained earnings, and cash flows for the one year then ended. The unaudited trial balance is in Exhibit 4.23–1 (Chapter 4).

1. In previous chapters you have worked on the audit of various account balances. Your instructor will give you directions about using the results of your work here to develop proposed adjustments. Some instructors may wish to direct you to use your previous results along with some hypothetical results from part 2, below. In this case students' "answers" may differ.

2. Without prejudice to your findings when working on Kingston assignments in other chapters, and disregarding the subsequent event information in assignment 13.25, you may assume the audit evidence showed the following:

a. When auditing the bank reconciliation, you found that cheques dated in December totalling $51,040 in payment of trade accounts payable were held until January 6, 1993, when they were mailed to creditors.

b. The audit of accounts receivable showed pricing and math errors in the total amount of $12,000 overstatement of receivables and sales. Apart from this amount, the allowance for doubtful accounts was considered large enough.

c. The audit of inventory revealed that some hardware costing $20,000 was found to be obsolete or damaged, with scrap value estimated anywhere from 20 percent to 40 percent of cost. The audit also revealed an unshipped customer hardware order (cost of $10,000) excluded from the December 31 inventory count and compilation, even though the customer was billed $16,000 in January. Also, a lumber shipment in transit ($3,000 cost, plus $500 shipping charges) was excluded from December 31 inventory even though title passed to Kingston before it was received in January.

d. The search of unrecorded liabilities revealed other unrecorded inventory purchases and unrecorded accounts payable of $75,000. These goods were in transit on December 31 and were not included in the inventory shown in the control account on December 31. Also, a December utility bill for $2,100 was not recorded until it was paid in January.

e. The 11 percent bank loan of $750,000 was obtained on July 1, 1992. Interest payable June 30, 1993, was not accrued as of December 31.

f. $200,000 of the long-term debt is due January 1, 1993.

g. Dividends of $50,000 were declared on December 31, payable on February 15, to shareholders of record December 31.

h. Buildings costing $300,000 and equipment costing $600,000 were placed in service on July 1, 1992. Amortization at the annual rates of 4 percent for the buildings and 10 percent for the equipment was not calculated and entered in the accounts. Also, costs of $7,310 that should have been capitalized as land cost was charged to miscellaneous expense, and $23,000 spent to overhaul and recondition some equipment on July 1, 1992, was charged to the repairs and maintenance expense.

i. Use an income tax rate of 40 percent for all income. The tax return and financial statement income are identical, so there are no deferred or prepaid income taxes resulting from timing differences. The trial balance shows no income taxes payable because Kingston paid the entire estimated amount before December 31.

Required:

a. Prepare a scoresheet working paper for the proposed adjusting journal entries (see Exhibit 13–9).

b. Prepare the balance sheet as of December 31, 1992, and the income statement for the year then ended.

c. Prepare a cash flow statement for the year ended December 31, 1992. (Use the comparative trial balance in Exhibit 4.23–1.)

d. Prepare an audit report to go with the financial statements. (Pretend that all the note disclosures are adequate.)

MULTIPLE-CHOICE QUESTIONS FOR PRACTICE AND REVIEW

13.27 When auditing the year-end balance of interest-bearing notes payable, the auditors are most likely to audit at the same time the company's:
a. Interest income.
b. Interest expense.
c. Amortization of goodwill.
d. Royalty revenue.

13.28 The main purpose of a written client representation letter is to:
a. Shift responsibility for financial statements from the management to the auditor.
b. Provide a substitute source of evidence for detail procedures auditors would otherwise perform.
c. Provide management a place to make assertions about the quantity and valuation of the physical inventory.
d. Impress upon management its ultimate responsibility for the financial statements and disclosures.

13.29 Which one of these procedures or sources is not used to obtain evidence about contingencies?
a. Scan expense accounts for credit entries.
b. Obtain a representation letter from the client's lawyer.
c. Read the minutes of the board of directors' meetings.

d. Examine terms of sale in sales contracts.

13.30 A Type II subsequent event involves subsequent information about a condition that existed at the balance sheet date. Subsequent knowledge of which of the following would cause the company to adjust its December 31 financial statements?
a. Sale of an issue of new shares for $500,000 on January 30.
b. Settlement of a damage lawsuit for a customer's injury sustained February 15 for $10,000.
b. Settlement of litigation in February for $100,000 that had been estimated at $12,000 in the December 31 financial statements.
b. Storm damage of $1 million to the company's buildings on March 1.

13.31 A. Griffin audited the financial statements of Dodger Magnificat Corporation for the year ended December 31, 1992. She completed the audit field work on January 30, and later learned of a stock split voted by the board of directors on February 5. The financial statements were changed to reflect the split, and she now needs to dual-date the audit report before sending it to the company. Which of the following is the proper form?

a. December 31, 1992, except as to Note X, which is dated January 30, 1993.

b. January 30, 1992, except as to Note X, which is dated February 5, 1993.

c. December 31, 1992, except as to Note X, which is dated February 5, 1993.

d. February 5, 1993, except for completion of field work, for which the date is January 30, 1993.

13.32 In connection with a company's filing a registration statement under most provincial securities acts, auditors have a responsibility to perform procedures to find subsequent events until:

a. The year-end balance sheet date.

b. The audit report date.

c. The date the registration statement and audit report are delivered to the provincial securities commission.

d. The "effective date" of the registration statement, when the securities can be offered for sale.

13.33 The auditing standards regarding "subsequent discovery of facts that existed at the balance sheet date" refers to knowledge obtained after:

a. The date the audit report was delivered to the client.

b. The audit report date.

c. The company's year-end balance sheet date.

d. The date interim audit work was complete.

13.34 Which two of the following are not required by U.S. auditing standards?

a. Client representation letter.

b. Lawyer's letter.

c. Management letter.

d. Engagement letter.

13.35 Which of these persons generally do not participate in writing the management letter (client advisory comments)?

a. Client's outside lawyers.

b. Client's accounting and production managers.

c. Audit firm's audit team on the engagement.

d. Audit firm's consulting and tax experts.

Exercises and Problems

13.36 Client Representation Letter. In connection with your audit, you request that management furnish you with a letter containing certain representations. For example:

(1) the client has satisfactory title to all assets;

(2) no contingent or unrecorded liabilities exist except as disclosed in the letter;

(3) no shares of the company's stock are reserved for options, warrants, or other rights; and

(4) the company is not obligated to repurchase any of its outstanding shares under any circumstances.

Required:

a. Explain why you believe a letter of representation should be furnished to you.

b. In what way, if any, do these client representations affect your audit procedures and responsibilities?

(AICPA adapted)

13.37 Engagement and Client Representation Letters. The two major written understandings between a PA and client, in connection with an audit of financial statements, are the engagement (arrangements) letter and the client representation letter.

Required:

a. (1) What are the objectives of the engagement (arrangements) letter?

(2) Who should prepare and sign the engagement letter?

(3) When should the engagement letter be sent?

(4) Why should the engagement letter be renewed periodically?

b. (1) What are the objectives of the client representation letter?

(2) Who should sign the client representation letter?

(3) When should the client representation letter be obtained?

(4) Why should the client representation letter be prepared for each examination?

c. A PA's responsibilities for providing accounting services sometimes involve an association with unaudited financial statements. Discuss the need in this circumstance for:

(1) An engagement letter.

(2) Client representation letter.

(AICPA adapted)

13.38 Client Representations Letter Omissions. During the audit of the annual financial statements of Amis Manufacturing, Inc., the company's president, Vance Molar, and Wayne Dweebins, the engagement partner, reviewed matters that were supposed to be included in a written representation letter. Upon receipt of the following representation letter, Dweebins contacted Molar to state that it was incomplete.

To John & Wayne, PAs:

In connection with your examination of the balance sheet of Amis Manufacturing, Inc., as of December 31, 1992, and the related statements of income, retained earnings, and cash flows for the year then ended, for the purpose of expressing an opinion on whether the financial statements present fairly the financial position, results of operations, and cash flows of Amis Manufacturing, Inc., in conformity with generally accepted accounting principles, we confirm, to the best of our knowledge and belief, the following representations made to you during your audit. There were no:

Plans or intentions that may materially affect the carrying value or classification of assets or liabilities.

Communications from regulatory agencies concerning noncompliance with, or deficiencies in, financial reporting practices.

Agreements to repurchase assets previously sold.

Violations or possible violations of laws or regulations whose effects should be considered for disclosure in the financial statements or as a basis for recording a loss contingency. Unasserted claims or assessments that our lawyer has advised are probable of assertion that must be disclosed in accordance with Statement of Financial Accounting Standards No. 5.

Capital stock purchase options or agreements or capital stock reserved for options, warrants, conversions, or other requirements.

Compensating balance or other arrangements involving restrictions on cash balances.

Vance Molar, President
Amis Manufacturing, Inc.
March 14, 1993

Required:

Identify the other matters that Molar's representation letter should specifically confirm.

(AICPA adapted)

13.39 Subsequent Events. You are nearing the completion of an examination of the financial statements of Jubilee, Inc., for the year ended December 31. You are concerned with ascertaining the occurrence of subsequent events that may require adjustment or disclosure essential to a fair presentation in conformity with generally accepted accounting principles.

Required:

a. Briefly explain what is meant by the phrase "subsequent event."

b. How do those subsequent events which require financial statement adjustment differ from those which require only financial statement disclosure?

c. What are the procedures that should be performed to ascertain the occurrence of subsequent events?

(AICPA adapted)

13.40 Subsequent Events and Contingent Liabilities. Crankwell, Inc., is preparing its annual financial statements and annual report to shareholders. Management wants to be sure that all of the necessary and proper disclosures are incorporated into the financial statements and the annual report. Two classes of items that have an important bearing on the financial statements are subsequent events and contingent liabilities. The financial statements could be materially inaccurate or misleading if proper disclosure of these items is not made.

Required:

a. With respect to subsequent events:
  (1) Define what is meant by a "subsequent event."
  (2) Identify the two types of subsequent events and explain the appropriate financial statement presentation of each type.

b. With respect to contingent liabilities:
  (1) Identify the essential elements of a contingent liability.
  (2) Explain how a contingent liability should be disclosed in the financial statements.

c. Explain how a subsequent event may relate to a contingent liability. Give an example to support your answer.

(CMA adapted)

13.41 Subsequent Events Procedures. You are in the process of "winding up" the field work on Top Stove Corporation, a company engaged in the manufacture and sale of kerosene space heating stoves. To date there has been every indication that the financial statements of the client present fairly the position of the company at December 31 and the results of its operations for the year then ended. Top Stove had total assets at December 31 of $4 million and a net profit for the year (after deducting federal and provincial income taxes) of $285,000. The principal records of the company are a general ledger, cash receipts record, voucher register, sales register, cheque register, and general journal. Financial statements are prepared monthly. Your field work will be completed on February 20, and you plan to deliver the report to the client by March 12.

Required:

a. Write a brief statement about the purpose and period to be covered in a review of subsequent events.

b. Outline the program you would follow to determine what transactions involving material amounts, if any, have occurred since the balance sheet date.

(AICPA adapted)

13.42 Subsequent Events—Cases. The following events occurred in independent cases, but in each instance the event happened after the close of the fiscal year under audit but before all members of the audit team had left the office of the client. State in each case what disclosure, if any, you would expect in the financial statements (and notes thereto). The balance sheet date in each instance is December 31.

1. On December 31, commodities handled by the company had been traded in the open market in which the company procures its supplies at $1.40 per pound. This price had prevailed for two weeks, following an official market report that predicted vastly enlarged supplies; however, no purchases were made at $1.40. The price throughout the preceding year had been about $2, which is the level experienced over several years. On January 18 the price returned to $2, following public disclosure of an error in the official calculations of the prior December—correction of which destroyed the expectations of excessive supplies. Inventory at December 31 had been valued on a lower-of-cost-or-market basis.

2. On February 1 the board of directors adopted a resolution accepting the offer of an investment banker to guarantee the marketing of $100 million of preferred shares.

3. On January 22 one of the three major plants of the client burned down, resulting in a loss of $50 million, which was covered to the extent of $40 million by insurance.

4. The client in this case is an investment company of the open-

end type. In January a wholly new management came into control. By February 20 the new management had sold 90 percent of the investments carried at December 31 and had purchased others of a substantially more speculative character.

5. This company has a wholly owned but not consolidated subsidiary producing oil in a foreign country. A serious rebellion began in that country on January 18 and continued beyond the completion of your audit work. The press in this country has carried extensive coverage of the progress of the fighting.

(AICPA adapted)

13.43 Subsequent Events—Cases. In connection with your examination of the financial statements of Olars Manufacturing Corporation for the year ended December 31, your post-balance sheet audit procedures disclosed the following items:

1. January 3: The provincial government approved a plan for the construction of an expressway. The plan will result in the appropriation of a portion of the land area owned by Olars Manufacturing Corporation. Construction will begin late next year. No estimate of the condemnation award is available.

2. January 4: The funds for a $25,000 loan to the corporation made by Mr. Olars on July 15 were obtained by him with a loan on his personal life insurance policy. The loan was recorded in the account loan payable to officers. Mr. Olars's source of the funds was not disclosed in the company records. The corporation pays the premiums on the life insurance policy, and Mrs. Olars, wife of the president, is the owner and beneficiary of the policy.

3. January 7: The mineral content of a shipment of ore en route on December 31 was determined to be 72 percent. The shipment was recorded at year-end at an estimated content of 50 percent by a debit to raw material inventory and a credit to accounts payable in the amount of $20,600. The final liability to the vendor is based on the actual mineral content of the shipment.

4. January 15: A series of personal disagreements have arisen between Mr. Olars, the president, and Mr. Tweedy, his brother-in-law, the treasurer. Mr. Tweddy resigned, effective immediately, under an agreement whereby the corporation would purchase his 10 percent share ownership at book value as of December 31. Payment is to be made in two equal amounts in cash on April 1 and October 1. In December the treasurer had obtained a divorce from Mr. Olars's sister.

5. January 31: As a result of reduced sales, production was curtailed in mid-January and some workers were laid off. On February 5 all the remaining workers went on strike. To date the strike is unsettled.

6. February 10: A contract was signed whereby Mammoth Enterprises purchased from Olars Manufacturing corporation all of the latter's capital assets (including rights to receive the proceeds of any property condemnation), inventories, and the right to conduct business under the name "Olars Manufacturing Division." The effective date of the transfer will be March 1. The sale price was $500,000, subject to adjustment following the taking of a physical inventory. Important factors contributing to the decision to enter into the contract were the policy of the board of directors of Mammoth Industries to diversify the firm's activities and the report of a survey conducted by an independent market appraisal firm, which revealed a declining market for Olars's products.

Required:

Assume that the above items came to your attention prior to completion of your audit work on February 15. For each of the above items:

a. Give the audit procedures, if any, that would have brought the item to your attention. Indicate other sources of information that may have revealed the item.

b. Discuss the disclosure that you would recommend for the item, listing all details that should be disclosed. Indicate those items or details, if any, that should not be disclosed. Give your reasons for recommending or not recommending disclosure of the items or details.

(AICPA adapted)

13.44 Subsequent Discovery of Fact. On June 1 Albert Faultless of A.J. Faultless & Co., CAs, noticed some disturbing information about his client, Hopkirk Company. A story in the local paper mentioned the indictment of Tony Baker, whom A.J. knew as the assistant controller at Hopkirk. The charge was mail fraud. A.J. made discreet enquiries with the controller at Hopkirk's headquarters and learned that Baker had been speculating in foreign currency futures. In fact, part of Baker's work at Hopkirk involved managing the company's foreign currency. Unfortunately, Baker had violated company policy, lost a small amount of money, then decided to speculate some more, lost some more, and eventually lost $7 million in company funds.

The mail fraud was involved in his attempt to cover his activity until he recovered the original losses. Most of the events were in process on March 1, when A.J. had signed and dated the unqualified report on Hopkirk's financial statements for the year ended on the previous December 31.

A.J. determined that the information probably would affect the decisions of external users and advised Hopkirk's chief executive to make the disclosure. She flatly refused to make any disclosure, arguing that the information was immaterial. On June 17 A.J. provided the subsequent information in question to a news reporter, and it was printed in the *Wall Street Journal* along with a statement that the fi-

nancial statements and accompanying audit report could not be relied on.

Required:
Evaluate the actions of Faultless & Co., PAs, with respect to the subsequent information discovered. What other action might Faultless & Co. have taken? What are the possible legal effects of the firm's actions, if any?

13.45 Omitted Audit Procedures. The following are independent situations that have occurred in your audit firm, Arthur Hurdman (AH):[*]

1. During the internal inspection review by the regional office of AH, one of your clients, Wildcat Oil Suppliers, was selected for review. The reviewers questioned the thoroughness of inventory obsolescence procedures, especially in light of the depressed state of the oil exploration industry at the time. They felt that specific procedures, which they considered appropriate, were not performed by your audit team.

2. Top Stove, one of your clients, installed a microcomputer in July 1992 to process part of the accounting transactions. You completed the audit of Top Stove's December 31, 1992 statements on February 15, 1993. During the April 1993 review work on Top Stove's first-quarter financial information, you discovered that during the audit of the 1992 statements only the manual records were investigated in the search for unrecorded liabilities.

3. AH belongs to the private companies practice section (PCPS) of the AICPA division of firms. In keeping with membership requirements of the PCPS, AH contracted with Haskin and Anderson (HA) to conduct a peer review of AH's audit quality control procedures. In HA's report to AH, the audit of Al's Store Organization (ASO) was criticized due to the letterhead on ASO's representation letter. Although the representation letter complied with the

---

[*] Situation derived from examples given in Thomas R. Weirich and Elizabeth J. Ringelberg, "Omitted Audit Procedures," *CPA Journal*, March 1984, p. 36.

requirements of SAS 19, it was prepared on the letterhead of the Palo Alto Garden Club. (Al's wife, Alice, had been president of the club during the period of the audit.)

Required:

a. Without regard to the specific situation given, answer the following questions:

(1) What are the proper steps auditors should take if it is discovered, after the report date, that an auditing procedure was omitted?

(2) How are auditors' decisions affected if, after review of the workpapers, it is determined that other audit procedures produced the necessary sufficient, appropriate evidence?

(3) If in subsequently applying the omitted procedure, the auditors become aware of material new information that should have been disclosed in the financial statements, how should they proceed?

b. Describe the proper action to take in each situation above, given the additional information provided below:

Case 1: You made a thorough consideration on the scope of the audit of Wildcat Oil Suppliers, and you made a detailed review of the working papers. You have concluded that compensating procedures were conducted sufficient to support the valuation of inventory.

Case 2: Your subsequent investigation of the microcomputer records of Top Stove revealed that material liabilities were not recorded as of December 31.

Case 3: You were requested to investigate the ASO alleged audit procedure deficiency. Your investigations revealed that ASO had a significant loan from the local bank that had received the AH report on ASO's financial statements. The loan is still outstanding, and indeed the representation letter was written on the garden club letterhead.

13.46 Second Partner Review and Dual Dating. You have been assigned to perform a review of a correspondent PA firm's audit of Oxford Millwork Company for the calendar year ending December 31. In the audited financial statements of Oxford Millwork Company, you find the following representations:

Common shares, $10 par value, 100,000 shares outstanding, 400,000 shares authorized (Note 1) $1,000,000

Note 1: Subsequent event (dated January 20). The board of directors approved a three-for-one stock dividend effective January 20. At the effective date, the par value of outstanding common shares is $3 million.

You have reviewed the correspondent PA firm's audit report and found the opinion dated "January 15, 1993, except as to Note 1 which is dated January 20, 1993."

Required:

a. What is the purpose of a second partner review?

b. What is the purpose of dual dating?

c. What recommendations would you make to the PA firm concerning presentation of the subsequent event?

Discussion Cases

13.47 Recognizing Income of a Purchased Subsidiary. The following brief dialogue occurred in a controversy wherein a plaintiff claimed that management backdated the effective date of an acquisition in order to pump up

earnings improperly. The independent auditors, Eastford and Redwood (E&R), are involved because they signed an unqualified report on the consolidated financial statements in question.

Plaintiff's lawyer: Plaintiff alleges that COSIF Company's purchase of 100 percent of the stock of Prosper, Inc., was effective on April 28, almost four months after the beginning of COSIF's fiscal year on January 1. However, COSIF included in consolidated income the results of Prosper's operations for the full 12 months ended December 31. This was improper accounting which failed to reflect the substance of the transaction.

Eastford and Redwood knew, or should have known, that the effective date was April 28. The evidence shown today proves that the first written agreement concerning the acquisition was a memorandum dated March 5, which set forth the general terms of the transaction. The final written agreement was signed and dated on April 28. Their unqualified opinion was improperly rendered.

Eastford and Redwood's lawyer: The issue is whether January 1 or some later date should have been used as the acquisition date for accounting purposes. E&R stipulate that the first written memorandum was dated March 5 and the final agreement April 28. However, we have also introduced into evidence written representations from the president of COSIF and COSIF's outside counsel that an oral agreement substantially equivalent to the March 5 memorandum agreement was reached on or about January 1. COSIF's outside counsel is one of the most highly regarded law firms in the Maritimes.

These representations were meaningful to E&R because we were not engaged as COSIF's auditors until November 14 and were not present when the actual negotiations took place.

Plaintiff alleges that applicable accounting principles were misapplied because no written agreement existed on January 1.

We insist that elements of the April 28 agreement, which made the acquisition effective as of January 1, show that the substance of the transaction supports our conclusion that January 1

was the proper accounting date. We cite the following:

1. COSIF and Prosper clearly intended an effective date of January 1.
2. The fixed portion of the purchase price depended on a minimum amount of Prosper's income through December 31 of the year preceding. (At March 5 the audit of Prosper's financial year had not yet been completed.)
3. The contingent portion of the purchase price depended on a minimum amount of Prosper's income for the year beginning January 1 and two years thereafter.
4. Warranties made by Prosper as to assets and liabilities were as of December 31 (just prior to the January 1 effective date).
5. Interest on COSIF's notes issued in the payment package ran from January 1.
6. The full amount of Prosper's earnings from January 1 inured to the benefit of COSIF.

Required:
What is the proper accounting date for COSIF's investment in Prosper?

13.48 Lawyer's Letter Responses. Omega Corporation is involved in a lawsuit brought by a competitor for patent infringement. The competitor is asking $14 million actual damages for lost profits and unspecified punitive damages. The lawsuit has been in progress for 15 months, and Omega has worked closely with its outside counsel preparing its defence. Omega recently requested its outside lawyers with the firm of Wolfe & Goodwin to provide information to the auditors.

The managing partner of Wolfe & Goodwin asked four different lawyers who have worked on the case to prepare a concise response to the auditors. They returned these:

1. The action involves unique characteristics wherein authoritative legal precedents bearing directly on the plaintiff's claims do not seem to exist. We believe the plaintiff will have serious problems establishing

Omega's liability; nevertheless, if the plaintiff is successful, the damage award may be substantial.

2. In our opinion, Omega will be able to defend this action successfully, and, if not, the possible liability to Omega in this proceeding is nominal in amount.

3. We believe the plaintiff's case against Omega is without merit.

4. In our opinion Omega will be able to assert meritorious defences and has a reasonable chance of sustaining an adequate defence, with a possible outcome of settling the case for less than the damages claimed.

Required:

a. Interpret each of the four responses separately. Decide whether each is (1) adequate to conclude that the likelihood of an adverse outcome is "remote," requiring no disclosure in financial statements, or (2) too vague to serve as adequate information for a decision, requiring more information from the lawyers or from management.

b. What kind of response do you think the auditors would get if they asked the plaintiff's counsel about the likely outcome of the lawsuit? Discuss.

13.49 Accounting for a Contingency— Lawyer's Letter Information. Central City was involved in litigation brought by MALDEF, a citizens' group, over the creation of single-member voting districts for city council positions. The auditor was working on the financial statements for the year ended December 31, 1992, and had almost completed the field work by February 12, 1993.

The court had heard final arguments on February 1 and rendered its judgment on February 10. The ruling was in favour of MALDEF and required the creation of certain single-member voting districts. While this ruling itself did not impose a monetary loss on Central City, the court also ruled that MALDEF would be awarded a judg-

ment of court costs and legal fees to be paid by Central City.

Local newspaper reports stated that MALDEF would seek a $250,000 recovery from the city. The auditor obtained a lawyer's representation letter dated February 15 that stated the following: "In my opinion the court will award some amount for MALDEF's legal fees. In regard to your enquiry about an amount or range of possible loss, I estimate that such an award could be anywhere from $30,000 to $175,000."

Required:

a. What weight should be given to the newspaper report of the $250,000 amount MALDEF might ask? What weight should be given to the lawyer's estimate?

b. How should this subsequent event be reflected in the 1992 financial statements of Central City? As an accounting adjustment of the amounts presented (Type I)? As a disclosure in the 1992 statements with accounting for the amounts in the 1993 financial statements (Type II)?

13.50 Contingencies. Northern Lights Pulp and Paper Company (NL) has been an audit client of Web & Web, Chartered Accountants, for several years. NL was provincially incorporated in 1965 and has operated two small pulp-and-paper mills in Northern Ontario since that time.

Hard hit by the recession, the company has experienced losses in its last three years, but current-year income projections are optimistic. Like its competitors in the forest industry, NL has managed to cut costs and increase productivity and predicts a significant profit for the year ended December 31, 1994.

It is August 1994. You have just been assigned as the senior-in-charge of NL since the previous senior accepted a position as controller in the private sector. The interim audit was completed by the previous senior. The partner has asked you to become familiar with the client by reviewing the permanent file, the interim file, and the many notes prepared by the previous senior. He would also like you to prepare a memo addressing audit issues you identify based on your review. You noted the following in performing your review of the files:

1. Current year (1994) projected net income is $5,000,000. Prior year (1993) losses were $1,200,000 (1992–$2,000,000, and 1991–$3,500,000). Industry statistics reported total annual losses of $1.4 billion in 1992 to under $200 million in 1993.

2. The controller who had been with the company for 12 years was fired in April 1994. A recently qualified chartered accountant was hired as the new controller.

3. The computerized system was converted during the first six months of the year. No parallel runs were performed since the software package purchased was common to the forest industry. At the interim audit, several accounts were not reconciled. The vice president, finance, believes that the balances were not transferred correctly and has promised to look into this before year-end.

4. A letter was received in May 1994 from the provincial government requiring the company to meet an individual contamination reduction target by 1995. To meet these targets, NL must build a new, secondary biological treatment plant. No action to meet these targets had been taken at the time of the interim audit. The company plans to begin construction of the new treatment plant in September 1994. The letter indicates that heavy fines will be imposed if the company does not comply by the due date.

5. In March 1994, a chemical engineer was hired to help the general manager of each mill establish due diligence standards. This action was taken in response to fears raised by the president, who became aware that Bata Industries and two of its directors were convicted of an environmental offence in 1992. The due diligence standards had not been developed at the time of the interim audit as the chemical engineer had been involved in establishing a way to reduce costs. In 1993, NL was fined $30,000 for failing to meet pollution emission standards.

6. Legal fees increased 150% during the first six months of 1994, in comparison to the first six months of 1993.

7. Over the period April to June 1994, NL issued cheques totalling $90,000 to the president and the chemical engineer. According to the new controller, the president and the chemical engineer each earned a $45,000 bonus for the first six months of the year due to the improved financial performance of the company. The president asked the controller to pay the bonus over a three-month period. Therefore, six cheques of $15,000 each were issued.

8. The minute book (shareholders' and directors' meetings) was not updated for the interim audit but is expected to be up to date for the year-end audit.

9. After much hesitation, the president finally agreed to sign the 1993 management representation letter.

Requiredplan:

Prepare the memo requested by the partner addressing audit issues and their impact on the 1994 audit. The memo should also address risk factors, materiality, and the overall audit approach for the 1994 audit.

(ICAO adapted)

13.51 Contingencies. You are the senior auditor in charge of the field work for the examination of the financial statements of ABC Chemical Corporation for the year ended December 31, 1995. The company produces chlorine and related products, which are used as bleaching agents, primarily by pulp-and-paper companies.

An analytical review of the company's operation for the current year reveals that recorded sales have increased about 10%, and net income about 20% relative to the previous year. This is surprising, since demand for the company's products has been weak because of a long and continuing recession in the North American pulp-and-paper industry.

The controller attributes the improvement to an aggressive marketing program directed at foreign companies. In addition, he claims that ABC Chemical has significantly reduced its production costs this year while still remaining, he thinks, within applicable pollution and commercial laws and regulations. He also requests that you not include any of the foreign accounts receivable at year-end in your confirmation sample, since "the practice is not normal in three countries, and is likely to harm our business relationship with these new customers." Finally, he mentions that because of the unusually good operating results and improving market conditions, the company sold $10,000,000 of common shares in November 1995.

Required:

a. As auditor, do you have any responsibility for determining whether the company actually complies with pollution control laws and regulations in its operations? Briefly explain.

b. Assume the foreign receivables are material in amount at December 31, 1995. Explain how you would deal with the restriction imposed by the controller and how the restriction could affect your auditor's report.

c. Explain how you would design a dollar unit sampling plan to determine the sample size for testing the foreign receivables at year-end. Be specific in identifying relative factors affecting sample size and their likely values (high, medium, or low). (Do not discuss selection or evaluation of the sample.)

d. List four audit procedures you would perform with respect to the sale of common shares during the year.

(CGAAC adapted)

13.52 Contingencies. A PA is performing an audit of financial statements of a publicly held company in accordance with generally accepted auditing standards and has completed all the appropriate audit steps up to and through the performance of substantive tests of details of transaction cycles and account balances. She is therefore in the final stages of completing the audit.

Required:

a. With what third parties (if any) is the PA likely to communicate at this stage of the audit process and what would be the purpose of such communication? Explain.

b. Discuss the PA's responsibilities (if any) with respect to subsequent events occurring after the balance sheet date.

c. Discuss the PA's responsibilities (if any) with respect to the MD&A portion of the company's annual report to shareholders.

d. Would it be appropriate to perform analytical procedures at this point in the audit? Explain.

(CGAAC adapted)

13.53 Evaluating Evidence. The purpose of substantive testing is to verify the assertions made by management in the financial statements. An auditor does this by using various evidence gathering methods including inspection, observation, enquiry, confirmation, computation, and analysis.

Consider the following six unrelated audit tests that a PA performed in conjunction with the examination of the financial statements of a client whose fiscal year ended December 31, 1994.

1. Sent negative confirmation requests to a sample of the client's customers with unpaid balances at November 30, 1994.

2. Requested statements as of December 31, 1994, from a large sample

of vendors with whom the client did business during 1994.

3. Examined invoice copies and shipping documents supporting the first 20 sales transactions recorded in January 1995.
4. Inspected share certificates associated with temporary investments in marketable securities, held in the client's safety deposit box on December 31, 1994.
5. Verified the mechanical accuracy of the "aged" listings, prepared by the chief accountant, of the client's accounts receivable at December 31, 1994.
6. Counted cash on hand at December 31, 1994.

Required:

For each of the six audit tests, list the management assertion(s) which is (are) primarily being verified and comment on the quality (appropriateness) of the evidence obtained. Organize your answer, in your examination booklet, as follows.

Management Assertion(s)	Quality of Evidence

(CGAAC adapted)

13.54 Related Party Transactions. Susan Sharp, PA, audited the financial statements of her continuing client, Octopos Industries, for the year ended December 31, 1993. Octopos is a publicly held company whose shares are traded on the Vancouver Stock Exchange. In discussing the property, plant, and equipment accounts with the controller, Sharp learned that a new machine costing $55,000,000 (a material amount) was constructed for the company during the year by an affiliated firm, of which the president of Octopos Industries is the sole shareholder.

In support of this transaction, Sharp examined an invoice from the vendor for $55,000,000 that was stamped "paid." She also examined a memo from the president to the controller of Octopos, authorizing the payment of the invoice. Given the sensitivity of the matter, the president of Octopos instructed the controller not to disclose the transaction in the company's financial statements.

No other problems or unusual situations were encountered during the audit, which was completed on February 25, 1994.

Required:

a. Describe the additional audit procedures (if any) that Sharp should have performed with respect to the machine acquired from the affiliated company.
b. Without prejudice to your answer to part (a), assume that Sharp had obtained sufficient, appropriate evidence with respect to the transaction. Prepare an auditor's report for the case, in good form. Sharp is the managing partner of a firm of PAs whose executive offices are in Vancouver.

(CGAAC adapted)

PART IV

PROFESSIONAL SERVICES AND RESPONSIBILITIES

CHAPTER 14

Learning Objectives

This chapter covers several areas of public accounting practice related to accountants' association with financial information other than complete, audited historical financial statements. PAs often perform work and give reports in these areas of practice:

- Unaudited Financial Statements: Review and Compilation.
- Review of Interim Financial Information.
- Special Reports—Other Comprehensive Bases of Accounting.
- Internal Accounting Control.
- Forecasts and Projections.
- Financial Statements to be Used outside Canada.

These topics involve assurance standards, auditing standards, and accounting and review services standards that were introduced or mentioned briefly in Chapter 2. Your learning objectives related to these topics are to be able to:

1. Write appropriate reports for review and compilation of unaudited financial statements, given specific fact circumstances.

2. List some interim information review procedures and write a report on a review of interim financial information.

3. Define, explain, and give examples of "another appropriate disclosed basis of accounting" (AADBA), distinguishing them from GAAP.

4. Explain the content of an auditor's report on supplementary current value financial statements in comparison to a standard report on historical cost financial statements.

5. Describe the various reports on internal control and their connection with public reporting and reporting to a client's audit committee.

6. Define the various financial presentations and levels of service involved in association with financial forecasts and projections, and write compilation and examination reports.

7. Describe the new umbrella standards for assurance engagements.

OTHER PUBLIC ACCOUNTING SERVICES AND REPORTS

INTRODUCTION

. . . .

Public accountants offer numerous assurance services on information other than the standard historical cost financial statements. These services grow from consumer demand for association by an objective expert. Naturally, business, government, and the public want the credibility that goes along with PAs' association. However, PAs need to be careful in their reports on such information that they will not suggest the addition of more credibility than is warranted. As you study the topics in this chapter, you will see the standards for PA association and the care with which reports are worded.

UNAUDITED FINANCIAL STATEMENTS

. . . .

LEARNING OBJECTIVE
1. Write appropriate reports for review and compilation of unaudited financial statements, given specific fact circumstances.

Many PA firms conduct practice in accounting and review services for small-business clients. These engagements include bookkeeping, financial statement preparation, and financial statement review to help small businesses prepare financial communications. Until the late 1970s, auditing standards concentrated on one level of assurance based on a full audit and appeared to deny small clients the full benefit of PAs' services.

The investigations by the Adams Committee in Canada and in the U.S. Congress during 1977–78 highlighted the problem by centring attention on the idea that auditing standards handicapped the business of small public accounting firms and their services to small-business clients. The argument has become known as the "Big GAAS–Little GAAS" question. Big GAAS was portrayed as the villain in the play, with the proposition that existing standards were enacted under the influence of large PA firms whose practice is centred on big business. Even though this proposition is not true, the fact is that small PA firms want to give, and small businesses want to receive, some level of assurance as a result of accountants' work even though an audit in accordance with GAAS is not performed.

A separate part of the *Handbook,* the 8000 sections, has been set aside to deal with these limited assurance engagements. The 8000 section deals with review engagements and the 9000 section deals with compilation engagements.

Review Services

The review services explained in this section apply specifically to accountants' work on the unaudited financial statements. In a review services engagement, an accountant performs some procedures to achieve a moderate level of assurance. This level is not the same that could be attained by performing an audit in accordance with GAAS. According to *Handbook Section* 8100.05:

Reviews are distinguishable from audits in that the scope of a review is less than that of an audit and therefore the level of assurance provided is lower. A review consists primarily of enquiry, analytical procedures and discussions related to information supplied to the public accountant by the enterprise with the limited objective of assessing whether the information is being reported on appropriate criteria. In this section, the word *plausible* is used in the sense of appearing to be worthy of belief based on the information obtained by the public accountant in connection with the review.

Section 8100.15 identifies standards applicable to a review engagement. They are stated as follows:

Standards Applicable to Review Engagements
General standard
The review should be performed and the review engagement report prepared by a person or persons having adequate technical training and proficiency in conducting reviews, with due care and with an objective state of mind.
Review standards
 (*i*) The work should be adequately planned and properly executed. If assistants are employed, they should be properly supervised.
 (*ii*) The public accountant should possess or acquire sufficient knowledge of the business carried on by the enterprise so that intelligent enquiry and assessment of information obtained can be made.
(*iii*) The public accountant should perform a review with the limited objective of assessing whether the information being reported on is plausible in the circumstances within the framework of appropriate criteria. Such a review should consist of:
 (*a*) Enquiry, analytical procedures and discussion; and
 (*b*) additional or more extensive procedures when the public accountant's knowledge of the business carried on by the enterprise and the results of the enquiry, and analytical procedures and discussion cause him or her to doubt the plausibility of such information.
Reporting standards
 (*i*) The review engagement report should indicate the scope of the review. The nature of the review engagement should be made evident and be clearly distinguished from an audit.
 (*ii*) The report should indicate, based on the review:
 (*a*) whether anything has come to the public accountant's attention that causes him or her to believe that the information being reported on is not, in all material respects, in accordance with appropriate criteria; or
 (*b*) that no assurance can be provided.
The report should provide an explanation of the nature of any reservations contained therein and, if readily determinable, the effect.

These standards suggest that auditors need special training and experience in conducting reviews, especially with respect to working within a plausibility framework. As can be seen by the second review standard, obtaining knowledge of the business is a critical part of the review engagement. Such knowledge is critical to determining whether the information obtained during the course of the engagement is plausible. Sufficient knowledge of the business (and industry) is required to make intelligent enquiries and a reasonable assessment of responses and other information obtained. However, the knowledge of business required for review engagements is normally less detailed than that required in an audit.

The review standards indicate that review work on unaudited financial statements consists primarily of enquiry and analytical procedures. The information gained thereby is similar to audit evidence; but the recommended limitation on procedures (listed below) does not suggest performance of typical auditing procedures of assessing control risk, conducting physical observation of tangible assets, sending confirmations, or examining documentary details of transactions.

- Obtain knowledge of the client's business. Know the accounting principles of the client's industry. Understand the client's organization and operations.
- Enquire about the accounting system and bookkeeping procedures.
- Perform analytical procedures to identify relationships and individual items that appear to be unusual.
- Enquire about actions taken at meetings of shareholders, directors, and other important executive committees.
- Read (study) the financial statements for indications that they conform with generally accepted accounting principles.
- Obtain reports from other accountants who audit or review significant components, subsidiaries, or other investees.
- Enquire of officers and directors about the following: Conformity with generally accepted accounting principles. Consistent application of accounting principles. Changes in the client's business or accounting practices. Matters about which questions have arisen as a result of applying other procedures (listed above). Events subsequent to the date of the financial statements.
- Perform any other procedures considered necessary if the financial statements appear to be incorrect, incomplete, or otherwise unsatisfactory.
- Prepare working papers showing the matters covered by the enquiry and analytical review procedures, especially the resolution of unusual problems and questions.
- Obtain a written representation letter from the owner, manager, or chief executive officer and from the chief financial officer.

Many firms will perform more detailed procedures such as bank reconciliations and bank confirmations to corroborate information obtained by enquiry. However, there is no requirement to perform such more detailed procedures under current review standards. Reviews have traditionally been supposed to provide negative assurance, or (in the words of the new assurance framework, to be discussed later in this chapter) a moderate level of assurance that indicates the financial information is "plausible" (*Section* 5025.12).

A review service does not provide a basis for expressing an opinion on financial statements. Each page of the financial statements should be conspicuously marked as being unaudited. The standards indicate that a report on a review services engagement should include the following:

- Statement on the scope of the review engagement and that a review service was performed in accordance with generally accepted standards for review engagement.
- Statement that a review consists primarily of enquiries of company personnel and analytical procedures applied to financial data.
- Statement that a review service does not constitute an audit, and that an opinion on financial statements is not expressed. (This is a disclaimer of any audit opinion.)

- Statement that the accountant is not aware of any material modifications that should be made; or, if aware, a disclosure of departure(s) from generally accepted accounting principles. (This is a negative assurance.)

When other independent accountants are involved in audit or review of parts of the business, the principal reviewer cannot divide responsibility by referring to the other accountants in the review report, unless the disclosure helps explain the reason for a reservation. You can follow the spirit of the auditing standards to write the form and content of the reference to the work and reports of other auditors (*Section* 6930.22–.23). An example of a review report is given in Exhibit 14–1.

Compilation Services

Compilation is a synonym for an older term—write-up work. Both terms refer to an accountant helping a client "write up" the financial information in the form of financial statements. A compilation service is accounting work in which an accountant performs few, if any, procedures, and it is substantially less than a review service. The description of a compilation of financial statements, according to *Handbook Section* 9200.03 is

> one in which a public accountant receives information from a client and arranges it into the form of a financial statements. The public accountant is concerned that the assembly of information is arithmetically correct, however the public accountant does not attempt to verify the accuracy or completeness of the information provided. Unlike an audit or review engagement in which the public accountant does sufficient work to issue a communication that provides assurance regarding the financial statements, no expression of assurance is contemplated in a compilation engagement.

Since no assurance credibility is provided by compilation engagements, the public accountant is limited in what action she or he can take. However, the public accountant also has a responsibility to not be associated with misleading information.

> When the public accountant is aware that there are matters which the public accountant believes would cause the financial statements to be false or misleading, she or he should request additional or revised information in order to complete the statements. If the client does not provide the information requested or agree with the statements, the public accountant should not release the statements and should withdraw from the engagement. (*Section* 9200.18)

E X H I B I T 14–1	**REVIEW ENGAGEMENT REPORT (from *Handbook Section* 8200.04)**

To (person engaging the public accountant)

I have reviewed the balance sheet of Client Limited as at ...., 19... and the statements of income, retained earnings and changes in financial position for the year then ended. My review was made in accordance with generally accepted standards for review engagements and accordingly consisted primarily of enquiry, analytical procedures and discussion related to information supplied to me by the company.

A review does not constitute an audit and consequently I do not express an audit opinion on these financial statements.

Based on my review, nothing has come to my attention that causes me to believe that these financial statements are not, in all material respects, in accordance with generally accepted accounting principles.

City   (signed) . . . .
Date   CHARTERED ACCOUNTANT

Financial statements may be compiled on a basis other than GAAP if in the auditor's judgment this other basis is appropriate for the circumstances of the engagement. This appropriate non-GAAP basis is referred to as "another appropriate disclosed basis of accounting" or AADBA in the literature. The best way to disclose AADBA statement is through the statement's title (e.g., "Statements Based on Income Tax Accounting") or in a note discussing the statements. The reasons for the compilation are also best achieved through notes to the statements or via the title.

In a compilation service, an accountant should understand the client's business, read (study) the financial statements looking for obvious clerical or accounting principle errors, and follow up on information that is incorrect, incomplete, or otherwise unsatisfactory. Each page of the financial statements should be marked **unaudited—see Notice to reader.** The report can be issued by an accountant who is not independent, provided the lack of independence is disclosed, as required by some professional bodies such as the ICAO, which requires disclosure in the Notice to Reader (see Exhibit 14–2). The report should contain the following (see Exhibit 14–2):

- Statement that the public accountant compiled the statement from information provided by management (or proprietor).

- Statement that the public accountant has not audited, reviewed, or otherwise attempted to verify the accuracy or completeness of such information.

- Caution to readers that the statement may not be appropriate for their purposes.

- No expression of any form of opinion or negative assurance.

Exhibit 14–2 illustrates that two kinds of reports on compiled financial statements can be given: (1) a report stating that the accountant is not independent (as in Exhibit 14–2); or (2) a report by an independent public accountant on financial statements prepared using an appropriate basis of accounting such as GAAP. In the second case, the basis of accounting may be an "appropriate disclosed basis of accounting other than GAAP," just like other kinds of accounting services, and reports can cover financial statements presented on such other bases of accounting. (Other appropriate bases of accounting are discussed later in this chapter.)

Although compilation engagements do not provide any attest assurance or credibility, they can be viewed as providing accounting credibility. A public accountant's compilation of the statements as opposed to a nonprofessional's must add some kind of credibility, otherwise there would be no reason to pay the extra cost of a PA to do the compilation.

E X H I B I T 14–2   **NOTICE TO READER (from *Handbook Section* 9200.24)**

I have compiled the balance sheet of Client Limited as at December 31, 19X1, and the statements of income, retained earnings and changes in financial position for the (period) then ended from information provided by management (the proprietor). I have not audited, reviewed or otherwise attempted to verify the accuracy or completeness of such information. Readers are cautioned that these statements may not be appropriate for their purposes.

I am not independent with respect to Client Limited.

City

Date

(printed or signed) . . . .

CHARTERED ACCOUNTANT

Note that the Notice to Reader is not a proper place to make non-GAAP AADBA disclosures because the Notice to Reader does not mention GAAP or any other basis of accounting.

Exhibit 14–3 summarizes the major differences between audit, review, and compilation engagements.

OTHER REVIEW AND COMPILATION TOPICS

There are several other aspects of review and compilation engagements and reports that differ from audit standards. These topics point out some of the different problems in dealing with unaudited financial statements.

Prescribed Forms

Industry trade associations, banks, government agencies, and regulatory agencies often use prescribed forms (standard reprinted documents) to specify the content and measurement of accounting information required for special purposes. Such forms may not request disclosures required by GAAP or may specify measurements that do not conform to GAAP.

When such forms are compiled (not when reviewed) by an accountant, the compilation report does not need to call attention to the GAAP departures or to GAAP disclosure deficiencies.

There's nothing in either *Section* 9200 or in the Guideline, "Compilation Engagements—Financial Statement Disclosures," requiring public accountants to disclose known departures from GAAP in either the compiled statements or the Notice to Reader. Moreover, in the latter the accountant specifically states that no attempt has been made to determine whether the statements contain GAAP departures. The reason for this is that disclosure of known departures could be confusing or even misleading. If such disclosures were required, readers might assume the accountant is responsible for disclosing *all* GAAP departures in the statements and that the only departures are the disclosed departures. Such a responsibility is beyond the scope of a compilation engagement.

E X H I B I T 14–3   **AUDIT VERSUS MAJOR NONAUDIT ENGAGEMENTS SUMMARY**

Compilations	Review	Audit
Prepared for internal use of restricted users	Plausibility, consistency	Conformity with GAAP
IC not evaluated	IC not evaluated	Eval. IC
No independent corroborating evidence	Some evidence	Independent corroborating evidence
Compilation, bookkeeping	Enquiry-based review, discussions, reasonableness	Substantive and compliance testing
Accounting credibility	Negative assurance	Positive assurance, audit credibility
Notice to reader	Accountant's comments or review engagement report	Auditor's report
IC = Internal control		

How then does the auditor deal with situations of known departures from GAAP or other AADBA? Well, for one thing the Notice to Reader contains a caution to readers that the financial statements may not be appropriate for their purposes. For another, compiled statements may not be appropriate for general purposes and, hence, are restricted in their use depending on the purpose of the engagement. For example, compiled statements are frequently prepared for management, and they are aware of the limitations. Moreover, "when the accountant is aware that the statements may be misleading for some users or purposes, then the public accountant may need to include appropriate disclosures (in the statements, themselves, not the Notice to Reader) to prevent them from being misleading. Of course, if management will not allow the disclosures considered necessary, he or she has clearly no alternative but to withhold the statements and withdraw from the engagement" (R.J. Johnston, *CA Magazine,* May 1988, p. 53.) Despite this responsibility, keep in mind that with the limited amount of work involved in compilations there is no assurance that the PA can determine whether the financial statements achieve the specified intended purpose.

Communications Between Predecessors and Successors

In the case of audits, successor auditors are required to make certain enquiries of predecessor auditors when a new client is obtained (e.g., Rule 302 of Professional Conduct of ICAO). Rule 302 and similar rules of other accounting bodies in fact apply to all public accounting engagements, including compilation and review work.

Interpretation to Rule 302 gives advice to accountants when communicating with the predecessor. First, the successor accountant should ask the new client to notify the predecessor (incumbent) accountant of the proposed change by the client. The successor should then enquire of the predecessor "whether there are any circumstances that should be taken in account which might influence the potential successors' decision whether or not to accept the appointment" (Interpretation 302). Normally, the successor should await the reply of the predecessor before commencing work for the new client. The Interpretation also requires that the predecessor reply promptly to the successor's queries. When enquiries are made, the successor must obtain the client's permission for the predecessor to disclose confidential information. When confidentiality is in doubt, legal advice should be obtained. An important issue is how much effort the predecessor should make in supplying information to the successor. The interpretation suggests a minimum of discussing with the successor "reasonable information of the work being assumed" and then gives advice on what constitute "reasonable."

In addition to the rules of professional conduct, PAs should be aware of any federal and provincial legislation, including securities legislation, regulating changes in professional appointments.

Personal Financial Plans

Personal financial planning has become a big source of business for PA firms. Most personal financial plan documentation includes personal financial statements. Ordinarily, an accountant associated with such statements would need to give the standard compilation report (disclaimer), which seems rather awkward in a personal financial planning engagement when the client is the only one using the statements. In Canada a PA who wishes to meet the requirements as a certified financial planner under the

Financial Planning Standards Council of Canada must satisfy that body's Rules of Conduct in disclosing any potential conflicts of interest to his or her clients. Although there is no distinction for compilation of personal financial information in Canada, U.S. standards exempt such personal financial statements from the reporting requirement. However, the following report must be given, with each page of the financial report marked "See accountant's report":

> The accompanying Statement of Financial Condition of Edward Beliveau, as of December 31, 1992, was prepared solely to help you develop your personal financial plan. Accordingly, it may be incomplete or contain other departures from generally accepted accounting principles and should not be used to obtain credit or for any purposes other than developing your financial plan. We have not audited, reviewed, or compiled the statements.

A Note on GAAP Departures and Review Engagement Reports

An accountants' report of known GAAP departures must be treated carefully in review reports.

As in audit reports, the accountant can and should add an explanatory paragraph pointing out known departures from GAAP, including omitted disclosures. The knowledge of GAAP departures means that the accountant must make exception to the departure in the negative assurance sentence, like this: "Except for the failure, as described in the preceding paragraph, to (describe the departure), based on my review nothing has come to my attention . . . "

A separate paragraph describing the departure in more detail would be inserted as the next to last paragraph in the Review Engagement Report. See Exhibit 14–4 for the complete report.

The range of review reports possible is similar to that for audit reports, and they arise for similar reasons. Exhibit 14–5 illustrates an adverse report resulting from a GAAP departure, and Exhibit 14–6 illustrates a denial of assurance report as a result of a newer scope limitation.

E X H I B I T 14-4   **QUALIFICATION RESULTING FROM A DEPARTURE FROM GENERALLY ACCEPTED ACCOUNTING PRINCIPLES WHEN THE EFFECTS ARE NOT READILY DETERMINABLE (from *Handbook Section* 8200.B, example A)**

REVIEW ENGAGEMENT REPORT

To (person engaging the public accountant)

I have reviewed the balance sheet of Client Limited as at ......, 19... and the statements of income, retained earnings and changes in financial position for the year then ended. My review was made in accordance with generally accepted standards for review engagements and accordingly consisted primarily of enquiry, analytical procedures and discussion related to information supplied to me by the company.

A review does not constitute an audit and consequently I do not express an audit opinion on these financial statements.

Note .... indicates that the investments in companies subject to significant influence have not been accounted for on the equity basis. The effects of this departure from generally accepted accounting principles on the unaudited financial statements have not been determined.

Except for the failure, as described in the preceding paragraph, to account for the investments on an equity basis, based on my review, nothing has come to my attention that causes me to believe that these financial statements are not, in all material respects, in accordance with generally accepted accounting principles

City

Date

(signed) . . . .
          CHARTERED ACCOUNTANT

E X H I B I T 14–5   **ADVERSE REPORT RESULTING FROM A DEPARTURE FROM GENERALLY ACCEPTED ACCOUNTING PRINCIPLES (from *Section* 8200.B, example B)**

REVIEW ENGAGEMENT REPORT

To (person engaging the public accountant)

I have reviewed the balance sheet of Client Limited as at ......, 19... and the statements of income, retained earnings and changes in financial position for the year then ended. My review was made in accordance with generally accepted standards for review engagements and accordingly consisted primarily of enquiry, analytical procedures and discussion related to information supplied to me by the company.

A review does not constitute an audit and consequently I do not express an audit opinion on these financial statements.

Note .... indicates that commencing this year the company ceased to consolidate the financial statements of its subsidiary companies because management considers consolidation to be inappropriate when there are substantial non-controlling interests. Under generally accepted accounting principles, the existence of such noncontrolling interests is not an acceptable reason for not consolidating the financial statements of subsidiary companies with those of the reporting enterprise. Had consolidated financial statements been prepared, virtually every account in, and the information provided by way of notes to, the accompanying financial statements would have been materially different. The effects of this departure from generally accepted accounting principles on the accompanying financial statements have not been determined.

My review indicates that, because the investment in subsidiary companies is not accounted for on a consolidated basis, as described in the preceding paragraph, these financial statements are not in accordance with generally accepted accounting principles.

City

Date

(signed) . . . .

CHARTERED ACCOUNTANT

E X H I B I T 14–6   **DENIAL OF ASSURANCE (from *Section* 8200.B, example D)**

REVIEW ENGAGEMENT REPORT

To (person engaging the public accountant)

I have reviewed the balance sheet of Client Limited as at ......, 19... and the statements of income, retained earnings and changes in financial position for the year then ended. My review was made in accordance with generally accepted standards for review engagements and accordingly consisted primarily of enquiry, analytical procedures and discussion related to information supplied to me by the company, except as explained below.

A review does not constitute an audit and consequently I do not express an audit opinion on these financial statements.

My review indicated serious deficiencies in the accounting records of the company. As a consequence, I was unable to complete my review. Had I been able to complete my review, I might have determined adjustments to be necessary to these financial statements.

Because of my inability to complete a review, as described in the preceding paragraph, I am unable to express any assurance as to whether these financial statements are, in all material respects, in accordance with generally accepted accounting principles.

City

Date

(signed) . . . .

CHARTERED ACCOUNTANT

R E V I E W
C H E C K P O I N T S

14.1 Explain what led to the creation of Review and Compilation Standards.

14.2 What considerations should a successor accountant make in accepting a new engagement?

14.3 How should a public accountant disclose misleading statements detected during a compilation engagement?

14.4 What is the difference between a review services engagement and a compilation service engagement regarding historical financial statements? Compare both of these to an audit engagement.

· ·

INTERIM FINANCIAL INFORMATION

· · · · · · · · · · · ·

LEARNING   OBJECTIVE

2. List some interim information review procedures and write a report on a review of interim financial information.

Accounting principles do not require interim financial information as a basic and necessary element of financial statements conforming to GAAP. When interim information is presented, however, it should conform to the accounting Recommendation in the *CICA Handbook* (*Section* 1750). Examples of situations where audited interim financial statements might be prepared are buy/sell situations for a business, or to fulfil financial reports required by regulatory authorities, particularly those Canadian companies whose securities are traded in U.S. capital markets and therefore must comply with SEC requirements.

A common type of review engagement is the review of interim financial statements or information.

A review of interim financial information differs considerably from an audit. According to *Section* 8200.03, on procedures for review of interim financial statements, a key objective of a review of interim financial statements is to assess whether accounting principles have been applied on a basis consistent with the annual report as well as to the corresponding interim financial statements of the previous year. In particular the auditor is concerned that interim financial statements are not misleading relative to the annualized report. The interim review requires neither a complete assessment of internal control risk each quarter nor the gathering of sufficient, appropriate evidential matter on which to base an opinion on interim financial statements. The nature, timing, and extent of review procedures explained below presume that the reviewer has a knowledge base of the company from the audit of the most recent annual financial statements. Note that the presumption of an existing audit knowledge base from the annual audit means there can be significantly more information guiding the review of interim statements than for a review without such a knowledge base. For this reason some observers feel that a review with an audit knowledge base provides more assurance than a review without an audit knowledge base. One significant difference, for example, is that the public accountant has more familiarity with the system of internal controls when there is an existing audit knowledge base.

Nature of Review Procedures

Review procedures consist mainly of enquiry and analytical procedures. *Section* 8200.02 suggests a checklist that includes the following:

- Enquire about the accounting system.
- Obtain an understanding of the system. Determine whether there have been any significant changes in the system used to produce interim information.
- Perform analytical procedures to identify relationships and individual items that appear to be unusual.
- Read the minutes of shareholder, board of director, and board committee meetings to identify actions or events that may affect interim financial information.
- Read (study) the interim financial information and determine whether it conforms with generally accepted accounting principles.

- Obtain reports from other accountants who perform limited reviews of significant components, subsidiaries, or other investees.
- Enquire of officers and executives about the following: Conformity with generally accepted accounting principles. Consistent application of accounting principles. Changes in the client's business or accounting practices. Matters about which questions have arisen as a result of applying other procedures (listed above). Events subsequent to the date of the interim information.
- Obtain written representations from management about interim information matters.

Timing of Review Procedures

Review procedures should be performed at or near the date of the interim information. Starting the engagement prior to the cutoff date will give auditors a chance to deal with problems and questions without undue deadline pressures.

Extent of Review Procedures

The accountant needs to acquire a sufficient knowledge of the client's business, just as if the engagement were a regular audit. Knowledge of strengths and deficiencies in the internal control system and of problem accounting areas obtained during the most recent audit is very useful in judging the extent of review procedures. Basically, the extent of review procedures depends on the accountant's professional judgment about problem areas in the system of internal control, the severity of unique accounting principles problems, and the errors that have occurred in the past. With knowledge of these areas, the accountant can direct and fine-tune the review procedures in the interest of improving the quality of the interim information.

Reporting on a Review of Interim Information

An accountant may report on interim information presented separately from audited financial statements, provided that a review has been satisfactorily completed. The basic content of the report is as follows (*Section* 8200.04):

- A statement that a review was made in accordance with standards established for review engagements.
- An identification of the interim information reviewed.
- A description of the review procedures.
- A statement that a review is not an audit.
- A denial of opinion on the interim information.
- Negative assurance about material conformity with the disclosed basis of accounting.
- Each page should be marked "unaudited."

An actual report on reviewed interim information presented in a quarterly report (not within an annual report) is shown in Exhibit 14–7.

When the interim information is presented in a note to audited annual financial statements as supplemental information and when it is presented voluntarily under GAAP and the client has requested a review, the auditors give the standard audit report without mentioning the reviewed interim information, unless there is a reason to take exception. Under this exception basis of reporting, interim information is mentioned in a modified standard audit report only if it departs from Section 1750 principles, or if management indicates the auditor performed procedures without also

EXHIBIT 14–7   REPORT ON INTERIM INFORMATION IN A COMPANY'S QUARTERLY REPORT

The Shareholders, XYZ Inc.:

At the request of the Board of Directors and Stockholders, we have made a review of the unaudited condensed balance sheets of Analog Devices, Inc., at April 28, 1990, and April 29, 1989, the related unaudited consolidated statements of income for the three- and six-month periods ended April 28, 1990, and April 29, 1989, and the unaudited consolidated statements of cash flows for the six-month periods ending April 28, 1990, and April 29, 1989, in accordance with standards established by the CICA.

A review of interim financial information consists principally of obtaining an understanding of the system for the preparation of the interim financial information, applying analytical review procedures to financial data, and making inquiries to persons responsible for financial and accounting matters. It is substantially less in scope that an examination in accordance with generally accepted auditing standards, the objective of which is the expression of an opinion regarding the financial statements taken as a whole. Accordingly, we do not express such an opinion.

Based on our review, nothing has come to our attention that causes us to believe that the accompanying financial statements are not in all material respects in accordance with generally accepted accounting principles.

Public Accountants
Montreal, Quebec
May 16, 1990

---

saying the auditor expresses no opinion, or if management fails to label interim information in the note to annual audited financial statements as "unaudited."

Additional Interim Information Communication

During the difficult economic times in the last decade, especially in financial institutions, auditors were criticized in the United States for taking no action when they became aware of material problems with interim financial information. The auditors responded that they were not required to take any action because they were not engaged to perform an interim review and issue a report.

Several regulatory agencies were distressed that some companies issued misleading interim information—sometimes their auditors knew about it—but nothing was done to inform the public or the regulators. Suggestions were conveyed to the AICPA Auditing Standards Board, and it responded with "Communication of Matters about Interim Financial Information Filed or to Be Filed with Specified Regulatory Agencies—An Amendment to SAS No. 36, Review of Interim Financial Information."

This AICPA standard requires that auditors do something when they learn that interim information filed or to be filed with certain specified agencies is probably materially misstated as a result of a departure from GAAP. The required action is to (*a*) discuss the matter with management as soon as possible, (*b*) inform the company's audit committee if management does not take appropriate and timely action, and (*c*) if the audit committee does not respond appropriately, decide whether to resign from the interim review engagement or resign as the company's auditor. However, auditing standards do not require resignation or direct communication to the "specified agencies." The auditing standard appears to be a compromise between regulators who probably wanted direct reporting and auditors who wanted to handle difficult problems within the affected companies. Again, this requirement only affects Canadian companies falling within the jurisdiction of the SEC.

. . . .

R E V I E W
CHECKPOINTS

14.5 Is interim financial information required to be presented in order for annual financial statements to be in conformity with GAAP?

14.6 In what respects is a review of the interim financial information similar to a review of the unaudited annual financial statements of a nonpublic company?

14.7 When interim information is presented in a note to annual financial statements, under what circumstances would an audit report on the annual financial statements be modified with respect to the interim financial information?

· ·

SPECIAL REPORTS AND AADBA

· · · · · · · · · · · · ·

LEARNING OBJECTIVE

3. Define, explain, and give examples of "another appropriate disclosed basis of accounting" (AADBA), distinguishing them from GAAP.

For a long time, a small war has been waged over the "Big GAAP–Little GAAP" controversy. Many accountants have been dismayed by the complexity of generally accepted accounting principles and have openly questioned their relevance to small businesses with uncomplicated operations. They believe that business managers and users of the financial statements care little about accounting for such things as pension obligations, capitalized leases, deferred taxes, and similar complicated topics. They characterize such topics as "standards overload" that may be necessary for "big business" but are largely superfluous for "small business."

For a while, the "little GAAP" advocates lobbied for formal GAAP exemptions for small businesses. However, resistance was encountered in the counterargument that there was a danger of creating "second-class GAAP" for small business while reserving "real GAAP" for big companies. Bankers and other users of financial statements were not nearly so eager to have "little GAAP" financial statements as some accountants wanted them to be. Anyway, many small businesses aspire to be large businesses, and their managers may not want to be stigmatized by "little GAAP" beginnings. Another reason to distinguish different bases of accounting is that in some industries, notably banks and other financial institutions, there is no GAAP for the industry other than that specified by regulation. For example, in April 1989 in response to the November 1988 CICA Exposure Draft "Banks," the Superintendent of Financial Institutions stated that "until a great deal more work is done my office will not accept the inclusion of banks within the scope of the *Handbook.*"[1]

In addition, there may be legislative reporting requirements that differ from the *Handbook;* for example, public sector reporting requirements to Parliament may deviate from those reflected in generally accepted public sector accounting principles. Also, some users of financial statements—limited groups of specified users—may have special information needs that necessitate reports deviating from GAAP: for example, financial statements in conformity with contractual requirements or buy/sell agreements. For all of these reasons, reports may be prepared on a basis other than GAAP using another appropriate basis of accounting (AADBA).

At the time of this writing (May 1997) the authoritative literature on AADBA is in the form of *Handbook Section* 5100.05-.06 and a CICA Exposure Draft, "Auditor's Report on Financial Statements Using a Basis of Accounting Other Than Generally Accepted Accounting Principles" issued in August 1996. The objective of this Exposure Draft is "to identify the special circumstances in which it is appropriate for the auditor's report on financial statements to refer to a basis of accounting other than generally accepted accounting principles and to provide guidance on the wording of the auditor's report." The Exposure Draft proposes to replace *Handbook Section* 5520 and Audit Guidelines AUG–12 and AUG–14. The Exposure Draft broadens AADBA to include "special information needs of specified users" when GAAP may not meet their needs. This requires the auditor to understand the purpose of the financial state-

---

[1] *Audit of the Allowance for Credit Losses,* CICA, 1993, p. 3.

ments for the identified users and to be satisfied that the AADBA meets their needs. The box on the next page outlines the AADBA report decision tree per the Exposure Draft.

Studies in the United States have shown that AADBA financial statements can be less expensive to produce and easier to interpret than full GAAP statements. Surveys report that 50 percent of AADBA financial statements for small businesses are on the "tax basis of accounting," and 49 percent are on the "cash basis." However, these studies also show that AADBA is only appropriate when it meets user needs.

Another Appropriate Disclosed Basis of Accounting

Companies that are not subject to securities regulations and filing requirements can choose to present financial information in accordance with a comprehensive basis of accounting other than GAAP. A comprehensive basis in this context refers to a coherent accounting treatment in which substantially all the important financial measurements are governed by criteria other than GAAP. Examples include (1) treatment applied by financial institutions to statements conforming to the accounting rules of the Office of the Superintendent of Financial Institutions (OFSI) that are not in accordance with GAAP (as discussed in AUG–14, para 8), (2) tax basis accounting, (3) cash basis accounting, and (4) some other fairly well-defined methods, such as constant-dollar, price-level-adjusted financial statements.

AADBA financial statements should not use the titles normally associated with GAAP statements, such as "balance sheet," "statement of financial position," "statement of operations," "income statement," and "statement of cash flows."[2] Even the titles are said to suggest GAAP financial statements. Instead, AADBA statements should use titles like the ones shown in the following box.

Some Non-GAAP Financial Statement Titles Used in Practice

Statement of Assets and Liabilities—Regulatory Basis.
Statement of Assets and Liabilities—Cash Basis.
Statement of Admitted Assets, Liabilities, and Surplus—Statutory Basis
   Required by the Insurance Superintendent of the Province.

Statement of Assets, Liabilities, and Capital—Income Tax Basis.
Statement of Income—Regulatory Basis.
Statement of Revenue and Expenses—Income Tax Basis.
Statement of Revenue Collected and Expenses Paid—Cash Basis.
Statement of Changes in Partners' Capital Accounts—Income Tax Basis.

AADBA statements can be audited, reviewed, or compiled like any other financial statements. All the general and field work auditing standards and the standards for review and compilation apply, just as they apply for GAAP financial statements. The reporting standards regarding consistency, adequate disclosure, and report responsibility (fourth reporting standard) also apply to AADBA statements. Disclosure

---

[2] The only exception would be if AADBA were the only available alternatives, such as with the banking industry in Canada. See "GAAP vs. AADBA" by D. Cockburn, *CA Magazine*, January 1992, pp. 35–37.

**CICA EXPOSURE DRAFT: AUDITOR'S REPORT ON FINANCIAL STATEMENTS
PREPARED USING A BASIS OF ACCOUNTING OTHER THAN GAAP—August 1996**

APPENDIX A—AUDITOR'S REPORT ON FINANCIAL STATEMENTS—DECISION TREE
(Note: This outline should be read in the context of the proposed new *Section* and is not a substitute therefor.)

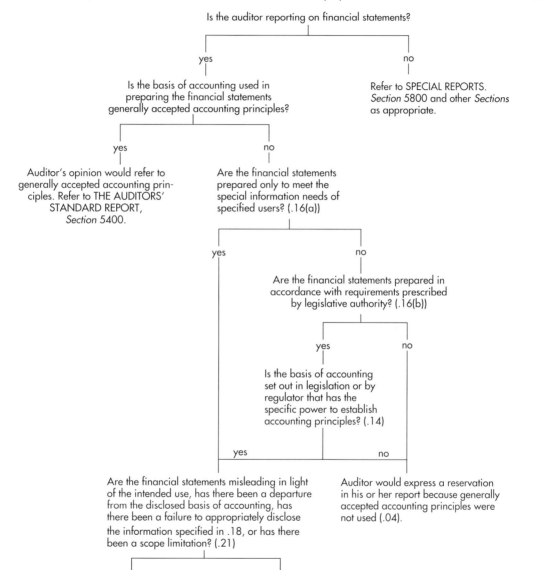

See the CICA Internet Site: http://www.cica.ca for additional information on this Exposure Draft.

requirements are not reduced by AADBA. However, the first reporting standard, which requires the audit report statement on whether the financial statements are presented in conformity with GAAP, is handled differently.

When a non-GAAP accounting method is used, the first reporting standard is satisfied by a sentence in the report that presents the AADBA basis of accounting; and the opinion sentence refers to the AADBA instead of to GAAP. Disclosures in the financial statements should (1) contain an explanation of the AADBA, and (2) describe in general how the AADBA differs from GAAP, but (3) the differences do not have to be quantified—that is, the AADBA does not need to be reconciled to GAAP with dollar amounts. For all practical purposes, the GAAP criteria are replaced by criteria applicable to the AADBA. (See *Handbook Section* 5701.14). An example of a special report on cash basis statements is in Exhibit 14–8.

GAAP, Other Than Historical Cost

You should be aware that GAAP sometimes is not historical cost. The prime examples are market value accounting for the assets in defined benefit pension plans, investment companies (e.g., venture capital companies, small business investment companies, mutual funds), and personal financial statements (e.g., individual or family). In these cases current value accounting is GAAP. The audit report on such financial statements gives an opinion that they are "in conformity with generally accepted accounting principles." No mention is made of an AADBA, because the current value accounting is GAAP and not an AADBA. Indeed, if such financial statements are prepared using the normal historical cost accounting, they contain departures from GAAP, and a qualified audit opinion would be given.

E X H I B I T 14–8   **SPECIAL REPORT ON NON-GAAP COMPREHENSIVE BASIS**

Independent Auditors' Report

To Trust North Bank Association (Trustee)
and the Unit Holders of the Mega Offshore Trust:

We have audited the accompanying statements of assets, liabilities, and trust corpus—cash basis, of the Mega Offshore Trust as of December 31, 1992 and 1991, and the related statements of changes in trust corpus—cash basis, for each of the three years in the period ended December 31, 1992. These financial statements are the responsibility of the Company's management. Our responsibility is to express an opinion on these financial statements based on our audits.

(Standard scope paragraph here)

As described in Note 2, these financial statements were prepared on the cash receipts and disbursements basis of accounting, which is a comprehensive basis of accounting other than generally accepted accounting principles.

In our opinion, the financial statements referred to above present fairly, in all material respects, the assets, liabilities, and trust corpus arising from cash transactions of the Mega Offshore Trust as of December 31, 1992 and 1991, and the related changes in trust corpus arising from cash transactions for each of the three years in the period ended December 31, 1992, on the basis of accounting described in Note 2.

/s/ Auditor signature
March 18, 1993

Note 2 describes a cash basis of accounting and concludes:

This basis for reporting royalty income is considered to be the most meaningful because distributions to the Unit holders for a month are based on net cash receipts for such month. However, it will differ from the basis used for financial statements prepared in accordance with generally accepted accounting principles because, under such accounting principles, royalty income for a month would be based on net proceeds for such month without regard to when calculated or received.

Another informally recognized basis of accounting that has no formal body of rules is "liquidation basis accounting." Some mention is made of this basis in the literature, but you will not find much official guidance. In fact there is some controversy as to whether the liquidation basis of accounting is GAAP or AADBA when the going concern assumption is no longer appropriate. One of the authors found that there is a split opinion on this within the CICA (as of May 1997). Nevertheless, auditors sometimes give reports on liquidation basis financial statements without referring to them as an AADBA. An excerpt is in the box below. (Be aware, however, that this type of opinion is not illustrated in any standard. It was invented in practice.)

Opinion Paragraph on Liquidation Basis Statements

In our opinion, the financial statements referred to above present fairly, in all material respects, the financial position of Canada Liquidating Corporation at December 31, 1992, and the excess of revenues over costs and expenses and its cash flows for the year then ended, in conformity with generally accepted accounting principles for a company in liquidation.

REVIEW CHECKPOINTS

14.8 Why does AADBA exist? Can AADBA financial statements be audited?

14.9 Why do you think standard setters have not created "little GAAP" by exempting small businesses from compliance with many complicated accounting standards?

14.10 What should auditors do about the fourth reporting standard when financial statements are presented on a comprehensive basis of accounting other than GAAP?

Current Value Financial Statements

LEARNING OBJECTIVE

4. Explain the content of an auditor's report on supplementary current value financial statements in comparison to a standard report on historical cost financial statements.

Accounting theorists have long favoured various measurements in current value accounting, including discounted present value of cash flows, entry values (replacement cost, current cost), and exit values (disposal value, current cash equivalent) for all types of companies and industries. Measurement by anything other than historical cost received little notice from the practising profession until the mid-1970s, when five things happened: (1) inflation accelerated in Canada and worldwide; (2) critics voiced loud discontent with historical-cost measurement; (3) British, Australian, Dutch, and other accountants started promoting accounting measurement alternatives; (4) the SEC issued Accounting Series Release No. 190 requiring disclosure of certain replacement cost information; and (5) the CICA moved into the phase of considering new measurement bases, including some kinds of current value accounting, which culminated in *Handbook Section* 4510 recommending the presentation of supplementary information on both a current cost and price level adjusted basis. (This section was dropped in the early 1990s.)

EXHIBIT 14–9 **REPORT ON CURRENT VALUE FINANCIAL STATEMENTS**

THE ROUSE COMPANY AND SUBSIDIARIES
Consolidated Cost Basis and Current Value Basis Balance Sheets
December 31, 1991 and 1990
(in thousands)

	1991		1990	
	Current Value Basis (note 1)	Cost Basis	Current Value Basis (note 1)	Cost Basis
Assets				
Property (notes 4, 5, 8 and 14):				
Operating properties:				
Current value	$3,638,801		$3,825,882	
Property and deferred costs of projects		$2,482,292		$2,424,003
Less accumulated depreciation and amortization		331,312		287,365
	3,638,801	2,150,980	3,825,882	2,136,638
Development operations:				
Construction and development in progress	59,513	54,290	56,186	49,890
Pre-construction costs, net	14,734	14,734	17,196	17,196
	74,247	69,024	73,382	67,086
Property held for development and sale . . .	192,195	158,472	166,616	125,387
Other property, net (note 14)	18,878	9,004	20,234	9,727
Other assets	87,843	87,843	78,338	78,338
Accounts and notes receivable (note 6) . . .	75,547	75,547	85,153	85,153
Investments in marketable securities	27,505	27,505	41,758	41,578
Cash and cash equivalents	59,077	59,077	70,790	70,790
Total	$4,174,093	$2,637,452	$4,362,153	$2,614,877

(continued)

Interest on the part of accountants in current value and inflation-adjusted financial statements virtually disappeared with the decline in the inflation rate after 1985. However, as the number of failures among banks and trust companies, brokerages, and financial services companies surged after 1984, regulators began to beat the drum for "mark to market" (current value) accounting for loans and securities held by financial institutions. In 1992 the FASB made some rules requiring disclosure of market values for financial institution assets. Many regulators also require disclosure of current market values on a supplemental basis.

In the past the real estate and the hotel/motel industries have been particularly interested in reporting the current value of real estate assets. One of the earliest disclosures of current asset values was by the Rouse Company, owners of several major mall developments. Excerpts from the balance sheet and the audit report are in Exhibit 14–9. You can see that the audit report contains an unqualified opinion on the historical cost financial statements. It also contains an explanatory paragraph, complete with cautions about the realization of the current values, and a special report opinion on the current value information.

Auditors can accept engagements to audit and report on current value financial statements as long as (1) the company's measurement and disclosure criteria are reasonable and (2) the measurements and disclosures are reasonably reliable. However, auditing standards do not acknowledge general current financial statements to

EXHIBIT 14–9   REPORT ON CURRENT VALUE FINANCIAL STATEMENTS (concluded)

Independent Auditors' Report

The Board of Directors and Shareholders,
The Rouse Company:

We have audited the accompanying consolidated cost basis balance sheets of The Rouse Company and subsidiaries as of December 31, 1991 and 1990, and the related consolidated cost basis statements of operations, common stock, and other shareholders' equity and cash flows for each of the years in the three-year period ended December 31, 1991. We have also audited the supplemental consolidated current value basis balance sheets of The Rouse Company and subsidiaries as of December 31, 1991 and 1990, and the related supplemental consolidated current value basis statements of changes in revaluation equity for each of the years in the three-year period ended December 31, 1991. These financial statements are the responsibility of the Company's management. Our responsibility is to express an opinion on these financial statements based on our audits.

We conducted our audits in accordance with generally accepted auditing standards. Those standards require that we plan and perform the audit to obtain reasonable assurance about whether the financial statements are free of material misstatement. An audit includes examining, on a test basis, evidence supporting the amounts and disclosures in the financial statements. An audit also includes assessing the accounting principles used and significant estimates made by management, as well as evaluating the overall financial statement presentation. We believe that our audits provide a reasonable basis for our opinion.

In our opinion, the aforementioned consolidated cost basis financial statements present fairly, in all material respects, the financial position of The Rouse Company and subsidiaries at December 3, 1991 and 1990, and the results of their operations and their cash flows for each of the years in the three-year period ended December 31, 1991, in conformity with generally accepted accounting principles.

As more fully described in note 1 to the consolidated financial statements, the supplemental consolidated current value basis financial statements referred to above have been prepared by management to present relevant financial information about The Rouse Company and its subsidiaries which is not provided by the cost basis financial statements and are not intended to be a presentation in conformity with generally accepted accounting principles. In addition, as more fully described in note 1, the supplemental consolidated current value basis financial statements do not purport to present the net realizable, liquidation, or market value of the Company as a whole. Furthermore, amounts ultimately realized by the Company from the disposal of properties may vary from the current values presented.

In our opinion, the aforementioned supplemental consolidated current value basis financial statements present fairly, in all material respects, the information set forth therein on the basis of accounting described in note 1 to the consolidated financial statements.

KPMG Peat Marwick
February 19, 1992

---

be a stand-alone AADBA. They regard the current value information as supplementary to the GAAP financial statements. (In this regard general current-value financial statements are different from current value as GAAP for defined benefit plans, investment companies, and personal financial statements, and also different from a stand-alone AADBA, such as cash basis accounting.)

. . . .

REVIEW
CHECKPOINTS

14.11 What are some examples of AADBA? of entities for which current value is GAAP? of current value financial statements that are supplementary to historical financial statements?

14.12 Insofar as the opinion paragraph in an audit report is concerned, what difference does the client's use of an AADBA make? What difference if the client is one for whom current value is GAAP? What difference if a real estate or manufacturing company presents supplementary current value information?

. . . .

Special Reports—Additional Topics

Auditors may perform a variety of services acting in the capacity of auditor (not as tax adviser or management consultant) that require a report, other than the standard unqualified audit report. Such services involve special reports issued in connection with:

- Engagements to report on specified elements, accounts, or items of a financial statement (*Section* 5805).
- Engagements to report on compliance with contractual agreements or regulatory requirements (*Section* 5815).
- Limited-scope engagements to perform procedures agreed on by the client (*Section* 5810).

Specified Elements, Accounts, or Items

Auditors may be requested to render special reports on such things as rentals, royalties, profit participations, or a provision for income taxes. The fourth CICA reporting standard does not apply because the specified element, account, or item does not purport to be a financial statement of financial position or results of operations. The consistency disclosure via footnotes should be made in all cases.

Special engagements with limited objectives enable auditors to provide needed services to clients. *Section* 5805 gives the standards for these engagements. Examples include grant application data, reports relating to amount of sales used in computing rental, reports relating to royalties, reports on a profit participation, and a report on the adequacy of a tax provision in financial statements. Exhibit 14–10 contains an illustrative report on a company's accounts receivable.

Compliance with Contractual Agreements or Regulatory Requirements

Clients may have restrictive covenants in loan agreements. Lenders may require a periodic report on whether the client has complied with such contractual agreements. Following a scope paragraph referring to the report on the audited financial statements, the auditor may give a negative assurance of the following type:

EXHIBIT 14–10   **EXAMPLE OF A REPORT ON A SCHEDULE OF ACCOUNTS RECEIVABLE (from** *Handbook Section 5805.19)*

AUDITOR'S REPORT
ON SCHEDULE OF ACCOUNTS RECEIVABLE

To the Directors of Client Limited

I have audited the schedule of accounts receivable of Client Limited as at ...., 19... This financial information is the responsibility of the management of Client Limited. My responsibility is to express an opinion on this financial information based on my audit.

I conducted my audit in accordance with generally accepted auditing standards. Those standards require that I plan and perform an audit to obtain reasonable assurance whether the financial information is free of material misstatement. An audit includes examining, on a test basis, evidence supporting the amounts and disclosures in the financial information. An audit also includes assessing the accounting principles used and significant estimates made by management, as well as evaluating the overall presentation of the financial information.

In my opinion, this schedule presents fairly, in all material respects, the accounts receivable of Client Limited as at ...., 19.. in accordance with generally accepted accounting principles.

City   (signed)   . . . .
Date   CHARTERED ACCOUNTANT

In connection with our audit, nothing came to our attention that caused us to believe that the company failed to comply with the terms, covenants, provisions, or conditions of sections 32 through 46 of the indenture dated January 1, 1988, with North Country Bank. However, our audit examination was not directed primarily toward obtaining knowledge of such noncompliance.

A similar negative assurance may be given with regard to federal and provincial regulatory requirements. Examples include limitations on investments for mutual funds, and provincial insurance commissioner regulations about the nature of insurance company investments. When the auditor is engaged to provide an audit opinion as to a client's compliance with criteria established by provisions of agreements statutes or regulations, *Section* 5815 provides the appropriate guidance. In this case positive assurance is provided and other than criteria and scope the auditor's report is similar to that for audits of financial statements. An example of an opinion on compliance given in a separate report is provided in Exhibit 14–11.

Regulatory agencies may seek to have auditors sign assertions in prescribed report language that go beyond acceptable professional reporting responsibilities and involve auditors in areas outside their function and responsibility. In such cases auditors should insert additional wording in the prescribed report language or write a completely revised report that reflects adequately their position and responsibility.

Applying Agreed-upon Procedures

In some cases clients may ask auditors to perform a specified set of procedures—the agreed-upon procedures—to examine a particular element, account, or item in a financial statement. Such work should not be considered an audit because the specified set of agreed-upon procedures is usually not sufficient to be considered in accordance with generally accepted auditing standards. These special-purpose engagements have a limited scope, so the second and third GAAS examination

---

E X H I B I T   14–11   **EXAMPLE OF AN OPINION ON COMPLIANCE GIVEN IN A SEPARATE REPORT** (from *Handbook Section* 5815.11)

AUDITOR'S REPORT
ON COMPLIANCE WITH AGREEMENT

To A Trust Company Limited

I have audited Client Limited's compliance as at December 31, 19X1 with the criteria established by (describe nature of provisions to be complied with) described in Sections ...... to ...... inclusive of (name of agreement) dated ...., 19... with (name of party to agreement) and the interpretation of such agreement as set out in note 1 attached. Compliance with the criteria established by the provisions of the agreement is the responsibility of the management of Client Limited. My responsibility is to express an opinion on this compliance based on my audit.

I conducted my audit in accordance with generally accepted auditing standards. Those standards require that I plan and perform an audit to obtain reasonable assurance whether Client Limited complied with the criteria established by the provisions of the agreement referred to above. Such an audit includes examining, on a test basis, evidence supporting compliance, evaluating the overall compliance with the agreement, and where applicable, assessing the accounting principles used and significant estimates made by management.

In my opinion, Client Limited is in compliance, in all material respects, with the criteria established by (the provisions to be complied with) described in Sections ...... to ...... of this agreement.

City   (signed) . . . .
Date   CHARTERED ACCOUNTANT

standards (control risk assessment and sufficient competent evidence for an opinion) and the GAAS reporting standards do not apply.

For example, a client may request procedures on the long-term debt of a company it plans to acquire—not an audit of the company's complete financial statements. *Section* 5810, "Special Reports—Applying Specified Auditing Procedures to Financial Information other than Financial Statements," gives an example report on such an engagement. The scope paragraph, quoted below in Exhibit 14–12, is clearly not a standard scope explanation describing an audit in accordance with generally accepted auditing standards:

The conclusions paragraph quoted earlier follows the recommendation in *Section* 5810 by (1) denying an audit opinion on the accounts and items, (2) giving a negative assurance as to "no exceptions," (3) listing the procedures, and (4) stating that the report is for restricted use only. You can see how the objectives of this kind of service are very limited and how the report conclusions are also very limited.

REPORTING ON INTERNAL CONTROL
. . . .

Managements and boards of directors have been encouraged to make public reports on internal control, and auditors have been encouraged by the regulators such as Quebec's inspector general of financial institutions to become associated with such reports. Many annual reports of public companies contain a "report from management" that includes brief commentary about internal control responsibilities. Apart from these brief reports, public reports on internal control are not commonplace.

The topic of internal control reports has led a topsy-turvy life. In 1980 the SEC expressed the belief that management's comments in its own report on controls were "other information" and that auditors had a responsibility to disclose any material deficiencies that management did not disclose. This event prompted the Auditing Standards Board to issue an interpretation stating that auditors are responsible for seeing whether a management report contains a material misstatement of fact or fails to be complete insofar as known material weaknesses in internal accounting control are concerned. In 1983 the SEC expressed satisfaction with management's tendency

---

E X H I B I T 14–12   **EXAMPLE OF A REPORT ON SPECIFIED AUDITING PROCEDURES CARRIED OUT ON LONG-TERM DEBT** (from *Handbook Section* 5810.10)

To A. Trustee Limited

As specifically agreed, I have performed the following procedures in connection with the above company's certificate dated ...., 19.... as to the amount of the company's Funded Obligations as at ...., 19....:
(list the procedures)

As a result of applying the above procedures, I found no (the following) exceptions (list of exceptions). However these procedures do not constitute an audit of the company's Funded Obligations and therefore I express no opinion on the amount of Funded Obligations as at ...., 19.....

This letter is for use solely in connection with the closing on ...., 19.... of the issue of .... securities of the company.

City   (signed) . . . .
Date   CHARTERED ACCOUNTANT

toward volunteering reports on internal accounting control and decided not to require such reports. At the same time, the SEC dropped its consideration of requiring some form of auditor association with management's comments on control. At the time the SEC was in a "deregulation mode" and loath to enact new requirements. In 1988 the SEC once again proposed a rule to require a management report on companies' internal control. Nothing came of this proposal. However, by 1991, with bank failures at an all-time high, Congress passed legislation requiring internal control reports by insured depository institutions. The Auditing Standards Board may delete its current standard on internal control reports and issue a related statement on assurance standards regarding management's report on internal control.

Meanwhile in Canada similar concerns about banks and trust and insurance companies prompted the CICA to issue the Auditing Guideline "Special Reports on Regulated Financial Institutions" in May 1992.

Regulated financial institutions such as banks, insurance and trust companies, pension funds, mutual funds, and investment dealers often include special reporting responsibilities beyond those for financial statements to shareholders. The auditor must sometimes communicate in writing transactions or conditions that come to his or her attention (i.e., negative assurance is provided). This form of communication is referred to as a derivative report. At other times the auditor is required to carry out procedures relating to the matters specified in addition to those required by GAAS. The required communication that reports on such specified procedures is referred to as a nonderivative report.

Especially in the case of derivative reporting, the audit firm should take steps to inform all staff providing services to the financial institution to be sensitized to this reporting responsibility and to be observant concerning potentially relevant transactions or conditions.

When considering an appointment as auditor of a financial institution, the public accountant should obtain an understanding of any special reporting responsibilities and if necessary contact the regulator or obtain interpretation of the regulatory responsibility from legal counsel.

The extent of management involvement will vary with the nature of the special reporting responsibility to the regulator. As a minimum, however, management will need to have an understanding of (*a*) the reporting responsibility, (*b*) the information, including management representation, that the auditor will need, and (*c*) the process the auditor will follow in issuing a report. All understanding should be documented in writing.

Normally, the auditor would send a copy of the report to the board of directors and other members of management before sending the report to the regulator. In some cases the auditor may wish to seek legal advice and report solely to the regulator.

A derivative report is a by-product of the financial statement audit. The only additional audit procedures are (1) understanding and clarifying the derivative reporting responsibility, (2) making all relevant parties aware of it, and (3) reporting separately to the regulator.

The auditor looks for evidence that affects the viability of the financial institution. Unfortunately, the legislation governing auditor's responsibilities often uses such general and subjective terms as "sound financial practices," and "well-being," which are left to the auditor's judgment, and this may differ from the regulator's interpretation (for example, see AUG–17). This may lead to varying interpretations of the matters specified by legislation and to inconsistencies in the types of transactions or conditions identified and reported by auditors.

As a result there are three limitations on the usefulness of derivative reports.

1. The auditor is not required to carry out procedures directed at providing positive assurance on the matters or reportable conditions specified in legislation.

2. There may be no comprehensive and precise interpretation of the matters or reportable conditions.

3. The financial statement audit may not be designed to address such matters.

In deciding on the types of matters or reportable conditions that should go into a derivative report, the auditor should consider not only the significance of individual transactions and conditions encountered, but also whether a combination of insignificant items should be included in the derivative report. The findings should be discussed with appropriate levels of management, including the audit committee.

The derivative report should be titled "Derivative Report by the Auditor." An illustration is given in the Exhibit 14–13.

A nonderivative reporting responsibility involves a reporting engagement separate from the audit of the financial statements. Unique features of such engagements are:

1. The auditor may be asked to provide an opinion without a specific assertion from management.

2. The auditor may be required to report directly to the regulator.

3. The matters are often subjective and thus open to different interpretations, and there may be no established criteria for evaluating the matters.

The Special Reports Recommendations can be applied to many of the nonderivative reporting responsibilities specified in legislation. For example, *Sections* 5805, 5810, 5815, 8500, and 8600 can all be relevant for specific nonderivative reporting engagements. AUG–13 focuses on the following nonderivative reporting engagement matters:

1. The methods of management concerning administration and safekeeping of property administered for others.

E X H I B I T   14–13   **DERIVATIVE REPORT BY THE AUDITOR (from CICA Guideline AUG–13, example A)**

To the Chief Executive Officer of X Financial Institution:

I have audited the financial statements of X Financial Institution as at December 31, 19X1 and for the year then ended, and reported thereon under date of February 19, 19X2.

Pursuant to the requirements of Section XXX of the Y Act (the Act), I am required to report to you any transactions or conditions encountered during the aforementioned audit that (describe matters specified in legislation). For the purposes of understanding the types of transactions or conditions that (describe matters specified in legislation), I have used the following interpretations developed from the following sources:

(Describe the interpretations used and the sources of such interpretations)

During the course of the aforementioned audit, based on the interpretations referred to above, I encountered no relevant transactions or conditions.

No procedures have been carried out in addition to those necessary to form an opinion on the financial statements.

This report has been prepared in accordance with the applicable Auditing and Related Services Guideline issued by The Canadian Institute of Chartered Accountants, and is to be used solely to satisfy the requirements of Section XXX of the Act and should not be referred to or used for any other purpose.

City   (signed) . . . .
Date   CHARTERED ACCOUNTANT

cc: Superintendent of Financial Institutions

2. The methods of management adopted by the company to comply with laws relating to self-dealing and conflicts of interest.

3. The procedures adopted by management to safeguard the interests of creditors and members.

Legislation may require an opinion on the adequacy of methods of management, the effectiveness of controls, or the adequacy of procedures. However, in order to do the job the auditor needs to understand a regulator's expectations. The auditor requires reasonable and attainable standards and criteria to serve as benchmarks for evaluating the adequacy of matters to be reported on. Most legislation does not specify the criteria to be used. The auditor may need to consult with the regulator. An agreement reached on appropriate criteria should be put in writing.

It is also desirable to put in writing any other terms of the engagement with the regulator, such as form of opinion and the period to be covered.

If criteria cannot be established in consultation with the regulator, the auditor may agree to (1) industry standards, (2) authoritative literature, (3) other specialists, and (4) management's view on the matters to be reported on. In all cases it is important for the auditor to describe in his or her report the criteria used and the source of the criteria.

The general and applicable examination standards of *Section* 5100 apply to nonderivative reports. The auditor should obtain an understanding of the policies and procedures established by the client to address the matters on which the auditor is to report. The auditor would also obtain sufficient evidence as to whether the policies and procedures existed and operated effectively throughout the period covered by the report; and evaluate the adequacy of policies and procedures against appropriate criteria.

The auditor should obtain a letter of representation from management concerning management's responsibility for the legislated matters and responsibility to inform the auditor of the status of policies and procedures that affect the legislated matters.

The auditor's report is addressed to the party specified in legislation and should be titled "Auditor's Report on [specify matters]." The report consists of an introductory paragraph, a scope paragraph, an opinion paragraph (that there is reasonable assurance that matters being reported on were adequate or effective), and a concluding paragraph stating that the report has been prepared in accordance with this guideline and is to be used solely to satisfy the legislative requirement. (An example of a nonderivative report is given in Exhibit 14-14.)

A reservation in a nonderivative report would be guided by the *Recommendations* in *Section* 5510.

Public and Restricted Reports

Several different kinds of reports on internal control based on a special study of controls have evolved in practice:

- Public reports on control in effect as of a specific date.
- Public reports on control in effect during a specified time period.
- Restricted use reports based on the control risk assessment work during an audit, not sufficient for expressing an opinion on control.
- Restricted use reports based on regulatory agencies' pre-established criteria.
- Restricted use reports based on a review without tests of controls or based on application of agreed-upon procedures.

EXHIBIT 14–14   **(from CICA Guideline AUG–13, example B)**

Example of a nonderivative report when:

(i) legislation require the auditor to report to the regulator directly on the adequacy of the procedures adopted to safeguard the interests of creditors and members; and

(ii) the auditor has decided on appropriate criteria.

AUDITOR'S REPORT ON PROCEDURES
TO SAFEGUARD THE INTERESTS OF
CREDITORS AND MEMBERS

To the Superintendent of Financial Institutions:

Pursuant to the requirements of Section XXX of the Act Respecting X Financial Institutions (the Act), I have audited the procedures employed by XYZ Financial Institution (the Company) to safeguard the interests of its creditors and members for the year ended December 31, 19XX. These procedures are the responsibility of the Company's management. My responsibility is to express an opinion on these procedures based on my audit.

I conducted my audit in accordance with generally accepted auditing standards. Those standards require that I plan and perform an audit to obtain reasonable assurance whether the procedures adopted by the Company were adequate to safeguard the interests of its creditors and members based on appropriate criteria. Such an audit includes obtaining an understanding of the procedures employed by management to safeguard the interests of creditors and members, obtaining sufficient appropriate audit evidence to determine whether these procedures operated effectively throughout the year and evaluating the adequacy of the procedures against appropriate criteria. I used the following criteria developed from the sources noted:

(Describe the criteria used and the sources of such criteria)

Because of the inherent limitations of any procedures adopted by a financial institution to safeguard the interests of its creditors and members, only reasonable assurance can be obtained with respect to the adequacy of such procedures.

In my opinion, based on the above criteria, there is reasonable assurance that the procedures adopted by the Company for the year ended December 31, 19XX were adequate to safeguard the interests of its creditors and members.

This report has been prepared in accordance with the applicable Auditing and Related Services Guideline issued by The Canadian Institute of Chartered Accountants, and is intended to be used solely to satisfy the requirements of Section XXX of the Act and should not be referred to or used for any other purpose.

City   (signed) . . . .
Date   CHARTERED ACCOUNTANT

cc: Senior company management

Some restricted use reports have been illustrated in Exhibits 14–13 and 14–14. Other restricted use internal control reports are covered in *Section* 5900, "Opinions on Control Procedures in Service Organizations," and in *Section* 5750. It is the public reports on internal controls for which we have little authoritative Canadian guidance currently. As an illustration of what we may expect, the Standard (Public) Report on Internal Control in the United States, which is based on a special study of internal controls, is provided in Exhibit 14–15. There, you can see that the last paragraph expresses positive assurance (opinion) on the controls. We will discuss general assurance engagements later in this chapter.

When reporting to a regulatory agency, reports modelled on this standard form may be acceptable. If not, a special report can be issued that, among other things, states the accountant's conclusions based on the agency's criteria and restricts use of the report to the agency (see Exhibit 14–14). Such reports most often are requested in connection with audits of financial institutions.

Other special-purpose reports on control systems can be issued, but their scope is generally limited. Such reports should (*a*) describe the scope of the engagement, (*b*) disclaim an opinion on the system as a whole, (*c*) state the accountant's findings, and (*d*) restrict the report to management or specified third parties (*Section* 5220).

EXHIBIT 14-15   REPORTING ON INTERNAL ACCOUNTING CONTROL

To the Company, Directors, Stockholders,
Management, a Regulatory Agency, or Specified Others:

We have made a study and evaluation of the system of internal accounting control of Anycompany and subsidiaries in effect at December 31, 1990. Our study and evaluation was conducted in accordance with standards established by the American Institute of Certified Public Accountants.

The management of Anycompany is responsible for establishing and maintaining a system of internal accounting control. In fulfilling this responsibility, estimates and judgments by management are required to assess the expected benefits and related costs of control procedures. The objectives of a system are to provide management with reasonable, but not absolute, assurance that assets are safeguarded against loss from unauthorized use or disposition, and that transactions are executed in accordance with management's authorization and recorded properly to permit the preparation of financial statements in accordance with generally accepted accounting principles.

Because of inherent limitations in any system of internal accounting control, errors or irregularities may occur and not be detected. Also, projection of any evaluation of the system to future periods is subject to the risk that procedures may become inadequate because of changes in conditions, or that the degree of compliance with the procedures may deteriorate.

In our opinion, the system of internal accounting control of Anycompany and subsidiaries in effect at December 31, 1990, taken as a whole, was sufficient to meet the objectives stated above insofar as those objectives pertain to the prevention or detection of errors or irregularities in amounts that would be material in relation to the consolidated financial statements.

/s/ Auditor signature, PA
February 18, 1991

A problem with the public report noted in Exhibit 14–15 relates to which internal controls should be evaluated. For example, should only accounting controls be evaluated? accounting controls plus operational controls? accounting controls plus operational plus management controls? These questions relate to what should be the internal control objectives for publicly issued internal control reports. Other questions in regard to issuing public general-purpose internal control reports relate to the criteria to be used in evaluating controls. (For example, is effectiveness of management and operating controls too subjective to be measured and evaluated? Current standards focus on accounting controls.) Also, what procedures should the auditors perform in support of such a report, and how should they distinguish between review and examination of internal controls? Some feel these issues can be addressed in a broader attestation/assurance framework rather than in a specific internal control framework.

In May 1990 the CICA sponsored a conference on "criteria of control." The conclusion was that in order to report on internal control the CICA needed to develop systems criteria for internal control similar to GAAP in accounting. Only with such criteria would auditors be able to address Recommendation 49 of the Macdonald Commission Report (1988) to evaluate and report on the design and functioning of internal control systems of financial institutions. With this goal in mind, the CICA's board of governors established the Criteria of Control Committee in 1992. The initial focus of this committee is on financial reporting controls, but an attempt will also be made to develop generic control principles that would also be applicable to operations.

In November 1995 the Criteria of Control Committee of the CICA issued its first publication in the control and governance series, "Guidance on Criteria on Control," or "COCO," for short. The executive summary of the exposure draft provides a useful perspective on the committee's work efforts so far and is therefore reproduced here in full.

The guidance describes and defines control and sets out criteria for its effectiveness. The guidance is applicable to all kinds of organizations, and to part of organizations.

The guidance adopts a broad understanding of control. It involves the coordination of activities toward the achievement of objectives, and includes the identification and mitigation of known risks, the identification and exploitation of opportunities, and the capacity to respond and adapt to the unexpected. Thus, control can provide assurance regarding a broad range of objectives in three general categories: the effectiveness and efficiency of operations, the reliability of financial and management reporting, and compliance with applicable laws and regulations and internal policies.

While people at all levels of an organization participate in control, the decisions and actions of senior management and the board of directors and their level of interest in control set the tone. Management is accountable for control, and therefore needs to assess its overall functioning.

The guidance sets out a control framework, which is a way of looking at an organization so that important aspects of control and relationships between them are apparent. The guidance acknowledges that no one control framework will be perfectly suited to all organizations. It also gives examples of how the criteria can be reorganized into other frameworks, and how other management approaches such as total quality management can be compared to the control framework.

The guidance sets out twenty-three control criteria, stated at a high level in order to be broadly applicable. They address areas such as the culture and values that support good control; objective-setting, risk assessment and planning; control activities that provide assurance that necessary actions are performed; and the monitoring of all aspects of performance to learn what improvements are required. Considerable judgment will be required in applying the criteria, for example, in interpreting them into actionable steps that can be integrated with other management activities; in identifying indicators or early-warning signs so that timely reporting about control can be integrated with reporting about other aspects of performance; and in deciding on the acceptability of risk remaining after control processes have been taken into account.

COCO is written in general, abstract terms in order to provide a flexible framework for future guidelines. The primary intended audience of the guidelines are "auditors who are asked to provide assurance on the reliability of assertions about effectiveness of controls." Control is defined as comprising "those elements of an organization (including its resources, systems, processes, culture, structure, and taxes) that, taken together, support people in the achievement of the organization's objectives."

According to the guidance, key concepts in evaluating controls are as follows:

1. Control is effected by people throughout the organization, including the board of directors or its equivalent,[3] management, and all other staff.

2. People who are accountable, as individuals or teams, for achieving objectives should also be accountable for the effectiveness of control that supports achievement of those objectives.

3. Organizations are constantly interacting and adapting.

4. Control can be expected to provide only reasonable assurance, not absolute assurance.

5. Effective control demands that a balance be maintained:

---

[3] The governing body of a government or not-for-profit entity may be called by a different name. In a unit within an organization, the equivalent to the board of directors is the senior management or other leadership group.

i) Between autonomy and integration—Keeping this balance often involves shifting between centralization and decentralization and between imposing constraints to achieve consistency and granting freedom to act.

ii) Between the statuus quo and adapting to change—Keeping this balance often involves shifting between demanding greater consistency to gain efficiency and granting greater flexibility to respond to change.

Perhaps the most important features of the guidelines are the 20 control criteria they identify. They are quite detailed but can be summarized by the following categories or components:

1. Purpose groups criteria, which provide a sense of the organization's direction. They address:
   - objectives (including mission, vision and strategy)
   - risks (and opportunities)
   - policies
   - planning
   - performance targets and indicators

2. Commitment groups criteria, which provide a sense of the organization's identity and values. They address:
   - ethical values, including integrity
   - human resource policies
   - authority, responsibility, and accountability
   - mutual trust

3. Capability groups criteria, which provide a sense of the organization's competence. They address:
   - knowledge, skills, and tools
   - communication processes
   - information
   - co-ordination
   - control activities

4. Monitoring and learning groups criteria, which provide a sense of the organization's evolution. They address:
   - monitoring internal and external environments
   - monitoring performance
   - challenging assumptions
   - reassessing information needs and information systems
   - follow-up procedures
   - assessing the effectiveness of control

The basic control framework consists of the definition of control and the criteria as summarized by the broad categories.

Reaction to the criteria appear to be favourable so far. They are consistent with the Canadian philosophy of developing guidelines that are not too detailed so that they resemble a "cookbook" approach to evaluating controls. The committee deliberately crafted the criteria at a high level so that they could be applied to all systems at all organizations. There is considerable scope for experimentation and creativity, and auditors will have to use considerable professional judgment in applying the criteria to specific situations.

There is a comparable effort in the United States titled Internal Control—An Integrated Framework (commonly referred to as COSO). Although both COCO and COSO have the same objective of providing guidance about control and criteria for control, COCO builds on COSO by expanding the notion of what control is and taking a particularly people-oriented approach.

At the present time the guidance will not be included in the *CICA Handbook*. The guidance therefore will not have the authority of *Handbook* accounting or auditing recommendations. A member's decision to use the control guidance to assess internal controls will depend on whether he or she finds the guidance useful and relevant. In this sense the guidance is somewhat experimental.

A second project of the CICA Criteria of Control Committee is the Guidance for Directors—Governance processes for control issued in December 1995. This is the second in a series addressing various aspects of control systems. The purpose of the document is to set out guidance on governance processes to meet the responsibilities of board of directors to control.

It identifies six key areas of board control responsibilities.

1. Establishing and monitoring the organization's ethical values.
2. Approval and monitoring of mission, vision, and strategy.
3. Overseeing external communication.
4. Evaluating senior management.
5. Monitoring management control systems.
6. Assessing the board's effectiveness.

The primary focus of the document and of Guidance on Criteria of Control is shown in Exhibit 14–16. This exhibit illustrates the evolving framework for evaluating management and operational controls as part of the internal control framework. To assist auditors in interpreting this guidance relative to other authoritative pronouncements, the Criteria of Control Committee prepared a degree of authoritativeness framework, which is presented in Exhibit 14–17. This exhibit makes clear that the control and governance series are not intended to become *Handbook* recommendations at the current time. Instead, the intent seems to be to get client organizations to experiment with the framework until a more fine-tuned standard can be developed. The resulting framework will probably first be used for internal reporting with an eventual goal of developing sufficiently articulated and supported standards for external reporting purposes. Because of the complexity and pervasiveness of internal controls, the due process for developing reporting and auditing standards on internal control will probably take considerably longer than is usual in developing *Handbook* recommendations.

Special Reports: Service Organizations

Occasionally, some clients' transactions are handled by a **service organization**—another business that executes or records transactions, or both, on behalf of the client. Examples of service organizations include computer data-processing service centres, trust departments of banks, insurers that maintain the accounting records for ceded insurance (reinsurance transactions), mortgage bankers and trust companies that service loans for owners, and transfer agents that handle the shareholder accounting for mutual and money market investment funds. An auditor may need information

E X H I B I T 14-16   (from CICA's Criteria of Control Guidance)

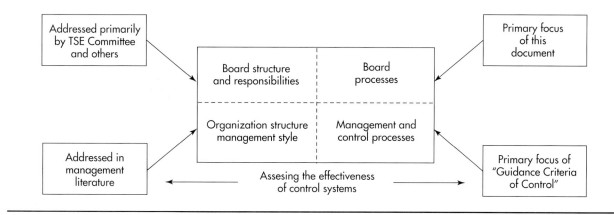

E X H I B I T 14-17   (from CICA's Criteria of Control Guidance)

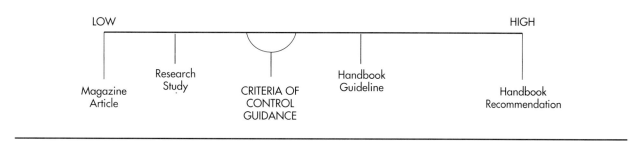

about the service organization's control over their mutual client's transactions. However, the auditor may not have access to do the work when the service organization is not an audit client. This situation is described in Exhibit 14–18.

In such situations all the parties concerned—the user auditor and its client organization, and the service auditor and its client (the service organization)—co-operate to try to enable the user auditor to obtain enough information about controls that affect the audit client's transactions. Certain special-purpose reports on internal accounting control (described more fully in *Section* 5900) can be relied on by the user auditor in connection with the assessment of control risk of the client organization. The reports provide opinions about the service organization's controls as they are applied to the client organization's transactions. Ordinarily, service auditors' reports are not public reports on internal controls. They are used mainly by other auditors.

Section 5900 describes the form of report under several conditions. In particular, the opinion paragraph should express an opinion on whether the stated internal control objectives were achieved and the control procedures exist either at a point in time or throughout the period covered by the service auditor. Exhibit 14–19 illustrates a report on control procedures at a specified point in time while Exhibit 14–20 illustrates a report on control effectiveness over a specified time period.

EXHIBIT 14–18

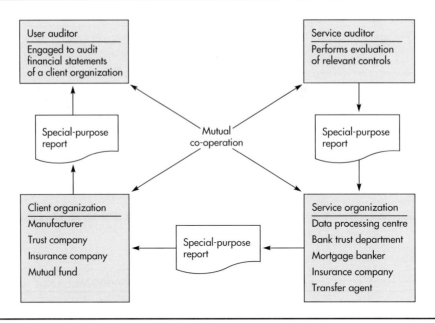

EXHIBIT 14–19   **AUDITOR'S REPORT ON CONTROL PROCEDURES** (from *Handbook Section* 5900.12)

To Y Service Organization

I have examined the accompanying description of the stated internal control objectives of X system of Y Service Organization and the control procedures designed to achieve those objectives and have performed tests of the existence of those control procedures as at June 30, 19X1. My examination was made in accordance with generally accepted auditing standards, and accordingly included such tests and other procedures as I considered necessary in the circumstances.

In my opinion, the control procedures included in the accompanying description were suitably designed to provide reasonable, but not absolute, assurance that the stated internal control objectives of the system described therein were achieved and the control procedures existed as at June 30, 19X1.

As I tested the existence of the control procedures only as at June 30, 19X1, I do not express an opinion on whether the control procedures existed at any other time.

City   (signed) . . . .
July 15, 19X1   CHARTERED ACCOUNTANT

Other Communication on Control and Other Matters

Regulators, Parliaments, and the public have been concerned about auditors' communication of internal control and other matters to high levels in public corporations, especially in banks and other financial institutions. In response, the CICA issued two Guidelines that address auditors' responsibilities to (1) communicate internal control matters noted in an audit (*Section* 5750), and (2) communicate certain matters to the audit committee of the board of directors (AUG–11, "Communications with Audit Committees (or equivalent)").

EXHIBIT 14–20   AUDITOR'S REPORT ON CONTROL PROCEDURES (from *Handbook Section* 5900.12)

To B Service Organization

I have examined the accompanying description of the stated internal control objectives of A system of B Service Organization and the control procedures designed to achieve those objectives and have performed tests of the effectiveness of those control procedures for the period from January 1, 19X1 to June 30, 19X1. My examination was made in accordance with generally accepted auditing standards, and accordingly included such tests and other procedures as I considered necessary in the circumstances.

In my opinion, the control procedures included in the accompanying description were suitably designed to provide reasonable, but not absolute, assurance that the stated internal control objectives of the system described therein were achieved, and the control procedures operated effectively from January 1, 19X1 to June 30, 19X1.

City   (signed) . . . .
July 15, 19X1   CHARTERED ACCOUNTANT

EXHIBIT 14–21   COMMUNICATION OF MATTERS IDENTIFIED DURING THE FINANCIAL STATEMENT AUDIT

During the course of my audit of . . . . for the year ended . . . . I identified matters which may be of interest to management. The objective of an audit is to obtain reasonable assurance whether the financial statements are free of material misstatement and it is not designed to identify matters that may be of interest to management in discharging its responsibilities. Accordingly an audit would not usually identify all such matters.

The matters identified were . . . .

This communication is prepared solely for the information of management and is not intended for any other purpose. I accept no responsibility to a third party who uses this communication.

Source: Handbook Section 5750.08

When performing an audit, auditors may notice **reportable matters.** These include significant deficiencies in the design or operation of the company's internal control structure, which could adversely affect the organization's ability to record, process, summarize, and report financial data in conformity with GAAP (AUG–13, "Special Reports on Regulated Financial Institutions"). Auditing standards do not require auditors to search for reportable matters, but they do require auditors to report the ones that come to their attention (*Section* 5750). The report, preferably in writing, is to be addressed to the management, or the board of directors or its audit committee. An illustration of such a report is in Exhibit 14–21.

Auditors often issue another type of report to management called a management letter. This letter may contain commentary and suggestions on a variety of matters in addition to internal control matters. Examples are operational and administrative efficiency, business strategy, and profit-making possibilities. These management letters are not required by auditing standards. They are a type of management advice rendered as a part of an audit. (An illustration of a management letter is shown in Chapter 13—Exhibit 13–10—in connection with completing the audit.)

The concern about reporting control-related matters within a company has spilled over into a set of other important matters that auditors are required to report to companies' audit committees (AUG–11, "Communications with Audit Committees [or equivalent]"). The purpose of these communications is to enhance the audit committees' ability to oversee the audit functions (external and internal) in a company. The auditors are responsible for informing the audit committee about these matters:

- Independent auditors' responsibilities regarding financial statements and other information in documents that include the audited financial statements (e.g., the annual report to shareholders, filings with the regulatory agencies such as the OSC or Superintendent of Financial Institutions).
- Management's significant accounting policies.
- Management judgments about accounting estimates used in the financial statements.
- Significant audit adjustments recommended by the auditors.
- Disagreements with management about accounting principles, accounting estimates, the scope of the audit, disclosures in the notes, and the wording of the audit report.
- The auditor's view on accounting matters on which management has consulted with other accountants.
- Major accounting and auditing issues discussed with management in connection with beginning or continuing an auditor-client relationship.
- Illegal acts.
- Difficulties with management encountered while performing the audit—delays in starting the audit or providing information, unreasonable time schedule, unavailability of client personnel, and failure of client personnel to complete data schedules.

Internal auditors also have responsibilities for reporting to a company's board of directors. Statement on Internal Auditing Standards No. 7 ("Communicating with the Board of Directors") states that the director of internal auditing should have direct communication with the board. In particular, significant findings about irregularities, illegal acts, errors, inefficiency, waste, ineffectiveness, conflicts of interest, and control deficiencies should be reviewed with the management, then communicated to the board of directors and its audit committee. As with the external auditors, these communications are designed to inform the board and the audit committee so that they can fulfil their responsibilities.

R E V I E W
CHECKPOINTS

14.13 Does the standard public report on internal control give the opinion known as "positive assurance?"

14.14 What reports on control and other matters are auditors required to give to a company's management, board of directors, or audit committee?

14.15 What two types of engagements can produce an auditor's written report on internal control intended for external use? Describe the reports in general terms.

FORECASTS AND PROJECTIONS

. . . .

LEARNING OBJECTIVE

6. Define the various financial presentations and levels of service involved in association with financial forecasts and projections, and write compilation and examination reports.

Accountants are associated with prospective financial information when a client requests them to help assemble or submit a report on a forecast or projection. Several provincial securities commissions have encouraged publication of forecasts. For example, the OSC has allowed forecasts since 1984. In September 1989 the CICA issued a new *Handbook* pronouncement (*Section* 4250), dealing with accounting issues involved with forecasts, or more generally, future-oriented financial information (FOFI). At the same time, an auditing and related services guideline was issued covering the examination of a financial forecast or projection included in a prospectus or other public offering document. In February 1993 the CICA issued an auditing guideline for compilation of a financial forecast or projection (AUG–16).

When accountants have compiled, examined, or helped prepare prospective financial statements, they should render a report on them. The characteristics of compilation and examination of prospective financial statements are explored later in this section.

Presentation Guides

Prospective financial statements can be completed in the same format as historical statements or less than complete, but in any event they must contain the following items (if applicable in the circumstances):

    a. Sales or gross revenue.

    b. Gross profit or cost of sales.

    c. Unusual or infrequently occurring items.

    d. Provision for income taxes.

    e. Discontinued operations or extraordinary items.

    f. Income from continuing operations.

    g. Net income.

    h. Primary and fully diluted earnings per share.

    i. Significant changes in financial position.

    j. Statement that assumptions are based on current information, with a warning that the prospective results may not be achieved.

    k. Summary of significant assumptions.

    l. Summary of significant accounting policies.

These items are what usually appear in historical financial statements for a future period, and so FOFI should be prepared in accordance with the accounting policies expected to be used in the future period (*Section* 4250.18).

Any presentation omitting one or more of the items (*a*) through (*l*) in this list is considered a partial presentation, not a prospective financial statement. Partial and pro forma presentations are not covered by the standards and not recommended for public use.

With the minimum items listed, the nature of prospective financial statements can be one of these:

1. **Financial forecast.** A forecast presents, to the best of the preparer's knowledge and belief, an entity's expected financial position, results of operations, and changes in financial position (cash flow). A forecast is based on assumptions about expected conditions and expected courses of action.

2. **Financial projection.** A projection is similar to a forecast, with the important exception that a projection depends on one or more **hypothetical assumption(s).** A hypothetical assumption expresses a condition and course of action the issuer expects could take place. A projection answers the questions: "What might happen if . . . ?" For example, a promoter trying to sell limited partnership interests in a new hotel project might present a cash flow projection based on the hypothetical assumption: "What will be the cash flow if annual hotel room occupancy averages 75 percent?" Financial projections may be multiple projections based on a range of hypothetical assumptions (e.g., hotel room occupancy of 50 percent, 75 percent, and 90 percent). A preparer should reasonably expect the future results to fall within the range, however.

Reporting on Prospective Financial Statements

Accountants can report on forecasts and projections three ways. The primary objective of association with forecasts and projections is to lend credibility to them—similar to the assurance objective related to historical financial statements.

1. **Examination of prospective financial statements.** An examination of a forecast or projection is a substantial task. For all practical purposes, it is the equivalent of an audit because the accountant is expected to:

- Evaluate the preparation of the prospective financial statements.

- Evaluate the support underlying the assumptions.

- Evaluate the presentation for conformity with *Section* 4250 presentation recommendations.

- Issue an examination report stating (*a*) whether the prospective financial statements are presented in conformity with CICA standards, (*b*) whether the assumptions provide a reasonable basis for the forecast or projection, and (*c*) a disclaimer as to achievability of the forecast.

Exhibit 14–22 organizes the forecast/projection examination guidelines. You should compare them to the assurance and GAAS standards in Exhibit 2–1.

2. **Compilation of prospective financial statements.** A compilation involves considerably less work than an examination. Compilation procedures mainly facilitate the mechanical preparation of the forecast or projection presentation. The accountants are not expected to gather a significant amount of supporting evidence. However, they are expected to notice assumptions that are obviously inappropriate in the circumstances. These compilation procedures are very similar to the ones specified for a compilation of unaudited historical financial statements.

3. **Application of agreed-upon procedures.** Clients can engage accountants for specified work on forecasts and projections by establishing the nature and scope of the work. In such arrangements (*a*) the users of the statements and accountant's report must take responsibility for the adequacy of the agreed-upon procedures for their purposes, (*b*) the report is to be restricted to these users, and (*c*) the prospective financial statements must contain a summary of significant assumptions. These engagements are the means of obtaining tailored services, so they can take a wide variety of specifications. The accountant's report is similarly tailored to the circumstances.

EXHIBIT 14–22   **FORECAST/PROJECTION GUIDELINES**

1. The examination should be performed by a person or persons having adequate technical training and proficiency to examine prospective financial statements.
2. In all matters related to the examination of prospective financial statements, the accountant should be independent.
3. Due professional care should be exercised in the performance of the examination and the preparation of the report.
4. The work should be adequately planned and assistants, if any, should be properly supervised.
5. Sufficient appropriate evidence should be obtained to provide a reasonable basis for the examination report.
6. The examination report should be given an opinion that the prospective financial statements are presented in conformity with presentation guidelines and that the underlying assumptions provide a reasonable basis for the forecast.
7. The report should give a caveat that the prospective results may not be achieved.
8. The examination report should identify the prospective financial statements and state that the examination of them was made in accordance with standards established by the CICA.
9. The report should contain a statement that the accountant assumes no responsibility to update the report for events and circumstances occurring after the date of the report.

EXHIBIT 14–23   **NOTICE TO READER ON THE COMPILATION OF A FINANCIAL FORECAST (from CICA Guideline AUG–16, February 1993, para. 22)**

To:.....

I have compiled the financial forecast of .... consisting of a balance sheet as at (date) and statements of income, retained earnings and changes in financial position for the (period) then ending using assumptions with an effective date of ...., and other information provided by management. My engagement was performed in accordance with the applicable guidance on compilation of a financial forecast issued by The Canadian Institute of Chartered Accountants.

A compilation is limited to presenting, in the form of a financial forecast, information provided by management and does not include evaluating the support for the assumptions or other information underlying the forecast. Accordingly, I do not express an opinion or any other form of assurance on the financial forecast or assumptions. Further, since this financial forecast is based on assumptions regarding future events, actual results will vary from the information presented and the variations may be material. I have no responsibility to update this communication for events and circumstances occurring after the date of this communication.

City   (signed) . . . .
Date   CHARTERED ACCOUNTANT

Reports on Prospective Financial Statements

Standard compilation and examination reports on forecasts are reproduced in Exhibits 14–23 and 14–24. The reports identify the financial statements and describe the accountant's work. The compilation report contains a disclaimer. It offers no conclusions or any other form of assurance. The examination report, in contrast, gives the accountant's conclusions about proper presentation and about the reasonableness of the assumptions.

In an engagement to examine (audit) and report on a forecast or projection, accountants can give opinions that are unqualified (see Exhibit 14–24), qualified, or adverse, or that are disclaimers resulting from scope limitations. The qualified or adverse opinions are given when the forecast or projection omits some information required to be presented by *Section* 4250. The adverse opinion is given when the presentation fails to disclose significant assumptions and when significant assump-

EXHIBIT 14–24   **AUDITOR'S REPORT ON FINANCIAL FORECAST (from CICA Guideline AUG–6, September 1989, para 43)**

To the Directors of ....

The accompanying financial forecast of .... consisting of a balance sheet as at (date) and the statements of income, retained earnings and changes in financial position for the (period(s)) then ending has been prepared by management using assumptions with an effective date of .... I have examined the support provided by management for the assumptions, and the preparation and presentation of this forecast. My examination was made in accordance with the applicable Auditing Guideline issued by The Canadian Institute of Chartered Accountants. I have no responsibility to update this report for events and circumstances occurring after the date of my report.

In my opinion:

- as at the date of this report, the assumptions developed by management are suitably supported and consistent with the plans of the Company, and provide a reasonable basis for the forecast;
- this forecast reflects such assumptions; and
- the financial forecast complies with the presentation and disclosure standards for forecasts established by the Canadian Institute of Chartered Accountants.

Since this forecast is based on assumptions regarding future events, actual results will vary from the information presented and the variations my be material. Accordingly, I express no opinion as to whether this forecast will be achieved.

City
Date

(signed) . . . .
CHARTERED ACCOUNTANT

---

tions are not reasonable. The disclaimer is given when necessary examination procedures are not performed.

An accountant should not write a report that may lead readers to believe that he or she attests to the achievability of the prospective results. You can see in Exhibit 14–24 that the accountant's report lends credibility and assurance to the forecast, but it does not attest to achievability. Accountants must be independent to give the examination report, and this independence includes independence from all promoters using the forecast to organize or market a venture as well as independence from the entity being promoted.

A recent OSC study found that forecasts issued in 1990 and 1991 were inaccurate by a larger margin than in previous surveys. According to this study, 77 percent of established firms surveyed overestimated their profit, compared with 71 percent in an earlier survey. Moreover, 62 percent overestimated profit by more than 20 percent, up from 51 percent who did so in the previous survey.

In a *Globe and Mail* article, portfolio manager John Saltz of Bolton Tremblay said that management is likely to be biased and optimistic. "I don't pay for stocks based on management's forecast of future earnings."

He also complained about the auditor's role. "The auditor says that the forecast is fine based on underlying assumptions but they don't comment on the underlying assumptions."

The OSC's acting head of corporate finance, Ram Ramachandran, said the audit requirement "may unconsciously add an element of respectability" and lead people to rely too much on the document. Auditors are working in a new area—forecasting—and "the process may not lend itself to crystal ball gazing. As a result, Ontario may ban forecasts altogether."[4]

A recent comprehensive study of financial statement user needs by the AICPA known commonly as the Jenkins Report found that "in general, users do not expect

---

[4] "Ontario may ban firm's profit forecasts," *The Globe and Mail*, March 1, 1994, p. B3.

management to provide forecasted financial statements. They are concerned about the reliability of the information and believe that forecasting financial performance is a function of financial analysis rather than business reporting."[5] Instead, users prefer improved disclosure of risks, uncertainties, and opportunities—key aspects on which to base forecasts. The Jenkins Report will probably have a major impact on reporting and ultimately auditing.

· ·

R E V I E W
C H E C K P O I N T S

14.16   How are prospective financial statements defined?

14.17   What are the similarities and differences between examination reports on forecasts and audit reports on historical financial statements? on compilation reports on forecasts? on compilation reports on historical financial statements?

14.18   Why is the OSC considering a ban on financial forecasts?

· ·

Financial Statements for Use in Other Countries
· · · · · · · · · · · · ·

LEARNING   OBJECTIVE
7. Describe the new umbrella standards for assurance engagements.

Auditors practising in Canada are more and more often being asked to report on a Canadian company's financial statements that are intended for use in other countries, especially the United States. Such financial statements may be used by foreign investors or by foreign parent companies for consolidation in foreign financial statements. For many years, American auditors have obtained financial statements of foreign companies and of subsidiaries of U.S.-based multinational companies for consolidation in a U.S. parent company's financial statements. These foreign statements have been prepared on the basis of U.S. GAAP by foreign managements and auditors, even while the foreign company's statements may also be prepared on the basis of foreign GAAP in other countries for use in those countries.

With increasing globalization of corporate ownership, the shoe is on the other foot, and many U.S. companies are owned by foreign parents. Now, the U.S. company's financial statements must be prepared on the basis of accounting principles used in other countries.

In engagements requiring use of foreign standards, Canadian auditors are expected to follow the Canadian general and field work auditing standards, just as they would in any audit. However, some differences in accounting may arise, and these will change some of the audit objectives. For example, some South American countries permit or require general price-level adjusted measurements (because of high rates of inflation), and these management calculations, applied to the Canadian company's account balances, will need to be audited. Likewise, some countries do not permit recognition of deferred taxes, so no deferred tax account balances will exist for audit. Clearly, the auditors must know the accounting principles applied in the country for which the financial statements are intended. The starting place is in

[5]   AICPA Special Committee on Financial Reporting, "Improving Business Reporting: A Customer Focus—Making the Information Needs of Investors and Creditors" (Jenkins Report), AICPA, 1994, pp. 11–15.

the International Accounting Standards established by the International Accounting Standards Committee.

In addition to knowing the foreign accounting principles, the Canadian auditor may be expected to apply foreign auditing standards and procedures. Some countries have codified their auditing standards in professional literature, like Canada, while others put their auditing standards in statutes and legal-like regulations. They may, in some cases, require more auditing of compliance with laws and regulations or other procedures than Canadian standards require. The audit report can take different forms, depending on the circumstances and the distribution of the foreign-GAAP financial statements:

A. Foreign-GAAP financial statements used only outside Canada. The options are:
  1. A Canadian-style report modified to refer to the GAAP of the other country (similar to an AADBA report).
  2. The report form used by auditors in the other country.

B. Foreign-GAAP financial statements that will have more than limited distribution in Canada. The options are:
  1. The CICA standard report, qualified or adverse for departures from Canadian GAAP, with another separate paragraph expressing an opinion on the fair presentation in conformity with the foreign GAAP.
  2. Both (*a*) the report form used by auditors in the other country (A2 above) or a Canadian-style report modified to refer to the GAAP of the other country (A1 above), and (*b*) the qualified or adverse Canadian standard report with an additional paragraph expressing an opinion on the foreign GAAP (B1 above).

C. Two sets of financial statements, foreign GAAP and Canadian GAAP, both of which may be distributed in the foreign country and in Canada. Report on each one:
  1. Report on the foreign-GAAP financial statements as in A1 above, with an additional paragraph notifying users that another report has been issued on Canadian GAP financial statements.
  2. Report on Canadian-GAAP financial statements as normally done for Canadian financial statements, but add a paragraph notifying users that another report has been issued on foreign-GAAP financial statements.

When a Canadian client must file with the U.S.'s SEC *and* when there is either a disclaimer due to uncertainty or an explanatory paragraph resulting from a change in accounting principle, a CICA Guideline on Canada–U.S. reporting conflicts should be followed. This Guideline recommends that a Canadian GAAS audit report be issued along with comments that should be added as additional information for American readers.

. . . .

R E V I E W
C H E C K P O I N T S

14.19 Why do you think a Canadian-style report on foreign-GAAP financial statements is similar to a report on AADBA financial statements?

14.20 What precautions should Canadian auditors take when reporting on foreign-GAAP financial statements that will be distributed in the United States?

. . . .

THE ASSURANCE FRAMEWORK

· · · · · · · · · · · ·

Many of the engagements discussed in the preceding sections fell under the new umbrella framework of the assurance engagements issued by the CICA as *Handbook Section* 5025 in April 1997. This standard was introduced in Chapter 2 and compared to GAAS. You should begin by reviewing the discussion there.

The fundamental concept of *Section* 5025 is that of an accountability relationship: "An accountability relationship exists when one party (the 'accountable party') is answerable to and/or responsible to another party (the 'user') for a subject matter or voluntarily chooses to report to another party on a subject matter" (*Section* 5025.04).

An assurance engagement can take place only when there is an accountability relationship. Therefore *Section* 5025.21 makes clear that the auditor needs to obtain evidence that such a relationship exists before taking on an assurance engagement. The usual form of this evidence is acknowledgment of the existence of the relationship by the accountable party, usually management. Failure to obtain such acknowledgment by the accountable party should be disclosed in the practitioner's report.

The existence of the accountability relationship is what distinguishes assurance engagements from other types of engagements such as tax planning and consulting work (*Section* 5025.15). In our discussions in the appendix to this chapter, and subsequent chapters, we will see that the distinctions between assurance and nonassurance engagements can be very fine indeed. Yet they are very important because assurance engagements with respect to financial statements are what distinguish the PA profession from other professional groups. Thus the assurance standards delineate the unique responsibilities of auditors (or, more generally now, the assurers).

The type of communication provided by the practitioner or assurer depends on the nature of the assurance engagement. The CICA envisions two major categories of assurance engagements. Attestation engagements are those in which the practitioner's (attestation) conclusion will be on a written assertion prepared by the accountable party. The assertion is used to evaluate, using suitable criteria, the subject matter for which the accountable party is responsible. The party making the assertion is sometimes referred to as the asserter.

The other category of assurance engagement is a direct reporting engagement. "In a direct reporting engagement, the practitioners' conclusion will evaluate directly using suitable criteria, the subject matter for which the accountable party is responsible" (*Section* 5025.05). By this definition the essential distinction between an assurance and a direct reporting engagement is that the assertions are written out by the asserter in an assurance engagement but may be only implied by the asserter in a direct reporting engagement. Despite this seemingly straightforward distinction, we will see that what exactly is meant by a written assertion is still considered by some to be a controversial matter in the current standard. We will discuss the ramifications of this in the appendix to this chapter, which covers outstanding issues that some consider remain with the standard.

In order to operationalize the above concepts, it is necessary to clarify additional concepts and relate them to the above assurance framework. This is shown in *Section* 5025.08–.13 as follows:

> The practitioner forms a conclusion concerning a subject matter by referring to suitable criteria. Criteria are benchmarks against which the subject matter and, in an attest engagement, mangement's written assertion on the subject matter, can be evaluated.

In an assurance engagement, the practitioner reduces engagement risk to a level that is appropriate for the assurance provided in his or her report. The term engagement risk is the risk that the practitioner may express an inappropriate conclusion. The three components of engagement risk are inherent risk, control risk and detection risk.

Practitioners should in theory be able to vary infinitely the level of assurance provided in assurance engagements. However, in order to help users understand the level of assurance being provided by the practitioner, the standards in this *Section* limit assurance to two distinct levels—a high level and a moderate level.

In an audit engagement, the practitioner provides a high, though not absolute, level of assurance by designing procedures so that in the practitioner's professional judgment, the risk of an inappropriate conclusion is reduced to a low level through procedures such as inspection, observation, enquiry, confirmation, computation, analysis and discussion. Use of the term "high level of assurance" refers to the highest reasonable level of assurance a practitioner can provide concerning a subject matter. Absolute assurance is not attainable as a result of factors such as the use of judgment, the use of testing, the inherent limitations of control and the fact that much of the evidence available to the practitioner is persuasive rather than conclusive in nature. Assurance will also be influenced by the degree of precision associated with the subject matter itself.

In a review engagement, the practitioner provides a moderate level of assurance by designing procedures so that, in the practitioner's professional judgment, the risk of an inappropriate conclusion is reduced to a moderate level through procedures which are normally limited to enquiry, analysis and discussion. Such risk is reduced to a moderate level when the evidence obtained enables the practitioner to conclude the subject matter is plausible in the circumstances.

Both attest engagements and direct reporting engagements can be completed with either a high or a moderate level of assurance. The level of assurance appropriate for a particular engagement will depend on the needs of users and the nature of the subject matter.

With these concepts and definitions it is now possible to develop meaningful standards for assurance engagements. These have already been listed in Chapter 2 and compared to GAAS. As noted there, the assurance standards are subdivided into (*a*) general standards that relate to attributes of the practitioner and the need for the practitioner to use suitable criteria in evaluating a subject matter (for example, criteria for control discussed in this chapter); (*b*) performance standards relating to obtaining sufficient appropriate evidence to support the practitioner's conclusion and documenting the basis for the conclusion including the concepts of significance (materiality) and engagement risk as used in assurance engagements; and (*c*) reporting standards prescribing the minimum requirements of the practitioner's report, including those for reservations and the conditions for issuing a reservation in an assurance engagement report.

The truly novel aspects of these standards deal with suitability of criteria, significance, engagement risk, and the increasing reliance on specialists contemplated by these standards. As we will see in Chapter 17, all of these concepts originated with public sector auditing standards. Given the varied nature of the engagements contemplated by this standard, it is expected that there could be far more reliance on specialists from other fields, and this creates responsibilities on the practitioner to understand the specialists' work to the extent necessary to fulfil the objectives of the engagement. There is an additional responsibility on the part of the specialist to understand the objectives of the engagement at least as to how they relate to the specialists' expertise (*Section* 5025.34). Thus the standards contemplate use of multidisciplinary audit team members to a significantly greater extent than in financial statement audits.

The concept of significance as used in the standard appears to have been influenced by public sector standards (covered in Chapter 17), which use the same concept. Significance can be viewed as an extension of materiality to include broader classes of users whose decisions may be influenced by nonfinancial factors such as, for example, the effectiveness of health care.

Engagement risk is defined in *Section* 5202 as:

> the risk that the practitioner will express an inappropriate conclusion in his or her report. This risk consists of (a) risks that are beyond the control of management and the practitioner (inherent risk), (b) the risks that are within control of management (control risk) and (c) risks that are within the control of the practitioner (detection risk). The extent to which the practitioner considers the relevant components of engagment risk will be affected by the nature of the subject matter and the level of assurance to be provided.

An interesting aspect of this definition of engagement risk and its components is that the risk is no longer limited to (*a*) risk of failing to detect significant misrepresentations or omissions, but also explicitly includes (*b*) the possibility that the practitioner may report significant items that in fact are not significant relative to the users. The traditional concept of audit risk is consistent with (*a*), but risk (*b*) has never before been explicitly considered in the audit risk model because it has been assumed this risk is self-correcting. In other words, if the auditor concludes erroneously that there is a material misstatement it's been assumed that additional work will always point out the error to the auditor. The reason risk (*a*) has traditionally been considered the more serious risk is that when this risk occurs the auditor has no evidence to support the proposition of material misstatement when in fact that is the case. Since the auditor's job can be characterized as finding material misstatements, control of risk (*a*) is the reason the auditor was hired in the first place. By extending the risk definition to include risks of the (*b*) type, the standard has potentially changed the risk model for generalized assurance engagements in a significant way that is not completely consistent with the traditional concept of audit risk. The justification for this perhaps is that in the significantly changed environment of assurance engagements auditors need to be explicitly aware of what should be considered significant for various subject matters. A more complete discussion of this risk definition is provided in the appendix.

Perhaps the most important change introduced by *Section* 5025 is the concept of suitable criteria. *Section* 5025.39 identifies five characteristics of suitable criteria: relevance, reliability, neutrality, understandability, and completeness. Since these criteria are supposed to apply to all assurance engagements including financial statement audits, these criteria introduce a potentially revolutionary link to accounting theory in that new characteristics of accounting information may now be contemplated. Notably, financial statement concepts listed in *Handbook Section* 1000 do not list completeness as a characteristic of financial statements. Currently, this does not create a problem in the standards because *Section* 5025.02 explicitly exempts existing *Handbook Recommendations* from the assurance engagement standard. But in the longer term it appears that some reconciliation may be necessary. Perhaps the most notable aspect of this development is that assurance and accounting standards are for the first time being linked, albeit in a tentative way. Perhaps this indicates a closer co-ordination between accounting and auditing standard setting in the future—a development some consider a long overdue in an increasingly complicated and interrelated business world. This also relates to the focus on accountability relations in assurance engagements, which also happens to be a primary objective of financial statements. In Chapter 17 we will see that suitable criteria and accountability relations are also central concepts in public sector auditing.

The introduction to the standard makes it clear that existing *Handbook Recommendations* override the current standard, but that nevertheless the long-term objective of the standard is to provide guidelines where standards currently do not exist and to provide future guidance on more specific recommendations in assurance engagements. In the scope of *Section 5025.01*, the long-term overall objective is described as follows:

> These standards establish a framework for all assurance engagements performed by practitioners and for the on-going development of related standards. The standards apply to:
>
> *(a)* engagements in the private and public sectors;
>
> *(b)* attest engagements and direct reporting engagements;
>
> *(c)* engagements designed to provide a high (i.e., audit) level of assurance; and
>
> *(d)* engagements designed to provide a moderate (i.e., review) level of assurance
>
> The assurance standard appendix makes it clear that the standards apply only when the practitioner provides a conclusion on a subject matter. The following services are not considered to provide a conclusion on a subject matter.
>
> *(a)* specified auditing procedure engagements (Section 9100)
>
> *(b)* compilation engagements (Section 9200)
>
> *(c)* derivative reporting (Section 5220); and
>
> *(d)* reports on the application of accounting principles, auditing standards, or review standards (Section 7600).

A good overview of the various services and the extent of the PA's involvement is provided as *Section 5020.B*, which is reproduced in the box that follows:

The purpose of this ... is to provide examples of information and the nature and extent of the public accountant's involvement with such information.

NOTE: In addition to the professional responsibilities outlined below, the public accountant would comply with the rules of professional conduct of his or her provincial Institute and would therefore, in all cases, exercise due professional skill and care in the work he or she carries out.

TYPE OF INFORMATION RESPONSIBILITIES	NATURE AND EXTENT OF INVOLVEMENT	NATURE AND EXTENT OF ASSOCIATION	PROFESSIONAL WORK	REPORTING
Information that is the subject matter of an assurance	Assurance engagement	The practitioner has associated himself or herself with the subject matter by virtue of the assurance engagement carried out (see paragraph 5020.04)	The practitioner discharges his or her responsibilities by complying with the Recommendations contained in STANDARDS FOR ASSURANCE ENGAGEMENTS, *Section 5025.*	Reporting section of STANDARDS FOR ASSURANCE ENGAGEMENTS, *Section 5025.*

Continued

TYPE OF INFORMATION RESPONSIBILITIES	NATURE AND EXTENT OF INVOLVEMENT	NATURE AND EXTENT OF ASSOCIATION	PROFESSIONAL WORK	REPORTING
Financial statements REPORT	Audit	The auditor has associated himself or herself with the financial statements by virtue of the audit work carried out (see paragraph 5020.04)	The auditor discharges his or her responsibilities by complying with the Recommendations contained in GENERALLY ACCEPTED AUDITING STANDARDS, *Section* 5100.	THE AUDITOR'S STANDARD *Section* 5400.
Financial statements	Review	The public accountant has associated himself of herself with the financial statements by virtue of the review carried out (see paragraph 5020.04).	The public accountant discharges his or her responsibilities by complying with the relevant Recommendations contained in GENERAL REVIEW STANDARDS, *Section* 8100, or REVIEWS OF FINANCIAL STATEMENTS, *Section* 8200.	GENERAL REVIEW STANDARDS, *Section* 8100, or REVIEWS OF FINANCIAL STATEMENTS, *Section* 8200.
Financial statements	Compilation	The public accountant has associated himself or herself with the financial statements by virtue of compiling the financial statements (see paragraph 5020.04).	The public accountant discharges his or her responsibilities by complying with the relevant Recommendations contained in COMPILATION ENGAGEMENTS, *Section* 9200.	COMPILATION ENGAGEMENTS, *Section* 9200
Financing document containing financial information extracted from the audited financial statements.	Consent to use of the auditor's name in the document in connection with the condensed financial information, by consenting to a statement in the document such as, "This condensed financial information has been extracted from the audited financial statements for the year ended December 31, 1986, previously reported on by our auditors ZYX & Co."	The auditor has associated himself or herself with the financial information by consenting to the use of his or her name in connection with that information (see 5020.04).	The auditor discharges his or her responsibilities by complying with paragraph 5020.13.	No reporting standard. See paragraph 5020.10.
Financing document containing financial information prepared by the client and not reported on by the auditor.	Consent to the inclusion of the auditor's name in the document by, for example, consenting to a factual statement in the document naming lawyers, auditors, etc.	The auditor does not associate himself or herself with the information contained in the document by merely consenting to the inclusion of his or her name in the document (see paragraphs 5020.04 and 5020.16).	The auditor discharges his or her responsibilities by complying with paragraph 5020.17.	No reporting standard. See paragraph 5020.10.
Financial statements	Typing or reproduction services.	The public accountant has associated himself or herself with the financial statements by virtue of the typing or reproduction services carried out (see paragraph 5020.04)	No professional responsibilities other than those discussed in the Note on the first page of this Appendix.	No reporting standard. See paragraph 5020.10.

Continued

TYPE OF INFORMATION RESPONSIBILITIES	NATURE AND EXTENT OF INVOLVEMENT	NATURE AND EXTENT OF ASSOCIATION	PROFESSIONAL WORK	REPORTING
Annual report containing audited financial statements.	To determine whether the financial statements and the auditor's report thereon are accurately reproduced in the annual report. To read the other information in the annual report and consider whether any of this information is inconsistent with the financial statements on which the auditor has reported.	The auditor has already associated himself or herself with the financial statements in the annual report by virtue of the audit work carried out. The auditor has also associated himself or herself with the other information in the annual report by virtue of the work carried out under *Section 7500* (see paragraph 5020.04).	The auditor discharges his or her responsibilities by complying with the Recommendations contained in THE AUDITOR'S INVOLVEMENT ANNUAL REPORT, *Section 7500.*	No reporting standard. See paragraph 5020.10.
Tax return and financial statements as attachments to the tax returns.	Preparation of tax return (financial statements were prepared by the client).	The public accountant has associated himself or herself with the tax return by virtue of preparing it and providing related tax advice (see paragraph 5020.04). The public accountant has not associated himself or herself with the financial statements because he or she has not performed services in respect of the financial statements or consented to the use of his or her name in connection with the financial statements (see paragraph 5020.04).	No professional responsibilities other than those discussed in the Note on the first page of this Appendix.	No reporting standard. See paragraph 5020.10.

Keep in mind that *Section* 5025 is intended to be broad enough to include most of the engagements covered in this chapter, and financial statement audits, as well as many other possible engagements, some of which are covered in later chapters. This is a tall order. Much experimentation and experience will be necessary before *Section* 5025 can be refined. The experience in implementing the standards may also suggest future adjustments to the framework itself. The appendix discusses in more detail some of the controversial aspects of the standards and where future adjustments and clarifications are likely. The appendix also reviews trends in the evolution of assurance standards in the United States and internationally.

For more current information on assurance engagements, the following websites may prove useful.

www.cia.ca	This is the CICA's general website containing all Exposure Drafts and related material outstanding.
www.tiesoft.net/jebcl/	This is a special CICA website for the task force on assurance services.
www.aicpa.org/assurance/ sitemap/index.htm	This the special AICPA website on the many facets of their ongoing assurance services project.

THE ASSOCIATION FRAMEWORK
· · · · · · · · · · · · ·

The public accounting services covered in this chapter are part of the broadest concept of auditor involvement with information about business enterprises—that of association. Compilation and review engagements are forms of association. *Association* is a term generally used within the profession to indicate a public accountant's involvement with an enterprise or with information issued by that enterprise. General standards for association are covered in *Section* 5020 of the *Handbook.*

"Association can arise in three ways:

"1. The public accountant associates himself or herself by some action on his or her part with information issued by the enterprise.

2. When the enterprise indicates that the public accountant was involved with information issued by the enterprises without the public accountant's knowledge or consent.

3. A third party assumes the public accountant is involved with information issued by an enterprise."

A public accountant by *Section* 5020.04 associates herself or himself with information when she or he:

"(*a*) performs services in respect of that information, or
(*b*) consents to use his or her name in connection with that information."

A public accountant's professional responsibilities when he or she is associated with information are the following:

"1. compliance with applicable standards in the *Handbook;*

2. compliance with the rules of professional conduct of his or her provincial institute; and

3. appropriate communication of the extent of his or her involvement with the information."

The public accountant should ensure that the information he or she is associated with is accurate, accurately reproduced, and not misleading. If the client attempts to make inappropriate use of the PA's name, the PA should amend the information or get legal advice.

Exhibit 14–25 provides a framework illustrating the relationships of various types of engagements and *Handbook* sections. As a result of the changes to public accounting brought on by *Section* 5025, the concept of association also had to be revised to incorporate the new assurance framework. The new association responsibilities are illustrated in *Section* 5020. A (see the box on page 652).

This revising of the concept of association has also necessitated changes to PA's responses to various client actions with respect to PA communications. The decision tree summarizing a PA's responsibilities with information or subject matters that he or she is inappropriately associated with is reproduced for *Section* 5020.A (see the box on page 653).

Exhibit 14–25 provides a fairly comprehensive association framework for all assurance engagements.

The CICA and provincial institutes are in the process of sorting out what is public accounting: specifically, should public accounting include or exclude compilations?

This is an important issue for CGAs and other practitioners because if a provincial public accountancy act excludes CGAs, then what CGAs can practise is determined by the definition of public accountancy. The trend appears to be to exclude compilation from the definition of public accountancy.

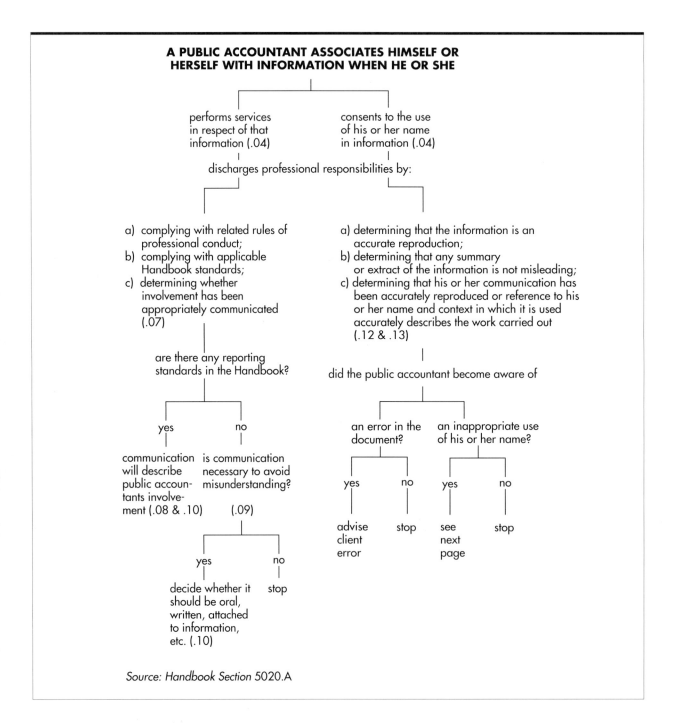

Source: Handbook Section 5020.A

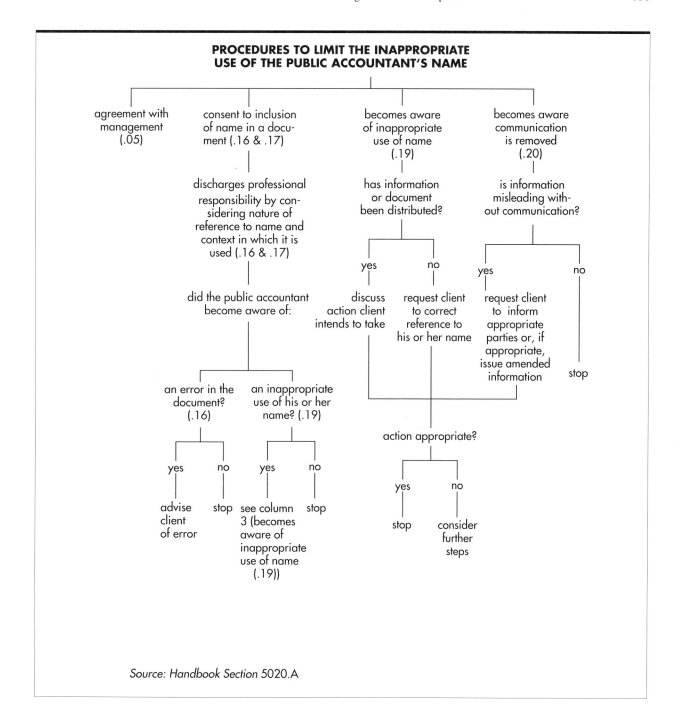

PROCEDURES TO LIMIT THE INAPPROPRIATE USE OF THE PUBLIC ACCOUNTANT'S NAME

agreement with management (.05)

consent to inclusion of name in a document (.16 & .17)

becomes aware of inappropriate use of name (.19)

becomes aware communication is removed (.20)

discharges professional responsibility by considering nature of reference to name and context in which it is used (.16 & .17)

has information or document been distributed?

is information misleading without communication?

did the public accountant become aware of:

yes — discuss action client intends to take

no — request client to correct reference to his or her name

yes — request client to inform appropriate parties or, if appropriate, issue amended information

no — stop

an error in the document? (.16)

an inappropriate use of his or her name? (.19)

yes — advise client of error

no — stop

yes — see column 3 (becomes aware of inappropriate use of name (.19))

no — stop

action appropriate?

yes — stop

no — consider further steps

Source: Handbook Section 5020.A

E X H I B I T   14–25   CURRENT FRAMEWORK FOR ASSOCIATION (as of March 1997)

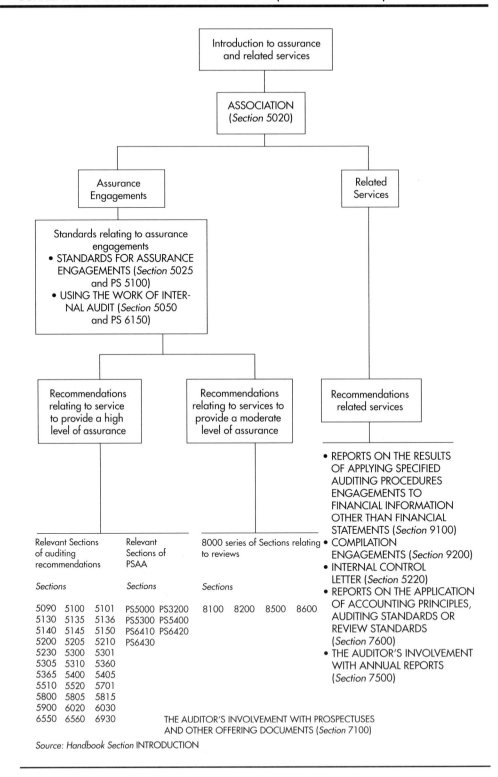

Source: Handbook Section INTRODUCTION

SUMMARY

· ·

Public accountants are highly regarded for assurance services. Many forms of services, in addition to audits of historical financial statements, have arisen or have been proposed. Managers of companies often develop innovative financial presentations, and they want to give the public some assurance about them, so they engage auditors. Regulators also often become interested in PAs' communication of information and press for assurance involvement.

Guided by auditing, accounting, and review services' standards and the general concepts of assurance, PAs offer services and render reports in several areas. These standards were summarized in Exhibit 14–25.

Unaudited financial statements have been around for a long time. Work on them is known in public practice as review and compilation. The difference lies in the amount of work performed and the level of assurance given in an accountant's report. Review engagements involve less work than an audit, and the report gives a low level of negative assurance instead of an audit opinion. Compilation engagements involve merely writing up the financial statements, which is less work than a review, and the report gives no assurance in the form of an outright denial.

Another type of review is accountants' review of interim financial information (e.g., quarterly financial reports). This review is technically similar to a review of unaudited financial statements, and the report on free-standing interim financial statements gives the negative assurance.

Not everyone wants to produce financial statements fully in conformity with generally accepted accounting principles. Managers have the option to prepare their statements for public use on an "another appropriate disclosed basis of accounting" (AADBA). Auditors can audit and report on such financial statements. This track gives managers an opportunity to avoid the complications of many of the GAAP rules. AADBA audits and reporting are in the auditing standards under the heading of "special reports." Other kinds of special audit reports can be given on parts of financial statements and on current value financial statements.

A special kind of engagement can result in a report on a company's internal control. This report is a positive assurance report on the internal control system. Regulators in some provinces, the SEC, and federal banking agencies have been interested in management reports and audit reports on internal control. This topic of reporting on internal control spills over into auditing standards designed to require auditors to report internally to managers and the board of directors in a company about internal control deficiencies and relations with management in connection with the annual audit.

Innovative managers and promoters frequently use forecasts and projections (known collectively as FOFI) to obtain investors and otherwise inform financial statement users about their estimates of future performance. Auditors can get involved with such presentations by examining or compiling forecasts and projections. In a report on an examination, which is similar to an audit, the accountant gives assurances about the reasonableness of the assumptions underlying the forecast or projection.

The next section in the chapter outlined auditors' responsibilities for reporting on financial statements prepared in accordance with the accounting principles generally accepted in other countries.

Next, the chapter covered the CICA's recent attempt to develop an umbrella framework for many of the PA services via the assurance engagement concept. The chapter concluded with a modified framework for all PA services resulting from introduction of the assurance engagement concept.

Multiple-choice Questions for Practice and Review

. . . .

14.21 Which of the following can be considered a prospective financial statement?
   a. Balance sheet based on current values of assets and liabilities.
   b. Interim-date balance sheet for the first quarter of the fiscal year.
   c. Forecasted income statement based on assumptions about expected conditions and expected conditions and expected courses of action.
   d. Forecasted valuation of securities held by a venture capital company.

14.22 Which of the following statements is correct?
   a. An examination report on prospective financial statements gives the same assurance as an audit report on historical financial statements.
   b. An examination report on prospective financial statements does not attest to the achievability of the forecast.
   c. In a compilation report on prospective financial statements, an accountant attests to the reasonableness of the underlying forecast assumptions.
   d. In reports on prospective financial statements, accountants undertake the obligation to update the reports for important subsequent events.

14.23 Under the Securities and Exchange Commission "safe harbour" rule regarding financial forecasts, persons connected with a company's forecast can be liable for monetary damages if:
   a. The plaintiffs are able to prove that the persons connected with the forecast showed lack of good faith and lack of a reasonable basis for belief in the forecast.
   b. The plaintiffs are able to prove that the persons connected with the forecast were merely negligent.
   c. The persons connected with the forecast had good faith and a reasonable basis for belief in its presentation.
   d. The persons connected with a forecast cannot sustain the burden of proof that they acted in good faith and with a reasonable basis for belief in the forecast.

14.24 In a current-value presentation of the balance sheet of a manufacturing company:
   a. The basis of valuation must always be explained in notes to the financial statements.
   b. The basis of valuation is well known as a "comprehensive basis of accounting other than GAAP."
   c. An auditor can attest to the fair presentation of financial position in conformity with GAAP.
   d. The company must follow the AICPA guides for presentation of a financial forecast.

14.25 Practice in connection with unaudited historical-cost financial statements is conducted by:
   a. International accounting firms only.
   b. Regional- and local-size PA firms.
   c. Local-size PA firms only.
   d. All PA firms.

14.26 The official CICA Recommendations for Compilation and Review services are applicable to practice with:
   a. Audited financial statements of public companies.
   b. Unaudited financial statements of some companies.
   c. Unaudited financial statements of all companies.
   d. Audited financial statements of nonpublic companies.

14.27 A review service engagement for an accountant's association with unaudited financial statements involves:
   a. More work than a compilation, and more than an audit.
   b. Less work than an audit, but more than a compilation.
   c. Less work than a compilation, but more than an audit.
   d. More work than an audit, but less than a compilation.

14.28 When an accountant is not independent, the following report can nevertheless be given:

a. Compilation report.

b. Standard unqualified audit report.

c. Examination report on a forecast.

d. Review report on unaudited financial statements.

14.29 An accountant is permitted to express "negative assurance" in which of the following types of reports.

a. Standard unqualified audit report on audited financial statements.

b. Compilation report on unaudited financial statements.

c. Review report on unaudited financial statements.

d. Adverse opinion report on audited financial statements.

14.30 When a company's financial statements in a review or compilation engagement contain a known material departure from GAAP, the accountant's report can:

a. Make no mention of the departure in a compilation report because it contains an explicit disclaimer of opinion.

b. Express the adverse conclusion: "The accompanying financial statements are not presented in conformity with generally accepted accounting principles."

c. Explain the departure as necessary to make the statements not misleading, then give the standard compilation report disclaimer.

d. Explain the departure as necessary to make the statements not misleading, then give the standard review report negative assurance.

14.31 When interim financial information is presented in a note to annual financial statements, the standard audit report on the annual financial statements should:

a. Not mention the interim information unless there is an exception the auditor needs to include in the report.

b. Contain an audit opinion paragraph that specifically mentions the interim financial information if it is not in conformity with GAAP.

c. Contain an extra paragraph that gives negative assurance on the interim information, if it has been reviewed.

d. Contain an extra explanatory paragraph if the interim information note is labelled "unaudited."

14.32 According to auditing standards, financial statements presented on an other comprehensive basis of accounting should not:

a. Contain a note describing the other basis of accounting.

b. Describe in general how the other basis of accounting differs from generally accepted accounting principles.

c. Be accompanied by an audit report that gives an unqualified opinion with reference to the other basis of accounting.

d. Contain a note with a quantified dollar reconciliation of the assets based on the other comprehensive basis of accounting with the assets based on generally accepted accounting principles.

14.33 For which of the following reports is an expression of negative assurance not permitted?

a. A review report on unaudited financial statements.

b. An audit report on financial statements prepared on a comprehensive basis of accounting other than GAAP.

c. A report based on applying selected procedures agreed upon by the client and the auditor.

d. A review report on interim financial information.

14.34 Which one of these events is an auditor not required to communicate to a company's audit committee or board of directors?

a. Management's significant accounting policies.

b. Management judgments about accounting estimates used in the financial statements.

c. Immaterial errors in processing transactions discovered by the auditors.

d. Disagreements with management about accounting principles.

EXERCISES AND PROBLEMS

14.35 Review of Forecast Assumptions. You have been engaged by the Dodd Manufacturing Corporation to attest to the reasonableness of the assumptions underlying its forecast of revenues, costs, and net income for the next calendar year, 1994. Four of the assumptions are shown below.

a. The company intends to sell certain real estate and other facilities held by Division B at an aftertax profit of $600,000; the proceeds of this sale will be used to retire outstanding debt.

b. The company will call and retire all outstanding 9 percent subordinated debentures (callable at 108). The debentures are expected to require the full call premium given present market interest rates of 8 percent on similar debt. A rise in market interest rates to 9 percent would reduce the loss on bond retirement from the projected $200,000 to $190,000.

c. Current labour contracts expire on September 1, 1994, and the new contract is expected to result in a wage increase of 5.5 percent. Given the forecasted levels of production and sales, aftertax operating earnings would be reduced approximately $50,000 for each percentage-point wage increase in excess of the expected contract settlement.

d. The sales forecast for Division A assumes that the new Portsmouth facility will be complete and operating at 40 percent of capacity on February 1, 1994. It is highly improbable that the facility will be operational before January of 1994. Each month's delay would reduce sales of Division A by approximately $80,000 and operating earnings by $30,000.

Required:

For each assumption, state the evidence sources and procedures you would use to determine the reasonableness.

14.36 Auditing a Current Value Balance Sheet. Your client, the Neighbourhood Paper Company (NPC), has a fiscal year-end of December 31. NPC needs to borrow money from a local bank and believes current value financial statements that report the appreciated value of its assets would be helpful. A loan is needed for working capital purposes.

NPC owns two paper-recycling processors. Old paper is chemically processed, reduced to a wet mass, and then pressed out into thick, semifinished paper mats. The mats are sold to customers who use them for packing material. Recycling processors are fairly complex pieces of integrated machinery and are built on a customized basis by a few specialized engineering companies.

NPC has owned one of the processors for five years. It was appraised last year at $135,000 by a qualified engineering appraiser. The second processor was purchased last month for $125,000—its appraised value—and $10,000 was spent in bringing certain maintenance up to date. Both processors have identical throughput production capabilities.

The other major asset is a nine-acre plot of land NPC bought four years ago when management thought the plant would be moved. The land was purchased for $195,000 and was appraised by a qualified appraiser at $250,000 only 20 months after the purchase date. The nine acres are located near a rapidly expanding industrial area.

Since the recycling processors were appraised/purchased so recently, management does not want to bear the expense of new appraisals this year. No plans have been made to obtain a new appraisal on the land. NPC, however, is a profitable operation. The unaudited income statement for the current year (historical-cost basis) shows net income of $46,000.

Required:

a. What practice standards are applicable to the engagement to review and report on the current value balance sheet?

b. What primary auditing procedures should you apply in addition to those necessary for the audit of the historical-cost financial statements?

c. Will any additional disclosures in footnotes be necessary?

d. Are there any evidential problems in the NPC situation that might prevent your rendering a report on the current value balance sheet?

14.37 Compilation Presentation Alternatives. Jimmy C operates a large service station, garage, and truck stop on Freeway 95 near Plainview. His brother, Bill, has recently joined as a partner, even though he still keeps a small PA practice. One slow afternoon, they were discussing financial statements with Bert, the local PA who operates the largest public practice in Plainview.

Jimmy: The business is growing, and sometimes I need to show financial statements to parts suppliers and to the loan officers at the bank.

Bert: That so.

Jimmy: Yea-boy, and they don't like the way I put 'em together.

Bert: That so.

Bill: Heck, Jimmy, I know all about that. I can compile a jim-dandy set of financial statements for us.

Jimmy: What does Jim Dan over at the café have to do with it?

Bert: Never mind, Jimmy. Bill can't do compiled financial statements for you. He's not independent.

Jimmy: I know, Momma didn't let him outa the house 'til he was 24. The neighbors complained.

Bert: That so.

Bill: Shucks.

Jimmy: But Bert, those fellas are always asking me about accounting policies, contingencies, and stuff like that. Said something about "footnotes." I don't want to fool with all that small print.

Required:

Think about the financial disclosure problems of Jimmy and Bill's small business. What three kinds of compiled financial statements can be prepared for them and by whom?

14.38 Negative Assurance in Review Reports. One portion of the report on a review services engagement is the following: Based on my review, I am not aware of any material modifications that should be made to the accompanying financial statements in order for them to be in conformity with generally accepted accounting principles.

Required:

a. Is this paragraph a "negative assurance" given by the PA?

b. Why is "negative assurance" generally prohibited in audit reports?

c. What justification is there for permitting "negative assurance" in a review services report on unaudited financial statements and on interim financial information?

14.39 Reporting on a Forecast. Kingston Company proposed to sell to investors limited partnership interests in 40 new hardware store buildings. Kingston Company would be the general partner. The deal was structured to raise funds for business expansion by offering a real estate investment. As part of the offering material, Kingston management produced a forecast based on the assumption of $1.5 million gross annual revenue for each new location. The lease income to the partnership is to be a base rental fee plus 10 percent of gross revenue in excess of $1 million. Kingston's existing stores have gross revenues ranging from $800,000 to $1.75 million. Kingston also produced related balance sheets and statements of changes in financial position, all in conformity with AICPA forecast presentation guidelines.

Kingston engaged Anderson, Olds & Watershed to examine the forecast and submit a report. One of the assistant accountants on the engagement drafted the opinion paragraph of the report as follows:

> In our opinion, the accompanying forecast is presented in conformity with guidelines for presentation of a forecast established by the American Institute of Certified Public Accountants, and the underlying assumption of $1.5 million average revenue per store is sufficient to cover the fixed and variable expenses of store maintenance, taxes, and insurance, which are the obligations of the limited partners. However, there will usually be differences between the forecasted and actual results because store revenues frequently do not materialize as expected, and the shortfall may be material. We have no responsibility to update this report for events and circumstances occurring after the date of this report.

Required:
Identify and explain the errors, if any, in this portion of the forecast examination report.

14.40 **Current Value Supplement.** Ms. Carboy (Kingston's controller) has prepared current cost information following the SFAS 89 guidelines. The information has been placed in a section at the front of the corporate annual report, apart from the audited financial statements. The section declares that Anderson, Olds & Watershed have not performed any review procedures on the information and does not express any opinion on it.

Kingston performs some welding work for customers and uses a ZB40-X-ray machine to inspect the strength of the welds. Kingston bought its ZB40 three years ago for $60,000. Most such X-ray machines last 10 years, so Kingston has recorded $6,000 amortization expense for the current year—the third year the machine has been used. A new ZB40 now costs $75,000. Kingston is planning to purchase a second one because it is the best on the market.

When Ms. Carboy prepared the supplementary current cost information, the BZ40 was reflected as follows:

> Current-year amortization expense $75,000
> Machinery and equipment $75,000
> Accumulated amortization 22,500
> Current-year amortization expense 7,500

Required:
a. Should the audit report contain a disclaimer on the current value supplementary information? Explain.
b. Does AOW have any responsibility regarding the current value information?
c. What audit procedures can be performed with regard to supplementary current value information? With reference to the ZB40 machine, explain the procedures.

Discussion Cases

14.41 **Prepare a Compilation Report.** You have been engaged by the Coffin Brothers to compile their financial schedules from books and records maintained by James Coffin. The brothers own and operate three auto parts stores in Central City. Even though their business is growing, they have not wanted to employ a full-time bookkeeper. James specifies that all he wants is a balance sheet, a statement of operations, and a statement of cash flows. He does not have time to write up footnotes to accompany the statement.

James directed the physical count of inventory on June 30 and adjusted and closed the books on that date. You find that he actually is a good accountant, having taken some night courses at the community college. The accounts appear to have been maintained in conformity with generally accepted accounting principles. At least you have noticed no obvious errors.

Required:

You are independent with respect to the Coffin brothers and their Coffin Auto Speed Shop business. Prepare a report on your compilation services engagement.

14.42 Reporting on Comparative Unaudited Financial Statements. Anson Jones, PA, performed a review service for the Independence Company in 1993. He wants to present comparative financial statements. However, the 1992 statements were compiled by Able and Associates, PAs, and Able does not want to co-operate with Jones by reissuing the prior-year compilation report. Jones has no indication that any adjustments should be made to either the 1993 or 1992 statements, which are to be presented with all necessary disclosures. However, he does not have time to perform a review of the 1992 statements. He completed his work on January 15, 1994, for the statement dated December 31, 1993.

Required:

Write Jones' review report and include the paragraph describing the report on the 1992 statements.

14.43 Erroneous Reporting on Interim Financial Information. The report in the box on this page was prepared by Baker & Baker, public accountants, on the interim financial information of Micro Mini Company. The interim financial information was presented in the first quarterly report for the three-month period ended March 31, 1993. No comparative quarterly information of the first quarter of the prior year was presented. Baker & Baker completed a review in accordance with standards established by the CICA and found that, to the best of their knowledge, the information was presented in conformity with CICA requirements. In an audit report dated January 21, 1993,

---

Report of Independent Auditors
The Board of Directors and Stockholders,
Micro Mini Company:

We have made a review of the balance sheet of Micro Mini Company at March 31, 1993, the related statement of income for the three-month period ended March 31, 1993, and the statement of cash flows for the three-month period ended March 31, 1993, in accordance with standards established by the Canadian Institute of Chartered Accountants.

A review of interim financial information consists principally of obtaining an understanding of the system for the preparation of the interim financial information, applying analytical review procedures to financial data, and making enquiries to persons responsible for financial and accounting matters.

In our opinion, the accompanying interim financial information presents fairly, in all material respects, the financial position of Micro Mini Company at March 31, 1993, and the results of its operations and its cash flows for the three-month period then ended in conformity with generally accepted accounting principles.

Baker & Baker, PAs
March 31, 1993

Baker & Baker had given a standard unqualified audit report on Micro Mini's 1992 and 1991 annual financial statements.

Required:
a. Review the report and list, with explanation, the erroneous portions in it.
b. Rewrite the report.

14.44 Report on Comprehensive Basis Other Than GAAP. The Brockville Life Insurance Company prepares its financial statements on a statutory basis in conformity with the accounting practices prescribed and permitted by the Commissioner of Insurance of the Province of Ontario. This statutory basis produces financial statements that differ materially from statements prepared in conformity with generally accepted accounting principles. On the statutory basis, for example, agents' first-year commissions are expensed instead of being partially deferred, and equity securities are reported at market value lower than cost, even if a "permanent impairment" of value is not evident.

The company engaged its auditors, Major and Major Associates, to audit the statutory basis financial statements and report on them. Footnote 10 in the statements contains a narrative description and a numerical table explaining the differences between the statutory basis and GAAP accounting. Footnote 10 also reconciles the statutory basis assets, liabilities, income, expense, and net income (statutory basis) to the measurements that would be obtained using GAAP.

Required:
Write the audit report appropriate in the circumstances. The year-end date is December 31, 1992, and the audit field work was completed on February 20, 1993. (The company plans to distribute this report to persons other than the department of insurance regulators.

14.45 Service Bureau Controls. Your firm has been engaged to render an opinion on control procedures at ABC Ser-

vices Ltd., which is a payroll service bureau.

Required:
a. What type of circumstances might arise that would prevent the auditor of a service organization from issuing an opinion without reservation on control procedures?
b. Identify the two types of engagements for a service bureau and compare and contrast the two types with respect to audit standards and procedures.

(CGAAC adapted)

14.46 Audits vs. Non-audits. Woo, PA, has been engaged to perform an audit of financial statements of FST Inc., which Smith, the owner-manager of FST, intends to submit to the bank in support of a loan application. Woo has applied the audit procedures he considered necessary in the circumstances and is "about halfway" through his collection of audit evidence when Smith informs him that since the bank has just indicated that a review engagement report is sufficient for its purposes, FST does not require a full audit.

Required:
a. Contrast the auditor's overall objective in the performance of an audit with the accountant's overall objective in the performance of a review engagement.
b. Considering that Woo has already applied some audit procedures to and obtained evidence regarding the financial statements of FST, what modifications should Woo make to the standard review engagement report?
c. What are the appropriate criteria against which the financial statements and related disclosures are measured in the case of:
   (1) an audit?
   (2) a review engagement?
   (3) a compilation engagement?

14.47 Special Reports. As well as engagements to examine financial statements in their entirety, a PA may be engaged to prepare other types of special reports for a client.

Required:

a. *Section* 5800 of the *CICA Handbook* provides for three types of special reports.
   (1) Identify each type of special report.
   (2) Identify the standards governing each type of examination.
   (3) Briefly explain how each of the resulting reports differs from an opinion on financial statements.

b. When the auditor is engaged to report on the design, effective operation, and continuity of control procedures at a service organization, what are the additional examination responsibilities of the auditor?

(CGAAC adapted)

14.48 Objectives of Different Engagements. Pierre Landret has recently started a landscaping and landscaping supply business. The business is incorporated, with the shareholders being Pierre and his wife. His educational background is a bachelor's degree in agricultural science, and he is unfamiliar with the accounting aspects of his new venture. He has come to you, a CGA, for advice. He says, "I want you to look at the records of my business for the past year. I understand that there are three different types of engagements that you can perform. What are the differences between them as they affect my business, and what purpose might each one serve for my business?

Required:

a. Draft a reply to Mr. Landret.

b. State the two matters that the public accountant must be satisfied about before accepting a review engagement.

c. State the three matters that the public accountant must be satisfied about before accepting a compilation engagement.

(CGAAC adapted)

APPENDIX 14A

A Critical Analysis of Section 5025

. . . .

Clearly, *Section* 5025 marks only the beginning of a long process of developing audit/assurance standards; it is also a significant attempt to keep auditing relevant as we enter the next century. There are bound to be changes to the section. In indicating possible future trends, we will start by pointing out some contentious areas over the seven years that it took for this section to evolve into its present form.

Section 5025 is the result of a long process that began in 1990, when a group was established to explore the concept of a broad umbrella framework for all assurance engagements. In 1992 the study group came out with a report, "Assurance Based Service Engagements." On the basis of the feedback it received about this report, the CICA in October 1995 issued an Exposure Draft on Standards for Assurance Engagements. This refined the earlier issues paper to create a better integration with public sector auditing standards; perhaps most importantly it also provided, in an extensive appendix, a series of example reports in diverse situations. However, several contentious issues were identified in the resulting feedback from this Exposure Draft so that the final standard was watered down somewhat. Most notably, the *Handbook* section on assurance engagements no longer has illustrations, and the linkage with public-sector auditing standards has been weakened. Nevertheless, this standard is a pioneering one for the profession globally, in that it is the first attempt to establish a coherent framework for all types of audit and audit-related services. The standard can be viewed as a good first step in the development of a reporting framework that will accommodate the needs and concerns of regulators and auditors and meet changing public expectations. Ultimately the framework should (a) clarify the roles and responsibilities of managers, regulators, and auditors, (b) outline how auditors discharge their responsibilities, and (c) set out appropriate criteria for use by auditors and regulators in fulfilling their responsibilities. In sum, the result should be a clearer accountability framework for the public and private sectors. It is this focus on an accountability framework that perhaps makes *Handbook Section* 5025 truly unique.

One important difference between the Exposure Draft and the final version of the standard is the lack of illustrative reports in the final version. The Exposure Draft had eight example reports in its Appendix B. Seven of these dealt with attestation engagements on internal control reports, and one was an example of a direct reporting engagement using a public sector illustration.

The box on the next page illustrates a high-level assurance attest engagement report without reservation, with additional information contained in an explanatory paragraph. Note why it was considered an attest engagement: the auditor was reporting on a written management assertion about the state of controls. Note also the use of the words "present fairly" on this new type of assertion and the use of the words "in all significant respects."

EXAMPLE REPORT 1

- High level of assurance.
- Attest engagement.
- Report without reservation.
- Additional information contained in explanatory paragraph.

AUDITORS' REPORT CONCERNING EFFECTIVENESS OF THE
SYSTEM OF INTERNAL CONTROL OVER FINANCIAL REPORTING[1]

To the Shareholders of ABC Company

We have audited management's assertion that ABC Company maintained an effective system of internal control over financial reporting as of December 31, 19XX in relation to the criteria [describe criteria or indicate source of criteria].[2] Management's assertion is included in the accompanying report [title of management report]. The maintenance of an effective system of internal control over financial reporting is the responsibility of management. Our responsibility is to express an opinion on management's assertion about the effectiveness of the internal control system based on our audit.

We conducted our audit in accordance with generally accepted auditing standards. Those standards require that we plan and perform an audit to obtain reasonable assurance that management's assertion is free from significant misstatements. An audit includes examining, on a test basis, evidence supporting the content and disclosures in management's assertion. An audit also includes assessing the criteria used and the significant judgments made by management, as well as evaluating the overall presentation of management's assertion.

In our opinion, management's assertion presents fairly, in all significant respects, the effectiveness of the system of internal control over financial reporting of ABC Company as of December 31, 19XX based upon the criteria referred to above.

Because of the inherent limitations in any internal control system, errors or irregularities may occur and not be detected. Also, projections of any evaluation of the internal control system over financial reporting to future periods are subject to the risk that the internal control system may become inadequate because of changes in conditions, or that the degree of compliance with the policies or procedures may deteriorate.[3]

City   . . . .
Date   Chartered Accountants

---

[1] In an attest engagement, the practitioner's report is directly on management's assertion on a subject matter; in a direct reporting engagement the report is directly on the subject matter.

[2] Alternatively, the description of criteria could be attached as an appendix to the report.

[3] Example of additional information and explanations neither required by statute nor intended as a reservation. As such, the opinion paragraph should precede that containing additional information or explanations.

This and the other examples were dropped, apparently because the CICA did not want to inhibit experimentation, particularly in preparing internal control reports in conformity with COCO.

As we noted in Chapter 14, there are currently no authoritative illustrations of public reports on internal control in Canadian standards. The closest thing we have is example report 1 above.

Perhaps the biggest concern with the current authoritative standard as reflected in comments to the Exposure Draft relates to the inconsistencies with existing review standards—specifically the need to make explicit the various risk assessments under 5025. In contrast, existing review standards are more procedurally oriented—for example, they do not require an assessment of internal controls. The chief reason for a risk-oriented framework in *Section* 5025 is that the risk model provides a better theoretical foundation by linking moderate risk to review attest engagements and low risk to audit attest engagements.

Other potential inconsistencies occur between *Section* 5025 and the review standards (5800 series), control procedures in service organizations (*Section* 5900), and public sector exception reporting standards (discussed in Chapter 17).

In addition, there are the inconsistencies explicitly recognized in Appendix A of *Section* 5025, as discussed in the chapter. The rationale for keeping out these engagements is that:

> assurance engagements are intended to provide a conclusion concerning a subject matter of interest to a user. In contrast, in an engagement to provide other services for which guidance is provided in the CICA Handbook, the practitioner communicates the nature of the work carried out with respect to a matter and the factual results of this work. The practitioner provides no conclusion concerning the subject matter. (*Section* 5025.A)

The fact that some users may choose to derive some assurance from the auditor's involvement in these excluded engagements, does not change the fact that the practitioner does not provide assurance consistent with 5025; hence these excluded engagements must have carefully worded reports that clearly communicate the nature of the auditors' involvement (*Section* 5025.A).

As we will see in Chapter 17, many public sector engagements involve a reporting of deficiencies that closely resemble derivative reporting engagements. According to *Section* 5025A, "derivative reporting is not an assurance engagement because the practitioner merely points out matters that have come to his or her attention during the engagement. The practitioner does not provide any assurance that these are the only matters which would be of interest to management, the audit committee, or the regulator."

This exclusion has potentially important ramifications for public sector auditors: many of their reports are exception or deficiency reports, and it is unclear whether these should be treated as only moderate assurance engagements or not included as assurance engagements at all. At least theoretically, this would suggest that no assurance is being provided by many public sector engagements. Public sector auditors would be very concerned with such an interpretation, especially considering that the assurance concept was extended primarily to incorporate the direct reporting nature of many public sector engagements. In fact, as noted in Chapter 17, a notable success of public sector auditing is in exception reporting of major waste, inefficiencies, or ineffectiveness in government operations. To exclude such obviously important public accountability engagements from the framework of assurance may suggest this framework is incomplete. In fact, *Section* 5025.15 was modified from the Exposure Draft version to specifically exclude mention of public sector mandates requiring legislative auditors. It would appear that some rethinking may be required on whether deficiency reports provide some assurance or not. After all, review engagements provide only negative assurance ("nothing has come to my attention" type of assurance), and yet they are considered assurance engagements by *Section* 5025. This relates, we feel, to the objectives of the engagement in the first place; we will have more to say about this shortly. It is clear that the interface between assurance standards and public sector standards will be an important aspect in the evolution of both sets of standards.

An interesting change in perspective that has taken place within the CICA with the evolution of the assurance engagement standards is that financial statement audits are now increasingly viewed as direct reporting engagements rather than assurance engagements. This is interesting, because the rest of the world views financial statement audits as assurance engagements, so the CICA may be developing a new concept for financial statement auditing. The classification hinges on whether financial statements are treated as written assertions (attest engagements) or as the subject matter of an audit (see D.J. Cockburn, "An Issue of Attestation," *CA Magazine,* November 1992, pp. 35–37). If financial statements are treated as subject matter of the audit, this question arises: What are the written assertions, if any? One may feel that a client representation letter may fulfil this requirement, but the problem here is that when *Section* 5025 refers to written assertions, they appear to mean a public declaration, not something that is just used to document audit working papers. The significance of this distinction is evident from the illustrations the CICA used in its 1995 Exposure Draft. There, all examples of attest engagements referred to a publicly written set of assertions by management (as in, for example, the box above), and only in attest engagements were the words "presents fairly" used in the practitioner's report. In the direct reporting engagement illustration, on the other hand, there was no mention of a client report and there was no use of the words "presents fairly." Perhaps this partly explains why the illustrations were dropped: they suggested a significant change in the nature of the financial statement auditor's report if in fact they were treated as direct reporting engagements. In addition, there would need to be consideration of the fact that suitable criteria may go beyond the current financial accounting framework of *Section* 1000 as noted in the chapter, and the combination of these two interpretations can effectively put the auditor in the position of setting accounting standards on each engagement. This was not likely the result that the CICA standard setters had in mind when they developed *Section* 5025. All of this helps illustrate the fundamental issues being raised by the concept of assurance standards.

The CICA recognizes these and other potential problems with the assurance standard. K. Duggan, in "To Assure or Not to Assure" (*CA Magazine,* January–February 1997, pp. 46–48), identified exception reporting, inconsistency with other *Handbook Sections,* lack of illustrative reports, and better clarification of the distinction between moderate and reasonable level of assurance as primary concerns of respondents to the 1995 Exposure Draft. Many of these concerns will be addressed by the CICA in the near future with additional guidelines and *Handbook Recommendations.* The next section provides a fairly complete listing of outstanding concerns raised by one of the respondents to the Exposure Draft, a subcommittee of the Canadian Academic Accounting Association (CAAA).

CAAA COMMITTEE INPUT ON THE ASSURANCE STANDARDS
· · · · · · · · · · · ·

In December 1995 a CAAA committee prepared comments on the Assurance Standards Exposure Draft. Some of the comments are still pertinent to *Section* 5025. Because of the importance of *Section* 5025, the relevant sections of the CAAA report, authored by Jean Bedard, Donald Cockburn, Morina Rennie, and the Canadian author of this textbook, are reproduced below to provide additional insight into the various paragraphs of this *Handbook Section.*

CLARIFICATION OF THE ASSURANCE ENGAGEMENT FRAMEWORK

The standard covers several types of existing engagements and is also intended to include engagements for which no current standards exist. Because of the comprehensive nature of this standard it may be desirable to include a figure such as the following in the introductory sections:

FIGURE 1

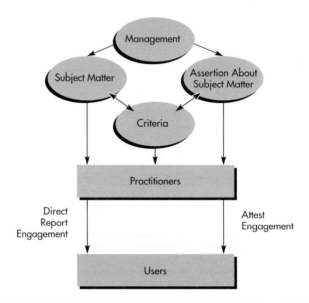

This type of chart should be helpful to the reader in understanding the relationships among the key components of assurance engagements.

The standard outlines four major types of engagements (high assurance/attest; high assurance/direct reporting; low assurance/attest; and low assurance/direct reporting). There is a lack of clarity when it comes to describing when some recommendations apply and when they do not. For example, it is not clear how engagement risk, significance, risk assessment, and evidence should vary according to the level of assurance required and the type of engagement.

One way to improve the clarity of the introductory sections would be to show how all existing engagements fit into the framework. For example, is the traditional financial statement audit intended to be a high-assurance: (1) attest engagement (with the financial statements being the "assertion" and the underlying economic events being the subject matter of the assertion); (2) direct reporting engagement (with the financial statements and the underlying economic events being viewed as the subject matter), or (3) attest engagement with an implied but unstated assertion by management that the financial statements are fairly presented? The Board's intent has direct implications for several of the proposed standards. For example if (1) above is the intent, then paragraphs .66(f) and .79 may need to be re-visited.

It would also be important to specify where 8100 and 7100 review engagements fit into the framework as well as various types of public sector engagements. Providing specific information to readers about where existing engagements fit in the framework will go a long way towards establishing a common understanding of the issues addressed in the standard.

ISSUES REGARDING THE WRITTEN ASSERTION

The ED is NOT explicit about what form the written assertion should take. Should it be assumed that management's assertion accompanies the report? Would there be situations for which the accountable party provides the assertion only to the assurance provider? For example, would an assertion such as "our internal control systems are appropriate" need to accompany the practitioner's conclusion? The Exposure Draft should provide an explicit description of what constitutes a written assertion by an accountable party.

The form of the written assertion causes particular difficulties if a financial statement audit is viewed as an attest engagement but where the financial statements are not considered to be this assertion (case (3) above)). If the assertion itself does not need to accompany the report, can it simply take the form of a representation letter? Or is the directors' signing of the financial statements considered to be an assertion that they are fair? Or should new requirements be proposed for management to make an explicit assertion regarding the fairness of presentation?

If an assertion always takes the form of a statement by the accountable party that the subject matter conforms to the criteria (perhaps with noted exceptions), is there, in substance, enough difference between an attest and direct reporting engagement to warrant the awkwardness this distinction introduces into the standard? Or should we be trying to cover both direct reporting and attest engagements in one standard?

OBJECTIVE(S) OF THE ENGAGEMENT

The objective of the engagement is a key concept underlying this proposed standard. Because the standard covers all assurance engagements, it is the objective of the engagement that will determine how this general standard and related specific standards will be applied. As a result of the potential growth in complexity of objectives for assurance engagements, we recommend that objectives be more explicitly and completely specified both in the introduction and in the proposed reporting standards of the ED. More specifically, we suggest the following:

1. In the section on Definitions and Underlying Concepts, the ED should describe "objective" in such a way that the concepts of "the subject matter," "the accountability relationship," and "the criteria" are included. If the exposure draft doesn't describe the concept of "objective", the discussion becomes somewhat unfocused—objective could mean anything.

A symptom of this problem is that the ED appears to use the terms "objective of the engagement" and "subject matter of the engagement" interchangeably. (For example, *Section* 5025.20.)

In all engagements it would appear that one of the objectives is to identify the subject matter of the engagement. So "objective of the engagement" is broader than "subject matter." It is possible that in less defined engagements such as environmental audits, auditors may fail to fully describe the subject matter, e.g., "biodiversity preservation," and leave it only implied thus causing the assurance report to be unnecessarily vague. Ideas that were implicit in traditional auditing may need to be made more explicit in many assurance engagements because of unique features of these engagements.

Another example of a difficulty created by an inadequate discussion of the term "objective" relates to interpretation of the characteristics of the criteria (paragraph .38). For example, relevant criteria are described as those that "contribute to findings and conclusions that meet the objective of the engagement." An explicit description of the term "objective" would help the reader assess whether this description is actually inconsistent with the concept of relevance found in GAAP (the criteria for financial statement audits), as it seems to be (with regard to users' needs).

Finally, an explicit description of what is meant by "objective of the engagement" may resolve an ambiguity in paragraph .20. That is, we are not sure what message the phrase "as it relates to the objective of the engagement" is intended to convey. Should it simply say "... subject matter of the engagement." The phrase "as it relates ..." is not used in paragraph .21.

The Board might consider a description such as the following:

> The objective of an engagement is to draw a conclusion, on the basis of sufficient, appropriate evidence, that provides the users in an accountability relationship with an agreed upon level of assurance regarding the conformity of a specified subject matter (or assertion) with stated criteria.

Objectives for specific engagements would identify the specific level of assurance provided that the particular accountability relationship, criteria and subject matter are relevant to that engagement. If necessary, the subject matter would also be defined.

2. Reporting standard, *Section* 5025.66(b) should be changed from "describe the objectives of the engagement" to "describe the objectives of the engagement including if necessary the accountability relationship, the criteria, and the subject matter."

   Paragraph .68 should similarly be adapted. Because no guidance is given in terms of the objective/purpose, the requirements of this paragraph to identify the objective of the engagement leave practitioners without help to determine what an appropriate description might include.

   Moreover, the example reports of the ED do not actually include a description of the purpose/objective of the engagement. The purpose may be inferred from a complete reading of the report. This is not the same as "a description of the purpose". Such an inference is possible for readers in these particular examples only because the subject matters and relationships are relatively well understood. In the case of less well defined assurance engagements such as environmental audits where auditors may need to rely on specialists in spelling out precisely what the subject matter is, however, the reporting obligation to describe the objectives may not be so clear cut. Therefore, the auditor (assurer) may need to actually define the subject matter (e.g., biodiversity), the criteria and the accountability relationship in order to properly describe the objective.

Examples 1–4:   The example reports use the term "presents fairly" to express the relationship, based on certain criteria, between the assertion and the subject matter. The Board should perhaps consider whether "presents fairly" would be the most appropriate term for all assurance engagements. Historically, "present fairly" has been used when the criteria are generally accepted and to designate that a reasonable choice has been made from among the set of generally accepted criteria. The Board might consider a concept such as "reasonably presented."

The last comment in the above report about fair presentation in accordance with GAAP has recently gained more urgency as result of a recent B.C. Court of Appeal decision criticizing auditors for "hiding behind GAAP." This is discussed more fully in Chapter 16.

The issue of properly clarifying the objectives of an assurance engagement cannot be overemphasized, since the objectives determine the relevance of the engagement for the users. For example, do auditors need to define the accountability relationship? the subject matter? This may not be evident in some of the newer assurance engagements. For example, in an environmental audit it may be necessary to define "biodiversity preservation" or "sustainable development" before verifying various data relating to these concepts. Such definitions help establish the warrants for the evidence providing the assurance and thus the relevance of the evidence to the conclusion. So there may be a need to develop a separate concept of the objective of an assurance engagement.

For example, assertions are generally more specific warrants [explanations] that are consistent with the stated criteria—like financial statement assertions are consistent with GAAP accounting. Given the close relationship between assertions and stated criteria, and the importance of establishing the relevance of stated criteria to the subject matter and the accountability relationship, perhaps all of these should be explicitly defined either in the assurer's report (in the case of direct reporting engagements), or as part of the asserter's written assertion report (in the case of an assurance engagement), or by reference to generally accepted criteria. This may be the only way to avoid confusing users and thus make the assurance engagement more relevant. Users, for example, may not agree with the assurer's definition of "biodiversity preservation," but at least with a definition they would have a better basis for understanding the report.

EVOLUTION OF THE ASSURANCE CONCEPT OUTSIDE OF CANADA
· · · · · · · · · · · ·

In the United States there currently are no assurance standards, although many AICPA groups are working on various aspects of assurance engagements. One of these groups, the Special Committee on Assurance Services (SCAS), has defined assurance services as "independent professional services that improve the quality of information, with context, for decision makers."

We see from this definition that the American concept may be broader than *Section 5025* because accountability decisions are but one class of decisions. In the SCAS's view, PAs must transform themselves from "certifiers" into "enhancers" of information. The word *quality* in the above definition is presumed to mean reliability and relevance for decision makers' needs. The context refers to how the information is presented in the practitioner's report. According to the SCAS, users can be the client or third parties and the true nature of the engagement is determined by the ultimate goal of the engagement. The SCAS foresees an overlap between assurance and consulting engagements, as indicated in the box below, but it explicitly excludes an overlap between assurance and tax services. In its view, the engagement letter is critical to determining the nature of the engagement.

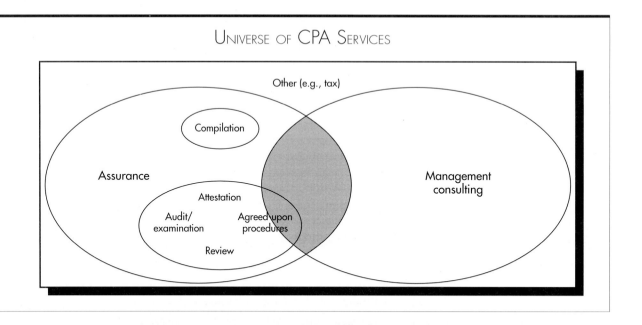

In the view of SCAS, assurance expands the traditional audit function in three major new directions: (1) meeting new needs of the existing client base—for example, risk assessment, performance measurement, and information systems reliability; (2) meeting needs of a new client base using existing service expertise—for example, process quality (ISO 9000), product quality, and World Wide Web assertions; and (3) providing new services for new clients—for example, elder care, electronic commerce assurance, and health care performance measures. The goal of the AICPA is to develop a new conceptual framework for all these areas that is flexible enough for practitioners to use on their own to identify additional assurance service opportunities.

Three boxes follow. The first illustrates a specific user-oriented service. The second provides a discussion of a recent AICPA-proposed assurance standard for Management Discussion & Analysis (MD&A) in annual reports. The third provides a recent overview of assurance services contemplated by the AICPA.

BENCHMARKING AT MOSS ADAMS

Neal West's firm, Moss Adams LLP, began doing benchmarking engagements some 10 years ago, with a pick-up in frequency over the last few. West, the firm's director of business assurance, is a member of the performance measurement task force of the AICPA assurance service committee, and he's ready to help other firms understand what these engagements are about and how to perform them. He told the *Journal* about some of his firm's experiences.

The original and still popular service starts with a cost of doing business survey for a trade association (for example, an association of marinas or fencing contractors). The association is the client, and its members, the subject of the survey, are the users of the information. The survey allows Moss Adams to create a set of "common size financial statements" based on financial data from all the surveyed members. Association members can compare their performances to the industry-wide performances. The engagement sometimes calls for stratifying the collective data by size of the surveyed entities into three or so sets of financial statements. Association members can compare their performance to the average for the industry or to the group they are closest to within the industry.

Sometimes the survey is used to gather nonfinancial performance data—typically, market, process or workforce data. But the purpose, again, is benchmarking. Another variation is to measure the performance of the top-performing segment of the industry. The data set a standard for association members: they know what is possible and can set targets. Associations can distribute the performance measures to members or provide them for a fee.

The intended use of the data by the associations is always clear when the engagement terms are settled. Many clients know what they want, but Moss Adams always considers what is best for the client's members and will be of most help. In those cases, Moss Adams is designing the engagements with clients by exploring their needs with them.

Moss Adams is doing a growing percentage of its benchmarking for individual firms. Why? Because not all firms fit neatly in an industry category. They may be uncommon in size or have unique geographic characteristics, for example. Moss Adams's Xemplar process, now under development, is designed to set a standard that individual firms of associations can use in such circumstances. Xemplar does not produce an average or an ideal, but an exception example, created in part from experts' views, against which a company can measure its operations.

West believes CPAs have the basic competencies to do this kind of work. They are skilled in financial analysis and use these techniques regularly on audits. What they need to do is use those analytical skills to create measurements clients can understand and to follow this up with assistance in helping clients improve their operations. Follow-on consulting services of this sort are a very important part of the assurance package, both in terms of benefits to the client and in terms of fees.

West gives this example: Suppose benchmarking shows that personnel turnover is adversely affecting sales and customer retention. Moss Adams would analyze the causes and help the client improve. As West puts it: "We're asking, 'Where are they? Where should they be? And why aren't they there?' Then we help them get there."

CPAs need to have a rich understanding of their clients' businesses and industries in order to do this work, but that is not a new type of demand on them. Basic analytical tools are taught in staff training at Moss Adams, and a synergy exists between analytical reviews that strengthen the audit and the analytical work needed to deliver benchmarking.

"It's a service that meets clients' needs and fits well with our skills base," West concludes.

Source: R.K. Elliott and D.M. Pallais, *Journal of Accountancy,* July 1997, p. 62.

PROPOSED ATTESTATION STANDARD ON MD&A

Out for exposure is a proposed Statement on Standards for Attestation Engagements (SSAE), *Management's Discussion and Analysis,* that would provide guidance for practitioners examining or reviewing management's discussion and analysis prepared according to Securities and Exchange Commission rules and regulations. "This is a voluntary, value added service auditors can offer their clients," said Richard Dieter, a task force member and partner of Arthur Andersen LLP.

"The scope of attestation engagements is increasing. People are looking for assurance on matters outside of historical financial statements," said Beth Schneider, a director at Deloitte & Touche LLP, who staffed the auditing standards board task force that drew up the exposure draft. Dieter added, "I think this proposed SSAE is important because it shows we are moving into more subjective and softer information, which includes disclosure of future demands and uncertainties that can face a business. The ASB views the MD&A attest service as a forerunner to some of the services CPAs are—and should be—performing." Emphasizing that such engagements are not required, Dieter said he does not expect the SEC to make it mandatory; he sees the demand for this service coming initially from underwriters in connection with securities offerings.

"The proposed standard also will provide a useful framework for future assurance services in that area."

Source: Journal of Accountancy, April 1997, p. 13.

The assurance services that show the most potential are those related to a given firm's existing expertise and client base. Thus, for example, elder care assurance engagements would be most successful as extensions of existing tax or permanent financial planning services. It seems that PAs have a competitive edge when there are tie-ins with existing services. In fact this has been the case traditionally with tax and consulting services, but with the concept now being extended to new assurance engagements. Note, however, that the issue of maintaining auditor independence may grow more complex as the distinctions between their various services become blurred, as is the case under some of the AICPA proposals. It may even become necessary to develop different independence criteria for different assurance engagements.

Where all of this leads is presently hard to tell, but it may be worthwhile to highlight the apparent differences between the CICA and AICPA approaches. The

A SAMPLE OF ASSURANCE SERVICE POSSIBILITIES

This list of services is taken from the special committee on assurance services survey of 21 large PA firms. (The full survey results, with over 200 entries, are available at www.aicpa.org/assurance/scas/newsvs/addlposs/index.htm.) The goal of the survey was to establish the breadth of assurance services already offered in practice.

- Assessment of ethics-related risks and vulnerabilities
- Controls over and risk related to investments
- Adequacy of controls and policies for derivatives
- Information systems security reviews
- Assessment of risk of accumulation, distribution and storage of digital information
- Fraud and illegal acts risk assessment
- Management/board salary benchmarking
- Internal audit quality assurance
- Adequacy of billing system compared to competitors
- Advertising rates to be paid vs. those charged
- Customer satisfaction surveys—reports/validations
- Review of compliance with investment policy
- Compliance with trading policies and procedures
- Compliance with royalty agreements (entertainment)
- Identification of critical items to monitor
- Examination of software specifications
- ISO 9000 certification
- Examination of hardware benchmark test results
- Newspaper circulation audits
- Annual environmental report
- Audit of milestone in long-term incentive plans
- Compliance with industry standards for additives test labs
- Verification of contributions under incentive plan
- Verification of construction costs for incentive grant

Source: R.K. Elliott and D.M. Pallais, *Journal of Accountancy,* July 1997, p. 63.

AICPA uses a broader concept of assurance that not only includes items specifically excluded by *Section* 5025, agreed upon procedure, compilation, and consulting engagements, but also does not limit itself to accountability frameworks. Whether this is good or bad depends on how well the AICPA will be able to distinguish between assurance and all other PA services. If they aren't able to do a better job, there is a risk that little will be accomplished with a new concept like assurance services, because all it may mean is that assurance services are little different from PA services in general (as discussed in Chapter 1). To further cloud the issue, the current AICPA position seems to treat all unwritten assertion engagements as consulting engagements.

It would appear from our perspective that it would be useful to clearly explain why tax services and some consulting services are not assurance engagements under the AICPA approach. Some indications of the CICA's views on this are given in *Section* 5020.B, reproduced in the chapter. The advantage of the CICA approach, with its focus on accountability, is the requirement that there be an asserter (the accountable party) whose explicit or implicit assertions are enhanced by the assurer. Thus, for example, one way to distinguish assurance from consulting and tax engagements is that in the latter situations the practitioner acts as an asserter and not as an assurer.

Such an interpretation is supported by the theory of argumentation in philosophy, which would view all PA services as types of dialogue. If the purpose of the argument in a dialogue is to support a conclusion about someone else's assertion, then we have an assurance engagement. If on the other hand we have an argument for the purpose of a different type of conclusion, then we have a non-assurance engagement. Purpose in turn is determined by the context of the dialogue, including the accountability relationship (e.g., see D. Walton, *Argument Structure, A Pragmatic Theory,* Toronto: University of Toronto Press, 1996, for more discussion of arguments and dialogue in philosophy). Thus, if we view PA services as part of a web of dialogue between the practitioner, the accountable party, and the users, the CICA approach may be on firmer philosophical ground because of its more precise assurance concept. Theories of philosophy suggest that context should determine the role the auditor plays, and the CICA approach appears to make a finer distinction between different contexts. However, as noted earlier, we need further clarifications on fundamental matters such as whether financial statements are written assertions or the subject matter of audit engagements. As in all dialogue, an agreement on the definition of the terms is a crucial starting point; and what the current controversies suggest is that existing definitions need clarification.

In August 1997 the International Auditing Practices Committee of the International Federation of Accountants (IFAC) issued an Exposure Draft (ED), "Reporting on the Credibility of Information." This ED essentially deals with assurance engagements as discussed here; however, the IFAC proposes to call them reporting service engagements (RSEs). The ED has four elements: (1) Motivation and Background, (2) The Framework, (3) General Principles, and (4) Example Reports.

The purpose of this ED is similar to that of the CICA's *Section* 5025—to provide a standards framework for current and future assurance services for practitioners who are carrying out assurance services where no specific standards exist. The ED appears to have been influenced particularly by *Handbook Section* 5025. The biggest differences between the two are as follows:

1. The assurance services can include those provided by internal as well as external auditors.

2. A much broader range of assurance is allowed, ranging from low to absolute.

3. The ED places more stress on getting the acknowledgment of the responsible party for the subject matter.

Generally, the ED is consistent with, and very similar to, *Section* 5025 except for the above. This is evident from the framework as well as from the general principles. For example, the ED framework specifically excludes the following engagements from the framework: agreed upon procedures where no conclusion is expressed; compilation of financial or other information; preparation of tax returns where no conclusion is expressed; and tax consultancy, management consulting, and other advisory services.

RSEs are defined as follows: services by PAs designed to report on the credibility of information, which is the responsibility of another party and which is referred to as the subject-matter, by evaluating that information against identified suitable criteria and expressing a conclusion.

The ED's framework consists of the above definition and the following elements of an assurance engagement (RSE):

(*a*) Professional accountant.

(*b*) Subject matter.

(*c*) Responsible party.

(*d*) Intended user.

(*e*) Criteria.

(*f*) Engagement process.

(*g*) Reporting.

The framework provides more details on each of the elements than does *Section* 5025—for example, on qualities of a PA (e.g., integrity, objectivity, condifidentiality). It also provides more illustrations of subject matters (e.g., human resource practices, corporate governance) and of the engagement process (e.g., planning, documentation, subsequent events). Interestingly, the criteria are virtually the same as the CICA's suitability criteria: relevance, reliability, neutrality, understandability, and completeness.

An interesting aspect of the IFAC's proposed framework is its definition of an assertion: "The assertion is the responsible party's conclusion about the subject matter based on suitable criteria. In a direct reporting engagement where there is no written assertion by the responsible party, the PA expresses a conclusion on the subject matter using suitable criteria" (ED, para. 31).

The IFAC's ED also provides a set of general principles that further clarify the framework. These principles start with a very important definition of the objective of an assurance engagement: "The objective of an [assurance engagement] RSE is to enable the professional accountant to report on the credibility of information, referred to as subject matter, that is the responsibility of another party, by evaluating the information against identified suitable criteria and expressing a conclusion about that subject matter" (ED, p. 24).

The general principle, like the general standard of financial statement auditing, refers to characteristics that the PA should have. The remaining principles deal with the following:

1. Accepting the Engagement.

2. Quality Control.

3. Planning and Conduct.

4. Evidence.

5. Documentation.

6. Subsequent Events.

7. Using the Work of an Expert.

8. Reporting.

9. Format of Report.

Some highlights of the differences between the CICA's *Section* 5025 and these principles include the following:

- The term "materiality" instead of "significance" is used for all assurance engagements.

- The risk model definition of the ED is more consistent with the traditional definition of the audit risk model.

- The ED explicitly states that the documentation "should include the PA's reasoning on all significant matters which require the exercise of professional judgment, together with the professional accountant's conclusion thereon. In areas involving difficult questions of principles or judgment, documentation will record the relevant facts that were known by the professional accountant at the time the conclusion was reached." The key test of this documentation principle appears to be: "What is necessary to provide another PA who has no previous experience with the engagement with an understanding of the work performed and the basis of the principal decisions taken but not the detailed aspects of the engagement?" (ED, p. 28).

The ED thus provides considerably more detailed guidance on what should be documented than the CICA's *Section* 5025.

Because of the greater range of assurances possible, the ED stresses the critical need to state clearly the assurance provided in the assurance report, and to include additional explanatory language relating to the following variables:

(*a*) The nature and form of the subject matter.

(*b*) The nature and form of the criteria applied to the subject matter.

(*c*) The nature and extent of the processes used to collect and evaluate evidence.

(*d*) The sufficiency and appropriateness of the evidence likely available.

It is clear that under the ED, PAs will have to put more care into the wording of these reports than under the two assurance systems that the CICA's *Section* 5025 envisages.

The ED ends with a discussion of the public sector perspective and some illustrative reports. The ED contends that the basic principles are the same in the public sector and that whatever the public sector mandate, a clear expression is necessary regarding the PA's conclusion about the subject matter. In other words, it is not enough to simply report instances of noncompliance as exceptions to due regard to economy, efficiency, and effectiveness. This clarifies that exception reports by themselves are not assurance engagements under the ED's criteria.

Perhaps the most interesting example that the ED provides is an assurance report with a "low" level of assurance (see the following box). There is nothing comparable contemplated in the current *Handbook Section* 5025.

IFAC's ED
EXAMPLE REPORT I

Title	Professional Accountant's Report
Addressee	To the Board of Directors AVP Company
Nature of the Engagement Responsible Party	The objective of this reporting service engagement is to report on AVP Company's Statement of Responses to the Defense Industry Questionnaire on Business Ethics and Conduct for the period .... to .... You, as directors, are responsible for the preparation of the Statement, and for the assertions made in the Statement.
Professional Accountant's Responsibility	Our responsibility is to express a conclusion on the Statement of Responses to the Defense Industry Questionnaire on Business Ethics and Conduct.
Limitation Cautionary Language	The nature of the subject matter (business ethics) imposes an inherent limitation on the assurance that can be provided, and because the nature of business ethics is dependent on the individual actions and the moral characteristics of individuals within the Company, the persuasiveness of the evidence available is limited. Accordingly, we have not evaluated whether the above mentioned policies and programs operated effectively to ensure compliance with the Company's Code of Business Ethics and Conduct on the part of the individual employees, or the extent to which the Company or its employees have compiled with federal procurement laws and we express no conclusion thereon. Furthermore, in accordance with the terms of this engagement, we have restricted our procedures to the inspection of relevant Company manuals and documents and discussion with management and other personnel. While these procedures provide less evidence than would be available by applying more extensive and comprehensive procedures, the evidence provides a basis for our conclusion, but the limited nature of the evidence restricts the assurance to a low level. Accordingly, this report should be used only in conjunction with other corroborative information about the Company's policies and programs.
Restriction on Use of Report	This report has been prepared for the directors of AVP Company; we disclaim any responsibility for any reliance on this report to any other party or for any purpose other than for which it was prepared.
Applicable Standards Criteria	This reporting service engagement has been undertaken in accordance with the International Standard on Reporting Service Engagements. This involved assessing the Company's policies and programs to determine that they are consistent with the production of the above mentioned Statement in conformity with the requirement of the Defense Industry Initiatives on Business Ethics and Conduct.
Conclusion	Based on our engagement procedures which were restricted, and recognizing the inherent limitations outlined above relating to the evidence collected, we conclude that the AVP Company Statement of Responses to the Defense Industry Questionnaire on Business Ethics and Conduct for the period .... to .... is, in all material respects, appropriately presented in accordance with the Defense Industry Initiatives on Business Ethics and Conduct.
	Name of Professional Accountant Date Location.

Note that the main reason for the low assurance is that for most user needs the report should be used in conjunction with other sources of information. This represents a more flexible approach to meeting user needs: explicit recognition that there are other information sources that users may have access to besides the auditor's report. This is an interesting extension of the CICA approach.

Assurance engagements will obviously be an important area of research, standard setting, and practitioner innovation in the foreseeable future. We hope this appendix has helped clarify the key issues to watch for in future developments. More detailed discussion of specific types of assurance engagements is provided in Chapters 17 and 18 and in the appendix on environmental auditing at the back of this book.

We conclude this appendix with two illustrative direct-reporting reports from AICPA-related publications. Exhibits 14A–1 and 14A–2 illustrate assurance reports on risk assessment and performance measurement respectively. Note how difficult it is to distinguish these reports from consulting engagements. The first report, on risk assessments, has more of an assurance orientation as defined by *CICA Handbook, Section* 5025, but it also contains components of what would normally appear in a management letter (see Chapter 13). The second report, on performance measurement, seems much more in line with that of a consulting engagement. Here the auditor appears to be acting more like an asserter than an assurer. However, keep in mind that in the United States there are no standards on assurance engagements yet, and that these reports should be viewed as tentative and experimental. In light of the issues discussed here, you can compare them with the CICA's ED report given earlier in this appendix, and with reports provided in later chapters. It is clear that assurance engagements have the potential to revolutionize the profession, and that this will be a very active area of experimentation and growth in the next few years.

E X H I B I T 14A–2   **ILLUSTRATIVE REPORT**

[CPA'S Letterhead]

[Date]

Mr. John Jones, President
Secure Dog Cages, Inc.
1000 South Drive
Anywhere, USA

Dear Mr. Jones:

We are pleased to report the completion of our engagement to assist you in identifying the critical business risks of Secure Dog Cages, Inc. The purpose of our engagement is to assist you in better monitoring and managing the risks that your Company faces on a day-to-day basis.

Identification of Specific Business Risks

Attached is a list of the risks we identified as being relevant to Secure Dog Cages. Based on our previous meetings, the top ten risks in order of priority to the Company are as follows:

1. **Competition Risk**—The Company operates in a highly competitive environment with two primary competitors operating in the same geographic area as the Company.
2. **Political and Social Risk**—The Company has recently received a great deal of negative publicity due to noncompliance with the Occupational Safety and Health Act (OSHA).
3. **Management Risk**—The Company's production manager lacks training and experience, which has recently caused numerous scheduling problems and frequent shortages in finished goods inventory.
4. **Mangement Risk**—The Company's production manager fails to communicate effectively with production shift supervisors, which in turn causes numerous inefficiencies in the scheduling process.

EXHIBIT 14A–2   (concluded)

5. **Lender Risk**—The Company has a strained relationship with its primary lender due to several individually minor events of noncompliance with the Company's debt covenants.
6. **Employee Risk**—The Company has an unusually high rate of employee turnover. This is believed to be primarily due to the low level of wages paid by the Company in comparison to its competitors.
7. **Supply Risk**—The Company appears to be overly dependent on one major supplier, ABC Supplies, Inc.
8. **Receivables Risk**—Although the Company does have stringent credit policies, there are frequent exceptions to these policies, often resulting in uncollectible receivables.
9. **Cash Maagement Risk**—The Company occasionally overinvests in long-term assets, resulting in working capital deficiencies.
10. **Cash Management Risk**—The Company frequently pays bills before their due date without receiving discounts.

Analysis of Existing Risk Management Procedures

As agreed, we have also evaluated the Company's procedures for monitoring and controlling the top three risks and have provided our recommendations as follows:

Competition Risk—Although the company operates in a highly competitive environment, the Company currently appears to be adequately monitoring and controlling this risk.

Political and Social Risk—Because the Company's production manager lacks training and experience, there are frequent scheduling problems and shortages of finished goods inventory. The Company may want to reconsider this position and whether additional training for the production manager will correct the situation.

Should you need assistance in implementing our recommendations, we will be glad to help. Once the Company has dealt with these risks, we would like to meet with you again and develop risk management procedures for additional risks.

Reliability of Information

As noted, the purpose of our engagement was to assist you in improving the process by which you monitor and manage the risks that face your Company.
However, it is ultimately your responsibility to assess the adequacy of your risk management system.

In performing our engagement, we relied on the accuracy and reliability of information provided by Company personnel. We have not audited, examined, or reviewed the information, and express no assurance on it.

Distribution of the Report

This report is intended solely for the information and use of the management of Secure Dog Cages, Inc. and should not be used for any other purpose.

We appreciated the opportunity to serve you and thank the individuals in your organization for their cooperation. Over time, it will be necessary to reassess your risks to ensure that they have not changed and to ensure that your risk management system is functioning properly. Through our ongoing involvement with you as a client and our knowledge of your business and its processes, we are in a unique position to assist you with that process. Please contact us at any time should you desire such services.

Sincerely,

[Firm Name]

Reprinted with permission of Practitioners Publishing Company from *Guide to Nontraditional Engagements*, 3rd Edition. Copies of this guide can be ordered by calling PPC at (800) 323-8724.

EXHIBIT 14A–3   **ILLUSTRATIVE REPORT**

[CPA's Letterhead]

(Date)

ABC Automotive Services, Inc.
4321 Long Road
Anywhere, USA

Dear Mr. Johnson:

We are pleased to report the completion of the initial phrase of our engagement to assist you in developing and monitoring performance measures for ABC Automotive Services, Inc.[1] The purpose of our engagement is to help you identify and increase the quality of the performance measures. We considered the Company's strengths and weaknesses, overall mission, and specific objectives and strategies. Based on our procedures, we believe the following performance measures are consistent with the Company's objectives and strategies.

Recommended Performance Measures

The following management reports are currently being prepared and analyzed on a regular basis, and this should continue:

- Weekly accounts receivable aging—This lists past due accounts by customer and is used as a means of identifying collection problems.
- Monthly operating budget—This report consists of projected monthly revenue and expenses. It is used for comparison to actual month-end results.
- Monthly cash flow projection—This projection is prepared based on projected revenues, cash collections, and cash outlays each month. It is used to monitor the company's cash position so that line-of-credit draws can be anticipated.

In addition, the Company's measurements of weekly margin on labor measurement should be replaced and supplemented with the following performance measures:

- Daily units turned per employee—This measure captures labor utilization on a daily, rather than weekly basis, allowing you to more quickly identify slack time or other inefficiencies. Monitoring of units turned, along with solicitation from your employees of ways to turn units more quickly, will allow management to identify potential cost-savings that can then be weighed against quality considerations. This measure relates both to cycle time (the time it takes to turn one unit) and waste (inefficient use of employee time).
- Average time spent in follow-up, weekly per employee—This measure will complement the preceding measure by allowing management to gauge work quality and customer satisfaction. This measure relates both to quality and waste (time spent in rework).
- Jobs completed within time promised to customer—This measure allows you to monitor customer satisfaction based on delivery as promised. It is influenced by two separate factors, efficiency of work performed and promises made to the customer.
- Jobs completed late (delivery)—This measure, when added with the preceding measure, yields total jobs completed each day. This sum should correlate with daily units turned by employees. A lack of correlation may indicate that finished units are sitting and waiting for an unacceptable time before being returned to the customer.

Reliability of Information

As noted, the purpose of our engagement was to assist you in increasing the quality of the performance measures that you use in your decision-making process. Quality of information is improved by increasing its reliability, relevance, or both; and increased relevance is often attained by accepting a lower level of reliability. It is ultimately your responsibility to assess whether the information is sufficiently reliable for your intended use.

In performing our engagement, we relied on the accuracy and reliability of information provided by Company personnel. We have not audited, examined, or reviewed the information, and express no assurance on it.

Methods for Capturing the Information

In developing the preceding performance measures, we have considered availability and cost of obtaining the data necessary to calculate them. We believe that the information can be accumulated in a cost-effective manner, as follows:

- Daily units turned per employee—This information can be obtained with only slight modification to the daily work recap that each technician completes daily.
- Average time spent in follow-up, weekly per employee—This can also be obtained from the daily work recap, with only slight modification so that the technician can indicate whether the job is new or rework.
- Jobs completed within time promised to customer, and jobs completed later—This information can be captured from the work tickets currently prepared for each customer.

The daily work recaps and work tickets are forwarded to your accountant twice daily.

E X H I B I T 14–27   (concluded)

Analysis of Existing Performance Measures

Based on our discussions with you, discussions with other company personnel, and our analysis of your existing management reporting system and underlying data, the following performance measures and management reports are currently being used to manage the company:

- Weekly margin on labor—This is a weekly summary of gross margin on labor divided by total labor charges to customer. Materials are billed customers at a standard mark-up, so margins on materials are not tracked weekly.

- Weekly accounts receivable aging.

- Monthly operating budget.

- Monthly cash flow projection.

We have recommended that all of these, other than the weekly margin on labor, be continued. The Company's purpose in measuring the weekly margin on labor was, at one time, to monitor the relative profitability of the various services the Company provided. Over the past five years, however, the Company has gained a reputation as a quality provider of transmission services, and over 90% of the Company's revenues now come from transmission repair. Because of this evolution in the Company's services, the weekly margin on labor has come to be used primarily as a way to monitor labor utilization. We believe this can be more effectively managed by tracking the more specific measure of units turned. To provide a balanced scorecard that also considers inefficiency and customer satisfaction, we have recommended the additional measures related to time spent in follow-up (or rework) and jobs completed on time.

Ongoing Monitoring

The primary benefit of developing performance measures is that they can be tracked over time to monitor improvement and progress toward management's objectives and strategies. We would be glad to work with you on an ongoing basis to interpret the performance results and provide recommendations for improvement. Attached is a graphic presentation of the recommended performance measures for activity from [date] to [date].

Distribution of the Report

This report is intended solely for the information and use of the management of ABC Automotive Services, Inc. and should not be used for any other purpose.

We appreciate the opportunity to serve you and thank the individuals in your organization for their cooperation. Over time, as certain of the Company's objectives and strategies are achieved or as priorities change, it will be necessary to update your performance measurement system. In accordance with our engagement letter dated [date], we will provide (quarterly) progress reports to assess how the Company is progressing in its action plan, provide our interpretations of results, offer recommendations, as appropriate, and, most importantly, work with you to revise your objectives, action plans, and performance measures if necessary to respond to changing conditions.[2]

Sincerely,

[Firm Name]

Notes:

[1] This is an example report on the first phase of performance measurement services engagement to assess the client's performance measures and recommend new or revised measures. It should be tailored as necessary for each client. A critical aspect of providing performance measurement services is that, in addition to the first phase, the practitioner provides ongoing services. As discussed in *Section* 1610, this can consist of periodic meetings, which include progress reports on the client's performance measures and may include analyses of financial results.

[2] If the engagement does include quarterly progress reports, the last paragraph can be replaced with the following:

> We appreciate the opportunity to serve you and thank the individuals in your organization for their cooperation. Over time, as certain of the Company's objectives and strategies are achieved or as priorities change, it will be necessary to update your performance measurement system. Through our ongoing involvement with you as a client and our knowledge of your business and its processes, we are in a unique position to assist you with that process. Please contact us at any time should you desire such services.

Reprinted with permission of Practitioners Publishing Company from *Guide to Nontraditional Engagements*, 3rd Edition. Copies of this guide can be ordered by calling PPC at (800) 323-8724.

CHAPTER 15

Learning Objectives

Previous chapters have focused on the theory and practice of auditing. This chapter tells you about the regulation of accountants and accounting practice. Regulation and discipline depend on published codes of ethics and on effective enforcement practices. Your objectives in this chapter on professional ethics are to be able to:

1. Reason through an ethical decision problem using the imperative, utilitarian, and generalization principles of moral philosophy.

2. Analyse fact situations and decide whether an accountant's conduct does or does not conform to a province's Rules of Professional Conduct.

3. Name and explain the various professional associations and government agencies that enforce rules of conduct and explain the types of penalties they can impose on accountants.

PROFESSIONAL ETHICS, AUDITOR RESPONSIBILITIES

As part of a privileged profession, auditors have a set of responsibilities to society. These responsibilities can be grouped into three categories: moral responsibilities, professional responsibilities, and legal responsibilities. Morality deals with character and "doing the right thing." What is right is determined largely by social norms. Thus, auditors have a responsibility to conform to social norms. However, social norms are changing and a study of ethics may be helpful in preparing for lifelong adaption. Auditor's moral responsibilities can be summarized as "a public accountant should be upright, not kept upright." Ethics relates to proper conduct in one's life. A study of ethics helps the auditor develop a set of principles by which to live.

The more formal ethical responsibilities auditors have are referred to here as professional responsibilities. Professional responsibilities or professional ethics are the rules and principles for the proper conduct of an auditor in his or her professional work. Professional ethics are necessary for a number of reasons: to get the respect and confidence of the public, to distinguish the professional from the general public, to attain order within the profession, and to provide a means of self-policing the profession. These professional responsibilities (as distinguished from moral responsibilities that everyone should adhere to) are largely captured in the Rules of Professional Conduct, which is the topic of this chapter. Legal responsibilities are the topic of the next chapter (Chapter 16).

GENERAL ETHICS

A pervasive sense of proper ethical conduct is very important for professional accountants. Two aspects of ethics operate in the professional environment—general ethics (the spirit) and professional ethics (the rules). Mautz and Sharaf have contributed the following thoughts to the linkage between general ethics and professional ethics:

> The theory of ethics has been a subject of interest to philosophers since the beginnings of recorded thought. Because philosophers are concerned with the good of all mankind, their discussions have been concerned with what we may call general ethics rather than the ethics of small groups such as the members of a given profession. We cannot look, therefore, to their philosophical theories for direct solutions to our special problems. Nevertheless, their work with general ethics is of primary importance to the development of an appropriate concept in any special field. *Ethical behavior in auditing or in any other activity is no more than a special application of the general notion of ethical conduct devised by philosophers for men generally. Ethical conduct in auditing draws its justification and basic nature from the general theory of ethics. Thus, we are well advised to give some attention to the ideas and reasoning of some of the great philosophers on this subject.* [Emphasis added]

Overview

What is ethics? Wheelwright defined ethics as "that branch of philosophy which is the systematic study of reflective choice, of the standards of right and wrong by which it is to be guided, and of the goods toward which it may ultimately be directed."[1] In this definition, you can detect three key elements: (1) ethics involves questions requiring reflective choice (decision problems); (2) ethics involves guides of right and wrong (moral principles); and (3) ethics is concerned with the consequences of decisions.

What is an ethical problem? A problem situation exists when you must make a choice among alternative actions, and the right choice is not absolutely clear. An ethical problem situation may be described as one in which the choice of alternative actions affects the well-being of other persons.

What is ethical behaviour? You can find two standard philosophical answers to this question: (1) ethical behaviour is that which produces the greatest good, and (2) ethical behaviour is that which conforms to moral rules and principles. The most difficult problem situations arise when two or more rules conflict or when a rule and the criterion of "greatest good" conflict. Some cases are given later in this chapter to illustrate these difficulties.

Why does an individual or group need a code of ethical conduct? While it has been said that a person should be upright and not be kept upright, a code serves a useful purpose as a reference and a benchmark for individuals. A code makes explicit some of the criteria for conduct peculiar to the profession. Thus codes of professional ethics are able to provide some direct solutions that may not be available in general ethics theories. Furthermore, an individual is better able to know what the profession expects. From the point of view of the organized profession, a code is a public declaration of principled conduct, and it is a means of facilitating enforcement of standards of conduct. Practical enforcement and professionwide internal discipline would be impossible if members were not first put on notice of the standards.

A Variety of Roles

While one of the main purposes of ethics is to guide the actions of decision makers, the role of decision maker does not fully describe a professional person's entire obligation. Each person acts not only as an individual but also as a member of a profession and as a member of society. Hence, accountants and auditors are also spectators (observing the decisions of colleagues), advisers (counselling with co-workers), instructors (teaching accounting students or new employees on the job), judges (serving on disciplinary committees of provincial institutes), and critics (commenting on the ethical decisions of others). All of these roles are important in the practice of professional ethics.

An Ethical Decision Process

In considering general ethics, your primary goal is to arrive at a set of acceptable methods for making ethical decisions. Consequently, an understanding of some of the general principles of ethics can contribute background for a detailed consideration of the behaviour directed by the Rules of Professional Conduct of your provincial institute.

---

[1] Philip Wheelwright, *A Critical Introduction to Ethics*, 3d ed. (Indianapolis, Ind.: Odyssey Press, 1959).

To Tell or Not to Tell?

In your work as an auditor, you discover that the cashier, who has custody over the petty cash fund, has forged several payment records in order to cover innocent mistakes and to make the fund balance each month when it is replenished. Your investigation reveals that the amount involved during the year is $240. The cashier is a woman, age 55, and the president of the company is a man who can tolerate no mistakes, intentional or otherwise, in the accounting records. In fact, he is unyielding in this respect. He asks you about the results of your audit. Not doubting that the cashier would be fired if the forgeries were known, should you remain silent and thus not tell the truth?

In the earlier definition of ethics, one of the key elements was reflective choice. This involves an important sequence of events beginning with the recognition of a decision problem. Collection of evidence, in the ethics context, refers to thinking about rules of behaviour and outcomes of alternative actions. The process ends with analysing the situation and taking an action. Ethical decision problems almost always involve projecting yourself into the future to live with your decisions. Professional ethics decisions usually turn on these questions: "What written and unwritten rules govern my behaviour?" and "What are the possible consequences of my choices?" Principles of ethics can help you think about these two questions in real situations.

PHILOSOPHICAL PRINCIPLES IN ETHICS
. . . .

LEARNING OBJECTIVE

1. Reason through an ethical decision problem using the imperative, utilitarian, and generalization principles of moral philosophy.

We could dispense with the following discussion of ethical theories if we were willing to accept a simple rule: "Let conscience be your guide." Such a rule is appealing because it calls on an individual's own judgment, which may be based on wisdom, insight, adherence to custom, or an authoritative code. However, it might also be based on caprice, immaturity, ignorance, stubbornness, or misunderstanding.

In a similar manner, reliance on the opinions of others or on the weight of opinion of a particular social group is not always enough. Another person or a group of persons may perpetuate a custom or habit that is wrong. (Think about the signboard that proclaimed: "Wrong is wrong, even if everybody is doing it.") To adhere blindly to custom or to group habits is to abdicate individual responsibility. Titus and Keeton summarized this point succinctly: "Each person capable of making moral decisions is responsible for making his own decisions. The ultimate locus of moral responsibility is in the individual."[2] Thus, the function of ethical principles is not to provide a simple and sure rule but to provide some guides for your individual decisions and actions. The situation presented earlier ("To Tell or Not to Tell?") and the one that follows show some problem situations that for most persons would present difficult choices. Consider them in light of the imperative, the utilitarian, and the generalization principles.

---

[2] Harold H. Titus and Morris Keeton, *Ethics for Today*, 4th ed. (New York: American Book-Stratford Press, 1966), p. 131.

CONFLICTING DUTIES

As a result of your fine reputation as a public accountant, you were invited to become a director of a local bank and were pleased to accept the position. While serving on the board for a year, you learned that a bank director is under a duty to use care and prudence in administering the affairs of the bank, and that failure to do so in such a way that the bank suffers for a financial loss means that the director(s) may be held liable for damages. This month, in the course of an audit, you discover a seriously weakened financial position in a client who has a large loan from your bank. Prompt disclosure to the other bank directors would minimize the bank's loss, but, since the audit report cannot be completed for another three weeks, such disclosure would amount to divulging confidential information gained in the course of an audit engagement (prohibited by confidentiality principles). You can remain silent and honour confidentiality principles (and fail to honour your duty as a bank director), or you can speak up to the other directors (thus violating confidentiality principles). Which shall it be?

The Imperative Principle

The imperative principle directs a decision maker to act according to the requirements of an ethical rule. Strict versions of imperative ethics maintain that a decision should be made without trying to predict whether an action will probably create the greatest balance of good over evil. Ethics in the imperative sense is a function of moral rules and principles and does not involve a situation-specific calculation of the consequences.[3]

The philosopher Immanuel Kant (1724–1804) was perhaps the foremost advocate of the imperative school. Kant was unwilling to rely solely on decision makers' inclinations and values for decisions in various circumstances. He strongly preferred rules without exceptions to the varied and frequently inconsistent choices of individuals. He maintained that reason and the strict duty to be consistent governed the formulation of his first law of conduct: "Act only on that maxim whereby you can at the same time will that it should become a universal law." (Act only as you think everyone should act all the time.) This law of conduct is Kant's first formulation of his categorical imperative, meaning that it specifies an unconditional obligation. One such maxim (rule), for example, is: "Lying is wrong."

Suppose you believed it proper to lie by remaining silent about the cashier's attempts to cover mistakes (or any other specific kind of lie). The Kantian test of the morality of such a lie is: Can this maxim be a moral rule which should be followed without exception by all persons when asked about the results of audit work? In order for all persons to follow a rule, all persons must know of it, and when everyone knows that the rule is to lie about the results of some audit work, then no one is fooled by the auditor's silence (or false response).

---

[3] I. Kant, *Foundations of the Metaphysics of Morals*, trans. Lewis W. Beck (Indianapolis, Ind.: Bobbs-Merrill, 1959; originally published in 1785).

A lie succeeds only when the hearer of it does not know it is a lie. The nature of the universal rule is universal knowledge of it. Therefore, any manner of lying is bound to fail the test because no one would believe the speaker of the lie. Thus, lying is wrong because, when made universal, no one could be believed and virtually all common communication would become impossible.

A decision maker who followed the imperative principle would be on the horns of a dilemma in the case of conflicting duties as bank director and auditor. To remain silent to the other directors could be construed as a lie, since a director's duty is to speak up. Yet, to speak up would mean that the auditor's implicit promise to the client not to divulge confidential information would be a lie. However, following the imperative, the auditor in the other illustration would tell the employer about the forged payment records. By this principle, it does not matter that the circumstances might be different (e.g., the cashier was a 22-year-old man and the amount was $24,000). Kant maintained that motive and duty alone define a moral act, not the consequences of the act. This reasoning places the highest "value" of maintaining believable communication, and a lower "value" on the fate of the cashier.

The general objection to the imperative principle is the belief that so-called universal rules always turn out to have exceptions. The general response to this objection is that if the rule is stated properly to include the exceptional cases, then the principle is still valid. The problem with this response, however, is that human experience is complicated, and extremely complex universal rules would have to be constructed to try to cover all possible cases.[4]

One value of the Kantian categorical imperative, with its emphasis on universal, unconditional obligations, is that it lets you know when you are faced with an ethical decision problem. When only one rule derived from the categorical imperative is applicable, you may have no trouble following it. When two rules or two duties are in conflict, a serious problem exists. Assume for the sake of illustration that another rule is: "Live up to all your professional duties." In the auditor/bank director illustration, two rules ("Lying is wrong" and "Live up to all your professional duties") may thus be in conflict. Such conflicts of rules and duties create difficult problems because adherence to one of the rules means breaking the other.

The Kantian imperative theory, however, does not provide an easy way to make the decision. Someone who is rule-bound may find himself or herself in a dilemma. Just this kind of dilemma is what prompts people to look for ways to weigh the consequences of actions, and one way is described by the principle of utilitarianism discussed in the section below.

Most professional codes of ethics have characteristics of the imperative type of theory. As a general matter, professionals are expected to act in a manner in conformity with the rules. However, society frequently questions not only conduct itself but the rules on which conduct is based. Thus, a dogmatic imperative approach to ethical decisions may not be completely sufficient for the maintenance of professional standards. Society may question the rules, and conflicts among them are always possible. A means of estimating the consequences of alternative actions may be useful.

---

[4] Several rules of professional conduct to be discussed shortly are explicitly phrased to provide exceptions to the general rules (for example, rules 210 and 204 of the ICAO Rules of Professional Conduct). Imperative rules also seem to generate borderline cases, so the ethics divisions of PA professional bodies issue interpretations and rulings to explain the applicability of the rules.

FOLLOWING THE RULES MAY NOT BE GOOD ENOUGH

Once upon a time, the AICPA Rules of Conduct permitted auditors to have financial connections with audit clients in the form of certain immaterial loans and secured loans.

In June 1991 the SEC criticized Ernst & Young in connection with the audits of Republic Bank Corporation. Partners of the accounting firm had $15.8 million in loans from the Dallas bank, which later failed. The FDIC has criticized KPMG Peat Marwick for partners' loans from the failed Penn Square Bank in the early 1980s. The accountants maintained that the loans were held within the requirements of the rules of conduct concerning auditor independence. The regulators think independence was impaired.

In a move designed to protect the independence of CPAs and the reputation of the profession, following considerable unfavourable publicity, the AICPA concluded that the current form of the rules was too flexible and the relationships might damage the appearance of independence. In 1991 the AICPA enacted new restrictions on loans from audit clients.

The Principle of Utilitarianism

The principle of utilitarianism maintains that the ultimate criterion of an ethical decision is the balance of good over evil consequences produced by an action.[5] The emphasis in utilitarianism is on the consequences of action, rather than on the following of rules. The criterion of producing the greater good is made an explicit part of the decision process. While the principle is very useful, note well that it does not specify the values that enable you to figure the good or evil of an action.

In **act-utilitarianism** the centre of attention is the individual act, as it is affected by the specific circumstances of a situation. An act-utilitarian's ethical problem may be framed in this way: "What effect will my doing this act in this situation have on the general balance of good over evil?" This theory admits general guides such as "Telling the truth is probably always for the greatest good." However, the emphasis is always on the specific situation, and decision makers must determine whether they have independent grounds for thinking that it would be for the greatest general good not to tell the truth in a particular case.

The general difficulty with act-utilitarianism is that it seems to permit too many exceptions to well-established rules. Because attention is focused on individual acts, the long-run effect of setting examples for other people appears to be ignored. If an act-utilitarian decision is to break a moral rule, then the decision's success usually depends on everyone else's adherence to the rule. For example, to benefit from tax evasion for a good reason depends on everyone else not having an equally good reason for not paying their taxes.

Rule-utilitarianism, on the other hand, emphasizes the centrality of rules for ethical behaviour while still maintaining the criterion of the greatest universal good. This kind of utilitarianism means that decision makers must first determine the rules that will promote the greatest general good for the largest number of people. The

---

[5] J. S. Mills, *Utilitarianism*, ed. Oskar Piest (Indianapolis, Ind.: Bobbs-Merrill, 1957; originally published in 1861).

Balancing Act

Consolidata, Inc., was a tax client of Alexander Grant & Company, PAs (AG). Consolidata prepared payrolls for 38 customers, received the customers' money, then paid the payrolls. AG learned that Consolidata was in serious financial difficulty and advised the company to inform its customers, but company officials did not do so. When AG learned that the company's officers and directors had resigned, AG telephoned 12 Consolidata customers who were also AG clients, told them of the situation, and advised them not to entrust further payroll funds to Consolidata. The 12 were spared the risk of losing their money, and Consolidata went out of business a month later.

Consolidata accused AG of breach of contract for breaking an obligation of confidentiality required by the AICPA Code of Professional Conduct. One SEC lawyer said she thought AG should have alerted all 38 customers, not just the 12 AG clients. Accountants and SEC officials viewed the situation as a balancing of confidentiality (AICPA rule) against the public interest (Consolidata customers who needed a warning).

---

initial question is not which action has the greatest utility, but which rule. Thus, the rule-utilitarian's ethical decision problem can be framed as follows: "What effect will everyone's doing this kind of act in this kind of situation have on the general balance of good over evil?" The principle of utility becomes operative not only in determining what particular action to take in a specific decision situation in which rules conflict but also in determining what the rules should be in the first place.

The statement of the rule-utilitarian's problem may be given a very commonsense expression: "What would happen if everybody acted this way?" In this form, the question is known as generalization.

The Generalization Argument

For all practical purposes, the **generalization argument** may be considered a judicious combination of the imperative and utilitarian principles. Stated succinctly, the argument is this: "If all relevantly similar persons acting under relevantly similar circumstances were to act in a certain way and the consequences would be undesirable, then no one ought to act in that way without a reason."[6] A more everyday expression of the argument is this question: "What would happen if everyone acted in that certain way?" If the answer to the question is that the consequences would be undesirable, then your conclusion, according to the generalization test, will be that the way of acting is unethical and ought not be done.

The key ideas in the generalization test are similar persons and similar circumstances. These features provide the needed flexibility to consider the many variations that arise in real problem situations. They also demand considerable judgment in determining whether persons and circumstances are genuinely different or are just arbitrarily rationalized as different so that a preconceived preference can be "explained" as right.

---

[6] Marcus G. Singer, *Generalization in Ethics* (New York: Atheneum, 1961, 1971), esp. pp. 5, 10–11, 61, 63, 73, 81, 105–22.

SERVICE VERSUS INDEPENDENCE

For many years a national PA firm had encouraged its professionals to become active members of the boards of directors of corporations. The purpose was to provide expertise to businesses in the metropolitan area and to enable the accounting firm to become well known and well respected. The firm changed its policy to prohibit such service after it had the opportunity to obtain some of these corporations as audit clients, but it was forced to refuse or delay the PA–client relationship. The firm's audit independence was considered impaired when a member of the firm had served in a director or management capacity during the period covered by the financial statements the corporations wanted the firm to audit. The generalization test was: If members of the firm serve on the boards of directors of all corporations that may become audit clients, none of these corporations can be accepted as audit clients—a result that is undesirable.

The problem over conflict of duties as a bank director and public accountant can arise only when accounting clients are customers of the bank. As long as circumstances of conflict do not exist, the question of "What if every PA served as a bank director of a bank with whom no accounting client did business?" is easily answerable. There is no problem because no conflict can arise. But when the potential for conflict exists, the question becomes, "What if every PA were exposed to conflict-of-duty situations like this one?" In this case, the results could be undesirable, and the conclusion would be that no PAs should serve as bank directors unless none of their accounting clients did business with the bank.

Another kind of conflict subject to the generalization test is illustrated by a PA firm's desire for service and need for independence.

This brief review of principles in ethics provides some guide to the ways that many people approach difficult decision problems. The greatest task is to take general notions of ethics—the imperative, utilitarianism, and generalization—and apply them to a real decision. Their application through codes of professional conduct is a challenge.

· ·

R E V I E W
CHECKPOINTS

15.1 What roles must a professional accountant be prepared to occupy in regard to ethical decision problems?

15.2 When might the rule "Let conscience be your guide" not be sufficient basis for your personal ethics decisions? for your professional ethics decisions?

15.3 Assume that you accept the following ethical rule: "Failure to tell the whole truth is wrong." In the textbook illustrations about (a) your position as a bank director and (b) your knowledge of the cashier's forgeries, what would this rule require you to do? Why is an unalterable rule like this classed as an element of imperative ethical theory?

15.4 How does utilitarian ethics differ from imperative ethics?

· ·

Rules of Professional Conduct and Code of Ethics

* * * * * * * * * * * *

LEARNING OBJECTIVE

2. Analyse fact situations and decide whether an accountant's conduct does or does not conform to a province's Rules of Professional Conduct.

Each of the PA bodies (CAs, CGAs, CMAs) has its own rules of professional conduct for its members, either provincially or nationally. Generally, these rules are published as a part of the member's *Handbook,* which identifies the various activities and regulations of the PA institute or association and includes a section on professional conduct. Codes of conduct need to develop a balance between very detailed rules and more general principles. The codes also need to be practical; as a result, they tend to have similar frameworks, as indicated in the box below.

The codes of professional conduct are usually organized hierarchically, with general principles at the beginning and with increasing detail and specifics as one goes from the rules to specific interpretations of the rules. The general principles are sometimes referred to as "ideal standards" and the more specific rules and related interpretations as "minimum standards."

The various codes of professional conduct are meant to apply to all members in public practice subject to certain exceptions for students and members not in public practice. Generally, for CAs and CMAs the issuance of codes is the responsibility of provincial institutes or societies. CGAs have a national code set by CGAAC; however, provincial associations of CGAs may add modifications to the national code. Recently, the CA provincial institutes have substantially harmonized their codes so that the CA code can be viewed as more of a national one.

As an illustration of a code, the ICAO *Member's Handbook* identifies the various activities and regulations of the Ontario Institute, and includes a section on professional conduct. The professional conduct section is divided into three parts: a Foreword, the Rules of Professional Conduct, and the Interpretation of the Rules. Many people consider the Foreword the most important part of the professional conduct regulations.[7] The reason is that the Foreword contains a set of principles that are intended to provide guidance in the absence of specific rules. In particular, unlike the rules that many people think of as "thou shalt nots"—a series of rules against—the Foreword sets out the broad principles providing guidance in the absence of specific rules. The Foreword is must reading for CAs and students because the *Members'*

Typical Framework for a Code of Conduct for Professional Accountants

- Introduction and purpose
- Fundamental principles and standards
- General rules
- Specific rules
- Discipline
- Interpretations of rules

Table 3.3 of L.J. Brooks, *Professional Ethics for Public Accountants,* West Publishing, 1995, p. 120.

---

[7] K. Gunning, "Required Reading," *CA Magazine,* November 1992, pp. 38–40.

Handbook specifically advises members that all the rules that follow "are to be read in the light of the Foreword to the rules."

The Foreword has some clearly defined sections. The first section sets out the purpose of the rules, which is to guide the profession in serving the public. The second section of the Foreword reviews the key characteristics that mark a profession and a professional, and concludes that "chartered accountancy is a profession."

The next section identifies the six "fundamental statements of accepted conduct" around which all the rules are centred. These six principles can be summarized as follows:

1. The member should act to maintain the profession's reputation.
2. The member should use due care and maintain his or her professional competence.
3. The member should maintain independence in the appearance as well as the fact of independence of his or her professional judgment.
4. The member should preserve client's confidentiality.
5. The member should base his or her reputation on professional excellence—in particular, advertising should inform, not solicit.
6. The member should show professional courtesy to other members at all times.

These principles can be interpreted as ideals to which every professional aspires. The rules themselves are more specific because they are intended as guides to action and to be enforceable. However, adherence to the rules represents only a minimum acceptable or floor level of performance for CAs. On the other hand, because they are more detailed, the rules allow the implementation of a code through the use of concrete benchmarks against which a member's performance can be compared.

The Foreword singles out for further discussion several of the principles that require additional guidance: (*a*) sustaining professional competence (related to principle 2 above), (*b*) avoiding conflicts of interest in respect of a client's affairs (related to principle 3), and (*c*) practice development based on professional excellence rather than self-promotion (related to principle 5). It will be evident from the space devoted to the rules themselves that these particular principles seem to require the most detailed guidance for members. However, as the Foreword makes clear, in a world where ethical decision-making is becoming more complex yet indispensable for maintaining the public interest, the absence of specific rules makes the principle that much more important. As a result, some writers have concluded that the six principles should be given much more prominence, and used more frequently.[8]

After the Foreword come the Rules of Conduct themselves. The ICAO Council also publishes "Council Interpretations of (Rules of Conduct)," which are detailed explanations of specific rules necessary to help members understand particular applications. Anyone who departs from Council interpretations has the burden of justifying that departure in any disciplinary hearing.

The CMAs have a similar set of provincial rules for each provincial society. For example, the Society of Management Accountants of Ontario (SMAO) *Handbook on*

---

[8] Ibid.

Ethics contains predominantly (20 of 26 pages) general principles of ethics; the more detailed rules and interpretations are covered in the remainder. Where CMAs have the right to perform assurance engagements, the rules require that they comply with local legislation.

The CGAs have a national code of conduct that provides the basic framework for the provincial association rules. The CGA code consists of a preamble that explains why a code is necessary and who is affected; a statement of ethical principles; Rules of Conduct, with guidance concerning their application to certain specific situations; and, finally, a set of definitions of terms used throughout the CGA code. There is much similarity in the general principles of all three professional codes, which are reviewed in the next section, along with the related rules.

Rules of Professional Conduct

The Rules of Professional Conduct derive their authority from the bylaws of the various PA professional bodies.

Members of the professional bodies (CAs, CGAs, CMAs) are held responsible for compliance with the rules by all persons associated with them in public practice, including employees and partners. In addition, members may not permit other people to carry out on their behalf acts which are prohibited by the rules.

As an illustration, an outline of the ICAO rules and their topics is presented below.

THE INSTITUTE OF CHARTERED ACCOUNTANTS OF ONTARIO
RULES OF PROFESSIONAL CONDUCT

Section 100—GENERAL

101	Compliance with bylaws, regulations and rules
102.1	Conviction of criminal or similar offences
102.2	Reporting disciplinary suspension, expulsion or restriction of right to practise
103	False or misleading applications
104	Requirement to reply in writing

Section 200—STANDARDS OF CONDUCT AFFECTING THE PUBLIC INTEREST

201	Maintenance of reputation of profession
202	Integrity and due care
203.1	Professional competence
.2	Co-operation with practice inspections and conduct investigations
204.1	Objectivity: audit engagements
.2	Objectivity: review engagements
.3	Objectivity: insolvency engagements
.4	Disclosure of conflicts

An authority on professional ethics, Len Brooks at the University of Toronto, has identified certain principles in codes of conduct that apply to all professional accountants. See the following box.

FUNDAMENTAL PRINCIPLES IN CODES OF CONDUCT FOR PROFESSIONAL ACCOUNTANTS

Members should:

- at all times maintain the good reputation of the profession and its ability to serve the public interest
- perform with:
  - integrity
  - objectivity
  - independence
  - professional competence
  - due care
  - confidentiality
- not be associated with any misleading information or misrepresentation

Table 3.4 of L.J. Brooks, *Professional Ethics for Public Accountants,* West Publishing, 1995, p. 121.

The rest of this chapter discusses Brooks's principles and related rules in more detail. However, the student should refer to the appropriate *Member's Handbooks* for CAs, CGAs, or CMAs for more extensive guidance on rules related to these professional groups.

Serving the Public Interest

The single most important principle is that accountants must serve the public interest; they can only do so if the profession maintains a good reputation at all times. The remaining principles all serve to support this first principle. "The phrase 'at all times' is significant because the public will view any serious transgression of a professional accountant including those outside business or professional activity, as a black mark against the profession as a whole. Consequently, if a professional accountant is convicted of a minimal offense or fraud, his or her certification is usually revoked" (L.J. Brooks, *Professional Ethics for Accountants,* West Publishing, 1995, p. 120.)

Integrity

Integrity is the duty to be honest and conscientious in performing professional services. Integrity relates to the basic character of the professional—a PA must "be upright" not "kept upright." Without the integrity of its members, the profession cannot maintain its good reputation and serve the public interest.

Independence and Objectivity

Independence and objectivity are closely related terms. The rather fine distinction is based mainly on the fact that independence is the term given to objectivity in the special case of assurance engagements, and that independence is a way of achieving objectivity.

The term objectivity is defined in the ICAO Rule 204 substantially as follows:

> In the performance of audit, review, or insolvency engagements, a member in public practice shall hold himself or herself free of any influence, interest, or relationship which, in respect of the engagement impairs the member's professional judgment or objectivity or which, in the view of a reasonable observer, would impair the member's professional judgment or objectivity. For all engagements the member should disclose all conflict of interest which may be seen by a reasonable observer to impair the member's professional judgment or objectivity.

The ICAO makes no reference to the term "independence" in its Code of Conduct. However, the term independence is used in the Canadian Business Corporations Act, in some provincial corporations acts, and in the SMA provincial Rules of Conduct. The key Canadian legislation requires that the auditor be "independent"—presumably, the fact of independence must be determined by the courts, especially if the term is not specifically codified in a PA's professional standards.

The Canadian Business Corporations Act, Section 161, defines independence as a key qualification of an auditor, as indicated in the following box:

---

161. **(1) Qualification of auditor.**—Subject to subsection (5), a person is disqualified from being an auditor of a corporation if he is not independent of the corporation, any of its affiliates, or the directors or officers of any such corporation or its affiliates.

(2) Independence.—For the purpose of this section,
  (a) independence is a question of fact; and
  (b) a person is deemed not to be independent if he or his business partner
     (I) is a business partner, a director, an officer or an employee of the corporation or any of its affiliates, or a business partner of any director, officer or employee of any such corporation or any of its affiliates;
     (II) beneficially owns or controls, directly or indirectly, a material interest in the securities of the corporation or any of its affiliates, or
     (III) has been a receiver-manager, liquidator or trustee in bankruptcy of the corporation or any of its affiliates within two years of his proposed appointment as auditor of the corporation.

(3) Duty to resign.—An auditor who becomes disqualified under this section shall, subject to subsection (5), resign forthwith after becoming aware of his disqualification.

The term independence is internationally recognized. For example, the International Federation of Accountants Technical Standard on Ethics, section 8, specifies that "professional accountants in public practice when undertaking a reporting assignment should be independent in fact and appearance." Similar wording is used in the SMAO's Code of Conduct with respect to the need for independence on assurance engagements.

It should be clear from all this that independence is an important concept for PAs. For this reason we discuss both independence and objectivity. However, the focus of this textbook is on audits, so our focus will be on independence.

The Canadian legislation referred to earlier requires independence for financial statement audit services. However, review services in connection with unaudited financial statements, engagements to report on prospective financial statements (forecasts and projections), other assurance services, and engagements to express opinions on representations other than financial statements (e.g., reports on internal control) all require independence. In this regard you should be aware of the definition of "public practice." A member is considered to be in the public practice of accounting if (1) he or she "holds out to be a PA," that is, lets it be known publicly that the member is a PA, and (2) offers to perform for clients the types of services rendered by other public accountants. The latter part of the definition is very broad because PAs perform a wide range of accounting, audit, taxation, and consulting services.[9] (Note that this CICA definition of public accounting is one of the few instances where the CICA uses the term "independence.") The result of this definition is that most PAs who seek to obtain clients from the general public are in the practice of public accounting. For example, the PAs who work for H&R Block, the tax preparation corporation, are in public practice if they let themselves be known as PAs, even though the company is not an accounting firm.

The concept of independence is the cornerstone of the public accounting profession. Since the purpose of independent financial auditing is to lend credibility to financial statements, auditors must in fact be impartial and unbiased with respect to both the client management and the client entity itself.

Not only must auditors be independent in fact, they must also appear independent to outside decision makers who rely on their assurance services. Independence, in fact, is a mental condition and is difficult to demonstrate by physical or visual means. Thus, some appearances of lacking independence may be prohibited in specific interpretations of the independence principle. The next box gives some interpretations used by CGAAC.

The interpretations in the box deal with the financial interests in a client. The time period of the prohibited activities depends on the circumstances. A member may divest a prohibited financial interest before the first work on a new client begins, after which it is improper to reinvest when the engagement will continue for future years. Direct or indirect financial interests are allowed up to the point of materiality (with reference to the member's wealth). This provision permits members to hold mutual fund shares and have some limited business transactions with clients so long as they do not reach material proportions.

Generally, the Rules of Conduct allow home mortgages, immaterial loans, and secured loans, all made under a client's normal lending procedures, terms, and requirements, if the client is a bank or other financial institution. However, in the United States a scandal broke out when some accountants apparently used their public accountant client relations with banks to obtain loans on real estate ventures

---

[9] The CICA's definition of public accountant in its *Terminology for Accountants*, 4th Ed (1992), is as follows: "1. The perfomance of services for clients, the purpose of which is to add credibility to financial information that may be relied upon by interested parties. 2. The performance of independent professional accounting and related services for clients. 3. Any service so defined by a particular statute or authority."

CGAAC Statement of Ethical Principles and Rules of Conduct

R202.5 Deemed Conflicts of Interest

If the member or the member's partners in a public accounting practice are engaged to provide audit or review services for a client, and any of the following circumstances are present or were present during the period being reported upon, a member is deemed to be not free of actual or potential conflict of interest:

(a) the member, any of the member's partners, or any employee of the member assigned to the engagement is a director, officer or employee of the client, or a person in the member's or the partners' immediate families is a director or officer of the client.

(b) the member, any of the member's partners, any employee of the member assigned to the engagement, or a person in the member's partners' or the employee's immediate families:

   (I) is indebted to the client, other than that obtained or granted in the normal course of business;

   (II) owns or controls, directly or indirectly, any interest in a debt obligation of the client, other than that obtained or granted in the normal course of business and which is immaterial to the individual and the member.

   (III) is appointed a trustee in bankruptcy, liquidator, receiver or receiver-manager, this Rule shall not apply to a solvent company provided that all the shareholders agree to the appointment; or

   (IV) is an executor, administrator or trustee of the client estate, trust, charitable foundation, pension or profit-sharing plan.

(c) any of the member's close relatives:

   (I) holds an interest in the client that is material to the holder, or is a director, officer or employee of the client who has the right or responsibility to make decisions significantly affecting the affairs of the client.

   (II) is an executor, administrator or trustee of the client estate, trust, charitable foundation, pension or profit-sharing plan.

   (III) is an executor, administrator or trustee of an estate, trust or charitable foundation which holds a material interest in the client.

Source: Extract from CGAAC Statement of Ethical Principles, published by the Certified General Accountants Association of Canada (©CGA–Canada, 1996, reprinted by permission).

---

and expensive homes, sometimes on prime rate terms that other similar borrowers could not obtain. When financial institutions failed and these loans became known, the newspaper stories and regulators' lawsuits brought a flood of unfavourable publicity. As noted earlier in "Following the Rules May Not Be Good Enough" (see page 690), the AICPA put an end to most loans from audit clients with a revised rule of their own. Currently there are no similar prohibitions in Canadian Rules of Conduct.

Other Permitted Loans

Independence is not considered impaired by a member obtaining these kinds of personal loans from assurance service clients: (*a*) auto loans and leases collateralized by the automobile, (*b*) insurance policy loans based on policy surrender value, (*c*) loans collateralized by cash deposits at the same financial institution, and (*d*) credit card balances and cash advances equivalent to other customers of the client in the normal course of business. Thus, an individual involved in the audit of a bank can have an auto loan at the bank, borrow money secured by cash in a certificate of deposit, and have the bank's credit card. For insurance company clients, the PA can borrow against the cash surrender value of a life insurance policy. However the loans should have the same terms as granted to other customers of the institution in the normal course of business. Potentially, these kinds of permitted loans could be abused in spirit, as apparently happened in the United States. The key ethical judgment is what is "the normal course of business" and, more basically, what types of loan could lead to at least the perception of impairment of auditor independence.

The Codes of Conduct collectively prohibit activities that amount to the ability to make decisions for the client or to act as management, broadly defined. The appearance of independence is impaired if such a connection existed at any time during the period covered by the financial statements, regardless of whether the association was terminated prior to the beginning of the audit work. The presumption is that members cannot be independent and objective when attesting to decisions in which they took part or with which they appeared to be connected.

In terms of ethics principles, these rules may be justified on a rule-utilitarian basis as far as direct financial interests are concerned. The logic is something like this: The greatest good is created by making a situation free of any suspicious circumstances, no matter how innocent they may be in truth. The goodwill of public reliance and respect is greater than the PA's sacrifice of the opportunity to invest in securities of clients or participate in their management. Note that this suggests that defining assurance engagements to overlap with consulting engagements as discussed in the appendix to Chapter 14 may create special problems with the Code of Conduct. Thus, the codes may require a clearer distinction between assurance and non-assurance engagements.

Other Issues Related to the Independence Principle

In addition to the issues discussed above, there are other aspects relevant to the independence principle, briefly described below.

Honorary Positions in Nonprofit Organizations (as per CGAAC Rule 202.4)

Ordinarily, independence is impaired if a PA serves on an organization's board of directors. However, members can be honorary directors of such organizations as charity hospitals, fund drives, symphony orchestra societies, and other nonprofit organizations so long as (1) the position is purely honorary, (2) the PA is identified as an honorary director on letterheads and other literature, (3) the only form of participation is the use of the PA's name, and (4) the PA does not vote with the board or participate in management functions. When all these criteria are satisfied, the PA/board member can perform assurance services because the appearances of independence will have been preserved.

Retired Partners

Independence problems do not end when partners retire, resign, or otherwise leave an accounting firm. A former partner can cause independence to be impaired in some circumstances in connection with his or her association with a client of the former firm. However, the problems are solved and independence is not impaired if (1) the person's retirement benefits are fixed, (2) the person is no longer active in the accounting firm (sometimes even retired partners remain "active"), and (3) the former partner is not held out to be associated with the accounting firm by a reasonable observer. Regulators may have stricter rules relating to former partners.

Accounting Services

If a PA performs the bookkeeping and makes accounting decisions for a company and the management of the company does not know enough about the financial statements to take primary responsibility for them, the PA cannot be considered independent for assurance services. The problem in this situation relates to the appearance of the PA having both prepared the financial statements or other data and given an audit report or other assurance on his or her own work. The PA can perform the bookkeeping and counsel the client management about the accounting principles choices, but in the final analysis, the management must be able to say, "These are our financial statements (or other data); we made the choices of accounting principles; we take primary responsibility for them." Again, regulators may have stricter rules relating to such bookkeeping services.

Actual or Threatened Litigation

Independence can be threatened by appearances of a PA trying to serve his or her own best interests. This condition can arise when a PA and a client move into an adversary relationship and away from the co-operative relationship needed in an assurance engagement. PAs are considered not independent when (1) company management threatens or actually starts a lawsuit against the PA alleging deficiencies in audit or other assurance work and (2) the PA threatens or starts litigation against the company management alleging fraud or deceit. Such cases may be rare, but auditors can find out a way out of such difficult audit situations by ending the assurance engagement. Essentially the PA–client relationship ends, and the litigation begins a new relationship.

Investor or Investee Relationships

In this context "investor" and "investee" have the same meaning as in the accounting rules about accounting for investments on the equity method (*Handbook Section* 3050). The *investor* is the party that has significant influence over a business, and the *investee* is the business in which the investor has the significant influence.

When the PA's client is the investor, a PA's direct or material indirect financial interest in a nonclient investee impairs the PA's independence. The reasoning for the basic rule is that the client investor, through its ability to influence a nonclient investee, can increase or decrease the PA's financial stake in the investee by an amount material to the PA, and, therefore, the PA may not appear to be independent. The exception is: If the nonclient investee is immaterial to the investor, independence is not considered impaired when the PA's financial interest in a nonclient investee is immaterial in relation to the PA's wealth.

When a PA has an investment in a nonclient investor: (*a*) independence with respect to a client investee that is material in the financial statements of the investor is impaired when the PA has any direct or material indirect financial interest in the nonclient investor; (*b*) independence with respect to a client investee that is not material in the financial statements of the investor is not impaired, even if the PA's investment is material to the PA, as long as the PA does not have significant influence over the actions of the nonclient investor; but (*c*) independence with respect to a client investee that is not material in the financial statements of the investor is impaired when the PA has a large enough investment to give the PA a significant influence over the actions of the nonclient investor, which then can influence (manage) affairs of the client investee. The reasoning underlying the independence impairment conclusions in these relationships is that the PA occupies a position similar to being a member of management of the client investee.

Effect of Family Relationships

The Code of Conduct and all the interpretations apply to "members," but you should not confuse being a member of a professional accounting institute, society, or association with the use of the word *member* in the rule. For purposes of independence, the terms *member* and *member's firm* generally include:

- All partners in the accounting firm.
- All professional employees participating in the engagement, including audit, tax, and management consulting personnel.
- All other manager-level employees located in a firm office that does a significant part of the audit.
- Any PA firm person formerly employed by or connected with the audit client in a managerial capacity unless the person (*a*) is disassociated from the client and (*b*) does not participate in the engagement.
- Any PA firm professional (e.g., partner, manager, staff) who is associated with the client in a managerial capacity and is located in an office of the PA firm that does a significant part of the engagement.

The term "member" excludes "students" registered under the bylaws of the professional body. However, the Codes of Conduct generally apply to students as well as members.

This enumeration permits (*a*) financial relationships by manager-level personnel located in offices not involved in the audit; (*b*) financial relationships by staff in offices not involved in the audit and in an office involved in the audit as long as they are not on the engagement itself; (*c*) former managerial relationships by partners, managers, and staff, provided they are now disassociated from the client and do not participate in the engagement; and (*d*) current managerial relationships by managers and staff, provided they do not participate in the engagement and are located in an office that does not do a significant part of the engagement. All this is rather complicated, but the bottom line is that it is rare for any partners/shareholders in the firm to be able to have any of the financial or managerial relationships. It is possible for managers and staff to have such relationships, provided they are far removed from the actual work on the audit engagement.

Financial interests of spouses and dependent persons (whether related or not) and some financial interests of close relatives are attributed to the member. (Close relatives include nondependent children, stepchildren, brothers, sisters, parents, grandparents, parents-in-law, and the spouses of each of these.) Thus, independence would be impaired if (*a*) a spouse or dependent grandfather of a member had a direct financial interest in an audit client or (*b*) a member on an engagement knew about a material financial interest of a nondependent daughter or brother in a client.

Employment relations of spouses, dependent persons, and close relatives can be attributed to a member. Positions that can exercise significant influences over the operating, financial, or accounting policies of the client are attributed to the member and impair independence. Positions that are "audit sensitive" (e.g., cashier, internal auditor, accounting supervisor, purchasing agent, inventory warehouse supervisor) are attributed to the member and impair independence. However, such employment poses no problem when it cannot influence the audit work (e.g., secretarial, non-financial) or is not audit-sensitive.

The Code of Conduct rules are minimum criteria relating to independence. PA firms can make more limiting rules. The anecdote in the next box shows some rules given to PA firm job applicants by a Big Six accounting firm.

IF EMPLOYED BY "ANONYMOUS FIRM," I UNDERSTAND THAT:

Professional staff members of the firm, their spouses, and dependents are prohibited from owning or controlling investments in any of our clients and certain related nonclients, and I will be required to dispose of any such investments before commencing employment with the firm.

I will be prohibited from disclosing nonpublic information regarding clients or other entities to anyone, other than for firm business, or using it for any personal purpose.

I will be expected to devote my energies to the firm to the fullest extent possible and refrain from other business interests that might require significant time or that could be considered a conflict of interest.

Neither an offer of employment nor employment itself carries with it a guarantee of tenure of employment, and my employment, compensation, and benefits can be terminated, with or without cause or notice, at any time at the option of the firm or myself.

Analysis

Generally, the Rules of Professional Conduct and corporation acts legislation imply a fine distinction between independence and integrity and objectivity. The spirit of the rules is that integrity and objectivity are required in connection with all professional services, and, in addition, independence is required for assurance services. In this context integrity and objectivity are the larger concepts, and "independence" is a special condition largely defined by the matters of appearance specified in the codes or their interpretations. "Conflicts of interest," as for example cited in ICAO Rule 204, refers to the need to avoid having business interests in which the accountant's personal financial relationships or the accountant's relationships with other clients might tempt the accountant to fail to serve the best interests of a client or the public that uses the results of the engagement.

Phrases such as "shall not knowingly misrepresent facts" and "[shall not] subor-dinate his or her judgment to others" emphasize conditions people ordinarily identify

---

Auditor's Downfall

MIAMI (March, 1987): Mr. G, former partner of a large PA firm, surrenders today to begin a 12-year prison term.

As auditor of ESM, Mr. G knowingly approved the company's false financial statements for five years, allowing the massive fraud to continue, ultimately costing investors $320 million.

Just days after being promoted to partner, two ESM officers told him about an accounting ruse that was hiding millions of dollars in losses. He had missed it in two previous audits. They said: "It's going to look terrible for you, a new partner."

Mr. G didn't want to face his superiors at the firm with the admission of the failed audits. He decided to go along with ESM because he thought they could make up the losses and get everybody out of it.

Mr. G: "I never evaluated a criminal side to what I was doing. It was a professional decision, a judgment decision that it would eventually work itself out. It's the only thing I never discussed with my wife."

ESM loaned Mr. G $200,000 to help out with his financial problems. "I never related my actions to the money. I just didn't want to face up that I had missed it originally."

On being prepared for prison: "I don't know. What can I bring, a typewriter, computer? I'd like to read and work on things."

Source: The Wall Street Journal, March 4, 1987.

---

with the concepts of integrity and objectivity. Accountants who know about a client's lies in a tax return, false journal entries, material misrepresentations in financial statements, and the like have violated both the spirit and the letter of the Rules of Conduct. However, in tax practice, an accountant can act as an advocate to resolve doubt in favour of a taxpayer-client as long as the tax treatment has a reasonable or justifiable basis.

Professional Competence and Due Care

The professional competence and due care principles of the Codes of Conduct can be summarized as follows:

A. *Professional competence.* Undertake only those professional services that the member or the member's firm can reasonably expect to be completed with professional competence.

B. *Due professional care.* Exercise due professional care in the performance of professional services.

C. *Planning and supervision.* Adequately plan and supervise the performance of professional services.

D. *Sufficient relevant data.* Obtain sufficient relevant data to afford a reasonable basis for conclusions or recommendations in relation to any professional services performed.

Analysis

The professional competence and due care principles are a comprehensive statement of general standards that accountants are expected to observe in all areas of practice. These are the principles that enforce the various series of professional standards. For example, there is usually a specific rule relating to compliance with professional standards.

Compliance with Professional Standards

A member engaged in the practice of public accounting shall perform his or her professional services in accordance with generally accepted standards of practice of the profession (from Rule 206 of ICAO).

Analysis

This rule may be viewed as an extension and refinement of the due care principle. It implies adherence to duly promulgated technical standards in all areas of professional service. These areas include review and compilation (unaudited financial statements), consulting tax, and "other" professional services. The practical effect of this rule is to make noncompliance with all technical standards subject to disciplinary proceedings. Thus, failure to follow auditing standards, accounting and review standards, and assurance, compilation, and professional conduct standards is a violation of this rule.

Accounting Principles.   The compliance rule requires adherence to official pronouncements of accounting principles, with an important exception relating to unusual circumstances where adherence would create misleading statements. The rule itself concedes that unusual circumstances may exist; it permits PAs to decide for themselves the applicability of official pronouncements and places on them the burden of an ethical decision. The rule is not strictly imperative, in that it allows PAs to exercise a utilitarian calculation for special circumstances. The compliance rule requires adherence to official pronouncements unless such adherence would be misleading. The consequences of misleading statements to outside decision makers would be financial harm, so presumably the greater good would be realized by explaining a departure.

As a result of the November 1997 Supreme Court of Canada ruling in *Kripps v. Touche Ross,* this compliance rule is likely to become more influential in the future. This is further discussed in Chapter 16.

Confidentiality

The general principle of confidentiality is as follows:

> A member in public practice shall not disclose any confidential information without the specific consent of the client.

This principle shall not be construed (1) to relieve a member of his or her professional obligations[10] to comply with a validly issued and enforceable subpoena or summons, (2) to prohibit a member's compliance with applicable laws and

---

[10] C. Chazen, R.L. Miller, and K.I. Solomon, "When the Rules Say: See Your Lawyer," *Journal of Accountancy,* January 1981, p. 70.

government regulations, (3) to prohibit review of a member's professional practice under *Member's Handbook* bylaws, or (4) to preclude a member from initiating a complaint with or responding to any enquiry made by the ethics division or trial board or a duly constituted investigative or disciplinary body of the members' professional group (CAs, CMAs, or CGAs).

Members of any of the bodies identified in (4) above and members involved with professional practice reviews identified in (3) above shall not use to their own advantage or disclose any member's confidential client information that comes to their attention in carrying out those activities. This prohibition shall not restrict members' exchange of information in connection with the investigative or disciplinary proceedings described in (4) above or the professional practice reviews described in (3) above.

Confidential information is information that should not be disclosed to outside parties unless demanded by a court or an administrative body having subpoena or summons power. Privileged information, on the other hand, is information that cannot even be demanded by a court. Common-law privilege exists for husband–wife, attorney–client, and physician–patient relationships. In all the recognized privilege relationships, the professional person is obligated to observe the privilege, which can be waived only by the client, patient, or penitent. (These persons are said to be the holders of the privilege.)

> The duty to keep a client's affairs confidential should not be confused with the legal concept of privilege. The duty of confidentiality precludes the member from disclosing a client's affairs without the knowledge or consent of the client. However, this duty does not excuse a member from obeying an order of a court of competent jurisdiction requiring the member to disclose the information.
>
> A court will determine whether or not a member should maintain the confidentiality of client information depending on the facts of each case. (ICAO Council Interpretation 210.1, paragraph 1)

Accountants and clients have attempted to establish privilege for tax file workpapers so as to shield them from Revenue Canada summons demands (tax file workpapers contain accountants' analyses of "soft spots" and potential tax liability for arguable tax positions) but have so far been unsuccessful.

The rules of privileged and confidential communication are based on the belief that they facilitate a free flow of information between parties to the relationship. The nature of accounting services makes it necessary for the accountant to have access to information about salaries, products, contracts, merger or divestment plans, tax matters, and other data required for the best possible professional work. Managers would be less likely to reveal such information if they could not trust the accountant to keep it confidential. If accountants were to reveal such information, the resultant reduction of the information flow might be undesirable, so no accountants should break the confidentiality rule without a good reason.

Difficult problems arise over auditors' obligations to "blow the whistle" on clients' shady or illegal practices. Generally, the codes indicate that confidentiality in such cases can be overridden by reason of obtaining or following legal advice. If a client refuses to accept an audit report that has been modified because of inability to obtain sufficient appropriate evidence about a suspected illegal act, failure to account for or disclose properly a material amount connected with an illegal act, or inability to estimate amounts involved in an illegal act, the audit firm should withdraw from the engagement and give the reasons in writing to the board of directors. In such an

IRS Informant

James C, CPA, was in hot water with the IRS. To get relief, he agreed to tell the IRS about tax cheating by his clients. After all, some of them were practising tax evasion, and James C. knew about it.

Steven N, a client, said: "It's every taxpayer's worst nightmare. I relied on my trusted accountant to keep me out of trouble with the IRS. James C often sat in my living room. We treated him like family. I even gave him power of attorney to represent me before the IRS."

But Steven N had skimmed untaxed income from his restaurant business and was indicted for tax evasion. An AICPA spokesman said: "The accountant's job is to point out errors to the client—not to the IRS."

Postscript: The Missouri State Board of Accountancy revoked James C's CPA certificate, saying: "His action is not only at odds with the role of the CPA, but acts to undermine the very foundation of the professional relationship between an accountant and client. Such duplicity cannot and will not be condoned."

Post Postscript: The U.S. Senate considered a bill making it a crime for federal agents to offer forgiveness of taxes to induce CPAs to inform on their clients. The U.S. Justice Department dropped the tax evasion charges against Steven N.

Source: The Wall Street Journal, February 2, 1990, August 31, 1990, and November 25, 1991.

---

extreme case, the withdrawal amounts to whistle blowing, but the action results from the client's decision not to disclose the information. For all practical purposes, information is not considered confidential if disclosure of it is necessary to make financial statements not misleading.

Auditors are not, in general, legally obligated to blow the whistle on clients. However, circumstances may exist where auditors are legally justified in making disclosures to a regulatory agency or a third party. Such circumstances include (1) when a client has intentionally and without authorization associated or involved a PA in its misleading conduct, (2) when a client has distributed misleading draft financial statements prepared by a PA for internal use only, or (3) when a client prepares and distributes in an annual report or prospectus misleading information for which the PA has not assumed any responsibility.

PAs should not view the rules on confidential information as a licence or excuse for inaction where action may be appropriate to right a wrongful act committed or about to be committed by a client. In some cases auditors' inaction may be viewed as part of a conspiracy or willingness to be an accessory to a wrong. Such situations are dangerous and potentially damaging. A useful initial course of action is to consult with a lawyer about possible legal pitfalls of both whistle blowing and silence. Then, decide for yourself.

Contingency Fees and Service Without Fees

ICAO Rule 215 states, "A member engaged in the practice of public accounting or a related function shall not offer or agree to perform a professional service for a fee payable only where there is a specified determination or result of the service ... A member engaged in the practice of public accounting or a related function shall not represent that he or she performs any professional service without fee except services of a charitable, benevolent or similar nature ..."

For a fee to be considered a contingency fee, two characteristics need to be met.

1. Its terms must be contracted for before any service area performed, and
2. The amount paid for the performance must be directly affected by the results obtained.

If one of these characteristics is not present, the fee is not a contingency fee and therefore does not violate the ICAO's Rule 215,[11] or similar rules by other accounting bodies (such as the CGAAC's Rule 802). Fees are not contingent if they are fixed by a court or other public authority or, in tax matters, determined as a result of the finding of judicial proceedings or the findings of government agencies; nor are fees contingent when they are based on the complexity or time required for the work. The current Rule 215 is quite restrictive, conflicting with some statutes such as the Federal Bankruptcy Act and Provincial Trustee Acts, which allow fees based on the results of the PA's work. Because of these conflicts with statutory law, some have called for modifications of the rules to apply to assurance engagements only.[12]

Rule 215 prohibits contingent fees in assurance engagements where users of financial information may be relying on the PAs' work. Acceptance of contingent fee arrangements during the period in which the member or the member's firm is engaged to perform any type of assurance engagement is considered an impairment of independence.

Fee Quotation

ICAO Rule 214 states that "a member shall not quote a fee for any professional services unless requested to do so by a client or prospective client, and no quote shall be made until adequate information has been obtained about the assignment." It is thus against Rule 214 to quote a fee "over the phone" or quote a fixed charge for all audits. There is extensive anecdotal evidence that particularly during economic downturns some firms practice "low balling" or charging a fee that is below cost in order to get an engagement. Low balling would appear to be in violation of at least the spirit of Rule 214 since presumably the need for the information about the assignment is to ensure that an adequate audit is done in which the costs are recovered (no service should be provided for free unless for charitable purposes). The real concern is that auditors may cut back on audit procedures to the point of reducing the quality of audits.[13]

Discreditable Acts

CGAAC's Rule 101 states that "a member shall not permit the member's firm name to be used with, participate in, or knowingly provide services to any practice, pronouncement, or act which would be of a nature to discredit the profession." We will refer to this and related rules as discreditable act rules.

---

[11] C. Schultz, "When Talk Turns to Contingency Fees," *CA Magazine*, May 1988, p. 29.
[12] Ibid. p. 33.
[13] M.C. Carscallen, "Fee completion hurts integrity of accounting services," *Bottom Line*, April 1991, p. 20.

Analysis

The discreditable acts rules may be called the morals clauses of the Codes, but they are only occasionally the basis for disciplinary action. Penalties usually are invoked automatically under the bylaws, which provide for expulsion of members found by a court to have committed any fraud, filed false tax returns, or been convicted of any criminal offence; or found by the Disciplinary Committee to have been guilty of an act discreditable to the profession. Discreditable acts can include (*a*) withholding a client's books and records when the client has requested their return; (*b*) practising employment discrimination in hiring, promotion, or salary practices on the basis of race, colour, religion, sex, or national origin; (*c*) failing to follow government audit standards and guides in governmental audits when the client or the government agency expects such standards to be followed; and (*d*) making, or permitting others to make, false and misleading entries in records and financial statements. An extreme example of an actual discreditable act is given in the box below.

EXTREME EXAMPLE OF A DISCREDITABLE ACT

The Enforcement Committee found that Respondent drew a gun from his desk drawer during a dispute with a client in his office in contravention of Section 501.41 [discreditable acts prohibition] of the [Texas] Rules of Professional Conduct. Respondent agreed to accept a private reprimand to be printed ... in the Texas State Board Report.

Source: Texas State Board Report, February 1986.

Advertising and Other Forms of Solicitation

The rules relating to solicitation state that a member shall not seek to obtain clients by advertising or other forms of solicitation in a manner that is false, misleading, or deceptive. Solicitation through coercion, overreaching, or harassing conduct is prohibited.

Analysis

The Rules permit advertising with only a few limitations. The current rules apply only to PAs practising public accounting and relate to their efforts to obtain clients. Basic guidelines about advertising include the following:

- Advertising may not create false or unjustified expectations of favourable results.
- Advertising may not imply the ability to influence any court, tribunal, regulatory agency, or similar body or official.
- Advertising may not contain a fee estimate when the PA knows it is likely to be substantially increased, unless the client is notified.
- Advertising may not contain any representation that is likely to cause a reasonable person to misunderstand or be deceived, or that contravenes professional good taste.

Advertising consists of messages designed to attract business that are broadcast widely (e.g., through print, radio, television, billboards) to an undifferentiated audience. The guidelines basically prohibit false, misleading, and deceptive messages.

Solicitation, on the other hand, generally refers to direct contact (e.g., in person, mail, telephone) with a specific potential client. In regard to solicitation, the rules basically prohibit extreme bad behaviour that tends to bring disrepute on the profession.

The advertising rule has undergone many changes over the last two decades. Long ago, all advertising by PAs was prohibited. Then, institutional-type advertising on behalf of PAs in general was permitted. Then, in 1979, in response to the Charter of Rights guarantee to members, the ICAO approved advertising "in good taste," with limitations on style, type size, and the like. The other professional bodies followed suit.

Most PAs carry out only modest advertising efforts, and many do no advertising at all. According to a recent article, advertising so far has been very precisely targeted—for example, at CFOs of wholesalers in the food industry. Firms have generally used local rather than national advertising. The biggest problem in advertising so far is that members may make claims they are not able to substantiate.

Firms rarely get new clients through advertising, but it can be effective in generating business in the form of new services for existing clients or from referrals. Overall, other than some isolated examples of creative advertising by some firms, the profession has not pursued advertising aggressively. Nevertheless, it is likely PAs will advertise more in the future.[14] This seems to be especially true as Internet Web sites by PA firms continue to proliferate (see Chapter 19) and the Internet becomes more popular as an advertising medium. Public practice is generally marked by decorum and a sense of good taste. However, there are exceptions, and they tend to get much attention—most of it disapproving from other PAs and the public in general. The danger in bad advertising is that the advertiser may develop an image as a professional huckster, which may backfire on efforts to build a practice.

THE ART OF ADVERTISING

In 1987, three charges were brought against "a partner of Ernst & Whinney" in Ontario under subsections (c), (a), and (d). The discipline committee found the member "not guilty" on the first charge, but "guilty" on the second and third. Both guilty charges concerned a 1985 ad he had placed in *The Globe and Mail* which stated, in part, "Canada's Fastest Growing Firm of Business Advisors Announces Its Newest Partners."

The committee found the ad misleading in two ways. First, "accountants do not have a monopoly on the term 'business advisors.'" Second, the claim was made on the basis of statistics that were "accurate as they relate to the participating chartered accountant firms [but] without disclosure of the necessary parameters or basis for the statement, it is misleading."

The member received a written reprimand, was assessed court costs of $6,000, and was fined $5,000.

Source: Tim Falconer, *CA Magazine*, October 1993, p. 46.

---

[14] T. Falconer, "The Art of Advertising," *CA Magazine*, October 1993, pp. 43–46.

Commissions and Referral Fees

A. Prohibited Commissions

A member in public practice shall not for a commission recommend or refer to a client any product or service, or for a commission recommend or refer any product or service to be supplied by a client, or receive a commission, when the member or the member's firm also performs for that client public accounting.

This prohibition applies during the period in which the member is engaged to perform public accounting services and the period covered by any historical financial statements involved in such services.

B. Permitted Commission

A member in public practice is not prohibited by this rule in receiving a commission from the sale or purchase of an accounting practice.

A **commission** is generally defined as a percentage fee charged for professional services in connection with executing a transaction or performing some other business activity. Examples are insurance sales commissions, real estate sales commissions, and securities sales commissions. The rules treat such fees as an impairment of independence when received from assurance engagement clients, just like ICAO's Rule 215 treats contingent fees.

However, many PAs perform financial planning for businesses and individuals, and they have seen commissions for insurance, securities, mergers and acquisitions, and other transactions go to other professionals. They want some of this action. The rules permit such commissions, provided the engagement does not involve assurance services.

Most of the commission fee activity takes place in connection with personal financial planning services. PAs often recommend insurance and investments to individuals and families. When the rule change was under consideration, critics pointed out that commission agents (e.g., insurance salespersons, securities brokers) cannot always be trusted to have the best interests of the client in mind when their own compensation depends in large part on clients' buying the product that produces commissions for themselves. These critics bemoaned the demise of the only advisers, PAs, who could not take commissions. They made the point that "fee-only" planning advisers, who do not work on commission, were more likely to have the best interests of the client in mind, directing them to investment professionals who handle a wide range of alternatives. In light of these matters, some PAs make it a point to provide financial planning services on a fee-only basis. This is also the position of the newly organized Financial Planners Standards Council of Canada, which is dedicated to creating a licensing system for certified financial planners (CFPs) in Canada beginning in June 1997. This organization is sponsored by the CICA, CGAAC, and SMAC, among other associations.

The rules also include fee arrangements related to commissions. Referral fees are (*a*) fees a PA receives for recommending another PA's services and (*b*) fees a PA pays to obtain a client. Such fees may or may not be based on a percentage of the amount of any transaction. Referral involves the practice of sending business to another PA and paying other PAs or outside agencies for drumming up business. These activities are banned by the Rules of Conduct on the basis that they impair the principle of objectivity.

Form of Organization and Name

General Rule Relating to Form of PA Organization

Each practice office shall be under the personal charge of a member who is a public accountant.

General Rule Relating to Name of PA Organization

A member shall not practice public accounting under a firm name that is misleading. Names of one or more past owners may be included in the firm name of a successor organization.

Analysis

The rules allow members to practise in any form of organization permitted by provincial laws and regulations—proprietorships, partnerships, professional corporations, limited liability partnerships, limited liability corporations, and ordinary corporations. Most provincial accountancy laws prohibit the general corporate form of organization for PAs; however, there has been a recent push for the limited liability partnership form of organization due to increased legal risks. Under the limited liability partnership form of organization, most partners do not have their personal assets at risk. The only partners with personal assets at risk are those involved in the litigated engagement; the rest of the partners risk only their investment in the partnership. In the traditional form of partnership, all partners' personal assets are at risk. Thus, the limited liability partnership is a great improvement at a time of increased litigation.

In 1992 the AICPA approved a move to permit PAs to practise in limited liability corporations and ordinary corporations like other businesses.

Public accountants have been beset by lawsuits for damages in which they and their insurers are the only persons left with any money (e.g., in cases of business failure), and multimillion-dollar damages have been awarded to plaintiffs against them. In the proprietorship, partnership, and professional corporation forms of business, all the business and personal assets of PAs are exposed to loss to such plaintiffs. Many accountants think the tort liability litigation process has gotten out of hand, and so they seek some protection through new forms of organization. See the following box for some consequences that can arise from an attempt at innovative forms of PA firm organization.

PAS (ALMOST) SELL SHARES TO PUBLIC

Nearman & Lents, a Florida PA firm, formed a corporation named Financial Standards Group, Inc., and filed a registration statement with the Securities and Exchange Commission to sell shares to the public. The accounting firm wanted to "go national on a large scale, and . . . raise $3 million or $4 million capital."

The registration became effective, and some shares were actually sold. However, Nearman & Lents withdrew the offering and gave the money back to the purchasers. Florida regulators had raised questions about the company practising public accounting without a license with non-PA ownership, which was prohibited. Financial Standards Group did not become the first publicly held PA firm.

The venture met resistance. Accounting traditionalists and lawyers who specialize in suing accountants for misconduct have generally frowned on letting accountants avail themselves of the limited legal liability provided by a corporation. Regulators have also discouraged accounting firms from issuing shares to outsiders for fear that outside equity partners might taint a firm's ability to judge [audit] a client's books impartially.

Source: New York Times (June 14, 1990) and SEC.

The rules of conduct effectively block persons who are not PAs from being owners. This rule section creates problems for tax and management consulting services personnel who are not PAs. They cannot be admitted to full partnership or become shareholders without causing the other owners who are PAs to be in violation of the rule. Thus, an accounting firm may employ non-PAs who are high on the organization chart, but these persons may not be unrestricted partners or shareholders under current rules.

Rules of Conduct and Ethical Principles

Specific rules in the Rules of Conduct may not necessarily be classified under one of the ethics principles. Decisions based on a rule may involve imperative, utilitarian, or generalization considerations, or elements of all three. The rules have the form of imperatives because that is the nature of a code. However, elements of utilitarianism and generalization seem to be apparent in the underlying rationale for most of the rules. If this perception is accurate, then these two principles may be utilized by auditors in difficult decision problems where adherence to a rule would produce a undesirable result.

REVIEW
CHECKPOINTS

15.5 What ethical responsibilities do members of the provincial institutes have for acts of nonmembers who are under their supervision (e.g., recent university graduates who are not yet PAs)?

15.6 Is an incorporated accounting practice substantially different from an accounting practice organized in the form of a partnership? in the form of a limited liability partnership?

15.7 Define what is meant by a contingency fee and explain how such fees apply to PAs. Do you feel a change is necessary to rules for contingency fees in Canada?

REGULATION AND QUALITY CONTROL

LEARNING   OBJECTIVE
3. Name and explain the various professional associations and government agencies that enforce rules of conduct and explain the types of penalties they can impose on accountants.

As a PA, you will be expected to observe rules of conduct published in several codes of ethics. If you are a PA and have a client who issues shares on U.S. stock exchanges, you will be subject to the following:

Source of Rules of Conduct	Applicable to:
Members' Handbook	Persons licensed by province to practise accounting or, if no licence required in province, persons belonging to provincial institutes, societies, or organizations
Business Corporations Acts and Securities Acts at federal and provincial levels	Public accountants (usually PAs performing public accounting services) within the various jurisdictions
U.S. Securities and Exchange Commission	Persons who practise before the SEC as accountants and auditors for SEC-registered companies (including auditors of many large Canadian corporations)

If you are an internal auditor, you will be expected to observe the rules of conduct of the Institute of Internal Auditors. As a management accountant, you will be expected to observe the Society of Management Accountants standards of ethical conduct for management accountants. Certified fraud examiners are expected to observe the Association of Certified Fraud Examiners' Code of Ethics.

Fraud Examiner Expelled for Fraud

Curtis C was expelled by the board of regents at its regular meeting on August 4, 1991. Mr. C, formerly an internal auditor employed by the City of S, was a member from February 1989 until his expulsion. He was the subject of an investigation by the trial board for falsifying information.

Mr. C wrongfully represented himself as a certified internal auditor, when in fact he did not hold the CIA designation. Such conduct is in violation of Article 1.A.4 of the CFE Code of Professional Ethics.

L. Jackson Shockey, CFE, CPA, CISA, chairman of the board of regents, said: "We are saddened that a member has been expelled for such conduct. However, in order to maintain the integrity of the CFE program, the trial board vigorously investigates violations of the Code of Professional Ethics. When appropriate, the board of regents will not hesitate to take necessary action."

Source: CFE News, September 1991.

Regulation and professional ethics go hand in hand. Codes of ethics provide the underlying authority for regulation. Quality control practices and disciplinary proceedings provide the mechanisms of self-regulation. Self-regulation refers to quality control reviews and disciplinary actions conducted by fellow PAs—professional peers. Elements of accountants' self-regulation have been explained in terms of the quality control standards (Chapter 2).

Self-Regulatory Discipline

Accounting firms as well as individuals are subject to the Rules of Professional Conduct of the institutes, associations, or societies only if they choose to join these organizations. But as a practical matter anyone wishing to practise public accounting finds that the added credibility of belonging to a professional group greatly improves the chances of establishing a successful practice. Thus, enforcement of the Rules of Conduct is an important means of regulating the profession. Regulators can suspend a member's activities on certain exchanges; the professional bodies can initiate other disciplinary proceedings.

An Illustration of Self-regulation: A Provincial Institute's Disciplinary Process
The provincial institutes' bylaws and rules of professional conduct in the *Member's Handbook* provide the basis for self-regulation. The institutes have a duty to investigate all written complaints received about their members and students, as well as information from the media that may indicate professional misconduct. The Professional Conduct Committee, which represents a broad cross-section of the member-

ship, investigates the complaint and decides whether further action is necessary. The committee considers the respondents' reply and all relevant data in making its decision.

Three conclusions are possible (as per ICAO):

1. The member did not breach the rules and the process is ended.
2. The member did or may have breached the rules, but the infraction is not serious enough to prosecute before the discipline committee; the respondent is informally admonished in writing or at a committee meeting.
3. Charges are laid and the matter is brought up before the discipline committee where a process similar to a civil trial procedure is followed. The discipline committee can reach a decision of not guilty or guilty. There is also an appeal process, which is headed by yet another committee, the Appeal Committee.

In a guilty verdict the penalties can include any one or more of the following (as per ICAO list):

*   The member or student be reprimanded.
*   The member or student be suspended from the institute.
*   The student be struck off the register of students.
*   The member be expelled from membership in the institute.
*   The member satisfactorily complete a professional development course(s) and/or an examination(s), and/or engage an advisor or tutor.
*   The member complete a period of supervised practice.
*   The member be reinvestigated by the professional conduct committee.
*   The member or student be charged costs and/or fined.
*   The member or student be disciplined in such other way as the committee may determine.
*   The decision and order(s) be publicized along with the member's or student's name.

The penalties listed above cover a range of severity. In many cases a discipline committee can admonish or suspend a PA and require a number of hours of continuing professional education (CPE) to be undertaken. The goal is to help the PA attain an appropriate level of professional competence and awareness. Although intended as a constructive resolution, the CPE requirement is similar to "serving time." Persons who fail to satisfy CPE conditions will find themselves charged with "actions detrimental to the profession" (violations of rules such as CGAAC's Rule 606 or ICAO's Rule 201) and expelled as "second offenders."

The expulsion penalty, while severe, does not prevent a PA from continuing to practice accounting. Membership in a professional group, while beneficial, is not required. However, a PA must have a valid licence in order to practise public accounting in certain provinces. CGAs are subject to disciplinary action for any offence that constitutes a breach of professional conduct. This disciplinary action is brought on by the member's association or professional corporation, or, if the action is outside these groups, by the board of directors of CGA-Canada (Rule 602.1, CGAAC).

EXAMPLE OF PUBLIC DISCIPLINARY NOTICE

Member Found Guilty of Breaching Rule of Professional Conduct 215
Re: Contingent Fees
A member has been found guilty of a charge of professional misconduct, laid by the professional conduct committee, under Rule of Professional Conduct 215, of agreeing to render professional services for a fee contingent on the results.

It was ordered that the member:
- be reprimanded in writing by the chairman of the hearing,
- be assessed costs of $1,500 to be paid within a specified time; and
- that the decision and order be published in Check Mark.

It was determined that the publication of the member's name was not necessary in the circumstances, as there was no evidence of any intent to breach the rules of professional conduct or moral turpitude on the part of the member, and that this was a matter of first instance.

Public Regulation Discipline

Provincial institutes of chartered accountants, provincial associations of CGAs, and provincial societies of CMAs are self-governing agencies. Depending on the province's Public Accounting Act, they issue licences to practise accounting in their jurisdictions or certificates indicating they have met the standards to be a PA. Most provinces require a licence or certification procedure to use the designation *CA* or *Chartered Accountant*, and some limit the assurance (audit) function to licenceholders. Most provinces do not regulate work in areas of management consulting, tax practice, or bookkeeping services.

Provincial institutes, associations, and societies, have rules of conduct and disciplinary processes as outlined above. Through the disciplinary process, the provincial institutes, associations, and societies, can admonish a licenceholder; but, more importantly, they can suspend or revoke the licence to practise in some provinces. Suspension and revocation are severe penalties because a person no longer can use the PA title and cannot sign audit reports. When candidates have successfully passed the PA examination or fulfilled other requirements and are ready to become PAs, some provincial institutes administer an ethics examination or an ethics course intended to familiarize new PAs with the rules of professional conduct.

According to a study by Brooks and Fortunato, most disciplinary actions by the ICAO stem from violating the standards affecting the public interest (200 level). Over a roughly three-year period (1988–90), most violations involved just four rules:

Rule 201: Good Reputation of Profession representing   36 violations
           20 percent of all violations

Rule 202: Integrity and Due Care representing   29 violations
           16 percent of all violations

Rule 205: False and Misleading Representations   20 violations
representing 11 percent of all violations

Rule 206: Expressing an Opinion Without Complying   21 violations
with GAAS representing 12 percent of all
violations[15]

This same study also found that "all but one of the ICAO convictions we examined resulted in disclosure of the convicted member's names, and 95% resulted in levying the costs of hearing on that person. Of those convicted 78% were reprimanded, of which 44% were also suspended; 17% of the total convicted were expelled from the profession." The average fine levied for these cases was $5,695.[16]

The national harmonization of the Rules of Professional Conduct has not only made the self-regulatory processes more comparable across the country for CAs but has also increased the examinability of the Rules of Professional Conduct in the UFE. The appearance of the Rules of Professional Conduct on the UFE in 1994 should serve to reinforce the importance of this topic. CGAAC's rules of conduct have always been national in scope, as noted earlier.

As noted in Chapter 2, the provincial securities commissions sometimes file complaints with the Professional Conduct Committees of the provincial institutes or associations. In addition, some securities commissions, notably the OSC, have been assertive in not accepting financial statements that they consider at odds with GAAP. The OSC now issues staff accounting communiqués (SACs) in which it highlights major problem areas. Any company attempting to use the disfavoured technique may find that its financial statements are unacceptable to the OSC even though there is no reservation in the auditor's report.

The OSC is going even further. "It has a plan to increase its supervision of auditors and other financial advisers and to gain the power to take disciplinary action against them. Although these proposals have yet to be enacted, the OSC already exerts some control over firms via out-of-court settlements, as indicated in the following box.

PREVENTIVE MEDICINE

"For example, in response to problems arising from the audit of National Business Systems, Inc., the OSC agreed that the partner in charge of that audit would not act as the senior or second partner in charge of the audit of a public company for a year. It was also agreed that procedures and systems would be reviewed by an auditor from another firm and that the results would be resubmitted to the OSC. Moreover, arrangement was made to have the Toronto office inspected by a partner from outside Canada to ensure professional standards were met. The firm agreed to pay $70,000 to cover OSC expenses."

Source: J. Bedard and L. LeBlanc, *CA Magazine*, November 1991, p. 42.

---

[15] L. Brooks and V. Fortunato, "Disciplines at the ICAO," *CA Magazine*, May 1991, p. 45.
[16] Ibid, pp. 42–43.

The SEC also conducts public regulation disciplinary actions. Its authority comes from its rules of practice, one of which, Rule 2(e) provides that the SEC can deny, temporarily or permanently, the privilege of practice before the SEC to any person found (1) not to possess the requisite qualifications to represent others, or (2) to be lacking in character or integrity or to have engaged in unethical or improper professional conduct, or (3) to have willfully violated any provision of the federal securities laws or their rules and regulations. When conducting a "Rule 2(e) proceeding," the SEC acts in a quasijudicial role as an administrative agency.

The SEC penalty bars an accountant from signing any documents filed by an SEC-registered company. The penalty effectively stops the accountant's SEC practice. In a few severe cases, Rule 2(e) proceedings have resulted in settlements barring not only the individual accountant but also the accounting firm or certain of its practice offices from accepting new SEC clients for a period of time.

The OSC and other Canadian regulators have been pushing to have similar disciplinary powers within their jurisdictions. Clearly, if the self-regulating process of the institutes is not sufficient to deter bad practices, regulators are willing to step in. In 1991 members of the ICAO approved a proposal giving the institute the power to subject firms to disciplinary action.

In the next chapter we will see how in reaction to a recent Supreme Court of Canada ruling in *Hercules v. Ernst & Young,* there are renewed calls in the Canadian press for new securities laws that will hold auditors firmly liable for any negligence in financial statements. Other recent regulatory developments include greater independence and enforcement powers for Ontario and Quebec securities commissions, and increased harmonization procedures between the Alberta and British Columbia commissions. These structural changes in the regulatory climate are likely to increase regulatory disciplinary actions against PAs in the future.

Revenue Canada can also discipline accountants as a matter of public regulation. Revenue Canada can suspend or disbar from practice before it any PA shown to be incompetent or disreputable or who has refused to comply with tax rules and regulations. Revenue Canada can also levy monetary fines for improper practices. The Revenue Ministry has made public its willingness to prosecute those accountants it suspects of "deliberate attempt to defraud the federal treasury."[17]

R E V I E W
C H E C K P O I N T S

15.8 What options does Revenue Canada have to discipline PAs?

15.9 What organizations and agencies have Rules of Conduct you must observe when practising public accounting? internal auditing? management accounting? fraud examination?

15.10 What penalties can be imposed by provincial institutes on CAs in their "self-regulation" of ethics code violators?

15.11 What penalties can be imposed by public regulatory agencies on PAs who violate rules of conduct?

---

[17] J. Middleniss, "Too many accountants guilty of fraud, Liberals vow crackdown on shady advisers," *Bottom Line,* March 1994, p. 1.

Consequences of Unethical/Illegal Acts

Ethics is serious business. Several sectors of professional and public life exist under general clouds of suspicion. Even though many practitioners of accounting, business management, finance, journalism, law, medicine, and politics conduct themselves in an exemplary fashion, generally unfavourable perceptions of them are held by some people. Fortunately, accountants generally rate near the top of trustworthy professions (along with the clergy.) Many people, however, think it is a necessity of business life to shade the formal and informal rules of behaviour in order to "get ahead" or "make a buck." Acting on this belief can have catastrophic consequences for the profession. Without the public's confidence, the accounting profession cannot meet the public interest.

However, conforming to rules of behaviour is not always easy because of potential conflicts in the rules. The most troublesome area lies in the potential conflict between rules related to confidentiality on the one hand, and the prohibition against association with misleading information on the other. Whenever there is a conflict of interest situation for the auditor there is a potential to create a threat to the auditor's independent state of mind. Brooks (1995, p. 126) identified the following deficiencies in professional Codes of Conduct.

- No or insufficient prioritization is put forward to resolve conflicting interests.
- Consultation on ethical matters is encouraged for some members, but is inhibited for others.
- A fair reporting/hearing process is not indicated, so members are uncertain whether to come forward.
- Protection is not offered to a whistle blower.
- Sanctions are often unclear, and their applicability is not defined.
- Resolution mechanisms for conflicts between professionals and firms, or employers, or employing corporations are not put forward.

According to an article in the November 13, 1997, issue of *The Finincial Post* by Sandra Rubin, the latest round of mergers among the accounting firms is making these deficiencies even more critical to the integrity of the financial reporting system. The problem is the perception of increased conflict of interest and the fact that the merged firms will be so big that no single nation (or national body) will be able to regulate them. The role of the International Organization of Securities Commissions (IOSCO) will likely increase the future regulation of the huge international PA firms.

Summary

This chapter began with considerations of moral philosophy, explained the provincial institutes' Rules of Professional Conduct, and ended with the agencies and organizations that enforce the rules governing PAs' behaviour.

Professional ethics for accountants is not simply a matter covered by a few rules in a formal Rule of Professional Conduct. Concepts of proper professional conduct permeate all areas of practice. Ethics and its accompanying disciplinary potential are the foundation for public accountants' self-regulatory efforts.

Your knowledge of philosophical principles in ethics—the imperative, the utilitarian, and generalization—will help you make decisions about the provincial Rules of Professional Conduct. This structured approach to thoughtful decisions is important not only when you are employed in public accounting but also when you work in government, industry, and education. The ethics rules may appear to be restrictive, but they are intended for the benefit of the public as well as for the discipline of PAs.

Public accountants must be careful in all areas of practice. Regulators' views on ethics rules may differ in several aspects from the provincial institute views. As an accountant, you must not lose sight of the nonaccountants' perspective. No matter how complex or technical a decision may be, a simplified view of it always tends to cut away the details of special technical issues to get directly to the heart of the matter. A sense of professionalism coupled with a sensitivity to the impact of decisions on other people is invaluable in the practice of accounting and auditing.

Finally, it should be noted that there is a strong link between codes of conduct and GAAS. In fact, codes of conduct can be viewed as a means of fulfilling auditor responsibilities for GAAS and assurance standards. For example, the first GAAS standard, which relates to the personal attributes of the auditor (see Chapter 2), closely corresponds to the ethical principles of integrity, objectivity, independence, professional competence, and due care discussed above. The dominance of ethic issues over accounting or auditing techniques is increasingly being recognized throughout the profession. Most audit failures appear to be attributable to poor professional judgment, at least in hindsight, that arise from improper consideration of conflicts of interest on various disclosure and measurement issues. In this regard, see L.J. Brooks, *Professional Ethics for Accountants,* West Publishing, 1995, p. 69; and S. Gunz and J. McCutcheon, "Some Unresolved Ethical Issues in Auditing," *Journal of Business Ethics,* 1991.

MULTIPLE-CHOICE QUESTIONS FOR PRACTICE AND REVIEW

15.12 Auditors are interested in having independence in appearance because:
a. They want to impress the public with their independence in fact.
b. They want the public at large to have confidence in the profession.
c. They need to comply with the standards of field work of GAAS.
d. Audits should be planned and assistants, if any, need to be properly supervised.

15.13 If a PA says she always follows the rule that requires adherence to CICA pronouncements in order to give a standard unqualified audit report, she is following a philosophy characterized by:
a. The imperative principle in ethics.
b. The utilitarian principle in ethics.
c. The generalization principle in ethics.

d. Reliance on one's inner conscience.

15.14 Which of the following "committees" have been authorized to discipline members in violation of the rules of professional conduct?
a. CICA Committee on Professional Ethics.
b. Appeals Committee.
c. Discipline Committee.
d. Professional Conduct Committee.

15.15 Which of the following bodies does not have any power to punish individual members for violations of the Rules of Professional Conduct?
a. CICA.
b. Revenue Canada.
c. OSC.
d. ICAO.

15.16 Phil Greb has a thriving practice in which he assists lawyers in preparing litigation dealing with accounting and auditing matters. Phil is "practising public accounting" if he:

a. Uses his CA designation on his letterhead and business card.

b. Is in partnership with another PA.

c. Practises in a limited partnership with other PAs.

d. Never lets his clients know that he is a PA.

15.17 The ICAO should remove its general prohibition against PAs' taking commissions and contingent fees because:

a. CAs prefer more price competition to less.

b. Commissions and contingent fees enhance audit independence.

c. The Charter of Rights will force the change anyway.

d. Objectivity is not always necessary in accounting and auditing services.

15.18 PA Smith is the auditor of Ajax Corporation. Her audit independence will not be considered impaired if she:

a. Owns a $1,000 worth of Ajax shares.

b. Has a husband who owns $2,000 worth of Ajax shares.

c. Has a sister who is the financial vice president of Ajax.

d. Owns $1,000 worth of the shares of Pericles Corporation, which is controlled by Ajax as a result of Ajax's ownership of 40 percent of Pericles's shares, and Pericles contributes 3 percent of the total assets and income in Ajax's financial statements.

15.19 When a client's financial statements contain a material departure from a *CICA Handbook* Accounting Recommendation and the PA believes that disclosure is necessary to make the statements not misleading:

a. The PA must qualify the audit report for a departure from GAAP.

b. The PA can explain why the departure is necessary, and then give an unqualified opinion paragraph in the audit report.

c. The PA must give an adverse audit report.

d. The PA can give the standard unqualified audit report with an unqualified opinion paragraph.

15.20 Which of the following would not be considered confidential information obtained in the course of an engagement for which the client's consent would be needed for disclosure?

a. Information about whether a consulting client has paid the PA's fees on time.

b. The actuarial assumptions used by a tax client in calculating pension expense.

c. Management's strategic plan for next year's labour negotiations.

d. Information about material contingent liabilities relevant for audited financial statements.

15.21 Which of the following would probably not be considered an "act discreditable to the profession":

a. Numerous moving traffic violations.

b. Failing to file the PA's own tax return.

c. Filing a fraudulent tax return for a client in a severe financial difficulty.

d. Refusing to hire Asian Canadians in an accounting practice.

15.22 The U.S. Securities and Exchange Commission would consider an audit firm's independence not impaired when:

a. A partner completed the client's audit in January, retired from the firm in March, and became a member of the former client's board of directors in August.

b. A partner who had been in charge of the firm's national audit coordination office retired in May 1990, and became a member of the board of directors of one of the firm's clients in August 1992.

c. A partner in the firm has a father-in-law who is the warehouse supervisor for an audit client.

d. The audit firm helped the client perform data processing for three months during the current year in connection with preparing financial statements to be filed with the SEC.

15.23 A PA's legal licence to practise public accounting can be revoked by:
- *a.* The CICA.
- *b.* Provincial Institute of PAs.
- *c.* Auditing Standards Board.
- *d.* Provincial securities commissions.

15.24 An auditor's independence would not be considered impaired if he had:
- *a.* Owned common shares of the audit client but sold them before the company became a client.
- *b.* Sold short the common shares of an audit client while working on the audit engagement.
- *c.* Served as the company's treasurer for six months during the year covered by the audit but resigned before the company became a client.

- *d.* Performed the bookkeeping and financial statement preparation for the company, which had no accounting personnel, and the president had no understanding of accounting principles.

15.25 When a PA knows that a tax client has skimmed cash receipts and not reported the income in the federal income tax return but signs the return as a PA who prepared the return, the PA has violated which Rule of Professional Conduct?
- *a.* Confidential Client Information.
- *b.* Integrity and Objectivity.
- *c.* Independence.
- *d.* Accounting Principles.

EXERCISES AND PROBLEMS

15.26 Independence, Integrity, and Objectivity Cases. Knowledge of the rules of conduct and related interpretations on independence, integrity, and objectivity will help you respond to the following cases. For each case, state whether the action or situation shows violation of the Rules of Professional Conduct, explain why, and cite the relevant rule or interpretation.

- *a.* PA R. Stout performs the audit of the local symphony society. Because of her good work, she was elected an honorary member of the board of directors.
- *b.* N. Wolfe, a retired partner of your PA firm, has just been appointed to the board of directors of Palmer Corporation, your firm's client. Wolfe is also an ex officio member of your firm's income tax advisory committee, which meets monthly to discuss income tax problems of the partnership's clients, some of which are competitors of Palmer Corporation. The partnership pays Wolfe $100 for each committee meeting attended and a monthly retirement benefit, fixed by a retirement plan policy, of $1,000.

(AICPA adapted)

- *c.* PA Archie Goodwin performs significant day-to-day bookkeeping services for Harper Corporation and supervises the work of the one part-time bookkeeper employed by Marvin Harper. This year, Marvin wants to engage PA Goodwin to perform an audit.
- *d.* PA Fritz's wife owns 20 percent of the common shares of Botacel Company, which wants Fritz to perform the audit for the calendar year ended December 31, 1997.
- *e.* Fritz's wife gave her shares to their 10-year-old daughter on July 1, 1997.
- *f.* Fritz's daughter, acting through an appropriate custodian, sold the shares to her grandfather on August 1, 1997. His purchase, as an accommodation, took one-half of his retirement savings.
- *g.* Fritz's father managed to sell the shares on August 15 to his brother, who lives in Brazil. The brother fled there 20 years ago and has not returned.
- *h.* Clyde Brenner is a manager in the Regina office of a large national PA firm. His wife, Bonnie, is assistant controller in ATC Corporation, a

client of the firm whose audit is performed by the New York office. Bonnie and Clyde live in Rhode Island and commute to their respective workplaces.

i. Clyde Brenner just received word that he has been admitted to the partnership.

j. The Rockhard Trust Company, a client of your firm, privately told your local managing partner that a block of funds would be set aside for home loans for qualified new employees. Rockhard's president is well aware that your firm experiences some difficulty hiring good people in the midsize but growing community and is willing to do what he can to help while mortgage money is so tight. Several new assistant accountants obtained home loans under this arrangement.

15.27 Independence, Integrity, and Objectivity Cases. Knowledge of the rules of conduct, interpretations thereof, and related rulings on independence, integrity, and objectivity will help you respond to the following cases. For each case, state whether the action or situation shows violation of the Rules of Professional Conduct, explain why, and cite the relevant rule or interpretation.

a. Your client, Contrary Corporation, is very upset over the fact that your audit last year failed to detect an $800,000 inventory overstatement caused by employee theft and falsification of the records. The board discussed the matter and authorized its lawyers to explore the possibility of a lawsuit for damages.

b. Contrary Corporation filed a lawsuit alleging negligent audit work, seeking $1 million in damages.

c. In response to the lawsuit by Contrary, you decided to start litigation against certain officers of the company, alleging management fraud and deceit. You are asking for a damages judgment of $500,000.

d. The Allright Insurance company paid Contrary Corporation $700,000 under fidelity bonds covering the employees involved in the inventory theft. Both you and Contrary Corporation have dropped your lawsuits. However, under subrogation rights, Allright has sued your audit firm for damages on the grounds of negligent performance of the audit.

e. Your audit client, Science Tech, Inc., installed a cost accounting system devised by the consulting services department of your firm. The system failed to account properly for certain product costs (according to management), and the system had to be discontinued. Science Tech management was very dissatisfied and filed a lawsuit demanding return of the $10,000 consulting fee. The audit fee is normally about $50,000, and $10,000 is not an especially large amount for your firm. However, you believe that Science Tech management operated the system improperly. While you are willing to do further consulting work at a reduced rate to make the system operate, you are unwilling to return the entire $10,000 fee.

f. A group of dissident shareholders filed a class-action lawsuit against both you and your client, Amalgamated, Inc., for $30 million. They allege there was a conspiracy to present misleading financial statements in connection with a recent merger.

g. PA Anderson, a partner in the firm of Anderson, Olds, and Watershed, (a professional accounting corporation), owns 25 percent of the common shares of Dove Corporation (not a client of AO&W). This year Dove purchased a 32 percent interest in Tale Company and is accounting for the investment using the equity method of accounting. The investment amounts to 11 percent of Dove's consolidated net assets. Tale Company has been an audit client of AO&W for 12 years.

h. Durkin & Panzer, PAs, regularly perform the audit of the North

Country Bank, and the firm is preparing for the audit of the financial statements for the year ended December 31, 1997.

i. Two directors of the North Country Bank became partners in D&P, PAs, on July 1, 1997, resigning their directorship on that date. They will not participate in the audit.

j. During 1997, the former controller of the North Country Bank, now a partner of D&P, was frequently called on for assistance regarding loan approvals and the bank's minimum chequing account policy. In addition, he conducted a computer feasibility study for North Country.

(AICPA adapted)

k. The Cather Corporation is indebted to a PA for unpaid fees and has offered to give the PA unsecured interest-bearing notes. Alternatively, Cather Corporation offered to give two shares of its common stock, after which 10,002 shares would be outstanding.

(AICPA adapted)

l. Johnny Keems is not yet a PA but is doing quite well in this first employment with a large PA firm. He's been on the job two years and has become a "heavy junior." If he passes the PA exam in September, he will be promoted to senior accountant. This month, during the audit or Row Lumber Company, Johnny told the controller about how he is remodelling an old house. The controller likes Johnny and had a load of needed materials delivered to the house, billing Johnny at a 70 percent discount—a savings over the normal cash discount of about $300. Johnny paid the bill and was happy to have the materials, which he otherwise would not have been able to afford on his meager salary.

m. PA Lily Rowan inherited $1 million from her grandfather, $100,000 of which was the value of shares in the North Country Bank. Lily practises accounting in Hamilton, and several of her audit clients have loans from the bank.

n. Groaner Corporation is in financial difficulty. You are about to sign the report on the current audit when your firm's office manager informs you that the audit fee for last year has not yet been paid.

o. Your audit client, Glow Company, is opening a plant in a distant city. Glow's president asks that your firm's office in that city recruit and hire a new plant controller and a cost accountant.

p. Colt & Associates, PAs, audit Gore Company. Ms. Colt and Bill Gore (president) found a limited real estate partnership deal that looked too good to pass up. Colt purchased limited partnership interests amounting to 23 percent of all such interests, and Gore personally purchased 31 percent. Unrelated investors held the remaining 46 percent. Colt and Gore congratulate themselves on the opportunity and agree to be passive investors with respect to the partnership.

15.28 General and Technical Rule Cases. Knowledge of the rules of conduct, interpretations thereof, and resolutions of Council related to general and technical standards will help you respond to the following cases. For each case, state whether the action or situation shows violation of the ICAO Rules of Professional Conduct, explain why, and cite the relevant rule or interpretation.

a. PA P. Stebbins helped Price Corporation prepare a cash flow forecast of hospital operations. The forecast was presented by Stebbins at a city council hearing for approval under the city's health services ordinance. Stebbins's report, which accompanied the forecast, consisted entirely of a full description of the sources of information used and the major assumptions made but did not include a disclaimer on the achievability of the forecast.

b. Kim Philby of Philby & Burgess, PAs, received a telephone call from his friend John, who is financial vice president of U.K. Auto Parts. U.K. distributes parts over a wide area and does about $40 million in business a year. U.K. is not a client but is audited by Olds & Watershed CAs, a venerable firm in the city. Kim has been hoping that John would switch auditors. Today John wants to get Kim's opinion about accounting for lease capitalizations related to a particularly complicated agreement with franchise dealers. Kim makes notes and promises to call John tomorrow.

c. PA Maclean gave a standard unqualified audit report on the financial statements of Anglo Korp. The annual report document did not contain supplementary oil and gas reserve information required by the *Handbook*.

d. Saul Panzer is a former university football player. Saul is a PA who works for Aggregate Corporation, which owns controlling interests in 42 other corporations. Theodolinda Bonner, president of Aggregate, has assigned Saul the task of performing audits of these corporations and submitting audit opinions directly to her for later presentation to the board of directors.

e. PA Blunt audits the Huber Hope Company. Huber's controller, also a PA, has conducted his own audit of Little Hope, Inc., Huber's single subsidiary, which amounts to 10 percent of the total assets, revenue, and income of the consolidated entity. Blunt has written an audit report that carefully explains reliance on "part of examination made by other independent auditors," with added language to explain the controller's role.

15.29 Responsibilities to Clients Cases. Knowledge of the rules of conduct and interpretations thereof on confidential client information and contingent fees will help you respond to the following cases. For each case, state whether the action or situation shows violation of the ICAO Rules of Professional Conduct, explain why, and cite the relevant rule or interpretation.

a. PA Sally Colt has discovered a way to eliminate most of the boring work of processing routine accounts receivable confirmations by contracting with the Cohen Mail Service. After the auditor has prepared the confirmations, Cohen will stuff them in envelopes, mail them, receive the return replies, open the replies, and return them to Sally.

b. Cadentoe Corporation, without consulting its PA, has changed its accounting so that it is not in conformity with generally accepted accounting principles. During the regular audit engagement, the PA discovers that the statements based on the accounts are so grossly misleading that they might be considered fraudulent. PA Cramer resigns from the engagement after a heated argument. Cramer knows that the statements will be given to John Cairncross, his friend at the Last National Bank, and knows that John is not a very astute reader of complicated financial statements. Two days later, Cairncross calls Cramer and asks some general questions about Cadentoe's statements and remarks favourably on the very thing that is misrepresented. Cramer corrects the erroneous analysis, and Cairncross is very much surprised.

c. A PA who had reached retirement age arranged for the sale of his practice to another public accountant. Their agreement called for the transfer of all working papers and business correspondence to the accountant purchasing the practice.

d. Martha Jacoby, PA, withdrew from the audit of Harvard Company after discovering irregularities in Harvard's income tax returns. One week later, Ms. Jacoby was telephoned by Jake Henry, PA, who explained that he had just been retained by Harvard Company to replace Ms. Jacoby. Mr. Henry asked Ms. Jacoby why she withdrew from the Harvard engagement. She told him.

e. David Moore, PA, offers a consulting service to clients in which he reviews their needs for computer-related supplies (magnetic tapes, disks, cards, paper, and so on) and places their orders with Computographics, Inc. This supplier offers a special discount price because of the volume of business generated by Moore. David is considering two alternative billing arrangements:

1. Charge the clients no fee and instead accept a 3 percent commission from Computographics, Inc.

2. Charge his regular consulting rate of $160 per hour.

f. Amos Fiddle, PA, prepared an uncontested claim for a tax refund on Faddle Corporation's amended tax return. The fee for the service was 30 percent of the amount that Revenue Canada rules to be a proper refund. The claim was for $300,000.

g. After Faddle had won a $200,000 refund and Fiddle collected the $60,000 fee, Jeremy Faddle, the president, invited Amos Fiddle to be the auditor for Faddle Corporation.

15.30 Other Responsibilities and Practices Cases. Knowledge of the rules of conduct and interpretations thereof regarding various other responsibilities and practices will help you respond to the following cases. For each case, state whether the action or situation shows violation or potential for violation of the ICAO Rules of Professional Conduct, explain why, and cite the relevant rule or interpretation.

a. PA R. Stout completed a review of the unaudited financial statements of Wolfe Gifts. Ms. Wolfe was very displeased with the report. An argument ensued, and she told Stout never to darken her door again. Two days later, she telephoned Stout and demanded he return (1) Wolfe's cash disbursement journal, (2) Stout's working paper schedule of adjusting journal entries, (3) Stout's inventory analysis working papers, and (4) all other working papers prepared by Stout. Since Wolfe had not yet paid her bill, Stout replied that provincial law gave him a lien on all the records and that he would return them as soon as she had paid his fee.

b. The PA firm of Durkin & Panzer had received promissory notes in payment of the Henshaw Hacksaw company tax return preparation fee. Six months after the notes were due, PA Durkin notified Dave Henshaw that the notes had been turned over to the North Country Bank for collection.

c. PA Panzer has been invited to conduct a course in effective tax planning for the City Chamber of Commerce. The C. of C. president said a brochure would be mailed to members giving the name of Panzer's firm, his educational background and degrees held, professional society affiliations, and testimonials from participants in the course held last year comparing his excellent performance with that of other PAs who have offered competing courses in the city.

d. PA Philby is a member of the provincial bar. Her practice is a combination of law and accounting, and she is heavily involved in estate planning engagements. Her letterhead gives the affiliations: Member, Provincial Bar of —, and Member, CICA.

e. The PA firm of Burgess & Maclean has made a deal with Cairncross & Company, a firm of management consulting specialists, for mutual business advantage. B&M agreed to recommend Cairncross to clients who need management consulting services. Cairncross agreed to recommend B&M to clients who need improvements in their accounting systems. During the year both firms would keep records of fees obtained by these mutual referrals. At the end of the year, Cairncross and B&M would settle the net differences based on a referral rate of 5 percent of fees.

f. Sturm & Drang, PAs, conduct an aggressive, growing practice in Middle City. The firm pays 20 percent of first-year fees to any staff member (below partner) who brings in a new client.

g. Jack Robinson and Archie Robertson (both PAs) are not partners, but they have the same office, the same employees, and a joint bank account, and they work together on audits. A letterhead they use shows both their names and the description "Members, ICAO."

h. PA Dewey retired from the two-person firm of Dewey & Cheatham. One year later, D&C merged practices with Howe & Company, to form a regional firm under the name of Dewey, Cheatham, & Howe Company.

i. Fritz Brenner, PA, died and widow Brenner inherited the interest he had in the PA firm of Brenner & Horstmann, P.C. Can widow Brenner share in the partnership as a passive investment? She is not a PA.

15.31 Rules of Professional Conduct

Required:

For each of the following completely independent situations, describe the rules of professional conduct that are relevant. Have they been violated? Support your conclusion.

Situation A

Randi Woode, PA, was working on the year-end audit of her client, Pads N' Pens (PNP). PNP is an office stationery retailer with a July 31 year-end. She was having difficulty completing the audit because some accounting records for the months of April and May had been destroyed in a fire.

She told the owner-manager of PNP, Joe Smith, that she might have to qualify her audit report because of her inability to substantiate some of the balances on the financial statements. Joe pointed out that he had been her client for eight years and that she knew him to be honest and trustworthy. He also said a qualified report would harm his negotiations with the bank for additional loans. After considering PNP's need for additional financing, as well as their long-standing relationship, Randi agreed to issue an unqualified report.

Situation B

Lori Wilkes is an audit senior with a large PA firm in Toronto. She has learned that one of her largest clients, Superior Motors Ltd. (SML), is planning to acquire Steelco Inc. SML is Canada's largest automobile manufacturer, and Steelco is one of SML's biggest steel suppliers. Lori is confident that SML's acquisition of Steelco will reduce SML's costs dramatically, and that as a result, SML's share price will rise. She has, therefore, encouraged her boyfriend, Tom, to buy some shares while being careful not to divulge the real reasons behind her recommendation.

Situation C

After obtaining his PA designation, Larry Wilde decided to set up his own public accounting practice. He reasoned that naming his practice "Quality Chartered Accountancy Services" would best attract new clients.

(ICAO adapted)

15.32 **Rules of Professional Conduct.** In mid-May, Aileen Macdonald, PA, received a phone call from one of her largest clients, a manufacturer. The client wanted to know more details about the impact that the GST would have on his 1991 operations and financial statements. When Aileen and the client had discussed the results of the 1989 audit last February, part of their conversation had dealt with the new tax. Aileen had indicated that she would be sending a newsletter about the tax by July 1.

Since February there had been more changes to the legislation, which Aileen and her partners hadn't had time to absorb. However, Aileen had registered for the annual June provincial conference, where she would attend the four technical sessions on the GST. She planned to ask questions about her client's situation during the question-and-answer periods that followed each session.

Aileen explained to the client that she would have more information within a month and would contact him then. At that time, she will ask the client for names of firms that might be interested in receiving her newsletter.

Required:

Which rules of professional conduct are relevant to the above situation? Discuss the rules with which Aileen Macdonald is in compliance as well as those she may have violated.

(ICAO adapted)

Discussion Cases

· ·

15.33 General Ethics. Is there any moral difference between a disapproved action in which you are caught and the same action that never becomes known to anyone else? Do many persons in business and professional society make a distinction between these two circumstances? If you respond that you do (or do not) perceive a difference while persons in business and professional society do not (or do), then how do you explain the differences in attitudes?

15.34 Ethics Decision Problem. You are treasurer of a church. A member approaches you with the following proposition: "I will donate shares to the church on December 31, if, on January 1, you will sell it back to me. All you will need to do is convey the certificate with your signature to me in return for my cheque, which will be for the asking price of the shares quoted that day without reduction for commissions."

The member's objective, of course, is to obtain the income tax deduction as of December 31, but he wants to maintain his ownership interest. The policy of the church board is not to hold any shares but to sell shares within a reasonably short time.

Consider:

a. Should the treasurer accommodate the member? Would you if you were treasurer?

b. Would your considerations and conclusions be any different if:

1. The church were financially secure and the gift were small in amount?
2. The church were financially secure and the gift were large?
3. The church would be in deficit position for the year were it not for the gift?

15.35 Competition and Audit Proposals. Accounting firms are often asked to present "proposals" to companies' boards of directors. These "proposals" are comprehensive booklets, accompanied by oral presentations, telling about the firm's personnel, technology, special qualifications, and expertise in hope of convincing the board to award the work to the firm.

Dena has a new job as staff assistant to Michael, chairman of the board of Granof Grain company. The company has a policy of engaging new auditors every seven years. The board will hear oral proposals from 12 accounting firms. This is the second day of the three-day meeting. Dena's job is to help evaluate the proposals. Yesterday, the proposal by Anderson, Olds & Watershed was clearly the best.

Then Dena sees Michael's staff chief, a brash go-getter, slip a copy of the AOW written proposal into an envelop. He tells Dena to take it to a friend who works for Hunt and Hunt, a PA firm scheduled to make its presentation tomorrow. He says: "I told him we'd let him glance at the best proposal."

Michael is absent from the meeting and will not return for two hours.

What should Dena do? What should PA Hunt do if he receives the AOW proposal, assuming he has time to modify the Hunt and Hunt proposal before tomorrow's presentation?

15.36 Engagement Timekeeping Records. A time budget is always prepared for audit engagements. Numbers of hours are estimated for various segments of the work—for example, internal control evaluation, cash, inventory, report review, and the like. Audit supervisors expect the work segments to be completed "within budget," and staff accountants' performance is evaluated in part on ability to perform audit work efficiently within budget.

Sarah is an audit manager who has worked hard to get promoted. She hopes to become a partner in two or three years. Finishing audits on time weighs heavily on her performance evaluation. She assigned the cash audit work to Craig, who has worked for the firm for 10 months. Craig hopes to get a promotion and salary raise this year. Twenty hours were budgeted for the cash work. Craig is efficient, but it took 30 hours to finish because the company had added seven new bank accounts. Craig was worried about his performance evaluation, so he recorded 20 hours for the cash work and put the other 10 hours under the internal control evaluation budget.

What do you think about Craig's resolution of his problem? Was his action a form of lying? What would you think of his action if the internal control evaluation work was presented "under budget" because it was not yet complete, and another assistant was assigned to finish that work segment later?

15.37 Audit Overtime. All accountants' performance evaluations are based in part on their ability to do audit work efficiently and within the time budget planned for the engagement. New staff accountants, in particular, usually have some early difficulty learning speedy work habits, which demand that no time be wasted.

Elizabeth started work for Anderson, Olds & Watershed in September. After attending the staff training school, she was assigned to the Rising Sun Company audit. Her first work assignment was to complete the extensive recalculation of the inventory compilation, using the audit test counts and audited unit prices for several hundred inventory items. Her time budget for the work was six hours. She started at 4 P.M. and was not finished when everyone left the office at 6 P.M. Not wanting to stay downtown alone, she took all the necessary working papers home. She resumed work at 8 P.M. and finished at 3 A.M. The next day, she returned to the Rising Sun offices, put the completed working papers in the file, and recorded six hours in the time budget/actual schedule. Her supervisor was pleased, especially about her diligence in taking the work home.

What do you think about Elizabeth's diligence and her understatement of the time she took to finish the work? What would you think of the case if she had received help at home from her husband? What would you think of the case if she had been unable to finish and had left the work at home for her husband to finish while he took off a day from his job interviews?

15.38 Form of Practice, Technical Standards, and Confidentiality. Knowledge of the rules of conduct and interpretations thereof will help you respond to this case problem.

Gilbert and Bradley formed a corporation called Financial Services, Inc. Each took 50 percent of the authorized common shares. Gilbert is a PA and a member of the provincial institute. Bradley is a CPCU (Chartered Property Casualty Underwriter). The corporation performs auditing and tax services under Gilbert's direction and insurance services under Bradley's supervision. The opening of the corporation's office was announced in a full-page advertisement in the local newspaper.

One of the corporation's first audit clients was the Grandtime Company. Grandtime had total assets of $600,000 and total liabilities of $270,000. In the course of the audit, Gilbert found that Grandtime's building with a book value of $240,000 was pledged as a security for a 10-year term note in the amount of $200,000. The client's statement did not mention that the building was pledged as security for the 10-year term note. However, as the failure to disclose the lien did not affect either the value of the assets or the amount of the liabilities, and the audit was satisfactory in all other respects, Gilbert rendered an unqualified opinion on Grandtime's financial statements. About two months after the date of his opinion, Gilbert learned that an insurance company was planning to loan Grandtime $150,000 in the form of a first-mortgage note on the building. Realizing the insurance company was unaware of the existing lien on the building, Gilbert had Bradley notify the insurance company of the fact that Grandtime's building was pledged as security for the term note.

Shortly after the events described above, Gilbert was charged with several violations of professional ethics.

Required:
Identify and discuss the Rules of Professional Conduct violated by Gilbert and the nature of the violations.

(AICPA adapted)

15.39 Rules of Professional Conduct. You and Laura Cooper are the two partners of a PA firm in Ottawa. After your two-week Caribbean vacation, you return to the office to discover that your secretary is busily preparing to mail some brochures. You have never seen the brochures before and your secretary explains that Laura had them printed during your absence. The brochures are colourful and glossy and the name of your firm is boldly displayed on the front cover. You pick up a brochure and notice that it describes your firm as "the PA firm where clients always come first." On the last page of the brochure, readers are advised that new audit cli-

ents will not be charged a fee for any management consulting services provided in the first full year.

You ask Laura about the brochures, and she tells you that she had them specially designed and printed in order to increase the firm's profile and competitiveness. She believes that mailing these brochures to all the top companies in Ottawa will not only increase the firm's client base but will also help it develop a high-quality image by getting a reputation for obtaining the "best clients." Furthermore, she plans to contact all recipients of the brochure in a few weeks to arrange a "follow-up" meeting to discuss their accounting and auditing needs.

Required:
Describe which rules of professional conduct may have been violated and indicate your professional responsibilities and course of action.

(ICAO adapted)

15.40 Conflict of Clients' Interests. Jon Williams, PA, has found himself in the middle of the real-life soap opera "Taxing Days of Our Lives."

The cast of characters:
Oneway Corporation is Jon's audit and tax client. The three directors are the officers and also the only three shareholders, each owning exactly one-third of the shares.

President Jack founded the company and is now nearing retirement. As an individual, he is also Jon's tax client.

Vice president Jill manages the day-to-day operations. She has been instrumental in enlarging the business and its profits. Jill's individual tax work is done by PA Phil.

Treasurer Bill has been a long-term, loyal employee and has been responsible for many innovative financial transactions and reports of great benefit to the business. He is Jon's close personal friend and also an individual tax client.

The conflict:
President Jack discussed with PA Jon the tax consequences to him as an individual of selling his one-third interest in Oneway Corporation to vice

president Jill. Later, meeting with Bill to discuss his individual tax problems, Jon learns that Bill fears that Jack and Jill will make a deal, put him in a minority position, and force him out of the company. Bill says: "Jon, we have been friends a long time. Please keep me informed about Jack's plans, even rumours. My interest in Oneway Corporation represents my life savings and my resources for the kids' university. Remember, you're little Otto's godfather."

Thinking back, Jon realized that vice president Jill has always been rather hostile. Chances are that Phil would get the Oneway engagement if Jill acquires Jack's shares and controls the corporation. Nevertheless, Bill will probably suffer a great deal if he cannot learn about Jack's plans, and Jon's unwillingness to keep him informed will probably ruin their close friendship.

Later, on a dark and stormy night:

Jon ponders the problem. "Oneway Corporation is my client, but a corporation is a fiction. Only a form. The shareholders personify the real entity, so they are collectively my clients, and I can transmit information among them as though they were one person. Right? On the other hand, Jack and Bill engage me for individual tax work, and information about one's personal affairs is really no business of the other. What to do? What to do?

Required:

Give Jon advice about alternative actions, considering the constraints of the ICAO's Rules of Conduct.

15.41 **Failure to Follow GAAS.** It's going to be a long night! First thing this morning, the senior partner of your three-partner firm, Peters, Peters and Paul ("PPP"), called you into her office to tell you that she had a confidential but exciting assignment for you. The firm has been retained to review the audit working papers of another firm in connection with its audit of TVB Software (TVB), a public company. That firm, Yeller, Louder and Soft (YLS), had performed the audit of TVB for the last two years, since the date it went public. It appears that the bank did not renew TVB's loan when it matured some six months ago and TVB was unable to obtain other financing. As a result, your firm's client lost a good portion of the $2 million he had invested in the shares of TVB. Your client is suing the auditors of TVB, alleging that they failed to perform the audit in accordance with generally accepted auditing standards (GAAS), and that as a result, your client relied on financial statements that were not correct when he made his decision to hold on to his TVB shares. The last audited statements are included in Exhibit 15.41–1.

Victoria Smyth, the partner, has reviewed the contents of YLS's working papers. Her notes are in Exhibit 15.41–2. You have been asked to review these notes and prepare a report identifying any departures from GAAS to support your client's view that the audit was not conducted in accordance with GAAS. In this regard, you should note whether each instance is a clear departure from GAAS or whether the matter is grey and, therefore, subject to potential challenge in court. Victoria is also concerned that your firm may have some professional responsibilities under the Rules of Professional Conduct in connection with this agreement. She would like you to identify these for her.

Required:

Prepare the report requested by Victoria Smyth.

(ICAO adapted)

E X H I B I T 15.41–1   **EXTRACTS FROM AUDITED FINANCIAL STATEMENTS**

TVB Software
Balance Sheet
As at December 31
(in thousands of dollars)

	19-3	19-2
Assets		
Current Assets		
Prepaids	$ 237	$ 410
Accounts receivable	6,146	5,410
Inventory	13,904	9,382
	20,287	15,202
Other Assets		
Fixed assets	13,640	14,975
Goodwill	4,084	4,310
Other assets	6,950	7,010
	24,674	26,295
	$44,961	$41,497
Liabilities and Shareholder Equity		
Current Liabilities		
Bank indebtedness	$ 4,940	$ 1,749
Accounts payable	10,641	5,940
Deferred revenue	140	3,643
Current portion of long-term debt	1,400	1,400
	17,121	12,732
Long-term Debt	18,210	19,990
Share capital	8,500	8,500
Retained Earnings	1,130	275
Total Liabilities and Capital	$44,961	$41,497

TVB Software
Income Statement
For the years ended December 31
(in thousands of dollars)

	19-3	19-2
Sales	$21,724	$31,490
Cost of Sales	15,908	20,130
Gross Margin	5,816	11,360
Sales and Administrative Expenses		
Salaries	1,760	3,170
Research costs	304	3,775
Marketing and sales	501	2,607
Interest	1,739	1,889
Other	657	16
	4,961	11,457
Net income before taxes	855	(97)
Income taxes	—	203
Net Income	$ 855	($ 300)

E X H I B I T   15.41–1   **EXTRACTS FROM NOTES TO FINANCIAL STATEMENTS (continued)**

TVB Software
For the year ended December 31, 19-3

From Note 1—Accounting Policies

 Goodwill

  Goodwill is amortized to income over its 40-year life.

From Note 7—Fixed Assets

 Fixed assets comprises.

	Cost	December 31, 19-3 Accumulated Debt	Book Value
Computer Equipment	$29,790	$26,100	$ 3,690
Furniture and Fixtures	10,650	7,700	2,950
Building	11,000	4,000	7,000
Total	$51,440	$37,800	$13,640

E X H I B I T   15.41–2   **TVB SOFTWARE**

"PRIVILEGED"

Victoria Smyth's notes on review of audit working papers of TVB Software prepared by Yeller, Louder & Soft

1. I reviewed YLS's working papers at their office. The audit report for the year ended December 31 19•3 was signed by YLS on February 20, 19•4.

    The working papers were neat and appeared to be well organized. All of the files have been prepared by audit staff and have been reviewed by a YLS junior audit partner, though not the one who signed the financial statements. This is the only public company audited by YLS.

    I asked to review the files of the previous year but was told that YLS only retains one year of files. The 19•2 files had been destroyed. I reminded YLS that the 19•2 files had now been subpoenaed by the Court.

2. The audit was staffed by two YLS CAs. Neither had performed audits of a software company before, but one of them had several years of auditing experience. The other CA had recently qualified and had spent the previous two years working for a government internal auditor's department. The audit partner told me that he wasn't concerned about this other CA because he was related to TVB's CFO and, hence, had a good knowledge of some of the workings of the company.

3. The audit was fully substantive in nature. All three of YLS's files contain working papers documenting the results of its substantive testing. Each section of the work contains a checklist of substantive tests. The tests appear to have been developed specifically for this assignment. The steps on the checklists appear to be signed off and cross-referenced to the appropriate working papers.

4. The first file is called the "TOP FILE" and contains several memos to file. The most significant of these are as follows:

    a) Materiality. A short memo sets materiality at $400,000. The memo notes that the company is not currently profitable although it is expected to be in the near future. As a result, it is more appropriate to use balance sheet numbers to determine materiality. Once the company becomes profitable, YLS would expect to use normalized income as a basis for materiality. Thus, one per cent of total assets is approximately $400,000.

    b) Plan. A short memo sets out that the audit will be fully substantive against a materiality of $400,000 and follow the approach used in the previous year, including the tailored audit programs developed that year.

    c) Engagement letter, signed by the client.

    d) Legal letters to each of TVB's lawyers, each with a standard reply.

E X H I B I T   15.41–2   **TVB SOFTWARE (continued)**

---

e) A standard management representation letter, containing no unusual or tailored paragraphs.

5. Prepaids. As these amounts were not material, YLS only compared this year's schedule to that of the previous year. There were no unusual items on either of the schedules.

6. Accounts receivable. The audit work in this section included a confirmation of the 15 largest accounts and 10 other accounts selected at random, covering 79% of the population. All but two of the confirmations (totalling $326,000) were received back with no problems noted. In view of the satisfactory result on the other confirmations, no additional procedures were carried out in relation to these two items.

   A review was done to identify subsequent payments, and as at the date of the audit opinion, 85% of the receivables had been collected. Of the remaining accounts, none were above $100,000, so no further work was carried out.

   Procedures were carried out to ensure that balances outstanding at year end related to shipments before year-end. These procedures included agreeing amounts to invoices and shipping documents.

7. Inventory. The inventory consisted of software packages, most of which were manufactured by TVB, and some purchased for modification and resale.

   YLS attended the inventory count at year-end and reviewed the procedures necessary to achieve a proper cut-off. As a result of these procedures, YLS found cut-off errors that resulted in an overstatement of sales of $182,500. They concluded that, as this amount was not material, no adjustment was necessary. They also reviewed the inventory valuation by reviewing the process for allocating costs to specific products. This is a very complex process and the audit work seems to be detailed and thorough with much recomputation and testing in the files. They concluded that the allocation methodology was appropriate in the circumstances. They did not identify any errors.

8. Fixed assets. YLS's work was limited to reviewing the schedule of purchases (there were none above $100,000) and recomputing the depreciation for the year.

9. Goodwill. YLS recomputed the amortization for the year.

10. Bank indebtedness. YLS confirmed the amount of the bank indebtedness and the long-term debt, which is also owing to the bank. The confirmation noted that the debt was up for renewal in June of the following year. There is a note in the file that company management was confident that the debt would be renewed for a five-year term. As well, the file contained copies of some internal TVB memoranda, written over a four-month period in 19●3, summarizing management's meetings with the bank and supporting the view that the debt would likely be renewed. On this basis, YLS concurred with management's view that the debt should continue to be classified as long-term debt.

11. Accounts payable. The files contained a confirmation of 100% of the accounts payable. All of the replies were in the file and all discrepancies had been followed up. As a result of these procedures, YLS concluded that accounts payable were understated by $232,000 but that, as this amount was immaterial, no adjustment was required.

12. Income taxes. Very detailed work was carried out in this section by a tax manager from YLS. The review appears very thorough and amounts are reconciled down to the penny.

13. Profit and loss. YLS carried out analytical procedures, comparing the current year's results to those of the previous year on an account-by-account basis. Explanations were obtained from management for all variances over $50,000 or 5 per cent of the previous year's balance.

    The file includes a detailed review of all invoices paid to outside consultants, including several other accounting firms, and copies of their reports. One of the assignments relates to a ''business review'' of TVB carried out at the request of the bank. The report for that assignment is not in the file.

15.42 CGA Code of Ethics. The issue of ethical conduct is becoming more and more important in the professional practice of PAs.

Required:

a. Identify the sequence of steps that have been proposed for an auditor to follow in attempting to resolve an ethical dilemma.

b. What are the two broad aims of the CGA Code of Ethics?

c. Briefly describe the three mechanisms by which the CGA Code of Ethics and Rules of Professional Conduct work.

(CGAAC adapted)

15.43 Independence. You are an audit manager with the firm of Wu, Potter and McKinley, PAs. You and Ray St. Claire, a manager with another PA firm, are having a discussion about auditor independence. Ray says, "On the one hand, the public seems to be demanding more and more assurance from us about more and more aspects of a client's operations, but to maintain our practice in today's environment we have to be competitive to be able to attract new clients."

Required:

a. Identify and briefly explain the competitive practice on the part of auditors to which Ray is referring.

b. Why is this perceived as a threat to auditor independence and the quality of audits?

c. With reference to parts *a.* and *b.*, what could a client do, at least in theory, to take advantage of this situation? What is the reason this strategy might not work?

d. What does the CGA-Canada Code of Ethics say about this issue?

(CGAAC adapted)

15.44 Audit Proposals. Smith and Mulberry (S&M) were asked by Behometh Ltd. to submit a proposal for its audit. This involved a 30-minute presentation to the board of directors and a written submission. The submission included a fixed fee quote for the first two years, a detailed outline of the proposed audit strategy, and a list of the qualifications of the audit team to be assigned. Five other PA firms were invited to bid on the engagement. S&M put in a "low-ball" bid because the partners saw this as a golden opportunity to get exposure in this industry.

Several weeks later, Edgar Brown, chairman of the board, telephoned Mike Mulberry, congratulating him on being awarded the audit. The conversation went as follows:

Edgar: I'm pleased to offer you the engagement, Mike, and I want you to know you weren't the lowest bid. What really impressed us was your attitude and promise to give us personal attention. It's so refreshing to find an auditor who openly states there needs to be a completely harmonious relationship between auditor and client.

Mike: We're really pleased to be your auditors, Edgar. We were a little apprehensive about not having any experience in your industry.

Edgar: Well Mike, since you did indicate you would hire someone experienced to oversee the engagement, I really see no problem. I certainly support your idea of Stan Biggs, since he knows the industry inside out. We're a little sorry to lose him. He had only been with us two years since obtaining his PA and was a fine controller.

Mike: Yes, his knowledge of your operations should allow us to complete the audit in the minimal time.

Edgar: There is one favour you can do us right away, Mike. We would like to start a national ad campaign that depicts our auditor slashing prices to the bone on our products. We would like you to be the auditor in that ad.

Mike: Acting's not really my strong suit, Edgar, but I'm sure we can accommodate you on that.

Edgar: By the way Mike, to show how much we value our auditors, I want to give you a key to the executive washroom, a special pass that allows you to park in restricted zones, and a letter that will give you folks an additional 25 percent off our employee store prices.

Mike: Thanks very much, Edgar.

(ICAO adapted)

The following week Mike went out to review the working papers of the predecessor auditors. He was shocked at the poor quality of work evident in these files. However, given the rule against criticism of fellow members, he believed it would be inappropriate to mention this to Behometh.

The audit went very smoothly. In fact, with Biggs in charge, S&M even managed to turn a profit on the job.

Several months later some information came to light, which Mike was not sure if he should worry about. Although Biggs had severed all employment ties with Behometh prior to joining S&M, apparently he still retained 1,000 shares of voting stock in the company.

Required:

Discuss the ethical issues in this case.

(ICAO adapted)

APPENDIX 15A

THE SEC ON INDEPENDENCE

. . . .

LEARNING OBJECTIVE

3. Identify and explain the major differences between AICPA and SEC views on auditors' independence.

The Securities and Exchange Commission was established in 1934 to administer the Securities Act of 1933, the Securities Exchange Act of 1934, and several other regulatory acts. In addition to administrative powers, the SEC has rule-making and judicial powers. The SEC relies heavily on the accounting profession and has a great interest in auditing standards and standards of professional conduct.

The SEC rule on independence is in Rule 2-01(b) of Regulation S-X. Except for differences in the choice of words, the content of the SEC rule appears to be very similar to Rules of Conduct. The SEC and provincial institutes define *member* essentially the same with reference to independence matters. However, these surface similarities mask some substantive differences in the ways the two agencies interpret their rules. The main differences are in the areas of bookkeeping, family relations, financial interests, and former partners.

BOOKKEEPING

. . . .

The SEC prohibits the combination of bookkeeping (accounting) and auditing services. The provincial institutes do not consider independence impaired if an accountant first prepares the client's books and then audits the financial statements prepared from them. However, the client must be able to accept responsibility for accounting decisions and for the financial statements. The SEC views the two services as incompatible, believing that an auditor cannot appear to be independent when auditing the bookkeeping work he or she has done. In the SEC's eyes, independence is impaired even if the PA keeps clients' books by offering computerized accounting services. However, exceptions can be made in the case of emergency, in other unusual situations, and when computer services for first-time registrants were merely routine and mechanical, and did not involve the most recent fiscal year in the financial statements.

FAMILY RELATIONS

. . . .

The SEC tends to go further than provincial institutes in attributing family relations to a "member." The SEC considers independence impaired in most cases when a spouse, dependent person, or someone else in the member's household has a direct or material indirect financial interest, or when nondependent close relatives (children, brothers, sisters, grandparents, parents, parents-in-law, and the spouses of each of the foregoing) have material direct financial interests or managerial relationships in an audit client. The provincial institutes make allowances for the "audit sensitivity" of a relative's employment, letting independence be considered intact if the position is not sensitive. However, the provincial institute interpretations warn members to be aware of the appearances no matter what the specific facts may be. Overall, the provincial institutes' position appears to be flexible and permits assessment of the circumstances in each case. In contrast, the SEC position tends to prohibit most relationships involving close relatives, especially when the relative holds an executive position or is in a position to influence the content of the financial statements.

FINANCIAL INTERESTS

The SEC tends to be stricter than the provincial institutes on matters of prohibited indirect financial interests. The tendency is to be conservative and to consider most financial relationships, investments in concert with client's officers and directors, and other joint business ventures as impairments of independence.

FORMER PARTNERS

The SEC is stricter than the provincial institutes about the effect of a retired or resigned partner's association with his or her former firm's appearance of independence. Broadly, the SEC considers the firm's independence impaired if (*a*) a former partner who was closely associated with an audit becomes a member of the board of directors of the auditee within two years after resignation or retirement, (*b*) a former partner who was "prominent in his or her firm" becomes a director of a client of the accounting firm within five years, and (*c*) a former partner becomes an executive of a client of the accounting firm without a total separation, including settlement of retirement benefits, from the firm. However, former partners can become directors of auditees and still receive retirement benefits from the accounting firm so long as the benefits were fixed at the time of retirement. The provincial institutes' rules are similar but do not contain the specific time limits.

SEC VIEWS

The SEC has emphasized an important facet of factual independence, saying: "Perhaps the most critical test of the actuality of an accountant's independence is the strength of his insistence upon full disclosure of transactions between the company and members of its management as individuals; accession to the wishes of management in such cases must inevitably raise a serious question [of] whether the accountant is, in fact, independent." The provincial institutes' rules do not emphasize this point. This SEC view casts a cloud of suspicion over the practice of negotiating with the client the nature and amount of financial statement adjustments proposed by auditors.

SEC interpretations on independence are made by staff members in the Office of the Chief Accountant. In the past, accountants presented fact situations and requested decisions about their independence in a particular situation. The staff prepared letters expressing case-specific conclusions. Periodically, some of these conclusions were compiled and published. At present, they can be found in Financial Reporting Release No. 1, Section 602, published by the SEC. These case decisions are used by accountants as analogies to new fact situations and as guides to figuring out the SEC position.

Accountants are always welcome to submit their independence questions to the chief accountant for a decision. It is much better to settle a question before an audit is conducted than to have an issue of independence raised later. Accountants' letters describing fact situations and letters containing SEC conclusions are routinely released to the public.

· ·

R E V I E W
C H E C K P O I N T S

15.45 Compare the ICAO and SEC views on independence. How are they similar? How do they differ?

· ·

CHAPTER 16

Learning Objectives

As noted in Chapter 15, auditors have three sources of responsibility: moral, professional, and legal.

The previous chapter on professional ethics dealt mainly with accountants' self-regulation. This chapter focuses on public regulation through the courts. The discussion will help you to understand accountants' legal liability for professional work. Your learning objectives are to be able to:

1. List some ways that auditors can get into civil and criminal legal trouble.

2. Specify the characteristics of accountants' liability under common law, and cite some specific case precedents.

3. Specify the characteristics of accountants' liability under statutory law.

Legal Liability

The Legal Environment

LEARNING OBJECTIVE

1. List some ways that auditors can get into civil and criminal legal trouble.

"Tort reform" has been a hot topic in the business and popular press. Record-setting damages have been awarded, and professional liability insurance premiums have increased dramatically, and in some cases insurance is difficult to obtain. Insurance premiums for small firms went from $64 per person in 1980 to more than $2,000 per person in 1992, for lower coverage!

The problems affect everyone, from manufacturers to rock concert promoters. Accountants are likewise affected. In the 1980s over $250 million was paid to settle litigation. Twenty-seven medium-sized accounting firms formed their own offshore captive insurance company in Bermuda to get adequate liability insurance.

Accountants are potentially liable for monetary damages and even subject to criminal penalties (e.g., under SEC rules), including fines and jail terms, for failure to perform professional services properly. They can be sued by clients, clients' creditors, investors, and the government. Exposure to large lawsuit claims is possible through class actions permitted under federal rules of court procedure in Canada and the United States. In a class action suit, a relatively small number of aggrieved plaintiffs with small individual claims can bring suit for large damages in the name of an extended class. After a bankruptcy, for example, 40 bondholders who lost $40,000 might decide to sue, and they can sue on behalf of the entire class of bondholders for all their alleged losses (say $40 million). In some jurisdictions, lawyers will take such suits on a contingency fee basis (a percentage of the judgment, if any). The size of the claim and the zeal of the lawyers make the class action suit a serious matter. In the United States this has become such a problem that it threatens the existence of many firms, and one regional firm has already been forced into bankruptcy as a result of litigation.

Lawsuit Causes and Frequency

One study of law cases showed that accountants' and auditors' legal troubles arose from five major types of errors. In 129 cases 334 errors were found, classified as follows: (1) 33 percent involved misinterpretation of accounting principles, (2) 15 percent involved misinterpretation of auditing standards, (3) 29 percent involved faulty implementation of auditing procedures, (4) 13 percent involved client fraud, and (5) 7 percent involved fraud by the auditor.[1] These data suggest that accountants' and auditors' exposure to liability for failure to report known departures from accounting principles, for failure to conduct audits properly, for failure to detect management fraud, and for actually being parties to frauds. Threat of lawsuits has

---

[1] K. St. Pierre and J. Anderson, "An Analysis of Audit Failures Based on Documented Legal Cases," *Journal of Accounting, Auditing, and Finance,* Spring 1982, pp. 236–37.

also affected how public accountants conduct their work in consulting services and tax practice. Lest you believe audit practice bears all the liability, be aware that about 35 percent of civil damage suits arise from tax practice disputes.

Another study of accountants' litigation showed how lawsuits against auditors have increased. During the 1960–72 period, 181 cases were found, compared to 291 cases during the 1973–85 period.

All litigation is serious and results in expenses for defence, but not all cases result in payments for damage. In fact, about 40 percent of the lawsuits in the 1960–85 period were dismissed or settled with no payment by the accounting firm. Another 30 percent were settled by payment of approximately $1 million or less. This leaves about 30 percent of the cases where the auditors paid significant damage awards. All these data relate to lawsuits over audit services, to the exclusion of lawsuits about nonaudit services and other matters.[2]

Audit Responsibilities

Many users of audit reports expect auditors to detect fraud, theft, and illegal acts, and to report them publicly. Auditors take responsibility for detecting material misstatements in financial statements; but they are very cautious about taking responsibility for detecting all manner of fraud, and are especially cautious about accepting a public reporting responsibility. Fraud and misleading financial statements loom large among the concerns of financial statement users. They are afraid of information risk, and they want it to be reduced, even eliminated. Some of their expectations are very high, and for this reason an expectation gap often exists between the diligence users expect and the diligence auditors are able to accept.

The audit responsibility for detection of fraud in financial statements is a complex topic, and Chapter 18 (Fraud Awareness Auditing) is devoted entirely to it. Auditors take some responsibility but not as much as many users expect (e.g., see *Handbook Sections* 5135 and 5136). This disparity leads to lawsuits, even when auditors have performed well.

. . . .

R E V I E W
CHECKPOINTS

16.1 What are class action lawsuits, and why should auditors be concerned about them?

16.2 What are some causes of auditors' involvement in lawsuits as defendants?

16.3 What proportion of lawsuits against accountants relate to tax practice?

. . . .

The next parts of this chapter cover accountants' legal liabilities under common law and statutory law. The principle of *stare decisis* or "to stand by a previous decision" is an important principle of common law. The practical problem in many cases, however, is whether the facts in a given case are similar enough to a precedent-setting one. It's rare that the facts are exactly the same. Common law is all the cases and precedents that govern judges' decisions in previous lawsuits. Common law is "common knowledge," in the sense that judges tend to follow the collective wisdom

[2] Zoe-Vonna Palmrose, "An Analysis of Auditor Litigation and Audit Service Quality," *Accounting Review*, January 1988, pp. 55–73.

of past cases decided by themselves and other judges. Common law is not enacted in statutes by a legislature. In contrast, statutory law is all the prohibitions enacted by a legislature—for example, the Canadian Business Corporation Acts and related provincial Corporation Acts.

Liability Under Common Law
· · · · · · · · · · · ·

LEARNING OBJECTIVE

2. Specify the characteristics of accountants' liability under common law, and cite some specific case precedents.

Legal liabilities of professional accountants may arise from lawsuits brought on the basis of the law of contracts or as tort actions for negligence. Breach of contract is a claim that accounting or auditing services were not performed in the manner agreed. This basis is most characteristic of lawsuits involving public accountants and their clients. Tort actions cover the civil complaints (e.g., fraud, deceit, and injury), and such actions are normally initiated by users of financial statements.

Tort refers to a private or civil wrong or injury. The rule of the law of torts is to compensate victims for harm suffered from the activities of others. The problem for tort law is to identify those actions which create a right to compensation. In doing so the law takes into account the fault or blame of the defendant (breach of duty) and whether the defendant's conduct could be considered the cause of the harm (causation). Both breach of a duty to the plaintiff and causation must be established in order for the defendant to be found liable for damages. However, the burden of proof for tort actions varies depending on social policy. For example, under "no fault" schemes the burden of compensation is spread widely to all automobile owners (Smith, Soberman, and Easson, *The Law and Business Administration in Canada,* 7th Edition, 1995, pp. 76–79).

Suits for civil damages under common law usually result when someone suffers a financial loss after relying on financial statements later found to be materially misleading. In the popular press, such unfortunate events are called audit failures. However, a distinction should be made between a business failure and an audit failure. A business failure is a bankruptcy or other serious financial difficulty experienced by an auditor's client. Business failures arise from many kinds of adverse economic events. An audit failure is an auditor's faulty performance, a failure to conduct an audit in accordance with generally accepted auditing standards (GAAS) with the result that misleading financial statements get published.

Characteristics of Common Law Actions

When an injured party considers himself or herself damaged by an accountant and brings a lawsuit, he or she generally asserts all possible causes of action, including breach of contract, tort, deceit, fraud, or whatever else may be relevant to the claim.

Burden of Proof on the Plaintiff

Actions brought under common law place most of the burdens of affirmative proof on the plaintiff, who must prove (1) that he or she was damaged or suffered a loss, (2) the necessary privity or beneficiary relationship, (3) that the financial statements were materially misleading or that the accountant's advice was faulty, (4) that he or she relied on the statements or advice, (5) that they were the direct cause of the loss, and (6) that the accountant was negligent, grossly negligent, deceitful, or otherwise responsible for damages. In the appendix dealing with U.S. securities acts, you will see that some of the U.S. statutes shift some of these burdens of affirmative proof to the professional accountant.

Clients may bring a lawsuit for breach of contract. The relationship of direct involvement between parties to a contract is known as *privity*. When privity exists, a plaintiff usually need only show that the defendant accountant was negligent. (Ordinary negligence—a lack of reasonable care in the performance of professional accounting tasks—is usually meant when the word *negligence* stands alone.) If negligence is proved, the accountant may be liable, provided the client has not been involved in some sort of contributory negligence in the dispute—that is, that it can be shown that the client contributed to his own harm.

Smith v. London Assurance Corp. (1905)

> This was the first American case involving an auditor. The auditor sued for an unpaid fee, and the company counterclaimed for a large sum that had been embezzled by one of its employees, which they claimed would not have occurred except for the auditor's breach of contract. The evidence indicated that the auditors indeed failed to audit cash accounts at one branch office as stipulated in an engagement contract. The court recognized the auditors as skilled professionals and held them liable for embezzlement losses that could have been prevented by nonnegligent performance under the contract.

Fifty years ago, it was very difficult for parties, other than contracting clients, to succeed in lawsuits against auditors. Other parties not in privity had no cause of action for breach of contract. However, the court opinion in the case known as *Ultramares* expressed the view that, if negligence were so great as to constitute gross negligence—lack of minimum care in performing professional duties, indicating reckless disregard for duty and responsibility—grounds might exist for concluding that the accountant had engaged in constructive fraud. Actual fraud is characterized as an intentional act designed to deceive, mislead, or injure the rights of another person.

Ultramares Corporation v. Touche (1931)

> The *Ultramares* decision stated criteria for an auditor's liability to third parties for deceit (a tort action). In order to prove deceit, (1) a false representation must be shown, (2) the tort-feasor must possess scienter—either knowledge of falsity or insufficient basis of information, (3) intent to induce action in reliance must be shown, (4) the damaged party must show justifiable reliance on the false representation, and (5) there must have been a resulting damage. The court held that an accountant could be liable when he did not have sufficient information (audit evidence) to lead to a sincere or genuine belief. In other words, an audit report is deceitful when the auditor purports to speak from knowledge when he has none. The court also wrote that the degree of negligence might be so gross, however, as to amount to a constructive fraud. Then the auditor could be liable in tort to a third-party beneficiary.

Another important result of the *Ultramares* case was that the accountants were not liable to third parties for ordinary negligence. This had two ramifications for public accountants: 1. auditors were not liable to third parties for the next 35 years and 2. this decision had a major impact on the U.S. Congress and influenced its passage of the SEC Acts of 1933 and 1934, creating a statutory responsibility to third parties where none existed under common law (see Appendix 16A).

Most auditor legal responsibilities arise from the law of negligence, which is the part of the common law known as the law of torts. Negligence is the failure to perform a duty with the requisite standard care (due care). The standard relates to one's public calling or profession.

Under the common law of torts for negligence (which is based on fault theory and causation as discussed above), all of the following four elements of negligence must be established by the plaintiff if she or he is to successfully sue the auditor:

I. FOUR ELEMENTS OF NEGLIGENCE

1. There must exist a legal duty of care to the plaintiff.
2. There must be a breach in that duty (e.g., failure to follow GAAS and GAAP).
3. There must be proof that damage resulted (otherwise the plaintiff is limited to the amount of audit fee).
4. There must be a reasonably proximate connection between the breach of duty and the resulting damage (e.g., losses must occur subsequent to firm's audit).

The auditor's defence is to demonstrate that at least one of the above elements is missing. The auditor may also use a contributory negligence argument that the plaintiff contributed to his own loss by, for example, not correcting internal control weaknesses. However, the contributory negligence defence applies only to parties having a contractual relationship with the auditor. Just to keep things straight the auditor is the first party, the contractual client (who hires the auditor for the audit engagement and thus has privity of contract with the auditor) is the second party, and other audited financial statement users are third parties.

II. DUE CARE TO WHOM?

A key issue in establishing liability against auditors is to whom do they owe a duty of care? The contractual client (the second party to the contract) is owed a duty of care due to privity of contract. The client is the organization that appoints the auditor, a corporation, a proprietorship, or a partnership. The engagement letter is critical in specifying the contractual obligation, particularly for nonaudit engagements. This explains the importance of having the engagement letter in the first place—it is the basis for establishing the liability of the auditor to second parties.

Under the *Foss* v. *Harbottle* (1842) principle, financial stakeholders cannot sue for losses suffered simply because the corporation in which they hold the stake has suffered losses. This is the flipside of the protection that the stakeholder gets from suits by the corporation's creditors. Just as a creditor can't sue the corporation's owners, the owners can't sue on behalf of the corporation. The corporation itself has to claim any damages. In the case of auditors, the owners are not viewed as having privity of contract with the auditors; only the corporation has privity of contract. Thus, shareholders can only take action as third parties, and then they must establish damages separate from that to the corporation. It turns out that the difficulty of establishing this latter point has greatly limited legal liability to Canadian accountants from shareholders (even though the auditors' report is addressed to the shareholders).

The most important source of liability to auditors, however, is from third parties. This relates to a principle of common law that got transplanted from third-party liability for acts causing injury or physical damage (*Heaven* v. *Pender*, 1883). Until recently, courts were unwilling to compensate for pure economic losses—that is, where there was no physical injury or damage to a plaintiff's person or property. However, that situation has changed dramatically. The *Ultramares* v. *Touche* case (1931) confirmed that there is no third-party liability for financial losses caused by ordinary auditor negligence. Only in the case of fraud or constructive fraud (gross negligence) could the auditor be held liable to third parties.

The leading case for extending tort law to cover pure economic loss is *Hedley Byrne v. Heller and Partners,* which is described in the following box:

HEDLEY BYRNE & CO. LTD. V. HELLER & PARTNERS LTD.
[1964] A.C. 562 (H.L.)

In *Hedley Byrne,* the National Provincial Bank telephoned and wrote to Heller & Partners on behalf of Hedley Byrne to find out whether Easipower Ltd., a customer of Heller & Partners, was of sound financial position and thus a company with which Hedley Byrne would want to do business. Heller & Partners, disclaiming all responsibility to both enquiries by National Provincial Bank, said Easipower Ltd. was of sound financial shape. Hedley Byrne, in reliance on those statements, entered into a contract with Easipower Ltd., which subsequently thereafter sought liquidation.

The House of Lords, in deciding that Heller & Partners Ltd. would have been liable except for the disclaimer, established the modern role governing liability for professional advisers whose negligence gives rise to economic loss. A professional adviser has an implied duty of care in making an oral or written statement to another person whom he or she knows or should know will rely on it in making a decision with economic consequences.

Source: L.J. Brooks. *Professional Ethics for Accountants,* West Publishing, 1995, p. 113. Reprinted with permission.

Another reason that *Hedley Byrne* v. *Heller* is so important to the public accounting profession is that it established the precedent of third-party liability for (ordinary) negligence to "reasonably foreseeable third-parties". These third parties would include eventually, as a result of subsequent cases, present shareholders and lenders as well as limited classes of prospective shareholders and prospective lenders.

This precedent-setting decision was upheld by the Supreme Court of Canada in *Haig v. Bamford* (1976). The Supreme Court concluded that auditors owe a duty to third parties of which they have "actual knowledge of the limited case that will use and rely on the statements." The details of this are given in the following box:

Haig v. Bamford et. al. (1976) 72 D.L.R. (3d) 68

In *Haig,* the Saskatchewan Development Corporation agreed to advance a $20,000 loan to a financially troubled company in part based on the conditional production of satisfactory audited financial statements. The company engaged Bamford's accountants to prepare the statements. The accountant knew that the statements would be used by Saskatchewan Development Corporation. Relying on the accountant's information, Saskatchewan Development Corporation advanced $20,000 to the company. Later investigation disclosed that a $28,000 prepayment on two uncompleted contracts had been treated as if the contracts had been completed, thereby showing a profit instead of a loss, and the accountants failed to spot the error. The court held that where an accountant has negligently prepared financial statements and a third party relies on them to his or her detriment, a duty of care in an action for negligent misstatement will arise in the following circumstances: the accountant knows that it will be shown to a member of a limited class of which the plaintiff is a member and which the accountant actually knows will use and rely on the statement; the statements have been prepared primarily for guidance of that limited class and in respect of a specific class of transactions for the very purpose for which the plaintiff did in fact rely on them; the fact that the accountant did not know the identity of the plaintiff is not material as long as the accountant was aware that the person for whose immediate benefit they were prepared intended to supply the statements to members of the very limited class of which the plaintiff is a member.

Source: L.J. Brooks, *Professional Ethics for Accountants,* West Publishing, 1995; p. 113. Reprinted with permission.

The contemporary *Toromont* v. *Thorne* case (1975) also upheld the *Hedley Byrne* precedent, as it applied to Canada, of liability to known third parties (in this case a prospective investor, Toromont). Auditor's liability in Canada was further extended to prospective investors (reasonably foreseeable third parties) in *Dupuis v. Pan American Mines* (1979), the details of which are given in the following box:

Dupuis v Pan American Mines

On June 15, 1971, a draft prospectus pertaining to Pan American Mines Ltd. and its wholly owned subsidiary, Central Mining Corporation, was filed with the Quebec Securities Commission. Included in the prospectus was a consolidated balance sheet of Pan Am and its subsidiary, which had been audited by the accounting firm of Thorne, Gunn, Helliwell & Christenson, and on which Thorne, Gunn had expressed an unqualified opinion. On June 16, 1971, the securities commission authorized trading in Pan Am shares and distribution of the prospectus. Pan Am was then listed on the Canadian Stock Exchange, but in

November 1971 trading in the shares was suspended, and in February 1972 Pan Am was delisted.

The plaintiff, Albert Dupuis, brought an action claiming that he had suffered a loss on shares of Pan Am purchased between the time the shares were listed and the time trading was suspended. His action was based on the alleged falsity of some of the information contained in the prospectus, including the auditors' report and the notes to the considated financial statement.

The judges' decision was worded in part as follows: "When an auditor prepares a balance sheet which he knows is going to be inserted in a company prospectus offering stock for sale, *I believe he has a duty to make sure that the contents of that balance sheet are accurate* so that prospective investors will not be led into error by it" (emphasis added).

In conclusion, the judge gave the plaintiff judgment against Thorne, Gunn for $89,266.91, with interest from October 15, 1971, and costs.

Source: H. Rowan, "Legal Cases," *CA Magazine,* August 1979, pp. 36–39.

In summary, through 1979 Canadian courts had gradually widened auditor's liability under common law to include limited classes of third parties.

The recent *Caparo Industries Plc. v. Dickman* case (1989) in the United Kingdom, however, has the potential to reverse this increasing liability to third parties, since it limits liability to those third parties of which auditors have knowledge.[3]

Caparo Industries plc. v. Pickman et al.
[1991] 2. W.L.R. 358 (H.L.)

Caparo, in its takeover of Fidelity plc, had Touche Ross & Co. audit the financial statements of Fidelity. Caparo later alleged that its purchase of shares and subsequent takeover were made in reliance on the accounts, which they claimed were misleading and inaccurate in that they showed a pre-tax profit of £1.3 million instead of a loss of £400,000. Caparo sued Touche Ross for negligence, maintaining that Touche Ross owed them a duty of care as shareholders and potential investors with respect to the audit and certification of the accounts.

The House of Lords decided that Touche Ross owed no duty of care to Caparo either as a potential investor before it was registered or as a shareholder thereafter, for the following reasons:

While there is no general principle that will determine the existence and scope of a duty of care in all cases, in order for a duty of care to arise, there must be: the harm said to result from the breach of duty must have been reasonably foreseeable;

[3] M. Paskelle-Mede, "Duty of Care Revisited," *CA Magazine,* December 1993, pp.34–35.

there must be a relationship of sufficient "proximity" between the party said to owe the duty and the party to whom it is said to be owed; and the situation must be one in which, on policy grounds, the court considers it fair, just and reasonable that the law should impose a duty of a given scope on the part of one party for the benefit of the other.

Source: L.J. Brooks, *Professional Ethics for Accountants,* West Publishing, 1995, pp. 113–114. Reprinted with permission.

A related Canadian case is given in the following box:

FLANDERS V. MITHA

In August 1992 Justice Holmes of the B.C. Supreme Court ruled in *Flanders v. Mitha* (1992) that "disgruntled investors sueing a BC accounting firm Buckett & Sharpley for negligently preparing a housing co-op's financial statements must show that they actually relied on those statements when making their investment decision." During the court proceedings none of the plaintiffs was found to have actually relied on the financial statements in purchasing an apartment. They either relied on the realtor or had made the purchase decision prior to requesting and receiving the financial statements from the realtor. *Flanders v. Mitha* (1992) thus limits the auditor's liability when his or her work is used by a client to solicit investments from the public.

The interesting questions are whether the Canadian Courts will continue to take this narrow approach (some other recent British Columbia decisions suggest so), and whether regulatory agencies such as the Ontario Securities Commission (OSC) will succeed in convincing legislatures to make companies, their directors, and auditors legally responsible to shareholders under revised securities acts for all misleading documents (as in the United States). Currently, Canadian auditors' legal liability to third parties follows from common law only. (The four elements of negligence above were identified in *Toromont v. Thorne et al.* [1975], in which the auditors were found negligent but the plaintiffs could not prove that they suffered losses as a result.) Nevertheless, some recent articles in the financial press make it clear that litigation against auditors in Canada is reaching alarming proportions.

In summary, the current status of auditor third-party legal liability appears to be as follows: The courts have attempted to strike a fair balance between reliable information for users of financial statements and unreasonable risk to the auditor. This balance has resulted in Canadian auditors currently being liable for negligent error to limited classes of third parties. Third parties are often classified in the following categories:

- Known third parties.
- Reasonably foreseeable third parties.
- All third parties relying on financial statements.

The trend in litigation suggests the courts will most likely draw the line between categories (*b*) and (*c*) for purposes of deciding to whom auditors owe a duty of care.

Fraudulent misrepresentation is a basis for liability in tort (established in *Haig v. Bamford*), so parties not in privity with the accountant may have causes of action when negligence is gross enough to amount to constructive fraud. These other parties include primary beneficiaries, actual foreseen and limited classes of persons, and all other injured parties.

State Street Trust Co. v. Ernst (1938)

> Accountants, however, may be liable to third parties, even without deliberate or active fraud. A representation certified as true to the knowledge of the accountants when knowledge there is none, a reckless misstatement, or an opinion based on grounds so flimsy as to lead to the conclusion that there was no genuine belief in its truth, are all sufficient upon which to base liability. A refusal to see the obvious, a failure to investigate the doubtful, if sufficiently gross, may furnish evidence leading to an inference of fraud so as to impose liability for losses suffered by those who rely on the balance sheet. In other words, heedlessness and reckless disregard of consequences may take the place of deliberate intention. In this connection we are to bear in mind the principle already stated, that negligence or blindness, even when not equivalent to fraud, it nonetheless evidence to sustain an inference of fraud. At least, this is so if the negligence is gross.

Primary beneficiaries are third parties for whose primary benefit the audit or other accounting service is performed. Such a beneficiary will be identified to, or reasonably forseeable by, the accountant prior to or during the engagement, and the accountant will know that his or her work will influence the primary beneficiary's decisions. For example, an audit firm may be informed that the report is needed for a bank loan application at the North Land Bank in the Kingston Company case (at the back of many of the chapters here). Many cases indicate that proof of ordinary negligence may be sufficient to make accountants liable for damages to primary beneficiaries.

CIT Financial Corp. v. Glover (1955)

> Auditors are liable to third parties for ordinary negligence if their reports are for the primary benefit of the third party. Thus, the privity criterion may not serve as a defense when third-party beneficiaries are known.

Accountants may also be liable to foreseeable beneficiaries—creditors, investors, or potential investors who rely on accountants' work. If the accountant is reasonably able to foresee a limited class of potential users of his or her work (e.g., local banks, regular suppliers), liability may be imposed for ordinary negligence. This, however, is an uncertain area, and liability in a particular case depends entirely on the unique facts and circumstances. Beneficiaries of these types and all other injured parties may recover damages if they are able to show that an accountant was grossly negligent and perpetrated a constructive fraud.

Rusch Factors, Inc. v. Levin (1968)

With respect to the plaintiff's negligence theory, this case held that an accountant should be liable in negligence for careless financial misrepresentations relied upon by actually foreseen and limited classes of persons. According to the plaintiff's complaint in the case, the defendant knew that his certification was to be used for, and had as its very aim and purpose, the reliance of potential financiers of the Rhode Island corporation.

Rosenblum, Inc. v. Adler (1983)

Giant Stores Corporation acquired the retail catalog showroom business owned by Rosenblum, giving stock in exchange for the business. Fifteen months after the acquisition, Giant Stores declared bankruptcy. Its financial statements had been audited and had received unqualified opinions on several prior years. These financial statements turned out to be misstated because Giant Stores had manipulated its books.

In finding for the plaintiffs on certain motions, the New Jersey Supreme Court held that Independent auditors have a duty of care to all persons whom the auditor should reasonably foresee as recipients of the statements from the company for proper business purposes, provided that the recipients rely on those financial statements ... It is well recognized that audited financial statements are made for the use of third parties who have no direct relationship with the auditor ... Auditors have responsibility not only to the client who pays the fee but also to investors, creditors, and others who rely on the audited financial statements.

[The case went back to the trial court for further proceedings.]

Defences of the Accountant

The defendant accountant in a common law action presents evidence to mitigate or refute the plaintiff's claims and evidence. For example, the accountant might offer evidence that the plaintiff was not in privity or not foreseen, that the financial statements were not misleading, or that the plaintiff contributed to the negligence. The primary defence against a negligence claim is to offer evidence that the audit had been conducted in accordance with GAAS with due professional care.

Some courts hold plaintiffs to a strict privity criterion to have a standing in court. In New York courts the general rule is that these conditions must be met: (1) the accountants must have been aware that the financial reports were to be used for a particular purpose, (2) the accountants must have known that a particular third party was going to rely on the reports, and (3) some action by the accountants must link them with the third party and must demonstrate that the accountants knew of the reliance on the reports. In response to these conditions, some users of financial statements have invented a request for a "reliance letter." Users have requested accountants to sign letters saying that they have been notified that a particular recipient of the financial statements and audit report intends to rely upon them for particular purposes.

The AICPA has warned accountants to be careful when signing such letters so that they do not become an automatic proof of users' actual reliance.

In several Canadian cases the auditors successfully argued that clients should not have relied on the financial statements to make their investment decision.[4] A good example is when banks claim that they have been mislead by the financial statements. A key issue in this instance is the fourth element of negligence: Did the banks' losses

---

4 "Auditing in Crisis," *Bottom Line*, March 1990.

follow from the auditor's breach of duty with regard to auditing the financial statements? Peskelle-Mede notes that "the courts carefully review the degree of reliance plaintiff bankers have on misleading financial statements. Banks usually have available to them not only their customers' financial statements but a great deal of other information as well. Their decision to continue a loan is very often based on considerations quite apart from any reliance they may place on the opinion of the customer's auditors. In these circumstances the auditors ought not to be found liable—or at least not entirely—for the bank's losses." In general, "it's refreshing to see a court carefully reviewing the degree of reliance plaintiff bankers place on misleading financial statements."[5]

Liability in Compilation and Review Services

You may find it easy to think about common law liability in connection with audited financial statements. Do not forget, however, that accountants also render compilation and review services and are associated with unaudited financial information (see Chapter 14). People expect public accountants to perform these services in accordance with professional standards, and courts can impose liability for accounting work judged to be substandard. Accountants have been assessed damages for work on such statements, as shown in *1136 Tenants' Corporation* v. *Max Rothenberg & Co.* Approximately 11 percent of losses in the AICPA professional liability insurance plan involve compilation and review engagements relating to unaudited financial statements.

1136 Tenants' Corporation v. Max Rothenberg & Co. (1967)

> Despite defendant's claims to the contrary, the court found that he was engaged to audit and not merely write up plaintiff's books and records. The accountant had, in fact, performed some limited auditing procedures including preparation of a worksheet entitled "Missing Invoices 1/1/63–12/31/63." These were items claimed to have been paid but were not. The court held that, even if accountants were hired only for write-up work, they had a duty to inform plaintiffs of any circumstances that gave reason to believe that a fraud had occurred (e.g., the record of "missing invoices"). The plaintiffs recovered damages of about $237,000.

One significant risk is that the client may fail to understand the nature of the service being given. Accountants should use a conference and an engagement letter to explain clearly that a compilation service ("write-up") involves little or no investigative work, and that it is lesser in scope than a review service. Similarly, a review service should be explained in terms of being less extensive than a full audit service. Clear understandings at the outset can enable accountants and clients to avoid later disagreements.

Yet even with these understandings, public accountants cannot merely accept client-supplied information that appears to be unusual or misleading. A court has held that a public accountant's preparation of some erroneous and misleading journal entries without sufficient support was enough to trigger common law liability for negligence, even though the accountant was not associated with any final financial statements. CICA standards for compilations require accountants to obtain additional information if client-supplied accounting data are incorrect, incomplete, or otherwise unsatisfactory. Courts may hold accountants liable for failure to obtain additional information in such circumstances.

---

[5] H. Rowan, "Are Banks Looking to Pin the Blame?" *CA Magazine*, June 1988.

When financial statements are reviewed, public accountants' reports state: "Based on my review, nothing has come to my attention that causes me to believe that these financial statements are not, in all material respects in accordance with generally accepted accounting principles" (*Handbook Section* 8200.04). Courts can look to the facts of a case and rule on whether the review was performed properly. Generally, the same four elements of negligence must be met for review engagements as for audit engagements. The only difference is that "due care' in review engagements should follow the standards for review engagements rather than the standards for audits. Generally, it would appear that third-party liability continues to flow to the same classes of persons who would be relying on the financial statements.[6] Some courts might decide an accountant's review was substandard if necessary adjustments or "material modifications" should have been discovered. These risks tend to induce more work by accountants beyond superficial looking-it-over and enquiry procedures.

A 1987 New York case, however, may create an attitude more favourable for PAs' review work on unaudited financial statements. In 1985 William Iselin & Company sued the Mann Judd Landau (MJL) accounting firm, claiming damages for having relied on financial statements reviewed by MJL. Iselin had used the financial statements of customers for its factoring–financing business. A customer had gone bankrupt and Iselin's loans became worthless. A New York appeals court dismissed the case, saying that third parties (Iselin) cannot rely on reviewed financial statements as they can on audited financial statements to assure themselves that a company is financially healthy. The court observed that MJL expressed no opinion on the reviewed financial statements. Iselin's lawyer was reported to have observed: "Accountants and their clients will find that reviews are useless, since no one can rely on them."

. . . .

R E V I E W
C H E C K P O I N T S

16.4   What must be proved by the plaintiff in a common law action seeking recovery of damages from an independent auditor of financial statements? What must the defendant accountant do in such a court action?

16.5   What legal theory is derived from the *Ultramares* decision? Can auditors rely on the *Ultramares* decision today?

16.6   Define and explain *privity*, *primary beneficiary*, and *foreseeable beneficiary* in terms of the degree of negligence on the part of an accountant that would trigger the accountant's liability.

16.7   What proportion of lawsuits against accountants relate to compilation and review (unaudited financial statements) practice?

. . . .

III. Due Care: Its Meaning
. . . .

A key aspect to the second element of negligence is the meaning of due care. What is it that the auditor must be breaching? Due professional care implies the careful application of all the standards of the profession (GAAS, GAAP) and observance of all the rules of professional conduct. The courts have interpreted due care to be that of a reasonably prudent practitioner, neither the extremes of the highest possible

---

[6]   "The Jury's Still Out on Review Engagement Liability," *CA Magazine*, June 1988.

standards nor the lowest acceptable or minimum standards would be considered due care. This suggests that looking at Rules of Professional Conduct or the Handbook may not always be sufficient in the view of the courts since these would be viewed as minimal standards. In fact, over the years the courts have helped shape audit practice by their interpretation of what is due care. For example, the concept of testing (less than 100 percent examination of the accounts) was first accepted as reasonable by the progressive decision in *London and General Bank* (1895). This case was also the first to acknowledge that there is some limit on the auditor's responsibility for the detection of fraud and the *duty* to take increased care in the presence of suspicious circumstances. This case influenced the development of later professional announcements and hundreds of subsequent cases (e.g., *1136 Tennants* [1967]).

Another example of the influence of the courts in setting auditing standards (and therefore influencing due care provisions) is the requirement that the auditor corroborate management assertions with his or her own evidence. The auditor can't just rely on words of management; he or she must justify reliance through checking, testing, and other audit procedures. This practice following from the third examination standard has been shaped by decisions in many court cases, such as *Continental Vending* (1969) and the Canadian *Toromont* v. *Thorne* (1975).

An obvious example of court influence in determining what constitutes auditor due care is *McKesson Robbins* (1939) (discussed in Appendix 16A). Which can be viewed as ultimately influencing the creation of *Handbook Sections* 5803 and 6030 (and similar sections in U.S. standards). In that case, the auditor failed to observe inventory or confirm receivables. It should thus be evident that the due care provision of negligence has significantly shaped and probably will continue to influence the development of audit standards. One impact of the *Continental Vending* case, for example, is that the courts did not accept the auditor's defence that they were following GAAP (i.e., the auditors were able to establish that the footnote in the financial statement was in accordance with GAAP); instead, the courts expected the auditor to use some higher standard of fairness in deciding on proper disclosure. This has led to much greater diligence on the part of standard setters when it comes to matters of disclosing various types of information.

A sense of urgency on this issue of fairness has recently been introduced to Canadian courts, as indicated in the following box:

ACCOUNTING PROFESSION HAS A DUTY TO SHAREHOLDERS

Before buying shares in a company, investors usually rely on an important safeguard—the auditor's opinion of its financial statements. And that opinion usually declares that the statements are both "presented fairly" and are "in accordance with generally accepted accounting principles (GAAP)." For decades, though, auditors have tried to duck legal liability to the investors they serve. Auditors appear to want what doesn't exist: authority without responsibility.

This spring two Canadian lawsuits promise to clarify the trust that investors can place in auditors. One case, *Stephen Kripps et al. v. Touche Ross* (now Deloitte Touche) *et al.,* emerged from the B.C. Court of Appeal last month. In 1985, Kripps et al. relied on the audited financial statements of a mortgage company to buy $1.9 million of its debentures. The company went into receivership and the investors lost $2.7 million including interest. The investors sued the auditor, lost in a lower court, and won at appeal.

A 2-to-1 appeal court majority ruled that "Touche had actual knowledge that a simple application of GAAP would ... lead to financial statements that could not be said to have fairly represented the financial position" of the company. "Auditors cannot hide behind [the formula] 'according to GAAP'" the court declared, "if the auditors know ... that the financial statements are misleading." It ruled against Touche. The court's point is correct—GAAP is too loose a standard to be a sufficient safeguard by itself. That's why the financial statements must also be "presented fairly," to use the actual language of the auditor's opinion. Despite the ruling's validity, some accountants want the Canadian Institute of Chartered Accountants (CICA) to support an appeal by Touche to the Supreme Court.

Postscript: On November 6, 1997, the Supreme Court of Canada denied Deloitte & Touche's right to appeal the negligence ruling against it by the B.C. Court of Appeal. The *Kripps v. Touche Ross* decision thus may make it easier for investors to sue Canadian auditors in the future. The other case referred to in the above editorial is discussed at the end of this chapter.

Source: Editorial, *The Financial Post*, May 20, 1997.

IV. OTHER ELEMENTS OF NEGLIGENCE

The two other elements of negligence have also proven to be material issues in various court cases. The third element requires that some damage must occur to the third party—otherwise, they are limited to recovering the audit fee only. This was the situation in *Toromont* v. *Thorne*. The last element of negligence requires that there be a causal link between the breach of duty and the resulting damage. Thus, for example, losses occur before the time of the audit, or it can be proven in some other way that the plaintiff did not rely on the audited information to any significant degree, the lawsuit will fail.

Perhaps at this point it is useful to note the relationship between joint and several liability and the fourth element of evidence. In Canada and the United States we have what's called joint and several liability, meaning any of several defendants that have caused part of the damages are liable to the plaintiffs for the entire amount of damages. This system was set up to protect plaintiffs from having to sue several different parties to recover the full amount of damages. Under joint and several liability, the courts can force the defendant with the "deepest pockets" to pay all the damages even though they may have contributed, say, only 1 percent to the losses. It is, of course, then up to the defendant auditor to recover from the other defendants its share of the losses. If the other defendants are in bankruptcy, however, this can leave the auditor stuck with all the losses. The box below, from a recent *Bottom Line* article, indicates the problems that joint and several liability is causing in Canada.

Low Coverage Limits Leave Major Firms Exposed

Major accountancies are in "near crisis" because of high deductibles and low coverage limits in their malpractice insurance.

"From the point of view of current planning, the (large) firms are looking at this as if there is really no insurance going to be available," said William Broadhurst, head of a national task force on accountants' professional liability.

No Canadian insurer is writing policies large enough. So the six largest Canadian accounting firms insure through international markets, usually as part of international groups.

They do not negotiate separately as Canadian firms.

Ten years ago, a typical deductible was about $2 million. Now it is around $50 million, according to Broadhurst.

Too Small

Consequently, all recent payouts in Canada on settlements and judgements have been too small to be covered by insurance.

"There may have been [some for] a couple of million [dollars] here and there," he said.

So far, there has been nothing even close to the settlements in 1988 and 1989 on the Alberta bank failures claims, "generally said to be in the order of $100 million."

Even if there is no payout on a claim, there are litigation costs.

"With this large deductible, you're into your own resources from dollar one, right up," Broadhurst said.

Until the mid-80s, coverage of $200 million was available, and the risks could be adequately provided for. Premiums, deductibles and coverage have all steadily worsened (senior CA partners are reportedly paying as much as $30,000 a year for limited professional insurance).

Now, there is no true, commercial insurance for more than $100 million. But even for the band of liability between $50 million and $100 million, coverage is now "spotty," said Broadhurst.

Different syndicates cover different "layers"—one for $50–60 million, say, and another for $60–75 million. The upshot is that a large firm is likely to be insured for about 50 percent of this whole range: only about $25–30 million.

As for the $100–$150 million range, there are two kinds of "self-insurance." First, international firms have formed "pools" for their various national components. Second, large Canadian firms have joined in a mutual fund.

But they can only draw out what they put in (plus interest). If the payouts exceed the pooled assets, they have to be pro-rated among the firms.

Beyond $150 million, there is no protection at all.

In Canada there are now two much larger sets of claims, "the only two of threatening size," as Broadhurst put it: one for about $900 million from the failure of Castor Holdings Ltd., the other concerning Standard Trust, for about $1.5 billion."

Warm Feeling

Broadhurst professed ignorance on the merits of these cases. But he said, "If they were substantially successful, the [defendant accounting] firms would not be able to deal with these numbers. Now, I make the assumption they won't be. But they don't give you a good warm feeling."

Hard numbers on Canadian settlements don't exist, said Broadhurst, and if they did, they might not be "hugely impressive."

The insurance market reflects international experience, and Canadian potential, not yet the actuality.

But according to Broadhurst, insurers rate Canada towards the high end of risk, close to the U.S., the U.K. and Australia. "Presumably in the underwriters' mind, there's no significant difference between us and the others ... The risks in Canada mirror [those] other jurisdictions."

The litigation environments of the U.S. and Canada do differ.

But Canada has fewer, larger financial institutions. The risk to the auditors increases with the size of the institution. Broadhurst concluded that the factors are all in place, for exposure to claims as big as in the U.S., U.K. and Australia.

"We view the insurance situation as basically a disaster," he said. On the other hand, he said, "We would have a hard time saying there's a disaster situation in Canada."

"We have a near-crisis situation ... It could turn into a crisis any day."

Crisis Any Day

"Do we have to have a bankruptcy of a major firm, before someone looks at the problem and decides whether or not there is some action required?"

"We're hoping we don't have to go that route."

Broadhurst saw no prospect for a turnaround in insurance, unless legislation limits auditors' liability to their proportion of fault.

Source: Gerald Owen, *The Bottom Line*, March 1995.

Auditor's Liability When Auditor Is Associated with Misleading Financial Information
• • • • • • • • • • • •

If the courts conclude that the auditor is associated with misleading financial statements, even if such statements are in conformity with GAAP, they may conclude that the auditors are fraudulently negligent. If auditors are found guilty of a fraudulent misrepresentation, then there are no limits on third-party liability. In U.S. courts the concepts of gross negligence–constructive fraud has been used to expand auditor liability to larger classes of third parties. This is done not only through U.S. common law but also in statutory law via the U.S. Securities Acts. As a result there have been several cases in the United States in which auditors have been found guilty of fraud when they otherwise would have been found to be only negligent (see, e.g., *Continental Vending* in Appendix 16A on page 770.

Interestingly, the Ontario Securities Commission appears to be interested in increasing auditors' legal responsibility to shareholders by revising the securities acts in Ontario. This may be a way of expanding auditor liability to wider classes of third parties in Ontario (e.g., see subsequent discussion of "Auditing in Crisis"). This combined with the increasing influence of Charter of Rights and Freedoms legislation on the courts may make the Canadian legal environment more comparable to that of the United States in the near future. In addition, class action legislation has recently been approved in Quebec (1979), Ontario (1993), and British Columbia (1995). Contingency fees are another issue being considered by the Ontario Law Society; implementing them would also make the Ontario environment more comparable to that of the United States. Thus many of the problems of high litigation rates and insurance premiums and costly court decisions may soon be imported to at least parts of the Canadian legal environment. Recent proposals to expand auditor responsibilities for detecting money-laundering schemes will further add to the liabilities burden.

Auditor's Liability Under Statutory Law

LEARNING OBJECTIVE
3. Specify the characteristics of accountants' liability under statutory law.

A great deal of liability for American auditors arises from statutory law under the SEC. These SEC laws give the SEC the legal right to decide what is GAAP. There is nothing comparable in Canadian legislation, yet increasingly the OSC and Quebec regulators are seeking more enforcement power over professionals such as accountants operating in the capital markets. We will discuss the latest developments at the time of this writing at the end of the chapter.

What is unique about Canadian statutory law is the Canadian Business Corporation Act (CBCA) and related provincial corporation acts.

The highlights of the CBCA are as follows (to be covered in more detail in your business law course).

1. The CBCA identifies conditions under which the auditor is not considered independent (Section 161).

2. It identifies conditions of appointing and retiring the auditor (Sections 162 and 163).

3. It identifies the auditor's rights and responsibilities (Section 168):
   (*a*) to attend shareholder meetings
   (*b*) to provide a written statement of reasons for a resignation
   (*c*) to make an audit examination unimpeded and gain access to data the auditor considers necessary

4. Sections 44–47 of the CBCA identify the financial statements subject to audit, and specify that the financial statements must be in conformity with the *CICA Handbook*.
   (Note that this represents a stark contrast with U.S. securities law, which allows the SEC to decide what is GAAP. The important point is that the ultimate authority in the United States is the SEC, whereas here in Canada the

ultimate authority on accounting issues is the CICA via the *Handbook*. This gives *Handbook* standards much higher legal status than comparable standards in the United States.)

5. Until 1994 the CBCA applied to all companies incorporated under the act, having revenues in excess of $10 million or assets greater than $5 million. Under amendments to the CBCA made in 1994, privately held companies are no longer required to have their financial statements audited or disclosed. The Ontario Business Corporations Act requires audits only for companies having $100 million of either assets or revenues; other provincial corporations acts vary in their reporting requirements.

Another potentially important Canadian statutory law is Bill 61, described in the next box.

"Proposed Federal Crime Legislation Puts Accountants at Risk of Being Prosecuted"

VANCOUVER: Amendments to Canada's Criminal Code could jeopardize unwary financial professionals, legal experts warn.

Bill C-61, known informally as the "proceeds of crime" legislation, is so sweeping that unsuspecting accountants could be guilty of a criminal offence for simply giving advice, the lawyers say.

The proceeds of crime legislation, which is now contained in Part XII.2 of the Criminal Code, is based on American antiracketeering statutes and is designed to deprive criminals of their ill-gotten gains.

But, although the new law may seem well intentioned, Bill C-61 is so broadly worded that, if accountants know or even suspect that a client has illegal profits, they could be guilty of a crime if they act for that client.

The amendments contained in the Bill create two new offences—money laundering and possessions of property derived through drug trafficking.

Money laundering is defined as dealing with any property with intent to conceal or convert it while knowing that it was derived as a result of a "designated drug offence" or an "enterprise crime."

The Criminal Code describes "designated drug offences" as virtually any drug infraction other than simple possession. "Enterprise crime" are generally profit-motivated offences and include things such as bribery, fraud, gambling and stock manipulation.

Under the criminal law doctrine of "wilful blindness," people are deemed to know they are dealing with the proceeds of crime if they are suspicious about the source of any property but choose to remain ignorant rather than make further inquiries.

The effect of the legislation is that accountants who accept any property, including fees, from a client, knowing or being wilfully blind to the fact the property was obtained illegally, could be charged with possession or laundering.

Problems could also arise if accountants become suspicious about a client's finances during an ongoing engagement. If they continue to act and their advice relates to property obtained through a crime, they could be committing an offence.

Accountants will be particularly vulnerable because they are often aware of the intimate details of a client's financial dealings.

Source: Brad Dusley, *The Bottom Line*, November 1990, p. 6. Reprinted with permission.

OTHER ISSUES

. . . .

Interestingly, the CICA has recently proposed an Exposure Draft on auditor responsibilities concerning money-laundering activities.

1. Fiduciary Duty of Accountants

According to an article by G. McLennan, a unique feature of Canadian common law that may precipitate a litigation crisis here is the expanding concept of fiduciary duty as it applies to accountants. An accountant may be a fiduciary in many different situations, including when he or she acts as a trustee, receiver, auditor, or simply an adviser to a peculiarly vulnerable client. Accountants may also be liable for simply assisting someone who is a fiduciary to another, although this would only be the case where a PA knows the fiduciary relationship and knows it is being dishonestly breached.

Allegations of a breach of fiduciary duty have become increasingly common in lawsuits against accountants in Canada. If a court concludes that an accountant is a fiduciary, he or she may be held responsible for damages, even though (1) the PA's conduct did not cause the damage, (2) the plaintiff failed to take reasonable steps to mitigate those damages, or (3) the plaintiff was partially at fault or other third parties contributed to the damages suffered. Thus, common defences to a negligence action, such as contributory negligence, remoteness of damages, failure to mitigate, and no duty of care, do not apply to an action in breach of fiduciary duty.

Literally, fiduciary means "trust-like" but the term has been used in so many contexts in the courts that it applied as if it related to, among other things, all breaches of duty by accountants.

The closest thing to legal definition is that set forth in the Supreme Court of Canada decision concerning *LAC Minerals* v. *Corona Resources*. In *LAC Minerals* the court stated there were three factors to consider when determining if a fiduciary duty exists:

1. The fiduciary has scope for the exercise of some discretion or power..

2. The fiduciary can unilaterally exercise that power or discretion so as to affect the beneficiary's legal or practical interests.

3. The beneficiary is peculiarly vulnerable to or at the mercy of the fiduciary who is holding the discretion or power.

Case law provides illustrations when such a duty exists; the article by M. Paskell-Mede reviews several of these cases. Generally, when an accountant acts as a receiver/manager or trustee in insolvency situations, he or she owes a fiduciary duty to creditors of an insolvent corporation. Where an accountant has an established relationship with one lender, it may be that it is a breach of fiduciary duty to also act as a trustee or receiver of the insolvent borrower. Accountants that act as financial advisers or tax advisers also have a fiduciary duty. Accountants that have successfully defended themselves in lawsuits involving breach of fiduciary duty have done so by showing that either factors 1 or 3 in the definition were not present.[7]

2. Confidentiality v. Misleading Financial Statements

In Chapter 15 we noted that there may be a potential conflict between rules dealing with confidentiality and rules dealing with association with misleading financial statements. There is a conflict between similar rules in the U.S. code that has been the focus of two court cases there: *Consolidata Services v. Alexander Grant* (1981) and *Fund of Funds v. Arthur Andersen* (1982). In *Consolidata* the courts ruled that auditors should have preserved confidentiality, and in *Fund of Funds* the courts ruled that the confidential information should have been used to prevent misleading reports. The inconsistent legal results from these two cases illustrate that the rules can be just as difficult to resolve for the courts as they are for practising auditors. In both cases, however, it was the auditors who lost—and paid. (The court awarded damages to Fund of Fund's shareholders in the amount of $80 million, the largest judgment ever made against a public accounting firm until that time.)

3. Legal Liability Implications for Auditor Practice

As a result of the increasingly litigious climate, auditors ought to

   (*i*) Be wary of what kind of clients are accepted.
   (*ii*) Know (thoroughly) the client's business (KNOB)
   (*iii*) Perform quality audits
      (*a*) use qualified personnel, properly trained and supervised, and motivated
      (*b*) obtain sufficient evidence (including proper elicitation of oral evidence and documentation of client's oral evidence)
      (*c*) prepare good working papers
      (*d*) obtain engagement and representation letters.

The increased litigation has also caused improvements in audit working paper files through:

   (*a*) use of forceful management letters that are "unambiguous and couched in terms of alarm with respect to problematic internal controls or sloppy bookkeeping;

   (*b*) use of detailed memos in the working papers describing the conversation with the client and accompanied by a follow-up letter to the client.

   (*c*) use of a letter to the client or note to the file documenting discussions to reduce audit fees or changing to a review engagement." (M. Pashell-Mede, "So Sue Me," *CA Magazine*, February 1991, pp. 36–38).

---

[7] G. McLennan, "Trust Not," *CA Magazine*, June-July, 1993, pp. 40–43 and M. Paskell-Mede, "Adviser Relationships," *CA Magazine*, May 1995, pp. 27–32.

Legal Liability for Failure to Disclose Illegal Acts

With the new *Handbook Section* 5136, "Misstatements—illegal acts," issued in December 1994, auditors now have expanded guidance on detecting and disclosing illegal acts or possibly illegal acts. One of the objectives of this *Handbook Section* is to reduce the auditor's exposure to legal liability. It does this (1) by reducing the risk that GAAS will be misinterpreted by auditors and the courts; (2) by establishing recommendations for the auditors to follow, such as that of obtaining written representation from management about illegal acts, that reduce the likelihood of an audit failing to detect a material misstatement arising from the consequences of an illegal act; and (3) by providing a defence for the auditor if he or she fails to detect a material misstatement despite conducting the audit in accordance with the standards.[8]

Illegal acts is another area where potential ethical and legal conflicts may now be expected to grow. According to an article by M. Paskell-Mede, the whistle-blowing responsibility of the auditor to third parties may be expected to grow even in the absence of a regulator since plaintiffs are raising the issues of association more frequently in lawsuits. It is Paskell-Mede's impression that plaintiffs whose lawyers recognize that their case is weak—as a result of inability to demonstrate either actual reliance on the financial statements or that a direct duty of care was owed with respect to those statements—are now compensating for this weakness by presenting the claim as one based on association. In such instances, the plaintiff's lawyer will argue that their client relied on the auditor's reputation. However, the courts so far have upheld the obligation for auditors to maintain client confidentiality. For example, in *Transamerica Financial Corporation, Canada v. Dunwoody & Company*, the judge decided that client confidentiality overrode whistle-blowing to a third-party plaintiff especially since the plaintiff was already aware of irregularities at the client. For Paskell-Mede this is evidence that the courts are becoming more careful about assigning blame to auditors—that they are becoming more sophisticated in analysing the causal connection between the illegal misrepresentation and damages.[9]

Is There an Auditor Liability Crisis in Canada?

Some people argue that there is no auditor's legal liability crisis in Canada. In a recent article M. Paskell-Mede takes this position and gives an updated review of the differences between the American and Canadian legal systems concerning auditors' legal liability. In the United States pending suits against auditors total about US$20 billion. There is a definite crisis there. Do we have a problem of the same magnitude in Canada?

The author doesn't think so and identifies important differences.

1. Jury trials are common in the United States for civil cases but "virtually extinct" for auditor liability suits in Canada. American juries tend to be more sympathetic to plaintiffs and swayed by factors other than the evidence. Judges are less influenced by the drama of the courtroom setting, and tend to be better experienced and better trained in dealing with commercial disputes.

---

[8]   V. Murusalu, "Drawing the Line," *CA Magazine*, Jan/Feb. 1995, pp. 68–69.

[9]   M. Paskell-Mede, "Tales of Sherwood Forest," *CA Magazine*, August 1994, pp. 47–48.

2. Punitive damages are not available in Canada for mere negligence. Moreover, any damages awarded are only a fraction of the compensatory damages assessed (instead of the multiples used in the United States).

3. In Canada the unsuccessful party must pay up to 50 to 60 percent of the legal fees of the opposing side and possible other costs (e.g., 1 percent of the amount claimed). This tends to discourage frivolous suits.

4. Class actions (a few suing on behalf of many) are much rarer in Canada because of the belief here that each plaintiff may rely on the accountant's work differently. But this may change, with more provinces allowing class actions, as noted earlier.

5. The U.S. national regulator, the SEC (nothing comparable in Canada), uses the "fraud on the market" theory, which assumes that the entire market for shares is affected by misrepresentations. This greatly increases the liability exposure of auditors of publicly traded companies.

"Faced with these differences it seems safe to assume that Canadian accountants will not face lawsuits of the same magnitude and frequency as those experienced by U.S. accountants, assuming no fundamental changes to our legal systems. On the other hand, lawsuits in Canada are getting larger and some CA firms may soon exceed their insurance limits and be forced into bankruptcy. Thus it may simply be a matter of time before we, too, face a liability crisis."[10]

Others argue that we already are facing a liability crisis. In a series of articles entitled "Auditing in Crisis" in the March 1990 issue of the *Financial Post*, the following points were made.

A vicious cycle had started by 1990 in that due to severe competition (partly caused by the many mergers in the 80s) audit fees had been lowered, resulting in lower-quality audits. This combined with more aggressive reporting resulted in more problem audits, which in turn increased lawsuits. Plaintiffs also were increasingly of the type that can litigate indefinitely (financial institutions, government agencies). This came at a time of increased policing of accounting firms by regulators such as the OSC. As a result, the total number of lawsuits increased dramatically starting in the 1980s. For example, there were 18 major lawsuits initiated between 1985 and 1990. Compare this to a total of 9 between 1917 and 1984. In addition to the increased lawsuits, the damage awards per lawsuit have increased dramatically. This, combined with an exponential growth in lawsuits in the United States, has greatly increased North American professional liability insurance premiums (premiums have risen by 10 percent per year).

The series of articles also provides much anecdotal evidence that there are serious problems in many auditor–client relationships. For example, according to a vice president of finance of a major Canadian company, "it's very easy for management to browbeat an auditor at any time in the audit," and "anything goes unless there is a rule to the contrary (in the *Handbook*)."

To combat these problems, key recommendations developed in an article by M.F. Murray were that the auditors report to a company's audit committee, that standard setters should reduce the number of accounting alternatives in GAAP, that auditors need more guidance on how to report on a company's ability to continue, and that auditors need to better document high-risk clients and be ready to take

---

[10]   M. Paskell-Mede, "What Liability Crisis," *CA Magazine*, May 1994, pp. 42–43.

immediate defensive measures. Some firms now even talk about "firing" their troublesome clients. Some warning signs of potentially troublesome clients include financial or organizational difficulty, involvement in suspicious transactions, uncooperativeness, fee pressures, refusal to sign engagement and representation letters, and frequent involvement in litigation.

Before accepting clients, PAs should ask why clients are changing accountants, visit the client's business, meet their accounting and tax personnel, and check their references. A useful client acceptance checklist could be used that documents whether a client should be accepted for an engagement. This form should be prepared before the engagement letter is submitted. If this screening does not result in rejection of an existing or prospective client, it may also be used to identify engagements that require extra precautions, such as very precise engagement letters and advance collection of fees.[11]

SOME VERY RECENT DEVELOPMENTS CONCERNING THE LIABILITY CRISIS
. . . .

In December 1995 the American accounting profession was successful in getting the U.S. Congress to pass (over President Clinton's veto) the Private Securities Litigation Reform Act, which changes auditor liability under SEC section 10b (discussed in the appendix). There are three objectives to the act. First, it is intended to "discourage abusive claims of investors' losses due to fraudulent misstatements or omissions by issuers of securities" (and professionals associated with the misstatements or omissions, such as auditors). Second, the act provides more protection against securities fraud. Third, the act increases the flow of forward-looking financial information." The act meets these objectives by imposing specific pleading requirements; by reducing the effectiveness of discovery in coercing settlements; by mandating sanctions for frivolous claims; by giving the plaintiff class far more control of class actions; by providing for proportionate liability except in cases of knowing fraud; by creating a safe harbour for forward-looking information; and by codifying auditor's responsibilities to search for and disclose fraud (A.R. Andrews and G. Simonette Jr., "Tort Reform Revolution," *Journal of Accountancy,* September 1996, p. 54).

For the purposes of this chapter, the most important feature of the act concerns the reform of "joint and several liability," which under SEC law now only applies to auditors who knowingly commit a violation of the security law. "A defendant (auditor) whose conduct is less culpable is liable only for a percentage of the total damages corresponding to the percentage of responsibility allocated to the defendant (auditor) by the jury ... Thus for example, if a PA firm is found 10% responsible for an injury and insolvent corporate management is allocated 90% the PA firm no longer will have to make up all of the management's share (as long as the PA firm did not engage in knowing fraud)" (Ibid., p. 50).

A recent Supreme Court of Canada decision may cause a dramatic shift in Canadian auditors' liability in the near future, as indicated in the following box.

---

[11]   M.F. Murray, "When a Client Is a Liability," *Journal of Accountancy,* September 1992, pp. 54–58.

Auditors Not Legally Liable to Investors, Top Court Rules

An auditor who signs a company's financial statements has no legal liability to shareholders or investors.

That's the thrust of a ruling by the Supreme Court of Canada brought down Thursday in the case of *Hercules Managements Ltd. et al. v. Ernst & Young et al.*

The court's concern, observers say, is to protect auditors from unlimited liability to thousands of investors who may use the audit opinion for many different purposes.

The annual financial statement is now a joke, says Al Rosen, a professor of accounting at York University in Toronto and a partner in Rosen & Vettese Ltd., forensic accountants.

"Public accountants may think this is a wonderful win for them," Rosen added. "But in the long run I see this as a disaster. Who really needs an audit of financial statements that are not useful for investor decision-making?"

The court's ruling was applauded by Michael Rayner, president of the Canadian Institute of Chartered Accountants. "The decision leaves the profession in a legal environment in which it can maximize its contribution to the capital markets," Rayner said yesterday.

The court has "tried to provide a reasonable amount of liability for auditors," he added.

"We believe the responsibility of auditors is important ... and there are still significant redresses available through the courts for auditors who are engaged in a situation where there is clear negligence on their part."

The effect of the court's ruling could be short-lived. Brenda Eprile, executive director of the Ontario Securities Commission—Canada's leading securities regulator—says provincial regulators are working on a legal framework that will re-establish the legal liability of auditors to investors.

Hercules Managements was the 80% shareholder of Manitoba-based Northguard Acceptance Ltd., which lent money on mortgages in the 1970s and early 1980s. Ernest & Young was the auditor.

In 1984, Northguard went into receivership. Hercules sued Ernst & Young, alleging negligence.

The action was dismissed by the Manitoba Court of Queen's Bench, and by the Manitoba Appeal Court. It was heard by the Supreme Court on December 6. The Canadian Institute of Chartered Accountants gained status with the court to argue in favor of protecting auditors from liability.

The court's ruling does not declare whether Ernst & Young was negligent.

On the issue of liability, the court said audited financial reports only call for "a duty of care" by the auditors when they are used "as a guide for the shareholders, as a group, in supervising or overseeing management."

For this reason, there appears to be no direct liability to the shareholders for any reduction in value of their equity, jointly or individually.

"The law in Canada in respect of the responsibility of auditors is basically consistent with the United Kingdom, the United States and many other countries," Rayner said.

"I feel that I have been run over by a truck," said Mark Schulman, of the Winnipeg law firm of Schulman and Schulman, who acted for Hercules.

He points out that one motions judge, three judges of the court of appeal and seven judges in the Supreme Court all ruled against Hercules, and thoroughly entrenched the principle of no general auditor liability.

Eprile pointed out that auditors are already liable, under securities acts to investors, in the narrow case when the audited financial statements appear in a prospectus.

"We are recommending that we amend our securities legislation ... to call for liability in the [entire] secondary market," she said.

That would mean that the public company, the auditor, the directors and possibly the underwriters would be liable for any negligent disclosure when investors buy a company's shares through a stock exchange.

The legislation has been drafted, Eprile said. It would be uniform across Canada and may take a year or two to get through provincial legislatures, she said.

Source: Philip Mathias, *The Financial Post,* May 24, 1997, p. 3.

If the comments of the OSC and similar views reflected in a *Financial Post* editorial of May 24, 1997, are indicative of what to expect in the near future, then the above Supreme Court ruling may have as significant an impact in Canada as *Ultramares* in the United States. For an indication of the type of statutory law liability the OSC and other provincial securities commissions may have in mind, refer to the appendix, where details are provided on existing statutory law liability in the United States under SEC law.

SUMMARY

Litigation against accountants has virtually exploded in the United States and to a lesser extent in Canada. Damage claims of hundreds of millions of dollars have been paid by PA firms and their insurers. Insurance is expensive and hard to obtain. A mid-sized national PA firm in the United States, Laventhol & Horwath, declared bankruptcy in 1990 as a result of losses from litigation. Accountants are not alone in this rash of litigation, which affects manufacturers, architects, doctors, and people in many other walks of life. The professional accounting organizations have joined with other interest groups pushing for "tort reform" of various types (e.g., limitation of damages, identification of liability) in an effort to stem the tide. Other effects of this climate take the form of changing the nature of organizations in which public accountants practice (thus, the push to limited liability partnership). Little seems to work.

Accountants' liability to clients and third parties under common law has expanded. Fifty years ago, a strict privity doctrine required other parties to be in a contract with and known to the accountant before they could sue for damages based on negligence.

Of course, if an accountant was grossly negligent in such a way that his or her actions amounted to constructive fraud, liability exists as it would for anyone who committed a fraud. Over the years the privity doctrine was modified in many jurisdictions, leading to liability for ordinary negligence to primary beneficiaries (known users) of the accountants' work product, then to liability based on ordinary negligence to foreseen and foreseeable beneficiaries (users not so easily known). While the general movement has been to expand accountants' liability for ordinary negligence, some jurisdictions have held closer to the privity doctrine of the past. The treatment can vary from province to province.

Accountants' liability under statutory law is also onerous, especially the potentially wide application of Bill C-61, which can label accountants as "racketeers." Regulatory laws in the United States greatly changed the obligations of public accountants. Canadian PAs whose clients obtain financing from the United States may be affected by these laws, and these laws also have had an influence on Canadian regulators such as those proposing Bill C-61. Also, there has been recent talk of creating a nationwide regulatory agency similar to the SEC in Canada. The key issue is whether the provinces will go along and how far.

Under common law a plaintiff suing an accountant had to bring all the proof of the accountant's negligence to the court and convince the judge or jury. In the case of a public offering of securities registered in a registration statement filed under a U.S. Securities Act, the plaintiff only needs to show evidence of a loss and that the financial statements were materially misleading. Case rested. Then, the accountant shoulders the burden of proof of showing that the audit was performed properly or that the loss resulted from some other cause. The burden of proof has thus shifted from the plaintiff to the defendant. The securities acts also impose criminal penalties in some cases. As indicated throughout the chapter, many commentators feel that the profession is in the midst of a liability crisis that has many causes and may take a long time to resolve.

Appendix 16A reviews U.S. statutory law in some detail because many court cases setting legal precedents for accountants were launched as a result of these statutory laws.

Multiple-choice Questions for Practice and Review
· ·

16.8 Under the Foreign Corrupt Practices Act of 1977:

  a. Companies must refrain from bribing foreign politicians for commercial advantage.

  b. Independent auditors must audit all elements of a company's internal control system.

  c. Companies must establish control systems to keep books, records, and accounts properly.

  d. Independent auditors must establish control systems to keep books, records, and accounts properly.

16.9 The management accountants employed by Robbins, Inc., wrongfully charged executives' personal expences to the overhead on a government contract. Their activities can be characterized as:

  a. Errors in the application of accounting principles.

b. Irregularities of the type of independent auditors should plan an audit to detect.

c. Irregularities of the type independent auditors have no responsibility to plan an audit to detect.

d. Illegal acts of a type independent auditors should be aware might occur in government contract business.

16.10 Which of these laws does the U.S. Securities and Exchange Commission not administer?

a. Securities Act of 1933.

b. Securities and Exchange Act of 1934.

c. Racketeer Influenced and Corrupt Organization Act.

d. Foreign Corrupt Practices Act of 1977.

16.11 Good Gold Company sold $20 million of preferred shares. The company should have registered the offering under the Securities Act of 1933 if it were sold to:

a. 150 accredited investors.

b. One insurance company.

c. 30 investors all resident in one state.

d. Diverse customers of a brokerage firm.

16.12 When a company registers a security offering under the Securities Act of 1933, the law provides an investor with:

a. An SEC guarantee that the information in the registration statement is true.

b. Insurance against loss from the investment.

c. Financial information about the company audited by independent PAs.

d. Inside information about the company's trade secrets.

16.13 A group of investors sued Anderson, Olds & Watershed, PAs, for alleged damages suffered when the company in which they held common shares went bankrupt. In order to avoid liability under the common law, AOW must prove which of the following?

a. The investors actually suffered a loss.

b. The investors relied on the financial statements audited by AOW.

c. The investors' loss was a direct result of their reliance on the audited financial statements.

d. The audit was conducted in accordance with generally accepted auditing standards and with due professional care.

16.14 The Securities and Exchange Commission document that governs accounting in financial statements filed with the SEC is:

a. Regulation D.

b. Form 8-K.

c. Form S-18.

d. Regulation S-X.

16.15 Able Corporation plans to sell $10 million common shares to investors. The company can do so without filing an S-1 registration statement under the Securities Act (1933) if Able sells the shares:

a. To an investment banker who then sells them to investors in its national retail network.

b. To no more than 75 investors solicited at random.

c. Only to accredited investors.

d. Only to 35 accredited investors and an unlimited number of unaccredited investors.

16.16 A "public company" subject to the periodic reporting requirements of the Exchange Act (1934) must file an annual report with the SEC known as the:

a. Form 10-K.

b. Form 10-Q.

c. Form 8-K.

d. Form S-3.

16.17 When investors sue auditors for damages under Section 11 of the Securities Act (1933), they must allege and prove:

a. Scienter on the part of the auditor.

b. That the audited financial statements were materially misleading.

c. That they relied on the misleading audited financial statements.

d. That their reliance on the misleading financial statements was the direct cause of their loss.

DISCUSSION CASES

· ·

16.18 Responsibility for Errors and Irregularities. Huffman & Whitman, a large regional PA firm, was engaged by the Ritter Tire Wholesale Company to audit its financial statements for the year ended January 31. Huffman & Whitman had a busy audit engagement schedule from December 31 through April 1, and they decided to audit Ritter's purchase vouchers and related cash disbursements on a sample basis. They instructed staff accountants to select a random sample of 130 purchase transactions and gave directions about the important deviations, including missing receiving reports. Boyd, the assistant in charge, completed the working papers, properly documenting the fact that 13 of the purchases in the sample had been recorded and paid without the receiving report (required by stated internal control procedures) being included in the file of supporting documents. Whitman, the partner in direct charge of the audit, showed the findings to Lock, Ritter's chief accountant. Lock appeared surprised but promised that the missing receiving reports would be inserted into the files before the audit was over. Whitman was satisfied, noted in the workpapers that the problem was solved, and did not say anything to Huffman about it.

Unfortunately, H&W did not discover the fact that Lock was involved in a fraudulent scheme in which he diverted shipments to a warehouse leased in his name and sent the invoices to Ritter for payment. He then sold the tires for his own profit. Internal auditors discovered the scheme during a study of slow-moving inventory items. Ritter's inventory was overstated by about $500,000 (20 percent)—the amount Lock has diverted.

Required:

a. With regard to the 13 missing receiving reports, does a material weakness in internal control exist? If so, does Huffman & Whitman have any further audit responsibility? Explain.

b. Was the audit conducted in a negligent manner?

16.19 Responsibility for Errors and Irregularities. Herbert McCoy is the president of McCoy Forging Corporation. For the past several years, Donovan & Company, PAs, has done the company's compilation and some other accounting and tax work. McCoy decided to have an audit. Moreover, McCoy had recently received a disturbing anonymous letter that stated: "Beware, you have a viper in your nest. The money is literally disappearing before your very eyes! Signed: A friend." He told no one about the letter.

McCoy Forging engaged Donovan & Company, PAs, to render an opinion on the financial statements for the year ended June 30, 1993. McCoy told Donovan he wanted to verify that the financial statements were "accurate and proper." He did not mention the anonymous letter. The usual engagement letter providing for an audit in accordance with generally accepted auditing standards (GAAS) was drafted by Donovan & Company and signed by both parties.

The audit was performed in accordance with GAAS. The audit did not reveal a clever defalcation plan. Harper, the assistant treasurer, was siphoning off substantial amounts of McCoy Forging's money. The defalcations occurred both before and after the audit. Harper's embezzlement was discovered by McCoy's new internal auditor in October 1993, after Donovan had delivered the audit report. Although the scheme was fairly sophisticated, it could have been detected if Donovan & Company had performed additional procedures. McCoy Forging demands reimbursement from Donovan for the entire amount of the embezzlement, some $40,000 of which occurred before the audit and

$65,000 after. Donovan has denied any liability and refuses to pay.

Required:
Discuss Donovan's responsibility in this situation. Do you think McCoy Forging would prevail in whole or in part in a lawsuit against Donovan under common law? Explain your conclusions.

(AICPA adapted)

16.20 Common Law Liability Exposure. A PA firm was engaged to examine the financial statements of Martin Manufacturing Corporation for the year ending December 31. Martin needed cash to continue its operations and agreed to sell its common share investment in a subsidiary through a private placement. The buyers insisted that the proceeds be placed in escrow because of the possibility of a major contingent tax liability that might result from a pending government claim against Martin's subsidiary. The payment in escrow was completed in late November. The president of Martin told the audit partner that the proceeds from the sale of the subsidiary's common shares, held in escrow, should be shown on the balance sheet as an unrestricted current account receivable. The president was of the opinion that the government's claim was groundless and that Martin needed an "uncluttered" balance sheet and a "clean" auditor's opinion to obtain additional working capital from lenders. The audit partner agreed with the president and issued an unqualified opinion on the Martin financial statements, which did not refer to the contingent liability and did not properly describe the escrow arrangement.

The government's claim proved to be valid, and, pursuant to the agreement with the buyers, the purchase price of the subsidiary was reduced by $450,000. This adverse development forced Martin into bankruptcy. The PA firm is being sued for deceit (fraud) by several of Martin's unpaid creditors who extended credit in reliance on the PA firm's unqualified opinion on Martin's financial statements.

Required:
a. What deceit (fraud) do you believe the creditors are claiming?
b. Is the lack of privity between the PA firm and the creditors important in this case?
c. Do you believe the PA firm is liable to the creditors? Explain.

(AICPA adapted)

16.21 Common Law Liability Exposure. Risk Capital Limited, an Alberta corporation, was considering the purchase of a substantial amount of treasury shares held by Sunshine Corporation, a closely held corporation. Initial discussions with the Sunshine Corporation began late in 1992.

Wilson and Wyatt, Sunshine's accountants, regularly prepared quarterly and annual unaudited financial statements. The most recently prepared financial statements were for the year ended September 30, 1992.

On November 15, 1992, after extensive negotiations, Risk Capital agreed to purchase 100,000 shares of no par, class A capital shares of Sunshine at $12.50 per share. However, Risk Capital insisted on audited statements for calendar year 1992. The contract that was made available to Wilson and Wyatt specifically provided:

Risk Capital shall have the right to rescind the purchase of said shares if the audited financial statements of Sunshine for the calendar year 1992 show a material adverse change in the financial condition of the corporation.

The audited financial statements furnished to Sunshine by Wilson and Wyatt showed no such material adverse change. Risk Capital relied on the audited statements and purchased the treasury shares of Sunshine. It was subsequently discovered that, as of the balance sheet date, the audited statements were incorrect and that in fact there had been a material adverse change in the financial condition of the corporation. Sunshine is insolvent, and

Risk Capital will lose virtually its entire investment.

Risk Capital seeks recovery against Wilson and Wyatt.

Required:

Assuming that only ordinary negligence is proved, will Risk Capital prevail:

a. Under the *Ultramares* decision?

b. Under the *Rusch Factors* decision?

16.22 Common Law Liability Exposure.

Smith, PA, is the auditor for Juniper Manufacturing Corporation, a privately owned company that has a June 30 fiscal year. Juniper arranged for a substantial bank loan, which was dependent on the bank receiving, by September 30, audited financial statements showing a current ratio of at least 2 to 1. On September 25, just before the audit report was to be issued, Smith received an anonymous letter on Juniper's stationery indicating that a five-year lease by Juniper, as lessee, of a factory building that was accounted for in the financial statements as an operating lease was in fact a capital lease. The letter stated that there was a secret written agreement with the lessor modifying the lease and creating a capital lease.

Smith confronted the president of Juniper, who admitted that a secret agreement existed but said it was necessary to treat the lease as an operating lease to meet the current ratio requirement of the pending loan and that nobody would ever discover the secret agreement with the lessor. The president said that, if Smith did not issue his report by September 30, Juniper would sue Smith for substantial damages that would result from not getting the loan. Under this pressure and because the working papers contained a copy of the five-year lease agreement supporting the operating lease treatment, Smith issued his report with an unqualified opinion on September 29. In spite of the fact that the loan was received, Juniper went bankrupt. The bank is suing Smith to recover its losses on the loan and the lessor is suing Smith to recover uncollected rents.

Required:

Answer the following, setting forth reasons for any conclusions stated:

a. Is Smith liable to the bank?

b. Is Smith liable to the lessor?

c. Was Smith independent?

(AICPA adapted)

16.23 Common Law Liability Exposure.

Farr and Madison, PAs, audited Glamour, Inc. Their audit was deficient in several respects:

1. Farr and Madison failed to audit properly certain receivables, which later proved to be fictitious.

2. With respect to other receivables, although they made a cursory check, they did not detect many accounts that were long overdue and obviously uncollectible.

3. No physical inventory was taken of the securities claimed to be in Glamour's possession, which in fact had been sold. Both the securities and cash received from the sales were listed on the balance sheet as assets.

There is no indication that Farr and Madison actually believed the financial statements were false. Subsequent creditors, not known to Farr and Madison, are now suing based on the deficiencies in the audit described above. Farr and Madison moved to dismiss the lawsuit against it on the basis that the firm did not have actual knowledge of falsity and therefore did not commit fraud.

Required:

May the creditors recover without demonstrating that Farr and Madison had actual knowledge of falsity? Explain.

16.24 Liability in a Review Engagement.

Mason and Dilworth, PAs, were the accountants for Hotshot Company, a closely held corporation owned by 30 residents of the area. M&D had been previously engaged by Hotshot to perform some compilation and tax work. Bubba Crass, Hotshot's president and holder of 15 percent of the shares, said he needed something more than these services. He told Mason, the partner in charge, that he wanted financial statements for internal use, primarily for management purposes, but also to obtain short-term loans from financial institutions. Mason recommended a "review" of the financial statements. Mason did not prepare an engagement letter.

During the review work, Mason had some reservations about the financial statements. Mason told Dilworth at various times he was "uneasy about certain figures and conclusions," but that he would "take Crass's word about the validity of certain entries since the review was primarily for internal use in any event and was not an audit." M&D did not discover a material act of fraud committed by Crass. The fraud would have been detected had Mason not relied so much on the unsupported statements made by Crass concerning the validity of the entries about which he had felt so uneasy.

Required:

a. What potential liability might M&D have to Hotshot Company and other shareholders?

b. What potential liability might M&D have to financial institutions that used the financial statements in connection with making loans to Hotshot Company?

(AICPA adapted)

16.25 Regulation D Exemption. One of your firm's clients, Fancy Fashions, Inc., is a highly successful, rapidly expanding company. It is owned predominantly by the Munster family and key corporate officials. Although additional funds would be available on a short-term basis from its bankers, this would only represent a temporary solution of the company's need for capital to finance its expansion plans. In addition, the interest rates being charged are not appealing. Therefore, John Munster, Fancy's chairman of the board, in consultation with the other shareholders, has decided to explore

the possibility of raising additional equity capital of approximately $15 million to $16 million. This will be Fancy's first public offering to investors, other than the Munster family and the key management personnel.

At a meeting of Fancy's major shareholders, its lawyers and a PA from your firm spoke about the advantages and disadvantages of "going public" and registering a share offering in the United States. One of the shareholders suggested that Regulation D under the Securities Act of 1933 might be a preferable alternative.

Required:

a. Assume Fancy makes a public offering for $16 million and, as a result, more than 1,000 persons own shares of the company. What are the implications with respect to the Securities Exchange Act of 1934?

b. What federal civil and criminal liabilities may apply in the event that Fancy sells the securities without registration and a registration exemption is not available?

c. Discuss the exemption applicable to offerings under Regulation D, in terms of two kinds of investors, and how many of each can participate.

(AICPA adapted)

16.26 Applicability of Securities Act and Exchange Act.

1. The partnership of Zelsch & Company, PAs, has been engaged to audit the financial statements of Snake Oil, Inc., in connection with filing an S-1 registration statement under the Securities Act (1933). Discuss the following two statements made by the senior partner of Zelsch & Company.

   a. "The partnership is assuming a much greater liability exposure in this engagement than exists under common law."

   b. "If our examination is not fraudulent, we can avoid any liability claims that might arise."

2. Xavier, Francis, & Paul is a growing, medium-sized partnership of PAs located in the Midwest. One of

the firm's major clients is considering offering its shares to the public. This will be the firm's first client to go public. State whether the following are true or false. Explain each.

   a. The firm should thoroughly familiarize itself with the securities acts, Regulation S-X, and Regulation S-K.

   b. If the client is unincorporated, the Securities Act (1933) will not apply.

   c. If the client is going to be listed on an organized exchange, the Exchange Act (1934) will not apply.

   d. The Securities Act (1933) imposes an additional potential liability on firms such as Xavier, Francis, & Paul.

   e. So long as the company engages in exclusively intrastate business, the federal securities laws will not apply.

16.27 Section 11 of Securities Act (1933) Liability Exposure. The Chriswell Corporation decided to raise additional long-term capital by issuing $20 million of 12 percent subordinated debentures to the public. May, Clark & Company, PAs, the company's auditors, were engaged to examine the June 30, 1993, financial statements, which were included in the bond registration statement.

May, Clark & Company completed its examination and submitted an unqualified auditor's report dated July 15, 1993. The registration statement was filed and became effective on September 1, 1993. On August 15 one of the partners of May, Clark & Company called on Chriswell Corporation and had lunch with the financial vice president and the controller. He questioned both officials on the company's operations since June 30 and enquired whether there had been any material changes in the company's financial position since that date. Both officers assured him that everything had proceeded normally and that the financial condition of the company had not changed materially.

Unfortunately, the officers' representation was not true. On July 30 a substantial debtor of the company failed to pay the $400,000 due on its account receivable and indicated to Chriswell that it would probably be forced into bankruptcy. This receivable was shown as a collateralized loan on the June 30 financial statements. It was secured by shares of the debtor corporation, which had a value in excess of the loan at the time the financial statements were prepared but was virtually worthless at the effective date of the registration statement. This $400,000 account receivable was material to the financial condition of Chriswell Corporation, and the market price of the subordinated debentures decreased by nearly 50 percent after the foregoing facts were disclosed.

The debenture holders of Chriswell are seeking recovery of their loss against all parties connected with the debenture registration.

Required:

Is May, Clark & Company liable to the Chriswell debenture holders under Section 11 of the Securities Act (1933)? Explain. (Hint: Review the *BarChris* case in Chapter 5.)

             (AICPA adapted)

16.28 Rule 10b-5 Liability Exposure under the Exchange Act (1934). Gordon & Groton, PAs, were the auditors of Bank & Company, a brokerage firm and member of a national stock exchange. G&G examined and reported on the financial statements of Bank, which were filed with the Securities and Exchange Commission.

Several of Bank's customers were swindled by a fraudulent scheme perpetrated by Bank's president, who owned 90 percent of the voting shares of the company. The facts establish that Gordon & Groton were negligent in the conduct of the audit but neither participated in the fraudulent scheme nor knew of its existence.

The customers are suing G&G under the antifraud provisions of Section 10(b) and Rule 10b-5 of the Exchange Act (1934) for aiding and abetting the fraudulent scheme of the president. The customers' suit for fraud is predicated exclusively on the negligence of G&G in failing to conduct a proper audit, thereby failing to discover the fraudulent scheme.

Required:

Answer the following, setting forth reasons for any conclusions stated:

a. What is the probable outcome of the lawsuit?

b. What might be the result if plaintiffs had sued under a common law theory of negligence? Explain.

(AICPA adapted)

16.29 Foreign Corrupt Practices Act. Major Manufacturing Company is a large diversified international corporation whose shares trade on the New York Stock Exchange. The U.S. Department of Justice and the SEC have investigated the Global Oil Well Equipment Company, a subsidiary of Major. The agencies allege that Global has engaged in activities clearly in violation of the Foreign Corrupt Practices Act.

Tobias (Global president), Wilton (vice president), and Clark (regional manager of operations in Nogoland) have conspired to make payments to influential members of Nogoland's Parliament in order to influence legislation in Global's favour. The agencies allege that Tobias, Wilton, and Clark met secretly in Geneva and decided to give inducements to Mr. Rock, the Speaker of Nogoland's Parliament. They made a $750,000 loan to Mr. Rock's manufacturing business at a 2 percent interest rate. They gave a $10,000 diamond to Mrs. Rock as a memento of the Rock's wedding anniversary. They paid Jeremy Rock's tuition to medical school. These expenditures were classified as investments, commissions, and promotion expenses in the Global financial statements. Their nature and purpose were not otherwise disclosed.

Required:

a. What provisions of the FCPA have apparently been violated by these actions by Global and its officers?

b. What penalties might be assessed on the corporation, if convicted? on Tobias, Wilton, and Clark?

(AICPA adapted)

16.30 Management Fraud Probability Assessment. This is an exercise designed to reveal some facts of reasoning and decision making. The "fraud involvement test" is fictional.

A team of accountants and psychologists has developed a procedure to test for the existence of management involvement in fraudulent activities. The procedure consists of developing a personality profile of key managers and relating this profile to a master profile compiled from interviews conducted by clinical psychologists with a substantial number of individuals who have admitted to perpetrating material frauds. If the manager's profile is sufficiently similar to the master profile, the test signals "fraud." If there is not sufficient similarity, the test signals "no fraud." In the last 18 months, the procedure has been tested extensively in the field by a national public accounting firm and it has found the following:

- If a key manager has been involved in a material fraud, the test procedure indicates "fraud" 8 times out of 10.
- If a key manager has not been involved in a material fraud, the test will nonetheless indicate "fraud" 20 times out of 100.
- The evidence indicates that about 10 key managers in 100 have been involved in material fraud.

Based on these results, what is your assessment of the probability that a key manager who receives a "fraud" test signal is actually involved in fraudulent activities?

16.31 Audit Report and Legal Liabilities. The auditor's report below was drafted by Smith, a staff accountant at the firm of Wong & Wilson, PAs, at the completion of the audit of the financial statements of PPC Ltd., a publicly held company, for the year ended March 31, 1993. The report was submitted to the engagement partner, who reviewed the audit working papers and properly concluded that an unqualified opinion should be issued. In drafting the report, Smith considered the following:

- During the fiscal year, PPC changed its amortization method for capital assets. The engagement partner concurred with this change in accounting principles and its justification, and Smith included an explanatory paragraph in the auditor's report.
- The 1993 statements are affected by an uncertainty concerning a lawsuit, the outcome of which cannot presently be estimated. Smith has included an explanatory paragraph in the auditor's report.
- The financial statements for the year ended March 31, 1992 are to be presented for comparative purposes. Wong & Wilson had previously audited these statements and expressed an unqualified opinion.

The report which Smith drafted appears below:

Independent Auditor's Report
To the Board of Directors
of PPC Ltd.:

We have audited the accompanying balance sheet of PPC Ltd., as of March 31, 1993 and 1992, and statements of income and retained earnings for the year then ended. These financial statements are the responsibility of the company's management.

We conducted our audits in accordance with generally accepted auditing standards. Those standards require that we plan and perform the audit to obtain reasonable assurance about whether the financial statements are fairly presented. An audit includes examining, on a test basis, evidence supporting the amounts and disclosures in the financial statements. An audit also includes assessing significant estimates made by management, as well as evaluating the overall financial statement presentation. We believe that our audits provide a basis for determining whether any material modifications should be made to the accompanying financial statements.

As discussed in Note X to the financial statements, the company changed its method of computing amortization in fiscal 1993.

In our opinion, except for the accounting change, with which we concur, the financial statements referred to above present fairly, in all material respects, the financial position of PPC Ltd. as of March 31, 1993, and the results of its operations for the year then ended in conformity with generally accepted accounting principles.

As discussed in Note Y to the financial statements, the company is a defendant in a lawsuit alleging infringement of certain copyrights. The company has filed a counteraction, and preliminary hearings on both actions are in progress. Accordingly, any provision for liability is subject to adjudication of this matter.

Wong & Wilson, PAs
May 5, 1993

Required:

Identify the deficiencies in the order in which they appear in the auditor's report as drafted by Smith. Do not redraft the report.

(CGAAC adapted)

16.32 Liability for Auditor Negligence. You have been called to testify as an expert witness in a negligence action brought against another public accounting firm, Muss, Tache & Co. (Muss). Briefly, the facts of the case are:

- Muss's client is insolvent.
- A major cause of the insolvency was overvaluation of the net assets of a wholly owned subsidiary, which led to its failure.
- The subsidiary was audited by another PA firm, Able & Co. (Able).

- The primary auditor (Muss) accepted the work of Able without examination of either the subsidiary's accounting records or Able's working papers.
- The action was initiated by the bank that was the primary creditor.
- Muss's defence hinged on these factors:
  - (a) There was no need to examine the other auditor's working papers, since the other firm was in good standing with the Institute.
  - (b) Since the subsidiary constituted only 12% of consolidated net income, it was not material anyway.

Required:

a. Discuss whether or not the bank will be successful in its suit for damages, with reference to the factors the court would consider in arriving at its decision.

b. If Muss, Tache & Co. had made an internal quality control review several weeks after the issue of the audit report and the review indicated that Muss should have performed some work on the subsidiary, what action should Muss, Tache & Co. have taken at the time? Assume that the review had occurred before Muss's client's insolvency became known and before that bank's negligence action was initiated.

c. Discuss the factors that Muss, Tache & Co. should have considered when determining the materiality for this engagement.

(ICAO adapted)

16.33 Liability in a Prospectus Engagement. Alex P. Keaton Jr. has just returned to the office after an exhausting "busy season." His partner, Malory Dowell, called Alex into her office.

"Alex, I have good news and bad news. First the good news! I've just returned from Expansion Exploration Ltd. and they are going public to help finance their Arctic activities. Therefore, you finally get a chance to work on a prospectus engagement! The bad news is that they want to have the prospectus and the underwriting agreement signed by next Friday, the 31st of March.

"Fortunately, we have been their auditors for the past five years, so we won't have any problems there. Also, I'm quite certain that all five years have had "clean" opinions.

"They have provided me with a copy of their interim financial statements for the five months ended February 28, 1989. As you may recall, their last year-end was September 30, 1988.

"What I would like you to do now, is to provide me with a memo for our planning file briefly outlining what our involvement is to be on this prospectus and describing what communications we are going to have to provide to the securities commission as a result of this involvement."

Required:

a. Assume the role of Alex P. Keaton Jr. and prepare the memo requested by Malory Dowell.

b. Indicate the parties to whom it could be shown that the auditors owe a legal duty of care in this particular situation, and discuss the implications.

(ICAO adapted)

16.34 Litigation Resulting from Bankruptcy of Client. A bank that lent considerable funds to a "high-flying" and, until its recent bankruptcy, highly successful real estate development company has hired your firm to investigate the company's long-time auditors, a medium-sized PA firm. The bank has claimed that the financial statements did not fairly represent the company's financial position. The senior partner in your firm in charge of the investigation has been provided with full access to the complete working papers of the initial auditor in order to complete the investigation. If the matter ultimately goes to court, the case will likely be very high in profile and will likely receive significant media coverage.

The senior partner in your firm has assigned you, a manager with considerable auditing experience, to assist him in evaluating the auditors' quality of work and actions.

Required:

a. Outline what you would do to help your senior partner prepare for the investigation. You should give details of those items he should consider in his preparation as well as the guidelines that would be used to develop an opinion as to the appropriateness of the auditors' actions.

b. On what basis (bases) will the court decide the auditors' liability in this situation?

(ICAO adapted)

Appendix 16A

U.S. Statutory Law

Appendix Objective
Acquaint students whose future clients may come under the jurisidiction of U.S. statutory and common law. Some influential U.S. cases are reviewed as well as the statutory law.

Two Important Laws

Numerous laws affect accountants and business people in the United States, but two of them deserve special mention. The Foreign Corrupt Practices Act of 1977 (FCPA) and the Racketeer Influenced and Corrupt Organization Act (RICO) have changed the landscape of much audit practice and have influenced the nature of lawsuits. These are the focus of this appendix. However, some recent developments perhaps should also be mentioned at this point. One is a change in SEC rules that requires the auditor to inform the SEC of material illegal acts if a client fails to inform the SEC within one business day of the auditor's discovery of the illegal acts. Another development (to be discussed in Chapter 18) is the increased global concern about corruption and auditors' responsibility to report on it. The United States was the first nation to make it illegal to bribe foreign officials. This was implemented through the landmark Foreign Corrupt Practices Act of 1977, discussed below.

Foreign Corrupt Practices Act of 1977

In 1976, under a program of voluntary disclosure, some 250 American companies notified the Securities and Exchange Commission (SEC) that they had made illegal or questionable payments in the United States and abroad. Millions of dollars were involved in some cases, as were high officials in the United States, Europe, and Japan. The pattern of payments involved contributions to American and foreign politicians, bribes to win overseas contracts, and under-the-table payments to expedite performance of services. Some payments were made with the apparent consent of chief executive officers, while others were authorized at lower management levels without the knowledge of top executives. Some disbursements came from general corporate funds and others from secret "slush funds" maintained off the books.

A rising tide of public indignation and impatience with wrongdoing prompted enactment of the Foreign Corrupt Practices Act of 1977 (FCPA). This law—an amendment of the Securities Exchange Act of 1934—makes it a criminal offence for American companies to bribe a foreign official, a foreign political party, or a candidate for foreign political office for the purpose of influencing decisions in favour of the business interests of the company. Companies may be fined up to $2 million; individuals may be fined up to $100,000 and imprisoned up to five years for violations.

The law also amended the Securities Exchange Act of 1934 to include some accounting and internal control standards. These provisions require companies registered with the SEC to keep books, records, and accounts which, in reasonable detail, accurately and fairly reflect the transactions and dispositions of the company's assets. Companies must also devise and maintain a system of internal accounting control. The effect of the Foreign Corrupt Practices Act of 1977 was to make a company's failure to establish and maintain a control system a violation of federal law in addition to being a mere matter of poor business practice. However, the monetary fines and prison terms that apply to bribes do not apply to violations of the accounting and internal control requirements.

The law gives the Securities and Exchange Commission another way to bring action against companies and accountants. Only three months after the law was passed, the SEC charged a company's officers with making false entries in the books and records and failing to maintain an adequate accounting control system. The case was settled with an injunction—the SEC's most frequent settlement method—in which the company, without admitting or denying a violation of law, agreed not to violate the law in the future. Accountant's disciplinary proceedings are also settled frequently with an injunction. You might think this kind of agreement is not a harsh penalty. However, the public notoriety of the proceedings singles out the defendants, and an injunction has some teeth. If a company or an accountant later breaks the law, the persons can be charged with criminal contempt of court. Penalties for such contempt can be severe.

When companies or accountants are taken to court with FCPA or other charges of securities acts violations, the case is litigated (decided by a judge). The SEC got its first litigated decision under FCPA in 1983 and won. However, the SEC is not interested in harassment or in unnecessarily expensive responses to internal control needs. In the first five years, the SEC brought only 26 FCPA cases against American companies, and the U.S. Justice Department brought only 8 cases. The principal purpose of FCPA is to reach knowing and reckless managerial misconduct and managers' efforts to "cook the books." As one judge put it, FCPA was enacted on the principle that reasonably accurate recordkeeping is essential to promote management responsiblity and thwart management misfeasance, misuse of corporate assets, and other conduct reflecting adversely on management's integrity.

The FCPA is a law directed at company managements. Independent auditors have no direct responsibility under the law. They may advise clients about faulty control systems, but they are under no express obligation to report on deficient systems. The law cast a spotlight on companies and their internal auditors. It had the effect of making internal audit departments more important and more professional. The internal auditors often got the assignment to see that their companies complied with FCPA.

Racketeer Influenced and Corrupt Organization Act

RICO is not a law administered by the Securities and Exchange Commission. It is a general federal law, and it has both civil and criminal features. Lawsuits are often characterized as "civil RICO" or "criminal RICO." The original intent of the law was to provide an avenue for criminal prosecution of organized crime activities. However, clever lawyers have found ways to apply it in other cases, including malpractice lawsuits against accountants. As noted in the chapter, this legislation appears to have influenced comaprable legislation initiatives in Canada (e.g., Bill C-61).

The civil RICO provisions permit plaintiffs to allege and attempt to prove (*a*) fraud in the sale of securities and (*b*) mail or wire (e.g., telephone) fraud related to audit or tax practice; but RICO provides a perverse twist. If the plaintiffs in a lawsuit can prove a "pattern of racketeering activity," they can, if successful, win triple damages, court costs, and legal fees' reimbursement. These potential losses raise considerably the risk of the lawsuit.

You might think that accountants may not be in great danger of being found to have participated in a "pattern of racketeering activity." Think again! Such a "pattern" can be established if a defendant accountant has engaged, whether convicted or not, in two racketeering acts—fraud in the sales of securities, mail fraud, wire fraud—within the past 10 years. An accounting firm can meet this test by losing a malpractice lawsuit that involved clients' mailing misleading financial statements and using the telephone during the audit. Since all the major PA firms have lost malpractice lawsuits, they are exposed to civil RICO lawsuits. In fact, RICO has been included among the charges in numerous lawsuits against accountants, and one accounting firm lost such a lawsuit resulting in a judgment of about $10 million.

RICO is hated and feared not only because of the monetary effect on a lawsuit. PAs do not wish to be characterized as "racketeers." It's not good for business. When the RICO threat is included in a lawsuit, PAs are more eager to settle with the plaintiffs before trial, paying damages that might not be won in a courtroom.

LIABILITY UNDER STATUTORY LAW

. . . .

Several federal statutes provide sources of potential liability for accountants, including the Federal False Statements Statute, Federal Mail Fraud Statute, Federal Conspiracy Statute, Securites Act of 1933 ("Securities Act"), and Securities and Exchange Act of 1934 ("Exchange Act").

The securities acts contain provisions defining certain civil and criminal liabilities of accountants. Because a significant segment of accounting practice is under the jurisdiction of the securities acts, the following discussion will concentrate on duties and liabilities under these laws. First, however, you should become familiar with the scope and function of the securities act and the Securities and Exchange Commission (SEC).

Federal securities regulation in the United States was enacted in 1933 not only as a reaction to the events of the early years of the Great Depression but in the spirit of the New Deal era and as a culmination of attempts at "blue-sky" regulation by the states. The Securities Act of 1933 and the Securities and Exchange Act of 1934 require disclosure of information needed for informed investment decisions. The securities acts and the SEC operate for the protection of investors and for the facilitation of orderly capital markets. Even so, no government agency, including the SEC, rules on the quality of investments. The securities acts have been characterized as "truth-in-securities" law. Their spirit favours the otherwise uninformed investing public, while caveat vendor is applied to the issuer—let the seller beware of violations.

SEC Regulation of Accountants and Accounting

The SEC has made rules governing the conduct of persons practising before it. Rule 2(e) of its Rules of Practice provides a means of public regulation discipline. Through these rules, the SEC can apply direct regulatory authority to individual accountants and accounting firms.

Both the Securities Act (1933) and the Exchange Act (1934) give the SEC power to establish accounting rules and regulations. Regulation S-X contains accounting requirements for audited annual and unaudited interim financial statements filed under both the Securities Act and the Exchange Act. Equally important, Regulation S-K contains requirements relating to all other business, analytical, and supplementary financial disclosures. In general, Regulation S-X governs the content of the financial statements themselves, and Regulation S-K governs all other disclosures in financial statement footnotes and other places in reports required to be filed.

For more than 50 years, the SEC has followed a general policy of relying on the organized accounting profession to establish generally accepted accounting principles (GAAP). However, the SEC makes its influence and power known in the standard-setting process. Its chief accountant monitors the development of FASB standards, meets with FASB staff, and decides whether a proposed pronouncement is reasonable. The SEC view is communicated to the FASB, and the two organizations try to work out major differences before a new Statement on Financial Accounting Standards (SFAS) is made final. Usually the two bodies reach agreement.

In the past, however, the SEC itself has made a few accounting rules because (1) the SEC could act faster when an emerging problem needed quick attention and (2) the SEC thought GAAP was deficient and wanted to prod the FASB to act. Consequently, GAAP and Regulation S-X differ in a few respects, but not many. Examples where Regulation S-X requires more than GAAP include nonequity classification of redeemable preferred shares separate presentation of some income tax details, and additional disclosures about compensating balances, inventories, and long-term debt maturities. Otherwise, "SEC accounting" is not fundamentally different from GAAP accounting. The spirit of the force and effect of accounting principles and the respective roles of FASB and SEC are explained by an early SEC policy statement as follows:[12]

1. When financial statements filed with the commission are prepared according to principles that have no authoritative support, they will be presumed to be misleading. Other disclosures or footnotes will not cure this presumption.

2. When financial statements involve a principle on which the commission disagrees but has promulgated no explicit rules or regulations, and the principle has substantial authoritative support, then supplementary disclosures will be accepted in lieu of correction of the statements.

3. When financial statements involve a principle that (*a*) has authoritative support in general, but (*b*) the commission has ruled against its use, then the statements will be presumed misleading. Supplementary disclosures will not cure this presumption.

The biggest difference between SEC practice and other accounting practice involves the disclosures required by Regulation S-K. These requirements are detailed, and accountants must be well aware of them. In many respects, Regulation S-K goes beyond GAAP because FASB pronouncements usually do not specify as much detail about footnote disclosures. Also, accountants must keep up to date on the SEC's Financial Reporting Releases (FRR—a new name for the Accounting Series Releases issued through 1982), which express new rules and policies about accounting and disclosure. Finally, accountants must keep up to date on the SEC's Staff Accounting Bulletins (SAB), which are unofficial but important interpretations of Regulation S-X and Regulation S-K.

Integrated Disclosure System

Under the integrated dislcosure system, companies must give annual reports to shareholders, file annual reports on Form 10-K (discussed later in this appendix), and file registration statements (also discussed later in this appendix) when securities are

---

[12] Accounting Series Release No. 4 (1938). Also, Accounting Series Release No. 150 (1973) affirmed that pronouncements of the FASB will be considered to constitute substantial authoritative support of accounting principles, standards, and practices (FRR No. 1, Section 101). Other sources of authoritative support are enumerated in SAS 5 (see Chapter 2, Exhibit 2–3).

offered to the public. However, companies can prepare the annual report to shareholders in conformity with Regulation S-X and Regulation S-K, and use it to provide most of the other information required for the Form 10-K annual report. Some companies can also use these reports as the basic reports required in a Securities Act registration statement because the integrated disclosure system basically has made the 10-K requirements the same as the registration statement disclosure requirements.

The integrated disclosure system is intended to simplify and co-ordinate various reporting requirements. It also has had the not-too-subtle effect of making most of Regulation S-X and Regulation S-K required in annual reports to shareholders, making them GAAP for companies that want to obtain the benefits of integration.

Regulation of Auditing Standards

In contrast to its concern for the quality of accounting principles, the SEC's involvement in auditing standards and procedural matters has been minimal since the developments of the McKesson and Robbins affair. Following an investigation of *McKesson*, the SEC ruled that auditors' reports must state that an audit was performed in accordance with "generally accepted auditing standards." At that time (1938) the 10 standards had not yet been issued by the AICPA. They were written and adopted soon afterward.

> McKesson & Robbins, Inc.
> An SEC investigation resulted in these conclusions expressed in Accounting Series Release No. 19 (1940): First, the auditors failed to employ that degree of vigilence, inquisitiveness, and analysis of the evidence available that is necessary in a professional undertaking and is recommended in all well-known and authoritative works on auditing. Meticulous verification was not needed to discover the inventory fraud. Second, although the auditors are not guarantors and should not be responsible for detecting all fraud, the discovery of gross overstatements in the accounts is a major purpose in an audit, despite the fact that every minor defalcation might not be disclosed.

The SEC's chief accountant also monitors the development of auditing standards by the AICPA Auditing Standards Board (ASB). A member of the chief accountant's staff attends ASB meetings, analyses new proposals, and decides whether an issue of relevance to SEC-registered public companies is involved. The chief accountant discusses differences of opinion with the ASB, and the two try to work them out. Ordinarily, the SEC does not get as involved with technical auditing standards and ASB proceedings as it does with accounting standards and FASB proceedings. The SEC has rules about audit reports that corresond with generally accepted auditing standards (GAAS), but the SEC has no body of technical rules similar to the Statements on Auditing Standards.

Regulation of Securities Sales

For the most part, the Securities Act (1933) regulates the issue of securities, and the Exchange Act (1934) regulates trading in securities. Neither these securities laws nor the SEC approves or guarantees investments. The laws and the SEC's regulation concentrate on disclosure of information to investors, who have the responsibility for judging investment risk and reward potential. The Securities Act provides that no person may lawfully buy, sell, offer to buy, or offer to sell any security by the means of interstate commerce unless a registration statement is "effective" (a legal term meaning, essentially, "filed and accepted"). This prohibition should be interpreted literally: No person can buy or sell any security by means of interstate commerce

ENTHUSIASM FOR PRIVATE STOCK OFFERINGS

Ariad Pharmaceuticals, Inc., raised $46 million in a private share sale. Specialists in small-company finance say the sale is a sign of growing interest in private financings that could benefit many companies.

Ariad's shares were offered only to a small number of wealthy investors. They had to attest that they had a net worth of at least $1 million (excluding homes) or otherwise met government tests (SEC Regulation D) aimed at protecting small investors. Ariad obtained about 21 percent from institutional investors and the rest from individuals.

Many companies prefer to sell shares privately to avoid the need for public disclosure about proprietary technology or trade practices.

Source: The Wall Street Journal, March 27, 1992.

GENERAL SEC DEFINITIONS

Nonpublic Offering ("Private Placement"). Sale of securities to a small number of persons or institutional investors (usually not more than 35), who can demand and obtain sufficient information without the formality of SEC registration.

Nonpublic Company. Company with less than $5 million in assets and fewer than 500 shareholders. Not required to register and file reports under the Exchange Act.

Accredited Investors. Financial institutions, investment companies, large tax-exempt organizations, directors and executives of the issuer, and individuals with net worth of $1 million or more or income of $200,000 or more.

(e.g., telephone, mail, highway, national bank) unless a registration statement is effective.

A registration statement must be filed and must be effective before a sale is lawful. The SEC has adopted a series of forms for use in registrations. The forms most commonly used for general public offerings are Forms S-1, S-2, and S-3. These forms are related to the integrated disclosure system discussed earlier. They are not sets of "forms" as in an income tax return, however. A "registration form" is a list of financial statement and disclosure requirements cross-referenced to Regulation S-X and Regulation S-K.

Form S-1 is the general registration form. It is available to all issuers but must be used by issuers who do not qualify to use Forms S-2 or S-3. A certain set of financial statements and disclosures (Part I) in an S-1 is known as the prospectus, which must be distributed to all purchasers. Investors can obtain the complete S-1, containing all the required information, from the SEC.

Form S-3 represents the SEC's acknowledgment of "efficient markets" for widely distributed information about well-known companies. Part I (the prospectus) can be concise—containing information about the terms of the securities being offered, the

---

Securities Act (1933) Registration Forms

Form S-1   General registration form available to all companies.
Form S-2   Registration form for small "seasoned" companies.
Form S-3   Registration form for large "seasoned" companies.
Form S-18 Registration form for relatively small initial public offerings (IPOs).

---

purpose and use of proceeds, the risk factors, and some other information about the offering. The remainder of the financial information is "incorporated by reference." Financial statements are not enclosed with the prospectus, but reference is merely made to reports filed earlier (10-K, 10-Q, and 8-K reports, which will be discussed later). The information in these reports is presumed to have been obtained and used by securities analysts and already impounded in current securities prices. Form S-3 can be used by companies that have made timely reports under the Exchange Act for 36 months, that have not recently defaulted on obligations, and that have $150 million of shares trading or $100 million of shares trading with annual trading volume of 3 million shares. These requirements describe reasonably large, "seasoned" companies.

There are other forms as well: S-2 is for smaller seasoned companies and S-18 is for smaller companies making an initial public offering (IPO). These forms are simpler and processed much faster in order to facilitate access to public securities markets by smaller companies.

Regulation of Periodic Reporting

The Exchange Act primarily regulates daily trading in securities and requires registration of most companies whose securities are traded in interstate commerce. Companies having total assets of $5 million or more and 50 or more shareholders are required to register under the Exchange Act. The purpose of these size and share criteria is to define securities in which there is a significant public interest. (From time to time, these criteria may be changed.)

For auditors and accountants, the most significant aspect of the Exchange Act is the requirement for annual reports, quarterly reports, and periodic special reports. These reports are referred to by the form numbers 10-K, 10-Q, and 8-K, respectively. Under the integrated disclosure system, a company's regular annual report to shareholders may be filed as a part of the 10-K to provide part or all of the information required by law. The 10-Q quarterly report is filed after each of the first three fiscal quarters, and its contents are largely financial statement information. Form 8-K, the "special events report," is required whenever certain significant events occur, such as changes in control, legal proceedings, and changes in accounting principles. These 8-K reports are "filed" with the SEC but are not usually sent to all shareholders and creditors. They can be obtained from the SEC and, therefore, are considered publicly available information. Frequently, 8-Ks consist of news releases distributed by the company. Commercial information services also obtain the filings and disseminate the information to clients and newsletter subscribers. Anyone can obtain the filings by requesting them and paying a fee.

One of the events considered significant for an 8-K report is a change of auditors. Companies that change auditors must report the reasons for the change. Most often they

---

EXCHANGE ACT (1934) PERIODIC REPORTS

Form 10-K Annual report.
Form 10-Q Quarterly report.
Form 8-K   Periodic report of selected special events.

---

cite personality conflicts, high fees, growth of the business and need for a larger audit firm, geographical expansion and need to have a firm with several offices, new international operations and need for a firm with foreign offices or affiliates, and other similar reasons. When companies grow and "go public" for the first time, investment bankers involved in the public offering often suggest changing to a Big Six firm for added credibility. This bias to large PA firms has long been a sore point with the other PA firms. They and the AICPA have declared that audits by firms other than the Big Six are professionally competent and that the investment bankers should recognize the fact. Nevertheless, large and growing companies often switch to the larger PA firms.

In the past some auditor changes have occurred for the purpose of getting an auditor who will agree with management's treatment of a troublesome revenue recognition or expense deferral treatment. Such changes are suspect, and a few of them have turned out to be cases of audit failure on the part of the new auditor. Thus, auditor changes in the context of a disagreement with management are thought to be of interest to investors. Whenever a company changes auditors, the company must report the fact and state whether in the past 24 months there has been any disagreement with the auditors concerning matters of accounting principles, financial statement disclosure, or auditing procedure. At the same time, the former auditor must submit a letter stating whether the auditor agrees with the explanation and, if the auditor disagrees, giving particulars. These documents are available to the public on request, and their purpose is to make information available about client–auditor conflicts that may have a bearing on financial presentations and consequent investment decisions. Reported disagreements have included disputes over recoverability of asset cost, revenue recognition timing, expense recognition timing, amounts to be reported as liabilities, and necessity for certain auditing procedures. These disclosures must also provide information about "opinion shopping" consultations with a new auditor.

LIABILITY PROVISIONS: SECURITIES ACT OF 1933

Section 11 of the Securities Act is of great interest to auditors because it alters significantly the duties and responsibilities otherwise required by common law. This section contains the principal criteria defining civil liabilities under the statute. Portions of Section 11 pertinent to auditors' liability are discussed next.

Section 11—General Liability

The Securities Act (1933) is applicable only when a company files a registration statement (e.g., S-1, S-2, S-3, S-18) to issue securities. The sections that follow explain the practical meaning of the act.

In Section 11 the accountant is considered the "expert" on the financial statements that are covered by the audit report and, therefore, must perform a reasonable investigation—an audit in accordance with GAAS using due professional care. All other people who might be included in a registration legal action do not need to prove that they made a "reasonable investigation" of the financial statements, since they relied on the authority of the expert (the accountant who provided the audit report). Thus, the other parties would like the accountant to expand the audit report to cover as much as possible, while the accountant must be careful to specify exactly which statements, including footnotes, are covered by the audit report.

The effect of Section 11 is to shift the major burdens of affirmative proof from the injured plaintiff to the expert accountant. Recall that under the common law, the plaintiff had to allege and prove damages, misleading statements, reliance, direct cause, and negligence. Under Section 11, the plaintiff still has to show that he or she was damaged and has to allege and show proof that financial statements in the registration statement were materially misleading, but here the plaintiff's duties essentially are ended. Exhibit 16A–1 summarizes these common-law and statutory duties.

Privity Not Required

The plaintiff does not have to be in privity with the auditor. Section 11 provides that any purchaser may sue the accountant. The purchaser–plaintiff does not need to prove that he or she relied on the financial statements in the registration statement. In

EXHIBIT 16A–1   **COMPARISON OF COMMON-LAW AND STATUTORY LITIGATION**

Under Common Law	Under Securities Act, Section 11	Under Exchange Act, Section 10(*b*)
Plaintiff		
Proves damages or loss.	Same as common law.	Same as common law.
Proves necessary privity or beneficiary relationship.	Any purchaser may sue the accountant.	Any purchaser or seller may sue the accountant.
Alleges, shows evidence, and the court decides whether financial statements were misleading.	Same as common law.	Same as common law.
Proves reliance on misleading statements.	Not required. *	Same as common law.
Proves misleading statements the direct cause of his loss.	Not required.	Same as common law.
Proves the requisite degree of negligence by the accountant.	Not required.	Must allege and prove that the accountant knew about the scheme or device to defraud.
Defendant Accountant		
Offers evidence to counter above, such as: no privity, statements not misleading, and that the audit was conducted in accordance with GAAS with due care. †	Must prove a reasonable investigation was performed (due diligence) †	Must prove acted in good faith and had no knowledge of the misleading statements. †

*Proof of purchaser's reliance may be required if a 12-month earnings statement had been issued.
†Upon failing to prove a proper audit, due diligence, or good faith, the accountant may try to prove that the plaintiff's loss was caused by something other than the misleading financial statements, for example, actions by the plaintiff such as contributory negligence or loss from some other cause.

fact, the purchaser may not have even read them.[13] The purchaser is not required to show that the misleading statements caused him or her to make an unwise decision and, thus, suffer a loss.

Section 11 was written with the protection of the investing public in mind, not the protection of the expert auditor. The first significant court case under Section 11 was *Escott et al. v. BarChris Construction Corporation et al.* The ruling in this case was that the auditors did not conduct a reasonable investigation and, thus, did not satisfy Section 11(b)(B).

> *Escott v. BarChris Construction Corp.* (1968)
>
> The court ruled that the auditors were the only experts under Section 11 and specifically ruled that the attorneys were not considered experts. In individual findings against all defendants (except the auditors), the court generally ruled that they had not conducted reasonable investigations to form a basis for belief and that they had not satisfied the diligence upon the portions of the prospectus expertised by the auditors [a lesser diligence requirement under Section 11(b)(C)]. The court ruled that the auditors had also failed to perform a diligent and reasonable investigation [Section11(b)(B)]. The court found that the auditor had spent "only" 20.5 hours on the subsequent events review, had read no important documents, and "He asked questions, he got answers that he considered satisfactory, and he did nothing to verify them ... He was too easily satisfied with glib answers to his inquiries." The court also said: "Accountants should not be held to a standard higher than that recognized in their profession. I do not do so here. The senior accountant's review did not come up to that standard. He did not take some of the steps [the] written program prescribed. He did not spend an adequate amount of time on a task of this magnitude."

Section 11 Exemption

Financial reporting has changed since 1933. The SEC now requires some larger companies to present interim financial statements and encourages the presentation of forecasts. To remove the legal liability barrier to auditor association with such information, the SEC has exempted auditors from Section 11 liability related to interim information and has enacted a "safe harbour" with respect to forecasts. (A *safe harbour* means that plaintiffs in a lawsuit must show that the auditor did not act in good faith when reporting on a forecast, effectively placing the burden of proof on the plaintiff.) The FASB requires some kinds of supplementary information outside the basic financial statements (oil and gas reserve information), and auditing standards require implicit reporting. (*Implicit reporting* means that auditors modify the standard audit report only when some exception is taken to the presentation of the supplementary information; otherwise, the report is silent.) The SEC has not exempted auditors' implicit reports on supplementary information from Section 11 liability exposure.

Statute of Limitations

Section 13 of the Securities Act defines the statute of limitations in such a way that suit is barred if not brought within one year after discovery of the misleading statement or omission, or in any event if not brought within three years after the public offering. These limitations and the reliance limitation related to a 12-month

---

[13]   This matter of reliance is modified by Section 11(a) to the extent that when enough time has elapsed and the registrant has filed an income statement covering a 12-month period beginning after the effective date, when the plaintiff must prove that he or she purchased after that time in reliance on the registration statement. However, the plaintiff may prove reliance without proof of actually having read the registration statement.

earnings statement restrict auditors' liability exposure to a determinable time span. Oftentimes, the statute of limitations is the best defence available to auditors. (In 1991 proposals were made to extend the time span to two years after discovery and five years after the fraudulent act occurred.)

Due Diligence Defence

Section 11 also states the means by which auditors can avoid liability. Section 11(b) describes the "due diligence" defence. If the auditor can prove that a reasonable examination was performed, then the auditor is not liable for damages. Section 11(c) states the standard of reasonableness to be that degree of care required of a prudent person in the management of his or her own property. In a context more specific to auditors, a reasonable investigation would be shown by the conduct of an audit in accordance with generally accepted auditing standards in both form and substance.

Section 11 also gives a diligence defence standard for portions of a registration statement made on the authority of an expert. Any person who relies on an "expert" is not required to conduct a reasonable investigation of his or her own, but only to have no reasonable grounds for disbelief. Thus, the auditor who relies on the opinion of an actuary or engineer need not make a personal independent investigation of that expert's area. Similarly, any officer, director, attorney, or underwriter connected with a registration has a far lesser diligence duty for any information covered by an auditor's expert opinion. In the *BarChris* judgment, officers, directors, attorneys, and underwriters were found lacking in diligence except with respect to audited financial statements.

Causation Defence

Section 11(e) defines the last line of defence available to an auditor when lack of diligence has been proved. This defence is known as the causation defence. Essentially, if auditors can prove that the plaintiff's damages (all or part) were caused by something other than the misleading and negligently prepared registration statement, then all or part of the damages will not have to be paid. This defence may create some imaginative "other reasons." In the *BarChris* case, at least one plaintiff had purchased securities after the company had gone bankrupt. The presumption that the loss in this instance resulted from events other than the misleading registration statement is fair, but this claim was settled out of court, so there is no judicial determination for reference.

Section 17—Antifraud

Section 17 of the Securities Act is the antifraud section. The wording and intent of this section is practically indentical to Section 10(b) and Rule 10b-5 under the Exchange Act. The difference between the two acts is the Securities Act references to "offer or sale" and the Exchange Act reference to "use the securities exchanges."

SECTION 24—CRIMINAL LIABILITY
· · · · · · · · · · · ·

Section 24 sets forth the criminal penalties imposed by the Securities Act. Criminal penalties are characterized by monetary fines or prison terms, or both. The key words in Section 24 are wilful violation and wilfully causing misleading statements to be filed.

United States v. Benjamin (1964)

The judgment in this case resulted in conviction of an accountant for willingly conspiring by use of interstate commerce to sell unregistered securities and to defraud in the sale of securities, in violation of Section 24 of the 1933 Securities Act. The accountant had prepared "pro forma" balance sheets and claimed that use of the words *pro forma* absolved him of responsibility. He also claimed that he did not know his reports would be used in connection with securities sales. The court found otherwise, showing that he did in fact know about the use of his reports and that certain statements about asset values and acquisitions were patently false and that the accountant knew they were false. The court made two significant findings: (1) that the wilfulness requirements of Section 24 may be proved by showing that due diligence would have revealed the false statements and (2) that use of limiting words such as *pro forma* does not justify showing false ownership of assets in any kind of financial statements.

LIABILITY PROVISIONS: SECURITIES AND EXCHANGE ACT OF 1934

Section 10 of the Exchange Act is used against accountants quite frequently. Like Section 17 of the Securities Act, Section 10 is a general antifraud section.

The *Fischer* v. *Kletz* ruling and the *Hochfelder* decisions have more to say about Section 10. An important point about Section 10 liability is that plaintiffs must prove scienter—that an accountant acted with intent to deceive—in order to impose liability under the rule. Mere negligence is not enough cause for liability. The basic comparison of Section 10 with common law and with Section 11 of the Securities Act is shown in Exhibit 16A–1.

> *Fischer* v. *Kletz* (popularly known as the "Yale Express" case, 1967)
> The judge ruled that "aiding and abetting" allegations were sufficient grounds for proceeding to trial on the merits of the lawsuit. This decision is the court's ruling to deny the defendant's motion to dismiss the suit. No other public record exists because the suit was later settled without trial. Plaintiff's allegations were based on common-law deceit, Section 18 of the Exchange Act, and Section 10(b), and Rule 10B-5 under the Exchange Act. The case was complicated by the accounting firm's involvement in a consulting services engagement after the financial statement audit.
>
> The court's findings dealt with the following subjects: (1) The accounting firm's role of consultant may have interfered with duties as statutory independent auditor; (2) silence and inaction rather than affirmative misrepresentations may be criteria for deceit; (3) "aiding and abetting" may trigger Section 10(b) and Rule 10b-5 liability; and (4) auditors may have public responsibilities in connection with unaudited interim financial statements.

> *Ernst & Ernst* v. *Hochfelder* (U.S. Supreme Court, 1976)
> The decision in this case established precedent for plaintiff's needs to allege and prove scienter—intent to deceive—to impose Section 10(b) liability under the Exchange Act. The point of law at issue in the case was whether scienter is a necessary element for a cause of action under 10(b) or whether negligent conduct alone is sufficient. "Scienter" refers to a mental state embracing intent to deceive, manipulate, or defraud. Section 10(b) makes unlawful the use or employment of any manipulative or deceptive device or contrivance in contravention of Securities and Exchange Commission rules. The respondents (*Hochfelder*) specifically disclaimed any allegations or fraud or intentional

misconduct on the part of Ernst & Ernst, but they wanted to see liability under 10(b) imposed for negligence.

The Court reasoned that Section 10(b) in its reference to "employment of any manipulative and deceptive device" meant that intention to deceive, manipulate, or defraud is necessary to support a private cause of action under Section 10(b), and negligent conduct is not sufficient. This decision is considered a landmark for accountants because it relieved them of liability for negligence under Section 10(b) of the Exchange Act and its companion SEC Rule 10b-5. Mere negligence is not enough. However, reckless professional work might yet be a sufficient basis for 10(b) liability even though scienter is not clearly established.

Section 18—Civil Liability

Section 18 sets forth pertinent civil liability definition under the Exchange Act.

Section 18, Securities and Exchange Act of 1934
Section 18(a): Any person who shall make or cause to be made any statement ... which ... was at the time and in the light of the circumstances under which it was made false or misleading with respect to any material fact shall be liable to any person (not knowing that such statement was false or misleading) who, in reliance upon such statement, shall have purchased or sold a security at a price which was affected by such statement, for damages caused by such reliance, unless the person sued shall prove that he acted in good faith and had no knowledge that such statement was false or misleading.

Good Faith Defence

Under Rule 10b-5 and Section 18, a plaintiff has to prove reliance on misleading statements and damages caused thereby—the same requirement as under common law. As a defence, the auditor must then prove action in good faith and no knowledge of the misleading statement. This requirement appears to be the *Ultramares* rule written into statute, to the extent that proving good faith is equivalent to showing that any negligence was no greater than ordinary negligence. (A note on the *Ultramares* decision was presented earlier in this chapter.)

Section 32—Criminal Liability

Section 32 states the criminal penalties for violation of the Exchange Act. Like Section 24 of the Securities Act, the critical test is whether the violator acted "willfully and knowingly."

The defendant accountants in the *Continental Vending* case (*United States v. Simon*) and in *United States* v. *Natelli* were charged with violation of Section 32.

United States v. Simon (popularly known as the "*Continental Vending* case, 1969)
The circumstances were judged to be evidence of willful violation of the Exchange Act. Generally accepted accounting principles were viewed by the judge as a persuasive but not necessarily conclusive criteria for financial reporting.

In affirming the conviction, the appeals court stated that it should be the auditor's responsibility to report factually whenever corporate activities are carried out for the benefit of the president of the company and when "looting" has occurred.

United States v. Natelli (popularly known as the "*National Student Marketing*" case, 1975)
Circumstances and actions on the part of accountants were construed to amount to wilful violation of the Exchange Act.

The court stated: "It is hard to probe the intent of a defendent ... When we deal with a defendant who is a professional accountant, it is even harder at times to distinguish between simple errors of judgment and errors made with sufficient criminal intent to support a conviction, especially when there is no financial gain to the accountant other than his legitimate fee."

Nevertheless, the court affirmed one accountant's conviction by the lower trial court because of his apparent motive and action to conceal the effect of some accounting adjustments. A footnote in particular, as it was written, failed to reveal what it should have revealed—the write-off of $1 million of "sales" (about 20 percent of the amount previously reported) and the large operating income adjustment ($210,000 compared to $388,031 originally reported). The court concluded that the concealment of the retroactive adjustments to the company's 1968 revenues and earnings were properly found to have been intentional for the very purpose of hiding earlier errors.

EXTENT OF LIABILITY

. . . .

You may be interested in knowing about who suffers exposure and penalties in lawsuits—the accounting firm, partners, managers, senior accountants, staff assistants, or all of these. Most lawsuits centre attention on the accounting firm and on the partners and managers involved in the audit or other accounting work. However, court opinions have cited the work of senior accountants, and there is no reason that the work of new staff assistant accountants should not come under review. All persons involved in professional accounting are exposed to potential liability.

U.S. Auditing Standards titled "Planning and Supervision" offer some important thoughts for accountants who question the validity of some of the work. Accountants can express their own positions and let the working paper records show the nature of the disagreement and the resolution of the question. SAS 22 expressed the appropriate action as follows:

> The auditor with final responsibility for the examination [partner in charge of the audit] and assistants should be aware of the procedures to be followed when differences of opinion concerning accounting and auditing issues exist among firm personnel involved in the examination. Such procedures should enable an assistant to document his disagreement with the conclusions reached if, after appropriate consultation, he believes it necessary to disassociate himself from the resolution of the matter. In this situation, the basis for the final resolution should also be documented.

CHAPTER 17

Learning Objectives

This chapter introduces governmental and internal auditing in the context of comprehensive auditing. These fields differ in important respects from financial statements auditing practiced by independent CAs in public accounting. However, you will find that all the fields of auditing share many similarities. The explanations and examples in this chapter will help you understand the working environment, objectives, and procedures that characterize governmental and internal auditing. Your learning objectives are to be able to:

1. Describe the public sector and internal audit institutions (II), and tell how public sector and internal audit work interacts with independent audits.

2. Define public sector auditing and internal auditing.

3. Compare aspects of public sector, internal, and external auditors' independence problems.

4. Specify the elements of expanded scope auditing in both public sector and internal audit practice.

5. Describe the coverage of public sector and internal audit standards.

6. Describe a sequence of work in governmental and internal audits in terms of preliminary survey, evaluation of administrative control, evidence-gathering field work, and report preparation.

7. Explain the function of standards and measurements in economy and efficiency and program results audits.

8. List and explain several requirements for public sector and internal audit reports.

Comprehensive Auditing: Public Sector and

Internal Audits

"External," Public Sector, and Internal Audits
. . . .

LEARNING OBJECTIVE

1. Describe the public sector and internal audit institutions (II), and tell how public sector and internal audit work interacts with independent audits.

Public sector and internal auditing is an extensive subject. This chapter explains some of the main features. Even though points of similarity and difference in comparison to "external" auditing would be useful, space does not permit presentation of a detailed comparison. Many such similarities and differences will be apparent, however, when you study this chapter after having studied Chapters 1 and 2.

Perhaps you have already noticed the reference to "external" auditing. Ordinarily, you can refer to public sector, internal, and independent auditors—the latter referring to CAs in public practice, or PAs. Yet labels are potentially confusing. Many public sector and internal auditors are PAs, and take pride in their independence in mental attitude. For purposes of this chapter, therefore, "external" auditing will be used to refer to auditing performed by PAs in public accounting firms and thereby to distinguish public practice from public sector and internal practice.

Internal Auditing

Internal auditing is practised by auditors employed by an organization, such as a bank, hospital, city government, or industrial company. The Institute of Internal Auditors (IIA) is the international organization that governs the standards, continuing education, and general rules of conduct for internal auditors as a profession. (The IIA Standards for the practice of internal auditing are summarized in Appendix 17A.) The IIA also sponsors research and development of practices and procedures designed to enhance the work of internal auditors wherever they are employed. For example, the IIA actively provides courses in numerous internal audit and investigation subjects and promotes its massive, multivolume Systems Auditability and Control guide for dealing with computerized information systems.

The IIA also controls the Certified Internal Auditor (CIA) program. This certification is a mark of professional achievement that has gained widespread acceptance throughout the world. To become a CIA, a candidate must hold a university degree and pass a two-day examination covering these areas: theory and practice of internal auditing; management, quantitative methods, and information systems; and accounting, finance, and economics. Candidates must also have two years of audit experience (internal audit or public accounting audit) obtained before or after passing the examination. Holders of masters' degrees need only one year of experience.

Public Sector Auditing

The public sector auditors discussed in this chapter are auditors employed by federal, provincial, and municipal levels of government.

The Office of the Auditor General (OAG) is headed by the Auditor General of Canada. In one sense OAG auditors are the highest level of internal auditors for the federal government as a whole. Provincial (and other federal agencies and other local governmental units) use the CICA Public Sector Standards to guide their audits. These standards are published separately from the *Handbook* and include accounting and auditing standards. We will use the acronym *PS* for public sector auditing standards developed by the CICA. Because of the wide adoption of the PSs, you will be introduced to them in this chapter.

Many provinces also have provincial auditors similar to the OAG. They answer to provincial legislatures and perform the same types of work described herein as OAG auditing. In another sense OAG and similar provincial agencies are really external auditors with respect to government agencies they audit because they are organizationally independent.

Many government agencies have their own internal auditors and auditor general. Well-managed local governments also have internal audit departments. For example, many federal agencies (Health Canada, Revenue Canada, Natural Resources Canada), provincial agencies (education, welfare, health), and local governments (cities, regions, townships) have internal audit staffs. In the private sector some huge industrial companies have revenues and assets as large as some governments, and the corporate internal auditors are in the same position relative to such a company as a whole as the auditor general is to the federal government. Both in matters of scale and the positions they occupy, governmental and internal auditors have much in common. The discussion in this chapter combines and compares their activities. The following box illustrates the unique influence that public sector auditors have in Canada.

Novatel, or the Chamber of Horrors

Provincial auditors' reports have always cited cases of waste, flagrant mismanagement and not-so-flagrant cover-ups as springboards for recommendations on better accounting and accountability systems. Typically, such disclosures give rise to a flurry of damning articles in the provincial press—not to speak of indignant reactions from the opposition. As horror tales go, however, few have been more politically charged, brought more coverage in the national media, or served as a greater catalyst for improvements to a government's accounting systems than that of Novatel Communications Ltd., as documented in a special 1992 report by Alberta auditor general Donald Salmon.

Novatel was a joint venture created in 1983 between government-owned Alberta Government Telephones (AGT) and energy giant Nova Corp. The company's cellular systems and subscriber equipment business were to serve as a mainstay for the province's high-technology industry—a safeguard for the day when the oil revenues ran dry. By the end of 1988, however, it had accumulated losses of $148.7 million. In 1990, it issued a forecast in which it predicted a second-half profit of $16.9 million—which it had to revise eight days later into a $4.1-million shortfall. Shortly thereafter plans to find a strategic partner were scuttled when the German company Robert Bosch GmbH backed off from an agreement to buy 50% of Novatel. The government ended up with the company on its own hands, and the drain continued. In May 1992, it finally sold off part of the business to Northern Telecom Ltd. and another part to Telexel Holding Ltd., admitting to a $566-million loss on the deal.

By this time, the need to determine exactly what went wrong over Novatel's nine-year history was painfully apparent to all. Conscious of the expense that a full public inquiry would entail, Alberta's Executive Council chose instead to ask Don Salmon to conduct a review. Although this decision was criticized by the opposition as a deliberate attempt on the government's part to avoid a full probe, Salmon promised that the report would speak for itself. And that it did. Issued in September 1992, two weeks after Premier Donald Getty announced his resignation, the 201-page document described in exacting detail the events that ultimately led to what Salmon calculated as a $614-million tab for Alberta's taxpayers. It showed how mismanagement, cronyism and lack of strategic direction ultimately turned the Conservative government's much-touted ticket to the future into an albatross of loss, and how this could have been prevented. More important, it offered broad recommendations designed to strengthen accountability systems in the province.

The recommendations were as follows:

1. The province should consider using the expertise of the public service commissioner to short-list suitable candidates for appointments to the boards of all provincial agencies and Crown corporations. The primary criterion should be "proven relevant expertise."

2. All provincial agencies and Crown-controlled organizations, including subsidiaries, should be required to prepare annual budgets as a basis for comparison with actual results.

3. The public accounts should include the financial statements of all provincial agencies and Crown-controlled organizations and their subsidiaries.

4. The public accounts committee should consider the reasons why actual results are significantly worse than budgeted results.

5. The definition of a Crown-controlled organization should be widened to include a 50% interest in, or equal control of, an organization.

Although Getty officially stepped down shortly after the report's release, Salmon says he nevertheless indicated that he "was pleased and accepted the recommendations." But the story did not quite end there: In January 1993, after Ralph Klein had taken over as premier, the AG had a further opportunity to admonish the government when he released his 1991–92 report. That report was rife with additional horror stories, including the fact that the government had lost $80.8 million on Gainers Inc. since it took the meatpacking plant over from Peter Pocklington in 1989. The stories were so numerous, in fact, that they prompted *Calgary Herald* columnist Don Braid to quip: "Salmon could truly destroy the government if he ever decided to get annoyed about the dismal facts in his reports ... [He] probably figures that the information in his reports is damning enough. If so, he's right."

Indeed, further developments tended to confirm Braid's assessment. In that same annual report, Salmon made eight main recommendations—five of which were the same as those put forward in the Novatel report. Klein, who was planning an election later in the year, hastened to accept virtually all of them. Salmon recalls: "So here for the first time we have a government that accepts all of our recommendations."

In Salmon's view, this link between the Novatel report and the ensuing acceptance of his recommendations is not a chance occurrence. He concludes in these terms: "In Alberta we were fortunate—we were given that special assignment on Novatel, which was much broader than our normal work. And because of the large loss in one organization we were able to then give some strong and broad recommendations. I think this has helped the government focus on financial accountability—and that, of course, is what we're interested in."

Source: M. Criag Bourdin, "On Guard for Thee," *CA Magazine,* January/February 1994, pp. 30–31.

Interaction with External Auditors

External auditors often find themselves working with internal auditors on an independent audit of a company's financial statements. They also often take engagements to perform audits in accordance with the CICA standards (PS 5000 to PS 5400 in the *CICA Public Sector Handbook*).

Considering the Internal Audit Function in an Independent Audit of Financial Statements

External auditors consider the internal audit function in two contexts: (1) internal audit is part of a company's control environment and external auditors must understand how it operates in order to gain an understanding of the company's control structure (second GAAS examination standard) and (2) internal auditors may help the external auditors gather evidence about internal control and about balances in accounts (third GAAS examination standard). External auditors can make their audits more efficient by utilizing the work of a company's internal auditors and, thereby, avoiding duplication of effort.

External auditors must obtain an understanding of a company's internal audit department and its program of work. This task is part of the understanding of the entire control structure. If a preliminary review of the internal audit function shows that the internal auditors have developed, monitored, and made recommendations about internal controls, the external auditors will probably decide that it will be efficient to use internal audit information to reduce their own work on the audit. When this decision is made, the external auditors are obligated to investigate the competence and objectivity of the internal auditors. These investigations become a part of the external auditors' work program.

Internal auditors' competence is investigated by obtaining evidence about their educational and experience qualifications, their certification (CIA) and continuing education status, the department's policies and procedures for work quality and for making personnel assignments, the supervision and review activities, and the quality of reports and working paper documentation. This evidence enables the external auditors to make an evaluation of internal auditors' performance.

Internal auditors' objectivity is investigated by learning about their organizational status and lines of communication in the company. The theory is that objectivity is enhanced when the internal auditors are responsible to high levels of management and can report directly to the audit committee of the board of directors. Objectivity is questioned when the internal auditors report to divisional management, line managers, or other persons with a stake in the outcome of their findings. Objectivity is especially questioned when managers have some power over the pay or job tenure of the internal auditors. Likewise, objectivity is questioned when individual internal auditors have relatives in audit-sensitive areas or are scheduled to be promoted to positions in the activities under internal audit review.

Favourable conclusions about competence and objectivity enable external auditors to accept the internal auditors' documentation and work on review, assessment, and monitoring of a company's internal control procedures. This information, combined with other evidence obtained through the external auditors' own work, leads to an assessment of control risk that is used in the remainder of the external audit planning.

Competent, objective internal auditors may also have performed some external audit–like procedures to obtain evidence about the dollar balances in accounts (substantive procedures). For example, they often confirm accounts receivable and make observations during interim counts of physical inventory. By relying in part on this work, external auditors may be able to relax the nature, timing, or extent of their own procedures in the same areas. Be careful to note, however, that this utilization of internal auditors' work may not be a complete substitute for the external auditors' own procedures and evidence related to accounting judgments and material financial statement balances.

The external auditors cannot share responsibility for audit decisions with the internal auditors and must supervise, review, evaluate, and test the work performed by the internal auditors. This requirement applies both to the work of obtaining an understanding of the internal control structure and to the work of using internal auditors' evidence about financial statement balances.

Compliance Auditing Applicable to Governmental Entities and Other Recipients of Governmental Financial Assistance

When independent accountants in public practice take engagements governed by the OAG audit standards, they are supposed to conduct the work in accordance with PSs. In fact, failure to follow PSs in such engagements is an "act discreditable to the profession." Some parliamentary regulatory laws require auditors to test and report on an entity's compliance with laws and regulations. This work is known as compliance auditing, and it has a special relevance in government-standard audit engagements.

External auditors have responsibilities under the CICA's generally accepted auditing standards for detecting material errors, irregularities, and certain illegal acts in connection with the independent audits of commercial and not-for-profit financial statements. These are detailed in the appendixes to Chapter 18 in this textbook. However, governmental entities and government fund recipients contend with many more laws and regulations, especially ones concerned with eligibility, procedure, and payment of amounts under various entitlements and programs. Auditors must study the laws and regulations and get the management to give a list of all the ones applicable in the circumstances. Auditors can then determine whether to perform specific procedures to obtain evidence about compliance with the laws and regulations.

The public sector sometimes requires reports on compliance. The auditors can give positive assurance on areas tested with compliance procedures and negative assurance on areas not tested. An example of part of a report on compliance test results is shown in the next box.

UNIVERSITY OF XYZ,
PROVINCE OF XYZ

University Student Loan Program:

Finding: Of the 50 student records tested for a total dollar amount of $94,181, 15 loan application forms were completed incorrectly ... These applications must be completed correctly to ensure that the students will not be overawarded. These errors resulted in 1 student being overawarded by a total amount of $1,387; 2 students being underawarded by a total of $631; and with no effect on the awarded amount for the remaining 12 students.

Recommendations: Management should ensure that the costs and estimates are calculated correctly. The loan applications should be reviewed.

University's response: The overaward resulted because one student's Student Aid Report was received late. The award was based on preliminary information from the Comprehensive Financial Aid Report. Underawards were the result of clerical errors. Management will monitor the completion of the loan applications more closely.

Some public sector agencies also require reports on internal control. (Some aspects of such reports for nongovernmental entities were discussed in Chapter 14.) The reports on internal control must describe the entity's control structure, report the scope of the auditors' work, and describe any reportable conditions and material control weaknesses. The requirements for such reports can be very detailed and go beyond the scope of this textbook.

REVIEW
CHECKPOINTS

17.1 What special professional certification is available for internal auditors? for OAG auditors?

17.2 What must external auditors do to use the work of internal auditors in the audit of a company's financial statements?

17.3 Why do you think special attention is paid to compliance auditing for governmental-type audits when independent PAs may perform compliance procedures in all types of audits anyway?

DEFINITIONS AND OBJECTIVES

LEARNING OBJECTIVE

2. Define public sector auditing and internal auditing.

The Institute of Internal Auditors (IIA) defined internal auditing and stated its objective as follows:

Internal auditing is an independent appraisal function established within an organization to examine and evaluate its activities as a service to the organization. The objective of internal auditing is to assist members of the organization in the effective discharge of their obligations. To this end, internal auditing furnishes them with analyses, appraisals, recommendations, counsel, and information concerning the activities reviewed.

Operational Auditing

Internal auditors perform audits of financial reports for internal use, much as external auditors audit financial statements distributed to outside users. Thus, much internal auditing work is similar to the auditing described elsewhere in this textbook. However, some internal auditing activity is known as **operational auditing**. Operational auditing (also known as **performance auditing** and **management auditing**) refers to auditors' study of business operations for the purpose of making recommendations about economic and efficient use of resources, effective achievement of business objectives, and compliance with company policies. The goal of operational auditing is to help managers discharge their management responsibilities and improve profitability. Operational auditing, thus, is included in the definition of internal auditing given above. In a similar context, an operational or effectiveness audit performed by independent PA firms is a distinct type of consulting service having the goal of helping a client improve the use of its capabilities and resources to achieve its objectives. So, internal auditors consider operational auditing an integral part of internal auditing, and external auditors define it as a type of consulting service offered by public accounting firms.

Independence

LEARNING OBJECTIVE
3. Compare aspects of public sector, internal, and external auditors' independence problems.

Internal auditors hold independence, and the objectivity thus obtained, as a goal. Although internal auditors cannot be disassociated from their employers in the eyes of the public, they seek operational and reporting independence. Operationally, internal auditors should be independent when obtaining evidence in the sense of being free from direction or constraint by the managers of the business unit under audit (e.g., program, division, subsidiary). Independence and objectivity are enhanced when internal auditors have the authority and responsibility to report to a high executive level and to the audit committee of the board of directors. The goal here is a measure of practical independence from the control or direct influence of operating managers whose functions, operations, and results they may be assigned to audit. Practical independence enables internal auditors to be objective in reporting findings without having to fear for their jobs. (See the IIA Code of Ethics in Appendix 17B.)

Public sector auditors, like external and internal auditors, hold independence as a goal. PS 5000.13 recommends that public sector auditors should adhere to established rules of professional conduct such as those embodied in the Rules of Conduct of each provincial institute. This relates to maintaining integrity and objectivity as well as to the independence-damaging appearance of financial and managerial involvement. As a public sector auditor, one must be aware that such personal factors as preconceived ideas about programs, political or social convictions, and loyalty to a level of government may impair the integrity and objectivity that is the foundation of real independence. Like internal auditors, public sector auditors must be alert to external sources of independence impairment, such as interference by higher-level officials and threats to job security.

Organizational separation from such influences is essential for independence so that auditors can report directly to top management without fear of job or compensation retribution. Auditors of governmental units are presumed independent when they are (1) free from sources of personal impairment, (2) free from sources of external impairment, (3) organizationally independent, (4) independent under Provincial Rules of Professional Conduct, (5) elected or appointed and reporting to a legislative body of government, or (6) auditing in a level or branch of government other than the one to which they are normally assigned.

On any particular assignment, public sector auditors may perform services for the benefit of several interested parties—the management of the auditee, officials of the agency requiring the audit, officials of one or more agencies that fund the auditee's programs, members and committees of local governments, a provincial legislature, and/or the national Parliament and the public. All such parties should receive the audit report unless laws or regulations restrict public distribution (e.g., for reasons of national security). In fact, the annual reports of the OAG and provincial auditors to their respective parliaments are widely reported media events—which suggests that public sector auditors do not face the expectations gap of external auditors. In contrast, standard audit reports on financial statements given by independent external auditors are addressed to the client and distributed only by the client to whomever the client wishes (except in the case of securities commission–registered companies, where the law usually requires the reports to be filed for public inspection).

Scope of Service

LEARNING OBJECTIVE

4. Specify the elements of expanded scope auditing in both public sector and internal audit practice.

The stated objective of internal auditing is phrased in terms of service to "the organization," not just to management or some narrow internal interest group. Internal auditors, exercising their objectivity, function for the benefit of the whole organization—whether it is represented by the board of directors, the chief executive officer, the chief financial officer, or other executives. The services provided by internal auditors include (1) audits of financial reports and accounting control systems; (2) reviews of control systems that ensure compliance with company policies, plans, and procedures and with laws and regulations; (3) appraisals of the economy and efficiency of operations; and (4) reviews of effectiveness in achieving program results in comparison to established objectives and goals. Internal auditors often make recommendations that result in additional profits or cost savings for their companies. In this capacity they function like management consultants.

The Office of the Auditor General of Canada shares with internal auditors these same elements of expanded-scope services. The OAG, however, emphasizes the accountability of public officials for the efficient, economical, and effective use of public funds and other resources. The OAG defines and describes expanded scope governmental auditing in terms of the types of government audits that can be performed, which are as follows:

1. Financial Statement Audits (PS 5200)
   a. Financial statement audits determine (1) whether the financial statements of an audited entity present fairly the financial position, results of operations, and cash flows or changes in financial position in conformity with generally accepted accounting principles and (2) whether the entity has complied with laws and regulations for transactions and events that may have a material effect on the financial statements.

INTERNAL AUDITORS PRODUCE INTEREST INCOME

During an audit of the cash management operations at branch offices, internal auditors found that bank deposits were not made until several days after cash and cheques were received. Company policy was to complete the bookkeeping before making the deposit.

The auditors showed branch managers a cost-efficient way to capture the needed bookkeeping information that would permit release of the cash and cheques. Management agreed to implement the timely deposit of cheques and transfer to headquarters through an electronic funds transfer system from local banks to the headquarters bank, performing the bookkeeping afterward.

The change resulted in additional interest income in the first year in the amount of $150,000.

---

2. Compliance Audits.

   According to Public Sector Auditing Standards PS 5300, "Auditing for Compliance With Legislative and Related Authorities," compliance audits are those in which audit mandates are required to do one or more of the following:

   a. Express an opinion on whether an entity complied with specified authorities or whether its transactions were carried out in compliance with specified authorities.

   b. Express an opinion on whether the transactions that have come to their notice in the cause of discharging their other audit responsibilities were carried out in compliance with specified authorities.

   c. Report instances of noncompliance with authorities observed in the course of discharging their audit responsibilities.

3. Value for Money (Performance) Audits (PS 5400)

   a. Economy and efficiency audits include determining (1) whether the entity is acquiring, protecting, and using its resources (such as personnel, property, and space) economically and efficiently; (2) the causes of inefficiencies or uneconomical practices; and (3) whether the entity has complied with laws and regulations concerning matters of economy and efficiency.

   b. Effectiveness or program audits include determining (1) the extent to which the desired results or benefits established by the legislature or other authorizing body are being achieved; (2) the effectiveness of organizations, programs, activities, or functions; and (3) whether the agency has complied with laws and regulations applicable to the program.

The audit of a governmental organization, program, activity, or function may involve one or more of these types of audits. The term "comprehensive audit" is used to describe engagements that include all three types of the audits described above. The OAG, however, and other public sector auditors do not require comprehensive audits. Most public sector engagements involve just one or two of the above three types of audits. The scope of the work is supposed to be determined according to the needs of the users of the audit results. However, the OAG recommends observance of PSAS standards in audits of governmental units by external auditors as well as by governmental auditors at federal, state, and local levels.

. . . .

17.4 What is operational auditing, and why can it be called a type of consulting service?

17.5 How can internal auditors achieve practical independence?

17.6 What general auditing services do internal auditors provide?

17.7 What general auditing services do governmental auditors provide?

17.8 What factors should governmental auditors consider in determining whether they are independent?

. . . .

INTERNAL AUDITING STANDARDS
. . . .

LEARNING   OBJECTIVE

5. Describe the coverage of public sector and internal audit standards.

The Standards for the Professional Practice of Internal Auditing were issued by the Institute of Internal Auditors (IIA) in 1978 (see Appendix 17A). The IIA now issues Statements on Internal Auditing Standards (SIAS) intended to provide authoritative interpretations of the 1978 standards.

The 1978 standards are classified into five major categories. Altogether, 25 different guiding standards are included, under the following headings:

1. Independence.
2. Professional Proficiency.
   a. The Internal Auditing Department.
   b. The Internal Auditor.
3. Scope of Work.
4. Performance of Audit Work.
5. Management of the Internal Auditing Department.

Students usually learn CICA generally accepted auditing standards (GAAS) first, then study other auditing standards. The IIA standards include the spirit of all the general and field work standards of the CICA generally accepted auditing standards. On the assumption that GAAS, including the CICA Statements on Auditing Standards, are familiar, we will look only at the IIA standards that are significantly different.

Internal auditors are expected to comply with the Institute of Internal Auditors' standards of professional conduct (see Appendix 17B). IIA audit standards are recommended and encouraged, but compliance with them depends on their acceptance, adoption, and implementation by practising internal auditors. The IIA standards require internal auditors to be skilled in dealing with people and in communicating effectively. Such a requirement may be considered implicit in GAAS related to training and proficiency, but little is said in GAAS about effective communication, perhaps because the audit report language is so standardized. External auditors tend to believe that the public has the responsibility to learn how to understand their audit reports, while internal auditors believe that it is their own responsibility to see that their reports are understood properly.

Three of the IIA standards call for (1) review of compliance with policies, plans, procedures, laws, and regulations; (2) review of economy and efficiency in the use of resources; and (3) review of the results of programs for effectiveness. These standards all go considerably beyond the requirements of generally accepted auditing standards and closely resemble those of two of the three types of public sector audits.

The IIA standards include a requirement for following up to ascertain that appropriate action is taken on reported audit findings or ascertaining that management or the board of directors has taken the risk of not taking action on reported findings. CICA standards have no comparable follow-up requirement because external audit reports do not make recommendations related to financial statements.

Ten of the IIA standards deal with the organization and management of the internal audit department. Accountants in public practice have similar standards, but their standards are in the quality control standards, rather than in GAAS. However, observance of quality control standards is considered essential for proper auditing practice in accordance with GAAS. The quality control standards are "incorporated by reference" in GAAS and enforced through practice inspections of provincial institutes and quality control reviews of accounting firms.

The four reporting standards are comprehensive insofar as audit reports on financial statements are concerned, but the related IIA standard merely says, "Internal auditors should report the results of their audit work." Since the details under this standard are similar to the public sector standards, further explanation will be given later in the discussion of the public sector standards.

PUBLIC SECTOR STANDARDS

The Public Sector Auditing Standards (PSs) incorporate the CICA generally accepted auditing standards as well as a number of ideas from the CICA Statements on Auditing Standards. However, public sector standards go beyond those of the *CICA Handbook* in several respects. Many external auditors accept engagements to audit government grants and programs that must follow not only GAAS but the public sector standards as well. Therefore, these standards are important to independent auditors. Indeed, these public sector standards control all the government audit work performed by PA firms. The four current Public Sector Auditing Statements (PSs) are as follows:

Public Sector Auditing Recommendation PS 5000: Auditing in the Public Sector

This first recommendation provides background information useful in interpreting the subsequent statements.

In the public sector legislatures and other elected or appointed bodies provide authority for the management of financial resources. Management is responsible for the administration of a government entity and is accountable to the governing body and ultimately to the public the governing body represents. In the federal and provincial governments, management consists of the executive (i.e., Cabinet) and appointed officials (e.g., deputy ministers). Similarly in local governments, management consists of various combinations of elected and appointed officials.

Responsibilities of management include measuring the effectiveness of programs, directing operations and activities with due regard for economy and efficiency, maintaining adequate systems of control, ensuring compliance with applicable authorities, selecting and applying appropriate accounting policies, and safeguarding assets.

To the extent required by their mandates, auditors help legislatures and other governing bodies to fulfill their responsibility by providing assurances as to the credibility of management reports, assessments of various administrative practices, and other information. In order to fulfill these responsibilities, auditors must be independent of those they audit. They must be qualified and have access to all information pertinent to their mandate. Auditors must respect the confidentiality and sensitivity of the information that comes to their attention.

Government and other entities in the public sector employ resources to achieve a variety of social and economic goals, and while their audited financial statements provide an accounting of their financial operations, these statements by themselves may not adequately report management performance. The governing bodies of such entities may therefore be interested in information relating to:

1. Compliance with legislative and related authorities.
2. Accounting for and safeguarding of assets.
3. Adequacy of management control systems.
4. Economy and efficiency in the administration of resources.
5. Effectiveness of programs.

Auditors of governments and other entities in the public sector may be directed to report to the government bodies on these matters. Management, however, may not be required to make public representations on them. In such circumstances auditors provide their own assessments to governing bodies rather than attesting to the credibility of representation by management. This kind of reporting is a unique feature of public sector auditing.

Auditors in the public sector report in accordance with their mandates. Audit mandates specify what is required of auditors and give them the authority to carry out their work. These mandates are either established by contract or included in legislation.

The audit and reporting requirements specified in audit mandates establish the audit objectives. These objectives vary in accordance with the concerns of legislatures or other governing bodies. Most require auditors to examine and express opinions on the financial statements. Some may also require auditors to examine and report on the information listed above. Audits that fulfill these broad-scope mandates are often referred to as comprehensive audits. Some jurisdictions authorize auditors to bring any other matters to their attention that in the auditor's judgment should be reported: for example, questionable or nonproductive payments, or the adverse effects of specific legal requirements on the financial statements. Some auditors in the public sector are required to report deficiencies on an exception basis. In such circumstances the auditor's report should describe the nature of the mandate and any mitigating factors or other relevant context of the exception.

Auditors in the public sector should adhere to established rules of professional conduct such as those embodied in the codes of each provincial institute. The *CICA Handbook* sets out GAAS when expressing opinions on financial statements. Public Sector Accounting and Auditing Standards supplement the *CICA Handbook* to recognize special circumstances in the public sector.

Summary of PS 5200:
Audit of Financial Statements in the Public Sector (May 1985)

This recommendation deals with the application of generally accepted auditing standards to audits of financial statements of governments and other entities in the public sector. The public sector auditor should use GAAS as set out in *Section* 5100 of the *CICA Handbook.*

In some circumstances the public sector financial statements may have information different from that set out in *Section* 5100 (e.g., comparison of expenditures in the period with limits established by legislation). In these situations appropriate modifications may be required in the wording of the auditor's report.

Many public sector entities such as governments do not use GAAP but rather another appropriate disclosed basis of accounting (AADBA) considered appropriate by management or specifically prescribed by legislation. In the absence of GAAP appropriate for the reporting entity, auditors should express a reservation of opinion on any accounting policies that they believe result in misleading financial statements together with the reasons and, when practicable, quantification of the effect on the financial statements. In applying this statement the auditor needs to be satisfied that the AADBA does not result in misleading statements. It is not sufficient for auditors to conclude only that alternatives to the AADBA result in more appropriate presentations.

The statement ends with a discussion of the use of the words *present fairly* in conjunction with AADBA. This statement discourages use of the words *present fairly* with accounting policies that arise from legislated requirements, unless the auditor can explain in the report the context in which the term *present fairly* is used. Effectively, this statement says that there are two opinions when using AADBA in the public sector: 1. an opinion on conformity with AADBA, and 2. an opinion on the fairness of AADBA. Theoretically, therefore, it is possible to have a reservation on only one of these two opinions. (This is sometimes referred to as a two-part opinion.)

Summary of PS 5300:
Auditing for Compliance with Legislative and Related Authorities (May 1986)

This statement provides guidance for audit mandates that are required to:

1. Express an opinion on whether an entity complied with specified authorities or whether its transactions were carried out in compliance with specified authorities.

2. Express an opinion on whether the transactions that came to the auditors' notice in the course of discharging their other audit responsibilities were carried out in compliance with specified authorities.

3. Report instances of noncompliance with authorities observed in the course of discharging audit responsibilities.

In this statement the word *authorities* refers to legislation, regulations, orders-in-council, directives, municipal bylaws, corporate bylaws, and other instruments through which powers are established and delegated. Governments and other entities in the public sector may be subject to numerous authorities. Auditors of such entities require knowledge and familiarity of the authorities that apply to the entity being audited and to the transactions for which the entity is responsible.

The same general and examination standards apply to opinions on compliance as to opinions on financial statements (see *Section* 5100). However, since an opinion on compliance does not relate specifically to financial statements, different reporting standards are required.

In an opinion on compliance, the words *in all significant respects* are used because there may be minor instances of noncompliance that either may not be detected by the audit or may not be worthy of inclusion in the report. Significance is closely related to the materiality concept, and both terms encompass a broader concept than solely quantitative considerations. Auditors must exercise professional judgment when assessing the significance of noncompliance.

Depending on their mandates, auditors may examine and report on only a portion of the entity such as a program, a class of transactions, or even a simple transaction. Accordingly, the auditor's report should clearly identify the entity or portion of its examination.

PS 5300 recommends that when expressing an opinion on compliance with specified authorities, the auditor's report should:

1. describe the scope of the audit by:
   (*a*) identifying the entity or portion thereof being reported on;
   (*b*) specifying the authorities against which compliance is being reported; and
   (*c*) stating that the examination was performed in accordance with generally accepted auditing standards, and accordingly included such tests and other procedures as the auditor considered necessary in the circumstances; and

2. include the auditor's opinion as to whether the entity or portion thereof has complied in all significant respects with the specified authorities. The report should provide adequate explanation with respect to any reservation contained in the opinion.

Public sector auditors may be required by their mandates to report instances of noncompliance with authorities which they have observed in the course of discharging their audit responsibilities. Such mandates require auditors to report only those matters which, in their opinion, do not comply with relevant authorities. Readers of the auditor's report need an appreciation of the context in which instances of noncompliance are observed. Consequently, the auditor's report should clearly describe the requirements of the audit mandate and the manner in which the auditor identified the instances reported.

The statement concludes with an appendix illustrating A. Opinions on Compliance with Specified Authorities, Exhibit 17–1; B. Opinions on Compliance Provided in Conjunction with the Auditor's Report on Financial Statements, Exhibit 17–2; and C. Reporting Instances of Noncompliance with Authorities, Exhibit 17–3.

Note that it is Exhibit 17–3 that would be considered most questionable under the new assurance engagement standard *Section* 5025 because it is more in the nature of an exception reporting engagement. Note also, however, in Exhibit 17–3 the use of the words "audit" and "examination," which suggest an assurance engagement. This is currently a controversial issue between public sector auditors and the CICA.

Summary of PS 5400:
"Value-For-Money Auditing Standards" (March 1988)

Value-for-money (VFM) auditing is identified as one of the three main elements of comprehensive auditing, the others being the audit of financial statements (covered in PS 5200) and auditing for compliance with legislative and related authorities

EXHIBIT 17-1   **OPINIONS ON COMPLIANCE WITH SPECIFIED AUTHORITIES AUDITOR'S REPORT (example 1 from CICA's PS 5300.B1)**

To the honourable Minister responsible for Entity Inc.

I have made an examination to determine whether Entity Inc. complied with the provisions of Part IV of the Government Agencies Act during the year ended March 31, 19-1. My examination was made in accordance with generally accepted auditing standards, and accordingly included such tests and other procedures as I considered necessary in the circumstances.

In my opinion, Entity Inc. has complied, in all significant respects, with the provisions of Part IV of the Government Agencies Act during the year ended March 31, 19-1.

City

Date   Chartered Accountant

EXHIBIT 17-2   **OPINIONS ON TRANSACTIONS COMING TO THE AUDITOR'S NOTICE IN THE COURSE OF DISCHARGING OTHER AUDIT RESPONSIBILITIES** (opinions on compliance provided in conjunction with auditor's report on the financial statements) (example 2 from CICA's PS 5300.B2)

Auditor's Report

To the honourable Minister responsible for ABC Crown corporation

I have examined the balance sheet of ABC Crown Corporation as at March 31, 19-1 and the statements of income, retained earnings and changes in financial position for the year then ended. My examination was made in accordance with generally accepted auditing standards, and accordingly included such tests and other procedures as I considered necessary in the circumstances.

In my opinion, these financial statements present fairly the financial position of the Corporation as at March 31, 19-1 and the results of its operations and the changes in its financial position for the year then ended in accordance with generally accepted accounting principles applied on a basis consistent with that of the preceding year.

Further, I have examined the transactions that came to my notice in the course of the above mentioned examination of the financial statements of ABC Crown Corporation for the year ended March 31, 19-1, to determine whether they were in accordance with Part XII of the Financial Administration Act, the regulations, the charter and bylaws of the corporation (and any directives given to the corporation pursuant to the Act). My examination of these transactions was made in accordance with generally accepted auditing standards, and accordingly included such tests and other procedures as I considered necessary in the circumstances. In my opinion, these transactions were, in all significant respects, in compliance with the authorities specified.

City

Date   Chartered Accountant

(covered in PS 5300). VFM auditing is a form of auditing that focuses on economical, efficient, and effective use of resources rather than rendering an opinion on financial statements. VFM's primary application is in the public sector, where almost all comprehensive auditing is conducted. However, VFM audits can also be performed in the private sector, where they are more commonly referred to as "program" or "management," or operational audits. VFM audits are those designed to examine and report on:

- Adequacy of management systems, controls and practice, including those intended to control and safeguard assets, to ensure due regard to economy, efficiency, and effectiveness.

E X H I B I T 17–3   REPORTING INSTANCES OF NONCOMPLIANCE WITH AUTHORITIES (although the mandate resulting in this report may apply to any auditor, this example report on observed instances of noncompliance with authorities is written on the premise of its inclusion in the annual report of a legislative auditor) (example 3 from CICA's PS 5300.B3)

Section 8 (B) of the Audit Act of the Province requires me to report instances that I have observed, in the course of my examinations, where:

(a) accounts were not properly kept or public money was not fully accounted for;
(b) essential records were not maintained or the rules and procedures applied were not sufficient to safeguard and control public property or to effectively check the assessment, collection and proper allocation of revenue or to ensure that expenditures were made only as authorized; or
(c) money was expended other than for the purposes for which it was appropriated.

In accordance with this provision of my Act, my Annual Report for the year ended March 31, 19–1, reports those instances that I have observed in the course of my audits of departments, funds and provincial agencies and that I consider to be significant. My examination of each of these matters was performed in accordance with generally accepted auditing standards, and accordingly included such tests and other procedures as I considered necessary in the circumstances. The instances reported should not be used as a basis for drawing conclusions as to compliance or noncompliance with respect to matters not reported. The instances that I have observed are described in this Report under the appropriate department, fund or agency. (Illustration of reporting the approach followed by the auditor in selection matters for examination in conjunction with a reported instance of noncompliance.)

Department of Health

Compliance with Authorities

In the course of my audit of the Department of Health, I reviewed the system of internal controls to ascertain that it provides appropriate measures to ensure compliance with the provisions of the Hospital Insurance Act (1985). A number of deficiencies in the controls were noted as reported in Chapter 15 of this Report. As a result of these deficiencies, selected transactions were examined to determine whether they were carried out in compliance with the Act. Only the following significant instance of noncompliance was noted.

On March 26, 19–1, a payment of $132,000 was made to General Hospital for out-patients support care under the authority of the Hospital Insurance Act. Section 5 (a) of the Act states that all payments in excess of $100,000 must have prior approval of Treasury Board. My examination of this matter indicated that such approval was not obtained. This payment was, in my opinion, not made in compliance with Section 5 (a) of the Hospital Insurance Act.

- The extent to which resources have been managed with due regard to economy and efficiency.
- The extent to which programs, operations, or activities of an entity have been effective.

VFM audits can be applied to any entity or portion of an entity, such as a program or management control system. The terms of the auditor's mandate specify the audit and reporting requirement. Many VFM mandates require the auditor to report on any deficiencies observed; others require the auditor to express an opinion with reasonable assurance that there are no significant deficiencies in the systems and practices examined. The auditor may also attest to written assertions prepared by management with respect to economy, efficiency, and/or effectiveness of their performance.

In this Statement:

- "Economy" refers to the acquisition of the appropriate quality and quantity of financial, human, and physical resources at the appropriate times and at the lowest cost.

- "Efficiency" refers to the use of financial, human, and physical resources such that outputs are maximized for any given set of resource inputs, or input is minimized for any given quantity and quality of output provided.
- "Effectiveness" refers to the achievement of the objectives or other intended effects of programs, operations, or activities.

I. General Standards

1. The person or persons carrying out the examination should possess or collectively possess the knowledge and competence necessary to fulfil the requirements of the particular audit. [Comment: The auditor is not expected to possess the expertise of specialists on the audit team but must have a level of knowledge sufficient to define the objectives and terms of references of work assigned to the specialists. The auditor should obtain reasonable assurance concerning the specialists' competence in their fields.]

2. The examination should be performed and the report prepared with due care and with an objective state of mind. [Comment: VFM audit reports often include recommendations to address identified deficiencies. The auditor should consider the effect that offering such advice may have on his or her objectivity in subsequent audits of the same entity. Detailed plans and implementation of changes are the responsibility of management.]

II. Examination Standards

1. The work should be adequately planned and properly executed. Audit team members should be properly supervised. [Comment: This is similar to the comparable GAAS standard except that in planning the VFM audits, the concept of significance is used. Significance and materiality are synonymous concepts; however, "significance" is the term often used in the public sector because it is embedded in legislation and practice. Significance is judged in relation to the reasonable prospect of a matter influencing the judgment of a user of the audit report. Both significance and materiality encompass qualitative as well as quantitative consideration.]

2. Criteria for evaluating the matters subject to audit should be identified, and the auditor should assess their suitability in the circumstances. [Comment: Auditors need criteria against which to evaluate matters subject to audit. Criteria are reasonable and attainable standards of performance and control against which the adequacy of systems and practices and the extent of economy, efficiency, and effectiveness of operations can be assessed. There are no generally accepted VFM audit criteria. Criteria may be developed from various sources such as legislation, and standards of good practice developed by professions and associations. Criteria identified from these sources may require interpretation and modification to ensure their relevance to the entity under audit.]

   The auditor has responsibility to assess whether identified criteria are suitable. Suitable criteria are those relevant to the matters being audited and appropriate in the circumstances. When management has developed criteria for assessing systems, practices, and operations, the auditor would use those criteria if they are suitable. In some mandates auditors are required to select suitable criteria with or without the agreement of management. In no circumstance should the auditor perform the audit and report on the basis of criteria that are unsuitable. If suitable criteria cannot be identified, the scope of the audit is reduced and the limitation in scope should be addressed in the report.

3. Sufficient appropriate audit evidence should be obtained to afford a reasonable basis to support the content of the auditor's report. [Comment: The auditor needs to minimize the risk of reporting erroneous findings or inappropriate conclusions. Sufficiency corresponds to quantity and appropriateness to the quality of evidence. Sufficiency of quantity of evidence will be influenced by its quality. Generally, evidence obtained directly by the auditor (for example, through observation or analysis) is more reliable than information obtained indirectly, and documentary evidence is more reliable than oral evidence. The auditor may need to rely on evidence that is persuasive rather than conclusive. Normally, the auditor seeks corroborating evidence from different sources or of a different nature in making assessments and forming conclusions.]

III. Reporting Standards

The auditor's report should:

1. Describe the objectives and scope of the audit including any limitations therein.
2. State that the examination was performed in accordance with the standards recommended in this Statement and accordingly included such tests and other procedures as the auditor considered necessary in the circumstances.
3. Identify the criteria and describe the findings which form the basis for the auditor's conclusion.
4. State the auditor's conclusions.

[Comments: There is no standard report in current VFM practice that is analogous to the auditor's standard report on financial statements. Any limitation of scope and reasons therefore should be described in the audit report. The report should clearly state the auditor's conclusions. Conclusions should be related to the objectives and scope of the audit and should follow logically from the description of the criteria and findings. Adequate explanation should be provided for any reservations contained in the opinion.]

Summary of the Differences between Traditional Auditing and VFM Auditing

1. In traditional audits, the objective is to render an opinion on the financial statements, and scope restrictions can result in qualification. In VFM audits, the auditor's mandate may provide the auditor with the discretion to establish the audit objectives and scope.

In most cases VFM audits have mandates established through legislation or contracts. These mandates specify what is required for the auditor.

2. In VFM audits the objectives and scope vary from one audit to another, depending on the function and characteristics of the organization being audited.

According to PS 6410.15, an auditor always has to use his or her professional judgment when faced with a broad mandate and define it in specific terms with specific objectives. In the case where the mandate is specific, an auditor must still assess the objectives' appropriateness.

3. In VFM audits much of the audit focuses on matters that are not necessarily financial, such as human resource management.

4. There is no body of standards analogous to GAAP. Standards may be management-defined, legislative, or defined by professions and associations.

5. The nature and sources of evidence may differ from those in financial statement auditing. PS 6410.31 states that "sufficient appropriate evidence should be obtained to afford a reasonable basis to support the content of the auditor's report."

   Since a VFM audit can be required to report deficiencies rather than to form an overall opinion, the amount of evidence needed may be lower.

   The fact that a VFM audit can focus more on processes than results also influences the nature of the evidence. Note that this creates some inconsistency with *Handbook Section* 5025 as discussed in Chapter 14.

6. A VFM audit will tend to use a multidisciplinary audit team with expertise in different areas (like economics, statistics, engineering). The make-up of the group will depend on the type of organization being audited, and the needs of the mandate.

7. VFM audits may not relate to a standard time period, such as a year-end.

8. There is no standard audit report for VFM audits. The form of the report will depend on the mandate, and can take the form of a report on deficiencies, or an overall opinion, or an attestation of management assertions. By contrast, an audit of the financial statements of an entity has a standard report prescribed by the *CICA Handbook*.

9. VFM audits use the concept of "significance" rather than materiality. Significance, broadly defined, will include the following considerations:

   a. *Financial magnitude.* Areas with larger dollar amounts will receive greater attention.

   b. *Importance.* Some programs, operations, and activities are more important than others in the entity's strategy to achieve its objectives.

   c. *Economic, social, and environmental impact.* A project or program with a small budget may have a significant impact on the population, or the environment.

   d. *Previous VFM recommendations.* The auditor may choose to emphasize deficient areas previously pointed out that appear not to have improved.

   e. *Express purpose of audit.* In some cases the mandate may clearly express the matter(s) requiring greater investigation.

   f. *Degree of centralized function in the entity.* The importance of these functions can be out of proportion to their size.

10. The concept of "audit risk" takes on unique meanings in a VFM audit. "Inherent risk" is the probability of lack of due regard to value-for-money. "Control risk" is the probability that a system, control, or practice designed to ensure that VFM will fail. "Detection risk" is the risk that the auditor will fail to detect significant errors.

In summary, there are many differences between traditional financial statement and VFM audits. However, as noted in Chapter 14, the new assurance engagement concept recently introduced in *Handbook Section* 5025 incorporates, with modifications, many of the concepts of VFM audits. This is understandable, since an objective of *Section* 5025 is to provide an umbrella framework for *all* audits, including VFM audits.

ECONOMY, EFFICIENCY, AND EFFECTIVENESS AUDITS

Economy and efficiency measures are fairly straightforward. Auditors can use these tools and techniques to evaluate them: financial and organizational analysis; computer-assisted data analysis and EDP testing; value analysis; productivity measurement and quantitative analysis; methods analysis using work study techniques; work measurement; and productivity–opportunity matrices. Economy is related to the price variance, while efficiency is related to the efficiency variance of standard variance analysis in managerial accounting for control. The products here, however, are usually services or activities instead of tangible goods, and thus it may not be possible to measure them as discrete units.

Effectiveness is more difficult to define and evaluate, but it may be helpful to view it as a type of "volume" or "capacity" variance where "volume(s)" are measured relative to some objective or objectives of the organization. The Canadian Comprehensive Auditing Foundation (CCAF) prepared a report called *Effectiveness Reporting and Auditing in the Public Sector* to deal with the question of effectiveness. The report enumerated 12 different "attributes" of effectiveness that the auditor must examine in performing a value-for-money audit. The attributes are:

1. *Management direction.* How well integrated are the organization's objectives and component programs with management decision making?
2. *Relevance.* Does the program still serve the originally intended purpose?
3. *Appropriateness.* Is the program's structure appropriate considering its purpose?
4. *Achievement of results.* Has the program realized its goals and objectives?
5. *Acceptance.* How well have constituents or customers received the service or output of the organization?
6. *Secondary impacts.* Has the organization caused any other intended or not-intended results?
7. *Costs and productivity.* How efficient has the organization been?
8. *Responsiveness.* Has the organization adapted well to changes in its environment?
9. *Financial results.* Has the organization accounted properly for revenues and expenses, and valued assets and liabilities properly?
10. *Working environment.* Is the work environment appropriate, given the organization's purpose, and does it promote initiative and achievement?
11. *Protection of assets.* Does the organization safeguard valuable assets?
12. *Monitoring and reporting.* Does the organization know where it stands with regard to key performance indicators?

Effectiveness can mean much more than the extent to which program objectives are being met and encompasses all the above characteristics.

When defining effectiveness, the client (Parliament or other legislative bodies) may have completely different perceptions than the stakeholder (the program recipient).

Audit mandates specify what is required of auditors and provide auditors with the authority to carry out their work and report. The amount of discretion an auditor has in establishing the objectives and scope of the VFM audit varies. Some VFM audit mandates embodied in legislation provide only general direction about objectives and scope. In such cases the auditor decides on audit objectives and scope for a particular VFM audit. Other legislated mandates, such as that for special examinations of federal Crown corporations, may be more specific in defining objectives and scope. In contractual mandates, audit objectives and scope are usually specified by the client. In such cases the auditor would assess the appropriateness of the audit objectives and scope before accepting the engagement.

VFM audit mandates also have different reporting requirements. Many mandates require direct reporting about the entity. For example, auditors may report deficiencies, or provide an opinion on whether there is reasonable assurance, based on specified criteria, that there are no significant deficiencies in the systems and practices examined. Auditors may be asked to attest to management assertions. When the mandate does not specify the reporting requirements, auditors would choose, often in consultation with their clients, how the results of the audit will be reported. The reporting requirements affect the nature and extent of work that must be performed in the audit.

Government audits require more work on compliance and reporting on internal control than external auditors normally do in an audit of financial statements of a private business. The reason is the public's concern for laws, regulations, and control of expenditures. One-third of the Canadian economy and over $100 billion of federal funds used is represented by the public sector, so the stakes are high.

· ·

R E V I E W   **17.9**   Identify the twelve attributes of effectiveness.
CHECKPOINTS
17.10 What is a comprehensive audit?

17.11 Explain the difference between compliance and VFM audits.

17.12 Compare and contrast economy, efficiency, and effectiveness measures of performance. Which of these is the hardest to audit? Explain.

· ·

Audit Assignments
· · · · · · · · · · · ·

One question you might ask is this: "How are public sector and internal auditors assigned to an audit job in the first place?" Herbert pointed out that government auditors are assigned as a result of:

- Specific statutory or policy requirements for audits.

- Legislative, audit committee, or executive department requests.

- Auditors' own initiative resulting from recognition of the importance of a program, activity, or organization because of the size of its revenues, expenditures, or investment in assets.

- Auditors' own initiative resulting from recognition of the potential importance of a new program or activity.
- Auditors' response to a request for proposal to audit a specific organization, program, activity, or function.[1]

Internal auditors undertake specific assignments for similar reasons. Corporate policy or the audit committee of the board of directors may require certain audits, or executives may request them. Also, a well-managed internal audit department will often take the initiative to recommend an agenda or schedule of audit assignments.

Accountants in public practice most often get involved in public sector audits as a result of responding to an agency's request for proposal (RFP). Well-prepared RFPs specify the audit work requested, making clear what extent of expanded scope auditing is needed. When responding to an RFP, a public accountant is effectively bidding for the job in competition with other respondents. The response to an RFP will specify the engagement objectives and nature of services, the engagement scope and limitations, the roles and responsibilities of the auditee's personnel and other consultants, the engagement approach and methods, the manner and timing of reporting, the work schedule, and the fee.

The process of getting the assignment is important because it includes an understanding and definition of the objectives of the audit. Auditors must know these objectives—whether they relate to financial reports, compliance audit, internal control review, or economy, efficiency, and effectiveness studies—in order to plan and manage the evidence-gathering activities. Governmental and internal auditors do not need to reply to an RFP but must take similar care in planning the assignment.

Evidence Gathering

LEARNING OBJECTIVE

6. Describe a sequence of work in governmental and internal audits in terms of preliminary survey, evaluation of administrative control, evidence-gathering field work, and report preparation.

The evidence-gathering field work can best be described in general terms as an application of a practical audit method for solving audit problems.

- *Problem recognition.* Ascertain the pertinent facts and circumstances. In addition to overall engagement objectives, identify specific objectives in detail. Define problem areas or opportunities for improvement. Define program goals.
- *Evidence collection.* Select and perform procedures designed to produce information related to problem areas, opportunities for improvement, or achievement of program goals.
- *Evidence evaluation.* Evaluate activities in terms of economy, efficiency, and goal achievement. Report findings and recommendations.[2]

Preliminary Survey

Most government and many internal audit engagements begin with a **preliminary survey**. A preliminary survey is an auditor's familiarization with the organization, program, or activity being audited, gained by gathering information, but without detailed investigation or verification procedures. It is designed to identify problem

---

[1] Adapted from Leo Herbert, *Auditing the Performance of Management* (Belmont, Calif.: Lifetime Learning Publications, 1979), p. 24.

[2] Adapted from *Guidelines for CPA Participation in Government Audits to Evaluate Economy, Efficiency, and Program Results*, MAS Guideline Series No. 6 (New York: AICPA, 1977), p. 19.

areas needing additional review in order to plan and accomplish the audit.[3] Sawyer has pointed out that the preliminary survey is a logical means of salvaging order out of a complex chaos of information by answering these questions: What is the job? Who does it? Why is it done? How is it done?[4] These questions require auditors to have a business sense about the audit objectives so that they can get the big picture.

Using interview techniques, auditors can learn about the nature of the entity under audit and its program goals, the organizational structure of the entity, its policies and procedures, its administrative and internal control systems, its financial data, and its nonfinancial measurement system. In many respects VFM audits depend on the administrative controls of the entity and the nonfinancial measures of its program results. For example, efficiency, economy, and effectiveness may be measured not only in terms of monetary expenditure but, more importantly, in terms of employee productivity, student educational achievement, medical service delivered, research and development achievement, environmental effectiveness, or other outputs.

As a part of the preliminary survey, auditors must determine the specific standards for economy, efficiency, and effectiveness results relevant in the circumstances. Some of these standards for government agencies can be found in laws, legislative committee reports, legislative or administrative orders and resolutions, local ordinances and resolutions, grant proposals, and contracts made by a grantee or agency. Similarly, business units may be under orders from the board of directors or may be undertaking a project resulting from an internal proposal that sets forth budgets and objectives.

Standards for economy and efficiency are sometimes hard to determine. Auditors' challenges are to determine the appropriate standards as objectively as possible. An increasing number of sources are available. For example, the publications of the Urban Institute, the International City Management Association, and the National Planning Association are sources of standards. These organizations have produced data about various city services and social services, transportation, energy, and environmental protection programs. Also, it would appear that the various publications of the Criteria for Control Committee of the CICA should provide useful guidance on control issues (see below). Auditors should not overlook available reference books and should also be able to apply good management principles to recognize underutilized facilities, nonproductive work, costly procedures, and over-staffing or understaffing in particular circumstances.

The preliminary survey should be an organized activity, with a written plan or program. It should not be a haphazard "get acquainted" activity conducted loosely. It should lead to a program for study and evaluation of the administrative controls of the business unit, program, activity, or function being audited.

Emphasis on Administrative Controls

Auditors have classified controls into two broad categories: administrative controls and internal accounting controls. **Administrative control** has been defined as the plan of organization and all methods and procedures that are concerned mainly with operational efficiency and adherence to managerial policies and that usually relate only indirectly to financial records. This management function is directly associated

---

[3] Adapted from *Public Sector Audit Guidelines #1: "Planning VFM Audits"* (March 1990).

[4] Lawrence B. Sawyer, *Sawyer's Internal Auditing* (Altamonte Springs, Fla.: The Institute of Internal Auditors, 1988), p. 129.

EXHIBIT 17–4   ACCOUNTING AND ADMINISTRATIVE CONTROLS

Accounting Control Techniques	Administrative Control Techniques
Cash	
Establish a control total of cash receipts as soon as they are received, so that subsequent deposits, journal entries, and ledger entries can be compared to the total.	Prepare timely forecasts of cash flow and provide for temporary borrowing to cover needs, or for temporary investment to generate interest income.
Accounts Receivable	
Reconcile customers' subsidiary ledger accounts with the control account total to control bookkeeping accuracy.	Prepare an aged trial balance of customer receivables for the credit manager's collection efforts.
Inventory	
Assign physical control responsibility to a storekeeper to safeguard inventory from theft or other unauthorized removal.	Co-ordinate inventory purchases with sales and production forecasts so that stockout losses and inventory carrying costs can be optimized.

with the responsibility for achieving the organization's objectives. It is the starting point for establishing accounting control of transactions. Administrative control sets the stage for detailed accounting control.

Another aspect of control is **internal accounting control**. It consists of the plan of organization and procedures designed to prevent, detect, and correct accounting errors that may occur and get recorded in ledger accounts and financial statements. The external auditors' assessment of control risk is a fairly complicated subject covered in Chapter 6 and other chapters in this textbook.

In connection with governmental and internal audits, however, auditors are very concerned with the administrative controls because they directly affect economy, efficiency, and effectiveness of activities. Administrative control is a broad concept involving all management activities, such as responsibilities for production, quality control, transportation, research and development, personnel relations, and many other areas. The focus is not limited to accounting-related activities. This breadth makes it difficult to express specific standards and objectives for administrative control.

The new guidance provided by the Criteria of Control Committee (discussed in Chapter 14) will be equally useful in evaluating administrative controls. The Control Criteria Study views internal controls much more broadly than previous recommendations and in particular includes behavioural factors, objective setting, values, visions, and ethics as part of the control system.[5]

Chapter 6 explained specific standards and objectives of internal control used by auditors of financial statements. As a reminder, you should think of accounting controls as being very specific and accounting-related and of administrative controls as being more general and management-related. Some examples illustrating the contrast are given in Exhibit 17–4.

One key question is this: Given the lack of specific standards, how can you cope with the need to study and evaluate administrative control? Answer: It is not easy! You need to rely on knowledge of marketing, management, production, finance, statistics, business law, economics, taxation, operations research, political science,

[5] B.J. Zimmerman, "Message in a Hologram," *CA Magazine*, June/July 1995, p. 52.

physical sciences, and other subjects. These are some of the nonaccounting courses you can take in your university curriculum. Such studies are important because they serve as a foundation for organizing your early practical experiences and your development of a common sense in business management. Last, but far from least, you will also need to be able to exercise imagination to adapt your classroom and on-the-job experience to specific audit engagement circumstances. You can expect very little to be routine in a study and evaluation of administrative control, and that is what makes governmental and internal audit assignments such exciting challenges.

Audit Procedures

LEARNING OBJECTIVE

7. Explain the function of standards and measurements in economy and efficiency and program results audits.

The general evidence-gathering procedures in governmental and internal audits are about the same as the ones used by external auditors in the audit of financial statements. These procedures are explained in general in Chapter 4 and in more specific terms in other chapters in this textbook. However, the audit problems are usually different in audits of economy, efficiency, and program results.

Governmental and internal auditors must be as objective as possible when developing conclusions about efficiency, economy, and effectiveness results. This objectivity is achieved by (1) finding standards for evaluation and (2) using measurements of actual results so that the actual results can be compared to the standards. Finding standards and deciding on relevant measurements takes imagination. Sawyer has presented two examples, one rather routine and the other very unusual, to illustrate the role of standards and measurements.[6]

Routine Problem.   Evaluate the promptness with which materials pass through a receiving inspection before being accepted and placed in inventory.

- *Source of a standard.* Management policy about acceptable delay between date of receipt and date of inspection approval.
- *Measurement unit.* Number of days between date of receipt and date of inspection approval.
- *Audit procedures.* Select a sample of inspection reports and record the two relevant dates and the number of elapsed days. Develop descriptive statistics of the sample data. Compare these measurements to the management policy standard. Report the findings and conclusions.

Unusual Problem.   Determine whether the company's test pilots are reporting aircraft defects properly.

- *Background information.* Test pilots fill out check sheets as they fly, recording such things as pressure instrument readings under various flight conditions. If a reading is outside acceptable limits, the pilot is supposed to prepare a report, which will trigger an investigation of the reason for the unacceptable instrument reading.
- *Source of a standard.* Engineering specifications of acceptable limits for pressure readings under specific flight conditions. For example, the fuel pressure at 20,000 feet and a power setting of 85 percent should be between 90 and 100 pounds.

---

[6] Lawrence B. Sawyer, *Sawyer's Internal Auditing* (Altamonte Springs, Fla.: The Institute of Internal Auditors, 1988), pp. 229–30.

- *Measurement unit.* Number of times an instrument reading is reported improperly by a test pilot.
- *Audit procedures.* Select a sample of check sheets and related test pilot reports. Compare each instrument reading on the check sheet to the engineering specifications. Read the test pilot's reports and look for no unfavourable mention of acceptable readings and for appropriate mention of unacceptable readings. Tally and describe all report deficiencies. Summarize the findings and report the conclusions. (Notice that the procedure involves reading the test pilot's reports for two possible deficiencies—inappropriate reporting of acceptable readings as well as failure to report unacceptable readings.)

When dealing with standards, measurements, and comparisons, auditors must keep inputs and outputs in perspective. Evidence about inputs—personnel hours and cost, materials quantities and cost, asset investment—are most important in connection with reaching financial audit conclusions. For economy, efficiency, and effectiveness conclusions, however, output measurements are equally important. Management has the responsibility for devising information systems to measure output. Such measurements should correspond to program objectives set forth in laws, regulations, administrative policies, legislative reports, and other such sources. Auditors must realize that output measurements are usually not expressed in financial terms—for example, water quality improvement, educational progress, weapons effectiveness, materials-inspection time delays, and test pilot reporting accuracy.

Many economy and efficiency audits and most effectiveness audits are output-oriented. Auditors need to be careful not to equate program activity with program success without measuring program results. (In contrast, with respect to financial statement audits, the auditor's primary concern is with reporting on the accounting for inputs.) An outstanding example of the difference is illustrated in the box below. It deals with a newspaper article by Thomas Walkom of the *Toronto Star* about a provincial auditor's report that shocked Ontario taxpayers several years ago. Part of what caused the media sensation was that it was not medical officers or health officials who made this discovery but auditors merely trying to assess effectiveness of nursing home care.

Auditor's Report a Life-and-Death Story

Provincial Auditor Douglas Archer has made a damning indictment of Ontario's social services system.

The auditor usually reports on areas where the government of the day has wasted money. That always provides interesting reading.

But money is just money, not usually a matter of life and death.

Yesterday, Archer's annual report was chillingly different.

The auditor's staff inspected six institutions which are supposed to care for developmental handicapped adults—those who used to be called retarded people. Three are operated by the government and three by nonprofit agencies.

Here is what the auditors found.

- In one nonprofit agency, 15 residents had died over two years as a result of problems associated with "feeding and nutrition."

That is three times the usual mortality rate for such institutions. When auditors attempted to check with the Ministry of Community and Social Services about the deaths, they found it blithely unworried.

Indeed, the ministry—which is responsible for inspection—could initially find written reports on only five of the 15 deaths. (It later found six more reports in another filing cabinet.)

Later, in the Legislature, Premier Bob Rae identified the institution as the Brantwood Residential Development Centre in Brantford.

- In another instance, auditors found residents in one non-profit agency had gone 10 years without vision or hearing checkups.

  In two of the three nonprofit agencies audited, residents had gone for more than a year without medical or dental examinations.

  All this occurred in spite of the fact that the agencies had been inspected by the ministry—and in spite of the fact that inspectors are required to ensure all residents receive annual checkups.

- Ministry inspection reports were misleading. Inspectors reported that all "serious occurrences" involving the care of residents at the nonprofit agencies were reported.

  But the auditors stated flatly that serious occurrences were "seldom reported."

- Abuse. The auditors said they had evidence to suggest that abuse of residents of provincially run institutions is more widespread than reported.

  The auditors say that statistics on abuse are "questionable" and found that in one year, 17 cases of abuse had not been reported.

  They add that staff members said they feared reprisals from their co-workers if they reported cases of abuse.

  Indeed, unlike nonprofit institutions, provincially run centres for adult developmentally handicapped people are not inspected at all.

  That's bad since, as the auditors note, residents of these institutions are "particularly susceptible and vulnerable to abuse."

- Inadequate inspection of old-age homes. These institutions for the care of the elderly are run by municipalities and charitable organizations but supervised by government.

However, the auditors found that inspections were carried out by bureaucrats rarely qualified to judge matters such as diet and nursing care.

Government inspectors made no effort to ensure that required fire safety and sanitary inspections were carried out.

Usually, homes were given too much advance notice of inspections, they were able to clean up their act beforehand, the report says.

All of this is disturbing information. What disturbs particularly is the way in which attempts to oversee these institutions seem to have failed.

In case of provincially run institutions for retarded adults, there simply is no outside inspection, beyond the usual ones required by, for instance, the fire code.

Here the ministry seems to think government operation provides its own safeguards.

In the case of government-regulated, nonprofit institutions, inspection seems to be haphazard at best.

The question of inspection is particularly crucial now. For the government has been engaged in an effort to shift people from large institutions—such as residences for the developmentally handicapped—into smaller, community-based group homes.

Done right, this could be of great advantage to the individual.

But to be done right, this so-called deinstitutionalization requires vigilant inspection. Society must be sure these people are not merely dumped and forgotten.

Given the inadequate way in which Queen's Park is able to monitor even its existing institutions, the future for this particular path does not look bright.

Source: Thomas Walkom, *The Toronto Star*, November 28, 1990, A23. Reprinted with permission—The Toronto Star Syndicate.

R E V I E W
CHECKPOINTS

17.13 What is a request for proposal (RFP)? And what significance does it have in a governmental audit engagement performed by an independent PA in public practice?

17.14 Specify and describe a general analytical approach that can be used in audits of economy, efficiency, and program results.

17.15 Which four major blocks of work characterize governmental and internal audit engagements?

17.16 What information can an auditor expect to obtain in a preliminary survey?

17.17 Where can an auditor expect to find information about economy, efficiency, and program results standards for governmental agencies? for business units? for municipal services and social programs?

17.18 What is administrative control? What does it accomplish?

17.19 How can governmental and internal auditors try to achieve objectivity when developing conclusions about economy, efficiency, or program results?

REPORTING

LEARNING OBJECTIVE

8. List and explain several requirements for public sector and internal audit reports.

Public sector and internal audit reports are not standardized like external auditors' reports on financial statements. Each report is different because governmental and internal auditors need to communicate findings on a variety of assignments and audit objectives. The key criterion for such a report is its ability to communicate clearly and concisely.

Public Sector Audit Report

Exhibit 17–5 contains an example of findings from a report by government auditors. This example is condensed from a more lengthy report in the *1994 Annual Report by the Office of the Provincial Auditor of Ontario.* It shows the nature and emphasis of a governmental audit report.

The emphasis is on the effectiveness of a drinking water surveillance program for Ontario. The general audit assignment was to assess how well the program was working. One feature of effectiveness is highlighted in the excerpts in Exhibit 17–5: priority should be given to those plants identified as having significant compliance

EXHIBIT 17–5   **QUALITY OF DRINKING WATER**
Drinking Water Surveillance Program

The Drinking Water Surveillance Program for Ontario was established to monitor and provide reliable current information on drinking water quality. The program was started in 1986 and is intended to eventually include all water treatment plants in Ontario.

The program tests water samples for the presence and levels of 180 substances including bacteria, inorganic chemicals, organic chemicals such as PCB and dioxin, and radioactive substance. Sampling frequency ranges from monthly for new plants to semi-annually for established plants with underground water sources. The Ministry publishes the results of this program annually.

As of December 31, 1993, 120 of the 490 (23 percent) water treatment plants were covered by the program. However, it should be noted that these two plants serve about seven million people or 70 percent of Ontario's population. The Ministry plans to extend this program to about 15 new plants every year. In general, the results have indicated that water treatment plants monitored to date by the program are producing water of acceptable quality.

Inspection Program

Water treatment plants collect samples of their intake and outflow for laboratory tests to assess the quality of their treatment processes. The Ministry inspects all treatment plants every two years to verify compliance with Ministry guidelines.

A 1992 summary report by the Ministry on the inspection of 490 water treatment plants indicated that over 120 of them had significant compliance problems, including:
- not performing sufficient sample testing for bacteria and toxic chemicals;
- not conforming with minimum guidelines for treating bacteria; and
- not meeting Ministry guidelines on treated water quality.

We observed that the plants with significant compliance problems were mainly smaller plants serving about 10 percent of Ontario's population. Furthermore, over 90 percent of these plants were not yet covered by the Drinking Water Surveillance Program.

Our review of 23 current water treatment inspection files indicated similar problems. We noted that problems which were not followed up at the time of our audit had been outstanding for approximately 17 months on average.

We are concerned about the lack of timely followup action on problems identified by inspection staff and the inadequate monitoring of plants not covered by the Drinking Water Surveillance Program.

Recommendations:

Instead of relying on a two-year inspection cycle of all water treatment plants, the Ministry should give priority to follow-up on those plants identified as having significant compliance problems.

Plants having significant compliance problems should be brought into the Drinking Water Surveillance Program as quickly as is practical.

Ministry Response

The Ministry has created a new, proactive inspections unit in each district that will be responsible for plant inspections along with other facilities. Inspection frequency will be based on risk assessment factors rather than routine cycles so that plants with historic problems will be inspected more frequently. Improved reporting and abatement followup is an important element of this new approach to inspections.

The correction of problems at water treatment plants often requires capital work, etc., which may take two or more years to complete. During this time, however, abatement work is ongoing and staff do not wait for the next scheduled inspection to follow-up.

Priority of additions to the Drinking Water Surveillance Program is now being given to plants presently not meeting the sampling guidelines.

Abatement staff will continue to work with plants to obtain conformance with provincial guidelines and policy.

Source: 1994 Annual Report by the Office of the Provincial Auditor of Ontario, pp. 80–81. © Queen's Printer for Ontario, 1994. Reproduced with permission of The Office of the Provincial Auditor of Ontario.

problems. The report consists of a general description of the objectives of the surveillance program, the objective of the audit, the resulting recommendations (which are numbered—here recommendation 3.06), and the ministry responses.

As noted in Chapter 14, such reports may not be considered assurance engagements under *Section* 5025 if all they do is report on deficiencies found. With exception reporting there is always the risk that readers may draw unwarranted conclusions (such as, for example in this case, concluding that the drinking water is unsafe). Therefore, it is important that a clear description of the specific objectives and scope of the particular audit be included in the report and that the report emphasize that deficiencies are reported in relation to them. "The more readers are told about what was done, for what purpose, and the results, the less likely they will be to reach unwarranted conclusions" (D. Hillier, "VFM Audit Standards," *CA Magazine,* October 1987, page 48). This seems to be the case with Exhibit 17–5, and therefore it likely meets the conditions of an assurance engagement as defined in *Section* 5025. Also see K. Duggan, "To Assure or Not to Assure," *CA Magazine,* January–February 1997, pp. 46–48.

Internal Audit Report

The reporting stage is the internal auditor's opportunity to capture management's undivided attention. To be effective, a report cannot be unduly long, tedious, technical, or laden with minutiae. It must be accurate, concise, clear, and timely. There is no standard form for internal audit reports, and there will likely never be one, given the diversity of assignments and the diversity of managers' abilities and interests. Unlike external audit reports, internal audit reports are usually considered "open" until a formal written reply to the recommendations is received from the management of the audited unit or department. This reply, which would also go to the same people as the audit report, such as the audit committee, would indicate which recommendations were implemented or which were considered not cost-efficient. Only after the written response is received is the audit considered closed. Another procedure unique to internal (and public sector) audit reporting is that the criticisms and recommendations are usually reviewed with the audit management before they are included in the final report.

Exhibit 17–6 contains an example of an internal audit report on the study of a transportation operation. The report begins with a summary or overall conclusion that conveys the essential findings and captures the reader's attention.

Consulting Engagement Reports by PAs

In contrast to the well-defined areas of audit and tax practice, public accountants' practice in consulting services can be described only by cataloguing a variety of such services. On a specific engagement basis, independent accountants, acting as management consultants, perform services in areas as diverse as those performed by governmental and internal auditors. Consultants may accent engagements to evaluate compliance, economy and efficiency, and program results. Consequently, consulting engagement reports exhibit the same characteristics as internal audit reports and public sector reports: The problem is identified, some explanation of the investigation is given, and the findings and recommendations are expressed clearly and concisely.

The consulting report in Exhibit 17–7 is the full text of an actual report. The assignment was a relatively uncomplicated one—evaluation of the system for controlling inventory—and the resultant report is a good example of clarity and direct communication.

E X H I B I T 17–6   **INTERNAL AUDIT REPORT (excerpts)**

XYZ /Corporation
Audit Project Rbx-18 August 16, 19XX

	Audit Highlights

Highway Transportation Department (A regularly scheduled review)	
Prior Audit	No deficiency findings
Audit Coverage	1. Equipment maintenance and vehicle dispatching.
	2. Fuel, parts, and repair services.
Overall Opinion	In general, the operation was functioning in a reasonably satisfactory manner.
	We found some control weaknesses. The most serious involved the lack of separation of duties in the procurement of parts and services. Steps are being taken to correct these weaknesses.
Executive Action Required	None

Summary Report

Foreward:

This report covers the result of our regularly scheduled review of the activities of the Highway Transportation Department. Our last review of the department's activities disclosed no deficiencies.

The department's primary responsibilities are (1) to transport personnel and materials and (2) to maintain and repair automotive equipment.

At the time of our review, about 50 employees were assigned to the department. Operating costs (not including labor) for equipment rental, repair parts and services, and fuel and oil are projected to reach about $900,000 for 19XX. Mileage for the year will total about 5 million miles.

During this review, we issued one progress report to bring to management attention certain matters requiring prompt corrective action.

Purpose:

We have made an examination of the Highway Transportation Department's principal activities to determine whether they were being controlled adequately and effectively. In performing our review, we examined the system of controls concerning the following activities.

1. Equipment maintenance and vehicle dispatching, including (a) scheduling preventive maintenance inspections, (b) performing regular maintenance and repairs, and (c) dispatching cars and trucks.
2. Ordering, receiving, and disbursing fuel and parts and obtaining automotive repair services.

Opinions and Findings:

We formed the opinion that adequate controls had been provided over the activities we reviewed, except for lack of separation of duties in the procurement of parts and services. (Some) other matters of lesser significance likewise involved control weaknesses.

We also formed the opinion that despite the control weaknesses we had discovered, the functions we reviewed were being performed in a generally satisfactory manner.

Our conclusions and findings on each of the groups of activities covered in our examination are summarized in the following paragraphs.

Equipment Maintenance and Vehicle Dispatching:

Adequate controls have been provided to make sure that (1) automotive equipment would receive inspection and preventive maintenance in accordance with manufacturers' recommendations and (2) truck and car dispatching would be accomplished in accordance with established procedures.

We examined preventive maintenance reports and related control records and satisfied ourselves that maintenance was being properly scheduled, monitored, and performed. We also examined documentation supporting vehicle dispatching and observed the dispatching operations; we concluded that dispatching was being adequately controlled and performed.

E X H I B I T 17–6   **(continued)**

Ordering, Receiving, and Disbursing Fuel and Parts, and Obtaining Vehicle Repair Services:

Controls had been provided to make sure that fuel, parts, and outside repair services were (1) ordered when needed, (2) recorded upon receipt, and (3) properly approved for payment, and that the disbursement of fuel and parts was adequately documented.

We found, however, (1) a lack of appropriate separation of duties in the procurement of parts and services, and (2) what we considered to be inadequate surveillance over the withdrawal of gas and oil by vehicle operators. These matters are discussed more fully in the Supplement to this Summary Report.

We examined representative samples of (1) reports, records, and blanket purchase orders covering the procurement and receipt of supplies and services, and (2) the logs and records covering fuel withdrawals. Despite the control weaknesses, we concluded on the basis of our tests that the functions were being performed in a reasonably satisfactory manner. We made an analysis of the fuel pump meter records and compared them with the amounts of fuel recorded by vehicle operators. The results showed little variance between the two, indicating that fuel withdrawals were being properly recorded.

The deficiency findings previously mentioned are discussed in the Supplement which follows and are summarized at the end of the Supplement, along with the referrals for completion of corrective action.
/s/Auditor-in-Charge
/s/Supervising Auditor
/s/Manager of Internal Auditing

Details of Deficiency Findings:

1. *There was no separation of functional authority in the procurement of parts and services, and effective administration of labor-hour agreements was beyond the Highway Transportation Department's resources.*
Blanket Purchase Orders (BPOs) have been issued for the procurement of parts and services. The . . . purchasing department has assigned to the Highway Transportation Department all authority and responsibility for controlling (a) release of orders under the BPOs to suppliers; (b) receipt, inspection, and acceptance upon delivery; and (c) approvals of invoices for payment.
In practice, all of these functions are performed by the department manager or by one or two people under his direct control and supervision. Thus, there is none of the protection normally afforded by the separation of such functions among personnel of independent departments, such as establishing requirements, ordering, receiving, inspection, and approving for payment.
Because of the lack of separation of duties, we made an extensive examination of the system and of transactions, but we found no basis for questioning any of the charges. Nevertheless, we recommend that branch management review this condition with a view toward implementing some reasonable control through assignment of some of the key functions to other departments.
We discussed this matter with management personnel, and they informed us they intend to review the methods used at other major divisions of the company to determine whether any of their practices may warrant adoption.

2. *Gasoline and oil were being withdrawn by company employees without adequate surveillance.*
Since our last examination, the department reassigned the service station attendant who had recorded gasoline and oil disbursements on the form provided for that purpose. Under present practice, the vehicle operator serves himself and records his own withdrawals of gasoline and oil, without surveillance. There is no assurance, therefore, that the records are maintained accurately or that the information is always entered. Hence, the dangers of misappropriations are increased. We estimate that the total yearly gasoline withdrawal will approximate 300,000 gallons at a cost of about $66,000.
We recognize that the benefits of control must be weighed against the costs of control. Nevertheless, we recommend that management consider some of means of surveillance—even on a spot-check basis—to provide minimum elements of control.
We discussed this matter with management personnel and they indicated that appropriate surveillance would be conducted over fuel pump operations.

Summary of Findings Requiring Corrective Action
The matters requiring corrective action are summarized as follows:

1. There was no separation of functional authority in the procurement of parts and services.
2. Gasoline and oil were being withdrawn by company employees without adequate surveillance.

Finding 1 is referred jointly to the management of the Procurement Department and the manager of the Highway Transportation Department for completion of corrective action. Finding 2 is referred to the manager of the Highway Transportation Department for completion of corrective action.

EXHIBIT 17–7   CONSULTING REPORT BY A PUBLIC ACCOUNTING FIRM

Mr. C. D. Derfin
Control Instruments, Inc.

Dear Mr. Derfin:

We have completed our review of the cost accounting system of Control Instruments, Inc., as outlined in our engagement letter to you. The primary objective of our review was to determine if your new system should be modified. Our conclusion is that the present system for controlling inventory is sound. It is simple, but it should provide for good control of inventory. The problem is one of improper utilization of the existing system.

We believe that control of inventory is vital to company operations. We understand there are numerous shortages of parts which delay the assembly process. However, we do not believe this problem is primarily due to a system weakness. We observed that additions to inventory are properly entered on the perpetual records when receiving reports are received by the inventory control clerk. Items are deducted from the records when they are pulled from the warehouse, and an adequate system exists for keeping track of material shortages. We believe that the warehouse operation is the primary source of inventory control problems. Our observations and recommendations in this area are summarized below.

Warehouse Operations

Warehouse personnel are currently taking cycle counts of raw materials to locate differences between perpetual records and actual quantities on hand. We noted there were many such discrepancies. In an attempt to find a reason for these discrepancies, we unpacked three pulled orders in the warehouse and compared actual items packed with the amounts indicated as being packed on the bills of material. In each case, we found discrepancies.

In order to identify the source of these errors, we recommended the warehouse be required to initial the bills of material for the orders they pull. They have already been instructed to do this. The production supervisor currently unpacks all pulled orders and counts the contents before the orders go to the production line. We believe he should take the additional step of reporting the exact discrepancies daily to John Roberts. Additional recommendations to improve the warehouse operation are summarized below. Some of these recommendations are already being implemented.

1. Continue the cycle count procedure, but take time to resolve differences daily. Report reasons for differences to John Roberts.
2. Temporarily assign a person full time to maintain inventory records.
3. Stock inventory in the correct locations or attach a note to the bin stating where additional items are located.
4. Adopt a "last bag" system for control of "C" items.
5. When an order for several units on the small line requires more than one box, pack all of one type of part in the same box.
6. When pulling an order for several units on the large line, pack as many complete units as possible and limit the shortages to the remaining units.
7. Require warehouse personnel to pack orders neatly, particularly general kits.
8. Adopt a daily routine in the warehouse as follows:
   a. Stock the items received.
   b. Fill short orders.
   c. Fill remaining orders.
   d. Work on special projects.

We noted that physical control of inventory has been substantially improved by constructing a chain-link fence around the warehouse area. Since access to the warehouse is now very limited, it will be difficult for unauthorized personnel to remove parts.

General Observation

While most of our time was spent in the warehouse, we also noted some opportunities to improve the general operation of the Control Instruments facility. Our recommendations are summarized below:

1. Revise the cost book to contain an accurate description and the current cost of each item.
2. Revise the Bills of Material to make them accurate and adopt a formal procedure for keeping them current.

EXHIBIT 17–7   (concluded)

3. Redesign the forms used for Bills of Material. They can be changed to indicate more clearly the number of items packed versus the number of item specified. They could also indicate which items are used in the electrical subassembly process, so these items could be packed together. These forms should be ordered as snap-out multiple part forms.
4. Redesign the "owe sheets" to make them consistent and easy to understand.
5. Assign part numbers to all purchased parts except common nuts and bolts.
6. Assign part numbers to sheet metal parts and include these parts in the cost book and Bills of Material.
7. Adopt a tag method for keeping track of labor-hours spent on individual units and revise labor time standards as appropriate.

Accounting Procedures

There is some confusion over exactly what accounting procedures have been employed in the past. We recommend the following procedures be used in the future to account for cost of materials and labor. We believe most of these procedures are already understood by accounting personnel and are being used.

1. Record raw materials purchased at standard cost and maintain a purchase price variance account. For internal financial statements, the variance can be treated as part of cost of goods sold.
2. Charge labor to cost of goods sold at standard time. Charge the difference between standard and actual to labor efficiency variance, which is part of cost of goods sold.
3. At the end of each month, count the finished goods inventory and estimate work-in-process inventory.

We would be pleased to discuss this letter further at your convenience.
We appreciate this opportunity to be of service to you.

Very truly yours,
Burr & Hamilton,
PAs

The consulting report, like the governmental and internal audit reports, gets to the main problem quickly, identifying the source of trouble as the warehouse operation. The consultants found and reported that the trouble was not the result of a basic system weakness. The report makes specific points and recommendations on inventory-handling procedures as well as on record-keeping procedures. This particular engagement required not only ordinary expertise as an accountant but also an ability to perceive some elementary materials-handling problems and offer good managerial solutions.

REVIEW CHECKPOINTS

17.20 What are the major differences between independent auditors' reports on financial statements and internal, public sector, and consulting reports on efficiency and economy and effectiveness audits?

17.21 Why do you think the public sector reporting standards permit the report to include "pertinent views of responsible officials" {of the auditee} concerning the auditor's findings, conclusions, and recommendations?

Summary

Governmental and internal auditing standards include the essence of the CICA generally accepted auditing standards (GAAS) and go much further by expressing standards for audits of economy, efficiency, and effectiveness of program results. In addition, the internal auditing standards contain many guides for the management of an internal audit department within a company.

All auditors hold independence as a primary goal, but internal auditors must look to an internal organization independence from the managers and executives whose areas they audit. Public sector auditors must be concerned about factual independence with regard to social, political, and level-of-government influence.

Public sector auditing is complicated by the special context of audit assignments intended to accomplish accountability by agencies that handle federal funds—grants, subsidies, welfare programs, and the like. The requirements of the public sector auditing standards impose on the audit function the responsibility for compliance audit work designed to determine agencies' observance of laws and regulations, of which there are many. Auditors must report not only on financial statements but also on internal control, violations of laws and regulations, fraud, abuse, and illegal acts. These elements are all part of Ottawa's oversight of federal spending, facilitated by auditors.

Audit engagements are an application of the practical audit method—essentially a fact-finding approach. Auditors start the work with an understanding of the audit objectives involved in the assignment and carry them out through the major blocks of work—preliminary survey, study and evaluation of administrative control, application of audit procedures, and reporting of the audit conclusions and recommendations. Auditors try to achieve objectivity by determining appropriate standards for economy, efficiency, and effectiveness of program results, by measuring their evidence, and by comparing their measurements to the standards in order to reach objective conclusions.

Public sector and internal audit reports and similar reports on public accountants' consulting services are not standardized like the GAAS reports on audited financial statements. Auditors must be very careful that their reports communicate their conclusions and recommendations in a clear and concise manner. The variety of assignments and the challenge of reporting in such a free-form setting contribute to making governmental auditing, internal auditing, and consulting services exciting fields for career opportunities.

One field in particular has expanded to the private sector—that of environmental auditing. This subfield is described in the appendix at the back of this textbook.

A useful website for this chapter is http://www.rutgers.edu/accounting/raw/IIA. This Institute of Internal Auditors site includes association news releases on ethics, professional standards, and membership options.

Multiple-choice Questions for Practice and Review

17.22 Which of the following is considered different and more limited in objectives than the others?

a. Operational auditing.
b. Performance auditing.
c. Management auditing.
d. Financial statement auditing.

17.23 A typical objective of an operational audit is for the auditor to:

a. Determine whether the financial statements fairly present the company's operations.

b. Evaluate the feasibility of attaining the company's operational objectives.

c. Make recommendations for achieving company objectives.

d. Report on the company's relative success in attaining profit maximization.

17.24 A government auditor assigned to audit the financial statements of the provincial highway department would not be considered independent if the auditor:

a. also held a position as a project manager in the highway department.

b. Was the provincial audit official elected in a general statewide election with responsibility to report to the legislature.

c. Normally works as a provincial auditor employed in the department of human services.

d. Was appointed by the provincial minister with responsibility to report to the legislature.

17.25 Government auditing can extend beyond audits of financial statements to include audits of an agency's efficient and economical use of resources and:

a. Constitutionality of laws and regulations governing the agency.

b. Evaluation of the personal managerial skills shown by the agency's leaders.

c. Correspondence of the agency's performance with public opinion regarding the social worth of its mission.

d. Evaluations concerning the agency's achievements of the goals set by the legislature for the agency's activities.

17.26 Which of the following best describes how the detailed audit program of the external auditor who is engaged to audit the financial statements of a large publicly held company compares with the audit client's comprehensive internal audit program?

a. The comprehensive internal audit program covers areas that would normally not be reviewed by the external auditor.

b. The comprehensive internal audit program is more detailed although it covers fewer areas than would normally be covered by the external auditor.

c. The comprehensive internal audit program is substantially identical to the audit program used by the external auditor because both review substantially identical areas.

d. The comprehensive internal audit program is less detailed and covers fewer areas than would normally be reviewed by the external auditor.

17.27 Which of the following would you not expect to see in an auditor's report(s) on the financial statements of an independent government agency?

a. A statement that the audit was conducted in accordance with generally accepted government audit standards.

b. A report on the agency's compliance with applicable laws and regulations.

c. Commentary by the agency's managers on the audit findings and recommendations.

d. A report on the agency's internal control structure.

17.28 Public Sector Auditing Standards require auditors to determine and report several things about provincial and local governments that receive federal funds. Which of the following is not normally required to be reported?

a. An opinion on the fair presentation of the financial statements in accordance with generally accepted accounting principles.

b. A report on the government's internal control structure related to the federal funds.

c. The government's performance in meeting goals set in enabling legislation.

d. A report on the government's compliance with applicable laws and regulations.

17.29 In government and internal performance auditing, which of the following is the least important consideration when performing the field work?

a. Determining the applicable generally accepted government accounting principles pronounced by the GASB.

b. Defining problem areas or opportunities for improvement and defining program goals.

c. Selection and performance of procedures designed to obtain evidence about operational problems and production output.

d. Evaluation of evidence in terms of economy, efficiency, and achievement of program goals.

17.30 Which of the following is the least important consideration for a government auditor who needs to be objective when auditing and reporting on an agency's achievement of program goals?

a. Measure the actual output results of agency activities.

b. Compare the agency's actual output results to quantitative goal standards.

c. Perform a comprehensive review of administrative controls.

d. Determine quantitative standards that describe goals the agency was supposed to achieve.

17.31 When an external auditor obtains an understanding of a client's internal control structure in connection with the annual audit of financial statements, the external auditor must obtain information and evaluate:

a. The competence and objectivity of the internal auditors.

b. The education, experience, and certification of the internal auditors.

c. The employment of internal auditors' relatives in management positions.

d. The internal audit department and its program of work.

17.32 Compliance auditing in audits performed in accordance with public sector auditing standards is necessary for an auditor's:

a. Report on the auditee's internal control, including reportable conditions and material weaknesses.

b. Opinion on the auditee's observance, or lack thereof, of applicable laws and regulations.

c. Opinion on the auditee's financial statements.

d. Report of a supplementary schedule of federal assistance programs and amounts.

Exercises and Problems

17.33 Identification of Audits and Auditors. Audits may be characterized as (*a*) financial statement audits, (*b*) compliance audits, (*c*) economy and efficiency audits, and (*d*) program results audits. The work can be done by independent (external) auditors, internal auditors, or governmental auditors (including Revenue Canada auditors and federal bank examiners). Below is a list of the purpose or products of various audit engagements.

1. Determining the equity of interest rates charged on federally guaranteed loans to students.

2. Determining the fair presentation in conformity with GAAP of an advertising agency's financial statements.

3. Study of Ministry of Natural Resources (MNR) policies and practices on grant-related income.

4. Determination of costs of municipal garbage pickup services compared to comparable service subcontracted to a private business.

5. Audit of tax shelter partnership financing terms.

6. Study of a private aircraft manufacturer's test pilot performance in reporting on the results of test flights.

7. Periodic Superintendent of Financial Institution examination of a bank for solvency.

8. Evaluation of the promptness of materials inspection in a manufacturer's receiving department.

9. Report of how better care and disposal of vehicles confiscated by drug enforcement agents could save money and benefit law enforcement.

10. Rendering a public report on the assumptions and compilation of a revenue forecast by a sports stadium/racetrack complex.

Required:

Prepare a three-column schedule showing (1) each of the engagements listed above; (2) the type of audit (financial statement, compliance, economy and efficiency, or program results); and (3) the kinds of auditors you would expect to be involved.

17.34 Organizing a Preliminary Survey. You are the director of internal auditing of a large municipal hospital. You receive monthly financial reports prepared by the accounting department, and your review of them has shown that total accounts receivable from patients has steadily and rapidly increased over the past eight months.

Other information in the reports shows the following conditions:

a. The number of available hospital beds has not changed.

b. The bed occupancy rate has not changed.

c. Hospital billing rates have not changed significantly.

d. The hospitalization insurance contracts have not changed since the last modification 12 months ago.

Your internal audit department audited the accounts receivable 10 months ago. The working paper file for that assignment contains financial information, a record of the preliminary survey, documentation of the study and evaluation of administrative and internal accounting controls, documentation of the evidence-gathering procedures used to produce evidence about the validity and collectibility of the accounts, and a copy of your report which commented favourably on the controls and collectibility of the receivables.

However, the current increase in receivables has alerted you to a need for another audit so that things will not get out of hand. You remember news stories last year about the manager of the city water system who got into big trouble because his accounting department double-billed all the residential customers for three months.

Required:

You plan to perform a preliminary survey in order to get a handle on the problem, if indeed a problem exists. Write a memo to your senior auditor listing at least eight questions he should use to guide and direct the preliminary survey. (Hint: The questions used in the last preliminary survey were organized under these headings: (1) Who does the accounts receivable accounting? (2) What data processing procedures and policies are in effect? and (3) How is the accounts receivable accounting done? This time, you will add a fourth category: What financial or economic events have occurred in the last 10 months?)

(CIA adapted)

17.35 Study and Evaluation of Administrative Control. The study and evaluation of administrative controls in a governmental or internal audit is not easy. First, auditors must determine the controls subject to audit. Then, they must find a standard by which performance of the control can be evaluated. Next, they must specify procedures to obtain the evidence on which an evaluation can be based. Insofar as possible, the standards and related evidence must be quantified.

Students working on this case usually do not have the experience or theoretical background to figure out control standards and audit procedures, so the description below gives certain information (in italics) that internal auditors would know about or be able to figure out on their own. Fulfilling the requirement thus amounts to taking some information from the scenario below and figuring out other things by using accountants' and auditors' common sense.

The Scenario: Ace Corporation ships building materials to more than a thousand wholesale and retail customers in a five-province region. The company's normal credit terms are net/30 days, and no cash discounts are offered. Fred Clark is the chief financial officer, and he is concerned about maintaining control over customer credit. In particular, he has stated two administrative control principles for this purpose.

1. Sales are to be billed to customers accurately and promptly. Fred knows that errors will occur but thinks company personnel ought to be able to hold quantity, unit price, and arithmetic errors down to 3 percent of the sales invoices. He considers an invoice error of $1 or less not to matter. He believes that prompt billing is important since customers are expected to pay within 30 days. Fred is very strict in thinking that a bill should be sent to the customer one day after shipment. He believes that he has staffed the billing department well enough to be able to handle this workload. The relevant company records consist of an accounts receivable control account; a subsidiary ledger of customers' accounts in which charges are entered by billing (invoice) date and credits are entered by date of payment receipts; a sales journal that lists invoices in chronological order; and a file of shipping documents cross-referenced by the number on the related sales invoice copy kept on file in numerical order.

2. Accounts receivable are to be aged and followed up to ensure prompt collection. Fred has told the accounts receivable department to classify all the customer accounts in categories of (*a*) current, (*b*) 31–59 days overdue, (*c*) 60–90 days overdue, and (*d*) more than 90 days overdue. He wants this trial balance to be complete and to be transmitted to the credit department within five days of each month-end. In the credit department, prompt follow-up means sending a different (stronger) collection letter to each category, cutting off credit to customers over 60 days past due (put-

ting them on cash basis), and giving the over-90-days accounts to an outside collection agency. These actions are supposed to be taken within five days after receipt of the aged trial balance. The relevant company records, in addition to the ones listed above, consist of the aged trial balance, copies of the letters sent to customers, copies of notices of credit cutoff, copies of correspondence with the outside collection agent, and reports of results—statistics of subsequent collections.

Required:

Take the role of a senior internal auditor. You are to write a memo to the internal audit staff to inform them about comparison standards for the study and evaluation of these two administrative control policies. You also need to specify two or three procedures for gathering evidence about performance of the controls. The body of your memo should be structured as follows:

1. Control: Sales are billed to customers accurately and promptly.
   a. Accuracy.
      (1) Policy standard ...
      (2) Audit procedures ...
   b Promptness.
      (1) Policy standard ...
      (2) Audit procedures ...

2. Control: Accounts receivable are aged and followed up to ensure prompt collection.
   a. Accounts receivable aging.
      (1) Policy standard ...
      (2) Audit procedures ...
   b. Follow-up prompt collection.
      (1) Policy standard ...
      (2) Audit procedures ...

17.36 Analytical Review of Inventory. External auditors usually calculate inventory turnover (cost of goods sold for the year divided by average inventory) and use the ratio as a broad indication of inventory age, obsolescence, or overstocking. External auditors are interested in evidence relating to the material accuracy of the financial statements taken as a whole. Internal auditors, on the other hand, calculate turnover by categories and classes of inventory in order to detect problem areas that might otherwise get overlooked. This kind of detailed analytical review might point to conditions of buying errors, obsolescence, overstocking, and other matters that could be changed to save money.

The data shown in Exhibit 17.36–1 are turnover, cost of sales, and inventory investment data for a series of four historical years and the current year. In each of the historical years, the external auditors did not recommend any adjustments to the inventory valuations.

Required:
Calculate the current year inventory turnover ratios. Interpret the ratio trends and point out what conditions might exist, and write a memo to the vice president for production explaining your findings and the further investigation that can be conducted.

17.37 PA Involvement in an Expanded-Scope Audit. A public accounting firm received an invitation to bid for the audit of a local food commodity distribution program funded by the Ministry of Agriculture. The audit is to be conducted in accordance with the public sector audit standards published by the CICA. The accountants have

EXHIBIT 17.36–1 **INVENTORY DATA**

	Inventory Turnover				Current-year Inventory (000)	
	19X1	19X2	19X3	19X4	Beginning	Ending
Total inventory	2.1	2.0	2.1	2.1	$3,000	$2,917
Materials and parts	4.0	4.1	4.3	4.5	1,365	620
Work in process	12.0	12.5	11.5	11.7	623	697
Finished products:						
Computer games	6.0	7.0	10.0	24.0	380	500
Floppy disk drives	8.0	7.2	7.7	8.5	64	300
Semiconductor parts	4.0	3.5	4.5	7.0	80	400
Electric typewriters	3.0	2.5	2.0	1.9	488	400

Additional Information

			Current Year (000)		
	Transfers	Sales	Cost of Goods Sold	Gross Profit	Compared to 19X4
Materials and parts	$3,970*	NA	NA	NA	
Work in process	7,988†	NA	NA	NA	
Computer games	2,320‡	$2,000	$2,200	$<200>	Sales volume declined 60%§
Floppy disk drives	2,236‡	3,000	2,000	1,000	Sales volume increased 35%
Semiconductor parts	2,720‡	4,000	2,400	1,600	Sales volume increased 40%
Electric typewriters	712‡	1,000	800	200	Sales volume declined 3%

NA means not available.
* Cost of materials transferred to Work in Process.
† Cost of materials, labour, and overhead transferred to Finished Goods.
‡ Cost of goods transferred from Work in Process to Finished Product Inventories.
§ Selling prices also were reduced and the gross margin declined.

become familiar with the public sector standards and recognize that the public sector standards incorporate the CICA generally accepted auditing standards (GAAS).

The public accounting firm has been engaged to perform the audit of the program, and the audit is to encompass both financial and performance audits that constitute the expanded scope of a public sector audit.

Required (See Appendix 17D):

a. The accountants should perform sufficient audit work to satisfy the financial and compliance element of the GAO standards. What is the objective of such audit work?

b. The accountants should be aware of general and specific kinds of uneconomical or inefficient practices in such a program. What are some examples?

c. What might be some standards and sources of standards for judging program results?

Discussion Cases

. . . .

17.38 Operational Audit: Customer Complaints. Danny Deck, the director of internal auditing for the Rice Department Stores, was working in his office one Thursday when Larry McMurray, president of the company, burst in to tell about a problem. According to Larry: "Customer complaints about delays in getting credit for merchandise returns are driving Sally Godwin up the wall! She doesn't know what to do because she has no control over the processing of credit memos."

Sally is the manager in charge of customer relations, and she tries to keep everybody happy. Upon her recommendation, the company adopted an advertising motto: "Satisfaction Guaranteed and Prompt Credit When You Change Your Mind." The motto is featured in newspaper ads and on large banners in each store.

Danny performed a preliminary review and found the following:

1. Sally believes that customers will be satisfied if they receive a refund cheque or notice of credit on account within five working days.

2. The chief accountant described the credit memo processing procedure as follows: When a customer returns merchandise, the sales clerks give a smile, a "returned merchandise receipt," and a promise to send a cheque or a notice within five days.

The store copy of the receipt and the merchandise is sent to the purchasing department, where buyers examine the merchandise for quality or damage to decide whether to put it back on the shelves, return it to the vendor, or hold it for the annual rummage sale. The buyers then prepare a brief report and send it with the returned merchandise receipt to the customer relations department for approval. The buyer's report is filed for reference and the receipt, marked for approval in Sally's department, is sent to the accounting department. The accounting department sorts the receipts in numerical order, checking the numerical sequence, and files them in readiness for the weekly batch processing of other transactions than sales and cash receipts, both of which are processed daily. When the customer has requested a cash refund, the cheques and cancelled returned merchandise receipt are approved by the treasurer, who signs and mails the cheque. When the credit is on a customer's charge account, it is shown on the next monthly statement sent to the customer.

3. The processing in each department takes two or three days.

Required:

a. Analyse the problem. How much time does it take the company to process the merchandise returns?

b. Formulate a recommendation to solve the problem. Write a brief report explaining your recommendation.

17.39 **Public Sector Auditor Independence (Study of Chapter 15 on Professional Ethics is recommended for this problem).** The public sector reporting standards for VFM audits state that each report should include "recommendations for action to correct the problem areas and to improve operations." For example, an audit of the Metropolitan Area Transit Authority found management decision deficiencies affecting some $230 million in provincial funds. The public sector auditors recommended that the transit authority improve its management control over subway car procurement through better enforcement of contract requirements and development of a master plan to test cars.

Suppose the transit authority accepted and implemented specific recommendations made by the OAG auditors. Do you believe these events would be enough to impair the independence of the OAG auditors in a subsequent audit of the transit authority? Explain, and tell if it makes any difference to you whether the same or a different person performs both the first and subsequent audits.

17.40 **Marketing Audit I.** During your eight years with a PA firm based in Winnipeg with offices in four other provinces, you had developed an increasing interest and reputation in the field of marketing. On one of your monthly trips to the Calgary office, you were invited to have lunch with James, the president and CEO of Vulcan Pharmaceuticals Inc. (VPI), which you knew as a strong competitor in a very competitive field. Your host came to the point over coffee:

"Your firm and your name were suggested to me by an executive at Chugalug Beverages, who credits your marketing recommendations with the turnaround in Chugalug's sales and profitability. It is no secret that the "drug game" is a competitive jungle. Products, distribution, prices, promotion, all have to be watched very carefully; otherwise you can wake up to discover you have been left behind by the competition. The picture at Vulcan is troubling. In 1993, we led the copetition with net income of $102 million on sales of $850 million; prospects seemed very rosy. But in 1994, sales dropped to $760 million and our net income to $48 million. I have just seen the forecast for 1995, and it is not good; specifically, the vice president finance is forecasting a further decline in sales to $680 million and net income just in the black at $10 million; I think he is being optimistic. The chairman is not happy at all, and neither am I.

"We have studied the problem at length, and remain convinced that we have the best research and franchise arrangements in Canada and that, building on these strengths, our products still lead the field. We are also convinced that our distribution arrangements are superior to those of all our major competitors. Where we seem vulnerable is in two areas: promotion, which is all advertising in this "game"; and pricing.

"I would like to make a presentation to our board, next week if possible, on how you would go about a management audit of marketing at VPI, including a brief outline of the sort of criteria you would use for advertising and pricing."

Required:

Prepare the marketing audit proposal to the board.

(CGAAC adapted)

17.41 Marketing Audit II. As director of management audit in the Ministry of Labour, Skills, and Employment Training, you had always been uneasy about the large contractual grants awarded for job training to the 67 provincial colleges and the large number of small training organizations—some commercial, some not-for-profit—that had recently been established. There was a rudimentary process of assessing applications, but essentially the ministry just paid the bill submitted by the training organizations. As a professional auditor, and, you hoped, a good public servant, you were very concerned about control and accountability.

There were two points of focus in your concern. First, you believed that current arrangements provided no incentives to efficiency in resource utilization or effectiveness in training program delivery. Second, while you considered that the required external financial audit by the provincial legislative auditor provided reasonable assurance of fiscal propriety, you also knew that the external auditors did not actually look for fraud, but only reported it if they came across it in the course of their audit of the financial statements. So you continued to have some concern about some scandal that would reflect on the ministry and your own department. To your surprise and relief, you found that the senior assistant deputy minister, who was also a PA, shared your concerns. Her note to you suggested a course of action:

> "I share your concerns about the hand-out program for job training. The colleges have a reasonable tradition of accountability, and I can live with that; it is the large number of small training organizations that concerns me. They are not accountable in any serious way to us, and, consequently, we cannot be accountable in any serious way to

Treasury Board for the resources we transfer to them—although we are sure to be blamed for something even though we cannot control it! The issue of the actual effectiveness of these programs is a matter I intend to avoid for the moment, but I would like to begin to deal with two accountability issues.

"The first issue relates to efficiency in resource utilization, and I would like you to work with two consultants who will arrive next week to write a planning memorandum for an efficiency audit of training programs in the large group of commercial and not-for-profit training organizations with which we had contractual arrangements. The part of the memorandum on which I want you to concentrate is the question of evidence. What constitutes evidence of efficiency in these organizations? How would you get that evidence?

"The second issue on which I would like to have your thoughts about the nature of evidence and how to get it, is with respect to fraud. I have received two unsigned notes over the last two months, and I got another one today, alleging that there is serious fraud in many of these training organizations, and that much of the information we get as justification for payment may be false. I want you to approach this matter as a confidential by-product of the efficiency audit and summarize your thoughts in a confidential memo. You should indicate what evidence would be needed and how it should be collected."

Required:

Prepare the two planning documents, one public, one confidential, as requested.

(CGAAC adapted)

17.42 DracuLab Inc. Six years as an audit manager in a PA firm, then five more as assistant director, management audit, in the provincial Ministry of Health had given you an appetite for new challeges in the health field. So you were pleased to be offered the position of executive director, management audit, reporting to the vice-president, finance and administration, in DracuLab Inc., a rapidly growing drug and medical equipment corporation with net income of $115 million on sales of $805 million in 1994. Your enthusiasm increased further during your first detailed briefing session with the vice-president:

"Welcome to DracuLab Inc. I have been arguing for a larger role for management audit for five years—your predecessor left in frustration when my attempt to increase her budget last year fell on stoney ground and the CEO and board have finally come around to my point of view (helped, I should add, by a note in the last management letter from our external auditor). You have a current staff of nine, consisting of seven accountants and two administrative people. I have secured a commitment for you to hire three more professional staff as soon as possible and to provide considerable flexibility to extend your staff on a contractual basis as needed over the next year.

"As you know, this is a very technical multiproduct corporation with a wide range of technical professional staff. My sense is that these people see management audit as simply a minor extension of the accounting department, and they doubt that you have the skills to say anything intelligent and helpful about their specialized tasks. And it is precisely in these technical areas that the external auditor and I have strong reservations about our management controls.

"While you are working on your staffing, I would also like you to take a first step towards building confidence in your area by coming to the executive meeting and making a presentation that focuses directly on the professional skills of your department, including the hiring of supplementary personnel and the use of specialists on a contractual basis."

Required:

Prepare the presentation for the Executive meeting.

(CGAAC adapted)

17.43 Natran Inc., a Crown Corporation. In your role as director of internal audit for Natran, Inc., a federal Crown corporation with revenues of $3 billion in 1993–94 and 37,000 employees across the country, you employed your 15 professional and six support staff in a variety of functions. In the last three years, the proportions of your work related to compliance with legislation and regulations, and to value-for-money questions, had risen to 30 percent and 40 percent, respectively. When the vice president summoned you to a meeting just after the presentation of your proposed audit plan and budget for the forthcoming year, you anticipated having to defend what you considered a barely sufficient audit plan in the light of the risks facing Natran. The vice president was concerned about audit budgets, but concern was focused on the soaring cost of the independent external audit that Natran was obliged by statute to undergo each year.

"I have always been unhappy with what I consider the ridiculously high fees we have to pay for the traditional external attest audit of our financial statements. But things are getting much worse. Now we are faced with much higher costs as the external auditor feels obliged not only to address the compliance issues that get a lot of public attention, but also, as a consequence of the revisions to the Financial Administration Act, to get into a host of value-for-money issues and to more or less insist that management prepare a set of auditable assertions on value for money, broadly defined. The proposed bill for all this work is staggering, and I need your advice on how we can minimize the costs of our external audit.

"Specifically, I want your advice on how we can co-ordinate the roles of internal audit and external audit to accomplish the total audit effort in the most effective and efficient way. The Financial Administration Act obliges the external auditor to use your work and to indicate the extent of reliance. What I want to see is a very large degree of reliance. I would like you to make a presentation to the audit committee of the board in a couple of weeks on the issue. You should introduce the topic by pointing to the benefits to Natran of coordinated audit work, and tell the committee what your Internal Audit Standards say on the topic. That should take about one-third of your presentation.

"For the balance of your presentation I would like you to present a proposal to maximize the potential usefulness of your department to the external auditor in his areas of responsibility. Indicate what you do now that would be helpful, and also indicate how you could adapt your work program using existing resources to be even more helpful since there is no way I can get you additional staff this year. I know the external auditor has the highest regard for you and your staff, and would almost certainly welcome more audit co-ordination. But the ball is, I believe, in our court. It is our responsibility to act. I look forward to your help in reducing this burden."

Required:
Prepare the requested presentation.

(CGAAC adapted)

17.44 TechNet, a Software Company. Your role as vice president, management audit, in TechNet, Inc., was always challenging and occasionally trying. TechNet had become the biggest software corporation in Canada three years ago when it took over two strong competitors. Profit in 1993–94 was $103 million on total revenue of just over $3 billion. The CEO's philosophy was that competitive pressure was essential both externally and internally. While the three major divisions representing the original TechNet and its two corporate acquisitions were carefully co-ordinated, they were also required to compete against one another. There were no entitlements at TechNet. Even within each division, the CEO had established a belief in competitive survival, and managers of staff areas were required to demonstrate that their services were the most cost-effective available. Your role was to monitor this highly competitive corporate environment with 14 professionals—accountants and engineers—and six administrative staff. The management audit department was used to introduce bright new managers to the whole corporate environment at TechNet and to offer occasional revitalization to executives after a period on the "front line."

In one of your recent performance audits, you had been quite severe on the vice president (marketing) in one of the divisions, and she had responded angrily, accusing you of bias. She re-enforced this claim by arguing that the management audit staff member who had led the audit had joined the audit staff only eight months previously from one of the other divisions. She and her colleagues had also been heard to remark that it was time your department was "outsourced"— the current term for "contracted out"! Your meeting with the CEO to discuss the matter ended with his making the following proposal:

"I think that our senior staff need to trust your department and we need to reassure them in this respect. I would therefore like you to come to the senior staff meeting and make a presentation about the independence of your operations. The statement could actually take the form of a departmental policy statement on independence. By all means include the usual information on organizational status, but spend at least half your time on that difficult but critical concept of objectivity. I would be pleased to comment on your draft."

Required:

Draft the proposed presentation.

(CGAAC adapted)

17.45 Health Care Audit. You are director of management audit in United Metro Hospitals (UMH), which is a group of four hospitals with a total of 800 acute care and long-term care beds. Your role has been really that of a troubleshooter. When a problem arose (usually a systems problem of some sort), you were dispatched to fix it. The new CEO had been appointed with a mandate to change things, and he came to the point with you quite quickly.

"I have just come from a group of hospitals in southern Ontario, where the head of management audit served as my eyes and ears on areas of corporate risk, kept a strong internal evaluative tone, and was my major source of suggestions for change. I want you to play the same sort of reflective role here. I would like you to start with a part of traditional management audit. We are all going to have to build a value-for-money culture in our primary services, but that is going to take some time. Where I want to start is with our support services, and, within that group, specifically the purchasing department. Excluding capital purchases, we spent nearly $15 million last year on the host of

items we need to keep the hospital running—drugs, minor equipment, food, and so on—and that figure has been growing by ten percent each year for the last four years. We have a Purchasing Department with an impressive director—Mary Thompson—four professionals, and two administrative support staff, who are responsible for making sure that all necessary items of the appropriate quality are obtained at the best prices in town. With our market clout, we should have no problems. But I have heard more complaints from administrative and clinical staff about the Purchasing Department than any other support area.

"Obviously, I discount the usual nonsense from those who claim that their brother-in-law working out of his basement can offer a better deal, but there is certainly a broad perception that something is wrong. So I want you to begin with Purchasing. Please come to the hospital executive committee next week with a presentation, which should include the following: first, a brief comment on the current role and main activities of purchasing in UMH; second, and as the core of your presentation, a discussion of the purchasing activities you propose to audit and the approach you would follow in conducting the audit (including some illustrative criteria); and, finally, some preliminary reflections (which might actually help you in suggesting audit criteria) on how purchasing might grow into sophisticated supply management at UMH. Frankly, I think we need to bring the department into the 1990s, and your audit should be designed with such changes in mind."

Required:

Prepare the requested presentation.

(CGAAC adapted)

APPENDIX 17A

SUMMARY OF GENERAL AND SPECIFIC STANDARDS FOR THE PROFESSIONAL PRACTICE OF INTERNAL AUDITING*

· ·

100 **Independence. Internal auditors should be independent of the activities they audit**.

    110 Organizational Status. The organizational status of the internal auditing department should be sufficient to permit the accomplishment of its audit responsibilities.

    120 Objectivity. Internal auditors should be objective in performing audits.

200 **Professional Proficiency. Internal audits should be performed with proficiency and due professional care**.

THE INTERNAL AUDITING DEPARTMENT
· · · · · · · · · · ·

    210 Staffing. The internal auditing department should provide assurance that the technical proficiency and educational background of internal auditors are appropriate for the audits to be performed.

    220 Knowledge, Skills, and Disciplines. The internal auditing department should possess or should obtain the knowledge, skills, and disciplines needed to carry out its audit responsibilities.

    230 Supervision. The internal auditing department should provide assurance that internal audits are properly supervised.

THE INTERNAL AUDITOR
· · · · · · · · · · ·

    240 Compliance with Standards of Conduct. Internal auditors should comply with professional standards of conduct.

    250 Knowledge, Skills, and Disciplines. Internal auditors should possess the knowledge, skills, and disciplines essential to the performance of internal audits.

    260 Human Relations and Communications. Internal auditors should be skilled in dealing with people and in communicating effectively.

    270 Continuing Education. Internal auditors should maintain their technical competence through continuing education.

    280 Due Professional Care. Internal auditors should exercise due professional care in performing internal audits.

300 Scope of Work. **The scope of the internal audit should encompass the examination and evaluation of the adequacy and effectiveness of the organization's system of internal control and the quality of performance in carrying out assigned responsibilities**.

310 Reliability and Integrity of Information. Internal auditors should review the reliability and integrity of financial and operating information and the means used to identify, measure, classify, and report such information.

320 Compliance with Policies, Plans, Procedures, Laws, and Regulations. Internal auditors should review the systems established to ensure compliance with those policies, plans, procedures, laws, and regulations which could have a significant impact on operations and reports and should determine whether the organization is in compliance.

330 Safeguarding of Assets. Internal auditors should review the means of safeguarding assets, and, as appropriate, verify the existence of such assets.

340 Economical and Efficient Use of Resources. Internal auditors should appraise the economy and efficiency with which resources are employed.

350 Accomplishment of Established Objectives and Goals for Operations or Programs. Internal auditors should review operations or programs to ascertain whether results are consistent with established objectives and goals and whether the operations or programs are being carried out as planned.

400 **Performance of Audit Work. Audit work should include planning the audit, examining and evaluating information, communicating results, and following up**.

410 Planning the Audit. Internal auditors should plan each audit.

420 Examining and Evaluating Information. Internal auditors should collect, analyze, interpret, and document information to support audit results.

430 Communicating Results. Internal auditors should report the results of their audit work.

440 Following Up. Internal auditors should follow up to ascertain that appropriate action is taken on reported audit findings.

500 **Management of the Internal Auditing Department. The director of internal auditing should properly manage the internal auditing department**.

510 Purpose, Authority, and Responsibility. The director of internal auditing should have a statement of purpose, authority, and responsibility for the internal auditing department.

520 Planning. The director of internal auditing should establish plans to carry out the responsibilities of the internal auditing department.

530 Policies and Procedures. The director of internal auditing should provide written policies and procedures to guide the audit staff.

540 Personnel Management and Development. The director of internal auditing should establish a program for selecting and developing the human resources of the internal auditing department.

550 External Auditors. The director of internal auditing should coordinate internal and external audit efforts.

560 Quality Assurance. The director of internal auditing should establish and maintain a quality assurance program to evaluate the operations of the internal auditing department.

APPENDIX 17B

THE INSTITUTE OF INTERNAL AUDITORS CODE OF ETHICS*

PURPOSE

A distinguishing mark of a profession is acceptance by its members of responsibility to the interests of those it serves. Members of The Institute of Internal Auditors (Members) and Certified Internal Auditors (CIAs) must maintain high standards of conduct in order to effectively discharge this responsibility. The Institute of Internal Auditors (Institute) adopts this Code of Ethics for Members and CIAs.

APPLICABILITY

This Code of Ethics is applicable to all Members and CIAs. Membership in The Institute and acceptance of the "Certified Internal Auditor" designation are voluntary actions. By acceptance, Members and CIAs assume an obligation of self-discipline above and beyond the requirements of laws and regulations.

The standards of conduct set forth in this Code of Ethics provide basic principles in the practice of internal auditing. Members and CIAs should realize that their individual judgement is required in the application of these principles.

CIAs shall use the "Certified Internal Auditor" designation with discretion and in a dignified manner, fully aware of what the designation denotes. The designation shall also be used in a manner consistent with all statutory requirements.

Members who are judged by the Board of Directors of The Institute to be in violation of the standards of conduct of the Code of Ethics shall be subject to forfeiture of their membership in The Institute. CIAs who are similarly judged also shall be subject of forfeiture of the "Certified Internal Auditor" designation.

STANDARDS OF CONDUCT

I.   Members and CIAs shall exercise honesty, objectivity, and diligence in the performance of their duties and responsibilities.

II. Members and CIAs shall exhibit loyalty in all matters pertaining to the affairs of their organizations or to whomever they may be rendering a service. However, Members and CIAs shall not knowingly be a party to any illegal or improper activity.

III. Members and CIAs shall not knowingly engage in acts or activities which are discreditable to the profession of internal auditing or to their organization.

IV. Members and CIAs shall refrain from entering into any activity which may be in conflict with the interest of their organization or which would prejudice their ability to carry out objectively their duties and responsibilities.

V. Members and CIAs shall not accept anything of value from an employee, client, customer, supplier, or business associate of their organization which would impair or be presumed to impair their professional judgment.

VI. Members and CIAs shall undertake only those services which they can reasonably expect to complete with professional competence.

VII. Members and CIAs shall adopt suitable means to comply with the Standards for the Professional Practice of Internal Auditing.

VIII. Members and CIAs shall be prudent in the use of information acquired in the course of their duties. They shall not use confidential information for any personal gain not in any manner which would be contrary to law or detrimental to the welfare of their organization.

IX. Members and CIAs, when reporting on the results of their work, shall reveal all material facts known to them which, if not revealed, could either distort reports or operations under review or conceal unlawful practices.

X. Members and CIAs shall continually strive for improvement in their proficiency, and in the effectiveness and quality of their service.

XI. Members and CIAs, in the practice of their profession, shall be ever mindful of their obligation to maintain the high standards of competence, morality, and dignity promulgated by The Institute. Members shall abide by the bylaws and uphold the objectives of The Institute.

APPENDIX 17C

ABRIDGED SUMMARY OF PUBLIC SECTOR AUDITING INTERPRETATION AND APPLICATION (PS 6410): PLANNING VFM AUDITS (MARCH 1990)

Like the guidelines in the *CICA Handbook*, these guides are developed to help auditors interpret and apply the PSs. This interpretation discusses planning considerations of the audit mandate, knowledge of the entity, audit objectives and scope, criteria, audit evidence, and the audit plan.

For purposes of this interpretation, the client may be a legislature or other elected or appointed governing body that delegates to management authority and responsibility for acquiring and using the entity's resources. Management may consist of various combinations of elected and appointed officials who are responsible for the administration of those resources and are accountable to the legislature or other governing body. The auditor is an independent third party who examines elements of management's performance and reports the results of the audit to the client.

Although both financial statement and VFM audits are based on an auditor examining and reporting information related to an accountability relationship between client and management, there are some important differences between the two types of audit. The distinctive features of VFM audits include the following:

- Audit mandates may provide the auditor with discretion in establishing the audit objectives and scope.

- Audit objectives and scope vary from one audit to another.

- Audits address a variety of matters that are not necessarily of a financial nature (e.g., human resource management).

- There is no body of generally accepted criteria analogous to GAAP for financial statement audits.

- The nature and sources of evidence may differ from those in financial statement audits.

- Multidisciplinary audit team members may be used to a greater extent than in financial statements audits.

- Audits may not relate to a standard time period, unlike financial statement audits, which generally relate to fiscal years of the entities audited.

- There is no generally accepted standard short-form report; auditors may use direct reporting, either by reporting deficiencies or providing an overall opinion, or they may attest to management assertions.

Audit mandates specify what is required of auditors and provide auditors with the authority to carry out their work and report. The amount of discretion an auditor has in establishing the objectives and scope of a VFM audit varies. Some VFM audit mandates embodied in legislation provide only general direction about objectives and scope. In such cases the auditor decides on audit objectives and scope for a particular VFM audit. Other legislated mandates, such as that for special examinations of federal Crown corporations, may be more specific in defining objectives and scope. In contractual mandates audit objectives and scope are usually specified by the client. In such cases the auditor would assess the appropriateness of the audit objectives and scope before accepting the engagement.

VFM audit mandates also have different reporting requirements. Many mandates require direct reporting about the entity. For example, auditors may report deficiencies, or provide an opinion on whether there is reasonable assurance, based on specified criteria, that there are no significant deficiencies in the system and practices examined. Auditors may be asked to attest to management assertions. When the mandate does not specify the reporting requirements, auditors would choose, often in consultation with their clients, how the results of the audit will be reported. The reporting requirements affect the nature and extent of work that must be performed in the audit.

Knowledge of the entity is important for audit planning. This knowledge is initially obtained on a first-time audit during the preliminary review of survey. On subsequent audits the preliminary review is a way of updating knowledge of the entity. The knowledge required in the preliminary review permits the auditor to identify the areas to be addressed in more depth later in the audit. The process of obtaining knowledge about the entity continues throughout the audit and subsequent information may have an effect on the initial planning decisions.

In conducting the preliminary review the auditor would examine the important features of the entity including (1) the nature of the entity, (2) accountability relation-ships, (3) program, operations, and activities, (4) performance (5) resources, (6) systems controls and practices, (7) work environment, (8) government priorities, (9) external environment, (10) risks, (11) constraints, and (12) constituents.

Each of these is discussed in the interpretation. In order to avoid possible misun-derstanding, it is desirable for auditors to communicate their understanding of the entity to management and, when possible, to their clients. This may be a verbal or written communication, such as a report of the preliminary review.

Audit objectives and scope must be established for all VFM audits to provide a framework for the audit. They are closely linked. Audit objectives relate to why the audit is being conducted and are based on the audit mandate. Audit scope is defined in terms of the entity or portion thereof, the matters, and the time period subject to audit.

Auditors generally consider factors such as significance, risk, auditability, re-source requirements, and timing when establishing or assessing the objectives and scope of a VFM audit. These factors are interrelated, and the sequence in which they are assessed depends on the circumstances of the audit.

Significance and Risk

In VFM auditing, significance (materiality) consists of qualitative and quantitative considerations, including (1) financial magnitude, (2) importance, (3) economic, social, and environmental impact, (4) management action with respect to important issues previously raised, (5) interest expressed in the matters, and (6) impact of centralized function. These are discussed in paragraph 19 of the interpretation.

In setting the objectives and scope of a VFM audit, the auditor needs to consider components of audit risk, including the likelihood of an occurrence of a lack of due regard for money (inherent risk) and the likelihood of an inadequacy in a system, control, or practice designed to ensure VFM (i.e., control risk).

Audit risk is affected by many factors, including (1) the diversity, consistency, and clarity of the entity's objectives and goals, (2) the complexity of operations, (3) the complexity and quality of management information and control systems and external reporting, (4) the nature and degree of change in the environment or within the entity, (5) the program delivery method, (6) and the nature of transactions. These are discussed in paragraph 21 of the interpretation.

The auditor should identify all areas of the entity that are significant and/or high risk when establishing or assessing the audit objectives and scope. In doing so significance and risk would be assessed together. The auditor should plan to examine significant areas where the risk is high and other areas that are significant in terms of achieving VFM, even where the risk is judged low. Insignificant areas, whether the risk is high or low, may be reviewed to confirm the auditor's judgment, but would not generally be examined in detail.

Auditability relates to whether an audit can be done. The auditor needs to assess whether an audit with the proposed objectives and scope can be conducted. To accomplish this the auditor would consider whether:

- There are relevant approaches, methodologies, and criteria available.
- The information or evidence required is likely to be available and can be obtained efficiently.

Criteria

Auditors need criteria against which to evaluate matters subject to audit. Criteria are reasonable and attainable standards of performance and control against which the adequacy of systems and practices and the extent of VFM can be assessed. Reasonable and attainable criteria are those that management can be realistically expected to meet.

Criteria must be suitable, or else inappropriate conclusions may be drawn. Suitable criteria are defined in paragraph 27 of PS 5400. Suitability of criteria depends on factors such as (1) the audit objectives, (2) the activity, and (3) the approach to audit.

Some characteristics of suitable criteria include:

1. reliability
2. objectivity (freedom from bias)
3. usefulness
4. understandability
5. acceptability
6. comparability
7. completeness

These characteristics are considered together in identifying criteria and assessing their suitability. The relative importance of the characteristics in different circumstances is a matter of professional judgment. The level of detail of the audit conclusions is affected by the level of detail at which audit criteria are specified. At the planning stage criteria may be identified at a relatively general level. However, more specific criteria would generally be identified for audit examination. Criteria can be developed from many sources but may require interpretation and modification to ensure their suitability.

Audit Evidence

When planning a VFM audit, it is important that the auditor identify the probable nature, sources, and availability of audit evidence required. Factors to consider include:

1. The effect of the audit approach.

2. The ability to integrate audit work with other audits or studies (e.g., work of internal auditors).

3. The effect of the reporting requirements. The amount of evidence required to form an overall opinion on an entity may be relatively greater than that needed to identify and report audit deficiencies.

4. The cost of obtaining evidence.

Audit Plan

The results of audit planning would be reflected in an audit plan. The audit plan documents key planning information and decisions such as:

- The auditor's understanding of the entity.
- The audit objectives.
- The scope of the audit (i.e., the entity or portion thereof, the matters and time period subject to audit).
- The planned criteria.
- The probable nature, sources, and availability of evidence.
- The resources required.
- The work schedule.
- The reporting requirements and timing of the report.

As additional information becomes available during the audit, the audit plan may need to be modified. Inclusion of the above information in the audit plan provides evidence of compliance with VFM auditing standards on planning.

There are many similarities between assurance engagements (*Section* 5025) and VFM engagements. An interesting feature of the Exposure Draft of *Section* 5025 was an illustration of a direct reporting engagement report using a VFM audit as an example. Although this illustration was dropped from the final version of 5025, we include it here as Exhibit 17C–1 to show what a VFM audit report might look like when characterized as an assurance engagement. Note that this is not just a report of deficiencies, since an overall conclusion on the "subject-matter" is also provided.

EXHIBIT 17C–1   CICA EXPOSURE DRAFT STANDARDS FOR ASSURANCE ENGAGEMENTS—
OCTOBER 1995 EXAMPLE REPORT 8

- long-form report
- high level of assurance
- direct report engagement
- significant weakness
- qualification
- additional information contained in explanatory paragraphs

(This report would be one of several value-for-money audits reported together in an Auditor General's report. A cover page to the report would show the addressee as the Members of the Legislative Assembly and would be signed by the Auditor General. The report might also include detailed explanations of recommended remedial action and the Ministry's responses to each of the recommendations.)

CHAPTER Y
Value-For-Money Audit
Ministry of XY-COMMERCIALIZATION OF INTELLECTUAL PROPERTY

Audit objectives

We had two objectives for this audit. First, we assessed whether the Ministry of XY adequately identified, protected and developed the commercial potential of intellectual property arising from its research and development activities. Second, we assessed whether the Ministry collected royalties owed to the Crown.

During the period of January 1 to November 1, 19XX, we examined all significant activities of the Ministry in this regard, in particular the work of its Commercialization Unit.

Audit Criteria

We assessed the Ministry's performance against the following criteria.

1. The Ministry should recognize the commercial potential of intellectual property as early as possible in the life cycle of a research project.
2. The Ministry's rights over intellectual property should be safeguarded.
3. The commercial application of intellectual property should be fully developed at least cost.
4. All royalties due the Crown should be collected.

These criteria are discussed more fully in the detailed findings following the conclusion paragraph.

Management's responsibilities

In 1993-94, the Ministry spent $250 million on research and development. Since 1985, it has been the policy of the Ministry to protect and exploit the commercial potential of the intellectual property arising from its research work. The Ministry's Commercialization Unit is responsible for:

(a) assisting in the identification of intellectual property with promising commercial potential;
(b) safeguarding the ownership of intellectual property resulting from research funded by the Ministry;
(c) developing commercial application of the Ministry's intellectual property; and
(d) collecting royalties.

Once intellectual property has been identified, the Unit works in partnership with private sector contractors to develop its commercial potential. The Ministry collects $15 million in royalties annually.

Auditor's responsibility

Our responsibility is to express an opinion on the Ministry's performance in carrying out these responsibilities. To do so, we examined a representative sample of research projects under way during our audit that were at various stages in their life cycle. We also examined relevant management processes and practices.

We conducted our audit in accordance with generally accepted auditing standards for value-for-money audit engagements promulgated by The Canadian Institute of Chartered Accountants. Those standards require that we plan and perform an audit to obtain reasonable assurance in support of our conclusion. An audit includes examining

evidence, on a test basis, in order to conclude on the audit objective based on the criteria. Our audit work was completed on December 31, 19XX.

Significant weakness

Our audit revealed that the Ministry was taking little action to systematically identify the commercial potential of its intellectual property. As a result, there was a considerable risk that the commercial potential of intellectual property was not recognized at all, or was recognized much later than it could have been.

Conclusion

In our opinion, except for the effect of the significant weakness described above, once the commercial potential of intellectual property had been recognized, the Ministry adequately protected and developed it, and adequately collected royalties due based on the criteria described above.

Detailed Findings

For the projects we examined, we found many instances where the Ministry had only recognized the commercial potential of its intellectual property several years after the discoveries had been made. There were also several instances where research papers had already been published although no assessment of the commercial potential had been done, thereby jeopardizing the possibility of protecting the Ministry's rights over any potential applications that might have resulted. There are two reasons for this. First, the Ministry does not consider whether a research project might result in intellectual property with commercial potential when these projects are initiated. Second, the Ministry does not attempt to monitor projects as they progress; for example, by assessing their commercial potential at pre-determined intervals. Instead, when commercial potential was identified, it was because a research team had recognized, or is recognized much later than it could be.

For those research projects that we examined where the potential for commercialization had been identified, we found that appropriate legal steps had been taken to protect the Ministry's legal rights. For the most part, this was accomplished through patent applications as well as license agreements and copyrights. We also found that appropriate security arrangements were in place. However, as discussed above, there may be other projects when protection might have been appropriate but had not been sought.

The Ministry contracts with private sector firms to develop the commercial application of intellectual property. If a commercial product results, the development firm receives an exclusive license to exploit it. The Ministry receives royalties in return (usually 30%). In this way, the Ministry passes on the cost, and the risk, of development to its partner. Although a high failure rate would normally be expected, we found that fully three-quarters of the intellectual property that contractors had attempted to develop had resulted in a marketable product.

We found that the Ministry collects the royalties owed to the Crown. The Ministry is exercising satisfactory control over this income. It receives an annual return from contractors on royalties due and takes appropriate action to verify these amounts are correct and are collected on a timely basis. [further background and elaboration of the findings]

Appendix 17D

Abridged Summary of U.S. Standards for Audit of Governmental Organizations, Programs, Activities, and Functions (1988 Revision)

. . . .

Scope of Audit Work
. . . .

Audits may have a combination of financial and performance audit objectives, or may have objectives limited to only some aspects of one audit type. Auditors should follow the appropriate generally accepted government audit standards (GAGAS) that are applicable to the individual objectives of the audit.

Financial Statement Audits.

a. Financial statement audits determine (1) whether the financial statements of an audited entity present fairly the financial position, results of operation, and cash flows or changes in financial position in accordance with generally accepted accounting principles, and (2) whether the entity has complied with laws and regulations for those transactions and events that may have a material effect on the financial statements.

2. Performance Audits.

a. Economy and efficiency audits include determining (1) whether the entity is acquiring, protecting, and using its resources (such as personnel, property, and space) economically and efficiently, (2) the causes of inefficiencies or uneconomical practices, and (3) whether the entity has complied with laws and regulations concerning matters of economy and efficiency.

b. Program audits include determining (1) the extent to which the desired results or benefits established by the legislature or other authorizing body are being achieved, (2) the effectiveness of organizations, programs, activities, or functions, and (3) whether the agency has complied with laws and regulations applicable to the program.

General Standards
. . . .

Qualifications. The staff assigned to conduct the audit should collectively possess adequate professional proficiency for the tasks required.

2. *Independence.* In all matters relating to the audit work, the audit organization and the individual auditors, whether government or public, must be free from personal and external impairments to independence, should be organizationally independent, and should maintain an independent attitude and appearance.

3. *Due professional care.* Due professional care should be used in conducting the audit and in preparing related reports.

4. *Quality Control.* Audit organizations conducting government audits should have an appropriate internal quality control system in place and participate in an external quality control review program.

FINANCIAL AUDITS

. . . .

Field Work Standards for Financial Audits

The GAGAS standards of field work incorporate the AICPA standards of field work for financial audits (GAAS) and prescribe supplemental standards to satisfy the unique needs of government financial audits.

2. Planning shall include consideration of the requirements of all levels of government.

3. A test should be made of compliance with applicable laws and regulations, including: (*a*) the auditor should design audit steps and procedures to provide reasonable assurance of detecting errors, irregularities, and illegal acts that could have a direct and material effect on the financial statement amounts or the results of financial related audits, and (*b*) the auditor should also be aware of the possibility of illegal acts that could have an indirect and material effect on the financial statements or the results of financial related audits.

4. A record of the auditors' work should be retained in the form of working papers, which should:
   a. Contain a written audit program cross-referenced to the working papers.
   b. Contain the objective, scope, methodology, and results of the audit.
   c. Contain sufficient information so that supplementary oral explanations are not required.
   d. Be legible with adequate indexing and cross-referencing, and include summaries and lead schedules, as appropriate.
   e. Restrict information included to matters that are materially important and relevant to the objectives of the audit.
   f. Contain evidence of supervisory reviews of the work conducted.

Reporting Standards for Financial Audits

The GAGAS standards of reporting incorporate the AICPA standards of reporting for financial audits (GAAS) and prescribe supplemental standards to satisfy the unique needs of government financial audits.

2. A statement should be included in the auditors' report that the audit was made in accordance with generally accepted government auditing standards (GAGAS).

3. The auditors should prepare a written report on their tests of compliance with applicable laws and regulations. This report should contain a statement of positive assurance on those items which were tested for compliance and negative assurance on those items not tested. It should include all material instances of noncompliance, and all instances or indications of illegal acts that could result in criminal prosecution.

4. The auditors should prepare a written report on their understanding of the entity's internal control structure and the assessment of control risk made as part of the financial statement audit, or a financial related audit. This report should include as a minimum: (*a*) the scope of the auditor's work, (*b*) the entity's significant internal controls or control structure including the controls

established to ensure compliance with laws and regulations that have a material impact on the financial statements, and (*c*) the reportable conditions, including the identification of material weaknesses identified as a result of the auditors' work in understanding and assessing the control risk.

5. Written reports are to be prepared giving the results of each financial-related audit regarding financial presentations other than complete financial statements.

6. If certain information is prohibited from general disclosure, the report should state the nature of the information omitted and the requirement that makes the omission necessary.

7. Written audit reports are to be submitted by the audit organization to the appropriate officials of the organization audited and to the appropriate officials of the organizations requiring or arranging for the audits, including external funding organizations, unless legal restrictions, ethical considerations, or other arrangements prevent it. Copies of the reports should also be sent to other officials who have legal oversight authority or who may be responsible for taking action and to others authorized to receive such reports. Unless restricted by law or regulation, copies should be made available for public inspection.

PERFORMANCE AUDITS

Field Work Standards for Performance Audits

Work is to be adequately planned.

2. Staff are to be properly supervised.

3. An assessment is to be made of compliance with applicable requirements of laws and regulations when necessary to satisfy the audit objectives: (*a*) Auditors should design the audit to provide reasonable assurance of detecting abuse or illegal acts that could significantly affect the audit objectives, and (*b*) auditors should be alert to situations or transactions that could be indicative of abuse or illegal acts.

4. An assessment should be made of applicable internal controls when necessary to satisfy the audit objectives.

5. Sufficient, competent, and relevant evidence is to be obtained to afford a reasonable basis for the auditors' judgments and conclusions regarding the organization, program, activity, or function under audit. A record of the auditors' work is to be retained in the form of working papers, which may include tapes, films, and disks.

Reporting Standards for Performance Audits

Written audit reports are to be prepared communicating the results of each government audit.

2. Reports are to be issued promptly so that the information is available for timely use by management, legislative officials, and other interested parties.

3. The report should include:

    a. A statement that the audit was made in accordance with GAGAS and disclose when applicable standards were not followed.

    b. A statement of the audit objectives and a description of the audit scope and methodology.

    c. A full discussion of the audit findings and, where applicable, the auditor's conclusions.

    d. A description of the cause of problem areas noted in the audit, and recommendations for actions to correct the problem areas and to improve operations when called for by the audit objectives.

    e. An identification of the significant internal controls that were assessed, the scope of the auditors' assessment work, and any significant weaknesses found during the audit.

    f. All significant instances of noncompliance and abuse and all indications or instances of illegal acts that could result in criminal prosecution that were found during or in connection with the audit.

    g. Pertinent views of responsible officials of the organization, program, activity, or function audited concerning the auditors' findings, conclusions, and recommendations, and what corrective action is planned.

    h. A description of any significant noteworthy accomplishments, particularly when management improvements in one area may be applicable elsewhere.

    i. A listing of any significant issues needing further study and consideration.

    j. A statement about any pertinent information that was omitted because it is deemed privileged or confidential. The nature of such information should be described, and the basis under which it is withheld should be stated.

4. The report should be complete, accurate, objective, and convincing, and be as clear and concise as the subject matter permits.

5. Written audit reports are to be submitted by the audit organization to the appropriate officials of the organization audited, and to the appropriate officials of the organizations requiring or arranging for the audits, including external funding organizations, unless legal restrictions, ethical consideration, or other arrangements prevent it. Copies of the reports should also be sent to other officials who may be responsible for taking action on audit findings and recommendations and to others authorized to receive such reports. Unless restricted by law or regulation, copies should be made available for public inspection.

CHAPTER 18

Learning Objectives

Fraud auditing can be very exciting. It has the aura of detective work—finding things people want to keep hidden. However, fraud auditing and examination are not easy and are not activities to be pursued without training, experience, and care. Fraud awareness, thus, is the focus of this chapter. Having worked through this chapter, you will have accomplished these learning objectives:

1. Define and explain the differences among several kinds of fraud, errors, irregularities, and illegal acts that might occur in an organization.

2. Explain the various auditing standards regarding external, internal, and governmental auditors' responsibilities with respect to detecting and reporting errors, irregularities, and illegal acts.

3. List and explain some conditions that can lead to frauds.

4. Describe ways and means for preventing frauds.

5. Describe some common employee fraud schemes and explain some audit and investigation procedures for detecting them.

6. Describe some common financial reporting fraud features and explain some audit and investigation procedures for detecting them.

7. Explain the use of some extended audit procedures for finding fraud.

8. Describe how PAs can assist in prosecuting fraud perpetrators.

Fraud Awareness Auditing

Introduction

. . . .

This chapter is not intended to make you a fraud examiner or fraud auditor. Its purpose is to heighten your familiarity with the nature, signs, prevention, detection, and reaction to fraud that can enable you to perform financial statement audits with awareness of fraud possibilities.

Users of audited financial statements generally believe that one of the main objectives of audits is fraud detection. External auditors know the issue is very complex, and they fear the general view that their work should ferret out all manner of major and minor fraud and misstatement in financial statements. This difference in viewpoints is one of the chronic "expectation gaps" between external auditors and users of published financial statements.

Part of the gap arises from the ability and expertise needed to be a fraud examiner or fraud auditor. Most of the trained and experienced fraud examiners come from government agencies, such as Revenue Canada, the Royal Canadian Mounted Police (RCMP), the Office of the Auditor General of Canada (OAG), provincial securities commissions (especially the OSC), the Minister of Justice, and various police departments. Alumni of these agencies often practise as consultants and fraud examiners, but few of them enter public accounting to become financial statement auditors. So, what are most financial statement auditors to do? One option is to become more aware of fraud possibilities so that they can perform a limited set of procedures and determine when it is necessary to call upon people with greater fraud examination expertise. Financial statement auditors need to understand fraud and potential fraud situations, and they need to know how to ask the right kinds of questions during an audit. We know this is not impossible because there has always been the odd investigative job to be done by accountants. For example, one of the best known of fraud auditors in Canada got started doing an investigative audit of a former owner of the Toronto Maple Leafs hockey team.

Definitions Related to Fraud

. . . .

LEARNING OBJECTIVE

1. Define and explain the differences among several kinds of fraud, errors, irregularities, and illegal acts that might occur in an organization.

There are several kinds of "fraud." Some are defined in laws, while others are matters of general understanding. Exhibit 18–1 shows some acts and devices often involved in financial frauds. Collectively, these are known as white-collar crime— the misdeeds done by people who wear ties to work and steal with a pencil or a computer terminal. In white-collar crime there are ink stains instead of bloodstains.

Fraud consists of knowingly making material misrepresentations of fact, with the intent of inducing someone to believe the falsehood and act upon it and, thus, suffer a loss or damage. This definition encompasses all the varieties by which people can lie, cheat, steal, and dupe other people.

EXHIBIT 18–1   AN ABUNDANCE OF FRAUDS

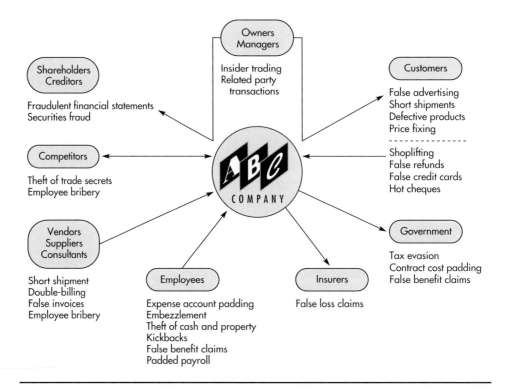

Employee fraud is the use of fraudulent means to take money or other property from an employer. It usually involves falsifications of some kind—false documents, lying, exceeding authority, or violating an employer's policies. It consists of three phases: (1) the fraudulent act, (2) the conversion of the money or property to the fraudster's use, and (3) the cover-up.

Embezzlement is a type of fraud involving employees' or nonemployees' wrongfully taking money or property entrusted to their care, custody, and control, often accompanied by false accounting entries and other forms of lying and cover-up.

Defalcation is another name for employee fraud and embezzlement. Technically, defalcation is the term used when somebody in charge of safekeeping the assets is doing the stealing.

Management fraud is deliberate fraud committed by management that injures investors and creditors through materially misleading financial statements. The class of perpetrators is management; the class of victims is investors and creditors; and the instrument of perpetration is financial statements.[1] Sometimes management fraud is called "fraudulent financial reporting." **Fraudulent financial reporting** was defined by the National Commission on Fraudulent Financial Reporting (1987) as intentional or reckless conduct, whether by act or omission, that results in materially misleading financial statements.

---

[1] R. K. Elliott and J. J. Willingham, *Management Fraud: Detection and Deterrence* (New York: Petrocelli Books, Inc., 1980), p. 4.

The *CICA Handbook Section* 5135.02–.03 defines fraud as follows:

Fraud and other irregularities'' refer to an intentional misstatement in financial state-ments, including an omission of amount or disclosure, or to a misstatement arising from theft of the entity's assets. Fraud also involves:

(*i*) the use of deception such as manipulation, falsification, or alteration of account-ing records or documentation;

(*ii*) misrepresentation or intentional omission of events, transactions, or other sig-nificant information; or

(*iii*) intentional misapplication of accounting principles relating to amount, classifi-cation, or manner of presentation of disclosure.

The word *fraud* is used in this section, although in practice the auditor will normally be concerned with a suspected rather than a proven fraud. Final determina-tion of whether fraud has occurred will probably be made by a court of law.

Errors are unintentional misstatements or omissions of amounts or disclosures in financial statements. Irregularities are intentional misstatements or omissions in financial statements, including fraudulent financial reporting (management fraud) and misappropriations of assets (defalcations). Direct-effect illegal acts are viola-tions of laws or government regulations by the company or its management or employees that produce direct and material effects on dollar amounts in financial statements.

Fraud auditing has been defined in courses conducted by the Association of Certified Fraud Examiners as a proactive approach to detect financial frauds using accounting records and information, analytical relationships, and an awareness of fraud perpetration and concealment schemes. A good overview of the nature and scale of the fraud problem in Canada is provided by KPMG's Annual Fraud Report, the latest of which is summarized in the following box.

Fraud Hits 62% of Top Firms, Survey Says

Nearly two-thirds of Canada's top businesses were hit by fraud last year, despite claims by most they know how such scams are carried out, a new survey says. The study, released yesterday by **KPMG Investigation and Security Inc.,** said 62% of companies fell victim to some form of fraud in 1996, up 10% from the year before.

However, 97% of respondents also said they had some degree of knowledge about how such crimes are executed.

The findings are drawn from a poll of the country's top 1,000 private and public firms as ranked by *The Financial Post.* The response rate was 22%. KPMG has conducted the survey annually since 1992, asking executives how fraud has affected their businesses.

Of those surveyed, 47% cited poor internal controls as the main reason for fraud taking place. Other top causes were the vulnerability of specific indus-tries, employee and third party collusion and management overriding internal controls.

Forty-five per cent of frauds were committed by people outside the companies in question. Of those taking place internally, 38% were blamed on employees and 17% were committed by management.

The most common form of management fraud involved expense accounts. Cheque forgery and counterfeiting were the most frequent forms of employee fraud, the study said.

Most of those held responsible for such scams had been employed by their companies for more than two years, according to the findings. The typical fraudster was a man aged 26 to 40 who earned less than $50,000 a year.

For the first time, the survey also asked respondents about money laundering—14% said they had been affected by this form of fraud.

Source: Terry Weber, *The Financial Post,* Wednesday, May 14, 1997, p. 13.

Characteristics of Fraudsters

White-collar criminals are not like typical bank robbers, who are often described as "young and dumb." Bank robbers and other strong-arm artists often make comic mistakes like writing the holdup note on the back of a probation identification card, leaving the getaway car keys on the convenience store counter, using a zucchini as a holdup weapon, and timing the holdup to get stuck in rush-hour traffic. Then there's the classic about the robber who ran into his own mother at the bank (she turned him in!).

Burglars and robbers average about $400–$500 for each hit. Employee frauds average $20,000, on up to $500,000 if a computer is used. Yet, employee frauds are not usually the intricate, well-disguised ploys you find in espionage novels. Who are these thieves wearing ties? What do they look like? Unfortunately, they "look like" most everybody else, including you and me. They have these characteristics:

- Likely to be married.
- Not likely to be divorced.
- Probably not tattooed.
- Member of a church.
- Educated beyond high school.
- No arrest record.
- Range in age from teens to over 60.
- Socially conforming.
- Employment tenure from 1 to 20 or more years.
- Usually act alone (70 percent of incidents).

White-collar criminals do not make themselves obvious, although there may be telltale signs, which will be described later as "red flags." Unfortunately, the largest frauds are committed by people who hold high executive positions, have long tenure with an organization, and are respected and trusted employees. After all, these are the people who have access to the largest amounts of money and have the power to give orders and override controls.

WHO DOES IT?

Alex W was a 47-year-old treasurer of a credit union. Over a seven-year period, he stole $160,000. He was a good husband and the father of six children, and he was a highly reputed official of the credit union. His misappropriations came as a stunning surprise to his associates. He owed significant amounts on his home, cars, university for two children, two side investments, and five different credit cards. His monthly payments significantly exceeded his take-home pay.

Source: National Association of Certified Fraud Examiners (NACFE), "Auditing for Fraud."

The Art of Fraud Awareness Auditing

Fraud examination work combines the expertise of auditors and criminal investigators. Fraud examiners are fond of saying that their successes are the result of accident, hunches, or luck. Nothing can be further from the reality. Successes come from experience, application of logic, and the ability to see things that are not obvious (as Sherlock Holmes noticed the dog that did not bark). Fraud awareness auditing, broadly speaking, involves familiarity with many elements: the human element, organizational behaviour, knowledge of common fraud schemes, evidence and its sources, standards of proof, and sensitivity to red flags.[2]

Independent auditors of financial statements and fraud examiners approach their work differently. While there are many differences, these are some of the most important and obvious ones:

- Financial auditors follow a program/procedural approach designed to accomplish a fairly standard job, while fraud examiners float in a mind-set of sensitivity to the unusual where nothing is standard.

- Financial auditors make note of errors and omissions, while fraud examiners focus as well on exceptions, oddities, and patterns of conduct.

- Financial auditors assess control risk in general and specific terms to design other audit procedures, while fraud examiners habitually "think like a crook" to imagine ways that controls could be subverted for fraudulent purposes.

- Financial auditors work to a level of materiality (dollar size big enough to matter) that is usually much higher than the amounts that fraud examiners consider worth pursuing. Financial auditors use materiality as a measure of importance one year at a time, whereas fraud examiners think in terms of cumulative materiality. (Theft of $20,000 per year may not loom large each year, but after a 15-year fraud career, $300,000 is a considerable loss.)

- Financial audits are based on theories of financial accounting and auditing logic, while fraud examination has a theory of behavioural motive, opportunity, and integrity.

---

[2] These and other aspects of the art of fraud auditing are more fully developed in G.J. Bologna and R.J. Lindquist, *Fraud Auditing and Forensic Accounting* (New York: John Wiley & Sons, 1987), pp. 27–42; W.S. Albrecht, M.B. Romney, D.J. Cherrington, I.R. Payne, and A.J. Roe, *How to Detect and Prevent Business Fraud* (New York: Prentice-Hall, 1982); R. White and W.G. Bishop, III, *The Role of the Internal Auditor in the Deterrence, Detection, and Reporting of Fraudulent Financial Reporting* (The Institute of Internal Auditors); and M.J. Barrett and R.N. Carolus, *Control and Internal Auditing* (The Institute of Internal Auditors).

THE CASE OF THE EXTRA CHECKOUT

The district grocery store manager could not understand why receipts and profitability had fallen and inventory was hard to manage at one of the largest stores in her area. She hired an investigator who covertly observed the checkout clerks and reported that no one had shown suspicious behaviour at any of the nine checkout counters. Nine? That store only has eight, she exclaimed! (The store manager had installed another checkout aisle, not connected to the cash receipts and inventory maintenance central computer, and was pocketing all the receipts from that register.)

External and internal auditors get credit for finding about 20 percent of discovered frauds. Larger percentages are discovered by voluntary confessions, anonymous tips, and other haphazard means. Fraud examiners have a higher success rate because they are called in for a specific purpose when fraud is known or highly suspected.

Some aspects of audit methodology make a big difference in the fraud discovery success experience. Financial auditors often utilize inductive reasoning—that is, they sample accounting data, derive audit findings, and project ("induct") the finding to a conclusion about the population of data sampled. Fraud examiners often enjoy the expensive luxury of utilizing deductive reasoning—that is, after being tipped off that a certain type of loss occurred or probably occurred, they can identify the suspects, make clinical observations (stakeouts), conduct interviews and interrogations, eliminate dead-end results, and concentrate on running the fraudster to ground. They can conduct covert activities that usually are not in the financial auditors' tool kit. The "expensive luxury" of the deductive approach involves surveying a wide array of information and information sources, eliminating the extraneous, and retaining the selection that proves the fraud.

· ·

R E V I E W
C H E C K P O I N T S

18.1 What are the defining characteristics of white-collar crime? employee fraud? embezzlement? defalcation? management fraud? errors? irregularities? illegal acts?

18.2 What does a fraud perpetrator look like? And how does one act?

18.3 Compare and contrast the type of work performed by external auditors (auditing financial statements to render an audit report) and fraud examiners.

· ·

AUDITORS' AND INVESTIGATORS' RESPONSIBILITIES
· · · · · · · · · · · ·

Audit standards from several sources explain the responsibilities for errors, irregularities, and illegal acts. The term "external auditors" refers to independent PAs who audit financial statements for the purpose of rendering an opinion; internal auditors and certified internal auditors are references to persons, who can be both independent and PAs, employed within organizations; "government auditors" refers to auditors whose work is governed by the public sector audit standards, whether they be audit employees of governments or public accounting firms engaged to perform government audits; and "fraud examiners" refers to people engaged specifically for fraud investigation work. Forensic or investigative accounting deals with the relationship and application of financial facts to legal problems, particularly in use of the findings at a trial. "The involvement of the forensic accountant is almost always on a reactive basis which distinguishes the forensic accountant from the fraud auditor, who more usually tends to be involved on an active basis with the aspects of prevention and detection in a corporate or regulatory environment.[3]

External Auditors' Responsibilities

The CICA auditing standards are rigorous. Relevant standards concern misstatements (*Section* 5135), misstatements due to illegal acts by clients (*Section* 5136), auditing accounting estimates (*Section* 5305), communication with audit committees or equivalent (AUG–11), and communication of matters identified during the financial statement audit (*Section* 5750).

Auditor's Responsibility to Detect and Report Errors and Irregularities

Section 5135 presents an extensive array of audit responsibilities. The details are in Appendix 18A. Basically, *Section* 5135 requires auditors to understand errors and irregularities, assess the risk of their occurrence, design audits to provide reasonable assurance of detecting material ones, and report on findings to management, directors, users of financial statements (sometimes), and outside agencies (certain conditions).

Illegal Acts by Clients

Section 5136 does not distinguish between the two kinds of illegal acts identified in U.S. standard SAS 53:

> (1) Direct-effect illegal acts produce direct and material effects on financial statement amounts (e.g., violations of tax laws and government contracting regulations for cost and revenue recognition), and they come under the same responsibilities as errors and irregularities; and (2) Indirect-effect illegal acts is the term used to refer to violations of laws and regulations that are far removed from financial statement effects (e.g., violations relating to insider securities trading, occupational health and safety, food and drug administration, environmental protection, and equal employment opportunity).

In the United States the far-removed illegal acts come under a responsibility for general awareness, particularly in matters of contingent liability disclosure, but not routine responsibility for detection and reporting. Details of U.S. standards are in Appendix 18A.

Section 5136, on the other hand, requires auditors to consider the consequences of the illegal acts and the best way of disclosing such consequences. If failures to disclose would result in a material misstatement, then the auditor should attempt to reduce this risk to an appropriately low level. *Section* 5136 acknowledges that illegal acts may be difficult to detect because of (1) efforts made to conceal them, and (2) questions about whether an act is illegal, which are complex and may only be

---

[3] G.J. Bologna and R.J. Lindquist, *Fraud Auditing and Forensic Accounting*, Wiley, 1987, p. 85.

resolved by a court of law. For these reasons *Section* 5136.10 recommends that the engagement letter inform management of limitations in detecting illegal acts through the audit.

The auditor should use knowledge of the business and make enquiries of management to identify laws and regulations that could result in material misstatements if violated and not reported (*Section* 5136.11). In addition, auditors should enquire and obtain representations about awareness and disclosure of possibly illegal acts (*Section* 5136.21). Discovery of material possibly illegal acts should be communicated to the audit committee and other appropriate levels of management. *Section* 5136.23 gives a list of circumstances that may indicate illegal acts.

Auditing Accounting Estimates

Section 5305 is related to fraudulent financial reporting because numerous fraud cases have involved manipulation of estimates. This area is difficult because an accounting estimate is an approximation of a financial statement element, item, or account made by an organization's management. (Examples include allowance for loan losses, net realizable value of inventory, percentage-of-completion revenue, and fair value in nonmonetary exchanges.)

Management is responsible for making the accounting estimates, and auditors are responsible for evaluating their reasonableness in the context of the financial statements taken as a whole. Auditors are supposed to keep track of the differences between (1) management's estimates and (2) the closest reasonable estimates supported by the audit evidence. And they are supposed to evaluate (1) the differences taken altogether for indications of a systematic bias and (2) the combination of differences with other likely errors in the financial statements found by other audit procedures.

Communication with Audit Committees

The *Guideline of Communication with Audit Committees* (or equivalent) (AUG–11) sets forth requirements intended to ensure that audit committees are informed about the scope and results of the independent audit. The auditing standards place great faith in audit committees and boards of directors, although their effectiveness has been questioned elsewhere.[4] *Section* 5750 requires external auditors to make oral or written communication on the following matters: (a) misstatements other than trivial errors; (b) fraud; (c) misstatements that may cause future financial statements to be materially misstated; (d) illegal or possibly illegal acts, other than ones considered inconsequential; and (e) significant weaknesses in internal control.

Appendix 18A provides additional details on these and related U.S. standards.

P.J. Cockburn, in an article titled "Closing the Gap" in the November 1993 issue of *CA Magazine* (pp. 31–32), noted that there is some inconsistency in the *Handbook* regarding responsibility to detect material misstatements due to error and those due to fraud. Specifically, *Section* 5000.04 states: "The auditor seeks reasonable assurance whether the financial statements are free of material misstatement" without qualifying the sources of misstatement, whereas the newer *Section* 5135.16 explains

---

[4] Wechsler reported the findings of the National Commission on Fraudulent Financial Reporting: that of the 120 fraudulent financial reporting cases brought by the SEC between 1981 and 1986, two-thirds involved companies that had audit committees. This caused Professor Briloff to remark: "Now I see that they are not functioning as they should." (D. Wechsler, "Giving the Watchdog Fangs," *Forbes*, November 13, 1989, p. 130.) However, these observations beg the question of the thousands of companies with and without audit committees that did not get involved in fraudulent financial reporting.

that an auditor is "less likely" (because of concealment) to detect misstatement arising from fraud than he or she would be to detect misstatement from error. In addition, *Section* 5136 suggests that some illegal acts such as building code violations may have an even lower chance of being detected by an external auditor. These would appear to correspond to indirect-effect illegal acts.

In contrast to these CICA Standards, the new AICPA Standard SAS No. 82, "Consideration of Fraud in a Financial Statement Audit" (effective for periods ending after December 15, 1997), requires U.S. auditors to take the same responsibility for detecting material misstatement due to fraud (intentional misstatement) as for material misstatement due to error (unintentional misstatement). SAS 82 requires auditors to specifically assess the risk of material misstatement due to fraud in every audit. The SAS identifies two types of fraud: fraudulent financial reporting and misappropriation of assets. When the auditor finds fraud, he or she needs to consider the implications for other aspects of the audit, arrange discussions with the appropriate level of management and the audit committee, and suggest that the client consult legal counsel for any regulatory requirements.

A recent study by American researchers provides more specific guidance on fraud warning signs. "The lack of awareness of the warning signs of fraud is a frequently cited cause of audit failure. If auditors better understood the signs and applied professional scepticism, they would decrease their risk of not detecting fraud. Knowing the most important warning signs should help auditors do a better job of assessing fraud risk." A survey of 130 auditors asked them to rank 30 commonly cited warning signals of fraud according to their relative importance. The auditors ranked client dishonesty as the most important factor. The survey revealed an interesting pattern. Auditors generally perceived "attitude" factors to be more important warning signs of fraud than "situational" factors.

The top 15 warning signs are listed in the box below.

AUDITORS' RANKING OF THE RELATIVE IMPORTANCE OF FRAUD WARNING SIGNS

Auditors' rankings	Fraud warning signs
1.	Managers have lied to the auditors or have been overly evasive in response to audit enquiries.
2.	The auditor's experience with management indicates a degree of dishonesty.
3.	Management places undue emphasis on meeting earnings projections or the quantitative targets.
4.	Management has engaged in frequent disputes with auditors, particularly about aggressive application of accounting principles that increases earnings.
5.	The client has engaged in opinion shopping.
6.	Management's attitude toward financial reporting is unduly aggressive.
7.	The client has a weak control environment.

8. A substantial portion of management compensation depends on meeting quantified targets.
9. Management displays significant disrespect for regulatory bodies.
10. Management operating and financial decisions are dominated by a single person or a few persons acting in concert.
11. Client managers display a hostile attitude toward the auditors.
12. Management displays a propensity to take undue risks.
13. There are frequent and significant difficult-to-audit transactions.
14. Key managers are considered highly unreasonable.
15. The client's organization is decentralized without adequate monitoring.

Source: V.B. Heiman-Hoffman, K.P. Morgan, and J.M. Patton, "The Warning Signs of Fraudulent Financial Reporting," *Journal of Accountancy,* October 1996, pp. 76–77.

Internal Auditors' Responsibilities

Internal auditors' attitudes about fraud responsibilities cannot be usefully generalized. Some hesitate to get involved because they believe that a watchdog role will damage their image and effectiveness as internal consultants. Others have flocked to the fraud investigation education programs run by the National Association of Certified Fraud Examiners because they want to add the fraud expertise dimension to their skills.

The scope-of-work sections of the internal audit standards (Appendix 17A in this book) give the basic charge to internal auditors for fraud awareness auditing: Internal auditors review the reliability and integrity of financial and operating information (section 310); review the systems established to ensure compliance with policies, plans, procedures, laws, and regulations (section 320); and review the means of safeguarding assets and verify the existence of assets (section 330). This charge was expanded in Statement on Internal Auditing Standards No. 3, "Deterrence, Detection, Investigation, and Reporting of Fraud." An abbreviated list of some specifications from SIAS 3 is in Appendix 18A.

The internal auditing standards appear to be carefully written to impose no positive obligation for fraud detection and investigation work in the ordinary course of assignments. However, internal auditors are encouraged to be aware of the various types of frauds, their signs (red flags), and the need to follow up the notice of signs and control weaknesses to determine whether a suspicion is justified; then, alert management to call in the experts. SIAS 3 cautions that internal auditors are not expected to guarantee that fraud will be detected in the normal course of most internal audit assignments.

Public Sector Auditing Standards

As discussed in Chapter 17, public sector standards are applicable for audits conducted by government employees and by public accounting firms engaged to perform audits on governmental organizations, programs, activities, and functions. Consequently, the public sector standards control a significant portion of audits by public accountants. The basic governmental audit requirements are to know the applicable laws and regulations, design the audit to detect abuse or illegal acts, and report to the proper level of authority. Some more detailed guidance from a variety of sources is provided in Appendix 18A.

Auditors are supposed to prepare a written report on their tests of compliance with applicable laws and regulations, including all material instances of noncompliance and all instances or indications of illegal acts that could result in criminal prosecution. (More discussion of compliance auditing and reports relating to laws and regulations is in Chapter 17.) Reports should be directed to the top official of an organization and, in some cases to an appropriate oversight body, including other government agencies and audit committees. Persons receiving the audit reports are responsible for reporting to law enforcement agencies.

The following box illustrates the dramatic impact that fraud can have in the public sector.

FORMER CHIEF MOUNTIE HIRED AFTER SUN EXPOSE BLITZ ON HEALTH-CARE FRAUD

Ontario Health Minister Jim Wilson contracted Inkster, now president of KPMG Investigation and Security, after widespread cheating was exposed by Sun columnist Christie Blatchford yesterday.

"The number of reported fraud cases quoted in (The) Toronto Sun are of great concern to me," Wilson said in a statement hand-delivered by aide Cynthia Janzen yesterday.

Blatchford revealed every single day, between 30 and 50 people show up at Ontario's hospitals and clinics seeking treatment with bogus health cards, and the government ignores it. In February, stolen health cards were presented for treatment 1,057 times, she wrote.

Despite promises to crack down on fraud in the 1995 throne speech and fall economic statement, Ontario's health ministry employs just one fraud investigator for every 1.6 million provincial residents. Wilson employs more political staff than enforcement officers in his $18-billion ministry, which has prosecuted only one case of fraud this year.

Janzen said Wilson was motivated after reading Blatchford's column. A 1993 internal governmental report found that fraud costs the health ministry $284 million a year. And, unfortunately, the Conservative government has failed in its promise to weed out health-care fraud, Tory and Liberal MPPs said.

"Basically, there is no enforcement," Tory MPP and Crown attorney Toni Skarica said in an interview.

"There are virtually no resources put into fraud investigations or prosecutions. As a result, we could get major frauds that undermine the economy," Skarica said.

Liberal critic Dominic Agostino said the province is losing "hundreds of millions a year" to illegitimate hucksters.

Source: Jeff Harder, *The Toronto Sun,* May 31, 1997, p. 5. Copyright 1997, *The Toronto Sun,* a division of Sun Media Corporation.

No Separation of Duties

An electronic data processing employee instructed the company's computer to pay his wife rent for land she had allegedly leased to the company by assigning her an alphanumeric code as a lessor and then ordering the payments. The control lesson: Never let a data entry clerk who processes payment claims also have access to the approved vendor master file for additions or deletions.

Source: G.J. Bologna and R.J. Lindquist, *Fraud Auditing and Forensic Accounting* (New York: John Wiley & Sons, 1987), p. 70–71.

Fraud Examiner Responsibilities

If you try to make an informal ranking of the strength of commitment to fraud matters, it appears that the external auditors (GAAS) come first, followed by the public sector auditors, then the internal auditors (SIAS 3). Of course, fraud examiners have the strongest spirit of fraud detection and investigation. They differ significantly from other kinds of auditors. When they take an assignment, fraud is already known or strongly suspected. They do not fish around for fraud while performing "normal" work. In fact, the Association of Certified Fraud Examiners teaches that assignments are not begun without predication, which means a reason to believe fraud may have occurred. (The Professional Standards and Practices for Certified Fraud Examiners are reproduced in Appendix 18B.)

Fraud examiners' attitudes and responsibilities differ from those of other auditors in two additional respects—internal control, and materiality. Their interest in internal control policies and procedures lies not so much in evaluating their strengths but in evaluating their weaknesses. Fraud examiners "think like crooks" to imagine fraud schemes for getting around an organization's internal controls. They imagine scenarios of white-collar crime in situations where controls are not in place.

Fraud examiners have a different attitude about "materiality." While other auditors may have a large dollar amount as a criterion for an error that is big enough to matter, fraud examiners have a much lower threshold. An oddity is an oddity no matter the amount of money involved, and small oddities ought not be passed by just because "$5,000 isn't material to the financial statements taken as a whole." External auditors comprehend materiality in relation to each year's financial statements, so that, for example, a $50,000 misstatement of income might not be big enough to matter. Fraud examiners think of materiality as a cumulative amount. A fraud loss of $20,000 this year may not be material to an external auditor, but $20,000 each year for a 15-year fraud career amounts to $300,000 in the fraud examiner's eyes—and it is big enough to matter!

. . . .

R E V I E W
CHECKPOINTS

18.4 What are the CICA auditing standards requirements regarding (*a*) awareness of fraud, (*b*) procedural audit work, (*c*) professional skepticism, and (*d*) reporting? Do these standards differ for (1) errors, irregularities, and direct-effect illegal acts; and (2) far-removed-effect illegal acts?

Money, Money, Money Case

Brian Money, a 29-year-old assistant branch manager and lending officer of a large downtown Toronto bank, defrauded the bank of some $10.2 million over a 20-month period. He fabricated loans to real and fictitious customers and gambled away the proceeds at an Atlantic City casino. Money was such a valued customer that the casino flew its corporate jet to Toronto to pick him up for weekend jaunts.

The defalcation came to light when Canadian law enforcement authorities arrested Money for a traffic violation on his return from a trip to Atlantic City. A search of his person disclosed that he was carrying about $29,000 in currency. That information was passed on to the bank, which then conducted an audit and found the fictional loans and transfers of funds to the casino. The bank is suing the casino to recover at least part of its loss.

Money used a *lapping scheme* to keep auditors off his trail—that is, he paid off earlier loans with subsequent loans so that no delinquencies would show. However, the fictional loan balances grew and grew. Money's superior at the branch had approved the larger loans because "he had no reason to mistrust him." The branch manager was subsequently suspended along with the assistant branch manager for administration, a credit officer, and an auditor.

Source: G.J. Bologna and R.J. Lindquist, *Fraud Auditing and Forensic Accounting* (2nd ed.), New York: John Wiley & Sons, 1995, pp. 230–231. Reprinted by permission of John Wiley & Sons, Inc.

18.5 To what extent would you say internal auditors include fraud detection responsibility in their normal audit assignments?

18.6 How does the requirement for design of audit procedures differ in public sector audit work from external auditors' work on financial statement audits (not involving governmental auditing)? Consider both errors/irregularities and illegal acts aspects.

18.7 Why might it be said that the order of strength of commitment to fraud matters is (1) government auditors, (2) external auditors, (3) internal auditors?

18.8 Why might fraud examiners have attitudes about control systems and materiality different from those of other auditors?

· ·

Conditions That Make Fraud Possible, Even Easy
· · · · · · · · · · · ·

LEARNING OBJECTIVE

3. List and explain some conditions that can lead to frauds.

When can fraud occur? Imagine the probability of fraud being a function of three factors—motive, opportunity, and lack of integrity. When one or two of these factors weigh heavily in the direction of fraud, the probability increases. When three of them lean in the direction of fraud, it almost certainly will occur.[5] As Bologna and

---

[5] For further reference, see D.R. Cressey, "Management Fraud, Accounting Controls, and Criminological Theory," pp. 117–47, and Albrecht et al., "Auditor Involvement in the Detection of Fraud," pp. 207–61, both in R.K. Elliott

---

I Couldn't Tell Anyone

An unmarried young woman stole $300 from her employer to pay for an abortion. Coming from a family that strongly disdained premarital sex, she felt that her only alternative was to have the secret abortion. Once she realized how easy it was to steal, however, she took another $86,000 before being caught.

Source: W.S. Albrecht, "How CPAs Can Help Clients Prevent Employee Fraud," *Journal of Accountancy*, December 1988, p. 113.

Lindquist put it: Some people are honest all the time, some people (fewer than the honest ones) are dishonest all the time, most people are honest some of the time, and some people are honest most of the time.[6]

Motive

A **motive** is some kind of pressure experienced by a person and believed unshareable with friends and confidants. Psychotic motivation is relatively rare; but is characterized by the "habitual criminal," who steals simply for the sake of stealing. Egocentric motivations drive people to steal to achieve more personal prestige. Ideological motivations are held by people who think that their cause is morally superior, and that they are justified in making someone else a victim. However, economic motives are far more common in business frauds than the other three.

The economic motive is simply a need for money, and at times it can be intertwined with egocentric and ideological motivations. Ordinarily honest people can fall into circumstances where there is a new or unexpected need for money, and the normal options for talking about it or going through legitimate channels seem to be closed. Consider these needs:

- Pay college tuition.
- Pay hospital bills for a parent with cancer.
- Pay gambling debts.
- Pay for drugs.
- Pay alimony and child support.
- Pay for high lifestyle (homes, cars, boats).
- Finance business or stock speculation losses.
- Report good financial results.

Opportunity

An **opportunity** is an open door for solving the unshareable problem in secret by violating a trust. The violation may be a circumvention of internal control policies and procedures, or it may be simply taking advantage of an absence or lapse of

---

and J.J. Willingham, *Management Fraud: Detection and Deterrence* (New York: Petrocelli Books, Inc., 1980).; J.K. Loebbecke, M.M. Eining, and J.J. Willingham, "Auditors' Experience with Material Irregularities: Frequency, Nature, and Detectability," *Auditing: A Journal of Practice and Theory*, Fall 1989, pp. 1–28.

[6] Bologna and Lindquist, *Fraud Auditing*, p. 8.

She Can Do Everything

Mrs. Lemon was the only bookkeeper for an electrical supply company. She wrote the cheques and reconciled the bank account. In the cash disbursements journal, she coded some cheques as inventory, but she wrote the cheques to herself, using her own true name. When the cheques were returned with the bank statement, she simply destroyed them. She stole $416,000 over five years. After being caught and sentenced to prison, she testified to having continuous guilt over doing something she knew was wrong.

Source: NACFE, "Auditing for Fraud."

---

control in an organization. We have no police state where every person is shadowed by an armed guard. Everyone has some degree of trust conferred for a job, even if it is merely the trust not to shirk and procrastinate. The higher the position in an organization, the greater the degree of trust; and, hence, the greater the opportunity for larger frauds. Here are some examples:

- Nobody counts the inventory, so losses are not known.
- The petty cash box is often left unattended.
- Supervisors set a bad example by taking supplies home.
- Upper management considered a written statement of ethics but decided not to publish one.
- Another employee was caught and fired, but not prosecuted.
- The finance vice president has investment authority without any review.
- Frequent emergency jobs leave a lot of excess material just lying around.

Lack of Integrity

Practically everyone, even the most violent criminals, knows the difference between right and wrong. Unimpeachable integrity is the ability to act in accordance with the highest moral and ethical values all the time. Thus, it is the lapses and occasional lack of integrity that permit motive and opportunity to take form as fraud. But people normally do not make deliberate decisions to "lack integrity today while I steal some money." They find a way to describe (rationalize) the act in words that make it acceptable for their self-image. Here are some of these rationalizations:

- I need it more than the other person (Robin Hood theory).
- I'm borrowing the money and will pay it back.
- Nobody will get hurt.
- The company is big enough to afford it.
- A successful image is the name of the game.
- Everybody is doing it.

THE MOST COMMON COMPUTER-RELATED CRIMES

Whereas computer hacking (pranksters breaking into computers) has received most of the recent media attention, the most prevalent computer crime is the fraudulent disbursement of funds, which is generally preceded by the submission of a spurious claim in the following forms:

- False vendor, supplier, or contractor invoice.
- False governmental benefit claim.
- False fringe benefit claim.
- False refund or credit claim.
- False payroll claim.
- False expense claim.

Fraudulent disbursement of funds usually requires a data entry clerk in accounts payable, payroll, or the benefits section, acting either alone or in collusion with an insider or outsider (depending on how tight the internal controls are). From an accountant's perspective, the claim is a false debit to an expense so that a corresponding credit can be posted to the cash account for the issuance of a cheque. Auditors assert that such disbursement frauds represent more than half of all frauds by lower-level employees.

At higher management levels, the typical fraud involves overstating profits by the fabrication of such data as sales, which are increased arbitrarily (sales booked before the sales transaction is completed), and the understatement of expenses, which are arbitrarily reduced or disguised as deferrals to the next accounting period. There are numerous variations on these two main themes: overstatement of sales, and understatement of expenses. One of the more common ploys to overstate profits is to arbitrarily increase the ending inventory of manufactured goods or merchandise held for sale. That ploy results in understating the cost of goods sold and thereby increasing the net profit.

The executive compensation system often provides the incentive to overstate profits. If bonus awards depend on profits, executives have an economic incentive to fudge the numbers. They may also be tempted to do so if they own a great many company shares, whose value depends on investors' perceptions of profitability. If profits are down, investors are unhappy and may rush to sell, thus causing a lowered share price and depressing the value of the executive's own shares.

Manipulations of this type often require line executives and personnel in accounting and data processing capacities to conspire together. Such conspiracies have become a recurring theme in business. The pressure on executives for high performance grows each year. We are therefore likely to see more such frauds in the future.

Source: G.J. Bologna and A.J. Lindquist, *Fraud Auditing and Forensic Accounting* (2nd Edition), Wiley, 1995, pp. 176–179. Reprinted by permission of John Wiley & Sons, Inc.

REVIEW
CHECKPOINTS

18.9   What are some of the pressures that can cause honest people to contemplate theft? List some egocentric and ideological ones as well as economic ones.

18.10 What kinds of conditions provide opportunities for employee fraud? for financial statement fraud?

18.11 Give some examples of "rationalizations" that people have used to excuse fraud. Can you use them?

· ·

FRAUD PREVENTION
· · · · · · · · · · ·

LEARNING OBJECTIVE
4. Describe ways and means for preventing frauds.

Accountants and auditors have often been exhorted to be the leaders in fraud prevention by employing their skills in designing "tight" control systems. This strategy is, at best, a short-run solution to a large and pervasive problem. Business activity is built on the trust that people at all levels will do their jobs properly. Control systems limit trust and, in the extreme, can strangle business in bureaucracy. Imagine street crime being "prevented" by enrolling half the population in the police force to control the other half! Managers and employees must have freedom to do business, which means giving them freedom to commit frauds as well.[7] Effective long-run prevention measures are complex and difficult, and involve the elimination of the causes of fraud by mitigating the effects of motive, opportunity, and lack of integrity.

Managing People Pressures in the Workplace

From time to time, people will experience financial and other pressures. The pressures cannot be eliminated, but the facilities for sharing them can be created. Some companies have "ethics officers" to serve this purpose. Their job is to be available to talk over the ethical dilemmas faced in the workplace and help people adopt legitimate responses. However, the ethics officers are normally not psychological counsellors.

Many companies have "hot lines" for anonymous reporting of ethical problems. Reportedly, the best kind of hot-line arrangement is to have the responding party be an agency outside the organization. In the United States some organizations are in the business of being the recipients of hot-line calls, co-ordinating their activities with the management of the organization.

The most effective long-run prevention, however, lies in the practice of management by caring for people. Managers and supervisors at all levels can exhibit a genuine concern for the personal and professional needs of their subordinates and fellow managers, and subordinates can show the same concern for one another and for their managers. The approach is idealistic and calls for the elimination of interpersonal competition, of climbing up over the bodies of colleagues, and of office "politics." Nevertheless, it is practised in many organizations in the form of staff meetings, personal counselling, and "quality circles" (groups of employees from all levels who plan production, selling, and administrative activities together). Some organizations have day care centres, alcohol and drug counselling, financial counselling, and other programs to help people share their problems with experts.

When external auditors are engaged in the audit of financial statements, they must obtain an understanding of the company's "control structure." The control structure includes the "control environment," which relates to the overall scheme of management activity in the company. Management that considers carefully the people pressures in the workplace, using some of the devices mentioned above, has a good control environment and the beginnings of a good control structure.

---

[7] Cressey, "Management Fraud," p. 124.

Dishonesty Is Bad Policy

Now be honest. When fixing your car following an accident, your body shop includes extra repairs and puts them on the insurance company's tab. Do you say thanks and let the insurer pay?

According to an ethics poll conducted recently for the **Canadian Coalition Against Insurance Fraud,** 25% of those surveyed said they'd go along with the mechanic's bill padding.

For the property and casualty insurers who make up the membership of the coalition, this ethical laxity adds up to an estimated $1.3-billion-a-year problem, including the cost of police and fire officials' investigations.

That's how much is lost on fraudulent claims relating to homes. Insurance fraud is second only to illegal drug sales as a source of criminal profit.

Put another way, fraud accounts for 10% to 15% of all claims paid out— money that ends up being covered by honest policyholders in the form of increased premiums.

The coalition is conducting a study to analyse the kinds of insurance fraud that are most frequently perpetrated, says executive director Mary Lou O'Reilly.

She says a link has been found between the ethical decisions people make in their everyday lives and opportunistic fraud.

"Fraud for the average Canadian is an opportunity to 'get back' some of what they feel is rightfully theirs when they have a legitimate claim."

Sometimes, for example, they inflate a claim to cover the deductible. "But these are not seasoned criminals," she says. "These are honest people who just don't recognize that fraud is a crime."

Or people who get clumsy when they veer from the straight and narrow. Insurers have dozens of anecdotes about people whose 12-inch televisions suddenly develop 29-inch screens once they're lost. Then there was the one about the policyholder with the damaged 20-foot boat that turned out to have been stored in an 18-foot garage.

The coalition has helped cut down on fraud through an alliance with Crime Stoppers, volunteer-run, privately funded, anonymous telephone-tip services operated in co-operation with local police forces.

Under the arrangement, a tip called in to Crime Stoppers about a possible fraud is relayed to the Insurance Crime Prevention Bureau and investigated. Police may also be called in.

If a claim is denied, Crime Stoppers receives 5% of the damage claim up to $1,500, which is then passed on to the tipster at the discretion of Crime Stoppers.

Source: Susan Yellin, *The Financial Post,* May 23, 1997, p. 10.

How to Encourage Fraud

Practice autocratic management.
Orient management to low trust and power.
Manage by crisis.
Centralize authority in top management.
Measure performance on a short-term basis.
Make profits the only criterion for success.
Make rewards punitive, stingy, and political.
Give feedback that is always critical and negative.
Create a highly hostile, competitive workplace.
Insist that everything be documented with a rule for everything.

Source: Adapted from G.J. Bologna and R.J. Lindquist, *Fraud Auditing and Forensic Accounting* (New York: John Wiley & Sons, 1987), pp. 47–49.

Control Procedures and Employee Monitoring

Auditors would be aghast at an organization that had no control policies and procedures, and rightly so. Controls in the form of job descriptions and performance specifications are indeed needed to help people know the jobs they are supposed to accomplish. Almost all people need some structure for their working hours. An organization whose only control is "trustworthy employees" has no control.[8] Unfortunately, "getting caught" is an important consideration for many people when coping with their problems. Controls provide the opportunity to get caught.

Without going into much detail about controls at this point, let it be noted that procedures for recognizing and explaining red flags are important for nipping frauds in the bud before they get bigger. Controls that reveal the following kinds of symptoms are necessary:[9]

- Missing documents.
- Second endorsements on cheques.
- Unusual endorsements.
- Unexplained adjustments to inventory balances.
- Unexplained adjustments to accounts receivable.
- Old items in bank reconciliations.
- Old outstanding cheques.
- Customer complaints.
- Unusual patterns in deposits in transit.

The problem with control systems is that they are essentially negative restrictions on people. The challenge is to have a bare minimum of useful controls and to avoid picky rules that are "fun to beat." The challenge of "beating the system," which can

---

[8] W.S. Albrecht, "How CPAs Can Help Clients Prevent Employee Fraud," *Journal of Accountancy*, December 1988, pp. 110–14.
[9] Ibid., pp. 113–14.

Regulators Unite to Fight Telemarketing Scams

Two Canadian securities commissions have joined regulators from 21 U.S. states and the U.S. Federal Trade Commission in an offensive on telemarketing scams that cost investors about $40 billion a year.

Securities regulators in Quebec and British Columbia are taking part in the campaign, "Project Field of Schemes," by publicizing some of the most significant cases of the past three months.

Frauds over the Internet are a new source of concern, an extension of the telemarketing campaigns that target old people.

"The Internet is like a huge classified ad section, with a money wanted column showing you where to invest, and it becomes a perfect medium for conveying investment offers," said Mark Griffin, president of the North American Securities Administrators Association.

The British Columbia Securities Commission supported the campaign because it knows all regulators deal with the same types of scams, often orchestrated by the same people.

"Frauds are similar wherever you go—and often the perpetrators have crossed jurisdictional boundaries so they can start fresh in a new place where they are not known," said Barbara Barry, communications manager at the BCSC.

"Basically, people and their greed are universal."

She noted a recent case involving a company called Goldman-Stanley consultants, which controlled four other firms. Its name was purposely similar to that of the well-known New York investment house and its stationery had a similar look.

"People who bought believed that Goldman-Stanley consultants were agents that were placing foreign exchange contract purchases for legitimate companies in other jurisdictions," Berry said.

Goldman-Stanley also used a storefront location to mimic a well-known Hong Kong investment firm in a successful attempt to solicit Asian clients.

Source: Ian Karleff, *The Financial Post,* July 3, 1997, p. 8.

lead to bigger and better things, is an invitation to fraudulent types of behaviour. (How many university students find ways to get into course registration before their scheduled times?)

Integrity by Example and Enforcement

The key to integrity in business is "accountability"—that is, each person must be willing to put his or her decisions and actions in the sunshine. There must be norms for these decisions and actions. Many organizations begin by publishing codes of conduct. Some of these codes are simple, and some are very elaborate. Government agencies and defence contractors typically have the most elaborate rules for employee conduct. Sometimes they work, sometimes they don't. A code can be effective if the "tone at the top" supports it. When the chairman of the board and the

---

WHERE DID HE COME FROM?

The controller defrauded the company for several million dollars. As it turned out, he was no controller at all. He didn't know a debit from a credit. The fraudster had been fired from five previous jobs where money had turned up missing. He was discovered one evening when the president showed up unexpectedly at the company and found a stranger in the office with the controller. The stranger was doing all of the accounting for the bogus controller.

Source: NACFE, "Auditing for Fraud."

---

president make themselves visible examples of the code, then other people will believe it is real. Subordinates will tend to follow the boss's lead.

Hiring and firing are important. Background checks on prospective employees are advisable. A new employee who has been a fox in some other organization's hen house will probably be a fox in a new place. Organizations have been known to hire private investigators to make these background checks. Fraudsters should be fired and, in most cases, prosecuted. They have a low rate of recidivism (repeat offences) if they are prosecuted, but they have a high rate if not.[10] Prosecution delivers the message that management does not believe that "occasional dishonesty" is acceptable.

REVIEW
CHECKPOINT

18.12 Make a two-column list with fraud-prevention management-style characteristics in one column and, opposite each of these, management-style characteristics that might lead to fraud.

FRAUD DETECTION

Since an organization cannot prevent all fraud, its auditors, accountants, and security personnel must be acquainted with some detection techniques. Frauds consist of the fraud act itself, the conversion of assets to the fraudster's use, and the cover-up. Catching people in the fraud act is difficult and unusual. The act of conversion is equally difficult to observe, since it typically takes place in secret away from the organization's offices (e.g., fencing stolen inventory). Many frauds are investigated by noticing signs and signals of fraud, then following the trail of missing, mutilated, or false documents that are part of the accounting records cover-up.

This chapter has already mentioned signs and signals in terms of red flags, oddities, and unusual events. Being able to notice these takes some experience, but this book can give some starting places.[11]

---

[10] Ibid., p. 114.

[11] Long lists of red flags can be found in Bologna and Lindquist, *Fraud Auditing*, pp. 49–56; Albrecht et. al., in *Management Fraud*, pp. 223–26; Statement on Auditing Standard 82; "Auditing for Fraud" courses of the Association of Certified Fraud Examiners; and courses offered by other organizations, such as the CICA and the Institute of Internal Auditors.

Red Flags

Employee Fraud.   Employee fraud usually, but not always, involves people below the top executive levels. Observation of persons' habits and lifestyle and changes in habits and lifestyle may reveal some red flags. Fraudsters in the past have exhibited these characteristics:

- Lose sleep.
- Take drugs.
- Can't relax.
- Can't look people in the eye.
- Go to confession (e.g., priest, psychiatrist).
- Work standing up.
- Drink too much.
- Become irritable easily.
- Get defensive, argumentative.
- Sweat excessively.
- Find excuses and scapegoats for mistakes.
- Work alone, work late.

Personality red flags are problematic because (1) honest people sometimes show them and (2) they often are hidden from view. It is easier to notice changes, especially when a person changes his or her lifestyle or spends more money than the salary justifies—for example, on homes, furniture, jewellery, clothes, boats, autos, vacations, and the like.

Often, telltale hints of the cover-up are visible. These generally appear in the accounting records. The key is to notice exceptions and oddities, such as transactions that are at odd times of the day, month, or season; too many or too few; in the wrong branch location; and in amounts too high, too low, too consistent, or too different. Exceptions and oddities can appear in these forms:

- Missing documents.
- Cash shortages and overages.
- Excessive voids and credit memos.
- Customer complaints.
- Common names or addresses for refunds.
- Adjustments to receivables and payables.
- General ledger that does not balance.
- Increased past due receivables.
- Inventory shortages.
- Increased scrap.
- Alterations on documents.
- Duplicate payments.
- Employees who cannot be found.
- Second endorsements on cheques.

High Style in the Mailroom

A female mailroom employee started wearing designer clothes (and making a big deal about it). She drove a new BMW to work. An observant manager, who had known her as an employee for seven years and knew she had no outside income, became suspicious. He asked the internal auditors to examine her responsibilities extra carefully. They discovered she had taken $97,000 over a two-year period.

Source: NACFE, "Auditing for Fraud."

- Documents being photocopied.
- Dormant accounts becoming active.

Management Fraud (fraudulent financial reporting)

LEARNING OBJECTIVE

6. Describe some common financial reporting fraud features and explain some audit and investigation procedures for detecting them.

Fraud that affects financial statements and causes them to be materially misleading often arises from the perceived need to "get through a difficult period." The difficult period may be characterized by a cash shortage, increased competition, cost overruns, and similar events. Managers usually view these conditions as "temporary," believing they can be overcome by getting a new loan, selling shares, or otherwise buying time to recover. In the meantime, falsified financial statements are used to "benefit the company." These conditions and circumstances have existed along with frauds in the past:

- Unfavourable industry conditions.
- Excess capacity.
- High debt.
- Profit squeeze.
- Strong foreign competition.
- Lack of working capital.
- Rapid expansion.
- Product obsolescence.
- Slow customer collections.
- Related party transactions.

By both fraud and "creative accounting," companies have caused financial statements to be materially misleading by (1) overstating revenues and assets, (2) understating expenses and liabilities, and (3) giving disclosures that are misleading or that omit important information. Generally, fraudulent financial statements show financial performance and ratios that are better than current industry experience or better than the company's own history. Sometimes the performance meets exactly the targets announced by management months earlier.

Because of the double-entry bookkeeping system, fraudulent accounting entries always affect two accounts and two places in financial statements. Since many frauds

Broker Vows to Repay Huge Client Losses

A former investment-market whiz kid facing multi-million-dollar lawsuits and fraud charges has vowed to reimburse client's losses, his lawyer says.

Mr. X faces 15 fraud charges totalling $22 million and lawsuits from more than 20 ex-clients claiming $10 million ...

Investors accused Mr. X, 33, of misrepresenting the value of their funds, negotiating without their knowledge and not repaying loans. His ex-employers and wife are also being sued.

After retirees, a taxi owner, a dentist, accountants, a builder and an actress told First Marathon Securities Ltd. and Midland Walwyn Capital Inc of unusual losses, Mr. X was fired and his licence suspended. Charged Monday in one of Canada's largest brokerage frauds, he was freed on bail.

Gone are the couple's Porsche, Jaguar and lavish parties, the couple's lawyer said. Their $1.3 million Forest Hill home and their Cobourg house are so heavily mortgaged "there might be no equity."

Two Toronto retirees claimed $582,121 U.S. was lost with Mr. X, court documents say.

Eight clients in million dollar claims cite Mr. X for "deceit, fraud ... negligence and breach of contract," said their lawyer, Neil Gross. "All of them have suffered devastating losses."

Source: Ian Robertson, *The Toronto Sun,* June 12, 1997, p. 2. Copyright 1997, *The Toronto Sun,* a division of Sun Media Corporation.

---

involve improper recognition of assets, there is a theory of the "dangling debit," which is an asset amount that can be investigated and found to be false or questionable. Frauds may involve the omission of liabilities, but the matter of finding and investigating the "dangling credit" is normally very difficult. It "dangles" off the books. Misleading disclosures also present difficulty, mainly because they involve words and messages instead of numbers. Omissions may be hard to notice, and misleading inferences may be very subtle.

A client's far-removed illegal acts may cause financial statements to be misleading, and external auditors are advised to be aware of circumstances that might indicate them. Below is a list of some signs and signals of the potential for illegal acts:

- Unauthorized transactions.
- Government investigations.
- Regulatory reports of violations.
- Payments to consultants, affiliates, employees for unspecified services.
- Excessive sales commissions and agent's fees.
- Unusually large cash payments.
- Unexplained payments to government officials.
- Failure to file tax returns, to pay duties and fees.

Overstated Revenue, Receivables, and Deferred Costs

Cali Computer Systems, Inc., sold franchises enabling local entrepreneurs to open stores and sell Cali products. The company granted territorial franchises, in one instance recording revenue of $800,000 and in another $580,000. Unfortunately, the first of these "contracts" for a territorial franchise simply did not exist, and the second was not executed and Cali had not performed its obligations by the time it was recorded. In both cases the imaginary revenue was about 40 percent of reported revenues. These franchises were more in the nature of business hopes than completed transactions.

Cali was supposed to deliver computer software in connection with the contracts and had deferred $277,000 of software development cost in connection with the programs. However, this software did not work, and the contracts were fulfilled with software purchased from other suppliers.

Source: SEC Accounting and Auditing Enforcement Release 190, 1988.

Bribery and Corruption: A New Global Social Concern

A recent article in the *White Paper* (May/June 1997), a publication of the Association of Certified Fraud Examiners, titled "The Global Explosion of Corruption—the Misuse of Public Power for Private Profit or Political Gain," identifies corruption as a major challenge in the new global, high-tech economy. A long section of the article talks about Transparency International, a unique organization dedicated to fighting global corruption. This section is reproduced in full below.

Transparency International Encourages Governments to Fight Corruption

In 1993, Dr. Peter Eigen, former World Bank director, founded Transparency International (TI) in Berlin as a not-for-profit, non-governmental organization, "to counter corruption ... in international business transactions," according to its mission statement.

The small group, which has organized over 60 chapters throughout the world, says that it encourages governments to establish laws, policies, and anti-corruption programs. TI is funded by multilateral groups (including the World Bank), national programs, and private companies.

TI says that corruption is causing vast sums of money to be misallocated by public officials in dozens of countries. The group says that funds which were originally earmarked for new schools, hospitals, and institutions to serve the most needy, are often channelled into projects of negligible social value by officials receiving kickbacks from commercial contractors.

Corruption is also the enemy of progress, TI says. Corrupt leaders cling to power, opposing efforts to open government, curbing personal freedoms, and abusing human rights, the group says. Also, the honest business person goes broke, the rules of a

The Corruption Scorecard

Corruption ranks in 1996, based on the level of corruption in a country perceived by employees of multinational firms and institutions (1 = most corrupt in survey, 54 = least corrupt)

1 Nigeria	19 Bolivia	37 Hong Kong
2 Pakistan	20 Argentina	38 Japan
3 Kenya	21 Italy	39 Austria
4 Bangladesh	22 Turkey	40 U.S.
5 China	23 Spain	41 Israel
6 Cameroon	24 Hungary	42 Germany
7 Venezuela	25 Jordan	43 Britain
8 Russia	26 Taiwan	44 Ireland
9 India	27 Greece	45 Australia
10 Indonesia	28 South Korea	46 Netherlands
11 Philippines	29 Malaysia	47 Switzerland
12 Uganda	30 Czech Rep.	48 Singapore
13 Columbia	31 Poland	49 Norway
14 Egypt	32 South Africa	50 Canada
15 Brazil	33 Portugal	51 Finland
16 Ecuador	34 Chile	52 Sweden
17 Mexico	35 Belgium	53 Denmark
18 Thailand	36 France	54 New Zealand

healthy economic system become twisted, and companies addicted to paying bribes become rotten, TI says.

The group says there are too many countries where corporations can pay bribes abroad and claim these as tax deductible expenses in their home countries. "We will do our best to get our house in order," said Ethiopian Prime Minister Meles Zenawi at an international conference a year ago, "but our Northern friends: please do not support the bribery by your exporters by giving them tax deductions for their bribes."

In 1996, a committee of the Organization for Economic Cooperation and Development (OECD) chaired by a Swiss professor at the University of Basel, Mark Pieth, published a report on corruption in international business, according to *The Wall Street Journal.*[12] The report said that only a third of 27 (now 29) member-governments in the OECD forbid outright domestic tax deduction for foreign bribes paid by their nationals. (These include the U.S., Canada, Britain, and Japan.)

Western countries whose tax regimes still allow or tolerate tax deductibility of foreign bribes as of October 1996, according to *The WSJ,* include Belgium, Luxembourg, France, Sweden, Greece, and Germany. In some nations, businesses claiming deductions can even write "bribe" or "extortion" on the relevant line in the tax form. Other nations, said *The WSJ,* dress their bribery in euphemism: on the German form such costs are called *nuetzliche Ausgaben*—"useful expenditures."

In mid-December 1996, the United Nations issued a "Declaration against corruption and bribery in international commercial transactions" which condemns all

---

[12] "Commercial Corruption," *The Wall Street Journal,* January 2, 1997.

corrupt practices, endorses work in curbing corruption, and calls for action by the U.N. itself. U.N. officials participated in some of the original planning sessions of TI.

"The mounting support for anti-corruption action in the international organizations is a vital requirement in raising this issue to highest political levels in governments around the globe," said Eigen. "But these initiatives only have an impact if they are followed up at the national level and if organizations like TI constantly monitor the official agencies to see their bold rhetoric is matched by meaningful action."

Electronic trading and funds transfer systems [see Chapter 19] combined with offshore banking havens and new financial instruments have facilitated the laundering of criminal and illegal funds. It has been estimated that up to 25% of financial instruments and foreign currency trading involves same kind of illegal money laundering scheme. Cross border capital flows now amount to $1.25 trillion per day. The illegitimate amounts are so huge that they threaten world financial markets. The only way to deal with money laundering of this scale is through international efforts. Unfortunately some major countries have been unwilling to cooperate. It is suspected that countries that have concentrations of huge banks such as in Japan have been reluctant to deter money laundering activities because of the huge profit involved. These banks quietly influence their governments to look the other way.

The only country to make it illegal to pay foreign bribes is the U.S. under its Foreign Corrupt Practices Act [see Chapter 16].

Key issues identified at an OECD conference in Paris in November 1997 include how broadly to define bribery (e.g., bribes to everyone or to public officials only), and a need for all countries to criminalize the acceptance of kickbacks.

As noted, however, the U.N. and other international organizations (such as the OECD) may soon make it possible with the use of sophisticated computerized accounting systems to more effectively fight international fraud.

In Canada more can be done to combat the global social ills caused by corruption. A recent article by V. Krishnan suggests that "Parliament has implicitly sanctioned the deductibility of payments to foreign government officials and employees. While it is illegal to bribe domestic officials to secure a contract or service, there is no prohibition against bribing foreign officials or employees. The only uncertainty is whether such payments are tax deductible."

This suggests that perhaps yet another type of assurance engagement may evolve in the future, the ethics audit, as indicated in the box below.

ETHICS AUDITS ON THE WAY, PROFESSOR SAYS

Within 10 years, some companies will give shareholders an "ethics audit" at annual meetings, says Wesley Cragg, a professor of business ethics at York University.

The independently prepared assessment of a company's ethical performance would join the financial audit, he told a seminar for corporate directors in Toronto yesterday.

Cragg said good ethical behavior is good business. "If you're going to be an efficient, modern corporation, you have no choice.

"Mining companies in this country have a very poor reputation, which they have acquired with some reason," but Vancouver gold miner **Placer Dome Ltd.,** for example, is trying to act ethically, even if it reduces profits.

Companies that put "social responsibility at the centre of their operations" are not dominant, but "they're out there."

They are partly driven by fear that if they fail to act, then governments may legislate standards. But they also see financial gains in ethical behavior, he said.

"Increasingly, boards are concerned about the ethical side of things, not what is legal but what is right," said lawyer Carol Hansell of Davies Ward & Beck.

Bribery is a big ethical problem, especially for companies operating in the Third World and the former Soviet Union. "You have a consultant and he's called the fixer. You don't ask what he does," a director said. "Many companies that I work with very closely ... say this is the sort of thing we have to do," Cragg agreed.

But he cited the case of a major Canadian mining company that has operated in Indonesia for 30 years and says it doesn't pay bribes. A spokesman for Toronto nickel giant Inco Ltd. initially said Inco was the company, but then withdrew the statement. He referred the question to his supervisor Dave Allen, who refused to respond to a direct question about whether Inco paid bribes.

Source: Dan Westel, *The Financial Post,* May 28, 1997, p. 12.

The box above suggests that in addition to international cooperation it is necessary to fight fraud by preventing it. A good way of achieving this is by an enforceable code of conduct. In fact a company without such a code suggests an improperly run company as far as protection of shareholders is concerned. This is why ethics audits may increasingly be demanded in the future. In addition, COCO Guidelines recommend such a code. The best way to fight fraud is to prevent it, and a code of ethics may be viewed as a type of preventive control.

A further illustration of the increased recognition that preventing frauds and bribery is becoming an important issue in Canada is given in *The Financial Post* editorial reprinted in the box below.

SUPPORT MOVE TO ESTABLISH WORLDWIDE ANTI-BRIBERY LAWS

The Canadian government should step up its encouragement of the Organization for Economic Cooperation & Development efforts to outlaw bribery. The worldwide set of fair and enforceable anti-bribery laws sought by the OECD is a beginning. But education is also necessary—the destructive effects of bribery must be well understood.

Bribery flourishes in Southeast Asia, the former Soviet Union, Latin America and Africa. And the ethical issues are by no means clear-cut. In Russia, for example, petty government officials routinely extort small bribes merely for doing the job they are poorly paid to do anyway. Is that bribery or an undeclared consumer fee for service? In other countries, bribery is outlawed, but there's more bribery there than in some nations that have no anti-bribery laws.

In enlightened Europe and North America, some aircraft manufacturers have corruptly paid millions of dollars to foreign government officials to get billion-dollar contracts. And European tax authorities often allow a foreign bribe to be deducted as a "commission" (no questions asked). This is not possible under Canadian tax law.

Canadian exporters may face acute dilemmas. Should a company depart from what is legal in Canada, and pay a bribe, or should it forfeit a lucrative order on the basis of what may be a very muddy ethical issue? Too often, a bribe is paid and the excuse is "everybody does it in that country."

The OECD initiative should be supported for three major reasons. First, bribery is an extra cost of doing business that should not have to be paid. Second, Canadian companies might find themselves at a direct disadvantage vis-à-vis manufacturers from other countries that are practised at the art of baksheesh.

Third, bribery damages the offshore economy by causing officials to make decisions based on how much silver crosses their palms rather than what is good for the economy. The cost of bribery is incorporated into the manufacturer's prices, which tends to punish local people who may already have a low living standard. And a weakened offshore economy is not good for the Canadian exporter. Mark Drake, senior vice-president of the Alliance of Manufacturers and Exporters Canada, says "More and more Canadian companies are recognizing that good ethics is good business."

International anti-bribery standards should have uniform characteristics. They should embody a realistic definition of bribery, one that excludes some of the sad practices of underpaid bureaucrats. Once bribery is defined, there should be no excuses taken from executives caught red-handed—the law must be applied equitably. And these standards must be applied consistently, worldwide. Canadian companies must not be placed at a disadvantage because they have higher standards than the competition.

Source: Editorial, *The Financial Post,* May 30, 1997.

R E V I E W
C H E C K P O I N T S

18.13   Is there anything odd about these situations? (1) Auditors performed a surprise payroll distribution, and J. Jones, S. Smith, and D. Douglas were absent from work. (2) A cheque to Larson Lectric Supply was endorsed with "Larson Lectric" above the signature of "Eloise Garfunkle." (3) Numerous cheques were issued dated January 1, May 19, July 4, September 2, October 13, and December 25, 1991.

18.14   What account could you audit to determine whether a company had recorded fictitious sales?

Internal Control

A study by KPMG showed that 50 percent of all frauds are detected by the internal control system. An important feature of internal control is the separation of these duties and responsibilities: (1) transaction authorization, (2) recordkeeping, (3) custody of, or access to, assets, and (4) reconciliation of actual assets to the accounting records. Generally, a person who, acting alone or in a conspiracy, can perform two or more of these functions also can commit a fraud by taking assets, converting them, and covering up. (Other control features were explained in Chapter 6.)

Fraud awareness auditing involves perceptions of the controls installed (or not installed) by a company, plus "thinking like a crook" to imagine ways and means of stealing. When controls are absent, the ways and means may be obvious. Otherwise, it may take some scheming to figure out how to steal from an organization.

THE TRUSTED EMPLOYEE

A small business owner hired his best friend to work as his accountant. The friend was given full unlimited access to all aspects of the business and was completely responsible for the accounting. Five years later, the owner finally terminated the friend because the business was not profitable. Upon taking over the accounting, the owner's wife found that cash receipts from customers were twice the amounts formerly recorded by the accountant "friend." An investigation revealed that the friend had stolen $450,000 in cash sales receipts from the business, while the owner had never made more than $16,000 a year. (The friend had even used the stolen money to make loans to the owner and to keep the business going!)

No Locks on the Door

Perini Corporation kept blank cheques in an unlocked storeroom, where every clerk and secretary had access. Also in the storeroom was the automatic cheque-signing machine. The prenumbered cheques were not logged and restricted to one person. The bookkeeper was very surprised to open the bank statement one month and find that $1.5 million in stolen cheques had been paid on the account.

Source: NACFE, "Auditing for Fraud."

WHEN YOUR IDENTITY IS STOLEN

Even your utility bills can be turned to fraudulent use.

A 22-year-old secretary realizes she's got an evil twin travelling around the country when Revenue Canada begins demanding she cough up unpaid taxes. Her imposter—who'd apparently applied for and received a social insurance number under her name years earlier—has been moving from job to job without paying taxes.

The names of children who died years ago are used to set up phony businesses that collect GST refunds. An Etobicoke man, who is eventually jailed for tax fraud, collected the names from tombstones.

Another con man opens a number of accounts at Vancouver-area banks using someone else's SIN and birth certificate. He defrauds the banks of more than $170,000 by depositing phony cheques and withdrawing the money from ATMs.

Identity thieves take over someone else's identity to commit fraud—either by applying for a credit card or loan, opening a bank account or using social insurance numbers to hide from the taxman.

These are some of the stories on the growing list of Canadian cases involving identity theft as identified by privacy commissioner Ann Cavoukian.

The victim often doesn't find out what's happened until months later and by that time his or her credit report is such a mess it can take years to sort out.

Cavoukian has just released a report on some of the steps she believes need to be taken to stop the crime. Some of the less obvious ones include the following:

Tips to prevent identity theft

- Shred or tear up sensitive documents before throwing them away. These include phone and utility bills, pre-approved credit applications and anything that provides credit card number, bank account number, tax information, your driver's license number or your birth date.

- Install a locked mailbox.

- Obtain a copy of your credit report regularly to check for fraudulent accounts and false address changes. Contact Equifax Canada Inc at 1-800-465-7166.

- Don't leave a paper record behind after using bank machines.

- Avoid writing your credit card number or SIN on a cheque.

- Don't give your credit card number out over the phone unless you know the company you're dealing with well. It's especially important not to provide personal information over cordless or cellular phones.

Source: Valeries Lawton, *Toronto Star,* July 6, 1997, B5. Reprinted with permission—The Toronto Star Syndicate.

REVIEW CHECKPOINTS

18.15 What could happen if a person could authorize medical insurance claims and enter them into the system for payment without supervisory review?

18.16 What could happen if the inventory warehouse manager also had responsibility for making the physical inventory observation and reconciling discrepancies to the perpetual inventory records?

SCHEMES AND DETECTION PROCEDURES
· · · · · · · · · · · ·

An article by J. Hall, titled "How to Spot Fraud," first printed in the October 1996 issue of *Journal of Accountancy,* is quoted in full in the following box:

---

1. Focus on Fraud Possibilities

Hard as it is to accept, most preventive controls can be beaten by a motivated thief. And when thieves are inside the organization, they may be part of the control effort itself.

Ask yourself how management steps such as reengineering, downsizing, outsourcing, computerization and globalization affect the reliability of controls—as well as the attitudes of those who have access to the assets.

Other places to look are industry resources. Many industry organizations maintain data on fraud cases. Since banks, insurers and others all support fraud prevention, contact your industry association's security professionals for guidance.

Keep files of news reports of fraud. These articles often contain enough detail to allow you to understand how the deed was done. But be careful not to get caught up in the drama of the fraud: Put less emphasis on the thieves and their reasons for stealing, focusing instead on the modus operandi.

Typical questions you should ask:

- What jobs are likely to provide opportunities for fraud?
- What opportunities exist for employees, executives, vendors, contractors' agents, customers and others?
- How could they get around approval or transaction confirmation controls?
- What general ledger account and cost center could the fraud be charged to?
- How could the thief deceive the manager in charge of those cost centers when the month-end reports are reviewed?

2. Know the Symptoms

Here's a short list of some fraud symptoms:

- Multiple endorsements on commercial cheques.
- The use of common or repetitive names for refunds—such as Smith or Jones or a commercial name that is very similar to one in your industry but is spelled slightly differently.
- Line items in standard reconciliations that don't go away.
- Customer complaints about having paid invoices for which they are being dunned.
- Adjustments to either inventory records or customer accounts.
- The addresses of vendors that are the same as employee addresses.
- No proceeds from the disposition of used assets.

When one of these symptoms appears, use caution. Often there are reasonable explanations and they usually don't lead to a thief—just an error or an ill-designed process. So don't jump to conclusions. Instead, track down the cause for the symptom.

Be especially cautious when reacting to a person's suspicious lifestyle. While such signs should sound an alarm, by themselves they prove nothing, but certainly more investigation is warranted.

3. Design Controls and Audit Procedures

In developing procedures, be sure to include specific steps calculated to look for fraud symptoms. And while measuring fraud exposure, assess the reliability of such controls.

4. Follow Through on All Symptoms Observed

Whoever finds a symptom of fraud—the external or internal auditor or a company manager—should resolve the situation before going on. Operate with an attitude of healthy professional skepticism. Beware of pressures to complete work within unreasonable deadlines. Be aware that the single symptom you are looking at may not be an isolated occurrence, it may be one of many.

If you believe the follow-up is beyond your capabilities, consider giving the problem to a professional investigator. There are legal liability dangers inherent in mishandling possible fraud cases."

The same article provides a case study reproduced in the following box:

THE REBATE SCAM

A construction company's project manager engineered a simple scam that earned him about $250,000 before he was unmasked. Here's how he did it—and how he was tripped up:

The project manager opened a bank account using a name very similar to the name of the construction project he was managing. He then approached three major suppliers and requested cash rebates in excess of normal industry practice. In exchange, he guaranteed each would be the sole source for their respective products. In addition, he promised they would be paid promptly for all materials delivered. He told them the rebates were due on the first of each month for all transactions of the proceeding month. The cheques were to be made payable to the name on the bogus bank account.

The suppliers agreed to the unusual terms in order to secure the business. None questioned the name on the cheques because it was close enough to the actual project name.

The arrangement worked smoothly for several months. Rebate cheques were delivered to the project manager each month and he deposited them into his account. After the cheques cleared, he withdrew most of the funds using cashier's cheques.

The scheme came to light when a supervisor in the construction company's accounts payable department questioned why prompt-payment discounts weren't being made to the three suppliers. She had just attended a fraud-awareness seminar and remembered that such an unusual arrangement might be a symptom of fraud. Rather than question either the project manager or the suppliers, she correctly referred the matter to the corporate audit department for investigation.

The auditors made simultaneous unannounced visits to all three suppliers. Two wouldn't talk, but the third explained the relationship and provided copies of the canceled rebate cheques.

Lessons learned from the case:

- It's relatively easy to open unauthorized bank accounts because most banks have limited ability to verify the identity of the person opening an account.
- Scam artists know how to cash cheques—to any payee, in any amount.
- Schemes that involve relationships with suppliers are particularly hard to prevent and detect.
- When contracting with suppliers, try to secure the right to review any appropriate records. While this is fairly common in the contracting environment, it's also something to consider for other relationships in which purchase orders are used.

In this section of the chapter, we will try a new approach: we will consider some "casettes" (little cases). They will follow a standard format in two major parts: (1) Case Situation, and (2) Audit Approach. Some problems at the end of the chapter will give the case situation, and you will be assigned to write the audit approach section. The first three casettes deal with employee fraud, and the last two deal with management fraud. With the first three casettes, you can practise on learning objective 5: Describe some common employee fraud schemes and explain some audit and investigation procedures for detecting them. With the last two casettes, you can practise on learning objective 6: Describe some common financial reporting fraud features and explain some audit and investigation procedures for detecting them.

Casette 18.1
Case of the Missing Petty Cash

Problem

Petty cash embezzlement.

Method

The petty cash custodian (1) brought postage receipts from home and paid them from the fund, (2) persuaded the supervisor to sign blank authorization slips the custodian could use when the supervisor was away, and using these to pay for fictitious meals and minor supplies, (3) took cash to get through the weekend, replacing it the next week.

Paper Trail

Postage receipts were from a distant post office station the company did not use. The blank slips were dated on days the supervisor was absent. The fund was cash short during the weekend and for a few days the following week.

Amount

The fund was small ($100), but the custodian replenished it about every two working days, stealing about $20 each time. With about 260 working days per year and 130 reimbursements, the custodian was stealing about $2,600 per year. The custodian was looking forward to getting promoted to general cashier and bigger and better things!

AUDIT APPROACH

Objective

Obtain evidence of the existence and validity of petty cash transactions.

Control

A supervisor is assigned to approve petty cash disbursements by examining them for validity and signing an authorization slip.

Test of Controls

Audit for transaction authorization and validity. Select a sample of petty cash reimbursement cheque copies with receipts and authorization slips attached; study them for evidence of authorization and validity (vouching procedure). Notice the nature and content of the receipts. Obtain supervisor's vacation schedule and compare dates to authorization slip dates.

Audit of Balance

On Friday count the petty cash and receipts to see that they add up to $100. Then, count the fund again later in the afternoon. (Be sure the second count is a surprise and that the custodian and supervisor sign off on the count working paper so the auditor will not be accused of theft.)

Discovery Summary

Knowing the location of the nearby post office branch used by the company, the auditor noticed the pattern of many receipts from a distant branch, which was near the custodian's apartment. Several authorizations were dated during the supervisor's vacation, and he readily admitted signing the forms in blank so his own supervisor "wouldn't be bothered." The second count on the same day was a real surprise, and the fund was found $35 short.

CASETTE 18.2
THE LAUNDRY MONEY SKIM

Problem

Stolen cash receipts skimmed from collection.

  Albert owned and operated 40 coin laundries around town. As the business grew, he could no longer visit each one, empty the cash boxes, and deposit the receipts. Each location grossed about $140 to $160 per day, operating 365 days per year. (Gross income about $2 million per year.)

Method

Four part-time employees each visited 10 locations, collecting the cash boxes and delivering them to Albert's office, where he would count the coins and currency (from the change machine) and prepare a bank deposit. One of the employees skimmed $5 to $10 from each location visited each day.

Paper Trail

None, unfortunately. The first paper that gets produced is Albert's bank deposit, and the money is gone by then.

Amount

The daily theft does not seem like much, but at an average of $7.50 per day from each of 10 locations, it was about $27,000 per year. If all four of the employees had stolen the same amount, the loss could have been about $100,000 per year.

AUDIT APPROACH

Objective

Obtain evidence of the completeness of cash receipts—that is, that all the cash received is delivered to Albert for deposit.

Control

Controls over the part-time employees were nonexistent. There was no overt or covert surprise observation and no times when two people went to collect cash (thereby needing to agree, in collusion, to steal). There was no rotation of locations or other indications to the employees that Albert was concerned about control.

Test of Controls

With no controls there are no test of control procedures. Obviously, however, "thinking like a crook" leads to the conclusion that the employees could simply pocket money.

Audit of Balance

The "balance" in this case is the total revenue that should have been deposited, and auditing for completeness is always difficult. Albert marked a quantity of coins with an etching tool and marked some $1 and $5 bills with ink. Unknown to the employees, he put these in all the locations, carefully noting the coins and bills in each.

Discovery Summary

Sure enough, a pattern of missing money emerged. When confronted, the employee confessed.

Casette 18.3
The Well-Padded Payroll

Problem

Embezzlement with fictitious people on the payroll.

Method

Maybelle had responsibility for preparing personnel files for new hires, approval of wages, verification of time cards, and distribution of payroll cheques. She "hired" fictitious employees, faked their records, and ordered cheques through the payroll system. She deposited some cheques in several personal bank accounts and cashed others, endorsing all of them with the names of the fictitious employees and her own.

Paper Trail

Payroll creates a large paper trail with individual earnings records, T-4 tax forms, payroll deductions for taxes and insurance, and payroll tax reports. Maybelle mailed all the T-4 forms to the same post office box.

Amount

Maybelle stole $160,000 by creating some "ghosts," usually three to five out of 112 people on the payroll, and paying them an average of $256 per week for three years. Sometimes the ghosts quit and were later replaced by others. But she stole "only" about 2 percent of the payroll funds during the period.

AUDIT APPROACH

Objective

Obtain evidence of the existence and validity of payroll transactions.

Control

Different people should be responsible for hiring (preparing personnel files), approving wages, and distributing payroll cheques. "Thinking like a crook" leads an auditor to see that Maybelle could put people on the payroll and obtain their cheques.

Test of Controls

Audit for transaction authorization and validity. Random sampling might not work because of the small number of ghosts. Look for the obvious. Select several weeks' cheque blocks, account for numerical sequence (to see whether any cheques have been removed), and examine cancelled cheques for two endorsements.

Audit of Balance

There may be no "balance" to audit, other than the accumulated total of payroll transactions, and

the total may not appear out of line with history because the fraud is small in relation to total payroll and has been going on for years. Conduct a surprise payroll distribution, follow up by examining prior cancelled cheques for the missing employees. Scan personnel files for common addresses.

Discovery Summary

Both the surprise distribution and the scan for common addresses provided the names of two or three exceptions. Both led to prior cancelled cheques (which Maybelle had not removed and the bank reconciler had not noticed), which carried Maybelle's own name as endorser. Confronted, she confessed.

Casette 18.4
False Sales, Accounts Receivable, and Inventory

Problem

Overstated sales and accounts receivable caused overstated net income, retained earnings, current assets, working capital, and total assets.

Method

Q.T. Wilson was a turnaround specialist who took the challenge at Mini Marc Corporation, a manufacturer of computer peripheral equipment. He set high goals for sales and profits. To meet these goals, managers shipped bricks to distributors and recorded some as sales of equipment to retail distributors and some as inventory out on consignment. No real products left the plant. The theory was that actual sales would grow, and the bricks would be replaced later with real products. In the meantime, the distributors may have thought they were holding consignment inventory in the unopened cartons.

Paper Trail

All the paperwork was in order because the managers had falsified the sales and consignment invoices, but they did not have customer purchase orders for all the false sales. Shipping papers were in order, and several shipping employees knew the boxes did not contain disk drives.

Amount

Prior to the manipulation, annual sales were $135 million. During the two falsification years, sales were $185 million and $362 million. Net income went up from a loss of $20 million to $23 million (income), then to $31 million (income); and the gross margin percent went from 6 percent to 28 percent. The revenue and profit figures outpaced the industry performance. The accounts receivable collection period grew to 94 days, while it was 70 days elsewhere in the industry.

AUDIT APPROACH

Objective

Obtain evidence about the existence and valuation of sales, accounts receivable, and inventory.

Control

Company accounting and control procedures required customer purchase orders or contracts evidencing real orders. A sales invoice was supposed to indicate the products and their prices, and shipping documents were supposed to indicate actual shipment. Sales were always charged to the customer's account receivable.

Test of Controls

There were no glaring control omissions such that "thinking like a crook" would have pointed to fraud possibilities. Sensitive auditors might have noticed the high tension created among employees by concentration on meeting profit goals. Normal selection of sales transactions with vouching to customer orders and shipping documents might turn up a missing customer order. Otherwise, the paperwork would seem to be in order. The problem lay in the managers' power to override controls and instruct shipping people to send bricks. Most auditors do not ask the question: "Have you shipped anything, other than company products, this year?"

Audit of Balance

Confirmations of distributors' accounts receivable might have elicited exception responses. The problem was to have a large enough confirmation sample to pick up some of these distributors or to be skeptical enough to send a special sample of confirmations to distributors who took the "sales" near the end of the accounting period. Observation of inventory should include some inspection of goods not on the company's premises.

The overstatements were not detected. The confirmation sample was small and did not contain any of the false shipments. Tests of detail transactions did not turn up any missing customer orders. The inventory out on consignment was audited by obtaining a written confirmation from the holders, who apparently had not opened the boxes. The remarkable financial performance was attributed to good management.

Casette 18.5
Overstate the Inventory, Understate the Cost of Goods Sold

Problem

Overstated inventory caused understated cost of goods sold, overstated net income and retained earnings, and overstated current assets, working capital, and total assets.

Method

A division manager at Doughboy Foods wanted to meet his profit goals and simply submitted overstated quantities in inventory reports. The manager (a) inserted fictitious count sheets in the independent auditors' working papers, (b) handed additional count sheets to the independent auditors after the count was completed saying "these got left out of your set," and (c) inserted false data into the computer system that produced a final inventory compilation (even though this ploy caused the computer-generated inventory not to match with the count sheets).

Paper Trail

In general, management reports should correspond to accounting records. The manager's inventory reports showed amounts larger than shown in the accounts. He fixed the problem by showing false inventory that was "not recorded on the books."

Amount

The food products inventory was overstated by $650,000. Through a two-year period, the false reports caused an income overstatement of 15 percent in the first year and would have caused a 39 percent overstatement the second year.

AUDIT APPROACH

Objective

Obtain evidence of the existence, completeness, and valuation of inventory.

Control

Inventory counts should be taken under controlled conditions, but not under the control of managers who might benefit from manipulation. (However, if these managers are present, auditors should nevertheless be prepared to perform the audit work.) Inventory-takers should be trained and follow instructions for recording quantities and condition.

Test of Controls

Auditors should attend the inventory-taker training sessions and study the instructions for adequacy. Observation of the inventory-taking should be conducted by managers and by auditors to ensure compliance with the instructions.

Audit of Balance

For evidence of existence, select a sample of inventory items from the perpetual records and test-count them in the warehouse. For evidence of completeness, select a sample of inventory items in the warehouse, test-count them, and trace them to the final inventory compilation. For evidence of valuation, find the proper prices of inventory for one or both of the samples, calculate the total cost for the items, and compare to their amounts recorded in the books. Compare book inventory amounts to management reports. Control the working papers so that only members of the audit team have access. Analytical procedures gave some signals. The particular manager's division had the lowest inventory turnover rate (6.3) among all the company divisions (comparable turnover, about 11.1) and its inventory had consistently increased from year to year (227 percent over the two-year period).

Discovery Summary

In the second year, when the manager handed over the count sheets "that got left out of your set," the

auditor thanked him, then went to the warehouse to check them out. Finding them inaccurate, she compared book inventories to his management reports and found an overstatement in the reports. This prompted further comparison of the computer-generated inventory with the count sheets and more evidence of overstated quantities on 22 of the 99 count sheets.

R E V I E W
C H E C K P O I N T S

18.17 If the petty cash custodian were replaced and the frequency of fund reimbursement decreased from every two days to every four days, what might you suspect?

18.18 Give some examples of control omissions that would make it easy to "think like a crook" and see opportunities for fraud.

18.19 If sales and income were overstated by recording a false cash sale at the end of the year, what "dangling debit" might give the scheme away?

18.20 What three general descriptions can be given to manipulations that produce materially misleading financial statements?

DOCUMENTS, SOURCES, AND "EXTENDED PROCEDURES"

References are often made in the auditing literature to "extended procedures," but these are rarely defined and listed. Authorities are afraid that a list will limit the range of such procedures, so "extended procedures" is generally left undefined as an open-ended set to refer vaguely to "whatever is necessary in the circumstances." This section describes some of the "extended procedures" with the proviso that (1) some auditors may consider them ordinary and (2) other auditors may consider them unnecessary in any circumstances. Even so, they are useful detective procedures in either event.

Content of Common Documents

Auditing textbooks often advise beginner auditors to "examine cheques," and to "check the employees on a payroll." It helps to know something about these common documents and the information that can be seen on them.

Information on a Cheque

Exhibit 18–2 describes the information found on a typical cheque. Knowledge of the codes for federal reserve districts, offices, states, and bank identification numbers could enable an auditor to spot a crude cheque forgery. Similarly, a forger's mistakes with the optical identification printing or the magnetic cheque number might supply a tipoff. If the amount of a cheque is altered after it has cleared the bank, the change would be noted by comparing the magnetic imprint of the amount paid to the amount written on the cheque face. The back of a cheque carries the endorsement(s) of the payees and holders in the due course; the date and the name and routing number of the bank where the cheque was deposited; and the date, identification of the federal reserve office, and its routing number for the federal reserve cheque clearing. (Sometimes there is no federal reserve clearing identification when local cheques are cleared locally without going through a federal reserve office.) Auditors can follow the path of a cancelled cheque by following the banks where it was deposited and cleared. This route may or may not correspond with the characteristics of the payee. (For example, ask why a cheque to a local business in Mississauga, Ontario, should be deposited in a small Missouri bank and cleared through the St. Louis federal reserve office.)

E X H I B I T 18–2   HOW TO READ A CANCELLED CHEQUE AND ENDORSEMENT

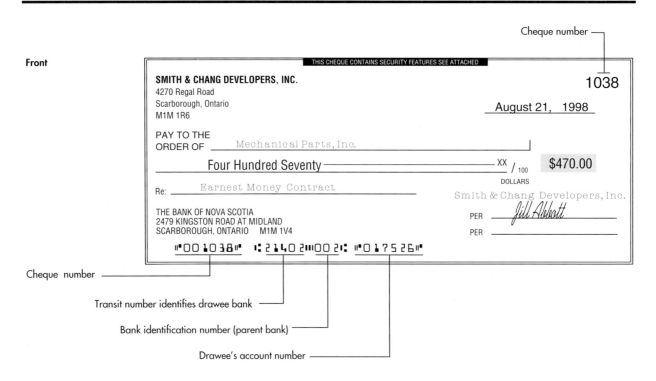

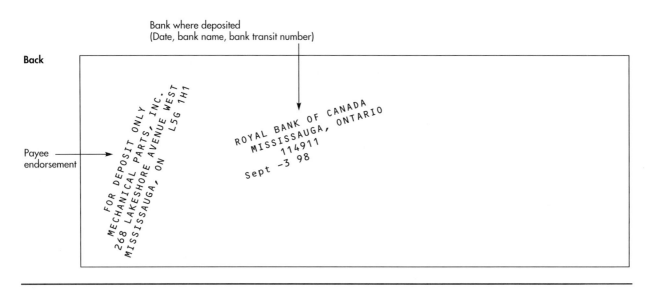

Information on a Bank Statement

Most of the information shown on the bank statement in Exhibit 18–3 is self-explanatory. However, auditors should not overlook the usefulness of some of the information: the bank's count and dollar amount of deposits and cheques can be compared to the detail data on the statement; the account holder's business identification number is on the statement, and this can be used in other databases (for individuals, this is a place to get a person's Social Insurance number); and the statement itself can be studied for alterations.

E X H I B I T 18–3   **SMALL BUSINESS BANK STATEMENT**

```
                                                                 27
      ⊠ North Country Bank

        MISSISSAUGA, ON                              ACCOUNT
        P.O. BOX 908                 ---         604017-526-5
        KINGSTON, ON  K5G 2H3        ---   ---
                                     ---             PAGE
                                     ---              1

        CAULCO INC                             SIN/TAX ID
        BLDG 1 OFFICE F                        74-2076251
        5450 BEE CAVE RD
        MISSISSAUGA, ON                        CYC MC FREQ
        L5G 1H2                                01 01 M0000

        **  YOUR CHECKING ACCOUNT      01-29-88 THRU 02-29-88 **

  TO YOUR PREVIOUS BALANCE OF - - - - - - - -      7,559.06
  YOU ADDED          1 DEPOSITS FOR  - - - - -      5,654.16
  YOU SUBTRACTED   26 WITHDRAWALS FOR - - - - -    10,838.29
  GIVING YOU A CURRENT BALANCE OF - - - - - - -     7,374.93

  NUMBER OF DAYS USED FOR AVERAGES  - - - - - -           31
  YOUR AVERAGE LEDGER BALANCE - - - - - - - - -      4,014.67
  YOUR LOW BALANCE OCCURRED ON 02-22 AND WAS  -      2,374.93

                      THANK YOU


  -----------------------------------------------------------
  -----------------------------------------------------------
                   DEPOSITS AND OTHER ADDITIONS

      DATE      AMOUNT
      0204      5654.16 ✔
  -----------------------------------------------------------
                   CHECKS AND OTHER WITHDRAWALS

  CHECK DATE    AMOUNT CHECK DATE    AMOUNT CHECK DATE     AMOUNT
  2201 0211     57.83✔ 2214 0203    403.92✔ 2225 0217   ✔ 182.77
    **                 2215 0203    135.59✔   **
  2205 0222     16.72✔ 2216 0216      6.16✔ 2231 0205   ✔ 254.37
  2206 0203    533.28✔ 2217 0217    138.43✔ 2232 0210   ✔  60.61
  2207 0203   1312.15✔ 2218 0217    131.92✔
    **                 2219 0217     82.97✔ 2234 0217   ✔  64.69
  2209 0203    247.10✔ 2220 0217     87.49✔ 2235 0218   ✔ 279.97
  2210 0203    249.98✔ 2221 0217     85.68✔   **
  2211 0203    255.26✔ 2222 0217     84.69✔ 2238 0219   ✔  90.00
  2212 0203    242.09✔   **
  2213 0203    384.91✔ 2224 0217    449.71✔
```

Valid Social Insurance Numbers

In Canada, Social Insurance Numbers (SINs) have become a universal identification number. They can be useful to auditors when checking the personnel files and the validity of people on the payroll. Here are some characteristics of SINs:[13]

- Every SIN consists of three groups of digits. Each group has three digits (XXX; XXX; XXX). No group contains consecutive zeros, so 000 XXX XXX, XXX 000 XXX, and XXX XXX 000 are not valid numbers.

- The first three digits gives the "area," indicating the province or territory where the number was issued. Numbers are usually issued at an early age, so the number may identify the province of birth. (Careful, however—Human Resources Development Canada may sometimes use numbers assigned to one geographic area for another.) In addition, some numbers are issued as a courtesy to foreign visitors and foreign students.

- Working with Human Resources Development Canada, an auditor may be able to detect fictitious SIN numbers.

· ·

R E V I E W
C H E C K P O I N T S

18.21 How could you tell whether the amount on a cheque had been raised after it was paid by a bank?

18.22 If a false Social Insurance Number of a new employee is entered in the payroll system, and the employee receives a paycheque, what control in the system is not being used? What's wrong with this number: 585 671 234 for Byron Middleton, born July 1, 1950, in Edmonton, Alberta?

· ·

Sources of Information

A wide variety of records and information is available for various kinds of investigations ranging from personal background checks to business enquiries. Our concern here is with public records and ways to get them. Only a few of the hundreds of sources are described briefly below.

General Business Sources

City and county tax assessor–collectors keep files on real property by address and legal description, owner, taxable value, improvements, and amount of taxes and delinquencies. Province (and some city) regulatory agencies have directories of liquor licences, and various professionals (e.g., PAs, dentists, doctors, plumbers, electricians). Provincial building ministries and ministers of public housing may have a central index file of appraisers, real estate brokers, and most components of the building industry. The industry and trade ministries have data on companies that apply for import and export licences. The federal Ministry of Transportation maintains files on the chain of ownership of all civil aircraft in Canada. Provincial

---

[13] Caution: Human Resources Development Canada periodically adds numbers that have been issued and may use numbers assigned to one geographic area for another. If the validity of an SIN becomes important in an audit, check with Human Resources Development Canada to ascertain the current status of numbers issued. For further reference, see M. L. Levy, "Financial Fraud: Schemes and Indicia," *Journal of Accountancy*, August 1985, p. 85; E. J. Pankau, *Check it Out* (Houston: Cloak & Data Press, 1990), pp. 20–27.

securities commissions have extensive financial information on registered companies and their properties, principal officers, directors, and owners. Local Better Business Bureaus keep information about criminal rackets, cons, and their operators, and can provide information about the business reputation of local businesses. Standard & Poor's Register of Corporations, Directors, and Executives lists about 37,000 public and private companies and the names and titles of over 400,000 officials. The Internet and various on-line information sources are becoming increasingly important not only in investigative accounting but as part of gaining familiarity with a new client in a normal audit.[14]

Business and Asset Identification Sources

According to Pankau, each region and province has a system for registering businesses—corporations, joint ventures, sole proprietorships, and partnerships. They keep files on registered "assumed names" (DBA, or "doing business as" names). Some businesses may be registered with a province and not a region, or with a region and not a province. All real corporations are chartered by a province or federal government, and each province's ministry of consumer and corporate affairs keeps corporate record information, such as the date of registration and the initial officers and owners. (Using these sources, you can find the assets or business "hidden" in the spouse's name.) Crooks often work through a labyrinth of business entities, and you can find all the registered ones in these sources. You can find phony vendor companies created by real employees to bilk employers with false billings. Banks, finance companies, and other creditors often file Uniform Commercial Code (UCC) records to record the interest of the creditor in assets used as collateral for a loan so that other parties cannot claim interest in the assets (e.g., boats, business equipment, appliances). UCCs are found in regional clerks' offices and in the province's office of the ministry of consumer and/or commercial affairs. (They are also on-line in some commercial data bases.)[15]

Federal and Provincial Revenue Agencies

Ever wonder how revenue agents find tax evaders? One accountant described the following sources of tips for possible big audit findings. (1) Police arrest records point to people who may have illicit unreported income. (2) Real estate sales records may identify people who "forget" to put their sales in a tax return. (3) Auto registrations of expensive cars point to people who have a lot of money to spend—maybe some unreported income. (4) Comparison of provincial sales tax returns with income tax revenue amounts may reveal discrepancies (depending on which tax collector is feared the most). (5) Agents have used university-town newspaper rental ads to identify people who rent rooms, garage apartments, duplex halves, and the like, but forget to report the income. The following boxes provide illustrations of procedures used in public sector auditing and by insurance fraud auditors, respectively.

---

[14] Hundreds of sources and directories under the categories of business, finance, people, property, and electronic databases are listed and described in the U.S. General Accounting Office publication *Investigators' Guide to Sources of Information* (GAO/OSI-88-1, March 1988, updated periodically).
Also, insider information is increasingly difficult to "keep under the lid" as investors form on-line investor forums to assist each other in passing on "hot tips." See J.A. Abbey, "Fools and Their Money," *Time*, June 17, 1996, pp. 51–54). Auditors may find these on-line services useful sources of information on risks and uncertainties facing their clients.

[15] These and other sources of business and personal information are described in Pankau, *Check It Out.*

QUOTA REPORTS FISHY?

HALIFAX—New recruits to the ranks of the federal fisheries enforcement program are to be given courses in accounting so they can net fishermen who have been cooking their books. And inspectors currently on the payroll of the Fisheries and Oceans Department will be given crash courses in audit procedures over the next several months that will teach them to focus on crooked practices in the fishing industry. A 1994 audit suggested that much of the fish caught on the country's coasts slips through the federal quota system as a result of misreporting of black market trading. The report by federal auditors was obtained by The Canadian Press news service under the *Access to Information Act.*

It is said the inspectors, who tend to concentrate on the mesh sizes of nets and the species and volumes of fish in a trawler's hold, should focus more on the records and catch reports maintained by fishermen. Authors of the report suggested the inspectors attend commercial-crime courses conducted by the RCMP. The audit pointed to some fishermen, provided with individual quotas, as possible villains who have taken advantage of procedural gaps in enforcement to cheat the quota system.

Over the last few years, individual quotas have replaced the shared quota system which set overall limits on catches within designated fisheries. The new system reduced competition for the total allowable catches and extended the season for fishermen who survived devastation of the east coast cod fishery. It was eventually extended to the west coast and Lake Erie fisheries.

Despite its shortcomings, however, the bureaucrats who reviewed the process hailed the individual quota system as a stabilizing factor in the fragile fishing industry.

Source: The Bottom Line, September 1996, p. 6.

FORENSICS ON FRONT LINES IN WAR ON INSURANCE FRAUDS

TORONTO—Forensic accountants play an increasingly important role in documenting, proving and reducing insurance fraud.

Insurance adjusters and lawyers have long used accountants to document clearly fraudulent claims. However, many insurance companies, concerned about huge losses to fraud—about $1.3 billion a year in property and casualty (P&C) claims alone—have recently set up their own fraud-busting Special Investigation Units (SIUs).

The SIUs, staffed mostly by ex commercial crime unit police officers, work proactively to reduce fraud by investigating all claims above a certain amount, as well as suspicious claims.

Once they have established the possibility of fraud, the SIUs (or insurance counsel, if the claim has already progressed to the litigation stage) turn to forensic accountants for the hard proof. "It's just starting to happen," said Ted

Baskerville of Lindquist Avey MacDonald Baskerville. "Our role up to now has always been to deal with claims that are overstated—or appear to be—or with arson, or staged theft."

In suspected arson or staged theft cases, Lindquist Avey's forensic specialists determine the insured's possible financial motive by looking at details of ownership or management, historical financial results, past and future obligations, profitability and cash flow.

They prepare a general profile of the company, including its relationship with creditors, and try to answer the following: Do owners have financial needs they can't satisfy legitimately through the business? What do the owners withdraw from the company, or how do they benefit from it in other ways?

In cases of possible theft, it's important to look at other businesses owned by the insureds; maybe they're trying to run down one business for the benefit of another.

The growing use of electronic document storage systems can have unexpected benefits for the forensic sleuth.

According to Ken Gibson of Mintz & Partners in Toronto, "people sometimes don't realize what they have stored." Many systems automatically back up computer communications like e-mail.

Aspiring fraud perpetrators may destroy the e-mail record in their own computers, but forget, or don't know, that investigators can read the backup disk.

Gibson typically deals with commercial damage claims—theft for example, where inventory appears to be gone, but there's little evidence of a break-in.

In those sorts of cases, he said, investigators try to establish whether anything is in fact missing and, if so, whether it had any real value.

Often, a line of goods, such as video or electronic products, isn't selling, and then it allegedly disappears.

The forensic investigator looks at sales figures, dealings with suppliers, and interviews employees or others involved.

Fraud by employees, leading to fidelity bond claims, is a growth industry, according to Ivor Gottschalk of Ernst & Young's Toronto-based forensic and litigation accounting group.

Often, an employee in a company's purchasing department orders an unnecessary or nonexistent material or service, and gets a kickback for the order.

Other types of fraud include setting up fake suppliers, fictitious employees on a payroll, or phony accounts payable.

"People are getting more and more creative," said Gottschalk.

"We're seeing fraud on the other side, where there's actually fraud in collusion with customers. Companies will normally control their purchasing departments quite closely because they're aware that purchasing is very vulnerable to outside forces.

"But generally, you wouldn't think of your accounts receivable clerk as being in a position to benefit somebody outside the company, writing off invoices to customers, for example."

Many forensic accountants are members of the Association of Certified Fraud Examiners, based in the U.S., but with more than 900 Canadian members in nine chapters.

18.23 Where could you find information about real estate valuation? aircraft ownership? names of licensed doctors? assumed (fictitious) business names? liens
on personal property?

Extended Procedures

LEARNING OBJECTIVE
7. Explain the use of some
extended audit proce-
dures for finding fraud.

The nature of extended procedures is limited only by an auditor's imagination and,
sometimes, the willingness of management to co-operate in extraordinary audit
activities. Next is a short series of extended procedures, with some brief explanations.[16]

Count the Petty Cash Twice in a Day
The second count is unexpected, and you might catch an embezzling custodian short.

Investigate Suppliers (vendors)
Check the Better Business Bureau for reputation, the telephone book for a listing and
address, and the provincial corporation records for owners and assumed names. You
may find fictitious vendors being used to make false billings or companies related to
purchasing department employees.

Investigate Customers
As with vendors, investigation may reveal companies set up by insiders, with billings
at below-list prices so that the insiders can "buy" goods and resell them at a profit.

Examine Endorsements on Cancelled Cheques
Look for second endorsements, especially the names of employees. Most business
payments are deposited with one endorsement. Be sure to include cheques payable to
"cash" or to a bank for purchase of cashiers' cheques. The second endorsee indicates
that the payee may not have received the benefit of the payment.

Add Up the Accounts Receivable Subsidiary
Cash payments on customer accounts have been stolen, with receipts given credit
entry to the customer account, but no cash deposit and no entry to the control
account.

Audit General Journal Entries
Experience has shown that the largest number of accounting errors requiring adjustment are found in nonroutine, nonsystematic journal entries. (Systematic accounting
is the processing of large volumes of day-to-day ordinary transactions.)

[16] Further explanation of these and other procedures can be found in the books and articles cited in preceding footnotes and in these sources: *AICPA Technical Practice Aids* (TPA 8200.02); D. Churbuck, "Desktop Forgery," *Forbes*,
November 27, 1989, pp. 246–254; O. Hilton, *Scientific Examination of Questioned Documents*, rev. ed. (New York:
Elsevier North Holland, 1982); A.C. Levinston, "40 Years of Embezzlement Tracking," *Internal Auditor*, April 1991,
pp. 51–55.

Match Payroll to Life and Medical Insurance Deductions

Ghosts on the payroll seldom elect these insurance coverages. Doing so reduces the embezzler's take and complicates the cover-up.

Match Payroll to Social Insurance Numbers

Fictitious SINs may be chosen at random; if so, the fraudster will have made the mistake of using an unissued number or one that does not match with the birthdate. Sort the payroll SINs in numerical order and look for false, duplicate, or unlikely (e.g., consecutive) numbers.

Match Payroll with Addresses

Look for multiple persons at the same address.

Retrieve Customers' Cheques

If an employee has diverted customer payments, the cancelled cheques showing endorsements and deposits to a bank where the company has no account are not available because they are returned to the issuing organization (customer). Ask the customer to give originals or copies, or to provide access for examination.

Use Marked Coins and Currency

Plant marked money in locations where cash collections should be gathered for turning over for deposit.

Measure Deposit Lag Time

Compare the dates of cash debit recording and deposit slip dates to dates credited by the bank. Someone who takes cash, then holds the deposit for the next cash receipts to make up the difference, causes a delay between the date of recording and the bank's date of deposit.

Document Examination

Look for erasures, alterations, copies where originals should be filed, telltale lines from a copier when a document has been pieced together, handwriting, and other oddities. Professional document examination is a technical activity that requires special training (e.g., RCMP), but crude alterations may be observed, at least enough to bring them to specialists' attention.

Enquire, Ask Questions

Be careful not to discuss fraud possibilities with the managers who might be involved. It gives them a chance to cover up or run. Wells described fraud audit questioning (FAQ) as a nonaccusatory method of asking key questions of personnel during a regular audit to give them an opportunity to furnish information about possible misdeeds. Fraud possibilities are addressed in a direct manner, so the FAQ approach must have the support of management. Example questions are "Do you think fraud is a problem for business in general?" "Do you think this company has any particular problem with fraud?" "In your department, who is beyond suspicion?" "Is there any information you would like to furnish regarding possible fraud within this organization?"[17]

---

[17] Joseph T. Wells, "From the Chairman: Fraud Audit Questioning," *The White Paper*, National Association of Certified Fraud Examiners, May-June 1991), p. 2. This technique must be used with extreme care and practice.

WANT TO FUDGE YOUR TAX DEDUCTIONS?

Don't try to turn that $300 receipt into $800 with the stroke of a ballpoint pen. The IRS has ultraviolet scanners, ink chromatographers, densitometers, and argon-ion lasers that can identify the brand of pen, the age of the paper, and the source of the paper. Something printed on a laser printer is harder, but they're working on it.

Source: D. Churbuck, "Desktop Forgery," *Forbes*, November 27, 1989, p. 252.

Covert Surveillance

Observe activities while not being seen. External auditors might watch employees clocking onto a work shift, observing whether they use only one time card. Travelling hotel auditors may check in unannounced, use the restaurant and entertainment facilities, and watch the employees skimming receipts and tickets. (Trailing people on streets and maintaining a "stakeout" should be left to trained investigators.)

Horizontal and Vertical Analyses

This is analytical review ratio analysis and is very similar to the preliminary analytical procedures explained in Chapter 5. Horizontal analysis refers to changes of financial statement numbers and ratios across several years. Vertical analysis refers to financial statement amounts expressed each year as proportions of a base, such as sales for the income statement accounts and total assets for the balance sheet accounts. Auditors look for relationships that do not make sense as indicators of potential large misstatement and fraud.

Net Worth Analysis

This is used when fraud has been discovered or strongly suspected, and the information to calculate a suspect's net worth can be obtained (e.g., asset and liability records, bank accounts). The method is to calculate the suspect's net worth (known assets minus known liabilities) at the beginning and end of a period (months or years), then try to account for the difference as (1) known income less living expenses and (2) unidentified difference. The unidentified difference may be the best available approximation of the amount of a theft.

Expenditure Analysis

This is similar to net worth analysis, except the data are the suspect's spending for all purposes compared to known income. If spending exceeds legitimate and explainable income, the difference may be the amount of a theft.

It should be noted that an analysis like this normally represents only indirect (circumstantial) evidence in a court of law and normally by itself it cannot prove the "guilt beyond a reasonable doubt" that is required in criminal cases.

Valuation Services

Forensic accounting and fraud auditing frequently involve quantification of economic losses resulting from illegal activities. This may require the specialized services of chartered business valuators. For example, see the CICA practice aid, *Investigative and Forensic Accounting Practice Issues* (1995).

R E V I E W
CHECKPOINTS

18.24   What is the difference between a "normal procedure" and an "extended procedure"?

18.25   What might be indicated by two endorsements on a cancelled cheque?

18.26   What three oddities might be found connected with ghosts on a padded payroll?

18.27   What can an auditor find using horizontal analysis? vertical analysis? net worth analysis? expenditure analysis?

AFTER DISCOVERING A FRAUD

Building a case against a fraudster is a task for trained investigators. Most internal and external auditors take roles as assistants to fraud examiners, who know how to conduct interviews and interrogations, perform surveillance, use informants, and obtain usable confessions. In almost all cases, the postdiscovery activity proceeds with a special prosecutorial assignment with the co-operation or under the leadership of management. A Crown attorney and police officials may be involved. Prosecution of fraudsters is advisable because, if left unpunished, they often go on to steal again. This is no place for "normal" auditing, but auditors have been given some guidelines related to relevant communications.

CICA and Internal Audit Standards

Standards for external auditors contain materiality thresholds related to reporting auditors' knowledge of errors, irregularities, and illegal acts. Immaterial errors are supposed to be reported to management at least one level above the people involved (*Section* 5135.19). The idea is that small matters can be kept in the management family. However, errors material to the financial statements must be adjusted and handled by management persons responsible for the financial statements to the satisfaction of auditors, or else the audit report will be qualified.

Irregularities get slightly different treatment, but there is still a materiality standard in effect. The auditors should inform the audit committee of the board of directors of all irregularities, except ones that are "clearly inconsequential." Irregularities involving senior management are never "inconsequential." In the CICA audit standards, room is always left for auditors' discretion in determining whether something is minor enough not to matter and not to report. However, management and directors must deal with irregularities to the satisfaction of the auditors. If uncertainties persist about the irregularities and management's actions, the audit report should be qualified, explaining all the unsavory reasons, or the auditors may withdraw from the engagement.

Clients' illegal acts also come under the "clearly inconsequential" materiality standard. Ones that amount to more than this should be reported to the organization's audit committee, and the financial statements should contain adequate disclosures about the organization's illegal acts (*Section* 5136.04). External auditors always have the option to withdraw from the engagement if management and directors do not take action satisfactory in the circumstances.

Under the CICA audit standards, disclosures of irregularities and clients' illegal acts to outside agencies are limited. If the auditors get fired, the firm can cite these matters in the letter attached to the provincial securities commission, which may require explanation of an organization's change of auditors. A fired auditor can tell the successor auditor about them when the successor makes the enquiries required by professional ethics.

Auditors must respond when answering a subpoena issued by a court or other agency with authority, which will happen in a lawsuit or prosecution. When performing work under public sector audit standards, auditors are required to report irregularities and illegal acts to the client agency under the audit contract, which may be an agency or office different from the organization audited.

SIAS No. 3 requires internal auditors to inform management of suspected wrongdoing. They are expected to report fraud findings to management, the board of directors, or the audit committee of the board, being careful not to report to persons who might be involved in a fraud scheme. But as the following box indicates, much can still be done to improve the fraud record of Canadian firms.

FIRMS SHOULD TAKE FRAUD SERIOUSLY

Company managers are increasingly aware of fraud and have taken initiatives to address its costly consequences, but there is no reason for complacency.

KPMG Investigation and Security Inc. says 62% of respondents to its survey of 1,000 of the country's largest companies as ranked by FP reported that fraud had taken place in their organization in the past year, up from 52% in the 1996 survey. Better detection is responsible for some of the rise, KPMG says, but a large part is attributable to an actual increase in the incidence of fraud.

Those surveyed see a host of factors as key in allowing fraud to take place, such as poor hiring practices, management override of internal controls and collusion between employees and third parties. However, poor internal controls are viewed as the leading factor.

Internal fraud remains a huge problem. The survey indicates that based on dollar losses 55% of all scams are from inside companies. Management accounts for 17% of all fraud—usually phoney expense accounts. Employee fraud—38%—is predominantly cheque forgery or counterfeiting. What is equally disturbing is that almost half the respondents conduct business in such a way as to be vulnerable to money laundering.

The sad fact is many companies—25% of those surveyed—haven't taken even basic measures to shrink the possibility of fraud. These include devising a corporate code of conduct and checking new employees. With the incidence of fraud rising, this is hardly a responsible way to manage a company.

Source: Editorial, *The Financial Post,* May 16, 1997, p. 14.

Consulting and Assisting

LEARNING   OBJECTIVE
8. Describe how PAs can assist in prosecuting fraud perpetrators.

While engaged in the audit work, auditors should know how to preserve the chain of custody of evidence. The chain of custody is the crucial link of the evidence to the suspect, called the "relevance" of evidence by lawyers and judges. If documents are lost, mutilated, coffee-soaked, or compromised (so that a defence lawyer can argue that they were altered to frame the suspect), they can lose their effectiveness for the prosecution. Auditors should learn to mark the evidence, writing an identification of the location, condition, date, time, and circumstances as soon as it appears to be a signal of fraud. This marking should be on a separate tag or page, the original document should be put in a protective envelope (plastic) for preservation, and audit work should proceed with copies of the documents instead of originals. A record should be made of the safekeeping and of all persons who use the original. Any eyewitness observations should be timely recorded in a memorandum or on tape (audio or video), with corroboration of colleagues, if possible. There are other features to the chain of custody relating to interviews, interrogations, confessions, documents obtained by subpoena, and other matters, but these activities usually are not conducted by auditors.

Independent PAs often accept engagements for litigation support and expert witnessing. This work can be termed forensic accounting, which means the application of accounting and auditing skills to legal problems, both civil and criminal. Litigation support can take several forms, but it usually amounts to consulting in the capacity of helping lawyers document cases and determine damages. Expert witness work involves testifying to findings determined during litigation support and testifying about accounting principles and auditing standards applications. The CICA and the Institute of Internal Auditors conduct continuing education courses for auditors who want to become experts in these fields.

FRAUD AUDITS AS ASSURANCE ENGAGEMENTS
. . . .

An obvious question is whether investigations and audits of the types discussed in this chapter are assurance or consulting engagements. Much depends on the nature of the engagement and whether there exists an accountability relationship. But if we view every employee including management as being accountable for resources entrusted to them by the company, many fraud audits would appear to be of the direct reporting types, with an implied assertion that defalcations are not occurring.

Currently, the only authoritative guidance on fraud audit reports is that developed by the Association of Certified Fraud Examiners in their Fraud Examiners Manual. Exhibit 18–4 illustrates a "clean" opinion on a fraud audit. Note, however, that although the term *opinion* is used, suggesting high assurance for the assertion "there is no fraud," the wording of the opinion paragraph is more in the nature of the moderate-assurance, "nothing came to our attention" type that is used in review engagements. This is probably because there is no agreed-upon set of standardized procedures such as GAAS that can provide high assurance for this particular type of assertion.

The equivalent of an adverse opinion, on the other hand, which is given in Exhibit 18–5, provides much higher assurance for the assertion that a fraud did occur (especially if there is a signed confession satisfying all legal requirements). But note

E X H I B I T 18–4

Investigation Appendix	Engagement Contracts/Opinion Letters

FRAUD EXAMINATION OPINION
(evidence does not support allegation)

[Date]

[   ], Esq.
[Law Department]
[Company Name]
[Address]
[City, State, Zip Code]

RE: [Fraud Examination]

Dear Mr./Mrs. [   ]:

We have conducted a fraud examination concerning a possible misappropriation of assets of the [Company Name]. This examination was predicted upon information resulting from a routine audit of the company's books by the company's internal auditors.

Our examination was conducted in accordance with lawful fraud examination techniques, which include, but are not limited to: examination of books and records; voluntary interviews of appropriate personnel; and other such evidence-gathering procedures as necessary under the circumstances.

Because concealment and trickery are elements of fraud, no assurance can be given that fraud does not exist. However, based on the results of our examination, we have found no evidence to indicate a violation of criminal and/or civil fraud-related statutes in connection with this matter.

Very truly yours,

Source: Fraud Examiner's Manual © 1993 Association of Certified Fraud Examiners, Austin, TX—Revised 10/1/93.

---

that the high assurance is provided in part because of the way the opinion is worded. The opinion does not state that the fraud can be proven legally—that is, "beyond a reasonable doubt," as would be required in a criminal court. Instead the conclusion is a much milder one—"if proven in a court of law," the actions would be considered fraudulent. In other words, the fraud auditor is not claiming that there is fraud beyond a reasonable doubt, which is something only the courts can decide. Rather, the auditor is saying that he or she is providing high assurance that a fraud may have taken place. Thus, by properly wording the conclusion the auditor can provide high assurance for the conclusion, and the use of the word "opinion" would appear to be warranted in this case under *Section* 5025.

There are two important lessons to be learned from these illustrative reports: one is that the level of assurance depends very much on the ability to identify suitable criteria—for example, a signed confession; the other is that the level of assurance depends very much on the specific phrasing of the conclusion. For example, if in Exhibit 18–5 the auditor had concluded that fraud had taken place, such an opinion would provide only low assurance because fraud is a legal matter that must be proven in the courts. In addition, because the fraud assertion has not yet been proven in the courts—and because fraud is a matter to be proven under criminal law—the auditor might even be found guilty of libel! There is the related issue that even if the auditor *does* have high assurance that a fraud has been perpetrated, high audit assurance does not necessarily equate to the "beyond a reasonable doubt" burden of proof that is required by the Criminal Code. On the other hand, under civil law, if, for example, the client's company is only expecting to recover damages or trying to obtain sufficient cause to fire the employee, then the burden of proof is considerably lower. In civil law the burden of proof is "on balance of probabilities" and an opinion such as in Exhibit

EXHIBIT 18–5

Investigation Appendix	Engagement Contracts/Opinion Letters

FRAUD EXAMINATION OPINION
(evidence supports allegation)

[Date]

[   ], Esq.
[Law Department]
[Company Name]
[Address]
[City, State, Zip Code]

RE: [Fraud Examination]

Dear Mr./Mrs. [   ]:

We have conducted a fraud examination concerning a possible misappropriation of assets of the [Company Name]. This examination was predicated upon information resulting from a routine audit of the company's books by the company's internal auditors.

Our examination was conducted in accordance with lawful fraud examination techniques, which include, but are not limited to: examination of books and records; voluntary interviews of appropriate witnesses/personnel; and other such evidence-gathering procedures as necessary under the circumstances.

During the pendency of this fraud examination, Mr. [   ] voluntarily furnished a signed statement indicating that he misappropriated $...................... to his personal benefit.

Based on the results of our examination and the confession of Mr. [   ], it is our opinion that his actions, if proven in a court of law, could constitute a violation of relevant criminal and/or civil fraud-related statutes.

Very truly yours,

Source: Fraud Examiner's Manual © 1993 Association of Certified Fraud Examiners, Austin, TX—Revised 10/1/93.

18–5 may very well satisfy this requirement. So the amount of assurance depends on the circumstances, and the wording should properly reflect the circumstances.

For example, since fraud is a legal term and legal conditions must be met before the term is assigned to anyone, a perhaps better term for use in an assurance report is "irregularities," which is a term defined by the PA profession. An auditor can then reach a conclusion about the likelihood of irregularities occurring (including but not limited to fraud) without being encumbered with legal definitions and the responsibilities inherent in using specific legal terms such as fraud. As long as there is ambiguity between the level of assurance provided by the assurance engagement, and legal assurance required by terms such as "on balance of probabilities" and "proof beyond a reasonable doubt," it is probably in the auditor's best interest to use terminology that does not have a precise legal meaning but instead reflects the standards of the PA profession. Otherwise the auditors will need to be very careful when the legal terms are used in the report, or risk being caught in libel suits.

Hopefully this section has illustrated some of the complexities of expanding assurance engagements into new areas not familiar to most PAs.

REVIEW
CHECKPOINTS

18.28 Why is prosecution of fraud perpetrators generally a good idea?

18.29 What are the CICA materiality guidelines for reporting errors, irregularities, and illegal acts?

18.30 Why must care be taken with evidence of fraudulent activity?

Summary

Fraud awareness auditing starts with knowledge of the types of errors, irregularities, illegal acts, and frauds that can be perpetrated. External, internal, and governmental auditors all have standards for care, attention, planning, detection, and reporting of some kinds of errors, irregularities, and illegal acts. Fraud examiners, on the other hand, have little in the way of standard programs or materiality guidelines to limit their attention to fraud possibilities. They float on a sea of observations of exceptions and oddities that may be the tip of a fraud iceberg.

Fraud may be contemplated when people have motives, usually financial needs, for stealing money or property. Motive, when combined with opportunity and a lapse of integrity, generally makes the probability of fraud or theft very high. Opportunities arise when an organization's management has a lax attitude about setting an example for good behaviour and about maintenance of a supportive control environment. The fear of getting caught by control procedures deters some fraudsters. Otherwise, attentive management of personnel can ease the pressures people feel and, thus, reduce the incidence of fraud.

Auditors need to know about the red flags, those telltale signs and indications that have accompanied many frauds. When studying a business operation, auditors' ability to "think like a crook" to devise ways to steal can help in the planning of procedures designed to determine whether fraud occurred. Often, imaginative "extended procedures" can be employed to unearth evidence of fraudulent activity. However, technical and personal care must always be exercised because accusations of fraud are always taken very seriously. For this reason, after preliminary findings indicate fraud possibilities, auditors should enlist the co-operation of management and assist fraud examination professionals in bringing an investigation to a conclusion.

For information on the Association of Certified Fraud Examiners (CFEs), visit their website at www.cfenet.com.

Multiple-choice Questions for Practice and Review

18.31 One of the typical characteristics of management fraud is:
   a. Falsification of documents in order to steal money from an employer.
   b. Victimization of investors through the use of materially misleading financial statements.
   c. Illegal acts committed by management to evade laws and regulations.
   d. Conversion of stolen inventory to cash deposited in a falsified bank account.

18.32 CICA auditing standards do not require auditors of financial statements to:
   a. Understand the nature of errors and irregularities.
   b. Assess the risk of occurrence of errors and irregularities.
   c. Design audits to provide reasonable assurance of detecting errors and irregularities.
   d. Report all finding of errors and irregularities to police authorities.

18.33 Which of the following types of auditors have the highest expectations in their audit standards regarding the detection of fraud?
   a. External auditors of financial statements.
   b. Government auditors of financial statements, programs, activities, and functions.

c. Internal auditors employed by companies.

d. Management advisory consultants engaged to design a company's information system.

18.34 Which two of the following characterize the work of fraud examiners and are different from the typical attitude of external auditors?

a. Analysis of control weaknesses for opportunities to commit fraud.

b. Analysis of control strengths as a basis for planning other audit procedures.

c. Determination of a materiality amount that represents a significant misstatement of the current-year financial statements.

d. Thinking of a materiality amount in cumulative terms—that is, as becoming large over a number of years.

18.35 When auditing with "fraud awareness," auditors should especially notice and follow up employee activities under which of these conditions?

a. The company always estimates the inventory but never takes a complete physical count.

b. The petty cash box is always locked in the desk of the custodian.

c. Management has published a company code of ethics and sends frequent communication newsletters about it.

d. The board of directors reviews and approves all investment transactions.

18.36 The best way to enact a broad fraud-prevention program is to:

a. Install airtight control systems of checks and supervision.

b. Name an "ethics officer" who is responsible for receiving and acting upon fraud tips.

c. Place dedicated "hot line" telephones on walls around the workplace with direct communication to the company ethics officer.

d. Practise management "of the people and for the people" to help them share personal and professional problems.

18.37 Which of the following gives the least indication of fraudulent activity?

a. Numerous cash refunds have been made to different people at the same post office box address.

b. Internal auditor cannot locate several credit memos to support reductions of customers' balances.

c. Bank reconciliation has no outstanding cheques or deposits older than 15 days.

d. Three people were absent the day the auditors handed out the paycheques and have not picked them up four weeks later.

18.38 Which of the following combinations is a good means of hiding employee fraud but a poor means of carrying out management (financial reporting) fraud?

a. Overstating sales revenue and overstating customer accounts receivable balances.

b. Overstating sales revenue and overstating bad debt expense.

c. Understating interest expense and understating accrued interest payable.

d. Omit the disclosure information about related party sales to the president's relatives at below-market prices.

18.39 Which of these arrangements of duties could most likely lead to an embezzlement or theft?

a. Inventory warehouse manager has responsibility for making the physical inventory observation and reconciling discrepancies to the perpetual inventory records.

b. Cashier prepared the bank deposit, endorsed the cheques with a company stamp, and took the cash and cheques to the bank for deposit (no other bookkeeping duties).

c. Accounts receivable clerk received a list of payments received by the cashier so that he could make entries in the customers' accounts receivable subsidiary accounts.

d. Financial vice president received cheques made out to suppliers and the supporting invoices, signed the cheques, and put them in the mail to the payees.

18.40 If sales and income were overstated by recording a false credit sale at the end of the year, where could you find the false "dangling debit?" In the:

a. Inventory?

b. Cost of goods sold?

c. Bad debt expense?

d. Accounts receivable?

18.41 Which of these is an invalid Social Insurance Number?

a. 462 003 335.

b. 473 09 7787.

c. 506 98 5529.

d. 700 051 135.

18.42 Public records from which of these sources could be used to find the owner of an office building?

a. Ministry of Industry and Trade export/import licence files.

b. Transport Canada records.

c. City and county tax assessor-collector files.

d. Securities commission filings.

18.43 Experience has shown that the largest number of accounting errors requiring adjustment are found in:

a. Systematic processing of large volumes of day-to-day ordinary transactions.

b. Payroll fraudsters' mistakes in using unissued Social Insurance numbers.

c. Petty cash embezzlements.

d. Nonroutine, nonsystematic journal entries.

18.44 The type of financial analysis that expresses balance sheet accounts as percentages of total assets is known as:

a. Horizontal analysis.

b. Vertical analysis.

c. Net worth analysis.

d. Expenditure analysis.

Exercises and Problems

18.45 Give Examples of Errors, Irregularities, and Frauds. This is an exercise concerning financial reporting misstatements, not employee theft. Give an example of an error, irregularity, or fraud that would misstate financial statements to affect the accounts as follows, taken one case at a time. (Note: "overstate" means the account has a higher value than would be appropriate under GAAP, and "understate" means it has a lower value.)

a. Overstate an asset, state another asset.

b. Overstate an asset, overstate shareholder equity.

c. Overstate an asset, overstate revenue.

d. Overstate an asset, understate an expense.

e. Overstate a liability, overstate an expense.

f. Understate an asset, overstate an expense.

g. Understate a liability, understate an expense.

18.46 Overall Analysis of Accounting Estimates. Oak Industries, a manufacturer of radio and cable TV equipment and an operator of subscription TV systems, had a multitude of problems. Subscription services in a market area, for which $12 million cost had been deferred, were being terminated, and the customers were not paying on time ($4 million receivables in doubt). The chances are 50–50 that the business will survive another two years.

An electronic part turned out to have defects that needed correction. Warranty expenses are estimated to range from $2 million to $6 million. The inventory of this part ($10 million) is obsolete, but $1 million can be recovered in salvage; or, the parts in inventory can be rebuilt at a cost of $2 million (selling price of the inventory on hand would then be $8 million, with 20 percent of selling price required to market and ship the products, and the normal profit expected is 5 percent of the selling price). If the inventory were scrapped, the company would manufacture a replacement inventory at a cost of $6 million, excluding marketing and shipping costs and normal profit.

The company has defaulted on completion of a military contract, and the government is claiming a $2 million refund. Company lawyers think the dispute might be settled for as little as $1 million.

The auditors had previously determined that an overstatement of income before taxes of $7 million would be material to the financial statements. These items were the only ones left for audit decisions about possible adjustment. Management has presented the analysis below for the determination of loss recognition:

Write-off deferred subscription costs	$3,000,000
Provide allowance for bad debts	4,000,000
Provide for expected warranty expense	2,000,000
Lower of cost or market inventory write-down	2,000,000
Loss on government contract refund	—
Total write-offs and losses	$11,000,000

Required:

Prepare your own analysis of the amount of adjustment to the financial statements. Assume that none of these estimates have been recorded yet, and give the adjusting entry you would recommend. Give any supplementary explanations you believe necessary to support your recommendation.

18.47 Select Effective Extended Procedures. Given below are some "suspicions," and you have been requested to select some effective extended procedures designed to confirm or deny the suspicion.

Required:

Write the suggested procedures for each case in definite terms so that another person can know what to do.

a. The custodian of the petty cash fund may be removing cash on Friday afternoon to pay for his weekend activities.

b. A manager has noticed that eight new vendors have been added to the purchasing department approved list since the assistant purchasing agent was promoted to chief agent three weeks ago. She suspects that all or some of them may be phony companies set up by the new chief purchasing agent.

c. The payroll supervisor may be stealing unclaimed paycheques of people who quit work and don't pick up the last cheque.

d. Although no customers have complained, cash collections on accounts receivable are down, and the counter clerks may have stolen customers' payments.

e. The cashier may have "borrowed" money, covering it by holding each day's deposit until cash from the next day(s) collection is enough to make up the shortage from an earlier day, then sending the deposit to the bank.

18.48 Horizontal and Vertical Analysis. Horizontal analysis refers to changes of financial statement numbers and ratios across two or more years. Vertical analysis refers to financial statement amounts expressed each year as proportions of a base, such as sales for the income statement accounts, and total assets for the balance sheet accounts. Exhibit 18.48–1 contains the Retail Company's prior year (audited) and current year (unaudited) financial statements, along with amounts and percentages of change from year to year (horizontal analysis) and common-size percentages (vertical analysis). Exhibit 18.48–2 contains selected financial ratios based on these financial statements. Analysis of these data may enable auditors to discern relationships that raise questions about misleading financial statements.

Required:

Study the data in Exhibits 18.48–1 and 18.48–2. Write a memo identifying

EXHIBIT 18.48–1　**RETAIL COMPANY**

	Prior Year Audited		Current Year		Change	
	Balance	Common Size	Balance	Common Size	Amount	Percent
Assets:						
Cash	$　600,000	14.78%	$　484,000	9.69%	(116,000)	−19.33%
Accounts receivable	500,000	12.32	400,000	8.01	(100,000)	−20.00
Allowance doubt accts.	(40,000)	−0.99	(30,000)	−0.60	10,000	−25.00
Inventory	1,500,000	36.95	1,940,000	38.85	440,000	29.33
Total current assets	$2,560,000	63.05	2,794,000	55.95	234,000	9.14
Capital assets	3,000,000	73.89	4,000,000	80.10	1,000,000	33.33
Accum. depreciation	(1,500,000)	−36.95	(1,800,000)	−36.04	(300,000)	20.00
Total assets	$4,060,000	100.00%	$4,994,000	100.00%	934,000	23.00%
Liabilities and equity:						
Accounts payable	$　450,000	11.08%	$　600,000	12.01%	150,000	33.33%
Bank loans, 11%	0	0.00	750,000	15.02	750,000	NA
Accrued interest	50,000	1.23	40,000	0.80	(10,000)	−20.00
Accruals and other	60,000	1.48	10,000	0.20	(50,000)	−83.33
Total current liab.	560,000	13.79	1,400,000	28.03	840,000	150.00
Long–term debt, 10%	500,000	12.32	400,000	8.01	(100,000)	−20.00
Total liabilities	1,060,000	26.11	1,800,000	36.04	740,000	69.81
Share capital	2,000,000	49.26	2,000,000	40.05	0	0
Retained earnings	1,000,000	24.63	1,194,000	23.91	194,000	19.40
Total liabilities and equity	$4,060,000	100.00%	$4,994,000	100.00%	934,000	23.00%
Statement of operations:						
Sales (net)	$9,000,000	100.00%	$8,100,000	100.00%	(900,000)	−10.00%
Cost of goods sold	6,296,000	69.96	5,265,000	65.00	(1,031,000)	−16.38
Gross margin	2,704,000	30.04	2,835,000	35.00	131,000	4.84
General expense	2,044,000	22.71	2,005,000	24.75	(39,000)	−1.91
Amortization	300,000	3.33	300,000	3.70	0	0
Operating income	360,000	4.00	530,000	6.54	170,000	47.22
Interest expense	50,000	0.56	40,000	0.49	(10,000)	−20.00
Income taxes (40%)	124,000	1.38	196,000	2.42	72,000	58.06
Net income	$　186,000	2.07%	$　294,000	3.63%	108,000	58.06%

NA means not applicable.

EXHIBIT 18.48–2　**RETAIL COMPANY**

	Prior Year	Current Year	Percent Change
Balance sheet ratios:			
Current ratio	4.57	2.0	−56.34%
Days' sales in receivables	18.40	16.44	−10.63
Doubtful accounts ratio	0.0800	0.0750	−6.25
Days' sales in inventory	85.77	132.65	54.66
Debt/equity ratio	0.35	0.56	40.89
Operations ratios:			
Receivables turnover	19.57	21.89	11.89
Inventory turnover	4.20	2.71	−35.34
Cost of goods sold/sales	69.96%	65.00%	−7.08
Gross margin %	30.04%	35.00%	16.49
Return on equity	6.61%	9.80%	48.26

and explaining potential problem areas where misstatements in the current year financial statements might exist. Additional information about Retail Company is as follows:

- The new bank loan, obtained on July 1 of the current year, requires maintenance of a 2:1 current ratio.
- Principal of $100,000 plus interest on the 10 percent long-term note obtained several years ago in the original amount of $800,000 is due each January 1.
- The company has never paid dividends on its common shares and has no plans for a dividend.

18.49 Expenditure Analysis. Expenditure analysis is used when fraud has been discovered or strongly suspected, and the information to calculate a suspect's income and expenditures can be obtained (e.g., asset and liability records, bank accounts). Expenditure analysis consists of establishing the suspect's known expenditures for all purposes for the relevant period, subtracting all known sources of funds (e.g., wages, gifts, inheritances, bank balances, and the like), and calling the difference the expenditures financed by unknown sources of income.

FORENSIC ACCOUNTING CONSULTING ENGAGEMENT 1

You have been hired by the law firm of Gleckel and Morris. The lawyers have been retained by Blade Manufacturing Company in a case involving a suspected kickback by a purchasing employee, E. J. Cunningham.

Cunningham is suspected of taking kickbacks from Mason Varner, a salesman for Tanco Metals. He has denied the charges, but Lanier Gleckel, the lawyer in charge of the case, is convinced the kickbacks have occurred.

Gleckel filed a civil action and subpoenaed Cunningham's books and records, including his last year's bank statements. The beginning bank balance January 1 was $3,463, and the ending bank balance December 31 was $2,050. Over the intervening 12 months, Cunningham's gross salary

was $3,600 per month, with a net of $2,950. His wife doesn't work at a paying job. His house payments were $1,377 per month. In addition, he paid $2,361 per month on a new Mercedes 500 SEL and paid a total of $9,444 last year toward a new Nissan Maxima (including $5,000 down payment). He also purchased new state-of-the-art audio and video equipment for $18,763, with no down payment, and total payments on the equipment last year of $5,532. A reasonable estimate of his household expenses during the period is $900 per month ($400 for food, $200 for utilities, and $300 for other items).

Required:
Using expenditure analysis, calculate the amount of income, if any, from "unknown sources."

18.50 Net Worth Analysis. Net worth analysis is used when fraud has been discovered or strongly suspected, and the information to calculate a suspect's net worth can be obtained (e.g., asset and liability records, bank accounts). The procedure is to calculate the person's change in net worth (excluding changes in market values of assets), and to identify the known sources of funds to finance the changes. Any difference between the change in net worth and the known sources of funds is called "funds from unknown sources," which may be ill-gotten gains.

FORENSIC ACCOUNTING CONSULTING ENGAGEMENT 2

C. Nero has worked for Bonne Consulting Group (BCG) as the executive secretary for administration for nearly 10 years. His dedication has earned him a reputation as an outstanding employee and has resulted in increasing responsibilities. C. Nero is a suspect in fraud.

This is the hindsight story. During Nero's first five years of employment, BCG subcontracted all of its feasibility and marketing studies through Jackson & Company. This relationship was terminated because Jackson & Company merged with a larger, more expensive consulting group. At the time of termination, Nero and his supervisor were forced to select a new firm to conduct BCG's market research. However, Nero never informed the accounting department that the Jackson & Company account had been closed.

Since his supervisor allowed Nero to sign the payment voucher for services rendered, Nero was able to continue to process cheques made payable to Jackson's account. Nero was trusted to be the only signature authorizing payments less than $10,000. The accounting department continued to write the cheques and Nero would take responsibility for

delivering them. Nero opened a bank account in a nearby city under the name of Jackson & Company, where he would make the deposit.

Required:
C. Nero's financial records have been obtained by subpoena. You have been hired to estimate the amount of loss by estimating Nero's "funds from unknown sources" that financed his comfortable lifestyle. Below is a summary of the data obtained from Nero's records.

NERO'S RECORDS

	Year One	Year Two	Year Three
Assets:			
Residence	$100,000	$100,000	$100,000
Shares and bonds	30,000	30,000	42,000
Automobiles	20,000	20,000	40,000
Certificate of deposit	50,000	50,000	50,000
Cash	6,000	12,000	14,000
Liabilities:			
Mortgage balance	90,000	50,000	—
Auto loan	10,000	—	—
Income:			
Salary		34,000	36,000
Other		6,000	6,000
Expenses:			
Scheduled mortgage payments		6,000	6,000
Auto loan payments		4,800	—
Other living expenses		20,000	22,000
Hint:			
Set up a working paper like this:			
	End Year 1	End Year 2	End Year 3

Assets (list)
Liabilities (list)
Net worth (difference)
Change in net worth
Add total expenses
= Change plus expenses
Subtract known income
= Funds from unknown sources

DISCUSSION CASES
. . . .

GENERAL INSTRUCTIONS FOR CASES 18.51–18.56:
These cases are designed like the ones in the chapter. They give the problem, the method, the paper trail, and the amount. Your assign-

ment is to write the Audit Approach portion of the case organized around these sections:

Objective: Express the objective in terms of the facts supposedly asserted in financial records, accounts, and statements.

Control: Write a brief explanation of desirable controls, missing controls, and especially the kinds of "deviations" that might arise from the situation described in the case.

Test of controls: Write some procedures for getting evidence about existing controls, especially procedures that could discover deviations from controls. If there are no controls to test, then there are no procedures to perform; go then to the next section. A "procedure" should instruct someone about the source(s) of evidence to tap and the work to do.

Audit of balance: Write some procedures for getting evidence about the existence, completeness, valuation, ownership, or disclosure assertions identified in your objective section above.

Discovery summary: Write a short statement about the discovery you expect to accomplish with your procedures.

18.51 Employee Embezzlement via Cash Disbursements and Inventory. Follow the instructions at the beginning of this Discussion Cases section.

STEALING WAS EASY

Problem: Cash embezzlement, inventory and expense overstatement.

Method: Lew Marcus was the only bookkeeper at the Ace Plumbing Supply Company. He ordered the supplies and inventory, paid the bills, collected the cash receipts and cheques sent by customers, and reconciled the bank statements. The company had about $11 million in sales, inventory of $3 million, and expenses that generally ran about $6–7 million each year. Nobody checked Lew's work, so sometimes when he received a bill for goods from a supplier (say, for $8,000) he would make an accounting entry for $12,000 debit to inventory, write an $8,000 cheque to pay the bill, then write a $4,000 cheque to himself. The cheque to Lew was not recorded, and he removed it from the bank statement when he prepared the bank reconciliation. The owner of the business considered the monthly bank reconciliation a proper control activity.

Paper trail: No perpetual inventory records were kept, and no periodic inventory count was taken. The general ledger contained an inventory control account balance that was reduced by 60 percent of the amount of each sale of plumbing fixtures (estimated cost of sales). The bank statements and reconciliations were in a file. The statements showed the cheque number and amount of Lew's cheques to himself, but the cheques themselves were missing. The cheques to vendors were in the amounts of their bills, but the entries in the cash disbursements journal showed higher amounts.

Amount: Over an eight-year period, Lew embezzled $420,000.

18.52 Employee Embezzlement via Cash Receipts and Payment of Personal Expenses. Follow the instructions at the beginning of this Discussion Cases section. In this case you can assume that you have received the informant's message.

THE EXTRA BANK ACCOUNT

Problem: Cash receipts pocketed and personal expenses paid from business account.

Method: The Ourtown Independent School District, like all others, had red tape about school board approval of cash disbursements. To get around the rules, and to make timely payment of some bills possible, the superintendent of schools had a school bank account that was used in the manner of a petty cash fund. The board knew about it and had given blanket approval in advance for its use to make timely payment of minor school expenses. The board, however, never reviewed the activity in this account. The business manager had sole responsibility for the account, subject to the annual audit. The account got money from transfers from other school accounts and from deposit of cafeteria cash receipts. The superintendent did not like to be bothered with details, and he often signed blank cheques so that the business manager would not need to run in for a signature all the time. The business manager sometimes paid her personal American Express credit card bills, charged personal items to the school's VISA account, and pocketed some cafeteria cash receipts before deposit.

Paper trail: An informant called the state education audit agency and told the story that this business manager had used school funds to buy hosiery. When told of this story, the superintendent told the auditor to place no credibility in the informant, who is "out to get us." The business manager had in fact used the account to write unauthorized cheques to "cash," put her own American Express bills in the school files (the school district had a VISA card, not American Express), and signed on the school card for gasoline and auto repairs during periods of vacation and summer when school was not in session. (As for the hosiery, she purchased $700 worth with school funds one year.) The superintendent was genuinely unaware of the misuse of funds.

Amount: The business manager had been employed for six years, was trusted, and stole an estimated $25,000.

18.53 Employee Embezzlement via Padded Payroll. Follow the instructions at the beginning of this Discussion Cases section. In this case your assignment is to analyse the payroll register and see if you can identify any of the ghosts.

GHOST RIDERS ON THE PAYROLL

Problem: Embezzlement with fictitious people on the payroll.

Method: Billy Joe had responsibility for preparing personnel files for new hires, approval of wages, verification of time cards, and distribution of payroll cheques. He "hired" fictitious employees, faked their records, and ordered cheques through the payroll system.

Paper trail: The payroll department produces a payroll register listing various items of information about employees. A selection from the register is in Exhibit 8.53–1. Reading the columns from left to right, it shows the employee identification number, employee name, employees' section number (retail store location), Social Insurance number, and bank addresses (account numbers for electronic funds transfer).

Amount: Billy Joe stole $160,000 over a three-year period.

Required:
Analyse the payroll register in Exhibit 18.53–1 and identify the questionable employees who might be ghosts on the payroll.

18.54 Employee Embezzlement: Medical Claims Fraud. Follow the instructions at the beginning of this Discussion Cases section.

DOCTOR! DOCTOR!

Problem: Fictitious medical benefit claims were paid by the company, which self-insured up to $50,000 per employee. The expense account that included legitimate and false charges was "employee medical benefits."

Method: As manager of the claims payment department, Martha Lee was considered one of Beta Magnetic's best employees. She never missed a day of work in 10 years, and her department had one of the company's best efficiency ratings. Controls were considered good, including the verification by a claims processor that (1) the patient was a Beta employee, (2) medical treatments were covered in the plan, (3) the charges were within approved guidelines, (4) the cumulative claims for the employee did not exceed $50,000 (if over $50,000 a claim was submitted to an insurance company), and (5) the calculation for payment was correct. After verification processing, claims were sent to the claims payment department to pay the doctor directly. No payments ever went directly to employees. Martha Lee prepared false claims on real employees, forging the signature of various claims processors, adding her own review approval, naming bogus doctors who would be paid by the payment department. The payments were mailed to various post office box addresses and to her husband's business address.

E X H I B I T 18.53–1   **PAYROLL REGISTER**

I.D. No.	Name	Sect.	Social Ins. Number	Address
5592	Annalee, Michele	1990	455411471	6205193611
8961	Avondale, Richard	1990	435315873	4723265701
186	Bryce, Sharon	1990	449435042	2763431893
3553	Gorman, Thalia	1990	459497264	1565644635
6521	Gordon, Marshall	1990	463355479	8999781365
6999	Harvey, Kevin	1990	396546363	7409894998
8920	Mazzini, Virgil	1990	461785493	2012719362
4534	Paperton, Karen	1990	453491250	6371802086
6204	Peterman, Jennifer	1990	473600914	7818539686
5481	Brione, Kimberly	2000	461635205	5622472908
5363	Brione, Douglas	2000	137567089	4286008036
7891	Jones, Jonothan	2000	464373412	3890567269
9491	Jones, Michael	2000	464373413	3890567269
527	Jones, Thomas	2000	464373413	4609659041
4042	Bull, Lisa	2000	466471495	2797567256
6041	Bushman, Jolle	2000	451355503	9103080617
590	Camp, Liana	2000	455690418	4237338557
3054	Cantraz, Luan	2000	460594645	7894813997
8063	Churchman, Matt	2000	466232740	6977367072
2964	Allford, Eric	2010	444782904	2935968014
9293	Altzheimer, Jeff	2010	453493495	6349921488
6729	Ameston, Jackie	2010	483889548	2722529584
3154	Arrgon, Mary	2010	452535653	8213209536
852	Bulling, John	2010	325462648	5587231055
7219	Chidid, Adam	2010	124491704	7443759037
9346	Chu, Song	2010	465350881	2171962355
5261	Cooker, Scott	2010	459983822	4634865235
4987	Coolman, Maury	2010	458531820	1291047566
1667	Daughterford, Debby	2010	461478070	8223680929
6145	Butterby, Laura	2020	462237424	3463748143
9265	Butterby, Leigh	2020	462236725	3463748143
1231	Butterby, L.A.	2020	462236726	3463748143
6919	Cevil, John	2020	453454988	9781429093
6840	Chung, Hihnno	2020	483113789	4888874664
7489	Cordon, Andy	2020	497605588	5129368143
9111	Coward, Clay	2020	452639707	49242627
4873	Cranehook, Mary	2020	275643410	1622537823
9362	Diercheski, Ward	2020	460496149	7641205905
378	Fineman, Bryan	2020	459679356	8703966421
4613	Deitrick, James	2025	135635583	6947113473
5361	Larson, Kermit	2025	221156649	6947113473
3276	Newman, Paul	2025	601669984	6947113473
3493	Robertson, Jack	2025	680623358	6947113473
8857	Rosingale, Patricia	2025	460654900	6609741958
7103	Ruhle, Mabry	2025	397804404	6940593886
7559	Ruffinio, Jill	2025	461394849	2874916590
8494	Rummsfell, Judith	2025	466539183	4621454720
43	Smith, Michael	2025	442641436	6504510060
1948	Shultze, Robert	2025	457020330	9202701679

Nobody ever verified claims information with the employee. The employees received no reports of medical benefits paid on their behalf. While the department had performance reports by claims processors, these reports did not show claim-by-claim details. No one verified the credentials of the doctors.

Paper trail: The falsified claim forms were in Beta's files, containing all the fictitious data on employee names, processor signatures, doctors' bills, and phony doctors and addresses. The cancelled cheques were returned by the bank and were kept in Beta's files, containing "endorsements" by the doctors. Martha Lee and her husband were somewhat clever: They deposited the cheques in various banks in accounts opened in the names and identification of the "doctors."

Martha Lee did not stumble on the paper trail. She drew the attention of an auditor who saw her take her 24 claims processing employees out to an annual staff appreciation luncheon in a fleet of stretch limousines.

Amount: Over seven years, Martha Lee and her husband stole $3.5 million, and, until the last, no one noticed anything unusual about the total amount of claims paid.

18.55 Financial Reporting: Overstated Sales and Profits. Follow the instructions at the beginning of this Discussion Cases section. For this case, give the recommended adjusting journal entry as well as the audit approach.

THANK GOODNESS IT'S FRIDAY

Problem: Overstated sales caused overstated net income, retained earnings, current assets, working capital, and total assets. Overstated cash collections did not change the total current assets or total assets, but they increased the amount of cash and decreased the amount of accounts receivable.

Method: Alpha Brewery Corporation has generally good control policies and procedures related to authorization of transactions for accounting entry, and the accounting manual has instructions for recording sales transactions in the proper accounting period. The company regularly closes the accounting process each Friday at 5 P.M. to prepare weekly management reports. The year-end date (cutoff date) is December 31, and in 1990 December 31 was a Monday. However, the accounting was performed through Friday as usual, and the accounts were closed for the year on January 4.

Paper trail: All the entries were properly dated after December 31, including the sales invoices, cash receipts, and shipping documents. However, the trial balance from which the financial statements were prepared was dated December 31, 1990. Nobody noticed the slip of a few days because the Friday closing was normal.

Amount: Alpha recorded sales of $672,000 and gross profit of $268,800 over the January 1–4 period. Cash collections on customers' accounts came in the amount of $800,000.

18.56 Financial Reporting: Overstated Inventory and Profits (duplicated in Chapter 10: Case 10.68). Follow the instructions at the beginning of this Discussion Cases section. For this case recalculate the income (loss) before taxes using the correct inventory figures. (Assume the correct beginning inventory two years ago was $5.5 million.)

THE PHANTOM OF THE INVENTORY

Problem: Overstated physical inventory caused understated cost of goods sold and overstated net income, current assets, total assets, and retained earnings.

Method: All Bright Company manufactured lamps. Paul M, manager of the State Street plant, was under pressure to produce profits so that the company could maintain its loans at the bank. The loans were secured by the inventory of 1,500 types of finished goods, work in process, and parts used

SCHEDULE FOR 18.56

	Two Years Ago	One Year Ago	Current Year
Sales	$25,000	$29,000	$40,500
Cost of goods sold	(20,000)	(22,000)	(29,000)
Expenses	(5,000)	(8,000)	(9,000)
Income (loss) before taxes	—	$ (1,000)	$ 2,500
Ending inventory	$ 6,000	$ 8,000	$10,200
Other current assets	9,000	8,500	17,500
Total assets	21,000	21,600	34,300
Current liabilities	5,000	5,500	13,000
Long-term debt*	5,500	6,600	9,300
Shareholder equity	10,500	9,500	12,000

*Secured by inventory pledged to the bank.

for making lamps (bases, shades, wire, nuts, bolts, and so on). Paul arranged the physical inventory counting procedures and accompanied the external audit team while the external auditors observed the count and made test counts after the company personnel had recorded their counts on tags attached to the inventory locations. At the auditors' request, Paul directed them to the "most valuable" inventory for their test counts, although he did not show them all of the most valuable types. When the auditors were looking the other way, Paul raised the physical count on inventory tags the auditors would not include in their test counts. When everyone had finished each floor of the multistory warehouse, all the tags were gathered and sent to data processing for computer compilation and pricing at FIFO cost.

Paper trail: All Bright had no perpetual inventory records. All the records of the inventory quantity and pricing were in the count tags and the priced compilation, which was produced by the data processing department six weeks later. The auditors traced their test counts to the compilation and did not notice the raised physical quantities on the inventory types they did not test-count. They also did not notice some extra (ficti-tious) tags Paul had handed over to data processing.

Amount: Paul falsified the inventory for three years before the company declared bankruptcy. Over that period the inventory was overstated by $1 million (17 percent, two years ago), $2.5 million (31 percent, one year ago), and $3 million (29 percent, current year). The financial statements showed the following (dollars in 000):

18.57 Role of Control, Analytical Procedures, and Extended Procedures in Fraud Detection

CORRUPT CAPERS IN THE CHICKEN BUSINESS

After fathering six children and completing 14 years of employment with a variety of federal law enforcement and regulatory agencies with whom I had served in audit, compliance, investigative, and supervisory capacities, I fell prey to the need to earn more money. So I accepted an executive position with a new fast-food chain in Nashville, Tennessee, then called Minnie Pearl Chicken Systems, Inc. The company bore the name of that great lady of Grand Old Opry fame, but she herself was only a small shareholder and inactive in day-to-day management. The year was 1969, and any celebrity with national name recognition was in the fast-food business. But that's another story.

I was given the job of managing a company division called Nashco Equipment and Supply. Nashco was organized as a profit centre. It supplied both company-owned and franchised restaurants with restaurant decor, furniture, cooking equipment and utensils, uniforms, signage, and ad specialties. Nashco's operations were located about a mile from corporate headquarters in a leased warehouse and office facility of some 60,000 square feet. Nashco's major functional components at that site included purchasing, inventory control, sales, and physical distribution.

Nashco's physical distribution function included warehousing, receiving, and shipping activities. The latter included a fleet of leased trucks used to deliver restaurant equipment, supplies, and certain construction materials to new restaurant sites throughout the United States and Canada.

On the day I arrived to take over the division, the president of the company briefed me on his expectations. In simple terms his demand was, "Make money." He didn't say "or else." But I instinctively knew the implications. I inferred that because he made it clear that the division had lost money the year before—about $500,000.

The profit-centre manager who had incurred the loss was still employed by the company. In fact he had been demoted and made an assistant—to me! However, the president suggested I could terminate him at any time if I so desired.

It seemed to me that terminating the poor man should have been handled by someone either above me or by the corporate personnel director. At any rate I was stuck with him for the time being, mainly because I didn't know what else to do.

When I did meet my assistant, he seemed like a pleasant-enough chap. His previous experience and his education were in aeronautical engineering—a little odd perhaps, since we

were in the fast-food business. I didn't give it much further thought. Why should I? What did I know about the restaurant business? I was as green as he was—greener! He had been with the company for nine months.

My first day on the job, after my "executive briefing" with the president, was spent meeting all the members of my staff. Most of these folks were also relatively new at their jobs and showed evidence of insecurity in their roles. The only people who seemed secure in job roles were the warehousing people—stevedores, truck drivers, and the traffic manager. They at least knew their jobs and their place. They even showed great deference to me when I met them. But I didn't know why. (Was it typical of Southern culture to show deference for the boss? Perhaps. But here it seemed more than just deference. They almost feigned servility when I met them.)

As it turned out these were no gentlemen of the South. They were crooks. The evidence of their scams began to surface after I had had enough time to become better educated in my job. I spent my first two months learning as much as I could about the fast-food industry, franchising restaurant layouts and designs, and restaurant equipment purchasing and sales. I finally moved through the area I knew least and began to concentrate on what I knew best—accounting, finance, audits, controls, investigations, management, and security.

My first effort to reverse the previous year's loss was to review the previous year's operating statements and search for causes. Two items glared at me. Cost of sales was out of line the year before because of a large inventory shrink. Inventory per books was $200,000 higher than the physical count had indicated. The variance was about 10 percent—far more than anyone had expected. But nothing had been done to investigate the loss. The outside auditors made the appropriate adjustments, and the matter was left at that.

Another item was the high cost of transportation expense. I divided the total cost of transportation by the number of miles Ryder Truck Systems had billed us during the previous year. The resultant cost per mile was about double the national average for that time period.

So I had two things to work on now that I was freed from learning how to run a fried-chicken restaurant.

The inventory control group that reported to me consisted of three young ladies, two recent high school graduates and a supervisor, a woman of about 25 who appeared bright and hard-working.

One day when things seemed quiet (which wasn't very often in the halcyon days of fast food in Nashville in 1969), I visited with the inventory control supervisor and asked that she give me a briefing on what she and her crew did. She explained she manually kept perpetual inventory control system to me as best she could, after apologizing that she really was neither an accountant nor an auditor. She said she took a year of high school bookkeeping and had worked in the office of a moving company for several years before we hired her. At Minnie Pearl her training consisted of a four-hour briefing given by a member of the controller's staff. She apologized for the condition of the inventory records, saying there was more work than she and her staff could handle on a timely basis. So she often had to work overtime to catch up (for which she said she was not paid).

A cursory review of her in-process work and a few inventory ledger cards made my knees feel weak. She had not yet entered shipments of goods made three weeks earlier. And her recording of inbound merchandise was about equally tardy. For all intents and purposes we had no real inventory control system. Some goods were received and shipped out two weeks before any entry was made on the appropriate inventory ledger card.

What was worse, I discovered that a number of ledger cards contained red-ink entries. She explained that the procedure was recommended by a member of the controller's staff who informed her that she should make such an entry whenever she went to the warehouse to make a spot check of certain inventory items. She hadn't fully understood the rationale for cycle counting of selected items, so whenever she noted a discrepancy—the balance shown on the card disagreed with her count—she merely made a red-ink entry on whichever side of the card the discrepancy favoured. But she never advised anyone of the discrepancy or investigated any further, and she never reconciled her pluses and her minuses to determine whether she had a net of more or less. At the year-end, however, she did total the minuses and pluses out, she said. But not during the working year.

On one such ledger card there was a succession of red-ink entries. The ledger card related to large electric chicken fryers that cost the company over $1,000 each. Each of our restaurants needed four fryers. I quickly tallied her pluses and minuses and found the minuses were ahead by some 40 units, or by over $40,000!

A little investigating showed that an equipment serviceman for the company occasionally called from the field and ordered a replacement fryer for one that was in such a state of disrepair it needed to be sent back to the manufacturer on a warranty-claim basis. The warehousemen, lacking any prohibiting instructions, accommodated him.

What the serviceman did in fact was repair the chicken fryer on site, and when the new one arrived he would tell the restaurant manager the warehouse erred, and he himself would return the fryer—no problem. However the fryer never got back to the warehouse. It ended up in his garage, which was filled with other company property as well—refrigerator cabinets, heated cabinets, and even a knocked-down walk-in cooler.

As soon as it became apparent that something was wrong by way of the ledger card for chicken fryers, I began calling franchises and asking them whether anyone had offered to sell them chicken fryers at reduced prices. On the fifth call a franchisee mentioned that the serviceman had offered to sell him several fryers for a new restaurant at very "reasonable" prices. The serviceman told him the fryers were brand new and still in the manufacturer's carton.

"Sure enough and so they were," said the franchisee.

"Where did he say he got them?" I asked.

"He didn't say and I didn't ask him," said the franchisee.

"But I know where he kept them."

"Where's that?" I asked.

"In his garage," he said.

Armed with the franchisee's statement and our garbled inventory card, we got a search warrant for the serviceman's garage. There we found a treasure trove of restaurant equipment and supplies that belonged to the company.

So first things first, we developed a real inventory control system and hired an experienced person to supervise the function.

Transportation costs were next on the agenda. Our transport costs were horrendous. I tried the "rant and rave" approach to reduce costs early on but saw no real reduction. After the theft matter had settled down, I tried to find why transportation costs were so high.

I found that our truck fleet, after making deliveries of restaurant equipment, deadheaded back to Nashville, bypassing equipment manufacturers along the route. I thought that was strange, so I talked to the traffic manager. He said it was illegal for us to pick up our own inbound freight, that we were not common carriers and restaurant equipment was not an exempt commodity like farm produce. Our ICC permits allowed us to handle our own goods only after title had passed to us, which he said occurred after we received them at our warehouse.

So I called several manufacturers who sold us equipment and asked whether we could pick up our equipment purchases at their plant sites with our own fleet. They each said they would accommodate us, but we should change our purchase orders to show FOB their plant sites so as to not run afoul of ICC regulations. Changing the shipment for FOB destination point to FOB origination point caused title to pass to us at their plant so we could haul our own merchandise back and thus save the freight-in charges.

Feeling buoyed by this cost-cutting discovery, I called in the traffic manager and told him to co-ordinate his driver's return trips with the purchasing director and to pick up our equipment along the routes back to Nashville.

A month went by. No real reduction in transportation costs. The traffic manager skirmished with the purchasing director whenever he was told to have a returning truck make a pickup.

Then information came our way that indicated our truck drivers were unhappy about the notation of return loads. It kept them on the road a day or two longer, and away from their wives and children—or so they claimed. At least four of our drivers sought union representation from the Teamsters, as did a half-dozen warehouse employees.

What I didn't fully grasp was that I was ruining something a lot of people had a financial stake in. The drivers didn't want to pick up chicken fryers in Dallas or stainless steel sinks in St. Louis on their way back from Los Angeles because they already had a load to carry. What they were carrying back to Nashville was head lettuce and other fresh fruits and vegetables from California.

Several things tripped up the scheme. The first was collect phone calls made by our drivers to the traffic manager from strange places in California, places where we had neither existing restaurants nor new ones under construction; for example, Salinas has been known for its head lettuce ever since William Saroyan and John Steinbeck made it famous for that.

The Salinas calls caught my attention first. But then when Bakersfield showed up (potatoes) and Ventura/Oxnard (oranges, lemons), I knew something strange was happening. We had no restaurants within miles of these places and they weren't exactly along the route back to Nashville from San Francisco and Los Angeles, where we did have a large number of restaurants.

The strange calls piqued my curiosity, but they weren't evidence of anything yet. My next move was to review the expense claims submitted by the drivers after their returns. That had been the responsibility of my assistant. When I asked that he send the vouchers directly to me from then on, he seemed miffed, as though I had insulted his integrity. He said it was a Mickey Mouse chore, better left to him or the traffic manager, who really knew how to check the excesses of truck drivers who crib on their expense vouchers. When I insisted, he pouted but agreed to send me the vouchers.

I then visited the controller's office at corporate headquarters and asked to see all documentation that supported truck driver expense reports for the preceding six months.

In reviewing the documents submitted by drivers, I noted a recurring oddity. Weight statements at entry points on the Arizona border coming in from California seemed to be smudged, erased, written over, or just plain undecipherable. I selected about a half-dozen examples, made copies of the statements, and returned to my office. I then sent copies to a friend who was an Arizona state trooper, and asked him to secure for me copies of the state's own originals of the weight slips. Sure enough, when I got them back, the weights written on our copies were 20,000 or more pounds lower, indicating that the truck was loaded with something on its way back home.

Next we made phone calls to the numbers in Salinas, Oxnard, and Bakersfield. They were offices of produce growers, merchants, and ship-pers. One claimed he sold lettuce to Minnie Pearl restaurants in St. Louis. When told we had opened no restaurants in Saint Louis yet, he stammered and hung up.

We thought we could piece together what had happened at that point, but we needed confirmation. Our theory of the case was that the traffic manager through contacts with produce merchants in Nashville and St. Louis and growers and shippers in California was doing a little moonlighting with our fleet.

Shipping fresh produce by rail or by truck from California is not cheap. But because the federal government has attempted to support agricultural economics by making special rules for farm products, such products are generally exempt commodities from the standpoint of certain ICC regulations. Truckers who haul farm products are subject to far fewer requirements and regulations.

But because California ships out so much more produce than it takes in, its growers are chronically short of transportation mediums. So growers and shippers are eager to find any poor and lonesome trucker heading east with excess capacity. A thriving bootleg trucking business therefore existed that utilized the trucks of companies that could not find legitimate return loads.

The Minnie Pearl trucks were "sleepers" and carried two drivers so as to expedite deliveries and returns. The typical bootleg arrangement consisted of a $400 fee paid in cash to the two drivers by the grower or shipper. The drivers in turn took $100 each and gave $200 to our traffic manager, who had brokered the deal to begin with.

We cracked the case by asking one pair of driver-partners to explain the discrepancy between the weight slips they had submitted with their expense vouchers and the originals of those slips that we had secured from the state of Arizona. They laid out the scheme and implicated other drivers, and the traffic manager as the mastermind. Both confessed mainly because they were on parole—a report of the incident to parole authorities might have caused them to complete their prison sentences.

The traffic manager then implicated several other managers in the company as deriving benefits from his scheme.

(Source: G.J. Bologna and R.J. Lindquist, Fraud Auditing and Forensic Accounting (New York: John Wiley & Sons, 1987), pp. 227–33. Reprinted with permission of the publisher.)

Required:
a. Identify any potential management or personnel problems that might contribute to or facilitate fraud.
b. Identify the analytical procedures and findings that raised signals for further investigation and management work.
c. Identify some detail (extended) procedures performed to give signals and definite information about operational and fraudulent problems in connection with the inventory write-downs (shrink).
d. Identify some detail (extended) procedures performed to give signals and definite information about operational and fraudulent problems in connection with the high transportation costs.

18.58 Bank Reconciliation. Chapter 18 covers a wide range of fraud topics. The audit of bank reconciliations is in Chapter 9. Discussion Case 9.63 deals with a manipulated bank reconciliation and refers to Exhibit 18–3 in Chapter 18. You may wish to use Case 9.63 as an assignment for Chapter 18.

18.59 Payroll Fraud. You had established a national reputation as head of management audit at Henry Vanier Inc., a food manufacturing and processing corporation based in Calgary, with 40,000 employees in eight plants across the country and profits in 1993–94 of $92 million on revenue of $900 million. Your reputation had been based on innovations inspired by your financial control system audits and your performance audits in such areas as investment in new technology, cost-

ing, and quality assurance. Vanier had also avoided the embarrassing public revelations of fraud suffered over the last two years by your major competitor—Top Brands, which is based in Montreal. You were due to present your updated three-year audit plan to the board meeting next month, and the CEO dropped into your office as you were pondering your draft presentation.

"I have been watching the debacle at Top Brands with dismay," he said. "I realize that they are our competitors, but this fraud business affects the whole industry. Your approach to fraud is, I understand from our previous chats, really to keep an eye open for any signs while you conduct your financial control, compliance, and performance audits, and, as far as we all know, that has kept us from serious problems. But I wonder if we should build on that good public record by actually taking a careful pre-emptive look at fraud, and possibly even adding to our mission statement what I would like to call our corporate 'fraud policy.' To this end, I would like you to take an additional hour at the forthcoming board meeting to do three things: first, I would like a short statement on the definition of fraud and the responsibilities of management and auditors; then you should give the board a brief overview, but with all the stages defined, on how you would conduct a fraud investigation at Vanier. Finally, for, say, the last third of your presentation, I would like you to present a draft of the components that could go into a fraud policy statement for consideration by the board. I would envisage that this statement would be given to all employees and board members, and indeed widely publicized."

While you were working on this presentation, you received a call from Susan, one of your staff. Apparently, in a routine review of the payroll system, she had encountered a possible case of fraud, and she wanted you to review her findings. As part of the routine review, Susan extracted payroll records for the last quarter from the mainframe computer into a dBASE file. She then used ACL to analyse the payroll records. The dBASE file contains the following fields that are of relevance for the audit:

EMPNUM	Employee number
NAME	Name of employee
ADDRESS	Address of employee
DEPT	Department
SUPRVSOR	Supervisor name
PERIOD	Payroll period (1 for January, 2 for February, and so on)
BANK	Bank for payroll deposit
BANKACCT	Account number of payroll deposit
PAY	Amount of payment

The following is a partial printout from the dBASE file that Susan found disturbing:

EMPNUM	BANK	BANKACCT
691023	BNS	71029-2
701932	HKB	8923-12
702595	BNS	78910-3
710941	RBC	81-234
711120	HKB	9012-15
720187	BNS	73015-2
720198	TDB	1-29305
729510	BOM	128-412
729102	BNS	71029-2
730194	RBC	81-234
732103	BNS	72076-3
732461	RBC	81-234
732518	BOM	128-412
732892	TDB	1-29305
733019	HKB	8923-12
740125	BNS	72076-3
742957	TDB	1-29305
744910	BOM	128-412
751025	BNS	78910-3
760120	HKB	9012-15

Required:

a. Prepare the presentation on fraud for the forthcoming meeting.

b. Explain what conclusions can be drawn from the partial ACL printout.

c. What additional computer-assisted audit techniques would you use to make the printout more useful? You do not need to provide the ACL commands.

d. What audit procedures are required to follow up these payroll records?

(CGAAC adapted)

Appendix 18A

Details of Various Audit Standards Concerning Errors, Irregularities, Illegal Acts, Fraud, Abuse, and Inefficiency

. . . .

Auditor's Responsibility to Detect and Communicate Misstatements (from *Section* 5135.09)

Because the auditor maintains an attitude of professional skepticism when performing the audit, he or she will consider whether circumstances encountered indicate the possibility of a material misstatement existing in the financial statements. Examples of circumstances which, either individually or in combination, may make the auditor suspect misstatements exist are:

a. Unrealistic time deadlines for audit completion imposed by management.

b. Reluctance by management to engage in frank communication with appropriate third parties, such as regulators and bankers.

c. Limitation in audit scope imposed by management.

d. Identification of important matters not previously disclosed by management.

e. Conflicting or unsatisfactory evidence provided by management or employees.

f. Unusual documentary evidence such as handwritten alterations to documentation or handwritten documentation that would usually be electronically printed.

g. Information provided unwillingly or after unreasonable delay.

h. Seriously incomplete or inadequate accounting records.

i. Unsupported transactions.

j. Unusual transactions, by virtue of their nature, volume, or complexity, particularly if they occurred close to the year-end.

k. Significant unreconciled differences between control accounts and subsidiary records, or between physical count and the related account balance, that were not appropriately investigated and corrected on a timely basis.

l. Inadequate control over computer processing. For instance, too many processing errors, or delays in processing results and reports.

m. Significant differences from expectations disclosed by analytical procedures.

n. Fewer confirmation responses than expected, or significant differences revealed by confirmation responses.

If the auditor confirms or is unable to dispel the suspicion that the financial statements are materially misstated, he or she needs to consider the implications for the audit. The auditor would refer to Materiality and Audit Risk in Conducting an Audit, *Section* 5130, Reservations in the Auditors' Report, *Section* 5510, and Communication of Matters Identified During the Financial Statement Audit, *Section* 5750, for guidance on the evaluation and disposition of misstatements and the effect on the auditor's report.

From AICPA, SAS 82, "Consideration of Fraud in a Financial Statement Audit." Numerous aspects of responsibility for detecting and reporting errors and irregularities include the following:

1. Understand the characteristic causes and signs of errors and fraud. Risk factors that relate to misstatements arising from fraudulent financial reporting may be grouped in the following three categories:

a. *Management's characteristics and influence over the control environment.* These pertain to management's abilities, style, and attitude relating to internal control and the financial reporting process.

b. *Industry conditions.* These involve the economic and regulatory environment in which the entity operates.

c. *Operating characteristics and financial stability.* These pertain to the nature and complexity of the entity and its transactions, the entity's financial condition, and its profitability.

2. Assess the risk that errors or fraud may cause a company's financial statements to contain a material misstatement.

3. Design the audit to provide reasonable assurance of detecting material errors and fraud.

4. Exercise due care in planning, performing, and evaluating the results of audit procedures.

5. Have the proper degree of professional skepticism, assuming neither dishonesty nor unquestioned honesty of management.

6. Assign significant engagement responsibilities to audit personnel with the experience and training indicated as needed by the risk assessment. (Higher risk requires more experienced auditors and more extensive supervision.)

7. Determine whether accounting policies (revenue recognition, asset valuation, capitalization versus expensing) are acceptable in the circumstances.

8. Audit large and unusual transactions, particularly those that occur at or near year-end.

9. Evaluate the quantitative and qualitative significance of differences between the accounting records and the underlying facts and circumstances.

10. Accumulate potential audit adjustments and summarize and evaluate the combined effect.

11. Report immaterial fraud to a level of management at least one level above the people involved.

12. Insist that financial statements affected by a material fraud be revised, or else give a qualified report explaining all the substantive reasons.

13. Withdraw from the engagement if uncertainties about fraud cannot be resolved and management co-operation is unsatisfactory, and communicate the reasons for withdrawal to the audit committee of the board of directors.

14. Inform the company's audit committee of frauds, except those that are clearly inconsequential. (Frauds involving senior management are never "inconsequential.")

15. Disclose fraud to outside agencies in limited circumstances by:

- Reporting a change of auditors on SEC Form K-8.
- Responding to a subpoena.
- Responding to a successor auditor's enquiries.
- Communicating with a funding or other agency when required in audits of entities that receive governmental financial assistance.
- Communicate to the SEC any detection of a fraudulent act if the client fails to do so.

External auditors are not responsible for:

- Authenticating documents (lack of training).
- Finding intentional misstatements concealed by collusion* when using procedures designed to find unintentional misstatements.
- Ensuring or guaranteeing that all material misstatements will be discovered.
- General reporting of fraud to outside agencies or parties.
- Detecting and reporting errors and fraud in areas outside the scope of an engagement limited to parts or elements of financial statements.

Section 5136, Illegal Acts by Clients. Auditors have these responsibilities regarding illegal acts:

1. *a.* The auditor should apply his or her knowledge of the entity's business and make enquiries of management to identify laws and regulations which, if violated, could reasonably be expected to result in a material mistatement in the financial statements.
   b. The auditor is more likely to identify such laws and regulations if they:
   - *(i)* Enter into the determination of financial statement amounts or disclosures, for example, the Income Tax Act for taxable entities or the Bank Act for chartered banks.
   - *(ii)* Have a fundamental effect on the entity's industry and its operations, for example, an environmental law or regulation for a company which produces toxic chemicals.
   c. The auditor should enquire whether management is aware of any such laws and regulations.
2. When performing procedures in the normal course of the audit, the auditor will be alert to the possible existence of laws and regulations which, if violated, could reasonably be expected to result in a material misstatement in the financial statements.
3. The auditors should assess inherent risk. Example procedures should include:
   a. Obtaining evidence by reading the minutes of meetings of the board of directors or from reading the response to an enquiry letter to a law firm.
   b. Enquiring of and obtaining a written representation from management.
   c. Identifying factors that could indicate the likelihood of violation is other than low. These include:
   - *(i)* Violations of such laws or regulations by the entity in the current or a prior period.
   - *(ii)* Recent, well-publicized violations of such laws or regulations by other entities within the industry.
   - *(iii)* Active monitoring of such laws or regulations by a regulatory agency or other groups.
   - *(iv)* The complexity of such laws or regulations.
   - *(v)* Management's lack of experience in interpreting or applying such laws or regulations, for example, because the law or regulation is unusual or recently enacted.

*****Collusion** is the circumstance in which two or more people conspire to conduct fraudulent activity in violation of an organization's internal control policies and procedures.

   d. If the auditor assessed inherent risk as above low, the procedures might include:

     (i) Obtaining a more detailed understanding of laws or regulations identified, for example, by enquiry of management, other knowledgeable employee or the entity's legal counsel or by reviewing the laws or regulations.

     (ii) Enquiring of management about policies and procedures implemented by management to help discharge its responsibility to prevent and detect illegal acts.

     (iii) Testing of controls of the policies and procedures implemented by management (if the auditor plans to assess control risk below maximum).

     (iv) Consulting with the entity's legal counsel or other specialists about the application of laws or regulations and the possible effect on the financial statements.

     (v) Reading correspondence and reports from a regulatory agency or other similar authority.

     (vi) Reading minutes of meetings of the board of directors or committees established to monitor compliance with those laws or regulations identified.

4. The auditor should enquire and obtain written representation from management to confirm that either:

   a. management is not aware of any illegal or possibly illegal acts; or

   b. management has disclosed to the auditor all facts related to illegal or possibly illegal acts.   [Jan. 1995]

5. When the auditor has obtained evidence that indicates an illegal or possibly illegal act, other than one considered inconsequential, may have occurred, the auditor should ensure that the audit committee and other appropriate levels of management are informed.

6. Auditors should also watch for the following:

   a. Comments made in the response letter obtained in accordance with COMMUNICATIONS WITH LAW FIRMS, *Section* 6560.

   b. Investigation by a government agency, an enforcement proceeding or payment of unusual fines or penalties.

   c. Violations of laws or regulations cited in correspondence and reports issued by regulatory agencies made available to the auditor.

   d. Unusually large cash receipts or payments, transfers to numbered bank accounts or accounts in financial institutions with which the entity does not normally do business.

   e. Unsupported payments.

   f. Increased or unusual legal or consulting fees.

   g. Allegations about illegal acts made by suppliers, creditors, or employees.

   h. Media comment.

External auditors are not responsible for:

- Final determination that a particular act is illegal (lack of legal, judicial expertise).
- Ensuring that illegal acts will be detected or that related contingent liabilities will be disclosed.

- Designing audit procedures to detect illegal acts in the absence of specific information brought to the auditors' attention.
- General reporting of illegal acts to outside agencies or parties.

Auditor Communications to the Audit Committee (AUG–11)

1. The audit committee may expect the auditor to communication such matters as:
   a. illegal acts;
   b. significant transactions that appear to be inconsistent with the ordinary course of business;
   c. unusual actions which significantly increase the risk of loss to the entity; and
   d. actions which, if they became public knowledge, might cause serious embarrassment to the entity, such as breaches of the corporate code of conduct.
2. The auditor's responsibility under generally accepted auditing standards and planning the audit include discussion of the following:
   a. the general approach to the audit, such as the cyclical coverage of branches and stock-taking in various locations;
   b. areas of the financial statements identified as having a high risk of material mistatement and the auditor's response thereto;
   c. the materiality and audit risk levels on which the audit is based (as noted in MATERIALITY AND AUDIT RISK IN CONDUCTING AN AUDIT, paragraph 5130.31, the question of whether to communicate these levels is a matter for the professional judgment of the auditor);
   d. weaknesses in internal control;
   e. fraud;
   f. significant accounting principles and policies;
   g. management judgments and accounting estimates;
   h. misstatements;
   i. disagreements with management;
   j. consultation with other accountants;
   k. major issues discussed that influence audit appointment; and
   l. difficulties encountered in performing the audit.

   Section 5750, *Communication of Matters Identified During the Financial Statement Audit.* The auditor has the responsibility to report during the course of the financial statement audit the following matters to the appropriate level of management.
   a. misstatements, other than trivial errors;
   b. fraud;
   c. misstatements that may cause future financial statements to be materially misstated;
   d. illegal or possibly illegal acts, other than ones considered inconsequential; and
   e. significant weaknesses in internal control.

   The type and significance of the matter to be communicated will determine the level of management to which the communication is directed.

The auditor would review matters communicated as a result of the previous financial statement audit. If, in the auditor's professional judgment, the matters have not been satisfactorily addressed, the auditor would consider recommunicating these matters and, when appropriate, communicating them to a higher level of management. Periodically, the auditor would consider whether because of changes in circumstances, such as a change in management, or simply because of the passage of time, it is appropriate to recommunicate matters communicated as a result of a previous financial statement audit.

The communication should preferably be in writing (para. 09) on a timely basis (para. 14). When no such matters have been identified there is no requirement to communicate the fact.

Appendix 18B

Professional Standards and Practices for Certified Fraud Examiners (December 31, 1994)

- -

I. GENERAL STANDARDS

A. **Independence and Objectivity**

CFEs are responsible for maintaining independence in attitude and appearance, approaching and conducting fraud examinations in an objective and unbiased manner, and assuring that examining organizations they direct are free from impairments to independence.

B. **Qualifications**

CFEs must possess skills, knowledge, abilities, and appearance needed to perform examinations proficiently and effectively. CFEs responsible for directing fraud examinations must assure they are performed by personnel who collectively possess the skills and knowledge necessary to complete examinations in accordance with these Standards. CFEs must maintain their qualifications by fulfilling continuing education requirements and adhering to the Code of Ethics of the Association of Certified Fraud Examiners.

C. **Fraud Examinations**

CFEs must conduct fraud examinations using due professional care, with adequate planning and supervision to provide assurance that objectives are achieved within the framework of these Standards. Evidence is to be obtained in an efficient, thorough, and legal manner; and reports of the results of fraud examinations must be accurate, objective, and thorough.

D. **Confidentiality**

CFEs are responsible for assuring they and the examining organizations they direct exercise due care to prevent improper disclosure of confidential or privileged information.

II. SPECIFIC STANDARDS

A. **Independence and Objectivity**

1. Attitude and Appearance

Independence of attitude requires impartiality and fairness in conducting examinations and in reaching resulting conclusions and judgments. CFEs must also be sensitive to the appearance of independence so that conclusions and judgments will be accepted as impartial by knowledgeable third parties. CFEs who become aware of a situation or relationship that could be perceived to impair independence, whether or not actual impairment exists, should inform management immediately and take steps to eliminate the perceived impairment, including withdrawing from the examination, if necessary.

2. Objectivity

To assure objectivity in performing examinations, CFEs must maintain an independent mental attitude, reach judgments on examination matters without undue influence from others, and avoid being placed in positions where they would be unable to work in an objective professional manner.

3. Organizational Relationship

The CFE's reporting relationship should be such that the attitude and appearance of independence and objectivity are not jeopardized. Organizational independence is achieved when the CFE's function has a mandate to conduct independent examinations throughout the organization, or by a reporting relationship high enough in the organization to assure independence of action.

B. **Qualifications**

1. Skills, Knowledge, Abilities, and Experience

CFEs cannot be expected to have an expert level of skill and knowledge for every circumstance that might be encountered in a fraud examination. Nevertheless, CFEs must have sufficient skill and knowledge to recognize when additional training or expert guidance is required. It is the responsibility of a CFE to assure that necessary skills, knowledge, ability, and experience are acquired or available before going forward with a fraud examination.

CFEs must be skilled in obtaining information from records, documents, and people; in analyzing and evaluating information and drawing sound conclusions; in communicating the results of fraud examinations, both orally and in writing; and in serving as an expert witness when appropriate.

CFEs must be knowledgeable in investigative techniques, applicable laws and rules of evidence, fraud auditing, criminology, and ethics.

2. Continuing Education

CFEs are required to fulfill continuing education requirements established by the Association of Certified Fraud Examiners. Additionally, CFEs are responsible for securing other education necessary for specific fraud examinations and related fields in which they are individually involved.

3. Code of Ethics

CFEs are to adhere to the Code of Professional Ethics of the Association of Certified Fraud Examiners.

C. **Fraud Examinations**

1. Due Professional Care

Due professional care is defined as exercising the care and skill expected of a prudent professional in similar circumstances. CFEs are responsible for assuring that there is sufficient predication for beginning a fraud examination; that said examinations are conducted with diligence and thoroughness; that all applicable laws and regulations are observed; that appropriate methods and techniques are used; and that said examinations are conducted in accordance with these Standards.

2. Planning and Supervision

CFEs must plan and supervise fraud examinations to assure that objectives are achieved within the framework of these Standards.

3. Evidence

CFEs must collect evidence, whether exculpatory or incriminating, that supports fraud examination results and will be admissible in subsequent proceedings, by obtaining and documenting evidence in a manner to ensure that all necessary evidence is obtained and the chain of custody is preserved.

4. Reporting

CFE reports of the results of fraud examinations, whether written or verbal, must address all relevant aspects of the examination, and be accurate, objective, and understandable.

In rendering reports to management, clients, or others, CFEs shall not express judgments on the guilt or innocence of any person or party, regardless of the CFE's opinion of the preponderance of evidence. CFEs must exercise due professional care when expressing other opinions related to an examination, such as the likelihood that a fraud has or has not occurred, and whether or not internal controls are adequate.

D. **Confidentiality**

CFEs, during fraud examinations, are often privy to highly sensitive and confidential information about organizations and individuals. CFEs must exercise due care so as not to purposefully or inadvertently disclose such information except as necessary to conduct the examination or as required by law.

Source: Association of Certified Fraud Examiners, 716 West Avenue, Austin, Texas, 78701.

PART V

SPECIALIZED TOPICS

CHAPTER 19

Learning Objectives

Chapter 8 covered the general issues of planning audit testing within a computer environment. This chapter covers audit planning and testing issues associated with more advanced EDP systems and the rapidly evolving world of electronic commerce, which is the generic term for all electronic messaging technology including electronic data interchange (EDI), electronic funds transfer (EFT), E-mail, fax, telex, videotape, and electronic filing with the government.

The chapter is subdivided into four parts: (1) characteristics and control considerations of advanced EDP systems, (2) audit tests of advanced EDP systems, (3) computer abuse and fraud, and (4) some audit considerations of electronic commerce.

After you study Chapter 19, you should be able to:

1. List and describe the four features that characterize "advanced" computer systems.

2. List and briefly describe several techniques applicable for auditing advanced computer systems.

3. Define and describe computer fraud and the controls that can be used to prevent it.

4. Define and describe electronic commerce, its impact on the business environment, and the major implication for auditors.

AUDIT OF ADVANCED SYSTEMS AND

ELECTRONIC COMMERCE

ADVANCED SYSTEMS: CHARACTERISTICS AND CONTROL CONSIDERATIONS

. . . .

LEARNING OBJECTIVE
1. List and describe the four features that characterize "advanced" computer systems.

Simple batch computer systems deal with one component of an organization at a time, such as payroll or billing. Advanced applications involve immediate update utilizing a companywide data base, performing multiple functions simultaneously (EDP Audit Guidelines: EDP Environments—on-line computer systems; and EDP Environments—database systems). Of course, you will encounter variations between simple batch and the most advanced systems. For example, terminals and workstations are commonly used for data entry; but the transactions collected on disks for batch update or terminals may be for enquiry about the status of balances (e.g., perpetual inventory), while update is still by batch. Further, while some processing may be updated immediately, such as order entry, other applications in the same company, such as payroll that has a natural periodic cycle, could be batch-processed.

Advanced systems have been described using many terms, such as time-sharing, on-line, real time, and distributed processing (see box). The problem with such terms from an audit point of view is that they describe hardware and software technology and do not focus on how accounting transactions are processed. For purposes of evaluating control, advanced systems are those systems (large or small) that possess one or more of the following characteristics:

- Data communication.
- Data integration.
- Automatic transaction initiation.
- Unconventional or temporary audit trial.

Data Communication

Data communication is a combination of electronic data transmission and the computer. The complexity of data communication networks may vary from a few remote terminals linked to a microcomputer to a complex network utilizing time-sharing, on-line, real time, and distributed processing systems (terms defined in the box). The main "advanced" feature is that programs, transactions, and data files can be introduced, maintained, modified, or accessed at locations distant from the central data processing installation.

Advanced Computer Terms

Time-sharing

Time-sharing is a computer system with a number of independent, relatively slow-speed terminal devices. The user has the impression that he or she is the sole user, due to the slowness of input/output, when in reality the computer is sharing its time with a number of users. Time-sharing may be owned or utilized by many organizations. (The company providing the service for many users is called a "service bureau.")

On-line

On-line is used with two different meanings. Data files are said to be on-line if they are electronically available to the central processor and can be accessed without operator intervention. On-line also refers to a user who is connected to the central processor as described above under time-sharing. Data processing also is termed on-line (or direct access or random) when transactions can be input into computer processing from the point of origin without first being sorted (EDP–5).

Real Time

Real time has a variety of meanings. Real time can refer to a quick response in a time-shared system, such as is necessary for airline reservations. Real time in an accounting and production sense means that the system evaluates information and feeds back (return signals) in time to take action.

Distributed Processing

Distributed processing refers to the situation where two or more computers handle the data processing. This is a form of extension of time-sharing, except that the terminals can be connected to one of a number of computers. Minicomputers may be located at a remote site to handle local processing and to maintain local files, with summary data transactions transmitted to a central location.

Advanced computer systems are said to be transaction driven or event driven because the individual transaction triggers the processing activity and updates all relevant files. In contrast a batch system could be said to be program driven because a specific program must be loaded into the computer to process all transactions that fit that program and its related files. In a transaction-driven system, the transaction-type identification code part of the transaction input is the most sensitive part because it initiates all subsequent actions.

Control Implications

Control standards in advanced communication systems are difficult to maintain, yet controls at all locations that can access the system are essential. Especially crucial are procedures for identification and authorization of all users (e.g., passwords). Control weaknesses at any one location may compromise the control structure elsewhere.

Data Integration

In batch processing, each application system has its own files. For example, the payroll processing utilizes the payroll master file. Some of the same information (such as employee numbers and pay rates) also may be maintained on personnel files and labour cost accounting files. Further, the master files in a batch system tend to become the property of a particular user department. Periodic review must be made of identical fields in various user department files to ensure that they are the same and to reconcile differences.

Advanced systems frequently include a new part of the system software called a database management system (DBMS) and an integrated "master file" called the data base (EDP–6). The database contains all the information formerly maintained in separate user department files. A particular piece of data, such as employee number, is stored only once (data integration), but through the DBMS it is made available to all programs (payroll, personnel, cost accounting) that need that data. Thus, data redundancy (same data stored in several separate files) is eliminated. Since the traditional files having all the same record format do not exist, the concept of a field in a record no longer applies. The individual pieces of information (employee number, address, pay rate, balance) are called data elements and are logically combined by the DBMS to provide programs with the records necessary for the particular processing. The information in the data base becomes a companywide resource, rather than belonging to a particular user department.

Control Implications

The DBMS contains controls that restrict access to the data base. The data base is composed of individual data elements, each with a unique storage space in the data base. The entire population of data elements is called the schema. Authorized users (including computer programs) can be limited to only those portions of the data base (called subschema) that are needed. Thus, authorized employees in the payroll department may be able to enter the weekly hours that update year-to-date gross pay, while being precluded from changing any pay rate.

Responsibility must be delegated for establishing, assigning, and maintaining the authorization procedures. This responsibility usually is assigned to a data base administrator (DBA) person. The DBA is responsible for determining who should have access to each data element (that is, for defining each user's subschema). Further, responsibility must be assigned by the DBA to users for each data element in the data base. The data base administrator should have the following responsibilities:

- Design the content and organization of the data base, including logical data relationships, physical storage strategy, and access strategy.
- Protect the data base and its software, including control over access to and use of the data and DBMS, and provide for backup and recovery in the case of errors or destruction of the data base.
- Monitor the performance of the DBMS and improve its efficiency.

- Communicate with the data base users, arbitrate disputes over data ownership and use, educate users about the DBMS, and consult users when problems arise.
- Provide standards for data definition and use and document the data base and its software.[1]

Since the DBA should have such extensive responsibilities, this function should be segregated from the other computer functions of systems development, programming, operations, and users described previously.

When auditors encounter a DBMS, the following control procedures should be evaluated:

DBMS Control Procedures	Audit Consideration
Segregation of data administration functions.	Segregation of data administrator from incompatible functions.
User data controls.	Segregation of duties within data administration, if possible. User responsibility for data. User review of all changes. Periodic review and comparison with physical counts and other evidence of correct data values.
Accuracy controls.	Use of standard data editing and validation procedures.
Error-correction controls.	Use of procedures for error correction.
Access controls.	Use of procedures to limit access to programs to authorized personnel only.

Source: Gordon B. Davis et al., *Auditing & EDP* (New York: AICPA, 1983), p. 111.

Automatic Transaction Initiation

Automatic transaction initiation, present in some batch systems, usually is more extensive in advanced systems. Transactions can be computer-initiated to write invoices, cheques, shipping orders, and purchase orders, without human review.

Control Implications
Without a human-readable document indicating the transaction event, the correctness of automatic transactions is difficult to judge. Authorization of transactions occurs when certain flags are installed in program or records (e.g., inventory quantity falling below reorder point). Therefore, authorization is more difficult to trace to the proper person. Control procedures must be designed into the system to ensure the genuineness and reasonableness of automatic transactions and to prevent or detect erroneous transactions.

Unconventional or Temporary Audit Trail

The audit trail of frequent printouts in simple systems and the hard-copy source documents supporting keyed data entry gradually disappear as systems become more advanced. They are replaced by sensor-based data collection input and microfilm or

---

[1]   Davis et al., *Auditing & EDP,* p. 109.

EXHIBIT 19–1   TRANSACTION-ORIENTED ENVIRONMENT

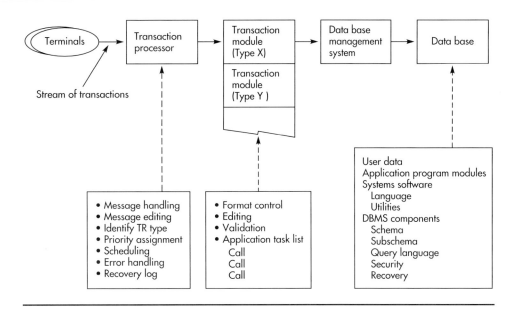

machine-readable output. All advanced systems need an audit trail in case of transmission interruption or power surge; however, the retention period may be short and the information available only in machine-readable form.

Control Implications

Audit and control specifications for an audit trail need to be established at the time a system is designed or evaluated for lease or purchase. The loss of hard-copy documents and reports and the temporary nature of the audit trail may require external auditors to alter both the timing and the nature of audit procedures. Greater co-operation and co-ordination are required between external and internal auditors.

A transaction-oriented environment is represented in Exhibit 19–1. The transaction processor keeps track of the remote input terminal sources of messages, performs preliminary message editing, checks authority, and identifies the transaction type. Based on the transaction code, a particular transaction module (such as the payroll update program) is initiated. These modules edit the transactions for input errors. A query-only transaction (no change to data elements in the data base) will involve less complex transaction modules. All transactions must pass through the DBMS, where access authorization is tested and certain data elements are made available for the return trip through the various steps. Such systems require complex hardware and software.

R E V I E W
CHECKPOINTS

19.1   Define an audit trail. How might a computer system audit trail in an advanced system differ from one in a simple system or a manual system?

19.2   What are the characteristics of advanced computer systems?

19.3 Why are advanced computer systems said to be "transaction driven," while batch systems are said to be "program driven"?

19.4 How can each department "own" its computer data files when data processing is accomplished in a simple batch system but lose ownership if a data base management system (DBMS) is used?

19.5 What are the responsibilities of the data base administration (DBA) function?

19.6 What control procedures should be evaluated when a data base is used instead of master files?

· ·

Tests of Computer Controls in Advanced Computer Systems

· · · · · · · · · · · ·

LEARNING OBJECTIVE
2. List and briefly describe several techniques applicable for auditing advanced computer systems.

As explained in the beginning of Chapter 8, the internal control audit objectives do not change when the environment changes from manual to computer data processing, or from simple batch computer processing to more advanced computer processing. Auditors must still assess the control risk. However, the audit techniques must be adapted to the different environment. The control features for advanced computer systems are summarized in the box below.

Control Features

To achieve the control objectives in an advanced computer environment, the system should be designed to provide the following features:

1. User identification. The system should have the capability to uniquely identify each of the persons using the system.
2. Request authorization. The system should be able to determine if the processing or information request of a user is authorized.
3. Activity logging. The system should be capable of recording all user activity (such as the number of attempted log-ons, enquiries, and the like), as well as recording information about the processes executed.

Source: AICPA, *Management, Control, and Audit of Advanced EDP Systems* (New York: AICPA, 1977), p. 11.

Audit Tools and Techniques

The audit of advanced computer systems usually involves computer audit specialists with advanced technical proficiency. However, "general" auditors (and you as a student of auditing) must possess some knowledge of the tools and techniques available in order to co-ordinate the specialist's work with the other procedures to achieve the audit objective of assessing control risks. Auditors also need to know the available techniques in order to advise clients of the control concerns and potential audit aids. Most of the tools and techniques discussed below need to be designed into the system. Auditors should become more involved in reviewing systems at the development stage to ensure that adequate controls are installed and that auditability is possible.

The tools and techniques applicable to auditing in an advanced computer environment can be classified as those that (1) operate on-line on a real-time basis with live data, (2) operate on historical data, (3) utilize simulated or dummy data, and (4) utilize programs analysis techniques.

Techniques Using Live Data

In most cases these techniques require that special audit modules be designed and coded into programs at the time of development. These **audit hooks** allow auditors to select specific transactions of audit interest before or during processing and save them for subsequent audit follow-up. (Program modules solely for audit or maintenance purposes are called audit hooks. The same concepts used for fraudulent purposes are called **trap doors**.)

Tagging Transactions.   Transactions selected by the auditor are "tagged" with an indicator at input. A computer trail of all processing steps of these transactions in the application system can be printed out or stored in computer files for subsequent evaluation.

Audit Files.   Auditor-selected transactions are written to a special file for later verification. Two methods may be employed. **Systems control audit review file (SCARF)** is a method by which auditors build into the data processing programs special limits, reasonableness, or other audit tests. These tests produce reports of transactions selected according to the auditor's criteria, and the reports are delivered directly to the auditor for review and follow-up. The SCARF procedure is especially attractive to internal auditors. A **sample audit review file (SARF)** technique is similar to SCARF, except that instead of programming auditors' test criteria, a random sampling selection scheme is programmed. The report of sample transactions can be reviewed by auditors after each production run. The SCARF method is efficient for producing representative samples of transactions processed over a period by the computer.

Snapshot.   A "picture" of main memory of transactions and data base elements is taken before and after computer processing operations have been performed. The picture is then printed out for auditor use. For example, the contents of an accounts receivable balance are saved before a sales transaction is posted, and the contents after posting are saved. These balances, along with the sales transaction, indicate whether update processing was correct. The auditor can trace and verify the decision process utilizing the results.

Monitoring Systems Activity.   Hardware and software are available to analyse activity within a computer. These monitors are designed to determine computer efficiency. However, they may be applied for financial audit purposes to determine who uses elements of the system and for what operations. For example, a record of passwords used to enter accounting transactions can be captured and compared to the list of personnel authorized to enter these transactions.

Extended Records.   Special programs provide an audit trail of an individual transaction by accumulating the results of all application programs that contributed to the processing of a transaction. The accumulated results are stored either as additional fields of the transaction record or in a separate audit file. For example, the snapshot example of accounts receivable balances before and after update processing could be added to the sales transaction, making an extended transaction record. Thus, auditors can follow the flow of a transaction without reviewing several files at various times and stages of processing.

Techniques Using Historical Data

These techniques generally are designed to give auditors access to machine-sensible files. The parallel simulation concept of reprocessing data and comparing results to original processing, explained previously, is included in this class of techniques. Also included is generalized audit software, which was discussed in Chapter 8. A particularly popular software for analysing data bases is Audit Command Language, or ACL.

Techniques Using Simulated or Dummy Data

The test data concept explained earlier is a technique that fits in this class, although it generally is used in simple batch computer systems. An extension of the test data concept has been expanded for use in advanced computer systems under the name of integrated test facility.

Integrated Test Facility (ITF).   This "minicompany" approach is a technique used by clients' program maintenance personnel, although it can be used by auditors. It involves creating a dummy department or branch complete with records of employees, customers, vendors, receivables, payables, and other accounts. The ITF has master file records (or data base records), carefully coded (such as "99"), included among the real master-file records. Simulated transactions (test data) are inserted along with real transactions, and the same application programs operate on both the test data and the real transactions. Since the auditor knows what the ITF output should be, the actual results of processing (output reports, error reports) can be reviewed to determine whether the application program is functioning properly. A great deal of care is required when ITF is used because the fictitious master-file records, the transactions, and the account outputs are placed in the actual accounting system and in the business records. The account amounts and other output data must be reversed or adjusted out of the financial statements. Also, care must be taken not to damage or misstate any of the real master-file records and account balances.

Program Analysis Techniques

Numerous software packages are used by computer technicians for documentation, debugging, and analysis. These tools also can be used for audit purposes in certain situations. Programs exist to take the source code (e.g., COBOL) and produce flowcharts or decision tables that can be used to understand the logic of an application program. **Cross-reference** programs provide printed listings of every occurrence of each name used in an application program or a list of every file used in an application system. Auditors can use these listings to follow the flow of transactions and identify significant data files. Program analysis software can be utilized by auditors to identify potential trapdoors created for fraudulent use.[2]

---

[2] This may be an oversimplification because computer systems may have multiple controls that create thousands of error combinations and possible test transactions. Computerized test data generators are available to help auditors overcome the magnitude of the test data creation task.

E X H I B I T 19–2   ADVANCED COMPUTER SYSTEMS AUDIT TOOLS AND TECHNIQUES

Technique	Capability Supplied by	Used by	Data Used	Purpose	Advantages	Disadvantages
Tagging transactions	Vendor or application system designer.	Auditors and managers.	Live accounting.	Test of controls and substantive audit.	Full range of selectivity.	Adds to overhead of system, special programming.
Audit files	Systems designer.	Auditors and control personnel.	Live accounting and system.	Test of controls and substantive audit.	Specified transactions logged for audit review.	Cost.
Snapshot	Systems designer.	Programmers and auditors.	Live system.	Review system, logic.	Aids understanding of flow of transaction processing.	Special programming.
Monitoring	Vendor.	Auditors and managers.	Live system.	Review actual system activity.	Shows what has happened.	Requires technical knowledge to interpret.
Generalized audit software	Vendor and systems designer, software house, manufacturer, or audit firm.	Auditors and managers.	Historical and live.	Test of controls and substantive audit. Perform wide variety of audit procedures.	Retrieves data for audit puposes. Relatively easy to use, not expensive.	Requires some programming knowledge by auditor. Presently limited to types of files that can be accessed.
Simulation	Auditors, internal and external with program copy.	Auditors.	Historical.	Determine accuracy of data processed tests of controls audit.	Permits comparison with real processing.	Extensive use can be large consumer of machine resources.
Extended records	Design of client applicaton.	Auditors and managers.	Historical.	Provide complete trail for audit and management purposes.	Provide complete account history.	Very costly use of machine resources at present
Integrated test facility	Auditors, mostly internal.	Auditors.	Simulated.	Test of controls audit.	Relatively inexpensive.	Must be "backed out" very carefully.
Program analysis techniques	Special software, contractor, or vendor.	Auditors and programmers.	Usually simulated.	Authentication of program operation. Check of key points in program execution.	Gives better understanding of application; gives assurance controls are functioning.	Needs auditor knowledge of programming; may be expensive; useful only in certain circumstances.

Source: Adapted from AICPA, *Management, Control, and Audit of Advanced EDP Systems* (New York: AICPA, 1977), p. 24.

These advanced computer systems audit tools and techniques are summarized in Exhibit 19–2. These audit tools and techniques should be studied carefully—especially the purposes, advantages, and disadvantages. The next section of this chapter will focus on how auditors can use the computer to assist in auditing historical computer accounting records, primarily to support substantive audit procedures to gather evidence on account balances.

· ·

R E V I E W
C H E C K P O I N T S

19.7   What are the names of the advanced control techniques that clients can imbed in computer systems, classified according to categories (e.g., live data, historical data, dummy data, program analysis techniques)?

19.8 What is the difference between the test data technique and the integrated test facility technique?

19.9 Which of the advanced audit tools and techniques would be used for test of controls audit procedures? for substantive audit procedures?

19.10 ''The use of the test data technique (or the integrated test facility technique) to test the client's application control procedures is unprofessional. We don't enter fake transactions into a client's manual system. Why should we do it in their computer system?'' Evaluate this position and question posed by an audit partner.

19.11 Evaluate the following statement made by a client's data processing manager: ''Who cares if we used identification numbers and passwords to access the inventory data base and the update programs as long as the computer maintains a transaction log?''

· ·

COMPUTER ABUSE AND COMPUTER FRAUD
· · · · · · · · · · · ·

LEARNING OBJECTIVE

3. Define and describe computer fraud and the controls that can be used to prevent it.

Computer fraud is a matter of concern for managers and investors as well as auditors. Experts in the field have coined two definitions related to computer chicanery: *computer abuse* is the broad definition, but *computer fraud* is probably the term used more often (see box below).

COMPUTER ABUSE AND COMPUTER FRAUD DEFINITIONS

Computer Abuse:
Any incident associated with computer technology in which a victim suffered or could have suffered a loss and a perpetrator by intention made or could have made a gain. (D.B. Parker, *Crime by Computer* (New York, Charles Scribner's Sons, 1976, p. 12.)

Computer Fraud:
Fraud is any intentional act designed to deceive or mislead another person with the result that the victim suffers a loss or the perpetrator achieves a gain.

Computer fraud is any fraud that involves electronic data processing in the perpetration or cover-up of the fraudulent acts.

Computer abuse and fraud includes such diverse acts as intentional damage or destruction of a computer, use of the computer to assist in a fraud, and use of the mystique of computers to promote business. Computers have been damaged by vandals—an abuse best prevented by physical security measures. A computer was used by the perpetrators of the Equity Funding financial fraud to print thousands of fictitious records and documents that otherwise would have occupied the time of hundreds of clerks. Some services (such as ''computerized'' dating services) promote business on the promise of using computers when none are actually used. In a business environment auditors and managers are concerned particularly with acts of computer theft or embezzlement of assets, and material misstatements in the financial statements. To perpetrate computer frauds, persons must have access to one or more of the following:

- The computer itself, or a terminal.
- Data files.
- Computer programs.
- System information.
- Time and opportunity to convert assets to personal use.

Computer financial frauds range from the crude to the complex. They hit financial institutions with alarming frequency, especially through credit card theft and abuse. They are apparently hard to detect in the ordinary course of business. The AICPA conducted a study of computer frauds in the banking and insurance industry and found that customer complaints were the leading clues to discovery of fraud, while routine audits were credited with discovery of 18 percent. Auditors have some success, but they are not infallible detectives. The box below gives the range of detection incidence.

How Fraud Is Detected in Financial Institutions

Customer complaint or enquiry	24%
Accident, tip-off, unusual perpetrator activity	22
Controls	18
Routine audit	18
Nonroutine study	8
Changes in operations, EDP, financial statements	6
Unidentified	5

Source: Report on the Study of EDP-Related Fraud in the Banking and Insurance Industries (AICPA, 84).

Control Protection

Organizations can install controls designed to prevent and detect computer frauds and to limit the extent of damage from them. These prevention, detection, and limitation controls are summarized in Exhibit 19–3.

Controls can be classified in three different levels. *Administrative controls* refer to general controls that affect the management of an organization's computer resources.

The *physical controls* affect the computer equipment itself and related documents. The "inconspicuous location" control simply refers to placing microcomputers, terminals, and data processing centres in places out of the way of casual traffic. Of course, the equipment used daily must be available in employees' workplaces, but access must be controlled to prevent unauthorized persons from simply sitting down and invading the system and its data files.

EXHIBIT 19–3   PROTECTING THE COMPUTER FROM FRAUD (selected controls)

	Objective of Control		
	Prevention	Detection	Limitation
Administrative controls:			
Security checks on personnel	X		
Segregation of duties	X		
Access and execution log records (properly reviewed)		X	
Program testing after modification		X	
Rotation of computer duties			X
Transaction limit amounts			X
Physical controls:			
Inconspicuous location	X		
Controlled access	X		
Computer room guard (after hours)		X	
Computer room entry log record		X	
Preprinted limits on documents (e.g., cheques)			X
Data backup storage			X
Technical controls:			
Encoding data	X		
Access control software and passwords	X		
Transaction logging reports		X	
Control totals (financial, hash)		X	
Program source comparison (comparing versions of programs)		X	
Range checks on permitted transaction amounts			X
Reasonableness check on permitted transaction amounts			X

Source: Computer Fraud, Ernst & Whinney, 1987.

Technical controls include some matters of electronic wizardry. "Encoding data" actually means converting it to scrambled form or code so that it can look like garbled nonsense when transmitted or retrieved from a file. Since the collapse of the Soviet Union and the lessened need for Cold War intelligence work, industrial spying is predicted to increase; businesses should assume that data transmitted by wire and airwaves (e.g., satellite transmission) will be intercepted by public and private intelligence services and analysed for the purpose of commercial advantage. Unscrupulous industrial spies may try to break into an organization's computer system, and elaborate password software will be necessary to thwart them. (Hackers have been known to program telephones to call random numbers to find a computer system, then try millions of random passwords to try to get in!) The range and reasonableness checks refer to computer monitoring of transaction processing to try to detect potentially erroneous or fraudulent transactions. These are the equivalent of the low-tech imprint you may have seen on some negotiable cheques: "Not negotiable if over $500," for example.

Embezzlement and Financial Statement Fraud

Computer experts generally agree that an ingenious programmer can commit theft or misappropriation of assets that will be difficult, if not impossible, to detect.

Nonetheless, such frauds usually produce an unsupported debit balance in some asset account. For example, someone might manipulate the computer to cause purchased goods to be routed to his own warehouse. In this case the business inventory balance probably would be overstated. One bank employee caused chequing account service charges to be credited to his own account instead of to the appropriate revenue account. In this case the service charge revenue account would be less than the sum of charges to the chequing account customers. Thorough auditing of accounting output records might result in detection of computer-assisted frauds such as these.

Noncomputer auditing methods, as well as some computer-assisted methods, may be employed to try to detect computer frauds. Direct confirmations with independent outside parties, analytical review of the output of the system for typical relationships, and comparison of output with independently maintained files may reveal errors and irregularities in computer-produced accounting records. However, all too often auditors and managers are surprised by computer frauds reported to them by conscious-stricken participants, anonymous telephone messages, tragic suicides, or other haphazard means. Nevertheless, auditors working in a computer environment are expected to possess the expertise required to identify serious computer control weaknesses. When such weaknesses are believed to exist, the best strategy is to use the services of a computer specialist to help plan and execute technical procedures for further study and evaluation of the computer control systems.

Frauds can be ingenious, and the changing technology may make them even more difficult to control. However, as the box below illustrates, careful clients can avoid suffering large losses. Chapter 18 in this textbook covered many topics related to auditors' awareness of fraud possibilities, including computer-assisted embezzlement and financial statement fraud. Awareness of fraud signs and the ability to invent methods of gathering evidence of them are very important for auditors. Fraud detection is potentially a valuable service to audit clients, and external auditors have not tried to exploit it as an audit product.

R E V I E W
C H E C K P O I N T S

19.12 What are the five things a person must use to commit a computer fraud?

19.13 What controls can a company use to protect computer systems from fraud?

19.14 What is "book entry" recordkeeping in the securities industry?

Electronic Commerce: Some Implications for Auditors

LEARNING OBJECTIVE
4. Define and describe electronic commerce, its impact on the business environment, and the major implication for auditors.

"Electronic commerce" is a term coined by Benjamin Wright in a landmark book titled *The Law of Electronic Commerce* that looks at the legal implications of the rapidly developing electronic managing technology. Benjamin Wright's work has influenced the CICA's Technology Task Force, and he has been invited to write a chapter in the second edition of *EDI for Managers and Auditors*.

"Electronic commerce" is a generic term for a new way of doing business and carrying out economic transactions. A recent *Wall Street Journal* article has this to say about the growing impact of electronic commerce on the economy. "Electronic

MUGGINGS ON THE INTERNET

OTTAWA—The information highway is proving to be a mean street for many careless Canadian businesses, according to a survey by Ernst & Young.

More than half the participants in the survey said they had been mugged on the Internet in the last year, and experienced security-related financial losses.

Twenty of the companies reported losses of more than $1 million. Most losses were in the $250,000 range.

Inadvertent errors were cited as the more frequent cause of losses. More than 80 percent said they were unable or unwilling to estimate the value of the loss in dollars.

A fifth of those who responded said hackers, former employees or crooked competitors had broken into or tried to crack their computer systems. Only three per cent said they incurred financial losses as a result of the break-in, but 27 per cent said some disruption was caused.

Break-ins

No less than 85 per cent are convinced that security risks on the Internet have increased, and almost a third claim the risks have grown at a faster rate than computing itself.

Most of the companies contracted by Ernst & Young confessed that they do not have adequate tools or properly trained staff to prevent security-related losses. Yet there is evidence that companies are becoming increasingly aware of the need to place a greater emphasis on security.

More than two-thirds of the companies surveyed also reported attacks by malicious computer viruses, but few caused significant financial losses or disruptions to their organizations.

Source: Rennie MacKenzie, *The Bottom Line,* February 1996, p. 6.

---

commerce is currently in its infancy. But as the links between computing and communications deepen, the automated electronic marketplace should grow. Analysts expect it to account for as much as 25 percent of all retail activity within a generation. That would affect a lot of sales clerks."[3] And it would also affect a lot of supporting industries that consumers don't deal with directly, such as manufacturing and wholesaling.

Electronic commerce includes such contentious new issues as information property rights and the regulation of electronic financial markets. However our scope here is restricted to the messaging technology and we will cover the major area in turn: EDI, fax, E-mail, and the Internet.

EDI

EDI stands for *Electronic Data Interchange*. It can be defined "as an exchange of electronic business documents between economic trading partners, computer to

---

[3] G. Pascal Zachory, "Worried Workers," *The Wall Street Journal,* June 8, 1995, p. 9.

computer, in a standard format."[4] What distinguishes EDI from other electronic exchanges such as fax or E-mail is the use of a standard format and the computer-to-computer exchange. These exchanges can take place between quite different computer environments and for this reason the EDI standard protocol is intended to be both hardware and software independent.

EDI is an increasingly popular form of business communication in which companies link their computer systems to swap documents electronically (invoices, purchase orders, credit notes).

Many large companies and Revenue Canada are already committed to EDI and so by default are the many companies and individuals trading with them. Typically an EDI network gets started when a dominant purchaser insists that all its suppliers get on the network if they wish to continue to do business with the purchaser.

EDI transforms the business environment by creating electronic exchanges of documents in real time, on-line. Effectively, transactions and contracts are created through two interacting computer systems. Public standards have been developed for EDI so that organizations with dissimilar computing environments can exchange electronic business documents without using paper. The chief benefits of EDI include enhanced customer service, increased reliability of information, and reinforcement of ties with business partners. However, these benefits come with costs: integration of client computer software with EDI, increased complexity associated with EDI technology, and trading partner agreements (TPAs). The rapid growth of EDI globally in many industries indicates that the benefits outweigh the costs for most clients. EDI fundamentally changes the ways organizations do business, and consequently it is having a pervasive impact on how the audit is conducted.

I. Nature of EDI

To send or receive an EDI message, a company needs three basic elements: a generally accepted business format or EDI standards, a translation capability or EDI software, and a mail service or value-added network.

Standards are agreements on how data are to be structured for electronic communications. They define the acceptable contents of EDI messages and techniques for structuring these messages into the electronic message equivalents of paper-based documents. The most commonly used EDI standard in North America is ANSI SSC X12, developed by the American National Standards Institute. Internationally, the United Nations–developed standards of EDIFACT are prevalent for global use.

EDI translation software performs three basic functions: file conversion, EDI formatting, and communications. File conversion software takes data stored in the company's business application and formats it for input into the formatting software. The formatting program operates on this input data to translate it into the desired EDI format. Finally, the communications software dials the trading partner or communications network and sends the EDI-formatted data using acceptable protocols. This process is repeated in the reverse order at the receiving end.

The communication between sending and receiving partners' computers can be direct or through a value-added network (VAN). In point-to-point communications, there is a direct access from the computer of the sender to the computer of the receiver. This access is commonly achieved through the use of telephone lines and a computer modem. This requires the trading partners to have the same communication protocols and, preferably, the same standard. A VAN serves as an electronic post

---

[4] *EDI for Managers and Auditors*, 2nd edition, CICA, 1993, Toronto, p. 3.

office. With a VAN the sender relays the electronic message to the VAN, which either relays it to the receiver or holds it for later receiver pickup. It is a security risk to have computers linked directly to each other. By using a network that acts as a buffer between trading partners, the risk is avoided. Besides, most networks keep an activity log showing what mail was sent, where it went, and what was deposited in the mailbox and its source. This activity log can be used by auditors as a useful audit trail.[5] The advantages of VAN are summarized in the box below.

Advantages of VAN

- It reduces communication and data protocol problems, since most VANs have the appropriate facilities to deal with different protocols; the fact that the sender and receiver are not directly connected eliminates the need for them to agree on and implement a common protocol.

- The mailbox facility of the VAN allows one trader to deal with many partners without establishing numerous point-to-point connections.

- It reduces scheduling problems, since sender and receiver do not directly communicate; the receiver can, at its convenience, request delivery of the information from the VAN.

- The VAN is more likely than an organization that runs a point-to-point system to provide a third-party report for its customers (pursuant to *Handbook Section* 5900, "Opinions on Control Procedures at a Service Organization," and AICPA SAS No. 70, *Reports on the Processing of Transactions by Service Organizations*).

- In some cases, the VAN provides value-added services, such as translating the application format to a standard format; the partner sending the data does not have to reformat.

- The VAN can provide increased security as it contributes to authentication of sender and recipient and can act as a network "firewall" to protect the entity.

Source: CICA, *Audit Implications of EDI,* CICA, 1996, p. 10.

II. Implementation of EDI

Three general levels of implementation of EDI have been identified. The level of implementation is associated with the degree of integration between EDI and the organization's existing processing applications.

Standard or "Door-to-Door" EDI.   This involves a stand-alone computer, such as a PC, that sends documents to the EDI trading partner in standard EDI format. This represents the lowest level of integration. When the EDI document is received, it is

---

[5]   D. Pirie and D. Sheehy, "Electronic Commerce," *CA Magazine,* June/July 1996, p. 47.

translated into company-specific format, and is then usually keyed in manually into the recipient's processing application.

Application Seamless Integration.   On this more complex level, documents are received, authenticated, and accepted into the "job stream" of the receiving computer applications. Careful attention must be given to which applications and business functions are affected by EDI.

Fully Engineered Business Processes in a Paperless Environment.   On this level the organization is designed to fully integrate business processes with EDI. Many of the conventional intermediate processes and steps are eliminated in such an environment. This creates somewhat of a shock for auditors because of the unavailability of paper documents, the dependence on computer-based information systems, and the effect of an employee in one entity being able to initiate a transaction in another organization. A special type of EFT called an electronic funds transfer (EFT) completes the automation of sales/collection and purchases/payments, as depicted in Exhibit 19–4.

III. Benefits of EDI

EDI is capable of delivering significant benefits. A 1992 survey conducted by the EDI Council of Canada identified the most significant benefits of EDI as reinforcement of ties with a business partner, enhanced customer service, reduction of errors, and increased reliability of information.

EXHIBIT 19–4   SAMPLE INTEGRATED EDI/EFT SYSTEM

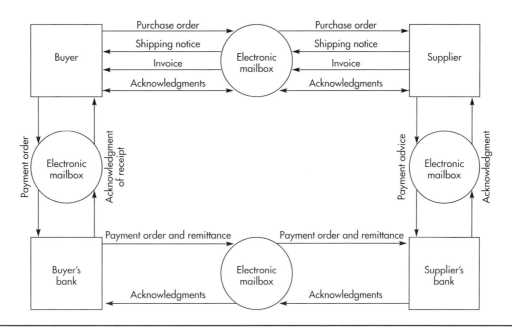

Source: Exhibit 1.1, *Audit Implications of EDI*, CICA, 1996, p. 2.

Business Survival.   EDI is fast becoming a requirement to remain competitive. The speed with which a company responds to a business opportunity holds the key to its success. Furthermore, as EDI becomes an industrial norm, those without it will be unable to compete. Even if EDI is not a "requirement" in a certain industry today, it is likely to become a requirement in the future. The ability to receive and send electronic transmissions has already become a necessity in a number of diverse industries. It is believed that EDI will eventually become a vendor selection criterion. Examples of this pressure can be found in the Buick Division of General Motors, which sent a letter to its suppliers saying that to continue to do business with Buick, suppliers would be required to implement EDI within a given period of time.

Cost Efficiencies.   There is a tremendous potential for cost savings. These savings result from the reduction in document processing tasks, better use of personnel, reduction in the cost of carrying and storing the inventory, and reduction of other costs such as premium freight and special handling. Also eliminated are manual sorting, matching, filing, reconciling, and similar tasks. A recent study showed that the cost of generating a traditional purchase order is about $10. If you use EDI, the cost for a similar transaction drops to less than $1.[6]

Improved Internal Processes.   Before it is possible to replace the manual system with electronic flows, the manual system must be understood. This usually results in an exhaustive review of the current operations and their organization as companies are forced to "take a hard look at themselves." The result of a review is not only better understanding of the operations but also elimination of unnecessary steps and streamlining of operations.

One of the first areas of implementation of EDI was purchasing. Due to near-instantaneous communication with vendors acting as trading partners, the purchasing process cycle time has been drastically reduced. Studies have shown that purchasing cycles can be reduced from 7 to 10 days down to less than a day. International business trading can experience greater cycle time reduction. As a direct result, EDI can be used to better plan purchasing requirements due to closer ties with vendors and reduced cycle time. Furthermore, the level of inventory can be reduced to a bare minimum, which frees up vital storage for more value-added activities and lays the foundation for the implementation of just-in-time (JIT) inventory management systems. Such a demand pull process also reduces the working capital requirement. If EFT is also used, the cash cycle can be improved as customers can pay quickly and billing time and errors can be reduced. The prolonged impact on a corporation's cash flow can be enormous. As the use of EDI spills over into other areas, further improvements will result, allowing companies to re-form strategic goals. For example, ICL in the United Kingdom reported over $200 million in inventory reductions and 70 percent reduction in administration costs due to JIT implementation through EDI. Refer to Exhibit 19–5 for a summary of the effects of a recent implementation of EDI at Canadian Tire.

Enhanced Customer Service.   Through EDI a company has access to much more accurate information, and has access to that information in a timely manner. Accordingly, management can use information on a real-time basis and can more effectively address the concerns of customers. Reduced billing errors and ease of payment are examples of tangible benefits available to customers. "EDI improves customer service by disseminating product information and taking orders through a wide EDI network (which) increases market penetration and distribution significantly."

---

[6]   A. Salmon, "It's Electronic Data Interchange or the Highway." *The Bottom Line,* September 1996, p. 8.

E X H I B I T 19–5   SUMMARY OF IMPLEMENTATION AND RESULTS AT CANADIAN TIRE CORPORATION

Implementation

- Implementation began January 1994.
- 419 stores linked to EDI system via satellite transmission.
- Mission statement of CTC, "to be the best at what our customers value most."
- Senior management fit their mission statement to EDI implementation.
- CTC goals include:
  1) reduced cycle times
  2) reduced "stock-outs"
  3) reduced supplier changing costs
  4) reduced manual errors
  5) elimination of paper
- The ANSI X12 standard was adopted and all CTC trade partners were mandated to abide by this standard.
- A forecasting model and JIT were integrated with EDI system.

Efficiency Improvements

1) *Cycle times*—Typical order-filling cycle time was 10 days. Following EDI implementation, cycle time reduced to an average of 3 days
2) *Reduced "stock-outs"*—EDI implementation allowed a 35% reduction in standing orders to be achieved
3) *Reduced supplier changing costs*—Changing suppliers no longer requires lengthy renegotiation of contracts and tedious paperwork. Now CTC accesses a menu and with a keystroke changes a vendor immediately.
4) *Reduced errors*—Due to the massive amount of human interaction in the traditional system, the potential for error was large. With EDI the elimination has decreased the occurrence of errors by approximately 75%.
5) *Elimination of paper*—The CTC/vendor partnerships that have converted to EDI have enjoyed a 100% elimination of paper in their product transfer programs.

Better Supply Chain Management.   Relationships with suppliers can be improved because the co-operation and co-ordination required to implement EDI tends to build trust between the trading partners. EDI also helps to reduce the number of vendors as the firm concentrates on few and long-term suppliers who are more responsive to the firm's needs.

Improved Ability to Compete Internationally.   Because of increased market segmentation, product proliferation, and shorter product life cycles, manufacturers must be able to respond to changes in the market and to introduce new products quickly. Concurrent product/process development helps manufacturers to respond quickly by cutting down the time it takes to get a new product to the market. For this type of development to work, EDI is necessary to help manufacturers and suppliers exchange information quickly and efficiently. Also, EDI allows for significant improvements in both accuracy and speed of processing international documentation involving numerous trading partners, ranging from freight forwarders, brokers, and banks to insurers, customs, and government agencies. Those organizations having mastered the correct technical infrastructure will find they have a definite competitive edge to enter global markets, and link up with new trading partners through common goals and business practice. "There are reports suggesting that the removal of trade barriers in Europe is likely to cause an explosion in EDI. Vendors are now talking in terms of global trading partners management and global software."[7]

---

[7]   CICA, *EDI for Managers and Auditors* (2nd Edition), CICA, 1993, p. 29.

Improved Planning and Forecasting.   Companies can better forecast and plan for receipt of goods and orders, which, in turn, streamlines the planning of manufacturing and assembling schedules. Financial aspects such as financing can be better timed and simplified by involving banks into the system. Furthermore, by capturing trading information directly from EDI transactions, companies can automatically produce a wealth of statistics for market research and strategic planning.

IV. Risks and Control

The objective of EDI to entice a large pool of economic partners into a fully integrated network exposes a business to greater interdependence and vulnerability. There will be more forward and backward integration with customers and suppliers with EDI. If there were to be a technical error in the system, the problem would extend beyond the business to the suppliers and customers. As a result, managers will have to establish contingency plans and auditors will have to monitor these plans by assessing reliance on controls to minimize the risk of mutual dependence among trading partners to an acceptable level.

When an auditor first encounters a client who has changed to EDI, there are many risk issues related to using EDI. Most have a bearing on the internal control structure. EDI alters the effectiveness of internal controls designed for processing transactions in a conventional way. New controls should be designed into an EDI system to effectively reduce the risks associated with using this type of data communication system. In particular, there is a loss in the paper audit trail.

Although EDI reduces paperwork, the loss of the traditional paper trail poses a problem to the auditor. In the past paper-source documents have provided substantive evidence of authorization and execution. Without this evidence there is a risk that unauthorized persons may approve or even tamper with transactions. Consequently, management must provide strict controls to ensure that automated transactions through EDI are properly adhered to. Furthermore, emphasis must be placed upon careful retention of records in magnetic media. If sufficient controls are not properly implemented, auditability of lost or contaminated data may be compromised.

Problems of Reorganization.   Introducing EDI successfully requires that all those who will be affected by it fully understand how it will change the way the company operates currently and how it will function in the future. Top management support, early user involvement, and organizationwide training are needed to develop EDI as a part of an overall change management strategy; otherwise, as an independent implementation, it will fail to achieve its full potential. Such a change strategy should include the corresponding arrangement of company structure, people, and processes as it implements what amounts to an organizationwide engineering effort. The commitment of top management is pivotal and sometimes is described as the crucial factor in the success of a proposed project—no support, no go. This implies that the starting point should be enquiry of top management of their planning, detailing the need and benefits of such a project. Furthermore, client employees need to be won over through information sessions, training seminars, and other similar steps. These are necessary to realize the full benefits of EDI technology.

In order to further minimize reorganization problems, management should research the hardware, software, standards, network, and communication needs. This can be done through groups, conferences, and affiliations with EDI councils and standards-setting bodies for the industry. The reorganization process should be an interactive and participative one.

The successful implementation of EDI is dependent upon a commitment from the entire organization. A co-operative atmosphere must be established between all stakeholders. Auditors, managers, third-party providers, and trade partners must all form project teams to carry out carefully prepared plans. Auditors should participate early in the planning stages of EDI development in order to have their views addressed early. There must be open communication and a creative freedom for all parties so that the new EDI system will be effective and accepted. Finally, it is paramount that the EDI implementation plan be marketed and integrated into the corporate strategic plan. In addition, however, there are risks to be addressed with a new EDI system. Just as a strategic plan must be formulated, an assessment of the risks must be analysed by all of the stakeholders.

Accuracy and Completeness.   The records and details of transactions are all initiated, transmitted, and retained in electronic media. In the absence of a comprehensive system of data validation and security, transmission and transaction error will happen without detection, and data could be subjected to unauthorized amendment or disclosure to third parties. Therefore, it would be difficult to have faith in the integrity of any document received. This could result in additional cost from inaccurate processing and loss of competitive advantage leading to potential financial loss. The risk is acute in EDI, especially when EDI involves the electronic transmission of payments, where there must be trust between the sender and the recipient of the payment transmission. In order to prevent loss, omission, or fraud, sufficient controls should be implemented to ensure the accuracy and completeness of input, processing, and transmission of messages. Guidelines should be set to ensure that only mandated personnel are authorized to originate the transmission. Adequate validation systems should be designed to validate a record's existence and authenticity, with exception reporting of irregularities at regular intervals.

Security.   Another major concern with EDI system is security. Obviously, access control becomes a greater concern when EDI is used, and this forces almost complete reliance on preventive controls. All confidential, significant data should be protected against unauthorized disclosure or modification during storage and transmission, and physical access to EDI equipment should be restricted.

Cryptographic security may be used to provide authorization control and audit trail of archives. There are two types of cryptographic security, which are supported by the X12 standard and are in use for EDI data. One is encryption that protects confidentiality of messages, and the other is authentication. Encryption is the coding of a message into unreadable data. The sender of the message should use a special data encryption standard (DES) algorithm or key to transform readable text into unreadable coded text. The unreadable coded text is transmitted to the trading partner, who uses the same DES algorithm to decode the message.

On the other hand, authentication protects the integrity of the message, since any modification of the data becomes obvious. With authentication, a DES algorithm is applied to an EDI message. The algorithm produces a coded, shortened version of the message, called a message authentication code (MAC). The MAC is usually a 32-bit string of data. The MAC is attached to the original message and both are sent to the trading partner. Upon receipt of the message with an MAC, the receiver recomputes the MAC using the original message and the DES algorithm key. If the two MACs are identical, the receiver knows that there has been no modification to the original message during transmission.

While the use of encryption and authentication can help to control transferring and validation of EDI data, additional controls are still needed to restrict physical access to EDI equipment. The use of authorization codes, passwords, and smart cards, for example, can help to prevent unauthorized use of physical equipment.

Application Failure.   Application failures or even systems downtime can have a significant negative effect on partners within the business cycle. The risk of failure of an application exposes the trading partners to potentially material losses unless effective contingency plans are in place to allow fast recovery. This is made worse where the EDI application is closely integrated with inventory management and production processing. Management should ensure that the appropriate backup, retention, and contingency plans are in place to minimize the domino effect of such failures on existing system or other trading partners along the EDI time line. Adequate contingency planning should include alternative methods of transmitting data and processing data during the application failure; management should also plan for recovering the EDI application within the tolerance period.

Risks of Integration.   Whenever information systems applications such as order processing become integrated with other business applications such as inventory management and production control, as in EDI, the risk of a domino effect resulting from errors, omissions, and failures is markedly increased. The speed of transactions and the lack of human intervention in EDI systems increases the magnitude of consequences several fold. Integrating signals a higher level of complexity, sophistication, dependency, vulnerability, and contingency. Therefore, cost is proportionately higher, unless adequate compensating controls and contingency plans are implemented along with EDI. Vigorous testing and auditor's early participation in the development is strongly recommended.

Interdependence and Cross Vulnerabilities.   EDI enlists a large number of partners into a wide data communication network to be used as a fully integrated tool to support transactions and business decisions. With an increased number of partners, there is a corresponding increase in the level of interdependence upstream from suppliers and downstream to customers. The mishaps of one partner within the EDI business cycle can start a chain reaction, making other trading partners vulnerable. The mutual reliance between trading partners exposes both parties to certain levels of uncontrolled risks, especially as EDI involves high speed and low human intervention. A proactive plan to identify and prevent problems becomes necessary. No longer can transactions simply be subject to the controls unique to one organization. Internal controls must be expanded in a co-ordinated and co-operative manner to include one's trading partners and even the value-added networks. Mutual control must ensure that transactions are initiated, transmitted over a public-switched network, and received in a manner that retains the integrity and confidentiality of the paper-based system.

Managing the trading partner in the value chain is also vital for competitive advantage. Companies have to ensure that they choose committed trading partners, who understand the benefits of EDI and whose internal processes and systems can be adapted to EDI technology. Care should be taken in selecting trading partners, and sufficient data should be gathered using tools such as questionnaires to ensure technological and strategic compatibility. It is a good idea to document the standards and guidelines in the trading partner and network agreements to ensure that there is a mutual understanding of respective responsibility and obligation. Besides, understanding the way your trading partner conducts business is crucial to enhancing partnership quality.

As the use of EDI grows in Canada, organizations will share more information with their trading partners. This merging of interorganizational data exposes organizations to substantial reliance between trading partners. To reduce the risk of exposing firms to a total paralysis in their interdependent systems, managers implementing EDI must make concerted efforts to understand their trading partners' business. It is no longer acceptable to withhold information and remain secretive. The level of interdependence between trading partners must be clearly understood. Performance measures including cost structures and market share must be shared, and improvements in efficiency must be set by all trading partners. An atmosphere of collaboration, co-operation, and mutual trust is required to make an EDI network successful. This illustrates that in the new electronic commerce economy that is evolving, interdependence may be a key characteristic for remaining competitive. This suggests that the economic dependence and related party transaction issues discussed in Chapter 13 will become more important in the new, interconnected global economy.

Risks of Third Party Network Providers.   EDI depends on numerous software and services supplied by third-party network providers. Using third-party network providers to transmit EDI transactions to trading partners gives rise to a number of potential risks. For example, confidential information could be disclosed to unauthorized third parties; unauthorized transactions could be introduced by third parties; transactions could be lost, causing business losses and inaccurate financial reporting; and audit trails could be lost.

Controls to deal with third-party relationships should be used, such as requesting an auditor's report on the overall control of the service organization, assessing the service provided, specifying each necessary obligation and responsibility in the third-party network contract, especially the confidentiality guarantee, and conducting regular meetings with third-party network providers to review problems and ensure appropriate corrective actions.

Uncertain Legal Status of EDI Contracts.   EDI technology has outpaced the legal system's ability to keep pace with technological change. Many legal disputes may be related to the electronic transactions of EDI (e.g., evidence, enforceability and liability). In most countries there is little legal precedent concerning responsibility and liability for transactions executed via EDI. Many jurisdictions have yet to decide on the legality of electronic documents and what effectively constitutes a legal electronic signature to bind parties to a contract.

The controls for potential legal risk that management can pursue include enlisting third-party arbitration, signing formal agreements, and understanding current documents, such as the EDI Model Trading Partner Agreement, the Canadian Payment Association Standards and Guidelines Applicable to EDI, and the EDI Payments Capable Guidelines.

According to J. Babe in "The Legal Pitfalls of EDI" (*The Lawyers Weekly,* May 23, 1997, p. 3): "The need for paper based contracts continues because the law is not there to otherwise regulate or interpret [a business] relationship, absent such contract." She continues:

> Businesses are advised to enter into "interchange agreements" or "trading partner agreements" at the start of their relationship, to document on paper the terms of their deal and the standards which will apply to their transmissions. These agreements

provide for not only the terms of the deal, but also for hardware and software issues such as transmission standards, deemed receipt, etc. ...

Drafters of these agreements should at least start with one of the standard forms of interchange agreements for that industry, or with the Uniform Rules for Conduct of International Trade Data Teletransmission, to ensure the coverage of the numerous legal and technical issues between the trading partners, and with any VAN or VANs linking the parties and their similar or dissimilar technologies.

Drafters can then use these standards as mandated by the customer or industry, and add custom drafting to tailor the deal as necessary.

The CICA Study *Audit Implications of EDI* outlines a model agreement as shown in the following box.

Trading Partner Agreement (TPA) Model

The following represents an outline model of the various clauses expected to be included in a typical TPA agreement. Generally, a TPA would cover these core clauses. It remains a matter of tailoring according to the specific local governing laws and adding whatever other clauses the contracting parties, assisted by legal counsel, would choose to include. This is the case for the American Bar Association (ABA) TPA model, the EDI Council of Canada TPA model (prepared by the Legal and Audit Committee), the Australian model, and various European models.

Outline

1. Identification of EDI standards.
2. Identification of third-party service providers.
3. Obligation to conduct EDI competently.
4. Adoption of signatures.
5. Place and time of message receipt.
6. Functional acknowledgments.
7. Application acknowledgments.
8. Garbled transmissions.
9. Trade terms and conditions.
10. Disclaimer of confidentiality.
11. Legal enforceability of transactions.
12. Termination of agreement.
13. Disclaimer of obligation to enter into transactions.
14. Limitation of liability.
15. Arbitration.

Source: CICA, *Audit Implications of EDI*, CICA, 1996, p. 23, Exhibit 3–3.

Babe also identifies rules of evidence as a crucial issue. Generally the rules relating to records or documents are that they will be accepted by the courts if they:

are from highly reliable sources, e.g., bank records, government records, and records of other public bodies which have no interest to the action and which prepared the record in the regular course of their work. Case law has endeavoured to apply these foregoing rules on records—formulated for paper-based documents—to electronically produced or stored records. Unhappily, these cases are not consistent (see *R. v. Bell,* [1985] 2 S.C.r., 287 and *R. v. McMullen* (1979), 25 O.R. (2d) 301 (C.A.) ... To provide certainty, New Brunswick enacted An Act to Amend the Evidence Act, which received Royal Assent on April 25, 1996.

Correct Approach?
Not everyone agrees that this legislation—which generically includes as evidence documents in electronic formats, if the original copy has been destroyed—was the correct approach. There are concerns about the lack of required proof of the software or electronic imaging system integrity in copying, storing or reproducing such documents. Altered electronic records are hard to spot. The validity of such electronic records relies largely on the systems used and security of those systems.

The Uniform Law Conference of Canada has published its Proposal for a Uniform Evidence Act. This proposal has been circulated for input from Canadian Bar Association members and other law reform conferences, and requires that evidence be given on methods and security for electronic records creation and storage. The Nova Scotia Law Reform Commission is also drafting new legislation for both electronic evidence and electronic signatures.

In short, business is progressing, but the law has a lot to do to catch up.

Auditability Issue.   The general implications for auditors relate to the loss of an audit trail resulting from the paperless environment and lack of human intervention, which in turn results in total dependence on the electronic system. All of this significantly increases risk, making control assurance the key objective for EDI environments. This in turn gives rise to a need for monitoring (EDI) controls throughout the period under audit.

Trading partner agreements frequently include an obligation to report and disclose compliance with a set of specified standards of EDI control. Increasingly, auditors will be asked to provide opinions on the EDI control environment, largely to satisfy the reliability requirements of the record-keeping system for legal purposes, as noted above. Eventually, such opinions are likely to be made mandatory and fully generalized. This will require further development of control standards and criteria. Also, auditors will have to be better trained in this emerging area of information technology (IT).

An audit trail can be defined as those documents, records, journals, ledgers, magnetic media transactions master files, and accounting reports that enable an auditor to trace a transaction from source document to summarized total in an accounting report and vice versa. EDI alters the traditional transaction audit trail, and thus there is a risk that unauthorized persons might initiate transactions or modify the transaction trail (refer to Exhibit 19–6). The control objective should be to maintain adequate audit trails with regard to transactions and the ability to preverify and adequately monitor electronic authorization controls and integrity controls.

E X H I B I T   19–6   **SUMMARY OF EDI'S IMPACT ON THE AUDIT TRAIL**

In using EDI, the audit trail is affected in the following ways:

1. Source documents are transcribed into machine-readable form and are difficult to access.
2. Traditional source documents may be eliminated.
3. Ledger summaries are replaced by master files.
4. The data processing file does not necessarily provide a transaction listing or journal.
5. Files are maintained in a magnetic medium and can only be read by computer.
6. Because processing activities are done inside the computer and through electronic media, the transaction trail cannot be directly observed.

Automated controls involving electronic signatures, approvals, and authorizations should be designed and implemented to establish effective operational control.

Since EDI extends beyond one company, it poses a serious problem for the auditor's evaluation of internal controls in an EDI system. It is difficult enough to focus on the internal controls of one separate entity. However, in an EDI system the auditor is faced with looking at how EDI affects the internal controls of the entity *and* the interconnected parties; this complicates how auditors examine internal control. In other words, the distinction between where one set of internal controls ends and another begins gets blurred in EDI systems. The box below summarizes the difference between EDI and more traditional computerized environments.

TRADITIONAL VERSUS EDI COMPUTERIZED ENVIRONMENTS

- The traditional computerized audit environment has boundaries between the audit client and other parties to the transactions. As a result of the boundaries, documents are produced as evidence of the transaction. In an EDI environment, transactions flow seamlessly from one party to another, with little or no physical evidence that the transaction has occurred.

- In an EDI environment, data security and controls need to include the protection of information that has physically left the entity and is en route to other trading partners. The information that is being sent must be protected against alteration, physical mishaps, sabotage, and theft.

- To evaluate EDI evidence that exists only in an electronic form may require the auditor to use data extraction tools that were not essential in a traditional computerized audit environment.

- In an EDI environment, authorization, completeness, and accuracy of transactions may not be as evident as in a more traditional environment. They may be expressed in the trading partner agreement and in program logic, and perhaps evidenced in cryptic digital authentication codes. To assess these application control objectives, the auditor is likely to need knowledge of the agreements and of system processes.

- In an EDI environment, the use of third-party service providers (such as VANs) is prevalent. These present separate audit considerations.

Source: Audit Implications of EDI, CICA, 1996, p. 26.

V. Internal Control in the Context of an Audit

1. Auditing Objective.   The objective of auditing is to obtain a level of assurance that management representation as expressed in financial statements is a fair representation of the actual economic activities of the organization. The general accepted auditing standards require that any opinion offered by the auditor be supported with sufficient persuasive evidence.

In arriving at an opinion, the auditor must obtain assurance regarding the overall control environment of the organization, identify the areas where there is risk, and identify the potential errors in the transaction cycles. This involves identifying and testing the controls in place to prevent the occurrence of errors and to ensure the detection of errors. The relative materiality of the transactions processed using EDI, the volume of the transactions, the impact of the environmental controls on the EDI platform, and the level of sophistication of the EDI system will impact the audit approach. An understanding of the EDI environment is mandatory before the risks can be analysed and determined. The identification of controls in EDI can then be conducted and the appropriate level of testing determined. In designing the audit approach, the auditor should keep in mind that the traditional audit tools may not be adequate to audit EDI.

While some form of substantive testing is required for year-end purposes, the level of testing is a direct function of the degree of reliance on the controls. There must be a cost-effective balance between the two. Recognizing the complexity of the technology affecting the transient nature of the audit trail, substantive procedures may not be an acceptable alternative. Where substantive procedures are not an alternative, the auditor must be able to rely on the systems. If insufficient assurance exists, the auditor should adjust the report accordingly.

2. Auditability.   With information systems, an organization should focus concurrently on three objectives: strategic support, control assurance, and cost effectiveness. In the EDI environment the transient nature of the audit trail, the resulting paperless environment, and the lack of human intervention combine to create a significant increase in risk. That is why control assurance should become the key objective for EDI environments.

With respect to the objective of control assurance, the key concern has to be the auditability of the EDI environment and associated system. As defined in the CICA's study, *EDI for Managers and Auditors* (2nd ed., p. 132): "Information is auditable in the context of modern information systems when it can be substantiated by tracing it to source documents, which can be based on paper or paperless media, or when reliance can be placed on preverified, certified, and continually monitored control processes." This means that management should implement adequate preverified and certified monitoring systems to ensure continued control functionality of the computer applications.

Auditors, on the other hand, are faced with a paperless trail and are dependent upon the system output that generates the financial statements. Auditors should be concerned about raising enough evidence necessary to support an opinion regarding the fairness of these financial statements. Furthermore, they need to constantly monitor the control environment through substantial compliance testing to provide assurance that these EDI financial statements are reliable. This is achieved by analysing and testing the application controls of the business. This creates a shift in traditional auditing. In the past auditors would have to focus on a point in time and perform significant substantive tests. EDI, on the other hand, requires operations review on a continuous basis. Hence, many auditors see EDI implementation shifting audits from a balance sheet focus to an operations/compliance approach. Also, there is even more reliance on environmental and general controls because of the "migration" of application controls to general control.

According to the CICA's study *Audit Implications of EDI* (1996, p. 33):

Because of the impact of EDI on the client's business, a substantive audit approach may no longer be cost-effective. It should be noted that effective application and general controls are important for effective EDI transaction processing. As a result, there should be a number of effective internal controls and the auditor should be able to assess control risk at below maximum.

To assess control risk below maximum, the auditor will need to be able to perform tests of controls. This involves knowledge of the controls that should be present and knowledge of the audit techniques that might be followed.

D. Pirie and D. Sheehy review the major audit techniques for EDI in their article "Electronic Commerce" (*CA Magazine,* June/July 1996, pp. 47):

An ITF is a fictitious entity on a live data file. It enables an auditor to enter test transactions into the system without corrupting the integrity of real operational or financial data. Most, if not all, EDI software vendors provide built in ITF capability. This is why it currently is the most popular EDI audit technique. An auditor can launch test transactions through the VAN to test controls that are part of the systems under evaluation. (The client would have to authorize the VAN to accept transactions from the auditor and forward them to the client's mailbox.) The auditor could launch these test transactions on a continuous or periodic basis and compare expected processing results. An alternative would be to set up audit transaction types (registered with the VAN) that duplicate current transactions and process these back to the auditor. The box below gives an illustration of an ITF.

Example—One example of an integrated test facility application is in a large health insurance organization that electronically receives and pays claims from hospitals. Using the auditor account at the VAN, or other access into the organization's system, the auditor submits a series of claims (e.g., dental claims, surgical claims, etc.) via EDI and reviews the claims register to determine which claims were paid and the amount of payment. The test claims include a variety of conditions, including claims both for individuals who are entitled to benefits and fictitious individuals. In addition, procedures such as heart surgery that are payable by the insurance company, and procedures such as cosmetic surgery that are not covered by insurance, as well as charges within and in excess of reimbursable limits, are tested. The test data go through the system and output is routed to the test division or dummy account. This file is then reviewed online by the auditor.

Embedded audit modules enable continuous monitoring and analysing of transaction processing, which is particularly effective in high-volume, real-time systems in which timeliness, completeness, accuracy and validity of transactions are essential. Embedded audit modules are often implemented for the applications that pose the highest risk, particularly when transactions files may not be available for subsequent analysis.

These modules allow the auditor to select samples at any time because the data are selected during the normal production process.

A concurrent audit tool, while similar in purpose to an embedded audit module, is designed and controlled by the auditor and linked into the organization's information system rather than being part of the system. It allows an auditor to evaluate the client's controls when a transaction is being processed without disrupting the client's normal operations. It can be linked into the system for a short time to perform tests and provide audit evidence. For client's with weak controls, a concurrent audit tool gives an auditor the opportunity to perform analytical procedures and substantive testing on data captured by the tool. When client controls are strong, the auditor can use the tool to test controls. The major application controls can be classified by major audit assertions.

In an EDI environment, there are no classic "batch total" control procedures for completeness. Therefore, the program must establish this control when a transaction is initiated or received. Controls can be built into any or all of the application, translation or communication levels of software to assure all transactions are complete. Some combination of sequentially numbering and computer matching EDI transactons is typically used. The auditor needs to know how the client tracks EDI transactions through its software layers and what reconciliation procedures are performed by the application software, or by special control programs that analyse the EDI transaction log files and other control files.

Message authentication allows each party to verify that data received are genuine and have not been altered (existence/occurrence).

Pricing or valuation information for a transaction may come from the EDI purchase order or a mutually controlled pricing catalogue maintained by trading partners.

The EDI trading partner agreement specifies measurement/ownership (rights and obligations) of goods, which is often independent of their physical flow.

In EDI audits, the extent of substantive testing may be minimal compared to compliance testing. Upon completing the testing of the EDI systems, the auditor must decide on the level of assurance that has been obtained. The testing may reveal the need to audit related systems of trade partners or affect the degree of testing of year-end balances. With respect to year-end testing, the appendix to Chapter 10 of this text has already considered the impact of EDI on auditing of payables. The 1996 CICA study *Audit Implications of EDI* has this say about auditing year-end balances electronically:

Confirmations may also be performed electronically between the auditor and the client's trading partners. To work successfully, however, trading-related applications may need to be modified to automatically retrieve the requested information, format it in an EDI transaction set, and transmit it to the requesting auditor. The development of EDI confirmation transaction depends, to a large extent, on the relevance of confirmations in future audits. In an integrated EDI environment, where the higher velocity of transactions could result in immaterial receivable and payable balances, confirmations may be unnecessary. Subsequent payment review would probably be more efficient ...

[However], because of the impact of EDI on the client's business, a substantive audit approach may no longer be cost-effective. It should be noted that effective application and general controls are important for effective EDI transaction processing. As a result, there should be a number of effective internal controls and the auditor should be able to assess control risk at below maximum.

To assess control risk at below maximum, the auditor will need to be able to perform tests of controls. This involves knowledge of the controls that should be present and knowledge of the audit techniques that might be followed. Appendix C [of this study] also sets out a general audit program that might be considered when performing tests of controls and conducting substantive tests in an EDI environment.

It is clear that the integrity of controls is the primary concern for the auditor in EDI systems. In addition to the application controls reviewed earlier, the auditor needs to consider such general controls as access controls for third-party trading partners, controls regarding program and file changes, controls of network service procedures, and appropriate retention, back-up, and contingency plans. As noted in Chapter 8, most auditors consider the general controls more important than application controls to the point that if general controls are weak, auditors are much less likely to place reliance on application controls. This audit strategy is even more true of advanced systems because as noted earlier, in advanced systems there tends to be a migration of controls from specific applications to more general controls.

The comprehensive guidance provided in Criteria for Control (COCO) discussed in Chapter 14 provides a consistent and comprehensive framework for evaluating the effectiveness of a company's internal control system, in particular challenges created by EDI systems. Auditors are being encouraged to apply the principles identified in COCO to all kinds of systems. With experience perhaps the impact of COCO on EDI system evaluation will become more evident. If, after the evaluation, there is high enough risk of serious weaknesses in the EDI control system, the auditor may need to issue an opinion reservation. In other words, the EDI controls may be so important that the auditor may not be able to get enough assurance without some reliance on them.

Other Issues

1. Institute's Role

a) Standard setting.   EDI is a new technology that is adding to the challenges facing the auditing profession. There is a need for PA professional groups in increase their own knowledge of EDI technology and issue guidelines, standards, and other technical assistance to auditors in the field attempting to cope with these activities. The existing CICA guidelines on advanced systems do not directly concern themselves with EDI.

However, recently there have been co-operative efforts with the AICPA on developing audit technique studies. These technique studies often precede any guidelines or standards that eventually appear in the *Handbook*. Two such recent studies are *Audit Implications of EDI* (1996) and *Audit Implications of Electronic Document Management* (1997).

b) Proper training.   The institute should provide proper training to the auditors so that they have the necessary knowledge and expertise to exert professional judgment to assess and report on the existence and effectiveness of internal control systems in the EDI context. To evaluate the adequacy of control, auditors must understand hardware and software control features such as cryptographic control techniques. Specialized audit technique studies are a useful beginning for such training.

2. Auditor's Expanding Role

a) Co-operate with internal auditors.   The external auditor has a responsibility toward the external users and therefore will have different overall objectives than the internal auditor. However, with regard to the review of the entity's internal control systems, the external auditor may place reliance on the work of the internal auditor. The external auditor would also need to consider the internal auditor's competence and objectivity and evaluate his or her work. In practice, the external auditor and internal auditor should work jointly in designing the audit procedures to be applied. The existence of the internal auditor does not relieve the external auditor of the responsibility to conduct such audit procedures as are considered necessary to support the audit opinion. The external auditor must have the competence and level of knowledge to be able to review the internal auditor's work and conclude on its adequacy in meeting the external auditor's objective. For additional details on reliance on the work of internal auditors, see Chapter 6.

b) Work as proactive consultant to the client.   "Some of the audit benefits of EDI include a compressed business cycle (thereby reducing year-end account balances for receivables, payables, and inventories), improved completeness of transaction data because of agreed-upon standards for messages and data transmission, and improved accuracy of transaction data because of the standardization of data formats and the absence of rekeying" (A. Pirie and D. Sheehy, "Electronic Commerce," *CA Magazine,* June/July 1996, p. 45). But such benefits are possible only when the EDI system is well designed. The auditor should act as a control consultant, assessing the viability of the compliance program or control self-assessment program as a way to implement the new controls required of the EDI system. Auditors should also be proactive in providing value-added input to the EDI project by assessing the adequacy of internal controls.

An auditor can provide valuable service to the EDI project management team by focusing on the following:

- Evidence of proactive planning versus reactive response.
- Existing manual controls that have been substituted with automated ones. The rule of thumb is that the new controls must be at least as good as the old ones.
- Controls differentiation between PC-based EDI systems and mainframe EDI.
- Definition of responsibilities for maintaining versions of standards and trading partner directory.
- Co-operative problem solving and relationship building with trading partners.
- Identification of qualified co-ordinator to deal competently with functional areas along the EDI time line.
- Industry affiliation and appropriate level of participation.
- Criteria for implementation sign-off by executives, if applicable, that include considerations transcending organizational boundaries.

c) Help in EDI system development.   From an audit standpoint the development and documentation of the EDI system is an important time in which to emphasize control. Application controls should be built in before the EDI system becomes operational, so that the system will be reliable at the outset. Some companies involve internal auditors at the systems development stage. However, there is controversy arising about the role of independent external auditors during EDI system development. One view favours a limited role for the external auditors at the development stage since it affects auditor's independence. The other view asserts that external auditors should contribute their knowledge to the design and testing of the system because of their expertise in the area of internal control.

The external auditor's role during the design and development of EDI systems is crucial for providing reasonable assurance to management that auditable and properly controlled systems are being developed. During the development of an EDI application, the auditor should perform a review of the design of the controls structure and provide input to the development effort. Any control weaknesses must be identified at the early stages of development, since the cost of modifying the systems after implementation can be prohibitive. The auditor should work with the development and implementation teams through to the acceptance testing stage. The auditors should not hesitate to specify and recommend adequate compensating controls given the nature of EDI environment.

3. Audit Implication of Legal Liability.   When EDI is only used to transmit informational data, legal issues do not normally arise. However, when EDI is used as a basis of forming a legally binding agreement such as a contract, legal concerns will come into play. Of all the components required for a legally enforceable contract, the requirement of writing and signing is the most pertinent to EDI. With an EDI transaction, the concern is that the agreement is not in writing and does not have a signature.

The courts have been accepting other forms of electronic transmission, such as telegrams and faxes, as acceptable when addressing the question of writing and signature. An EDI purchase order or contract could be purely electronic, however, while the other forms of electronic transmission all result in a physical document. As no court ruling has yet examined a completely electronic transmission under the writing and signing provision, there is still room for argument over whether EDI will qualify under the writing and signing requirements for a valid contract. For this reason, many companies use a trading partner agreement to specifically address this issue. The writing issue can be solved by expressing in the trading partner agreement that the EDI messages shall be deemed written and would become fixed in a tangible medium of expression. Likewise, the parties can agree in the trading partner agreement that a particular identification code or message authentication code will be accepted as a signature between the two parties.

Another area of EDI activity that often raises legal questions is the liability of EDI third-party vendors, particularly value-added networks. As with the other EDI issues, no specific EDI case has yet been brought before the courts. Nevertheless, cases involving the other forms of electronic transmission can be considered. In the case of *Postal Telegraph Cable Co. v. Lathrop*, the telegraph carrier was liable for the damages suffered by the innocent party caused by its proven negligence. This seems to suggest that a VAN that has a close relationship with its customer and is likely to be aware of the potential for damages could be liable for consequential damages in the case of a failure on the part of the network. As a result, most VANs require that customers sign a contract that significantly limits the VAN's liability. The warranty and contract remedy disclaimer clauses that are commonly used are generally effective.

In assessing the risk of the clients and the planned level of audit risk, auditors should examine the trading partner agreement to evaluate the enforceability of the electronic transmitted message, and the probability of bearing the legal liability if things go wrong with the transaction.

In the United States legislation is pending that places the onus on banks, financial institutions, and corporations to prove the audit trail in electronic environments such as EDI. Under the legislation EDI users are required to take reasonable security measures to protect their messages. The court will assign legal liability to the party that breaks the audit trail. It is likely that a similar law will soon find application in Canadian courts. As noted earlier, New Brunswick has already enacted legislation, and there is a proposal before the Canadian Bar Association to amend legal rules of evidence with respect to electronic documents. It may be that a client's risk of being successfully sued will be higher as a result of failing to maintain an adequate audit trail. Accordingly, the disclosure of the risk and contingent liability in the financial statements may be necessary.

VII. Impact of EDI on the Audit Profession

There are a number of factors which, taken together in the context of EDI, will have serious implications for the auditing profession. These factors include an increasingly litigious society, the widening technology gap, the growing expectation gap, and the increasing vulnerability of complex technological systems. These kinds of developments in combination can create a powder keg for the auditing industry. A single high-profile incident could jeopardize the accounting profession's reputation, the financial viability of one or more accounting firms, and the privileged right to audit.

In fact, according to a report to the CICA's Auditing Standards Committee by its Computer Advisory Subcommittee, the technology gap is widening between the changing requirements of the audit and the profession's ability to adapt, both in terms of the skills required and in terms of the development of advanced audit tools and techniques. With the emergence of EDI technology, audit firms must make a choice about their approach to achieving the goal of being technologically competent and competitive. The PA profession should develop and implement a Managed Technology Adaptation Process (MTAP) that will, over an appropriate time frame, enhance the technology-related knowledge base of the majority of partners and staff, and ensure that all audits effectively and efficiently meet their objectives.

The MTAP approach involves six related strategies or areas of effort that together will create the direction and momentum necessary for a firm to reach its stated goal. The six areas are (1) develop an advanced audit technology framework, (2) develop and implement an integrated multilevel professional development program, (3) develop and implement computer-based auditing tools and aids, (4) implement an online audit restructuring program, (5) initiate a hardware acquisition program, and (6) implement a technology adaptation monitoring process.

The audit profession's ability to respond to technological advancement will determine the profession's future. On a more hopeful note, technology offers unparalleled opportunities for the profession to increase the overall quality of its services and to fulfil a very real need in the corporate community. In time, technology may allow auditiors to implement the many new assurance engagements that will evolve as electronic commerce revolutionizes the way businesses function.

Fax

Although fax technology has been around for decades, its use skyrocketed in the 1980s. Fax is sometimes referred to as telecopy, and it is a form of electronic transmission that conforms to facsimile standards of telegraph and telephone companies. The typical fax machine scans a paper document and converts it to a digital signal that is then sent through the telephone system. The fax machine can also receive signals and print the image on a sheet of paper. The cheaper, older systems print on thermal paper that archives poorly. The newer machines print on plain paper. Faxes can be configured with computers but there is no widely available system that can store the fax as alphanumeric information just like any other computer record.

According to Wright [1991; pp. 19–20], many businesses use faxes for legal transactions, including contracts. Bidding is sometimes done by fax, orders can be made, and bills can be sent by fax.[8]

The major use of faxes in auditing is to obtain confirmations. However, according to a *CA Magazine* article, "Fax Magic" (May 1993), by D.J. Cockburn, the increasing use of fax machines to obtain confirmations results in insufficient audit evidence. The problem is that a dishonest client can easily falsify a confirmation through use of photocopies of the appropriate letterhead and signature. The faxed copy can't distinguish between a photocopy and an original. Hence, without proof of origin, confirmations by fax cannot be held as totally reliable audit evidence.

---

[8]   B. Wright, *The Law of Electronic Commerce*, Little Brown & Co., 1991.

This problem can be avoided by having the call initiated by the receiver rather than the sender. Since not all machines are equipped with this "pull" capability, the next best procedure is to call the purported sender to ensure that the confirmation received was valid. Optimally, faxed confirmations should be used as backup of interim evidence until the original confirmations are received. Many faxes tend to fade anyway so that photocopies of the fax should be filed, rather than or in addition to the original fax document.

E-mail

Electronic mail (E-mail) is the telecommunication of messages between computers. The link is usually through a special network, the most famous being the Internet. The most popular form of message is simple text and informal messages, and E-mail is rapidly replacing mail service as it requires no paper. The messages can be stored in computer memory on magnetic disk or printed on paper; however, the communication can also be made with no record of the message.

Wright [1991, p. 20] notes that traders frequently use E-mail to negotiate and conclude deals. In such applications the auditor would be concerned that at least an electronic audit trail be maintained, recording transactions in chronological order on magnetic media. Like EDI, fax and E-mail present challenges to the legal profession as to what constitutes writings and signature in electronic messaging environments. A client should create trading partner agreements with all parties with whom it has extensive electronic commercial dealings.

The Internet

"The use of public networks such as CompuServe, Prodigy, and the Internet to transmit EDI transactions is an emerging new alternative to VANs and proprietary networks."[9]

The Internet in particular is growing at an explosive rate, roughly doubling in size every year. It promises to revolutionize the business world and turn it into electronic commerce in its broadest sense. According to *Journal of Accountancy:*

> The Internet is a public communication system [that is] universally accessible and unregulated. It is a worldwide network of computers that communicate with each other over phone lines and fibre optic cables. The Internet itself is free. However access to the Internet involves some costs, either what it costs you to build your own access or the fees you pay an Internet service provider (ISP) for access.
>
> The World Wide Web (WWW) or Web is a part of the Internet in which users can exchange graphics and video as well as the more traditional text and databases that were part of the original Internet. Users can create their own sites that other users can tap into to share data. Many users of the Web employ an ISP at a low monthly rate for unlimited access.[10]

The Web is at the heart of the Information Highway that is being discussed just about everywhere. The Internet already profoundly affects PAs. One of the most important ways is that it can bring vast amounts of information to the computer screen. For example, available on the 'Net are regulatory filings, legislative proceedings, legal information, information on client companies (provided either by the

---

[9] *Audit Implications of EDI,* CICA, 1996, p. 11.
[10] *Journal of Accountancy,* March 1997, p. 51.

companies themselves or by stock trader information hot lines such as Motley Fool), currency exchange rates, software downloads, university research materials, and professional forums for exchanging information—and this is just a few of the resources for PAs. (We have indicated useful on-line information sources for PAs in the end covers and in various chapters throughout this textbook.) To take full advantage of the Internet's information potential, PAs need to make use of browser software such as Netscape Navigator or Internet Explorer, which allow searches on the Internet. A search engine is a more intelligent piece of software that allows searches for specific information using titles or document headers, entire documents, or directories. This has been made necessary because of rapid proliferation, abandonment, and obsolescence of Websites.

Big 5 Embrace Net in an "Electronic Bear Hug"

CANADIAN banks and other financial institutions have embraced the Internet's World Wide Web in an electronic bear hug. Each of the Big Five now has a Web presence and many smaller financial institutions are also represented.

In common with most commercial Web sites, you'll find the expected commercial plugs. But most banks are experimenting with innovative Net applications. Some of these applications could be viewed as encroaching upon services often provided by financial planners and some accountants.

Of course, online business banking services are widely available. However, you must use a direct dial-up connection to the bank's private data network.

Banks are leery of allowing full Internet access to customer accounts, largely due to the relatively insecure nature of the Net. Data transmitted between your computer and the bank's server can pass through many virtual hands. It's possible for unscrupulous individuals on the Net to "sniff" packets of information not intended for their eyes.

However, this problem is being addressed.

Developments in the encryption of data transmitted over the Net and improvements in the security of Web browser and server software will make Net banking a reality.

Links mentioned in this article are available online at (http/www.hookup.net/-richa rdm/bankweb.html).

A number of factors have made the Internet a viable alternative to private networks and thus half of the online services in Canada utilize the Internet to access accounts. Some of these factors include the growth of the Net and number of Net users, the improved security of the newest releases of the most popular Web browsers and, most importantly, new protocols and agreements on how to exchange financial data.

Although there are still some who are concerned about Internet security, great effort has been made to bring powerful encryption and other techniques to the exchange of financial data on the Net. It is still foolish to include your credit-card information in a plain text email message, but Internet online banking is much more secure than that. Hey, if the bankers are satisfied ...?

Source: Richard Morochove.

However, our focus here is on how the Internet affects electronic commerce. A recent supplement, "Electronic Commerce," in the May 10, 1997, issue of *The Economist* (henceforth EC) provides a good overview of many of the issues. The text-based Internet had been around as a research tool for many years and even then was doubling in use every year. However, it wasn't until the release of Mosaic, the first of the graphical browsers, in 1993, and until IBM began to tout its computers as "entrance ramps" to the "Information Superhighway," that the Internet was discovered by the general public. By that point the Internet had over one million users—a "critical mass." "Worldwide, some 23 million households are now connected to the Internet, which translates into around 55m users. Some estimates, taking a broad definition of Internet use, say that by 2000 the number will grow to 550 m, or 10% of the world's population" (EC, p. 5).

It's the exponential growth of users to form a huge potential marketplace, and their interconnectivity—and the Internet's potential as a relatively costless way of doing business (what MicroSoft's Bill Gates terms "frictionless capitalism")—that has generated the enthusiasm for a broad electronic marketplace in virtual cyberspace. The idea was to create store and mall sites on the Internet that would in effect put them anywhere at any time. The actual physical location of a business no longer made a difference. Theoretically, this would allow the smallest companies to compete directly with the largest on a level playing field. But in practice it's not quite turning out that way. An article, "The Great Equalizer?" in the *Toronto Star's* Fast Forward section of June 19, 1997, suggests that Web sites are turning out to be like advertising: the bigger the company, the more elaborate and attractive the Web site. Creativity however, makes it possible for small businesses to target very specific market niches in a unique way, allowing them to distinguish themselves from thousands of similar sites. Many PA firms now have their own Web sites, which offer helpful advice in a variety of areas including tax and technology (including electronic commerce), as well as summaries of various legal issues and regulations, many dealing with on-line filing and on-line commerce.

EC, pp. 9–10, talks about one of the great success stories on the Internet: Amazon, a virtual bookstore with 2.5 million titles, of which only the top-selling 400 titles are kept in stock. Most other requests are routed directly to publishers. As a result, costs are 10–40% lower than in other bookstores. In addition, through use of sophisticated software Amazon is able to maintain "a vast database of customers' preferences and buying patterns tied to their e-mail and postal addresses," giving Amazon a competitive advantage over traditional bookstores. "Businesses such as Motley Fool (a personal-finance site), Firefly's Big Note (a music store) and Amazon have thrived by turning their customers into a community" (EC, p. 6). "The key seems to be for the online merchant to offer something better than their physical counterpart" (EC, p. 9). But this seems to be surprisingly difficult to achieve: most on-line stores are losing money, and despite the growth of Internet users, electronic markets have had surprising difficulty in becoming viable, especially at the retail level. It seems that outside of making hotel reservations, and buying computer software, airline tickets, CDs, and videos, there is great resistance to using the Internet to buy anything at the retail level (EC, p. 11). Instead, it seems that the Internet is becoming primarily another advertising and marketing medium.

Even so, the impact on intermediaries between producers and ultimate consumers has been great. The Internet is providing shoppers with an abundance of information to help them make more informed decisions and is forcing intermediaries to provide more value-added services. For example, in the financial service industry "brokers have justified their high fees by pointing to the quality of their advice. But now knowledgeable amateurs and industry experts can trade stock tips for no charge in popular personal investing sites such as Motley Fool. Are they sometime biased, and often wrong? Yes, just like pros (EC, p. 11). A recent article by Suzanne Craig in *The Financial Post* (see the following box) illustrates the effect that more knowledgable brokers and Internet access is having in Canada.

INTERNET TRADES SEEN PUTTING SQUEEZE ON BROKERAGE FEES

Whistler, B.C.—Internet securities trading has created a new breed of investor who will drive transaction fees down, said the head of a Canadian electronic trading firm.

Colleen Moorehead, president of Toronto-based Versus Brokerage Services Inc., estimates it costs $756 to sell 2,000 shares of a Canadian bank through a full-service firm. Selling the same shares through an Internet brokerage account costs as little as $60.

She told a conference of investment dealers here that full-service investment houses must start telling retail investors how much the trade costs and how much their advice costs.

"Technology will continue to drive transaction revenues lower," she said. "Execution and advice must be unbundled to allow investors to see what they are paying for each of these services relative to their perception of value for each."

Some banks have launched Internet trading services in the last year and competition has slowly begun to force prices down. In April, for instance, Toronto Dominion Bank, which runs Green Line Investor Services, Inc., dropped its fee for personal computer or Internet trading to a flat $29 rate for buy and sell orders of up to 1,000 shares.

"As these investors get advice and market information from many sources other than full-price brokers, they are willing to pay premium to trade," Moorehead said.

This has forced brokers to compete not on price but on the quality of advice they offer, he said. "Brokers simply must learn to transform their client relationships away from a series of unconnected product transactions, to a more educative, comprehensive, advisory and professional financial services practice," he said.

Source: Suzanne Craig, *The Financial Post,* June 17, 1997, p. 6.

Increasingly newspapers are putting their classified ads for jobs, real estate, and automobiles on line.

Another example of the Internet affecting commerce relates to retail car sales, as indicated in this excerpt from EC, p. 12:

A few years ago most people would have laughed at the idea of buying a car online. Now those who try it are more likely to sigh with relief. Instead of spending a loathsome afternoon with a salesman, customers of Auto-by-Tel, the leading Internet car-buying service, simple tell the service what kind of car they want, and wait for nearby dealerships to make their best offer. Customers report prices up to 10% lower than their best face-to-face haggling efforts could achieve, without having to step into a dealership until it is time to pay and pick up the car. The reason: it costs a dealer only about $25 to respond to an Auto-By-Tel lead, instead of hundreds of dollars to advertise and sell a car the conventional way.

Last year 2m of the 15m cars sold in America went to customers who set foot in the dealership only to pick up the car. Chrysler, which put its Internet sales last year at just 1.5% of the total, reckons that in four years' time the figure will be 25%. Manufacturers are thrilled by this trend; they generally consider dealers a necessary evil, just as airlines do travel agents. But a creative dealership, which can set up its own Web site, can also use the Internet to expand its franchise.

The way intermediaries such as brokers react to competition from the Internet will determine how the marketplace evolves. There are several factors that have retarded the growth of the electronic marketplace. One is that in order to protect their market niches, intermediaries such as brokers and auto dealers are resisting sharing information. Another relates to security concerns about making payments over the Internet. "Even though there is not a single documented fraud involving credit-card numbers stolen over the Internet, a poll showed that 95% would not give their credit card numbers online ... The main threat is not that some hackers will swag numbers as they travel through the network, but that thieves will set up bogus shopfronts online to collect credit-card numbers" (EC, p. 14). Since it is conceivably impossible to tell which storefronts are legitimate other than perhaps by brand name, this suggests that some mechanisms will have to evolve to certify both merchants and consumers. A recent law enforcement conference indicates that the greatest risk may come from international crime syndicates, which have the resources to crack all electronic barriers, electronically steal from accounts, and use scrambled communications to avoid detection. Some experts feel the potential for future electronic crimes is "scary" and will only be combatted through international efforts by law enforcement agencies. Other barriers to the growth of Internet commerce identified by EC include the issue of the most efficient payment schemes (which might include e-money, subscription fees, or advertising fees), and the generally slow consumer acceptance of buying physical goods on-line. It seems that at the retail level at least, information and services are more readily sold on the Internet than most physical goods.

A major concern with Internet commerce continues to be lack of security, as indicated in the following box on e-crime:

Cyber Cops Believe Transborder Enforcement Is the Best Way to Tackle E-crime

Unlimited income. Make money fast. Excellent assay results. Do these Web site offers sound too good? Maybe they are. As any good cyber cop can tell you, electronic criminal activity—e-crime—is rife on the Net.

"The Net poses some new sorts of twists," says Hugh Stevenson, assistant director of the U.S. Federal Trade Commission marketing practices division.

"People making certain offerings can reach a very large audience with a single posting in a way they couldn't with a single phone call."

The types of crimes are not new, says Michael Duncan, a management analyst with the Royal Canadian Mounted Police's technological crime section in Ottawa. "Many of the crimes now committed on the Internet are simply variations of age-old schemes."

The RCMP's Duncan says he gets three or four reports daily about illegal chain letters or pyramid schemes on the Net—frequently from vigilants who cruise the Net searching for the latest scams.

Many customers do not report fraud—often because they are too embarrassed.

Earlier this year, the FTC recovered US$2.8 million from Fortuna Alliance LLC, a Bellingham, Wash., firm that raised an estimated US$13 million from more than 25,000 Net users. Several were from Prince Edward Island's brokerage community. Investors were promised a return of more than US$5,000 a month from a US$250 investment. When Fortuna got the money, it was wired to offshore trust accounts in Antigua.

Watch out for illegal gambling, job placement scams, and "pump and dump" chat rooms that promote the sale of near-worthless shares, several involving listings on the Alberta and Vancouver stock exchanges.

"The Internet creates novel opportunities to create crimes," says Tom Pownall, computer crime program analyst for the RCMP.

International co-operation is key to curbing crime on the Net, says Pownall. The prosecution of economic crime is "geared for the paper-based crime ... Now we need mutual legal assistance treaties so we can freeze data instantly."

Top 10 Internet Scams

- Pyramids or illegal multilevel marketing schemes.
- Sales of computer equipment and software—either not delivered or misrepresented.
- Sales of Internet services and products.
- Business opportunities with misleading earnings potential.
- Work-at-home plans, including sale of computer graphics software packages that often don't work.
- Buyers' club memberships that misrepresent savings.
- Magazine sales by people unconnected to the magazine.
- Investments of all types, such as near-worthless securities.
- Scholarship services.
- Prize offers.

Source (article): Margaret Brady, *The Financial Post,* July 19, 1997, pp. 18–19.

Source (list): National Fraud Information Centre, Washington, D.C., Phone 1-800-876-7060. Web site: www.fraud.org., E-mail: fraudinfosint.com.

Because of this concern for security, in October 1997 the CICA and AICPA announced joint development of assurance for Internet transactions. The goal is to develop electronic commerce principles that reduce business risks of electronic commerce to an acceptable level. See http://www.cia.ca for more details.

There are also tax uncertainties, as summarized in the following box.

INTERNET BLURS TAX BOUNDARIES

The explosive growth of electronic commerce conducted over the Internet has sent tax authorities around the world back to the drawing board. Their objective is to determine whether the existing tax rules, most of which were written decades ago, are flexible enough to handle this new means of conducting business or whether new regulations are needed.

While the Finance Department recently began a review of the issues, its U.S. counterpart, the U.S. Treasury Department, issued a detailed discussion paper on electronic commerce last November. The document suggests taxation remain neutral, and that no additional taxes be created that would impede the growth of electronic commerce. But it seeks to ensure that companies conducting business over the Internet do not avoid taxation and gain a fiscal advantage over existing channels of commerce.

Many companies use the Internet as a global advertising medium by setting up a home page to display their products or services. Prospective customers around the world can view these products and place an order. The product is shipped to the customer using conventional means.

The technology drastically reduces the cost of participating in global markets and has allowed many companies—especially those selling consumer goods—to significantly expand their sales territories.

From a taxation perspective, this type of activity should not create any additional complexities, since the advertising could be viewed as analogous to advertising in a newspaper or magazine. Furthermore, it should not be relevant where the Internet server happens to be located, if all it is being used for is to display and describe products and services.

However, issues can arise when products or services are transmitted electronically, such as software, music, videos or online publications. Customers can download the product from anywhere in the world, eliminating the need for a worldwide network of sales offices or warehouses. It is this type of activity that has created a problem for tax authorities because it effectively eliminates national borders and blurs the source and characterization of income.

What further complicates matters is that Internet servers can be located anywhere in the world. For example, a Canadian software company can be selling electronically into the U.S. market by using a server located there, or perhaps even in a third country.

The U.S. taxes companies earning income that is "effectively connected with a U.S. trade or business" and also taxes other U.S. source income, such as royalties. However, the Canada-U.S. tax treaty limits the U.S.'s right to tax Canadian-based businesses to income earned through a permanent establishment in the U.S. A permanent establishment is traditionally thought of as a physical facility such as an office or a plant.

With electronic commerce, the question arises as to whether, for example, an Internet server located in the U.S. would constitute a permanent establishment or simply a warehouse, which generally would not constitute a permanent establishment under the Canada-U.S. tax treaty. The Treasury Department paper suggests it is possible that no permanent establishment exists if the activities are limited to a server being maintained in the U.S ...

The application of other taxes—including sales taxes, customs, duties, and provincial and state income taxes—to Internet users also requires review ...

The questions surrounding who has the right to tax what may shift the emphasis from the traditional concept of source-based taxation—levying tax on income in the jurisdiction where it is earned—to that of residence-based taxation, or taxing where the seller is based. This may also create a range of tax-planning opportunities.

Source: By David Leslie, FCA, and Charles Chaho, CA, CPA, Ernst & Young. Full text of this article first appeared in *The Financial Post,* May 27, 1997.

Revenue Canada is already losing significant revenues because enforcing GST in virtual versions of *Time* magazine and some newspapers is proving to be impossible.

In the United States the tendency is to exercise jurisdiction over foreign Web sites, but there is a legal battle as to what level of government has the jurisdiction. There is a struggle between local, state, and federal governments, and a tendency to treat electronic transactions the same as those on most ordered goods. In fact, as EC points out (p. 17), one can think of "catalogue shopping as a sort of a Victorian virtual market." So in some senses virtual shopping may not be all that novel.

It's a different story in the industrial marketplace, thanks to the growth of EDI systems (see following box).

IT'S ELECTRONIC DATA INTERCHANGE OR THE HIGHWAY: COMPANIES DROPPING SUPPLIERS WHO LACK EDI

EDI transactions have traditionally been handled over private networks (VANs). Major providers of this service include Advantis, GE Information Systems Inc., and EDS. EDI participants rely on the VANs to provide a secure, reliable clearing house for sending data from one business to another. VANs are also responsible for keeping logs and backups of all messages. The down side to the VANs is the cost of doing EDI business.

They are not cheap and as a result EDI still is used primarily by larger businesses.

Many companies are moving EDI services to the Internet—a comparatively inexpensive EDI solution. Using the Net will provide small business with the advantages of EDI without the high costs involved in hardware, software and data transmission through a VAN.

Using the Internet as an EDI medium automatically increases the potential number of EDI business partners. But assuring secure and reliable transmission is more difficult on the Net than through a private network. EDI transaction information is extremely sensitive since it reveals key corporate financial information. As a result EDI software encrypts or scrambles information sent between trading partners.

Another problem is that forgeries can be difficult to detect since Internet protocols don't provide any guarantee of data transmitted. By using public key cryptography techniques, EDI software can encrypt data so it cannot be intercepted and misused.

At the same time, it provides digital signature on the data being transmitted.

This type of secure transaction is only now becoming available on the Internet.

Source: Written by Alan Salmon, Technology Editor, *The Bottom Line,* September 1996, p. 8.

One efficiency the Internet has allowed in EDI is the casting of a wider net of suppliers so that companies like GE, which has specialized bidding software, can invite bids from all over the world. This has lowered the cost of goods by 5–20%. The potential economic benefits of this can affect EDI itself, as summarized in EC, p. 17, as follows:

EDIcating business

Today, an estimated 95% of Fortune 1,000 companies use EDI in one way or another. GE says its EDI business with these firms grew 50% last year. But much as EDI has changed some industries, it has three serious flaws. It usually requires an expensive private network connection between two trading partners; the two parties must have a pre-existing relationship to give them time to set up the network; and it is not interactive. Computers typically generate orders when needed—picking suppliers from static price lists—and receive answers from other computers; there is no opportunity for negotiation and discussion. Because of the high cost of setting up EDI networks, the system has typically been limited to large firms; only 2% of America's 6m companies are using it, and then only with the companies they trade with most frequently.

Now companies, including GE, are experimenting with EDI over the Internet. It may not offer quite the same security and reliability as dedicated networks, but it is much cheaper and more flexible, since there is no need for a prior network connection. This alone opens it to many more and smaller firms. Eventually it will have a more profound effect. EDI networks are typically set up as a hub with spokes, with a big buyer at the hub and its suppliers at the spokes. The spokes cannot communicate among themselves, and any changes must be made from the hub. Because the Internet replaces much of this limited network with its own ubiquitous links, companies will be able to connect more freely, forming virtual trading communities and moving easily between them. If EDI can evolve to become as flexible as the Internet itself, it will keep a place in electronic commerce; if it cannot, there are plenty of transaction technologies that could take its place.

Some of these other transactions technologies include payment with electronic tokens, subscriptions covering various services or products, and either smart debit or smart credit cards with stored values.

As with the original EDI, Internet commerce raises unique legal problems. We have already noted the ones related to tax law. A recent conference in Toronto on the future of law and business on the Internet was reported by Monique Conrod in *The Lawyer's Weekly*. Two topics reported on in the article were contracts and jurisdiction: "Three basic goals must be met to make online contracts viable: providing authentication of the parties (which is impeded by the anonymous nature of the Internet), ensuring the integrity of the contents of the document in transmission, and guaranteeing enforceability through legal requirements such as signatures." This article is further excerpted in the following box.

Law Playing Catch-up with Internet

A digital signature should not be confused with a digitized handwritten signature [Ms. Perdue said].

A "digitized signed" document is one transmitted using public and private key encryption codes, which enable the recipient to verify the authenticity and integrity of the contents.

If such a document is tampered with in transmission the message will be received as gibberish.

A number of U.S. states now have digital signature legislation pending, and the U.N. Committee on International Trade Law is currently drafting model legislation on the subject.

Another growing area of concern is juridiction: Does a Web site confer jurisdiction everywhere?

"It depends," [said Ms. Perdue].

In the U.S. decisions have tended to come down in favour of exercising jurisdiction over foreign Web sites, she said.

One of the biggest problems faced by business is the "wild west mentality" inherent in the Net, she added.

"There are a lot of individuals with no respect for authority" who do not want to see the Net regulated, she explained.

Source: M. Conrod, *The Lawyer's Weekly,* April 25, 1997, p. 9. Reprinted with permission.

Despite these problems, "business-to-business electronic commerce is currently estimated at $70 billion and it is speculated to grow to US$150 billion by 2000. While these figures are highly speculative, there is a broad consensus within the computer industry that electronic commerce will be huge and that it will bring fundamental changes in which businesses use information technology" (L. Kehoe, "Caught in the Web of Electronic Commerce," *The Financial Post,* May 17, 1997, p. 23.) These figures may also be suggestive of the impact the Internet will have on future forms of assurance services.

Summary of Electronic Commerce

In summary, electronic commerce is fundamentally restructuring the way business is conducted. For auditors the implications are significant and pervasive. There are unique new risks associated with electronic commerce; electronic commerce greatly complicates the internal control system, yet forces the auditor to rely on controls, especially preventive controls, more than ever before. And finally the new risks may result in new contingencies which the auditor needs to consider for proper disclosure in the financial statements, for example, contingent liabilities as a result of failing to maintain an adequate audit trail.

Electronic commerce is here to stay because its benefits far outweigh the risks. These benefits include moving goods, money, and information much more efficiently. For example, according to a recent *Financial Post* article entitled, "EDI is forcing accountants to rethink traditional roles," Wal-Mart Stores is used as an example of how EDI can be used strategically to overcome competition. "Without question, they're one of the most powerful (EDI) systems—maybe in the world, in managing inventory and accounting in order to meet consumer demand." Some argue that stores such as Wal-Mart were "virtually created by EDI, even though EDI was originally started by the trucking industry in the 1970s. Wal-Mart stores use the EDI technology to link their suppliers directly to their stock data bases, so suppliers are automatically notified, and authorized to send shipment, when shelves are bare" (EC, p. 17).

That's one of the reasons they operate as efficiently as they do. Despite increasing competition from discount retailers, K-Mart is in the process of attempting to further exploit its EDI technology. A recent article on management changes at K-Mart, "Discounting the Naysayers," by Z. Olijnyk in the July 2, 1997, issue of *The Financial Post,* has this to say about K-Mart's innovations: "Heller [the new president of K-Mart Canada] admits he and the owners will have to get a better handle on exactly who shops at K-Mart and why. Through the use of the company's extensive computerized data base, he says that K-Mart must build a better profile of 'who comes in to buy $100-worth of items at a time and who only comes in once in a while.'" This type of "data mining" is currently the hottest area in software development.

It is clear that EDI and electronic commerce will become an established part of the business environment and that auditors will have to learn to deal with it. However, not only are new audit concerns being raised, but on a more general level there is increasing concern that data mining and related developments are beginning to erode the individual's right to privacy. Thus, privacy audits may become yet another new type of assurance engagement in the future.

SUMMARY

· ·

The technical work in a computer environment can take different forms. Auditors can try to audit "around" the computer, and act like it does not exist except as a very fast and accurate manual accounting processor. They can adopt computer expertise and audit "through" the computer to test its control features. They can audit "with" the computer to assess control risk and obtain substantive evidence, thus taking full advantage of its power and versatility.

Auditors must assess the control risk in a client's organization, no matter what technology is used for preparing the financial statements. This means that general and application computer controls will need to be studied and tested for compliance with the company's control procedures (if the detail test of controls is necessary in the circumstances). Tests of controls are described in the chapter for advanced systems. When advanced systems are used by a client, auditors can make use of some equally advanced techniques and devices. Among them are the live date techniques (audit hooks, tagging transactions, SCARF, SARF, snapshot, monitoring systems activity, and extended records), the historical data techniques (parallel processing and generalized software applications), the simulated data processing (test data and

ITF), and the program analysis techniques (computerized program flowcharting and cross reference programs). The chapter explains these advanced methods briefly.

Using the computer to obtain substantive evidence is explained in the context of generalized audit software (GAS). Its advantages and phases of application are described in Chapter 8. The future no doubt holds significant promise for developments in decision aids and expert systems.

The chapter also provides coverage of computer-oriented auditing with a section on computer-related fraud considerations. Controls and potential problems are discussed. A review of Chapter 8 (Fraud Awareness Auditing) is recommended. It covers a variety of fraud considerations that are relevant to both computer and noncomputer fraud detection.

Chapter 19 concludes with a review of issues associated with the rapidly evolving world of electronic commerce focusing on EDI, Fax, E-mail, and the Internet. It is clear that continued rapid growth in electronic commerce will revolutionize the way the majority of audits are conducted and greatly influence the types of assurance engagements that may evolve in the future.

CASE STUDY   KINGSTON COMPANY

Kingston Case Assignments

19.15   Kingston Company: Preparation of Test Data.   You have gathered the information regarding the sales invoices, which are entered on-line but not processed until they are batch balanced and validated. The information entered includes a transaction code, batch number and date, invoice date, invoice number, sales tax code, customer number, inventory item numbers and quantities shipped, bill of lading number, and total invoice amounts (sales). The sales total is a check figure computed by hand to be compared to the total of the extensions of individual inventory items. The computer multiplies the quantity entered by the price from a product price master file, enters the amount in the final invoice, and sums these extensions. There are some problems with this program.

Test data transactions are going to be used to test the validation programs for the following items:

1. No customer number (missing data test).
2. Invalid customer number (incorrect check digit for customer number entered; error may be in the number entered or in the check digit).
3. No bill of lading number (missing data test).
4. Sales greater than $25,000 (limit test).
5. Zero sales (missing data test).
6. Negative sales (reasonableness test).

The audit manager has prepared the decision logic table, shown in Exhibit 19.15–1, to indicate the 15 test transactions that should be prepared. Note that you will have to compute only one customer number with the wrong check digit (use for test transactions 2, 11–14) and one customer number with the correct check digit (use for test transactions 3–7, and 15). Also note that you should compute the total sales value of your test transactions as a batch control total.

E X H I B I T   19.15–1   **DECISION LOGIC TABLE**

Conditions				Test Data Transactions												
	(1)	(2)	(3)	(4)	(5)	(6)	(7)	(8)	(9)	(10)	(11)	(12)	(13)	(14)	(15)
Customer code number in field	n	y	y	y	y	y	y	n	n	n	y	y	y	y	y
Customer number is valid		n	y	y	y	y	y				n	n	n	n	y
Bill of lading document number in field	y	y	n	y	y	y	y	n	y	y	n	y	y	n	y
Sales amount < 25,000	y	y	y	n 25,500		y	y	y	n 25,501	y	y	y 24,999		n 27,000	y
Sales amount = 25,000					n 25,000							n 25,000			
Sales amount = 0						n 0									
Sales amount < 0							n –100			n –5,000					
Actions															
Error messages	X	X	X	X	X	X	X	X	X	X	X	X	X	X	
No error message															X

Document count control total = 15.
Sales dollar batch control for test = $? positive amounts.
                      ?   negative amounts.
                  $?

y = valid condition.
n = invalid condition.

Required:

a. Prepare the data for 15 simulated transactions for using test data to evaluate the input validation controls over sales invoices listed above.

To keep this problem reasonable, you are directed to prepare simulated test data for only the following input items:

- Customer number—5 digits plus check digit (using modules 11 prime number method illustrated in Chapter 11).
- Bill of lading number—3 digits.
- Total sales values—6 digits with no cents.

Present the 15 transactions in a schedule like this:

Transaction No.	Customer No.	BOL No.	Sales Value
1.			
2.			
·			
·			
·			
15			

b. Assume that when the test data were run through Kingston's validation program, test transactions (3), (8), (11), and (14) failed to produce an error message that no bill of lading number was in the field. What effect could this weakness (noncompliance with a desired control) have on the audit? In other words, what financial statement accounts would be affected that would require changing the nature, timing, or extent of substantive audit procedures?

19.16   Kingston Company: GAS and On-Line Controls.   The Kingston Company maintains the accounts receivable subsidiary ledger in a computer data base. Assume that Anderson, Olds & Watershed has a generalized audit software package that will operate on the Hewlett-Packard minicomputer. The audit partner has decided to stratify the accounts receivable population of 1,506 accounts and send positive confirmations to the 6 accounts with the largest balances and send negative confirmations to a random sample of 93 of the remaining accounts.

Required:

a. Assume you are going to use the GAS package to select the customer accounts and prepare the confirmations. List the steps (in general terms) required in the following phases: defining the audit objective, planning, and application design.

b. Since the Kingston company has converted the sales order, billing, and shipping system to a computer system, Jonathan Roberts, Kingston's internal audit department director, is concerned about ongoing auditability of the system. He has heard of something called integrated test facility and asks you to explain it to him. Draft a memo to him describing, in general terms, what ITF is and how it might be utilized in Kingston's accounts receivable accounting system.

19.17   Kingston Company: Use of the Microcomputer as an Audit Tool.   Anderson, Olds & Watershed recently has obtained several portable microcomputers but has not used them on any audit to date. Dalton Wardlaw has called you to his office again because he has learned that you used microcomputers in your accounting courses at The Big University. As you know, Dalton is not too comfortable with computers but is eager to learn and is most interested in using the latest technology. He asks you to describe how the microcomputer might be used on the Kingston Company engagement.

Required:

Prepare a memo to Dalton Wardlaw explaining how the microcomputer could be used in the audit of the Kingston Company. Be specific about what correspondence, memos, and auditing working papers (covered in the textbook) could be prepared and maintained on the microcomputer. Explain how this could save audit time as well as make the audit easier for Wardlaw to supervise and review.

Multiple-choice Questions for Practice and Review

19.18 Which of the following client computer systems generally can be audited without examining or directly testing the computer programs of the system?

    a. A system that performs relatively uncomplicated processes and produces detailed output.

    b. A system that affects a number of master files and produces a limited output.

    c. A system that updates a few master files and produces no other printed output than final balances.

    d. A system that performs relatively complicated processing and produces very little detailed output.

19.19 Control procedures within the computer system may leave no visible evidence indicating that the procedures were performed. In such instances the auditor should test these computer controls by:

    a. Making corroborative inquiries.

    b. Observing the separation of duties of personnel.

c. Reviewing transactions submitted for processing and comparing them to related output.

d. Reviewing the run manual.

19.20 An auditor will use the test data method to gain certain assurances with respect to the computer:

a. Input data.

b. Machine capacity.

c. Control procedures contained within the program.

d. General control procedures.

19.21 After obtaining a preliminary understanding of a client's computer control structure, an auditor may decide not to perform test of controls auditing related to the control procedures within the computerized portion of the client's control system. Which of the following would not be a valid reason for choosing to omit tests of controls auditing?

a. The client's computer control procedures duplicate manual control procedures existing elsewhere in the system.

b. There appear to be major weaknesses that indicate a higher control risk.

c. The time and dollar costs of testing exceed the time and dollar savings in substantive work if the tests of computer controls show the controls to operate effectively.

d. The client's control procedures appear adequate enough to justify a low control risk assessment.

19.22 Which of the following is likely to be of least importance to an auditor when obtaining an understanding of the computer control procedures in a company with a computerized accounting system?

a. The segregation of duties within the computer function.

b. The control procedures over source documents.

c. The documentation maintained for accounting applications.

d. The cost/benefit ratio of computer operations.

19.23 Which of the following would lessen internal control in a computer system?

a. The computer librarian maintains custody of computer program instructions and detailed listings.

b. Computer operators have access to operator instructions and detailed program listings.

c. The control group is solely responsible for the distribution of all computer output.

d. Computer programmers write and debug programs that perform routines designed by the systems analyst.

19.24 Assume an auditor estimates that 10,000 cash disbursement cheques were issued during the accounting period. If a computer application control, which performs a limit check for each cheque request, is to be subjected to the auditor's test-data approach, the same should include:

a. Approximately 1,000 test items.

b. A number of test items determined by the auditor to be sufficient under the circumstances.

c. A number of test items under the circumstances.

d. One transaction.

19.25 When an on-line, real-time (OLRT) computer system is in use, the computer control procedures can be strengthened by:

a. Providing for the separation of duties between data input and error listing operations.

b. Attaching plastic file protection rings to reels of magnetic tape before new data can be entered on the file.

c. Preparing batch totals to provide assurance that file updates are made for the entire input.

d. Making a validity check of an identification number before a user can obtain access to the computer files.

19.26 When auditing a computerized accounting system, which of the following is not true of the test data approach?

a. Test data are processed by the client's computer programs under the auditor's control.

b. The test data must consist of all possible valid and invalid conditions.

c. The test data need consist of only those valid and invalid conditions in which the auditor is interested.

d. Only one transaction of each type need be tested.

19.27 A primary advantage of using generalized audit packages in the audit of an advanced computer system is that it enables the auditor to:

a. Substantiate the accuracy of data through self-checking digits and hash totals.

b. Utilize the speed and accuracy of the computer.

c. Verify the performance of machine operations which leave visible evidence of occurrence.

d. Gather and store large quantities of supportive evidential matter in machine-readable form.

19.28 Which of the following is an advantage of generalized computer audit packages?

a. They are all written in one identical computer language.

b. They can be used for audits of clients that use differing computer equipment and file formats.

c. They have reduced the need for the auditor to study input controls for computer-related procedures.

d. Their use can be substituted for a relatively large part of the required testing.

19.29 An auditor cannot test the reliable operation of computerized control procedures by:

a. Submission at several different times of test data for processing

on the computer program the company uses for actual transaction processing.

b. Manual comparison of detail transactions internal auditors used to test a program to the program's actual error messages.

c. Programming a model transaction processing system and processing actual client transactions for comparison to the output produced by the client's program.

d. Manual reperformance of actual transaction processing with comparison of results to the actual system output.

19.30 An auditor can get evidence of the proper functioning of password access control to a computer system by:

a. Writing a computer program that simulates the logic of a good password control system.

b. Selecting a random sample of the client's completed transactions to check the existence of proper authorization.

c. Attempting to sign onto the computer system with a false password.

d. Obtaining written representations from the client's computer personnel that the password control prevents unauthorized entry.

19.31 An auditor would most likely use generalized audit software (GAS) to:

a. Make copies of client data files for controlled reprocessing.

b. Construct a parallel simulation to test the client's computer controls.

c. Perform tests of a client's hardware controls.

d. Test the operative effectiveness of a client's password access control.

EXERCISES AND PROBLEMS

· ·

19.32 Audit "Around" Versus Audit "Through" Computers. PAs may audit "around" or "through" computers

in the examination of financial statements of clients who utilize computers to process accounting data.

Required:

a. Describe the auditing approach referred to as auditing "around" the computer.

b. Under what conditions does the PA decide to audit "through" the computer instead of "around" the computer?

c. In auditing "through" the computer, the PA may use "test data."
  (1) What is the "test data" test of controls audit procedure?
  (2) Why does the PA use the "test data" procedure?

d. How can the PA be satisfied that the computer program tested by him or her actually is being used by the client to process its accounting data?

(AICPA adapted)

19.33 Payroll Audit Procedures, Computer, and Sampling. You are the senior auditor in charge of the annual audit on Onward Manufacturing Corporation for the year ending December 31. The company is of medium size, having only 300 employees, but the payroll system work is performed by a computer. All 300 employees are union members paid by the hour at rates set forth in a union contract, a copy of which is furnished to you. Job and pay rate classifications are determined by a joint union–management conference, and a formal memorandum is placed in each employee's personnel file.

Every week, clock cards prepared and approved in the shop are collected and transmitted to the payroll department. The total of labour hours is summed on an adding machine and entered on each clock card. Batch and hash totals are obtained for the following: (1) labour hours and (2) last four digits of Social Insurance numbers. These data are keyed into a disk file, batch balanced, and converted to tape storage for batch processing. The clock cards (with cost classification data) are sent to the cost accounting department.

Payroll cheques are written by the computer. As each person's payroll record is processed, the Social Insurance number is matched to a table (in a separate master table file) to obtain job classification and pay rate data, then the pay rate is multiplied by the number of hours and the cheque is printed. (Ignore payroll deductions for the following requirements.)

Required:

a. What audit procedures would you recommend to obtain evidence that payroll data are accurately totalled and transformed into machine-readable records? What deviation rate might you expect? What tolerable deviation rate would you set? What "items" would you sample? What factors should be considered in setting the size of your sample?

b. What audit procedures would you recommend to obtain evidence that the pay rates are appropriately assigned and used in figuring gross pay? In what way, if any, would these procedures be different if the gross pay were calculated by hand instead of on a computer?

19.34 GAS Application—Phases and Documentation. The phases and documentation of developing a GAS application are very similar to the phases and documentation when the client develops a new computer system. Refer to Chapter 8 and prepare a table of phases and the related documentation when the client develops a new system. Based on the material in Chapter 19, prepare a table of the phases and the related documentation when the auditor develops a GAS application. Organize your answer as follows:

Client's System Development		Auditor's GAS Application	
Phases	Documentation	Phases	Documentation

19.35 GAS Application—Receivables Confirmation. You are using generalized audit software to prepare accounts receivable confirmations during the annual audit of the Eastern Sunrise Services Club. The company has the following data files:

Master file—debtor credit record.
Master file—debtor name and address.
Master file—account detail.
Ledger number.
Sales code.
Customer account number.
Date of last billing.
Balance (gross).
Discount available to customer (memo account only).
Date to last purchase.

The discount field represents the amount of discount available to the customer if the customer pays within 30 days of the invoicing date. The discount field is cleared for expired amounts during the daily updating. You have determined that this is properly executed.

Required:

List the information from the data files shown above that you would include on the confirmation requests. Identify the file from which the information can be obtained.

19.36 GAS Application—Fixed Assets. You are supervising the audit field work of Sparta Springs Company and need certain information from Sparta's fixed asset records, which are maintained on magnetic disk. The particular information is (1) net book value of assets, so that your assistant can reconcile the subsidiary ledger to the general ledger control accounts (the general ledger contains an account for each asset type at each plan location), and (2) sufficient data to enable your assistant to find and inspect selected assets.

Record layout of the fixed asset master file:
Asset number.
Description.
Asset type.
Location code.
Year acquired.
Cost.
Accumulated amortization, end of year (includes accumulated amortization at the beginning of the year plus amortization for year to date).
Amortization for the year to date.
Useful life.

Required:
a. From the data file described above, list the information needed to verify correspondence of the subsidiary detail records with the general ledger accounts. Does this work complete the audit of fixed assets?
b. What additional data are needed to enable your assistant to inspect the assets?

19.37 GAS Application—Inventory. Your client, Boos & Becker, Inc., is a medium-sized manufacturer of products for the leisure-time activities market (camping equipment, scuba gear, bows an arrows, and the like). During the past year, a minicomputer system was installed and inventory records of finished goods and parts were converted to computer processing. Each record of the inventory master file contains the following information:
Item or part number.
Description.
Size.
Quantity on hand.
Cost per unit.
Total value of inventory on hand, at cost.
Date of last sale or use.
Quantity used or sold this year.
Reorder point (quantity).
Economic order quantity.
Code number of major vendor.
Code number of secondary vendor.

In preparation for year-end inventory, the client has two identical sets of preprinted, prepunched inventory cards prepared from the master file. One set is for the client's inventory counts, and the other is for your use to make audit test counts. The following information has been keypunched into the cards and printed on their face:
Item or part number.
Description.
Size.
Unit of measure code.

In taking the year-end count, the client's personnel will write the actual counted quantity on the face of each card. When all counts are complete, the counted quantity will be processed against the master file, and quantity-on-hand figures will be adjusted to reflect the actual count. A computer listing will be prepared to show any missing inventory count cards and all quantity adjustments of more than $100 in value. These items will be investigated by client personnel and all required adjustments will be made. When adjustments have been completed, the final year-end balances will be computed and posted to the general ledger.

Your firm has available a generalized audit software package that will run on the client's computer and can process both cards and disk master files.

Required:

a. In general and without regard to the facts above, discuss the nature of generalized audit software packages and list the various audit uses of such packages.

b. List and describe at least five ways a GAS package can be used to assist in all aspects of the audit of the inventory of Boos & Becker, Inc. (For example, the package can be used to read the inventory master file and list items and parts with a high unit cost or total value. Such items can be included in the test counts to increase the dollar coverage of the audit verification.) Hint: Think of the normal audit procedures in gathering evidence on inventory when the client makes a periodic count, then think of how the GAS could help in this particular client situation.

(AICPA adapted)

Discussion Cases

. . . .

19.38 Roche Island Quarry—Evidence Collection in an On-line System. Your firm has audited the Roche Island Quarry Company for several years. Roche Island's main revenue comes from selling crushed rock to construction companies from several quarries owned by the company in Quebec and Ontario. The rock is priced by weight, quality, and crushed size.

PAST PROCEDURE

Trucks owned by purchasing contractors or by Roche Island needed to display a current certified empty weight receipt or be weighed in. The quarry yard weighmaster recorded the empty weight on a hand-written "scale ticket" along with the purchasing company name, the truck number, and the date. After the truck was loaded, it was required to leave via the scale where the loaded weight and rock grade were recorded on the "scale tickets." The scale tickets were sorted weekly by grade and manually recorded on a summary sheet, which was forwarded to the home office. Scale tickets were prenumbered and accounted for in the home office.

Revenue (and receivables) audit procedures involved evaluating the controls at selected quarries (rotated each year) and vouching a statistical sample of weight tickets to weekly summaries. Weekly summaries were traced through pricing and invoicing to the general ledger on a sample basis, and general ledger entries were vouched back to weekly summaries on a sample basis. Few material discrepancies were found.

NEW PROCEDURES

At the beginning of the current year, Roche Island converted to a distributed network of microcomputers to gather the information formerly entered manually on the "weight ticket." This conversion was done with your knowledge but without your advice or input. Now, all entering trucks must weigh in. The yard weighmaster enters NEW on the terminal keyboard, and a form appears on the screen that is similar to the old scale ticket, except the quarry number, transaction number, date, and incoming empty weight are automatically entered. Customer and truck numbers are keyed in. After the weigh-in, the weighmaster enters HOLD through the terminal. The weight ticket record is stored in the microcomputer until weigh-out.

When a truck is loaded and stops on the scale, the weighmaster enters OLD and a directory of all open transactions appears on the screen. the weighmaster selects the proper one and enters OUT. The truck out-weight and the rock weight are computed and entered automatically. The weighmaster must enter the proper number for the rock grade. The weighmaster cannot change any automatically entered field. When satisfied that the screen weight ticket is correct, the weighmaster enters SOLD and the transaction is automatically transmitted to the home office computer, and the appropriate accounting data-base elements are updated.

One copy of a scale ticket is printed and given to the truck driver. There is no written evidence of the sale kept by Roche Island.

Required:
It is now midyear for Roche Island and you are planning for this year's audit.
a. What control procedures (manual and computer) should you expect to find in this system for recording quarry sales?
b. The computer programs that process the rock sales and perform the accounting reside at the home office and at the quarries. What implications does this have on your planned audit procedures?
c. What are you going to do to gather substantive audit evidence now that there are no written "scale tickets"?

19.39 Auditor Control of GAS Software. Two audit partners were discussing computerized audit techniques. One said: "We should not leave the firm's generalized audit software on the client's computer system. This would be no different from leaving our audit

program with the client. Likewise, we should not rely on the client's generalized audit software package."

Required:
Evaluate and discuss the partner's statement.

19.40 Discovering Intentional Financial Misstatements in Transactions and Account Balances—Using the Computer. AMI International was a large office products company. Headquarters management imposed pressure on operating division managers to meet profit forecasts. The division managers met these profit goals using several accounting manipulations involving the record-keeping system, which maintained all transactions and account balances on computer files. Employees who operated the computer accounting system were aware of the modifications of policy and managers ordered to accomplish the financial statement manipulations. The management and employees carried out these activities:
1. Inventory write-downs for obsolete and damaged goods were deferred.
2. The sales entry system was kept open after the quarterly and annual cutoff dates, recording sales of goods shipped after the cutoff dates.
3. Transactions coded as leases of office equipment were recorded as sales.
4. Shipments to branch offices were recorded as sales.
5. Vendors' invoices for parts and services were not recorded until later, but the actual invoice date was faithfully entered according to accounting policy.

Required:
Describe one or more procedures that could be performed with generalized audit software to detect signs of each of these transaction manipulations. Limit your answer to the actual work accomplished by the computer software.

CHAPTER 20

Learning Objectives

Chapter 20 contains more mathematical–statistical details related to the test of controls sampling introduced in Chapter 7. In fact, Chapter 20 is like a technical appendix on test of controls sampling and substantive testing. In Chapter 20 you will find more specific explanation of how to do statistical sampling in the test of controls phase of the control risk assessment work and for substantive tests of details. After studying this chapter in conjunction with Chapter 7, you should be able to:

PART I

1. Explain the role of professional judgment in assigning numbers to risk of assessing control risk too low, risk of assessing control risk too high, and tolerable deviation rate.

2. Use statistical tables or calculations to determine test of controls sample sizes.

3. Calculate the effect on test of controls sample sizes of subdividing a population into two relevant populations.

4. Use your imagination to overcome difficult sampling unit selection problems.

5. Use tables and calculations to compute statistical results (UEL, the computed upper error limit) for evidence obtained with detail test of controls procedures.

6. Use the discovery sampling evaluation table for assessment of audit evidence.

7. Choose a test of controls sample size from among several equally acceptable alternatives.

PART II

8. Calculate a risk of incorrect acceptance, given judgments about inherent risk, control risk, and analytical procedures risk, using the audit risk model in the Handbook Guideline on Materiality and Audit Risk (paragraph 23).

9. Explain the considerations in controlling the risk of incorrect rejection.

10. Explain the characteristics of dollar-unit sampling and its relationship to attribute sampling.

11. Calculate a dollar-unit sample size for the audit of the details of an account balance.

12. Describe a method for selecting a dollar-unit sample, define a "logical unit," and explain the stratification effect of dollar-unit selection.

13. Calculate an upper error limit for the evaluation of dollar-value evidence, and discuss the relative merits of alternatives for determining an amount by which a monetary balance should be adjusted.

STATISTICAL SAMPLING CONCEPTS FOR TESTS OF CONTROLS AND TESTS OF BALANCES

PRELIMINARY CONCEPTS

How Risk and Materiality Are Used in Statistical Auditing

Materiality and risk are key concepts in statistical sampling and in auditing. This is illustrated by the *Handbook Section* 5130.25 quote that "Decisions concerning materiality and audit risk are the most significant made in the course of an audit because they form the basis for determining the extent of the auditing procedures to be undertaken." Hence, professional judgment concerning these concepts is critical to audit practice.

In order to better understand why this is so, it's useful to imagine what the audit would be like if it were a purely scientific endeavour in which the management assertions were treated as hypotheses which had to be either supported (verified) or contradicted by the evidence. Perhaps a good analogy, but one not to be taken too literally, is to think of auditor opinions as being similar to the opinion polls one frequently encounters in the media.

A recent opinion poll in *The Toronto Star* reported that a mayoral candidate M.L. led candidate B.H. with 51 percent and 46 percent support, respectively, of decided voters. This poll was the result of surveying 400 Toronto residents. A sample of this size is considered accurate to within 5 percentage points, 19 times out of 20. In other words, due to the uncertainties associated with the representatives of the sample of 400, the best the statistician can conclude about M.L.'s prospects is that there is a 95 percent confidence level that his actual support is in the range 51% + or − 5% = 46% to 56%. The width of this band around the best point estimate (the 51%) is frequently referred to as sampling precision, which is related to materiality, and the confidence level is related to the amount of audit assurance.

Conceptually, an auditor can make a similar statement about financial statements. For example, after audit testing the auditor may conclude that a client's net income number is 200,000 + or − 10,000, 19 times out of 20. It would be possible for the auditor to make this kind of statement if the appropriate statistical samples were drawn from all the various accounting components making up net income. In this statistical sampling framework, materiality is compared to the degree of accuracy or precision of the sample (i.e., the + or − 10,000 for the client or + or − 5 percent of the *Star* poll); and audit assurance is related to the statistical confidence (the 19 times out of 20 statement, which means the same as 95 percent = 19/20). Thus, if a purely statistical interpretation were to be put on the auditor's report, "presents fairly in all material respects" means that the difference between the audit estimate (the audit value or AV) based on audit testing and the reported amount (the book value or BV) is less than material. The level of audit assurance is assumed to be captured by the words *in our opinion* in the auditor's report. The standard audit report supplies the highest, but unspecified, level of assurance with the adverse opinion the lowest level of assurance that the financial statements are fairly presented in accordance with GAAP.

The standard audit report can therefore be interpreted to mean there is a high level of assurance that there are no material misstatements in the financial statements. Conversely, we can look at the complement of assurance, which is audit risk (*Section* 5130.02), and interpret the standard audit report to mean there is a low level of risk that there are material misstatements in the financial statements after the audit.

In terms of a statistical sampling framework, the auditor's decision on the form of this report will be based on doing a sufficient amount of testing so that the auditor will be able to construct a confidence interval around his or her best estimate AV such that if BV is included in this interval *and* this interval is smaller than materiality, the auditor will have achieved the planned level of assurance from his or her testing. An equivalent but perhaps more intuitive approach can be developed which constructs an interval of possible errors around BV and if this precision is smaller than materiality, then the auditor has achieved the stated confidence that there is no material error. For example, assume the auditor has done enough testing at a client with a reported net income of $198,000 to conclude that the auditor has 95 percent confidence (assurance) that GAAP income is in the interval 198,000 + or − 10,000. Assume materiality is set at 8 percent of reported income so that materiality equals .08 * 198,000 = 15,840. Since the achieved precision of 10,000 is less than materiality of 15,840, the auditor can conclude with at least 95 percent assurance that there is no material error in the reported net income of $198,000.

In order that the auditor can reach such a conclusion, he or she will have to plan the testing so that achieved precision is no larger than materiality. Note that if BV − AV is greater than materiality, then the auditor has not obtained the 95 percent assurance from testing and will either have to do more audit work or insist on an adjustment. The details of this are discussed in the rest of the chapter. We begin by discussing the concepts of sampling risks and hypothesis tests.

How Sampling Risks Are Controlled in Statistical Auditing

When using statistical sampling concepts in auditing, we need to develop a decision rule, which must be used consistently if we are to control risks objectively. It is the assumption of the consistent use of a strict decision rule that allows the risks to be predicted and thus controlled via the sample size. The decision rule is frequently referred to as a hypothesis test, and the auditor is typically interested in distinguishing between two hypotheses:

Hypothesis 1: There exists a material misstatement in the total amount recorded for the accounting population (e.g., accounts receivable file).
Hypothesis 2: There exists no misstatement in the amount recorded for the accounting population.

The decision rule the auditor uses in statistical auditing is to select one of these two simplified hypotheses based on the results of the statistical sample. The mechanics of this will be discussed later in this chapter. For now we are interested in depicting what happens to sampling risk (risk that arises when testing only a portion

F I G U R E 20–1

of the population statistically) when a consistent decision rule is used. This is when the concept of a probability of acceptance curve becomes useful.

Probability of Acceptance Curve (or acceptance curve, for short)

Consider Figure 20–1, which plots the probability of acceptance of the recorded amount against total misstatement within the recorded amount of some accounting population, such as aggregate accounts receivable. The horizontal axis reflects total misstatement while the vertical axis reflects probability.

In a perfect world of no uncertainty, auditors would want to have a zero probability of accepting a recorded amount having material misstatement (MM). However, the concept of testing or sampling only a part of a population requires the auditor to be willing to accept some uncertainty concerning the total population value. This is reflected in the fact that the probability of acceptance cannot be zero at MM with sampling. However, the auditor can, or course, design his or her audit so that this probability is appropriately low (see "X" in Figure 20–1).

An auditor using a consistent decision rule selecting one of the hypotheses discussed above with a given sample size over a range of possible errors will experience varying probabilities of acceptance, as indicated in Figure 20–2. This is what we mean by a probability of acceptance curve.

Note an important feature of this curve: as the error amount increases (in the direction of the arrow), the probability of acceptance goes down (as one would expect). How fast it drops depends on a variety of factors including the statistical model, the sample size, and the error pattern.

Concepts of Sampling Risk

The probability of acceptance curve is useful for depicting the full range of sampling risks that the auditor may experience with a given test. This is summarized in Figure 20–3.

To understand these risks, let's consider some scenarios. First, assume there is an immaterial amount of misstatement (i.e., to the left of MM in Figure 20–3), say ½ MM. The probability of acceptance curve in Figure 20–3 tells us what the probability is of accepting any given amount of misstatement (including .5MM).

Is acceptance the correct decision with this amount of misstatement? The answer is yes because the amount of misstatement is less than material. Thus, the probability of acceptance gives us the probability of making the correct decision at .5MM. Since the only other alternative in this simple framework is to reject the reported amount, an incorrect decision, this probability of making the incorrect decision must then be

FIGURE 20–2

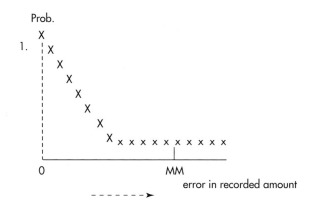

one minus the probability of acceptance. This risk of incorrect decision when there is less than material misstatement is referred to as the alpha risk in auditing.

A completely different error is possible when there happens to be a material misstatement, that is, at or to the right of MM in Figure 20–3. Now, accepting the reported amount is the incorrect decision and the probability of accepting the recorded amount is thus the risk of accepting a material misstatement. This risk of accepting a material misstatement is referred to in auditing as the beta risk. The correct decision is to reject the reported amount when there is a material misstatement and this equals one minus the probability of accepting the reported amount when there is a material misstatement, or one minus beta risk.

To recap: alpha risk can only occur when there is less than material misstatement and alpha risk = one minus the probability of acceptance when there is less than material misstatement. On the other hand, beta risk can only take place when there is a material misstatement and beta risk = the probability of acceptance of the recorded amount when there is material misstatement.

Another important thing to note is that as error increases, the probability of acceptance decreases and therefore, beta risk decreases. The maximum beta risk is thus at the smallest amount of material misstatement, which is at the point MM itself. That is, maximum beta risk is at MM. Hence if the auditor controls beta risk at a specified level at MM, he or she automatically controls it at a lower level for errors greater than MM.

This is not true for alpha risk, however. An analysis of Figure 20–3 should make clear that as probability of acceptance decreases with increasing errors in the immaterial error range, alpha risk is increasing. Maximum alpha risk therefore occurs at just below MM and equals (at the limit) one minus beta risk at MM. For a numerical example assume beta risk is controlled at .05 at MM. Then we know that maximum alpha risk = 1 − .05 = .95. In practice, alpha risk is frequently controlled only at zero

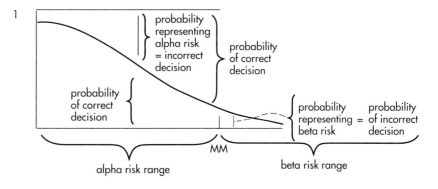

errors by controlling alpha risk at its minimum level. Note that this concept of risk control is completely different from that of beta risk control, which is always controlled via the beta risk's maximum value.

Positive and Negative Approaches and Confidence Level

In the statistical literature there is frequent reference to the concept of confidence level of a statistical test. How does this relate to alpha and beta risks as used in auditing?

The answer is, it all depends.

It depends on the way the hypothesis tests are constructed. Confidence level is related to the primary or null hypothesis of the test. Specifically, confidence level equals one minus risk of rejecting the null hypothesis when it is true. Thus, confidence level is dependent on the null hypothesis used. In auditing a distinctive statistical terminology has evolved over the years. If hypothesis 1 above is the null hypothesis, then we are using the negative approach to hypothesis testing, and if hypothesis 2 is the null hypothesis, then we are using the positive approach to hypothesis testing.

Under the negative approach, confidence level equals one minus beta risk while under the positive approach, confidence level equals one minus alpha risk.

The negative approach is the more important and common approach in auditing. In particular, it underlies all attribute sampling tables and formulas. Dollar unit sampling always uses the negative approach. The positive approach frequently underlies formulas using the normal distribution assumption; this is briefly discussed at the end of the chapter. Because of its simplicity and straightforward relationship to audit objectives, the negative approach is used throughout the remainder of the chapter. However, it should be noted that the positive approach is much more important in the sciences, and, in particular, the alpha risk when associated with the null hypothesis of "no difference" is the more important risk of the sciences. In contrast, the beta risk is more important in auditing because it is related to the more important hypothesis of "material misstatement" or "significant difference," which it is the auditor's job to detect. In fact, some have characterized the purpose of the auditing profession as that of "controlling beta risk" associated with financial statements. For this reason beta risk is associated with audit effectiveness.

F I G U R E 20–4   ACCEPTANCE CURVES FOR DUS

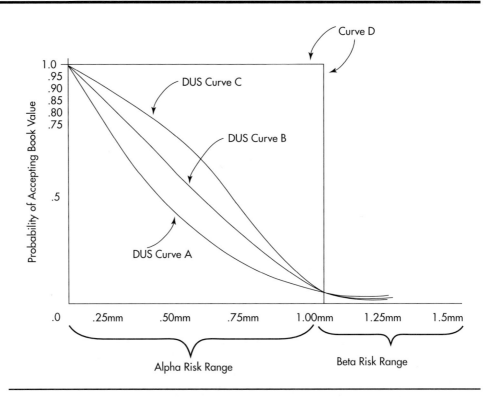

Effect of Changing the Sample Size under the Negative Approach

Under the negative approach, the confidence level = 1 − beta risk. Under some interpretations auditors can equate the confidence level with audit assurance, and so these auditors work with assurance or confidence factors rather than risk factors. The underlying principles remain essentially the same, however, whether the auditor works with risk or confidence levels.

What if the auditor varies the sample size while keeping the confidence level constant?

Figure 20–4 illustrates what happens: Curve A is the probability of acceptance with the smallest sample size possible for given beta risk, Curve B results from using twice the Curve A sample size, and Curve C results from four times the Curve A sample size, whereas Curve D represents a "perfect acceptance curve" with no sampling risk. Curve D occurs when a population is examined 100 percent. From Figure 20–4 it is evident that if confidence level (and thus beta risk under the negative approach) and MM are held constant while changing the sample size, it is the alpha risk that changes with the sample size—specifically, alpha risk is reduced throughout its range when the sample size is increased, and the converse. This illustrates that if the auditor wishes to reduce alpha risk while keeping beta risk and MM unchanged, then a larger sample size needs to be used. In fact, if any one of alpha risk, beta risk, or MM were to be reduced, sample size would need to be increased, and the converse.

Curve A reflects the acceptance curve with the smallest sample size possible with dollar unit sampling for a given beta risk. This smallest sample size is called a discovery sample. If the auditor wishes to control alpha risk to a lower level than indicated by Curve A, the sample size should be increased. Sample size increases in practice are normally implemented through formulas by one of two major approaches: 1. increase the number of errors to be accepted by the sample, or 2. increase the planned expected error rate in computing the sample size. Sometimes a combination of the two approaches is used in computing the sample size. More rigorous methods are available for controlling alpha risk for an explicit amount of expected errors, but we will not cover these methods here because the additional complexity does not change the nature of the basic judgments that must be made and the necessary cost-benefit tradeoffs that are required. The concepts of beta risk, alpha risk, and their relationship to confidence level described here applies with some modification to all statistical procedures. In this sense they are very general, and Figures 20–1 to 20–4 are suggestive of sampling risk associated with all statistical hypothesis testing. Auditors have developed their own terminology for the risks associated with different audit procedures. As we review various statistical procedures, we will identify new risk terms associated with these procedures, but we will see that for the most part these risks relate to the more important sampling risk in auditing, that of beta risk.

PART I: TEST OF CONTROLS WITH ATTRIBUTE SAMPLING RISK AND RATE QUANTIFICATIONS

· · · · · · · · · · · ·

LEARNING OBJECTIVE

1. Explain the role of professional judgment in assigning numbers to risk of assessing control risk too low, risk of assessing control risk too high, and tolerable deviation rate.

The quantification of sampling risk is an exercise of professional judgment. When using statistical sampling methods, auditors must quantify the two risks of decision error. The risk of assessing control risk too low is generally considered more important than the risk of assessing control risk too high. Auditors must also exercise professional judgment to determine the extent of deviation allowable (tolerable rate) in assessing control risk.

Tolerable Deviation Rate: A Professional Judgment

Auditors should have an idea about the correspondence of rates of deviation in the population with control risk assessments. Perfect control compliance is not necessary, so the question is: What rate of deviation in the population signals control risk of 10 percent? 20 percent? 30 percent? and so forth, up to 100 percent? To answer this question, you need to relate material misstatement of an account to a tolerable deviation rate for the control procedures affecting that account.

Assume that material dollar misstatement of $30,000 is used in planning the audit of accounts receivable for possible overstatement. This amount is relevant to the audit of control over sales transactions because uncorrected errors in sales transactions misstate the financial statements by remaining uncorrected in the accounts receivable balance. In other words, we test the controls over sales transaction processing in order to determine the control risk relevant to our audit of the accounts receivable balance. Therefore, if sales transactions are in error by $30,000 or more, the accounts receivable balance may be materially misstated.

However, a deviation in a sales transaction (e.g., one unsupported by shipping documents) does not necessarily mean the transaction amount is totally in error.

EXHIBIT 20-1   ILLUSTRATIVE CONTROL RISK AND TOLERABLE RATE RELATIONSHIPS

Tolerable Rate	Control Risk	Control Risk
1% (anchor)	0.05	
2	0.10	
4	0.20	Low control risk.
6	0.30	
8	0.40	
10	0.50	Moderate control risk.
12	0.60	
14	0.70	
16	0.80	Control risk slightly below maximum.
18	0.90	
20	1.00→	Maximum control risk.

Note: The tolerable rate increases 1 percentage point for each additional 0.05 control risk in this example.

After all, missing paperwork may be the only problem. Perhaps a better example is a mathematical accuracy deviation: If a sales invoice is computed incorrectly to charge the customer $2,000 instead of $1,800, there is a 100 percent control deviation (the inaccuracy), but it does not describe a 100 percent dollar error. Therefore, more than $30,000 in sales transactions can be "exposed" to control deviation without generating $30,000 dollar error in the sales and the accounts receivable balances. This "exposure" is sometimes called the **smoke/fire concept**, meaning that there can be more exposure to error (smoke) than actual error (fire), just as in a conflagration.

Smoke/fire thinking produces a multiplier to apply to the tolerable dollar misstatement assigned to the account balance, $30,000 in our example. We know that a multiplier of 1 is not reasonable (i.e., $30,000 on invoices with deviations produces $30,000 of misstatement in the accounts receivable), and a multiplier of 100 or 200 is probably also not reasonable (too large). Some auditors say a multiplier of 3 is reasonable, having no other basis than a mild conservatism. Some PA firms have sampling policies with implicit multipliers that range from 3 to 14. A multiplier of 3 has the practical effect of producing the conclusion that $90,000 on sales invoices could be exposed to control deviations. If the total gross sales on all invoices is $8.5 million, the implied **tolerable deviation** rate is $90,000/$8.5 million = 0.0106, or approximately 1 percent.

This 1 percent tolerable deviation rate now represents a theoretical anchor. It is the deviation rate that marks low control risk (say, 0.05 control risk). When this tolerable deviation rate seems too low for practical audit work, auditors can "accept" a higher tolerable rate. The only thing that happens is that auditors are implicitly saying that a higher control risk is ultimately satisfactory for the audit of the account balance. Higher tolerable rates signal greater control risk in this scheme of thinking, like the example in Exhibit 20–1.

The point in this demonstration of smoke/fire and tolerable rate thinking is to show that tolerable rate is a decision criterion that helps auditors assess a control risk. The association of tolerable rates with different control risks is the important point. To achieve a low control-risk assessment (e.g., 10 percent), the sample size of transactions will be very large, but the sample size required to obtain a moderate control risk assessment (e.g., 50 percent) can be much smaller. Therefore, sample size varies inversely with the tolerable rate—the lower the rate (and the lower the

EXHIBIT 20–2   CONTROL RISK INFLUENCE ON SUBSTANTIVE BALANCE-AUDIT SAMPLE SIZE

Control Risk Categories	(1) Possible Control Risk Assessments (CR)	(2) Related Risk of Incorrect Acceptance (RIA)*	(3) Number of Balance Items to Select for Substantive Audit
Low control risk	0.10	0.50	51
	0.20	0.25	81
	0.30	0.167	96
Moderate control risk	0.40	0.125	107
	0.50	0.10	117
	0.60	0.083	125
Control risk slightly below the maximum	0.70	0.071	130
	0.80	0.0625	136
	0.90	0.0556	140
Maximum control risk	1.00	0.05	143

*Assuming AR = 0.05, IR = 1.0, AP = 1.0. Therefore, RIA = 0.05/(1.0 × CR × 1.0).

"desired control risk assessment"), the larger the sample size. Some auditors express the tolerable rate as a number (necessary for statistical calculations of sample size), while others do not put a number on it.

The audit strategy is to think about the audit plan, including a consideration of the sample size of balances the team wants to audit. For example, Exhibit 20–2, column 3, shows various numbers of customer accounts. Suppose the audit manager plans to select 107 for confirmation and other procedures. This decision suggests that control risk needs to be as good as 40 percent (Exhibit 20–2, column 1), and the tolerable rate for this assessment is 8 percent (Exhibit 20–1). Thus, the auditors need to select a sample of sales transactions for test of controls audit sufficient to justify a decision about an 8 percent tolerable rate.

Risk of Erroneous Control Risk Assessments: Another Professional Judgment

Assessing control risk too low causes auditors to rely on control too much (overreliance) and audit the related account balances less than is necessary. The risk in "risk of assessing control risk too low" relates to the effect of the erroneous control evaluation. This effect is produced in the substantive audit by influencing the sample size for auditing the account balances related to the controls being evaluated.

Internal control is evaluated, and control risk is assessed, on the environment, the accounting system, and the client control procedures related to particular account balances. For example, auditors will evaluate control over the processing of sales and cash receipts transactions because these are the transactions that produce the debits and credits to the customer accounts receivable. Some other examples are shown in Exhibit 20–3. The ultimate purpose of the control risk assessment is to decide how much work to do when auditing the general ledger accounts—for example, cash accounts receivable, inventory, sales revenue, and expenses. The question of "how much work" relates directly to the sample size of the general ledger account details to audit—for example, how many bank accounts to reconcile, how many customer accounts receivable to

EXHIBIT 20–3   EXAMPLES OF CLASSES OF TRANSACTIONS FLOWING INTO GENERAL
LEDGER BALANCES

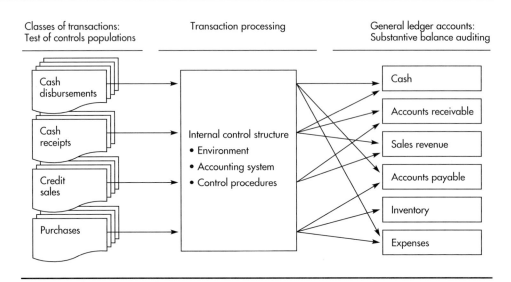

confirm, how many inventory items to count and recalculate for correct costing. The control risk assessment provides supporting information for the balance-audit work. We will proceed, using the audit of accounts receivable as an occasional example.

When planning the audit of the accounts receivable balance, auditors make judgments and estimates of the overall risk of failing to detect material misstatements in the balance (AR, audit risk related to the receivables audit), the probability that errors entered the accounts (IR, inherent risk), and the effectiveness of their analytical procedures for detecting material errors in the receivables (APR, analytical procedures risk). At this stage the remaining elements of the risk model are the control risk (CR) and the substantive sample risk of incorrect acceptance (RIA). The internal control evaluation task is directed to assessing the control risk, and the risk of incorrect acceptance is then derived using the expanded risk model: RIA = AR/(IR × CR × APR). As the acronym indicates, RIA is the same as beta risk discussed earlier in this chapter.

Since control risk is the probability that the client's controls will fail to detect material misstatements, provided any enter the accounting system in the first place, control risk itself can take on values ranging from very low probability (say, 0.10) to maximum probability (1.0). Using the audit risk model (Handbook Auditing Guideline: Applying Materiality and Audit Risk Concepts in Conducting An Audit), there exists a risk of incorrect acceptance (RIA, also known in the literature as "test of details risk") for every possible control risk assessment (CR). These RIAs affect the sample sizes for the substantive audit work on the account balances.

Exhibit 20–2 shows a range of possible control risk assessments in column (1). To their left are some labels commonly used in public accounting practice. (PA firms deal with a few control risk categories instead of a full range of control risk probabilities.)[1] Column (2) contains the risks of incorrect acceptance (RIA) derived

---

[1] PA firms that use quantitative test of controls sampling policies have quantified probabilities underlying their categories, and they fall in the ranges indicated in Exhibit 20–1.

from the audit risk model for the balance-audit substantive sample, and column (3) shows the substantive sample sizes based on these RIAs. The sample sizes in column (3) are the substantive balance-audit sample sizes (e.g., number of customer accounts, number of inventory items), not the test of controls samples. (The actual calculation of these substantive sample sizes is explained later in this chapter.)

These relationships are evident in Exhibit 20–2: (1) for higher control risk, the related RIA is lower; (2) for lower RIAs, the substantive samples are larger; and (3) therefore, the higher the control risk, the larger the substantive sample size required for the audit of the related balance sheet account. These are the relationships suggested by the second examination standard—that is, the understanding of the control structure and the assessment of control risk is for the purpose of planning the nature, timing, and extent of substantive tests to be performed.

Erroneous decisions leading to assessing control risk too high also should be avoided in the interest of audit efficiency.

For the following explanation, you need to be introduced to the concept of the upper error limit (UEL). The UEL is a statistical estimate of the population deviation rate computed from the test of controls sample evidence. It consists of the actual sample deviation rate (number of deviations found in the sample divided by the test of controls sample size) plus a statistical allowance for sampling error. The UEL is similar to the upper confidence limit of a statistical confidence interval. (You probably studied confidence intervals in your statistics course.) It is used in statistical evaluation of test of controls sample results as the estimate of the population deviation rate. It is compared to the tolerable deviation rate when auditors assess the control risk.

If the number of deviations in a test of controls sample causes the UEL to be higher than the tolerable deviation rate, when the population deviation rate is actually equal to or lower than the tolerable deviation rate, the auditors may assess control risk too high. This causes them to perform more substantive audit work on the related account balance than they would have performed had they obtained better information about the control risk.

Conversely, if achieved sample UEL is too low (specifically below tolerable error), the auditor may assess control risk too low. This causes the auditor to do less substantive audit work on the related account balance than she or he would have performed had he or she obtained better information on the control risk. This is a much more serious risk for the auditor because it ultimately relates to audit effectiveness. Note also that since this risk affects adversely the auditor's ability to detect material misstatement, assessing control risk too low is the beta risk associated with tests of control.

PA firms frequently use a risk of assessing control risk too low of 10 percent. This is a rather arbitrary policy that eases the burden of the number of judgments auditors need to make. The implication is that auditors are willing to take a 1 in 10 chance of assessing control risk too low and suffer the consequences of auditing a substantive sample smaller than they would have audited had the decision error not been made. However, less arbitrary methods can be devised that link CR missassessments to the extent of substantive testing of details. These refined methods are not discussed here.

. . . .

R E V I E W
C H E C K P O I N T S

20.1 If inherent risk (IR) is assessed as 0.90 and the detection risk (DR) implicit in an audit plan is 0.10, what audit risk (AR) is implied when the assessed level of control risk is 0.10? 0.50? 0.70? 0.90? and 1.0?

20.2 What general considerations are important when an auditor decides on an acceptable risk of assessing control too high?

20.3 What general considerations are important when an auditor decides on an acceptable risk of assessing control risk too low?

20.4 What considerations are important when an auditor decides on an acceptable risk of assessing control risk too high? What is the probability of finding one or more deviations in a sample of 100 if the population deviation rate is actually 2 percent?

20.5 What is the probability of finding one or more deviations in a sample of 100 units if the deviation rate in the population is only 0.5 percent?

20.6 What is the connection between possible assessments of control risk and a judgment about tolerable rate, both considered prior to performing test of controls audit procedures?

20.7 What is the connection between material dollar misstatement assigned for the substantive audit of a balance and tolerable deviation rate used in a test of controls sample?

20.8 What professional judgment and estimation decisions must be made by auditors when applying statistical sampling in test of controls audit work?

. . . .

SAMPLE SIZE DETERMINATION
. . . .

We will use the simplest formulas and tables to plan and evaluate statistical sampling in auditing. These formulas are based on dollar unit sampling (DUS) theory. One of the advantages of DUS is that the same formula and tables can be used for planning sample sizes for tests of controls (attribute sampling) as well as substantive tests of details. The key formula is $R = nP$. Solving for n in this formula: $n = R/P$ yields the sample size that would be used with DUS. In this formula R is the (beta) risk factor or, equivalently, the confidence level factor, P is the precision, and n is the sample size. This same formula is used for sample planning and evaluation: if the formula is used to solve n, then it is being used for sample planning; if the formula is used to solve for P, then it is being used for sample evaluation.

The risk level factor, R, is unique for each combination of risk level (or, equivalently, confidence level) and number of errors. Since we are using the negative approach, confidence level $= 1 - $ beta risk. The less serious alpha risks are frequently controlled indirectly in practice through the number of errors that are considered acceptable. For a given RIA and MM, the greater the number of errors to be considered acceptable by a sample, the greater the sample size required (and, as discussed earlier, the lower the alpha risk). In case you are interested, R is the mean of a Poisson distribution with a Poisson process that captures the essence of the attributes sampling distribution underlying DUS theory. Here we are using the Poisson distribution to approximate the binomial or hypergeometric distributions that underlie the attribute sampling theory that forms the basis for statistical tests of controls. This approximation is quite good for most audit applications, and so we can exploit the simplifications possible with the Poisson distribution.

P stands for precision and is referred to as planned precision at the sample determination stage. In tests of controls, P is tolerable error or some fraction of it at the sample determination stage. P is also referred to as the planned upper error limit (or planned UEL) at the sample determination stage. The auditor must use professional judgment in specifying the number of errors, RIA, and P in planning sample sizes for tests of controls using the formula and Appendix 20A.

To illustrate the calculation of sample size for tests of controls, assume the following:

1. Your risk of assessing control risk too low is 1 percent. That is, beta risk for tests of controls is 1 percent.

2. Your tolerable rate is 6 percent. That is, the P value in the formula is 6 percent = .06.

3. Your expected population deviation rate is zero, so we expect zero errors in the sample.

4. Your sample size is 77 calculated using the formula $R = nP$ and Appendix 20A as follows:

    Sample size = $n = R/P$ = using Poisson risk factor for zero errors and beta risk of .01, divided by tolerable deviation rate = 4.61/.06 = 77 (to be conservative always round up to the nearest integer).

The sample sizes using the formula are reliable in that they closely approximate but do not understate the sample sizes necessary to achieve audit objectives. (This is because the Poisson is a conservative approximation of the binomial and hypergeometric distributions on which attribute sampling is based.) However, since it is much easier to work with the Poisson table of R values, we will base all our calculations on Appendix 20A.

We can now also illustrate control of alpha risk. If we wish to reduce alpha risk, one method is to use a higher number of errors—that is, let errors = 1 in Appendix 20A and all else in the illustration remains unchanged. Then sample size (n) = 6.64/ .06 = 111. Be sure you can confirm this using the formula and Appendix 20A. Since beta risk is still the same (1 percent) and so is tolerable deviation rate (6 percent), what we get for the increased sample size is a reduction in alpha risk (as illustrated in Figure 20–4). The auditor can make this alpha risk control explicit by using more complex formulas, but most firms follow a policy of controlling alpha risk indirectly based on subjectively estimating the number of errors or using a planned precision P that is less than the tolerable deviation rate.

The effect of using a lower planned precision in sample determination can also be illustrated. Let's assume the auditor uses a planned precision of 3 percent rather than the tolerable error rate of 6 percent. Now we get a sample size n = 4.61/.03 = 154. Again, beta risk is 1 percent, tolerable error rate is still 6 percent (it will be used in the sample evaluation decision rule for deciding if the sample error rate is acceptable) so that what the auditor obtains with the increased sample size is, again, a reduction in alpha risk. Since sample size can be increased to virtually any amount, most audit firms put a restriction on planned precision by not letting it get below one half the tolerable deviation rate.

· ·

R E V I E W
C H E C K P O I N T S

20.9 What facts, estimates, and judgments do you need to figure a test of controls sample size using the Appendix 20A tables? What other relevant judgment is not used?

20.10   Test yourself to see whether you can get the sample size of 87 from Appendix 20A with these specifications: beta risk = 5 percent, tolerable deviation rate = 9 percent, expected errors = 3.

20.11   What facts, estimates, and judgments do you need to figure a test of controls sample size using the Appendix 20A Poisson risk factors? What other relevant judgment is not used?

20.12   Test yourself to see whether you can get the sample size of 70 using the Poisson risk factor equation with these specifications: beta risk = 5 percent, tolerable deviation rate = 9 percent, expected errors = 2.

. . . .

MORE ABOUT DEFINING POPULATIONS: STRATIFICATION
. . . .

LEARNING OBJECTIVE

3. Calculate the effect on test of controls sample sizes of subdividing a population into two relevant populations.

Auditors can exercise flexibility when defining populations. Accounting populations are often **skewed**, meaning that much of the dollar value in a population is in a small number of population units. For example, the **80/20 "rule"** is that 80 percent of the value tends to be in 20 percent of the units. Many inventory and accounts receivable populations have this skewness. Sales invoice, cash receipt, and cash disbursement populations may be skewed, but usually not as much as inventory and receivables balances.

Theoretically, a company's control procedures should apply to small-dollar as well as to large-dollar transactions. Nevertheless, many auditors believe that evidential matter is better when more dollars are covered in the test of controls part of the audit. This inclination can be accommodated in a sampling plan by subdividing (stratifying) a population according to a relevant characteristic of interest. For example, sales transactions might be subdivided into foreign and domestic; accounts receivable might be subdivided into sets of customers with balances of $5,000 or more and those with smaller balances; payroll transactions might be subdivided into supervisory payroll (salaried) and hourly payroll.

Nothing is wrong with this kind of stratification. However, you must remember that (1) an audit conclusion based on a sample applies only to the population from which the sample was drawn and (2) the sample should be representative—random for statistical sampling. If 10,000 invoices represent 2,000 foreign sales and 8,000 domestic sales, and you want to subdivide the population this way, you will have two populations. You can establish decision criteria of acceptable risk of assessing control risk too low and tolerable deviation rate for each population. You also can estimate an expected population deviation rate for each one. Suppose your specifications are these:

	Foreign	Domestic
Risk of assessing control risk too low	5%	10%
Tolerable deviation rate	5	5
Expected population deviation rate	2	1
Then, sample size (Appendix 20A and assume P is adjusted for expected error rate, e.g., foreign $P = .05 - .02 = .03$).	100	58

You can evaluate each sample separately using the appropriate risk of assessing control risk too low, or you can combine the sample. To combine the sample sizes effectively, one would have to make the most conservative assumptions among the strata objectives. In the illustration this means using an overall combined risk of assessing control risk too low of 10 percent and an expected combined population (strata) deviation rate of 1 percent so that both alpha and beta risks are at the lower of the two sample sizes.

Interestingly, if the population had not been stratified but treated as one population of 10,000 invoices, and the criteria had been beta risk = 10 percent, tolerable deviation rate = 5 percent, expected error rate = 1 percent, the sample size would be 58. Subdividing in two a population subject to test of controls sampling has the practical effect of doubling the extent of sampling. This is the price we pay for being able to make separate statistical statements about each strata—so the audit issue is how important is it to evaluate the strata separately.

A Little More About Sampling Unit Selection Methods

LEARNING OBJECTIVE
4. Use your imagination to overcome difficult sampling unit selection problems.

Audit sampling can be wrecked on the shoals of auditors' impatience. Planning an imaginative selection method takes a little time, and auditors are sometimes in a big hurry to grab some units and audit them. A little imagination goes a long way. For example, suppose an auditor of a newspaper publishing client needs to audit the controls over the completeness of billings—specifically, the control procedure designed to ensure that customers were billed for classified ads printed in the paper. You have seen classified ad sections, so you know they consist of different-size ads, and you know that ad volume is greater on weekends than on weekdays. How can you get a random sample that can be considered representative of the printed ads?

The physical frame of printed ads defines the population. You probably cannot obtain a population count (size) of the number of ads. However, you know that the paper was printed on 365 days of the year, and the ad manager can probably show you a record of the number of pages of classified ads printed each day. Using this information, you can determine the number of ad pages for the year, say 5,000. For a sample of 100 ads, you can choose 100 random numbers between 1 and 5,000 to obtain a random page. Then you can choose a random number between 1 and 10 to identify one of the 10 columns on the page, and another random number between 1 and 500 (the number of lines on a page). The column-line co-ordinate identifies any ad on the random day. (This method approximates randomness because larger ads are more likely to be chosen than smaller ads. In fact, the selection method probably approximates a sample selection stratified by the size of the ads.)

You can judge the representativeness by noticing the size of the ads selected. Also, since you will know the number of Friday-Saturday-Sunday pages (say, 70 percent of the total, or 3,500 pages), you can expect about 70 of the ads to come from weekend days.

Random Number Table

The most accurate although most time-consuming sampling unit selection device is a table of random digits. (See Appendix 20B.) This table contains rows and columns of digits from 0 to 9 in random order. When items in the population are associated with numbers in the table, the choice of a random number amounts to choice of a sampling unit, and the resulting sample is random. Such a sample is called an **unrestricted random sample**. For example, in a population of 10,000 sales invoices, assume the first invoice in the year was 32071 and the last one was 42070. By obtaining a random start in the table and proceeding systematically through it, 100 invoices may be selected for audit.[2] Assume that a random start is obtained at the five-digit number in the second row, 50 column—number 29094—and that the reading path in the table is down to the bottom of the column, then to the top of the next column, and so on. The first usable number and first invoice is 40807, the second is 32146, and so forth. Note that several of the random numbers were skipped because they did not correspond with the invoice number sequence.[3] A page of random digits like the one in Appendix 20A can be annotated and made into your sample selection working paper to document the selection, as shown in Exhibit 20–4.

Systematic Random Selection

Another selection method used commonly in auditing because of its simplicity and relative ease of application is **systematic selection**. This method is employed when direct association of the population with random numbers is cumbersome. Systematic selection consists of (*a*) dividing the population size by the sample size, obtaining a quotient k (a "skip interval"); (*b*) obtaining a random start in the population file; and (*c*) selecting every kth unit for the sample. A file of credit records provides a good example. These may be filed alphabetically with no numbering system. Therefore, to select 50 from a population of 5,000, first find $k = 5,000/50 = 100$, then obtain a random start in the first 100 of the set of physical files and pull out every 100th one thereafter, progressing systematically to the end of the file and returning to the beginning of the file to complete the selection. This method only approximates randomness, but the approximation can be improved by taking more than one random start in the process of selection. When more than one start is used, the interval k is changed. For example, if five starts are used, then every 500th item would be selected. Five random starts give you five systematic passes through the population, and each pass produces 10 sampling items, for a total of 50.

Auditors usually require five or more random starts. You can see that when the number of random starts equals the predetermined sample size, the "systematic" method becomes the same as the unrestricted random selection method. Multiple random starts are a good idea because a population may have a nonrandom order that could be embedded in a single-start systematic method.

Computerized Selection

Most audit organizations have computerized random number generators available to cut short the drudgery of poring over printed random number tables. Such routines can print a tailored series of numbers with relatively brief turnaround time. Even so, some advance planning is required, and knowledge of how a random number table works is useful.

---

[2] A random start in a table may be obtained by poking a pencil at the table, or by checking the last four digits on your $10 bill to give row and column co-ordinates for a random start.

[3] Most auditors will not allow the same sample item to appear twice in a selection—duplicate selections are counted only once. Strictly speaking, this amounts to sampling without replacement and the hypergeometric probability distribution is appropriate instead of the binomial distribution. The binomial probabilities are exact only when each sample item is replaced after selection, thus giving it an equally likely chance of appearing in the sample more than once. For audit purposes the practice of ignoring the distribution is acceptable because the difference is mathematically insignificant.

E X H I B I T 20–4   RANDOM NUMBER TABLE USED AS AUDIT WORKING PAPER

Index _____	**Kingston Company**	Prepared by _____
	Random Selection of Sales Invoices	Reviewed by _____
	12/31/92	

Population: 10,000 invoices numbered 32071-42070.
Method: unrestricted selection of 5-digit random invoice numbers.
Random Start: _____

(32942)	95416	42339	59045	26693	49057	87496	20624	14819
07410	99859	83828	21409	29094	65114	36701	25762	12827
59981	68155	45673	76210	58219	45738	29550	24736	09574
46251	25437	69654	99716	11563	08803	86027	51867	12116
65558	51904	93123	27887	53138	21488	09095	78777	71240
99187	19258	86421	16401	19397	83297	(40111)	49326	81686
(35641)	00301	16096	(34775)	21562	97983	45040	19200	16383
14031	00936	81518	48440	02218	04756	19506	60695	88494
60677	15076	92554	26042	23472	69869	62877	19584	(39576)
66314	05212	67859	89356	20056	30648	87349	20389	53805
20416	87410	75646	64176	82752	63606	(37011)	57346	69512
28701	56992	70423	62415	(40807)	98086	58850	28968	45297
74579	(33844)	(33426)	07570	00728	07079	19322	56325	84819
62615	52342	82968	75540	80045	53069	20665	21282	07768
93945	06293	22879	08161	01442	75071	21427	94842	26210
75689	76131	96837	67450	44511	50424	82848	(41975)	71663
02921	16919	(35424)	93209	52133	87327	95897	65171	20376
14295	(34969)	14216	03191	61647	30296	66667	10101	63203
05303	91109	82403	(40312)	62191	67023	90073	83205	71344
57071	90357	12901	08899	91039	67251	28701	03846	94589
78471	57741	13599	84390	(32146)	00871	09354	22745	65806
89242	79337	59293	47481	07740	43345	25716	70020	54005
14955	59592	97035	80430	87220	06392	79028	57123	52872
42446	(41880)	(37415)	47472	04513	49494	08860	08038	43624
18534	22346	54556	17558	73689	14894	05030	19561	56517

Selection path: down each column to bottom, top next right column, then to top of column at left.
(⬭) Sampling unit selection.

You can also use random number generators in popular electronic spreadsheet programs, like LOTUS 1–2–3e. The @RAND function in 1–2–3 takes specifications for the number of digits desired in the random number, then generates a list of random numbers in a desired range. A custom list using an electronic spreadsheet or another random number generator can eliminate the problem of numerous discards (unusable numbers) that is encountered when a printed random number table is used. (Notice the numerous discards skipped in the procedure shown in Exhibit 20–4.)

DANGER IN SYSTEMATIC SELECTION

Western Products Company has a stable payroll of 50 hourly employees, paid weekly, for a total of 2,600 pay transactions in the year under audit. The auditors decided to select a systematic sample of 104 paycheques for detail test of controls audit procedures. The skip interval was $k = 2600/104 = 25$. The auditors carefully chose a random start in the first week at ?3 on the payroll register (Wyatt Earp) and selected every 25th payroll entry thereafter. They got 52 entries for Wyatt Earp and 52 entries for Bat Masterson. The audit manager was disgusted over the failure to get a representative sample!

R E V I E W
C H E C K P O I N T S

20.13 When you subdivide a population into two populations for attribute sampling, how do the two samples compare to the one sample that would have been drawn if the population had not been subdivided?

20.14 Are you required to use all five digits of a random number when you have a random number table like the one in Appendix 20B?

20.15 What steps are involved in selecting a sample using the systematic random selection method?

STATISTICAL EVALUATION

LEARNING OBJECTIVE

5. Use tables and calculations to compute statistical results (UEL, the computed upper error limit) for evidence obtained with detail test of controls procedures.

To accomplish a statistical evaluation of test of controls audit evidence, you must know the tolerable rate and the acceptable beta risk. These are your **decision criteria**—the standards for evaluation in the circumstances. You also need to know the size of the sample that was audited and the number of deviations. Now you can use Appendix 20A in making the evaluation. Again you use the Poisson risk factors in Appendix 20A except now you use the $R = nP$ formula to solve for P to get achieved precision = computed upper error limit = UEL: $P = R/n$. You already know n since now you already have selected the sample; R is obtained from Appendix 20A with your knowledge of the number of errors found and planned beta risk.

For example, suppose you audited a sample of 90 sales transactions and found 2 of them without proper shipping documents. Previously, you had decided a beta risk of 5 percent was appropriate.

Using the formula above, UEL = Poisson risk factor for number of errors, beta risk divided by sample size.

For example: The Poisson risk factor for beta risk = 5 percent and 2 errors (deviations) found in a sample is 6.30; thus, with a sample of 90: UEL = 6.30/90 = 0.07, or 7 percent.

TEST OF CONTROLS DECISION RULE

If UEL (computed upper error limit) is less than your tolerable deviation rate, you can conclude that the population deviation rate is low enough to meet your tolerable rate decision criterion, and you can assess the control risk at the level associated with the tolerable deviation rate. (Alternatively, you can assess the control risk at the level associated with the UEL, or you can calculate a probability associated with the tolerable deviation rate based on the sample data.)

If UEL exceeds your tolerable deviation rate, you can conclude that the population deviation rate may be higher than your decision criterion, and you should assess a higher control risk—for example, the control risk associated with the UEL.

Applying a Decision Rule

After you calculate the UEL, you can compare it to your previously determined tolerable deviation rate and apply an appropriate decision rule. Note you don't compare the computed UEL to the planned precision that you used in determining the sample size if the planned precision was less than the tolerable rate. As discussed earlier, the sole reason for using a planned precision less than tolerable was to control for alpha risk through a larger sample size. In sample evaluation the planned precision has no role to play because we use the achieved precision resulting from the actual sample results obtained.

A higher control risk assessment decision is not the same as a "rejection" decision. You can take the UEL derived from your sample and use it to assess the control risk. For example, assume you audited 30 sales transactions (tolerable deviation rate criterion of 8 percent, a beta risk criterion of 10 percent, and an expectation of zero deviations) to try to evaluate control risk at 0.40 (see Exhibit 20–5) and justify the audit of 107 customer accounts in the accounts receivable total (see Exhibit 20–6). You can achieve this control risk assessment if you find no deviations in the sample of 30 transactions (see Appendix 20A). If you find one actual deviation in the sample of 30, your computed upper error limit is 14 percent (see Appendix 20A and use the formula), and according to the decision rule, you should not assess control risk at 0.40. However, you can take UEL = 14 percent, assess a higher control risk (0.70 according to Exhibit 20–1), and audit a sample of 130 customer accounts, which is appropriate for control risk of 0.70, instead of the sample of 107 appropriate if control risk had been assessed at 0.40.

The **computed upper error limit** is a statistical calculation that takes sampling error into account. You know that a sample deviation rate (number of actual deviations in the sample divided by sample size) cannot be expressed as the exact population deviation rate. According to common sense and statistical theory, the actual but unknown population rate might be lower or higher. Since auditors are mainly concerned with the risk of assessing control risk too low (because it relates to the more serious beta risk), the higher limit is calculated to show how high the estimated population deviation rate may be.

Auditing standards tell you to "consider the risk that your sample deviation rate can be lower than your tolerable deviation rate for the population, even though the actual population rate exceeds the tolerable rate." In statistical evaluation you accomplish this consideration by holding the risk of assessing the control risk too low constant at the acceptable level while computing UEL, then comparing UEL to your tolerable deviation rate. In short, if achieved UEL > tolerable error for tests of controls, then reject reliance at planned level; otherwise you can rely. How much reliance depends on the auditor's judgment and the decision rule he or she uses. (Exhibit 20–1 is an example of such a decision rule.)

Example of Satisfactory Results

Suppose you selected 200 recorded sales invoices and vouched them to supporting shipping orders. You found no shipping orders for one invoice. When you followed up, no one could explain the missing documents, but nothing about the sampling unit appeared to indicate an intentional irregularity. You have already decided that a 10 percent risk of assessing control risk was too low—that is, beta risk for test of controls = 10 percent, and a 3 percent tolerable deviation rate, adequately define your decision criteria for the test of controls audit. Calculate UEL using the $R = nP$ formula and Appendix 20A. From $R = nP$ solve for P: $P = R/n$. From Appendix 20A find the appropriate value for R using beta risk = 10 percent and 1 error: $R = 3.89$. so the calculated upper error limit = UEL = 3.89/200 = 1.945 percent.

Audit conclusion: The probability is 10 percent that the population deviation rate is greater than 2 percent. This finding (UEL of 2 percent, less than tolerable rate of 3 percent) satisfies your decision criteria, and you can assess control risk as you had originally planned.

Example of Unsatisfactory Results

The situation is the same as above, except you found four invoices with missing shipping orders. Now, $P = R/n = 8/200 = 4$ percent = computed upper error limit = UEL.

Audit conclusion: The probability is 10 percent that the population deviation rate is greater than 4 percent. This UEL finding exceeds your tolerable rate criterion of 3 percent, and you ought to assess a higher control risk than you had originally planned.

Discovery Sampling—Fishing for Fraud

LEARNING OBJECTIVE

6. Use the discovery sampling evaluation table for assessment of audit evidence.

Discovery sampling is essentially another kind of sampling design directed toward a specific objective. However, discovery sampling statistics also offer an additional means of evaluating the sufficiency of audit evidence in the event that no deviations are found in a sample.

A discovery sampling table is obtainable from Appendix 20A by simply reading the entries for the zero errors line. That is, no errors are considered acceptable in the sample—as indicated in Figure 20–4, this results in the highest alpha risk over the range of immaterial errors. A discovery sampling plan deals with the following kind of question: If I believe some important kind of error or irregularity might exist in the records, what sample size will I have to audit to have assurance of finding at least one example? Ordinarily, discovery sampling is used for designing procedures to search for such things as examples of forged cheques or intercompany sales improperly classified as sales to outside parties. However, discovery sampling may be used effectively whenever a low deviation rate is expected. Auditors must quantify a desired **probability of at least one occurrence** when the specified tolerable deviation rate occurs. In discovery sampling the tolerable deviation rate is frequently referred to as the **critical rate of occurrence**. Generally, the critical rate is very low because the deviation is something very sensitive and important, such as a sign of fraud.

The probability in this case represents the desired probability of finding at least one occurrence (example of the deviation) in a sample. In Appendix 20A you can read across the zero errors column for the desired beta risk (the beta risk in the zero errors row represents the probability of at least one occurrence), and critical rate is simply the P value in our formula: $R = nP$.

To illustrate, suppose that in the test of controls audit of recorded sales, you are especially concerned about finding an example of a deviation of as few as 50 outright fictitious sales (intentional irregularities) existed in the population of 10,000 recorded invoices (a critical rate of 0.5 percent). Furthermore, suppose you want to achieve at least 0.99 probability (or in percentage terms, 99 percent probability) of finding at least one. Appendix 20A and our formula indicate a required sample size of 922 recorded sales invoices, as follows: $n = R/P = 4.61/0.005 = 922$. If a sample of this size were audited and no fictitious sales were found, you could conclude that the actual rate of fictitious sales in the population was less than 0.5 percent with 0.99 probability of being right.

This feature of discovery sampling evaluation provides the additional means of evaluating the sufficiency of audit evidence whenever an attribute sample turns up zero deviations. You can scan across the different beta risk tables in Appendix 20A until you find an R value in the zero errors row that comes just below the one associated with the lowest beta risk. As an illustration, suppose 200 sales invoices were audited and no deviations of missing shipping orders were found. Appendix 20A shows that, if the population deviation rate were 2 percent, the probability of including at least 1 deviation in a sample of 200 is 0.98 (i.e., $R = nP = 200 * 0.02 = 4$—the highest R value in the zero errors rows of Appendix 20A not exceeding 4 occurs with beta risk = 0.02—the complement of this risk is the probability of finding more than zero errors). None was found, so, with 0.98 probability, you can believe that the occurrence rate of missing shipping orders is 2 percent or less.

. . . .

R E V I E W
CHECKPOINTS

20.16 What is the auditing interpretation of the sampling error-adjusted deviation rate (UEL)?

20.17 What is the UEL for these data: sample size audited = 46, actual deviations found = 3, beta risk = 35 percent?

20.18 What is the proper interpretation of the probability in discovery sampling?

. . . .

Putting It All Together

To this point, you have learned some of the theoretical details about defining populations, perceiving control risk (CR) as a probability ranging from low (e.g., 0.10) to high (e.g., 1.0), using smoke/fire multiple thinking to determine an anchor tolerable deviation rate, and using tables and Poisson risk factor calculations to determine the test of controls sample size (n). You also learned about an assignment of successively higher tolerable deviation rates to successively higher CRs as a means of identifying each control risk level with a tolerable deviation rate.

You also have learned about the links that connect tests of controls sampling for control risk assessment to substantive sampling for the audit of an account balance. These links are (1) the smoke/fire multiplier judgment that relates tolerable dollar misstatement in the substantive balance-audit sample to the anchor tolerable deviation rate in the test of controls sample and (2) methods that relate an audit judgment of risk of incorrect acceptance for the substantive balance-audit sample to the risk of incorrect acceptance consequences of assessing control risk too low. There is one more link: (3) considering the cost of the substantive balance-audit sample to decide the test of controls sample size and the planned control risk assessment. The **planned control risk assessment**, with the emphasis on *planned*, is the auditors' selection of a control risk level for which they want to justify a control risk assessment after completing the test of controls audit work. Conceptually, the auditor should pick that strategy of control testing combined with substantive tests of detail that minimizes total audit cost. This can be done formally through use of explicit cost assumptions or informally, for example, as in Exhibit 20–6. Most firms use the informal approach, probably to help facilitate implementation and a certain consistency and audit quality across all clients, and because cost estimates may not be that accurate.

20.19 What are the links that connect test of controls sample planning with substantive balance-audit sample planning?

20.20 When you have several alternative test of controls sample sizes to choose from, how do you choose the one to audit?

SUMMARY OF SAMPLING FOR TESTS OF CONTROLS

Statistical sampling for attributes in test of controls auditing provides quantitative measures of deviation rates and risks of assessing control risk too low. The statistics support the auditors' professional judgments involved in control risk assessment. The most important judgments are the numbers assigned to the tolerable rate of deviation, the risk of assessing control risk too low, and the risk of assessing control risk too high. With these specifications and an estimate of the deviation rate in the population, a preliminary sample size can be predetermined. However, nothing is magic about a predetermined sample size. It will turn out to be too few, just right, or too many, depending on the evidence produced by it and the control risk assessment supported by it.

The easy part of attribute sampling is the statistical evaluation. The hard parts are (1) specifying the controls for audit and defining deviations, (2) quantifying the decision criteria, (3) using imagination to find a way to select a random sample, and (4) associating the quantitative evaluation with the assessment of control risk. The structure and formality of the steps involved in statistical sampling force auditors to plan the procedures exhaustively. This same structure and formality also contribute to good working paper documentation because they clearly identify the things that should be recorded in the working papers. Altogether, statistical sampling facilitates auditors' plans, procedures, and evaluations of defensible evidence.

Part II: Audit of an Account Balance
· · · · · · · · · · · ·

Most of the account balances that appear in financial statements consist of numerous subsidiary accounts, some more numerous than others. Many of these accounts may be audited with sampling methods—auditing less than 100 percent of the subsidiary accounts within a control account balance or financial statement total for the purpose of determining the fair presentation of one or more of the financial statement assertions. Some examples of such accounts include:

- Cash: Usually not audited by sampling because there are few accounts. Might be sampled if a company has a large number of bank accounts.
- Accounts receivable: Usually audited by sampling when there are a modest to large number of customers.
- Inventory: Usually audited by sampling when there are a modest to large number of different inventory items.
- Fixed assets: Sampling may be used to audit numerous additions or an "inventory-taking" of fixed assets.
- Accounts payable: Some sampling used, but normally a judgment sample for missing payables.
- Notes payable: Usually not audited by sampling because of small number.

This short list and description of accounts, however, is not a description of relevant data populations for all assertions. For example, you would select a sample from the recorded accounts receivable to audit for the existence, rights, valuation, and presentation and disclosure assertions, but not for the completeness assertion. To audit for missing accounts receivable, the recorded ones are the wrong population! (A selection of shipping documents to determine whether receivables from customers had been recorded, or an audit of cash receipts in the period after year-end to detect receipts applicable to the prior year, could be proper samples for auditing for accounts receivable completeness.) Likewise, a selection of recorded accounts payable does not produce evidence of completeness of liabilities recordings. After all, the unrecorded liabilities are not in that population. (A selection of cash disbursements made after the year-end to identify ones applicable to year-end liabilities could be one proper sample for auditing for liability completeness.)

The audit of an account balance with dollar-value sampling has a different objective than test of controls auditing with attribute sampling. Test of controls sampling has the main objective of producing evidence about the rate of deviation from company control procedures for the purpose of assessing the control risk. Measuring the dollar effect of control deviations is a secondary consideration. On the other hand, a test of an account balance has the objective of producing direct evidence of dollar amounts of error in the account. This is called dollar-value sampling to indicate that the important unit of measure is dollar amounts. Sometimes, dollar-value sampling is called variables sampling just to distinguish it from attributes sampling and the control risk assessment objective.

There are two main types of dollar-value sampling. The one most frequently used in financial auditing is called dollar-unit sampling. This method is the subject covered here. The other method is known as classical sampling—a name attached merely to distinguish it from dollar-unit sampling. Classical sampling is discussed briefly at the end of this chapter. The method is called "classical" because it was used before dollar-unit sampling was developed, and because it depends on the well-known statistical mathematics of the normal distribution. Dollar-unit sampling, by contrast, does not depend upon the normal distribution statistics.

Before we get to the techniques of dollar-unit sampling, however, two topics of common application need to be expanded—the risk of incorrect acceptance and the risk of incorrect rejection.

RISK OF INCORRECT ACCEPTANCE

LEARNING OBJECTIVE
8. Calculate a risk of incorrect acceptance, given judgments about inherent risk, control risk, and analytical procedures risk, using the audit risk model in the Handbook Guideline on Materiality and Audit Risk (paragraph 23).

In Chapter 7 you saw the audit risk model expanded to include these terms:

$$AR = IR \times CR \times APR \times RIA$$

Dollar-value sampling for account balance auditing is primarily concerned with the risk of incorrect acceptance (RIA) in the risk model. The RIA is also called the test of details risk because it is the sampling risk of failing to detect a materiality magnitude of monetary error with audit procedures applied to the details (subsidiary units) in a control account. The other elements of the model are products of auditors' professional judgment.

The audit risk (AR) is the overall risk the auditor is willing to take of failing to discover material misstatement in the account. PA firms that quantify this risk usually set it at 0.05 or 0.10. Their policies are somewhat arbitrary because there is no overall theory acceptable in the practice world to justify any particular quantification of the audit risk. Five percent and 10 percent just seem to work adequately.

The inherent risk (IR) is the auditors' assessment of general factors relating to the probability of erroneous transactions entering the accounting system in the first place. It is hard to assess, often consisting of auditors' memory of no problems in previous audits or other aspects of the knowledge of the business. Some PA firms have questionnaires to document the findings of the know-the-business procedures and to translate them into an inherent risk assessment. PA firms that quantify this risk assign values from 0.30 to 1.00.

Analytical procedures were introduced in Chapter 4. They basically consist of all evidence-gathering procedures other than direct audit of account details. They are substantive procedures, as are the substantive tests of details, but they are not applied on a sample basis. Thus, there is frequently no mathematical way to measure their risk of failure. The analytical procedures risk in the model (APR) is the auditors' judgment of the probability that these nondetail procedures will fail to detect misstatement in the amount of tolerable misstatement in the account. PA firms that quantify this risk assign values from 0.30 to 1.0.

The control risk (CR) is the auditors' assessment of the quality of the client's control structure. Control risk assessment was explained in detail in Chapters 6 and

7. Some PA firms combine the inherent risk judgment and the control risk assessment into one factor.

These risk elements are considered independent, meaning that their combined risk can be a product (multiplication). While theoretical arguments of the validity of the model rage, several PA firms have built it into their sampling plans. They determine the risk of incorrect acceptance for a sampling application by first making AR, IR, CR, and APR judgments and assessments, then calculate the RIA:

$$\text{Maximum RIA} = 0.50, \text{if the equation produces RIA} > 0.50.$$

However, be forewarned: Not all PA firms or other audit organizations use the model in this fashion. Some quantify RIA for statistical sampling in the context of the client situation without reference to the model. Some say they do sampling without quantifying RIA. Some say they do audit sampling, but not statistical sampling. Practice varies.

The risk of incorrect acceptance influences statistical sample size calculations, and thus it is a prime determinant of the extent of substantive audit work. Exhibit 20–2 was presented to emphasize the effect of the audit risk model and its production of RIA on the substantive balance-audit sample sizes, as affected by the range of possible control risk assessments.

Notice the nonlinear change in sample size in relation to the evenly spaced (linear) control risk levels. From CR = 0.10 to CR = 0.20, the sample size increases by 30 sampling units (81 − 51), but from CR = 0.90 to CR = 1.00, the sample size increases by only 3 sampling units (143 − 140). The sample sizes are based on dollar-unit calculations for an account balance of $300,000 with a tolerable misstatement of $10,000.

· ·

R E V I E W
C H E C K P O I N T S

20.21 What is the objective of test of controls auditing with attribute sampling? test of a balance with dollar-value sampling?

20.22 Does use of the audit risk model to calculate RIA remove audit judgment from the risk determination process?

20.23 Is there any benefit to be gained from using the audit risk model to calculate RIA?

20.24 If audit risk (AR) is 0.015, inherent risk (IR) is 0.50, control risk (CR) is 0.30, and analytical procedures risk (APR) is 0.50, what risk of incorrect acceptance (RIA) is suggested by the expanded risk model?

· ·

RISK OF INCORRECT REJECTION
· · · · · · · · · · · ·

LEARNING OBJECTIVE
9. Explain the considerations in controlling the risk of incorrect rejection.

The other risk auditors accept in audit sampling is to decide that an account balance is misstated by more than the material misstatement when, in fact, but unknown to the auditors, it is not misstated by that much. Note this is the alpha risk. This can happen when the sample is not actually representative of the population from which it was drawn. An initial incorrect rejection decision will create an audit inefficiency because additional work will be done to determine the amount of an adjustment, and the auditors ordinarily will discover that the recorded amount was not materially misstated all along. The planning goal is to keep the risk of incorrect rejection low and also to keep the cost of the audit work within reasonable bounds. When planning the size of an audit sample, the judgment about the acceptable risk of incorrect rejection amounts to an incremental cost analysis.

You can minimize the risk of incorrect rejection by auditing a large sample—spending time and effort at the beginning with the initial sample size. Alternatively, you can take a smaller sample size and save time and cost; but this strategy will increase the risk of incorrect rejection. Taking more risk of incorrect rejection increases the likelihood of "rejection," in which case you may need to expand the sample or otherwise perform work later that you could have performed at the beginning with the initial sample. Thus, your cost trade-off relationship involves (*a*) the cost saved by taking a smaller initial sample, reduced by (*b*) the probability-weighted expected cost of needing to expand the sample or perform other types of audit procedures. These two elements taken together are the expected cost saving from taking more risk of incorrect rejection. Taking a chance on needing to expand the sample is important only if the cost (per item) is lower in the initial sample and higher (per item) when sample units are added later. (If these costs were equal, you could simply audit sample items one at a time until you reached a justifiable conclusion.)

The cost trade-off is based on probabilities, and these sometimes are hard to estimate. An audit manager may prefer to incur the additional cost in the first phase of work to avoid any possibility of additional cost of subsequent work. Cost aside, the auditors may not have time to select and audit additional items before the report deadline. For example, auditors may not have time to mail additional accounts receivable confirmations and wait two weeks for replies. Assessment of the risk of incorrect rejection also depends on the audit manager's preferences for cost and certainty, and on the time deadlines for completing the audit.

The risk of incorrect rejection pertains to audit efficiency. However, GAAS does not present a model or method for determining or thinking about this risk. GAAS also does not have anything to say about a "base RIR" or an "alternative RIR" used in planning a dollar-value audit sample.

. . . .

R E V I E W
CHECKPOINTS

20.25 Why is the risk of incorrect acceptance considered more critical than the risk of incorrect rejection in connection with audit decisions about an account balance?

20.26 What considerations are important for determining the risk of incorrect rejection?

20.27 What position is taken in generally accepted auditing standards with respect to the risk of incorrect rejection?

. . . .

DOLLAR-UNIT SAMPLING FOR ACCOUNT BALANCE AUDITING
. . . .

LEARNING OBJECTIVE
10. Explain the characteristics of dollar-unit sampling and its relationship to attribute sampling.

Dollar-unit sampling (DUS) is a modified form of attributes sampling that permits auditors to reach conclusions about dollar amounts as well as compliance deviations. Variations are called combined attributes-variables sampling (CAV), cumulative monetary amount sampling (CMA), monetary unit sampling (MUS), and sampling with probability proportional to size (PPS).

Recall the discussion of the point that the test of controls audit of control procedures based on attribute statistics did not directly incorporate dollar measurements. Hence, conclusions were limited to decisions about the rate of control deviations, which helped auditors assess the control risk. DUS is a sampling plan that attaches dollar amounts to attribute statistics. DUS is used widely by many accounting firms and other audit organizations for account balance auditing (variables sampling).

The unique feature of DUS is its definition of the population as the number of dollars in an account balance or class of transactions. Thus, in our example of auditing accounts receivable with a recorded amount (book value) of $300,000, the population is defined as 300,000 dollar units instead of as 1,500 customer accounts for classical sampling applications.

With this definition of the population, the audit is theoretically conducted on a sample of dollar units, and each of these sampling units is either right or wrong. This is the type of treatment given to control procedures in attribute sampling: a control procedure is either performed or not performed and there is either a deviation or no deviation, thus a rate of deviation is the statistical measure. However, DUS sampling adopts a convention for assigning dollar values to the deviations, and we will cover these calculations a little later in this chapter.

DUS was significantly enhanced for audit practice by Canadian practitioners, who wrote the first widely published manual on the techniques.[4] It is now the first choice of auditors throughout their domestic and international practices.

Use of Dollar-Unit Sampling (DUS)

All dollar-value sampling methods, including DUS, require basic audit judgments for audit risk (AR), inherent risk (IR), control risk (CR), and analytical procedures risk (APR) for the purpose of deriving the risk of incorrect acceptance (RIA). All these sampling methods, including DUS, require an audit judgment of material dollar misstatement (MM) for the account and an estimate of the misstatement (EM) the auditors think might exist in the account.

DUS has advantages in the form of overcoming some of the difficulties inherent in classical sampling plans, such as:

- An accurate estimate of a normal distribution standard deviation is required for classical sampling. DUS does not require this estimate because the statistical basis is the binomial distribution.

- Classical statistics estimators suffer problems of bias because a sufficient number of errors may not be found in a sample to permit proper use. DUS imposes no requirements for a minimum number of errors.

- Large sample sizes: DUS sample sizes are generally smaller than classical sampling sample sizes. (Smaller sample sizes are considered more efficient in most situations.)

- Complicated stratification plans: DUS sample selection methods accomplish stratification by automatically selecting a large proportion of high-value items.

There are still some critics of DUS, and here is their purported list of disadvantages (along with rebuttals to their arguments):

---

[4]   D.A. Leslie, A.D. Teitlebaum, and R.J. Anderson, *Dollar-Unit Sampling: A Practical Guide for Auditors* (Toronto: Copp Clark Pitman, 1979).

- Criticism: The DUS assignment of dollar amounts to errors is conservative (high) because rigorous mathematical proof of DUS upper error limit calculations has not yet been accomplished. Rebuttal: On the other hand, this provides the auditor with assurance that achieved RIA < planned RIA, and this helps ensure that actual or achieved audit risk is within the planned level. In fact, some practitioners treat this feature of DUS as an advantage because they know their primary objective of risk control is virtually guaranteed of being met.

- Criticism: DUS is not designed to evaluate financial account understatement very well. Rebuttal: On the other hand, no sampling estimator is considered very effective for understatement error. Auditors control this problem the same way that they control for the completeness assertion—through audits of related populations such as subsequent payments or subsequent collections.

The use of DUS in account balance auditing can be inferred from the advantages and disadvantages indicated above. DUS is clearly the best method to use when auditors expect to find few or no errors, and where the greatest risk of error is the risk that the book value is overstated. DUS has also been found to be a reliable estimator in more varied situations where there are more errors, and modifications are available for dealing with both understatement and overstatement of book values. As in any formal techniques, care is needed in using the procedure to make sure the formal requirements of the model are satisfied.

R E V I E W
CHECKPOINTS

20.28 What are some of the other names for types of dollar-unit sampling (DUS)?

20.29 What is the unique feature of dollar-unit sampling?

20.30 What are the advantages and disadvantages of DUS?

20.31 In what way does dollar-unit sampling resemble attribute sampling for control deviations?

DUS Sample Size Calculation

LEARNING OBJECTIVE
11. Calculate a dollar-unit sample size for the audit of the details of an account balance.

The same formula is used for substantive testing of details as for testing of controls: $n = R/P$. The only adjustment is that planned precision must be converted from a dollar amount to a rate or percentage as is used in control testing. This is achieved by simply dividing the planned precision in dollars by the recorded amount of the account balance.

The basic equation for calculating a DUS sample size for substantive testing of details is:

$$n = (RA * RF) / MM$$

where:

RA = Total recorded amount (book value) of the account balance.
RF = Poisson risk factor appropriate for the risk of incorrect acceptance (RIA).
MM = Material misstatement for the account balance.

Note that the above formula follows from $n = R/P$ if we let $P = MM/RA$. That is, planned precision P is represented as a rate in testing of details by dividing material misstatement by the reported amount of the account balance.

The recorded amount (RA) is the book balance of the account under audit—for example, a $300,000 accounts receivable total for 1,500 customers, subject to auditing by sampling.

The concept of material misstatement was covered in Chapter 5.

As in attributes sampling, alpha risk (RIR) is usually controlled indirectly following either or both of the following approaches: (*a*) select a number of errors greater than zero, and/or (*b*) use a planned precision that has been reduced by the amount of expected misstatement. For example, in using approach (*b*) assume that expected misstatement is EM, then planned precision to be used in the denominator in sample determination would be $(MM/RA - EM/RA) = (MM - EM)/RA$. Auditors that use this technique don't allow planned precision to get below one half of MM/RA. Note that firms using this rule and setting the number of errors = zero in Appendix 20A never plan higher than twice the discovery sample for the given RIA (RIA = 1 – confidence level). To illustrate, assume as before in Chapter 7 that MM = $10,000. Then a discovery sample size (the smallest possible for RIA = 1 percent) is $n = 4.61/(10000/300000) = 4.61/0.0334 = 139$ (round up to be conservative). If the auditor wishes to accept a sample with one error and all else remains unchanged, the sample size will be $n = 6.64/0.0334 = 199$. Note that since RIA and materiality are the same, what the auditor gets for this increased work is a reduction in RIR. (Remember Figure 20–4.)

The other way to reduce RIR is by adjusting planned precision P for expected misstatements (*EM*). As an illustration, assume $EM = 4000$, then sample size can be increased to $n = 4.61/((10000 - 4000)/300000) = 4.61/(0.0334 - 0.0134) = 4.61/0.02 = 231$.

Note that in the numerator we use the R value with zero errors since we are already controlling RIA through the tighter precision (0.02 vs. 0.0334) in the denominator. There is thus little need to combine the adjustment of planned precision approach with the zero errors approach in controlling RIR with DUS.

More formal, explicit approaches are available for controlling RIR and RIA simultaneously, but since the basic principles are the same, we do not cover these refinements here.

. . . .

R E V I E W
CHECKPOINTS

20.32 All other factors remaining the same, will DUS sample size be larger, smaller, or the same for a larger book balance?

20.33 All other factors remaining the same, will DUS sample size be larger, smaller, or the same for a larger risk of incorrect acceptance?

20.34 All other factors remaining the same, will DUS sample size be larger, smaller, or the same for a larger expected misstatement?

20.35 All other factors remaining the same, will DUS sample size be larger, smaller, or the same for a larger tolerable misstatement?

. . . .

Selecting the Sample

LEARNING OBJECTIVE

12. Describe a method for selecting a dollar-unit sample, define a "logical unit," and explain the stratification effect of dollar-unit selection.

DUS sampling unit selection is a type of systematic selection, very similar to the systematic selection method introduced for attribute sampling.

However, before sampling is started, auditors usually take some defensive auditing measures. They identify the individually significant units in the whole population and remove them for a 100 percent audit. In our example of auditing the $400,000 accounts receivable in the balance sheet of Kingston Company, the auditors could identify the six customer accounts over $10,000 (total amount of $100,000) and set them aside for audit. The cutoff size of $10,000 in this case corresponds to the material misstatement assigned to the accounts receivable audit. By being sure to audit each customer account whose balance exceeds the material misstatement, the auditors guard against the possibility of missing a material misstatement that might exist in a single subsidiary account. This leaves the remaining $300,000 of accounts receivable as the dollar value population (RA) subject to auditing by sampling.

To carry out a systematic DUS selection, you must calculate the sample size (n), then divide the population size (RA) by 1 minus the sample size to get a "skip interval" (k):

$$k = RA/(n - 1).$$

For example, in the audit of the Kingston Company accounts receivable, if the sample is 96 the skip interval is:

$$k = \$300,000/95 = \$3,157.90 \text{ (rounded to 3158)}$$

You use $n - 1$ as the denominator because the method of choosing the first and last random selections adds 1 to the sample size.

With one random start, you select every 3,158th dollar unit. Each time a $1 unit is selected, it hooks the logical unit that contains it. A **logical unit** is the ordinary accounting subsidiary unit that contains the dollar unit selected in the sample. In this example the logical unit is a customer's account. Obviously, all customer accounts with balances of $3,158 or more will be selected, and the larger units have a proportionately larger likelihood of selection than the smaller units. These phenomena of the selection method give DUS its high degree of stratification, with automatic selection of the high-value logical units. DUS samplers say the DUS selection hooks the largest logical units and places them in the sample.

In contrast, the classical sampling methods define the population as 1,500 logical units and gives each of them an equal likelihood of being selected for the sample. Thus, very large and very small customer balances will be in a classical sample of customer accounts receivable. On average, the number of dollars of the account balance in a classical sample will be smaller than the number hooked in a DUS sample. Indeed, the DUS systematic selection guarantees that all customer accounts larger than the skip interval (k) will be in the sample, but classical sampling selection of logical units carries no such guarantee. In our Kingston example all customers with balances over $3,158 will be in the sample. Furthermore, each logical unit has a probability of being in the sample in proportion to its size. That is, a $500 customer balance has twice the probability of selection as a $250 customer balance.

A mini-example of DUS selection is shown in the box below.

MINI-EXAMPLE OF DUS SYSTEMATIC SAMPLE SELECTION

This example is a takeoff on the Kingston Company example. Everything is reduced so that you can see the entire sample selection.

Assume Kingston II has $30,000 accounts receivable in 15 customer accounts, and you want to select a sample of 10 dollar units, which gives you a skip interval, $k = 30,000/9 = 3,333$.

We still start with a random number between 1 and 3,333, say 722, and this random number identifies the first sampled dollar. (The first one will not necessarily fall in the first account.)

You identify subsequent logical units by starting an "accumulator." The accumulator first takes a value of zero minus the starting number. In our example the accumulator is zero $- 722 = - 722$.

You then add the next logical unit account balances to the accumulator until it turns into a positive number. On the first round, when the balance in the second account is added, the accumulator turns positive: $- 722 + 3,500 = 2,778$. When the accumulator turns positive, the logical unit contains a dollar for the sample.

On the next round, you go to the "modified accumulator" by subtracting the skip interval; then add the subsequent logical unit balances until the accumulator turns positive again. The modified accumulator is $2,778 - 3,333 = - 555$, then the accumulator next becomes $- 555 + 1,965 = 1,410$, and this positive number identifies another sample dollar. (See the table in the next box.)

The process is repeated.

If the modified accumulator remains positive after subtracting the sampling interval, as it does at account #12, you have selected two dollar units in the same logical unit. Subtract the skip interval again before adding the next account balance.

20.36 What effect does the identification of individually significant logical units have on the size of the recorded amount population for dollar-unit sampling (DUS)?

20.37 How does DUS sample selection produce an automatic stratification of choosing the high-value logical units in a control account balance?

20.38 What happens when two dollar units for the sample fall in the same logical unit?

Account Number	Account Balance	Accumulator	Modified Accumulator	Dollar Selected	Logical Unit
1	$ 750	− 722		1st	$ 750
2	3,500	2,778	− 555	3,334th	3,500
3	1,965	1,410	−1,923	6,667th	1,965
4	2,400	477	−2,856	10,000th	2,400
5	949	−1,907			
6	563	−1,344			
7	1,224	− 120			
8	3,211	3,091	− 242	13,333rd	3,211
9	2,961	2,719	− 614	16,666th	2,961
10	1,622	1,008	−2,325	19,999th	1,622
11	7,200	4,875	1,542	23,332*	7,200
			−1,791	26,665*	
12	1,199	− 592			
13	1,000	408	−2,925	29,998th	1,000
14	500	−2,425			
15	956	−1,469			_____
	$30,000				

Total of logical units in the sample of 10 dollar units $24,609

*Two dollar units in the same logial unit.

The "dollar selected" column starts with the random start at 722 and adds 3,333 each time a dollar is selected in the sample.

*Two dollar units in the same logical unit.

This is a selection routine for manual application. It may seem complicated at first glance, but it is really not hard to do with a calculator. When populations are on computer files, a routine like this one can be programmed to make the sample selection.

EXPRESS THE ERROR EVIDENCE IN DOLLARS

LEARNING OBJECTIVE
13. Calculate an upper error limit for the evaluation of dollar-value evidence, and discuss the relative merits of alternatives for determining an amount by which a monetary balance should be adjusted.

The problem with attribute sampling is how to express the results in terms of a deviation rate instead of in dollars. In an audit context, expressing results in dollars is more meaningful when the audit objective is a decision about the fair presentation of a balance expressed in dollars. Therefore, dollar-unit sampling adopts some conventions for expressing the error evidence in dollars.

The first step is to determine of an average sampling interval. This amount is slightly different from the sample selection skip interval. The **average sampling interval (ASI)** is:

$$ASI = \frac{RA}{n}$$

In our example of the audit of Kingston Company's accounts receivable with a sample of 96 customer accounts:

$$ASI = \$300,000/96 = \$3,125$$

You can work with ASI instead of the skip interval if you remember that the first random dollar is selective from the first interval of dollar units (in this case, 3125 dollar units) and then simply add 3125 a total of $n - 1$ times (in this case 95 times) to select $n - 1$ additional dollar units.

Calculate an Upper Error Limit (UEL): The No-error Case

The upper error limit (UEL) is a statistical estimate of the greatest amount of dollar error that might exist in an account balance, with a likelihood (risk of incorrect acceptance) that the actual amount of error might be even greater. The easiest UEL calculation arises when the sample is audited and no dollar misstatements are discovered. Then the calculation is:[5]

$$UEL = ASI * RF$$

In our example suppose the auditors audited 96 of Kingston's customers' accounts and found nothing wrong, no misstatements or arguments. If the auditors wish to evaluate the "greatest amount of error that might exist" at a risk of incorrect acceptance of 0.17, they will find the Poisson risk factor for RIA = 0.17 and zero errors in Appendix 20A, which is 1.77, and calculate the upper error limit:

$$UEL = ASI * RF$$
$$= \$3,125 * 1.77$$
$$= \$5,531$$

This calculation follows from our basic formula $R = n * P$, except now we solve for P instead of for n as we do at the sample size determination stage. That is, $P = R/n = 1.77/96 = 0.0184375$. This is the achieved UEL represented as a rate or percentage (keep in mind the attributes sampling theory basis for DUS). How do we convert this to a dollar amount? Simple! Multiply by RA: 0.0184375 * $300,000 = $5,531. Remember we divided by RA to convert precision to a percentage. So now we must multiply by RA to convert UEL to a dollar amount.

The risk of incorrect acceptance (RIA) represented by the choice of the Poisson risk factor should be the RIA derived from the risk model the auditor uses to plan the audit work. This RIA is one of the auditors' decision criteria for accepting the book value as materially accurate or for rejecting it as appearing to contain a material misstatement. The calculated upper error limit is similar to an attribute sampling computed upper error limit (that's why we represent both by UEL). The auditor can say: "Based on the quantitative evidence, I estimate the greatest amount of error in the population is UEL (rate of deviation for UEL), with a likelihood of RIA [beta risk] that the amount of misstatement error [or in the case of attitude sampling, the rate of deviation] might be greater." The RIA represents the risk associated with DUS. Of course, there are other sources of evidence that may have been used to derive a particular RIA that is less than AR. The risk model reflects these other sources. So, although 1 − RIA reflects the

---

[5] There are other methods for calculating a dollar-unit sampling UEL. They are more complicated and require a computer.

assurance provided by DUS, the total assurance from control-reliance, analytical-review procedures as well as DUS is 1 − AR.

The UEL must have a reference point for meaning something. The reference point is the material misstatement (MM) assigned to the account, and it is the other decision criterion. You can use it with an "upper error limit decision rule," as expressed in the box.

UPPER ERROR LIMIT DECISION RULE

Using actual sample data, calculate the upper error limit of monetary misstatement. Compare this UEL to the material misstatement decision amount. If the UEL is larger, make the "rejection" decision. If the UEL is smaller, make the "acceptance" decision. Note the decision is based on the amount considered material, MM, not the planned precision, which may be less than material in order to control RIR.

Using this UEL decision rule in our Kingston Company example, where the RIA is 0.17 and the tolerable misstatement is $10,000, the decision is that the evidence shows the $300,000 accounts receivable does not appear to contain a material misstatement. The UEL of $5,531 at RIA = 0.17 is less than the material misstatement.

The phenomenon of measuring a UEL amount of misstatement when no errors were found in the sample is a reflection of the partial knowledge given by a sample from the population instead of knowledge of the entire population. Similarly, in attribute sampling for detail test of controls, a UEL greater than zero is expressed even when no deviations are found in a sample. This kind of measurement of sampling error is frequently called further misstatement remaining undetected in the balance. Auditors can take it into account by calculating the UEL measurement.

The zero-error UEL measurement is actually a reflection of the sufficiency of audit evidence as represented by the size of the sample audited. If the sample size is very small, indicating limited knowledge of the population, the ASI will be large, and the UEL will be high. In these circumstances, the failure of the upper error limit decision rule (i.e., UEL greater than MM) is an indication of not enough evidence (sample size too small).

Calculate an Upper Error Limit (UEL): When Errors Are Found

When a dollar-unit sample is audited, the auditors determine (1) the dollar amount of difference between the book value and the audit value of the logical unit—the account or invoice—that contains the sampled dollar, and (2) the ratio of this difference to the recorded amount of the logical unit. This ratio is called the **tainting percentage or taint %**:

$$\text{Taint \%} = (\text{Book value} - \text{Audit value})/(\text{Book value})$$

The tainting percentage is the DUS device for departing from the all-or-nothing, error-no-error measurement of attribute sampling. The theory is that a $1 unit is

E X H I B I T 20–5   THREE ILLUSTRATIVE ERRORS

Customer	Book Value	Audit Value	Difference	Taint Percent
1,425	$1,000	$200	$ 800	80%
310	3,000	300	2,700	90
963	2,000	500	1,500	75

E X H I B I T 20–6   UEL CALCULATION (RIA = 0.17)

	Basic Error Likely Error and PGW Factors	×	Tainting Percentage	×	Average Sampling Interval	=	Dollar Measurement
1. Basic error (0)	1.77		100.00%		$3,125		$ 5,531
2. Most likely error:							
First error	1.00		90.00		3,125		$2,813
Second error	1.00		80.00		3,125		2,500
Third error	1.00		75.00		3,125		2,344
Projected likely error							7,657
3. Precision gap widening:							
First error	0.44		90.00		3,125		1,238
Second error	0.32		80.00		3,125		800
Third error	0.27		75.00		3,125		633
							2,671
Total upper error limit (0.17 risk of incorrect acceptance)							$15,859

being audited, but each $1 unit is imbedded in a larger logical unit. A logical unit can be partially in error, and this part is attributed to all the dollars in the unit, including the "sampling unit dollar." Thus, a sampling unit dollar can be wrong in part—the tainting percentage.

Look at the three illustrative errors from the audit of Kingston's accounts receivable in Exhibit 20–5. The first account had a book value of $1,000, but the auditors determined that the recorded amount should be $200. The customer's account is overstated by 80 percent (tainted with error), and so is the $1 sampling unit in it. The other two errors reflect 90 percent and 75 percent overstatement errors. The Taint % for a particular account is represented as t_1 where the subscript **1** refers to a specific account or line item.

The calculation of UEL when errors are found is a combination of Poisson risk factors (RF), tainting percentages t_1, and the average sampling interval (ASI). Exhibit 20–6 shows a UEL calculation assuming an audit of 96 dollar units from Kingston Company's $300,000 accounts receivable, when the three errors in Exhibit 20–5 were found.

The "basic error," calculated using the RF for the zero-error case, is the underlying sampling error associated with the sample size. It is weighted by a 100 percent tainting under the assumption that the maximum overstatement of a dollar unit is its recorded amount.

Next, the errors are put in descending order of their tainting percentages, the largest first and the smallest last. These are given a "likely error" factor of 1.0. The sum of 1.0 × respective tainting percentages × ASI for the errors is called the "projected likely error." This is the auditor's estimate of error based on the actual errors discovered ($5,000 = $800 + $2,700 + $1,500) projected to the population as $7,657.

The "precision gap widening (PGW)" is in addition to the sampling error generated by finding errors in the sample. These factors are in Appendix 20A. They bear a direct relationship to the Poisson risk (UEL) factors in Appendix 20A. Each PGW is the difference between the risk (UEL) factor for the error number and the risk (UEL) factor for the error number that preceded it minus 1.0 (the risk factor assigned to the actual error). Thus, the PGW for the first error at RIA = 0.17 is 0.44 = 3.21 − 1.77 − 1.00.

In terms of our UEL decision rule test of the accounts receivable, it appears that Kingston's $300,000 accounts receivable may contain more than $10,000 material misstatement because the UEL of $15,859 is greater than $10,000 at risk of incorrect acceptance of 0.17. In other words, there is a 0.17 probability that overstatement in the receivables exceeds $15,859, when the auditors wanted to achieve a probability of 0.17 that misstatement could exceed only $10,000. We therefore have the "rejection" decision.

Exhibit 20–6 calculations can be summarized by the following formula: $(1/n) * (R_0 + ((R_1 − R_0) * t_1) + ((R_2 − R_1) * t_2) + ((R_3 − R_2) * t_3)) * RA = (1/n) * (R_0 + ((1 + PGW_1) * t_1) + ((1 + PGW_2) * t_2) + ((1 + PGW_3) * t_3)) * RA = (1/n) * RA * (R_0 + t_1 + t_2 + t_3 + PGW_1 * t_1 + PGW_2 * t_2 + PGW_3 * t_3) = ((RA/n) * R) + ((RA/n) * (t_1 + t_2 + t_3)) + ((RA/n) * ((PGW_1 * t_1) + (PGW_2 * t_2) + (PGW_3 * t_3))) =$ Basic Error + Most Likely Error + Precision Gap Widening where Basic Error $= ((RA/n) * R_0)$, Most Likely Error $= ((RA/n) * (t_1 + t_2 + t_3))$, and Precision Gap Widening $= ((RA/n) * ((PGW_1 * t_1) + (PGW_2 * t_2) + (PGW_3 * t_3)))$. Note that (RA/n) is the Sampling Interval.

Although the above calculations may look rather complicated, they follow from the same evaluation formula used in testing of controls. Recall that achieved UEL in testing of controls for k errors found in the sample is $P = R/n$ where R is the Poisson risk factor for the specified beta risk and "k" errors using Appendix 20A. This can be rewritten as follows:

$$R/n = (1/n) * (R_0 + \sum_{i=1}^{K} (R^1 − R_{i-1}) * 1) = \text{achieved UEL as a rate}$$

In variables sampling, instead of just working with 0 and 1 values of attribute sampling (i.e., in the formula above there were k errors, or k "1" values, which determined the achieved UEL), one replaces the "1s" with the concept of taintings. That is, instead of 1 use a tainting:

$$t_i = (BV_i − AV_i) / BV_i$$

It's through the concept of the tainting or fractional error that DUS is converted from a pure attributes sampling model to a variable sampling model that measures the total possible dollar error in a population.

The tainting concept has an interesting history. When DUS was first developed by Dutch statistician Dr. Van Heerden, he viewed it as a purely attributes sampling model applied to monetary units. There is no limit to how small the monetary unit can be, so the initial idea was to apply it to the smallest denomination, say the penny. In penny unit sampling you can apply strict attribute sampling because monetary error recorded is reducible only to the nearest penny. Thus, either a penny is in error or not. For example, suppose we have an accounts receivable recorded balance of 543.37, and we confirm that the actual amount is 347.85. Thus, under penny unit sampling, 34,285 of the recorded pennies are "correct" while 54,337 − 34,785 = 19,552 of the pennies are completely in error—that is, there is a 19,552/54,337 = 36 percent recorded penny deviation rate in the account. From this perspective we can view the entire accounts receivable population as having a certain attributes deviation rate and attributes sampling is perfectly appropriate under such an interpretation. The only thing the auditor would have to do is develop a convention to decide which penny of Account A has been selected: one of the 19,552 pennies in error, or one of the 34,785 not in error. On selecting Account A and determining the error, the auditor would have to use a consistent convention—for example, the in-error pennies can be assumed always at the head of the sequence of recorded pennies, such as the first 19,552 recorded pennies are considered in error, not the last or the ones in the middle. Any consistent convention will do as long as the pennies in error continue having the same probability of being selected. Under such a convention there would be no need to modify any of the formulas used in testing of controls.

The difficulty with such an approach is that it may be impractical. For instance, if on following the convention the auditor knows of the $195.52 error but because of the convention he or she happens to select a penny not considered in error, the auditor would have to ignore this error. The auditor would be hard put to defend such an action in court!

The problem is that although such a convention is statistically valid, it is so in the long-term frequency sense, and the auditor has to consider the evidence in the specific case. So as a compromise auditors have developed the convention that when an account error is selected the errors are presumed averaged in every monetary unit in the account. For this reason the tainting is calculated and assumed to apply to every dollar-unit, or penny-units, or whatever, in the misstated account. This approach maximizes the information obtained from the sample. While this latter convention makes the treatment of errors in a given situation more acceptable to the auditor, and it closely approximates the "pure" convention of Van Heerden, it does deviate from pure attribute sampling theory. Nevertheless, much research has shown this approach to result in conservative DUS bounds (the actual RIA is less than the planned level, or to put it another way the actual confidence level of DUS is greater than planned). This bias is acceptable and even considered preferable by many auditors because it means that the assurance they're getting from DUS is actually somewhat higher than what the formulas indicate.

Calculate the Projected Likely Misstatement

The whole point of quantitative evidence evaluation is to extend the findings from the sample to the entire population. The first step is to calculate the **projected likely misstatement**, which is the auditors' best estimate of misstatement based on the errors found in the sample. You can see the projected likely misstatement (PLM) of $7,657 in the middle of Exhibit 20–6.

Auditors are supposed to think about the amount of PLM in relation to the material misstatement (MM) and consider whether there may be "further misstatement remaining undetected." The difference between UEL and PLM ($8,202 = $15,859 − $7,657) is the DUS quasi-statistical measurement of sampling error and the "further misstatement remaining undetected."

The PLM measurement plays a significant role in the auditors' problem of deciding upon an amount to recommend for adjustment when they have made a "rejection" decision.

Determine the Amount of an Adjustment

The problem of determining the amount to recommend for adjustment is troublesome because auditors usually do not know the exact amount of misstatement in an account. When the evidential base is a random sample, the three measurable aspects of monetary misstatement are (1) known misstatement, (2) projected likely misstatement, and (3) possible misstatement—the "further misstatement remaining undetected."

Quantitative Considerations

The known misstatement is the sum of the actual dollar error found in the sample. The projected likely misstatement is a calculation based on the known misstatements. Neither of these is affected by the auditors' risk of incorrect acceptance criterion. However, the possible misstatement may be large or small depending upon the RIA specification. This makes "possible misstatement" a slippery concept.

In our example of the audit of Kingston's accounts receivable, we have:

$$\text{Known misstatement} = \$5,000$$

$$\text{Projected likely misstatement} = \$7,657$$

$$\text{Possible misstatement} = \$8,202 \ (\text{at RIA} = 0.17)$$

The calculation of these components was illustrated earlier via the basic framework.

Auditing standards and practice contain no hard and fast rules for determining the amount of adjustment in sampling situations. Several measures of adjustment amounts can be derived from the data. Various sources have suggested the following:

- Adjust the amount of the known misstatement, in this case $5,000. Usually, the actual amount of known misstatement is smaller than the material misstatement. Often, this adjustment is too small and leaves too much potential for remaining error (in this case $10,859 = $15,859 − $5,000) is left unadjusted.

- Adjust the amount of the projected misstatement, in this case $7,657. The point estimate of likely misstatement is considered the best single-value measurement available for recommending an adjustment to the client.

- In addition to adjusting for the projected likely misstatement amount, also adjust the amount of the possible misstatement, in this case another $8,202. This sum is the largest one an auditor can measure using the risk of incorrect acceptance in the audit plan. It contains an element of statistical measurement that auditors and clients may or may not be willing to accept for adjustment purposes.

- Adjust by the amount of material misstatement when the sum of projected and possible misstatement exceeds material misstatement, in this case $10,000. This kind of rule is somewhat arbitrary and is subject to question when the sum exceeds $2 \times$ material misstatement.

- Adjust by the amount that the sum of projected and possible misstatement exceeds material misstatement, in this case $5,859 ($15,859 − $10,000). The theory here is that the amount of misstatement left in the account balance after adjustment will not exceed material misstatement ($10,000). This measure is somewhat arbitrary.

Statistical projections are used for adjustment recommendations. Adjustments for known misstatements or projected misstatement have the most empirical and theoretical support. It can be shown that for any amount of error, sample size can be increased sufficiently so that adjusting for projected misstatements will always reduce the remaining error to less than a material amount at the stated confidence level. Of course, if the auditor cannot increase the sample size sufficiently, then the theoretically best available adjustment is not an option and the auditor may have to rely on other audit procedures to determine the amount of adjustment or to make the appropriate reservation in the auditor's report.

Not too much is known about PA firms' use of statistical adjustments in financial audits, but, as noted in the next box, tax auditors may use such measures.

STATISTICAL SAMPLING BECOMES A TOOL IN AUDITS OF MULTINATIONAL CONCERNS

The IRS often tries to save resources in audits by projecting tax errors from samples of company data. It does this for travel and entertainment deductions. Now, the IRS is using sampling in challenging prices that a company charges for items sold to foreign subsidiaries. In such cases the IRS claims that a parent company is avoiding U.S. tax by undercharging its foreign units.

In a tax court dispute, Halliburton Company says the IRS was seeking to raise its income by $62.5 million for alleged underbilling; $29.5 million of the amount is from "adjustment for statistical sampling population." The pending case shows that the IRS is using sampling more aggressively.

Source: The Wall Street Journal, February 18, 1987.

As noted above, research suggests that adjusting for projected misstatement is a valid way of maintaining objective control of sampling risk after adjustment. For example, in Exhibit 20–6 after adjusting accounts receivable for projected likely error of 7657, a legitimate post-adjusted UEL with an RIA of 17 percent is 15859 − 7657 = 8202—which would be an acceptable UEL under our decision rule.

What happens if the difference between UEL and projected likely error is greater than material? Then, clearly an adjustment based on projected likely error would not be sufficient. One way to develop an objective adjustment is to increase sample size. It can be shown that no matter how much error there is in the population, the difference between UEL and projected likely error will be reduced as the sample size is increased. This means that theoretically there is a large enough sample size so that adjusting for projected likely error will ensure that adjusted UEL is less than material and thus acceptable at the stated RIA level (or equivalently at a confidence level of 1 − RIA). Of course, as noted above, the auditor may not always be able to increase sample size as much as he or she needs.

Nonquantitative Considerations

You can see that much latitude exists for determining the amount of an adjustment to recommend. Often the amount recommended for one account depends on adjustment amounts recommended for other accounts. Auditors typically consider the findings in other audit areas when recommending adjustments.

The special characteristics of the accounts also must be considered. For example, in some cases the actual misstatement (overstatement in our Kingston accounts receivable example) may consist of overcharges to customers and undercharges from sales that were underbilled or simply not invoiced to customers (understatements). Management may make a policy decision not to try to recover the underbilled or unbilled amounts, so the audit manager then must deal with all the overstatement error instead of a smaller net overstatement. Other accounts may be different. For example, both overstatements and understatements in an inventory valuation may be adjustable simply by correcting the records, and no one needs to take customer relations into account.

Even though the lack of a definitive rule on "how to figure the amount of an adjustment" has revealed the lack of science in auditing, we can close the discussion with a more definite statement: As a general rule, all actual misstatements discovered in accounts audited completely should be adjusted, provided the amounts are material. The *CICA Handbook* provides additional guidance, but first we must consider the case of both overstatement and understatement in the sample results.

. . . .

R E V I E W
C H E C K P O I N T S

20.39 Suppose you have audited a $600,000 recorded amount of inventory with a sample of 100 dollar units and their logical units, and found no errors. What is the UEL at RIA = 0.05? RIA = 0.10? RIA = 0.25? RIA = 0.50?

20.40 What is the risk-related interpretation of each of the UELs you calculated in 13.39 above?

20.41 What is the UEL for the audit of 96 dollar units from the $300,000 accounts receivable, given the errors shown in Exhibit 20–6, for RIA = 0.48? for RIA = 0.05? What interpretation can you give to these UELs?

20.42 If you had to pick the one best measure for an amount to recommend for adjustment based on a sample, which one would you choose?

20.43 Why do you think the auditing profession has no definite rules for deciding the amount of an adjustment?

. . . .

Overstatement and Understatement

When both overstatement and understatement errors are discovered, you need to combine them properly. The calculations are not difficult.[6] According to Leslie, Teitlebaum, and Anderson:

---

[6] The purpose of these calculations is to take into account both overstatement and understatement errors. It is not valid to (*a*) net the sample errors themselves and project the net error or (*b*) net the two total upper error limits to arrive at a net upper error limit. Actually, the calculations described in this chapter are the simplest of other more complex calculations.

1. Calculate separately the gross projected likely error (GPLEO) and the total upper error limit (TUELO) for overstatements, using an array of error taints only of the overstatement errors, ignoring understatement errors.

2. Calculate separately the gross projected likely error (GPLEU) and the total upper error limit (TUELU) for understatements, using an array of error taints only of the understatement errors, ignoring overstatement errors.

3. Calculate the net projected likely error (PLEN) by finding the net amount of the two gross projected likely error amounts, keeping track of whether the net amount is overstatement or understatement.

$$PLEN = GPLEO - GPLEU$$

4. Calculate the net upper limits (NUELO for overstatement and NUELU for understatement) by reducing each gross upper error limit (GUEL) by the gross projected likely error (GPLE) of the opposite direction of misstatement, that is:

$$NUELO = TUELO - GPLEU$$

$$NUELU = TUELU - GPLEO$$

The following example uses the overstatement amounts calculated in the preceding Kingston accounts receivable example and some hypothetical understatement amounts.

	Projected Likely Error	Upper Error Limit
Gross errors:		
Overstatements	$7,657	$15,859
Understatements	5,000	10,000
Net errors:		
Overstatements	2,657	10,859
Understatements	N/A = 0	2,343

NA means not applicable.

Now you can say that with risk of incorrect acceptance equal to the risk used to calculate both overstatement and understatement estimates, (1) the most likely misstatement amount is PLEN = $2,657 overstatement, but (2) the misstatement could be between NUELO = $10,859 overstatement and NUELU = $2,343 understatement. Since material misstatement for the receivables is $10,000, the total $300,000 appears to be materially misstated because the net upper error limit for overstatement exceeds $10,000.

With this background we can now develop operational guidelines for DUS adjustments consistent with the *Handbook*.

Audit Adjustments as per *Handbook*

According to *Handbook Section* 5130.37, the auditor should estimate a *likely* aggregate misstatement by aggregating:

    a. Known errors on other than representative samples.

    b. Projection of misstatements on representative (e.g., statistical) samples (i.e., PLENs in DUS).

    c. Disagreements with accounting estimates.

    d. Net effect of uncorrected misstatements in opening equity. (Note that this can include *projections* of misstatements in some accounts, e.g., beginning inventory.)

As noted in *Handbook Section* 5130.35, the above types of errors are aggregated in stages: in each stage the auditor determines whether the misstatement for each balance or class of transactions is material. If not, the auditor proceeds until the highest level of aggregation (net income, net assets) is reached.

If at any stage the auditor estimates a material likely aggregate misstatement, then the auditor should:

    a. Arrange for the client to recheck the areas that contain the largest misstatements. OR

    b. Perform additional audit procedures (expand audit testing). OR

    c. Insist on an adjustment. OR

    d. Issue a report reservation (*Handbook Section* 5130.36–.41).

An illustration of an adjustment based on known errors is given in Chapter 13. This example, however, does not consider projections or representative sample results.

The general rule in developing an adjustment policy for projections of errors based on statistical sampling is as follows (using the terminology in DUS mechanics):

1. If PLEN > materiality (situation 3 of guideline), the auditor should insist on adjustment or, failing that, qualify the report. Note that PLEN is the same as = "Likely aggregate misstatement" (LAM) of the Risk and Materiality Guideline in the *Handbook*.

2. If UEL net > materiality, but PLEN < materiality (situation 2 of guideline), then the auditor will normally have to do further audit work in order to obtain more persuasive evidence that material errors do not exist. Under this condition it is already improbable that (PLEN) material errors exist (since most likely errors projection lies below materiality) and so qualification may not be justified. But it is *not sufficiently improbable* without further work to justify a clear opinion (unless management agrees to some adjustments). Net UELs are also referred to as possible errors and in the risk and materiality guideline as further possible misstatements (less those due to nonsampling error). Since by definition nonsampling error is impossible to measure objectively (e.g., the degree to which auditors inaccurately "take a random sample"), they are not explicitly considered in any formula.

The types of adjustments possible include the following:

1. Adjust for known errors only.
   Note this can be applied to reduce both PLEN and UEL by the known errors. The auditor can then use the above decision rules to decide if the population is acceptable after adjustment.

2. Adjust for PLEN.

Note this reduces adjusted PLEN to zero and likely brings UEL to below materiality as well. If that is the case, the auditor can then accept the population after the adjustment.

3. Adjust for anything between zero and PLEN, depending on negotiations with client.

    Note that this is going to be influenced by factors such as the degree of leverage the auditor has over management, and the degree to which auditors incur nonsampling error. (e.g., how many of the "sample errors" do they decide to "isolate" and therefore ignore in making projections?) So, as you can see, significant professional judgment is involved in making adjustment decisions.

4. No adjustment necessary: situation 1 of the Guideline is comparable to the case UEL < materiality.

DISCLOSURE OF SAMPLING EVIDENCE
· · · · · · · · · · · ·

Generally accepted auditing standards do not require independent auditors to disclose anything about their audit sampling applications in their reports on audited financial statements. Auditors' determinations of risk, materiality, tolerable misstatement, sample selection, sample coverage of the population, and other details are

---

XYZ ORGANIZATION

Schedule of Findings and Questioned Costs

	Department of Energy: Heating Assistance for for Low-income Persons	Department of Health and Human Services: ABC Program
Number of items in population	234	1
Number of items tested	30	1
Number of items not in compliance	1	1
Dollar amount of population	$53,330	$ 2,826
Dollar amount of items tested	9,210	$ 2,826
Dollar amount of items not in compliance	$ 202	$ 2,826
Amount of questioned costs	$ 202	$ 2,176

Department of Energy:

   Documentation of verification of low-income status of one grant recipient could not be located. The cost of the assistance may be disallowed.

Department of Health and Human Services:

   The organization exceeded the approved advertising budget ($65), received an oral authorization, but did not request a written budget modification ($2,176). The program has agreed to accept the overexpenditure.

Source: CPA firm accounting and auditing bulletin, May 1991.

private auditor information. Consequently, users of financial reports are unable to judge the appropriateness of auditors' decision criteria and evidence evaluation.

However, the Office of Management and Budget audit report requirements (OMB Circular A-133) in the United States include some very interesting sampling disclosures. Among the information required to be reported is a "Schedule of Findings and Questioned Costs" related to government grant programs. The format shown in the next box is an illustration of the OMB requirement for the disclosure of sampling information. The XYZ Organization (e.g., a state agency) uses funds from two federal programs.

This illustration offers some information for statistical analysis. Although the schedule does not tell users whether the sample was random, assume that it was a dollar-unit (DUS) sample. (The average sampling unit was $307 = $9,210/30, whereas the average population item amount was $228 = $53,330/234, indicating a DUS-type weighting toward the higher-valued units.)

A user could derive the following:

$$\text{Average sampling interval (ASI)} = \$53,330/30 = \$1,778$$

$$\text{Actual errors} = \text{one } 100\% \text{ error of lack of documentation}$$

The projected likely error (lack of documentation and possible disallowed cost), applying the sample evidence to the whole population, is $1,778 = UEL weight (1.0) × tainting percentage (100%) × ASI ($1,778).

Calculation of the UEL requires an assumption about the risk of incorrect acceptance. Assume that 0.05 is appropriate, then:

	UEL Factor	×	Taint Percent	×	ASI	=	Dollar Amount
Basic error	3.00		100%		$ 1,778		$5,334
PLM	1.00		100		1,778		1,778
Precision gap widening (PGW)	0.75		100		1,78		1,334
Upper error limit at 0.05 risk							$8,446

Note: The illustrative disclosure does not suggest that the auditors projected the sample findings to the population. The disclosure suggests that a minor amount of cost ($202) was questioned in the Department of Energy program. However, government auditors, like the IRS auditors cited earlier, will not stop at the seemingly minor amount of actual error discovered in a sample. They want to know the amount that might be wrong with the entire population, and in this case the amount could be large. A sample-based projection might become the basis for a claim for refund of federal funds. Then the XYZ Organization could try to defend its proper control and stewardship over federal grants!

A Canadian example of the usefulness of statistical sampling is given in the following box.

PROVINCE CHARGES UNIVERSITY WITH LACK OF FISCAL CARE

The University of Toronto is careless in the control of its assets, says the 1990 provincial audit.

According to the annual report, the university could not account for 40 percent of its $310 million inventory, and lost money in the disposal of several assets.

The UofT comptroller's ledger gave no location or an unspecific location for $127 million worth of the university's equipment and furniture, said Rudolph Chiu, who managed the audit for the province. A location such as "Simcoe Hall," which has over 100 offices, was considered too vague.

The university could not find one-third of a sample of 73 items which were identified by room number, serial number, or model number. Missing items included video recorders, personal computers, cameras, and electronic equipment.

One department signed a statement verifying its possession of a computer, but would not allow the auditor to follow-up with an on-site inspection. The department claimed "it had just thrown it away the day before," said Chiu.

The University Vice-President of Administration said that the estimate of a 40 percent loss was invalid because the sample from which the percentage was derived was too small.

There's no question we do not have an adequate way of checking inventory, he added, "But it would cost us over a million dollars a year to hire someone to go out and physically check the equipment." Budget reductions in 1979 forced the university to eliminate the three accounting positions responsible for checking inventory.

The report also criticized the university for failing to adhere to its own policy in the sale of equipment. The policy requires that the item be advertised and that a fair price be determined by the university purchasing department. If the sale is to an employee or relative of an employee, the sale must be approved by a university vice-president.

In one case, a six-month-old truck was sold unadvertised to a university employee at a 45 percent discount. One year later, the value of the truck was still higher than the sale price.

Criddle faulted an Ottawa truck dealer who had given the purchasing department too low a price on the truck. "The words [the auditor] chose give the wrong impression," he said.

"It's not a question of the university being careless," he said, "It's a question of people not following policy. That doesn't surprise me. In a place this size there are a lot of procedures people don't realize exist."

He emphasized that the audit did not criticize the university for losing money, only for failing to adhere to its procedures.

Source: Kate Zernike, *The Newspaper,* December 5, 1990. Reprinted with permission from *The Newspaper,* University of Toronto's Independent Community newspaper.

An interesting statistical question raised by the preceding article relates to the quote by the university vice-president that the 40 percent loss is invalid because the sample size is too small. There are several ways to analyse this comment for its validity. One is to compute a DUS sample size based on, say, 95 percent confidence level and a materiality percentage of 40 percent. This yields, using Appendix 20A, and our formula:

$$n = \frac{R}{P} = \frac{3.0}{.4} = 7.5 \text{ or } 8.$$

for a discovery sample size. Doubling this to control for alpha risk still leaves a sample size well under what the internal auditors used.

Another approach is to solve for the amount of error that would be considered material at sample size of 73 and 95 percent confidence level (i.e., RIA = .05), and working backwards solve $73 = 3.0/P$. This yields a materiality of $P = 3.0/73 = .041$. In other words the sample size was sufficient to detect an error rate of 4.1 percent or higher at 95 percent confidence level. Several other analytical approaches could be followed, but they all point to the same consistent conclusion: the provincial auditor is likely correct and the 40 percent loss estimate is not invalid. Or, to put it in a more intuitive way, if you lost 40% of your belongings in a burglary you would realize it much more quickly than if, say, 1% of your belongings were missing.

There are a number of other statistical issues discussed in Appendix 20C. They include use of statistical regression in analytical review, use of DUS for compliance testing, and a more statistical interpretation of the audit risk model. It should be clear by now, however, that statistical auditing can help put auditing on a more scientific basis.

Summary

Statistical sampling requires knowledge of the underlying statistical calculations and relationships and a certain amount of faith in the mathematics. Auditors are entitled to hold a statistical result at arm's length and study it for its face validity. However, deciding to disregard an adverse statistical result because it does not give an auditor a good "feeling" is dangerous. Auditors must make decisions about account balances with care and with the best evidential base reasonably obtainable. It is not enough to develop a conclusion about the sampled units from a population. An auditor must project the sample evidence for a conclusion about the whole population—the dollar amount of the account under audit.

Applying statistical sampling is not technically difficult. However, making good sense of the judgments and estimates involved in sampling is hard. These are the facts, estimates, and judgments auditors should use when applying dollar-unit (DUS) sampling for the substantive audit of an account balance:

Fact

Recorded amount (book value, population value) of the account.

Estimate

Expected dollar misstatement in the account.

Judgments

Audit risk as it relates to the account.

Inherent risk as it relates to the account.

Control risk as it relates to the controls over transactions that create the account balance (co-ordinated with the control risk assessment work).

Analytical procedures risk related to other substantive procedures designed to obtain substantive evidence about the account balance.

Risk of incorrect acceptance (can be derived from the other risk judgments).

Risk of incorrect rejection (can be derived from the cost relationships). Material misstatement—the materiality used for the account.

The chapter incorporated all these elements in the application of dollar-unit sampling. They were used for explanations of procedures for calculating a sample size, selecting a dollar-unit sample, and evaluating the quantitative evidence obtained from a sample. The quantitative evidence measurements were integrated in a discussion of the problem of determining an amount to recommend for adjustment when the evidence is based on a sample.

Audit sampling is not just theory for textbooks; tax auditors, public sector auditors, and independent auditors who perform audits of government programs all use sampling for regulatory purposes. Tax and public sector audit applications were illustrated.

CASE STUDY   # KINGSTON COMPANY

This portion of the Kingston Company case expands the problem requirements in Chapter 7 to include statistical calculations for test of controls auditing. The auditors, Jack and Fred, are planning the audit of some of the controls related to accounting for sales charged to customers' accounts receivable. The purpose of the work is to evaluate control risk to help set the stage for the sample-based audit of the accounts receivable. The assessment of control risk is important because it will influence the sample size for the audit of the customer accounts receivable balances.

You have written an audit program for part of the test of controls auditing (Problem 7.26; refer to the first procedure in the audit program in Chapter 7 if you did not prepare a program for 7.26). You have also defined deviations related to the recorded sales (Problem 7.27; refer to the deviations listed in Problem 7.47 if you did not list them for 7.27).

Kingston Case Assignments

20.44   Determine a Test of Controls Sample Size.   The dialogue below contains the information necessary for using the smoke/fire multiplier concept related to tolerable deviation rate (TDR) determination and Roberts's method for calculating the risk of assessing control risk too low (RACRTL). These are used to figure sample sizes and costs. Essentially Roberts's method is a way to systematically minimize the combined costs of testing of controls and the related substance testing of details by adding up various combinations of costs of controls testing to the related substantive testing costs.

There are two separate sets of requirements: (1) the basic analysis uses certain information from the dialogue to formulate a plan and (2) the alternative analysis uses other variables that indicate differences of judgment. One or both of the sets can be assigned. The alternative set facilitates a demonstration of the differences in outcomes created by different judgments. In both sets the requirements are in the order of the stages of analysis. They can be assigned separately or all together.

Planning Dialogue

Fred: We need to plan the audit of the accounts receivable balance. Depending on our assessment of control risk, we could audit anywhere from 51 to 143 customer balances. I prepared a schedule similar to Exhibit 20–2.

Jack: That's a big difference.

Fred: Yes, it is. And each customer account will cost about $8 in billable audit time to complete. Should we try to assess control risk at 0.10 and justify auditing the smallest sample of customer accounts?

Jack: That depends. Ten thousand sales invoices were processed during the year ended December 31, starting with number 32071 and ending with number 42070. Last year the audit team assessed control risk high and audited a large sample of customer accounts.

Fred: That's interesting. By my estimate, we could audit the sales transactions for compliance with control procedures fairly quickly. It would cost only about $3 each to do a test of controls. We have already tested the controls over cash receipts and decided that the control risk is low.

Jack: Yes, but if we make a mistake assessing control risk too low, we might audit too few customer accounts and unknowingly have a risk of incorrect acceptance larger than we planned.

Fred: I don't think we would get in any trouble if we accepted only 0.01 additional risk from that kind of mistake.

Jack: Gee, Fred, I thought you were liberal. I was going to say we can afford to have another 0.02 risk of incorrect acceptance.

Fred: I voted PC, just like you! Anyway, we need to figure out a tolerable deviation rate for the detail test of controls over the accounting for the sales transactions. I think as much as $85,000 of the $8.5 million in sales could be exposed to control deviation and not cause the accounts receivable to contain material error.

Jack: I see where you're coming from. The tolerable misstatement for the accounts receivable audit is $10,000, and you are applying a smoke/fire multiplier of 8.5. But look at it this way: The company already has given allowance for some errors through the sales returns and allowances account to the tune of $400,000, for the year, so I think the multiplier could be as much as 17.

Fred: And you call me liberal!

Jack: Let's assign those new assistant accountants over there to figure this out. Tell them to make a first pass assuming we find no deviations in the test of controls sample.

(1) Required (for basic analysis):

a. Use Fred's smoke/fire multiplier of 8.5 to figure TDR at CR = 0.05; assign TDRs to the other control risk levels of adding one percentage point for each 0.05 increment in the control risk.

b. Use Fred's judgment of an incremental risk of incorrect acceptance of 0.01 for the substantive balance-audit of the accounts receivable to figure the RACRTLs for each control risk level. (Round to two decimal places.)

c. Calculate the test of controls sample sizes ($n[c]$) for each control risk level.

d. Calculate the total cost of the test of controls sample and the substantive balance-audit sample and determine the size of the test of controls sample to audit.

(2) Required (for alternative analysis):

a. Use Jack's smoke/fire multiplier of 17 to figure TDR at CR = 0.05; assign TDRs to the other control risk levels by adding 1 percentage point for each 0.05 increment in the control risk.

b. Use Jack's judgment of an incremental risk of incorrect acceptance of 0.02 for the substantive balance-audit of the accounts receivable to figure the RACRTLs for each control risk level. (Round to two decimal places.)

c. Calculate the test of controls sample sizes ($n[c]$) for each control risk level.

d. Calculate the total cost of the test of controls sample and the substantive balance-audit sample and determine the size of the test of controls sample to audit.

e. Assuming you have done requirement set (1), discuss the difference(s) in the audit plan suggested by the alternative analysis.

20.45 Quantitative Evaluation of Control Compliance Evidence.
To perform quantitative evaluation of compliance evidence, you need to complete a sampling data sheet. (Make a copy of Exhibit 7.27–1, or obtain one from your instructor.) If you worked problem 7.27, you will already have this data sheet. If not, review problem 7.27 and fill in the client name and the period covered, specify objectives of your work, describe the population to be sampled, and describe the sample selection process. Under the column headed "definition of deviations," write a brief statement of the deviations of interest. (You can find these deviations listed in problem 7.47.) Decide a sample size to audit. Choose one of these sample sizes—30, 60, 80, 90, 120, 160, 220, 240, 260, 300—to facilitate your instructor's presentation of solutions.

Required:

a. In addition to the information for the sampling data sheet described above, enter the statistical information: risk of assessing control risk too low, tolerable rate, and estimated deviation rate. Then enter your sample size. Next, "audit" your sample according to the instructions in problem 7.28, using the simulated data in Exhibit 7.28–1. Record the number of deviations, calculate the sample deviation rate, and calculate the computed upper limit (use the Appendix 20B tables or the Poisson risk factor equation for CUL).

b. Use the computed upper limit information to assign an evaluation to internal control risk related to the probability of sales overstatement errors being in the accounts receivable balances. For this requirement, assume a tolerable deviation rate of 4 percent and a risk of assessing control risk too low of 5 percent.

MULTIPLE-CHOICE QUESTIONS FOR PRACTICE AND REVIEW: PART I

20.46 When auditors plan a test of controls and think about several control risk assessments that could be made, they also can think about:
  a. One relevant tolerable deviation rate.
  b. Two relevant tolerable deviation rates.
  c. Three relevant tolerable deviation rates.
  d. Many relevant tolerable deviation rates.

20.47 When auditors plan a test of controls and decide they want to assess one control risk level (say, control risk of

0.40), they should think about decision criteria that include:

a. One relevant tolerable deviation rate.

b. Two relevant tolerable deviation rates.

c. Three relevant tolerable deviation rates.

d. Many relevant tolerable deviation rates.

20.48 An audit manager decided the possible control risk assessments listed in the left column could be relevant to the audit plan. What is wrong with the tolerable deviation rates associated with each control risk?

Control Risk	Tolerable Deviation Rate
0.20	0.06
0.50	0.04
0.80	0.02

a. The control risks are too widely spaced, ignoring possible assessments of 0.10, 0.30, 0.40, 0.60, 0.70, 0.90, and 1.00.

b. Nothing is wrong with the tolerable deviation rates associated with the possible control risk assessments.

c. All the tolerable deviation rates are too low.

d. The tolerable deviation rate relationships are reversed because the lowest rate (0.02) should be associated with the lowest risk (0.20) and the highest rate (0.06) should be associated with the highest risk (0.80).

20.49 Hershiser, an audit manager, made the judgments that his test of controls of the company's 50,000 purchase transactions should be based on a tolerable deviation rate of 0.06, a risk of assessing control risk too low of 0.05, and an expected deviation rate of 3 percent. His statistical sample size should be:

a. 100.

b. 360.

c. 160.

d. 50.

20.50 An audit manager decided the possible control risk assessments listed in the left column were relevant when thinking about control over sales transactions. The sample sizes for the subsequent substantive audit of the customer accounts receivable are shown to the right of each control risk. What risk of assessing control risk too low could be assigned for tests of controls at each control risk level?

Control Risk	Accounts Receivable Sample	Risk of Overreliance
0.20	190	2
0.50	350	2
0.80	390	2
0.90	400	0.10

a. From top to bottom: 5%, 10%, 1%.

b. From top to bottom: 10%, 1%, 5%.

c. From top to bottom: 1%, 10%, 5%.

d. From top to bottom: 1%, 5%, 10%.

20.51 Assume that audit manager Lasorda found two deviations in a sample of 90 transactions. The computed upper limit at 5 percent risk of assessing control risk too low is:

a. 10%.

b. 7%.

c. 6%.

d. 84%.

20.52 The auditing interpretation of the sampling error-adjusted deviation rate (computed upper limit, UEL) in a test of controls sample is:

a. The estimated worst likely deviation rate in the population with probability = risk of assessing control risk too low that the actual deviation rate is even higher.

b. The estimated lowest likely deviation rate in the population with probability = risk of assessing control risk too low that the actual deviation rate is even lower.

c. The estimated lowest likely deviation rate in the population with certainty that the actual deviation rate is even lower.

d. The estimated worst likely deviation rate in the population with certainty that the actual deviation rate is even higher.

20.53 If an auditor tested 100 transactions and found one deviation from an important control procedure, the audit conclusion could be that control risk can be assessed at the associated control risk level when:

a. The relevant tolerable deviation rate is 0.02.

b. The relevant tolerable deviation rate is 0.03.

c. The relevant tolerable deviation rate is 0.04.

d. More information about decision criteria is available.

20.54 If an auditor calculated a UEL of 5 percent when she had a tolerable deviation rate criterion of 4 percent, both at the same risk of assessing control risk too low:

a. Control risk should be assessed at the level associated with the 4 percent tolerable deviation rate.

b. Control risk should be assessed at the level associated with the 5 percent tolerable deviation rate.

c. Control risk should be assessed at the maximum level (100 percent) because the company's performance failed the test.

d. Control risk should be assessed at the minimum level (10 percent) because the statistics are close enough.

20.55 If an auditor calculated a UEL of 2 percent when she had a tolerable deviation rate criterion of 4 percent, both at the same risk of assessing control risk too low:

a. Control risk should be assessed at the level associated with the 4 tolerable deviation rate.

b. Control risk should be assessed at the level associated with the 2 percent tolerable deviation rate.

c. Control risk should be assessed at the maximum level (100 percent) because the company's performance failed the test.

d. Control risk should be assessed at the minimum level (10 percent) because the statistics are close enough.

20.56 What is the evaluation conclusion from a statistical sample of internal control attributes when a test of 125 documents results in five deviations if the tolerable deviation rate is 5 percent, the expected population deviation rate is 2 percent, and the allowance for sampling risk is 3 percent?

a. Accept the sample results as suitable support for assessing a low control risk because the tolerable rate less the allowance for sampling risk is less than the expected population deviation rate.

b. Use the evidence to assess a higher control risk than planned because the sample deviation rate plus the allowance for sampling risk exceeds the tolerable deviation rate.

c. Use the evidence to assess a higher control risk than planned because the tolerable deviation rate plus the allowance for sampling risk exceeds the expected population deviation rate.

d. Accept the sample results as suitable support for assessing a low control risk because the sample deviation rate plus the allowance for sampling risk exceeds the tolerable deviation rate.

20.57 An auditor designed a statistical test of controls sample that would provide a 1 percent risk of assessing control risk too low that not more than 7 percent of sales invoices lacked credit approval. From previous audits, the auditor expected about 2.5 percent rate of lack of approval in the population. The auditor selected 200 invoices, and 9 were found to lack credit approval. The achieved (computed) upper limit UEL of the deviation rate was:

a. 2.5%.

b. 3.5%.

c. 4.5%.

d. 7.0%.

20.58 Based on the same information in 20.57, the allowance for sampling error was:

a. 1.0%.

b. 3.5%.

c. 4.5%.

d. 5.5%.

EXHIBIT 20.59-1

	Case 1		Case 2		Case 3		Case 4		Case 5	
Sample A or B	A	B	A	B	A	B	A	B	A	B
Number of invoices examined	75	200	150	25	250	100	100	125	225	200
Number of deviations found in sample	1	4	2	0	6	2	1	3	7	4
Percentage (%) of sample invoices with deviations	1.3	2.0	1.3	0.0	2.4	2.0	1.0	2.4	3.1	2.0

EXERCISES AND PROBLEMS

· ·

20.59 Deciding the Best Evidence Representation. Assume you are working on the audit of a small company and are examining purchase invoices for the presence of a "received" stamp. The omission of the stamp is thus a deviation. The population is composed of approximately 4,000 invoices, which were processed by the company during the current year.

You decide that a deviation rate in the population as high as 5 percent would not require any extended audit procedures. However, if the population deviation rate is greater than 5 percent, you would want to assess a higher control risk and do more audit work.

In each case in Exhibit 20.59–1, write the letter of the sample (A or B) which, in your judgment, provides the better evidence that the deviation rate in the population is 5 percent or less. (Assume that each sample observation is selected at random.)

20.60 Estimating a Frequency. A local industrial company has two departments. In the larger department, about 45 sales invoices are completed each day; in the smaller department, about 15 invoices are completed each day. About 50 percent of all sales invoices completed in each department specify discounts from the company's list prices. However, the exact percentage varies from day to day. Sometimes it may be higher than 50 percent, sometimes lower.

For a period of one year, and for each department, a member of the audit staff kept track of the number of days on which more than 60 percent of the sales invoices specified discounts. Which department do you think showed the greater number of such days?

a. The larger department.
b. The smaller department.
c. About the same.

20.61 Risk of Assessing Control Risk Too High. When you audited Kingston Company's performance of its control procedures (in problem 20.45), you found four deviations of "wrong quantity billed" in a sample of 80 invoices. At the risk of assessing control risk too low of 5 percent, this finding showed a CUL of 12 percent, which is more than your tolerable rate of 4 percent. This quantitative evidence indicating control deficiency now subjects you to a risk of assessing control risk too high if you decide internal control risk is high and you should do more audit work on the accounts receivable.

Required:
Calculate the risk of assessing control risk too high based on the presumption that only 4 percent of invoices in the population actually have billed the wrong quantity to customers.

20.62 Sample Size Relationships. For the specifications of acceptable risk of assessing control risk too low, tolerable deviation rate, and expected population deviation rate shown below, prepare tables showing the appropriate sample sizes. (Use the evaluation tables in Appendix 20A or the Poisson risk factor equation as given in the solution to 20.61).

a. Tolerable deviation rate = 0.05. Expected population deviation rate = 0. Acceptable risk of assessing control risk too low = 0.01, 0.05, 0.10.

b. Acceptable risk of assessing control risk too low = 0.10. Expected population deviation rate = 0.01. Tolerable deviation rate = 0.10, 0.08, 0.05, 0.03, 0.02.

c. Acceptable risk of assessing control risk too low = 0.10. Tolerable deviation rate = 0.01, 0.02, 0.04, 0.07, 0.09.

d. Place a second sample size column in *a*, *b*, and *c*, and figure the sample size when the population contains only 500 units.

20.63 Exercises in Sample Selection.

a. Sales invoices beginning with number 0001 and ending with number 5000 are entered in a sales journal. You want to choose 50 invoices for a test of controls. Start at row 5, column 3, of the random number table in Appendix 13A and select the first five usable numbers, using the first four digits in the column.

b. There are 9,100 numbered cheques in a cash disbursements journal, beginning with number 2220 and ending with number 11319. You want to choose 100 disbursements for a test of controls. Start at row 11, column 1, of the table of random digits in Appendix 13A and select the first five usable numbers.

c. During the year the client wrote 45,200 vouchers. Each month, the numbering series started over with number 00001, prefixed with a number for the month (January = 01, February = 02, and so on), so the voucher numbers had seven digits, the last five of which were in overlapping series. You want to choose 120 vouchers for audit. Evaluate each of the following suggested selection methods:

(1) Choose a month at random and select 120 at random in that

month by association with a five-digit random number.

(2) Choose 120 usable seven-digit random numbers.

(3) Select 10 vouchers at random from each month.

d. Explain how you could use systematic sampling to select the first five items in each case above. For case (*c*), assume the random start is at voucher 03-01102.

20.64 Imagination in Sample Selection. The text illustrated a problem of selecting a sample of classified ads printed in a newspaper. Auditors often need to be imaginative when figuring out how to obtain a random sample. For each of the cases below, explain how you could select a sample having the best chance of being random.

a. You need a sample of recorded cash disbursements. The client used two bank accounts for general disbursements. Account number 1 was used during January-August and issued cheques numbered 3633–6632. Account number 2 was used during May-December and issued cheques numbered 0001–6000. (Hint: For purposes of random number selection and cheque identification, convert one of the numerical sequences to a sequence that does not overlap the other.) In Appendix 13A, start at row 1, column 2, and select the first five random cheques, reading down column 2.

b. You need a sample of purchase orders. The client issued pre-numbered purchase orders in the sequence 9000–13999 (5,000 of them). You realize if you just select five-digit random numbers from a table, looking for numbers in this sequence, 95 percent of the random numbers you scan will be discards because a table has 100,000 different five-digit random numbers. (The computer is down today!) How can you fiddle with this sequence to reduce the number of discards? (Hint: You can reduce discards to zero.) In Appendix 13A, start at row 30, column 3, and select the first five random purchase orders, reading down column 3.

c. You need a sample of perpetual inventory records so that you can go to the warehouse and count the quantities while the stockclerks take the physical inventory. The perpetual records have been printed out in a control list showing location, item description, and quantity. You have a copy of the list. It is 75 pages long, with 50 lines to a page (40 lines on the last page). Find an efficient way to select 100 lines for your test of controls audit of the client's counting procedure.

d. You need to determine whether an inventory compilation is complete. You plan to select a sample of physical locations, describe and count the inventory units, and trace the information to the inventory list. The inventory consists of tools, parts, and other hardware material shelved in a large warehouse. The warehouse contains 300 rows of 75-foot-long shelves, each of which has 10 tiers. The inventory is stored on these shelves. Find an efficient way to select 100 sampling units of physical inventory for count and tracing to the inventory listing.

20.65 UEL Calculation Exercises. Using the tables in Appendix 20A and the Poisson risk factor equation, find the computed upper limit (UEL) for each case below:

	(a)	(b)	(c)
Risk of assessing control risk too low	0.01	0.05	0.10
Sample size	300	300	300
Deviations	6	6	6
Sample deviation rate	—	—	—
Computed upper limit	—	—	—

	(d)	(e)	(f)
Risk of assessing control risk too low	0.05	0.05	0.05
Sample size	100	200	400
Deviations	2	4	8
Sample deviation rate	—	—	—
Computed upper limit	—	—	—

	(g)	(h)	(i)
Risk of assessing control risk too low	0.05	0.05	0.05
Sample size	100	100	100
Deviations	10	6	0
Sample deviation rate	—	—	—
Computed upper limit	—	—	—

20.66 Discovery Sampling. Using the discovery sampling theory and tables in Appendix 20A, fill in the missing data in each case below.

	(a)	(b)	(c)
Critical rate of occurrence	0.4%	0.5%	1.0%
Required probability	99	99	99
Sample size (minimum)	—	—	—

	(d)	(e)	(f)
Critical rate of occurrence	2.0%	1.0%	0.5%
Required probability	—	—	—
Sample size (minimum)	240	240	240

	(g)	(h)	(i)
Critical rate of occurrence	—	—	—
Required probability	70	85	95
Sample size (minimum)	300	460	700

DISCUSSION CASES

20.67 Tom's Misapplied Application. Tom Barton, an assistant accountant with a local PA firm, has recently graduated from the Other University. He studied statistical sampling for auditing in university and wants to impress his employers with his knowledge of modern auditing methods.

He decided to select a random sample of payroll cheques for the test of controls, using a tolerable rate of 5 percent and an acceptable risk of assessing control risk too low of 5 percent. The senior accountant told Tom that 2 percent of the cheques audited last year had one or more errors in the calculation of net pay. Tom decided to audit 100 random cheques. Since supervisory personnel had larger paycheques than production workers, he selected 60 of the larger cheques and 40 of the others. He was very careful to see that the selections of 60 from the April payroll register and 40 from the August payroll register were random.

The audit of this sample yielded two deviations, exactly the 2 percent rate experienced last year. The first was the deduction of federal income taxes based on two exemptions for a supervisory employee. The other was payment to a production employee at a rate for a job classification one grade lower than his actual job. The worker had been promoted the week before, and Tom found that in the next payroll he was paid at the higher correct rate.

When he evaluated this evidence, Tom decided that these two findings were really not control deviations at all. The withholding of too much tax did not affect the expense accounts, and the proper rate was paid the production worker as soon as the clerk caught up with his change orders. Tom decided that having found zero deviations in a sample of 100, the computed upper limit at 5 percent risk of assessing control risk too low was 3 percent, which easily satisfied his predetermined criterion.

The senior accountant was impressed. Last year he had audited 15 cheques from each month, and Tom's work represented a significant time savings. The reviewing partner on the audit was also impressed because he had never thought that statistical sampling could be so efficient, and that was the reason he had never studied the method.

Required:

Identify and explain the mistakes made by Tom and the others.

20.68 Determine a Test of Controls Sample Size. N. Wolfe, PA, is planning the audit of Goodwin Manufacturing Company's inventory. Wolfe plans to audit the inventory by selecting a sample of items for physical observation and counting, followed by price testing. The price testing part of the work takes a large portion of the time on each sampling unit because the company's costing method is complex. The estimated cost of auditing each sampling unit in this substantive balance-audit sample is estimated at $25.

Because this detail substantive work is expensive, Wolfe would like to minimize the sample size by assessing a low control risk. She decided that control over accurate pricing of purchases (additions to the inventory) would be the control attribute most appropriate. The reasoning is that inventory balance misstatements could arise from either or both of miscounting or erroneous pricing and costing calculations. If the basic purchase pricing were accurate, then that would leave the inventory count accuracy and the difficult inventory costing calculations as the remaining source for error and audit attention. The estimated cost to audit a purchase transaction for pricing accuracy is estimated to be $12. She thinks the client's staff makes few, if any, errors in pricing the purchase transactions.

For the audit of the inventory balance, Wolfe accepted the accounting firm's policy of setting audit risk at 0.05. Since business activity in the client company had been hectic lately, she decided to be conservative and set inherent risk at 1.0. However, certain analytical procedures will be performed by comparing the inventory balance to prior years, the company budget, and certain historical statistics, and these procedures might have a 10 percent chance of detecting material misstatements of the balance.

The book-recorded amount of the inventory is $72 million, spread among 3,345 different kinds of inventory items. Purchases for the year amounted to $467 million in about 6,000 separate purchase transactions.

Wolfe believes the inventory balance can be misstated by as much as $2 million without causing the financial

EXHIBIT 20.68–1   GOODWIN MANUFACTURING COMPANY

Control Risk Categories	CR	TDR	RIA	RACRTL	Test of Control n[c]	Cost	Balance-Audit n[s]	Cost	Total
Low control risk	0.10 0.20 0.30						25 46 60		
Moderate control risk	0.40 0.50 0.60						71 80 87		
Control risk below maximum	0.70 0.80 0.90						91 96 101		
Maximum risk	1.00						101		

RIA = Risk of incorrect acceptance for the substantive balance-audit sample.

statements as a whole to be materially misstated. The overall materiality judgment is $8 million misstatement of operating income before taxes, and $2 million is the amount assigned to the audit of the inventory balance.

The audit staff recently attended a training session where Wolfe learned about the concepts of a smoke/fire multiplier and an incremental risk of incorrect acceptance used to judge the risk of assessing control risk too low. Inventory purchase pricing errors can be numerous, yet not affect the dollar amounts very much, so Wolfe decided that a smoke/fire multiplier of 7 was appropriate. (The firm's policy is to use the multiplier to figure an anchor tolerable deviation rate for control risk = 0.05, and round the anchor up to 1 percent if the multiplier produces an anchor less than 1 percent. After that, each tolerable deviation rate is 1 per-

centage point higher for each 0.05 control risk level increment.)

The firm's policy about an incremental risk of incorrect acceptance resulting from assessing control risk too low has not yet been published, but Wolfe thinks that a 0.02 change should not make much difference.

The problem is deciding the size of the test of controls sample for the audit of the purchase-pricing transactions. Wolfe partially completed the worksheet shown in Exhibit 20.68–1. She handed it over to you.

Required:
Copy the worksheet. Complete it and decide the size of the sample for the detail test of accuracy control over the pricing of purchases (additions to the inventory). [Round the risk of incorrect acceptance and risk of assessing control risk too low probabilities to two decimal places.]

CASE STUDY   KINGSTON COMPANY (CONT.)

Statistical Sampling: Auditing the Trade Accounts Receivable Balance

The Kingston Company assignments that follow cover both the dollar-unit sampling (DUS) method and the classical sampling method. The assignment headings identify them. The dialogue immediately below provides the basic planning information for both sampling methods. Some of the planning information will be ignored, depending upon the sampling method used in the assignment. (Students will need to be able to identify the relevant information and disregard the irrelevant.)

Jack and Fred, the auditors, are getting ready to audit Kingston's trade accounts receivable.

Jack: Where's the trial balance?

Fred: Here it is. Kingston lists 1,506 customer balances totalling $400,000. The balances range from $1 to $25,000.

Jack: Yesterday, we decided the tolerable misstatement in receivables could be $10,000. That is, we want to audit for sales and receivables overstatement so we won't miss more than $10,000, if that much misstatement is in the account.

Fred: Monetary misstatements are a possibility. Last year, we audited 500 customer accounts selected at random and found $2,000 in overstatement. That computed to a projected likely overstatement of $4,000. We proposed a $3,000 adjustment to the gross receivables, but the partner passed the adjustment when he got the treasurer to agree to increase the allowance for doubtful accounts by $10,000. Even though the total receivables are down $100,000, maybe we ought to play it safe and figure $4,000 misstatement might be in the total. That makes the average misstatement expected about $2.67.

Jack: What was the standard deviation in last year's sample?

Fred: About $40. It was 10 times the average monetary misstatement.

Jack: Mmmmm (*thoughtfully*). Any individually big balances this year?

Fred: Kingston shows six balances over $10,000 for a total of $100,000. We ought to pull them out of the population for complete audit.

Jack: Agreed. No use taking chances.

Fred: Our analytical procedures related to receivables doesn't show much. The total is down, consistent with the sales decline, so the turnover is up a little. If any misstatement is in the receivables total, it may be too small to be obvious in the ratios.

Jack: That's good news if the problems are immaterial. Too bad we can't say analytical procedures reduce our audit risk. What about internal control?

Fred: We were successful in assessing control risk at 0.30 according to the analysis of our minimum cost samples. The company's control procedures seem to be performed well. I call that a low control risk situation. Incidentally, I can't separate the inherent risk assessment from the control risk assessment, so I think we should lump them together for a 0.30 combination.

Jack: According to the audit program, we will confirm a sample of customer accounts, send second requests after a week, then chase down all the nonrespondents by vouching all the charges and credits in the account to supporting documents or vouching to the customers' payments in January. I'm worried about the time it takes and our audit cost of doing these procedures.

Fred: I am, too. The fixed cost of getting confirmations out is the same, no matter whether we send 100 or 1,000. Of course, it costs money to process the returns. I estimate the variable cost per account in the initial sample to be about $8—that's a weighted average of the cost of confirmation and the cost of alternative procedures to chase down the nonrespondents. The cost of handling the nonrespondents is about $19 each, which is the cost we will incur to add to the sample if our first sample is not large enough. We won't have time to send more confirmations, so adding accounts to the sample means we will need to audit them the same way we audit nonrespondents.

Jack: Let's take a chance of needing to add to the sample. If it all works out all right, we'll save a lot of time and meet our time budget for the work. How about a 40 percent risk of incorrect rejection?

Fred: Well, the team took only a 15 percent risk last year. Let's think about it. (*Later.*)

Fred: Here's the results of the audit of the six largest customer accounts.

Account Number	Balance	Confirmation and Document Examination
109	$12,337	Wrong quantity billed on invoice 042042, December 28. Overcharged $600.
458	12,129	No error.
859	25,000	No error.
863	16,129	Arithmetic error on invoice 42065, December 29. Overcharged $450.
1092	15,005	No error.
1456	19,400	No error.

Kingston Case Assignments

20.69   Kingston Company: Dollar-Unit Sampling Audit of Accounts Receivable.

Jack and Fred decided to take a dollar-unit sample of Kingston's account receivable that was not removed for 100 percent audit. They thought about the risk of incorrect rejection but only got headaches for their trouble. They decided to use the Poisson risk factor method for determining the DUS sample size.

They audited the sample and discovered the errors in Exhibit 20.69–1. In the column headings: "Wrong Quant'y" means that Kingston billed the customer for more units than were actually shipped according to the shipping documents, "Wrong Math" means a computational error was made on the invoice, and "Wrong Date" means that the sale was recorded in the year under audit (1992) but the goods were not shipped until January the next year.

EXHIBIT 20.69–1   **ERRORS DISCOVERED IN THE SAMPLE OF ACCOUNTS RECEIVABLE**

Acct #	Book Balance	Wrong Quant'y	Wrong Math	Wrong Date	Audited Amount
25	$ 503			$115	$ 388
366	$ 492			112	$ 380
465	$ 507	$136			$ 371
623	$ 195	$ 63			$ 132
741*	$3,698		$100		#3,598
741*	$3,698		$100		$3,598
774	$ 517			$140	$ 377
1206	$ 524			$119	$ 405
1352	$ 700			$400	$ 300
1466	$ 351			$ 59	$ 292

*Selected twice for two dollar units.

Required:

a. Derive the risk of incorrect acceptance from the information in the auditors' dialogue.

b. Decide how many errors to estimate for using the Poisson risk factor method calculation of the DUS sample size. Assume that you audit this sample size.

c. Calculate the projected likely error and the upper error limit based on the errors in the sample (Exhibit 20.69–1).

d. Decide whether to "accept" the recorded amount without adjustment or to "reject" the recorded amount as an accurate balance with respect to the tolerable misstatement the auditors will allow.

20.70   Kingston Company: Determine the Amount of a Recommended Adjustment—Dollar-Unit Sampling.
Assume that you have audited the Kingston Company accounts receivable and have reached a conclusion about the materially accurate presentation of the $400,000 recorded amount.

Required:

Using your results from your sample in assignment 20.70, prepare a proposed adjusting journal entry. (Hint: When you reviewed the Kingston unaudited financial statements, you found that the company was reporting cost of goods sold at 65 percent of sales dollars.)

Alternative:

Without regard to your sample results in assignment 20.70, assume you calculated the DUS results in Exhibit 20.70–1 from the audit of the accounts receivable. All the error amounts are accounts receivable overstatements. Prepare a proposed adjusting journal entry. (Hint: When you reviewed the Kingston unaudited financial statements, you found that the company was reporting cost of goods sold at 65 percent of sales dollars.)

EXHIBIT 20.70–1   ASSUMED ACCOUNTS RECEIVABLE DUS CALCULATIONS

Type of Error	Known Error	Projected Likely Error	Upper Error Limit
Wrong quantity:			
Six large accounts	$ 600		
Sampled accounts	199	$1,848	$ 8,091
Wrong arithmetic			
Six large accounts	450		
Sampled accounts	100	168	5,763
Wrong date:			
Sampled accounts	945	5,292	12,486
All error:			
Six large accounts	1,052		
Sampled accounts	1,244	7,308	14,897

MULTIPLE-CHOICE QUESTIONS FOR PRACTICE AND REVIEW: PART II

20.71 When audit risk (AR) is 0.015, inherent risk (IR) is 0.50, control risk (CR) is 0.30, and analytical procedures risk (AP) is 0.50, the risk of incorrect acceptance (RIA) is:

a. 0.20.

    b. 0.02.
    c. 2.00.
    d. Not determinable.

20.72 Which of the following elements in the audit risk model is/are a product of the auditors' professional judgment?
    a. Control risk.
    b. Analytical procedures risk.
    c. Test of details risk of incorrect acceptance.
    d. All the above.

20.73 When making a sample-based decision about the dollar amount in an account balance, the incorrect acceptance decision error is considered more serious than the incorrect rejection decision error because:
    a. The incorrect rejection decision impairs the efficiency of the audit.
    b. Auditors will do additional work and discover the error of the incorrect decision.
    c. The incorrect acceptance decision impairs the effectiveness of the audit.
    d. Sufficient, competent evidence will not have been obtained.

20.74 "Overauditing" can be defined as:
    a. Auditing too small a sample size.
    b. Auditing a larger sample size than necessary.
    c. Taking more risk than is professionally acceptable.
    d. Giving an inappropriate unqualified report on financial statements.

20.75 The characteristic(s) that distinguishes dollar-unit sampling (DUS) from classical variables sampling is (are):
    a. Classical sampling requires an estimate of the standard deviation and DUS does not.
    b. Classical sampling depends upon the statistics of the normal distribution and DUS does not.
    c. DUS is not concerned with the audit of logical units in the population as is classical sampling.
    d. Classical sampling requires calculation of an upper limit of dollar error.

Dollar-Unit Sampling Questions

20.76 The unique feature of dollar-unit sampling (DUS) insofar as sample design is concerned is:
    a. Sampling units are not chosen at random.
    b. A dollar unit selected in a sample is not replaced before the sample selection is completed.
    c. Auditors need not worry about the risk of incorrect acceptance decision error.
    d. The population is defined as the number of $1 units in an account balance or class of transactions.

20.77 When calculating a dollar-unit (DUS) sample size, an auditor does not need to make a judgment or estimate of:
    a. Audit risk.
    b. Tolerable misstatement.
    c. Estimate misstatement.
    d. Standard deviation of misstatement.

20.78 Which of these combinations will produce the largest DUS sample size:

	RIA	Errors	Recorded Amount	Tolerable Misstatement
a.	0.03	2	$1,000,000	$50,000
b.	0.03	1	1,000,000	35,000
c.	0.06	0	1,500,000	65,000
d.	0.10	4	1,500,000	65,000

20.79 Which of the following statements is correct about dollar-unit sampling (DUS)?
    a. The risk of incorrect acceptance must be specified.
    b. Smaller logical units have a greater probability of selection in the sample than larger units.
    c. The systematic sampling "skip interval" is the same as the "average sampling interval" used for quantitative evaluation.
    d. Projected likely misstatement cannot be calculated in the quantitative evaluation when one or more errors are discovered.

20.80 One of the primary advantages of dollar-unit sampling (DUS) is the fact that:

a. It is a good method of sampling for evidence of understatement in asset accounts.

b. The sample selection automatically achieves high-dollar selection and stratification.

c. The sample selection provides for including a representative number of small-value population units.

d. Expanding the sample for additional evidence is very easy.

Exercises and Problems

20.81 Selecting a Dollar-Unit Sample. You have been assigned the task of selecting a dollar-unit sample from the Whitney Company's detail inventory records as of September 30, 1992. Whitney's controller has given you a list of the 23 different inventory items and their recorded book amounts. The senior accountant has told you to select a sample of 10 dollar units and the logical units that contain them.

Required:

Prepare a working paper showing a systematic selection of 10 dollar units and the related logical units. (Arrange the items in their numerical identification number order, and take a random starting place at the 1,210th dollar.)

ID	Amount	ID	Amount	ID	Amount	ID	Amount
1	$1,750	7	$1,255	13	$ 937	19	$2,577
2	1,492	8	3,761	14	5,938	20	1,126
3	994	9	1,956	15	2,001	21	565
4	629	10	1,393	16	222	22	2,319
5	2,272	11	884	17	1,738	23	1,681
6	1,163	12	729	18	1,228		

20.82 When Acceptable Risk Exceeds 50 Percent. Write an explanation of the auditing theory and generally accepted auditing standards regarding sampling plans when the risk model causes the calculation of RIA (acceptable risk of incorrect acceptance) to exceed 50 percent.

Discussion Cases

20.83 Relation of Dollar-Unit Sample Sizes to Audit Risk Model. Prepare tables like the one in Exhibit 20–1 under different assumptions for the three combinations given below. Calculate dollar-unit sample sizes using the Poisson risk factors for a dollar value of the balance of $300,000 and a tolerable misstatement of $10,000. Assume zero expected misstatement. (These are the recorded amount and tolerable misstatement underlying Exhibit 20–1.) Round your RIAs to two decimal places to use the Poisson risk factor tables.

1. AR = 0.10, IR = 1.00, AP = 1.00
2. AR = 0.05, IR = 0.50, AP = 1.00
3. AR = 0.05, IR = 1.00, AP = 0.50

Required:

Explain the differences or similarities among the different or same sample sizes produced by your calculations.

20.84 Determining an Efficient Risk of Incorrect Rejection (DUS). Your audit firm is planning the audit of a company's accounts receivable, which consists of 1,032 customer accounts with a total recorded amount (book value) of $300,000. You have already decided that the accounts receivable can be overstated by as much as $10,000, and the financial statements would not be considered materially misstated. Judging by the experience of past audits on this client, only a negligible amount of misstatement is expected to exist in the account.

Preliminary calculations of sample sizes have been made for several possible control risk levels. These calculations were based on a "base" risk of incorrect rejection of 0.01. Minimum sample sizes based on the alternative risks of incorrect rejection shown below also were calculated.

Audit work on the accounts will cost $8 per sampling unit when the accounts are selected for the initial sample. However, if the sample indicates a rejection (material overstatement) decision, the audit of additional sampling units will cost $19 each.

Control Risk	"Base" Sample	Alternative RIR	Alternative (minimum) Sample
0.20	80	0.02	41
0.30	96	0.02	53
0.40	107	0.03	62
0.50	116	0.03	68
0.60	122	0.03	74
0.70	128	0.03	78
0.80	133	0.03	82
0.90	137	0.03	86
1.00	141	0.03	89

Required:

For each of the control risk levels shown above, calculate the expected cost savings from auditing the initial alternative (minimum) sample. Assume that the action in the event of a rejection decision is to expand the work by selecting additional units up to the number in the base sample. Discuss the potential audit efficiencies and possible inefficiencies from beginning the audit work with the alternative (minimum) sample size.

20.85 Different Sampling Methods Compared. The trial balance of 50 of Kingston Company's accounts receivable ("balance" column) in Exhibit 20.85–1 was extracted from the population of 1,506 customer accounts you have seen in previous assignments. (However, the customer account numbers have been changed to run consecutively from 1 to 50.) This small population represents the accounts kept by a division of the company, although they are included in

the population of 1,506 for financial statement presentation. The small population normally would not be audited separately and normally would not be treated by statistical sampling methods. However, it is presented here to enable you to try out some of the sample selection methods and calculations. You also are given hypothetical audit findings for all the accounts, as if all of the errors in them were known. The requirements below are a kind of "final exam" on account balance audit sampling.

Required:

a. Select an unrestricted random sample (without replacement) of the customer accounts by associating account numbers with random numbers. Start in the first row, first column, of the Table of Random Digits in Appendix 20A. Use two-digit random numbers, reading down the first column until you have identified 10 customer accounts.

b. Select a systematic random sample of 10 customer accounts using two random starts. Select a random number between 1 and 10 and select every 10th account, then select another random number between 1 and 10 and select every 10th account again. (Your instructor's solution is based on random starts of 3 and 5.)

c. Select a systematic random dollar-unit sample of 10 dollars, identifying the associated logical units. For the given sample size of 10, the average sampling interval is $1,947 ($17,523/9). Select a random number between 1 and 1,947. (Your instructor's solution is based on a random starting number of 0741. At the end of the population you will need to cycle back to the beginning to get the 10th selection.)

d. Which customer account(s) in the trial balance will always be included in a systematic dollar-unit sample of 10?

e. Prepare a table comparing the results of each of the samples in a, b, and c above. The columns should be titled (a) Random Unit Sample,

E X H I B I T 20.85–1   **POPULATION OF 50 ACCOUNTS RECEIVABLE**

Account No.	Balance	Wrong Quantity	Wrong Math	Wrong Date	Monetary Error	Audit Amount
1	$ 141				$ 0	$ 141
2	346				0	346
3	1,301				0	1,301
4	683				0	683
5	1,555			$ 600	600	955
6	105				0	105
7	1,906	$ 200			200	1,706
8	102				0	102
9	634				0	634
10	116				0	116
11	77				0	77
12	51				0	51
13	320				0	320
14	178				0	178
15	188				0	188
16	482			137	137	345
17	183	59			59	124
18	130		$ 8		8	122
19	683				0	683
20	141				0	141
21	57				0	57
22	161				0	161
23	145				0	145
24	210				0	210
25	461	111			111	350
26	508			136	136	372
27	656				0	656
28	193		11		11	182
29	98				0	98
30	177				0	177
31	103				0	103
32	503			115	115	388
33	500			107	107	393
34	104				0	104
35	157				0	157
36	388				0	388
37	98				0	98
38	621	106			106	515
39	394				0	394
40	134				0	134
41	80				0	80
42	91				0	91
43	65				0	65
44	10				0	10
45	470			117	117	353
46	156				0	156
47	703				0	703
48	378			72	72	306
49	312				0	312
50	268				0	268
Number	50	$ 4	2	7	13	50
Total	$17,523	$ 476	$ 19	$ 1,284	$1,779	$15,744
Average	$350.46	$119.00	$9.50	$183.43	$35.58	$314.88
Standard deviation	$374.28				$94.31	$320.88

(*b*) Systematic Unit Sample, and (*c*) Dollar-Unit Sample. Label the rows for the following data and calculations: Population size, population dollar total, sample size, recorded amount in sample, number of error accounts in sample, projected likely misstatement (difference method, ratio method, dollar-unit method). Produce all the values for the rows for each kind of sample.

f. Calculate the upper error limit (finitely corrected) for the 2.0 percent risk of incorrect acceptance for each sample. Add a line for UEL to the table you started in (*e*) above. Assume the relevant standard deviations are standard deviation of random unit sample and systematic unit sample difference amounts = $181.

APPENDIX 20A

R VALUE TABLES

. . . .

POISSON RISK FACTORS (for calculating upper error limits of overstatement and understatement)

BETA RISKS

	50%		45%		40%		35%	
Errors	UEL	PGW	UEL	PGW	UEL	PGW	UEL	PGW
0	0.70	—	0.80	—	0.92	—	1.05	—
1	1.70	0.00	1.84	0.04	2.02	0.10	2.22	0.17
2	2.70	0.00	2.88	0.04	3.11	0.09	3.35	0.13
3	3.70	0.00	3.92	0.04	4.18	0.07	4.45	0.10
4	4.70	0.00	4.95	0.03	5.24	0.06	5.55	0.10
5	5.70	0.00	5.97	0.02	6.29	0.05	6.63	0.08
6	6.70	0.00	7.00	0.03	7.34	0.05	7.71	0.08
7	7.70	0.00	8.02	0.02	8.39	0.05	8.78	0.07
8	8.70	0.00	9.04	0.02	9.43	0.04	9.85	0.07
9	9.70	0.00	10.06	0.02	10.47	0.04	10.91	0.06
10	10.70	0.00	11.08	0.02	11.51	0.04	11.97	0.06
11	11.70	0.00	12.10	0.02	12.55	0.04	13.03	0.06
12	12.70	0.00	13.12	0.02	13.59	0.04	14.09	0.06
13	13.70	0.00	14.14	0.02	14.62	0.03	15.14	0.05
14	14.70	0.00	15.15	0.01	15.66	0.04	16.19	0.05
15	15.70	0.00	16.16	0.01	16.69	0.03	17.24	0.05
16	16.70	0.00	17.18	0.02	17.72	0.03	18.29	0.05
17	17.70	0.00	18.19	0.01	18.75	0.03	19.33	0.04
18	18.70	0.00	19.21	0.02	19.78	0.03	20.38	0.05
19	19.70	0.00	20.22	0.01	20.81	0.03	21.42	0.04
20	20.70	0.00	21.24	0.02	21.84	0.03	22.47	0.05

	30%		25%		20%		19%	
Errors	UEL	PGW	UEL	PGW	UEL	PGW	UEL	PGW
0	1.21	—	1.39	—	1.61	—	1.66	—
1	2.44	0.23	2.70	0.31	3.00	0.39	3.06	0.40
2	3.62	0.18	3.93	0.23	4.28	0.28	4.36	0.30
3	4.77	0.15	5.11	0.18	5.52	0.24	5.61	0.25
4	5.90	0.13	6.28	0.17	6.73	0.21	6.82	0.21
5	7.01	0.11	7.43	0.15	7.91	0.18	8.01	0.19
6	8.12	0.11	8.56	0.13	9.08	0.17	9.19	0.18
7	9.21	0.09	9.69	0.13	10.24	0.16	10.35	0.16
8	10.31	0.10	10.81	0.12	11.38	0.14	11.51	0.16
9	11.39	0.08	11.92	0.11	12.52	0.14	12.65	0.14
10	12.47	0.08	13.03	0.11	13.66	0.14	13.79	0.14
11	13.55	0.08	14.13	0.10	14.78	0.12	14.92	0.13
12	14.63	0.08	15.22	0.09	15.90	0.12	16.04	0.12
13	15.70	0.07	16.31	0.09	17.02	0.12	17.17	0.13
14	16.77	0.07	17.40	0.09	18.13	0.11	18.28	0.11
15	17.84	0.07	18.49	0.09	19.24	0.11	19.39	0.11
16	18.90	0.06	19.57	0.08	20.34	0.10	20.50	0.11
17	19.97	0.07	20.65	0.08	21.44	0.10	21.61	0.11
18	21.03	0.06	21.73	0.08	22.54	0.10	22.71	0.10
19	22.09	0.06	22.81	0.08	23.64	0.10	23.81	0.10
20	23.15	0.06	23.89	0.08	24.73	0.09	24.91	0.10

BETA RISKS

Errors	18%		17%		16%		15%	
	UEL	PGW	UEL	PGW	UEL	PGW	UEL	PGW
0	1.71	—	1.77	—	1.83	—	1.90	—
1	3.13	0.42	3.21	0.44	3.29	0.46	3.38	0.48
2	4.44	0.31	4.53	0.32	4.63	0.34	4.73	0.35
3	5.70	0.26	5.80	0.27	5.90	0.27	6.02	0.29
4	6.92	0.22	7.03	0.23	7.15	0.25	7.27	0.25
5	8.12	0.20	8.24	0.21	8.36	0.21	8.50	0.23
6	9.31	0.19	9.43	0.19	9.57	0.21	9.71	0.21
7	10.48	0.17	10.61	0.18	10.75	0.18	10.90	0.19
8	11.64	0.16	11.78	0.17	11.92	0.17	12.08	0.18
9	12.79	0.15	12.93	0.15	13.09	0.17	13.25	0.17
10	13.93	0.14	14.08	0.15	14.24	0.15	14.42	0.17
11	15.07	0.14	15.23	0.15	15.39	0.15	15.57	0.15
12	16.20	0.13	16.36	0.13	16.54	0.15	16.72	0.15
13	17.33	0.13	17.49	0.13	17.67	0.13	17.86	0.14
14	18.45	0.12	18.62	0.13	18.80	0.13	19.00	0.14
15	19.57	0.12	19.74	0.12	19.93	0.13	20.13	0.13
16	20.68	0.11	20.87	0.13	21.06	0.13	21.26	0.13
17	21.79	0.11	21.98	0.11	22.17	0.11	22.39	0.13
18	22.90	0.11	23.09	0.11	23.29	0.12	23.51	0.12
19	24.00	0.10	24.20	0.11	24.40	0.11	24.63	0.12
20	25.10	0.10	25.30	0.10	25.52	0.12	25.74	0.11

Errors	14%		13%		12%		11%	
	UEL	PGW	UEL	PGW	UEL	PGW	UEL	PGW
0	1.97	—	2.04	—	2.12	—	2.21	—
1	3.46	0.49	3.56	0.52	3.66	0.54	3.77	0.56
2	4.83	0.37	4.94	0.38	5.06	0.40	5.18	0.41
3	6.13	0.30	6.25	0.31	6.39	0.33	6.53	0.35
4	7.39	0.26	7.53	0.28	7.67	0.28	7.83	0.30
5	8.63	0.24	8.77	0.24	8.93	0.26	9.09	0.26
6	9.85	0.22	10.00	0.23	10.17	0.24	10.34	0.25
7	11.05	0.20	11.21	0.21	11.38	0.21	11.57	0.23
8	12.24	0.19	12.41	0.20	12.59	0.21	12.78	0.21
9	13.41	0.17	13.59	0.18	13.78	0.19	13.99	0.21
10	14.58	0.17	14.77	0.18	14.97	0.19	15.18	0.19
11	15.75	0.17	15.94	0.17	16.14	0.17	16.36	0.18
12	16.90	0.15	17.10	0.16	17.31	0.17	17.54	0.18
13	18.05	0.15	18.26	0.16	18.47	0.16	18.70	0.16
14	19.19	0.14	19.41	0.15	19.63	0.16	19.87	0.17
15	20.33	0.14	20.55	0.14	20.78	0.15	21.02	0.15
16	21.46	0.13	21.69	0.14	21.92	0.14	22.18	0.16
17	22.59	0.13	22.83	0.14	23.07	0.15	23.33	0.15
18	23.72	0.13	23.96	0.13	24.21	0.14	24.47	0.14
19	24.84	0.12	25.09	0.13	25.34	0.13	25.61	0.14
20	25.97	0.13	26.21	0.12	26.47	0.13	26.75	0.14

BETA RISKS

Errors	10%		5%		4%		3%	
	UEL	PGW	UEL	PGW	UEL	PGW	UEL	PGW
0	2.31	—	3.00	—	3.22	—	3.51	—
1	3.89	0.58	4.75	0.75	5.01	0.79	5.36	0.85
2	5.33	0.44	6.30	0.55	6.60	0.59	6.98	0.62
3	6.69	0.36	7.76	0.46	8.09	0.49	8.51	0.53
4	8.00	0.31	9.16	0.40	9.51	0.42	9.96	0.45
5	9.28	0.28	10.52	0.36	10.89	0.38	11.37	0.41
6	10.54	0.26	11.85	0.33	12.24	0.35	12.75	0.38
7	11.78	0.24	13.15	0.30	13.57	0.33	14.10	0.35
8	13.00	0.22	14.44	0.29	14.87	0.30	15.42	0.32
9	14.21	0.21	15.71	0.27	16.16	0.29	16.73	0.31
10	15.41	0.20	16.97	0.26	17.43	0.27	18.02	0.29
11	16.60	0.19	18.21	0.24	18.69	0.26	19.30	0.28
12	17.79	0.19	19.45	0.24	19.94	0.25	20.57	0.27
13	18.96	0.17	20.67	0.22	21.18	0.24	21.83	0.26
14	20.13	0.17	21.89	0.22	22.42	0.24	23.08	0.25
15	21.30	0.17	23.10	0.21	23.64	0.22	24.32	0.24
16	22.46	0.16	24.31	0.21	24.86	0.22	25.56	0.24
17	23.61	0.15	25.50	0.19	26.07	0.21	26.78	0.22
18	24.76	0.15	26.70	0.20	27.27	0.20	28.00	0.22
19	25.91	0.15	27.88	0.18	28.47	0.20	29.22	0.22
20	27.05	0.14	29.07	0.19	29.67	0.20	30.42	0.20

Errors	2%		1%	
	UEL	PGW	UEL	PGW
0	3.91	—	4.61	—
1	5.83	0.92	6.64	1.03
2	7.52	0.69	8.41	0.77
3	9.08	0.56	10.05	0.64
4	10.58	0.50	11.61	0.56
5	12.03	0.45	13.11	0.50
6	13.44	0.41	14.58	0.47
7	14.82	0.38	16.00	0.42
8	16.17	0.35	17.41	0.41
9	17.51	0.34	18.79	0.38
10	18.83	0.32	20.15	0.36
11	20.13	0.30	21.49	0.34
12	21.42	0.29	22.83	0.34
13	22.71	0.29	24.14	0.31
14	23.98	0.27	25.45	0.31
15	25.24	0.26	26.75	0.30
16	26.50	0.26	28.04	0.29
17	27.74	0.24	29.31	0.27
18	28.98	0.24	30.59	0.28
19	30.22	0.24	31.85	0.26
20	31.42	0.20	33.11	0.26

Appendix 20B

TABLE OF RANDOM DIGITS

32942	95416	42339	59045	26693	49057	87496	20624	14819
07410	99859	83828	21409	29094	65114	36701	25762	12827
59981	68155	45673	76210	58219	45738	29550	24736	09574
46251	25437	69654	99716	11563	08803	86027	51867	12116
65558	51904	93123	27887	53138	21488	09095	78777	71240
99187	19258	86421	16401	19397	83297	40111	49326	81686
35641	00301	16096	34775	21562	97983	45040	19200	16383
14031	00936	81518	48440	02218	04756	19506	60695	88494
60677	15076	92554	26042	23472	69869	62877	19584	39576
66314	05212	67859	89356	20056	30648	87349	20389	53805
20416	87410	75646	64176	82752	63606	37011	57346	69512
28701	56992	70423	62415	40807	98086	58850	28968	45297
74579	33844	33426	07570	00728	07079	19322	56325	84819
62615	52342	82968	75540	80045	53069	20665	21282	07768
93945	06293	22879	08161	01442	75071	21427	94842	26210
75689	76131	96837	67450	44511	50424	82848	41975	71663
02921	16919	35424	93209	52133	87327	95897	65171	20376
14295	34969	14216	03191	61647	30296	66667	10101	63203
05303	91109	82403	40312	62191	67023	90073	83205	71344
57071	90357	12901	08899	91039	67251	28701	03846	94589
78471	57741	13599	84390	32146	00871	09354	22745	65806
89242	79337	59293	47481	07740	43345	25716	70020	54005
14955	59592	97035	80430	87220	06392	79028	57123	52872
42446	41880	37415	47472	04513	49494	08860	08038	43624
18534	22346	54556	17558	73689	14894	05030	19561	56517
39284	33737	42512	86411	23753	29690	26096	81361	93099
33922	37329	89911	55876	28379	81031	22058	21487	54613
78355	54013	50774	30666	61205	42574	47773	36027	27174
08845	99145	94316	88974	29828	97069	90327	61842	29604
01769	71825	55957	98271	02784	66731	40311	88495	18821
17639	38284	59478	90409	21997	56199	30068	82800	69692
05851	58653	99949	63505	40409	85551	90729	64938	52403
42396	40112	11469	03476	03328	84238	26570	51790	42122
13318	14192	98167	75631	74141	22369	36757	89117	54998
60571	54786	26281	01855	30706	66578	32019	65884	58485
09531	81853	59334	70929	03544	18510	89541	13555	21168
72865	16829	86542	00396	20363	13010	69645	49608	54738
56324	31093	77924	28622	83543	28912	15059	80192	83964
78192	21626	91399	07235	07104	73652	64425	85149	75409
64666	34767	97298	92708	01994	53188	78476	07804	62404
82201	75694	02808	65983	74373	66693	13094	74183	73020
15360	73776	40914	85190	54278	99054	62944	47351	89098
68142	67957	70896	37983	20487	95350	16371	03426	13895
19138	31200	30616	14639	44406	44236	57360	81644	94761
28155	03521	36415	78452	92359	81091	56513	88321	97910
87971	29031	51780	27376	81056	86155	55488	50590	74514
58147	68841	53625	02059	75223	16783	19272	61994	71090
18875	52809	70594	41649	32935	26430	82096	01605	65846
75109	56474	74111	31966	29969	70093	98901	84550	25769
35983	03742	76822	12073	59463	84420	15868	99505	11426

Source: The Rand Corporation, *A Million Random Digits with 100,000 Normal Deviates* (Glencoe: Free Press, 1955), p. 102.

Appendix 20C

Other Topics in Statistical Auditing: Regression for Analytical Review

Auditors sometimes use statistical models with analytical review procedures. The most common such statistical model is regression. In a regression model a linear mathematical relationship is assumed between one dependent variable and one or more independent variables based on a set of values for these variables. An illustration of a relationship that may be used in auditing is to set the dependent variable equal to sales, the independent variable to cost of sales. The data set may consist of monthly recorded amounts for each of the 36 months preceding the current year. A scatter graph of these variables may suggest a linear relationship, which the auditor might exploit in order to get audit assurance from such a relationship.

The simple regression model assumes a linear relationship and "fits" a line that reflects this relationship and estimates two parameter values necessary to model the line. The regression model is represented as follows:

$$y = a + bx + E$$

where y = the dependent variable values, e.g., sales values, which vary depending on the independent variable.

where x = the independent variable, e.g., cost of sales, which is the variable assumed "to explain" the dependent variable. From an audit point of view it can be any variable that plausibly provides an explanation for the dependent variable based on past historical relationships.

where a = a constant and represents one of the parameters, the intercept (value of y when $x = 0$), estimated by the regression of the linear equation; where b = another constant estimated by the regression model called the coefficient of the independent variable and represents the slope of the regression line. Both constants a and b are needed to define the regression line mathematically.

where E = the residual unexplained difference and reflects the fact that the regression line is not a perfect predictor of y given the x variable. If this residual gets too large for any given month observation it is termed an *outlier.*

After constructing a regression line statistically with one or more independent variables, the auditor can use this model to predict the adequacy of the reported amount for the dependent variable for the months covering the current audit period.

For an illustration we use an example from an influential book on statistical regression by K.W. Stringer and J.R. Steward of the former Deloitte Haskins Sells.[7] Their Gamma Company example used data from the 36 months preceding the current fiscal year to estimate a linear equation using regression of the following form:

$$y = -366.46 + .8906\, x1 + 1.3578\, x2$$

where y here represents revenues for a software firm
$x1$ = programming hours at standard and
$x2$ = expenses

---

[7] K.W. Stringer and J.R. Stewart, *Statistical Techniques for Analytical Review (STAR)*, Deloitte, Haskins & Sells, New York, 1985.

Assume also that the model has successfully passed the usual tests for regression, e.g., *t* test and *F* test, and the usual diagnostics that are normally built into the software used by auditing firms. With such a model the auditor can develop expectations for the current audit period on revenues by month; for example, say the client reports revenues of 2,698 for June and the auditor wishes to get some assurance on the accuracy of this amount. The above regression model can be used to make a prediction about what revenues should be, given historical relationships. So, plugging standard hours of 2013 for June and expenses of 1157 for June into the equation, we get predicted revenues of:

$$y = -336.96 + .8906\,(2013) + 1.3578\,(1157) = 3027$$

The difference between the expected amount provided by the model and the actual amount proposed by the client (3027 − 2698 = 329) is the amount of variation unexplained by expected relationships. If the auditor feels this difference is significant he or she would investigate revenue for the month of June in more detail. Note how regression can be used to identify problem areas and to help plan the audit of the revenue amount in this case.

GRAPH OF TYPICAL REGRESSION APPLICATION

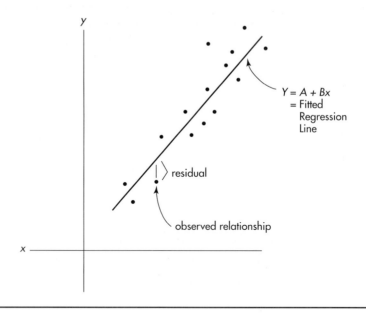

Several technical implementation issues have to be addressed in developing models like the one above. First, and most importantly, the auditor has to determine plausible business relationships for use in the regression to determine expectations for the amounts being audited. This includes identifying the appropriate dependent and independent variables to use in the model. The auditor would start by using his/her professional judgment in selecting the variables to use in the model. This can be supplemented by various statistical tests to further refine the model. For example, the initial set of independent variables considered for this regression included hours worked by programmer, senior programmer, and analysts as well as the hourly rates for each of these groups, and expenses charged to clients and cost of services.

It takes a high level of audit judgment and good knowledge of the client's business to develop cost-effective regression models for analytical procedures. Such statistical models are used primarily at the planning stage, when they are of most use to the auditor. As noted in Chapter 10, analytical procedures have proven to be very effective procedures for detecting material errors in audits. And they can be used for a variety of accounts, particularly when sufficiently desegregated monthly data are conveniently available from the client.

However, caution is advisable since research has also shown that while statistical analytical review can be used to provide some audit assurance for client accounts, it should not be used to provide a high level or the sole amount of assurance for anything other than immaterial amounts.

Another caution is that because of the sensitivity of the regression results to materiality, the planned level of assurance (essentially the confidence level), and the need to use the negative approach, auditors need to develop a special interface in applying regression models to audit practice. In other words, you can't just take a regression package available from, say, LOTUS and apply it to your audit data. Keep in mind that audit assurance is related to 1-RIA, not 1-RIR. Specifically, in most scientific applications the null hypothesis relates to there being no difference because the scientist is usually interested in the effects of some experimental treatment. In auditing because the crucial null hypothesis assumes there is a material difference, the confidence level is the complement of the opposite risk that is normally used in the sciences. Specifically, in the sciences (and therefore in most statistical tables) it is the positive approach that is used rather than the negative approach that is relevant to the auditor.

As a result special adjustments normally need to be made for classical statistical estimators, and that includes the regression model. That is why audit firms have developed a special audit interface to be used with the regression models. And you should be aware of the need for such an interface before applying off-the-shelf regression packages to audit applications. In fact it's far better to obtain a package specially tailored for auditor use. Most of the large firms already have such packages, thus making use of statistical analytical procedures very feasible.

DUS for Tests of Controls

Although we have noted that DUS formulas can be used for tests of controls applications, we implicitly assumed in all our illustrations that the test of controls sampling was based on physical unit selection. Some auditors argue that a more appropriate way of evaluating controls is to use dollar unit sampling rather than physical unit selection. The reason for this is that automatic stratification of the population results from DUS and the evaluation of controls can then be based on the maximum proportion of dollars (rather than maximum proportion of physical units) in the population that is likely to contain errors. Research has shown that compliance deviation rates per recorded dollar can be substantially different from compliance deviation rates for physical units such as sales invoices or shipping documents.

For example, in the stratification example in Chapter 7 compliance deviations for strata 3, 4, 5 may be much higher than for the high valued items, in strata 1 and 2. The auditor can incorporate such differences judgmentally or let the sampling technique DUS automatically account for this effect in evaluating controls. Note such differences in controls for different strata could affect auditor strategies as noted in Exhibit 13–2. In fact, we can take the position that unstratified physical units sampling for attributes ignores possible differing strengths of controls based on the value of items recorded—unstratified physical unit sampling for tests of controls implicitly assumes controls are equally strong for high-value items and low-value items. Limited empirical evidence on this issue suggests this is not the case in practice. Nevertheless, unstratified physical units is the most commonly used method in practice currently. A recent Canadian research study has called for a change in this practice and increased reliance on DUS for control testing.[8] As the importance of auditor reports on internal controls increases, perhaps this issue will gain increasing prominence.

We can now try to summarize all the various sampling risks with the audit risk model.

SAMPLING RISKS AND THE AUDIT RISK MODEL
· · · · · · · · · · · · ·

The basic goal of the audit can be characterized as providing a high degree of assurance that there are no material errors, where:

Level of assurance = Probability that there is no material error after the audit = 1 − Probability of material error existing after the audit = 1 − Audit risk, and where audit risk according to the *Handbook* can be represented as audit risk = IR * CR * DR where IR = inherent risk, CR = control risk, and DR = detective risk. DR in turn is sometimes split up into a substantive testing of details risk (RIA) and risk of other audit procedures including analytical review (APR). Some auditors prefer to stress the audit assurance aspect provided by these various sources so that they refer to assurance from substantive testing of details risk (= 1 − RIA) or assurance from analytical procedures (= 1 − APR). This is just a different way of looking at these factors, and the amount of work would not be affected since the assessments are still the same.

Now, how do all these risks relate to sampling risk?

IR = inherent risk has nothing to do with sampling risk, but note it relates to risk of having material errors, i.e., the negative approach null hypothesis underlying beta risk.

RIA = beta risk for substantive tests of details.

CR = beta risk for tests of control under some approaches; however, since there are usually several tests of control, CR does not automatically equal a beta for a given test. Professional judgment is also required in combining the results of several procedures on internal control (some statistical, some not) to assess CR for a given application.

APR = beta risk for regression equations for analytical review, but if combined with other nonstatistical analytical procedures (which is normally the case), additional professional judgment is required to assess APR.

Now we can better appreciate why same practitioners say "minimization of the overall beta risk is the reason for the existence of the public accounting profession." Statistical auditing provides a more objective means of controlling these beta risks for different procedures. Note moreover that alpha risk is not directly considered anywhere in the risk model. Perhaps this explains why auditors are less likely to directly quantify alpha risk in practice.

---

[8] D.A. Leslie, *Materiality, The Concept and Its Application to Auditing*, CICA, 1985, Ch. 8.

Appendix

Environmental Auditing

Introduction

Environmental auditing is a relatively new concept with most developments occurring within the last decade or so. Much of the interest seems to have arisen as a result of environmental "accidents" such as the *Exxon Valdez* oil spill in Alaska and the Union Carbide toxic gas explosion in Bhopal, India, which killed or injured over 200,000 people. These highly publicized catastrophes raised public consciousness to the point that considerable legislation has been passed which makes it increasingly impossible for companies to ignore environmental issues. In fact, the increasing awareness of environmental issues is leading to a redefinition of the objectives of economic growth and development, which in turn is leading to a reconsideration of the principles underlying the accounting reporting model. Changes in the financial reporting model and controls associated with environmental effects and adherence to environmental legislation have an impact in turn on auditing for these new assertions.

This appendix reviews the present state of environmental auditing and reporting. The current role of PAs is assessed, along with the opportunities for the profession as environmental auditing and reporting practices evolve to meet the new demands of stakeholders—demands which in some cases involve conflicting duties and thus can raise new ethical issues in auditing and reporting. In fact, in some cases environmental audits can be viewed as a part of broader ethics audits.[1]

The Evolving Demands of Corporate Stakeholders

Traditionally, a company's shareholders were normally defined as the providers of capital, creditors, and shareholders. Corporate reporting developed to meet the needs of these shareholders, providing them with financial information. The objective of financial reporting was, and largely still is today, the primary means of holding management accountable to the providers of capital.

Under the broader stakeholder concept of environmental auditing, however, accountability is linked to the concept of sustainable development introduced in the 1987 report of the U.N. World Commission on Environment and Development. The term refers to development that "meets the needs of the present without compromising the ability of future generations to meet their needs." The concept of stakeholder is, therefore, extended to include future generations.

[1] L.J. Brooks, *Professional Ethics for Accountants*, 1995, West Publishing, p. 256.

As sustainable development has become an increasingly important policy objective of governments and peoples of the world, other stakeholders are coming to exert more and more influence on companies. Communities, environmental groups, consumers, and employees are some of the "new" stakeholders to which companies are increasingly being held accountable. Sustainable development has redefined the notion of economic growth. Governments throughout the world and the people they serve have come to demand economic growth without compromise to the environment. Any investment or business activity may come under close scrutiny from environmentalists and other stakeholders. Stakeholders, such as communities in which companies operate, are demanding that companies comply with environmental regulations, practise sound environmental policies, and have systems and controls in place to manage their environmental policies.

The combination of heightened environmental awareness and stricter environmental regulations throughout the world has made environmental liabilities an increasingly important aspect of a company's financial position. Providers of capital, as the primary financial statement users, have come to demand greater disclosure of possible environmental liabilities and a company's policies and practices with regards to environmental systems. Thus, interest in environmental accounting is spreading, but there is little agreement about who should get such information, and what it should consist of—in qualitative or quantitative terms.

There are also no generally accepted conventions for the presentations and disclosure of such information. (Even for financial statements, more clarification is needed on how to define environmental costs and risks, and how to disclose them.)

There is also confusion about different types of environmental audit, their purpose and scope.

There is no agreement about who should perform such audits. (Many different disciplines and service providers are involved.)

There is little agreement on what auditing standards should be applied or developed.

Present-day Requirements for Environmental Reporting
• • • • • • • • • • • •

The increase in liabilities and obligations relating to environmental matters has led to an ever-increasing body of legislation governing financial disclosure and reporting. There has also been the formulation of public policy documents such as the *Valdez Principles* (see following box). The development of legislation has been driven primarily by securities commissions that have sought to increase disclosure of environmental liabilities to investors. The overall objective is to ensure the efficient operation of financial markets by ensuring that information concerning environmental liabilities and contingencies is adequately disclosed.

The Valdez Principles

1. **Protection of the Biosphere**
   We will minimize and strive to eliminate the release of any pollutant that may cause environmental damage to the air, water, or earth or its

inhabitants. We will safeguard habitats in rivers, lakes, wetlands, coastal zones, and oceans and will minimize contributing to the greenhouse effect, depletion of the ozone layer, acid rain, or smog.

2. **Sustainable Use of Natural Resources**

   We will make sustainable use of renewable natural resources, such as water, soils, and forests. We will conserve non-renewable natural resources through efficient use and careful planning. We will protect wildlife habitat, open spaces, and wilderness, while preserving biodiversity.

3. **Reduction and Disposal of Waste**

   We will minimize the creation of waste, especially hazardous waste, and whenever possible recycle materials. We will dispose of all wastes through safe and responsible methods.

4. **Wise Use of Energy**

   We will make every effort to use environmentally safe and sustainable energy sources to meet our needs. We will invest in improved energy efficiency and conservation in our operations. We will maximize the energy efficiency of products we produce or sell.

5. **Risk Reduction**

   We will minimize the environmental, health, and safety risks to our employees and the communities in which we operate by employing safe technologies and operating procedures and by being constantly prepared for emergencies.

6. **Marketing of Safe Products and Services**

   We will sell products or services that minimize adverse environmental impacts and that are safe as consumers commonly use them. We will inform consumers of the environmental impacts of our products and services.

7. **Damage Compensation**

   We will take responsibility for any harm we cause to the environment by making every effort to fully restore the environment and to compensate those persons who are adversely affected.

8. **Disclosure**

   We will disclose to our employees and to the public incidents relating to our operations that cause environmental harm or pose health or safety hazards. We will disclose potential environmental, health, or safety hazards posed by our operations, and we will not take any action against employees who report any condition that creates a danger to the environment or poses health and safety hazards.

9. **Environmental Director and Managers**

   We will commit management resources to implement the Valdez Principles, to monitor and to sustain a process to ensure that the Board of Directors and Chief Executive Officer are kept informed of and are fully responsible for all environmental matters. We will establish a Committee of the Board of Directors with responsibility for environmental affairs. At least one member of the Board of Directors will be a person qualified to represent environmental interests to come before the company.

10. **Assessment and Annual Audit**

    We will conduct and make public an annual self-evaluation of our

> progress in implementing these Principles and in complying with all applicable laws and regulations throughout our worldwide operations. We will work toward the timely creation of independent environmental audit procedures which we will complete annually and make available to the public.
>
> *Source:* Coalition for Environmentally Responsible Economies, USA, 1989, in CICA (1992), *Environmental Auditing and the Role of the Accounting Profession.*

The SEC in the United States requires environmental disclosure as part of the statutory filings of publicly traded companies. The following disclosures are required:

- Material effects of compliance with environmental law on earnings, capital expenditures, and competitive position.
- Estimates of current and future environmental expenditures.
- Pending and possible environmental legal proceedings.
- Any environmental problems likely to have a material effect.

In Canada the Ontario and Quebec Securities commissions require annual information forms that disclose the *cost of compliance* with environmental protection requirements for both current and future periods.

Present-day environmental disclosure is also embodied in the general accepted accounting principles of GAAP. Current *Handbook* requirements in Canada cover provision and contingent losses directly applicable to environmental matters. The *Handbook Section* 3290 on contingencies requires the accrual of any liabilities that are likely to come to bear and can be reasonably estimated. *Those that cannot be reasonably estimated with respect to amount and maturity should be disclosed.* A relatively new *CICA Handbook* section on capital assets requires the recognition in the financial statements of future site removal and restoration costs, through accumulated provision and a charge to income.

> When reasonably determinable, provision should be made for future removal and site restoration costs, net of expected recoveries, in a rational and systematic manner by charges to income. [*Section* 3060.39]
>
> Future removal and site restoration costs include costs, net of expected recoveries, for dismantling and abandoning a property. Provisions are needed to accrue the liability for future removal and site restoration costs, when the likelihood of their occurrence is established as a result of environmental law, contract, or because the enterprise has established a policy to restore site, and when such costs can reasonably be determined. Provisions are recorded as liabilities and are not classified with accumulated amortization [*Section* 3060.40]

In addition to financial disclosure of environmental matters that are required by exchange commissions and accounting standards, there are also nonfinancial disclosures that are required by various government and regulatory agencies. The U.S. Toxic Release Inventory (TRI) is probably one of the most significant of these nonfinancial reporting requirements. The legislation requires any company employing more than 10 people to provide information on emissions of its operations.

EXAMPLES OF ENVIRONMENTAL LEGISLATION FROM SIX JURISDICTIONS IN CANADA
(AS AT APRIL 30, 1992)

Federal
Canadian Environmental Protection Act,
  Guidelines and Regulations
Canada Water Act & Guidelines
Fisheries Act, Guidelines and Regulations
Transportation of Dangerous Goods Act
Northern Inland Water Act
Environmental Contaminants Act and
  Regulations
Canada Shipping Act & Regulations

Quebec
Environment Quality Act & Regulations
Pesticides Act
Conservation and Development of Wildlife Act
Ecological Reserves Act
Highway Safety Code-Transportation of
  Dangerous Substance Regulations
Transport Act and Transport of Waste Regulation

Alberta
Clean Air Act
Clean Water Act
Forest and Prairie Protection Act
Hazardous Chemical Act
Land Surface Conservation and Reclamation Act
Oil and Gas Conservation Act
Transportation of Dangerous Goods Act
Wilderness Areas Ecological Reserves and
  Natural Areas Act
Coal Conservation Act

New Brunswick
Clean Environment Act and Regulations
Clean Water Act and Regulations
Pesticides Control Act and General Regulation
Transportation of Dangerous Goods Act and
  General Regulation
Endangered Species Act

Ontario
Environmental Protection Act and Regulations
Dangerous Goods Transportation Act
Gasoline Handling Act
Ontario Water Resources Act
Environmental Assessment Act
Pesticides Act
Municipal Act
Endangered Species Act
Mining Act

British Columbia
Waste Management Act and Regulations
Transport of Dangerous Goods Act
Pesticide Control Act
Motor Vehicles Act—Air Pollution Control
  Regulations
Hazard Waste Management Corporation Act
Environment & Land Use Act

Source: CICA (1992), *Environmental Auditing and the Role of the Accounting Profession CICA, 1992.*

This information is provided in an annually filed report, which is available to the public.

Regulatory reporting requirements are more geared to the information needs of the "nontraditional" stakeholders than those of investors and creditors, although information provided is also of use to these stakeholders. The objective of these reports ties into the sustainable development concept. The proliferation of guidelines, legal precedents, and laws (see the box above for a sample Canadian listing for illustrative purposes) in the last 20 years means that the environment can no longer be ignored by business.

Legal Environment

To further complicate the issue, pollutants do not always stay at the site where they are produced. It is possible for the pollutants to travel by air or make their way to the underground water supply. Due to the pollutants' "ability to travel," the real damage can be a considerable distance from the immediate site of contamination. In addition, the effect of the pollution may take years to become noticeable. The contaminant's "ability to travel" and the "time-delay" nature of its effect make it very difficult to track down the origin of the pollutants. As a result, the legislation is purposely designed to make it easier for all the affected parties to sue and retrieve damages.

Generally, the legal liabilities will rest on the current owner of the property. Plaintiffs will sue, under tort, the current owner of the property that stores/emits the pollutants causing the damage. As a result, the business community and stakeholders (such as banks, creditors, and shareholders) are becoming very careful in purchasing properties or extending mortgages. The following box illustrates why Canadian banks now require a loan approval environmental checklist (which is equivalent to a Phase I Site Assessment, to be discussed later). In addition, company directors, officers, and other personnel can be held liable for environmental law violations. Penalties could range from fines to restitutions. For example, both the United States and Canada have enacted environmental protection laws that can levy fines of up to $2 million a day in the United States and $1 million a day in Canada, as well as personal fines and jail terms for the executives.[2]

In 1985 North Country Bank took a mortgage on commercial property after lending Company X $4 million to buy the property. The property had held fuel storage tanks in the 1930s and 1940s. In 1988 Company X refused to continue payments on the mortgage and North Country Bank took possession of the property. In 1989 environmental legislation was passed making owners of property legally liable to clean up certain carcinogenic compounds, including the petroleum residues that contaminated Property Y. Not only did North Country lose its $4 million loan, but as current owner it incurred an additional $12 million in clean-up costs!

As a result of this relatively hostile environment, businesses increasingly turned to the various types of environmental assessments to identify and avoid environmental problems. This allowed them to demonstrate "due diligence" in cases where it is a valid defence. This interest in "due diligence" started in the United States when a judge indicated the above fines could be reduced to $50,000 per day if an effective "due diligence" program could be shown to be in place at the corporation. The interest of many large companies was immediately stimulated to find out about such programs and how to implement them to make it effective. Not surprisingly, one of

---

[2] Ibid., p. 135.

the fundamental elements in this process is the organization's code of conduct, which sets out behavioural expectations for all employees.[3]

Given the potential magnitude of environmental liabilities, this information is becoming increasingly important to lenders and creditors. Information on a company's environmental policies and on its environmental systems designed to achieve these policies can provide creditors and shareholders with an indication of how successful a company will be in discharging its environmental responsibilities and avoiding environmental liabilities.

These legal and bad-publicity threats are getting management's attention. It's become increasingly clear that management has to manage operations with the new accountability expectations in mind. Furthermore, they have to report appropriately to the stakeholder, within an accountability framework, on how the entity performs to meet those expectations. This forces the management to look for and develop new ways to report to the internal and external stakeholders on environmental performance in both financial and nonfinancial turns.

In addition, some companies are beginning to expect more from environmental assessments than the basic regulatory compliance. They expect them to contribute to a continuous improvement in environmental performance and related cost management practices. They also want to have an emergency response plan and an environmental assessment/planning process in place. An illustration of some of these objectives is given in the box below.

SUSTAINABLE FOREST MANAGEMENT CERTIFICATION

Throughout the 1990s, sustainable forest management standards were being developed in a number of countries. We believe that such standards can be a welcome addition to forest management practices, as well as a way to assure the public that the forests are in capable hands. Regrettably, in some markets, these standards are being used to block trade. Certification should be voluntary, not mandated. Companies that follow the certification path will win in the long run by giving their customers another good reason to choose them as a preferred supplier.

A Sustainable Forest Management (SFM) system is being developed by the Canadian Standards Association (CSA), in cooperation with the forest industry, government, universities, non-governmental organizations, and aboriginal groups. Companies will voluntarily establish their own sustainable forest management system, and will apply to be certified according to the CSA Standard.

An audit will be required prior to certification. Although the SFM system was not scheduled to be introduced until 1996, Abitibi-Price decided to conduct its own pre-certification audits in two of its forestry operations in 1995.

Over the next years our sustainable forestry activities will be wide-ranging. We will do more comprehensive planning (greater detail, with more public input), and increase monitoring (documentation of what is being done and how it compares to standards). Our environmental awareness training will also continue, to ensure that all of our employees are familiar with our evolving

---

[3] Ibid., p. 135.

sustainable forest management practices. Often, such training is only the beginning. Our people's growing knowledge and respect for the natural world has an impact on the entire company.

The audits have allowed us to compare our practices against the developing standards to determine where we need to improve our practices. We will be auditing, then applying to have all of our forestry operations certified in 1997.

Auditing Our Forestry Operations

In August of 1995, Abitibi-Price's Newfoundland forest operations were audited by Price Waterhouse, an international accounting and management consulting firm which has developed considerable expertise in forest management auditing (forest scientists and academics are closely involved in the field-level audits). Our objective was to establish where we stood in relation to the Canadian Standards Association's Sustainable Forest Management system draft criteria. Price Waterhouse evaluated us on our silviculture, planning, harvesting, road construction, wildlife habitat, and biodiversity activities.

The audit report described our Newfoundland forests as "healthy and vigorous," and noted that our Fibre Resources division (serving both our Grand Falls and Stephenville mills) is to be commended for its proactive approach to sustainability. Our environmental awareness and compliance ratings compared favourably with other forest companies across Canada, our relations with the relevant regulatory agencies are good, and our environmental training efforts are excellent. We have prepared an action plan to implement recommended improvements in such areas as record-keeping, water quality and the inclusion of non-timber values.

Source: Abitibi-Price, *1994–95 Progress Report on the Environment,* pp. 16–17.

These various services are sometimes referred to as audits by the users. However, many other terms are used (see the following box).

Examples of Names of Environmental Audit and Similar-sounding Services

Environmental Audit	Environmental Liability Audit
Corporate Greening Audit	Environmental Impact Assessment
Waste Management Audit	Energy Audit
Emissions Audit	Environmental Risk Audit
Prepurchase Audit	Procurement Audit
Property Transfer Audit	Real Estate Audit
Site Clean-up Investigation	Water Conservation Audit
Environmental Compliance Audit	Supplier Audit
Environmental Management Audit	Product Life-cycle Audit

Source: Environmental Auditing and the Role of the Accounting Profession, CICA, 1992, p. 23.

The Investment Community

The SEC in the United States and the provincial securities commissions in Canada require specific disclosures on cost and effects of environmental protection and restoration measures. The commissions also encourage that general business risk and uncertainty be properly disclosed. This form of corporate reporting requires an examination of the company's conformity with the new accounting and reporting standards on environmental management systems. To allow comparability between different companies' financial statements, a commonly accepted criterion for the evaluation of environmental management systems is needed. However, this is made difficult by the existence of many providers of environmental services.

Service Providers

At present, there are many people who are qualified to provide environmental services. For example:

- Large, well-established engineering and scientific consulting firms.
- Management consulting divisions of some public accounting firms.
  - Their primary focus is on finance, management systems, and strategy, rather than on direct provision of technical, scientific assessment services.
- Small, specialty environmental consulting firms.
  - They typically having a strong engineering scientific and operational orientation. They tend to offer their professional services on site cleanup and facility compliance assessment.
- Internal corporate environmental audit functions.
- Law firms.

The services of law firms are requested when due diligence reviews or client–solicitor privilege is sought. Lawyers have an advantage over PAs. When PAs are providing the environmental engagement, they are bound by the client confidentiality but not the client–solicitor privilege. An ethical dilemma may occur when the service in question reveals violations of environmental laws and the PA is called upon to testify against his/her client.

For the PAs to obtain the solicitor–client privilege, a legal counsel is required. The counsellor will direct the environmental assessment, using specialist services needed. The resulting report to the senior management will then be on a restrictive basis (i.e., not for general internal use). In other words, the report will not be admissible in court as evidence and the PA will not be called to verify the report in court. This reduces the chance of the company (which calls for the report) incriminating itself through external parties being able to gain access to the report.

The PAs' Role and Their Concerns in Environmental Audit

The role of the PA profession in society has traditionally been derived from the social expectation that corporations are accountable to those who provide the funds for doing business. PAs provide an assurance to the stakeholders that the financial statements and financial information, prepared and provided by the entity, meet the established reporting standards and can be relied upon. The PA profession also sets the attestation standards for their role as they are providing this type of service.

The setting of the standards for financial reporting and for attestation of entities' financial reports is a quasilegal responsibility borne by the PA profession. An effect of this is to add credibility to the information provided by the management and the board of the shareholder.

On the other hand, many of the environmental laws and regulations are scientific and technical in nature. As a result, to conduct the environmental services the service providers have to have a significant amount of engineering and scientific expertise. Due to this unique nature of the engagement, "environmental audits" often involve the technical expertise of other professionals (such as lawyers and engineers). Currently, these professions and individuals can provide environmentally related audit and consulting services on their own. In other words, it is perfectly legal, and technically feasible, to carry out an "environmental audit" without the involvement of the PA profession. For example, some internal auditing activities were already including environmental protection elements in their health and safety programs. It is very often the case that even their in-house accountants are left out of the development process.

Recently, some organizations (e.g., the Institute of Environmental Auditors, based in Washington, D.C.) have begun to promote environmental audit as a distinct professional discipline. Their aim is to establish generally accepted standards for performing environmental audits as well as accreditation programs for those who conduct them.

This represents a potential problem. The term *audit* is generally and widely associated with the work of the PA profession. The close association may unfairly imply PAs' involvement. In addition, the public may perceive and expect the same level of assurance in a financial statement audit. As a result, the PA profession is increasingly concerned with the following questions.

1. Who wants the environmental audits, why, and what are they expecting?
2. What use is made of the results, by whom, for what purposes or decisions?
3. What is the subject matter of the environmental audits, who does them, and what disciplines and skills are involved?
4. How are they carried out, what do reports communicate, and what standards and methods are employed?
5. What is their history, how are they likely to evolve in the future, and what is the role of PAs in any of this?

Due to the increasing interest in the environmental movement by the general public and private sector, a large number of commissioned studies, reviews, investigations, and assessments are placed under the broad banner of "environmental audit." Although the issue has been looked into by a significant number of people, there is still no general accepted definition for the term *environmental audit*.

Nonetheless, methodologies and checklists, for various types of the environmental audit, have been drawn up by some companies for in-house use. This has also been done by some industry associations for member company use. Outside specialist firms have also published methodologies in this area as tools for quality assurance, service efficiency, and staff training. As a consequence, there are as many methodologies as the number of people developing them. Since different methodologies have been developed for different purposes and different perspectives, an "environmental audit" can represent different activities and services to different people.

In a nutshell, environmental auditing in Canada is not mandatory, and it is still in its infancy.

ACCOUNTING ASPECTS OF ENVIRONMENTAL REPORTING ISSUES
. . . .

An article by Longworth and Montano deals with accounting issues related to environmental costs.[4] A study group of the CICA has concluded that a new section to the *Handbook* should be added to deal specifically with recognition, measurements, and disclosure of environmental costs. The group feels current *Handbook Sections* 3060 on capital assets and 3290 on contingencies are deficient, especially in the conflict created between asset write-down under 3060 and accruals for a contingent loss (which can be reversed) under 3290.

One issue is that future cleanup costs do not represent obligations to other entities and thus create a new type of liability. This liability would set up a related deferred charge, which would be amortized over the useful life of the site.

Another issue is whether to capitalize or expense environmental costs incurred. Although there may be no economic benefits, there definitely are environmental benefits and the fundamental issue is whether the framework of financial reporting should be extended from shareholders to much broader classes of stakeholders. Being allowed to recognize costs as assets could play an important motivational role for management in improving the environment.

Generally, the study group found that the current reporting framework offers little guidance on accounting for environmental costs. Issues such as losses resulting from expected legislation, regulation, or public pressure should be disclosed, yet guidance is lacking for disclosing major environmental risks that can jeopardize a client's sustained existence. For this reason the study group proposed a separate section of the *Handbook* to deal with these specialized concerns.

Wolfe gives some background on standard setting for environmental auditing based on ISO (International Organization for Standardization).[5] ISO's mission is to develop international standards that will facilitate the exchange of goods and services and foster mutual co-operation in important areas of human endeavour—intellectual, scientific, technological, and economic. To date there are more than 8,500 ISO standards on topics ranging from product, program, and testing standards to telecommunications components. Conformance to these standards is becoming an increasingly necessary prerequisite to two-party contractual negotiations at the national and international levels. As a result many audit firms are finding lucrative work in performing compliance audits of ISO standards in many industries.

Canadian PAs are actively involved in the activities of the ISO with respect to the development of guidelines for environmental auditing and environmental management systems. The article notes the impact of the Canadian Standards Association on the development of the environmental program and management frameworks. Although the standards are not completed yet, it is clear that Canada will be very influential in setting environmental ISO standards.

---

[4] J. Longworth and K. Montano, "Cleaning Up the Books," *CA Magazine*, July 1993, pp. 55–58.
[5] J. Wolfe, "Standard Bearers," *CA Magazine*, June/July 1994, pp. 50–53.

ENVIRONMENTAL AUDITS

· · · · · · · · · · · ·

The main purpose of an environmental audit is to evaluate a company's operations and performance in terms of their conformity with federal, provincial, and municipal laws and regulations, and to identify the risks of any noncompliance. It is used to compile and report all pertinent information related to the environment. Also, such audits can help develop remedial plans aimed at mitigating environmental risks. Specifically, the results can be used to:

- Make managers and employees accountable for the environmental consequences of their activities.
- Assure the public and employees that environmental hazards are being adequately managed.
- Meet requirements of financial institutions and insurance companies.
- Evaluate compliance with government standards and legislation, and present a defence of due care if the company can show it took all reasonable precautions to avoid committing the offence in relation to environmental issues.

The actual environmental audit report will vary according to the specific terms of the mandate, the scope and complexity of the audit, and the audit findings. Although no standard guidelines exist in this field, every company should define its audit objectives and scope according to its own particular mandate, short- and long-term goals, and corporate culture. Some basic elements should be taken into consideration, such as:

- The size of the company and its operation, and their effects on the environment.
- The possibility of lawsuits.
- The company's role and image in the community.
- The extent of management's commitment to environmental concerns.
- Government environmental laws and regulations affecting the company's operations.

Since the scope of an environmental audit is so broad, a multidisciplinary audit team should be carefully selected. Their knowledge of the industry and of equipment used in the industry must be taken into account, as well as their training, experience, communication skills, and investigative techniques.

At the initial planning stage, the auditors should gather preliminary documentation on the client's business and prepare analytical studies of the company's activities and operations in order to assess the inherent risk of misstatement in the financial statements resulting from environmental damage caused by the client. Moreover, the auditors should determine the audit objectives and evaluation criteria, and prepare an audit program. The audit itself is a pragmatic process of compiling factual information about hazardous behaviour or situations by inspection of the site and enquiries of management and employees.

In addition, the audit team should examine the efforts made by the company to provide reasonable prevention and control of the environmental risks, and to ensure that environmental responsibilities have been appropriately assigned within the organization. By comparing the evidence gathered with the criteria determined on the basis of legal requirements and the company's policies and management practices, the auditors should be able to express an opinion on an audit report as to whether environmental matters are fairly presented in the financial statements. This report must be accurate and concise and point out the problems detected, and its evaluations should be sufficiently and appropriately justified by the working papers.

Depending on the results of the audit, the audit team may be subsequently asked to prepare action plans, monitoring structures, directives, or recommendations, and discuss them with management or with an advisory committee. In essence, environmental auditing appears to conform to the characteristics of a VFM audit, especially the effectiveness characteristic.

A wide range of services have come to be described as environmental auditing. All these environmentally related services, however, can be categorized under four headings:

A. Environmental Consulting Services

B. Site Assessments

C. Operational Compliance Assessments

D. Environmental Management System Assessments

Before considering these new areas, however, we first consider the audit of environmental issues in existing financial statements. This is covered in the AUG–19 Guideline of the *CICA Handbook*. AUG–19 provides guidance on "(a) planning considerations related to knowledge of the entity's business, assessing inherent risk, obtaining an understanding of internal control and designing audit procedures; (b) circumstances which may make the auditor suspect the financial statements are materially misstated; and (c) using the work of a specialist" (AUG–19, para. 4). This Guideline is largely summarized in "The Green Team," by K. Bewley, *CA Magazine*, September 1993, pp. 44–46. According to this article, audit of potential environment costs is becoming an essential task. This article proposes an audit strategy for proper disclosure of environmental costs consistent with *Handbook Section* 3060, "Capital Assets," and *Handbook Section* 3290, "Contingencies," which consider environmental matters.

At the initial planning stage, the auditor uses his or her knowledge of the client's business to assess the inherent risk of misstatement in the financial statements resulting from environmental damage caused by the client. The auditor would consider the various lines of business, the physical processes and products involved, and the sites used, as well as whether any environmental damage has resulted or could result from these activities. If the auditor believes there is a significant inherent risk that the client's activities will result in costs due to environmental damage, it will be necessary to make the further enquiries.

The auditor should then ask the client whether it or other companies in similar industries have been charged with violating any environmental laws, whether site assessments have been conducted, and whether the client has any insurance coverage for environmental risks. The auditor should also ask if the company has any policy on environmental matters.

If the auditor believes, based on his or her knowledge of the client and enquiries of management, that the client's operations present a high risk of environmental damage, he or she should enquire whether environmental management systems and controls are in place to monitor compliance with company policies and regulations. If available, the auditor may wish to review environmental management reports and/or special questionnaires to determine environmental risks.

Armed with this knowledge, the auditor then assesses inherent risk of material misstatement because of failure to recognize significant liabilities from environmental damage caused by the client. If the auditor is satisfied the risk is acceptably low, he or she has probably exercised due care and no additional procedure will be required. Alternatively, if the auditor finds evidence that a potential environmental liability or contingent liability exists with a material effect on the financial statement, further audit procedures will be necessary.

Examples of procedures that could be used to confirm or dispel the auditor's suspicions include:

- Additional enquiries of management, particularly management directly responsible for environmental matters.
- Consultation with entity's legal counsel or other specialists.
- Consultation with regulators.*
- Obtaining additional evidence by using the work of a specialist.

If the client has a system in place to develop accounting estimates for environmental liabilities, then the accepted procedures for auditing accounting estimates would apply. For example, the auditor would evaluate the system and expertise used to make the estimate, perhaps relying on the work of a specialist to corroborate the estimate. In addition, the auditor would consider whether there are industry data relating to the matter. If the information is available, the estimate could also be compared to the cost of past cleanup operations of a similar nature. As companies comply with the new *Handbook* regulation on site restoration costs, such data should be more readily available in the future.

The completeness assertion of environmental liabilities can be corroborated by the auditor's knowledge of the industry (e.g., Have environmental charges been made against other companies in the industry?) and the usual procedures of enquiries of management, lawyers, and review of minutes of director's meetings and correspondence from environmental regulators. Although auditors are not experts on environmental engineering, through the use of appropriate audit techniques and reliance on specialists they are able to form an opinion on whether environmental matters are appropriately presented in the financial statements. Generally, the assertions that are most affected by environmental factors in financial statement audits are the following:

- Completeness of liabilities and contingencies.
- Valuation of liabilities and contingencies.
- Valuation of assets.
- Completeness and valuation of commitments (AUG–19, Appendix).

AUG–19 and the Bewley article deal with the audit of environmentally related financial statement components, which are part of mainstream auditing. The four

---

*The auditor should obtain management's agreement before consulting with third parties, such as specialists or regulators.

environment service categories mentioned earlier, however, represent major departures from the traditional audit. These new types of services are discussed next.

Environmental Consulting Services

The primary objective of this type of engagement is to assist management in their operations. Due to the explanatory, analytical, or problem-solving nature of the assignment, there is no need to compare the subject matter to any pre-established criteria. As discussed in Chapter 14, under *Section* 5025 consulting services are not considered a form of assurance engagement.

Environmental consulting services tend to require extensive scientific, engineering, and operational expertise. In some situations external data are used to communicate how well the company's environmental responsibilities are being fulfilled. Furthermore, the external data can be used to determine whether the system is designed to sufficiently capture and report environmental performance data. In this service capacity PAs may be able to add value, although the lack of generally accepted standards on how to conduct such services and lack of accreditation makes it open to just about any consultant who wishes to pursue and compete for such engagements.

Site Assessment

This service is usually a one-time project that produces technical statements of findings for the users of varying detail depending on the terms of the engagements. The primary concern here is to investigate and determine whether the land (or the site) is suitable for a specific use and/or whether it contains any form of contaminant, toxic material, or waste. These contaminants will, sooner or later, require remedial and cleanup action. This implies that the current, or potential, site owner will incur the related costs in the future.

The choice of service provider, external or internal, is strictly a question of the risk acceptance of the user. When the report is for internal use, the users will prefer to have a candid opinion on the subject matter. As a result, the demand of independence and objectivity of the report subject matter will be less important. This situation changes when the user's primary concern is to satisfy the external requirements of lenders, buyers, insurers, or regulatory bodies. External information users normally expect the person conducting the investigations to be objective and independent of the current site owners and management. On the other hand, the services may originate internally through the concerns of owners, managers, or directors as internal matters. The internal report may then be requested by external users. In this case the service providers' independency and objectivity become more important.

The service providers may pay considerable attention to the evidence collected. The evidence becomes the basis for the establishment of reliability of the report. However, there are no generally accepted standards on the amount and type of evidence needed. The next box illustrates the three types of site assessment.

Some site assessments require a lot of scientific knowledge and may not fit into the PAs' range of expertise. The value-added of PAs is likely to be fairly minimal with

---

Overview of Steps Included in Typical Site Assessment

Phase I—Preliminary Assessment

Historical Review, for example:

>   Land title and ownership history
>   Aerial photographs
>   Municipal directories and records
>   Regulatory governmental agency file
>   Personnel histories (on and off site)

Walkthrough inspection, for example:

>   Process and operations
>   Material and waste handling and storage
>   Neighbouring properties
>   Underground storage tanks
>   Soil and vegetation damage

Phase II—Detailed Investigation

Sub-surface surveying (soil stratigraphy and hydrogeology)
Sample collection (solids, liquids, gases)
Sample analysis (field instruments and laboratories)
Data interpretation

Phase III—Remediation Alternatives

Determination of clean-up requirements, standards
Identification of remediation alternatives
Evaluation and testing of alternatives
Cost estimation
Work plan and scheduling

Source: Environmental Auditing and the Role of the Auditing Profession, CICA, 1992, p. 25.

---

regard to Phase II and Phase III assessments. This issue is discussed in more detail later in this appendix.

Operational Compliance Assessments

The primary focus is on the current adherence of specific operating plants and facilities, or all of the company's operations, with applicable environmental laws and regulations. The reports are of typical findings rather than the expression of an overall opinion as to compliance. This scope of the service can be extended to cover not only legal and regulatory compliances, but also compliance with internal company policies and procedures. (Exhibit 17–5 is an illustration of this type of compliance assessment.)

As with site assessment, the users can be internal or external users. Nonetheless, this type of service is frequently required by buyers and lenders (i.e., external users). Their concerns typically extend beyond the site cleanup liability to the overall compliance with the law and regulations in the daily operations. The users are interested in whether the operation is causing, or likely to cause, any violations of environmental laws and regulations. These violations can result in costly fines, penalties, jail terms, or suspension of the operations. In some situations the government may order the operation to install costly new equipment or to modify the operations to cut down the impact. To the buyers and lenders, this represents a significant risk factor.

Consequently, the users will require the service providers to be independent with respect to the subject matter and its management. Due to the need for a candid opinion, even the internal service providers are expected to provide the services with an independent state of mind.

The services are provided under a predetermined criterion. This criterion can be either applicable laws/regulations or specific company policies/procedures, or both. Nonetheless, some individual firms and internal service providers have well-developed methodologies regarding the collection and evaluation of evidence. There is no generally accepted standard on how to carry out the engagement. In addition, there is no standard on how to conduct an operational compliance assessment.

Unlike site assessment, which only deals with a "point in time," this service also addresses the overall compliance within a *specific period*. However, for compliance over a period of time, relevant historical evidence/records must be available. As a result, assertions over time cannot be achieved without a system to record various types of operational data. In such assessments the assertions can only be a "point in time" assessment, or of an investigatory fact-finding nature.

There would appear to be a significant role for PAs in public practice to provide and direct operational compliance assessments as an assurance-based service, provided there are verifiable assertions about compliance and about the effectiveness of systems to maintain compliance. This requires that appropriate management systems and records be in place to monitor compliance over time. However, this also requires the PAs to either possess a significant amount of knowledge on environmental matters or to use the work of the appropriate specialists. More importantly, the criteria used on such examinations would have to be as objective and specific as possible. This suggests the importance and urgency of establishing generally accepted standards for such assurance engagements.

Environmental Management System Assessment

This is an independent examination of the effectiveness and efficiency of the overall environmental management system. It is meant to provide information and assurance as to the effectiveness of systems, controls, and procedures to comply with corporate environmental policies. This includes risk identification, emergency response measures, employee training, "whistle blowing," recording, reporting, and follow-up on findings. The potential value to management is in the comfort that a reliable system is always in place. As a result, this type of service really resembles a comprehensive audit.

The engagement consists of an examination of the systematic documentation, periodic and objective evaluation of how well environmental organization, management, and equipment are performing, with the aim of helping to safeguard the environment. It is a continuous program or function rather than a one-time assignment. Nonetheless, the underlying assumption of the environmental management system assessment is the *preexistence* of a recordkeeping system, similar to the existing accounting system, that provides documentations. If this assumption is questionable, the engagement will have to settle for a "point in time" assessment.

Results are usually presented as reports of conclusions and detailed findings. Overall conclusions are usually expressed about conformity with the criteria. The main purposes for such reports are to provide an independent assurance that the environmental management systems and procedures can be relied upon for their stated purpose. The environmental management system assessment usually recommends, or at least triggers, follow-up actions. This feedback loop provides assistance to the immediate level of management, as well as to the board of directors, in improving the operation in question.

As mentioned above, the primary users of this service include boards of directors, their committees, and owner-managers. As with operational compliance assessments, the users (mostly internal) require a candid opinion. Therefore, the service can be provided internally, or externally. However, when the services are provided by an independent service provider, objectivity is usually enhanced. The only exception occurs when the examiners are the same people that designed and implemented the system in question. If the examination is conducted internally, it is usually conducted by a team drawn up to be independent of the entity, unit, function, or system being audited and to report through appropriate internal reporting arrangements. When a board or committee is formed to conduct the examination, independence will likely be enhanced.

The criteria used are drawn from several sources, since there are no commonly accepted criteria. Until the development of a commonly accepted standard, the assessment will continue to be based on the existing protocol approach using "yardsticks," which include those that reflect "best management practice." There is no standard or ground rule to ensure the clarity and usefulness of the examination in addressing the users' needs. The lack of a standard represents a serious limitation on the usefulness, reliability, and consistency of assessments. It could result in wide disparities between services, costs, and coverage of similar services.

However, in the assessment report there is usually no reference to any generally accepted standards for carrying out the review. Therefore, the opinion does not convey assurance as to the degree of conformity with the established criteria. The report might be taken by the user (especially the external user) to be a form of assurance, even if it is not meant to be one. This creates the possibility of an expectation gap. It may also suggest a serious liability problem to the service providers.

The CICA study *Environmental Auditing and the Role of the Accounting Profession* (1992, pp. 39–40) summarizes the issues with respect to environmental management systems assessments as follows:

> Many environmental service providers developed methodologies for gathering and evaluating evidence, but these are not based on generally accepted standards as to the nature and extent of evidence needed to achieve consistency and reliability of conclusions ... The lack of generally accepted standards for the conduct of these services

presents a serious limitation on their usefulness, reliability, and consistency, and results in wide disparities among service providers and costs.

A type of report issued by a consulting firm (see next box) appears at first glance to be similar to an auditor's report on financial statements. Some important differences should however be noted:

a. The scope of the examination ("review") is described, but specific criteria for assessing the subject-matter are not available. The "review" (assessment) was entirely by reference to the examiner's own experience and judgment.

b. There is no reference to generally accepted standards for carrying out such a "review."

c. The opinion expressed is to the effect that the company is the leader in its industry (in terms not defined), and that in some respects the company's practices are "state of the art" and place the company "among the leaders of industry as a whole ..."

These differences demonstrate the difficulties of providing assurance to users about subject-matter, when:

a. Generally accepted or specifically stated criteria do not exist for assessing the subject-matter.

b. Generally accepted standards for the conduct of the services (review, assessment, audit, or whatever) do not exist.

c. The opinion does not convey assurance as to the degree of subject-matter conformity with the established criteria. (How much comfort can the reader in fact take from such an opinion?)

Notwithstanding the above comments, it is difficult not to gain a positive impression about the company's practices from such a report.

However, problems of issuing such reports include the wording of any reservation, and the liabilities associated with issuing such a report.

In general, the study (p. 78) stated that currently environmental audits do not satisfy the PA profession's definition of audit for the following reasons:

First, in many cases it would not be possible for a verifiable assertion to be prepared, since there are no records of events and operations to examine. Findings have to be developed from direct investigation at a point in time and collection of such evidence as the examiner sees necessary for the purpose of the assessment in question. This is especially true of site and operational compliance assessments being carried out for the first time.

Second, the concept of evidence has not evolved to the extent that different examiners carrying out the same assessment separately would necessarily carry out similar procedures or require the same amount or types of evidence in order to develop their findings. This reflects a lack of generally recognized standards for the conduct of such services, and a lack of consistency in the procedures of those who perform them.

Third, there are no generally recognized standards for systems and controls to serve as criteria in evaluating environmental management systems (although in some industries, principles and preferred practices have been enunciated that go some way to providing criteria for companies in the industries in question, for example, the

---

Arthur D. Little   **Arthur D. Little, Inc.**
                                              Acorn Park
                                              Cambridge, Massachusetts
                                              02140—2390
                                              USA

February 4, 1991   Telephone 617 555 5770
                                             Telefax 617 555 5830
                                             Telex 921436

Ms. Joan Z. Bernstein
Vice President
Environmental Policy and Ethical Standards
Waste Management, Inc.
3003 Butterfield Road
Oak Brook, Illinois
60521

Dear Ms. Bernstein:

We have reviewed the appropriateness and quality of the environmental
management systems and environmental policies and procedures in place
during 1990 at Waste Management, Inc., and its principal operating subsidiaries, as well as the appropriateness and quality of Waste Management,
Inc.'s corporate Environmental Audit Program. We conducted our review
relying upon our judgment based upon our extensive consulting experience
in this area as well as our familiarity with similar programs established by
many other corporations.

In our opinion, Waste Management, Inc.'s corporate and subsidiary environmental management systems, policies and procedures, and its corporate
environmental audit program establish the Company as the leader in the U.S.
waste management industry. Furthermore, certain features of these systems,
policies and procedures, and audit program reflect approaches that are state
of the art and place Waste Management, Inc., firmly among the leaders of
industry as a whole with regard to corporate environmental management.

Arthur D. Little, Inc.
February 4, 1991

(*Source:* Waste Management Inc. 1990 Annual Environmental Report Summary)

---

guidelines issued by the Canadian Petroleum Association and Canadian Chemical
Producers Association).

Fourth, the results of such assessments are typically expressed as detailed reports
of findings and deficiencies, rather than as overall conclusions as to the extent that
stated subject-matter conforms with criteria. This reflects a fact-finding, investigatory type of service, as distinct from an assurance-providing or attestation service,
which is at the heart of auditing as defined.

In order to remedy these problems, the PA profession needs more training and proficiency. The study (p. 79) identified the primary knowledge and skills as follows:

Literature on environmental auditing indicates that the primary areas of knowledge and skill are:

- Environmental law and regulations.
- Operations, facilities and processes.
- Environmental sciences and technologies.
- Management systems and practices.
- Auditing and verification techniques.
- Relevant industry (peer facility) knowledge.

Nevertheless, even with these skills the study group concluded (p. 40):

the absence of either generally accepted or specifically stated (and agreed) criteria for assessing subject matter is a key determining factor in deciding what is and what is not an audit. A second key factor is the existence or otherwise of a basis for making a verifiable assertion about the subject matter. In summary therefore:

- Environmental Consulting Services are not audits as defined in this report.
- Site Assessments are not audits as defined.
- Operational Compliance Assessments are generally not audits as defined, but, under certain circumstances (particularly as to verifiable assertion), could be conducted as such.
- Environmental Management System Assessments are generally not audits in that sense, but, under certain circumstances (particularly as to criteria and verifiable assertions), could be conducted as such.
- There are no generally accepted standards at present for the conduct of the above assessment services nor for the consulting services.

However with the more comprehensive guidance now provided by *Section* 5025 it may be time to re-examine some of these conclusions reached back in 1992. For example, Dominique Barker in her University of Toronto research project [1996] noted that since the CICA study was published in 1992, the Canadian Standards Association (CSA) has published a comprehensive section on environmental site assessments. It turns out that the CSA standard for Phase I environmental site assessments (ESAs) appears to have all the basic elements of an assurance engagement of the direct reporting type. The standard has four components, outlined as follows:

1. A record review: the assessor collects data on past activities at the site. This includes documentation from sources (like confirmations in auditing).
2. A site visit: the CSA standard states that the assessor shall look for storage tanks, storage containers, unidentified substances, property use, strong odors, etc ... Note how this is not rocket science! Although there are procedures that are "technical" (aerial photographs, describing the heating and cooling system, material waste handling and storage), it is the kind of stuff that can be learned on the job, and that is becoming common knowledge. Note that when there are technically difficult areas, the auditor could ask the client for information and corroborate this with a specialist.
3. Interviews—CSA.

4. Evaluation of information and reporting: this has already been described, and has been compared to auditor opinion paragraphs.

The resulting report should have the following elements:

The standard says that the conclusions should be addressed as follows:

  a) the report shall have a conclusion section that states that the Phase I ESA has revealed
   (I) no evidence of contamination in connection with the property;
   (II) evidence of potential contamination in connection with the property (listed and described);
   (III) evidence of actual and potential contamination in connection with the property (listed and described).

  b) The Assessor shall
   (I) present the conclusions in a manner designed to help the Client understand their significance;
   (II) describe methods to reduce the level of uncertainty (e.g., confirm, refute, or delineate contamination); and
   (III) provide rationale for proposing such methods.

Note that the first element looks like it provides a moderate level of assurance similar to that of a review engagement as contemplated in *Section* 5025. Note also use of the word "significance" in the written criteria specified by the CSA, which we can assume are generally accepted by environmentalists. Thus it appears that the criteria for a direct reporting engagement of moderate-level assurance are met by using the CSA and *Section* 5025 standard. The remaining issue is whether the auditor has the training and competence to appropriately carry out the engagement by gathering the necessary evidence to support the conclusion. Fortunately, as Barker (1996) pointed out in discussing the four components of Phase I ESA, the site does not normally involve specialized expertise (for example, it should not take much expertise to observe physical obstructions, storage containers, stains, pits, lagoons, septic system and cesspools, and stressed vegetation). In the few instances when specialized expertise may be needed (e.g., search for specific substances such as PCBs) a multidisciplinary team should be competent in making a proper appraisal. Remember, this is a moderate assurance engagement. Phase II and Phase III would be the more specialized, technical-type site assessments providing higher assurance. In fact the purpose of Phase I is to obtain evidence of whether there is a reasonable need for higher-level assurance. As noted earlier, Phase I assurance is currently in high demand by Canadian financial institutions that are loaning money for purchasing property. Clearly there is a market need to be met, and this is a type of assurance service that PA firms could be providing. This conflicts with the recommendations of the 1992 CICA study, primarily because CSA standards had not yet been promulgated and thus there were no established criteria at the time. As Barker (1996, p. 7) concludes:

Phase I Environmental Site Assessments often lead to Phase II and III Site Assessments. These are technical, and should not be considered as work done by the accounting profession. If a Phase I leads to a Phase II and III, the work should only be done by a specialist (i.e., engineer).

   In conclusion, a Phase I Environmental Site Assessment meets the criteria of an Assurance Engagement, and provides a new source of work for auditors that is currently being done at engineering firms. Phase I assessments cost between $3000 and $6000, and are not as technical as many people think. In fact, at a very renowned engineering consulting firm, this work is not considered engineer's work: it is considered technician's work. Accounting firms should reconsider Phase I ESA as their area of expertise.

And, it will be added, as an important way of responding to user needs for different types of assurance services.

Finally, it should be stressed that environmental services do not always neatly fall into one of the four basic categories identified by the CICA 1992 Study Group: environmental consulting, site assessment, operational compliance assessment, and environmental management system assessment. A client may not be interested only in strict legal compliance. Many forward-looking companies attempt to also meet broader social needs, as in the Abitibi-Price example given earlier. The way this is done in a particular instance may result in a mixture of elements in the four categories. However, the need for an independent outside assessment is becoming more apparent even in the public sector, as a recent *Globe and Mail* editorial made clear. See the box below.

AN ENVIRONMENTAL AUDITOR

In these environmentally parlous times, the Show Boat song asserting that "fish gotta swim, birds gotta fly" might well be amended to add: "And politicians gotta try to make them fish swim here, and those birds fly there."

We croon thus because everywhere we look, we see our elected leaders neck deep in nature-management experiments in which good politics and good ecology apparently war.

How else do you explain why the East Coast cod didn't realize that Canadian politicians and bureaucrats had decided it was the patriotic duty of Canadian fish to multiply faster than all the world's fishermen could catch them? And it is not yet clear how well heavily logged British Columbia forests understand they are politically required to grow back in a manner both environmentally healthy and economically sustainable.

Theoretically, government scientists should mitigate these conflicts by objectively presenting nature's apolitical point of view. However, as a recent paper which appeared in the Canadian Journal of Fisheries and Aquatic Sciences has pointed out, all sorts of political and economic pressures can militate against the independence of government scientists.

After documenting what it said were abuses in the objective evaluation of the East Coast cod and West Coast salmon fisheries, the paper's three university based authors suggested that some kind of arm's-length relationship should separate the government's fish-science divisions from its fish-policy branch. They also recommended that both the available fish data and the scientific discussions surrounding them should be released so the public could see for themselves whether a given policy decision was scientifically defensible.

Not surprisingly, the Department of Fisheries and Oceans has challenged the veracity of the paper's central thesis. While we don't know precisely how conformist DFO's corporate culture is, our mouths don't exactly gape at the notion that even the most scrupulous government scientists would feel pressure to interpret data in a way which favoured voting fishermen over non-voting fish.

The question is what to do about it. The professors' arms-length suggestion seems a basically sound one to us. But there is no reason to restrict its application to the fisheries. Maybe all government scientists working in environmentally sensitive areas should work in quasi-independent organizations. However, even with that, we are not sure that the person on the street is going to be able to determine when good politics is also good science.

Therefore, we suggest that the federal government, in conjunction with the provinces, set up something we are calling an Environmental Auditor-General. What we want is for someone to have the mandate to—how shall we put this delicately—cut through the crap. In the same way that the Auditor-General presents a yearly report which regularly astounds us with examples of governmental stupidity and waste, so too we want an environmental b.s. detector.

We envision this office as even-handedly acerbic. If it makes no ecological sense to fly thousands of Toronto geese to New Brunswick where they may freeze to death in winter, let's hear it. If we are constructing wildlife refuges big enough to please local landowners but too small to sustain endangered populations, let's hear it.

We won't suggest who the first Environmental Auditor-General should be, but we are certain Mark Twain's Pudd'n-head Wilson has already enunciated the office credo: "When in doubt tell the truth."

Source: Editorial, *The Globe and Mail,* June 25, 1997, A18. Reprinted with permission from *The Globe and Mail.*

This editorial further illustrates the importance of maintaining independence in assurance engagements and why it may be necessary to maintain a clear distinction between consulting and assurance engagements—and, in a broader sense, the accountability relationship that assurance engagements are intended to preserve. This is yet another challenge that needs to be addressed as we more fully develop an assurance engagement framework that will be useful in the private and public sectors of the future.

KEY TERMS

account analysis identification of each important item and amount in an account followed by document vouching and enquiry to determine whether amounts should be classified elsewhere. *(Chapter 13)*

account balance audit program a specification (list) of procedures designed to produce evidence about the assertions in financial statements. *(Chapter 6)*

accounting (as a control objective) a general category concerned with ensuring that the accounting process for a transaction is completely performed and in conformity with GAAP. *(Chapter 6)*

accounting estimate an *approximation* of a financial statement element, item, or account made by an organization's management. *(Chapters 13 and 18)*

accounting system (as element of a control structure) an organization of policies and procedures for recording transactions properly *(Chapter 6)*

accuracy (as a control objective) refers to ensuring that dollar amounts are figured correctly. *(Chapter 6)*

act-utilitarianism (in moral philosophy) emphasis on the individual act is it is affected by the specific circumstances of a situation. *(Chapter 15)*

administrative control the plan of organization and all methods and procedures that are concerned mainly with operational efficiency and adherence to managerial policies and usually relate only indirectly to financial records. *(Chapter 17)*

adverse opinion the opposite of an unqualified opinion, stating that financial statements are *not* in conformity with GAAP. *(Chapter 2)*

analytical procedures audit evaluation of financial statement accounts by studying and comparing relationships among financial and nonfinancial data. *(Chapters 4 and 13)*

analytical procedures risk (AP) the probability that analytical procedures will *fail* to detect material errors. *(Chapter 7)*

application description (in computer system documentation) system flowcharts, description of all inputs and outputs, record formats, lists of computer codes, and control features. *(Chapter 8)*

associated with financial statements circumstance in which a PA's name is used in connection with financial statements, or a PA has prepared the statements, even if the PA's name is not used in any written report. *(Chapter 3)*

attest function common reference to independent audits of financial statements, but also refers to review services, association with forecasts and projections, and compilation services where lack of independence is not noted. *(Chapter 1)*

attestation the lending of some credibility to financial or other information by professional auditors who serve as objective intermediaries. *(Chapter 1)*

attestation standards a general set of standards intended to guide attestation work in areas other than audits of financial statements. *(Chapter 2)*

attributes sampling another name for test of controls audit sampling. *(Chapter 7)*

audit objective expression of a financial statement *assertion* for which evidence needs to be obtained. *(Chapter 9)*

audit of balances ordinary and extended *substantive procedures designed to find signs* of errors, irregularities, and frauds in account balances and classes of transactions. *(Chapter 7)*

audit procedure (nature) actions described as the general audit procedures of recalculation, physical observation, confirmation, verbal enquiry, document examination, scanning, and analytical review. *(Chapter 7)*

audit procedures   particular and specialized actions auditors take to obtain evidence in a specific audit engagement. *(Chapter 2)*

audit program   a list of the audit procedures believed necessary to obtain sufficient, competent evidence that will serve as the basis for the audit report. *(Chapters 2, 4, and 5)*

audit risk (global)   the probability that an auditor will give an inappropriate opinion on financial statements. *(Chapter 5)*

audit risk (account level)   probability that an auditor will fail to find misstatement equal to, or greater than, the tolerable misstatement assigned to an account. *(Chapter 5)*

audit standards   audit quality guides that remain the same through time and for all audits, including audits of computerized accounting systems. *(Chapter 2)*

auditee   the company or other entity whose financial statements are being audited. *(Chapter 1)*

auditing around the computer   auditors' attempt to isolate the computer and to find audit assurance by vouching data from output to source documents and by tracing from source documents to output. *(Chapter 8)*

auditing through the computer   auditors' actual evaluation of the hardware and software to determine the reliability of operations that cannot be viewed by the human eye. *(Chapter 8)*

auditing with the computer   audit techniques such as the use of the client's computer hardware and software to process real or simulated transactions or the use of specialized audit software to perform other audit tasks. *(Chapter 8)*

auditing without the computer   using visible evidence such as the input source data, the machine-produced error listings, the visible control points and the detailed printed output. *(Chapter 8)*

authorization (as a control objective)   ensuring that transactions are approved before they are recorded. *(Chapter 6)*

average sampling interval (ASI)   the recorded dollar amount of a population being sampled divided by the sample size. *(Chapter 20)*

backup   a retention system for files, programs, and documentation so that master files can be reconstructed in case of accidental loss and processing can continue at another site if the computer centre is lost to fire or flood. *(Chapter 8)*

batch control totals   totals of dollar numbers, nonsense numbers, or count of documents. *(Chapter 6)*

batch processing (also **serial** or **sequential processing**) all records to be processed are collected in groups (batches) of like transactions before computer processing. *(Chapter 8)*

bill of materials   a specification of the materials authorized for production; the source of authorization for the preparation of materials requisitions. *(Chapter 11)*

block sampling   choosing segments of contiguous transactions for a sampling application. *(Chapter 7)*

breach of contract   a claim that accounting or auditing services were not performed in the manner agreed. *(Chapter 16)*

capital budget   management document that contains the plans for asset purchases and business acquisitions. *(Chapter 12)*

cash flow forecast   forecast that informs the board of directors and management of the business plans, the prospects for cash inflows, and the needs for cash outflows. *(Chapter 12)*

categorical imperative (in moral philosophy)   Kant's specification of an unconditional obligation. *(Chapter 15)*

Certified General Accountants   persons who have met the Certified General Accountants Association of Canada criteria for CGA credentials. *(Chapter 1)*

Certified Internal Auditors   persons who have met the Institute of Internal Auditors' criteria for professional CIA credentials. *(Chapter 18)*

Certified Management Accountants   persons who have met the Society of Management Accountants of Canada criteria for CMA credentials. *(Chapter 1)*

chain of custody   the crucial link of the evidence to the suspect, called the "relevance" of evidence by lawyers and judges. *(Chapter 18)*

check digit   an extra number, precisely calculated, that is tagged onto the end of a basic identification number, such as an employee number. *(Chapter 6)*

cheque kiting   the illegal practice of building up apparent balances in one or more bank accounts based on uncollected (float) cheques drawn against similar accounts in other banks. *(Chapter 9)*

class of transactions   a group of transactions having common characteristics, such as cash receipts or cash disbursements, but which are not simply added together and presented as an account balance in financial statements. *(Chapter 7)*

classification (as a control objective)   ensuring that transactions are recorded in the right accounts, charged or credited to the right customer (including classification of sales to subsidiaries and affiliates) entered in the correct segment product line or inventory description, and so forth. *(Chapter 6)*

client   person (company, board of directors, agency or some other person or group) who retains the auditor and pays the fee. *(Chapter 1)*

collusion   circumstance in which two or more people conspire to conduct fraudulent activity in violation of an organization's internal control policies and procedures. *(Chapter 18)*

commission   a percentage fee charged for professional services in connection with executing a transaction or performing some other business activity. *(Chapter 15)*

common law   all the cases and precedents that govern judges' decisions in lawsuits for monetary damages. Common law is "common knowledge" in the sense that judges tend to follow the collective wisdom of past cases decided by themselves and other judges. *(Chapter 16)*

compensating control   a control feature used when a standard control procedure (such as strict segregation of functional responsibilities) is not specified by the company. *(Chapter 12)*

competent (characteristic of evidence)   evidence that is valid, relevant, and unbiased. *(Chapter 4)*

completeness (as a control objective)   ensuring that valid transactions are *not omitted entirely* from the accounting records. *(Chapter 6)*

computed upper limit (CUL)   a statistical estimate of the population deviation rate computed from the test of controls sample evidence. *(Chapter 20)*

conflict of interest   any relationship whereby an individual or his or her relative may benefit from a transaction within the individual's business relations where he or she has influenced the transaction or relationship. *(Chapter 1)*

contingent fee   a fee established for the performance of any service in an arrangement in which no fee will be charged unless a specific finding or result is attained, or the fee otherwise depends on the result of the service. *(Chapter 15)*

control environment   a set of characteristics that defines good management control features other than accounting policies and control procedures. *(Chapter 6)*

control procedures   specific error-checking routines performed by company personnel. *(Chapter 6)*

control risk   the probability that a material misstatement (error or irregularity) could occur and not be prevented or detected on a timely basis by the company's internal control structure policies and procedures *(Chapters 2, 5, and 6)*

internal control structure   consists of a company's control environment, accounting system, and control procedures. The existence of a satisfactory internal control structure reduces the probability of errors and irregularities in the accounts. *(Chapter 2)*

controlled reprocessing (also **parallel simulation**)   auditors' determination of whether output from the computer program the client actually used in processing data produces satisfactory accounting output when compared to the output from the auditors' controlled copy of the program. *(Chapter 19)*

cross-reference computer program   provide printed listings of every occurrence of each name used in an application program or a list of every file used in an application system. *(Chapter 19)*

cutoff bank statement   auditors' information source for vouching the bank reconciliation items; a complete bank statement including all paid cheques and deposit slips received directly by the auditors. *(Chapter 9)*

cycle   set of accounts and business activities that go together in an accounting system. *(Chapter 4)*

database administrator (DBA) person responsible for determining who should have access to data elements. *(Chapter 19)*

data elements individual pieces of information such as employee number, address, pay rate, balance in a computer system. *(Chapter 19)*

data redundancy indicates the same data stored in several separate files. *(Chapter 19)*

decision criteria standards for decision and evaluation in specific circumstances. *(Chapter 20)*

defalcation another name for employee fraud and embezzlement. *(Chapter 18)*

detail test of control procedure consists of (1) identification of the data population from which a sample of items will be selected for audit and (2) an expression of the action that will be taken to produce relevant evidence. In general, the *actions* in detail test of control audit procedures involve vouching, tracing, observing, scanning, and recalculating. *(Chapters 9, 10, and 11)*

detection rate ratio of the number of exceptions reported to auditors to the number of account errors. *(Chapter 9)*

detection risk the probability that audit procedures will fail to produce evidence of material misstatement, provided any have entered the accounting system in the first place and have not been detected and corrected by the client's control policies and procedures. *(Chapter 5)*

deviation (as in **control failure,** also *error, occurrence,* and *exception*) refers to a departure from a prescribed internal control procedure in a particular case. *(Chapter 7)*

direct-effect illegal acts violations of laws or government regulations by the company or its management or employees that produce direct and material effects on dollar amounts in financial statements. *(Chapter 18)*

direct personal knowledge audit evidence obtained by eyewitness and physical inspection. *(Chapter 4)*

disclaimer of opinion lowest level of assurance; "no assurance." Auditors explicitly state that they give no opinion and no assurance, thus taking no responsibility for a report on the fair presentation of financial statements in conformity with GAAP. *(Chapters 2 and 3)*

dollar-value estimation objective in statistical sampling the job of helping a client obtain an estimate of an amount. *(Chapter 20)*

dual-purpose procedure an audit procedure that simultaneously serves the *substantive* purpose (obtain direct evidence about the dollar amounts in account balances) and the *test of controls* purpose (obtain evidence about the company's performance of its own control procedures). *(Chapter 9)*

echo check a magnetic read after each magnetic write, "echoing" back to the sending location and comparing results. *(Chapter 8)*

80/20 "rule" the rule of thumb about population skewness that 80 percent of the value tends to be in 20 percent of the units. *(Chapter 20)*

embezzlement a type of fraud involving employees' or nonemployees' wrongfully taking money or property entrusted to their care, custody, and control, often accompanied by false accounting entries and other forms of lying and coverup. *(Chapter 18)*

employee fraud the use of fraudulent means to take money or other property from an employer. *(Chapter 18)*

engagement letter letter from the auditor to the management of an audit client setting forth the terms of the engagement. *(Chapter 4)*

errors (as in **errors and irregularities**) unintentional misstatements or omissions of amounts or disclosures in financial statements. *(Chapter 18)*

error (as in **control failure,** also **deviation, occurrence,** and **exception**) refers to a departure from a prescribed internal control procedure in a particular case. *(Chapter 7)*

error analysis investigation of each deviation from a prescribed control procedure to determine its nature, cause, and probable effect on financial statements. *(Chapter 7)*

event driven (also **transaction driven**) computer data processing system that is started with each transaction event; individual transactions trigger the processing activity and all relevant files are updated. *(Chapter 8)*

evidence all the influences upon the minds of auditors which ultimately guide their decisions. *(Chapter 2)*

exception (as in **control failure,** also **deviation, error,** and **occurrence**)   a departure from a prescribed internal control procedure in a particular case. *(Chapter 7)*

expectation about the population deviation rate   an estimate of the ratio of the number of expected deviations to population size. *(Chapter 7)*

extending the audit conclusion   performing substantive-purpose audit procedures on the transactions in the remaining period and on the year-end balance to produce sufficient competent evidence for a decision about the year-end balance. *(Chapter 7)*

extent (of audit procedures)   refers to the *amount* of work done when the procedures are performed. *(Chapters 6 and 7)*

existence (as a **financial statement assertion**)   management representation that assets, liabilities, equities, revenue, and expenses exist in reality. *(Chapter 4)*

expanded scope governmental auditing   auditing that goes beyond an audit of financial reports and compliance with laws and regulations to include economy and efficiency and program results audits. *(Chapters 1 and 17)*

expert witness   testifying to findings determined during litigation support and testifying as to accounting principles and auditing standards applications. *(Chapter 18)*

external auditors   independent PAs who audit financial statements for the purpose of rendering an opinion. *(Chapter 18)*

external evidence   documentary evidence obtained directly from independent external sources. *(Chapter 4)*

external-internal evidence   documentary evidence that has originated outside the client's data processing system but which has been received and processed by the client. *(Chapter 4)*

fidelity bond   an insurance policy that covers most kinds of cash embezzlement losses. *(Chapter 9)*

financial forecast   presents, to the best of the preparer's knowledge and belief, an entity's expected financial position, results of operations, and changes in financial position; based on assumptions about expected conditions and expected courses of action. *(Chapter 14)*

financial projection   similar to a forecast, with the important exception that a projection depends on one or more hypothetical assumptions. *(Chapter 14)*

financial reporting   broad-based process of providing statements of financial position (balance sheets), statements of results of operations (income statements), statements of changes in financial position (cash flow statements), and accompanying disclosure notes (footnotes) to outside decision makers who have no internal source of information like the management of the company has. *(Chapter 1)*

Financial Reporting Releases (FRR)   SEC publications of rules and policies about accounting and disclosures. *(Chapter 16)*

finitely corrected   sample size calculation that incorporates the population size in such a way that sample sizes larger than the population size cannot be produced. *(Chapter 20)*

forensic accounting   application of accounting and auditing skills to legal problems, both civil and criminal. *(Chapter 18)*

foreseeable beneficiaries   creditors, investors, or potential investors who rely on accountant's work. *(Chapter 16)*

fraud   action of knowingly making material misrepresentations of fact with the intent of inducing someone to believe the falsehood and act upon it and thus suffer a loss or damage. *(Chapter 18)*

fraud auditing   a pro-active approach to detect financial frauds using accounting records and information, analytical relationships, and an awareness of fraud perpetration and concealment efforts (ACFE). *(Chapter 18)*

fraud examiners   people engaged specifically for fraud investigation work. *(Chapter 18)*

fraudulent financial reporting (see also **management fraud**)   intentional or reckless conduct, whether by act or omission, that results in materially misleading financial statements (National Commission on Fraudulent Financial Reporting, 1987). *(Chapter 18)*

generalization argument (in moral philosophy)   a judicious combination of the imperative and utilitarian principles. *(Chapter 15)*

generalized audit software (GAS) set of software functions that may be utilized to read, compute, and operate on machine-readable records. *(Chapter 8)*

government auditors auditors whose work is governed by the GAO audit standards, whether they be audit employees of governments or public accounting firms engaged to perform government audits. *(Chapter 17)*

gross negligence lack of even minimum care in performing professional duties, indicating reckless disregard for duty and responsibility. *(Chapter 16)*

haphazard selection any unsystematic way of selecting sample units. *(Chapter 7)*

harmonization accountants' and regulators' interest in making accounting and auditing standards coordinated, if not uniform, throughout the world. *(Chapter 2)*

horizontal analysis study of changes of financial statement numbers and ratios across two or more years. *(Chapters 5 and 18)*

hypothesis testing auditors hypothesize that an account balance is materially accurate as to existence, ownership and valuation and test the hypothesis with sample-based evidence. *(Chapter 7)*

hypothetical assumption expression of a condition and course of action the issuer of a financial projection expects could take place. *(Chapter 14)*

illegal acts violations of laws and regulations that are *far removed* from financial statement effects. *(Chapter 18)*

information risk risk (probability) that the financial statements distributed by a company will be materially false and misleading. *(Chapter 1)*

inherent risk probability that material misstatements have occurred in transactions entering the accounting system used to develop financial statements. *(Chapter 5)*

injunction legal settlement in which a person or company, without admitting or denying a violation of law, agrees not to violate the law in the future. *(Chapter 16)*

inspection (as in **test of controls procedures**) auditors look to see whether the documents were marked with an initial, signature, or stamp to indicate they had been checked. *(Chapter 6)*

integrity ability to act in accordance with the highest moral and ethical values all the time. *(Chapter 18)*

interim audit work procedures performed several weeks or months before the balance sheet date. *(Chapter 4)*

interim date a date some weeks or months before the auditee's fiscal year-end. *(Chapters 2 and 7)*

internal accounting control the plan of organization and procedures designed to prevent, detect, and correct accounting errors that may occur and get recorded in ledger accounts and financial statements. *(Chapter 17)*

internal auditors persons employed within organizations for audit assignments. *(Chapters 1, 17, and 18)*

internal auditing (see also **management auditing, operational auditing, performance auditing**) study of business operations for the purpose of making recommendations about the economic and efficient use of resources, effective achievement of business objectives, and compliance with company policies. *(Chapters 1 and 17)*

internal control questionnaire a checklist used in a formal interview with knowledgeable managers. *(Chapter 6)*

internal evidence documents that are produced, circulated, and finally stored with the client's information system. *(Chapter 4)*

irregularities intentional misstatements or omissions in financial statements, including fraudulent financial reporting (management fraud) and misappropriations of assets (defalcations). *(Chapter 18)*

known misstatement the actual monetary error found in a sample. *(Chapter 7)*

levels of assurance standard unqualified report with opinion on financial statements, review report with negative assurance, and compilation report with no expression of opinion or assurance. *(Chapter 3)*

likely misstatement the projected amount of misstatement in a population based on sample evidence. *(Chapter 7)*

litigated settlement of a controversy by a judge in the civil justice system. *(Chapter 16)*

litigation support consulting in the capacity of helping lawyers document cases and determine damages. *(Chapter 18)*

logical unit ordinary accounting subsidiary unit that contains the dollar unit selected in a dollar-unit sample. *(Chapter 20)*

management auditing (see also **internal auditing, operational auditing, performance auditing**) study of business operations for the purpose of making recommendations about the economic and efficient use of resources, effective achievement of business objectives, and compliance with company policies. *(Chapters 1 and 17)*

management fraud (see also **fraudulent financial reporting**) deliberate fraud committed by management that injures investors and creditors through materially misleading financial statements. *(Chapter 18)*

material weakness in internal control condition in which the design or operation of the specific internal control structure elements (environment, accounting system, control procedures) does not reduce to a relatively low level the risk that errors or irregularities in amounts that would be material to the financial statements being audited may occur and may not be detected within a timely period by employees in the normal course of performing their assigned functions. *(Chapter 6)*

materials requisitions requests that create authorizations for the inventory custodian to release raw materials and supplies to the production personnel; documents that are the inventory recordkeepers' authorizations to update the raw materials inventory files to record reductions of the raw materials inventory. *(Chapter 11)*

mathematical computations (as **audit evidence**) auditors' own calculations. *(Chapter 4)*

mitigating factors elements of financial flexibility (salability of assets, lines of credit, debt extension, dividend elimination) available as survival strategies in circumstances of going concern uncertainty which may reduce the financial difficulty problems. *(Chapter 3)*

motive (with reference to fraud) pressure experienced by a person and believed to be unsharable with friends and confidants. *(Chapter 18)*

nature (of audit procedures) refers to the seven general procedures: recalculation, physical observation, confirmation, verbal enquiry, document examination, scanning, and analytical procedures. *(Chapter 6)*

negative assurance "Based on our review, we are not aware of any material modifications that should be made to the accompanying financial statements in order for them to be in conformity with generally accepted accounting principles;" permitted in reviews of unaudited financial statements, letters to underwriters, and reviews of interim financial information. *(Chapter 3)*

negative confirmations confirmation letter that requests a reply only if the account balance is considered incorrect. *(Chapter 4)*

nonpublic company company with less than $5 million in assets and fewer than 500 shareholders. Not required to register and file reports under the Exchange Act. *(Chapter 16)*

nonpublic offering (see also **private placement**) sale of securities to a small number of persons or institutional investors (usually not more than 35), who can demand and obtain sufficient information without the formality of registration. *(Chapter 16)*

nonsampling risk all risk other than sampling risk. *(Chapter 7)*

nonstatistical sampling audit sampling in which auditors do not utilize statistical calculations to express the results. *(Chapter 7)*

occurrence (as in **control failure,** also **deviation, error,** and **exception**) refers to a departure from a prescribed internal control procedure in a particular case. *(Chapter 7)*

operational auditing (see also **internal auditing, management auditing, performance auditing**) study of business operations for the purpose of making recommendations about the economic and efficient use of resources, effective achievement of business objectives, and compliance with company policies. *(Chapter 1)*

opportunity (with reference to fraud) an open door for solving the unshareable problem in secret by violating a trust. *(Chapter 18)*

ordinary negligence lack of reasonable care in the performance of professional accounting tasks. *(Chapter 16)*

overreliance (obsolete term)   the result of assessing control risk too low and restricting other audit procedures when they actually should perform more work. *(Chapter 7)*

ownership (as a financial statement assertion)   another name for the *rights* assertion, suggesting auditee's possession of legal title to assets. *(Chapter 4)*

paper trail   set of telltale signs of erroneous accounting, missing or altered documents, or a "dangling debit" (the false or erroneous debit that results from an overstatement of assets). *(Chapters 9, 10, 11, and 12)*

parallel simulation   reprocessing live data to test program controls. *(Chapter 19)*

parity check   electronic function that ensures the coding of data internal to the computer does not change when it is moved from one internal storage location to another. *(Chapter 8)*

payroll accounting   preparation of individual paycheques, pay envelopes, or electronic transfers using rate and deduction information supplied by the personnel function and base data supplied by the timekeeping-supervision functions. *(Chapter 11)*

payroll distribution (as an employer's procedure)   control of the delivery of pay to employees so that unclaimed cheques, cash, or incomplete electronic transfers are not returned to persons involved in any of the other payroll functions. *(Chapter 11)*

peer review   study of a firm's quality control policies and procedures, followed by a report on a firm's quality of audit practice. *(Chapters 1 and 13)*

performance auditing (see also **internal auditing, management auditing, operational auditing**)   study of business operations for the purpose of making recommendations about the economic and efficient use of resources, effective achievement of business objectives, and compliance with company policies. *(Chapter 1)*

personnel or **labor relations department**   function having transaction initiation authority to add new employees to the payroll, delete terminated employees, obtain authorizations for deductions (such as insurance, saving bonds, and withholding tax exemptions on federal forms), and transmit authority for pay rate changes to the payroll department. *(Chapter 11)*

physical observation (as an audit procedure)   auditors' actual eyewitness inspection of tangible assets and formal documents. *(Chapter 4)*

physical representation of the population   auditor's frame of reference for selecting a sample. *(Chapter 7)*

planned control risk assessment   emphasis on *planned*; the auditors' selection of a control risk level for which they *want* to justify a control risk assessment after completing the test of controls audit work. *(Chapter 20)*

planning materiality   the largest amount of uncorrected dollar misstatement the auditors believe could exist in published financial statement without causing them to be considered materially misleading. *(Chapter 5)*

population   set of all the elements that constitute an account balance or class of transaction. *(Chapter 7)*

population unit   one element in a population. *(Chapter 7)*

positive confirmation   confirmation letter requesting a reply in all cases, whether the account balance is considered correct or incorrect. *(Chapter 4)*

possible misstatement   the further misstatement remaining undetected in units not selected in a sample. *(Chapter 7)*

predication   (with reference to fraud examination) a reason to believe fraud may have occurred. *(Chapter 18)*

preliminary survey   an internal auditor's familiarization with the organization, program, or activity being audited, gained by gathering information, but without detailed investigation or verification procedures. *(Chapter 17)*

primary beneficiaries   third parties for whose primary benefit an audit or other accounting service is performed. *(Chapter 16)*

private placement (see also **nonpublic offering**)   sale of securities to a small number of persons or institutional investors (usually not more than 35), who can demand and obtain sufficient information without the formality of registration. *(Chapter 16)*

privity   the relationship of direct involvement between parties to a contract. *(Chapter 16)*

problem-recognition (as an audit method phase)　phase of formulating an audit objective related to a financial assertion. *(Chapter 7)*

pro forma financial date　presentation of financial statements "as if" an event had occurred on the date of the balance sheet. *(Chapter 13)*

production orders　internal documents that specify the materials and labour required and the timing for the start and end of production. *(Chapter 11)*

program description (computer program documentation)　contains a program flowchart, a listing of the program source code (such as COBOL), and a record of all program changes. *(Chapter 19)*

program driven　computer data processing system that is started when a specific program is loaded into the computer to process all transactions that fit that program and its related files; characterized by batch processing. *(Chapter 8)*

projected likely misstatement (PLM)　auditors' best estimate of misstatement based on the errors found in a sample. *(Chapter 20)*

prospectus　set of financial statements and disclosures distributed to all purchasers in an offering registered under Securities Law. *(Chapter 16)*

qualified audit report　audit report other than the standard unqualified audit report; contains an opinion paragraph that does not give the positive assurance that everything in the financial statements is in conformity with GAAP. *(Chapter 3)*

quality review　study of a firm's quality control policies and procedures; an "audit" of a firm's quality of audit practice. *(Chapter 1)*

racketeering acts　engagement in illegal activities such as fraud in the sales of securities, mail fraud, wire fraud. *(Chapter 16)*

random sample　set of sampling units chosen so that each population item has an *equal likelihood* of being selected in a sample. *(Chapter 7)*

reasonable assurance　concept that recognizes that the cost of any entity's internal control structure should not exceed the benefits that are expected to be derived. *(Chapter 6)*

referral fees　(a) fees a CPA receives for recommending another CPA's services and (b) fees a CPA pays to obtain a client. Such fees may or may not be based on a percentage of the amount of any transaction. *(Chapter 15)*

registrar　fiduciary who keeps the shareholder list and from time to time determines the shareholders eligible to receive dividends (shareholders of record on a dividend record date) and those entitled to vote at the annual meeting. *(Chapter 12)*

relative risk　conditions of more or less inherent risk. *(Chapter 5)*

reperformance (in test of controls procedure)　auditors perform again the arithmetic calculations and the comparisons the company people were supposed to have performed. *(Chapter 6)*

replication　process of reperforming a selection procedure and getting the same sample units. *(Chapter 7)*

reportable condition　significant deficiency in the design or operation of a company's internal control structure which could adversely affect the organization's ability to record, process, summarize, and report financial data in conformity with GAAP. *(Chapter 14)*

representative sample　sample that mirrors the characteristics of the population. *(Chapter 7)*

response rate　for positive confirmations is the proportion of the number of confirmations returned to the number sent, generally after the audit team prompts recipients with second and third requests. Research studies have shown response rates ranging from 66 to 96 percent. *(Chapter 9)*

review services　accountant performs some procedures lesser in scope than an audit for the purpose of giving a negative assurance report on financial statements. *(Chapter 14)*

risk model　$AR = IR \times CR \times DR$ (Chapter 12); $AR = IR \times CR \times AP \times RIA$. *(Chapter 20)*

risk of assessing the control risk too high　probability that the test of controls (compliance) evidence in the sample indicates high control risk when the actual (but unknown) degree of compliance would justify a *lower* control risk assessment. *(Chapter 7)*

risk of assessing the control risk too low   probability that the test of controls (compliance) evidence in the sample indicates low control risk when the actual (but unknown) degree of compliance does *not* justify such a low control risk assessment. *(Chapter 7)*

risk of incorrect acceptance (RIA)   probability that test of detail procedures will *fail* to detect material errors. *(Chapter 7)*

risk of incorrect rejection   probability that test of detail procedures will indicate that a balance *is* materially misstated when, in fact, it *is not. (Chapter 7)*

rule-utilitarianism (in **moral philosophy**)   emphasis on the centrality of rules for ethical behaviour while still maintaining the criterion of the greatest universal good. *(Chapter 15)*

run-to-run   sequential computer processing operations (runs) using the same data. *(Chapter 6)*

safe harbour   plaintiffs in a lawsuit must show that the auditor did not act in good faith when reporting on a forecast, effectively placing the burden of proof on the plaintiff. *(Chapter 15)*

sales forecast   estimated future sales. *(Chapter 11)*

sample   set of sampling units. *(Chapter 7)*

sample audit review file (SARF)   technique similar to SCARF, except instead of programming auditors' test criteria, a random sampling selection scheme in programmed. *(Chapter 19)*

sampling error   amount by which a projected likely misstatement amount could differ from an actual (unknown) total as a result of the sample not being exactly representative. *(Chapter 7)*

sampling error-adjusted upper limit   sample deviation rate adjusted upward to allow for the idea that the actual population rate could be higher. *(Chapter 7)*

sampling risk   probability that an auditor's conclusion based on a sample might be different from the conclusions based on an audit of the entire population. *(Chapter 7)*

sampling unit   one logical unit from a population, such as a customer's account, an inventory item, a debt issue, a cash receipt, a cancelled cheque, and so forth. *(Chapter 7)*

schema   entire set of data elements in a computerized data base. *(Chapter 19)*

scienter   person's action with knowing intent to deceive. *(Chapter 16)*

scope limitation   condition in which the auditors are unable to obtain sufficient competent evidence. *(Chapter 3)*

search for unrecorded liabilities   set of procedures designed to yield audit evidence of liabilities that were not recorded in the reporting period. *(Chapter 10)*

second audit partner   one who reviews the work of the audit team. *(Chapter 4)*

second partner review   working papers and financial statements, including footnotes, are given a final review on large engagements by a partner not responsible for client relations. *(Chapter 13)*

self-checking number   a basic code number with its check digit. *(Chapter 6)*

service organization   another business that executes and/or records transactions on behalf of the client. *(Chapter 14)*

simple extension   calculation of projected likely misstatement based on sample evidence using the difference and ratio methods. *(Chapter 20)*

skewness   concentration of a large proportion of the dollar amount in an account in a small number of the population items. *(Chapter 7)*

smoke/fire concept   means there can be more exposure to error (smoke) that actual error (fire), in analogy to test of controls sampling determination of a tolerable deviation rate. *(Chapter 20)*

specialists   persons skilled in fields other than accounting and auditing who are not members of the audit team. *(Chapter 4)*

standard deviation   a measure of population variability. *(Chapter 7)*

statistical sampling audit sampling that uses the laws of probability for selecting and evaluating a sample from a population for the purpose of reaching a conclusion about the population. *(Chapter 7)*

statutory law all the prohibitions enacted by a legislature. *(Chapter 16)*

stratification in relating to account balances and audit sampling, refers to subdividing a population. *(Chapter 7)*

subschema certain portions of a computerized database. *(Chapter 19)*

substantive audit procedures transaction detail audit and analytical procedures designed to detect material misstatements in account balances and footnote disclosures. *(Chapters 5 and 6)*

substantive-purpose audit program list of account balance-related procedures designed to produce evidence about assertions in financial statements. *(Chapter 7)*

substantive tests of details auditing performance of procedures to obtain direct evidence about the dollar amounts and disclosures in financial statements. *(Chapter 7)*

supervision (in payroll processing) authorization of all pay base data (hours, job number, absences, time off allowed for emergencies, etc.) by an employee's immediate supervisor. *(Chapter 11)*

systematic random sample random sample chosen by calculating a skip interval and selecting every *k*th population unit in a frame. *(Chapter 7)*

systems control audit review file (SCARF) method in which auditors build into the data processing programs special limit, reasonableness, or other audit tests for selection of transactions for audit. *(Chapter 19)*

systems development and documentation standards manual computer documentation containing standards that ensure (1) proper user involvement in the systems design and modification process, (2) review of the specifications of the system, (3) approval by user management and data processing management, and (4) controls and auditability. *(Chapter 8)*

tainting percentage ratio of misstatement in a sampling unit to the recorded amount of the sampling unit. *(Chapter 20)*

test data auditor-produced transactions used to audit programmed control procedures with simulated data. *(Chapter 19)*

test deck sample of one of each possible combination of data fields that may be processed through the client's actual computer system. *(Chapter 19)*

test of controls ordinary and extended procedures designed to produce evidence about the effectiveness of client controls that should be in operation. *(Chapters 6, 7, 9, 10, 11, and 12)*

timing (of audit procedures) refers to *when* procedures are performed: at "interim" before the balance sheet date, or at "year-end" shortly before and after the balance sheet date. *(Chapters 6 and 7)*

timekeeping payroll function of producing time cards or time sheets that provide the basis for payment to hourly workers. *(Chapter 11)*

tolerable deviation rate decision criterion of the frequency of control failure for assessing control risk. *(Chapter 7)*

tolerable misstatement decision criterion of the amount of dollar misstatement that can exist undetected in an account and not cause financial statements to be considered materially misleading. *(Chapter 5)*

tort legal action covering civil complaints other than breach of contract; normally initiated by users of financial statements. *(Chapter 16)*

tracing auditor selects sample items from basic source documents and proceeds forward through the accounting and control system to find the final recording of the accounting transactions. *(Chapter 4)*

transaction driven (also **event driven**) computer data processing system that is started with each transaction event; individual transactions trigger the processing activity and all relevant files are updated. *(Chapter 19)*

transfer agent fiduciary who handles the exchange of shares, cancelling the shares surrendered by sellers and issuing new certificates to buyers. *(Chapter 12)*

trap doors unauthorized computer program modules used solely for fraudulent purposes. *(Chapter 19)*

underreliance (obsolete term) the result of assessing control risk too high and expanding other audit procedures, performing more audit work when less work would suffice. *(Chapter 7)*

unrestricted random sample items in a population are associated with numbers in a random number table or computer program for selection of a sample; no population stratification. *(Chapter 20)*

upper error limit (UEL) largest amount of monetary misstatement that can be calculated, using the coefficient for the decision criterion risk of incorrect acceptance. *(Chapter 20)*

validity (as a control objective) ensuring that *recorded* transactions are ones that *should* have been recorded. *(Chapter 6)*

verbal and written representations (audit evidence) responses to audit enquiries given by the client's officers, directors, owners, and employees. *(Chapter 4)*

vertical analysis study of financial statement amounts expressed each year as proportions of a base such as sales for the income statement accounts and total assets for the balance sheet accounts. *(Chapters 5 and 18)*

vouching auditor selects sample items from an account and goes backward through the accounting and control system to find the source documentation that supports the item selected. *(Chapter 4)*

walk-through act of following one or a few transactions through the accounting system and control system in order to obtain a general understanding of the client's systems. *(Chapter 7)*

white collar crime misdeeds done by people who wear ties to work and steal with a pencil or a computer terminal. *(Chapter 18)*

year-end audit work audit procedures performed shortly before and after the balance sheet date. *(Chapter 4)*

INDEX